INDIANA

United States History

Growth and Development: Beginnings to 1914

William Deverell
Deborah Gray White

HOLT McDOUGAL
a division of Houghton Mifflin Harcourt

Authors

William Deverell

William Deverell is Professor of History at the University of Southern California. He is the author of *Railroad Crossing: Californians and the Railroad, 1850-1910* and *Whitewashed Adobe: The Rise of Los Angeles and the Remaking of the Mexican Past*. He is the editor of the *Blackwell Companion to the American West*. With Greg Hise, he co-authored *Eden by Design: The 1930 Olmsted-Bartholomew Plan for the Los Angeles Region* and co-edited *Land of Sunshine: The Environmental History of Metropolitan Los Angeles*. He is the former chairman of the California Council for the Humanities.

Deborah Gray White

Deborah Gray White, a former New York City school teacher, is Distinguished Professor of History at Rutgers University in New Brunswick, New Jersey. A specialist in American history and the history of African Americans, she is the author of several books, including: *Ar'n't I A Woman? Female Slaves in the Plantation South; Too Heavy a Load: Black Women in Defense of Themselves, 1894-1994*; and *Let My People Go, African Americans 1804-1860*, Volume 4 in the *Young Oxford History of African Americans*.

Copyright © 2010 by Holt McDougal, a division of Houghton Mifflin Harcourt Publishing Company

All rights reserved. No part of this publication may be reproduced or transmitted in any form or by any means, electronic or mechanical, including photocopy, recording, or any information storage and retrieval system, without permission in writing from the publisher.

Requests for permission to make copies of any part of the work should be mailed to the following address: Permissions Department, Holt McDougal, 10801 N. MoPac Expressway, Building 3, Austin, Texas 78759.

For acknowledgments, see page R110, which is an extension of the copyright page.

HOLT MCDOUGAL is a trademark of Houghton Mifflin Harcourt Publishing Company.

Printed in the United States of America

ISBN-13: 978-0-55-401664-1

ISBN-10: 0-55-401664-8

3 4 5 6 7 8 9 0868 12 11 10 09

Program Consultants

Contributing Author

Kylene Beers, Ed.D.
Senior Reading Advisor to
    Secondary Schools
Teachers College Reading and
    Writing Project
Columbia University
New York City, New York

A former middle school teacher, Dr. Beers has turned her commitment to helping struggling readers into the major focus of her research, writing, speaking, and teaching. She is the former editor of the National Council of Teachers of English (NCTE) literacy journal *Voices from the Middle*. Currently serving NCTE as vice president, she will assume the presidency in 2008. Her published works include *When Kids Can't Read: What Teachers Can Do* (Heinemann, 2002).

General Editor

Frances Marie Gipson
Secondary Literacy
Los Angeles Unified School
    District
Los Angeles, California

In her current position, Frances Gipson guides reform work for secondary instruction and supports its implementation. She has designed curriculum at the district, state, and national levels. Her leadership of a coaching collaborative with Subject Matter Projects of the University of California at Los Angeles evolved from her commitment to rigorous instruction and to meeting the needs of diverse learners.

Senior Literature and Writing Specialist

Carol Jago
English Department Chairperson
Santa Monica High School
Santa Monica, California

An English teacher at the middle and high school levels for 26 years, Carol Jago also directs the reading and literature project at UCLA and writes a weekly education column for the Los Angeles Times. She has been published in numerous professional journals and has authored several books, including *Cohesive Writing: Why Concept is Not Enough* (Boynton/Cook, 2002).

Consultants

Martha H. Ball, M.A.
Religion Consultant
Utah 3Rs Project Director
Utah State Office of Education
Salt Lake City, Utah

John Ferguson, M.T.S., J.D.
Senior Religion Consultant
Assistant Professor
Political Science/Criminal Justice
Howard Payne University
Brownwood, Texas

J. Frank Malaret
Senior Consultant
Dean, Downtown and West
    Sacramento Outreach Centers
Sacramento City College
Sacramento, California

Kimberly A. Plummer, M.A.
Senior Consultant
History-Social Science Educator/
    Advisor
Holt, Rinehart & Winston

Andrés Reséndez, Ph.D.
Senior Consultant,
Assistant Professor
Department of History
University of California at Davis
Davis, California

Indiana Teacher Advisory Panel

Sam Fies
History and Geography of the
    Eastern Hemishere
Highland Middle School
Shererville, Indiana

Jill Anne Hahn
Government and Economics
Central High School
Evansville, Indiana

Todd A. Kendrick
U.S. and World History
Franklin Central High School
Indianapolis, Indiana

Mary Jane Smith
Psychology
Warren Central High School
South Greenfield, Indiana

Academic Reviewers

Anne C. Bailey, Ph.D.
Spelman College
Atlanta, Georgia

Albert Camarillo, Ph.D.
Department of History
Stanford University

Larry Conyers, Ph.D.
Department of Anthropology
University of Denver

Willard Gatewood, Ph.D.
Emeritus Alumni Distinguished
    Professor, Department of
    History
University of Arkansas

Christopher Hendricks, Ph.D.
Department of History
Armstrong Atlantic State
    University
Savannah, Georgia

Skip Hyser, Ph.D.
Department of History
James Madison University
Harrisonburg, Virginia

Yasuhide Kawashima
Department of History
University of Texas at El Paso

Brenda E. Stevenson, Ph.D.
Department of History
UCLA
Los Angeles, California

David Switzer, Ph.D.
Department of Social Studies
Plymouth State University
Plymouth, New Hampshire

Jessica Wang, Ph.D.
Department of History
UCLA
Los Angeles, California

Nan Woodruff, Ph.D
Department of History
Pennsylvania State University

Craig Yirush, Ph.D.
Department of History
UCLA
Los Angeles, California

Educational Reviewers

Nelson Acevedo
New York City Alternative
    Schools and Programs
New York, New York

Henry Assetto
Twin Valley High School
Elverson, Pennsylvania

John Bilsky
Linton Middle School
Penn Hills, Pennsylvania

Julie Chan, Ed.D.
Director, Literacy Instruction
Newport-Mesa Unified School
    District
Costa Mesa, California

Kermit Cummings
Cockeysville Middle School
Baltimore County Public Schools
Baltimore, Maryland

Katherine A. DeForge
Social Studies Chair
Marcellus Central School
Marcellus, New York

Sandra Eades
Ridgely Middle School
Lutherville, Maryland

Ed Felten
Coopersville Public School
    District
Coopersville, Michigan

Tim Gearhart
Daniel Lewis Middle School
Paso Robles, California

Stacy Goldman
Lincoln Middle School
Berwyn, Illinois

Joseph P. Macary
Supervisor of Social Studies
Waterbury Public Schools
Waterbury, Connecticut

Carol Eiler Moore
Dundalk Middle School
Dundalk, Maryland

Tina Nelson
Baltimore County Public School
    District
Baltimore, Maryland

Ann-Jean Paci
Sheepshead Bay High School
Brooklyn, New York

Anthony Powell
Edmund W. Miles Middle School
Amityville, New York

Linda Prior
Floyd T. Binns Middle School
Culpeper County, Virginia

Wendy Schanberger
Hereford Middle School
Monkton, Maryland

Sue A. Shinn
Culpeper Middle School
Culpeper, Virginia

Kathleen Torquata
Lincoln Middle School
Berwyn, Illinois

Contents

UNIT 1 Our Colonial Heritage (BEGINNINGS–1783)

CHAPTER 1 The World before the Opening of the Atlantic (BEGINNINGS–1500)

CHAPTER 2 New Empires in the Americas (1400–1750)

Canal zone
Canal route
Railroad
Locks
0   10   20 Miles
0   10   20 Kilometers

Features

History Close-up

See how people lived and how places looked in the past by taking a close–up view of history.

BIOGRAPHIES

Meet the people who have influenced history and learn about their lives.

History and Geography

Explore the relationships between history and geography.

THE IMPACT TODAY

Understand how events from the past have had an impact on our world today.

LINKING TO TODAY

Link people and events from the past to the world you live in today.

QUICK FACTS

Examine key facts and concepts quickly and easily with graphics.

Charts, Graphs, and Tables

Analyze information presented visually to learn more about history.

CHARTS

INFOGRAPHICS
Analyze and interpret information from graphics.

TIME LINES

See how key events are related in time.

Points of View

See how different people have interpreted historical issues in different ways.

Historic Documents

Examine key documents that have shaped U.S. history.

Literature in History

Learn about the beliefs and experiences of people who lived in other times and places through literature pieces.

Social Studies Skills

Learn, practice, and apply the skills you need to study and analyze history.

Reading Social Studies

Learn and practice skills that will help you read your social studies lesson.

FOCUS ON WRITING AND SPEAKING

Use writing and speaking to study and reflect on the events and people who made history.

Writing Workshop

Learn to write about history.

Political Cartoons

Interpret political cartoons to learn about U.S. history.

Supreme Court Decisions

Study the impact of Supreme Court decisions on U.S. history.

Interdisciplinary Connections

Learn history through connections to other disciplines.

Primary Sources

Read and analyze the exact words of important people and documents as related to the study of U.S. history.

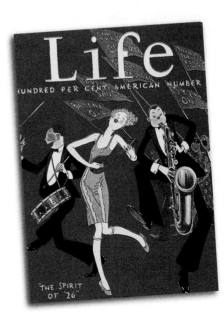

Maps

Interpret maps to see where important events happened and analyze how geography has influenced history.

Interactive Maps

Program Maps

Reading
like a Historian

Historians use paintings along with many other tools to help understand the past. The famous painting on the next page, *Washington Crossing the Delaware*, captures the determination of Patriot leaders and soldiers to endure brutal conditions in the hope of winning their struggle for liberty. As you study United States history, you too will learn how to use different historical sources to **Read like a Historian.**

To find out more about reading like a historian and the historical sources that follow, visit

go.hrw.com
More Online
KEYWORD: HISTORIAN

By Frances Marie Gipson
Secondary Literacy Coordinator
Los Angeles Unified School District, Los Angeles, California

What Does It Mean to Read like a Historian?

In your history class you will be doing a lot of reading, thinking, and problem-solving. Much of your reading and thinking will center on different types of texts or materials. Since you are in a history class reading all sorts of things, a question to consider is, "What does it mean to think, read, and solve problems like a historian?"

Historians work with different types of sources to understand and learn from history. Two categories of sources are **primary** and **secondary** sources.

Primary Sources are historical documents, written accounts by a firsthand witness, or objects that have survived from the past. A study of primary sources might include letters, government documents, diaries, photographs, art objects, stamps, coins, and even clothing.

Secondary Sources are accounts of past events created by people some time after the events happened. This textbook and other books written about historical events are examples of secondary sources.

As you learn more about your work as a historian, you will begin to ask questions and analyze historical materials. You will be working as a detective, digging into history to create a richer understanding of the mysteries of the past.

How to Analyze Written Sources

"Spain's Victory of Peace"

To five hundred thousand Cubans starved or otherwise murdered have been added an American battleship and three hundred American sailors lost as the direct result of the dilatory [delaying] policy of our government toward Spain. If we had stopped the war in Cuba when duty and policy alike urged us to do the *Maine* would have been afloat today, and three hundred homes, now desolate, would have been unscathed [safe from harm].

– New York Journal, February 17, 1898

Asking questions can help you determine the relevance and importance of written primary sources, such as this newspaper editorial about the sinking of an American warship. As you analyze the primary source above and the primary and secondary sources included in this textbook, ask yourself questions like the ones below.

- Who created the source and why?

- Did the writer have firsthand knowledge of the event, or does he report what others saw or heard?

- Was the writer a neutral party, or did the author have opinions or interests that might have influenced what was recorded?

- Did the writer wish to inform or persuade others?

- Was the information recorded during the event, immediately after the event, or after some lapse of time?

The Attack on Lawrence, Kansas

"Sheriff Jones, again at the head of an army of Missourians, marched into Lawrence. In broad daylight, they threw the printing presses of two newspapers into a river. They burned down the Free State Hotel and other buildings. Antislavery Kansans seethed with rage. Here is how one eyewitness described the attack: *Sheriff Jones, after looking at the flames rising from the hotel and saying that it was 'the happiest day of his life,' dismissed the troops and they began their lawless destruction.*"

–John A. Garraty, from *The Story of America*, 1994

When reading secondary sources, such as the description of the attack on Lawrence, Kansas, historians ask additional questions to seek understanding. They try to source the text, build evidence, and interpret the message that is being conveyed. For historians, reading is a quest to find evidence to answer or challenge a historical problem. As you study secondary sources, ask questions like the ones below.

- Who is the author? What do I know about this author?
- Did the author have firsthand information? What is the author's relationship to the event?
- What might be the author's motivation in writing this piece?
- What type of evidence did the author look at?
- Are any assumptions or biases present?
- How does this document fit into the larger context of the events I am studying?
- What kind of source is it?
- Is the source an original?
- Is the content probable or reasonable?
- What does the date tell me about the event?
- What do I already know about this topic that will help me understand more of what I am reading?

How to Analyze an Artifact

Artifacts, such as this phonograph invented by Thomas Edison, take many forms. They might be coins, stone tools, pieces of clothing, or even items found in your backpack. As you study artifacts in this textbook, ask yourself questions like the ones below.

- Why was this object created?

- When and where would it have been used?

- What does the artifact tell me about the technology available at the time it was created?

- What can it tell me about the life and times of the people who used it?

- How does the artifact help to make sense of the time period?

How to Analyze a Historical Map

Maps, such as this one from 1719 of New France, are symbolic representations of places shown in relation to one another. All maps necessarily include some details and leave out others. As you study maps in this textbook, ask questions like the ones below.

- When and where was the map produced?
- What details has the mapmaker chosen to include (or exclude) on this map?
- Why was the map drawn?
- How can I determine if the map is accurate?
- How are maps used to analyze the past, present, and future?

How to Analyze a Photograph

Photographs, like the one above of African American soldiers during the Civil War, are another important source for historians. One way to study a photograph is to write down everything you think is important about it. Then divide the image into four sections and describe the important elements from each section. As you study photographs in this textbook, ask questions like the ones below.

- **What is the subject of the photograph?**
- **What does the image reveal about its subject?**
- **What is the setting for the photograph?**
- **What other details can I observe?**
- **When and where in the past was the photograph created?**
- **How can I describe the photographer's point of view?**

How to Analyze a Political Cartoon

In 1871 Thomas Nast published this cartoon—"Who Stole the People's Money?"—poking fun at corruption in politics. As you study political cartoons in this textbook, use the following helpful tips and questions.

- List the parts of the political cartoon and the importance of each part.

- Describe the focus or significance of the political cartoon.

- Do the captions and call-out boxes clarify the political cartoon's purpose?

- Does the cartoon help me understand the information that I am studying in my textbook better?

Become an Active Reader

by Dr. Kylene Beers

Did you ever think you would begin reading your social studies book by reading about reading? Actually, it makes better sense than you might think. You would probably make sure you learned some soccer skills and strategies before playing in a game. Similarly, you need to learn some reading skills and strategies before reading your social studies book. In other words, you need to make sure you know whatever you need to know in order to read this book successfully.

Tip #1
Use the Reading Social Studies Pages

Take advantage of the two pages on reading at the beginning of every chapter. Those pages introduce the chapter themes; explain a reading skill or strategy; and identify key terms, people, and academic vocabulary.

Themes

Why are themes important? They help our minds organize facts and information. For example, when we talk about baseball, we may talk about types of pitches. When we talk about movies, we may discuss animation.

Historians are no different. When they discuss history or social studies, they tend to think about some common themes: Economics, Geography, Religion, Politics, Society and Culture, and Science and Technology.

Reading Skill or Strategy

Good readers use a number of skills and strategies to make sure they understand what they are reading. These lessons will give you the tools you need to read and understand social studies.

Key Terms, People, and Academic Vocabulary

Before you read the chapter, review these words and think about them. Have you heard the word before? What do you already know about the people? Then watch for these words and their meanings as you read the chapter.

Tells which theme or themes are important in the chapter

Explains a skill or strategy good readers use

Gives you practice in the reading skill or strategy

Identifies the important words in the chapter

Tip #2
Read like a Skilled Reader

You will never get better at reading your social studies book—or any book for that matter—unless you spend some time thinking about how to be a better reader.

Skilled readers do the following:

- They preview what they are supposed to read before they actually begin reading. They look for vocabulary words, titles of sections, information in the margin, or maps or charts they should study.

- They divide their notebook paper into two columns. They title one column "Notes from the Chapter" and the other column "Questions or Comments I Have."

- They take notes in both columns as they read.

- They read like **active readers**. The Active Reading list below shows you what that means.

- They use clues in the text to help them figure out where the text is going. The best clues are called signal words.

  Chronological Order Signal Words: *first, second, third, before, after, later, next, following that, earlier, finally*

  Cause and Effect Signal Words: *because of, due to, as a result of, the reason for, therefore, consequently*

  Comparison/Contrast Signal Words: *likewise, also, as well as, similarly, on the other hand*

Active Reading

Successful readers are **active readers**. These readers know that it is up to them to figure out what the text means. Here are some steps you can take to become an active, and successful, reader.

Predict what will happen next based on what has already happened. When your predictions don't match what happens in the text, reread the confusing parts.

Question what is happening as you read. Constantly ask yourself why things have happened, what things mean, and what caused certain events.

Summarize what you are reading frequently. Do not try to summarize the entire chapter! Read a bit and then summarize it. Then read on.

Connect what is happening in the part you're reading to what you have already read.

Clarify your understanding. Stop occasionally to ask yourself whether you are confused by anything. You may need to reread to clarify, or you may need to read further and collect more information before you can understand.

Visualize what is happening in the text. Try to see the events or places in your mind by drawing maps, making charts, or jotting down notes about what you are reading.

Tip #3
Pay Attention to Vocabulary

It is no fun to read something when you don't know what the words mean, but you can't learn new words if you only use or read the words you already know. In this book, we know we have probably used some words you don't know. But, we have followed a pattern as we have used more difficult words.

Key Terms and People

At the beginning of each section you will find a list of key terms or people that you will need to know. Be on the lookout for those words as you read through the section.

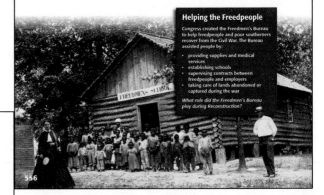

men's Bureau

In 1865 Congress established the **Freedmen's Bureau**, an agency providing relief for freed-people and certain poor people in the South.

Freedmen's Bureau
In 1865 Congress established the **Freedmen's Bureau**, an agency providing relief for freed-people and certain poor people in the South. The Bureau had a difficult job. At its high point, about 900 agents served the entire South. Bureau commissioner Oliver O. Howard eventually decided to use the Bureau's limited budget to distribute food to the poor and to provide education and legal help for freed-people. The Bureau also helped African American war veterans.

The Freedmen's Bureau played an important role in establishing more schools in the South. Laws against educating slaves meant that most freedpeople had never learned to read or write. Before the war ended, however, northern groups, such as the American Missionary Association, began providing books and teachers to African Americans. The teachers were mostly women who were committed to helping freedpeople. One teacher said of her students, "I never before saw children so eager to learn . . . It is wonderful how [they] . . . can have so great a desire for knowledge, and such a capacity for attaining [reaching] it."

After the war, some freedpeople organized their own education efforts. For example, Freedmen's Bureau agents found that some African Americans had opened schools in abandoned buildings. Many white southerners continued to believe that African Americans should not be educated. Despite opposition, by 1869 more than 150,000 African American students were attending more than 3,000 schools. The Freedmen's Bureau also helped establish a number of universities for African Americans, including Howard and Fisk universities.

Students quickly filled the new classrooms. Working adults attended classes in the evening. African Americans hoped that education would help them to understand and protect their rights and to enable them to find better jobs. Both black and white southerners benefited from the effort to provide greater access to education in the South.

READING CHECK Analyzing How did the Freedmen's Bureau help reform education in the South?

Helping the Freedpeople
Congress created the Freedmen's Bureau to help freedpeople and poor southerners recover from the Civil War. The Bureau assisted people by:
- providing supplies and medical services
- establishing schools
- supervising contracts between freedpeople and employers
- taking care of lands abandoned or captured during the war

What role did the Freedmen's Bureau play during Reconstruction?

556

Damaged South
Tired southern soldiers returned home to find that the world they had known before the war was gone. Cities, towns, and farms had been ruined. Because of high food prices and widespread crop failures, many southerners faced starvation. The Confederate money held by most southerners was now worthless. Banks failed, and merchants had gone bankrupt because people could not pay their debts.

Former Confederate general Braxton Bragg was one of many southerners who faced economic hardship. He found that *"all, all* was lost, except my debts." In South Carolina, Mary Boykin Chesnut wrote in her diary about the isolation she experienced after the war. "We are shut in here . . . All RR's [railroads] destroyed—bridges gone. We are cut off from the world."

Lincoln's Plan
President Abraham Lincoln wanted to reunite the nation as quickly and painlessly as possible. He had proposed a plan for readmitting the southern states even before the war ended. Called the **Ten Percent Plan**, it offered southerners amnesty, or official pardon, for all illegal acts supporting the rebellion. To receive amnesty, southerners had to do two things. They had to swear an oath of loyalty to the United States. They also had to agree that slavery was illegal. Once 10 percent of voters in a state made these pledges, they could form a new government. The state then could be readmitted to the Union.

Louisiana quickly elected a new state legislature under the Ten Percent Plan. Other southern states that had been occupied by Union troops soon followed Louisiana back into the United States.

Wade-Davis Bill
Some politicians argued that Congress, not the president, should control the southern states' return to the Union. They believed that Congress had the power to admit new states. Also, many Republican members of Congress thought the Ten Percent Plan did not go far enough. A senator from Michigan expressed their views.

"The people of the North are not such fools as to . . . turn around and say to the traitors, 'all you have to do [to return] is . . . take an oath that henceforth you will be true to the Government.'"
—Senator Jacob Howard, quoted in *Reconstruction: America's Unfinished Revolution, 1863–1877, by Eric Foner*

Two Republicans—Senator Benjamin Wade and Representative Henry Davis—had an alternative to Lincoln's plan. Following **procedures** of the Wade-Davis bill, a state had to meet two conditions before it could rejoin the Union. First, it had to ban slavery. Second, a majority of adult males in the state had to take the loyalty oath.

ACADEMIC VOCABULARY
procedure
a series of steps taken to accomplish a task

War destroyed Richmond, Virginia, once the capital of the Confederacy.

553

ACADEMIC
VOCABULARY

procedure
a series of steps taken to accomplish a task

Academic Vocabulary

When we use a word that is important in all classes, not just social studies, we define it in the margin under the heading *Academic Vocabulary.* You will run into these academic words in other textbooks, so you should learn what they mean while reading this book.

READING SOCIAL STUDIES

Words to Know

As you read this social studies textbook, you will be more successful if you know or learn the meanings of the words on this page. There are two types of words listed here. The first list contains academic words, the words we discussed at the bottom of the previous page. These words are important in all classes, not just social studies. The second list contains words that are special to this particular topic of social studies, U.S. history.

Academic Words

abstract	expressing a quality or idea without reference to an actual thing
acquire	to get
advocate	to plead in favor of
agreement	a decision reached by two or more people or groups
aspects	parts
authority	power, right to rule
circumstances	surrounding situation
classical	referring to the cultures of ancient Greece or Rome
complex	difficult, not simple
concrete	specific, real
consequences	the effects of a particular event or events
contemporary	existing at the same time
criteria	rules for defining
develop/development	1. the process of growing or improving 2. creation
distinct	separate
effect	the results of an action or decision
efficient/efficiency	productive and not wasteful
element	part
establish	to set up or create
execute	to perform, carry out
explicit	fully revealed without vagueness
facilitate	to bring about
factor	causes
function	use or purpose
implement	to put in place
implications	effects of a decision
implicit	understood though not clearly put into words
incentive	something that leads people to follow a certain course of action
influence	change, or have an effect on
innovation	a new idea or way of doing something
motive	a reason for doing something
neutral	unbiased, not favoring either side in a conflict
primary	main, most important
principle	basic belief, rule, or law
procedure	a series of steps taken to accomplish a task
process	a series of steps by which a task is accomplished
reaction	a response
role	1. a part or function 2. assigned behavior
strategy	a plan for fighting a battle or war
structure	the way something is set up or organized
vary/various	1. to be different 2. of many type

Social Studies Words

AD	refers to dates after Jesus's birth
BC	refers to dates before the birth of Jesus
BCE	refers to "Before Common Era," dates before the birth of Jesus
CE	refers to "Common Era," dates after Jesus's birth
century	a period of 100 years
civilization	the culture of a particular time or place
climate	the weather conditions in a certain area over a long period of time
culture	the knowledge, beliefs, customs, and values of a group of people
custom	a repeated practice; tradition
democracy	governmental rule by the people, usually on a majority rule principle
economy	the system in which people make and exchange goods and services
geography	the study of the earth's physical and cultural features
independence	freedom from forceful rule
monarchy	governmental rule by one person, a king or queen
North	the region of the United States sometimes defined by the states that did not secede from the Union during the Civil War
rebellion	an organized resistance to the established government
society	a group of people who share common traditions
South	the region of the United States sometimes defined by the states that seceded from the Union to form the Confederate States of America

Mapping the Earth

A **globe** is a scale model of the earth. It is useful for showing the entire earth or studying large areas of the earth's surface.

A pattern of lines circles the globe in east-west and north-south directions. It is called a **grid**. The intersection of these imaginary lines helps us find places on the earth.

The east-west lines in the grid are lines of **latitude**. Lines of latitude are called **parallels** because they are always parallel to each other. These imaginary lines measure distance north and south of the **equator**. The equator is an imaginary line that circles the globe halfway between the North and South Poles. Parallels measure distance from the equator in **degrees**. The symbol for degrees is °. Degrees are further divided into **minutes**. The symbol for minutes is ´. There are 60 minutes in a degree. Parallels north of the equator are labeled with an N. Those south of the equator are labeled with an S.

The north-south lines are lines of **longitude**. Lines of longitude are called **meridians**. These imaginary lines pass through the Poles. They measure distance east and west of the **prime meridian**. The prime meridian is an imaginary line that runs through Greenwich, England. It represents 0° longitude.

Lines of latitude range from 0°, for locations on the equator, to 90°N or 90°S, for locations at the Poles. Lines of longitude range from 0° on the prime meridian to 180° on a meridian in the mid-Pacific Ocean. Meridians west of the prime meridian to 180° are labeled with a W. Those east of the prime meridian to 180° are labeled with an E.

Lines of Latitude

Lines of Longitude

Northern Hemisphere

The equator divides the globe into two halves, called **hemispheres**. The half north of the equator is the Northern Hemisphere. The southern half is the Southern Hemisphere. The prime meridian and the 180° meridian divide the world into the Eastern Hemisphere and the Western Hemisphere. However, the prime meridian runs right through Europe and Africa. To avoid dividing these continents between two hemispheres, some mapmakers divide the Eastern and Western hemispheres at 20°W. This places all of Europe and Africa in the Eastern Hemisphere.

Our planet's land surface is divided into seven large landmasses, called **continents**. They are identified in the maps on this page. Landmasses smaller than continents and completely surrounded by water are called **islands**.

Geographers also organize Earth's water surface into parts. The largest is the world ocean. Geographers divide the world ocean into the Pacific Ocean, the Atlantic Ocean, the Indian Ocean, and the Arctic Ocean. Lakes and seas are smaller bodies of water.

Southern Hemisphere

Western Hemisphere

Eastern Hemisphere

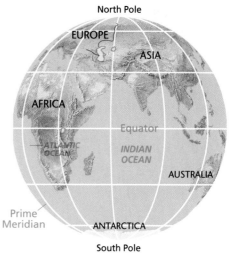

Mapmaking

A **map** is a flat diagram of all or part of the earth's surface. Mapmakers have created different ways of showing our round planet on flat maps. These different ways are called **map projections**. Because the earth is round, there is no way to show it accurately in a flat map. All flat maps are distorted in some way. Mapmakers must choose the type of map projection that is best for their purposes. Many map projections are one of three kinds: cylindrical, conic, or flat-plane.

Paper cylinder

Mercator projection

Cylindrical Projections

Cylindrical projections are based on a cylinder wrapped around the globe. The cylinder touches the globe only at the equator. The meridians are pulled apart and are parallel to each other instead of meeting at the Poles. This causes landmasses near the Poles to appear larger than they really are. The map below is a Mercator projection, one type of cylindrical projection. The Mercator projection is useful for navigators because it shows true direction and shape. However, it distorts the size of land areas near the Poles.

Conic Projections

Conic projections are based on a cone placed over the globe. A conic projection is most accurate along the lines of latitude where it touches the globe. It retains almost true shape and size. Conic projections are most useful for showing areas that have long east-west dimensions, such as the United States.

Paper cone

Conic projection

Flat-Plane Projections

Flat-plane projections are based on a plane touching the globe at one point, such as at the North Pole or South Pole. A flat-plane projection is useful for showing true direction for airplane pilots and ship navigators. It also shows true area. However, it distorts the true shapes of landmasses.

Flat plane

Flat-plane projection

Map Essentials

Maps are like messages sent out in code. Mapmakers provide certain elements that help us translate these codes. These elements help us understand the message they are presenting about a particular part of the world. Of these elements, almost all maps have titles, directional indicators, scales, and legends. The map below has all four of these elements, plus a fifth—a locator map.

❶ Title

A map's **title** shows what the subject of the map is. The map title is usually the first thing you should look at when studying a map, because it tells you what the map is trying to show.

Battles in the East

Legend	
	Union state
	West Virginia (Separated from Virginia in 1861 and joined the Union in 1863)
	Confederate state
→	Union forces
✺	Union victory
→	Confederate forces
✺	Confederate victory

0   15   30 Miles
0   15   30 Kilometers

PENNSYLVANIA

Antietam Sep. 1862

MARYLAND

WEST VIRGINIA

Shenandoah Valley

Potomac River

LEE

McCLELLAN

POPE

Washington

Manassas Junction

Bull Run July 1861 & Aug. 1862

LEE

Chesapeake Bay

Fair Oaks May – June 1862

LEE

Richmond

James River

York R.

McCLELLAN

Seven Days June 1862

Yorktown

N W E S

VIRGINIA

ATLANTIC OCEAN

❷ Compass Rose

A directional indicator shows which way north, south, east, and west lie on the map. Some mapmakers use a "north arrow," which points toward the North Pole. Remember, "north" is not always at the top of a map. The way a map is drawn and the location of directions on that map depend on the perspective of the mapmaker. Most maps in this textbook indicate direction by using a compass rose. A **compass rose** has arrows that point to all four principal directions, as shown.

❸ Scale

Mapmakers use scales to show the distances between points on a map. Scales may appear on maps in several different forms. The maps in this textbook provide a bar **scale**. Scales give distances in miles and kilometers.

To find the distance between two points on the map, place a piece of paper so that the edge connects the two points. Mark the location of each point on the paper with a line or dot. Then, compare the distance between the two dots with the map's bar scale. The number on the top of the scale gives the distance in miles. The number on the bottom gives the distance in kilometers. Because the distances are given in large intervals, you may have to approximate the actual distance on the scale.

❹ Legend

The **legend**, or key, explains what the symbols on the map represent. Point symbols are used to specify the location of things, such as cities, that do not take up much space on the map. Some legends, such as the one shown here, show colors that represent certain elevations. Other maps might have legends with symbols or colors that represent things such as roads. Legends can also show economic resources, land use, population density, and climate.

❺ Locator Map

A locator map shows where in the world the area on the map is located. The area shown on the main map is shown in red on the locator map. The locator map also shows surrounding areas so the map reader can see how the information on the map relates to neighboring lands.

Working with Maps

The Atlas at the back of this textbook includes both physical and political maps. Physical maps, like the one you just saw and the one below, show the major physical features in a region. These features include things like mountain ranges, rivers, islands, and plains. Political maps show the major political features of a region, such as countries and their borders, capitals, and other important cities.

Topographic Maps

Some maps are topographic maps. A topographic map, like this one, shows the shape of the earth's surface using contour lines. Contour lines are imaginary lines connecting points of the same elevation above sea level. The distance between the lines represents the distance between points on the earth's surface. If the lines are close together, the feature is more steep than if the lines are far apart. Symbols on topographic maps represent natural and manmade features such as rivers, mountains, roads, and even buildings. Name five symbols you see on this topographic map.

Dale, Indiana

Lake/pond, perennial
Elevation contour
Highway, primary
Highway, dual
Railroad, single track
Road, light-duty, paved
Road, minor
Stream, perennial

0   0.5   1 Mile
0   0.5   1 Kilometer

The Louisiana Purchase

U.S. states and territories in 1804
Louisiana Purchase
Disputed by United States and Britain

Lewis and Clark's Expedition, 1804–1806
Pike's Expedition, 1806–1807

0   200   400 Miles
0   200   400 Kilometers

Fort Clatsop
CASCADE RANGE
Bitterroot Mtns.
LEWIS'S RETURN
Fort Mandan
CLARK'S RETURN
OREGON COUNTRY (Claimed by Britain, Russia, Spain, and the United States)
Columbia River
Snake River
LOUISIANA PURCHASE (Purchased in 1803)
LEWIS AND CLARK'S EXPEDITION
Missouri River
Platte River
GREAT PLAINS
Pikes Peak 14,110 ft. (4,301 m)
Arkansas River
Santa Fe
Red River
Continental Divide
SPANISH TERRITORY
PIKE'S EXPEDITION
PACIFIC OCEAN
BRITISH TERRITORY
Lake Superior
Lake Michigan
Lake Huron
Lake Erie
Lake Ontario
St. Lawrence River
Mississippi River
MICHIGAN TERRITORY
INDIANA TERRITORY
St. Charles
St. Louis
OH
Ohio River
KY
TN
APPALACHIAN MOUNTAINS
MISSISSIPPI TERRITORY
New Orleans
SPANISH FLORIDA
ATLANTIC OCEAN
Gulf of Mexico

40°N
35°N
30°N
25°N
95°W 90°W 85°W 80°W 75°W

N W E S

Historical Map

In this textbook, most of the maps you will study are historical maps. Historical maps, such as this one, are maps that show information about the past. This information might be which lands an empire controlled or where a certain group of people lived. Often colors are used to indicate the different things on the map. What does this map show?

Route Map

One special type of historical map is called a route map. A route map, like the one above, shows the route, or path, that someone or something followed. Route maps can show things like trade routes, invasion routes, or the journeys and travels of people. If more than one route is shown, several arrows of different colors may be used. What does this route map show?

The maps in this textbook will help you study and understand history. By working with these maps, you will see where important events happened, where people moved, and how the United States grew and changed. In studying these maps, you will learn how geography has influenced history.

Geographic Dictionary

OCEAN
a large body of water

CORAL REEF
an ocean ridge made up of
skeletal remains of tiny sea animals

GULF
a large part of
the ocean that
extends into land

PENINSULA
an area of land that sticks
out into a lake or ocean

BAY
part of a large
body of water
that is smaller
than a gulf

ISLAND
an area of land
surrounded entirely
by water

ISTHMUS
a narrow piece of land
connecting two larger
land areas

DELTA
an area where a
river deposits soil
into the ocean

STRAIT
a narrow body of
water connecting two
larger bodies of water

SINKHOLE
a circular depression
formed when the roof
of a cave collapses

WETLAND
an area of land
covered by
shallow water

RIVER
a natural flow of
water that runs
through the land

LAKE
an inland body
of water

FOREST
an area of densely
wooded land

COAST
an area of land
near the ocean

MOUNTAIN
an area of rugged
land that generally
rises higher than
2,000 feet

VALLEY
an area of low
land between
hills or mountains

GLACIER
a large area of
slow-moving ice

VOLCANO
an opening in Earth's crust
where lava, ash, and gases erupt

CANYON
a deep, narrow valley
with steep walls

HILL
a rounded, elevated
area of land smaller
than a mountain

PLAIN
a nearly
flat area

DUNE
a hill of sand
shaped by wind

OASIS
an area in the
desert with a
water source

DESERT
an extremely dry area with
little water and few plants

PLATEAU
a large, flat,
elevated
area of land

The Five Themes of Geography

Geography is the study of the world's people and places. As you can imagine, studying the entire world is a big job. To make the job easier, geographers have created the Five Themes of Geography. They are: **Location, Place, Human-Environment Interaction, Movement,** and **Region**. You can think of the Five Themes as five windows you can look through to study a place. If you looked at the same place through five different windows, you would have five different perspectives, or viewpoints, of the place. Using the Five Themes in this way will help you better understand the world's people and places.

❶ **Location** The first thing to study about a place is its location. Where is it? Every place has an absolute location—its exact location on Earth. A place also has a relative location—its location in relation to other places. Use the theme of location to ask questions like, "Where is this place located, and how has its location affected it?"

❷ **Place** Every place in the world is unique and has its own personality and character. Some things that can make a place unique include its weather, plants and animals, history, and the people that live there. Use the theme of place to ask questions like, "What are the unique features of this place, and how are they important?"

❸ **Human-Environment Interaction** People interact with their environment in many ways. They use land to grow food and local materials to build houses. At the same time, a place's environment influences how people live. For example, if the weather is cold, people wear warm clothes. Use the theme of human-environment interaction to ask questions like, "What is this place's environment like, and how does it affect the people who live there?"

❹ **Movement** The world is constantly changing, and places are affected by the movement of people, goods, ideas, and physical forces. For example, people come and go, new businesses begin, and rivers change their course. Use the theme of movement to ask questions like, "How is this place changing, and why?"

❺ **Region** A region is an area that has one or more features that make it different from surrounding areas. A desert, a country, and a coastal area are all regions. Geographers use regions to break the world into smaller pieces that are easier to study. Use the theme of region to ask questions like "What common features does this area share, and how is it different from other areas?"

1 LOCATION

The United States is located in the Western Hemisphere. Forty-eight of the states are located between Mexico and Canada. This location has good farmland, many resources, and many different natural environments.

Canada

United States

Mexico

2 PLACE

New York City is one of the most powerful cities in the world. The people of New York also make the city one of the most ethnically diverse places in the world.

3 HUMAN-ENVIRONMENT INTERACTION

People near Las Vegas, Nevada, transform the desert landscape by building new neighborhoods. Americans modify their environment in many other ways—by controlling rivers, building roads, and creating farmland.

5 REGION

The United States is a political region with one government. At the same time, smaller regions can be found inside the country, such as the Badlands in South Dakota.

4 MOVEMENT

People, goods, and ideas are constantly moving to and from places such as Seattle, Washington. As some places grow, others get smaller, but every place is always changing.

How to Make This Book Work for You

Studying U.S. history will be easy for you using this textbook. Take a few minutes to become familiar with the easy-to-use structure and special features of this history book. See how this U.S. history textbook will make history come alive for you!

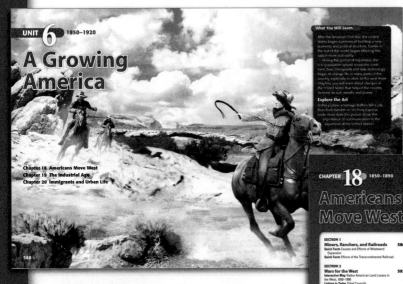

Unit

Each chapter of this textbook is part of a unit of study focusing on a particular time period. Each unit opener provides an illustration, painting, or photograph that gives you an overview of the exciting topics that you will study in the unit.

Chapter

Each chapter begins with a chapter-opener introduction where the sections of the chapter are listed out, and ends with Chapter Review pages and a Standardized Test Practice page.

Reading Social Studies These chapter-level reading lessons teach you skills and provide opportunities for practice to help you read the textbook more successfully. Within each chapter there is a point-of-reference *Focus on Reading* note in the margin to demonstrate the reading skill for the chapter. There are also questions in the Chapter Review activity to make sure that you understand the reading skill.

Social Studies Skills The Social Studies Skills lessons, which appear at the end of each chapter, give you an opportunity to learn and use a skill that you will most likely use again while in school. You will also be given a chance to make sure that you understand each skill by answering related questions in the Chapter Review activity.

Section

The Section opener pages include: Main Idea statements, an overarching Big Idea statement, and Key Terms and People. In addition, each section includes the following special features.

If You Were There . . . introductions begin each section with a situation for you to respond to, placing you in the time period and in a situation related to the content that you will be studying in the section.

Building Background sections connect what will be covered in this section with what you studied in the previous section.

Short sections of content organize the information in each section into small chunks of text that you should not find too overwhelming.

The **Taking Notes** feature allows you to write down the most important information from the section in a usable format.

SECTION 1

Miners, Ranchers, and Railroads

What You Will Learn...

Main Ideas

1. A mining boom brought growth to the West.
2. The demand for cattle created a short-lived Cattle Kingdom on the Great Plains.
3. East and West were connected by the transcontinental railroad.

The Big Idea

As more settlers moved West, mining, ranching, and railroads soon transformed the western landscape.

Key Terms

frontier, p. 586
Comstock Lode, p. 587
boomtowns, p. 588
Cattle Kingdom, p. 589
cattle drive, p. 589
Chisholm Trail, p. 589
Pony Express, p. 590
transcontinental railroad, p. 590

TAKING NOTES As you read the following section, take notes on the kinds of economic opportunities that people found in the West. Organize your notes in a table like the one below.

Opportunities in the West

If YOU were there...

You are a cowboy in Texas in 1875. You love life on the open range, the quiet nights, and the freedom. You even like the hard work of the long cattle drives to Kansas. But you know that times are changing. Homesteaders are moving in and fencing off their lands. Some of the older cowboys say it's time to settle down and buy a small ranch. You hope that they're not right.

What would make you give up a cowboy's life?

BUILDING BACKGROUND In the years following the Civil War, the U.S. population grew rapidly. Settlements in the West increased. More discoveries of gold and silver attracted adventurers, while the open range drew others. Thousands of former Civil War soldiers also joined the move West.

Mining Boom Brings Growth

During the years surrounding the War, most Americans had thought of the Great Plains and other western lands as the Great American Desert. In the years following the Civil War, Americans witnessed the rapid growth of the U.S. population and the spread of settlements throughout the West. With the admission of the state of California to the Union in 1850, the western boundary of the American **frontier**—an undeveloped area—had reached the Pacific Ocean.

The frontier changed dramatically as more and more people moved westward. Settlers built homes, fenced off land, and laid out ranches and farms. Miners, ranchers, and farmers remade the landscape of the West as they adapted to their new surroundings. The geography of the West was further changed by the development and expansion of a large and successful railroad industry that moved the West's natural resources to eastern markets. Gold and silver were the most valuable natural resources, and mining companies used the growing railroad network to bring these precious metals to the East.

Northwest Territory

Congress had to decide what to do with the western lands now under its control and how to raise money to pay debts. It tried to solve both problems by selling the western lands. Congress passed the **Land Ordinance of 1785**, which set up a system for surveying and dividing western lands. The land was split into townships, which were 36 square miles divided into 36 lots of 640 acres each. One lot was reserved for a public school, and four lots were given to veterans. The remaining lots were sold to the public.

To form a political system for the region, Congress passed the **Northwest Ordinance of 1787**. The ordinance established the **Northwest Territory**, which included areas that are now in Illinois, Indiana, Michigan, Ohio, Minnesota, and Wisconsin. The Northwest Ordinance created a system for bringing new states into the Union. Congress agreed that the Northwest Territory would be divided into several smaller territories with a

governor appointed by Congress. When the population of a territory reached 60,000, its settlers could draft their own constitution and ask to join the Union.

In addition, the law protected civil liberties and required that public education be provided. Finally, the ordinance stated that "there shall be neither slavery nor involuntary servitude [forced labor] in the . . . territory." This last condition banned slavery in the Territory and set the standard for future territories. However, slavery would continue to be a controversial issue.

READING CHECK Analyzing Information
How did the Northwest Ordinance of 1787 affect the United States?

SUMMARY AND PREVIEW The Northwest Ordinance settled the future of the Northwest Territory. In the next section you will read about other challenges the new government faced.

FOCUS ON INDIANA
When Ohio became the first state admitted from the Northwest Territory, the remaining area was renamed the Indiana Territory. Governor William Henry Harrison attempted to suspend the antislavery laws for the territory, but Congress would not allow it.

THE IMPACT TODAY
Townships remained the unit of local government after the Northwest Territory was divided into states. Many of these townships still exist today.

Focus on Indiana features cover events from Indiana history or point out how information on the page relates to the Indiana Social Studies.

Reading Check questions end each section of content so that you can test whether or not you understand what you have just studied.

Summary and Preview statements connect what you have just studied in the section to what you will study in the next section.

Section Assessment boxes provide an opportunity for you to make sure that you understand the main ideas of the section. We also provide assessment practice online!

Section 1 Assessment

go.hrw.com
Online Quiz
KEYWORD: SF7 HP5

Reviewing Ideas, Terms, and People

1. **a. Identify** What documents influenced ideas about government in the United States?
   b. Draw Conclusions What impact did the **Virginia Statute for Religious Freedom** have on the U.S. government?
   c. Elaborate Why is the separation of government powers a requirement for a society to be free?
2. **a. Identify** What was the **Articles of Confederation**?
   b. Summarize What powers were granted to Congress by the Articles of Confederation?
   c. Predict What are some possible problems that might result from the lack of a national court system?
3. **a. Describe** How were public lands in the West divided by the **Land Ordinance of 1785**?
   b. Evaluate In your opinion, what was the most important element of the **Northwest Ordinance of 1787**? Why?
   c. Elaborate What does the assignment of township lots reveal about values of Americans at this time?

Critical Thinking

4. **Categorizing** Review your notes on the Articles of Confederation. Copy the chart below and use it to show the strengths and weaknesses of the new government.

Articles of Confederation	
Strengths	Weaknesses

FOCUS ON WRITING

5. **Thinking about the Articles of Confederation** Make a list of powers the Articles of Confederation gave the national government. Which ones seem strong? Can you think of any important powers that are missing?

FORMING A GOVERNMENT **155**

Indiana

Indiana Academic Standards

What are the Indiana Academic Standards?

Academic Standards are simply the things you are expected to know, understand, and be able to do as a result of your education. In Indiana, the Academic Standards are organized by subject matter and subdivided into more specific ideas called Performance Indicators. So the Academic Standards and Performance Indicators for your United States history course focus on the knowledge and skills you will need to gain in this class.

In this section you will find the social studies standards and performance indicators that have been approved by the Indiana Board of Education. You will probably notice that some of the subjects in the standards are familiar to you. This course is meant to build on the skills and knowledge you already have. It will also help build a foundation for the more advanced studies you will begin in high school.

How can the Indiana Academic Standards and Performance Indicators help me?

These standards and indicators are helpful because they give you a clear picture of what you will be expected to learn. This can help you to focus on key material. You can think of the stan-dards as a kind of checklist of important subjects and skills. Another advantage of becoming familiar with the standards is that teachers often base lesson plans and tests on these standards. That means that the standards can give you a preview of what to expect in this course.

United States History – Growth and Development
In Grade 8, students focus upon United States history, beginning with a brief review of early history, including the Revolution and founding era, and the principles of the United States and Indiana constitutions, as well as other founding documents and their applications to subsequent periods of national history and to civic and political life. Students then study national development, westward expansion, social reform movements, and the Civil War and Reconstruction.

The Indiana's K – 8 academic standards for social studies are organized around four content areas. The content area standards and the types of learning experiences they provide to students in Kindergarten are described below. On the pages that follow, age-appropriate concepts are listed underneath each standard. Skills for thinking, inquiry, and participation in a democratic society including the examination of individuals, society, and culture are integrated throughout. Specific terms are defined and examples are provided when necessary.

La Porte

Standard 1 — History

Students will examine the relationship and significance of themes, concepts, and movements in the development of United States history, including review of key ideas related to the colonization of America and the revolution and founding era. This will be followed by emphasis on social reform, national development and westward expansion, and the Civil War and Reconstruction period.

Standard 2 — Civics and Government

Students will explain the major principles, values, and institutions of constitutional government and citizenship, which are based on the founding documents of the United States and how three branches of government share and check power within our federal system of government.

Standard 3 — Geography

Students will identify the major geographic characteristics of the United States and its regions. They will name and locate the major physical features of the United States, each of the states, and major cities, and use geographic skills and technology to examine the influence of geographic factors on national development.

Standard 4 — Economics

Students will identify, describe, and evaluate the influence of economic factors on national development from the founding of the nation to the end of Reconstruction.

Suspension bridge, Columbus

 # Standard 1

History Students will examine the relationship and significance of themes, concepts, and movements in the development of United States history, including review of key ideas related to the colonization of America and the revolution and founding era. This will be followed by emphasis on social reform, national development and westward expansion, and the Civil War and Reconstruction period.

Historical Knowledge
The American Revolution and Founding of the United States: 1754 to 1801

8.1.1 Identify major Native American Indian groups of eastern North America and describe early conflict and cooperation with European settlers and the influence the two cultures had on each other. **(Individuals, Society, and Culture)**

Example: Mohawk, Iroquois, Huron, and Ottawa; French and Native American Indian alliances; French and Indian War; British alliances with Native American Indians; settler encroachment on Native American Indian lands; Native American Indian participation in the Revolutionary War.

8.1.2 Explain the struggle of the British, French, Spanish, and Dutch to gain control of North America during settlement and colonization.

8.1.3 Identify and explain the conditions, causes, consequences, and significance of the French and Indian War (1754 – 1763), and the resistance and rebellion against British imperial rule by the thirteen colonies in North America (1761 – 1775).

8.1.4 Identify fundamental ideas in the Declaration of Independence (1776) and analyze the causes and effects of the Revolutionary War (1775 – 1783), including enactment of the Articles of Confederation and the Treaty of Paris.

8.1.5 Describe the development of sub-Saharan civilizations in Africa, including the kingdoms of Ghana, Mali, and Songhai, and the importance of political and trading centers, such as Timbuktu.

Example: The enactment of state constitutions, the Constitutional Conventions, ratifying conventions of the American states, and debate by Federalists versus Anti-Federalists regarding approval or disapproval of the 1787 Constitution (1787 – 1788).

8.1.6 Identify the steps in the implementation of the federal government under the United States Constitution, including the First and Second Congresses of the United States (1789 – 1792).

8.1.7 Describe the origin and development of political parties, the Federalists and the Democratic - Republicans, (1793 – 1801) and examine points of agreement and disagreement between these parties.

8.1.8 Evaluate the significance of the presidential and congressional election of 1800 and the transfer of political authority and power to the Democratic – Republican Party led by the new president, Thomas Jefferson (1801).

8.1.9 Describe the influence of important individuals on social and political developments of the time such as the Independence movement and the framing of the Constitution. (Individuals, Society, and Culture)

Example: James Otis, Mercy Otis Warren, Samuel Adams, Thomas Paine, George Washington, John Adams, Abigail Adams, Patrick Henry, Thomas Jefferson, James Madison, Alexander Hamilton, and Benjamin Banneker.

8.1.10 Compare differences in ways of life in the northern and southern states, including the growth of towns and cities in the North and the growing dependence on slavery in the South. (Individuals, Society, and Culture)

National Expansion and Reform: 1801 to 1861

8.1.11 Explain the events leading up to and the significance of the Louisiana Purchase (1803) and the expedition of Lewis and Clark (1803–1806).

Example: Feudalism, shogunate, court life.

8.1.12 Describe worldwide voyages of exploration and discovery.

Example: Marbury v. Madison (1803), McCulloch v. Maryland (1819), and Gibbons v. Ogden (1824).

8.1.13 Explain the causes and consequences of the War of 1812, including the Rush-Bagot Agreement (1818).

8.1.14 Examine the international problem that led to the Monroe Doctrine (1823) and assess its consequences.

8.1.15 Explain the concept of Manifest Destiny and describe its impact on westward expansion of the United States. (Individuals, Society, and Culture)

Example: Louisiana Purchase (1803), purchase of Florida (1819), Mexican War and the annexation of Texas (1845), acquisition of Oregon Territory (1846), Native American Indian conflicts and removal, California gold rush.

8.1.16 Describe the abolition of slavery in the northern states; conflict and compromises associated with westward expansion of slavery, such as the Missouri Compromise (1820), The Compromise of 1850, Kansas-Nebraska Act (1854); and the continued resistance to slavery by people such as Frederick Douglas, Harriet Tubman, William Lloyd Garrison, and Harriet Beecher Stowe.

8.1.17 Identify the key ideas of Jacksonian democracy and explain their influence on political participation, political parties, and constitutional government.

8.1.18 Analyze different interests and points of view of individuals and groups involved in the abolitionist, feminist and social reform movements, and in sectional conflicts. (Individuals, Society, and Culture)

Example: Jacksonian Democrats, John Brown, Nat Turner, Sojourner Truth, and the Seneca Falls Convention.

8.1.19 Explain the influence of early individual social reformers and movements. (Individuals, Society, and Culture)

Example: Elizabeth Cady Stanton, Horace Mann, Dorothea Dix, Lucretia Mott, Robert Owen, abolition movement, temperance movement, utopian movements.

The Civil War and Reconstruction Period: 1850 to 1877

8.1.20 Analyze the causes and effects of events leading to the Civil War, including development of sectional conflict over slavery.

Example: The Compromise of 1850, furor over publication of Uncle Tom's Cabin (1852), Kansas-Nebraska Act (1854), the Dred Scott Case (1857), the Lincoln-Douglas Debates (1858), and the presidential election of 1860.

8.1.21 Describe the importance of key events and individuals in the Civil War

Example: The battles of Manassas, Antietam, Vicksburg, and Gettysburg, and the Emancipation Proclamation and Gettysburg Address (1861–1865); Jefferson Davis, Stephen A. Douglas, Abraham Lincoln, Robert E. Lee, Ulysses S. Grant, William T. Sherman, Thaddeus Stevens.

8.1.22 Explain and evaluate the policies, practices, and consequences of Reconstruction, including the Thirteenth, Fourteenth, and Fifteenth Amendments to the Constitution.

8.1.23 Describe the conflicts between Native American Indians and settlers of the Great Plains. (Individuals, Society, and Culture)

8.1.24 Identify the influence of individuals on political and social events and movements such as the abolition movement, the Dred Scott case, women rights, and Native American Indian removal. (Individuals, Society, and Culture)

Example: Henry Clay, Harriet Tubman, Harriet Beecher Stowe, Henry Ward Beecher, Roger Taney, Frederick Douglass, John Brown, Clara Barton, Andrew Johnson, Susan B. Anthony, Sitting Bull, Ralph Waldo Emerson, Henry David Thoreau.

8.1.25 Give examples of how immigration affected American culture in the decades before and after the Civil War, including growth of industrialism in the North; religious differences; tensions between middle-class and working-class people, particularly in the Northeast; and intensification of cultural differences between the North and the South. (Individuals, Society, and Culture)

8.1.26 Give examples of the changing role of women and minorities in the northern, southern, and western parts of the United States in the mid-nineteenth century, and examine possible causes for these changes. (Individuals, Society, and Culture)

8.1.27 Give examples of scientific and technological developments that changed cultural life in the nineteenth-century United States, such as the use of photography, growth in the use of the telegraph, the completion of the transcontinental railroad, and the invention of the telephone. (Individuals, Society, and Culture)

Chronological Thinking, Historical Comprehension, Analysis and Interpretation, Research, and Issues-Analysis and Decision-Making

8.1.28 Recognize historical perspective and evaluate alternative courses of action by describing the historical context in which events unfolded and by avoiding evaluation of the past solely in terms of present-day norms.)

Example: Use Internet-based documents and digital archival collections from museums and libraries to compare views of slavery in slave narratives, northern and southern newspapers, and present day accounts of the era.

8.1.29 Differentiate between facts and historical interpretations recognizing that the historian's narrative reflects his or her judgment about the significance of particular facts.

8.1.30 Formulate historical questions by analyzing primary sources* and secondary sources* about an issue confronting the United States during the period from 1754 – 1877.

Example: Analyze and interpret the Virginia Statute for Religious Freedom (1786), President George Washington's Farewell Address (1796), the First Inaugural Address by Thomas Jefferson (1801), the Declaration of Sentiments and Resolutions of the Seneca Falls Convention (1848), and the Second Inaugural Address by Abraham Lincoln (1865).

8.1.31 Obtain historical data from a variety of sources to compare and contrast examples of art, music, and literature during the nineteenth century and explain how these reflect American culture during this time period. (Individuals, Society, and Culture)

Example: Art: John James Audubon, Winslow Homer, Hudson River School, Edward Bannister, Edmonia Lewis, Henry Ossawa Tanner; Writers: Louisa May Alcott, Washington Irving, James Fennimore Cooper, Walt Whitman, Frederick Douglass, Paul Dunbar, George Caleb Bingham.

* information resources: print media, such as books, magazines, and newspapers; electronic media, such as radio, television, Web sites, and databases; and community resources, such as individuals and organizations

* primary source: developed by people who experienced the events being studied (i.e., autobiographies, diaries, letters, government documents)

* secondary source: developed by people who have researched events but did not experience them directly (i.e., articles, biographies, Internet sources, nonfiction books)

Standard 2

Civics and Government Students will explain the major principles, values, and institutions of constitutional government and citizenship, which are based on the founding documents of the United States and how three branches of government share and check power within our federal system of government.

Foundations of Government

8.2.1 Identify and explain essential ideas of constitutional government, which are expressed in the founding documents of the United States, including the Virginia Declaration of Rights, the Declaration of Independence, the Virginia Statute for Religious Freedom, the Massachusetts Constitution of 1780, the Northwest Ordinance, the 1787 U.S. Constitution, the Bill of Rights, the Federalist and Anti-Federalist Papers, *Common Sense*, Washington's Farewell Address (1796), and Jefferson's First Inaugural Address (1801).

Example: The essential ideas include limited government, rule of law, due process of law, separated and shared powers, checks and balances, federalism, popular sovereignty, republicanism, representative government, and individual rights to life, liberty, property, and freedom of conscience.

8.2.2 Identify and explain the relationship between rights and responsibilities of citizenship in the United States.

Example: The right to vote and the responsibility to use this right carefully and effectively. The right to free speech and the responsibility not to say or write false statements.

8.2.3 Explain how and why legislative, executive, and judicial powers are distributed, shared, and limited in the constitutional government of the United States.

Example: Examine key Supreme Court cases and describe the role each branch of the government played in each of these cases.

8.2.4 Examine functions of the national government in the lives of people.

Example: Purchasing and distributing public goods and services, coining money, financing government through taxation, conducting foreign policy, providing a common defense, and regulating commerce.

Functions of Government

8.2.5 Compare, and contrast the powers reserved to the federal and state government under the Articles of Confederation and the United States Constitution.

8.2.6 Distinguish among the different functions of national and state government within the federal system by analyzing the United States Constitution and the Indiana Constitution.

Example: Identify important services provided by state government, such as maintaining state roads and highways, enforcing health and safety laws, and supporting educational institutions. Compare these services to functions of the federal government, such as defense and foreign policy.

Roles of Citizens

8.2.7 Explain the importance in a democratic republic of responsible participation by citizens in voluntary civil associations/nongovernmental organizations that comprise civil society.
Example: Reform movements such as the abolitionist movement, women's suffrage, the Freedman's Bureau.

8.2.8 Explain ways that citizens can participate in political parties, campaigns, and elections.
Example: Local, state, and national elections; referendums; poll work; campaign committees; voting.

8.2.9 Explain how citizens can monitor and influence the development and implementation of public policies at local, state, and national levels of government.
Example: Joining action groups, holding leaders accountable through the electoral process, attending town meetings, staying informed by reading newspapers and Web sites, watching television news broadcasts.

8.2.10 Research and defend positions on issues in which fundamental values and principles related to the United States Constitution are in conflict, using a variety of information resources*.
Example: Powers of federal vs. powers of state government.

* information resources: print media, such as books, magazines, and newspapers; electronic media, such as radio, television, Web sites, and databases; and community resources, such as individuals and organizations

Standard 3

Geography Students will identify the major geographic characteristics of the United States and its regions. They will name and locate the major physical features of the United States, each of the states, and major cities, and use geographic skills and technology to examine the influence of geographic factors on national development.

The World in Spatial Terms

8.3.1 Read maps to interpret symbols and determine the land forms and human features that represent physical and cultural characteristics* of areas in the United States.
* cultural characteristics: human features, such as population characteristics, communication and transportation networks, religion and customs, and how people make a living or build homes and other structures

Indianapolis at night

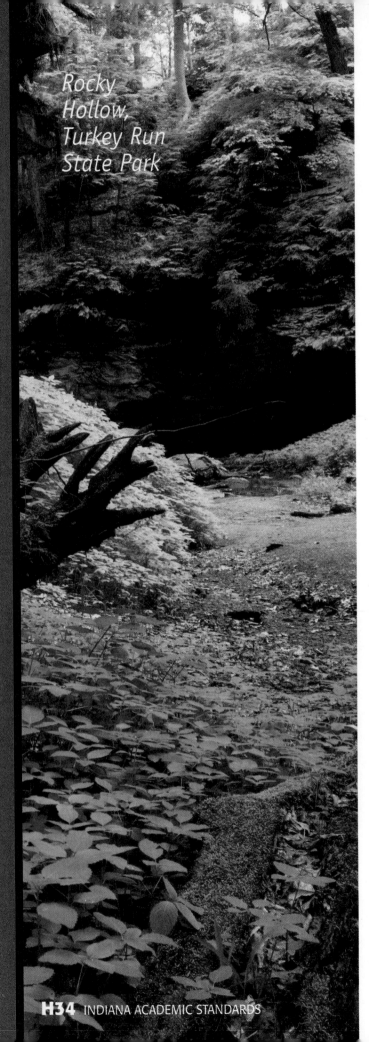

Rocky Hollow, Turkey Run State Park

Places and Regions

8.3.2 Identify and create maps showing the physical growth and development of the United States from settlement of the original thirteen colonies through Reconstruction (1877) including transportation routes used during the period.

Physical Systems

8.3.3 Identify and locate the major climate regions in the United States and describe the characteristics of these regions.

8.3.4 Name and describe processes that build* up the land and processes that erode* it and identify places these occur.

Example: The Appalachian Mountains are a formation that has undergone erosion. The Mississippi Delta is made up almost entirely of eroded material.

8.3.5 Describe the importance of the major mountain ranges and the major river systems in the development of the United States.

Example: Locate major U.S. cities during this time period such as Washington D.C., New York, Boston, Atlanta, Nashville, Charleston, New Orleans, Philadelphia, and Saint Louis and suggest reasons for their location and development.

* building: forces that build up Earth's surface include mountain building and deposit of dirt by water, ice, and wind

* erosion: the process by which the products of weathering* are moved from one place to another

* weathering: the breaking down of rocks and other materials on Earth's surface by such processes as rain or wind

Human Systems

8.3.6 Identify the agricultural regions of the United States and be able to give reasons for the type of land use and subsequent land development during different historical periods.

Example: Cattle industry in the West, cotton industry in the South.

8.3.7 Give examples and describe the formation of important river deltas, mountains, and bodies of water in Africa, Asia, and the Southwest Pacific.

Example: Westward expansion, impact of slavery, Lewis and Clark exploration, new states added to the union, Spanish settlement in California and Texas.

8.3.8 Gather information on ways people changed the physical environment of the United States in the nineteenth century using primary sources* and secondary sources* including digitized photo collections and historic maps.

8.3.9 Analyze human and physical factors that have influenced migration and settlement patterns and relate them to the economic development of the United States.

Example: Growth of communities due to the development of the railroad, development of the west coast due to ocean ports and discovery of important mineral resources, presence of a major waterway influences economic development and the workers who are attracted to that development.

* primary source: developed by people who experienced the events being studied (i.e., autobiographies, diaries, letters, governmental documents)

* secondary source: developed by people who have researched events but did not experience them directly (i.e., articles, biographies, Internet resources, nonfiction books)

Environment and Society

8.3.10 Create maps, graphs, and charts showing the distribution of natural resources — such as forests, water sources, and wildlife — in the United States at the beginning of the nineteenth century and give examples of how people exploited these resources as the country became more industrialized and people moved westward.

8.3.11 Identify ways people modified the physical environment as the United States developed and describe the impacts that resulted.

Examples: Identify urbanization*, deforestation*, and extinction* or near extinction of wildlife species; development of roads and canals.

* urbanization: a process in which there is an increase in the percentage of people living/working in urban places as compared to rural places.

* deforestation: the clearing of trees or forests

* extinction: the state in which all members of a group of organisms, such as a species, population, family or class, have disappeared from a given habitat, geographic area, or the entire world

[IN] Standard 4

Economics Students will identify, describe, and evaluate the influence of economic factors on national development from the founding of the nation to the end of Reconstruction.

8.4.1 Identify economic factors contributing to European exploration and colonization in North America, the American Revolution, and the drafting of the Constitution of the United States.

Example: The search for gold by the Spanish, French fur trade, taxation without representation.

8.4.2 Identify economic connections between the local community and the countries of Africa, Asia, or the Southwest Pacific.

8.4.3 Evaluate how the characteristics of a market economy have affected the economic and labor development of the United States.

Example: Characteristics include the role of entrepreneurs, private property, markets, competition, and self-interest.

8.4.4 Trace the development and change over time of the economic systems of various cultures, societies, or nations in Africa, Asia, and the Southwest Pacific. (Individuals, Society, and Culture)

Example: How trading networks grew into regional trading centers such as Timbuktu, Zimbabwe, Canton, and Hong Kong.

8.4.5 Explain how banks and other financial institutions use savings deposits to help borrowers and investors.

8.4.6 Compare and contrast the standard of living of various countries in Africa, Asia, and the Southwest Pacific using Gross Domestic Product (GDP)* per capita as an indicator.

8.4.7 Describe ways that people can increase individual human capital*.

Example: Acquiring knowledge and skills through education or training.

8.4.8 Identify ways that societies deal with helpful "spillovers*" (e.g. education) or harmful "spillovers" (e.g. pollution).

Example: Government support of public education, governments taxing or regulating pollution.

8.4.9 Explain how saving and investing help increase productivity and economic growth and examine how individual savings can grow through regular saving and the power of compound interest.

Example: Triangular trade routes, regional exchange of resources.

8.4.10 Examine the importance of borrowing and lending (the use of credit) in the United States economy and list the advantages and disadvantages of using credit.

8.4.11 Use a variety of information resources* to compare and contrast job skills needed in different time periods in United States history.

* economic systems: the ways that people allocate economic resources, goods, and services

* traditional economy: an economy in which resources are allocated based on custom and tradition

* command economy: an economy in which resources are allocated by the government or other central authority

* market economy: an economy in which resources are allocated by individuals and businesses responding to changes in prices

* mixed economy: an economy in which resources are allocated by some combination of traditional, command, or market systems

* Gross Domestic Product (GDP): the value of all goods and services produced in a country in a year

* human capital: the skills and expertise people acquire from education and training

* spillover: the impact of an activity (positive or negative) on the well-being of a third party

Multiple Choice

A multiple-choice test item is a question or an incomplete statement with several answer choices. To answer a multiple-choice test item, select the choice that best answers the question or that best completes the statement.

Learn

Use these strategies to answer multiple-choice test items:

1 Carefully read the question or incomplete statement.

2 Look for words that affect the meaning, such as *all, always, best, every, most, never, not,* or *only.* For example, in Item 1 to the right, the word *all* tells you to look for the answer in which all three choices are correct.

3 Read *all* the choices before selecting an answer—even if the first choice seems right.

4 In your mind, cross off any of the answer choices that you know for certain are wrong.

5 Consider the choices that are left and select the *best* answer. If you are not sure, select the choice that makes the most sense.

Read the questions and write the letter of the best response.

1 Which of the following are *all* physical features of geography?

A landforms, climates, people
B landforms, climates, soils
C landscapes, climates, plants
D landscapes, communities, soils

2 A region is an area that has

A one or more common features.
B ~~no people living in it.~~
C few physical features.
D set physical boundaries.

Practice

Read the questions and write the letter of the best response.

1 Which is one reason a weak central government was created by the Articles of Confederation?

A Many Americans were suspicious of distant power.

B It made it easier to collect revenue from the states.

C Foreign countries wanted to negotiate with individual states.

D It contributed to the country's economic stability.

2 During the Civil War the Union's main goal switched from reuniting the country to ending slavery. Which event best reflects that change?

A the Union's victory at the Battle of Gettysburg

B the Union's defeat at the First Battle of Bull Run.

C the issuance of the Emancipation Proclamation.

D the assassination of President Abraham Lincoln.

3 During the 1820s the Democratic Party under the leadership of Andrew Jackson dominated American politics. Which change helped shape a national identity based on political equality during this era?

A the elimination of voting and office holding restrictions

B the establishment of an official state religion

C allowing slavery to spread to all parts of the country

D encouraging American Indians to settle near white Americans

4 Ordinary citizens are most involved in the decision making process of which form of government?

A dictatorship

B direct democracy

C representative democracy

D monarchy

5 Many Americans settled in Northwest Territory because its physical geography made it an ideal place for which economic activity?

A mining

B plantation agriculture

C family farming

D manufacturing

6 Which social reformer helped write one of the founding documents of the women's rights movement?

A Frederick Douglass

B John Brown

C Elizabeth Cady Stanton

D Sojourner Truth

7 Where did the U.S. ranching industry start?

A the grasslands of west Texas

B the Great Basin of Utah

C the Pacific Northwest's rain forests

D the Rocky Mountains

8 Which describes a military aspect of the American Revolution?

A The Americans won the war by repeatedly engaging in direct attacks on the British.

B The battles started in New England and moved to the South by the end of the war.

C The Americans won the war with the help of hired Hessian troops.

D The British signed an alliance with France but it was too late to help them win.

9 Which of the following contributed to the ratification of the U.S. Constitution?

A start of the War of 1812

B petitions introduced by the Sons of Liberty

C compromise concerning a national bank

D publication of the Federalist Papers

10 Which statement best describes the Reconstruction era after the Civil War?

A The federal government gave all freedmen forty acres of land

B The South temporarily had a political system that blacks could participate in.

C Southern whites passed laws protecting freedmen's political rights.

D Sharecropping was outlawed by the federal government.

Primary Sources

Primary sources are materials, often called documents, created by people who lived during the times you are reading about. Examples of primary sources include text documents, such as letters and diaries, and visual documents, such as photographs.

Learn

Use these strategies to answer test questions about primary sources:

❶ Note the document's title and source line. This information can tell you the document's author, date, and purpose.

❷ Skim the document. Get an idea of its main focus.

❸ Read the question about the document. Note what information you are being asked to find.

❹ Read or examine the document carefully. As you do, identify the main idea and key details.

❺ Compare the question and answer choices to the document. Look for similar words. Then read between the lines. Use your critical-thinking skills to draw conclusions.

❻ Review the question and select the best answer.

Read the passage below. Use the passage to select the best answer to the question that follows.

Geography for Life

"Geography is a field of study that enables us to find answers to questions about the world around us—about where things are and how and why they got there…With a strong grasp of geography, people are better equipped to solve issues at not only the local level but also the global level."

— from *Geography for Life*, by the Geography Education Standards Project

1 Which statement below *best* summarizes the main idea of the above passage?

A Geography helps people to read and make maps.

B Geography helps people to get where they are going.

C Geography helps people to understand the world better and to solve problems.

D Geography helps people explore Earth.

Practice

Read the passage from the primary source, "The Charter of the United Nations," in Chapter 4. Use the passage to answer the following questions.

1 What does the passage state is a central goal of the United Nations?

A democracy

B peace

C power

D war

2 Based on the passage, why might the UN send troops into a region?

A to punish a country

B to conquer a country

C to obtain valuable resources

D to protect a member country

The Travels of Marco Polo
"...[T]he Great Khan hath distributed the territory of Manzi [China]...into nine kingdoms. To each of these kingdoms a king is appointed who...every year renders [gives] the [tax] accounts of his kingdom to the fiscal [financial] office at the capital..."
—from *The Travels of Marco Polo* 1300 A.D.

1 Which event made the writing of this European traveler's description possible?

A outbreak of the Black Death

B opening of the Silk Road

C fall of the Roman Empire

D founding of the African slave trade

Common Sense
"To the evil of monarchy we have added that of hereditary succession... For all men being originally equals, no one by birth could have a right to set up his own family in perpetual preference to all others for ever, and though himself might deserve some decent degree of honors... his descendants might be far too unworthy to inherit them."
—*Common Sense; of Monarchy and Hereditary Succession*

2 The quote describes which group's attitude toward King George III just prior to the signing of the Declaration of Independence?

A Loyalists

B neutral colonists

C Patriots

D British officials

"Slaves often escaped by borrowing papers from a friend...Among...[my] friends was a sailor...[with papers.]...This was borrowed; sailor's clothes were purchased, and on Monday morning, [I]...jumped on the train...The flight was a bold and perilous one; but here I am, in the great city of New York...A free state around me, and a free earth under my feet! What a moment was this to me!" — Frederick Douglass

3 This excerpt is typical of the writings which led some Americans to join which social movement?

A abolitionism

B temperance

C women's rights

D Second Great Awakening

4 The excerpt is from an 1830 U.S. Senate debate.

"The gentleman asserts that the Creeks are... [an] independent nation, by treaties made, first with Georgia, and lastly with the United States... I will ask...[him to look at] the treaty of Galphinton...:

"Article 1. The said Indians...within the limits of the State of Georgia, have been, and now are, ...[citizens of Georgia]..."
—21 Congress 1 Session: Volume 6, Part 1, Columns 325-39 [Senate, April 15, 1830]

Why, according to the excerpt, were the Creeks not an independent nation?

A Only the United States can negotiate and sign treaties.

B Only states can be sovereign.

C The Creeks had signed a treaty.

D The Creeks had repeatedly attacked white settlers.

Charts and Graphs

Charts and graphs are tables or drawings that present and organize information or data. Some standardized tests include questions about charts and graphs. These questions require you to interpret the information or data in the chart or graph to answer the question.

Learn

Use these strategies to answer test questions about charts and graphs:

❶ Read the title of the chart or graph. Identify the subject and purpose of the information shown.

❷ Read all the other labels. Note the types of information the chart or graph is showing and how the information is organized.

❸ Analyze the information or data. Look for patterns, changes over time, and similarities or differences. For example, in the graph at right, world population growth rises dramatically after 1900.

❹ Read the question carefully. Note key words in the question.

❺ Review the chart or graph to find the correct answer.

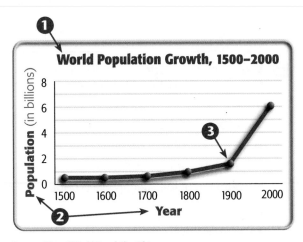

Source: *Atlas of World Population History*

1 Based on the graph above, during which period did the world population <u>increase</u> the <u>most</u>?

A 1600 to 1700
B 1700 to 1800
C 1800 to 1900
D 1900 to 2000

Practice

Examine the chart at right. Use the chart to answer the question below.

1 Which of the following statements accurately describes a difference between direct democracies and republics?

A Citizens vote on important issues in republics.

B Citizens vote for representatives in direct democracies.

C Citizens are not allowed to vote in republics.

D Citizens vote for representatives in a republic.

Democracy and Republic — QUICK FACTS

Direct democracies and republics are similar forms of government in which the people rule. There are some slight differences, though.

Direct Democracy	Republic
• Every citizen votes on every issue. • Ideas are debated at an assembly of all citizens.	• Citizens elect representatives to vote on issues. • Ideas are debated at an assembly of representatives.

2 Approximately how many slaves were in the English colonies in 1750

- **A** none
- **B** 240,000
- **C** 240
- **D** 50,000

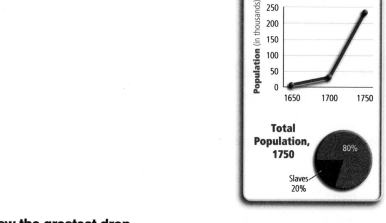

**Slave Populations
in the Colonies**

**Total
Population,
1750**

80%

Slaves
20%

3 Which period saw the greatest drop in upstream river shipping rates?

- **A** 1800 to 1810
- **B** 1810 to 1820
- **C** 1820 to 1830
- **D** 1805 to 1810

Upstream River Rates

4 Which group of immigrants saw the most dramatic increase between 1860 and 1900?

- **A** northern and western European
- **B** eastern and southern European
- **C** North and South American
- **D** Asian

**Shifting Patterns
of Immigration**

Where
Immigrants
Came
From,
1840–1860   1%
1%
2%
3%

Where
Immigrants
Came
From,
1880–1900   .5%
1.5%
6%

- ■ Northern and western Europe
- ■ Eastern and southern Europe
- ■ North and South America
- ■ Asia
- ■ All other areas

Maps

Standardized tests may include questions that refer to information in maps. These maps might show political features such as cities and states, physical features such as mountains and plains, or information such as climate, land use, or settlement patterns.

Learn

Use these strategies to answer questions about maps.

1 Read the map title to identify the map's subject and purpose. The map below shows levels of government freedom around the world.

2 Study the legend. It explains information in the map, such as what different colors or symbols mean.

3 Note the map's direction and scale. The scale shows the distance between points in the map.

4 Examine the map closely. Read all the labels and study the other information, such as colors, borders, or symbols.

5 Read the question about the map.

6 Review the map to find the answer.

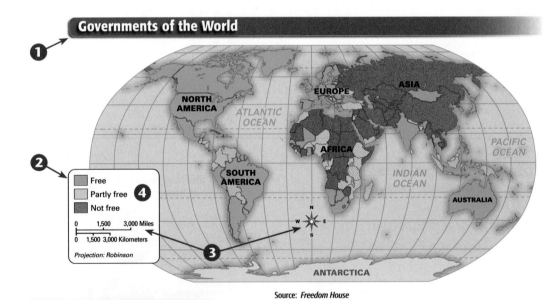

Source: *Freedom House*

Practice

Examine the map above. Use the information in the map to answer the following questions.

1 Which two continents have the least government freedom?

  A Africa and Asia

  B Africa and Europe

  C Australia and Europe

  D Europe and Asia

2 The continents with the most freedom are Australia and

  A Africa.

  B Europe.

  C North America.

  D South America.

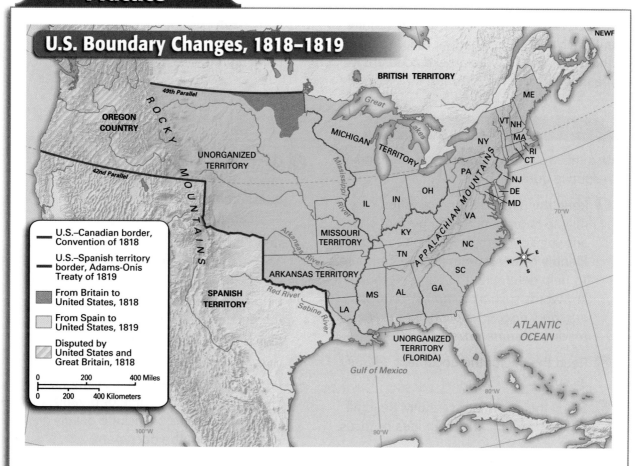

U.S. Boundary Changes, 1818–1819

Legend:
- U.S.–Canadian border, Convention of 1818
- U.S.–Spanish territory border, Adams-Onís Treaty of 1819
- From Britain to United States, 1818
- From Spain to United States, 1819
- Disputed by United States and Great Britain, 1818

0   200   400 Miles
0   200   400 Kilometers

3 According to the map, when was the 49th Parallel chosen as a boundary between the United States and British territory?

A 1817

B 1818

C 1819

D 1820

4 According to the map, which country ceded Florida to the United States in 1819?

A Canada

B Great Britain

C Russia

D Spain

Extended Response

Extended response questions usually require you to examine a document, such as a letter, chart, or map. You then use the information in the document to write an extended answer, often a paragraph or more in length.

Learn

Use these strategies to answer extended response questions:

1 Read the directions and question carefully to determine the purpose of your answer. For example, are you to explain, identify causes, summarize, or compare? To help determine the purpose, look for key words such as *compare, contrast, describe, discuss, explain, interpret, predict,* or *summarize.*

2 Read the title of the document. Identify its subject and purpose.

3 Study the document carefully. Read all the text. Identify the main idea or focus.

4 If allowed, make notes on another sheet of paper to organize your thoughts. Jot down information from the document that you want to include in your answer.

5 Use the question to create a topic sentence. For example, for the practice question below, a topic sentence might be, "Earth's tilt and revolution cause the seasons to change at about the same time each year in the Northern Hemisphere."

6 Create an outline or graphic organizer to help organize your main points. Review the document to find details or examples to support each point.

7 Write your answer in complete sentences. Start with your topic sentence. Then refer to your outline or organizer as you write. Be sure to include details or examples from the document.

8 Last, proofread your answer. Check for correct grammar, spelling, punctuation, and sentence structure.

Practice

Read question 1 and write your own well-constructed extended response.

1 **Extended Response** Britain's North American colonies relied on overseas trade. Describe the natural resources available in New England and Virginia during the colonial era and explain how those resources shaped each region's role in international trade.

_____

_____

_____

_____

_____

2 What is Manifest Destiny and how did it contribute to the political tensions that led to the Civil War?

_____

_____

_____

_____

_____

3 Classical Greek civilization developed a new system of government. Identify and describe that system of government and explain its long term political impact.

_____

_____

_____

_____

_____

4 Identify the civilizations which came into conflict during the Crusades and explain how the conflict was over territory that was culturally important to both civilizations.

_____

_____

_____

_____

_____

5 What was Shays's Rebellion and how did it contribute to the effort to revise the Articles of Confederation?

_____

_____

_____

_____

_____

6 Identify the issue that divided the Federalists and Anti-Federalists during the ratification debate over U.S. Constitution and explain how adding the Bill of Rights helped resolve the issue.

_____

_____

_____

_____

_____

Essays

Essay questions ask you to describe or discuss a topic based on your knowledge of the topic. Answers to essay questions should include a well-organized and well-written display of your knowledge.

Learn

Use these strategies to answer extended response questions:

❶ Read the directions and question carefully to determine the structure of your essay answer. What knowledge are you being asked to write about? Is it a cause-and-effect relationship, a description of an event or idea, or perhaps your own opinion on a subject?

❷ Make short notes about what you want to say in your essay. Write down important ideas, people, or events that you know should be included in your essay.

❸ Organize the information that you want to include in your essay in a way that explains the answer to the question being asked.

❹ In your introductory paragraph or sentence, use your own word to restate the question that you will be answering. This

helps the reader of your essay determine what information you will be providing in your essay.

❺ In the body of your essay, use specific facts to support your answer. Offer the reader of your essay proof that your answer is correct.

❻ In the last paragraph or sentence of your essay, restate in clear terms your answer to the question.

❼ Be sure to write your answer in complete sentences and use correct punctuation.

❽ Finally, proofread your answer and check for correct grammar, spelling, punctuation, and sentence structure.

Practice

Read the questions and write your own well-constructed essay answers.

1 Describe how the U.S. Constitution protects the rights of U.S. citizens. Include two examples

_____
_____
_____
_____
_____

2 Discuss the causes and effects of the westward expansion of the United States.

_____
_____
_____
_____
_____

Test-Taking Tips

1 Master the question

Have you ever said, "I knew the answer, but I thought the question asked something else"? Be very sure that you know what a question is asking. Read the question at least twice before reading the answer choices. Approach it as you would a mystery story or a riddle. Look for clues. Watch especially for words like not and except—they tell you to look for the choice that is false or different from the other choices or opposite in some way.

2 Track your time

Use all the time you are given to take a test in order to avoid making errors. Here are some checkpoints to help you monitor your time.

- How many questions should be completed when one quarter of the time is gone? When half the time is gone?

- What should the clock read when you are halfway through the questions?

- If you find yourself behind your checkpoints, you can speed up.

- If you are ahead, you can—and should—slow down.

3 Negatives do not fit

Be sure to watch for negative words in the questions such as *never, unless, not*, and *except*. When a question contains one of these negative words, look for the answer that does not fit with the other answers.

4 Jot it down quick

You might have made a special effort to memorize some information for the test. If you are worried you will forget as soon as the testing period begins, jot it down on the back of your test or on your scratch paper as soon as the teacher begins the test. Then go on and work on the test itself.

5 Anticipate the answers

Before you read the answer choices, answer the question yourself. Then read the choices. If the answer you gave is among the choices listed, it is probably correct.

6 How much do I write?

If a writing question contains the following terms, you will need several sentences for a complete answer:

- describe
- write
- justify
- why
- explain

7 In your own words

Sometimes the wording of a passage might be a bit different than the language you are used to using. Read the question and restate the question in your own words to make sure you are very comfortable with what is being asked.

8 I'm done!

When you think you are finished with your test you still need to check it. First, take a look at the clock and see how much time you have left. Go back and review your answers for any careless mistakes you may have made such as leaving a question blank or putting two answers to one question. Be sure to erase any stray marks, review the hardest questions you answered, and turn the test in at the end of the time period. There is nothing to be gained from finishing first—or last, for that matter.

Indiana and the United States

What do you have in common with students in New York, Texas, Idaho, and California? People in every state in the United States contribute to the future of the nation. To better understand how life in Indiana relates to life in the United States, we can look at four key areas in which Hoosiers are tied to the United States—history, civics and government, geography, and economics.

History

The study of history is the study of past events. Usually events are studied in chronological order, but it is also important to understand the connections between events. Often one event can have many causes and many effects.

Life in Indiana today has been affected by events of the past. For example, the county boundaries that exist today were heavily influenced by the decisions of the first government of the United States more than 200 years ago. These counties were first surveyed and mapped in the late 1700s when Indiana was part of the Northwest Territory. The residents of the region successfully petitioned for statehood in 1816. Indiana was a part of the West in the early United States. The state was widely known for its agricultural products before the Civil War. During the Industrial Revolution, Indiana became a center of innovation and industry.

Important events that took place in the state, such as the Battle of Fallen Timbers and the Battle of Tippecanoe, have affected the course of United States history. With the defeat of Native American forces in these battles, more western territory was opened to American settlers.

Residents of Indiana have fought in every war with which the United States has been involved, and the state has contributed inventors, entrepreneurs, politicians, entertainers, and writers that have shaped the lives of all Americans. Two Indiana politicians, Schuyler Colfax and Dan Quayle, have served as vice president of the United States. William Henry Harrison and his grandson Benjamin Harrison, both of whom served as president, began their political careers in Indiana as well.

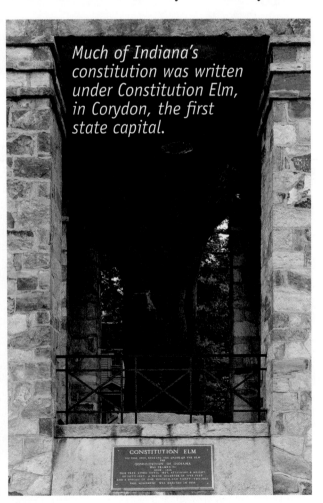

Much of Indiana's constitution was written under Constitution Elm, in Corydon, the first state capital.

Activity

Choose a historical event that took place in your city or county. Research the causes and effects of this event. Identify how the event was shaped by ideas or events in the rest of the United States. Then write a newspaper article about the importance of the event to Indiana and the United States.

Civics and Government

In the United States the authority of the government is based on several key documents that express the rights and responsibilities of citizens as well as people in government. The United States and Indiana both have constitutions, or documents that organize the government and assign powers to different parts. Both Indiana and the United States have three branches of government: legislative, executive, and judicial.

Indiana's state constitution was created by a committee of delegates in 1851. It has been amended, or officially changed, several times since then. Although Hoosiers are allowed to have almost any laws that they want, none of their state laws can contradict national laws. This system of power, in which national laws can override state laws, is called federalism. As a result, the national government is often referred to as the federal government.

Just as the state of Indiana cannot have laws that contradict federal laws, local governments in Indiana cannot have laws that contradict state laws. When there is disagreement about what a law means or whether a law is permitted by the constitution, the judicial branch of government decides the matter. Most such court cases begin in local courts, but may also go through state courts and federal courts.

While the government creates and enforces laws, citizens of Indiana can help influence what laws say. Both the United States and Indiana are run by democracies, or governments in which people rule themselves. Citizens of Indiana can vote in local, state, and national elections to choose leaders who will represent them in government and to decide what laws should be passed.

Activity

Research how local, state, and federal governments affect your community. Create a table that shows examples of what each level of government provides for your town or county.

Indiana State House, Indianapolis

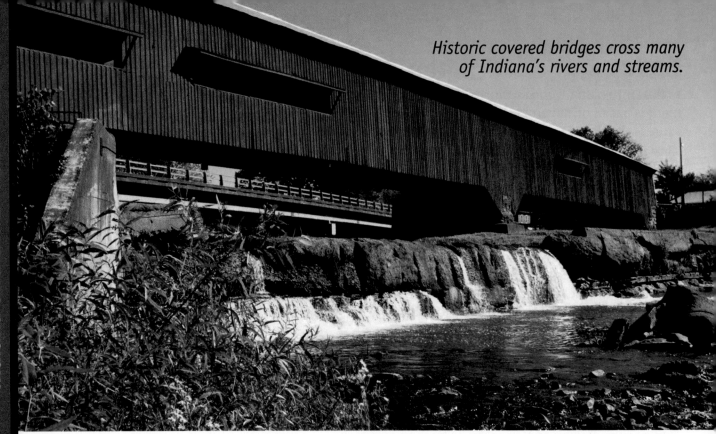

Historic covered bridges cross many of Indiana's rivers and streams.

Geography

The region of land known as the United States has experienced dramatic changes during the several billion years of Earth's history. Mountains have been pushed up and worn away, large oceans have appeared and disappeared, and glaciers have carved out large, deep lakes. The current positions of mountains, plains, rivers, and lakes, along with weather trends, have shaped the types of plant and animals that can survive naturally in different areas of the United States. People have also caused significant changes in the geography of the region.

Native Americans living in different regions of the United States hunted, gathered, farmed, and fished to survive. The natural resources of the various regions shaped the culture of the Native Americans who lived there. As European and American settlers moved into different areas of North America and the United States, they brought new tools and techniques that allowed them to use the land differently than the Native Americans had.

Deep rivers, dense forests, fertile soils, ocean harbors, and plentiful resources have greatly influenced the lives and cultures of the people in the United States. The physical geography of Indiana and much of the surrounding area has been largely shaped by the huge glaciers that once covered the region. The Great Lakes, including Lake Michigan, were carved out of the sedimentary rock by the enormous weight of glacial ice. As the most recent glaciers retreated, rich soil was left behind that provides Indiana with excellent farmland. The presence of many rivers, including the Wabash River in central Indiana and the Ohio River along the southern border of the state, has been important in linking Hoosiers and their products to the wider world.

Activity

Research the ways in which the location of rivers, plains, hills, and lakes have influenced the ways in which Hoosiers make their livings. Ask yourself what might be different about Indiana if the location of any major landform was different. Then create a poster that describes how the physical geography of Indiana shapes life in the state.

Economics

Indiana produces many agricultural and industrial products for export and imports millions of dollars worth of products from other states and countries. This movement of goods is part of the economy of the state. However, many businesses in Indiana do not create products but instead provide services such as medical care or banking. These companies are also a part of the Indiana economy.

During the first years of statehood, Indiana's economy relied heavily on agricultural products such as corn and wheat. By the time of the Civil War, the state was linked by railroads with the rest of the United States, and many factories began producing supplies for the Union troops. The late 1800s and early 1900s saw a dramatic increase in industrial manufacturing in the state. Most recently, Indiana and surrounding areas have been termed the "Rust Belt" to indicate the decline of heavy manufacturing in the area.

Today, the economy of Indiana is still heavily reliant on agriculture. As in the rest of the United States, service industry jobs are increasing as more and more manufacturing is moved to locations overseas. Still, the decline of manufacturing has hurt the state. In the 1990s, unemployment in the state rose. During the early 2000s, the economy of the state grew at a slower pace than that of the United States. Business and political leaders have been challenged to maintain the state's traditionally high standard of living.

Activity

As the economy of Indiana has changed, so have the jobs available to Hoosiers. Choose three of the following periods of Indiana history and research what jobs were available during those periods: early statehood, Civil War, Great Depression, late 1900s, present. Make a chart with lists of skills that would have been needed for a particular job during the periods you have chosen.

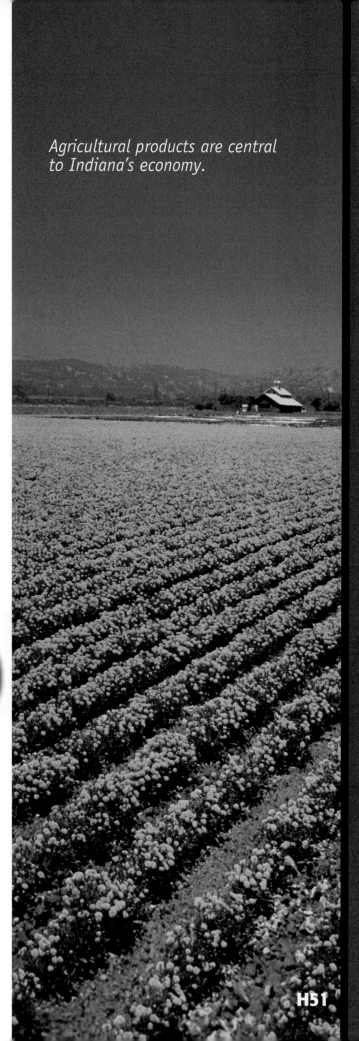

Agricultural products are central to Indiana's economy.

Our Colonial Heritage

North and South America were populated by Native American societies before Europeans arrived and began to colonize them. During the colonial period, Europeans came to the Americas to make new homes and gain wealth. Many people did so using slave labor from Africa.

As England's colonies in North America became more successful, they began to have conflicts with neighboring colonies, Native American people, and the British government. In the first four chapters, you will learn about the world before and after Columbus, and how the American colonies gained their independence.

Explore the Art

This painting by William Halsall shows the *Mayflower*, the ship that brought the Pilgrims to North America, in Plymouth Harbor. What might the Pilgrims have encountered when they first arrived at Plymouth?

The World before the Opening of the Atlantic

Indiana Standards

Social Studies Standards

8.1.1 Identify major Native American Indian groups of eastern North America and describe early conflict and cooperation with European settlers and the influence the two cultures had on each other.

8.1.2 Explain the struggle of the British, French, Spanish, and Dutch to gain control of North America during settlement and colonization.

8.3.1 Read maps to interpret symbols and determine the land forms and human features that represent physical and cultural characteristics of areas in the United States.

8.3.3 Identify and locate the major climate regions in the United States and describe the characteristics of these regions.

go.hrw.com
Indiana
KEYWORD: SF10 IN

FOCUS ON WRITING ✏

A Travelogue People who make long trips often write travelogues that describe their journeys. A travelogue allows people who did not make the trip to experience some of the same sights, sounds, and thoughts that the traveler did. In this chapter, you will gather information about different regions of the world and then write a travelogue describing what a place in one of these regions might have been like.

CHAPTER EVENTS

c. 38,000– 10,000 BC Paleo-Indians migrate to the Americas.

38,000 BC

WORLD EVENTS

What You Will Learn...

Buffalo graze on the plains in South Dakota. Millions of these animals used to roam lands from Canada to Texas. In this chapter you will learn about the first peoples in the Americas, some of whom relied on buffalo to survive.

c. AD 1100
Native Americans of the Mississippian culture begin living in the Angel Mounds settlement in southern Indiana.

c. 5000 BC
Communities in Mexico cultivate corn.

c. 1200 BC
Olmec begin their civilization in Mesoamerica.

1492 Christopher Columbus and his crew reach the Americas on October 12.

5000 BC

1000 BC

AD 1500

c. 2600 BC
The Great Pyramid is built at Giza, Egypt, as the tomb for the pharaoh Khufu.

c. 1350 New ideas begin to spread through Europe during the Renaissance.

3

Reading Social Studies

by Kylene Beers

| Economics | Geography | Politics | Society and Culture | Science and Technology |

Focus on Themes This chapter explains the early development of Mesoamerica and North America. You will read about early explorers from Europe, learn about early American settlements, and discover why the Spanish, the English, and the French all wanted a part of this new land. As you read the chapter, you will see how **geography** affected exploration and will learn about the **economic** issues that influenced growth and settlement.

Specialized Vocabulary of Social Studies

Focus on Reading If you flipped through the pages of this book, would you expect to see anything about square roots or formulas? How about petri dishes or hypotheses? Of course you wouldn't. Those are terms you'd only see in math and science books.

Specialized Vocabulary Like most subjects, social studies has its own specialized vocabulary. Included in it are words and phrases you will see over and over as you read social studies materials. The charts below list some terms you may encounter as you read this book.

Terms that deal with time	
Decade	a period of 10 years
Century	a period of 100 years
Era	a long period marked by great events, developments, or figures
BC	a term used to identify dates that occurred long ago, before the birth of Jesus Christ, the founder of Christianity; it means "before Christ." BC dates get smaller as time passes, so the larger the number, the earlier the date.
AD	a term used to identify dates that occurred after Jesus's birth; it comes from a Latin phrase that means "in the year of our Lord." Unlike BC dates, AD dates get larger as time passes, so the larger the number, the later the date.
BCE	another way to refer to BC dates; it stands for "before the common era"
CE	another way to refer to AD dates; it stands for "common era"

Terms that deal with government and society	
politics	the art of creating government policies
economics	the study of the creation and use of goods and services
movement	a series of actions that bring about or try to bring about a change in society
campaign	an effort to win a political office, or a series of military actions
colony	a territory settled and controlled by a country

You Try It!

The following passage shows you how some specialized vocabulary is defined in context.

Migration to the Americas

Native Americans in the Pacific Northwest carved images on **totems**—ancestor or animal spirits—on tall, wooden poles. Totem poles held great religious and historical significance for Native Americans of the Northwest. Feasts called potlatches were another unique, or unusual, aspect of these Native Americans' culture.

From Chapter 1, p. 12

Use the clues to understand meaning.

1. Find the word *totems.* The phrase after the **dash** is the definition. Often in this book, specialized vocabulary words are defined after a dash. So be on the lookout for dashes.

2. The word *potlatch* is defined in the third sentence. The clue to finding this definition is the word **called**. Words like **called** and **known as** can indicate that a definition is coming up. In this case, the word *feasts* is a definition of potlatch.

3. In the first sentence, you see a term that is in boldface print. You should recognize that word from seeing it in the section opener. The definition is **highlighted**. Why do you think some specialized vocabulary words are in boldface print, while others are not?

4. The word *unique* is defined in the final sentence. The clue to finding this definition is the **comma** followed by the word **or**. So be on the lookout for commas followed by *or.*

As you read Chapter 1, keep track in your notebook of the specialized vocabulary you learn.

Key Terms and People

Chapter 1

Section 1
Bering Land Bridge *(p. 6)*
Paleo-Indians *(p. 6)*
migration *(p. 6)*
hunter-gatherers *(p. 6)*
environments *(p. 7)*
culture *(p. 7)*

Section 2
pueblos *(p. 11)*
kivas *(p. 11)*
totems *(p. 12)*
teepees *(p. 14)*
matrilineal *(p. 14)*
Iroquois League *(p. 14)*

Section 3
Berbers *(p. 16)*
Mansa Musa *(p. 18)*
hajj *(p. 18)*
mosques *(p. 19)*
Askia the Great *(p. 19)*

Section 4
Socrates *(p. 22)*
Plato *(p. 22)*
Aristotle *(p. 22)*
reason *(p. 22)*
democracy *(p. 23)*
knights *(p. 24)*
Black Death *(p. 25)*
Michelangelo *(p. 26)*
Leonardo da Vinci *(p. 26)*
Johannes Gutenberg *(p. 27)*
joint-stock companies *(p. 27)*

Academic Vocabulary

Success in school is related to knowing academic vocabulary—the words that are frequently used in school assignments and discussions. In this chapter, you will learn the following academic words:

develop *(p. 8)*
classical *(p. 23)*

The Earliest Americans

If YOU were there...

You are living in North America about 10,000 years ago, close to the end of the Ice Age. For weeks, your group has been following a herd of elk across a marshy landscape. This trip has taken you far from your usual hunting grounds. The air is warmer here. There are thick grasses and bushes full of berries. You decide to camp here for the summer and perhaps stay a while.

How would settling here change your way of life?

BUILDING BACKGROUND The first settlers to the Americas probably came in small groups from Asia. Over thousands of years, they moved into nearly every region of North and South America. In the Americas, these people encountered, and adapted to, many different climates and types of land.

First Migration to the Americas

Many scientists believe that the first people arrived in North America during the last Ice Age. At the start of the Ice Age, Earth's climate became intensely cold. Large amounts of water froze into huge, moving sheets of ice called glaciers. As a result, ocean levels dropped more than 300 feet lower than they are today. When the sea level fell, a land bridge between northeastern Asia and present-day Alaska was exposed. Geographers call this strip of land the **Bering Land Bridge**. Although no one knows exactly when or how people crossed into North America, evidence suggests that people called **Paleo-Indians** crossed this bridge into Alaska between 38,000 and 10,000 BC.

This **migration**—a movement of people or animals from one region to another—took place over a long time. It is believed that Paleo-Indians traveled south into Canada, the United States, and Mexico following herds of animals. Over time, their descendants went as far as the southern tip of South America. These people were **hunter-gatherers**, people who hunted animals and gathered wild plants for food.

Land Migrations of Early Peoples

ASIA

180°
170°W
160°W
150°W
140°W
130°W

Bering Strait

ALASKA

Mammoth skeleton

LAURENTIDE ICE SHEET

Kernels of maize

NORTH AMERICA

120°W

30°N

Gulf of Mexico

90°W

110°W

MESOAMERICA   20°N

100°W

Maya pyramid, Chichén Itzá, Mexico

SOUTH AMERICA

About 8000 BC, Earth's climate grew warmer, and the Ice Age ended. Rising temperatures melted glaciers. Water levels in the oceans rose, and the Bering Land Bridge was covered with water.

The warmer climate at the end of the Ice Age created new **environments**, climates and landscapes that surround living things. Large herds of animals such as buffalo and deer ate new short grasses that thrived in the warm climate. As the number of these animals grew, Paleo-Indians hunted these animals for survival.

Varied environments influenced the development of different Native American societies, or groups that share a culture. **Culture** is a group's set of common values and traditions, including language, government, and family relationships.

Like all societies, Native American groups changed over time. People planted seeds, and eventually they learned to breed animals, farm, and grow plants. Maize, or corn, was one of their most important early crops. Later, they learned to grow beans and squash. Farming allowed people to stop moving around looking for food and to settle in one place. With adequate food supplies, settlements could support larger populations. As populations grew, more advanced societies began to develop.

READING CHECK **Drawing Conclusions** How did climate change affect early peoples' migrations?

GEOGRAPHY SKILLS **INTERPRETING MAPS**

1. **Movement** In what general direction did early peoples migrate?
2. **Human-Environment Interaction** What natural features affected the route people took from Alaska to southern North America?

Early Mesoamerican and South American Societies

Some of the earliest American cultures arose in Mesoamerica, a region that includes the southern part of what is now Mexico and the northern parts of Central America.

Olmec and Maya

Around 1200 BC the Olmec **developed** the earliest known civilization in Mesoamerica. The Olmec are known for their use of stone in architecture and sculpture. They built the first pyramids in the Americas, and they created sculptures of huge stone heads. When their civilization ended around 400 BC, trade had spread Olmec culture throughout the region.

Like the Olmec, the Maya grew maize and other crops and lived in small villages. These villages traded goods with each other, and by about AD 200, the Maya were building large cities.

Maya cities had pyramids, large stone temples, palaces, and bridges. The Maya also paved large plazas for public gatherings and built canals to control the flow of water through the cities.

In the 900s Maya civilization began to collapse. Historians are still not sure what caused this great civilization's decline.

Aztec

The Aztec were fierce warriors, and their superior military ability was key to their success. Around the mid-1100s AD, the Aztec migrated south to central Mexico. They conquered many towns, made alliances to build their empire, and controlled a huge trade network.

In AD 1325, the Aztec founded their capital, Tenochtitlán (tay-nawch-teet-LAHN), on an island in Lake Texcoco. It became the greatest city in the Americas and one of the world's largest cities. The city's island location made travel and trade difficult, so the Aztec built raised roads to connect the island to the shore.

Trade and tribute paid by conquered people in the form of cotton, gold, and food made the Aztec rich. By the early 1500s, they ruled the most powerful state in Mesoamerica.

Inca

The Inca began as a small tribe in the Andes Mountains of South America. They named their capital city Cuzco (KOO-skoh). In the

The ancient Maya city of Palenque was a major power on the border between the Maya highlands and lowlands. Its great temples and plazas were typical of the Classic Age of Maya civilization.

mid-1400s, the Inca began to expand their territory. By the 1500s the empire stretched along the Pacific coast from what is now northern Ecuador to central Chile. In time, the empire was home to about 12 million people. The Inca formed a strong central government with a king as ruler. The official language of the empire was Quechua. Because there was no written language, records were kept on a system of knotted strings called *quipu*.

The Inca are known for building and for art. Massive buildings and forts were made of huge stone blocks. An advanced system of highways ran the length of the empire. Paved roads and rope bridges connected all parts of Inca territory. This enabled the Inca to communicate with and control their large empire.

READING CHECK **Summarizing** What early civilizations existed in Mesoamerica and South America?

SUMMARY AND PREVIEW Early people migrated into North and South America and developed societies. In the next section you will learn about Native American cultures in North America.

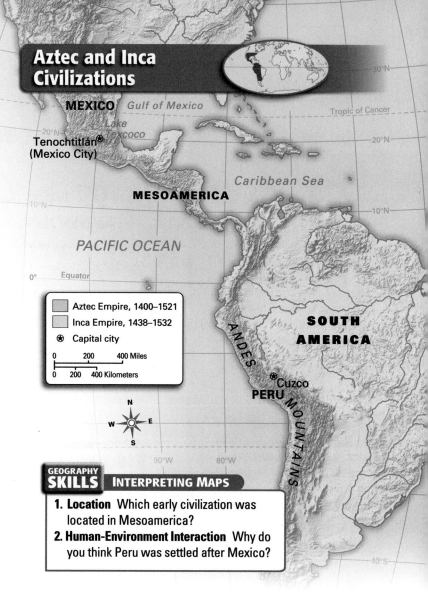

Aztec and Inca Civilizations

MEXICO Gulf of Mexico

Tropic of Cancer

Lake Texcoco

Tenochtitlán (Mexico City)

Caribbean Sea

MESOAMERICA

PACIFIC OCEAN

Equator

	Aztec Empire, 1400–1521
	Inca Empire, 1438–1532
✴	Capital city

0   200   400 Miles
0   200   400 Kilometers

ANDES

SOUTH AMERICA

Cuzco

PERU

MOUNTAINS

N E S W

GEOGRAPHY SKILLS **INTERPRETING MAPS**

1. **Location** Which early civilization was located in Mesoamerica?
2. **Human-Environment Interaction** Why do you think Peru was settled after Mexico?

go.hrw.com
Online Quiz
KEYWORD: SF7 HP1

Section 1 Assessment

Reviewing Ideas, Terms, and People

1. a. **Recall** What was the Ice Age?
   b. **Summarize** Why were early peoples able to use the **Bering Land Bridge**?
   c. **Predict** Why do you think early peoples in the Americas **migrated** south?
2. a. **Identify** What is the earliest known civilization in the Americas, and where was it located?
   b. **Analyze** How did the Aztec build such a powerful, rich state?
   c. **Draw Conclusions** Which of the four civilizations discussed do you think was the most highly developed?

Critical Thinking

3. **Categorizing** Review your notes on the migration of early peoples and their societies. Then copy the table below and use it to identify the accomplishments of early American civilizations.

	Rise	Significant Accomplishments
Olmec		
Maya		
Aztec		
Inca		

FOCUS ON WRITING

4. **Understanding Ancient Peoples** Use the descriptions of the earliest Americans found in this section to list some similarities and differences between the lives of ancient peoples and your life today.

Native American Cultures

What You Will Learn...

Main Ideas

1. Several early societies developed in North America long before Europeans explored the continent.
2. Geographic areas influenced Native American cultures.
3. Native American cultures shared beliefs about religion and land ownership.

The Big Idea

Many diverse Native American cultures developed across the different geographic regions of North America.

Key Terms and People

pueblos, *p. 11*
kivas, *p. 11*
totems, *p. 12*
teepees, *p. 14*
matrilineal, *p. 14*
Iroquois League, *p. 14*

 TAKING NOTES As you read, take notes on early societies. Write your notes in a chart like the one below.

Early Societies	
Culture Areas	
Beliefs	

 8.1.1, 8.3.3

If YOU were there...

You live in the North American Southwest about 1,000 years ago. You've been working in the fields for several hours today. The maize crop looks good this summer, and you are hoping for a successful harvest. After finishing your work, you walk home. The opening to your house is in a cliff wall 30 feet above a canyon floor. You must use ladders to get to the opening.

Do you like the location of your home? Why?

BUILDING BACKGROUND After crossing the land bridge from Asia during the Ice Age, hunter-gatherer groups spread into every region of North America. Many diverse cultures formed as Native Americans adapted to their different environments.

Early Societies

The earliest people in North America were hunter-gatherers. After 5000 BC some of these people learned how to farm, and they settled in villages. Although less populated than South America and Mesoamerica, North America had many complex societies long before Europeans reached the continent.

Anasazi

By 1500 BC the people who lived in the North American Southwest, like those who lived in Mesoamerica, were growing maize. One of the early farm cultures in the Southwest was the Anasazi (ah-nuh-SAH-zee). The Anasazi lived in the Four Corners region, where present-day Arizona, Colorado, New Mexico, and Utah meet. Anasazi farmers adapted to their dry environment and grew maize, beans, and squash. Over time, they began to use irrigation to increase food production. By the time the Anasazi settled in the area, they were already skilled basket makers. They wove straw, vines, and yucca to make containers for food and other items, and they eventually became skilled potters as well.

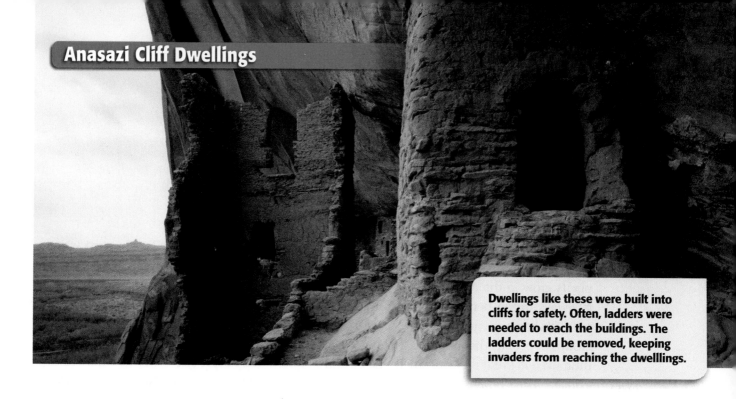

Anasazi Cliff Dwellings

Dwellings like these were built into cliffs for safety. Often, ladders were needed to reach the buildings. The ladders could be removed, keeping invaders from reaching the dwelllings.

The early Anasazi lived in pit houses dug into the ground. After about AD 750 they built **pueblos**, or aboveground houses made of a heavy clay called adobe. The Anasazi built these houses on top of each other, creating large multistoried complexes. Some pueblos had several hundred rooms and could house 1,000 people.

The Anasazi often built their houses in canyon walls and had to use ladders to enter their homes. These cliff dwellings provided a strong defense against enemies. The Anasazi also built **kivas**, underground ceremonial chambers, at the center of each community. Kivas were sacred areas used for religious ceremonies. Some of these rituals focused on the life-giving forces of rain and maize.

The Anasazi thrived for hundreds of years. After AD 1300, however, they began to abandon their villages. Scholars believe that drought, disease, or raids by nomadic tribes from the north may have caused the Anasazi to move away from their pueblos.

Mound Builders

Several farming societies developed in the eastern part of North America after 1000 BC. The Hopewell lived along the Mississippi, Ohio, and lower Missouri river valleys.

They supported their large population with agriculture and trade. They built large burial mounds to honor their dead.

The Hopewell culture had declined by AD 700. Another culture, the Mississippian, began to thrive in the same area. Skilled farmers and traders, the Mississippian built large settlements. Their largest city, Cahokia, was located near present-day Saint Louis, Missouri. It had a population of 30,000.

The Mississippian built hundreds of mounds for religious ceremonies. Cahokia alone had more than 100 temple and burial mounds. These mounds had flat tops, and temples were built on top of the mounds. Many of the mounds were gigantic. Monks Mound, near Collinsville, Illinois, for example, was 100 feet high and covered 16 acres.

Several other mound-building cultures thrived in eastern North America. More than 10,000 mounds have been found in the Ohio River valley alone. Some of these mounds are shaped like birds and snakes. The mound-building cultures had declined by the time European explorers reached the Southeast. Their societies no longer existed by the early 1700s.

READING CHECK **Summarizing** Why did some Native American groups build mounds?

Native American Culture Areas

Researchers use culture areas—the geographic locations that influenced societies—to help them describe ancient Native American peoples. North America is divided into several culture areas.

North and Northwest

The far north of North America is divided into the Arctic and Subarctic culture areas. Few plants grow in the Arctic because the ground is always frozen beneath a thin top layer of soil. This harsh environment was home to two groups of people, the Inuit and the Aleut. The Inuit lived in present-day northern Alaska and Canada. Their homes were igloos, hide tents, and huts. The Aleut, whose home was in western and southern Alaska, lived in multifamily houses that were partially underground. The two groups shared many cultural features, including language. Both groups survived by fishing and hunting large mammals. The Aleut and Inuit also depended on dogs for many tasks, such as hunting and pulling sleds.

South of the Arctic lies the Subarctic, home to groups such as the Dogrib and Montagnais peoples. While they followed the seasonal migrations of deer, these peoples lived in shelters made of animal skins. At other times, they lived in villages made up of log houses. Farther south, the Kwakiutl and the Chinook thrived, thanks to the rich supply of game animals, fish, and wild plants that allowed large populations to increase without the need for farming.

Native Americans in the Pacific Northwest carved images of **totems**—ancestor or animal spirits—on tall, wooden poles. Totem poles held great religious and historical significance for Native Americans of the Northwest. Feasts called potlatches were another unique, or unusual, aspect of these Native Americans' culture. At these gatherings, hosts, usually chiefs or wealthy people, gave away most of their belongings as gifts. In this way, the hosts increased their social importance.

FOCUS ON READING
What is the definition of **totems** according to this sentence?

West and Southwest

Farther south along the Pacific coast was the California region, which included the area between the Pacific and the Sierra Nevada mountain range. Food sources were plentiful, so farming was not necessary. One major plant food was acorns, which were ground into flour. People also fished and hunted deer and other game. Most Native Americans in the California region lived in groups of families of about 50 to 300. Among these groups, including the Hupa, Miwok, and Yokuts, more than 100 languages were spoken.

The area east of the Sierra Nevada Mountains, the Great Basin, received little rain. To survive, Native Americans adapted to the drier climate by gathering seeds, digging roots, and trapping small animals for food. Most groups in this area, including the Paiute, Shoshone, and Ute, spoke the same language.

The Southwest culture region included the present-day states of Arizona and New Mexico, and parts of Colorado and Texas. Pueblo groups, such as the Hopi and Zuni, lived there. Like the Anasazi, these Native Americans also adapted to a dry climate. The Pueblo irrigated the land and grew maize, squash, and beans. These crops were vital to southwestern peoples. The Pueblo religion focused on two key areas of Pueblo life, rain and maize. The Pueblo performed religious rituals hoping to bring rain and a successful maize crop to their peoples.

Pueblo peoples were settled and built multistoried houses out of adobe bricks. Over time their towns grew larger, and some towns had more than 1,000 residents. Pueblo peoples made fine pottery that featured beautifully painted designs.

Bering Sea

Native American Culture Areas

Arctic		Northeast	
Subarctic		Great Basin	
Northwest Coast		California	
Plateau		Southwest	
Great Plains		Southeast	

0   250   500 Miles
0 250 500 Kilometers

Human-hand carving, Great Plains culture area

Beaver-shaped pipe, Northeast culture area

Inuit
Ingalik
Han
Eyak
Tagish
Tlingit
Tongass
Haisla
Haida
Heiltsuk
Kwakiutl
Nootka
Squamish
Makah Nooksack
Chimakum
Coast
Salish Columbia
Chinook Spokane
Yakima
Klickitat
Walla Walla
Yaquina
Molala
Umpqua
Tolowa Modoc
Hupa Achomawi
Washo
Yuki Maidu
Wappo
Miwok
Costanoan
Esselen
Yokuts
Chumash

Saschutkenne
Dogrib
Carrier

Shuswap

Blackfoot

Nez
Percé Crow
Northern
Paiute
Northern
Shoshone

Western
Shoshone

Mono
Kawaiisu

Ute

ROCKY MOUNTAINS

Mohave
Yuma
Nakipa
Pima
Cochimi Seri
Ignacieno Yaqui

Hopi (Pueblo)
Navajo
Zuni (Pueblo)
Apache

Apache

Suma
Jumano

Tarahumara

Waicura

Lagunero
Guachichil

MESOAMERICA

Inuit

Chipewyan

Swampy
Cree

Hudson
Bay

**NORTH
AMERICA**

Montagnais

Micmac

Plains
Cree Plains
Ojibway

Mandan

Teton Sioux
Cheyenne
Omaha
Pawnee
Arapaho

Santee
Sioux Sauk
Fox

Iowa

Missouri
Cahokia
Osage

Kansas

Kiowa

Comanche

Wichita
Caddo
Tonkawa

Karankawa

Algonquian
Ottawa
Huron

Great
Lakes

Potawatomi
Kickapoo
Miami

Illinois

Shawnee

Chickasaw
Tuskegee
Creek
Alabama
Choctaw Apalachee
Mobile

Gulf of Mexico

Beothuk

Massachuset

Iroquois Mohawk
Oneida
Onondaga
Cayuga
Seneca

Wampanoag
Narragansett
Pequot
Mohegan

Delaware
Susquehanna

Powhatan

**ATLANTIC
OCEAN**

Cherokee
Cheraw
Cusabo

Seminole
Calusa

Tropic of Cancer
Taino

*Caribbean
Sea*

Human figure, Southwest culture area

PACIFIC OCEAN

**GEOGRAPHY
SKILLS** | **INTERPRETING MAPS**

1. **Region** Why did some culture areas have fewer groups of people than other culture areas did?
2. **Human-Environment Interaction** What natural features served as boundaries between culture areas?

Iroquois Longhouse

Northeastern Native Americans such as the Iroquois lived in longhouses made of tree bark. The drawing shows the longhouses in one Iroquois village.

Why do you think a fence was placed around the longhouses?

The Apache and Navajo also lived in the Southwest. These groups were nomadic—they moved from place to place hunting small animals and foraging for food. The Apache and Navajo also supported themselves by raiding the villages of the Pueblo and others.

Great Plains

The huge Great Plains region stretches south from Canada into Texas. This culture area is bordered by the Mississippi Valley on the east and the Rocky Mountains on the west. The Plains were mainly grassland, home to millions of buffalo. Deer, elk, and other game also thrived there.

Most Great Plains peoples were nomadic hunters. Many groups hunted buffalo using bows and spears. Blackfoot and Arapaho hunters sometimes chased the animals over cliffs, drove them into corrals, or trapped them in a ring of fire. Native Americans used buffalo skins for shields, clothing, and coverings for their **teepees**—cone-shaped shelters.

Some Plains groups were farmers. The Mandan and Pawnee settled in villages and grew corn, beans, and squash. The Pawnee lived in round lodges made of dirt. Like some other Native American groups, Pawnee society was **matrilineal**. This means that people traced their ancestry through their mothers, not their fathers.

Northeast and Southeast

Eastern North America was rich in sources for food and shelter. Animals, plant foods, fish, and wood for housing were plentiful in the region's woodlands and river valleys.

Most southeastern groups, including the Cherokee, Creek, and Seminole, lived in farming villages governed by village councils. In the Northeast, groups like the Algonquian survived by hunting and gathering plants. Those in the south farmed, hunted, gathered plants, and fished. Many tribes used strings of beads known as wampum for money.

To the east of the Ottawa and Algonquian lived the Iroquois (or Haudenosaunee). They were farmers, hunters, and traders who lived in longhouses, or rectangular homes made from logs and bark, that housed 8 to 10 families.

The Iroquois created the **Iroquois League**. This confederation, or alliance, was established by the Cayuga, Mohawk, Oneida, Onondaga, and Seneca. The league waged war against and made peace with non-Iroquois peoples. Its goal was to strengthen the alliance against invasion. The league helped the Iroquois become one of the most powerful Native American peoples in North America.

READING CHECK **Generalizing** How did environment influence Native American cultures in North America?

Shared Beliefs

Although they were different culturally and geographically, Native American groups of North America shared certain beliefs. The religion of most Native American peoples, for example, was linked to nature. Native Americans believed that spiritual forces were everywhere, dwelling in heavenly bodies and in sacred places on the earth. Spirits even lived within animals and plants. Native Americans tried to honor the spirits in their daily lives.

Ceremonies maintained the group's relationship with Earth and Sky, which were believed to be the sustainers of life. In addition, individuals who wanted help prayed to their spirit protector.

Native Americans also shared beliefs about property. They believed that individual ownership only applied to the crops one grew. The land itself was for the use of everyone in the village, and a person's right to use it was temporary. Native Americans also thought they should preserve the land for future generations. These beliefs contrasted sharply with those of Europeans— a difference that would cause conflict.

Despite their shared beliefs, the diverse culture groups of North America had little interest in joining together into large political units. As a result, Native Americans on the North American continent did not form large empires like the Aztec and Inca of Meso- and South America did.

READING CHECK **Identifying Points of View** What religious beliefs did Native American groups share?

SUMMARY AND PREVIEW People of North America formed many complex societies. In the next section you will read about societies in West Africa.

Section 2 Assessment

Reviewing Ideas, Terms, and People

1. **a. Recall** Why did the Anasazi build **kivas**?
   b. Summarize What different types of housing were built by the Anasazi?
   c. Draw Conclusions Why do you think that some mounds were built in the shape of birds and snakes?

2. **a. Identify** What are culture areas?
   b. Contrast How did food sources for Native Americans of the North and Northwest differ from those of Native Americans living in the West and Southwest?
   c. Elaborate Why was the formation of the **Iroquois League** considered to be a significant political development?

3. **a. Recall** How did Native Americans view land ownership?
   b. Analyze What role did religion play in the lives of Native Americans?
   c. Predict Why do you think most Native American groups did not form large empires like the Aztec and the Inca did?

Critical Thinking

4. **Comparing and Contrasting** Review your notes on early societies and culture areas. Then use a Venn diagram like this one to identify similarities and differences among Native American culture groups.

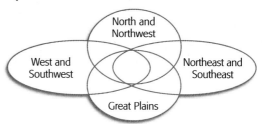

FOCUS ON WRITING

5. **Describing Culture** Look back through this section to discover ways in which a group's beliefs, environment, and practices can be described. Write down phrases that you think are especially useful in understanding Native American cultures.

Trading Kingdoms of West Africa

What You Will Learn...

Main Ideas

1. West Africa developed three great kingdoms that grew wealthy through their control of trade.
2. Slaves became a valuable trade item in West Africa.

The Big Idea

Using trade to gain wealth, Ghana, Mali, and Songhai were West Africa's most powerful kingdoms.

Key Terms and People

Berbers, *p. 16*
Mansa Musa, *p. 18*
hajj, *p. 18*
mosques, *p. 19*
Askia the Great, *p. 19*

TAKING NOTES As you read, take notes on the rise of early African kingdoms and the role of trade in their development. Use a chart like the one below.

Kingdom	Rise	The Role of Trade
Ghana		
Mali		
Songhai		

If YOU were there...

You are a trader's assistant from the Middle East, traveling in a caravan headed for West Africa. The caravan carries many goods, but the most precious is salt. Your job is to trade the salt for gold and return the gold to your employer immediately. Your boss never meets the traders face to face.

Why is your boss so secretive?

BUILDING BACKGROUND The continent of Africa was luxuriously rich in resources. West Africa had both fertile soils and valuable minerals, especially gold and iron. Ancient trade routes had connected Africa with the Middle East and Asia for hundreds of years. Over time, trade developed between regions with different resources. Trade and abundant resources led to the growth of several great kingdoms in West Africa.

West Africa's Great Kingdoms

For hundreds of years, trade routes crisscrossed West Africa. For most of that time, West Africans did not profit much from the Saharan trade because the routes were run by **Berbers**, a group of people from northern Africa. Eventually, that situation changed. A succession of three great kingdoms came to power as their peoples gained control of valuable trade routes in West Africa. Ghana (GAH-nuh) was the first of these empires, followed by the kingdoms of Mali (MAH-lee) and Songhai (SAWNG-hy).

Kingdom of Ghana

Historians think the first people in Ghana were farmers along the Niger River. Sometime after AD 300 these farmers, the Soninke (soh-NING-kee), were threatened by nomadic herders. The herders wanted to take the farmers' water and pastures. For protection, groups of Soninke families began to band together. This banding together was the beginning of Ghana.

Ghana's rulers grew wealthy by controlling trade in salt and gold. Salt came from the north in large slabs, and gold came from the south.

What does the photo to the left suggest about the amount of salt traded in a market?

Ghana was in an ideal position to become a trading center. To the north lay the vast Sahara, the source of much of the salt. Ghana itself was rich in gold. People wanted gold for its beauty, but they needed salt in their diets to survive. Salt, which could be used to preserve food, also made bland food tasty. These qualities made salt very valuable. In fact, Africans sometimes cut up slabs of salt and used the pieces as money.

As trade in gold and salt increased, Ghana's rulers gained power. Eventually, they built up armies equipped with iron weapons that were superior to the weapons of nearby people. Over time, Ghana took control of trade from merchants. Merchants from the north and south then met to exchange goods in Ghana.

By 800 Ghana was firmly in control of West Africa's trade routes. Nearly all trade between northern and southern Africa passed through Ghana. With so many traders passing through their lands, Ghana's rulers looked for ways to make money from them. One way they raised money was by forcing traders to pay taxes. Every trader who entered Ghana had to pay a special tax on the goods he carried. Then he had to pay another tax on any goods he took with him when he left. Ghana's rulers gained incredible wealth from trade, taxes on traders and on the people of Ghana, and their own personal stores of gold. They used their wealth to build an army and an empire.

Islam in Ghana

Extensive trade routes brought the people of Ghana into contact with people of many different cultures and beliefs. As the kingdom of Ghana extended into the Sahara, increased contact with Arab traders from the east brought the religion of Islam to Ghana.

Islam was founded in the 600s by an Arab named Muhammad. Muslims, followers of Islam, believe that God had spoken to Muhammad through an angel and had made him a prophet, someone who tells of God's messages. After Muhammad's death, his followers wrote down his teachings to form the book known as the Qur'an. Islam spread quickly through the Arabian Peninsula.

In the 1060s, a Muslim group called the Almoravids (al-muh-RAH-vuhdz) attacked Ghana in an effort to force its leaders to

Empires of West Africa, 800–1500

Legend:
- Ghana, 1000
- Mali, 1400
- Songhai, 1500
- Settlement
- Trade route
- Trade goods

0   250   500 Miles
0   250   500 Kilometers

GEOGRAPHY SKILLS   **INTERPRETING MAPS**

1. **Location** On what river are Timbuktu and Gao located?
2. **Region** Which empires ruled Timbuktu and Gao?

convert to Islam. The Almoravids weakened Ghana's empire and cut off many trade routes. Without its trade, Ghana could not support its empire, and the empire eventually fell. The influence of Islam, however, remained strong. By the late 1400s Islam would become the most practiced religion in the region.

Kingdom of Mali

Like Ghana, Mali lay along the upper Niger River. This area's fertile soil helped Mali grow. In addition, Mali's location on the Niger allowed its people to control trade on the river. Through this control of trade, the empire grew rich and powerful. According to legend, Mali's rise to power began under a ruler named Sundiata. Sundiata won back his country's independence and conquered nearby kingdoms, including Ghana.

Mali's most famous ruler, however, was a Muslim king named **Mansa Musa** (MAHN-sah moo-SAH). Under his leadership, Mali reached the height of its wealth, power, and fame.

Mansa Musa ruled Mali for about 25 years, from 1312 to 1337. During that time, Mali added many important trade cities, including Timbuktu (tim-buhk-TOO), Djenné (je-NAY), and Gao (GOW), to its empire. Traders came to Timbuktu from the north and the south to trade for salt, gold, metals, shells, and many other goods.

Religion was also very important to Mansa Musa. In 1324 he left Mali on a **hajj**, or pilgrimage to Mecca. Making this journey once in their lives is the spiritual duty of all Muslims. As he traveled to Mecca, Mansa Musa introduced his empire to the world. The stories of Mali's wealth and religion spread far and wide. Because of Mansa Musa's influence, Islam spread through a large part of West Africa.

Mansa Musa wanted all Muslims to be able to read the Qur'an. Therefore, he stressed the importance of learning to read and write the Arabic language. He sent scholars to study in Morocco. These scholars later set up schools in Mali for studying the Qur'an.

To encourage the spread of Islam in West Africa, Mansa Musa brought back artists and architects from other Muslim countries to build **mosques**, or buildings for Muslim prayer, throughout his lands.

The architectural advances in cities like Timbuktu as well as an organized government, an emphasis on education, and expansion of trade all combined to make Mansa Musa Mali's most successful ruler. Much of Mali's success depended on strong leaders. After Mansa Musa died, poor leadership weakened the empire. By 1500 nearly all of the lands the kingdom once ruled were lost. Only a small area of Mali remained.

Songhai Empire

In the 1300s Mansa Musa had conquered a rival kingdom of people called the Songhai, who also lived along the Niger River. As the Mali Empire weakened in the 1400s, the Songhai grew in strength. They took advantage of Mali's decline, regained their independence, and eventually conquered most of Mali.

One of Songhai's greatest rulers was Muhammad Ture, who chose the title *askia*, a title of military rank. He became known as **Askia the Great**. Like Mansa Musa, Askia the Great was a devout Muslim who supported education and learning. Under his rule, the cities of Gao and Timbuktu flourished. They contained great mosques, universities, schools, and libraries. People came from all parts of West Africa to study mathematics, science, medicine, grammar, and law.

Askia understood that an empire needed effective government. He created a professional army, and to improve the government, he set up five provinces within Songhai. He removed local leaders and appointed new governors who were loyal to him. He also created specialized departments to oversee various tasks, much like modern-day government offices do.

THE IMPACT TODAY

Some of the mosques built by Mansa Musa can still be seen in West Africa today.

Music from Senegal to Memphis

Did you know that the music you listen to today may have begun with the griots, musicians from West Africa? From the 1600s to the 1800s, many people from West Africa were brought to America as slaves. In America, these slaves continued to sing the way they had in Africa. They also continued to play traditional instruments such as the kora, shown here being played by Senegalese musician Soriba Kouyaté (far right). Over time, this music developed into a style called the blues, made popular by such artists as B. B. King (near right). In turn, the blues shaped other styles of music, including jazz and rock. So, the next time you hear a Memphis blues song or a cool jazz tune, listen for its ancient African roots.

ANALYSIS SKILL **ANALYZING INFORMATION**

How did West African music affect modern American music?

Soon after Askia the Great lost power, the empire of Songhai declined. Songhai was invaded by the Moroccans, the kingdom's northern neighbors. The Moroccans wanted to control the Saharan salt mines. They had superior military power and were able to take over Timbuktu and Gao. Changes in trade patterns completed Songhai's fall.

READING CHECK **Comparing** What did Ghana, Mali, and Songhai have in common?

West African Slave Trade

The practice of slavery had existed in Africa and in many parts of the world for centuries. Traditionally, slavery in West Africa mostly involved only black Africans, who were both slaveholders and slaves. This changed in the 600s when Arab Muslims, and later Europeans, became slave traders. Though Europeans had long traded resources with Africa, they became more interested in the growing slave trade.

People who were captured by warring groups during battle could be sold into slavery. In addition, criminals were sometimes sold as slaves. Other enslaved people were captured during raids on villages, and sometimes even the relatives of people who owed money were sold into slavery as payment for debts. Enslaved Africans were often bought to perform menial labor and domestic chores. In some cultures, having slaves raised the status of the slaveholder.

The market for West African slaves increased as Muslim traders bought or seized black Africans to sell in North Africa. West Africa was also home to many enslaved Africans brought to the Americas.

Over time, the slave trade became even more important to the West African economy. Kings traded slaves for valuable goods, such as horses from the Middle East and textiles and weapons from Europe. The trans-Saharan slave trade contributed to the power of Ghana, Mali, and Songhai.

READING CHECK **Drawing Inferences** Why did the slave trade in West Africa continue to grow?

SUMMARY AND PREVIEW Trade was important to the kingdoms of West Africa. In the next section you will learn about European trade.

Section 3 Assessment

go.hrw.com
Online Quiz
KEYWORD: SF7 HP1

Reviewing Ideas, Terms, and People

1. **a. Identify** How did West African kingdoms grow wealthy through trade?
   b. Describe How did **Mansa Musa** introduce his empire to the world?
   c. Elaborate Why was trade crucial to the survival of Ghana, Mali, and Songhai?
2. **a. Describe** How did some people become slaves in West Africa?
   b. Analyze What role did geography play in the development of the slave trade?
   c. Judge Why did the value of slaves as an export increase over time?

Critical Thinking

3. **Comparing and Contrasting** Review your chart on African kingdoms and trade. Then copy the diagram below and use it to show the similarities and differences in the fall of each kingdom.

Fall of Ghana, Mali, and Songhai	Similarities	Differences

FOCUS ON WRITING

4. **Gathering Information on Economies** Make a list of things that were important to the economies of the kingdoms of West Africa. Include your ideas about what seems most important to West Africans and things that you did not know about before reading this section.

Mansa Musa

How could one man's travels become a historic event?

When did he live? the late 1200s and early 1300s

Where did he live? Mali

What did he do? Mansa Musa, the ruler of Mali, was one of the Muslim kings of West Africa. He became a major figure in African and world history largely because of a pilgrimage he made to the city of Mecca.

Why is he important? Mansa Musa's spectacular journey attracted the attention of the Muslim world and of Europe. For the first time, other people's eyes turned to West Africa. During his travels, Mansa Musa gave out huge amounts of gold. His spending made people eager to find the source of such wealth. Within 200 years, European explorers would arrive on the shores of western Africa.

Identifying Points of View How do you think Mansa Musa changed people's views of West Africa?

KEY FACTS

According to chroniclers of the time, Mansa Musa was accompanied on his journey to Mecca by some 60,000 people. Of those people,

- **12,000** were servants to attend to the king.

- **500** were servants to attend to his wife.

- **14,000** were slaves wearing rich fabrics such as silk.

- **500** carried staffs heavily decorated with gold. Historians have estimated that the gold Mansa Musa gave away on his trip would be worth more than $100 million today.

This Spanish map from 1375 shows Mansa Musa sitting on his throne.

21

Europe before Transatlantic Travel

What You Will Learn...

Main Ideas

1. The Greeks and Romans established new forms of government.
2. During the Middle Ages, society eventually changed from a feudal system to a system with a middle class of artisans and merchants.
3. The Renaissance was a time of rebirth in the arts and in learning.

The Big Idea

New ideas and trade changed Europeans' lives.

Key Terms and People

Socrates, *p. 22*
Plato, *p. 22*
Aristotle, *p. 22*
reason, *p. 22*
democracy, *p. 23*
knights, *p. 24*
Black Death, *p. 25*
Michelangelo, *p. 26*
Leonardo da Vinci, *p. 26*
Johannes Gutenberg, *p. 27*
joint-stock companies, *p. 27*

TAKING NOTES As you read, take notes on the changes in society during the periods listed. Write your notes in a chart like this one.

Period of Time	Major Changes
Ancient Greece	
Roman Republic	
Middle Ages	
Renaissance	

If YOU were there...

You are a peasant in the Middle Ages, living on the land of a noble. Although you and your family work very hard from sunrise to sundown, much of the food you grow goes to the noble. Your house is very small and has a dirt floor. Your parents are tired and weak, and you wish you could do something to improve their lives.

Is there any way you could change your life?

BUILDING BACKGROUND Hard work was a constant theme in the lives of peasants in the Middle Ages. Nobles were not free to live as they chose, either. As the Middle Ages ended, the Renaissance brought new ways of thinking, and the growth of cities brought big changes to the way people lived and worked.

Greek and Roman Government

During the Renaissance, European thinkers and artists rediscovered the traditions of Greece and Rome. Ancient Greek and Roman texts were translated, and their ideas began to revolutionize European societies.

Greek Philosophers and Government

Ancient Greeks valued human reason and believed in the power of the human mind to think, explain, and understand life. Three of the greatest Greek thinkers, or philosophers, were **Socrates**, **Plato**, and **Aristotle**. Socrates, a great teacher, wanted to make people think and question their own beliefs. Plato, a philosopher and teacher, wrote a work called *The Republic*. It describes an ideal society based on justice and fairness for everyone. Aristotle taught that people should live lives based on **reason**, or clear and ordered thinking.

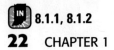

Greek scientists and mathematicians also gained fame for their contributions to geometry and for accurately calculating the size of Earth. Doctors studied the human body to understand how it worked. One Greek engineering invention that is still used today is a water screw, which brings water to farm fields.

One of the Greeks' most lasting contributions, however, is their political system. During the time known as the **Classical** Period, around the fifth and fourth centuries BC, Greece was organized into several hundred independent city-states, which became the foundation for Greek civilization. Athens was the first Greek city-state to establish **democracy**—a form of government in which people rule themselves. All male citizens in Athens had the right to participate in the assembly, a gathering of citizens, to debate and create the city's laws. Because all male citizens in Athens participated directly in government, we call the Greek form of government a direct democracy.

Roman Law and Government

Later, Rome followed Greece's example by establishing a form of democratic government. The Roman Republic was created in 509 BC. Each year Romans elected officials to rule the city. These officials had many powers, but they only stayed in power for one year. This early republic was not a democracy. Later, the Romans changed their government into one with three parts. These three parts were made up of elected representatives who protected the city and its residents.

Roman laws were written and kept on public display so all people could know them. Roman concepts of equality before the law and innocent until proven guilty protected Roman citizens' rights.

The political ideas of Greece and Rome survived to influence governments around the world, including that of the United States. In the U.S. political system, citizens vote for representatives, making the nation a democratic republic.

READING CHECK **Analyzing** How did Roman and Greek governments influence the United States?

Democracy and Republic QUICK FACTS	
Direct democracies and republics are similar forms of government in which the people rule. There are some slight differences, though.	
Direct Democracy	**Republic**
• Every citizen votes on every issue. • Ideas are debated at an assembly of all citizens.	• Citizens elect representatives to vote on issues. • Ideas are debated at an assembly of representatives.

THE IMPACT TODAY

Many of the geometry rules we learn in school today come straight from the Greek mathematician Euclid. Many doctors recite the Hippocratic Oath, named after the Greek doctor Hippocrates.

ACADEMIC VOCABULARY

classical referring to the cultures of ancient Greece or Rome

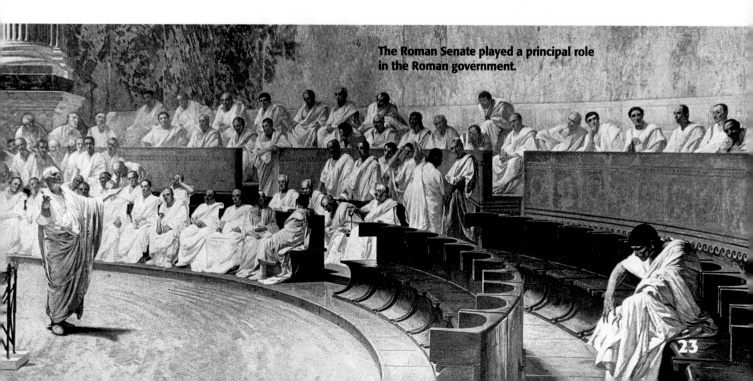

The Roman Senate played a principal role in the Roman government.

Middle Ages

As the Roman Empire fell, groups from the north and east moved into former Roman lands. By the early 500s Europe was divided into many small kingdoms. This marked the beginning of the Middle Ages, a period that lasted about a thousand years.

Feudalism

In the 480s a powerful group called the Franks conquered Gaul, the region we now call France. The Franks created a huge empire in Europe. When invaders began to attack European settlements in the 800s, the Frankish kings could not defend their empire. Because they could not depend on protection from their kings, nobles had to defend their own lands. As a result, the power of European nobles grew, and kings became less powerful. Although these nobles remained loyal to the king, they ruled their lands as independent territories.

Nobles needed soldiers to defend their lands. Nobles gave **knights**, warriors who fought on horseback, land in exchange for military service. Nobles who gave land to knights so that the knights would defend the land were called lords. A knight who promised to support the noble in battle was called a vassal. This system of promises between lords and vassals is known as feudalism.

Peasants owned no land, so they were not part of the feudal system. They did, however, need to grow food to live. As a result, a new economic system developed. Knights allowed peasants to farm land on their large estates, called manors. In return, the peasants had to give the knights food or other goods as payment.

Because of its structure, feudalism promoted the separation of territories and people. The Catholic Church, however, served as a strong unifying force among the states and people of Europe. During the Middle Ages, nearly everyone in Europe was Christian. Life revolved around the local church with markets, festivals, and religious ceremonies.

The Crusades

In the late 1000s, a long series of wars called the Crusades began between the European Christians and Muslims in Southwest Asia.

Time Line

Key Events in Europe

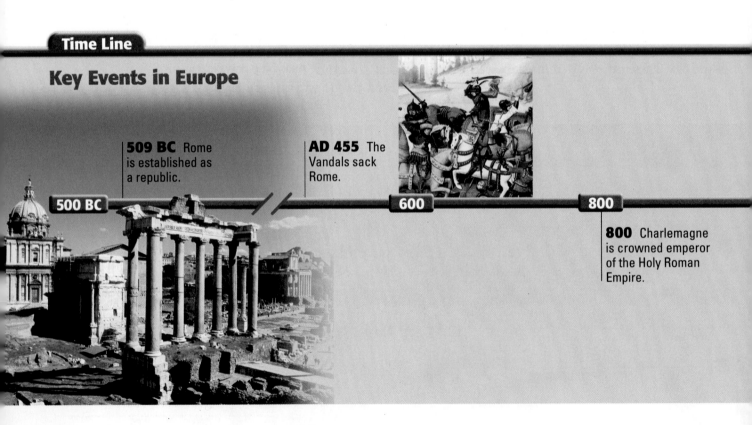

509 BC Rome is established as a republic.

AD 455 The Vandals sack Rome.

500 BC   600   800

800 Charlemagne is crowned emperor of the Holy Roman Empire.

The Turks had captured Palestine, the Holy Land where Jesus had lived. Christians no longer felt safe to travel there on pilgrimages. Christians were called upon to go to war with the Turks to recapture Palestine.

Although the Crusades failed, they changed Europe forever. Trade between Europe and Asia began to grow, introducing Europeans to new products such as apricots, rice, and cotton cloth, as well as the ideas of Muslim thinkers.

Travel, Trade, and Towns

In the Middle Ages, towns were small. After about 1000, this situation began to change. New technology meant farmers could produce larger harvests. As farmers grew more food, the population increased.

Travel became safer as increased protection from stronger rulers kept larger territories secure. Over time, kingdoms became nation-states—organized political units with central governments. This development provided even more protection to merchants.

The rulers of the Mongols made routes like the Silk Road, a caravan route that started in China and ended at the Mediterranean Sea,

safe for travelers and traders. Among these traders was Marco Polo. In 1271 he journeyed from Europe to China along part of the old Silk Road. He spent 20 years living and traveling in Asia. When Marco Polo returned to Europe, he brought back stories of spices, coal, and paper money.

Trade routes spread all across Europe. Merchants brought goods from Asia and Africa to sell in European markets. Their ships also brought back rats infected with the plague. The disease, known as the **Black Death**, spread across Europe, killing an estimated 25 million people. The European economy was dramatically affected by the shortage of workers. Peasants and serfs could now demand payment for their labor. They began to move to cities, which began to grow in size.

In time, the growth of trade led to the decline of feudalism and the manor system. A new middle class of artisans and merchants emerged, and trade cities became commercial centers. Trade associations called guilds became an influential part of European life.

READING CHECK **Drawing Conclusions** How did travel and trade affect the feudal system?

1215 Nobles force King John to sign Magna Carta.

1347 The Black Death arrives in Europe, eventually killing millions.

c. 1350 The Renaissance begins.

1000   1200   1400

1066 England is conquered by the Norman king William the Conqueror.

1436 Johannes Gutenberg perfects his invention of the printing press.

ANALYSIS
SKILL **READING TIME LINES**

What two factors on the time line most helped spread literacy in Europe?

Major cities like Venice and Florence became centers of commerce and banking during the 1300s. The trading of cloth, spices, and other goods renewed the European economy during the Renaissance.

How does this picture show a thriving economy?

Renaissance

The Renaissance period brought new ways of thinking to Europe, weakening the old feudal system even more. The word *Renaissance* means "rebirth" and refers to the period that followed the Middle Ages in Europe. This movement began in Italy and eventually spread to other parts of Europe.

During the Renaissance, European rulers began to increase their power over the nobles in their countries. Fewer invasions from outside forces helped bring a period of order and stability to Europe.

Search for Knowledge

Love of art and education was a key feature of the Renaissance. As Turks conquered much of the Byzantine Empire in the East, scholars fled to Italy. They brought ancient classical writings with them. Some of the works were by Greek thinkers like Plato.

Excited by the discoveries brought by Turkish scholars, European scholars went looking for ancient texts in Latin. They discovered many Latin texts in monasteries, which had preserved works by Roman writers. As Italian scholars read these ancient texts, they rediscovered the glories of Greece and Rome.

The search for knowledge and learning spread to all fields, including art, literature, science, and political thought. The Renaissance emphasized the importance of people rather than focusing on religion. This new focus on human value and the study of humanities was called humanism. People's interest in the humanities led them to respect those who could write, create, or speak well. During the Middle Ages, most people had worked only to glorify God.

Italian artists created some of the most beautiful paintings and sculptures in the world. Their art reflected the basic Renaissance idea—the value of human beings. **Michelangelo** and **Leonardo da Vinci** are two of the greatest Renaissance artists. They are known for their work in painting, sculpture, and architecture. Da Vinci was also an inventor, engineer, and mapmaker.

Italian writers also penned great works of literature. Dante Alighieri was a politician and poet. Before Dante, most authors wrote in Latin, the language of the church. But Dante chose to write in Italian, the common language of the people. This gave ordinary people the opportunity to read Dante's work.

Many texts that Europeans rediscovered in the 1300s dealt with science. After reading these works, Renaissance scholars went on to make their own scientific advances. They also studied ancient math texts and built on the ideas they read about. For example, they created symbols for the square root and for positive and negative numbers. Astronomers discovered that Earth moves around the sun. Other scientists used measurements and made calculations to create better, more accurate maps.

The development of the printing press was a giant step forward in spreading new ideas. In the mid-1400s, a German man, **Johannes Gutenberg** (GOOT-uhn-berk), developed a printing press that used movable type. This allowed an entire page to be printed at once. For the first time in history, thousands of people could read the same books and share ideas about them.

Economic Changes Affect Trade

The growth in trade and services at the beginning of the Renaissance sparked a commercial revolution. This also brought a rise in mercantilism. Mercantilism is an economic system that unifies and increases the power and wealth of a nation.

Four northern Italian cities, Florence, Genoa, Milan, and Venice, developed into important trading centers. These cities played two major roles in trade. They served as ports along the Mediterranean Sea. They also served as manufacturing centers and specialized in certain crafts. This economic activity made some families in these cities very wealthy.

As trade and commerce grew, the need for banks arose. Bankers in Florence, Italy, kept money for merchants from all over Europe. The bankers also made money by charging interest on funds they loaned to merchants. The greatest bankers in Florence were from the Medici family. Although Florence was already wealthy from trade, banking increased that wealth.

During this time, merchants began to create **joint-stock companies**, or businesses in which a group of people invest together. In a joint-stock company, the investors share in the companies' profits and losses. Forming joint-stock companies allowed investors to take fewer risks.

READING CHECK Drawing Conclusions How did the Renaissance lead to trade and a commercial revolution?

SUMMARY AND PREVIEW Greek and Roman traditions provided new ways for people to govern themselves. In the next chapter you will read about how the Renaissance paved the way for exploration of the Americas.

THE IMPACT TODAY
The demand for more books led to improvements in printing and binding that have made modern books affordable.

Section 4 Assessment

Reviewing Ideas, Terms, and People

1. **a. Identify** What is the difference between a direct democracy and a republic?
   b. Elaborate What is the importance of having a written law code?
2. **a. Describe** What is the relationship between **knights** and nobles?
   b. Elaborate How did the Crusades affect the feudal system?
3. **a. Identify** What does the term *Renaissance* mean?
   b. Analyze What is the relationship among trade, banking, and **joint-stock companies**?
   c. Elaborate What do you think was the greatest accomplishment of the Renaissance?

Critical Thinking

4. **Supporting a Point of View** Review your notes on the major changes that took place in Europe during the periods discussed in the section. In a chart like the one below, identify which period you think was most important, and explain why.

Most Important	Why

FOCUS ON WRITING

5. **Organizing a Chronology** Make a list of important events in Europe during the time discussed in this section. Reorder them from earliest to most recent.

The Black Death

"And they died by the hundreds," wrote one man who saw the horror, "both day and night." The Black Death had arrived. The Black Death was a series of deadly plagues that hit Europe between 1347 and 1351, killing millions. People didn't know what caused the plague. They also didn't know that geography played a key role in its spread—as people traveled to trade, they unknowingly carried the disease with them to new places.

EUROPE

Kaffa

CENTRAL ASIA

CHINA

AFRICA

The plague probably began in central and eastern Asia. These arrows show how it spread into and through Europe.

This ship has just arrived in Europe from the East with trade goods—and rats with fleas.

The fleas carry the plague and jump onto a man unloading the ship. Soon, he will get sick and die.

The plague is so terrifying that many people think it's the end of the world. They leave town for the country, spreading the Black Death even further.

People dig mass graves to bury the dead. Often, so many people are infected that there is no one left to bury them.

The garbage and dirty conditions in the town provide food and a home for the rats, allowing disease to spread even more.

So many people die so quickly that special carts are sent through the streets to gather the bodies.

GEOGRAPHY SKILLS | INTERPRETING MAPS

1. **Movement** How did the Black Death reach Europe from Asia?
2. **Human-Environment Interaction** What helped spread the plague throughout Europe?

Social Studies Skills

Analysis | Critical Thinking | Civil Participation | Study

Interpreting Diagrams

Understand the Skill

Diagrams are drawings that use lines and labels to explain or illustrate something. Different types of diagrams have different purposes. *Pictorial diagrams* show an object in simple form, much like it would look if you were viewing it. *Cutaway diagrams* show the "insides" of an object. *Component diagrams* show how an object is organized by separating it into parts. Such diagrams are sometimes also called *schematic drawings*. The ability to interpret diagrams will help you to better understand a historical object, its function, and how it worked.

Learn the Skill

Use these basic steps to interpret a diagram:

1. Determine what type of diagram it is.

2. Read the diagram's title or caption to find out what the diagram represents.

3. Look for any labels and read them carefully. Most diagrams include text that identifies the object's parts or explains relationships between the parts.

4. If a legend is present, study it to identify and understand any symbols and colors that are used in the diagram.

5. Look for numbers or letters that might indicate a sequence of steps. Also, look for any arrows that might show direction or movement.

An Early Castle

Pulley · Oven · Chapel · Fireplaces · Windows · Drawbridge · Moat · Well

Practice and Apply the Skill

Interpret the diagram of an early castle, and answer the following questions.

1. What type of diagram is this?

2. What labels in the diagram suggest how the castle was heated?

3. What was the purpose of the pulley?

4. Of what materials was the castle made?

5. What features of the castle helped make it secure against attack?

Chapter Review

HOLT
History's Impact
▶ video series
Review the video to answer the closing question:
Why do some American exports often depend on imported goods?

Visual Summary

QUICK FACTS

Use the visual summary below to help you review the main ideas of the chapter.

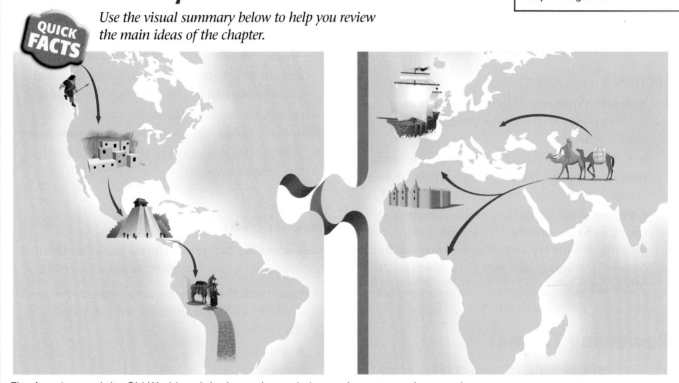

The Americas and the Old World each had complex societies, trade routes, and economies.

Reviewing Vocabulary, Terms, and People

Complete each sentence by filling in the blank with the correct term or person.

1. During the Ice Age, a narrow strip of land called the _____ was exposed.

2. The _____ of Paleo-Indians from North to South America took thousands of years.

3. Native Americans living in the Pacific Northwest carved _____ on tall poles.

4. The first political confederation of Native Americans in North America was the _____.

5. The most famous ruler of Mali was _____.

6. While Mali's leader was on a _____, or pilgrimage, to Mecca, he introduced his empire to the world.

7. The most famous ruler of Songhai took the name _____.

8. _____ describes an ideal society based on justice in *Republic*.

Comprehension and Critical Thinking

SECTION 1 *(Pages 6–9)*

9. **a. Describe** How did early peoples in the Americas get their food?

   b. Analyze What led to the development of different culture groups in the Americas?

   c. Elaborate What features did the early civilizations of Mesoamerica and South America have in common?

SECTION 2 *(Pages 10–15)*

10. **a. Identify** Which early Native American society built cliff dwellings, and which built mounds?

   b. Analyze How did Native Americans' religious beliefs affect their lives in North America?

   c. Evaluate Do you think it was easier for Native Americans to live in the dry climates of the Southwest, where rainfall was unpredictable, or in the North, where the cold climate presented a constant challenge?

11. a. Describe How did geography contribute to Ghana's wealth?

b. Compare What characteristics did Mansa Musa and Askia the Great have in common?

c. Elaborate How did West Africa develop a large slave-trade network?

SECTION 4 *(Pages 22–27)*

12. a. Recall What role did Greek and Roman traditions play in the development of the United States?

b. Summarize How did the Crusades in Southwest Asia and the travels of Marco Polo in Asia contribute to the growth of trade in Europe?

c. Evaluate Which do you think contributed the most to the advances in learning that occurred during the Renaissance—writing in the common language of a people or inventing the printing press?

Reviewing Themes

13. Geography How did changes in climate lead to migration to the Americas?

14. Economics Describe the development of the European economy during the Middle Ages.

Using the Internet   go.hrw.com   KEYWORD: SF7 CH1

15. Activity: Compare and Contrast What causes large groups of people to migrate? Factors that influence why people migrate can be labeled as "push" and "pull." Poor climate and lack of resources "pushed" Paleo-Indians to North America. This activity will help you understand factors of migration. Enter the activity keyword, then compare and contrast push-pull factors involved in Paleo-Indian migration with the factors influencing immigration to the United States today. Create an illustrated chart to display your research.

Reading Skills

Specialized Vocabulary of Social Studies *Use the Reading Skills taught in this chapter to answer the question about the reading selection below.*

> To encourage the spread of Islam in West Africa, Mansa Musa brought back artists and architects from other Muslim countries to build **mosques**, or buildings for Muslim prayer, throughout his lands. (p. 19)

16. What is the definition of the word *mosques* in the sentence above?

Social Studies Skills

Understanding Diagrams *Use the Social Studies Skills taught in this chapter to answer the question below.*

17. Look back at the diagram on page 30. Which of the following is the main way to enter the castle?

a. well

b. moat

c. drawbridge

d. windows

FOCUS ON WRITING

18. Writing Your Travelogue. You have read about many cultures across a long span of history. Pick one area that you found the most interesting in the chapter. Organize your thoughts about the kinds of people you would have met and the kind of things you would have done if you had traveled there during the time discussed.

Try to include information about a culture's history, customs, beliefs, practices, economies, political systems, and natural environments. Write a paragraph about what you might have liked or disliked about your trip. Be sure to include a main idea sentence and several sentences that support the main idea with evidence.

Standardized Test Practice

IN 8.1.1, 8.1.2, 8.3.1, 8.3.3

DIRECTIONS: Read each question and write the letter of the best response.

1 **Before the arrival of Europeans, the most advanced Native American societies were located in what is now**

 A California.

 B the eastern United States.

 C the American Southwest.

 D Mexico.

2 **The trade in gold, salt, and slaves is closely related to**

 A the Inca Empire.

 B the Roman Empire.

 C West Africa.

 D the Renaissance.

3 **Which of the following statements *best* describes the cause of increased trade between Europe and Asia in the late Middle Ages?**

 A The interruption of trade caused by the Crusades led many merchants to travel to Asia in search of trade partners.

 B European merchants traded with Asia due to a lack of valuable natural resources in Europe.

 C The growth of towns during the Middle Ages led to an increased demand for Asian trade goods.

 D Marco Polo's stories of Asia's great wealth led many Europeans to seek out Asian goods.

4 **How did the societies of North America differ from those of Central and South America?**

 A Societies in North America did not create political units like those in Central and South America.

 B North American culture groups lacked the diversity of those in Central and South America.

 C North American societies were significantly more advanced than those to the south.

 D Culture groups in North America worshipped many gods, while those in Central and South America were monotheistic.

5 **A result of Johannes Gutenberg's printing press was that**

 A the Renaissance began.

 B more people could read the same books and share ideas.

 C European trade and commerce grew.

 D overseas trade and travel became more popular.

6 **The exposure of a land bridge between Asia and present-day Alaska during the last Ice Age resulted in**

 A the introduction of new plants and animals to Asia and Europe.

 B the development of farming in the Americas.

 C the migration of people into the Americas.

 D the establishment of advanced cultures in North America.

7 **Examine the following passage by Marco Polo about his travels through China. Then answer the question that follows.**

> *"*Upon leaving Ta-in-fu, we traveled for seven days through a fine county in which there were many cities, where commerce and manufactures [goods] prevailed. We reached a large city named Pi-an-fu, which is very famous. Like Ta-in-fu, this city contains numerous merchants and artisans. Silk is produced here also in great quantity.*"*
>
> —Marco Polo, from the *Travels of Marco Polo: The Venetian*

Document-Based Question **What is the main idea of this passage?**

New Empires in the Americas

Indiana Standards

Social Studies Standards

8.1.2 Explain the struggle of the British, French, Spanish, and Dutch to gain control of North America during settlement and colonization.

8.1.30 Formulate historical questions by analyzing primary resources about an issue confronting the United States during the period from 1754-1877.

8.3.7 Using maps identify changes influenced by growth, economic development, and human migration in the eighteenth and nineteenth centuries.

8.4.1 Identify economic factors contributing to European exploration and colonization in North America, the American Revolution, and the drafting of the Constitution of the United States.

go.hrw.com
Indiana
KEYWORD: SF10 IN

FOCUS ON WRITING

Writing a Letter Long before telephones and e-mails, most people communicated with friends and family far away by letter. As you read this chapter, you will learn about different groups of people who came to the Americas. You will pretend to be a member of one of these groups and write a letter home to tell your friends and family about the people you meet and the experiences you have in the Americas.

WORLD

1416
Prince Henry the Navigator establishes a center for naval exploration at Sagres, Portugal.

1400

History's Impact
▶ video series
Watch the video to understand the impact of different cultures.

What You Will Learn...

The ships of explorer Christopher Columbus sail again in the form of these replicas. Columbus discovered land where Europeans did not expect land to be. The news excited Europe and set off the great Age of Exploration. The Americas and Europe—and the world—would never be the same again. In this chapter you will learn more about the Europeans who colonized North America.

1679
Rene-Robert Cavelier de La Salle becomes the first European to explore the region now known as Indiana.

1492
Christopher Columbus lands in the Bahamas.

1609
Henry Hudson makes his first voyage to North America.

1619
The first Africans in North America arrive at Jamestown, Virginia.

1500

1600

1700

1533
Francisco Pizarro and his men kill Inca leader Atahualpa.

1609
Galileo Galilei becomes the first person to use a telescope to view the heavens.

1644
The Qing dynasty begins in China and rules until 1912.

NEW EMPIRES IN THE AMERICAS **35**

Reading Social Studies

by Kylene Beers

| Economics | Geography | Politics | Society and Culture | Science and Technology |

Focus on Themes In this chapter you will read about European exploration of the sea and of North and South America. As you read, you will learn about how **politics** encouraged the desire to explore new trade routes and lands. You will also read about how **geography** affected the race for empires in the New World. European nations began exploring the newly discovered continents in an effort to establish colonies.

Outlining and History

Focus on Reading How can you make sense of all the facts and ideas in a chapter? One way is to take notes in the form of an outline.

Outlining a Chapter Here is an example of a partial outline for Section 4 of this chapter. Compare the outline to the information on pages 52–57. Notice how the writer looked at the headings in the chapter to determine the main and supporting ideas.

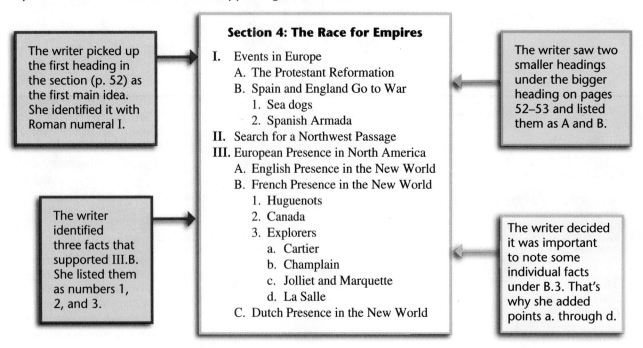

The writer picked up the first heading in the section (p. 52) as the first main idea. She identified it with Roman numeral I.

The writer saw two smaller headings under the bigger heading on pages 52–53 and listed them as A and B.

Section 4: The Race for Empires

I.   Events in Europe
   A. The Protestant Reformation
   B. Spain and England Go to War
      1. Sea dogs
      2. Spanish Armada
II. Search for a Northwest Passage
III. European Presence in North America
   A. English Presence in the New World
   B. French Presence in the New World
      1. Huguenots
      2. Canada
      3. Explorers
         a. Cartier
         b. Champlain
         c. Jolliet and Marquette
         d. La Salle
   C. Dutch Presence in the New World

The writer identified three facts that supported III.B. She listed them as numbers 1, 2, and 3.

The writer decided it was important to note some individual facts under B.3. That's why she added points a. through d.

Outlining a Few Paragraphs When you need to outline only a few paragraphs, you can use the same outline form. Just look for the main idea of each paragraph and give each one a Roman numeral. Supporting ideas within the paragraph can be listed with A, B, and so forth. You can use Arabic numbers for specific details and facts.

You Try It!

Read the following passage from this chapter. Then fill in the blanks to complete the outline below.

Conquest of the Aztec Empire

Chapter 2, (p. 46)

Moctezuma ruled the Aztec Empire, which was at the height of its power in the early 1500s. Moctezuma's capital, Tenochtitlán, was built in the middle of Lake Texcoco, near the present-day site of Mexico City. Tenochtitlán was a large city with temples, a palace, and buildings that were built on an island in the middle of the lake. The buildings and riches of the city impressed the Spaniards. They saw the Aztec Empire as a good source of gold and silver. They also wanted to convert the Aztec to Christianity.

The Aztec had thousand of warriors. In contrast, Cortés had only 508 soldiers, about 100 sailors, 16 horses, and some guns. Cortés hoped that his superior weapons would bring him victory.

Complete this outline based on the passage you just read.

I. Moctezuma and the Aztec Empire were at the height of power in the 1500s.

    A. Tenochtitlán was the capital

        1. Built in Lake Texcoco

        2. _____

    B. The buildings and riches impressed the conquistadors

        1. _____

        2. Christianity

II. _____

    A. Cortés had fewer soldiers

    B. _____

Key Terms and People

Chapter 2

Section 1
Leif Eriksson *(p. 38)*
Henry the Navigator *(p. 39)*
astrolabe *(p. 40)*
caravels *(p. 40)*

Section 2
Christopher Columbus *(p. 42)*
Line of Demarcation *(p. 44)*
Treaty of Tordesillas *(p. 44)*
Ferdinand Magellan *(p. 44)*
circumnavigate *(p. 44)*
Columbian Exchange *(p. 45)*

Section 3
conquistadors *(p. 46)*
Hernán Cortés *(p. 46)*
Moctezuma II *(p. 46)*
Francisco Pizarro *(p. 47)*
encomienda system *(p. 50)*
plantations *(p. 50)*
Bartolomé de Las Casas *(p. 51)*

Section 4
Protestant Reformation *(p. 53)*
Protestants *(p. 53)*
Spanish Armada *(p. 53)*
Northwest Passage *(p. 54)*
Jacques Cartier *(p. 54)*
charter *(p. 54)*

Section 5
immune *(p. 58)*
Middle Passage *(p. 59)*
African Diaspora *(p. 60)*

Academic Vocabulary

Success in school is related to knowing academic vocabulary—the words that are frequently used in school assignments and discussions. In this chapter, you will learn the following academic words.

effect *(p. 40)*
structure *(p. 59)*

Europeans Set Sail

What You Will Learn...

Main Ideas

1. Vikings were skilled sailors, and they were the first Europeans to reach North America.
2. Prince Henry the Navigator established a school for sailors and provided financial support that enabled the Portuguese to start exploring the oceans.
3. Portuguese sailors sailed around Africa and found a sea route to Asia.

The Big Idea

Europeans explored the world, searching for new lands and new trade routes.

Key Terms and People

Leif Eriksson, *p. 38*
Henry the Navigator, *p. 39*
astrolabe, *p. 40*
caravels, *p. 40*

TAKING NOTES As you read, take notes on European exploration. List the countries that explored the world and the places they explored. Write your notes in a chart like the one below.

Countries	Places Explored

If YOU were there...

You are a sailor living in Portugal in the mid-1400s. Several of your friends are excited about joining an expedition to sail to new lands. Although Portuguese navigators have made improvements to sailing ships and advancements in ocean travel, you have heard about the dangers other sailors have faced on the open seas.

Will you join the expedition or stay behind? Why?

BUILDING BACKGROUND Europeans were interested in the goods of Africa and Asia. In order to find new routes to these goods and to find new lands to settle, many European nations sent explorers on voyages.

Viking Sailors Reach North America

The Vikings were the first Europeans to make contact with North America. They came from Scandinavia, a peninsula that includes the present-day countries of Denmark, Norway, and Sweden. The Vikings were skilled sailors who developed a new style of ship, called the longship, that curved up at both ends. Viking vessels traveled the rough North Atlantic seas better than earlier ships because their designs were more stable.

The Vikings raided countries throughout Europe, but they also developed large trading networks. Viking ships sailed to the British Isles and the Mediterranean and Black seas. Eventually, the Vikings sailed west into the North Atlantic. There they founded a settlement on the island of Iceland in about 874. More than 100 years later, Viking Erik the Red left Iceland to settle Greenland.

Leif Eriksson, the son of Erik the Red, shared his father's love of adventure. In the year 1000, he was sailing from west Norway to Greenland when strong winds blew his ship off course and carried his ship all the way to the North American coast.

Eriksson and his crew landed on the Labrador Peninsula in present-day Canada. The Vikings then sailed farther south to the island of Newfoundland, and perhaps to what is now New England. According to their myths, Vikings saw forests, meadows, and rivers that held "larger salmon than they had ever seen."

Eriksson settled in a coastal area he called Vinland, but the Vikings left after only a few years. Attacks by Native Americans posed a constant threat, and the area may have been too far from other Viking settlements to be supported.

After the Vikings left North America, Europeans did not return to the continent for centuries. In the 1400s, however, a growing interest in discovery and exploration spread across Europe.

READING CHECK Sequencing List the stages of exploration that led to the Vikings' landing in North America.

Prince Henry the Navigator

In the early 1400s Portugal became a leader in world exploration. One man in particular, Prince **Henry the Navigator**, was responsible for advances that would make exploration more successful. Although he never set out on a voyage himself, Henry greatly advanced Portugal's exploration efforts.

In the early 1400s Prince Henry built an observatory and founded a school of navigation to teach better methods of sailing. He also financed research by mapmakers and shipbuilders. Finally, he paid for expeditions to explore the west coast of Africa.

Riches in Asia

During the 1400s, Europeans had several reasons to explore the world. First, they wanted Asian spices. They hoped to bypass the merchants who had a monopoly on, or economic control of, the Asian products that reached the Mediterranean. If a sea route to Asia could be found, countries could buy spices and other items directly.

Second, religion played a role in exploration. Christians in Europe wanted to convert more people to their faith. Third, many Europeans had become interested in Asian cultures. Explorer Marco Polo's book about his travels throughout Asia remained popular in Europe long after his death in 1324. Many Europeans wanted to learn more about Asia and its cultures.

History Close-up

The Caravel

A special type of ship called the caravel became the work-horse of many European explorers. Though small, caravels were sturdy. They could sail across huge oceans and up small rivers. Caravels featured important advances in sailing technology.

The smooth, rounded hull handled high seas well.

The large center rudder made quick turns possible.

Triangular sails enabled the caravel to sail into the wind.

ANALYSIS SKILL ANALYZING VISUALS

What features made the caravel an excellent sailing ship?

Causes and Effects of the Discovery of a Sea Route to Asia

Several factors led to the discovery of a sea route from Europe to Asia.

Causes

- Financial backing from Prince Henry the Navigator
- New technology (caravel and mariner's astrolabe)
- Seeking trade with Asia and financial gain
- Converting people to Christianity
- Curiosity

Effects

- Discovery of a sea route to Asia
- Face-to-face contact with traders in distant lands
- Awareness of different cultures and ways of life

ANALYSIS SKILL **ANALYZING INFORMATION**

Why was trade with Asia so important to Europeans?

ACADEMIC VOCABULARY

effect the result of an action or decision

FOCUS ON READING

Make an outline for the heading "A Sea Route to Asia."

Technological Advances

New technology played a major role in advancing world exploration. Sailors began to use tools such as the magnetic compass and the **astrolabe**, a device that enabled navigators to learn their ship's location by charting the position of the stars. Better instruments made it possible for sailors to travel the open seas without landmarks to guide them.

The Portuguese also made advances in shipbuilding. They began designing ships that were smaller, lighter, and easier to steer than the heavy galleons they had used before. These new ships, called **caravels** (ker-uh-velz), used triangular sails that, unlike traditional square sails, allowed ships to sail against the wind. By placing rudders at the back of the ship, the Portuguese also improved the steering of ships.

READING CHECK **Analyzing** How did Henry the Navigator promote exploration?

A Sea Route to Asia

By the 1400s Portugal had several motives, financial support, and the technology necessary for exploration. Portuguese explorers set out to find new lands.

Rounding Africa

Even with new technology, travel on the open seas was dangerous and difficult. One person described the **effect** on sailors of a voyage south from Portugal.

"Those which survived could hardly be recognized as human. They had lost flesh and hair, the nails had gone from hands and feet . . . They spoke of heat so incredible that it was a marvel that ships and crews were not burnt."
–Sailor, quoted in *World Civilizations*, edited by Edward McNall Burns, et al.

In spite of the dangers, Portuguese explorers continued sailing south, setting up trading posts along the way.

In 1488 Portuguese navigator Bartolomeu Dias led an expedition from Portugal southward along the African coast. A storm blew his ships around the southern tip of Africa. This point became known as the Cape of Good Hope. Dias wanted to continue his voyage, but his men did not. Since supplies were very low, Dias decided to call off the voyage and return to Portugal.

Later, King Manuel of Portugal sent another explorer, Vasco da Gama, on an expedition around the Cape of Good Hope. Da Gama left Lisbon, Portugal, in July 1497 and arrived in southwestern India the next year. Portugal had won the European race for a sea route to Asia.

When da Gama reached the Indian port of Calicut, Muslim traders met him and his men. The Muslims surprised the sailors by speaking to them in Portuguese. Soon da Gama and his crew learned that the people of India had been trading with Muslim and Italian merchants who knew Portuguese. Da Gama made two more trips back to India. He even governed a small colony there.

Results of Exploration

Portugal's explorations would have major results, including the start of the Atlantic slave trade. As Portuguese sailors explored the west coast of Africa, they negotiated for gold, ivory, and slaves. The slave trade devastated African communities. It led to increased warfare among kingdoms and broke up many families. The Portuguese sent many enslaved Africans to Europe and to islands in the Atlantic, where they lived and worked under brutal conditions.

The other nations of Europe watched as new trade routes brought increased wealth and power to Portugal. They soon launched voyages of exploration to find their own water routes to Asia.

READING CHECK **Predicting** How would continued exploration affect Africans?

SUMMARY AND PREVIEW In the 1400s, the Portuguese started a new era of exploration. In the next section you will learn how Europeans reached the American continents.

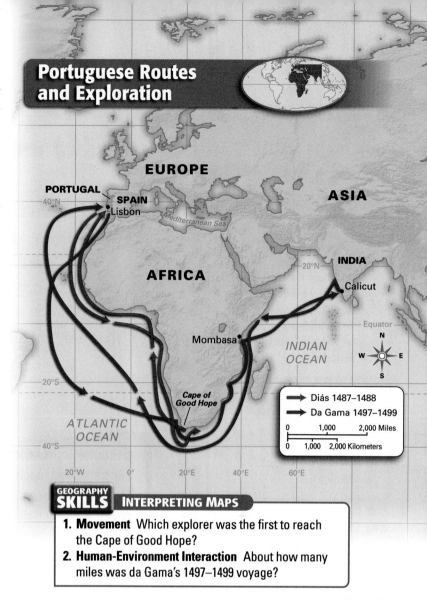

Portuguese Routes and Exploration

Legend:
→ Diás 1487–1488
→ Da Gama 1497–1499
0   1,000   2,000 Miles
0   1,000   2,000 Kilometers

GEOGRAPHY SKILLS **INTERPRETING MAPS**

1. **Movement** Which explorer was the first to reach the Cape of Good Hope?
2. **Human-Environment Interaction** About how many miles was da Gama's 1497–1499 voyage?

Section 1 Assessment

go.hrw.com
Online Quiz
KEYWORD: SF7 HP2

Reviewing Ideas, Terms, and People

1. **a. Identify** Who was **Leif Eriksson**?
   b. Summarize How did the Vikings eventually establish Vinland?
   c. Draw Inferences Why do you think the Vikings did not try to colonize the Americas?
2. **a. Identify** Who was Prince **Henry the Navigator**?
   b. Compare Why were **caravels** able to sail against the wind while other ships could not?
3. **a. Recall** Who was the first explorer to find a sea route from Europe to Asia?
   b. Explain How did Muslims living in India learn Portuguese?
   c. Draw Conclusions How did the slave trade affect West Africa?

Critical Thinking

4. **Summarizing** Review your notes on European exploration. Then copy the chart below and use it to explain the reason for the explorations, the technology that made explorations possible, and the results of the explorations.

Reason
Technology → Results

FOCUS ON WRITING

5. **Taking Notes on Early Explorers** As you read this section, take notes on groups of explorers. Make sure to note the differences and similarities between the groups, where they traveled, and why.

Europeans Reach the Americas

What You Will Learn...

Main Ideas

1. Christopher Columbus sailed across the Atlantic Ocean and reached a continent that was previously unknown to him.
2. After Columbus's voyages, other explorers sailed to the Americas.

The Big Idea

Christopher Columbus's voyages led to new exchanges between Europe, Africa, and the Americas.

Key Terms and People

Christopher Columbus, *p. 42*
Line of Demarcation, *p. 44*
Treaty of Tordesillas, *p. 44*
Ferdinand Magellan, *p. 44*
circumnavigate, *p. 44*
Columbian Exchange, *p. 45*

TAKING NOTES As you read, take notes on the explorers, their journeys, and the effects of European voyages to the Americas. Write your notes in a chart like the one below.

Explorer	Sponsored by	Traveled to

Effects of Journeys

If YOU were there...

You are a European explorer who just returned to your home-land from the Americas. While you were gone, you tried new and different foods, including corn, potatoes, and cocoa. You have brought some of these foods back with you. You want your friends and family to sample these items, but they resist.

What will you say about these new foods?

BUILDING BACKGROUND Europeans, Africans, and Asians had traded with each other for centuries using land and sea routes. Native American groups also knew of each other through trade routes. Although sailors often explored new areas, before 1492 the two worlds had no communication with each other.

Columbus Sails across the Atlantic

Stories of fabulous kingdoms and wealth in Asia captured the imagination of **Christopher Columbus**, a sailor from Genoa, Italy. Columbus was convinced that he could reach Asia by sailing west across the Atlantic Ocean.

The Journey Begins

Columbus asked King Ferdinand and Queen Isabella of Spain to pay for an expedition across the Atlantic. He promised them great riches, new territory, and Catholic converts. It took Columbus several years to convince the king and queen, but they finally agreed to help finance the journey. Ferdinand and Isabella ordered Columbus to bring back any items of value and to claim for Spain any lands he explored.

On August 3, 1492, Columbus's three ships set sail. The *Niña* and the *Pinta* were caravels. Columbus sailed in the larger *Santa María*. The ships carried about 90 sailors and a year's worth of supplies. They made a stop in the Canary Islands, and then on September 6, they resumed their journey. Soon, they passed the limits of Columbus's

Columbus's Voyages, 1492–1504

NORTH AMERICA

Gulf of Mexico

The Bahamas

San Salvador

ATLANTIC OCEAN

Tropic of Cancer

Cuba

20°N

Hispaniola

Puerto Rico

Jamaica

MESOAMERICA

Caribbean Sea

80°W

70°W

60°W

10°N

Trinidad

SOUTH AMERICA

First voyage, 1492–1493
Second voyage, 1493–1496
Third voyage, 1498
Fourth voyage, 1502–1504
Land seen by Columbus or crew members

0   250   500 Miles
0   250   500 Kilometers

Transatlantic Travel

ATLANTIC OCEAN

EUROPE

NORTH AMERICA

40°N

PORTUGAL

Azores

SPAIN

Canary Islands

20°N

AFRICA

Equator 0°

SOUTH AMERICA

20°S

Treaty of Tordesillas, 1494

GEOGRAPHY SKILLS INTERPRETING MAPS

1. **Place** Where did Columbus first land?
2. **Human-Environment Interaction** Why do you think Columbus saw only the coastal area of Mesoamerica?

maps and sailed into uncharted seas. After more than a month with no sight of land, the crew grew restless.

Soon the crew saw signs of land—birds and floating tree branches. Columbus promised a reward "to him who first sang out that he saw land." On October 12, 1492, a lookout cried, "Land! Land!" ending the long journey from the Canary Islands.

The ships landed on an island in the Bahamas. Columbus thought he had found a new route to Asia. Instead, he had reached another continent that was unknown to him. Columbus called the island San Salvador, which means "Holy Savior." Columbus also visited another island he called Hispaniola. There he met the Taino (TY-noh). At that time Europeans called Asia the Indies, so Columbus, believing he was in Asia, called these Native American people Indians.

The Taino lived in small farming communities. In his journal, Columbus wrote that the Taino were "so generous . . . that no

one would believe it who has not seen it." However, Columbus and his crew were not interested in Taino culture, but in gold. After three months of exploring, looking for gold, and collecting exotic plants and animals, Columbus returned to Spain.

Columbus made three more journeys to the Americas during his lifetime. In 1504 he returned to Spain in poor health. Columbus died two years later, still believing that he had reached Asia.

Impact of Columbus's Voyages

The voyages of Columbus changed the way Europeans thought of the world and their place in it. A new era of interaction between Europe and the Americas had begun.

Columbus's discovery also created conflict between European countries. Both Spain and Portugal wanted to add these lands to their growing empires. In 1493, Pope Alexander VI, originally from Spain, issued a decree that drew a new boundary for Spain and Portugal.

LETTER
Christopher Columbus, 1494

Two years after discovering the island of Hispaniola, Columbus wrote a letter to the Spanish king and queen outlining his ideas of its colonization.

Most High and Mighty Sovereigns,

In the first place, as regards the Island of Espanola: Inasmuch as the number of colonists who desire to go thither [there] amounts to two thousand, owing to the land being safer and better for farming and trading . . .

1. That in the said island there shall be founded three or four towns . . .

2. That for the better and more speedy colonization of the said island, no one shall have liberty to collect gold in it except those who have taken out colonists' papers . . .

3. That each town shall have its alcalde [Mayor] . . .

4. That there shall be a church, and parish priests or friars to administer the sacraments, to perform divine worship, and for the conversion of the Indians.

–Christopher Columbus,

letter to the king and queen of Spain, 1494

ANALYSIS SKILL **ANALYZING PRIMARY SOURCES**

What were Columbus's main concerns in founding a colony on Hispaniola?

This imaginary **Line of Demarcation** divided the Atlantic Ocean. Spain could claim all land west of the line.

The Portuguese king believed that this arrangement favored Spain. To prevent war, the leaders of the two nations signed the **Treaty of Tordesillas**, which moved the Line of Demarcation 800 miles further west. This gave Portugal more opportunity to claim lands unexplored by other Europeans.

READING CHECK **Identifying Points of View**
Why did Columbus want to sail across the Atlantic?

Other Explorers Sail to the Americas

Columbus's discoveries inspired others to sail across the Atlantic Ocean. In 1501 explorer Amerigo Vespucci (vuh-SPOO-chee) led a Spanish fleet to the coast of present-day South America. He was convinced the land he reached was not Asia. Instead, Vespucci believed he had found a "new world." A German mapmaker labeled the continents across the ocean *America* in honor of Vespucci. Europeans began using the names North America and South America for these lands.

In a Spanish settlement in present-day Panama, another explorer, Vasco Núñez de Balboa (NOON-yays day bahl-BOH-uh), heard stories from local Native Americans about another ocean farther west. Balboa set out to find it. For weeks he and his men struggled through thick jungle and deadly swamps. In 1513 they reached the top of a mountain. From this spot Balboa saw a great blue sea—the Pacific Ocean—stretching out before him.

In 1519, **Ferdinand Magellan** (muh-JEHL-uhn), a Portuguese navigator, set out with a Spanish fleet to sail down the east coast of South America. After sailing around the southern tip of the continent, Magellan continued into the Pacific even though his ships were dangerously low on food and fresh water.

Magellan's fleet sailed across the Pacific Ocean. In the Philippines, Magellan was killed in a battle with native peoples. Down to three ships, the expedition continued sailing west into the Indian Ocean. In 1522 the voyage's only remaining ship returned to Spain. Only 18 members of Magellan's original crew survived. These sailors were the first people to **circumnavigate**, or go all the way around, the globe. Their entire journey was some 40,000 miles long.

European explorers and settlers took plants and animals with them to the Americas. They also brought back a variety of new plants and animals to Europe, Asia, and Africa.

This transfer became known as the **Columbian Exchange** because it started with Columbus's explorations. The Columbian Exchange dramatically changed the world.

European explorers found many plants in the Americas that were unknown to them, including corn, potatoes, tobacco, and cocoa. They brought these items to Europe, where they were highly valued. The explorers also introduced horses, cattle, and pigs to the Americas. Native Americans came to use these animals for food and transportation. They also started to farm European grains such as wheat and barley.

Without intending to do so, the explorers also introduced deadly new diseases to the Americas. Native Americans had no natural resistance to European diseases and often died as a result of their exposure to them.

Over time, a trading pattern involving the exchange of raw materials, manufactured products, and slaves developed among Europe, Africa, and the Americas. Europeans shipped millions of enslaved Africans to work in the colonies in the New World.

READING CHECK **Evaluating** What were the negative aspects of the Columbian Exchange?

The Columbian Exchange

Items brought from the Americas
Cocoa
Corn
Potatoes
Squash
Tobacco
Turkeys

Items brought from Europe
Cattle
Citrus Fruits
Diseases
Grains
Horses
Sugarcane

ANALYSIS SKILL
Which side of the Atlantic did cattle come from? Potatoes? Sugarcane?

SUMMARY AND PREVIEW Columbus's voyages to America inspired other Europeans to explore the "New World." This led to new exchanges between both sides of the Atlantic. In the next section you will learn about Spain's empire in the Americas.

Section 2 Assessment

go.hrw.com
Online Quiz
KEYWORD: SF7 HP2

Reviewing Ideas, Terms, and People

1. **a. Recall** What agreement did **Christopher Columbus** make with Queen Isabella and King Ferdinand of Spain?
   b. Explain Where did Columbus think he had landed when he reached the Bahamas?
   c. Evaluate How did Columbus's voyage lead to a dispute between Spain and Portugal?
2. **a. Identify** Who was the first European explorer to see the Pacific Ocean?
   b. Summarize What route did **Ferdinand Magellan**'s ships take to **circumnavigate** the globe?
   c. Draw Conclusions How did the **Columbian Exchange** and the slave trade affect the economies and the people of Europe, Africa, and the Americas?

Critical Thinking

3. **Supporting a Point of View** Review your notes on European exploration. Then copy the graphic organizer below and use it to rank, in order, the two most important results of European voyages to the Americas. Explain your choices in the "Why" column.

Most Important	Why

FOCUS ON WRITING

4. **Understanding Christopher Columbus** As you read this section, pay attention to what life might have been like for Columbus and his crew as they sailed across the Atlantic. Note ways in which their voyage changed life for many Europeans.

Spain Builds an Empire

What You Will Learn...

Main Ideas

1. Spanish conquistadors conquered the Aztec and Inca empires.
2. Spanish explorers traveled through the borderlands of New Spain, claiming more land.
3. Spanish settlers treated Native Americans harshly, forcing them to work on plantations and in mines.

The Big Idea

Spain established a large empire in the Americas.

Key Terms and People

conquistadors, *p. 46*
Hernán Cortés, *p. 46*
Moctezuma II, *p. 46*
Francisco Pizarro, *p. 47*
encomienda system, *p. 50*
plantations, *p. 50*
Bartolomé de Las Casas, *p. 51*

TAKING NOTES Create a chart like the one below. As you read, take notes on Spanish conquest and settlement in the Americas.

Spanish Conquest and Settlement	
Aztec Empire	
Inca Empire	
Borderlands—Southeast	
Borderlands—Southwest	

 8.3.7, 8.4.1

If YOU were there...

You are an Aztec warrior living in central Mexico in the 1500s. You are proud to serve your ruler, Moctezuma II. One day several hundred foreigners arrive on your shores. They are pale, bearded men, and they have strange animals and equipment.

From where do you think these strangers have come?

BUILDING BACKGROUND Spain sent many expeditions to the Americas. Like explorers from other countries, Spanish explorers claimed the land they found for their country. Much of this land was already filled with Native American communities, however.

Spanish Conquistadors

The Spanish sent **conquistadors** (kahn-kees-tuh-DAWRS), soldiers who led military expeditions in the Americas. Conquistador **Hernán Cortés** left Cuba to sail to present-day Mexico in 1519. Cortés had heard of a wealthy land to the west ruled by a king named **Moctezuma II** (mawk-tay-SOO-mah).

Conquest of the Aztec Empire

Moctezuma ruled the Aztec Empire, which was at the height of its power in the early 1500s. Moctezuma's capital, Tenochtitlán, was built in the middle of Lake Texcoco, near the present-day site of Mexico City. Tenochtitlán was a large city with temples, a palace, and buildings that were built on an island in the middle of the lake. The buildings and riches of the city impressed the Spaniards. They saw the Aztec Empire as a good source of gold and silver. They also wanted to convert the Aztec to Christianity.

The Aztec had thousands of warriors. In contrast, Cortés had only 508 soldiers, about 100 sailors, 16 horses, and some guns. Cortés hoped that his superior weapons would bring him victory. Cortés also sought help from enemies of the Aztec. An Indian woman named Malintzin (mah-LINT-suhn) helped Cortés win allies.

At first Moctezuma believed Cortés to be a god and welcomed him. Cortés then took Moctezuma prisoner and seized control of Tenochtitlán. Eventually, Tenochtitlán was destroyed and Moctezuma was killed. Smallpox and other diseases brought by the Spanish quickened the fall of the Aztec Empire.

Conquest of the Inca Empire

Another conquistador, **Francisco Pizarro** (puh-ZAHR-oh), heard rumors of the Inca cities in the Andes of South America. The Inca ruled a large territory that stretched along the Pacific coast from present-day Chile to northern Ecuador.

Pizarro had fewer than 400 men in his army. But the Inca, like the Aztec, had no weapons to match the conquistadors' swords and guns. Though outnumbered, Pizarro's troops captured the great Inca capital at Cuzco in present-day Peru and killed the Inca leaders. By 1534 Pizarro and his Native American allies had conquered the entire Inca Empire.

In only a few years, the Spanish had conquered two great American empires. During the conquest, the Spanish and their allies killed thousands of Inca and Aztec and looted their settlements. Moreover, possibly more than three-quarters of the Aztec and Inca populations were killed by the diseases the Europeans brought.

Spanish Settlements

The Spanish began to settle their vast empire, which they called New Spain. Spain's government wanted to control migration to the Americas. Most of the emigrants were Spanish, though a few non-Spanish subjects of the king also migrated. Jews, Muslims, and non-Christians were forbidden to settle in New Spain. At first, most emigrants were men. The government then encouraged families to migrate. Eventually, women comprised one-quarter of the total emigration from Spain.

Spain ruled its large American empire through a system of royal officials. At the top was the Council of the Indies, formed in 1524 to govern the Americas from Spain. The Council appointed two viceroys, or royal governors. The Viceroyalty of Peru governed most of South America. The Viceroyalty of New Spain governed all Spanish territories in

LINKING TO TODAY

Armored Warfare

The armor of the Spanish conquistadors helped them defeat the Aztec and Inca. Spanish soldiers and their horses wore armor made of steel. The steel protected the soldiers from enemy weapons but was heavy and hard to wear. Armored weapons of today's soldiers include tanks and other large vehicles. Inside these vehicles, soldiers are safer from enemy gunfire.

ANALYSIS SKILL **ANALYZING INFORMATION**

1. Why did armor need to be heavy?
2. Why do modern armies still use armor?

Central America, Mexico, and the southern part of what is now the United States.

The Spanish established three kinds of settlements in New Spain. Pueblos served as trading posts and sometimes as centers of government. Priests started missions where they converted local Native Americans to Catholicism. The Spanish also built presidios, or military bases, to protect towns and missions.

To connect some of the scattered communities of New Spain, Spanish settlers built *El Camino Real*, or "the Royal Road." This network of roads ran for hundreds of miles, from Mexico City to Santa Fe. The roads later stretched to settlements in California.

READING CHECK Analyzing How did the Spanish conquer the great Aztec and Inca empires?

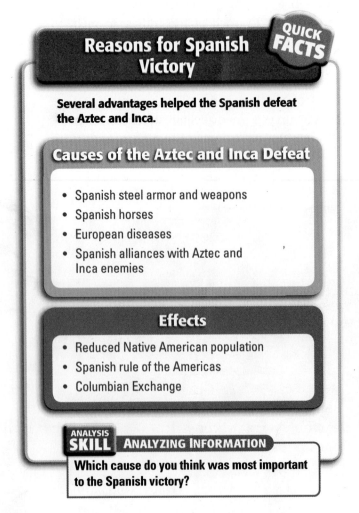

Reasons for Spanish Victory QUICK FACTS

Several advantages helped the Spanish defeat the Aztec and Inca.

Causes of the Aztec and Inca Defeat

- Spanish steel armor and weapons
- Spanish horses
- European diseases
- Spanish alliances with Aztec and Inca enemies

Effects

- Reduced Native American population
- Spanish rule of the Americas
- Columbian Exchange

ANALYSIS SKILL **ANALYZING INFORMATION**
Which cause do you think was most important to the Spanish victory?

Exploring the Borderlands of New Spain

Spain's American empire was not limited to lands taken from the conquered Aztec and Inca empires. Many other Spanish explorers came to North America. They explored the borderlands of New Spain and claimed many new lands for the Spanish crown.

Exploring the Southeast

In 1508 explorer Juan Ponce de León landed on the Caribbean island of Puerto Rico. By 1511 he had conquered the island for Spain and founded the city of San Juan. De León also discovered gold on Puerto Rico. Spanish officials appointed him governor of the colony.

In 1512 de León discovered the coast of present-day Florida. The next year he searched Florida for a mythical Fountain of Youth. Though he never found the fabled fountain, Ponce de León acquired royal permission to colonize Florida. However, he failed in his quest to colonize the area.

Two decades later another explorer traveled through Florida. Royal officials gave Hernando de Soto permission to explore the coastal region of the Gulf of Mexico. In 1539 his expedition landed in an area near the present-day city of Tampa Bay, Florida.

De Soto then led his men north through what is now Georgia and the Carolinas. The expedition then turned west and crossed the Appalachian Mountains. De Soto discovered the Mississippi River in 1541. The explorers then traveled west into present-day Oklahoma. De Soto died in 1542 on this journey.

Exploring the Southwest

The Spanish also explored what is now the southwestern United States. In 1528 explorer Álvar Núñez Cabeza de Vaca joined conquistador Pánfilo de Narváez on an expedition to North America. Their group of 300 men first landed on the Florida coast. They faced many severe problems, including a shortage of food.

The group built boats, which made it possible for them to travel around the Florida panhandle. The explorers continued along the Gulf Coast and eventually reached the Mississippi River. Severe weather hit this group hard, and many members of the expedition died. De Vaca's boat shipwrecked on what is now Galveston Island in Texas. Only de Vaca and three other men survived. One survivor was a Moroccan-born slave named Estevanico. His Spanish slaveholder also survived.

Each of the four survivors was captured and enslaved by Native American groups living in the area. After six years of captivity, the men finally escaped. They journeyed on foot throughout the North American Southwest, receiving help from Native Americans they met along the way. In 1536, after turning south, the group reached Spanish settlements in Mexico.

Soon after their journey ended, Estevanico's slaveholder sold him to a Spanish viceroy. The viceroy assigned Estevanico to serve as a guide for a new expedition he was sending into the Southwest. Native Americans killed the enslaved African in 1539.

De Vaca eventually returned to Spain, where he called for better treatment of Native Americans. De Vaca later wrote about his experiences in the first European book exclusively devoted to North America. De Vaca's book increased Spanish interest in the New World. His writings fueled the rumors that riches could be found in North America.

"For two thousand leagues did we travel, on land, and by sea in barges, besides ten months more after our rescue from captivity; untiringly did we walk across the land,…During all that time we crossed from one ocean to the other,… We heard that on the shores of the South there are pearls and great wealth, and that the richest and best is near there."

–Cabeza de Vaca, *The Journey of Álvar Núñez Cabeza de Vaca*

De Vaca's account inspired other explorers to travel to North America. In 1540 Francisco Vásquez de Coronado set out to

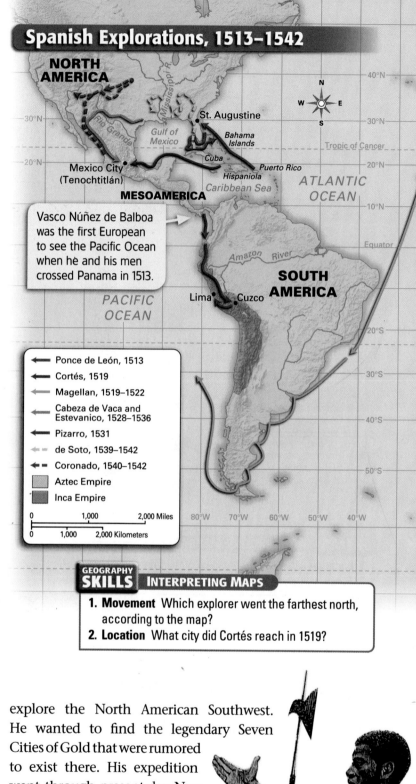

Spanish Explorations, 1513–1542

Vasco Núñez de Balboa was the first European to see the Pacific Ocean when he and his men crossed Panama in 1513.

- Ponce de León, 1513
- Cortés, 1519
- Magellan, 1519–1522
- Cabeza de Vaca and Estevanico, 1528–1536
- Pizarro, 1531
- de Soto, 1539–1542
- Coronado, 1540–1542
- Aztec Empire
- Inca Empire

0   1,000   2,000 Miles
0   1,000   2,000 Kilometers

GEOGRAPHY SKILLS INTERPRETING MAPS

1. **Movement** Which explorer went the farthest north, according to the map?
2. **Location** What city did Cortés reach in 1519?

explore the North American Southwest. He wanted to find the legendary Seven Cities of Gold that were rumored to exist there. His expedition went through present-day New Mexico and Arizona, where a group of his men discovered the Grand Canyon. Coronado trekked through Texas

Estevanico was an enslaved African who traveled with Cabeza de Vaca.

Spanish Viceroyalties, c. 1650

NORTH AMERICA

St. Augustine

Gulf of Mexico

Bahama Islands

Tropic of Cancer

Cuba

Puerto Rico

Mexico City (Tenochtitlán)

Hispaniola

Caribbean Sea

ATLANTIC OCEAN

MESOAMERICA

Equator

Amazon River

PACIFIC OCEAN

Lima

SOUTH AMERICA

ANDES MOUNTAINS

Buenos Aires

Tropic of Capricorn

Viceroyalty of New Spain
Viceroyalty of Peru
⊛ Capital of viceroyalty

0   1,000   2,000 Miles
0   1,000   2,000 Kilometers

Tierra del Fuego
Cape Horn

GEOGRAPHY SKILLS INTERPRETING MAPS

1. **Location** What was the capital of the Viceroyalty of Peru?
2. **Place** Which viceroyalty included modern-day Mexico?

THE IMPACT TODAY

Roman Catholicism is still the most commonly practiced religion in Latin America. More than 80 percent of the population is Catholic.

and Oklahoma, going as far north as Kansas before turning around. He never found the fabled cities of gold.

READING CHECK **Comparing** How were the expeditions of Ponce de León and Coronado similar?

Spanish Treatment of Native Americans

The journeys of the Spanish explorers allowed Spain to claim a huge empire in the Americas. Spain's American colonies helped make the country very wealthy. From 1503 to 1660, Spanish fleets loaded with treasure carried 200 tons of gold and 18,600 tons of silver from the former Aztec and Inca empires to Spain. Mexico and Peru also grew food to help support Spain's growing empire. However, these gains came with a price for Native Americans. Native peoples suffered greatly at the hands of the Spanish.

Forced Labor

By 1650 the Spanish Empire in the Americas had grown to some 3 to 4 million people. Native Americans made up about 80 percent of the population. The rest were whites, Africans, and people of mixed racial background. Settlers who came from Spain were called *peninsulares* (pay-neen-soo-LAHR-ays) and usually held the highest government positions. To reward settlers for their service to the Crown, Spain established the **encomienda** (en-koh-mee-EN-duh) **system**. It gave settlers the right to tax local Native Americans or to make them work. In exchange, these settlers were supposed to protect the Native American people and convert them to Christianity. Instead, most Spanish treated the Native Americans as slaves. Native Americans were forced to work in terrible conditions. They faced cruelty and desperate situations on a daily basis.

The Spanish operated many **plantations**, large farms that grew just one kind of crop. Plantations throughout the Caribbean colonies made huge profits for their owners. It took many workers to run a plantation, however, so colonists forced thousands of Native Americans to work in the fields. Indians who were taken to work on haciendas, the vast Spanish estates in Central and South America, had to raise and herd livestock. Other Native Americans were forced to endure the backbreaking work of mining gold and silver. The forced labor and harsh treatment killed many native people in New Spain.

The Role of the Catholic Church

The Catholic Church played a major role in the interactions of the Spanish with Native Americans. The Spanish king commanded priests to convert the local people to the Christian faith. Some Native Americans combined Spanish customs with their own. Others rejected Spanish ideas completely.

Some European settlers in the Americas protested the terrible treatment of Native Americans. A priest named **Bartolomé de Las Casas** said that the Spanish should try to convert Native Americans to Christianity by showing them love, gentleness, and kindness. The Spanish monarchs agreed, but the colonists did not always follow their laws.

READING CHECK **Finding Main Ideas** How did the encomienda system strengthen Spanish rule?

SUMMARY AND PREVIEW In the 1500s Spain built a vast empire in the Americas. The Spanish treated the Native Americans harshly in their new empire. In the next section you will learn about other European empires in the Americas.

Primary Source

BOOK
Brief Account of the Devastation of the Indies

Bartolomé de Las Casas, a Catholic priest in New Spain, encouraged better treatment of Native Americans.

"When they [Spaniards] have slain all those who fought for their lives or to escape the tortures they would have to endure, that is to say, when they have slain all the native rulers and young men (since the Spaniards usually spare only the women and children, who are subjected to the hardest and bitterest servitude [slavery] ever suffered by man or beast), they enslave any survivors. With these infernal [devilish] methods of tyranny they debase and weaken countless numbers of those pitiful Indian nations."

–Bartolomé de Las Casas,

from *Brief Account of the Devastation of the Indies*

ANALYSIS SKILL **ANALYZING POINTS OF VIEW**

How did Las Casas's view of the treatment of Native American groups differ from the views of other Spaniards?

Section 3 Assessment

Reviewing Ideas, Terms, and People

1. **a. Identify** Who was **Moctezuma II**?
   b. Analyze How was **Hernán Cortés** able to conquer the Aztec Empire?
   c. Elaborate What advantages did the Spanish have over Native Americans?

2. **a. Recall** Which Spanish explorer received permission to colonize Florida?
   b. Analyze Why do you think Cabeza de Vaca wrote of great riches that could be found in the Americas?
   c. Evaluate Why do you think de Vaca called for better treatment of Native Americans after having been held prisoner by them?

3. **a. Identify** What was the **encomienda system**?
   b. Analyze Why do you think the king of Spain commanded Catholic priests to teach Native Americans about Christianity?

Critical Thinking

4. **Categorizing** Review your notes on Spanish conquest and settlement in the Americas. Then copy the following graphic organizer and use it to explain the impact Spain had on the Americas.

Spanish America	
government	
religion	
labor	

FOCUS ON WRITING

5. **Taking Notes on the Spanish Empire** Take notes on the Spanish conquest of the Aztec Empire and the founding of the Spanish Empire. How did this empire affect Native Americans?

The Race for Empires

What You Will Learn...

Main Ideas

1. Events in Europe affected settlement of North America.
2. Several explorers searched for a Northwest Passage to the Pacific Ocean.
3. European nations raced to establish empires in North America.

The Big Idea

Other European nations challenged Spain in the Americas.

Key Terms and People

Protestant Reformation, *p. 53*
Protestants, *p. 53*
Spanish Armada, *p. 53*
Northwest Passage, *p. 54*
Jacques Cartier, *p. 54*
charter, *p. 54*

TAKING NOTES As you read, take notes on the reasons for European voyages to North America, the search for a Northwest Passage, and the development of European empires in North America.

Reasons for Voyages	Explorers' Search for a NW Passage	European Empires

8.1.1, 8.1.2, 8.3.7, 8.4.1

If YOU were there...

The people of your village in France have always belonged to the same church. Now in the 1600s, your village is divided over religious beliefs. You have heard about the Dutch colony of New Netherland in America, where people can practice any religion freely. You would like to leave for America, but your parents are unwilling to leave their home.

How would you persuade your family to emigrate?

BUILDING BACKGROUND During the 1400s, the Catholic Church was one of the most powerful institutions in Europe. Not everyone agreed with all of its teachings, however. Disagreement, and sometimes violence, led some people to search for new places to settle.

Events in Europe

Many significant events took place in Europe in the 1500s. Disagreements about religion threw Europe into turmoil. Some of these disagreements eventually led to wars. At the same time, several European nations began to compete for land and power overseas.

Key Events in European History, 1450–1588

c. 1450

Johannes Gutenberg develops his movable-type printing press.

The Protestant Reformation

In 1517 a German priest named Martin Luther publicly criticized the Roman Catholic Church. Luther charged that the church was too wealthy and that it abused its power. Criticisms like Luther's started the **Protestant Reformation**. This religious movement began in small German towns but quickly spread to most of Europe. It became a part of many political disputes as well. The **Protestants** were reformers who protested some of the Catholic Church's practices. Many Protestants believed God meant for religion to be simple.

The printing press—a machine that produces printed copies using movable type—helped spread the ideas of the Reformation. Protestants printed large numbers of Bibles as well as short essays explaining their ideas. This let more people read and think about the Bible on their own, rather than relying solely on the teachings of a priest.

Conflicts between Catholics and Protestants took place throughout Europe, often leading to civil war. In the late 1500s French Catholics fought French Protestants, known as Huguenots (HYOO-guh-nahts). Many Huguenots eventually emigrated to the Americas in search of religious freedom.

In 1534 King Henry VIII founded the Church of England, or the Anglican Church. By making himself the head of the church, Henry challenged the authority of the pope and angered Catholics. Political issues soon became mixed with the religious struggles.

Spain and England Go to War

In the late 1500s King Philip II used Spain's great wealth to lead a Catholic Reformation against the Protestant movement. He hoped to drive the Protestants out of England. Standing in his way was the Protestant English queen Elizabeth I and her sea dogs. Sea dogs was the name given to English sailors who raided Spanish treasure ships. The most successful and daring was Sir Francis Drake.

Philip was angered by English piracy. He began gathering the **Spanish Armada**, a huge fleet of warships meant to end English plans. The Armada had about 130 ships and some 27,000 sailors and soldiers. This mighty fleet was launched to invade England and overthrow Queen Elizabeth and the Anglican Church. But in July 1588, the smaller, but faster, English fleet defeated the Armada in a huge battle.

The Armada's defeat shocked the Spanish. In addition to the naval defeat, Spain's economy was in trouble. The gold and silver that Spain received from the Americas caused high inflation. Inflation is a rise in the price of goods caused by an increase in the amount of money in use. Economic problems in Spain combined with the defeat of the Spanish Armada led countries such as England, France, and the Netherlands to challenge Spanish power overseas.

READING CHECK Analyzing
What led to the decline of the Spanish Empire?

1517
Martin Luther nails his ninety-five theses to the door of a church in Wittenberg, Germany.

1588
The English defeat the Spanish Armada. The loss greatly weakens Spain, allowing other European countries to claim land in North America.

Search for a Northwest Passage

Europeans wanted to find a **Northwest Passage**, a water route through North America that would allow ships to sail from the Atlantic to the Pacific. The English began sending explorers to find it.

Italian sailor John Cabot knew that the king of England wanted to find such a route. Cabot offered to pay for his own expedition, asking only that the king of England grant him a royal charter to any lands he found. The king agreed, and Cabot made voyages to North America for England in 1497 and 1498.

Cabot sailed to North America, but he left very few records of his journeys. It is believed that he traveled along the coast of present-day Newfoundland in Canada. Although Cabot did not find a passage to the Pacific Ocean, his voyages were successful. They became the basis of England's claim to land in North America.

In 1524 France sent an Italian captain, Giovanni da Verrazano (vayr-raht-SAHN-oh), to seek a Northwest Passage. Verrazano sailed along the coast of North America from present-day North Carolina to Maine. **Jacques Cartier** (kahr-tyay), a French sailor, led France's next major exploration of North America. He made two trips to what is now Canada. Cartier sailed into the Saint Lawrence River and traveled all the way to present-day Montreal, claiming the areas he explored for France.

The Dutch also entered the race. They hired English captain Henry Hudson to find a Northwest Passage. Hudson first sailed to present-day New York in 1609. The following year Hudson returned to North America, sailing under the English flag. He traveled far to the north. Eventually he reached a strait that he hoped would lead to the Pacific Ocean. Instead, it led into a huge bay, later named Hudson Bay.

None of these explorers ever found a Northwest Passage. Their explorations, however, led to increased European interest in North America.

READING CHECK **Finding Main Ideas** Why did European explorers seek a Northwest Passage?

European Presence in North America

The Spanish and the Portuguese were the early leaders in overseas exploration. They dominated the colonization of the New World through the 1500s. However, Spain and Portugal focused on Central America, the Caribbean, and South America. They left much of North America unexplored. The English, French, and Dutch explored North America. These nations then sought to expand their own empires there.

English Presence in the New World

In the late 1500s England decided to set up a permanent settlement in North America. This colony was to establish an English presence in the New World. Sir Walter Raleigh received a **charter**, a document giving him permission to start a colony. In 1584 he sent an expedition that landed in present-day Virginia and North Carolina. Raleigh named the entire area Virginia.

The following year, Raleigh sent another group to found a colony on Roanoke Island, off the coast of North Carolina. The English colonists at Roanoke found life hard. They fought with Native Americans and had trouble finding and growing food. After only a year, the remaining colonists returned to England.

John White, a talented artist, and 150 colonists resettled Roanoke in the spring of 1587. White's granddaughter, Virginia Dare, was the first English colonist born in North America. After a few months, White went back to England to get more supplies. War with Spain prevented White from returning for three years. When he came back, White found the colony deserted. The only clue he found to the fate of the colonists was the word *Croatoan*, the name of a nearby island, carved into a post. Did the colonists try to escape a Native American attack by fleeing to the island? White never found out. To this day, no one is certain what happened to the "lost colony" at Roanoke.

Northwest Passage

HUDSON 1610–11

CABOT 1497–98

CARTIER

Hudson Bay

1535–36

1534

NORTH AMERICA

HUDSON 1609

ATLANTIC OCEAN

VERRAZANO 1524

Dutch exploration
English exploration
French exploration
Spanish exploration
New Spain, 1492–1682

0 150 300 Miles
0 150 300 Kilometers

GEOGRAPHY SKILLS | **INTERPRETING MAPS**

1. Movement According to the map, which explorer made two voyages to find a Northwest Passage?
2. Place Which explorer started farthest south in searching for a Northwest Passage?

French Presence in the New World

France built its first North American settlement in Florida, when Huguenots started a few small colonies there in 1564. The Spanish soon destroyed these settlements and drove out the French. Religious wars in France slowed further French efforts to colonize North America. When the fighting ended, the French renewed efforts to settle present-day eastern Canada. The explorations of Jacques Cartier and Samuel de Champlain gave France a claim to this region.

Nearly 70 years after Cartier sailed up the Saint Lawrence, French sailor Samuel de Champlain began exploring North America. He recorded his ideas about European exploration in his journal.

"Through [exploration] we gain knowledge of different countries, regions and kingdoms; through it we attract and bring into our countries all kinds of riches; through it ...Christianity [is spread] in all parts of the earth."

–Samuel de Champlain, quoted in *The Canadian Frontier, 1534–1760*, by W. J. Eccles

Champlain followed Cartier's old paths. Over the years he made many journeys along the Saint Lawrence River. He also visited the Great Lakes, led by Native American guides.

In 1608 Champlain founded a small colony on the Saint Lawrence River. He named the colony Quebec. This trading post opened fur-trading routes for the French throughout the region. Champlain's explorations became the basis of France's claim to much of Canada.

In the late 1600s the French began spreading out from the Saint Lawrence River. Calling their North American territory New France, French fur traders, explorers, and missionaries were all on the move.

In the 1650s French missionaries told stories about "a beautiful river, large, broad, and deep." In 1673 explorer Louis Jolliet (jahl-ee-ET) and missionary Jacques Marquette set out to find this great river, the Mississippi. (Hernando de Soto was the first European to find the Mississippi River, in 1541.) They reached the river and traveled down it as far as present-day Arkansas.

Nine years later René-Robert de La Salle followed the Mississippi River to the Gulf of

FOCUS ON INDIANA

Shortly before any French explorers made their way to the regioon that is now Indiana, Simon Daumont de Saint-Lusson had claimed the territory as part of the large region called Louisiana.

European Exploration of the Americas, 1492–1682

Interactive Map

Legend:
- Dutch exploration
- English exploration
- French exploration
- Spanish exploration
- New Spain, 1492–1682

0   150   300 Miles
0   150   300 Kilometers

Hudson's search for a Northwest Passage led him to the bay that still bears his name.

La Salle sailed down the Mississippi to its mouth and claimed for France all the land along the river and its tributaries.

Juan Ponce de León became the first European in Florida when he arrived in 1513.

Spanish explorers boldly pushed overland into North America's interior.

Map labels: Hudson Bay, NORTH AMERICA, Great Lakes, Mississippi River, Colorado River, Rio Grande, Gulf of Mexico, Tropic of Cancer, Caribbean Sea, ATLANTIC OCEAN, Newfoundland, Nova Scotia, Lake Champlain, Quebec, New York, Roanoke Island, St. Augustine, Bahama Islands, Cuba, Hispaniola, Puerto Rico, México City (Tenochtitlán)

Route labels: HUDSON 1610-11, CABOT 1497-98, CARTIER 1534-35, CARTIER 1534, CARTIER 1535-36, HUDSON 1609, CHAMPLAIN 1603-1615, CHAMPLAIN 1609, LA SALLE 1679-82, CORONADO 1540-42, DE SOTO 1539-42, CABEZA DE VACA AND ESTEVANICO 1528-36, PONCE DE LEÓN 1513, CORTÉS 1519

60°N, 50°N, 40°N, 30°N, 20°N, 110°W, 100°W, 80°W, 70°W

go.hrw.com
Interactive Map
KEYWORD: SF7 CH2

GEOGRAPHY SKILLS   INTERPRETING MAPS

1. **Region** Explorers from what country explored the Great Lakes region?
2. **Region** In what regions did Spanish explorers travel?

Mexico. He claimed the Mississippi Valley for King Louis XIV of France. To honor the king, La Salle named the region Louisiana.

Starting in the 1700s, the French built new outposts. These included Detroit on the Great Lakes and Saint Louis and New Orleans along the Mississippi River. Most towns in the French territory were small. As late as 1688 there were only about 12,000 French settlers in New France. Its small population and the value of the fur trade led French settlers to ally and trade with local Native American groups.

Because of their close trading relationships, the French treated the Native Americans with more respect than some other European settlers had done. Many French settlers learned Native American languages, and they even adopted their ways of life.

Dutch Presence in the New World

The English and the French were not the only European powers to seek an empire in North America. The Dutch, who had merchant fleets around the world, came in search of trade. They claimed the land between the Delaware and Hudson rivers and called it New Netherland. This area included parts of what is now New York, New Jersey, Connecticut, and Delaware. In 1624 the newly formed Dutch West India Company sent about 30 families to settle in New Netherland. Two years later Peter Minuit bought Manhattan Island from local Native Americans for about $24. Minuit then founded the town of New Amsterdam, today called New York City. To attract colonists, the Dutch allowed members of all religions to settle in their colony.

Minuit also helped Swedish settlers found New Sweden along the Delaware River. The first settlement, Fort Christina, was begun in 1638. The Swedish settlement was small, but the Dutch felt that it threatened Dutch lands and fur trading. The two sides fought a series of battles. Finally, the governor of New Netherland, Peter Stuyvesant (STY-vi-suhnt),

conquered New Sweden in 1655. He allowed the Swedes to continue their colony, but he called it the "Swedish Nation."

READING CHECK Drawing Conclusions
Were the French explorers in North America successful? Explain.

SUMMARY AND PREVIEW The English, French, Dutch, and Swedish explored the North American continent and later established colonies there. In the next section you will learn about the establishment of slavery in the Americas.

go.hrw.com
Online Quiz
KEYWORD: SF7 HP2

Section 4 Assessment

Reviewing Ideas, Terms, and People

1. **a. Identify** What was the **Protestant Reformation**?
   b. Explain What role did the printing press play in the Protestant Reformation?
   c. Summarize What were Martin Luther's reasons for protesting the Catholic Church?
2. **a. Identify** Who was the first European to search for the **Northwest Passage**?
   b. Describe Which French and Dutch explorers tried to find the Northwest Passage?
3. **a. Recall** What happened to the first English settlements in North America?
   b. Evaluate Which European empire in North America do you think was most successful? Why?

Critical Thinking

4. **Sequencing** Review your notes on European exploration and settlement. Then create a time line like the one below and place the four events you think were most important to the development of European empires in North America on the time line. Be sure to include the date of the event, as well as a description of it and its significance.

FOCUS ON WRITING

5. **Learning about the French Empire and Other Settlements** Take notes about the French, Dutch, Swedish, and English people who settled in America. Why did they come? What did they want and need in their new home?

Beginnings of Slavery in the Americas

What You Will Learn...

Main Ideas

1. European diseases wiped out much of the Native American population, causing colonists to look for a new labor force.
2. Europeans enslaved millions of Africans and sent them to work in their colonies.
3. Slaves in the Americas created a distinct culture.

The Big Idea

Europeans forced millions of African slaves to work in their colonies.

Key Terms and People

immune, *p. 58*
Middle Passage, *p. 59*
African Diaspora, *p. 60*

TAKING NOTES As you read, take notes on slavery in the Americas. Use a chart like the one below.

The Slave Trade		
Need for Workers		
Slave Trade		
Slave Culture		

8.1.1, 8.1.30, 8.3.1, 8.3.7, 8.4.1

If YOU were there...

You are an enslaved African living in North America. Your family is all that you have. You help each other, and your family provides some relief from the forced labor and harsh life on the plantation. Still, you long for your freedom. A fellow slave has told you of a plan to escape.

Will you stay with your family or try to flee?

BUILDING BACKGROUND European settlers in the Americas relied on support from their home countries to establish trade and provide protection. In return, the colonies were expected to produce money for the home country. Many colonies did this through plantations, mines, and other ventures that required a large labor force.

The Need for a New Labor Force

European diseases had a devastating effect on the Native American population. Measles, smallpox, and typhus were common in Europe. As a result, most adult Europeans were **immune**, or had a natural resistance, to them. Native Americans, however, had never been exposed to such diseases and had no immunity to them. As a result, many Native Americans became terribly sick after their first encounters with Europeans. Millions of them died in the years after Columbus reached the New World.

No one knows exactly how many Native Americans died from European diseases, but the loss of life was staggering. Spanish author Fernández de Oviedo reported in 1548 about the destruction of the Native Americans of Hispaniola. He reported that, of the estimated 1 million Indians who had lived on the island in 1492, "there are not now believed to be at the present time ... five hundred persons [left]." In North America the Native American population north of Mexico was about 10 million when Columbus arrived. This number would drop to less than a million. The drop in the native population played a major role in the emerging need for an alternative labor force.

Plantation agriculture was a mainstay of the colonial economic **structure**. Spain and Portugal established sugar plantations that relied on large numbers of native laborers. In the 1600s English tobacco farmers in North America also needed workers for their plantations. With a lack of Native American workers, they, too, needed another source of labor. Plantation owners in both North and South America wanted a cheap work force.

Some colonists, including Spanish priest Bartolomé de Las Casas, suggested using enslaved Africans as workers. Africans had already developed immunity to European diseases. The colonists soon agreed that slaves from West Africa could be the solution to their labor needs.

READING CHECK Analyzing How did disease contribute to the slave trade?

The Slave Trade

In 1510 the Spanish government legalized the sale of slaves in its colonies. The first full cargo ship of Africans arrived in the Americas eight years later. Over the next century, more than a million enslaved Africans were brought to the Spanish and Portuguese colonies in the New World. The Dutch and English also became active in the slave trade.

Middle Passage

Enslavement was a horrible experience for the slaves. Most enslaved people had been captured in the interior of Africa, often by Africans who profited from selling slaves to Europeans. The captives were chained around the neck and then marched to the coast. This journey could be as long as 1,000 miles.

The **Middle Passage** was the voyage across the Atlantic Ocean that enslaved Africans were forced to endure. Africans were packed like cargo in the lower decks of the slave ships. The slaves were chained together and crammed

ACADEMIC VOCABULARY
structure the way something is set up or organized

Primary Source

LETTER
King Afonso to King Joao III

King Afonso of the African nation of Kongo wrote a letter to the king of Portugal in 1526 asking him to do what he could to stop the practice of taking African slaves.

Sir, Your Highness should know how our Kingdom is being lost in so many ways . . . [M]erchants are taking every day our natives, sons of the land and the sons of our noblemen and vassals and our relatives, because the thieved and men of bad conscience grab them . . . [T]hey grab them and get them to be sold; and so great, Sir, is the corruption and licentiousness [law breaking] that our country is being completely depopulated, and Your Highness should not agree with this nor accept it as in your service. And to avoid it we need from those

(your) Kingdoms no more than some priests and a few people to teach in schools, and no other goods except wine and flour for the holy sacrament [religious service].

–**King Afonso of Kongo,**
letter to the king of Portugal, 1526

ANALYSIS SKILL **ANALYZING PRIMARY SOURCES**

1. Why does Afonso ask the Portuguese king to help stop the slave trade?
2. What does Afonso request from the king?

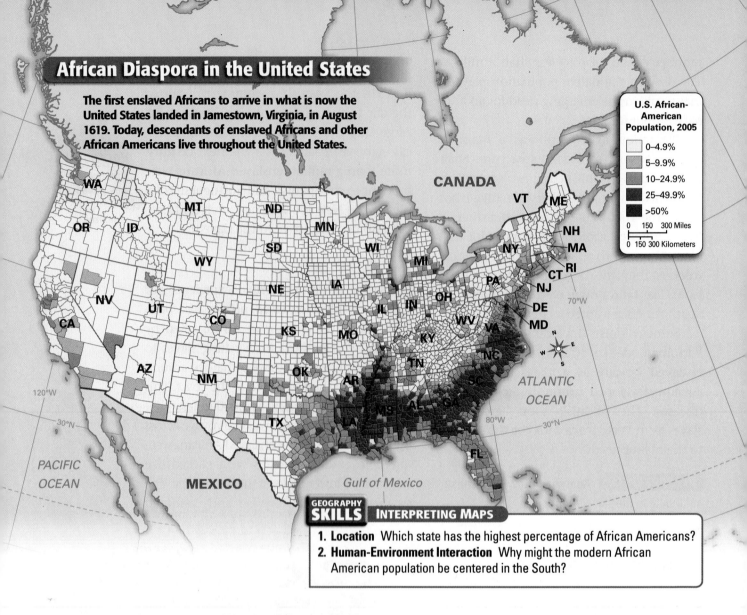

African Diaspora in the United States

The first enslaved Africans to arrive in what is now the United States landed in Jamestown, Virginia, in August 1619. Today, descendants of enslaved Africans and other African Americans live throughout the United States.

U.S. African-American Population, 2005

	0–4.9%
	5–9.9%
	10–24.9%
	25–49.9%
	>50%

0   150   300 Miles
0 150 300 Kilometers

GEOGRAPHY SKILLS INTERPRETING MAPS

1. **Location** Which state has the highest percentage of African Americans?
2. **Human-Environment Interaction** Why might the modern African American population be centered in the South?

into spaces about the size of coffins. The height between the decks was sometimes only 18 inches.

In this confinement, disease spread quickly, killing many Africans. Others suffocated or died from malnutrition. Some slaves took their own lives to end their suffering. It is estimated that one out of every six Africans died during the Middle Passage.

African Diaspora

Between the 1520s and 1860s about 12 million Africans were shipped across the Atlantic as slaves. More than 10 million of these captives survived the voyage and reached the Americas. The slave trade led to the **African Diaspora**. (A diaspora is the scattering of a people.) Enslaved Africans were sent all across the New World.

More than a third of the enslaved Africans, nearly 4 million people, were sent to Brazil. Most of those slaves were forced to work on Portuguese sugar plantations. Nearly 2 million slaves went to the colonies of New Spain. Some worked on plantations in the Caribbean, while others were taken to the mines of Peru and Mexico. Some 3 million slaves worked in British and French colonies in the Caribbean and Latin America. More than 600,000 slaves went to Britain's North American colonies that later became the United States.

Colonial leaders across the Americas developed laws that regulated slave treatment and behavior. Slaves were given few rights in the colonies. The law considered enslaved Africans to be property. In some colonies, a slaveholder was not charged with

THE IMPACT TODAY

Almost half of Brazil's current population is of African descent.

murder if he killed a slave while punishing him. Enslaved Africans, on the other hand, received harsh penalties for minor offenses, such as breaking a tool. Runaways were often tortured and sometimes killed.

The treatment of enslaved Africans varied. Some slaves reported that their masters treated them kindly. To protect their investment, some slaveholders provided adequate food and clothing for their slaves. However, severe treatment was very common. Whippings, brandings, and even worse torture were all part of American slavery.

READING CHECK **Generalizing** How were enslaved Africans treated in the Americas?

Slave Culture in the Americas

Slaves in the Americas came from many different parts of Africa. They spoke different languages and had different cultural backgrounds. But enslaved Africans also shared many customs and viewpoints. They built upon what they had in common to create a new African American culture.

Families were a vital part of slave culture. Families provided a refuge—a place not fully under the slaveholders' control. However, slave families faced many challenges. Families were often broken apart when a family member was sold to another owner. In Latin America, there were many more enslaved males than females. This made it difficult for slaves there to form stable families.

Religion was a second refuge for slaves. It gave enslaved Africans a form of expression that was partially free from their slaveholders' control. Slave religion was primarily Christian, but it included traditional elements from African religions as well. Religion gave slaves a sense of self worth and a hope for salvation in this life and the next. Spirituals were a common form of religious expression among slaves. Slaves also used songs and folktales to tell their stories of sorrow, hope, agony, and joy.

Many slaves expressed themselves through art and dance. Dances were important social events in slave communities. Like most elements of slave culture, art and dance were heavily influenced by African traditions.

READING CHECK **Identifying Points of View** Why was religion important to slaves in the Americas?

SUMMARY AND PREVIEW After disease wiped out much of the Native American population, colonists turned to slave labor. In the next chapter you will learn about English colonies in the Americas.

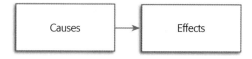

Section 5 Assessment

Reviewing Ideas, Terms, and People

1. **a. Recall** Why did so many Native Americans die after coming into contact with Europeans?
   b. Summarize Why did plantation owners turn to enslaved Africans as a labor force?
2. **a. Identify** What was the **Middle Passage**?
   b. Describe Explain how enslaved Africans were treated after they reached the colonies in the Americas.
3. **a. Explain** What are spirituals?
   b. Analyze How did religion and family provide a refuge from the harsh life enslaved Africans were forced to endure?

Critical Thinking

4. **Identifying Cause and Effect** Review your notes on the slave trade. Use a chart like the one below to explain the causes and the effects of the slave trade.

   | Causes | → | Effects |

FOCUS ON WRITING

5. **Writing about Slavery** Add information about the beginnings of slavery in the Americas to your notes. Include notes about slave culture. What refuges did enslaved people have from their suffering?

The Atlantic Slave Trade

The slave system that arose in the American colonies was strongly influenced by geographic forces. The climate of the southern colonies was suited to growing certain crops, like cotton, tobacco, and sugarcane. These crops required a great deal of labor to grow and to process. To meet this great demand for labor, the colonists looked to one main source—enslaved Africans.

Boston
Newport

40° N

NORTH AMERICA

Charleston

ATLANTIC OCEAN

Tropic of Cancer

Colonial Slave Ports Slave ships sailed to slave ports, where they unloaded their human cargo. Slave ports like Boston, Newport, and Charleston were located near farming areas and the mouths of rivers.

20° N

MIDDLE PASSAGE

WEST INDIES

SOUTH AMERICA

Equator

20° S

The Middle Passage
The terrifying and deadly voyage across the Atlantic was known as the Middle Passage. Enslaved Africans were chained and crowded together under ships' decks on this long voyage, as this drawing shows.

The West Indies Africans were brought to the West Indies to work on large sugar plantations. Sugarcane thrived in the West Indies, but it required huge amounts of labor to grow.

40° S

140° W   120° W   100° W   80° W   0

60° S

Slave forts began as trading posts. They were built near river mouths to provide easy access to both the sea and inland areas.

AFRICA

- St. Luis de Senegal
- James Fort
- Accra
- Elmina
- Whydah
- Assinie

New England traders exchanged goods for slaves on the West African coast and then transported the slaves to the American colonies or to the West Indies.

Elmina slave fort, West Africa

20° N

AFRICA

Kidnapped and Taken to a Slave Ship

Mahommah G. Baquaqua was captured and sold into slavery as a young man. In this 1854 account, he recalls being taken to the African coast to board a slave ship.

"I was taken down to the river and placed on board a boat; the river was very large and branched off in two different directions, previous to emptying itself into the sea . . . We were two nights and one day on this river, when we came to a . . . place . . . [where] the slaves were all put into a pen, and placed with our backs to the fire . . . When all were ready to go aboard, we were chained together, and tied with ropes round about our necks, and were thus drawn down to the sea shore."

Slaves Brought to the Americas, 1493–1810

Number of slaves (in millions)

Years	
1493–1600	~0.1
1601–1700	~1.4
1701–1810	~6.1

20° S

Tropic of Capricorn

40° S

GEOGRAPHY SKILLS INTERPRETING MAPS

1. **Location** Why were slave forts located where they were?
2. **Human-Environment Interaction** What geographic factors influenced the development of the Atlantic slave trade?

0° E   40° E   60° E   80° E   100° E

60° S

Social Studies Skills

Analysis | Critical Thinking | Civic Participation | Study

Framing Historical Questions

Define the Skill

One of the most valuable ways that people gain knowledge is by asking effective questions. An effective question is one that obtains the kind of information the person asking the question desires. The ability to frame, or construct, effective questions is an important life skill as well as a key to gaining a better understanding of history. Asking effective historical questions will aid you in studying history and in conducting historical research.

Learn the Skill

Effective questions are specific, straightforward, and directly related to the topic. When we do not obtain the information we want or need, often it is because we have asked the wrong questions. Asking effective questions is not as easy as it seems. It requires thought and preparation. The following guidelines will help you in framing effective questions about history and other topics as well.

1. Determine exactly what you want to know.

2. Decide what questions to ask and write them down. Having written questions is very important. They will help guide your study or research and keep you focused on your topic and goal.

3. Review each of your questions to make sure it is specific, straightforward, and directly related to your topic.

4. Rewrite any questions that are vague, too broad, or biased.

Questions that are vague or too broad are likely to produce information not directly related to what you want to know. For example, if you wanted to know more about trade and the voyages of exploration that are discussed in Chapter 2, "What were the voyages of exploration?" may not be a good question to ask. This question is too broad. Its answer would not give you the information you want.

Asking "Why was trade the most important cause of the voyages of exploration?" would not be an effective question either. This question is biased because it *assumes* trade was the main reason for the voyages, when that might not have been true. Good historical investigation assumes nothing that is not known to be fact. A more effective question, which would get the information you want, is "Were trade and the voyages of exploration connected, and, if so, in what ways?" Do you see now why wording is so important in asking effective questions and why you should write out and review your questions beforehand?

Practice the Skill

Reread the information about Cortés and the Aztec on pages 46–47, then complete the activities below.

1. Suppose you wanted to learn more about Cortés's defeat of the Aztec. Decide whether each of the following would be an effective question to ask about this topic. Explain why or why not.

   a. What happened when the Aztec and the Spanish met?

   b. Why did other Indians betray the Aztec?

   c. What resources did Cortés have that helped him conquer the Aztec?

2. Frame five questions that would be effective in helping you to learn more about this topic.

Chapter Review

Visual Summary

QUICK FACTS

Use the visual summary below to help you review the main ideas of the chapter.

Early Exploration and Settlement

Effects
• Destruction of Native American empires
• Columbian Exchange
• Colonies in the Americas
• Slavery in the Americas

Causes
• Competition between nations
• Desire for wealth
• Spread of Christianity

Reviewing Vocabulary, Terms, and People

1. The first Europeans to reach the east coast of North America were the _____.

2. _____ established a navigation school and financed expeditions to the west coast of Africa.

3. One of the most important European explorers was _____, who was the first person to claim lands in the Americas for Spain.

4. The first voyage that sailed completely around the world was headed by _____.

5. Sir Walter Raleigh founded the colony of Virginia after receiving a _____, a grant to set up a colony, from the queen of England.

6. Large farms or _____, that specialize in growing one type of crop for profit, were common in Spanish America.

Comprehension and Critical Thinking

SECTION 1 *(Pages 38–41)*

7. a. Recall On which two islands did the Vikings establish settlements before coming to North America?

b. Analyze What factors led Europeans to begin their voyages of exploration?

c. Evaluate What do you think motivated sailors to sign on for voyages of exploration?

SECTION 2 *(Pages 42–45)*

8. a. Recall Why was Columbus's first voyage important?

b. Summarize Explain the conflict that emerged between Spain and Portugal over their empires in the Americas and how it was resolved.

c. Evaluate Do you think the Columbian Exchange improved life or made life worse in the Americas? Explain your answer.

SECTION 3 *(Pages 46–51)*

9. a. Identify What territories in the Americas did Spain control?

b. Analyze What factors enabled the Spanish to defeat the Aztec and the Inca?

c. Elaborate Why was the encomienda system important to Spanish settlers?

SECTION 4 *(Pages 52–57)*

10. a. Describe What were the results of the defeat of the Spanish Armada?

b. Contrast How did French settlements in the Americas differ from the English and Spanish settlements?

c. Predict What problems might arise among the different empires with settlements in North America?

SECTION 5 *(Pages 58–61)*

11. a. Explain Why did the Spanish turn to enslaved Africans as a labor force in the Americas?

b. Analyze In what ways did enslaved Africans create their own unique culture in the Americas?

c. Evaluate What effects do you think slavery had on the populations and cultures of West African countries?

Reviewing Themes

12. Geography What geographic features in North America helped and hindered the exploration and colonization of the continent?

13. Politics In what way were the expansions of empires motivated by the politics among European nations?

Using the Internet go.hrw.com KEYWORD: SF7 CH2

14. Activity: Illustrated Map Columbus's successful return from the New World sparked an interest in exploration that resulted in an explosion of explorers. Each explorer mapped his route and the lands that he explored. Our knowledge of the New World increased quickly as explorers made maps and kept detailed logs to catalog what they found. Enter the activity keyword. Then choose a group of explorers and research

the routes these sailors took from the country of origin to the place upon which they landed. Present your research in an annotated and illustrated map or log book. Write from the point of view of an explorer and include information about the areas explored.

Reading Skills

Outlining and History *Use the Reading Social Studies Skill taught in this chapter to answer the following question.*

15. Make a short but complete outline of the section on pages 50–51 under the heading "Spanish Treatment of Native Americans."

Social Studies Skills

Framing Historical Questions *Use the Social Studies Skill taught in this chapter to answer the following question.*

16. Write a historical question for each of the five sections of this chapter.

FOCUS ON WRITING

17. Writing Your Letter First, review your notes and decide which group you want to write about. Which details from your notes will your friends and family be most interested in? Which do you find most important? What do you want to tell your family and friends about the Americas?

Standardized Test Practice

8.1.2, 8.1.30, 8.3.7, 8.4.1

DIRECTIONS: Read each question and write the letter of the best response.

1 Which of the following best illustrates the process known as the Columbian Exchange?

A Christopher Columbus sailed west to reach Asia and encountered the Americas.

B Corn and tomatoes were introduced to Europe from America.

C Asian goods moved long distances along the Silk Road to reach Europe.

D Advances in technology allowed sailors to better navigate on the open seas.

2 The decimation of the native population of the Americas and the need for plantation labor resulted in the

A encomienda system.

B establishment of religious tolerance.

C transatlantic slave trade.

D Columbian Exchange.

3 The desire to convert people to Christianity and the demand for Asian trade goods led to

A increased interest in exploration.

B the Renaissance.

C the conquest of the Americas.

D efforts to end the slave trade.

4 Spain's empire in the Americas included which of the following?

A South America

B Virginia.

C Mexico.

D Florida.

5 Which of the following established colonies in North America?

A the Portuguese.

B the Dutch.

C the English.

D the French.

6 The voyage of enslaved Africans across the Atlantic to the Americas was known as the

A Northwest Passage.

B African Diaspora.

C triangular trade.

D Middle Passage.

7 Examine the following passage from Bernal Díaz del Castillo's account of an Aztec marketplace. Then answer the question below.

> "The bustle and noise caused by this large crowd of people was so great that it could be heard more than four miles away. Some of our men, who had traveled through Italy, said that they never had seen a marketplace that covered so large an area, which was so well regulated, and so crowded with people as this one at Mexico."
>
> —Bernal Díaz del Castillo, adapted from *The Memoirs of the Conquistador Bernal Díaz del Castillo*

Document-Based Question What is the author's impression of the Aztec marketplace? How can you tell?

The English Colonies

IN Indiana Standards

Social Studies Standards

8.1.3 Identify and explain the conditions, causes, consequences, and significance of the French and Indian War (1754–1763), and the resistance and rebellion against British imperial rule by the thirteen colonies in North America (1761–1775).

8.1.4 Identify fundamental ideas in the Declaration of Independence (1776) and analyze the causes and effects of the Revolutionary War (1775–1783), including enactment of the Articles of Confederation and the Treaty of Paris.

8.3.5 Describe the importance ofthe major mountain ranges and the major river systems in the development of the United States.

8.4.9 Explain and evaluate examples of domstic and international interdependence throughout United States history.

go.hrw.com
Indiana
KEYWORD: SF10 IN

FOCUS ON WRITING

Writing an Infomercial What if television had been invented during the time that the English colonies were being founded in North America? Instead of relying on printed flyers and word of mouth to attract settlers, the founders of colonies might have made infomercials. In this chapter you will read about life in the American colonies during different times. You will choose one time period and colony and write an infomercial encouraging English citizens to settle in the colony of your choice.

UNITED STATES

1620
The Pilgrims sign the Mayflower Compact.

1620

WORLD

1648
Work is finished on India's Taj Mahal.

Mayflower Compact courtesy of the Pilgrim Society, Plymouth, Massachusetts.

What You Will Learn...

Plymouth Colony thrives again in this highly accurate re-creation. The original colonists came to North America in 1620 in search of religious freedom. By 1627, the year this scene re-creates, the colonists were well established. Their success encouraged others. In this chapter you will learn about English settlements that dotted the east coast of North America.

1732
Post Vincennes is established by the British.

1681
William Penn establishes the colony of Pennsylvania.

1763
Pontiac, an American Indian, leads a rebellion on the western frontier.

1773
Patriots stage the Boston Tea Party.

1670

1720

1770

1682
Peter the Great becomes czar of Russia.

1768
British explorer James Cook sets sail on his first trip to the South Pacific, meeting people like this Sandwich Islander.

THE ENGLISH COLONIES **69**

Reading Social Studies

| Economics | Geography | Politics | Society and Culture | Science and Technology |

Focus on Themes In this chapter you will read about the people who settled the early colonies of North America. You will learn about the problems they faced as they felt the tug between their homeland and their new land. You will see how they settled political differences (sometimes peacefully, other times not) and learned how to trade goods and grow crops to establish a thriving economy. You will discover that the **economy** often influenced their **politics**.

Vocabulary Clues

Focus on Reading When you are reading your history textbook, you may often come across a word you do not know. If that word isn't listed as a key term, how do you find out what it means?

Using Context Clues Context means surroundings. Authors often include clues to the meaning of a difficult word in its context. You just have to know how and where to look.

Clue	How It Works	Example	Explanation
Direct Definition	Includes a definition in the same or a nearby sentence	In the late 1600s England, like most western European nations, mercantilism, *a system of creating and maintaining wealth through carefully controlled trade.*	The phrase "a system of creating and maintaining wealth through carefully controlled trade" defines *mercantilism.*
Restatement	Uses different words to say the same thing	The British continued to keep a standing, *or permanent,* army in North America to protect the colonists against Indian attacks.	The word *permanent* is another way to say *standing.*
Comparisons or Contrasts	Compares or contrasts the unfamiliar word with a familiar one	*Unlike legal traders,* smugglers did not have permission to bring goods into the country.	The word *unlike* indicates that smugglers are different from legal traders.

You Try It!

The following sentences are from this chapter. Each uses a definition or restatement clue to explain unfamiliar words. See if you can use the context to figure out the meaning of the words in italics.

Context Clues Up Close

1. In 1605 a company of English merchants asked King James I for the right to *found*, or establish, a settlement. *(p. 72)*

   From Chapter 3

2. The majority of workers were *indentured servants*. These servants signed a contract to work for four to seven years for those who paid for their journey to America. *(p. 74)*

3. In New England, the center of politics was the *town meeting*. In town meetings people talked about and decided on issues of local interest, such as paying for schools. *(p. 91)*

Answer the questions about the sentences you read.

1. In example 1, what does the word *found* mean? What hints did you find in the sentence to figure that out?

2. In example 2, where do you find the meaning of *indentured servants*? What does this phrase mean?

3. In example 3, you learn the definition of *town meeting* in the second sentence. Can you combine these two sentences into one sentence? Try putting a dash after the word *meeting* and replacing "In town meetings" with "a place where . . ."

As you read Chapter 3, look for context clues that can help you figure out the meanings of unfamiliar words or terms.

Key Terms and People

Chapter 3

Section 1
Jamestown *(p. 72)*
John Smith *(p. 73)*
Pocahontas *(p. 73)*
indentured servants *(p. 74)*
Bacon's Rebellion *(p. 74)*
Toleration Act of 1649 *(p. 75)*
Olaudah Equiano *(p. 77)*
slave codes *(p. 77)*

Section 2
Puritans *(p. 78)*
Pilgrims *(p. 78)*
immigrants *(p. 78)*
Mayflower Compact *(p. 79)*
Squanto *(p. 79)*
John Winthrop *(p. 80)*
Anne Hutchinson *(p. 82)*

Section 3
Peter Stuyvesant *(p. 85)*
Quakers *(p. 86)*
William Penn *(p. 86)*
staple crops *(p. 87)*

Section 4
town meeting *(p. 91)*
English Bill of Rights *(p. 91)*
triangular trade *(p. 93)*
Great Awakening *(p. 94)*
Jonathan Edwards *(p. 94)*
Enlightenment *(p. 95)*
John Locke *(p. 95)*
Pontiac *(p. 97)*

Section 5
Samuel Adams *(p. 99)*
Committees of Correspondence *(p. 99)*
Stamp Act of 1765 *(p. 100)*
Boston Massacre *(p. 101)*
Tea Act *(p. 102)*
Boston Tea Party *(p. 102)*
Intolerable Acts *(p. 102)*
Quartering Act *(p. 102)*

Academic Vocabulary

In this chapter, you will learn the following academic words:

authority *(p. 73)*
factors *(p. 74)*

The Southern Colonies

What You Will Learn...

Main Ideas

1. Jamestown was the first permanent English settlement in America.
2. Daily life in Virginia was challenging to the colonists.
3. Religious freedom and economic opportunities were motives for founding other southern colonies, including Maryland, the Carolinas, and Georgia.
4. Farming and slavery were important to the economies of the southern colonies.

The Big Idea

Despite a difficult beginning, the southern colonies soon flourished.

Key Terms and People

Jamestown, *p. 72*
John Smith, *p. 73*
Pocahontas, *p. 73*
indentured servants, *p. 74*
Bacon's Rebellion, *p. 74*
Toleration Act of 1649, *p. 75*
Olaudah Equiano, *p. 77*
slave codes, *p. 77*

TAKING NOTES As you read, take notes in a chart like the one below on the founding of the southern colonies.

Colony	Year	Why Founded

8.1.1, 8.1.2, 8.3.2, 8.3.6, 8.4.1

If YOU were there...

A year ago, in 1609, you moved to the colony of Virginia. Life here has been hard. During the winter many people died of cold or sickness. Food is always scarce. Now it is spring, and a ship has come from England bringing supplies. In a week it will sail home. Some of your neighbors are giving up and returning to England. They ask you to come, too.

Would you take the ship back to England?

BUILDING BACKGROUND Several European nations took part in the race to claim lands in the Americas. Their next step was to establish colonies in the lands that they claimed. The first English colonies were started in the late 1500s but failed. Even in successful colonies, colonists faced hardships and challenges.

Settlement in Jamestown

In 1605 a company of English merchants asked King James I for the right to found, or establish, a settlement. In 1606 the king granted the request of the company to settle in a region called Virginia.

Founding a New Colony

The investors in the new settlement formed a joint-stock company called the London Company. This allowed the group to share the cost and risk of establishing the colony. On April 26, 1607, the first 105 colonists sent by the London Company arrived in America. On May 14, about 40 miles up the James River in Virginia, the colonists founded **Jamestown**, the first permanent English settlement in North America.

A lack of preparation cost a lot of the colonists their lives. Most of the men who came to Jamestown were adventurers with no farming experience or useful skills such as carpentry. Jamestown was surrounded by marshes full of disease-carrying mosquitoes. By the time winter arrived, two-thirds of the original colonists had died.

Jamestown Colony

Williamsburg

Williamsburg was founded in 1633 as Middle Plantation by settlers from Jamestown.

The forest could provide wood for building and for fuel.

The waters provided fish for food. But the water, so near the sea, was salty.

Jamestown 1607

Marsh

James River

ATLANTIC OCEAN

James River

Jamestown

Roanoke

Jamestown was located with defense in mind. Enemy Spanish ships would have to pass through a narrow channel to reach Jamestown, making the ships easy marks for the settlers' cannons.

Smith's Fort

GEOGRAPHY SKILLS INTERPRETING MAPS

1. **Human-Environment Interaction** What were the advantages and disadvantages of locating Jamestown on a river?
2. **Human-Environment Interaction** What do you think would have been a commonly used method of transportation for people in this region?

Powhatan Confederacy

Jamestown fared better under **John Smith,** who took control of the colony and built a fort in 1608. He forced the settlers to work harder and to build better housing by creating rules that rewarded harder workers with food. The colonists received help from the powerful Powhatan Confederacy of Native Americans after Smith made an agreement with them. The Powhatan brought food to help the colonists and taught them how to grow corn.

In 1609 some 400 more settlers arrived in Jamestown. That winter, disease and famine once again hit the colony. The colonists called this period the starving time. By the spring of 1610, only 60 colonists were still alive. Jamestown failed to make a profit until colonist John Rolfe introduced a new type of tobacco that sold well in England.

War in Virginia

John Rolfe married **Pocahontas**, daughter of the Powhatan leader, in 1614. Their marriage helped the colonists form more peaceful relations with the Powhatan. However, Pocahontas died three years later in England, which she was visiting with Rolfe.

In 1622, colonists killed a Powhatan leader. The Powhatan responded by attacking the Virginia settlers later that year. Fighting between the colonists and the Powhatan continued for the next 20 years. Because the London Company could not protect its colonists, the English Crown canceled the company's charter in 1624. Virginia became a royal colony and existed under the **authority** of a governor chosen by the king.

READING CHECK Finding Main Ideas What problems did the Jamestown colonists face?

ACADEMIC VOCABULARY

authority power, right to rule

Daily Life in Virginia

In early Virginia, people lived on scattered farms rather than in towns. Tobacco farmers established large farms called plantations. Tobacco was so valuable that it was sometimes used as money.

Headright System

These plantations were made possible in part by the headright system, which was started by the London Company. Under this system, colonists who paid their own way to Virginia received 50 acres of land. A colonist could earn another 50 acres for every additional person brought from England. Rich colonists who brought servants or relatives to Virginia gained large amounts of land.

ACADEMIC VOCABULARY

factors
causes

Primary Source

LETTER
A Note from Virginia

In this 1619 letter, the secretary of the Virginia colony, John Pory, encouraged people to move to Virginia.

"As touching the quality of this country, three things there be, which in few years may bring this colony to perfection; the English plow, vineyards, & cattle . . . All our riches for the present do consist in tobacco, wherein one man by his own labor has in one year, raised to himself to the value of 200 pounds sterling; and another by the means of six servants has cleared at one crop a thousand pound English. These be true, yet indeed rare examples, yet possible to be done by others."

—from *The Power of Words*, edited by T. H. Breen

ANALYSIS SKILL **ANALYZING PRIMARY SOURCES**

How does this letter indicate the importance of tobacco in Virginia?

Labor in Virginia

Colonists in Virginia suffered very high death rates, which led to labor shortages. The majority of workers were **indentured servants**. These servants signed a contract to work for four to seven years for those who paid for their journey to America.

Expansion of Slavery

Not all laborers in Virginia came from Europe. A Dutch ship brought the first Africans to Virginia in 1619. Some Africans were servants; others had been enslaved. Some African servants became successful farmers when their contracts ended.

The demand for workers was soon greater than the supply of people willing to work as indentured servants. Over time, the cost of slaves fell. These **factors** led some colonists to turn to slave labor. By the mid-1600s most Africans in Virginia were being kept in life-long slavery.

Bacon's Rebellion

As plantations grew, the economy of Jamestown began to expand. Soon, colonial officials began to ask for more taxes. During the mid-1600s poor colonists protested the higher taxes. They were also upset about the governor's policies toward Native Americans. They thought the colony was not well protected against attack. In 1676 a group of former indentured servants led by Nathaniel Bacon attacked some friendly American Indians. Bacon opposed the governor's policies promoting trade with American Indians. He also thought the colonists should be able to take the Indians' land. When the governor tried to stop him, Bacon and his followers attacked and burned Jamestown in an uprising known as **Bacon's Rebellion**.

At one point, Bacon controlled much of the colony. He died of fever, however, and the rebellion soon ended.

READING CHECK **Analyzing** What factors led to the increased use of slave labor in Virginia?

Colonists overcame tough beginnings to create large and wealthy settlements like this one in Virginia. Churches were often the first major buildings in a growing town.

How does the large church in the picture show Virginia's wealth?

Colonial Williamsburg Foundation

Other Southern Colonies

As Jamestown was developing in Virginia, new groups of colonists began planning their move to America. Many English Catholics came to America to escape religious persecution. English Catholics had long been against England's separation from the Roman Catholic Church. For this reason they were not allowed by the Church of England to worship freely. English leaders also feared that English Catholics would ally with Catholic countries such as France and Spain in conflicts.

Maryland

In the 1620s George Calvert, the first Lord Baltimore, asked King Charles I for a charter establishing a new colony in America for Catholics. In 1632 Charles issued the charter to Calvert's son, Cecilius, who took over the planning of the colony. Cecilius, known as the second Lord Baltimore, named the colony Maryland in honor of England's queen, Henrietta Maria. It was located just north of Virginia in the Chesapeake Bay area. Calvert intended for the colony to be a refuge for English Catholics. It would also be a proprietary colony.

This meant that the colony's proprietors, or owners, controlled the government.

In 1634 a group of 200 English Catholics came to Maryland. Included in the group were wealthy landowners, servants, craftspeople, and farmers. Settlers in Maryland benefited from the lessons learned by the Jamestown colonists. They spent their time raising corn, cattle, and hogs so that they would have enough to eat. Before long, many colonists also began growing tobacco for profit.

Although Catholics founded Maryland, a growing number of Protestants began moving there in the 1640s. Soon, religious conflicts arose between Catholics and Protestants in the colony. To reduce tensions, Lord Baltimore presented a bill to the colonial assembly that became known as the **Toleration Act of 1649**. This bill made it a crime to restrict the religious rights of Christians. This was the first law supporting religious tolerance passed in the English colonies.

The Toleration Act did not stop all religious conflict. However, it did show that the government wanted to offer some religious freedom and to protect the rights of minority groups.

Slave Populations in the Colonies

Population (in thousands)

250
200
150
100
50
0

1650   1700   1750

Total Population, 1750

80%

Slaves
20%

Charles Town was founded in 1670. South Carolina's large land grants encouraged plantation owners to bring in thousands of slaves.

James Oglethorpe tried to prevent slavery in Georgia. But slaves soon provided the labor for the colony's many rice plantations.

VIRGINIA

NORTH CAROLINA

SOUTH CAROLINA

GEORGIA

Charles Town

Savannah

SPANISH FLORIDA

ATLANTIC OCEAN

Southern Colonies

34°N

78°W

80°W

32°N

N
W   E
S

ANALYSIS SKILL **INTERPRETING CHARTS**

About how many slaves lived in the English colonies in 1700 and in 1750?

The Carolinas and Georgia

Colonies were also established south of Virginia. In 1663 the English king, Charles II, gave much of the land between Virginia and Spanish Florida to eight of his supporters. At first Carolina was a single colony. However, the settlements were far apart, and it was hard to govern them. In 1712 the colony separated into North and South Carolina.

Most of the colonists in North Carolina were farmers who had moved south from Virginia. Colonists primarily from Europe settled South Carolina. Those who paid their own way received large grants of land, and some brought enslaved Africans with them. By 1730 about 20,000 enslaved Africans were living in the colony, compared to some 10,000 white settlers.

South Carolina's proprietors managed the colony poorly, and in 1719 the proprietary government was overthrown. The Crown then purchased North and South Carolina in 1729, making them royal colonies.

In 1732 King George II granted a charter to James Oglethorpe and other trustees to found Georgia. The king hoped that Georgia would shield Britain's other colonies from Spanish Florida. Oglethorpe wanted the new colony to be a place where debtors, who had been jailed for their debts in England, could make a new start. In 1733 Oglethorpe and 120 colonists, mostly from England, founded the city of Savannah.

Oglethorpe did not want Georgia to have large plantations owned by a few wealthy individuals. He wanted many small farmers. To reach this goal, Oglethorpe outlawed slavery and limited the size of land grants. Soon, however, the settlers grew unhappy with Oglethorpe's strict rules. In 1752 the British government made Georgia a royal colony with new laws. Coastal Georgia was soon filled with large rice plantations worked by thousands of slaves.

READING CHECK **Finding Main Ideas** What were some of the reasons colonists came to the southern colonies?

Economies of the Southern Colonies

The economies of the southern colonies depended on agriculture. They also exported materials for building ships, such as wood and tar. Some colonies traded with local Indians for deerskins to sell.

The colonies had many small farms and some large plantations. Farms did well because the South enjoyed a warm climate and a long growing season. Many farms grew cash crops that were sold for profit. Tobacco, rice, and indigo—a plant used to make blue dye—were the most important cash crops.

The southern colonies' cash crops required a great deal of difficult work to grow and harvest. This meant a large workforce was needed. By the 1700s enslaved Africans, rather than indentured servants, had become the main source of labor.

Slavery was a viciously brutal condition for many inhabitants of the southern colonies. One former slave named **Olaudah Equiano** recorded his experiences.

"Tortures, murder, and every other imaginable barbarity … are practiced upon the poor slaves with impunity [no punishment]. I hope the slave-trade will be abolished."

—Olaudah Equiano, from *The Interesting Narrative of the Life of Olaudah Equiano, or Gustavus Vassa, the African*

Most of the southern colonies passed **slave codes**, or laws to control slaves. Colonies with large numbers of slaves had the strictest slave codes. For example, South Carolina's slaveholders feared that slaves would revolt. As a result, South Carolina's code said slaves could not hold meetings or own weapons. Some colonies did not allow slaveholders to free their slaves.

READING CHECK **Summarizing** What role did slavery play in the southern plantation economy? How was it regulated?

SUMMARY AND PREVIEW In this section you read about life in the southern colonies. In the next section you will learn about the New England colonies.

Section 1 Assessment

go.hrw.com
Online Quiz
KEYWORD: SF7 HP3

Reviewing Ideas, Terms, and People

1. **a. Describe** How did **John Smith** improve conditions in **Jamestown**?
   b. Explain What events led to a conflict between the Jamestown settlers and the Powhatan Confederacy?
2. **a. Recall** Why were **indentured servants** necessary in Virginia?
   b. Evaluate What do you think was the most serious problem faced by settlers in Virginia? Why?
3. **a. Identify** Which colony was the first to promote religious tolerance?
   b. Analyze Why did more enslaved Africans live in South Carolina than did white settlers?
   c. Predict How might the colony of Georgia have been different if Oglethorpe's plan had succeeded?
4. **a. Recall** What was the purpose of **slave codes**?
   b. Analyze Why were slaves in high demand in the southern colonies?

Critical Thinking

5. **Summarizing** Review your notes on the southern colonies. Then add a new column to your chart that summarizes the successes and/or failures of each colony.

Colony	Year	Why Founded	Successes/Failures

FOCUS ON WRITING

6. **Gathering Some Ideas** As you read this section, take notes on the early colonies of Virginia, Maryland, the Carolinas, and Georgia. Be sure to note what advantages they offered to settlers and what difficulties settlers faced. Start to think about the people who would be most likely to settle in the southern colonies.

The New England Colonies

What You Will Learn...

Main Ideas

1. The Pilgrims and Puritans came to America to avoid religious persecution.
2. Religion and government were closely linked in the New England colonies.
3. The New England economy was based on trade and farming.
4. Education was important in the New England colonies.

The Big Idea

English colonists traveled to New England to gain religious freedom.

Key Terms and People

Puritans, *p. 78*
Pilgrims, *p. 78*
immigrants, *p. 78*
Mayflower Compact, *p. 79*
Squanto, *p. 79*
John Winthrop, *p. 80*
Anne Hutchinson, *p. 82*

TAKING NOTES As you read, identify the reasons English colonists came to New England. Use a chart like the one below for your notes.

Reasons for Coming to New England	
Pilgrims	
Puritans	

 8.3.6

If YOU were there...

You live in a town near London in the early 1700s. Some of your neighbors are starting new lives in the American colonies. You would like to go with them, but you cannot afford the cost of the trip. There is one way you can go, though. You can sign a paper promising to work as a servant for five years. Then you would be free—and in a new country!

Would you sign the paper and go to America?

BUILDING BACKGROUND England's first successful colonial settlements were in Virginia. They were started mainly as business ventures. Other colonists in North America had different reasons for leaving their homes. Many, like the Pilgrims and Puritans, came to have freedom to practice their religious beliefs. Others, like the person above, simply wanted a new way of life.

Pilgrims and Puritans

Religious tensions in England remained high after the Protestant Reformation. A Protestant group called the **Puritans** wanted to purify, or reform, the Anglican Church. The Puritans thought that bishops and priests had too much power over church members.

Pilgrims on the Move

The most extreme English Protestants wanted to separate from the Church of England. These Separatists formed their own churches and cut all ties with the Church of England. In response, Anglican leaders began to punish Separatists.

The **Pilgrims** were one Separatist group that left England in the early 1600s to escape persecution. The Pilgrims moved to the Netherlands in 1608. The Pilgrims were **immigrants**—people who have left the country of their birth to live in another country.

The Pilgrims were glad to be able to practice their religion freely. They were not happy, however, that their children were learning the Dutch language and culture. The Pilgrims feared that their children would forget their English traditions. The Pilgrims decided to leave Europe altogether. They formed a joint-stock company with some merchants and then received permission from England to settle in Virginia.

On September 16, 1620, a ship called the *Mayflower* left England with more than 100 men, women, and children aboard. Not all of these colonists were Pilgrims. However, Pilgrim leaders such as William Bradford sailed with the group.

The Mayflower Compact

After two months of rough ocean travel, the Pilgrims sighted land far north of Virginia. The Pilgrims knew that they would thus be outside the authority of Virginia's colonial government when they landed. Their charter would not apply. So, they decided to establish their own basic laws and social rules to govern the colony they would found.

On November 21, 1620, 41 of the male passengers on the ship signed the **Mayflower Compact**, a legal contract in which they agreed to have fair laws to protect the general good. The Compact represents one of the first attempts at self-government in the English colonies.

In late 1620 the Pilgrims landed at Plymouth Rock in present-day Massachusetts. The colonists struggled through the winter to build the Plymouth settlement. Nearly half died during this first winter from sickness and the freezing weather.

Pilgrims and Native Americans

In March 1621 a Native American named Samoset walked boldly into the colonists' settlement. He spoke in broken English. Samoset had learned some English from the crews of English fishing boats. He gave the Pilgrims useful information about the peoples and places of the area. He also introduced them to a Patuxet Indian named **Squanto**. Squanto had at one time lived in Europe and spoke English as well.

HISTORICAL DOCUMENT
The Mayflower Compact

In November 1620, Pilgrim leaders aboard the Mayflower *drafted the Mayflower Compact. This excerpt from the Mayflower Compact describes the principles of the Pilgrim colony's government.*

We whose names are underwritten . . . having undertaken, for the glory of God, and advancement of the Christian faith, and the honour of our King and country, a voyage to plant the first colony in the northern parts of Virginia, do by these presents solemnly and mutually in the presence of God, and one of another, covenant and combine ourselves together into a civil body politic for our better ordering and preservation and furtherance of the ends aforesaid; and by virtue hereof, to enact, constitute, and frame such just and equal laws, ordinances, acts, constitutions, and offices . . . as shall be thought most meet and convenient for the general good of the colony unto which we promise all due . . . obedience.

> The Pilgrims describe the reasons they want to form a colony in North America.

> The Pilgrims promise to obey laws that help the whole colony.

by these presents: by this document	**aforesaid:** mentioned above
covenant: promise	**virtue:** authority
civil body politic: group organized to govern	**ordinances:** regulations
	meet: fitting

ANALYSIS SKILL — ANALYZING PRIMARY SOURCES

1. Why do you think the colonists felt the need to establish a government for themselves?
2. How do you think the Mayflower Compact influenced later governments in America?

From Squanto the Pilgrims learned to fertilize the soil with fish remains. Squanto also helped the Pilgrims establish relations with the local Wampanoag Indians. Conditions in the Plymouth colony began to improve.

The Pilgrims invited Wampanoag chief Massasoit and 90 other guests to celebrate their harvest. This feast became known as the first Thanksgiving. For the event, the Pilgrims killed wild turkeys. This event marked the survival of the Pilgrims in the new colony.

Pilgrim Community

Although the Pilgrims overcame many problems, their small settlement still struggled. Most Pilgrims became farmers, but the farmland around their settlement was poor. They had hoped to make money by trading furs and by fishing. Unfortunately, fishing and hunting conditions were not good in the area. Some colonists traded corn with American Indians for beaver furs. The Pilgrims made little money but were able to form a strong community. The colony began to grow stronger in the mid-1620s after new settlers arrived and, as in Jamestown, colonists began to have more rights to farm their own land.

The Pilgrims' settlement was different from Virginia's in that it had many families. The Pilgrims taught their children to read and offered some education to their indentured servants. Families served as centers of religious life, health care, and community well-being.

All family members worked together to survive during the early years of the colony. Women generally cooked, spun and wove wool, and sewed clothing. They also made soap and butter, carried water, dried fruit, and cared for livestock. Men spent most of their time repairing tools and working in the fields. They also chopped wood and built shelters.

Women in the Colony

In Plymouth, women had more legal rights than they did in England. In England women were not allowed to make contracts, to sue, or to own property. In America, Pilgrim women had the right to sign contracts and to bring some cases before local courts. Widows could also own property.

From time to time, local courts recognized the ways women helped the business community. Widow Naomi Silvester received a large share of her husband's estate. The court called her "a frugal [thrifty] and laborious [hardworking] woman."

Puritans Leave England

During the 1620s England's economy suffered. Many people lost their jobs. The English king, Charles I, made the situation worse by raising taxes. This unpopular act led to a political crisis. At the same time, the Church of England began to punish Puritans because they were dissenters, or people who disagree with official opinions. King Charles refused to allow Puritans to criticize church actions.

Great Migration

These economic, political, and religious problems in England led to the Great Migration. Between 1629 and 1640 many thousands of English men, women, and children left England. More than 40,000 of these people moved to English colonies in New England and the Caribbean. In 1629, Charles granted a group of Puritans and merchants a charter to settle in New England. They formed the Massachusetts Bay Company.

In 1630 a fleet of ships carrying Puritan colonists left England for Massachusetts to seek religious freedom. They were led by **John Winthrop**. The Puritans believed that they had made a covenant, or promise, with God to build an ideal Christian community.

A New Colony

The Puritans arrived in New England well prepared to start their colony. They brought large amounts of tools and livestock with them. Like the Pilgrims, the Puritans faced little resistance from local American Indians. Trade with the Plymouth colony helped them too. In addition, the region around Boston had a fairly healthful climate. Thus, few Puritans died from sickness. All of these things helped the Massachusetts Bay Colony do well. By 1691, the Massachusetts Bay Colony had expanded to include the Pilgrims' Plymouth Colony.

READING CHECK **Summarizing** What role did religion play in the establishment of the Massachusetts Bay Colony?

History Close-up
Plymouth Colony

Plymouth Colony
New England Colonies
70°W
ATLANTIC OCEAN

Several years later, the second colony, Duxbury, was founded.

Plymouth Bay

The Pilgrims landed in a region of forests, streams, and rocky soil.

Plymouth Colony was surrounded by stakes that formed a wall of protection. Outside the wall were colonists' crop fields.

INDIAN TRAIL

Abandoned Indian Village

Plymouth Colony (1620)

N W E S

ANALYSIS SKILLS ANALYZING VISUALS

In what ways were Plymouth Colony and the Indian village similar and different?

Religion and Government in New England

Massachusetts Bay Colony had to obey English laws. However, its charter provided more independence than did the royal charter of Virginia. For example, it created a General Court to help run the Massachusetts colony.

The Puritan colonists turned this court into a type of self-government to represent the needs of the people. Each town sent two or three delegates to the Court. After John Winthrop served as the colony's first governor, the General Court elected the governor and his assistants. In 1644 the General Court became a two-house, or bicameral, legislature.

Politics and religion were closely linked in Puritan New England. Government leaders were also church members, and ministers often had a great deal of power in Puritan communities. Male church members were the only colonists who could vote. Colonists became full members in the church by becoming what the Puritans called God's "elect," or chosen. Reaching this status was a difficult process. Individuals had to pass a public test to prove that their faith was strong.

BIOGRAPHY

Anne Hutchinson
1591–1643

In 1634 Anne Hutchinson emigrated with her family from England to the Massachusetts Bay Colony. After settling in Boston, she worked as a nurse and midwife. She also hosted a Bible-study class that met in her home. Over time, Hutchinson began to question the teachings of the local ministers. Meanwhile, her popularity grew.

After being banished from the colony, Hutchinson settled in Rhode Island and, later, Long Island. She died in an American Indian attack. Today we remember her as a symbol of the struggle for religious freedom.

Drawing Conclusions Why do you think church leaders disliked Hutchinson's ideas?

Church and State
QUICK FACTS

Religion Affected Government
- Government leaders were church members.
- Ministers had great authority.

Government Affected Religion
- Government leaders outlawed certain religions.
- Government leaders punished dissenters.

In 1636 minister Thomas Hooker and his followers left Massachusetts to help found Connecticut, another New England colony. In 1639 Hooker wrote the Fundamental Orders of Connecticut. This set of principles made Connecticut's government more democratic. For example, the Orders allowed men who were not church members to vote. As a result, some historians call Hooker the father of American democracy. The Fundamental Orders of Connecticut also outlined the powers of the general courts.

Not all Puritans shared the same religious views. Minister Roger Williams did not agree with the leadership of Massachusetts. He called for his church to separate completely from the other New England congregations. Williams also criticized the General Court for taking land from American Indians without paying them.

Puritan leaders worried that Williams's ideas might hurt the unity of the colony. They made him leave Massachusetts. Williams took his supporters to southern New England. They formed a new settlement called Providence. This settlement later developed into the colony of Rhode Island. In Providence, Williams supported the separation of the church from the state. He also believed in religious tolerance for all members of the community.

In Boston, an outspoken woman also angered Puritan church leaders. **Anne Hutchinson** publicly discussed religious ideas that some leaders thought were radical. For example, Hutchinson believed that people's relationship with God did not need guidance from ministers.

Hutchinson's views alarmed Puritans such as John Winthrop. Puritan leaders did not believe that women should be religious leaders. Puritan leaders put Hutchinson on trial for her ideas. The court decided to force her out of the colony. With a group of followers, Hutchinson helped found the new colony of Portsmouth, later a part of the colony of Rhode Island.

Perhaps the worst community conflicts in New England involved the witchcraft trials of the early 1690s. The largest number of trials were held in Salem, Massachusetts. In Salem a group of girls had accused people of casting spells on them. The community formed a special court to judge the witchcraft cases. The court often pressured the suspected witches to confess. Before the trials had ended, the Salem witch trials led to 19 people being put to death.

READING CHECK **Identifying Cause and Effect** What led to religious disagreements among the Puritans, and what was the result?

New England Economy

Connecticut, Massachusetts, New Hampshire, and Rhode Island were very different from the southern colonies. The often harsh climate and rocky soil meant that few New England farms could grow cash crops. Most farming families grew crops and raised animals for their own use. There was thus little demand for farm laborers. Although some people held slaves, slavery did not become as important to this region.

Merchants

Trade was vital to New England's economy. New England merchants traded goods locally, with other colonies, and overseas. Many of them traded local products such as furs, pickled beef, and pork. Many merchants grew in power and wealth, becoming leading members of the New England colonies.

Fishing

Fishing became one of the region's leading industries. The rich waters off New England's coast served as home to many fish, including cod, mackerel, and halibut. Merchants exported dried fish. Colonists also began hunting for whales that swam close to shore. Whales were captured with harpoons, or spears, and dragged to shore. Whaling provided valuable oil for lighting.

Shipbuilding

Shipbuilding became an important industry in New England for several reasons. The area had plenty of forests that provided materials for shipbuilding. As trade—particularly in slaves—in the New England seaports grew, more merchant ships were built. The fishing industry also needed ships. New England shipyards made high-quality, valuable vessels. Ship owners sometimes even told their captains to sell the ship along with the cargo when they reached their destination.

Skilled Craftspeople

The northern economy needed skilled craftspeople. Families often sent younger sons to learn skilled trades such as blacksmithing, weaving, shipbuilding, and printing. The young boys who learned skilled trades were known as apprentices.

Apprentices lived with a master craftsman and learned from him. In exchange, the boys performed simple tasks. Apprentices promised to work for a master craftsman for a set number of years. They learned trades that were essential to the survival of the colonies. Apprentices received food and often clothing from the craftsmen. Gabriel Ginings, for example, was an apprentice in Portsmouth, Rhode Island. He received "sufficient food and raiment [clothing] suitable for such an apprentice," as his 1663 contract stated.

After a certain amount of time had passed, apprentices became journeymen. They usually traveled and learned new skills in their trade. Eventually they would become a master of the trade themselves.

READING CHECK **Categorizing** What types of jobs were common in the New England colonies?

THE IMPACT TODAY

Fishing remains an important industry in New England, earning hundreds of millions of dollars each year.

Education in the Colonies

Education was important in colonial New England. Mothers and fathers wanted their children to be able to read the Bible. The Massachusetts Bay Colony passed some of the first laws requiring parents to provide instruction for their children.

Public Education

To be sure that future generations would have educated ministers, communities established town schools. In 1647 the General Court of Massachusetts issued an order that a school be founded in every township of 50 families.

Schoolchildren often used the *New England Primer,* which had characters and stories from the Bible. They learned to read at the same time that they learned about the community's religious values.

The availability of schooling varied in the colonies. There were more schools in New England than in the other colonies where most children lived far from towns. These children had to be taught by their parents or by private tutors. Most colonial children stopped their education after the elementary grades. Many went to work, either on their family farm or away from home.

THE IMPACT TODAY

Public schools remain the primary source of education for most U.S. children. Total enrollment today is around 55 million students.

Higher Education

Higher education was also important to the colonists. In 1636 John Harvard and the General Court founded Harvard College. Harvard taught ministers and met the colony's need for higher education. The second college founded in the colonies, William and Mary, was established in Virginia in 1693.

By 1700 about 70 percent of men and 45 percent of women in New England could read and write. These figures were much lower in Virginia, where Jamestown was the only major settlement.

READING CHECK **Analyzing** Why was education important to the New England colonies?

SUMMARY AND PREVIEW In this section you learned about the role that religion played in the New England colonies. In the next section you'll learn about New York, New Jersey, and Pennsylvania.

Section 2 Assessment

go.hrw.com
Online Quiz
KEYWORD: SF7 HP3

Reviewing Ideas, Terms, and People

1. **a. Recall** Why did the **Pilgrims** and **Puritans** leave Europe for the Americas?
   b. Elaborate Do you think the Pilgrims could have survived without the assistance of **Squanto** and Massasoit? Explain your answer.
2. **a. Describe** What role did the church play in Massachusetts?
   b. Analyze Why did some colonists disagree with the leaders of Massachusetts?
3. **a. Identify** Describe the economy in the New England colonies.
   b. Analyze Why do you think New England merchants became leading members of society?
4. **a. Describe** What steps did the Massachusetts Bay Colony take to promote education?
   b. Predict What are some possible benefits that New England's emphasis on education might bring?

Critical Thinking

5. **Identifying Cause and Effect** Review your notes on the reasons English colonists came to New England. Then copy the diagram below and use it to show how the colonists' experiences caused them to build certain types of colonies.

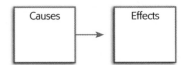

Causes → Effects

FOCUS ON WRITING

6. **Comparing Colonies** Take notes on the early New England colonies. Be sure to note what advantages they offered to settlers and what difficulties settlers faced. Put a star beside the colony or colonies you might use in your infomercial.

The Middle Colonies

If **YOU** were there...

You are a farmer in southern Germany in 1730. Religious wars have torn your country apart for many years. Now you hear stories about a place in America where people of all religions are welcome. But the leaders of the colony—and many of its people—are English. You would not know their language or customs. Still, you would be free to live and worship as you like.

How would you feel about moving to a country full of strangers?

BUILDING BACKGROUND The middle section of the Atlantic coast offered good land and a moderate climate. Several prominent English people established colonies that promised religious freedom. To people like the settler above, these colonies promised a new life.

New York and New Jersey

The Dutch founded New Netherland in 1613 as a trading post for exchanging furs with the Iroquois. The center of the fur trade in New Netherland was the town of New Amsterdam on Manhattan Island. Generous land grants to patroons, or lords, and religious tolerance soon brought Jews, French Huguenots, Puritans, and others to the colony. Director General **Peter Stuyvesant** (STY-vuh-suhnt) led the colony beginning in 1647.

Peter Stuyvesant was forced to surrender New Amsterdam to the English in 1664.

Social	Economic
• New York: Dutch influence	• successful farming of staple crops
• New Jersey: diverse population	• work force of slaves and indentured servants
• Pennsylvania: founded by Quakers	• active trade with Britain and West Indies

In 1664 an English fleet captured the undefended colony of New Amsterdam without firing a single shot. New Netherland was renamed New York, and New Amsterdam became New York City.

THE IMPACT TODAY

Today New York City is the largest city in the United States, with more than 8 million people.

Soon after the English conquest in 1664, the Duke of York made Sir George Carteret and Lord John Berkeley proprietors of New Jersey. This colony occupied lands between the Hudson and Delaware rivers. It had a diverse population, including Dutch, Swedes, Finns, and Scots. The fur trade was important to the economies of New York and New Jersey through the end of the 1600s.

READING CHECK **Comparing** How were New York and New Jersey similar?

BIOGRAPHY

William Penn
1644–1718

William Penn was born in London as the son of a wealthy admiral. Penn joined the Quakers in 1666 and became an active preacher and writer of religious works. He supported toleration of dissenters.

In 1681 he received a charter to establish a new colony called Pennsylvania. There, Penn put his beliefs into practice. He insisted on fair dealings with local American Indians, welcomed immigrants, and promised religious toleration.

Making Generalizations How did Penn's ideas influence the rules of the colony?

Penn's Colony

The Society of Friends, or the **Quakers**, made up one of the largest religious groups in New Jersey. Quakers did not follow formal religious practices and dressed plainly. They believed in the equality of men and women before God. They also supported nonviolence and religious tolerance for all people. At the time, many Quaker beliefs and practices shocked most Christians. As a result, Quakers were persecuted in both England and America.

One proprietor of the New Jersey colony was a Quaker named **William Penn**. Penn wished to found a larger colony under his own control that would provide a safe home for Quakers. In 1681 King Charles II agreed to grant Penn a charter to begin a colony west of New Jersey.

Penn's colony, known as Pennsylvania, grew rapidly. Penn limited his own power and established an elected assembly. He also promised religious freedom to all Christians. His work made Pennsylvania an important example of representative self-government— a government that reflects its citizens' will— in the colonies.

Penn named the capital of his colony Philadelphia, which means "the city of brotherly love." In 1682 the Duke of York sold Penn a region to the south of Pennsylvania. This area, called Delaware, remained part of Pennsylvania until 1776.

READING CHECK **Finding Main Ideas** Why did William Penn establish Pennsylvania, and how did he influence its government?

Economy of the Middle Colonies

The middle colonies combined characteristics of the New England and southern colonies. With a good climate and rich land, farmers there could grow large amounts of **staple crops**—crops that are always needed. These crops included wheat, barley, and oats. Farmers also raised livestock.

Slaves were somewhat more important to the middle colonies than they were to New England. They worked in cities as skilled laborers, such as blacksmiths and carpenters. Other slaves worked on farms, onboard ships, and in the growing shipbuilding industry. However, indentured servants largely filled the middle colonies' growing labor needs. Between 1700 and 1775 about 135,000 indentured servants came to the middle colonies. About half of them moved to Pennsylvania. By 1760 Philadelphia had become the largest British colonial city. Other cities in the middle colonies, such as New York City, also grew quickly.

Trade was important to the economy of the middle colonies. Merchants in Philadelphia and New York City exported colonial goods to markets in Britain and the West Indies. These products included wheat from New York, Pennsylvania, and New Jersey.

Throughout the colonies, women made important contributions to the economy. They ran farms and businesses such as clothing and grocery stores, bakeries, and drugstores. Some women also practiced medicine and worked as nurses and midwives. However, colonial laws and customs limited women's economic opportunities.

Most colonial women worked primarily in the home. Married women managed households and raised children. Sometimes they earned money for their families by selling products like butter. They also provided paid services such as washing clothes.

FOCUS ON READING
You can tell **staple crops** means "crops that are always needed" because of the dash between the vocabulary term and the definition.

READING CHECK Finding the Main Idea
On what were the economies of the middle colonies based?

SUMMARY AND PREVIEW In this section you learned about the middle colonies. In the next section you will read about colonial government, the slave trade, and conflicts that arose in the English colonies.

Section 3 Assessment

go.hrw.com
Online Quiz
KEYWORD: SF7 HP3

Reviewing Ideas, Terms, and People

1. **a. Describe** Name the middle colonies. Where were they located?
   b. Draw Inferences What led to the diverse populations of New York and New Jersey?
2. **a. Identify** Who are the **Quakers**?
   b. Analyze How did **William Penn** attempt to create a colonial government that would be fair to all?
3. **a. Describe** What different types of jobs did slaves in the middle colonies hold?
   b. Evaluate In what ways were women essential to the middle colonies?

Critical Thinking

4. **Sequencing** Review your notes about which nation founded each middle colony. Then complete the time line below by listing the event that occurred on each of the dates on the time line.

| 1613 | 1647 | 1664 | 1681 |

FOCUS ON WRITING

5. **Comparing Colonies** You've just read about early colonies in New York, New Jersey, and Pennsylvania. Think about the advantages they offered to settlers and what difficulties settlers faced. In your notes, put a star beside one of the colonies you might use in your infomercial.

America's Growth 1760

The English colonies in 1760 were located between the Atlantic Ocean and the Appalachian Mountains. The total population of the colonies was around 1.8 million. Soon, however, the colonies began to grow both in size and in population.

In 1763 Great Britain and France signed the Treaty of Paris, giving Britain control over all lands east of the Mississippi River. With the stroke of a pen, the colonies increased enormously in size. The westward expansion of the English colonies—soon to be the United States—had begun.

A Wall of Mountains The 1,500-mile-long Appalachian Mountain range formed a natural barrier to westward expansion. The Appalachians' dense forests and steep terrain made passage on foot or by horse difficult.

America's Population, 1760: 1.8 million

Ethnic Groups, 1760
- White/European
- African American
- Native American
- Other

70%
18%
11%
1%

Religions, 1760
- Protestant
- Catholic
- Jewish
- Other

92%
5%
2%
>1%

Natural Harbors The largest cities in the colonies, such as Philadelphia, New York, and Boston, grew where the best natural ports were. Ships were vital to the colonies: for the growing fishing industry, for overseas trade, and to bring more settlers to the new land.

Boston Harbor provided natural protection for ships.

ME
(part of MA)

NH

NY

MA

Boston, population 16,000

CT

RI

PA

NJ

New York, population 25,000

MD

DE
(part of PA)

Philadelphia, population 25,000

40° N

VA

ATLANTIC OCEAN

APPALACHIAN MOUNTAINS

NC

Mississippi River

SC

GA

A Flood of People The colonial population doubled between 1750 and 1770. Roughly half of the immigrants to the colonies were English. But the second-largest group of immigrants had no choice in the matter—they were enslaved people from Africa.

New England colonies
Middle colonies
Southern colonies

0   150   300 Miles
0   150   300 Kilometers

N
W   E
S

GEOGRAPHY SKILLS **INTERPRETING MAPS**

1. **Location** Where were the colonies' largest cities located at this time?
2. **Human-Environment Interaction** How did mountains and seas influence the location of the colonies?

Tropic of Cancer

90° W

70° W

Life in the English Colonies

What You Will Learn...

Main Ideas

1. Colonial governments were influenced by political changes in England.
2. English trade laws limited free trade in the colonies.
3. The Great Awakening and the Enlightenment led to ideas of political equality among many colonists.
4. The French and Indian War gave England control of more land in North America.

The Big Idea

The English colonies continued to grow despite many challenges.

Key Terms and People

town meeting, *p. 91*
English Bill of Rights, *p. 91*
triangular trade, *p. 93*
Great Awakening, *p. 94*
Jonathan Edwards, *p. 94*
Enlightenment, *p. 95*
Pontiac, *p. 97*

 TAKING NOTES As you read, take notes on how the following developments affected the growing colonies.

Development	Effects
Establishment of local government	
Political change in England	
Trade laws	
Great Awakening/ Enlightenment	
French and Indian War	

 8.1.1, 8.1.2, 8.1.3, 8.1.4, 8.2.8, 8.2.9, 8.3.1, 8.3.2, 8.3.5, 8.4.2, 8.4.9

If YOU were there...

Your family migrated to America in the 1700s and started a small farm in western Pennsylvania. Now, more and more people are moving in. You would like to move farther west, into the Ohio River valley. But a new law says you cannot move west of the mountains because it is too dangerous. Still, you are restless and want more land and more freedom.

Why might you decide to break the law and move west?

BUILDING BACKGROUND When they moved to America, the English colonists brought their ideas about government. They expected to have the same rights as citizens in England. However, many officials in England wanted tight control over the colonies. As a result, some colonists, like this family, were unhappy with the policies of colonial governments.

Colonial Governments

The English colonies in North America all had their own governments. Each government was given power by a charter. The English monarch had ultimate authority over all of the colonies. A group of royal advisers called the Privy Council set English colonial policies.

Colonial Governors and Legislatures

Each colony had a governor who served as head of the government. Most governors were assisted by an advisory council. In royal colonies the English king or queen selected the governor and the council members. In proprietary colonies, the proprietors chose all of these officials. In a few colonies, such as Connecticut, the people elected the governor.

In some colonies the people also elected representatives to help make laws and set policy. These officials served on assemblies. Each colonial assembly passed laws that had to be approved first by the advisory council and then by the governor.

Established in 1619, Virginia's assembly was the first colonial legislature in North America. At first it met as a single body, but it was later split into two houses. The first house was known as the Council of State. The governor's advisory council and the London Company selected its members. The House of Burgesses was the assembly's second house. The members were elected by colonists.

In New England the center of politics was the **town meeting**. In town meetings people talked about and decided on issues of local interest, such as paying for schools.

In the southern colonies, people typically lived farther away from one another. Therefore, many decisions were made at the county level. The middle colonies used both county meetings and town meetings to make laws.

Political Change in England

In 1685 James II became king of England. He was determined to take more control over the English government, both in England and in the colonies.

James believed that the colonies were too independent. In 1686 he united the northern colonies under one government called the Dominion of New England. James named Sir Edmund Andros royal governor of the Dominion. The colonists disliked Andros because he used his authority to limit the powers of town meetings.

English Bill of Rights

Parliament replaced the unpopular King James and passed the **English Bill of Rights** in 1689. This act reduced the powers of the English monarch. At the same time, Parliament gained power. As time went on, the colonists valued their own right to elect representatives to decide local issues. Following these changes, the colonies in the Dominion quickly formed new assemblies and charters.

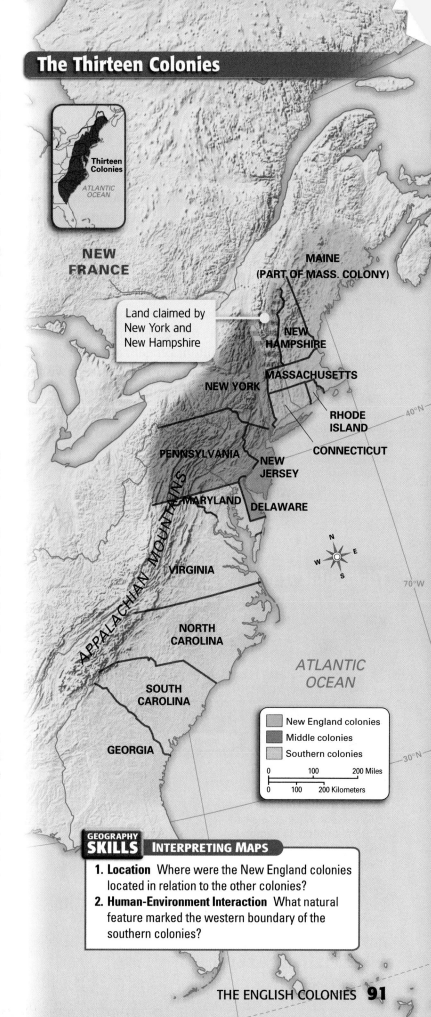

The Thirteen Colonies

Thirteen Colonies
ATLANTIC OCEAN

NEW FRANCE

MAINE (PART OF MASS. COLONY)

Land claimed by New York and New Hampshire

NEW HAMPSHIRE

MASSACHUSETTS

NEW YORK

RHODE ISLAND

CONNECTICUT

PENNSYLVANIA

NEW JERSEY

MARYLAND

DELAWARE

APPALACHIAN MOUNTAINS

VIRGINIA

NORTH CAROLINA

ATLANTIC OCEAN

SOUTH CAROLINA

GEORGIA

40°N

70°W

30°N

New England colonies
Middle colonies
Southern colonies

0   100   200 Miles
0 100   200 Kilometers

GEOGRAPHY SKILLS | **INTERPRETING MAPS**

1. **Location** Where were the New England colonies located in relation to the other colonies?
2. **Human-Environment Interaction** What natural feature marked the western boundary of the southern colonies?

Colonial Courts

Colonial courts made up another important part of colonial governments. Whenever possible, colonists used the courts to control local affairs. In general, the courts reflected the beliefs of their local communities. For example, many laws in Massachusetts enforced the Puritans' religious beliefs. Laws based on the Bible set the standard for the community's conduct.

Sometimes colonial courts also protected individual freedoms. For example, in 1733 officials arrested John Peter Zenger for printing a false statement that damaged the reputation of the governor of New York. Andrew Hamilton, Zenger's attorney, argued that Zenger could publish whatever he wished as long as it was true. Jury members believed that colonists had a right to voice their ideas openly and found him not guilty.

THE IMPACT TODAY

Like the colonies and Great Britain, nations today are economically interdependent. They rely on one another to buy and sell goods and services to keep their economies healthy. Communications technology has increased this interdependence, as huge sums of money can change hands each day with ease.

READING CHECK Analyzing Information
Why were colonial assemblies and colonial courts created, and what did they do?

English Trade Laws

One of England's main reasons for founding and controlling its American colonies was to earn money from trade. In the late 1600s England, like most western European nations, practiced mercantilism, a system of creating and maintaining wealth through carefully controlled trade. A country gained wealth if it had fewer imports—goods bought from other countries—than exports—goods sold to other countries.

To support this system of mercantilism, between 1650 and 1696 Parliament passed a series of Navigation Acts limiting colonial trade. For example, the Navigation Act of 1660 forbade colonists from trading specific items such as sugar and cotton with any country other than England. The act also required colonists to use English ships to transport goods. Parliament later passed other acts that required all trade goods to pass through English ports, where duties, or import taxes, were added to the items.

Triangular Trade

Trade between Britain and its colonies took a triangular shape. Different goods were transported on the routes of the triangles and traded at ports for local goods.

GEOGRAPHY SKILLS INTERPRETING MAPS

1. **Movement** Why is the movement of goods shown on the map called the triangular trade?
2. **Location** A farmer who wanted to grow sugar cane would most likely live where?

England claimed that the Navigation Acts were good for the colonies. After all, the colonies had a steady market in England for their goods. But not all colonists agreed. Many colonists wanted more freedom to buy or sell goods wherever they could get the best price. Local demand for colonial goods was small compared to foreign demand.

Despite colonial complaints, the trade restrictions continued into the 1700s. Some traders turned to smuggling, or illegal trading. They often smuggled sugar, molasses, and rum into the colonies from non-English islands in the Caribbean. Parliament responded with the Molasses Act of 1733, which placed duties on these items. British officials, however, rarely carried out this law.

By the early 1700s English merchants were trading around the world. Most American merchants traded directly with Great Britain or the West Indies. By importing and exporting goods such as sugar and tobacco, some American merchants became wealthy.

Triangular Trade

Trade between the American colonies and Great Britain was not direct. Rather, it generally took the form of **triangular trade**—a system in which goods and slaves were traded among the Americas, Britain, and Africa. There were several routes of the triangular trade. In one route colonists exchanged goods like beef and flour with plantation owners in the West Indies for sugar, some of which they shipped to Britain. The sugar was then exchanged for manufactured products to be sold in the colonies. Colonial merchants traveled great distances to find the best markets.

BIOGRAPHY

Olaudah Equiano
1745–1797

Olaudah Equiano claimed to have been born in Africa in present-day Nigeria. His autobiography told the story of his enslavement. According to his autobiography, Equiano survived the Middle Passage, traveling in a slave ship across the Atlantic. After arriving in the colonies, a Virginia planter purchased him and again sold him to a British naval officer. While working as a sailor, Equiano eventually earned enough money to purchase his own freedom in 1766. Equiano later settled in England and devoted himself to ending slavery.

Analyzing Information How did Equiano gain his freedom?

"I received such a salutation [smell] in my nostrils, as I had never experienced in my life; . . . I became so sick and low that I was not able to eat . . . The groans of the dying, rendered [made] the whole a scene of horror almost inconceivable [unbelievable]."

—Olaudah Equiano, from *The Interesting Narrative of the Life of Olaudah Equiano, or Gustavus Vassa, the African*

The Great Awakening

George Whitefield gives a powerful sermon during the Great Awakening. Ministers like Whitefield emphasized personal religious experiences over official church rules. They also allowed ordinary church members—whatever their race, class, or gender—to play a role in services. The value placed on individuals of all types during the Great Awakening helped shape American political ideas about who should have a say in government.

How do you think religious freedom led to political freedom?

Middle Passage

One version of the triangular trade began with traders exchanging rum for slaves on the West African coast. The traders then sold the enslaved Africans in the West Indies for molasses or brought them to sell in the mainland American colonies.

The slave trade brought millions of Africans across the Atlantic Ocean in a voyage called the Middle Passage. This was a terrifying and deadly journey that could last as long as three months.

Enslaved Africans lived in a space not even three feet high. Slave traders fit as many slaves as possible on board so they could earn greater profits. Thousands of captives died on slave ships during the Middle Passage. In many cases, they died from diseases such as smallpox. As farmers began to use fewer indentured servants, slaves became even more valuable.

READING CHECK **Identifying Cause and Effect** What factors caused the slave trade to grow? How did this affect conditions on the Middle Passage?

Great Awakening and Enlightenment

In the early 1700s revolutions in both religious and nonreligious thought transformed the Western world. These movements began in Europe and affected life in the American colonies.

Great Awakening

After years of population growth, religious leaders wanted to spread religious feeling throughout the colonies. In the late 1730s these ministers began holding revivals, emotional gatherings where people came together to hear sermons.

Many American colonists experienced "a great awakening" in their religious lives. This **Great Awakening**—a religious movement that swept through the colonies in the 1730s and 1740s—changed colonial religion. It also affected social and political life. **Jonathan Edwards** of Massachusetts was one of the most important leaders of the Great Awakening. His dramatic sermons told sinners to seek forgiveness for their sins or face punishment in Hell forever. British minister George Whitefield held revivals from Georgia to New England.

The Great Awakening drew people of different regions, classes, and races. Women, members of minority groups, and poor people often took part in services. Ministers from different colonies met and shared ideas with one another. This represented one of the few exchanges between colonies.

The Great Awakening promoted ideas that may also have affected colonial politics. Sermons about the spiritual equality of all people led some colonists to begin demanding more political equality. Revivals became popular places to talk about political and social issues. People from those colonies with less political freedom were thus introduced to more democratic systems used in other colonies.

Enlightenment

During the 1600s Europeans began to re-examine their world. Scientists began to better understand the basic laws that govern nature. Their new ideas about the universe began the Scientific Revolution. The revolution changed how people thought of the world.

Many colonists were also influenced by the **Enlightenment**. This movement, which took place during the 1700s, spread the idea that reason and logic could improve society. Enlightenment thinkers also formed ideas about how government should work.

Some Enlightenment thinkers believed that there was a social contract between government and citizens. Philosophers such as John Locke thought that people had natural rights such as equality and liberty. Ideas of the Scientific Revolution and the Enlightenment eventually influenced colonial leaders.

READING CHECK **Summarizing** How did the Great Awakening and the Enlightenment influence colonial society?

French and Indian War

By the 1670s tensions had arisen between New England colonists and the Wampanoag. Metacomet, a Wampanoag leader also known as King Philip, opposed the colonists' efforts to take his people's lands. In 1675 these tensions finally erupted in a conflict known as King Philip's War. The colonial militia—civilians serving as soldiers—fought American Indian warriors. Both sides attacked each other's settlements, killing men, women, and children. The fighting finally ended in 1676, but only after about 600 colonists and some 3,000 Indians had been killed, including Metacomet.

Native American Allies

Some Native Americans allied with the colonists to fight against Metacomet and his forces. These Indians had developed trade relations with colonists. They wanted tools, weapons, and other goods that Europeans could provide. In exchange, the colonists wanted furs, which they sold for large profits in Europe. As a result, each side came to depend upon the other.

French colonists traded and allied with the Algonquian and Huron. English colonists traded and allied with the Iroquois League. This powerful group united American Indians from six different groups. Many American Indians trusted the French more than they did the English. The smaller French settlements were less threatening than the rapidly growing English colonies. No matter who their allies were, many Indian leaders took care to protect their people's independence. As one leader said:

“We are born free. We neither depend upon [the governor of New France] nor [the governor of New York]. We may go where we please … and buy and sell what we please.”

—Garangula, quoted in *The World Turned Upside Down*, edited by Colin G. Calloway

FOCUS ON INDIANA

During most of the colonial period, Indiana remained under French rule, and life there was very different from life in the English colonies. Although there were some French settlements in the area, they were mainly military and trading outposts.

North American Empires before and after the Treaty of Paris

1754

Unclaimed

ARCTIC OCEAN

PACIFIC OCEAN

Hudson Bay

Quebec

Fort Detroit
Fort Necessity

New France

Thirteen Colonies

Florida

ATLANTIC OCEAN

Gulf of Mexico

New Spain

West Indies

Tropic of Cancer

■ British	▨ Disputed by Britain and France	
■ Spanish	▨ Disputed by Britain and Spain	
■ French	■ Disputed by Britain, Spain and Russia	
■ Russian	▭ 13 Colonies boundary	
--- Boundary of the Iroquois League		

0   500   1,000 Miles
0   500   1,000 Kilometers

1763

Unclaimed

Hudson Bay

PACIFIC OCEAN

Disputed

Canada

Quebec

French

Fort Detroit
Fort Necessity

Louisiana

Thirteen Colonies

ATLANTIC OCEAN

Florida

Gulf of Mexico

New Spain

West Indies

Tropic of Cancer

GEOGRAPHY SKILLS **INTERPRETING MAPS**

go.hrw.com
Interactive Map
KEYWORD: SF7 CH3

1. **Regions** Which countries gained North American territory between 1754 and 1763?
2. **Human-Environment Interaction** What natural feature helped form the boundary between British and Spanish territory in 1763?

War Erupts

Until the mid-1700s, France and Great Britain struggled for control of territory in North America. British colonists wanted to settle in the Ohio River valley, where they could take advantage of the valuable fur trade. The French believed this settlement would hurt their fur trade profits. A standoff developed in the Ohio Valley where the French had built three forts. Fighting erupted in 1753 as the British military moved to take over the valley.

When a young Virginian named George Washington arrived with more soldiers, he found the area under French control. Washington and his troops built a small, simple fort that he named Fort Necessity. After his troops suffered many casualties—captured, injured, or killed soldiers—Washington finally surrendered. His defeat in 1754 was the start of the French and Indian War. Leaders from the colonies met to discuss defense. The convention produced a plan for uniting the colonies called the Albany Plan. Meanwhile, in 1756 fighting began in Europe, starting what became known as the Seven Years' War.

Treaty of Paris

The turning point of the war came in 1759. That year British general James Wolfe captured Quebec, gaining the advantage in the war. However, the war dragged on for four more years. Finally, in 1763 Britain and France signed the Treaty of Paris, officially ending the war.

The terms of the treaty gave Canada to Britain. Britain also gained all French lands east of the Mississippi River except the city of New Orleans and two small islands in the Gulf of St. Lawrence. From Spain, which had allied with France in 1762, Britain received Florida. In an earlier treaty, Spain had received Louisiana, the land that France had claimed west of the Mississippi River. The Treaty of Paris changed the balance of power in North America. Soon British settlers began moving west to settle new lands.

Western Frontier

Most colonial settlements were located along the Atlantic coast. Colonial settlers, or pioneers, slowly moved into the Virginia and Carolina backcountry and the Ohio River valley.

Indian leaders like Chief **Pontiac** opposed British settlement of this new land. Pontiac's Rebellion began in May 1763 when his forces attacked British forts on the frontier. Within one month, they had destroyed or captured seven forts. Pontiac then led an attack on Fort Detroit. The British held out for months.

British leaders feared that more fighting would take place on the frontier if colonists kept moving onto American Indian lands. To avoid more conflict, King George III issued the Proclamation of 1763. This law banned British settlement west of the Appalachian Mountains. The law also ordered settlers to leave the upper Ohio River valley.

READING CHECK **Summarizing** Why did George III issue the Proclamation of 1763?

SUMMARY AND PREVIEW In this section you read about colonial governments, the slave trade, and the conflicts with foreign countries and with Native Americans that the colonies faced as they grew. In the next section you'll learn about the increasing tension between the colonies and Great Britain that led to independence.

Section 4 Assessment

Reviewing Ideas, Terms, and People

1. **a. Describe** How were colonial governments organized?
   b. Analyze How did political change in England affect colonial governments?
2. **a. Explain** What is **mercantilism**?
   b. Analyze How did the Navigation Acts support the system of mercantilism?
   c. Evaluate Did the colonies benefit from mercantilism? Why or why not?
3. **a. Identify** What was the **Great Awakening**?
   b. Compare How was the **Enlightenment** similar to the Great Awakening?
4. **a. Explain** What caused the French and Indian War?
   b. Evaluate Defend the British decision to ban colonists from settling on the western frontier.

Critical Thinking

5. **Summarizing** Review your notes on the developments in the colonies during the late 1600s to mid-1700s. Then add a box to the bottom of your chart in which you briefly summarize how the colonies grew and changed during the period, as well as the challenges they faced.

Development	Effects
Establishment of local government	
Political change in England	
Trade laws	
Great Awakening/Enlightenment	
French and Indian War	

How the colonies grew and changed and challenges faced

FOCUS ON WRITING

6. **Reviewing the Information** This section focused on what life was like in all the English colonies discussed so far. Does this information give you any new ideas about the colony you'll use in your infomercial?

Conflict in the Colonies

What You Will Learn...

Main Ideas

1. British efforts to raise taxes on colonists sparked protest.
2. The Boston Massacre caused colonial resentment toward Great Britain.
3. Colonists protested the British tax on tea with the Boston Tea Party.
4. Great Britain responded to colonial actions by passing the Intolerable Acts.

The Big Idea

Tensions developed as the British government placed tax after tax on the colonies.

Key Terms and People

Samuel Adams, *p. 99*
Committees of Correspondence, *p. 99*
Stamp Act of 1765, *p. 100*
Boston Massacre, *p. 101*
Tea Act, *p. 102*
Boston Tea Party, *p. 102*
Intolerable Acts, *p. 102*

TAKING NOTES As you read, take notes in a chart like the one below on each of the new laws passed by the British government.

Law
1.
2.
3.
4.
5.

 8.1.1, 8.1.3, 8.1.4, 8.1.9, 8.1.29, 8.1.30, 8.2.9, 8.4.1

If YOU were there...

You live in the New England colonies in the 1700s. Recently, British officials have placed new taxes on tea—your favorite beverage. You've never been very interested in politics, but you're beginning to think that people far across the ocean in Britain shouldn't be able to tell you what to do. Some of your friends have joined a group that refuses to buy British tea.

Would you give up your favorite drink to join the boycott?

BUILDING BACKGROUND As the British colonies grew and became prosperous, the colonists got used to running their own lives. Britain began to seem very far away. At the same time, officials in Britain still expected the colonies to obey them and to earn money for Britain. Parliament passed new laws and imposed new taxes. But the colonists found various ways to challenge them.

Great Britain Raises Taxes

Great Britain had won the French and Indian War, but Parliament still had to pay for it. The British continued to keep a standing, or permanent, army in North America to protect the colonists against Indian attacks. To help pay for this army, Prime Minister George Grenville asked Parliament to tax the colonists. In 1764 Parliament passed the Sugar Act, which set duties on molasses and sugar imported by colonists. This was the first act passed specifically to raise money in the colonies.

British officials also tried harder to arrest smugglers. Colonial merchants were required to list all the trade goods they carried aboard their ships. These lists had to be approved before ships could leave colonial ports. This made it difficult for traders to avoid paying duties. The British navy also began to stop and search ships for smuggled goods.

Voice of Protest

Leaders like Patrick Henry made speeches that encouraged colonists to protest the British government. Here, Henry is shown protesting the Crown's control of religion in front of a Virginia court.

Why were public speeches so important to protesting British rule?

Parliament also changed the colonies' legal system by giving greater powers to the vice-admiralty courts. These courts had no juries, and the judges treated suspected smugglers as guilty until proven innocent. In regular British courts, accused persons were treated as innocent until proven guilty.

Taxation without Representation

Parliament's actions upset many colonists who had grown used to being independent. The rising merchant class thought the taxes were unfair and hurt business. Many believed that Great Britain had no right to tax the colonies at all without popular consent.

James Otis argued that the power of the Crown and Parliament was limited. Otis said they could not "take from any man any part of his property, without his consent in person or by representation." Colonial assemblies had little influence on Parliament's decisions. In addition, the colonists had no direct representatives in Parliament. The colonists were subjects of the Crown instead of citizens of England.

At a Boston town meeting in May 1764, local leader **Samuel Adams** agreed with Otis. He believed that Parliament could not tax the colonists without their permission. The ideas of Otis and Adams were summed up in the slogan "No Taxation without Representation," which spread throughout the colonies.

Adams helped found the **Committees of Correspondence**. Each committee got in touch with other towns and colonies. Its members shared ideas and information about the new British laws and ways to challenge them.

A popular method of protest was the boycott, in which people refused to buy British goods. The first colonial boycott started in New York in 1765. It soon spread to other colonies. Colonists hoped that their efforts would hurt the British economy and might convince Parliament to end the new taxes.

Stamp Act

The British government continued to search for new ways to tax the American colonies, further angering many colonists. For example, Prime Minister Grenville proposed the **Stamp Act of 1765**. This act required colonists to pay for an official stamp, or seal, when they bought paper items. The tax had to be paid on legal documents, licenses, newspapers, pamphlets, and even playing cards. Colonists who refused to buy stamps could be fined or sent to jail.

Grenville did not expect this tax to spark protest. After all, in Britain people already paid similar taxes. But colonists saw it differently. The Stamp Act was Parliament's first attempt to raise money by taxing the colonists directly, rather than by taxing imported goods.

Protests against the Stamp Act began almost immediately. Colonists formed a secret society called the Sons of Liberty. Samuel Adams helped organize the group in Boston. This group sometimes used violence to frighten tax collectors. Many colonial courts shut down because people refused to buy the stamps required for legal documents. Businesses openly ignored the law by refusing to buy stamps.

In May 1765 a Virginia lawyer named Patrick Henry presented a series of resolutions to the Virginia House of Burgesses. These resolutions stated that the Stamp Act violated colonists' rights. In addition to taxation without representation, the Stamp Act denied the accused a trial by jury. Henry's speech in support of the resolutions convinced the assembly to support some of his ideas.

Repealing the Stamp Act

In Boston the members of the Massachusetts legislature called for a Stamp Act Congress. In October 1765, delegates from nine colonies met in New York. They issued a declaration that the Stamp Act was a violation of their rights and liberties.

Pressure on Parliament to repeal, or do away with, the Stamp Act grew quickly. A group of London merchants complained that their trade suffered from the colonial boycott. Parliament repealed the Stamp Act in 1766.

Members of Parliament were upset that colonists had challenged their authority. Thus, Parliament issued the Declaratory Act, which stated that Parliament had the power to make laws for the colonies "in all cases whatsoever." The Declaratory Act further worried the colonists. The act stripped away much of their independence.

Townshend Acts

In June 1767 Parliament passed the Townshend Acts. These acts placed duties on glass, lead, paints, paper, and tea. To enforce the Townshend Acts, British officials used writs of assistance. These allowed tax collectors to search for smuggled goods. Colonists hated the new laws because they took power away from colonial governments.

The colonists responded to the Townshend Acts by once again boycotting many British goods. Women calling themselves the Daughters of Liberty supported the boycott. In February 1768 Samuel Adams wrote a letter arguing that the laws violated the legal rights of the colonists. The Massachusetts legislature sent the letter to other colonies' legislatures, who voted to join the protest.

At the same time, tax collectors in Massachusetts seized the ship *Liberty* on suspicion of smuggling. This action angered the ship's owner and the Sons of Liberty. They attacked the houses of customs officials in protest. In response, the governor broke up the Massachusetts legislature. He also asked troops to restore order. British soldiers arrived in Boston in October 1768.

READING CHECK **Sequencing** What series of events led to the arrival of British troops in Boston in 1768?

NEWSPAPER ARTICLE
The Boston Massacre

An account of the Boston Massacre appeared in the Boston Gazette and Country Journal *soon after the event.*

"The People were immediately alarmed with the Report of this horrid Massacre, the Bells were set a Ringing, and great Numbers soon assembled at the Place where this tragical Scene had been acted; their Feelings may be better conceived than expressed; and while some were taking Care of the Dead and Wounded, the Rest were in Consultation what to do in these dreadful Circumstances.

But so little intimidated were they [Bostonians], notwithstanding their being within a few Yards of the Main Guard, and seeing the 29th Regiment under Arms, and drawn up in King street; that they kept their Station and appeared, as an Officer of Rank expressed it, ready to run upon the very Muzzles of their Muskets."

—*Boston Gazette and Country Journal,* March 12, 1770

ANALYSIS SKILL **ANALYZING PRIMARY SOURCES**

Why do you think the people described were not intimidated by the soldiers?

Boston Massacre

Many Bostonians saw the presence of British troops as a threat by the British government against its critics in Massachusetts. Some colonists agreed with Samuel Adams, who said, "I look upon [British soldiers] as foreign enemies." The soldiers knew that they were not welcome. Both sides resented each other, and name-calling, arguments, and fights between Bostonians and the soldiers were common.

The tension exploded on March 5, 1770. A lone British soldier standing guard had an argument with a colonist and struck him. A crowd gathered around the soldier, throwing snowballs and shouting insults. Soon a small number of troops arrived. The crowd grew louder and angrier by the moment. Some yelled, "Come on you rascals . . . Fire if you dare!" Suddenly, the soldiers fired into the crowd, instantly killing three men, including sailor Crispus Attucks. "Half Indian, half negro, and altogether rowdy," as he was called, Attucks is the best-remembered casualty of the incident. Two others died within a few days.

Samuel Adams and other protesters quickly spread the story of the shootings. They used it as propaganda—a story giving only one side in an argument—against the British. Colonists called the shootings the **Boston Massacre**. Paul Revere created an elaborate color print titled "The Bloody Massacre perpetrated in King Street" (above).

The soldiers and their officer, Thomas Preston, were charged with murder. Two Boston lawyers, Josiah Quincy and John Adams—Samuel Adams's cousin—agreed to defend the soldiers. They argued that the troops had acted in self-defense. The Boston jury agreed, finding Preston and six soldiers not guilty. Two soldiers were convicted of killing people in the crowd by accident. These men were branded on the hand and released. The trial helped calm people down, but many were still angry at the British.

READING CHECK **Analyzing** What was the significance of the Boston Massacre?

FOCUS ON INDIANA

While many revolutionaries wrote newspaper articles and pamphlets against British policies, one woman, Mercy Otis Warren, wrote a play. The play depicted the British governor of Massachusetts as intent on destroying the rights of citizens. Warren went on to write the first official history of the Revolutionary War.

The Road to Revolution

QUICK FACTS

Colonists reacted to British laws with anger and violence. Parliament continued to pass tax after tax.

British Actions

Colonists' Reactions

1764 The Sugar Act

The Sugar Act is passed to raise money from the colonies for Britain.

Samuel Adams founds the Committees of Correspondence to improve communication among the colonies.

1765 The Stamp Act

The Stamp Act taxes newspapers, licenses, and colonial paper products.

A series of resolutions is published stating that the Stamp Act violates the rights of colonists.

The Boston Tea Party

To reduce tensions in the colonies, Parliament repealed almost all of the Townshend Acts. However, it kept the tax on tea. British officials knew that the colonial demand for tea was high despite the boycott. But colonial merchants were smuggling most of this imported tea and paying no duty on it.

The British East India Company offered Parliament a solution. The company had huge amounts of tea but was not allowed to sell it directly to the colonists. If the company could sell directly to the colonists, it could charge low prices and still make money. Cheaper tea might encourage colonists to stop smuggling. Less smuggling would result in more tax money.

Parliament agreed and passed the **Tea Act** in 1773, which allowed the British East India Company to sell tea directly to the colonists. Many colonial merchants and smugglers feared that the British East India Company's cheap tea would put them out of business.

Three ships loaded with tea from the British East India Company arrived in Boston Harbor in 1773. Members of the Sons of Liberty demanded that the ships leave. But the governor of Massachusetts would not let the ships leave without paying the duty. Unsure of what to do, the captains waited in the harbor.

On the night of December 16, 1773, colonists disguised as Indians sneaked onto the three tea-filled ships and dumped over 340 tea chests into Boston Harbor. This event became known as the **Boston Tea Party**. Soon the streets echoed with shouts of "Boston harbour is a teapot tonight!"

READING CHECK **Summarizing** What factors led to the Boston Tea Party?

The Intolerable Acts

Lord North, the new British prime minister, was furious when he heard the news. Parliament decided to punish Boston. In the spring of 1774 it passed the Coercive Acts. Colonists called these laws the **Intolerable Acts**. The acts had several effects.

1. Boston Harbor was closed until Boston paid for the ruined tea.
2. Massachusetts's charter was canceled. The governor decided if and when the legislature could meet.
3. Royal officials accused of crimes were sent to Britain for trial. This let them face a more friendly judge and jury.
4. A new **Quartering Act** required colonists to house British solders.
5. The Quebec Act gave a large amount of land to the colony of Quebec.

1770 The Boston Massacre

British soldiers fire into a crowd of colonists, killing five men.

Colonists protest and bring the soldiers to trial.

1773 The Boston Tea Party

The Tea Act is passed, making British tea cheaper than colonial tea.

Colonists protest by dumping shipments of British tea into Boston Harbor.

1774 The Intolerable Acts

Boston Harbor is closed, and British troops are quartered.

Colonists' resentment toward Britain builds.

ANALYSIS SKILL ANALYZING VISUALS

In what year did the conflict between Britain and the colonists turn violent?

6. General Thomas Gage became the new governor of Massachusetts.

The British hoped that these steps would bring back order in the colonies. Instead they simply increased people's anger at Britain.

READING CHECK **Analyzing** What was the purpose of the Intolerable Acts?

SUMMARY AND PREVIEW In this section you learned about the increasing dissatisfaction between the colonists and Great Britain. In the next chapter you'll learn about the result of these conflicts—the American Revolution.

go.hrw.com
Online Quiz
KEYWORD: SF7 HP3

Section 5 Assessment

Reviewing Ideas, Terms, and People

1. **a. Explain** Why did Great Britain raise taxes in its American colonies?
   b. Evaluate Which method of protesting taxes do you think was most successful for colonists? Why?
2. **a. Describe** What events led to the **Boston Massacre**?
   b. Elaborate Why do you think John Adams and Josiah Quincy agreed to defend the British soldiers that were involved in the Boston Massacre?
3. **a. Recall** What was the purpose of the **Tea Act**?
   b. Draw Conclusions What message did the **Boston Tea Party** send to the British government?
4. **a. Explain** Why did Parliament pass the **Intolerable Acts**?
   b. Draw Conclusions Why do you think the colonists believed that these laws were "intolerable"?

Critical Thinking

5. **Identifying Cause and Effect** Review your notes on the laws passed by the British government.

Then add a new column to your chart and identify the laws' results.

Law	Result
1.	
2.	
3.	
4.	
5.	

FOCUS ON WRITING

6. **Gathering Information** Now you have some information about the political situation in Boston in the late 1700s. Why might someone from Britain want to immigrate to Boston at this time? Would you consider the city of Boston, rather than a whole colony, for the subject of your infomercial?

THE ENGLISH COLONIES **103**

Social Studies Skills

Analysis   Critical Thinking   Civic Participation   Study

Interpreting Time Lines

Define the Skill

Knowing the sequence, or order, in which historical events took place is important to understanding these events. Time lines visually display the sequence of events during a particular period of time. They also let you easily see time spans between events, such as how long after one event a related event took place—and what events occurred in between. In addition, comparing time lines for different places makes relationships between distant events easier to identify and understand.

Learn the Skill

Follow these guidelines to read, interpret, and compare time lines.

1 Determine each time line's framework. Note the years it covers and the periods of time into which it is divided. Be aware that a pair of time lines may not have the same framework.

2 Study the order of events on each time line. Note the length of time between events. Compare what was taking place on different time lines around the same time period.

3 Look for relationships between events. Pay particular attention to how an event on one time line might relate to an event on another.

Practice the Skill

Interpret the time lines below to answer the following questions.

1. What is each time line's framework?

2. How long was England without a king?

3. What event in England allowed the colonists to get rid of the Dominion of New England in 1689?

4. Massachusetts's independence had troubled English officials for many years. What do the time lines suggest about why this colony was allowed to remain independent until 1686?

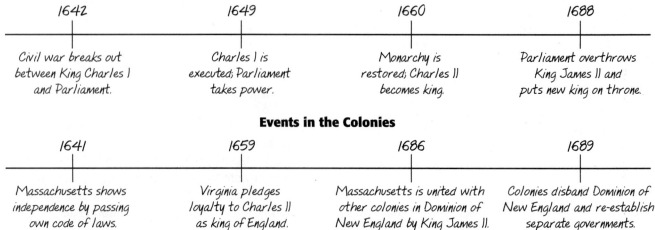

Events in England

1642	1649	1660	1688
Civil war breaks out between King Charles I and Parliament.	Charles I is executed; Parliament takes power.	Monarchy is restored; Charles II becomes king.	Parliament overthrows King James II and puts new king on throne.

Events in the Colonies

1641	1659	1686	1689
Massachusetts shows independence by passing own code of laws.	Virginia pledges loyalty to Charles II as king of England.	Massachusetts is united with other colonies in Dominion of New England by King James II.	Colonies disband Dominion of New England and re-establish separate governments.

Chapter Review

HOLT
History's Impact
▶ video series
Review the video to answer the closing question:
How does the value that Americans place on religious freedom limit government actions?

Visual Summary

Use the visual summary below to help you review the main ideas of the chapter.

Increasing tensions between the colonies and Britain led many colonists to consider cutting ties to Britain.

- Taxation without representation
- Acts of Parliament
- Violence between colonists and British troops

Reviewing Vocabulary, Terms, and People

Match the words in the left column with the correct definition in the right column.

1. Committees of Correspondence
2. Jonathan Edwards
3. mercantilism
4. immigrants
5. indentured servants
6. William Penn
7. Pocahontas
8. Quakers
9. staple crops
10. town meeting

a. colonists who received free passage to North America in exchange for working without pay for a certain number of years

b. created in Massachusetts, these groups helped towns and colonies share information about resisting the new British laws

c. crops that are continuously in demand

d. daughter of Powhatan chief whose marriage to colonist John Rolfe eased tensions between the Powhatan and the colonists

e. one of the leaders of the Great Awakening, he urged sinners to seek forgiveness

f. Protestant sect founded in England that believed salvation was available to all people

g. people who move to another country after leaving their homeland

h. political gathering at which people make decisions on local issues

i. Quaker leader who established a colony with the goal of fair government for all

j. system of creating and maintaining wealth through controlled trade

Comprehension and Critical Thinking

SECTION 1 *(Pages 72–77)*

11. a. Explain What problems did the settlers of Virginia face?

b. Draw Conclusions Why was Maryland's Toleration Act of 1649 important?

c. Predict How might the southern colonies' reliance on slave labor eventually cause problems?

SECTION 2 *(Pages 78–84)*

12. a. Describe On what was the economy of the New England colonies based?

b. Compare and Contrast How were the Pilgrim and Puritan colonies similar and different?

c. Evaluate Explain why you think the close ties between church and state in Massachusetts helped or hurt its government.

SECTION 3 *(Pages 85–87)*

13. a. Identify What types of crops were grown in the middle colonies?

b. Draw Conclusions Why did the middle colonies have a more diverse population than either New England or the South?

c. Elaborate Why would immigrants have chosen to live in the middle colonies?

SECTION 4 *(Pages 90–97)*

14. a. Identify What challenges did the English colonies face?

b. Analyze What effect did the Great Awakening and the Enlightenment have on the colonies?

c. Evaluate Explain which you think had a greater impact on colonial government—the passage of the English Bill of Rights or the Great Awakening.

SECTION 5 *(Pages 98–103)*

15. a. Recall Why did the British believe it was necessary to raise taxes on the American colonists?

b. Draw Conclusions How did the Boston Massacre and the Boston Tea Party affect relations between Great Britain and the colonies?

c. Evaluate Did the British government overreact to colonial protests by issuing the Intolerable Acts? Why or why not?

Reviewing Themes

16. Politics What political influences shaped the governments of the British colonies?

17. Economics How did mercantilism affect the economies of Great Britain and the colonies?

Reading Skills

Vocabulary Clues *Use the Reading Skills taught in this chapter to answer the question about the reading selection below.*

> A popular method of protest was the boycott, in which people refused to buy British goods. *(p. 99)*

18. According to the reading selection above, what is the best definition of *boycott*?

a. a popular method

b. buying British goods

c. people refusing

d. protest in which people refuse to buy goods

Social Studies Skills

Interpreting Time Lines *Use the Social Studies Skills taught in this chapter to answer the questions about the time lines on page 104.*

19. How many years after the English Civil War did Parliament overthrow King James II?

20. How many years did the Dominion of New England last?

a. 41

b. 18

c. 3

d. 6

FOCUS ON WRITING

21. Writing Your Infomercial Choose a colony and time period. Review your list of reasons why English citizens might want to live there. Then write an infomercial with at least four scenes. Each scene should have video and a voice-over telling one of the reasons for immigrating.

Standardized Test Practice

8.1.3, 8.1.4, 8.3.5, 8.4.9

DIRECTIONS: Read each question and write the letter of the best response.

1 Use the map below to answer the following question.

The red box on this map indicates which early colonial settlement?

A Plymouth

B Massachusetts Bay

C New Amsterdam

D Jamestown

2 Ideas about spiritual, social, and political equality arose in the colonies in the 1700s in a religious movement called

A Separatism.

B the Enlightenment.

C the Great Awakening.

D Puritanism.

3 How did Parliament's passage of the English Bill of Rights in 1689 affect England's North American colonies?

A Colonists became more interested in being governed by representatives they elected.

B Several colonies decided to unite and formed the Dominion of New England.

C The Great Awakening took place.

D A movement to end slavery developed.

4 What was the central issue in the dispute between Britain and its American colonies?

A the restrictions Parliament placed on trade

B the presence of British troops in the colonies

C the colonists' right to religious freedom

D the power to tax the colonists

5 Which side did Native Americans take in the French and Indian War?

A the British

B the French

C different groups sided with each country

D Native Americans did not fight in the French and Indian War

6 Examine the following passage from an early colonist's journal and then use it to answer the question below.

> *"An Indian came to us from the chief, the great Powhatan, with the word of peace. He said that Powhatan greatly desired our friendship, and that chiefs Pasyaheigh and Tapahanagh wanted to be our friends. Powhatan said that we would be able to sow and reap our crops in peace or else he would make war upon our enemies. This message turned out to be true, for these chiefs have ever since remained in peace and continued to trade with us. We rewarded the messenger with many small gifts, which were great wonders to him."*
>
> —Edward Maria Wingfield, from *A Discourse on Virginia*

Document-Based Question Why do you think Native American chiefs wanted to make peace with early English colonists?

The American Revolution

Indiana Standards

Social Studies Standards

8.1.4 Identify fundamental ideas in the Declaration of Independence (1776) and analyze the causes and effects of the Revolutionary War (1775–1783), including enactment of the Articles of Confederation and the Treaty of Paris.

8.1.9 Describe the influence of important individuals on social and political developments of the time such as the Independence movement and the framing of the Constitution.

8.1.28 Recognize historical perspective and evaluate alternative courses of action by describing the historical context in which events unfolded and by avoiding evaluation of the past solely in terms of present-day norms.

8.1.29 Differentiate betweenfacts and historical interpretations recognizing that the historian's narrative reflects his or her judgment about the significance of particular facts.

8.2.1 Identify and explain essential ideas of constitutional government, which are expressed in the founding documents of the United States, including the Virginia Declaration of Rights, the Declaration of Independence, the Virginia Statute for Religious Freedom, the Massachusetts Constitution of 1780, the Northwest Ordinance, the 1787 U.S. Constitution, the Bill of Rights, the Federalist and Anti-Federalist Papers, Common Sense, Washington's Farewell Address (1796), and Jefferson's First Inaugural Address (1801).

go.hrw.com
Indiana
KEYWORD: SF10 IN

FOCUS ON SPEAKING

Giving an Oral Report The Revolutionary War was a very exciting time in our history, a time filled with deeds of courage and daring and ending with an amazing victory for the underdog. As you read this chapter, you will learn about the great events and heroic people of that time. Then you will prepare and give an oral report on the history of the American Revolution.

UNITED STATES

1774 The First Continental Congress meets.

1775 The Revolutionary War begins with the fighting at Lexington and Concord.

1774

WORLD

What You Will Learn...

Soldiers fight with single-shot muskets in this re-enactment of the Revolutionary War. The men in the colonial militias did not have regular uniforms like the British soldiers did. They wore their own clothes and often used their own supplies. In this chapter you will learn about the American War for Independence.

1776 On July 4 the thirteen colonies issue the Declaration of Independence and break away from Great Britain.

1779 George Rogers Clark and his Patriot army capture Fort Sackville for the second time.

1781 The British surrender to George Washington at Yorktown.

1783 The Treaty of Paris is signed, ending the war.

1777

1780

1783

1778 France allies with the Americans and joins the war against Great Britain.

1779 Spain declares war against Great Britain.

1783 Simon Bolívar is born in present-day Venezuela.

THE AMERICAN REVOLUTION **109**

Focus on Themes In this chapter you will read about the events of the Revolutionary War, the war by which the United States won its independence. You will learn about some of the major battles that occurred between the American colonists and the British army and how **geography** sometimes affected their outcomes. You will also read the Declaration of Independence, one of the most important **political** documents in all of American history.

Main Ideas in Social Studies

Focus on Reading When you are reading, it is not always necessary to remember every tiny detail of the text. Instead, what you want to remember are the main ideas, the most important concepts around which the text is based.

Identifying Main Ideas Most paragraphs in history books include main ideas. Sometimes the main idea is stated clearly in a single sentence. At other times, the main idea is suggested, not stated. However, that idea still shapes the paragraph's content and the meaning of all of the facts and details in it.

Topic: The paragraph is about the pamphlet *Common Sense* by Thomas Paine.

+

News of the work spread throughout the colonies, eventually selling some 500,000 copies. Paine reached a wide audience by writing as a common person speaking to common people. *Common Sense* changed the way many colonists viewed their king. *(p. 118)*

Facts and Details:
• Many people from different colonies read the pamphlet.
• *Common Sense* eventually sold 500,000 copies.
• Thomas Paine's writing style was easy for the common people to read.

Main Idea: The pamphlet *Common Sense* shaped the way some colonists thought about their rulers.

Steps in Identifying Main Ideas

1. Read the paragraph. Ask yourself, "What is this paragraph mostly about?" This will be the topic of the paragraph.

2. List the important facts and details that relate to that topic.

3. Ask yourself, "What seems to be the most important point the writer is making about the topic?" Or ask, "If the writer could say only one thing about this paragraph, what would it be?" This is the **main idea** of the paragraph.

You Try It!

The following passage is from the chapter you are about to read. Read it and then answer the questions below.

The Treaty of Paris

After Yorktown, only a few small battles took place. Lacking the money to pay for a new army, Great Britain entered into peace talks with America. Benjamin Franklin had an influential role in the negotiations.

From Chapter 4, p. 139

Delegates took more than two years to come to a peace agreement. In the Treaty of Paris of 1783, Great Britain recognized the independence of the United States. The treaty also set America's borders. A separate treaty between Britain and Spain returned Florida to the Spanish. British leaders also accepted American rights to settle and trade west of the original thirteen colonies.

After you have read the passage, answer the following questions.

1. The main idea of the second paragraph is stated in a sentence. Which sentence expresses the main idea?

2. What is the first paragraph about? What facts and details are included in the paragraph? Based on your answers to these questions, what is the main idea of the first paragraph?

As you read Chapter 4, identify the main ideas of the paragraphs you are reading.

Key Terms and People

Chapter 4

Section 1
First Continental Congress *(p. 112)*
Patriots *(p. 113)*
minutemen *(p. 114)*
Redcoats *(p. 114)*
Second Continental Congress *(p. 114)*
Continental Army *(p. 114)*
George Washington *(p. 114)*
Battle of Bunker Hill *(p. 115)*

Section 2
Common Sense (p. 118)
Thomas Paine *(p. 118)*
Declaration of Independence *(p. 119)*
Thomas Jefferson *(p. 119)*
Loyalists *(p. 119)*

Section 3
mercenaries *(p. 128)*
Battle of Trenton *(p.129)*
Battle of Saratoga *(p. 130)*
Marquis de Lafayette *(p. 131)*
Baron Friedrich von Steuben *(p. 131)*
Bernardo de Gálvez *(p. 131)*
John Paul Jones *(p. 133)*
George Rogers Clark *(p. 133)*

Section 4
Francis Marion *(p. 136)*
Comte de Rochambeau *(p. 137)*
Battle of Yorktown *(p. 137)*
Treaty of Paris of 1783 *(p. 139)*

Academic Vocabulary

Success in school is related to knowing academic vocabulary—the words that are frequently used in school assignments and discussions. In this chapter, you will learn the following academic words:

reaction *(p. 114)*
strategy *(p. 129)*

The Revolution Begins

What You Will Learn...

Main Ideas

1. The First Continental Congress demanded certain rights from Great Britain.
2. Armed conflict between British soldiers and colonists broke out with the "shot heard 'round the world."
3. The Second Continental Congress created the Continental Army to fight the British.
4. In two early battles, the army lost control of Boston but then regained it.

The Big Idea

The tensions between the colonies and Great Britain led to armed conflict in 1775.

Key Terms and People

First Continental Congress, *p. 112*
Patriots, *p. 113*
minutemen, *p. 114*
Redcoats, *p. 114*
Second Continental Congress, *p. 114*
Continental Army, *p. 114*
George Washington, *p. 114*
Battle of Bunker Hill, *p. 115*

TAKING NOTES As you read, take notes on the events that occurred in the early days of the American Revolution. Write your notes in a graphic organizer like the one below.

First Continental Congress	Battles	Second Continental Congress

If YOU were there...

You are a member of the British Parliament in the 1770s. Some members say that the Americans are defying the king. Others point out that the colonists are British citizens who have certain rights. Now the king must decide to punish the rebellious colonists or listen to their complaints.

What advice would you give the king?

BUILDING BACKGROUND Taxes and harsh new laws led some colonists to protest against the British. In some places, the protests turned violent. The British government refused to listen, ignoring the colonists' demands for more rights. That set the stage for war.

First Continental Congress

To many colonists the closing of Boston Harbor was the final insult in a long list of abuses. In response to the mounting crisis, all the colonies except Georgia sent representatives to a meeting in October 1774. This meeting, known as the **First Continental Congress**, was a gathering of colonial leaders who were deeply troubled about the relationship between Great Britain and its colonies in America. At Carpenters' Hall in Philadelphia, the leaders remained locked in weeks of intense debate. Patrick Henry and others believed that violence was unavoidable. On the other hand, delegates from Pennsylvania and New York had strict orders to seek peace.

Wisely, the delegates compromised. They encouraged colonists to continue boycotting British goods but told colonial militias to prepare for war. Meanwhile, they drafted the Declaration of Rights, a list of 10 resolutions to be presented to King George III. Included was the colonists' right to "life, liberty, and property."

The First Continental Congress did not seek a separation from Britain. Its goal was to state the colonists' concerns and ask the king to correct the problems. But before they left Philadelphia, the delegates agreed to meet in 1775 if the king refused their petition.

Patrick Henry returned from the Congress and reported to his fellow Virginians. To encourage them to support the Patriot cause,

Paul Revere's Ride

Battle at Lexington

Battle at Concord

PAUL REVERE'S RIDE

Revere captured

North Church

Boston

Boston Harbor

0   2   4 Miles
0   2   4 Kilometers

Henry voiced these famous words:

> "They tell us, Sir, that we are weak; unable to cope with so formidable an adversary. But when will we be stronger? Gentlemen may cry, Peace, Peace—but there is no peace. I know not what course others may take; but as for me, give me liberty or give me death."
>
> —Patrick Henry, quoted in *Eyewitnesses and Others*

In time many colonists came to agree with Henry. They became known as **Patriots**—colonists who chose to fight for independence from Great Britain.

READING CHECK Identifying Cause and Effect

Why did the delegates attend the First Continental Congress? What were the results?

"Shot Heard 'round the World"

The Continental Congress planned to meet again in 1775. Before it could, the situation in the colonies had changed—for the worse.

The Ride of Paul Revere

British military leaders in the colonies grew uneasy when local militias seemed to be preparing for action. The governor of Massachusetts, Thomas Gage, learned that a stockpile of weapons was stored in Concord, about 20 miles from Boston. In April 1775 he decided to seize the supplies.

Gage thought he had kept his plan a secret. However, Boston was full of spies for the Patriot cause. They noticed the British were preparing for action and quickly informed the Patriots. Unsure of how the British would strike, Sons of Liberty member Paul Revere enlisted the aid of Robert Newman. Newman was to climb into the steeple of the Old North Church and watch for British soldiers. If they advanced across land, Newman would display one lantern from the steeple. If they rowed across the Charles River, Newman would display two lanterns.

When Revere and fellow Patriot William Dawes saw two lights shine, they set off on horseback. Using two different routes out of Boston, they sounded the alert. As the riders advanced, drums and church bells called out the local militia, or **minutemen**—who got their name because they were ready to fight at a minute's notice.

Battles at Lexington and Concord

At dawn on April 19, the British troops arrived at the town of Lexington, near Concord, where 70 armed minutemen waited. Patriot captain John Parker yelled to his troops, "Don't fire unless fired upon." Suddenly a shot rang out. To this day, no one knows who fired this "shot heard 'round the world."

The battle at Lexington ended in minutes with only a few volleys fired. When the smoke cleared, 8 of the badly outnumbered minutemen lay dead, and 10 were wounded. The British, with only one soldier wounded, marched on to Concord.

Although Revere had been arrested, the citizens of Concord were warned by another rider, Samuel Prescott. Most of the weapons in Concord had already been hidden, but the few that were left were now concealed. Some of the British troops, frustrated because the stockpile had disappeared, set fire to a few buildings. In **reaction** the minutemen charged forward.

ACADEMIC VOCABULARY
reaction
response

For the skilled colonial marksmen of Concord, the British soldiers made an easy target. They were wearing the British military uniform with its bright red jacket. For some time the colonists had called the British soldiers **Redcoats** because of these jackets. The British were forced to retreat to Boston, suffering many casualties along the way.

READING CHECK Drawing Inferences Why did the Patriots need several riders? Why did they take different routes?

Second Continental Congress

King George III had refused to address the concerns listed in the Declaration of Rights. In May 1775, delegates from 12 colonies met again in Philadelphia for the **Second Continental Congress**. This second group of delegates from the colonies was still far from unified, but represented the first attempt at a Republican government in the colonies.

Some of the delegates called for a war, others for peace. Once again they compromised. Although the Congress did not openly revolt, delegates showed their growing dissatisfaction. They sent word to colonial authorities asking for new state constitutions. States set up conventions to write them. They also authorized the Massachusetts militia to become the **Continental Army**. This force would soon include soldiers from all colonies and would carry out the fight against Britain. Congress named a Virginian, **George Washington**, to command the army.

As Washington prepared for war, the Congress pursued peace. On July 5 the delegates signed the Olive Branch Petition as a final attempt to restore harmony. King George refused to read it. Instead, he looked for new ways to punish the colonies.

READING CHECK Summarizing What did the Second Continental Congress accomplish?

Early Battles

While the Congress discussed peace, the Massachusetts militia began to fight. Boston was a key city in the early days of the war. Both Patriots and the British fought to hold it.

Bunker Hill

Desperate for supplies, leaders in Boston sent Benedict Arnold and a force of 400 men to New York State. Their objective was to attack the British at Fort Ticonderoga. In May 1775, Arnold captured the fort and its large supply of weapons.

Meanwhile, the poorly supplied Patriots kept the British pinned down inside Boston. Although British leaders were trying to form a battle plan, they awoke on June 17 to a stunning sight. The colonial forces had quietly dug in at Breed's Hill, a point overlooking north Boston. The Redcoats would have to cross Boston Harbor and fight their way uphill.

As the British force of 2,400 advanced, 1,600 militia members waited. Low on gunpowder, the commander ordered his troops not to fire "until you see the whites of their eyes." As they climbed the exposed hillside with their heavy packs, the British soldiers were cut down. Twice they retreated. Stepping over the dead and wounded, they returned for a third try. The colonists were now out of ammunition, and eventually they had to retreat.

This famous conflict is now known as the **Battle of Bunker Hill**, although it was actually launched from Breed's Hill. While the Patriots lost, they proved they could take on the Redcoats. For the British, the battle was a tragic victory. To win, they had sacrificed about double the number of Patriot soldiers.

★ Interactive Map

Battles for Boston, 1775–76

The colonists were forced to retreat from Breed's Hill, but the British suffered heavy losses during the battle.

Boston
THIRTEEN COLONIES
ATLANTIC OCEAN

Bunker Hill

Breed's Hill ☆

HOWE JUNE 1775

Charles River

Boston

42°22'N

71°06'W

71°04'W

Boston Harbor

Nook's Hill

General Washington arrived two weeks later and took command of 14,000 troops. In 1776 they drove the British from Boston.

Dorchester Heights

- ▬ American advance
- ▬▪ American retreat
- 🧍 American troops
- ▬ British advance
- ▬▪ British retreat
- 🧍 British troops
- ☆ British victory

0   .5   1 Mile
0   .5   1 Kilometer

GEOGRAPHY SKILLS **INTERPRETING MAPS**

go.hrw.com
Interactive Map
KEYWORD: SF7 CH4

1. **Place** What geographic advantage did control of Boston provide?
2. **Movement** How did British troops retreat from Boston? How can you tell?

Dorchester Heights

Shortly after the Battle of Bunker Hill, General Washington arrived in Boston to command the Continental Army. Washington knew that he would need heavier guns to drive the British out of Boston, and he knew where to get them—Fort Ticonderoga. Colonel Henry Knox was assigned to transport the captured cannons from Fort Ticonderoga to Boston. He successfully brought the heavy guns over 300 miles of rough terrain in the middle of winter. When Knox delivered the cannons, Washington was ready to regain control of Boston.

On March 4, 1776, Washington moved his army to Dorchester Heights, an area that overlooked Boston from the south. He stationed the cannons and his troops on Nook's Hill overlooking British general William Howe's position. When Howe awoke the next morn-

ing and saw the Patriots' well-positioned artillery, he knew he would have to retreat. "The Rebels have done more in one night than my whole army could do in months," Howe declared. On March 7 Howe retreated from Boston to Canada. The birthplace of the rebellion was now in Patriot hands.

READING CHECK **Drawing Inferences** Why was the geography of the Boston area important in forming a battle plan?

SUMMARY AND PREVIEW Some colonial leaders became convinced that they could not avoid war with Great Britain. In the next section you will read about another step toward war—the writing of the Declaration of Independence.

---

go.hrw.com
Online Quiz
KEYWORD: SF7 HP4

Section 1 Assessment

Reviewing Ideas, Terms, and People

1. **a. Identify** What was the **First Continental Congress**?
   b. Make Inferences Why did the First Continental Congress send the Declaration of Rights to the king?
   c. Elaborate Why did King George III refuse to consider the colonists' declaration?

2. **a. Identify** Who warned the colonists of the British advance toward Lexington and Concord?
   b. Analyze Why did the British army march on Lexington and Concord?
   c. Elaborate What is meant by the expression "shot heard 'round the world"?

3. **a. Describe** What was the purpose of the **Second Continental Congress**?
   b. Draw Conclusions Were the delegates to the Second Continental Congress ready to revolt against George III? Explain.
   c. Evaluate Defend George III's response to the Declaration of Rights and the Olive Branch Petition.

4. **a. Identify** What leader captured Fort Ticonderoga?
   b. Draw Conclusions How was the **Continental Army** able to drive British forces out of Boston?
   c. Evaluate How would you evaluate the performance of the Continental Army in the early battles of the war? Explain.

Critical Thinking

5. **Categorizing** Review your notes on the early battles of the Revolution. Then copy the graphic organizer below and use it to categorize events in the early days of the Revolution. Some events will be attempts at peace; others will be movement toward war.

Attempts at Peace	Movement toward War

FOCUS ON SPEAKING

6. **Thinking about the Beginning** You'll have about five minutes for your report and only a minute or two to talk about the beginning of the war. What are the one or two most important things you want to say?

George Washington

What would you do if you were asked to lead a new country?

When did he live? 1732–1799

Where did he live? George Washington was a true American, born in the Virginia colony. As president, he lived in New York City and Philadelphia, the nation's first two capitals. When he retired, he returned to his plantation at Mount Vernon.

What did he do? Although Washington was a wealthy farmer, he spent most of his life in the military and in politics. Leading the colonial forces to victory in the Revolutionary War, he then helped shape the new government of the United States. On April 30, 1789, he was sworn in as the first president of the United States.

Why is he so important? George Washington inspired Americans and helped to unite them. One of his great accomplishments as president was to keep the peace with Britain and France. Upon leaving the presidency, he urged Americans to avoid becoming politically divided.

Drawing Conclusions How might Washington's leadership in the Revolutionary War have prepared him for his role as president?

KEY EVENTS

1775 Serves in Second Continental Congress; selected commander of the Continental Army

1789 Inaugurated as president

1793 Begins second term as president

1796 Publishes his Farewell Address and retires to his plantation at Mount Vernon

1799 Dies at Mount Vernon; his will frees his slaves

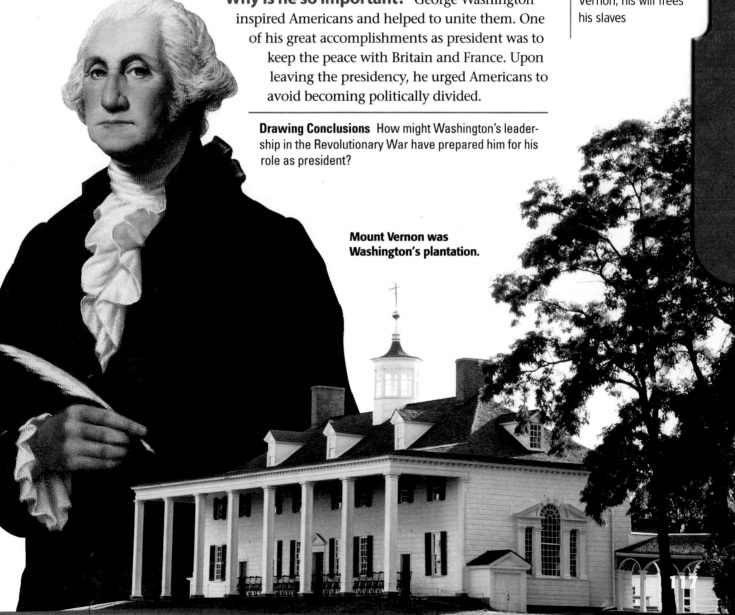

Mount Vernon was Washington's plantation.

117

Declaring Independence

What You Will Learn...

Main Ideas

1. Thomas Paine's *Common Sense* led many colonists to support independence.
2. Colonists had to choose sides when independence was declared.
3. The Declaration of Independence did not address the rights of all colonists.

The Big Idea

The colonies formally declared their independence from Great Britain.

Key Terms and People

Common Sense, p. 118
Thomas Paine, p. 118
Declaration of Independence, p. 119
Thomas Jefferson, p. 119
Loyalists, p. 119

TAKING NOTES As you read, take notes on the Declaration of Independence. Write your notes in a graphic organizer like the one below.

Influence of *Common Sense* on Declaration	Main Ideas of Declaration	People Not Included

8.1.1, 8.1.3, 8.1.4, 8.1.9, 8.1.28, 8.1.29, 8.1.30, 8.2.1

If YOU were there...

You live on a farm in New York in 1776. The conflicts with the British have torn your family apart. Your father is loyal to King George and wants to remain British. But your mother is a fierce Patriot, and your brother wants to join the Continental Army. Your father and others who feel the same way are moving to British-held Canada. Now you must decide what you will do.

Would you go to Canada or support the Patriots?

BUILDING BACKGROUND The outbreak of violence at Lexington, Concord, and Boston took some colonists by surprise. Many, like the father above, opposed independence from Britain. Those who supported freedom began to promote their cause in many ways.

Paine's *Common Sense*

"[There] is something very absurd in supporting a continent to be perpetually [forever] governed by an island." This plainspoken argument against British rule over America appeared in *Common Sense*, a 47-page pamphlet that was distributed in Philadelphia in January 1776. *Common Sense* was published anonymously—that is, without the author's name. The author, **Thomas Paine**, argued that citizens, not kings and queens, should make laws. At a time when monarchs ruled much of the world, this was a bold idea.

News of the work spread throughout the colonies, eventually selling some 500,000 copies. Paine reached a wide audience by writing as a common person speaking to common people. *Common Sense* changed the way many colonists viewed their king. It made a strong case for economic freedom and for the right to military self-defense. It cried out against tyranny—that is, the abuse of government power. Thomas Paine's words rang out in his time, and they have echoed throughout American history.

READING CHECK Supporting a Point of View Would you have agreed with Thomas Paine? Explain.

Independence Is Declared

Many colonial leaders agreed with Paine. In June 1776 the Second Continental Congress formed a committee to write a document declaring the colonies' independence. A committee also created a seal for the new country with the Latin motto "*E pluribus unum*" or "out of many, one." This motto recognized the new union of states.

A New Philosophy of Government

The **Declaration of Independence** formally announced the colonies' break from Great Britain. In doing so, it expressed three main ideas. First, **Thomas Jefferson**, the document's main author, argued that all people possess unalienable rights, including the rights of "life, liberty, and the pursuit of happiness."

Next, Jefferson asserted that King George III had violated the colonists' rights by taxing them without their consent. Jefferson accused the king of passing unfair laws and interfering with colonial governments. He also believed that stationing a large British army within the colonies was a burden.

Third, Jefferson stated that the colonies had the right to break from Britain. Influenced by the Enlightenment ideal of the social contract, he maintained that governments and rulers must protect the rights of citizens. In exchange, the people agree to be governed. Jefferson argued that King George III had broken the social contract.

On July 4, 1776, the Continental Congress approved the Declaration of Independence. This act broke all ties to the British crown. The United States of America was born.

Choosing Sides

The signing of the Declaration made the rebellion a full-scale revolt against Britain. Those who supported it would be considered traitors. Colonists who chose to side with the British were known as **Loyalists**—often called Tories.

FOCUS ON INDIANA

Throughout the colonies, conventions of delegates met to reorganize their governments. In 1776, Virginia delegates issued the Virginia Declaration of Rights, which stated that people had the right to rebel against inadequate government. Parts of the text are still a part of Virginia's state constitution today.

THE IMPACT TODAY

The Continental Congress voted for independence on July 2. However, because the Declaration was not approved until July 4, the fourth is celebrated today as Independence Day.

Primary Source

POINTS OF VIEW
Choosing Sides

When Ben Franklin's son William was a child, he helped his father experiment with lightning. But by the time William had grown and the Revolution started, the two men viewed the conflict differently. They exchanged letters on the subject.

"I am indeed of the opinion, that the parliament has no right to make any law whatever, binding on the colonies . . . I know your sentiments differ from mine on these subjects. You are a thorough government man, which I do not wonder at, nor do I aim at converting you. I only wish you to act uprightly and steadily."

–Benjamin Franklin,
quoted in *The Writings of Benjamin Franklin Vol. III*

"I think that all laws until they are repealed ought to be obeyed and that it is the duty of those who are entrusted with the executive part of government to see that they are so."

–William Franklin,
quoted in *Benjamin and William Franklin* by Sheila L. Skemp

ANALYSIS SKILL **ANALYZING PRIMARY SOURCES**

How did the two men view the British government differently?

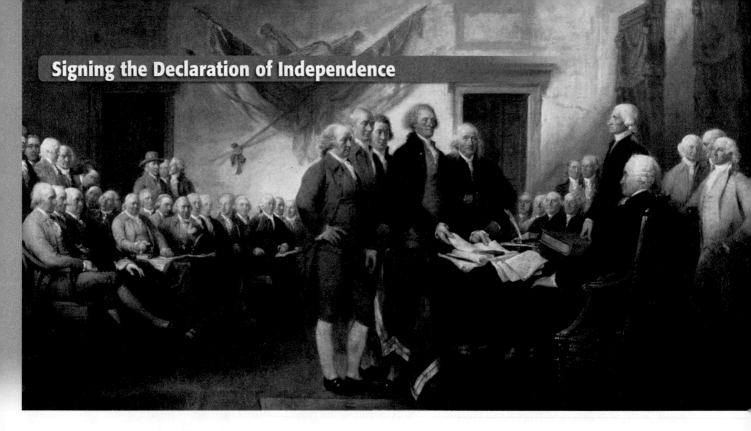

Signing the Declaration of Independence

Historians estimate that 40 to 45 percent of Americans were Patriots, while 20 to 30 percent were Loyalists. The rest were neutral.

Because of persecution by Patriots, more than 50,000 Loyalists fled the colonies during the Revolution. Most went to Canada, where Britain allowed them more self-rule after the Revolution. In doing so, they abandoned their homes and property. Divided allegiances tore apart families and friendships—even Benjamin Franklin became separated from his Loyalist son William.

Native Americans were at first encouraged by both sides to remain neutral. By the summer of 1776, however, both Patriots and the British were aggressively recruiting Indian fighters. Most sided with the British. In northern New York, four of the six Iroquois nations fought for the British. However, the Oneida and Tuscarora helped the Patriots, even delivering food to the soldiers at Valley Forge.

READING CHECK **Drawing Conclusions** Why would Native Americans have lost out no matter who won the war?

Unfinished Business

Today we recognize that the Declaration of Independence excluded many colonists. While it declared that "all men are created equal," the document failed to mention women, enslaved Africans, or Native Americans. The rights of these minorities would be subject to the rule of the majority.

Women

Although many women were Patriots, the Declaration did not address their rights. At least one delegate's wife, Abigail Adams, tried to influence her husband, John, to include women's rights in the Declaration. In a failed effort, she expressed her concerns:

❝ Remember the Ladies, and be more generous and favorable to them than your ancestors. Do not put such unlimited power into the hands of the Husbands ... If particular care and attention is not paid to the Ladies we are and will not hold ourselves bound by Laws in which we have no voice, or Representation. ❞

—Abigail Adams, quoted in *Notable American Women*

- ❶ John Adams
- ❷ Roger Sherman
- ❸ Robert Livingston
- ❹ Thomas Jefferson
- ❺ Benjamin Franklin
- ❻ Charles Thomson
- ❼ John Hancock

The Declaration of Independence was adopted on July 4, 1776. This painting shows 47 of the 56 signers of the document. The man sitting on the right is John Hancock, who was the president of the Second Continental Congress. He is accepting the Declaration from the committee that wrote it.

How realistic do you think this painting is?

African and Native Americans

The Declaration did not recognize the rights of enslaved Africans, either. The authors had compared life under British rule to living as an enslaved people. The obvious question arose: Why did any form of slavery exist in a land that valued personal freedom? Even Thomas Jefferson, the main author of the Declaration, was a slaveholder.

In July 1776 slavery was legal in all the colonies. By the 1780s the New England colonies were taking steps to end slavery. Even so, the conflict over slavery continued long after the Revolutionary War.

The Declaration of Independence also did not address the rights of Native Americans to life, liberty, or property. Despite the Proclamation of 1763, American colonists had been quietly settling on lands that belonged to Native Americans. This tendency to disregard the rights of Native Americans would develop into a pattern after the colonists won their independence from Great Britain.

READING CHECK Finding Main Ideas What groups were unrepresented in the Declaration of Independence?

SUMMARY AND PREVIEW In 1776 the colonists declared their independence. To achieve their goal, however, they would have to win a war against the British army. In the next section you will learn about some of the battles of the Revolutionary War. For a time, it seemed as if the British would defeat the colonists.

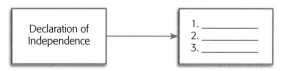

go.hrw.com
Online Quiz
KEYWORD: SF7 HP4

Section 2 Assessment

Reviewing Ideas, Terms, and People

1. **a. Identify** Who was **Thomas Paine**?
   b. Make Inferences Why do you think Thomas Paine originally published *Common Sense* anonymously?
   c. Elaborate Do you think that most colonists would have supported independence from Britain without Thomas Paine's publication of *Common Sense*? Explain.
2. **a. Identify** What two sides emerged in response to the **Declaration of Independence**? What did each side favor?
   b. Explain What arguments did the authors of the Declaration of Independence give for declaring the colonies free from British control?
   c. Predict How might some groups use the Declaration of Independence in the future to gain rights?
3. **a. Identify** Who urged her husband to "remember the ladies"?
   b. Making Inferences Why did the authors of the Declaration of Independence fail to address the rights of women, Native Americans, and African Americans in the document?

Critical Thinking

4. **Analyzing** Review your notes on the Declaration of Independence. Then copy the graphic organizer below and use it to identify three results of the Declaration of Independence.

```
┌──────────────┐        ┌──────────────┐
│ Declaration of│───────▶│ 1. _____ │
│ Independence  │        │ 2. _____ │
└──────────────┘        │ 3. _____ │
                        └──────────────┘
```

FOCUS ON SPEAKING

5. **Gathering Ideas about the Declaration of Independence** You are living at the time of the American Revolution. What is new and surprising about the colonists' actions? In one or two minutes, what is the most important thing you can say about the colonies' declaring independence?

The Declaration of Independence

EXPLORING THE DOCUMENT Thomas Jefferson wrote the first draft of the Declaration in a little more than two weeks. **How is the Declaration's idea about why governments are formed still important to our country today?**

Vocabulary

impel force

endowed provided

usurpations wrongful seizures of power

evinces clearly displays

despotism unlimited power

tyranny oppressive power exerted by a government or ruler

candid fair

In Congress, July 4, 1776
The unanimous Declaration of the thirteen united States of America,

When in the Course of human events, it becomes necessary for one people to dissolve the political bands which have connected them with another, and to assume among the Powers of the earth, the separate and equal station to which the Laws of Nature and of Nature's God entitle them, a decent respect to the opinions of mankind requires that they should declare the causes which **impel** them to the separation.

We hold these truths to be self-evident, that all men are created equal, that they are **endowed** by their Creator with certain unalienable Rights, that among these are Life, Liberty, and the pursuit of Happiness. That to secure these rights, Governments are instituted among Men, deriving their just powers from the consent of the governed, That whenever any Form of Government becomes destructive of these ends, it is the Right of the People to alter or to abolish it, and to institute new Government, laying its foundation on such principles and organizing its powers in such form, as to them shall seem most likely to effect their Safety and Happiness. Prudence, indeed, will dictate that Governments long established should not be changed for light and transient causes; and accordingly all experience hath shown, that mankind are more disposed to suffer, while evils are sufferable, than to right themselves by abolishing the forms to which they are accustomed. But when a long train of abuses and **usurpations**, pursuing invariably the same Object **evinces** a design to reduce them under absolute **Despotism**, it is their right, it is their duty, to throw off such Government, and to provide new Guards for their future security.—Such has been the patient sufferance of these Colonies; and such is now the necessity which constrains them to alter their former Systems of Government. The history of the present King of Great Britain is a history of repeated injuries and usurpations, all having in direct object the establishment of an absolute **Tyranny** over these States. To prove this, let Facts be submitted to a **candid** world.

He has refused his Assent to Laws, the most wholesome and necessary for the public good.

He has forbidden his Governors to pass Laws of immediate and pressing importance, unless suspended in their operation till his Assent should be obtained; and when so suspended, he has utterly neglected to attend to them.

EXPLORING THE DOCUMENT Here the Declaration lists the charges that the colonists had against King George III. **How does the language in the list appeal to people's emotions?**

He has refused to pass other Laws for the accommodation of large districts of people, unless those people would **relinquish** the right of Representation in the Legislature, a right **inestimable** to them and **formidable** to tyrants only.

He has called together legislative bodies at places unusual, uncomfortable, and distant from the depository of their Public Records, for the sole purpose of fatiguing them into compliance with his measures.

He has dissolved Representative Houses repeatedly, for opposing with manly firmness his invasions on the rights of the people.

He has refused for a long time, after such dissolutions, to cause others to be elected; whereby the Legislative Powers, incapable of **Annihilation**, have returned to the People at large for their exercise; the State remaining in the mean time exposed to all the dangers of invasion from without, and **convulsions** within.

He has endeavored to prevent the population of these States; for that purpose obstructing the Laws of **Naturalization of Foreigners**; refusing to pass others to encourage their migration hither, and raising the conditions of new **Appropriations of Lands**.

He has obstructed the Administration of Justice, by refusing his Assent to Laws for establishing Judiciary Powers.

He has made Judges dependent on his Will alone, for the **tenure** of their offices, and the amount and payment of their salaries.

He has erected **a multitude of** New Offices, and sent hither swarms of Officers to harass our people, and eat out their substance.

He has kept among us, in times of peace, Standing Armies without the Consent of our legislature.

He has affected to render the Military independent of and superior to the Civil Power.

He has combined with others to subject us to a jurisdiction foreign to our constitution, and unacknowledged by our laws; giving his Assent to their Acts of pretended legislation:

For **quartering** large bodies of armed troops among us:

For protecting them, by a mock Trial, from Punishment for any Murders which they should commit on the Inhabitants of these States:

For cutting off our Trade with all parts of the world:

For imposing taxes on us without our Consent:

For depriving us in many cases, of the benefits of Trial by Jury:

Mum Bett, a Massachusetts slave, believed that the words "all men are created equal" should apply to her and other enslaved Africans. She successfully sued for her freedom in 1781.

arbitrary not based on law

render make

abdicated given up

foreign mercenaries soldiers hired to fight for a country not their own

perfidy violation of trust

insurrections rebellions

petitioned for redress asked formally for a correction of wrongs

unwarrantable jurisdiction unjustified authority

magnanimity generous spirit

conjured urgently called upon

consanguinity common ancestry

acquiesce consent to

EXPLORING THE DOCUMENT Here the Declaration calls the king a tyrant. **What do you think *tyrant* means in this passage?**

For transporting us beyond Seas to be tried for pretended offences:

For abolishing the free System of English Laws in a neighboring Province, establishing therein an **Arbitrary** government, and enlarging its Boundaries so as to **render** it at once an example and fit instrument for introducing the same absolute rule into these Colonies:

For taking away our Charters, abolishing our most valuable Laws, and altering fundamentally the Forms of our Governments:

For suspending our own Legislature, and declaring themselves invested with Power to legislate for us in all cases whatsoever.

He has **abdicated** Government here, by declaring us out of his Protection and waging War against us.

He has plundered our seas, ravaged our Coasts, burnt our towns, and destroyed the lives of our people.

He is at this time transporting large armies of **foreign mercenaries** to complete the works of death, desolation and tyranny, already begun with circumstances of Cruelty & **perfidy** scarcely paralleled in the most barbarous ages, and totally unworthy the Head of a civilized nation.

He has constrained our fellow Citizens taken Captive on the high Seas to bear Arms against their Country, to become the executioners of their friends and Brethren, or to fall themselves by their Hands.

He has excited domestic **insurrections** amongst us, and has endeavored to bring on the inhabitants of our frontiers, the merciless Indian Savages, whose known rule of warfare, is an undistinguished destruction of all ages, sexes and conditions.

In every stage of these Oppressions We have **Petitioned for Redress** in the most humble terms: Our repeated Petitions have been answered only by repeated injury. A Prince, whose character is thus marked by every act which may define a Tyrant, is unfit to be the ruler of a free People.

Nor have We been wanting in attention to our British brethren. We have warned them from time to time of attempts by their legislature to extend an **unwarrantable jurisdiction** over us. We have reminded them of the circumstances of our emigration and settlement here. We have appealed to their native justice and **magnanimity**, and we have **conjured** them by the ties of our common kindred to disavow these usurpations, which, would inevitably interrupt our connections and correspondence. They too have been deaf to the voice of justice and of **consanguinity**. We must, therefore, **acquiesce** in the necessity, which denounces our Separation, and hold them, as we hold the rest of mankind, Enemies in War, in Peace Friends.

We, therefore, the Representatives of the united States of America, in General Congress, Assembled, appealing to the Supreme Judge of the world for the **rectitude** of our intentions, do, in the Name, and by Authority of the good People of these Colonies, solemnly publish and declare, That these United Colonies are, and of Right ought to be Free and Independent States; that they are Absolved from all Allegiance to the British Crown, and that all political connection between them and the State of Great Britain, is and ought to be totally dissolved; and that as Free and Independent States, they have full Power to levy War, conclude Peace, contract Alliances, establish Commerce, and to do all other Acts and Things which Independent States may of right do. And for the support of this Declaration, with a firm reliance on the Protection of Divine Providence, we mutually pledge to each other our Lives, our Fortunes and our sacred Honor.

John Hancock	Benjamin Harrison	Lewis Morris
Button Gwinnett	Thomas Nelson, Jr.	Richard Stockton
Lyman Hall	Francis Lightfoot Lee	John Witherspoon
George Walton	Carter Braxton	Francis Hopkinson
William Hooper	Robert Morris	John Hart
Joseph Hewes	Benjamin Rush	Abraham Clark
John Penn	Benjamin Franklin	Josiah Bartlett
Edward Rutledge	John Morton	William Whipple
Thomas Heyward, Jr.	George Clymer	Samuel Adams
Thomas Lynch, Jr.	James Smith	John Adams
Arthur Middleton	George Taylor	Robert Treat Paine
Samuel Chase	James Wilson	Elbridge Gerry
William Paca	George Ross	Stephen Hopkins
Thomas Stone	Caesar Rodney	William Ellery
Charles Carroll of Carrollton	George Read	Roger Sherman
	Thomas McKean	Samuel Huntington
George Wythe	William Floyd	William Williams
Richard Henry Lee	Philip Livingston	Oliver Wolcott
Thomas Jefferson	Francis Lewis	Matthew Thornton

Vocabulary

rectitude rightness

EXPLORING THE DOCUMENT Here is where the document declares the independence of the colonies. **Whose authority does the Congress use to declare independence?**

EXPLORING THE DOCUMENT The Congress adopted the final draft of the Declaration of Independence on July 4, 1776. A formal copy, written on parchment paper, was signed on August 2, 1776. **From whom did the Declaration's signers receive their authority to declare independence?**

EXPLORING THE DOCUMENT The following is part of a passage that the Congress removed from Jefferson's original draft: "He has waged cruel war against human nature itself, violating its most sacred rights of life and liberty in the persons of a distant people who never offended him, captivating and carrying them into slavery in another hemisphere, or to incur miserable death in their transportation thither." **Why do you think the Congress deleted this passage?**

The Struggle for Liberty

What You Will Learn...

Main Ideas

1. Many Americans supported the war effort.
2. The Patriots both won and lost battles during the years 1775–1777.
3. France and Spain helped the Patriots fight the British.
4. The winter at Valley Forge tested the strength of Patriot troops.
5. The war continued at sea and in the West.

The Big Idea

Patriot forces faced many obstacles in the war against Britain.

Key Terms and People

mercenaries, *p. 128*
Battle of Trenton, *p. 129*
Battle of Saratoga, *p. 130*
Marquis de Lafayette, *p. 131*
Baron Friedrich von Steuben, *p. 131*
Bernardo de Gálvez, *p. 131*
John Paul Jones, *p. 133*
George Rogers Clark, *p. 133*

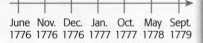 Create a time line like the one below. As you read, identify and describe the events occurring on each of the dates listed on your time line.

June   Nov.   Dec.   Jan.   Oct.   May   Sept.
1776   1776   1776   1777   1777   1778   1779

 8.1.1, 8.1.3, 8.1.4, 8.1.9, 8.1.30

If **YOU** were there...

You are a serving maid at an inn in New York City. British soldiers often stop at the inn for a meal. You sometimes overhear their conversations, though they don't notice you. Now a Patriot leader has asked you to bring him any information you hear. You want to help the Patriot cause but wonder what will happen if you are caught spying.

Would you agree to spy for the Patriots?

BUILDING BACKGROUND Many colonists struggled for the Patriot cause. Men, women, and children all made important contributions. They fought, kept farms and shops running, and provided food and supplies. In spite of their efforts, winning the war was a great challenge.

Supporting the War Effort

George Washington's chief task as the Continental Army's commander in chief was to raise troops. During the war, more than 230,000 soldiers served in the Continental Army, and another 145,000 enlisted in local militias. The typical soldier was young, often under the legal age of 16, and had little money or property. The army offered low pay, harsh conditions, and a big chance of becoming a casualty. Yet the Patriots knew they were fighting for their homes and their freedom.

Finding and keeping dedicated soldiers would be a constant challenge throughout the war. In time, the Continental Congress required states to supply soldiers. Men who could afford it often paid others, such as slaves or apprentices, to fight in their places.

One question facing General Washington was whether to recruit African Americans. Many white southerners opposed the idea, and at first Washington banned African Americans from serving. When the British promised freedom to any slave who fought on their side, however, thousands of African Americans joined the Redcoats.

Battles in the Middle Colonies, 1776–77

Major Battles

1. New York, August 1776
2. Trenton, December 1776
3. Princeton, January 1777
4. Brandywine, September 1777

Colonial Forces	British Forces
Strengths	**Strengths**
• Fought for a cause they believed in	• Well-trained, well-equipped soldiers
• Got help from European nations	• Large, powerful navy
Weaknesses	**Weaknesses**
• Untrained, poorly equipped soldiers	• Had to cross Atlantic Ocean
• Small navy	• Used mercenaries as soldiers

Legend:
- British advance
- British victory
- Colonial advance
- Colonial victory
- Proclamation Line of 1763

go.hrw.com
Interactive Map
KEYWORD: SF7 CH4

GEOGRAPHY SKILLS INTERPRETING MAPS

1. **Movement** About how far was Washington's march from Boston to New York?
2. **Human-Environment Interaction** How did geography affect the British advance on Philadelphia?

In response, the Continental Army began allowing free African Americans to serve.

While men served as soldiers, many women ran farms and businesses. Others helped the army by raising money for supplies or making clothing. Women served as messengers, nurses, and spies. A Massachusetts man noted:

❝ At every house Women and children [are] making Cartridges, running Bullets … and at the same time animating [encouraging] their Husbands and Sons to fight. ❞

—Anonymous, quoted in *Born for Liberty*, by Sara M. Evans

Perhaps the best known woman to fight in the war was Mary Ludwig Hays. She was called Molly Pitcher because she brought water to the troops. When her husband was wounded in a 1778 battle, she took his place loading cannons. Another woman, Deborah Sampson, dressed as a man and fought in several battles.

READING CHECK **Summarizing** How did various groups contribute to the war effort?

Defeats and Victories

As the Revolution gathered steam, it became more deadly. At first the Continental Army suffered a number of defeats. In time, though, the Patriots' patience began to pay off.

THE IMPACT TODAY

Women are still banned from ground combat. But in Operation Iraqi Freedom, women operated warships and flew combat jets and helicopters for the first time in a major air-ground conflict.

Canada

In part because the army was short on supplies, many Patriot leaders favored fighting a defensive war. Others wanted to invade British-controlled Canada and make it the "14th colony."

Patriot troops led by General Richard Montgomery captured Montreal in November 1775. The next major target was the city of Quebec. Benedict Arnold, now a general, led his troops north on a remarkable trek through the rough backcountry of Maine. He reached Quebec around the same time that Montreal fell to Montgomery. Since his first attempt to take the city failed, Arnold waited for Montgomery's troops to join his.

Taking an immense chance, the combined armies attacked during a fierce blizzard on New Year's Eve. They were quickly defeated. The Americans had suffered a crushing loss, and the Patriots' hopes of taking Canada faded.

New York

New York City became the next battleground. General Washington had moved his troops to New York, expecting the British arrival. Sure enough, in June 1776, a fleet of British ships approached New York Bay. Led by General William Howe, the British forced the Continental Army off Long Island.

Howe's 32,000 soldiers were much better equipped than Washington's 23,000 men, most of whom were militia. The Patriot general had to use all of his skills just to save his army.

In a series of battles, Howe pounded the Continental Army, forcing it to retreat farther and farther. The Redcoats captured Patriots as well as supplies. Eventually, the British pushed Washington across the Hudson River into New Jersey. Howe's revenge for his defeat at Boston was complete.

During the New York campaigns, a young Connecticut officer named Nathan Hale went behind British lines to get secret information. Seized by the British with documents hidden in the soles of his shoes, Hale was ordered to be hanged. Before his execution, he is said to have declared, "I regret that I have but one life to lose for my country."

FOCUS ON READING

What is the main idea of the third paragraph under "New York"?

Crossing the Delaware

George Washington and his troops crossed the partially frozen Delaware River on the night of December 25, 1776. This daring act led to a key Patriot victory at the Battle of Trenton. German American artist Emanuel Leutze created this famous painting in 1851. A version of Leutze's *Washington Crossing the Delaware* hangs in the Metropolitan Museum of Art in New York City.

What feelings do you think Leutze wanted to inspire with this painting?

New Jersey

In November 1776 the tattered Continental Army was on the run. Washington's remaining 6,000 men were tired and discouraged. The one-year contract for many of them would end on December 31. Who would re-enlist in this losing army, and who would replace the soldiers who left? Washington's army was in danger of vanishing.

Thinking the rebellion would end soon, Howe left New Jersey in the hands of soldiers from the German state of Hesse. The Hessians were **mercenaries**—foreign soldiers who fought not out of loyalty, but for pay.

On December 7 Washington retreated across the Delaware River into Pennsylvania. Even with 2,000 fresh troops, the Patriots were near the end. "These are the times that try men's souls," wrote Thomas Paine in *The American Crisis*, a series of pamphlets he began publishing in late 1776.

Without a convincing victory, Washington knew he would lose his army. He decided to take a big chance and go on the offensive. The Americans would attack the Hessians at Trenton, New Jersey.

On Christmas night, 1776, with a winter storm lashing about them, Washington and 2,400 soldiers silently rowed across the ice-clogged Delaware River. As morning broke, the men, short on supplies and many with no shoes, marched through the snow to reach the enemy camp.

The Hessians, having celebrated the holiday the night before, were fast asleep when the Patriots sprang upon them. The **Battle of Trenton** was an important Patriot victory. American soldiers took more than 900 prisoners.

British general Charles Cornwallis rushed to stop Washington as he marched northeast to Princeton. On the night of January 2, 1777, the Patriots left their campfires burning, then slipped into the darkness and circled behind the British troops. In the morning, Washington attacked. A local resident witnessed it:

"The battle was plainly seen from our door … and the guns went off so quick and many together that they could not be numbered … Almost as soon as the firing was over, our house was filled and surrounded with General Washington's men."
—Anonymous, quoted in *Voices of 1776* by Richard Wheeler

As Washington watched the Redcoats flee Princeton, he cheered, "It is a fine fox chase, my boys!" Now, new soldiers joined the chase. Others re-enlisted. The army—and the Revolution—was saved.

Saratoga

The two quick defeats stung the British. In the spring of 1777, they wanted a victory.

British general John Burgoyne decided to push through New York State and cut off New England from the other colonies. The **strategy** required perfect timing. According

ACADEMIC VOCABULARY

strategy a plan for fighting a battle or war

to the plan, Burgoyne's army would invade from Canada, recapture Fort Ticonderoga, and sweep south to Albany. General Howe, in New York City, would sail up the Hudson River to meet him, strangling New England.

Indeed, Burgoyne took Ticonderoga in early July and headed toward Albany. Here, the timing went wrong for the British. Unknown to Burgoyne, Howe had left New York, sailed up the Chesapeake Bay, and captured Philadelphia. Delegates to the Continental Congress were forced to flee.

Meanwhile, Burgoyne's army bogged down in thick forests. The Patriots had chopped down large trees and dammed rivers to create obstacles. All along the route, the militia swarmed out of nowhere to attack the Redcoats. As Burgoyne neared Saratoga, New York, he found himself surrounded. On October 17, 1777, he was forced to surrender his entire army to General Horatio Gates.

The **Battle of Saratoga** in New York was the turning point of the Revolutionary War. It was the greatest victory yet for the American forces. Morale soared. Patriot James Thacher wrote, "This event will make one of the most brilliant pages of American history."

READING CHECK Summarizing
Why was the Battle of Saratoga a turning point in the war?

Help from Europe

The French and Indian War had drastically changed the balance of power in North America. The French and Spanish had lost a large expanse of valuable land to the British. Both countries were delighted to see their powerful rival experiencing trouble in its American colonies.

The victory at Saratoga gave the Patriots something they had been desperately seeking: foreign help. Not surprisingly, it came from Britain's enemies, France and Spain. Even Britain's old ally, Holland, joined the fight on the side of the Patriots.

Battle of Saratoga

➡	British advance
✶	British victory
➡	Patriot advance
✶	Patriot victory

0   50   100 Miles
0   50   100 Kilometers

October 17, 1777 British forces under General John Burgoyne marched south, heading for Albany. They were crushed by Patriot forces under General Horatio Gates at Saratoga.

Time Line

The Patriots Gain Ground

December 26, 1776
Patriots win the Battle of Trenton.

1776   1777

January 3, 1777
Patriots win the Battle of Princeton.

July 27, 1777 Marquis de Lafayette arrives in Philadelphia to offer his assistance to the Patriot cause.

Two Remarkable Europeans

"The welfare of America is closely bound up with the welfare of mankind," declared a wealthy young Frenchman, the **Marquis de Lafayette**. Inspired by the ideas of the Revolution, Lafayette bought his own ship and arrived in America in 1777. He brought with him a group of well-trained soldiers and volunteered to serve in the Continental Army himself without pay.

Lafayette spoke little English and had never seen battle. However, he quickly became a skillful commander, earning the title of major general. Lafayette led 2,000 Patriots to successfully pursue 6,000 Redcoats throughout Virginia during 1780–81. He gave $200,000 of his own money to support the Revolution and wrote many letters home to powerful friends and family asking their aid for the Patriot cause.

In February 1778 another European came to serve heroically under Washington. **Baron Friedrich von Steuben**, an experienced military officer from Prussia, led with a combination of respect and fear. He started training the American troops, focusing on basic military drills. Soon he turned the Continental Army into a finely tuned fighting force. A historian called von Steuben's feat "perhaps the most remarkable achievement in rapid military training in the history of the world."

Help from France

Benjamin Franklin, a skilled and experienced diplomat, had gone to France in 1776 to ask for support from King Louis XVI. Finally, the Battle of Saratoga in 1777 persuaded the French king that the colonists could win the war. Not until then did the king agree to an alliance with the Patriots.

In May 1778 the Continental Congress ratified the treaty of support with France. The French had been helping the Patriots all along with supplies and ammunition. After the treaty became official, the French increased the level of supplies and agreed to provide soldiers and ships. The French naval support would be a key ingredient in defeating the British.

Help from Spain

Spain, also a bitter enemy of Britain, joined the war in 1779. **Bernardo de Gálvez**, the governor of Spanish Louisiana, became a key ally to the Patriots. Gálvez gathered a small army of Spanish soldiers, French Americans, colonists, and Native Americans. Together they made their way east from Louisiana. Gálvez seized British posts all the way to Pensacola, Florida.

READING CHECK **Summarizing** How did France and Spain help the Patriots?

February 1778
Baron Friedrich von Steuben begins training Patriot soldiers.

June 21, 1779
Spain declares war against Britain.

1778   1779   1780

May 1778 France joins the Patriots in an alliance.

March 14, 1780 Bernardo de Gálvez, the governor of Spanish Louisiana, captures the British stronghold of Fort Charlotte at present-day Mobile, Alabama.

ANALYSIS SKILL **READING TIME LINES**

Which nations joined the Patriot cause?

JOURNAL ENTRY
Valley Forge

A surgeon at Valley Forge, Albigence Waldo kept a journal of what he saw during the winter of 1777–78.

"The Army which has been surprisingly healthy hitherto, now begins to grow sickly from the continued fatigues they have suffered this Campaign. Yet they still show a spirit of Alacrity [cheerful readiness] and Contentment not to be expected from so young Troops. I am Sick—discontented—and out of humour. Poor food—hard lodging—Cold Weather—fatigue—Nasty Cloaths [clothes]—nasty Cookery . . . smoke and Cold—hunger and filthyness—A pox on my bad luck."

—Albigence Waldo, from *Diary of Surgeon Albigence Waldo of the Connecticut Line*

ANALYSIS SKILL ANALYZING PRIMARY SOURCES

Why did Waldo seem surprised by the soldiers' attitude?

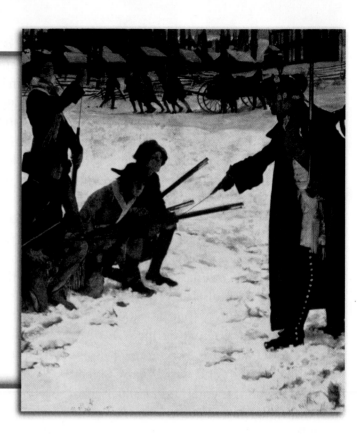

Winter at Valley Forge

The entry of France and Spain into the war came at a crucial moment. The Continental Army was running very low on food and clothing. In December 1777, Washington settled his 12,000 men at Valley Forge, north of Philadelphia.

To this day, the name of Valley Forge brings to mind suffering—and courage. Yet no battles took place here. The only enemy was the brutal winter of 1777–78.

Washington's men lacked even the most basic protections against shin-deep snows. In spite of the general's repeated requests for supplies, conflicts over funding between state authorities and Congress kept supplies from coming. Washington wrote in a letter:

"To see men without clothes . . . without blankets to lie upon, without shoes . . . without a house or hut to cover them until those could be built, and submitting without a murmur, is a proof of patience and obedience which, in my opinion, can scarcely be paralleled [matched]."

—George Washington, quoted in *George Washington: A Collection*

As winter roared in, soldiers quickly built crude shelters that offered little protection against the weather. Some soldiers had no shirts. Others had marched the shoes off their feet. At their guard posts, they stood on their hats to keep their feet from touching the freezing ground. One soldier wrote that getting food was the "business that usually employed us."

During that terrible winter, some 2,000 soldiers died of disease and malnutrition. Amazingly, the survivors not only stayed—they drilled and marched to the orders of Baron von Steuben, becoming better soldiers.

While the soldiers suffered through the winter at Valley Forge, the British lived a life of luxury in Philadelphia. Most of the Patriots had fled the city, leaving only Loyalists and British soldiers. Together they enjoyed the city's houses, taverns, and theaters, and held parties and balls.

READING CHECK **Finding Main Ideas** What challenges did the Continental Army face at Valley Forge?

War at Sea and in the West

While some Americans struggled against the British on land in the former colonies, others fought at sea and on the western frontier. Each area posed tough challenges.

War at Sea

The entry of the French navy into the war greatly aided the colonists. Many people had thought that the mighty British navy would crush the much smaller American fleet. However, the British failed to use their powerful navy effectively during the war.

In the fall of 1775, the Continental Congress made plans to build four American warships. Soon afterward the Congress formally established the marines and the Continental Navy. By adapting merchant vessels, the navy had eight fighting ships ready for combat by February 1776.

That month the tiny American navy launched a major offensive to damage the operating ability of the British fleet located off the Carolina coast. Rather than attack the fleet directly, the Patriots went after the British supply base on Nassau, in the Bahamas.

The American troops seized the main supply fort on the island. They then raised the newly created flag of the American Revolution over Nassau. After that campaign, the American navy focused on seizing British supply ships and weakening Britain's naval forces in the West Indies.

John Paul Jones

The Patriots owed much of their success on the seas to naval hero **John Paul Jones**. Jones had once been considered an outlaw. He was born John Paul in Scotland and began working on ships at a young age. After accidentally killing the leader of a mutiny, he fled to America and added Jones to his name.

When the war broke out, Jones volunteered his services to the newly created navy. He quickly established himself as a brave and clever sailor. Considered a pirate by the British, Jones captured many British supply ships. The French greatly admired Jones. When France entered the war in 1778, French leaders presented him with a small fleet of seven vessels to command. He named his flagship *Bonhomme Richard* ("Gentleman Richard") in honor of Benjamin Franklin's *Poor Richard's Almanac*.

One of Jones's most famous victories was the capture of the British warship *Serapis* on September 23, 1779. Early in the battle, the British knocked out the heaviest artillery on the *Bonhomme Richard*. Captain Richard Pearson of the *Serapis* then called out to Jones, "Has your ship struck [surrendered]?" Jones replied, "I have not yet begun to fight!" The battle continued for more than two hours. Finally the Americans wore down the British, who surrendered at 10:30 p.m.

The Continental Navy used fewer than 100 ships over the course of the war. Yet the British lost more than 200 ships to the small but effective American naval force.

War in the West

The lands west of the Appalachian Mountains were controlled by Native American nations. Both the British and the Patriots tried to enlist these groups in their cause.

George Rogers Clark volunteered to lead the western campaign. Clark had been a surveyor along the Ohio and Kentucky rivers. By the time the war broke out, he knew the lands of the Midwest well. Clark created an army from the scattered settlements in the area. One of the best-known groups was the Over Mountain Men, a band of settlers from present-day Tennessee.

Determined to weaken British support systems, Clark targeted trading villages. Following the Ohio River to the Tennessee, Clark's force set out on a 120-mile overland trek to Kaskaskia, in present-day Illinois. The village's leaders learned of the attack and surrendered. Other Patriots took Cahokia without a fight.

In February 1779 Clark launched a surprise attack on Fort Sackville near the town

FOCUS ON INDIANA

During the Revolutionary War Indiana was on the western frontier of the British colonies. Britain tried to control these lands with help from Native Americans. George Rogers Clark and his Patriot and French soldiers won Fort Sackville from the British, and the victory helped bring the large frontier region under Patriot control.

War in the West, 1778–79

Lake Michigan

Fort Detroit

Lake Erie

THIRTEEN COLONIES

Fort Pitt

BRITISH

Wabash River

Vincennes (Ft. Sackville)

CLARK

Ohio River

VA

APPALACHIAN MOUNTAINS

Cahokia

Kaskaskia

Fort Massac

Mississippi River

Tennessee River

→ British forces
→ Patriot forces
✶ Patriot victory

0   50   100 Miles
0   50 100 Kilometers

GEOGRAPHY SKILLS **INTERPRETING MAPS**

1. **Movement** How far did the Patriots march to get to Vincennes?
2. **Human-Environment Interaction** Why did military forces follow river routes?

of Vincennes. The attack was unexpected because the nearby Wabash River was icy and flooded. Despite overflowing riverbanks, Clark's force of 150 men endured an 18-day march through freezing water. They also managed to bring enough Patriot flags for an army of hundreds. The flags were displayed near the fort, and the skilled pioneers sustained enough musket fire to indicate a much larger army. Falling for the ruse, the commander of Fort Sackville surrendered.

In general the British were more successful at winning over the Native Americans. But Clark's many campaigns undermined British support in the West.

READING CHECK **Finding Main Ideas** How did Jones and Clark help the Patriots' war effort?

SUMMARY AND PREVIEW The Patriots faced hardships as the war continued. In the next section, you will see how they finally achieved their goal of independence.

Section 3 Assessment

go.hrw.com
Online Quiz
KEYWORD: SF7 HP4

Reviewing Ideas, Terms, and People

1. **a. Identify** What groups supported the Patriot war effort? How did each group contribute?
   b. Analyze Why was it difficult to find and keep soldiers in the Continental Army?

2. **a. Describe** What early defeats did the Patriots face?
   b. Elaborate Was it a mistake for the British to use **mercenaries** to help them fight the war? Why or why not?

3. **a. Elaborate** Why do you think European nations supported the colonists rather than Great Britain?
   b. Evaluate Do you think that the Patriots would have won the war without help from France and Spain? Why or why not?

4. **a. Describe** What difficulties did the Patriots face at Valley Forge?
   b. Elaborate How might weather conditions affect the outcome of a battle?

5. **a. Identify** Who was **John Paul Jones**?
   b. Compare In what ways was Jones's naval strategy like that of the Continental Army?

Critical Thinking

6. **Drawing Conclusions** Review the events on your time line. Copy the chart below and use it to identify the region in which the events took place and how the events reflected the Patriots' successes and failures.

Region	Patriot Problems	Patriot Successes

FOCUS ON SPEAKING

7. **Thinking about the Struggle for Liberty** Why was this period of the war so difficult for the Patriots? How did they struggle through? What are the one or two points that are the most important about this period of the war?

Independence!

If YOU were there...

You have grown up on a farm in South Carolina. You know every inch of the woods and marshes around your home. You are too young to join the Continental Army, but you have heard stories about a brave group of soldiers who carry out quick raids on the British, then disappear into the woods. These fighters get no pay and live in constant danger.

Would you consider joining the fighters? Why?

BUILDING BACKGROUND As the war moved to the South, American forces encountered new problems. They suffered several major defeats. But American resistance in the southern colonies was strong. Backwoods fighters confused and frustrated the British army.

War in the South

The war across the ocean was not going the way the British government in London had planned. The northern colonies, with their ragged, scrappy fighters, proved to be tough to tame. So the British switched strategies and set their sights on the South.

The British hoped to find support from the large Loyalist populations living in Georgia, the Carolinas, and Virginia. As they moved across the South, the British also planned to free enslaved Africans and enlist them as British soldiers. Under the leadership of a new commander, General Henry Clinton, the strategy paid off—for a while.

Brutal Fighting

The southern war was particularly brutal. Much more than in the North, this phase of the war pitted Americans—Patriots versus Loyalists—against one another in direct combat. The British also destroyed crops, farm animals, and other property as they marched through the South. One British officer, Banastre Tarleton, sowed fear throughout the South by refusing to take prisoners and killing soldiers who tried to surrender.

What You Will Learn...

Main Ideas
1. Patriot forces faced many problems in the war in the South.
2. The American Patriots finally defeated the British at the Battle of Yorktown.
3. The British and the Americans officially ended the war by signing the Treaty of Paris of 1783.

The Big Idea
The war spread to the southern colonies, where the British were finally defeated.

Key Terms and People
Francis Marion, *p. 136*
Comte de Rochambeau, *p. 137*
Battle of Yorktown, *p. 137*
Treaty of Paris of 1783, *p. 139*

TAKING NOTES As you read, take notes on the major events that led to the British defeat. Write your notes in a graphic organizer like the one below.

8.1.1, 8.1.3, 8.1.4, 8.1.9, 8.1.28, 8.1.29, 8.1.30, 8.2.1, 8.3.2

Georgia, the last colony to join the Revolution, was the first to fall to the British. A force of 3,500 Redcoats easily took Savannah in 1778 and soon put in place a new colonial government.

Britain's next major target was Charleston, South Carolina. In early 1780 General Clinton landed a force of 14,000 troops around the port city. With a minimal cost of about 250 casualties, the British scored one of their biggest victories of the war. The Patriots surrendered Charleston in May, handing over four ships and some 5,400 prisoners.

A Failed Attack

In August 1780, Patriot forces led by Horatio Gates tried to drive the British out of Camden, South Carolina. The attack was poorly executed, however. Gates had only half as many soldiers as he had planned for, and most were tired and hungry. In the heat of battle, many panicked and ran. The Patriot attack quickly fell apart. Of some 4,000 American troops, only about 700 escaped.

General Nathanael Greene arrived to reorganize the army. As he rode through the southern countryside, he was discouraged by the devastation. He later wrote, "I have never witnessed such scenes."

Guerrilla Warfare

The southern Patriots switched to swift hit-and-run attacks known as guerrilla warfare. No Patriot was better at this style of fighting than **Francis Marion**. He organized Marion's Brigade, a group of guerrilla soldiers.

Marion's Brigade used surprise attacks to disrupt British communication and supply lines. Despite their great efforts, the British could not catch Marion and his men. One frustrated general claimed, "As for this . . . old fox, the devil himself could not catch him." From that point on, Marion was known as the Swamp Fox.

READING CHECK **Sequencing** List the events of the war in the South in chronological order.

Battle of Yorktown

In early 1781 the war was going badly for the Patriots. They were low on money to pay soldiers and buy supplies. The help of their foreign allies had not brought the war to a quick end as they had hoped. The British held most of the South, plus Philadelphia and New York City. The Patriots' morale took another blow when Benedict Arnold, one of America's most gifted officers, turned traitor.

Regrouped under Nathanael Greene, the Continental Army began harassing British general Charles Cornwallis in the Carolinas. Hoping to stay in communication with the British naval fleet, Cornwallis moved his force of 7,200 men to Yorktown, Virginia. It was a fatal mistake.

General Washington, in New York, saw a chance to trap Cornwallis at Yorktown. He ordered Lafayette to block Cornwallis's escape by land. Then he combined his 2,500 troops

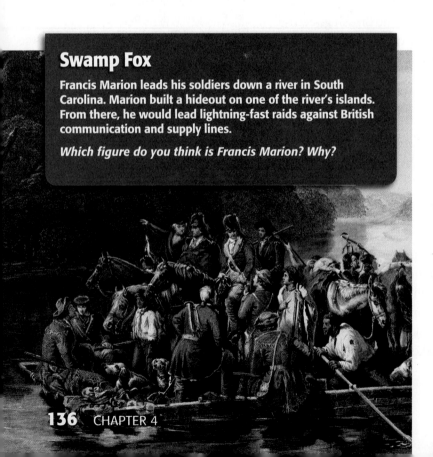

Swamp Fox

Francis Marion leads his soldiers down a river in South Carolina. Marion built a hideout on one of the river's islands. From there, he would lead lightning-fast raids against British communication and supply lines.

Which figure do you think is Francis Marion? Why?

Battle of Yorktown

The British scuttled, or purposely sank, dozens of their ships. This formed a barrier that kept the French ships from coming too close.

THIRTEEN COLONIES
Yorktown
ATLANTIC OCEAN

American troop positions
French troop positions
British troop positions
British defensive lines

0   0.5   1 Mile
0   0.5   1 Kilometer

In October 1781, American and French troops surrounded British forces and defeated them in the Battle of Yorktown.

ANALYSIS SKILLS | **ANALYZING VISUALS**

Human-Environment Interaction How did American and French forces trap the British at Yorktown?

with 4,000 French troops commanded by the **Comte de Rochambeau** (raw-shahn-BOH). Washington led the French-American force on a swift march to Virginia to cut off the other escape routes. The Patriots surrounded Cornwallis with some 16,000 soldiers. Meanwhile, a French naval fleet seized control of the Chesapeake Bay, preventing British ships from rescuing Cornwallis's stranded army.

The siege began. For weeks, the fighting steadily wore down the British defenses. In early October, Washington prepared for a major attack on the weakened British troops.

Facing near-certain defeat, on October 19, 1781, Cornwallis sent a drummer and a soldier with a white flag of surrender to Washington's camp. The Patriots took some 8,000 British prisoners—the largest British army in America.

The **Battle of Yorktown** was the last major battle of the American Revolution. Prime Minister Lord North received word of the Yorktown surrender in November. In shock he declared, "It is all over!"

READING CHECK **Drawing Conclusions** Why did the victory at Yorktown end the fighting?

PAMPHLET

Sentiments of an American Woman

The Continental Army received aid from female Patriots led by Esther DeBerdt Reed and Sarah Franklin Bache, the daughter of Benjamin Franklin. In 1780 these women organized a campaign that raised $300,000 for soldiers' clothing. The following pamphlet, written by the campaign's leaders, announced the campaign. In it, the authors used images of women helping with war efforts of the past to gain support for their cause.

A female spy passes news to a colonial officer.

"On the **commencement** of actual war, the Women of America **manifested** a firm resolution to contribute . . . to the deliverance of their country. Animated by the purest patriotism they are sensible of sorrow at this day, in not offering more than barren wishes for the success of so glorious a Revolution. They aspire to **render** themselves more really useful; and this sentiment is universal from the north to the south of the Thirteen United States. Our ambition is kindled by the fame of those heroines of **antiquity**, who . . . have proved to the universe, that . . . if opinion and manners did not forbid us to march to glory by the same paths as the Men, we should at least equal, and sometimes surpass them in our love for the public good. I glory in all that which my sex has done great and **commendable**. I call to mind with enthusiasm and with admiration, all those acts of courage, of constancy and patriotism, which history has transmitted to us . . ."

"So many famous sieges where the Women have been seen . . . building new walls, digging trenches with their feeble hands, furnishing arms to their defenders, they themselves darting the missile weapons of the enemy, resigning the ornaments of their apparel, and their fortune, to fill the public treasury, and to hasten the deliverance of their country; burying themselves under its ruins; throwing themselves into the flames rather than submit to the disgrace of humiliation before a proud enemy."

"Born for liberty, **disdaining** to bear the irons of a **tyrannic** Government, we associate ourselves . . . [with those rulers] who have extended the empire of liberty, and **contented** to reign by sweetness and justice, have broken the chains of slavery, forged by tyrants."

1. **commencement**: start 2. **manifested**: presented
3. **render**: make 4. **antiquity**: ancient times
5. **commendable**: praiseworthy 6. **disdaining**: refusing
7. **tyrannic**: unjust 8. **contented**: determined

The women declare that they would fight if they were allowed.

The authors list ways in which women have helped fight wars in the past.

In this phrase, the women link themselves to great women rulers of the past.

ANALYSIS SKILL **ANALYZING PRIMARY SOURCES**

1. What do the writers "call to mind" in asking women to join the Patriots' cause?
2. With whom do the writers associate themselves?

The Treaty of Paris

After Yorktown, only a few small battles took place. Lacking the money to pay for a new army, Great Britain entered into peace talks with America. Benjamin Franklin had a key role in the negotiations.

Delegates took more than two years to come to a peace agreement. In the **Treaty of Paris of 1783**, Great Britain recognized the independence of the United States. The treaty also set America's borders. A separate treaty between Britain and Spain returned Florida to the Spanish. British leaders also accepted American rights to settle and trade west of the original thirteen colonies.

At the war's end, Patriot soldiers returned to their homes and families. The courage of soldiers and civilians had made America's victory possible. As they returned home, George Washington thanked his troops for their devotion. "I . . . wish that your latter days be as prosperous as your former ones have been glorious."

READING CHECK **Summarizing** Explain how the War for Independence finally came to an end.

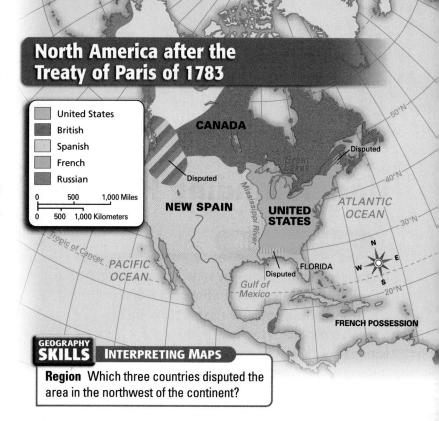

North America after the Treaty of Paris of 1783

- United States
- British
- Spanish
- French
- Russian

0   500   1,000 Miles
0   500   1,000 Kilometers

CANADA

Disputed

Disputed

NEW SPAIN

UNITED STATES

ATLANTIC OCEAN

50°N
40°N
30°N
20°N

Tropic of Cancer

PACIFIC OCEAN

Mississippi River

FLORIDA

Disputed

Gulf of Mexico

FRENCH POSSESSION

GEOGRAPHY SKILLS **INTERPRETING MAPS**

Region Which three countries disputed the area in the northwest of the continent?

SUMMARY AND PREVIEW Americans won their independence from Great Britain in 1783. In the next chapter you will learn how the new nation formed its first government.

go.hrw.com
Online Quiz
KEYWORD: SF7 HP4

Section 4 Assessment

Reviewing Ideas, Terms, and People

1. **a. Describe** What problems did the Patriots experience in the war in the South?
   b. Analyze What advantages did the southern Patriots have over the British in the South?
2. **a. Describe** What was the Patriots' strategy for defeating the British at Yorktown?
   b. Elaborate Why do you think General Cornwallis decided to surrender at the **Battle of Yorktown**?
3. **a. Identify** Who helped to negotiate the **Treaty of Paris** for the Americans?
   b. Predict How might relations between Great Britain and its former colonies be affected by the war?

Critical Thinking

4. **Evaluating** Review your notes on the events that led to the end of the war. Then copy the graphic organizer below and use it to identify and describe the most important event in turning the war in the Patriots' favor.

Event	Importance to end of war

FOCUS ON SPEAKING

5. **Thinking About the Revolution's End**
   After reading this section, you have a picture of the whole war. In your talk, what do you want to say about how the war ended? Were there any moments that were especially trying for the colonists?

Social Studies Skills

Understanding Historical Interpretation

Define the Skill

Historical interpretations are ways of explaining the past. They are based on what is known about the people, ideas, and actions that make up history. Two historians can look at the same set of facts about a person or event of the past and see things in different ways. Their explanations of the person or event, and the conclusions they reach, can be very different. The ability to recognize, understand, and evaluate historical interpretations is a valuable skill in the study of history.

Learn the Skill

When people study the past, they decide which facts are the most important in explaining why something happened. One person may believe certain facts to be important, while other people may believe other facts are more important. Therefore, their explanation of the topic, and the conclusions they draw about it, may not be the same. In addition, if new facts are uncovered about the topic, still more interpretations of it may result.

Asking the following questions will help you to understand and evaluate historical interpretations.

1 What is the main idea in the way the topic is explained? What conclusions are reached? Be aware that these may not be directly stated but only hinted at in the information provided.

2 On what facts has the writer or speaker relied? Do these facts seem to support his or her explanation and conclusions?

3 Is there important information about the topic that the writer or speaker has dismissed or ignored? If so, you should suspect that the interpretation may be inaccurate or deliberately slanted to prove a particular point of view.

Just because interpretations differ, one is not necessarily "right" and others "wrong." As long as a person considers all the evidence and draws conclusions based on a fair evaluation of that evidence, his or her interpretation is probably acceptable.

Remember, however, that trained historians let the facts *lead* them to conclusions. People who *start* with a conclusion, select only facts that support it, and ignore opposing evidence produce interpretations that have little value for understanding history.

Practice the Skill

Two widely accepted interpretations exist of the causes of the American Revolution. One holds that the Revolution was a struggle by freedom-loving Americans to be free from harsh British rule. In this view the colonists were used to self-government and resisted British efforts to take rights they claimed. The other interpretation is that a clash of economic interests caused the Revolution. In this view, the war resulted from a struggle between British and colonial merchants over control of America's economy.

Review Sections 4 and 5 of Chapter 3 and Sections 1 and 2 of Chapter 4. Then answer the following questions.

1. What facts in the textbook support the economic interpretation of the Revolution? What evidence supports the political interpretation?

2. Which interpretation seems more convincing? Explain why.

Chapter Review

HOLT
History's Impact
▶ video series
Review the video to answer the closing question:
Why do you think African Americans, women, and young adults under 21 fought for the vote?

Visual Summary

QUICK FACTS

Use the visual summary below to help you review the main ideas of the chapter.

Speeches and protests ignited revolutionary feelings.

Patriots fought Loyalists in the Revolutionary War.

The American colonies gained independence and became the United States.

Reviewing Vocabulary, Terms, and People

1. What were American colonists who remained loyal to Great Britain called?

  a. Whigs   **c.** Royalists

  b. Loyalists   **d.** Democrats

2. What was the name of the battle in which the Patriots finally defeated the British?

  a. Battle of Saratoga   **c.** Battle of Yorktown

  b. Battle of New Jersey   **d.** Battle of Valley Forge

3. What was the name for the colonial military force created to fight the British?

  a. mercenaries   **c.** Hessians

  b. Redcoats   **d.** Continental Army

4. Who was the French nobleman who helped the Patriots fight the British?

  a. Bernardo de Gálvez   **c.** Baron von Steuben

  b. Marquis de Lafayette   **d.** Lord Dunmore

Comprehension and Critical Thinking

SECTION 1 *(Pages 112–116)*

5. a. Recall What actions did the First and Second Continental Congresses take?

  b. Analyze How did the events at Lexington and Concord change the conflict between Great Britain and the colonies?

  c. Elaborate Why do you think that control of Boston early in the Revolutionary War was important?

SECTION 2 *(Pages 118–121)*

6. a. Identify Why is July 4, 1776, a significant date?

  b. Draw Conclusions What effect did *Common Sense* have on colonial attitudes toward Great Britain?

  c. Predict How might the content of the Declaration of Independence lead to questions over the issue of slavery?

SECTION 3 (Pages 126–134)

7. a. Describe What difficulties did the Patriots experience in the early years of the war?

b. Analyze How did the Patriots turn the tide of the war?

c. Elaborate Could the Patriots have succeeded in the war without foreign help? Explain.

SECTION 4 (Pages 135–139)

8. a. Recall Why did the British think they might find support in the southern colonies?

b. Make Inferences Why did it take more than two years for the British and the Americans to agree to the terms of the Treaty of Paris?

c. Evaluate In your opinion, what was the most important reason for the Patriots' defeat of the British?

Social Studies Skills

Understanding Historical Interpretation *Use the Social Studies Skills taught in this chapter to answer the questions about the reading selection below.*

In a series of battles, Howe pounded the Continental Army, forcing it to retreat farther and farther. The Redcoats captured Patriots as well as supplies. Eventually, the British pushed Washington across the Hudson River into New Jersey. Howe's revenge for his defeat at Boston was complete. (p. 128)

9. Which statement from the passage is an interpretation of historical facts?

a. The Redcoats captured Patriots as well as supplies.

b. Eventually, the British pushed Washington across the Hudson River into New Jersey.

c. Howe's revenge for his defeat at Boston was complete.

10. What might a different interpretation of the facts be?

Reviewing Themes

11. Politics What are three important rights listed in the Declaration of Independence?

12. Geography What role did geography play in the fighting that took place in the West?

Reading Skills

Main Ideas in Social Studies *Use the Reading Skills taught at the beginning of the chapter to answer the question about the reading selection below.*

(1) Native Americans were at first encouraged by both sides to remain neutral. (2) By the summer of 1776, however, both Patriots and the British were aggressively recruiting Indian fighters. (3) Most sided with the British. (4) In northern New York, four of the six Iroquois nations fought for the British. (p. 120)

13. Which sentence contains the main idea of the paragraph?

a. Sentence 1

b. Sentence 2

c. Sentence 3

d. Sentence 4

Using the Internet   go.hrw.com   KEYWORD: SF7 CH4

14. Activity: Researching The Battle of Saratoga showed the world that the Patriots were capable of defeating the British. This victory gave Benjamin Franklin the chance to use his fame as a scientist and diplomat to convince France to aid the Patriots. Enter the activity keyword and explain how these factors led to a Patriot victory and how the American Revolution affected France.

FOCUS ON SPEAKING

15. Prepare Your Oral Report Review your notes and be sure you've identified one or two important ideas, events, or people for each period of the war. Now, start to prepare your oral report by writing a one-sentence introduction to your talk. Then write a sentence or two about each period of the war. Write a concluding sentence that makes a quick connection between the Revolutionary War and our lives today. Practice your talk until you can give it with only a glance or two at your notes.

Standardized Test Practice

IN 8.1.4, 8.1.9, 8.1.28, 8.1.29, 8.2.1

DIRECTIONS: Read each question and write the letter of the best response.

1 What action would a Loyalist have been likely to take during the Revolution?

A attend the Continental Congress

B support the Olive Branch Petition

C support the Declaration of Independence

D join the Continental Army

2 Which of the following events took place *last*?

A The Declaration of Independence was issued.

B The Second Continental Congress met.

C The battles at Lexington and Concord occurred.

D The Battle of Bunker Hill took place.

3 Why was the victory at the Battle of Saratoga so important to the Patriot cause?

A It allowed the Declaration of Independence to be issued.

B It forced the British army to retreat from Boston.

C It convinced France to aid the colonies in their fight.

D It caused the British government to give up the war.

4 The most brutal and destructive fighting of the war probably occurred

A in the southern colonies.

B at Valley Forge.

C in New England.

D at Lexington and Concord.

5 The Declaration of Independence's claim that people have a right to "life, liberty, and the pursuit of happiness" shows the influence of what Enlightenment thinker from Europe?

A Jonathan Edwards

B John Locke

C King George III

D Thomas Paine

6 In what way was Clark's battle strategy the same as John Paul Jones's strategy?

A They both were badly outnumbered by the British.

B They both knew the colonial midwest region well.

C They both aimed to weaken the British by attacking their supply lines.

D They both survived the winter at Valley Forge.

7 Read the following passage from Thomas Paine's *The Crisis* and use it to answer the question below.

> *"*These are the times that try men's souls. The summer soldier and the sunshine patriot will, in this crisis, shrink from the service of his country, but he that stands it now, deserves the love and thanks of man and woman. Tyranny . . . is not easily conquered, yet we have this consolation with us, that the harder the conflict, the more glorious the triumph.*"*
>
> —Thomas Paine, *The Crisis,* 1776

Document-Based Question What point is Paine trying to make in this passage?

Assignment

Write a biographical narrative about a person who lived in the early Americas before or during the colonial period.

A Biographical Narrative

You have been listening to and telling narratives all your life. A biographical narrative, a form of historical writing, is a true story about an event or brief period in a person's life.

1. Prewrite

Getting Started

- Think of all the people you read about in this unit. Which ones interested you most?
- What particular events and situations in these people's lives seem most exciting or significant?

Pick one of these events or situations as the subject of your narrative.

Creating an Interesting Narrative

Make your narrative lively and interesting by including

- **Physical descriptions** of people, places, and things, using details that appeal to the five senses (sight, hearing, touch, smell, taste)
- **Specific actions** that relate directly to the story you are telling
- **Dialogue** between the people involved or direct **quotations**
- **Background information** about the place, customs, and setting
- **All relevant details and information** needed to relate the events of the story and how they affected the person (and perhaps history)

Organize the events in your narrative in chronological order, the order in which they occurred.

2. Write

You can use this framework to help you draft your narrative.

TIP **Asking Questions** Try using the *5W-How?* questions (*Who? What? When? Where? Why? How?*) to help you think of descriptive details. Ask questions such as, **Who** was this person? **What** was he or she doing? Exactly **where** and **when** did the event occur? **How** did the person or other people react to the event?

A Writer's Framework

Introduction	Body	Conclusion
■ Grab your reader's attention with a striking detail or bit of dialogue. ■ Introduce the historical person and setting, using specific details. ■ Set the scene by telling how the event or situation began.	■ Present actions and details in the order in which they occurred. ■ Connect actions with transition words like *first, then, next,* and *finally.* ■ Provide specific details to make the person and the situation come alive.	■ Wrap up the action of the narrative. ■ Tell how the person was affected by what happened. ■ Explain how the event or situation was important in the person's life and how it affected history.

3. Evaluate and Revise

Evaluating

Read through your completed draft to make sure your narrative is complete, coherent, and clear. Then look for ways to improve it.

Evaluation Questions for a Biographical Narrative

- Does your introduction grab the reader's attention? Do you introduce the historical person and tell how the event or situation began?
- Do you include details to make the person, place, and event seem real?
- Are the actions in the story in the order in which they occurred?

- Have you included all of the actions and details a reader would need to understand what happened?
- Does the conclusion tell how the event or situation affected the person and history?

TIP **Showing Sequence** A clear sense of the sequence of events is important in any narrative. Here is a list of words that show those relationships.

after	next
before	now
finally	soon
first	still
(second, etc.)	then
last	when
later	while

Revising

When you revise your narrative, you may need to add transition words. Transition words help you link ideas between sentences and paragraphs. Notice the words in bold in the following sentences.

> **After** Cabeza de Vaca and the other adventurers left the beach and started inland, they separated into different groups. **Later,** Cabeza de Vaca heard that many of the others had died. **Still,** he never lost faith that he would reach his fellow Spaniards in Mexico.

4. Proofread and Publish

Proofreading

Throughout your narrative, you used transition words to link events. Make sure that you have spelled the words correctly and have not confused them with other words. For example, be sure to use two *l*'s in *finally* and not to mistake the transition word *then* for the comparative word *than*.

Publishing

One good way to share your biographical narrative is to exchange it with one or more classmates who have written about the same person you have. After reading each other's narratives, you can compare and contrast them. How are your stories similar? How do they differ?

5. Practice and Apply

Use the steps and strategies outlined in this workshop to write your biographical narrative.

A New Nation

After the Revolutionary War, much needed to be done in the new United States. The ideas of the Revolution had to be preserved in the country's new government.

During the first years of the United States, political leaders met and discussed the form that the government should take. Often, people disagreed about how the new nation should be organized. Debates still take place about the framework of the U.S. government, which is written in the Constitution.

In the next three chapters, you will learn about the creation of the Constitution and how that document affects us today.

Explore the Art

In this scene, a teenaged printer's devil, or apprentice, is shown reading about the recent approval of the Constitution. How does the art show citizens' ideas about the Constitution?

CONSTITUTION RATIFIED!

Wednesday, March 4, 1789

THE UNITED STATES CONSTITUTION

Forming a Government

Indiana Standards

Social Studies Standards

8.1.5 Identify and explain key events leading to the creation of a strong union among the thirteen original states and in the establishment of the United States as a federal republic.

8.2.3 Explain how and why legislative, executive, and judicial powers are distributed, shared, and limited in the constiutional government of the United States.

8.2.5 Compare, and contrast the powers reserved to the federal and state government under the Articles of confederation and the United States Constitution.

8.4.9 Explain and evaluate examples of domstic and international interdependence throughout United States history.

go.hrw.com
Indiana
KEYWORD: SF10 IN

FOCUS ON WRITING

A Newspaper Editorial It is 1788 and you're writing an editorial for a local newspaper. You want to convince your readers that the new Constitution will be much better than the old Articles of Confederation. In this chapter you'll find the information you need to support your opinion.

UNITED STATES

1777
The Continental Congress approves the Articles of Confederation on November 15.

1775

WORLD

1778
The United States and France become allies.

What You Will Learn . . .

This photo shows Speaker of the House Dennis Hastert swearing in the 108th Congress, the legislative branch of the U.S. government. In this chapter, you will learn about the nation's earliest government, the Articles of Confederation, and its failures to achieve national unity. You will also read about the writing of the Constitution and how it attempted to solve the problems of the Articles by creating a new system of government with three branches.

1783
The Treaty of Paris ends the Revolutionary War and gives the territory northwest of the Ohio River, including Indiana, to the United States.

1781
On March 1 the Articles of Confederation go into effect after being ratified by all 13 states.

1786
Shays's Rebellion breaks out in Massachusetts.

1787
On May 14, state delegates begin to arrive at the Constitutional Convention in Philadelphia.

1791
The Bill of Rights is ratified by the states in December.

1780

1785

1790

1782
Spain completes its conquest of British Florida.

1787
The Ottoman Empire declares war on Russia.

1791
The *Lady Washington* becomes the first U.S. ship to reach Japan.

Reading Social Studies

by Kylene Beers

Focus on Themes Visualize a row of dominoes, lined up one after the other. Push over the first one, and—one after the other—all eventually fall. In this way, the events in this chapter are like dominoes that cause each other to occur. These events, one after another, finally led to the formation of a new government and a new **society**. If you read closely, you will see that **political** disagreements started the entire process.

Understanding Chronological Order

Focus on Reading Like falling dominoes, historical events can create huge chains of results, often stretching over many years. To understand history and events, therefore, we often need to see how they are related in time.

Understanding Chronological Order The word *chronological* means "related to time." Events discussed in this history book are discussed in **sequence**, in the order in which they happened. To understand history better, you can use a sequence chain to take notes about events in the order they happened.

Sequence Chain

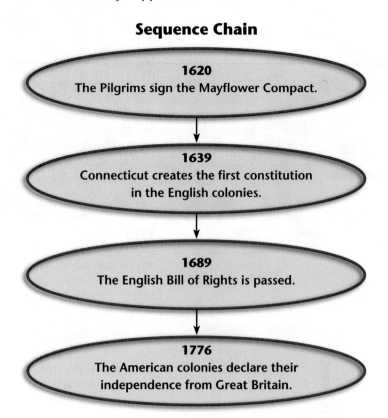

1620
The Pilgrims sign the Mayflower Compact.

1639
Connecticut creates the first constitution in the English colonies.

1689
The English Bill of Rights is passed.

1776
The American colonies declare their independence from Great Britain.

> **Tip:** Writers sometimes signal chronological order, or sequence, by using words or phrases like these:
>
> *first, before, then, later, soon, after, before long, next, eventually, finally*

You Try It!

Read the following passage and answer the questions that follow.

Farmers Rebel

In August 1786, farmers in three western counties began a revolt. Bands of angry citizens closed down courts in western Massachusetts. Their reasoning was simple—with the courts shut down, no one's property could be taken. In September a poor farmer and Revolutionary War veteran, Daniel Shays, led hundreds of men in a forced shutdown of the Supreme Court in Springfield, Massachusetts. The state government ordered the farmers to stop the revolt under threat of capture and death. These threats only made Shays and his followers more determined. The uprising of farmers to protest high taxes and heavy debt became known as Shays's Rebellion.

From Chapter 5, p. 161

Shays's forces were defeated by state troops in January 1787. By February many of the rebels were in prison. During their trials, 14 leaders were sentenced to death. However, the state soon freed most of the rebels, including Shays.

After you have read the passage, answer the following questions.

1. Which happened first—citizens closing courts in western Massachusetts or Shays shutting down the Supreme Court? How can you tell?

2. What happened after Shays's forces were defeated by state troops?

3. Draw a sequence chain that shows the effects of Shays's Rebellion in the order they occurred.

Before you read Chapter 5, look for clues that signal the order in which events occurred.

Academic Vocabulary

In this chapter, you will learn the following academic word:

advocate (p. 171)

The Articles of Confederation

What You Will Learn...

Main Ideas

1. The American people examined many ideas about government.
2. The Articles of Confederation laid the base for the first national government of the United States.
3. The Confederation Congress established the Northwest Territory.

The Big Idea

The Articles of Confederation provided a framework for a national government.

Key Terms and People

Magna Carta, *p. 152*
constitution, *p. 153*
Virginia Statute for Religious Freedom, *p. 153*
suffrage, *p. 153*
Articles of Confederation, *p. 154*
ratification, *p. 154*
Land Ordinance of 1785, *p. 155*
Northwest Ordinance of 1787, *p. 155*
Northwest Territory, *p. 155*

 TAKING NOTES As you read, take notes on the new American government in a chart like this one.

New American Government	
1. Influences on new government	
2. Structure of the Articles of Confederation	

 8.1.4, 8.1.5, 8.1.16, 8.1.30, 8.2.8, 8.2.9, 8.3.1, 8.3.2, 8.3.7

If YOU were there...

You live in a town in New England during the 1770s. In the town meeting, people are hotly debating about who will have the right to vote. Most think that only men who own property should be able to vote. Some think that all property owners—men and women—should have that right. A few others want all free men to have the vote. Now it is time for the meeting to decide.

How would you have voted on this issue?

BUILDING BACKGROUND At the time of the Revolution, each of the 13 states had its own government. The rights of citizens varied from state to state. In their town meetings, people often argued about exactly what those rights ought to be. Solving such issues was one step in moving toward a national government.

Ideas about Government

The American colonies had taken a bold step in declaring their independence from Great Britain in July 1776. Their next political goal was to form a new government. To do so, the American people drew from a wide range of political ideas.

English Laws and the Enlightenment

One source of inspiration was the rule of law. This rule makes even government officials subject to law. England had limited the power of its kings and queens in two documents. These were Magna Carta and the English Bill of Rights. **Magna Carta**, a document signed by King John in 1215, made the king subject to law. The English Bill of rights, passed in 1689, declared the supremacy of Parliament. It kept the king or queen from changing laws without Parliament's consent. As a result, the people's representatives had a strong voice in England's government.

Many Americans were also influenced by the Enlightenment—a philosophical movement that emphasized the use of reason to examine old ideas and traditions. Philosopher John Locke believed that a social contract existed between political rulers and the people they ruled. Baron de Montesquieu argued that the only way to achieve liberty was through the separation of governmental powers.

American Models of Government

Americans had their own models of self-government to follow, like town meetings, the Virginia House of Burgesses, and the Mayflower Compact. In 1639 the people of Connecticut drew up the English colonies' first written **constitution**. A constitution is a set of basic principles and laws that states the powers and duties of the government. In addition, the Declaration of Independence clearly set forth the beliefs on which Americans thought government should be based.

To keep individual leaders from gaining too much power, the new state constitutions created limited governments, or governments in which all leaders have to obey the laws. Most state constitutions had rules to protect the rights of citizens or those accused of

crimes. Some banned slavery. The Massachusetts constitution of 1780 is the oldest state constitution still in effect.

Thomas Jefferson's ideas about religious freedom were included in the **Virginia Statute for Religious Freedom**. This document declared that no person could be forced to attend a particular church or be required to pay for a church with tax money.

Right to Vote

Under British rule, only free, white men that owned land could vote. Many states' constitutions expanded **suffrage**, or the right to vote, by allowing any white man who paid taxes to vote. In every state, however, only landowners could hold public office. Some states originally allowed women and free African Americans to vote, but these rights were soon taken away. Suffrage would not be restored to these groups for decades to come.

READING CHECK **Comparing** What two principles were common to state constitutions written during the Revolutionary War?

Women's Suffrage

New Jersey allowed women to vote when it first joined the United States. This right was taken away by 1807.

Why do you think women were not allowed to vote in the early United States?

The Land Ordinances of 1785 and 1787

CANADA

Surveying the West
In 1785 the Northwest Territory was organized into lots that could be sold, and in 1787 a government was organized.

WISCONSIN 1848

MICHIGAN 1837

NORTHWEST TERRITORY

ILLINOIS 1818

INDIANA 1816

OHIO 1803 Area of first survey

One section = 1 square mile

Half section 320 acres

Quarter section 160 acres

6	5	4	3	2	1
7	8	9	10	11	12
18	17	16	15	14	13
19	20	21	22	23	24
30	29	28	27	26	25
31	32	33	34	35	36

One township = 36 square miles

Each township contained 36 sections. Each section was one square mile.

0   100   200 Miles
0   100   200 Kilometers

GEOGRAPHY SKILLS **INTERPRETING MAPS**

1. **Location** Which states were formed out of the Northwest Territory?
2. **Region** Into how many sections was a township divided?

FOCUS ON INDIANA

Under the Articles of Confederation, each state had its own constitution. Some of these stayed in effect even after the Articles were replaced by the U.S. Constitution. The Massachusetts Constitution of 1780, the last state constitution to be written by the original 13 states, is still in effect today.

Articles of Confederation

The Second Continental Congress was organized to create a national government. The Continental Congress appointed a Committee of Thirteen, with one member from each colony. This group was assigned to discuss and draft the Articles of Confederation, the new national constitution.

Under the **Articles of Confederation**, Congress would become the single branch of the national government, but it would have limited powers in order to protect the liberties of the people. Each state had one vote in the Congress. Congress could settle conflicts among the states, issue coins, borrow money, and make treaties with other countries and with Native Americans. Congress could also ask the states for money and soldiers. However, states had the power to refuse these requests. The government did not have a president or a national court system.

The Second Continental Congress passed the Articles of Confederation on November 15, 1777. Then it sent the Articles to each state legislature for **ratification**, or official approval, before the new national government could take effect.

Conflicts over claims to western lands slowed the process, but by 1779 every state except Maryland had ratified the Articles. Maryland's leaders refused to ratify until other states gave up their western land claims. Thomas Jefferson assured Maryland that western lands would be made into new states, rather than increasing territory for existing states. Satisfied with this condition, in March 1781 Maryland ratified the Articles. This put the first national government of the United States into effect.

READING CHECK **Summarizing** What were two weaknesses of the new national government?

Northwest Territory

Congress had to decide what to do with the western lands now under its control and how to raise money to pay debts. It tried to solve both problems by selling the western lands. Congress passed the **Land Ordinance of 1785**, which set up a system for surveying and dividing western lands. The land was split into townships, which were 36 square miles divided into 36 lots of 640 acres each. One lot was reserved for a public school, and four lots were given to veterans. The remaining lots were sold to the public.

To form a political system for the region, Congress passed the **Northwest Ordinance of 1787**. The ordinance established the **Northwest Territory**, which included areas that are now in Illinois, Indiana, Michigan, Ohio, Minnesota, and Wisconsin. The Northwest Ordinance created a system for bringing new states into the Union. Congress agreed that the Northwest Territory would be divided into several smaller territories with a governor appointed by Congress. When the population of a territory reached 60,000, its settlers could draft their own constitution and ask to join the Union.

In addition, the law protected civil liberties and required that public education be provided. Finally, the ordinance stated that "there shall be neither slavery nor involuntary servitude [forced labor] in the . . . territory." This last condition banned slavery in the Territory and set the standard for future territories. However, slavery would continue to be a controversial issue.

READING CHECK Analyzing Information
How did the Northwest Ordinance of 1787 affect the United States?

SUMMARY AND PREVIEW The Northwest Ordinance settled the future of the Northwest Territory. In the next section you will read about other challenges the new government faced.

FOCUS ON INDIANA
When Ohio became the first state admitted from the Northwest Territory, the remaining area was renamed the Indiana Territory. Governor William Henry Harrison attempted to suspend the antislavery laws for the territory, but Congress would not allow it.

THE IMPACT TODAY
Townships remained the unit of local government after the Northwest Territory was divided into states. Many of these townships still exist today.

Section 1 Assessment

go.hrw.com
Online Quiz
KEYWORD: SF7 HP5

Reviewing Ideas, Terms, and People

1. **a. Identify** What documents influenced ideas about government in the United States?
   b. Draw Conclusions What impact did the **Virginia Statute for Religious Freedom** have on the U.S. government?
   c. Elaborate Why is the separation of government powers a requirement for a society to be free?

2. **a. Identify** What was the **Articles of Confederation**?
   b. Summarize What powers were granted to Congress by the Articles of Confederation?
   c. Predict What are some possible problems that might result from the lack of a national court system?

3. **a. Describe** How were public lands in the West divided by the **Land Ordinance of 1785**?
   b. Evaluate In your opinion, what was the most important element of the **Northwest Ordinance of 1787**? Why?
   c. Elaborate What does the assignment of township lots reveal about values of Americans at this time?

Critical Thinking

4. **Categorizing** Review your notes on the Articles of Confederation. Copy the chart below and use it to show the strengths and weaknesses of the new government.

Articles of Confederation

Strengths	Weaknesses

FOCUS ON WRITING

5. **Thinking about the Articles of Confederation** Make a list of powers the Articles of Confederation gave the national government. Which ones seem strong? Can you think of any important powers that are missing?

History and Geography

Origins of the Constitution

The U.S. Constitution created a republican form of government based on the consent of the people. The framers of the Constitution blended ideas and examples from both the American colonies and from England to write this lasting document.

THE MAYFLOWER COMPACT, 1620

The *Mayflower*, shown here in an illustration, sailed to America in 1620. Aboard the ship, 41 men signed the Mayflower Compact, the first document in the colonies to establish guidelines for self-government. The signers agreed that they and their families would combine to form a "civil body politic," or community.

COLONIAL ASSEMBLIES

The British Parliament's two-chamber structure also influenced colonial governments. In Article I, Section 1, of the Constitution, the framers continued the practice of a two-chamber legislature.

"All legislative powers . . . shall be vested in a Congress of the United States, which shall consist of a Senate and House of Representatives."
—Article I, Section 1, U.S. Constitution

VIRGINIA STATUTE FOR RELIGIOUS FREEDOM, 1786

Classical liberal principles such as the written protection of citizens' personal liberties were reflected in the addition of the Bill of Rights. The First Amendment's freedom of religion clauses were based on Thomas Jefferson's Virginia Statute for Religious Freedom. The document, which was accepted by the Virginia legislature in 1786, ensured the separation of church and state in Virginia.

"Congress shall make no law respecting an establishment of religion, or prohibiting the free exercise thereof . . ."
—First Amendment, U.S. Constitution

American colonies

MAGNA CARTA, 1215

In this painting King John of England is signing Magna Carta, or the Great Charter, which established that the king was subject to the law just like everyone else. It also declared that people could not be deprived of their lives, liberty, or property *"except by the lawful judgment of [their] peers, or by the law of the land."* Compare this language to that of the Fifth Amendment to the Constitution.

"No person shall be . . . deprived of life, liberty, or property, without due process of law . . ."
—Fifth Amendment, U.S. Constitution

THE ENGLISH BILL OF RIGHTS, 1689

This painting shows King William and Queen Mary of England. Before taking the throne, William and Mary had to accept the English Bill of Rights. The English Bill of Rights took even more power away from the monarch than did Magna Carta. It also protected the rights of English citizens. These ideas would later influence the U.S. Constitution.

"Excessive bail ought not be required, nor excessive fines imposed; nor cruel and unusual punishments inflicted."
—English Bill of Rights

THE ENLIGHTENMENT, 1700s

Enlightenment thinkers such as English philosopher John Locke supported the movement toward self-government. Locke argued in his writings that government could exist only with *"the consent of the governed."* The framers of the Constitution looked to Locke for inspiration when writing the Constitution, as you can see from its very first words.

"We the people of the United States . . . "
—Preamble, U.S. Constitution

England

ANALYSIS
SKILL **ANALYZING INFORMATION**

1. What documents did the framers look to when writing the Constitution?

2. How did the English Parliamentary system affect the kind of government the framers created?

The New Nation Faces Challenges

What You Will Learn...

Main Ideas

1. The United States had difficulties with other nations.
2. Internal economic problems plagued the new nation.
3. Shays's Rebellion pointed out weaknesses in the Articles of Confederation.
4. Many Americans called for changes in the national government.

The Big Idea

Problems faced by the young nation made it clear that a new constitution was needed.

Key Terms and People

tariffs, *p. 159*
interstate commerce, *p. 160*
inflation, *p. 161*
depression, *p. 161*
Daniel Shays, *p. 161*
Shays's Rebellion, *p. 161*

TAKING NOTES As you read, use a graphic organizer like the one below to identify problems faced by the new nation.

Problems of the New Nation

8.4.1, 8.4.9

If YOU were there...

You own an orchard in Maryland in the 1780s. When you sell apples and apple pies in the market, people pay you with paper money. But now the tax collector says you must pay your taxes in gold or silver coins, not paper money. You and the other farmers are furious. Is this the liberty you fought a war for?

What would you do to protest these taxes?

BUILDING BACKGROUND Americans surprised the world by winning their independence from Great Britain. But the 13 new states were far from being a strong nation. Internal problems, especially with taxes and the economy, led to protests and rebellion. The government also had trouble with foreign trade and treaties.

Relations with Other Countries

Under the Articles of Confederation, Congress could not force states to provide soldiers for an army. The Continental Army had disbanded, or dissolved, soon after the signing of the Treaty of Paris of 1783. Without an army, the national government found it difficult to protect its citizens against foreign threats.

Trouble with Britain

It was also difficult to enforce international treaties such as the Treaty of Paris of 1783. The United States found it especially hard to force the British to turn over "with all convenient speed" their forts on the American side of the Great Lakes. The United States wanted to gain control of these forts because they protected valuable land and fur-trade routes. Still, Britain was slow to withdraw from the area. A British official warned against the United States trying to seize the forts by force. He said that any attempt to do so would be opposed by the thousands of British soldiers who had settled in Canada after the Revolution "who are ready to fly to arms at a moment's warning."

The United States Faces Trade Barriers

0   150   300 Miles
0   150   300 Kilometers

AMERICAN TRADE ROUTE
Spain closed the lower Mississippi River to U.S. shipping, hurting western trade with eastern markets.

EXPORTS TO BRITAIN
High British tariffs discouraged American exports to Britain.

BLOCKADE

ATLANTIC OCEAN

30°N

WEST INDIES TRADE
Britain closed many ports to American ships.

BLOCKADE

• New Orleans

Gulf of Mexico

BLOCKADE

Tropic of Cancer

80°W   70°W   20°N

WEST INDIES

GEOGRAPHY SKILLS INTERPRETING MAPS

1. **Movement** Along what river did trade goods reach the port of New Orleans?
2. **Location** Along what three routes did U.S. trade face foreign barriers?

Trade with Britain

The United States also faced problems trading with Great Britain. After the signing of the Treaty of Paris, Britain closed many of its ports to American ships. Before the Revolutionary War, colonial ships had traded a great deal with the British West Indies and stopped there on their way to other destinations. This travel and trading stopped after 1783.

In addition, Britain forced American merchants to pay high **tariffs**—taxes on imports or exports. The tariffs applied to goods such as rice, tobacco, tar, and oil that were grown or mined in the United States and then sold in Britain. Merchants had to raise prices to cover the tariffs. Ultimately, the costs would be passed on to customers, who had to pay higher prices for the goods. The economic condition of the country was getting worse by the day.

Trade with Spain

In 1784 Spanish officials closed the lower Mississippi River to U.S. shipping. Western farmers and merchants were furious because they used the Mississippi to send goods to eastern and foreign markets. Congress tried to work out an agreement with Spain, but the plan did not receive a majority vote in Congress. The plan could not be passed. As a result, Spain broke off the negotiations.

Many state leaders began to criticize the national government. Rhode Island's representatives wrote, "Our federal government is but a name; a mere shadow without substance [power]." Critics believed that Spain might have continued to negotiate if the United States had possessed a strong military. These leaders believed that the national government needed to be more powerful.

Impact of Closed Markets

The closing of markets in the British West Indies seriously affected the U.S. economy. James Madison of Virginia wrote about the crisis.

> "The Revolution has robbed us of our trade with the West Indies . . . without opening any other channels to compensate [make up for] it. In every point of view, indeed, the trade of this country is in a deplorable [terrible] condition."
>
> —James Madison, quoted in *Independence on Trial* by Frederick W. Marks III

Farmers could no longer export their goods to the British West Indies. They also had to hire British ships to carry their goods to British markets, which was very expensive. American exports dropped while British goods flowed freely into the United States.

This unequal trade caused serious economic problems for the new nation. British merchants could sell manufactured products in the United States at much lower prices than locally made goods. This difference in prices hurt American businesses.

The Confederation Congress could not correct the problem because it did not have the authority either to pass tariffs or to order the states to pass tariffs. The states could offer little help. If one state passed a tariff, the British could simply sell their goods in another state. Most states did not cooperate in trade matters. Instead, states worked only to increase their own trade rather than working to improve the trade situation for the whole country.

In 1785 the situation led a British magazine to call the new nation the Dis-United States. As a result of the trade problems with Britain, American merchants began looking for other markets such as China, France, and the Netherlands. Despite such attempts, Britain remained the most important trading partner of the United States.

READING CHECK **Analyzing** Why was the Confederation Congress unable to solve America's international trade problems?

Economic Problems

In addition to international trade issues, other challenges soon appeared. Trade problems among the states, war debts, and a weak economy plagued the states.

Trade among States

Because the Confederation Congress had no power to regulate **interstate commerce** — trade between two or more states—states followed their own trade interests. As a result, trade laws differed from state to state. This situation made trade difficult for merchants whose businesses crossed state lines.

Inflation

After the Revolutionary War, most states had a hard time paying off war debts and struggled to collect overdue taxes. To ease this hardship, some states began printing large amounts of paper money. The result was inflation. This money had little

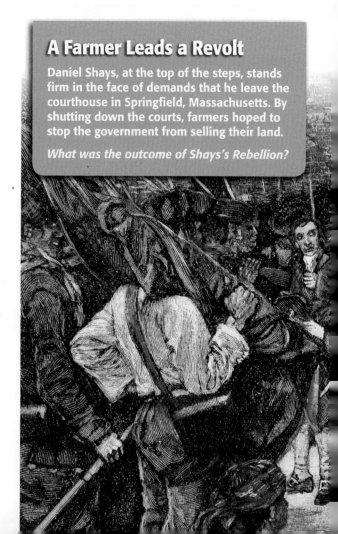

A Farmer Leads a Revolt

Daniel Shays, at the top of the steps, stands firm in the face of demands that he leave the courthouse in Springfield, Massachusetts. By shutting down the courts, farmers hoped to stop the government from selling their land.

What was the outcome of Shays's Rebellion?

or no real value, because states did not have gold or silver reserves to back it up. **Inflation** occurs when there are increased prices for goods and services combined with the reduced value of money. Congress had no power to stop states from issuing more paper money and thus stop inflation.

Weak Economy

In Rhode Island the state legislature printed large amounts of paper money worth very little. This made debtors—people who owe money—quite happy. They could pay back their debts with paper money worth less than the coins they had borrowed. However, creditors—people who lend money—were upset. Hundreds of creditors fled Rhode Island to avoid being paid back with worthless money.

The loss of trade with Britain combined with inflation created a **depression**. A depression is a period of low economic activity combined with a rise in unemployment.

READING CHECK **Summarizing** What economic problems did the new nation face?

Shays's Rebellion

Each state handled its economic problems differently. Massachusetts refused to print worthless paper money. It tried to pay its war debts by collecting taxes on land.

Heavy Debts for Farmers

Massachusetts's tax policy hit farmers hard. As landowners, they had to pay the new taxes. However, farmers had trouble paying their debts. The courts began forcing them to sell their property. Some farmers had to serve terms in debtors' prison; others had to sell their labor.

Many government leaders in the state did not care about the problems of poor farmers, however. In some cases, farmers actually owed these leaders money.

Farmers Rebel

In August 1786, farmers in three western counties began a revolt. Bands of angry citizens closed down courts in western Massachusetts. Their reasoning was simple—with the courts shut down, no one's property could be taken. In September a poor farmer and Revolutionary War veteran, **Daniel Shays**, led hundreds of men in a forced shutdown of the Supreme Court in Springfield, Massachusetts. The state government ordered the farmers to stop the revolt under threat of capture and death. These threats only made Shays and his followers more determined. The uprising of farmers to protest high taxes and heavy debt became known as **Shays's Rebellion**.

Shays's Defeat

Shays's forces were defeated by state troops in January 1787. By February many of the rebels were in prison. During their trials, 14 leaders were sentenced to death. However, the state soon freed most of the rebels, including Shays. State officials knew that many citizens of the state agreed with the rebels and their cause.

READING CHECK **Finding Main Ideas** What led to Shays's Rebellion?

Calls for Change

In the end, Shays's Rebellion showed the weakness of the Confederation government. It led some Americans to admit that the Articles of Confederation had failed to protect the ideals of liberty set forth in the Declaration of Independence.

When Massachusetts had asked the national government to help put down Shays's Rebellion, Congress could offer little help. More Americans began calling for a stronger central government. They wanted leaders who would be able to protect the nation in times of crisis.

Earlier in 1786 the Virginia legislature had called for a national conference. It wanted to talk about economic problems and ways to change the Articles of Confederation. The meeting took place in Annapolis, Maryland, in September 1786.

Nine states decided to send delegates to the Annapolis Convention but some of their delegates were late and missed the meeting. Connecticut, Georgia, Maryland, and South Carolina did not respond to the request at all and sent no delegates.

Because of the poor attendance, the participants, including James Madison and Alexander Hamilton, called on all 13 states to send delegates to a Constitutional Convention in Philadelphia in May 1787. They planned to revise the Articles of Confederation to better meet the needs of the nation.

READING CHECK Finding Main Ideas
Why did some people believe the national government needed to change?

SUMMARY AND PREVIEW Many Americans believed that Shays's Rebellion was final proof that the national government needed to be changed. In the next section you will read about the Constitutional Convention.

QUICK FACTS

Weaknesses of the Articles of Confederation

- Most power held by states
- One branch of government
- Legislative branch has few powers
- No executive branch
- No judicial system
- No system of checks and balances

Section 2 Assessment

go.hrw.com
Online Quiz
KEYWORD: SF7 HP5

Reviewing Ideas, Terms, and People

1. **a. Summarize** What problems did the United States experience with Spain and Great Britain?
   b. Predict What are some possible results of the growing problems between the United States and Great Britain? Why?

2. **a. Describe** What difficulties were involved with **interstate commerce**?
   b. Analyze What was the cause of **inflation** in the new nation, and how could it have been prevented?

3. **a. Explain** How did Massachusetts's tax policy affect farmers?
   b. Evaluate Defend the actions of **Daniel Shays** and the other rebels.

4. **a. Recall** Why did Madison and Hamilton call for a Constitutional Convention?
   b. Analyze How did **Shays's Rebellion** lead to a call for change in the United States?

Critical Thinking

5. **Categorizing** Review your notes on the problems faced by the new nation. Then identify those problems as either domestic or international in a graphic organizer like the one shown below.

Domestic Problems	International Problems

FOCUS ON WRITING

6. **Identifying Problems** In this section you learned about several problems of the young United States. Were any of those problems made worse by the powers that the Articles of Confederation did or did not give the national government?

Creating the Constitution

If YOU were there...

You are a merchant in Connecticut in 1787. You have been a member of your state legislature for several years. This spring, the legislature is choosing delegates to a convention to revise the Articles of Confederation. Delegates will meet in Philadelphia. It means leaving your business in others' hands for most of the summer. Still, you hope to be chosen.

Why would you want to go to the Constitutional Convention?

BUILDING BACKGROUND It did not take long for people to realize that the Articles of Confederation had many weaknesses. By the mid-1780s most political leaders agreed that changes were needed. To make those changes, they called on people with experience in government.

Constitutional Convention

In February 1787 the Confederation Congress invited each state to send delegates to a convention in Philadelphia. The goal of the meeting was to improve the Articles of Confederation.

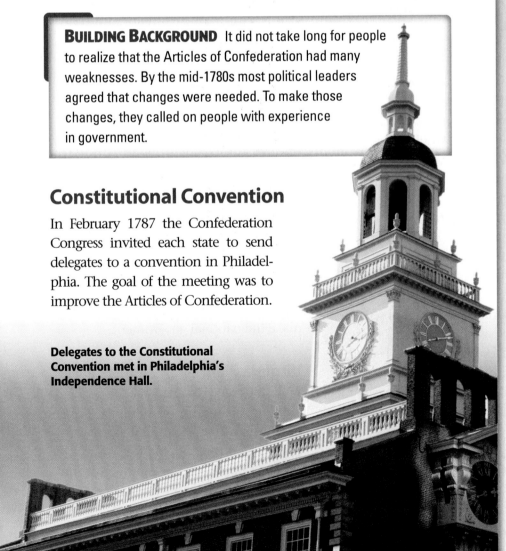

Delegates to the Constitutional Convention met in Philadelphia's Independence Hall.

What You Will Learn ...

Main Ideas

1. The Constitutional Convention met to improve the government of the United States.
2. The issue of representation led to the Great Compromise.
3. Regional debate over slavery led to the Three-Fifths Compromise.
4. The U.S. Constitution created federalism and a balance of power.

The Big Idea

A new constitution provided a framework for a stronger national government.

Key Terms and People

Constitutional Convention, *p. 164*
James Madison, *p. 164*
Virginia Plan, *p. 164*
New Jersey Plan, *p. 165*
Great Compromise, *p. 165*
Three-Fifths Compromise, *p. 166*
popular sovereignty, *p. 167*
federalism, *p. 167*
legislative branch, *p. 167*
executive branch, *p. 167*
judicial branch, *p. 167*
checks and balances, *p. 167*

TAKING NOTES As you read, take notes on the conflicts that arose during the Constitutional Convention and the compromises reached.

Conflicts	Compromises

8.1.5, 8.1.9, 8.1.28, 8.1.30,
8.2.1, 8.2.3, 8.2.5, 8.2.6, 8.4.1

Signing of the Constitution

Roger Sherman   **James Madison**   **James Wilson**

The **Constitutional Convention** was held in May 1787 in Philadelphia's Independence Hall to improve the Articles of Confederation. However, delegates would leave with an entirely new U.S. Constitution. This decision angered some of the participants.

Most delegates were well educated, and many had served in state legislatures or Congress. Benjamin Franklin and **James Madison** were there. Revolutionary War hero George Washington was elected president of the Convention.

Several important voices were absent. John Adams and Thomas Jefferson could not attend. Patrick Henry chose not to attend because he did not want a stronger central government. Women, African Americans, and Native Americans did not take part because they did not yet have the rights of citizens.

READING CHECK Summarizing What was the purpose of the Constitutional Convention?

Great Compromise

Several issues divided the delegates to the Constitutional Convention. Some members wanted only small changes to the Articles of Confederation, while others wanted to rewrite the Articles completely.

Those delegates who wanted major changes to the Articles had different goals. For example, small and large states had different ideas about representation, economic concerns such as tariffs, and slavery. In addition, delegates disagreed over how strong to make the national government.

Virginia Plan

After the delegates had met for four days, Edmund Randolph of Virginia presented the **Virginia Plan**. He proposed a new federal constitution that would give sovereignty, or supreme power, to the central government. The legislature would be bicameral—made

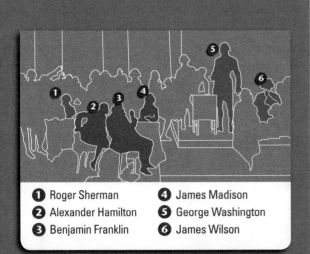

1 Roger Sherman   **4** James Madison
2 Alexander Hamilton   **5** George Washington
3 Benjamin Franklin   **6** James Wilson

This painting shows the signing of the Constitution on September 17, 1787. James Madison, number 4 on the diagram, became known as the "Father of the Constitution" for his ideas about government and his ability to lead the delegates to agreement. *Which person did the artist choose to make the focus of this painting? Why do you think that is?*

up of two houses, or groups of representatives—and chosen on the basis of state populations. Larger states would thus have more representatives than would smaller states. Delegates from the smaller states believed that it would give too much power to the larger states.

New Jersey Plan

The smaller states came up with a plan to stop the larger states from getting too much power. New Jersey delegate William Paterson presented the small-state or **New Jersey Plan**, which called for a unicameral, or one-house, legislature. The plan gave each state an equal number of votes, and thus an equal voice, in the federal government. The plan gave the federal government the power to tax citizens in all states, and it allowed the government to regulate commerce.

Compromise Is Reached

After a month of debate, the delegates were unable to agree on how states should be represented. The convention reached a deadlock.

Finally, Roger Sherman of Connecticut proposed a compromise plan. The legislative branch would have two houses. Each state, regardless of its size, would have two representatives in the Senate, or upper house. This would give each state an equal voice, pleasing the smaller states. In the House of Representatives, or lower house, the number of representatives for each state would be determined by the state's population. This pleased the larger states. The agreement to create a two-house legislature became known as the **Great Compromise**. James Wilson, a great speaker, saw his dream of a strong national government come true.

READING CHECK **Contrasting** How did the Virginia Plan and New Jersey Plan differ?

THE IMPACT TODAY

All U.S. states but one modeled their legislative branches on the federal one, with a House of Representatives and a Senate. Nebraska has a unicameral legislature.

QUICK FACTS

Great Compromise

Virginia Plan
- Gave more power to national government
- Bicameral legislature
- Number in both houses based on population

Great Compromise
- Bicameral legislature
- Number of representatives based on state populations in lower house
- Number of representatives equal from each state in upper house

New Jersey Plan
- Gave more power to state governments
- Unicameral legislature
- Number of representatives equal from each state

POINTS OF VIEW
Compromise and the Slave Trade

The issue of slavery highlighted the growing division between the North and the South. Gouverneur Morris of New York spoke with much emotion against the Three-Fifths Compromise. Also, the idea of banning the foreign slave trade prompted southerners such as John Rutledge of South Carolina to defend the practice.

❝If the Convention thinks that North Carolina, South Carolina, and Georgia will ever agree to the plan [to prohibit the slave trade], unless their right to import slaves be untouched, the expectation is vain [useless].❞

—**John Rutledge,**
quoted in *The Atlantic Monthly,* February 1891, by Frank Gaylord Cook

❝The admission of slaves into the Representation . . . comes to this: that the inhabitant of [a state] who goes to the coast of Africa and . . . tears away his fellow creatures from their dearest connections and damns them to the most cruel bondage [slavery], shall have more votes in a Government [established] for protection of the rights of mankind.❞

—**Gouverneur Morris,**
quoted in *Founding the Republic,* edited by John J. Patrick

ANALYSIS SKILL **ANALYZING PRIMARY SOURCES**

Finding Main Ideas How did these two views of slavery differ?

Three-Fifths Compromise

The debate over representation also involved regional differences. Southern delegates wanted enslaved Africans to be counted as part of their state populations. This way they would have more representatives, and more power, in Congress. Northerners disagreed. They wanted the number of slaves to determine taxes but not representation.

To resolve this problem, some delegates thought of a compromise. They wanted to count three-fifths of the slaves in each state as part of that state's population to decide how many representatives a state would have. After much debate, the delegates voted to accept the proposal, called the **Three-Fifths Compromise**. Under this agreement only three-fifths of a state's slave population would count when determining representation.

Another major issue was the foreign slave trade. Some of the delegates believed slavery was wrong and wanted the federal government to ban the slave trade. Others said that the southern states' economies needed the slave trade. Many southern delegates said they would leave the Union if the Constitution immediately ended the slave trade. Also at issue was Congress's ability to tax imports and exports.

Worried delegates reached another compromise. The Commerce Compromises allowed Congress to levy tariffs on imports, but not exports, and allowed the importation of slaves until the end of 1807. The delegates omitted, or left out, the words *slavery* and *slave* in the Constitution. They referred instead to "free Persons" and "all other Persons."

READING CHECK **Summarizing** What compromise was reached over the issue of the slave trade?

The Living Constitution

Most Convention delegates wanted a strong national government. At the same time, they hoped to protect **popular sovereignty**, the idea that political authority belongs to the people. Americans had boldly declared this idea in the Declaration of Independence.

Federalist Government

The delegates also wanted to balance the power of the central government with the power of the states. Therefore, the delegates created **federalism**. Federalism is the sharing of power between a central government and the states that make up a country. Under the previous confederal system, states were loosely joined together without a strong central government.

Under the Constitution, each state must obey the authority of the federal, or national, government. States have control over government functions not specifically assigned to the federal government. This includes control of local government, education, the chartering of corporations, and the supervision of religious bodies. States also have the power to create and oversee civil and criminal law. States, however, must protect the welfare of their citizens.

Checks and Balances

The Constitution also balances the power among three branches, each responsible for separate tasks. The first is the **legislative branch**, or Congress. Congress is responsible for proposing and passing laws. It is made up of two houses, as created in the Great Compromise. The Senate has two members from each state. In the House of Representatives each state is represented according to its population.

The second branch, the **executive branch**, includes the president and the departments that help run the government. The executive branch makes sure the law is carried out. The third branch is the **judicial branch**. The judicial branch is made up of all the national courts. This branch is responsible for interpreting laws, punishing criminals, and settling disputes between states.

The framers of the Constitution created a system of **checks and balances**, which keeps any branch of government from becoming too powerful. For example, Congress has the power to pass bills into law. The president has the power to veto, or reject, laws that Congress passes. However, Congress can override the president's veto with a two-thirds

LINKING TO TODAY

Legislative Branch

When it first met in 1789, the U.S. House of Representatives had just 65 members. As the nation's population grew, more members were added. Today, the number has been set at 435, to prevent the size of the House from growing unmanageable. Though the numbers of women and minorities in Congress are still unrepresentative of the population as a whole, Congress has become more diverse. Linda and Loretta Sanchez, pictured here, are the first sisters to serve in Congress at the same time.

ANALYZING INFORMATION

How is the change in makeup of the legislative branch shown through Linda and Loretta Sanchez?

The Constitution Strengthens the National Government

Strengths of the Constitution	Weaknesses of the Articles of Confederation
✔ most power held by national government	• most power held by states
✔ three branches of government	• one branch of government
✔ legislative branch has many powers	• legislative branch has few powers
✔ executive branch led by president	• no executive branch
✔ judicial branch to review the laws	• no judicial system
✔ firm system of checks and balances	• no system of checks and balances

majority vote. The Supreme Court has the power to review laws passed by Congress and strike down any law that violates the Constitution by declaring it *unconstitutional.*

The final draft of the Constitution was completed in September 1787. Only 3 of the 42 delegates who remained refused to sign. The signed Constitution was sent first to Congress and then to the states for ratification. The delegates knew that the Constitution was not a perfect document, but they believed they had protected the ideas of republicanism.

READING CHECK **Comparing and Contrasting** What are the differences between monarchies, federal systems, and confederal systems?

SUMMARY AND PREVIEW The Constitution balanced power among three branches of the federal government but was only written after many compromises. In the next section you will read about Antifederalist and Federalist views of the Constitution, and the struggle to get it approved by the states.

Section 3 Assessment

go.hrw.com
Online Quiz
KEYWORD: SF7 HP5

Reviewing Ideas, Terms, and People

1. **a. Recall** Why did the Confederation Congress call for a **Constitutional Convention**?
   b. Elaborate Why do you think it was important that most delegates had served in state legislatures?
2. **a. Identify** What was the **Great Compromise**?
   b. Draw Conclusions How did state issues lead to debate over structure of the central government?
3. **a. Explain** What was the debate between North and South over counting slave populations?
   b. Contrast How did delegates' views differ on the issue of the foreign slave trade?
4. **a. Recall** Why did the framers of the Constitution create a system of **checks and balances**?
   b. Evaluate Did the Constitution resolve the weaknesses in the Articles of Confederation? Explain your answer.

Critical Thinking

5. **Identifying Cause and Effect** Review your notes on the Constitutional Convention compromises. Then copy the graphic organizer below and use it to show how the compromises affected the framework of the new government.

Compromise	→	Effect

FOCUS ON WRITING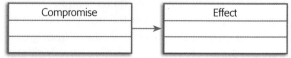

6. **Thinking about the Constitution** Look back through what you've just read and make a list of important features of the Constitution. Be sure to note important compromises.

Benjamin Franklin

How did one man accomplish so much?

When did he live? 1706–1790

Where did he live? Benjamin Franklin was born in Boston but ran away to Philadelphia at age 17 and made it his home. He also crossed the Atlantic Ocean eight times and visited 10 countries.

What did he do? What *didn't* he do! He was a printer, publisher, creator of the first circulating library, the first president of the University of Pennsylvania, inventor, scientist, philosopher, musician, economist, and the first U.S. Postmaster General. In politics he was a leading revolutionary, signer of the Declaration of Independence, head of an antislavery organization, delegate to the Constitutional Convention, and diplomat.

Why is he important? Benjamin Franklin, son of a candlemaker, became a celebrity in his own time, both in America and in Europe. Few people have mastered so many fields of knowledge and accomplished so much. He invented many useful objects, from bifocal glasses to the lightning rod. One of the oldest founding fathers, Franklin inspired younger revolutionaries such as Thomas Jefferson. Franklin believed strongly that people should volunteer and be in public service.

Finding Main Ideas How did Benjamin Franklin's life reflect his belief in public service?

KEY EVENTS

1729
Becomes owner and publisher of the *Pennsylvania Gazette*

1732–1758
Publishes *Poor Richard: An Almanack*

1752
Performs famous experiment using a kite to show that electricity exists in storm clouds

1775
Submits the Articles of Confederation

1779
Appointed minister to France

1782
Helps negotiate the Treaty of Paris with Britain

Poor Richard, 1734.
AN
Almanack
For the Year of Christ
1 7 3 4,
Being the second after LEAPYEAR

Ratifying the Constitution

What You Will Learn . . .

Main Ideas

1. Federalists and Antifederalists engaged in debate over the new Constitution.
2. The *Federalist Papers* played an important role in the fight for ratification of the Constitution.
3. Ten amendments were added to the Constitution to provide a Bill of Rights to protect citizens.

The Big Idea

Americans carried on a vigorous debate before ratifying the Constitution.

Key Terms and People

Antifederalists, *p. 170*
George Mason, *p. 170*
Federalists, *p. 170*
Federalist Papers, p. 171
amendments, *p. 173*
Bill of Rights, *p. 173*

TAKING NOTES As you read, take notes on the differing views of the U.S. Constitution.

Federalists		Antifederalists
	vs.	

8.1.5, 8.1.9, 8.1.28, 8.1.29, 8.1.30, 8.2.1, 8.2.5, 8.2.6, 8.4.1

If YOU were there...

You are a newspaper editor in Philadelphia. During colonial rule, officials sometimes closed down your newspaper because you had criticized the governor. Now you are one of many Americans who want to be sure the new Constitution will guarantee individual rights. You are writing an editorial in your paper explaining what you want.

What rights would you want the Constitution to protect?

BUILDING BACKGROUND The new Constitution did not make everyone happy. Even its framers knew they had not made a perfect document. Many people were afraid a strong national government would become as tyrannical as the British government had been. Before approving the Constitution, they wanted to be sure that their rights would be protected.

Federalists and Antifederalists

When the Constitution was made public, a huge debate began among many Americans. **Antifederalists**—people who opposed the Constitution—thought that the Constitutional Convention should not have created a new government. Others thought the Constitution gave too much power to the central government. For some Antifederalists, the main problem was that the Constitution did not have a section that guaranteed individual rights. Delegate **George Mason** became an Antifederalist for this reason.

Many Antifederalists were small farmers and debtors. Some Patriots were also strong Antifederalists, including Samuel Adams and Patrick Henry. Antifederalists were challenged by those who believed that the United States needed a stronger central government.

Federalists, supporters of the Constitution, included James Madison, George Washington, Benjamin Franklin, and Alexander Hamilton. Most Federalists believed that the Constitution offered a good balance of power between various political views. Many

Federalists vs. Antifederalists — QUICK FACTS

Alexander Hamilton
Federalist
- Supported the Constitution as an excellent plan for government
- Defended his views in the *Federalist Papers*

George Mason
Antifederalist
- Opposed the Constitution
- Believed the Constitution needed a section guaranteeing individual rights

Federalists were wealthy planters, farmers, and lawyers. However, others were workers and craftspeople.

Federalists and Antifederalists debated whether the new Constitution should be approved. They made speeches and printed pamphlets **advocating** their views. Mercy Otis Warren, an ardent Patriot during the war, wrote a pamphlet entitled *Observations on the New Constitution*, in which she criticized the lack of individual rights it provided. The Federalists had to convince people a change in the structure of government was needed. To do this, they had to overcome people's fears that the Constitution would make the government too powerful.

READING CHECK **Comparing and Contrasting**
Explain the similarities and differences between the Antifederalists and the Federalists.

Federalist Papers

One of the most important defenses of the Constitution appeared in a series of essays that became known as the **Federalist Papers**. These essays supporting the Constitution were written anonymously under the name Publius. They were actually written by Hamilton, Madison, and Jay.

The authors of the *Federalist Papers* tried to reassure Americans that the new federal government would not overpower the states. In *Federalist Paper* No. 10, Madison argued that the diversity of the United States would prevent any single group from dominating the government.

The *Federalist Papers* were widely reprinted in newspapers around the country as the debate over the Constitution continued. Finally, they were collected and published in book form in 1788.

FOCUS ON READING
Take notes on the chronological order of this section. Which was written first, the *Federalist Papers* or the Bill of Rights?

ACADEMIC VOCABULARY
advocate
to plead in favor of

HISTORIC DOCUMENT
Federalist Paper No. 10

In November 1787, Number 10 in the series called the Federalist Papers *was written in support of the Constitution. In it, James Madison describes the way federalism will overcome disagreements within society.*

> Madison believes that lawmakers are responsible for regulating the many competing concerns that make up society.

> **"**A landed interest, a manufacturing interest, a mercantile [trading] interest, a moneyed interest, with many lesser interests, grow up of necessity in civilized nations, and divide them into different classes, actuated [moved] by different sentiments and views. The regulation of these various and interfering interests [opinions] forms the principal task of modern legislation, and involves the spirit of party and faction [group] in the necessary and ordinary operations of the government . . .
>
> The federal Constitution forms a happy combination . . . the great . . . interests being referred to the national [legislature]; the local and particular to the state legislatures . . . The influence of factious leaders may kindle [start] a flame within their particular states, but will be unable to spread a general conflagration [large fire] through the other states.**"**
>
> —James Madison, quoted in *Living American Documents*,
> edited by Isidore Starr, et al.

> The federal government will handle issues affecting the nation as a whole; state and local governments will handle those concerning local issues.

ANALYSIS SKILL | **ANALYZING PRIMARY SOURCES**

Why does Madison think federalism will prevent disagreement?

The Constitution needed only 9 states to pass it. However, to establish and preserve national unity, each state needed to ratify it. Every state except Rhode Island held special state conventions that gave citizens the chance to discuss and vote on the Constitution.

Paul Revere served on a committee supporting ratification. He wrote of the Constitution, "The proposed . . . government, is well calculated [planned] to secure the liberties, protect the property, and guard the rights of the citizens of America." Antifederalists also spoke out in state conventions, and wrote articles and pamphlets that became known as the Antifederalist Papers. In New York, one citizen said, "It appears that the government will fall into the hands of the few and the great."

On December 7, 1787, Delaware became the first state to ratify the Constitution. It went into effect in June 1788 after New Hampshire became the ninth state to ratify it.

Political leaders across America knew the new government needed the support of the large states of Virginia and New York, where debate still raged. Finally, Madison and fellow Virginia Federalists convinced Virginia to ratify it in mid-1788. In New York, riots had occurred when the draft of the Constitution was made public. At the state convention in Poughkeepsie to discuss ratification, Hamilton argued convincingly against the Antifederalists led by DeWitt Clinton. When news arrived of Virginia's ratification, New York ratified it as well. Rhode Island was the last state to ratify the Constitution in May 1790.

READING CHECK **Drawing Conclusions**
Why were Virginia and New York important to the ratification of the Constitution?

Bill of Rights

Several states ratified the Constitution only after they were promised that a bill protecting individual rights would be added to it. Many Antifederalists did not think that the Constitution would protect personal freedoms.

Some Federalists said that the nation did not need a federal bill of rights because the Constitution itself was a bill of rights. It was, they argued, written to protect the liberty of all U.S. citizens.

James Madison wanted to make a bill of rights one of the new government's first priorities. In Congress's first session, Madison encouraged the legislators to put together a bill of rights. The rights would then be added to the Constitution as **amendments**, or official changes. In Article V of the Constitution, the founders had provided a way to change the document when necessary in order to reflect the will of the people. The process requires that proposed amendments must be approved by a two-thirds majority of both houses of Congress and then ratified by three-fourths of the states before taking effect.

Legislators took ideas from the state ratifying conventions, the Virginia Declaration of Rights, the English Bill of Rights, and the Declaration of Independence to make sure that the abuses listed in the Declaration of Independence would be illegal under the new government. In September 1789 Congress proposed 12 amendments and sent them to the states for ratification. By December 1791 the states had ratified the **Bill of Rights**—10 of the proposed amendments intended to protect citizens' rights.

These 10 amendments set a clear example of how to amend the Constitution to fit the needs of a changing nation. The flexibility of the U.S. Constitution has allowed it to survive for more than 200 years.

READING CHECK **Summarizing** Why is being able to amend the Constitution important?

SUMMARY AND PREVIEW Early disagreements over individual rights resulted in the Bill of Rights. In the next chapter you will learn about the structure of the Constitution.

THE IMPACT TODAY

In 1789, Madison suggested an amendment limiting Congress's power over its own salary. This amendment was not passed until 1992.

Section 4 Assessment

go.hrw.com
Online Quiz
KEYWORD: SF7 HP5

Reviewing Ideas, Terms, and People

1. **a. Identify** Who were the **Federalists** and the **Antifederalists**?
   b. Draw Conclusions What was the main argument of the Antifederalists against the Constitution?
   c. Elaborate Do you agree with the Antifederalists or the Federalists? Explain your position.
2. **a. Recall** When did the Constitution go into effect?
   b. Draw Conclusions Why was it important that all 13 states ratify the Constitution?
   c. Elaborate Do you think that the *Federalist Papers* played an essential role in the ratification of the Constitution? Explain your answer.
3. **a. Recall** Why did Congress add the **Bill of Rights**?
   b. Explain From where did legislators' ideas for the Bill of Rights come?
   c. Elaborate Do you think the process for amending the Constitution is too difficult? Explain your position.

Critical Thinking

4. **Analyzing** Review your notes on Federalist and Antifederalist views. Then identify the outcome of the debate in a graphic organizer like the one below. Be sure to mention the Bill of Rights.

FOCUS ON WRITING

5. **Organizing Your Evidence** In this section you learned how the Bill of Rights was an important addition to the Constitution. You now have all your evidence about the difference between the Articles of Confederation and the Constitution. Choose two or three of the most important points and prepare to defend the Constitution, just like Alexander Hamilton and James Madison did in the *Federalist Papers*.

Social Studies Skills

Analysis   Critical Thinking   Civic Participation   Study

Determining Different Points of View

Define the Skill

A *point of view* is a person's outlook or attitude. It is the way that he or she looks at a topic or thing. Each person's point of view is shaped by his or her background. Because people's backgrounds are different, their points of view are too. Since a person's point of view shapes his or her opinions, knowing that point of view helps you understand and evaluate those opinions. Being able to detect differences in point of view is important to understanding differences in people's opinions and actions in history.

Learn the Skill

When you encounter someone's beliefs, opinions, or actions in your study of history, use the following guidelines to determine his or her point of view.

1. Look for information about the person's background.

2. Ask yourself what factors in the person's background might have influenced his or her opinion or action concerning the topic or event.

3. Be aware that sometimes the person's opinions or actions themselves will provide clues to his or her point of view.

Benjamin Lincoln led the troops that put down Shays's Rebellion in Massachusetts. He was also a state politician and a general during the Revolution. Lincoln offered this explanation of Shays's uprising.

" Among [the main causes] I rank the ease with which ... credit was obtained ... in the time of [the Revolution] ... The moment the day arrived when all discovered that things were fast returning [to normal], ... and that the indolent [lazy persons] and improvident [unwise persons] would soon experience the evils of their idleness and sloth, many startled [panicked] ... and ... complained ... of the weight of public taxes ... and at the cruelty of ... creditors [those to whom money is owed] to call for their just dues [rightful payment] ... The disaffected [unhappy people] ... attempted ... to stop the courts of law, and to suspend the operations of government. This they hoped to do until ... an end should thereby be put to public and private debts. "

Lincoln's background as a general, state official, and leader against the rebels likely gave him a negative point of view on the revolt. His reference to the rebels as lazy and unwise also provides clues to his attitude. You should weigh such factors when evaluating the accuracy of his statement.

Practice the Skill

The following statement about Shays's Rebellion came from a Massachusetts farmer. Read it and apply the guidelines to answer the questions.

" I have labored hard ... all my days. I have been ... obliged to do more than my part in the [Revolution], been loaded with ... rates [taxes], ... have been ... [abused] by sheriffs ... and [debt] collectors ... I have lost a great deal ... [T]he great men are going to get all we have, and I think it is time for us to ... put a stop to it. "

1. From what point of view is this person commenting on the revolt? What is his opinion of it?

2. How does his view of himself differ from Lincoln's view of people like him?

3. Is this view of the revolt likely to be more accurate than Lincoln's view? Why or why not?

Chapter Review

HOLT

History's Impact
▶ video series
Review the video to answer the closing question:
Why would adding more U.S. territory have been appealing in the 1700s and 1800s?

Visual Summary

QUICK FACTS

Use the visual summary below to help you review the main ideas of the chapter.

The Articles of Confederation
• first government of United States
• weak union of states
• weaknesses led to Shays's Rebellion

The Constitution
• framework of today's government
• strengthened national government
• three branches
• checks and balances

Bill of Rights
• first 10 amendments
• ensures basic rights

Reviewing Vocabulary, Terms, and People

Match the numbered person or term with the correct lettered definition.

1. Bill of Rights
2. checks and balances
3. constitution
4. Constitutional Convention
5. *Federalist Papers*
6. inflation
7. Northwest Territory
8. George Mason
9. tariffs
10. Three-Fifths Compromise

a. agreement that stated that each slave would be counted as three-fifths of a person when determining representation

b. delegate to the Constitutional Convention who became an Antifederalist

c. increased prices for goods and services combined with the reduced value of money

d. area including present-day Illinois, Indiana, Michigan, Ohio, Wisconsin, and part of Minnesota

e. meetings held in Philadelphia at which delegates from the states attempted to improve the existing government

f. series of essays in support of the Constitution

g. set of basic principles that determines the powers and duties of a government

h. system that prevents any branch of government from becoming too powerful

i. taxes on imports or exports

j. the first 10 amendments to the Constitution

Comprehension and Critical Thinking

SECTION 1 *(Pages 152–155)*

11. a. Describe What powers did the Articles of Confederation give the national government?

b. Summarize What did the Confederation Congress do to strengthen the United States?

c. Evaluate Which document or institution do you think had the greatest influence on the development of the United States? Why?

SECTION 2 *(Pages 158–162)*

12. a. Recall What was Shays's Rebellion?

b. Draw Conclusions What was the general attitude of foreign nations toward the new government of the United States? Why?

c. Evaluate Of the problems experienced by the Confederation Congress, which do you think was the most harmful? Why?

SECTION 3 *(Pages 163–168)*

13. a. Describe In what ways did the Constitution strengthen the central government?

b. Explain How did the two compromises reached during the Constitutional Convention satisfy competing groups?

c. Elaborate In your opinion were there any weaknesses in the Constitution? Explain your answer.

SECTION 4 *(Pages 170–173)*

14. a. Recall Why was the Bill of Rights added to the Constitution?

b. Draw Conclusions Why were some Americans opposed to the Constitution?

c. Evaluate Would you have supported the Federalists or the Antifederalists? Explain your answer.

Reviewing Themes

15. Politics What political problems resulted from a weak central government under the Articles of Confederation?

16. Politics How did political disagreements lead to important compromises in the creation of the Constitution?

Reading Skills

Understanding Chronological Order *Use the Reading Skills taught in this chapter to answer the question below.*

17. Organize the following events chronologically according to the chapter.

a. The *Federalist Papers* are published.

b. The Constitution is ratified.

c. The Articles of Confederation are ratified.

d. Shays's Rebellion occurs.

e. The Constitutional Convention meets in Philadelphia.

Social Studies Skills

Determining Different Points of View *Use the Social Studies Skills taught in this chapter to answer the question below.*

18. List three differences between the Virginia Plan and the New Jersey Plan.

FOCUS ON WRITING

19. Writing Your Editorial You should start your editorial with a strong statement of your opinion about the Constitution. Then write two sentences about each of your main points of support— a weakness of the Articles of Confederation and/or a strength of the Constitution. End your editorial with a call to action: Ask the delegates to the Constitutional Convention to ratify the Constitution. Remember that you are trying to convince people to make a very important decision for our country—be persuasive.

DIRECTIONS: Read each question and write the letter of the best response.

1 **Which term would *best* describe the newly independent nation in the 1780s?**

A strong

B united

C troubled

D confident

2 **Under the Articles of Confederation, the greatest amount of power was in the hands of the**

A Congress.

B American people.

C national government.

D states.

3 **The structure of the U.S. Congress was created at the Constitutional Convention by the**

A Virginia Plan.

B Great Compromise.

C New Jersey Plan.

D Three-Fifths Compromise.

4 **The nation's most widespread problems under the Articles of Confederation involved**

A trade.

B suffrage.

C slavery.

D rebellion.

5 **The main objective of the Northwest Ordinance of 1787 was to**

A establish a national government with limited powers.

B create a system for bringing new states into the Union.

C settle border disputes between the United States and Canada.

D regulate interstate commerce and curb inflation.

6 **Which of the following documents influenced the system of government established by the U.S. Constitution?**

A Bill of Rights

B Mayflower Compact

C Federalist Papers

D Olive Branch Petition

7 **Read the following passage from one of the *Federalist Papers* and use it to answer the question below.**

> *"*The powers delegated by the proposed Constitution to the federal government are few and defined. Those which are to remain in the State governments are numerous and . . . will extend to all objects which . . . concern the lives, liberties, and properties of the people . . . The operations of the federal government will be most extensive and important in times of war and danger; those of the State governments in times of peace and security.*"*
>
> —James Madison, *Federalist Paper* No. 45

Document-Based Question **What point was Madison making about the system of government created by the proposed U.S. Constitution?**

Citizenship and the Constitution

Indiana Standards

Social Studies Standards

8.1.9 Describe the influence of important individuals on social and political developments of the time such as the Independence movement and the framing of the Constitution.

8.2.1 Identify and explain essential ideas of constitutional government, which are expressed in the founding documents of the United States, including the Virginia Declaration of Rights, the Declaration of Independence, the Virginia Statute for Religious Freedom, the Massachusetts Constitution of 1780, the Northwest Ordinance, the 1787 U.S. Constitution, the Bill of Rights, the Federalist and Anti-Federalist Papers, Common Sense, Washington's Farewell Address (1796), and Jefferson's First Inaugural Address (1801).

8.2.2 Identify and explain the relationship between rights and responsibilities of citizenship in the United States.

8.2.4 Examine functions of the national government in the lives of people.

8.2.6 Distinguish among the different functions of national and state government within the federal system by analyzing the United States Constitution and the Indiana Constitution.

8.2.8 Explain ways that citizens can participate in political parties, campaigns, and elections.

go.hrw.com
Indiana
KEYWORD: SF10 IN

FOCUS ON WRITING

A Pamphlet Everyone in the United States benefits from our Constitution. However, many people don't know the Constitution as well as they should. In this chapter you will read about the Constitution and the rights and responsibilities it grants to citizens. Then you'll create a four-page pamphlet to share this information with your fellow citizens.

UNITED STATES

1788
The Constitution goes into effect after New Hampshire becomes the ninth state to ratify it.

1787 ——————————— 1800

1791 The Bill of Rights becomes part of the Constitution on December 15.

What You Will Learn...

In this chapter you will learn about the U.S. Constitution, the Bill of Rights, and what it means to be an American citizen. Young citizens like the ones pictured here must be informed in order to fulfill the rights and responsibilities of citizenship.

1851
Indiana voters approve a new constitution, which is still in effect along with its amendments.

1942
The Fair Employment Act bans discrimination in the workplace.

1971
The Twenty-sixth Amendment is ratified, giving the right to vote to all U.S. citizens 18 years or older.

BALLOTS

1930   1950   1970   1990

1954 In *Brown* v. *Board of Education*, the Supreme Court declares segregation in public schools to be unconstitutional.

1990
The Americans with Disabilities Act is passed.

HIGH COURT BANS SEGREGATION IN PUBLIC SCHOOLS

CITIZENSHIP AND THE CONSTITUTION   **179**

Reading Social Studies

by Kylene Beers

Economics Geography **Politics** Society and Culture Science and Technology

Focus on Themes In this chapter you will read about the three branches of government, the Bill of Rights, and the duties and responsibilities of a United States citizen. As you read about each of these topics, you will see the American **political system** at work—not only in the Bill of Rights, but also through the responsibilities U.S. citizens have as they vote for leaders and work to help their communities and nation.

Summarizing Historical Texts

Focus on Reading History books are full of information. Sometimes the sheer amount of information they contain can make processing what you read difficult. In those cases, it may be helpful to stop for a moment and summarize what you've read.

Writing a Summary A summary is a short restatement of the most important ideas in a text. The example below shows three steps used in writing a summary. First underline important details. Then write a short summary of each paragraph. Finally, combine these paragraph summaries into a short summary of the whole passage.

The Constitution

Article II, Section 1

1. The <u>executive Power</u> shall be vested in a <u>President of the United States of America</u>. He shall hold his Office during the Term of <u>four Years</u>, and, together with the <u>Vice President</u>, chosen for the same Term, be <u>elected</u>, as follows:

2. <u>Each State shall appoint</u>, in such Manner as the Legislature thereof may direct, a Number of <u>Electors</u>, equal to the whole <u>Number of Senators and Representatives</u> to which the State may be entitled in the Congress; but no Senator or Representative, or Person holding an Office of Trust or Profit under the United States, shall be appointed an Elector.

Summary of Paragraph 1
The executive branch is headed by a president and vice president, each elected for four-year terms.

Summary of Paragraph 2
The electors who choose the president and vice president are appointed. Each state has the same number of electors as it has members of Congress.

Combined Summary
The president and vice president who run the executive branch are elected every four years by state-appointed electors.

You Try It!

The following passage is from the U.S. Constitution. As you read it, decide which facts you would include in a summary of the passage.

The Constitution

Article I, Section 2

1. The House of Representatives shall be composed of Members chosen every second Year by the People of the several States, and the Electors in each State shall have the Qualifications requisite for Electors of the most numerous branch of the State Legislature.

2. No person shall be a Representative who shall not have attained to the Age of twenty five years, and been seven Years a Citizen of the United States, and who shall not, when elected, be an Inhabitant of the State in which he shall be chosen.

After you read the passage, answer the following questions.

1. Which of the following statements best summarizes the first paragraph of this passage?

   a. Congress has a House of Representatives.

   b. Members of the House of Representatives are elected every two years by state electors.

2. Using the steps described on the previous page, write a summary of the second paragraph of this passage.

3. Combine the summary statement you chose in Question 1 with the summary statement you wrote in Question 2 to create a single summary of this entire passage.

Academic Vocabulary

Success in school is related to knowing academic vocabulary— the words that are frequently used in school assignments and discussions. In this chapter, you will learn the following academic words:

distinct *(p. 183)*
influence *(p. 224)*

As you read Chapter 6, think about what details you would include in a summary of each paragraph.

Understanding the Constitution

What You Will Learn...

Main Ideas

1. The framers of the Constitution devised the federal system.
2. The legislative branch makes the nation's laws.
3. The executive branch enforces the nation's laws.
4. The judicial branch determines whether or not laws are constitutional.

The Big Idea

The U.S. Constitution balances the powers of the federal government among the legislative, executive, and judicial branches.

Key Terms and People

federal system, *p. 182*
impeach, *p. 184*
veto, *p. 184*
executive orders, *p. 185*
pardons, *p. 185*
Thurgood Marshall, *p. 186*
Sandra Day O'Connor, *p. 186*

 TAKING NOTES As you read, take notes on the structure of each of the branches of government in a chart like the one below.

Branch	Structure
Legislative	
Executive	
Judicial	

 8.1.5, 8.1.9, 8.1.28, 8.1.30, 8.2.1, 8.2.3, 8.2.4, 8.2.6

If YOU were there...

You have just been elected to the U.S. House of Representatives. You know that committees do much of the work in Congress. They deal with many different fields such as foreign policy, agriculture, national security, science, and education. You would like to ask for a spot on a committee whose work interests you.

Which committee would you ask to serve on?

BUILDING BACKGROUND When the framers of the Constitution met in Philadelphia in 1787, they created a national government with three branches that balance one another's powers.

The Federal System

The framers of the Constitution wanted to create a government powerful enough to protect the rights of citizens and defend the country against its enemies. To do so, they set up a **federal system** of government, a system that divided powers between the states and the federal government.

The Constitution assigns certain powers to the national government. These are called delegated powers. Among them are the rights to coin money and to regulate trade. Reserved powers are those kept by the states. These powers include creating local governments and holding elections. Concurrent powers are those shared by the federal and state governments. They include taxing, borrowing money, and enforcing laws.

Sometimes, Congress has had to stretch its delegated powers to deal with new or unexpected issues. A clause in the Constitution states that Congress may "make all Laws which shall be necessary and proper" for carrying out its duties. This clause, called the elastic clause—because it can be stretched (like elastic)—provides flexibility for the government. The federal government has used this clause to provide public services such as funding for the arts and humanities.

READING CHECK **Summarizing** How is power divided between the federal and state governments?

Separation of Powers

U.S. Constitution

Legislative Branch (Congress)

- Writes the laws
- Confirms presidential appointments
- Approves treaties
- Grants money
- Declares war

Executive Branch (President)

- Proposes laws
- Administers the laws
- Commands armed forces
- Appoints ambassadors and other officials
- Conducts foreign policy
- Makes treaties

Judicial Branch (Supreme Court)

- Interprets the Constitution and other laws
- Reviews lower-court decisions

Legislative Branch

The federal government has three branches, each with **distinct** responsibilities and powers. This separation balances the branches and keeps any one of them from growing too powerful. The first branch of government is the legislative branch, or Congress. It makes the nation's laws. Article I of the Constitution divides Congress into the House of Representatives and the Senate.

With 435 members, the House of Representatives is the larger congressional house. The U.S. Census, a population count made every 10 years, determines how many members represent each state. A system called apportionment keeps total membership at 435. If one state gains a member, another state loses one. Members must be at least 25 years old, live in the state where they were elected, and have been U.S. citizens for seven years. They serve two-year terms.

The Senate has two members, or senators, per state. Senators represent the interests of the whole state, not just a district. They must be at least 30 years old, have been U.S. citizens for nine years, and live in the state they represent. They serve six-year terms. The senior senator of a state is the one who has served the longer of the two. Members of Congress can serve an unlimited number of terms in office.

The political party with more members in each house is the majority party. The one with fewer members is the minority party. The leader of the House of Representatives, or Speaker of the House, is elected by House members from the majority party.

The U.S. vice president serves as president of the Senate. He takes no part in Senate debates but can vote to break ties. If he is absent, the president pro tempore (pro tem for short) leads the Senate. There is no law for how the Senate must choose this position, but it traditionally goes to the majority party's senator who has served the longest.

Congress begins sessions, or meetings, each year in the first week of January. Both houses do most of their work in committees. Each committee studies certain types of bills, or suggested laws. For example, all bills about taxes begin in the House Ways and Means Committee.

ACADEMIC VOCABULARY
distinct
separate

READING CHECK Comparing and Contrasting
What are the similarities in requirements for members of the House of Representatives and the Senate? What are the differences?

Checks and Balances
QUICK FACTS

Executive Branch (President)
Checks on:
Legislative Branch
- May adjourn Congress in certain situations
- May veto bills

Judicial Branch
- Appoints judges

Legislative Branch (Congress)
Checks on:
Executive Branch
- May reject appointments
- May reject treaties
- May withhold funding for presidential initiatives
- May impeach president
- May override a veto

Judicial Branch
- May propose constitutional amendments to overrule judicial decisions
- May impeach Supreme Court justices

Judicial Branch (Supreme Court)
Checks on:
Executive Branch
- May declare executive actions unconstitutional

Legislative Branch
- May declare laws unconstitutional

Executive Branch

Article II of the Constitution lists the powers of the executive branch. This branch enforces the laws passed by Congress.

President and Vice President

As head of the executive branch, the president is the most powerful elected leader in the United States. To qualify for the presidency or vice presidency, one must be a native-born U.S. citizen at least 35 years old. The president must also have been a U.S. resident for 14 years.

Americans elect a president and vice president every four years. Franklin D. Roosevelt, who won four times, was the only president to serve more than two terms. Now, the Twenty-second Amendment limits presidents to two terms. If a president dies, resigns, or is removed from office, the vice president becomes president for the rest of the term.

The House of Representatives can **impeach**, or vote to bring charges of serious crimes against, a president. Impeachment cases are tried in the Senate. If a president is found guilty, Congress can remove him from office. In 1868 Andrew Johnson was the first president to be impeached. President Bill Clinton was impeached in 1998. However, the Senate found each man not guilty.

Working with Congress

The president and Congress are often on different sides of an issue. However, they must still work together.

Congress passes laws. The president, however, can ask Congress to pass or reject bills. The president also can **veto**, or cancel, laws Congress has passed. Congress can try to override, or undo, the veto. However, this is difficult since it takes a two-thirds majority vote. To carry out laws affecting the Constitution, treaties, and statutes, the president issues **executive orders**. These commands have the power of law. The president also may grant **pardons**, or freedom from punishment, to persons convicted of federal crimes or facing criminal charges.

The president also commands the armed forces. In emergencies, the president can call on U.S. troops. Only Congress, however, can declare war. Other executive duties include conducting foreign relations and creating treaties. Executive departments do most of the executive branch work. As of 2004 there were 15 such departments. The president chooses department heads, who are called secretaries, and the Senate approves them. The heads make up the cabinet, which advises the president.

READING CHECK ▶ **Drawing Conclusions**
What is the president's most important power?

Judicial Branch

The third branch of government, the judicial branch, is made up of a system of federal courts headed by the U.S. Supreme Court. The Constitution created the Supreme Court, but the Judiciary Act of 1789 created the system of lower district and circuit courts.

Article III generally outlines the courts' duties. Federal courts can strike down a state or federal law if the court finds a law unconstitutional. Congress can then try to revise the law to make it constitutional.

District Courts

The president makes appointments to federal courts. In an effort to keep federal judges free of party influence, the judges are given life appointments. The lower federal courts are divided according to cases over which they have jurisdiction, or authority. Each state has at least one of the 94 district courts.

THE IMPACT TODAY

In 2002 the new Department of Homeland Security was given cabinet-level status to protect against terrorism.

SUPREME COURT DECISIONS

Background of the Court
The rest of the Supreme Court decisions you see in this book will highlight important cases of the Court. But in this first one, we'll discuss the history of the Court.

The first Supreme Court met in 1790 at the Royal Exchange in New York City. The ground floor of this building was an open-air market. When the national government moved to Philadelphia, the Court met in basement rooms in Independence Hall. Once in Washington, the Court heard cases in the Capitol building until the present Supreme Court building was completed in 1932.

Circuit Riding
Today the Supreme Court holds court only in Washington, D.C. In the past, however, the justices had to travel through assigned circuits, hearing cases together with a district judge in a practice known as riding circuit.

The justices complained bitterly about the inconvenience of travel, which was often over unpaved roads and in bad weather. This system was not just inconvenient to the justices, however. Some people worried about the fairness of a system that required justices who had heard cases at trial to rule on them again on appeal. Other people, however, thought that the practice helped keep the justices in touch with the needs and feelings of the average citizen. Eventually,

circuit riding interfered so much with the increased amount of business of the Supreme Court that Congress passed a law ending the practice in the late 1800s.

Path to the Supreme Court
When a case is decided by a state or federal court, the losing side may have a chance to appeal the decision to a higher court. Under the federal system, this higher court is called the court of appeals. A person who loses in that court may then appeal to the Supreme Court to review the case. But the Supreme Court does not have to accept all appeals. It usually chooses to hear only cases in which there is an important legal principle to be decided or if two federal courts of appeals disagree on how an issue should be decided.

ANALYSIS SKILL **ANALYZING INFORMATION**
1. What are two reasons why the practice of circuit riding ended?
2. Why do you think the Supreme Court does not hear every case that is appealed to it?

FOCUS ON
READING

Jot down a short summary of the appeals process after reading this paragraph.

Courts of Appeals

If someone convicted of a crime believes the trial was unfair, he or she may take the case to the court of appeals. There are 13 courts of appeals. Each has a panel of judges to decide if cases heard in the lower courts were tried appropriately. If the judges uphold, or accept, the original decision, the original outcome stands. Otherwise, the case may be retried in the lower court.

Supreme Court

Supreme Court rulings can have dramatic effects on the nation, as in *Bush* v. *Gore*, which decided the outcome of the 2000 presidential election.

After a case is decided by the court of appeals, the losing side may appeal the decision to the Supreme Court. Thousands of cases go to the Supreme Court yearly in the hope of a hearing, but the Court has time to hear only about 100. Generally, the cases heard involve important constitutional or public-interest issues. If the Court declines to hear a case, the court of appeals decision is final.

Nine justices sit on the Supreme Court. The chief justice of the United States leads the Court. Unlike the president and members of Congress, there are no specific constitutional requirements for becoming a justice.

In recent decades, the Supreme Court has become more diverse. In 1967 **Thurgood Marshall** became the first African American justice. **Sandra Day O'Connor** became the first female Court justice after her 1981 appointment by President Ronald Reagan.

READING CHECK **Summarizing** Describe the structure and responsibilities of the judicial branch.

SUMMARY AND PREVIEW In this section you learned about the balance between the different branches of the federal government. In the next section you will learn about the Bill of Rights.

Section 1 Assessment

Reviewing Ideas, Terms, and People

1. a. Describe What type of government did the Constitution establish for the United States?
   b. Contrast What is the difference between delegated, reserved, and concurrent powers?

2. a. Recall What role does the vice president serve in the legislative branch?
   b. Compare and Contrast In what ways are the Senate and the House of Representatives similar and different?
   c. Elaborate Why do you think the requirements for serving in the Senate are stricter than those for serving in the House of Representatives?

3. a. Describe What powers are granted to the president?
   b. Make Generalizations Why is it important that the president and Congress work together in resolving governmental issues?
   c. Evaluate What do you think is the most important power granted to the president? Why?

4. a. Explain What is the main power of the judicial branch?
   b. Evaluate Which branch of government do you feel is most important? Explain your answer.

Critical Thinking

5. Categorizing Review your notes on the branches of government. Then copy the web diagram below and use it to show two powers of each branch of government.

FOCUS ON WRITING

6. Gathering Information about the Constitution Look back through what you've just read about the Constitution. Make a list of four or five of the most important features of the Constitution. You'll put that list on the second page of your pamphlet.

James Madison

What would you do to create a brand-new government?

When did he live? 1751–1836

Where did he live? Like several of the founding fathers, James Madison was a Virginian. He grew up in the town of Montpelier, and he kept a home there for his whole life.

What did he do? Through the persuasive power of his writing, Madison helped create the foundations of the U.S. government.

Why is he important? Madison is known as the Father of the Constitution. A brilliant thinker, he provided many of the basic ideas in the Constitution. He argued tirelessly for a strong national government, for separate branches of government, and for rights such as freedom of religion. He then rallied support for adoption of the Constitution and the Bill of Rights. In 1809 Madison became the fourth president of the United States. As president, he led the country through another war with Britain, the War of 1812. He and his wife, Dolley, were forced to flee Washington temporarily when the British invaded the capital and set fire to the White House.

Summarizing Why is Madison known as the Father of the Constitution?

KEY EVENTS

1780
Madison serves in the Continental Congress.

1787
Madison keeps a written record of the Constitutional Convention.

1787–1788
Madison helps write the *Federalist Papers*, urging support for the Constitution.

1801–1809
Madison serves as secretary of state under President Thomas Jefferson.

1809–1817
Madison serves two terms as president.

James Madison was an important force in the writing of the Constitution.

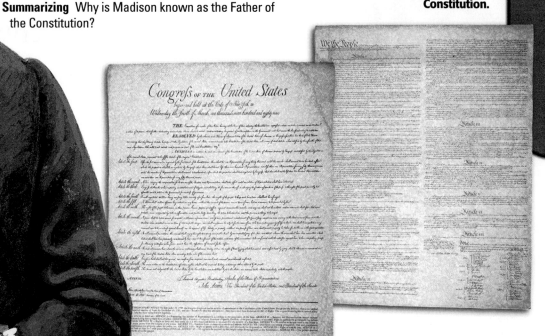

The Constitution of the United States

Preamble
The short and dignified preamble explains the goals of the new government under the Constitution.

We the People of the United States, in Order to form a more perfect Union, establish Justice, insure domestic Tranquility, provide for the common defense, promote the general Welfare, and secure the Blessings of Liberty to ourselves and our Posterity, do ordain and establish this Constitution for the United States of America.

Note: The parts of the Constitution that have been lined through are no longer in force or no longer apply because of later amendments. The titles of the sections and articles are added for easier reference.

Article I The Legislature

Section 1. Congress

All legislative Powers herein granted shall be vested in a Congress of the United States, which shall consist of a Senate and House of Representatives.

Section 2. The House of Representatives

1. Elections The House of Representatives shall be composed of Members chosen every second Year by the People of the several States, and the Electors in each State shall have the Qualifications requisite for Electors of the most numerous Branch of the State Legislature.

2. Qualifications No Person shall be a Representative who shall not have attained to the Age of twenty five Years, and been seven Years a Citizen of the United States, and who shall not, when elected, be an Inhabitant of that State in which he shall be chosen.

3. Number of Representatives Representatives and direct Taxes shall be apportioned among the several States which may be included within this Union, according to their respective Numbers, ~~which shall be determined by adding to the whole Number of free Persons, including~~ **those bound to Service**[1] ~~for a Term of Years, and excluding Indians not taxed, three fifths of~~ **all other Persons**.[2] The actual **Enumeration**[3] shall be made within three Years after the first Meeting of the Congress of the United States, and within every subsequent Term of ten Years, in such Manner as they shall by Law direct. The Number of Representatives shall not exceed one for every thirty Thousand, but each State shall have at Least one Representative; ~~and until such enumeration shall be made, the State of New Hampshire shall be entitled to choose three, Massachusetts eight, Rhode-Island and Providence Plantations one, Connecticut five, New-York six, New Jersey four, Pennsylvania eight, Delaware one, Maryland six, Virginia ten, North Carolina five, South Carolina five, and Georgia three.~~

4. Vacancies When vacancies happen in the Representation from any State, the Executive Authority thereof shall issue Writs of Election to fill such Vacancies.

5. Officers and Impeachment The House of Representatives shall choose their Speaker and other Officers; and shall have the sole Power of impeachment.

Legislative Branch

Article I explains how the legislative branch, called Congress, is organized. The chief purpose of the legislative branch is to make laws. Congress is made up of the Senate and the House of Representatives.

The House of Representatives

The number of members each state has in the House is based on the population of the individual state. In 1929 Congress permanently fixed the size of the House at 435 members.

Vocabulary

[1] **those bound to Service** indentured servants

[2] **all other Persons** slaves

[3] **Enumeration** census or official population count

Section 3. [The Senate]

1. Number of Senators The Senate of the United States shall be composed of two Senators from each State, ~~chosen by the Legislature thereof,~~ for six Years; and each Senator shall have one Vote.

2. Classifying Terms Immediately after they shall be assembled in Consequence of the first Election, they shall be divided as equally as may be into three Classes. The Seats of the Senators of the first Class shall be vacated at the Expiration of the second Year, of the second Class at the Expiration of the fourth Year, and of the third Class at the Expiration of the sixth Year, so that one third may be chosen every second Year; ~~and if Vacancies happen by Resignation, or otherwise, during the Recess of the Legislature of any State, the Executive thereof may make temporary Appointments until the next Meeting of the Legislature, which shall then fill such Vacancies.~~

3. Qualifications No Person shall be a Senator who shall not have attained to the Age of thirty Years, and been nine Years a Citizen of the United States, and who shall not, when elected, be an Inhabitant of that State for which he shall be chosen.

4. Role of Vice President The Vice President of the United States shall be President of the Senate, but shall have no Vote, unless they be equally divided.

5. Officers The Senate shall choose their other Officers, and also a President **pro tempore**,[4] in the Absence of the Vice President, or when he shall exercise the Office of President of the United States.

6. Impeachment Trials The Senate shall have the sole Power to try all **Impeachments**.[5] When sitting for that Purpose, they shall be on Oath or Affirmation. When the President of the United States is tried, the Chief Justice shall preside: And no Person shall be convicted without the Concurrence of two thirds of the Members present.

7. Punishment for Impeachment Judgment in Cases of Impeachment shall not extend further than to removal from Office, and disqualification to hold and enjoy any Office of honor, Trust or Profit under the United States: but the Party convicted shall nevertheless be liable and subject to Indictment, Trial, Judgment and Punishment, according to Law.

The Vice President

The only duty that the Constitution assigns to the vice president is to preside over meetings of the Senate. Modern presidents have usually given their vice presidents more responsibilities.

EXPLORING THE DOCUMENT If the House of Representatives charges a government official with wrongdoing, the Senate acts as a court to decide if the official is guilty. **How does the power of impeachment represent part of the system of checks and balances?**

Vocabulary

[4] **pro tempore** temporarily

[5] **Impeachments** official accusations of federal wrongdoing

---

Federal Office Terms and Requirements — QUICK FACTS

Position	Term	Minimum Age	Residency	Citizenship
President	4 years	35	14 years in the U.S.	natural-born
Vice President	4 years	35	14 years in the U.S.	natural-born
Supreme Court Justice	unlimited	none	none	none
Senator	6 years	30	state in which elected	9 years
Representative	2 years	25	state in which elected	7 years

Section 4. Congressional Elections

1. Regulations The Times, Places and Manner of holding Elections for Senators and Representatives, shall be prescribed in each State by the Legislature thereof; but the Congress may at any time by Law make or alter such Regulations, except as to the Places of choosing Senators.

2. Sessions ~~The Congress shall assemble at least once in every Year, and such Meeting shall be on the first Monday in December, unless they shall by Law appoint a different Day.~~

Section 5. Rules/Procedures

1. Quorum Each House shall be the Judge of the Elections, Returns and Qualifications of its own Members, and a Majority of each shall constitute a **Quorum**[6] to do Business; but a smaller Number may **adjourn**[7] from day to day, and may be authorized to compel the Attendance of absent Members, in such Manner, and under such Penalties as each House may provide.

2. Rules and Conduct Each House may determine the Rules of its Proceedings, punish its Members for disorderly Behaviour, and, with the Concurrence of two thirds, expel a Member.

3. Records Each House shall keep a Journal of its Proceedings, and from time to time publish the same, excepting such Parts as may in their Judgment require Secrecy; and the Yeas and Nays of the Members of either House on any question shall, at the Desire of one fifth of those Present, be entered on the Journal.

4. Adjournment Neither House, during the Session of Congress, shall, without the Consent of the other, adjourn for more than three days, nor to any other Place than that in which the two Houses shall be sitting.

Section 6. Payment

1. Salary The Senators and Representatives shall receive a Compensation for their Services, to be ascertained by Law, and paid out of the Treasury of the United States. They shall in all Cases, except Treason, Felony and Breach of the Peace, be privileged from Arrest during their Attendance at the Session of their respective Houses, and in going to and returning from the same; and for any Speech or Debate in either House, they shall not be questioned in any other Place.

2. Restrictions No Senator or Representative shall, during the Time for which he was elected, be appointed to any civil Office under the Authority of the United States, which shall have been created, or the **Emoluments**[8] whereof shall have been increased during such time; and no Person holding any Office under the United States, shall be a Member of either House during his **Continuance**[9] in Office.

Vocabulary

[6] **Quorum** the minimum number of people needed to conduct business

[7] **adjourn** to stop indefinitely

[8] **Emoluments** salary

[9] **Continuance** term

EXPLORING THE DOCUMENT The framers felt that because members of the House are elected every two years, representatives would listen to the public and seek its approval before passing taxes. **How does Section 7 address the colonial demand of "no taxation without representation"?**

EXPLORING THE DOCUMENT The veto power of the president is one of the important checks and balances in the Constitution. **Why do you think the framers included the ability of Congress to override a veto?**

Section 7. [How a Bill Becomes a Law]

1. Tax Bills All **Bills**¹⁰ for raising Revenue shall originate in the House of Representatives; but the Senate may propose or concur with Amendments as on other Bills.

2. Lawmaking Every Bill which shall have passed the House of Representatives and the Senate, shall, before it become a Law, be presented to the President of the United States: If he approve he shall sign it, but if not he shall return it, with his Objections to that House in which it shall have originated, who shall enter the Objections at large on their Journal, and proceed to reconsider it. If after such Reconsideration two thirds of that House shall agree to pass the Bill, it shall be sent, together with the Objections, to the other House, by which it shall likewise be reconsidered, and if approved by two thirds of that House, it shall become a Law. But in all such Cases the Votes of both Houses shall be determined by yeas and Nays, and the Names of the Persons voting for and against the Bill shall be entered on the Journal of each House respectively. If any Bill shall not be returned by the President within ten Days (Sundays excepted) after it shall have been presented to him, the Same shall be a Law, in like Manner as if he had signed it, unless the Congress by their Adjournment prevent its Return, in which Case it shall not be a Law.

3. Role of the President Every Order, Resolution, or Vote to which the Concurrence of the Senate and House of Representatives may be necessary (except on a question of Adjournment) shall be presented to the President of the United States; and before the Same shall take Effect, shall be approved by him, or being disapproved by him, shall be repassed by two thirds of the Senate and House of Representatives, according to the Rules and Limitations prescribed in the Case of a Bill.

How a Bill Becomes a Law

❶ A member of the House or the Senate introduces a bill and refers it to a committee.

❷ The House or Senate Committee may approve, rewrite, or kill the bill.

❸ The House or the Senate debates and votes on its version of the bill.

❹ House and Senate conference committee members work out the differences between the two versions.

❺ Both houses of Congress pass the revised bill.

Section 8.

Powers Granted to Congress

1. Taxation The Congress shall have Power To lay and collect Taxes, **Duties**,[11] **Imposts**[12] and **Excises**,[13] to pay the Debts and provide for the common Defense and general Welfare of the United States; but all Duties, Imposts and Excises shall be uniform throughout the United States;

2. Credit To borrow Money on the credit of the United States;

3. Commerce To regulate Commerce with foreign Nations, and among the several States, and with the Indian Tribes;

4. Naturalization and Bankruptcy To establish an uniform **Rule of Naturalization**,[14] and uniform Laws on the subject of Bankruptcies throughout the United States;

5. Money To coin Money, regulate the Value thereof, and of foreign Coin, and fix the Standard of Weights and Measures;

6. Counterfeiting To provide for the Punishment of counterfeiting the **Securities**[15] and current Coin of the United States;

7. Post Office To establish Post Offices and post Roads;

8. Patents and Copyrights To promote the Progress of Science and useful Arts, by securing for limited Times to Authors and Inventors the exclusive Right to their respective Writings and Discoveries;

9. Courts To constitute Tribunals inferior to the supreme Court;

10. International Law To define and punish Piracies and Felonies committed on the high Seas, and Offences against the Law of Nations;

LINKING TO TODAY

Native Americans and the Commerce Clause

The commerce clause gives Congress the power to "regulate Commerce with . . . the Indian Tribes." The clause has been interpreted to mean that the states cannot tax or interfere with businesses on Indian reservations, but that the federal government can. It also allows American Indian nations to develop their own governments and laws. These laws, however, can be challenged in federal court. Although reservation land usually belongs to the government of the Indian group, it is administered by the U.S. government.

Drawing Conclusions How would you describe the status of American Indian nations under the commerce clause?

Vocabulary

[11] **Duties** tariffs

[12] **Imposts** taxes

[13] **Excises** internal taxes on the manufacture, sale, or consumption of a commodity

[14] **Rule of Naturalization** a law by which a foreign-born person becomes a citizen

[15] **Securities** bonds

6 The president signs or vetoes the bill.

7 Two-thirds majority vote of Congress is needed to approve a vetoed bill. Bill becomes a law.

ANALYSIS SKILL **ANALYZING INFORMATION**

Why do you think the framers created this complex system for adopting laws?

Vocabulary

16 Letters of Marque and Reprisal documents issued by governments allowing merchant ships to arm themselves and attack ships of an enemy nation

11. War To declare War, grant **Letters of Marque and Reprisal,**[16] and make Rules concerning Captures on Land and Water;

12. Army To raise and support Armies, but no Appropriation of Money to that Use shall be for a longer Term than two Years;

13. Navy To provide and maintain a Navy;

14. Regulation of the Military To make Rules for the Government and Regulation of the land and naval Forces;

15. Militia To provide for calling forth the Militia to execute the Laws of the Union, suppress Insurrections and repel Invasions;

16. Regulation of the Militia To provide for organizing, arming, and disciplining, the Militia, and for governing such Part of them as may be employed in the Service of the United States, reserving to the States respectively, the Appointment of the Officers, and the Authority of training the Militia according to the discipline prescribed by Congress;

17. District of Columbia To exercise exclusive Legislation in all Cases whatsoever, over such District (not exceeding ten Miles square) as may, by Cession of particular States, and the Acceptance of Congress, become the Seat of the Government of the United States, and to exercise like Authority over all Places purchased by the Consent of the Legislature of the State in which the Same shall be, for the Erection of Forts, Magazines, Arsenals, dock-Yards, and other needful Buildings;—And

18. Necessary and Proper Clause To make all Laws which shall be necessary and proper for carrying into Execution the foregoing Powers, and all other Powers vested by this Constitution in the Government of the United States, or in any Department or Officer thereof.

The Elastic Clause

The framers of the Constitution wanted a national government that was strong enough to be effective. This section lists the powers given to Congress. The last portion of Section 8 contains the so-called elastic clause.

The Elastic Clause

The elastic clause has been stretched (like elastic) to allow Congress to meet changing circumstances.

Section 9. Powers Denied Congress

1. Slave Trade ~~The Migration or Importation of such Persons as any of the States now existing shall think proper to admit, shall not be prohibited by the Congress prior to the Year one thousand eight hundred and eight, but a Tax or duty may be imposed on such Importation, not exceeding ten dollars for each Person.~~

2. Habeas Corpus The Privilege of the **Writ of Habeas Corpus**[17] shall not be suspended, unless when in Cases of Rebellion or Invasion the public Safety may require it.

3. Illegal Punishment No **Bill of Attainder**[18] or **ex post facto Law**[19] shall be passed.

4. Direct Taxes No **Capitation**,[20] or other direct, Tax shall be laid, unless in Proportion to the Census or enumeration herein before directed to be taken.

5. Export Taxes No Tax or Duty shall be laid on Articles exported from any State.

6. No Favorites No Preference shall be given by any Regulation of Commerce or Revenue to the Ports of one State over those of another; nor shall Vessels bound to, or from, one State, be obliged to enter, clear, or pay Duties in another.

7. Public Money No Money shall be drawn from the Treasury, but in Consequence of Appropriations made by Law; and a regular Statement and Account of the Receipts and Expenditures of all public Money shall be published from time to time.

8. Titles of Nobility No Title of Nobility shall be granted by the United States: And no Person holding any Office of Profit or Trust under them, shall, without the Consent of the Congress, accept of any present, Emolument, Office, or Title, of any kind whatever, from any King, Prince, or foreign State.

Section 10. Powers Denied the States

1. Restrictions No State shall enter into any Treaty, Alliance, or Confederation; grant Letters of Marque and Reprisal; coin Money; emit Bills of Credit; make any Thing but gold and silver Coin a Tender in Payment of Debts; pass any Bill of Attainder, ex post facto Law, or Law impairing the Obligation of Contracts, or grant any Title of Nobility.

2. Import and Export Taxes No State shall, without the Consent of the Congress, lay any Imposts or Duties on Imports or Exports, except what may be absolutely necessary for executing it's inspection Laws: and the net Produce of all Duties and Imposts, laid by any State on Imports or Exports, shall be for the Use of the Treasury of the United States; and all such Laws shall be subject to the Revision and Control of the Congress.

3. Peacetime and War Restraints No State shall, without the Consent of Congress, lay any Duty of Tonnage, keep Troops, or Ships of War in time of Peace, enter into any Agreement or Compact with another State, or with a foreign Power, or engage in War, unless actually invaded, or in such imminent Danger as will not admit of delay.

 EXPLORING THE DOCUMENT Although Congress has implied powers, there are also limits to its powers. Section 9 lists powers that are denied to the federal government. Several of the clauses protect the people of the United States from unjust treatment. **In what ways does the Constitution limit the powers of the federal government?**

Vocabulary

[17] Writ of Habeas Corpus a court order that requires the government to bring a prisoner to court and explain why he or she is being held

[18] Bill of Attainder a law declaring that a person is guilty of a particular crime

[19] ex post facto Law a law that is made effective prior to the date that it was passed and therefore punishes people for acts that were not illegal at the time

[20] Capitation a direct uniform tax imposed on each head, or person

Article II | The Executive

Section 1. | The Presidency

1. Terms of Office The executive Power shall be vested in a President of the United States of America. He shall hold his Office during the Term of four Years, and, together with the Vice President, chosen for the same Term, be elected, as follows:

2. Electoral College Each State shall appoint, in such Manner as the Legislature thereof may direct, a Number of Electors, equal to the whole Number of Senators and Representatives to which the State may be entitled in the Congress: but no Senator or Representative, or Person holding an Office of Trust or Profit under the United States, shall be appointed an Elector.

3. Former Method of Electing President ~~The Electors shall meet in their respective States, and vote by Ballot for two Persons, of whom one at least shall not be an Inhabitant of the same State with themselves. And they shall make a List of all the Persons voted for, and of the Number of Votes for each; which List they shall sign and certify, and transmit sealed to the Seat of the Government of the United States, directed to the President of the Senate. The President of the Senate shall, in the Presence of the Senate and House of Representatives, open all the Certificates, and the Votes shall~~

The Electoral College

11 Number of Electors

WA 11
OR 7
MT 3
ND 3
MN 10
ID 4
SD 3
WI 10
MI 17
NH 4
VT 3
ME 4
NY 31
MA 12
RI 4
CT 7
NJ 15
PA 21
WY 3
NE 5
IA 7
IL 21
IN 11
OH 20
WV 5
VA 13
DE 3
MD 10
NV 5
UT 5
CO 9
KS 6
MO 11
KY 8
NC 15
CA 55
AZ 10
NM 5
OK 7
AR 6
TN 11
SC 8
Washington, D.C. 3
MS 6
AL 9
GA 15
TX 34
LA 9
FL 27
AK 3
HI 4

GEOGRAPHY SKILLS INTERPRETING MAPS

Place What two states have the most electors?

then be counted. The Person having the greatest Number of Votes shall be ~~the President, if such Number be a Majority of the whole Number of Electors appointed; and if there be more than one who have such Majority, and have an equal Number of Votes, then the House of Representatives shall immediately choose by Ballot one of them for President; and if no Person have a Majority, then from the five highest on the List the said House shall in like Manner choose the President. But in choosing the President, the Votes shall be taken by States, the Representation from each State having one Vote; A quorum for this purpose shall consist of a Member or Members from two thirds of the States, and a Majority of all the States shall be necessary to a Choice. In every Case, after the Choice of the President, the Person having the greatest Number of Votes of the Electors shall be the Vice President. But if there should remain two or more who have equal Votes, the Senate shall choose from them by Ballot the Vice President.~~

4. Election Day The Congress may determine the Time of choosing the Electors, and the Day on which they shall give their Votes; which Day shall be the same throughout the United States.

5. Qualifications No Person except a natural born Citizen~~, or a Citizen of the United States, at the time of the Adoption of this Constitution~~, shall be eligible to the Office of President; neither shall any Person be eligible to that Office who shall not have attained to the Age of thirty five Years, and been fourteen Years a Resident within the United States.

6. Succession In Case of the Removal of the President from Office, or of his Death, Resignation, or Inability to discharge the Powers and Duties of the said Office, the Same shall devolve on the Vice President, and the Congress may by Law provide for the Case of Removal, Death, Resignation or Inability, both of the President and Vice President, declaring what Officer shall then act as President, and such Officer shall act accordingly, until the Disability be removed, or a President shall be elected.

7. Salary The President shall, at stated Times, receive for his Services, a Compensation, which shall neither be increased nor diminished during the Period for which he shall have been elected, and he shall not receive within that Period any other Emolument from the United States, or any of them.

8. Oath of Office Before he enter on the Execution of his Office, he shall take the following Oath or Affirmation:—"I do solemnly swear (or affirm) that I will faithfully execute the Office of President of the United States, and will to the best of my Ability, preserve, protect and defend the Constitution of the United States."

EXPLORING THE DOCUMENT The youngest elected president was John F. Kennedy; he was 43 years old when he was inaugurated. (Theodore Roosevelt was 42 when he assumed office after the assassination of McKinley.) **What is the minimum required age for the office of president?**

Presidential Salary

In 1999 Congress voted to set future presidents' salaries at $400,000 per year. The president also receives an annual expense account. The president must pay taxes only on the salary.

Commander in Chief

Today the president is in charge of the army, navy, air force, marines, and coast guard. Only Congress, however, can decide if the United States will declare war.

Appointments

Most of the president's appointments to office must be approved by the Senate.

The State of the Union

Every year the president presents to Congress a State of the Union message. In this message, the president introduces and explains a legislative plan for the coming year.

Section 2. | Powers of Presidency |

1. Military Powers The President shall be Commander in Chief of the Army and Navy of the United States, and of the Militia of the several States, when called into the actual Service of the United States; he may require the Opinion, in writing, of the principal Officer in each of the executive Departments, upon any Subject relating to the Duties of their respective Offices, and he shall have Power to grant **Reprieves**[21] and **Pardons**[22] for Offences against the United States, except in Cases of Impeachment.

2. Treaties and Appointments He shall have Power, by and with the Advice and Consent of the Senate, to make Treaties, provided two thirds of the Senators present concur; and he shall nominate, and by and with the Advice and Consent of the Senate, shall appoint Ambassadors, other public Ministers and Consuls, Judges of the supreme Court, and all other Officers of the United States, whose Appointments are not herein otherwise provided for, and which shall be established by Law: but the Congress may by Law vest the Appointment of such inferior Officers, as they think proper, in the President alone, in the Courts of Law, or in the Heads of Departments.

3. Vacancies The President shall have Power to fill up all Vacancies that may happen during the Recess of the Senate, by granting Commissions which shall expire at the End of their next Session.

Section 3. | Presidential Duties |

He shall from time to time give to the Congress Information of the State of the Union, and recommend to their Consideration such Measures as he shall judge necessary and expedient; he may, on extraordinary Occasions, convene both Houses, or either of them, and in Case of Disagreement between them, with Respect to the Time of Adjournment, he may adjourn them to such Time as he shall think proper; he shall receive Ambassadors and other public Ministers; he shall take Care that the Laws be faithfully executed, and shall Commission all the Officers of the United States.

Section 4. | Impeachment |

The President, Vice President and all civil Officers of the United States, shall be removed from Office on Impeachment for, and Conviction of, Treason, Bribery, or other high Crimes and Misdemeanors.

Article III   The Judiciary

Section 1.   Federal Courts and Judges

The judicial Power of the United States shall be vested in one supreme Court, and in such inferior Courts as the Congress may from time to time ordain and establish. The Judges, both of the supreme and inferior Courts, shall hold their Offices during good Behavior, and shall, at stated Times, receive for their Services a Compensation, which shall not be diminished during their Continuance in Office.

Section 2.   Authority of the Courts

1. General Authority The judicial Power shall extend to all Cases, in Law and Equity, arising under this Constitution, the Laws of the United States, and Treaties made, or which shall be made, under their Authority;—to all Cases affecting Ambassadors, other public Ministers and Consuls;—to all Cases of admiralty and maritime Jurisdiction;—to Controversies to which the United States shall be a Party;—to Controversies between two or more States —between a State and Citizens of another State; —between Citizens of different States;—between Citizens of the same State claiming Lands under Grants of different States, and between a State, or the Citizens thereof, and foreign States, Citizens or Subjects.

2. Supreme Authority In all Cases affecting Ambassadors, other public Ministers and Consuls, and those in which a State shall be Party, the supreme Court shall have original Jurisdiction. In all the other Cases before mentioned, the supreme Court shall have appellate Jurisdiction, both as to Law and Fact, with such Exceptions, and under such Regulations as the Congress shall make.

Federal Judicial System   QUICK FACTS

Supreme Court
Reviews cases appealed from lower federal courts and highest state courts

Courts of Appeals
Review appeals from district courts

District Courts
Hold trials

> ## Judicial Branch
>
> The Articles of Confederation did not set up a federal court system. One of the first points that the framers of the Constitution agreed upon was to set up a national judiciary. In the Judiciary Act of 1789, Congress provided for the establishment of lower courts, such as district courts, circuit courts of appeals, and various other federal courts. The judicial system provides a check on the legislative branch: it can declare a law unconstitutional.

3. Trial by Jury The Trial of all Crimes, except in Cases of Impeachment, shall be by Jury; and such Trial shall be held in the State where the said Crimes shall have been committed; but when not committed within any State, the Trial shall be at such Place or Places as the Congress may by Law have directed.

Section 3. Treason

1. Definition Treason against the United States, shall consist only in levying War against them, or in adhering to their Enemies, giving them Aid and Comfort. No Person shall be convicted of Treason unless on the Testimony of two Witnesses to the same overt Act, or on Confession in open Court.

2. Punishment The Congress shall have Power to declare the Punishment of Treason, but no Attainder of Treason shall work **Corruption of Blood**,[23] or Forfeiture except during the Life of the Person attainted.

Vocabulary

[23] **Corruption of Blood** punishing the family of a person convicted of treason

The States

States must honor the laws, records, and court decisions of other states. A person cannot escape a legal obligation by moving from one state to another.

EXPLORING THE DOCUMENT The framers wanted to ensure that citizens could determine how state governments would operate. **How does the need to respect the laws of each state support the principle of popular sovereignty?**

Article IV Relations among States

Section 1. State Acts and Records

Full Faith and Credit shall be given in each State to the public Acts, Records, and judicial Proceedings of every other State. And the Congress may by general Laws prescribe the Manner in which such Acts, Records and Proceedings shall be proved, and the Effect thereof.

Section 2. Rights of Citizens

1. Citizenship The Citizens of each State shall be entitled to all Privileges and Immunities of Citizens in the several States.

2. Extradition A Person charged in any State with Treason, Felony, or other Crime, who shall flee from Justice, and be found in another State, shall on Demand of the executive Authority of the State from which he fled, be delivered up, to be removed to the State having Jurisdiction of the Crime.

3. Fugitive Slaves ~~No Person held to Service or Labour in one State, under the Laws thereof, escaping into another, shall, in Consequence of any Law or Regulation therein, be discharged from such Service or Labour, but shall be delivered up on Claim of the Party to whom such Service or Labour may be due.~~

Federalism QUICK FACTS

National

- Declare war
- Maintain armed forces
- Regulate interstate and foreign trade
- Admit new states
- Establish post offices
- Set standard weights and measures
- Coin money
- Establish foreign policy
- Make all laws necessary and proper for carrying out delegated powers

Shared

- Maintain law and order
- Levy taxes
- Borrow money
- Charter banks
- Establish courts
- Provide for public welfare

State

- Establish and maintain schools
- Establish local governments
- Regulate business within the state
- Make marriage laws
- Provide for public safety
- Assume other powers not delegated to the national government nor prohibited to the states

ANALYSIS SKILL — **ANALYZING INFORMATION**

Why does the power to declare war belong only to the national government?

Section 3. New States

1. Admission New States may be admitted by the Congress into this Union; but no new State shall be formed or erected within the Jurisdiction of any other State; nor any State be formed by the Junction of two or more States, or Parts of States, without the Consent of the Legislatures of the States concerned as well as of the Congress.

2. Congressional Authority The Congress shall have Power to dispose of and make all needful Rules and Regulations respecting the Territory or other Property belonging to the United States; and nothing in this Constitution shall be so construed as to Prejudice any Claims of the United States, or of any particular State.

Section 4. Guarantees to the States

The United States shall guarantee to every State in this Union a Republican Form of Government, and shall protect each of them against Invasion; and on Application of the Legislature, or of the Executive (when the Legislature cannot be convened), against domestic Violence.

EXPLORING THE DOCUMENT In a republic, voters elect representatives to act in their best interest. **How does Article IV protect the practice of republicanism in the United States?**

EXPLORING THE DOCUMENT America's founders may not have realized how long the Constitution would last, but they did set up a system for changing or adding to it. They did not want to make it easy to change the Constitution. **By what methods may the Constitution be amended? Under what sorts of circumstances do you think an amendment might be necessary?**

National Supremacy

One of the biggest problems facing the delegates to the Constitutional Convention was the question of what would happen if a state law and a federal law conflicted. Which law would be followed? Who would decide? The second clause of Article VI answers those questions. When a federal law and a state law disagree, the federal law overrides the state law. The Constitution and other federal laws are the "supreme Law of the Land." This clause is often called the supremacy clause.

Article V   Amending the Constitution

The Congress, whenever two thirds of both Houses shall deem it necessary, shall propose Amendments to this Constitution, or, on the Application of the Legislatures of two thirds of the several States, shall call a Convention for proposing Amendments, which, in either Case, shall be valid to all Intents and Purposes, as Part of this Constitution, when ratified by the Legislatures of three fourths of the several States, or by Conventions in three fourths thereof, as the one or the other Mode of Ratification may be proposed by the Congress; Provided that ~~no Amendment which may be made prior to the Year One thousand eight hundred and eight shall in any Manner affect the first and fourth Clauses in the Ninth Section of the first Article; and that no State, without its Consent, shall be deprived of its equal Suffrage in the Senate.~~

Article VI   Supremacy of National Government

All Debts contracted and Engagements entered into, before the Adoption of this Constitution, shall be as valid against the United States under this Constitution, as under the Confederation.

This Constitution, and the Laws of the United States which shall be made in Pursuance thereof; and all Treaties made, or which shall be made, under the Authority of the United States, shall be the supreme Law of the Land; and the Judges in every State shall be bound thereby, any Thing in the Constitution or Laws of any State to the Contrary notwithstanding.

The Senators and Representatives before mentioned, and the Members of the several State Legislatures, and all executive and judicial Officers, both of the United States and of the several States, shall be bound by Oath or Affirmation, to support this Constitution; but no religious Test shall ever be required as a Qualification to any Office or public Trust under the United States.

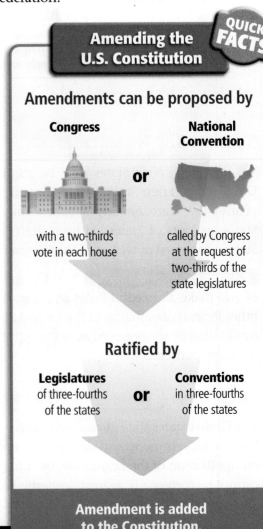

QUICK FACTS

Amending the U.S. Constitution

Amendments can be proposed by

Congress
with a two-thirds vote in each house

or

National Convention
called by Congress at the request of two-thirds of the state legislatures

Ratified by

Legislatures
of three-fourths of the states

or

Conventions
in three-fourths of the states

Amendment is added to the Constitution.

Article VII Ratification

The Ratification of the Conventions of nine States, shall be sufficient for the Establishment of this Constitution between the States so ratifying the Same.

Done in Convention by the Unanimous Consent of the States present the Seventeenth Day of September in the Year of our Lord one thousand seven hundred and Eighty seven and of the Independence of the United States of America the Twelfth In witness whereof We have hereunto subscribed our Names,

George Washington—
President and deputy from Virginia

Delaware

George Read
Gunning Bedford Jr.
John Dickinson
Richard Bassett
Jacob Broom

Maryland

James McHenry
Daniel of
 St. Thomas Jenifer
Daniel Carroll

Virginia

John Blair
James Madison Jr.

North Carolina

William Blount
Richard Dobbs Spaight
Hugh Williamson

South Carolina

John Rutledge
Charles Cotesworth
 Pinckney
Charles Pinckney
Pierce Butler

Georgia

William Few
Abraham Baldwin

New Hampshire

John Langdon
Nicholas Gilman

Massachusetts

Nathaniel Gorham
Rufus King

Connecticut

William Samuel Johnson
Roger Sherman

New York

Alexander Hamilton

New Jersey

William Livingston
David Brearley
William Paterson
Jonathan Dayton

Pennsylvania

Benjamin Franklin
Thomas Mifflin
Robert Morris
George Clymer
Thomas FitzSimons
Jared Ingersoll
James Wilson
Gouverneur Morris

Attest:
William Jackson,
Secretary

Constitutional Amendments

Note: The first 10 amendments to the Constitution were ratified on December 15, 1791, and form what is known as the Bill of Rights.

Amendments 1–10. The Bill of Rights

Amendment I

Congress shall make no law respecting an establishment of religion, or prohibiting the free exercise thereof; or abridging the freedom of speech, or of the press; or the right of the people peaceably to assemble, and to petition the Government for a redress of grievances.

Amendment II

A well regulated Militia, being necessary to the security of a free State, the right of the people to keep and bear Arms, shall not be infringed.

Amendment III

No Soldier shall, in time of peace be **quartered**[24] in any house, without the consent of the Owner, nor in time of war, but in a manner to be prescribed by law.

Amendment IV

The right of the people to be secure in their persons, houses, papers, and effects, against unreasonable searches and seizures, shall not be violated, and no **Warrants**[25] shall issue, but upon probable cause, supported by Oath or affirmation, and particularly describing the place to be searched, and the persons or things to be seized.

Amendment V

No person shall be held to answer for a capital, or otherwise **infamous**[26] crime, unless on a presentment or **indictment**[27] of a Grand Jury, except in

Fundamental Liberties

Freedom of Religion   Freedom of Speech

cases arising in the land or naval forces, or in the Militia, when in actual service in time of War or public danger; nor shall any person be subject for the same offence to be twice put in jeopardy of life or limb; nor shall be compelled in any criminal case to be a witness against himself; nor be deprived of life, liberty, or property, without due process of law; nor shall private property be taken for public use, without just compensation.

Amendment VI

In all criminal prosecutions, the accused shall enjoy the right to a speedy and public trial, by an impartial jury of the State and district wherein the crime shall have been committed, which district shall have been previously **ascertained**[28] by law, and to be informed of the nature and cause of the accusation; to be confronted with the witnesses against him; to have compulsory process for obtaining witnesses in his favor, and to have the Assistance of Counsel for his defence.

Amendment VII

In suits at common law, where the value in controversy shall exceed twenty dollars, the right of trial by jury shall be preserved, and no fact tried by a jury, shall be otherwise reexamined in any Court of the United States, than according to the rules of the common law.

Amendment VIII

Excessive bail shall not be required, nor excessive fines imposed, nor cruel and unusual punishments inflicted.

Amendment IX

The enumeration in the Constitution, of certain rights, shall not be construed to deny or disparage others retained by the people.

Amendment X

The powers not delegated to the United States by the Constitution, nor prohibited by it to the States, are reserved to the States respectively, or to the people.

Trials

The Sixth Amendment makes several guarantees, including a prompt trial and a trial by a jury chosen from the state and district in which the crime was committed.

Vocabulary

[28] **ascertained** found out

EXPLORING THE DOCUMENT The Ninth and Tenth Amendments were added because not every right of the people or of the states could be listed in the Constitution. **How do the Ninth and Tenth Amendments limit the power of the federal government?**

Freedom of the Press

Freedom of Assembly

MR. PRESIDENT HOW LONG MUST WOMEN WAIT FOR LIBERTY

Freedom to Petition the Government

ANALYSIS SKILL ANALYZING INFORMATION

Which amendment guarantees these fundamental freedoms?

Amendments to the U.S. Constitution

The Constitution has been amended only 27 times since it was ratified more than 200 years ago. Amendments help the structure of the government change along with the values of the nation's people. Read the time line below to learn how each amendment changed the government.

1870
Amendment 15
Prohibits national and state governments from denying the vote based on race

1791
Bill of Rights
Amendments 1–10

1865
Amendment 13
Bans slavery

1790   1820   1870

1795
Amendment 11
Protects the states from lawsuits filed by citizens of other states or countries

1804
Amendment 12
Requires separate ballots for the offices of president and vice president

1868
Amendment 14
Defines citizenship and citizens' rights

Amendments 11–27

Amendment XI

Passed by Congress March 4, 1794. Ratified February 7, 1795.

The Judicial power of the United States shall not be **construed**[29] to extend to any suit in law or equity, commenced or prosecuted against one of the United States by Citizens of another State, or by Citizens or Subjects of any Foreign State.

Amendment XII

Passed by Congress December 9, 1803. Ratified June 15, 1804.

The Electors shall meet in their respective states and vote by ballot for President and Vice-President, one of whom, at least, shall not be an inhabitant of the same state with themselves; they shall name in their ballots the person voted for as President, and in distinct ballots the person voted for as Vice-President, and they shall make distinct lists of all persons voted for as President, and of all persons voted for as Vice-President, and of the number of votes for each, which lists they shall sign and certify, and transmit sealed to the seat of the government of the United States, directed to the President of the Senate;—the President of the Senate shall, in the presence of the

Vocabulary

[29] **construed** explained or interpreted

President and Vice President

The Twelfth Amendment changed the election procedure for president and vice president.

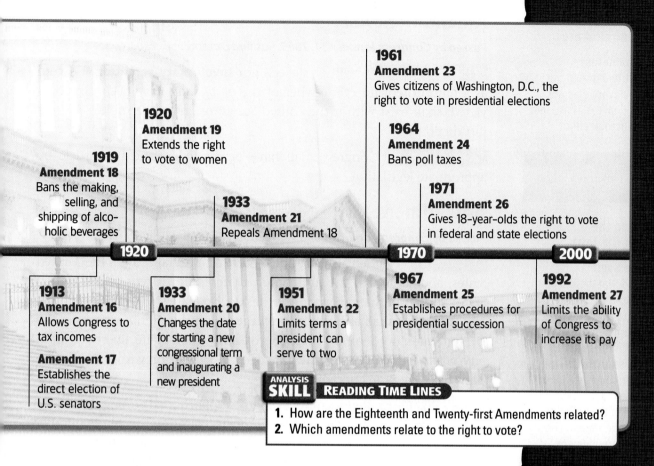

1961
Amendment 23
Gives citizens of Washington, D.C., the right to vote in presidential elections

1920
Amendment 19
Extends the right to vote to women

1964
Amendment 24
Bans poll taxes

1919
Amendment 18
Bans the making, selling, and shipping of alcoholic beverages

1933
Amendment 21
Repeals Amendment 18

1971
Amendment 26
Gives 18-year-olds the right to vote in federal and state elections

1920

1970

2000

1913
Amendment 16
Allows Congress to tax incomes

Amendment 17
Establishes the direct election of U.S. senators

1933
Amendment 20
Changes the date for starting a new congressional term and inaugurating a new president

1951
Amendment 22
Limits terms a president can serve to two

1967
Amendment 25
Establishes procedures for presidential succession

1992
Amendment 27
Limits the ability of Congress to increase its pay

ANALYSIS SKILL | **READING TIME LINES**

1. How are the Eighteenth and Twenty-first Amendments related?
2. Which amendments relate to the right to vote?

Senate and House of Representatives, open all the certificates and the votes shall then be counted;—The person having the greatest number of votes for President, shall be the President, if such number be a majority of the whole number of Electors appointed; and if no person have such majority, then from the persons having the highest numbers not exceeding three on the list of those voted for as President, the House of Representatives shall choose immediately, by ballot, the President. But in choosing the President, the votes shall be taken by states, the representation from each state having one vote; a quorum for this purpose shall consist of a member or members from two-thirds of the states, and a majority of all the states shall be necessary to a choice. ~~And if the House of Representatives shall not choose a President whenever the right of choice shall devolve upon them, before the fourth day of March next following, then the Vice-President shall act as President, as in case of the death or other constitutional disability of the President.~~—The person having the greatest number of votes as Vice-President, shall be the Vice-President, if such number be a majority of the whole number of Electors appointed, and if no person have a majority, then from the two highest numbers on the list, the Senate shall choose the Vice-President; a quorum for the purpose shall consist of two-thirds of the whole number of Senators, and a majority of the whole number shall be necessary to a choice. But no person constitutionally ineligible to the office of President shall be eligible to that of Vice-President of the United States.

Amendment XIII

Passed by Congress January 31, 1865. Ratified December 6, 1865.

1. Slavery Banned Neither slavery nor **involuntary servitude**,[30] except as a punishment for crime whereof the party shall have been duly convicted, shall exist within the United States, or any place subject to their jurisdiction.

2. Enforcement Congress shall have power to enforce this article by appropriate legislation.

Amendment XIV

Passed by Congress June 13, 1866. Ratified July 9, 1868.

1. Citizenship Defined All persons born or naturalized in the United States, and subject to the jurisdiction thereof, are citizens of the United States and of the State wherein they reside. No State shall make or enforce any law which shall abridge the privileges or immunities of citizens of the United States; nor shall any State deprive any person of life, liberty, or property, without due process of law; nor deny to any person within its jurisdiction the equal protection of the laws.

2. Voting Rights Representatives shall be apportioned among the several States according to their respective numbers, counting the whole number of persons in each State, ~~excluding Indians not taxed~~. But when the right to vote at any election for the choice of electors for President and Vice-President of the United States, Representatives in Congress, the Executive and Judicial officers of a State, or the members of the Legislature thereof, is denied to any of the ~~male~~ inhabitants of such State, ~~being twenty-one years of age~~, and citizens of the United States, or in any way abridged, except for participation in rebellion, or other crime, the basis of representation therein shall be reduced in the proportion which the number of such ~~male~~ citizens shall bear to the whole number of ~~male~~ citizens ~~twenty-one years of age~~ in such State.

3. Rebels Banned from Government No person shall be a Senator or Representative in Congress, or elector of President and Vice-President, or hold any office, civil or military, under the United States, or under any State, who, having previously taken an oath, as a member of Congress, or as an officer of the United States, or as a member of any State legislature, or as an executive or judicial officer of any State, to support the Constitution of the United States, shall have engaged in insurrection or rebellion against the same, or given aid or comfort to the enemies thereof. But Congress may by a vote of two-thirds of each House, remove such disability.

4. Payment of Debts The validity of the public debt of the United States, authorized by law, including debts incurred for payment of pensions and

The Reconstruction Amendments

The Thirteenth, Fourteenth, and Fifteenth Amendments are often called the Reconstruction Amendments. This is because they arose during Reconstruction, the period of American history following the Civil War. The country was reconstructing itself after that terrible conflict. A key aspect of Reconstruction was extending the rights of citizenship to former slaves.

The Thirteenth Amendment banned slavery. The Fourteenth Amendment required states to respect the freedoms listed in the Bill of Rights, thus preventing states from denying rights to African Americans. The Fifteenth Amendment gave African American men the right to vote.

African Americans participate in an election.

ANALYSIS SKILL **ANALYZING INFORMATION**

Why was the Thirteenth Amendment needed?

bounties for services in suppressing insurrection or rebellion, shall not be questioned. But neither the United States nor any State shall assume or pay any debt or obligation incurred in aid of insurrection or rebellion against the United States, ~~or any claim for the loss or emancipation of any slave;~~ but all such debts, obligations and claims shall be held illegal and void.

5. Enforcement The Congress shall have the power to enforce, by appropriate legislation, the provisions of this article.

Amendment XV

Passed by Congress February 26, 1869. Ratified February 3, 1870.

1. Voting Rights The right of citizens of the United States to vote shall not be denied or abridged by the United States or by any State on account of race, color, or previous condition of servitude.

2. Enforcement The Congress shall have the power to enforce this article by appropriate legislation.

Amendment XVI

Passed by Congress July 2, 1909. Ratified February 3, 1913.

The Congress shall have power to lay and collect taxes on incomes, from whatever source derived, without apportionment among the several States, and without regard to any census or enumeration.

Amendment XVII

Passed by Congress May 13, 1912. Ratified April 8, 1913.

1. Senators Elected by Citizens The Senate of the United States shall be composed of two Senators from each State, elected by the people thereof, for six years; and each Senator shall have one vote. The electors in each State shall have the qualifications requisite for electors of the most numerous branch of the State legislatures.

2. Vacancies When vacancies happen in the representation of any State in the Senate, the executive authority of such State shall issue writs of election to fill such vacancies: *Provided*, That the legislature of any State may empower the executive thereof to make temporary appointments until the people fill the vacancies by election as the legislature may direct.

3. Future Elections This amendment shall not be so construed as to affect the election or term of any Senator chosen before it becomes valid as part of the Constitution.

Amendment XVIII

Passed by Congress December 18, 1917. Ratified January 16, 1919. Repealed by Amendment XXI.

1. Liquor Banned After one year from the ratification of this article the manufacture, sale, or transportation of intoxicating liquors within, the importation thereof into, or the exportation thereof from the United States and all territory subject to the jurisdiction thereof for beverage purposes is hereby prohibited.

2. Enforcement The Congress and the several States shall have concurrent power to enforce this article by appropriate legislation.

3. Ratification This article shall be inoperative unless it shall have been ratified as an amendment to the Constitution by the legislatures of the several States, as provided in the Constitution, within seven years from the date of the submission hereof to the States by the Congress.

EXPLORING THE DOCUMENT The Seventeenth Amendment requires that senators be elected directly by the people instead of by the state legislatures. **What principle of our government does the Seventeenth Amendment protect?**

Prohibition

Although many people believed that the Eighteenth Amendment was good for the health and welfare of the American people, it was repealed 14 years later.

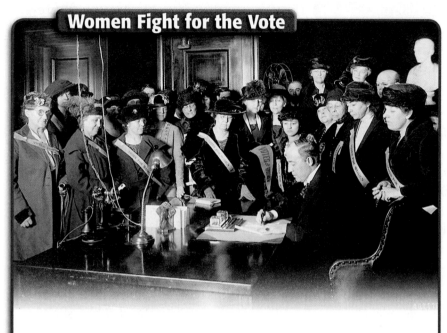

Women Fight for the Vote

To become part of the Constitution, a proposed amendment must be ratified by three-fourths of the states. Here, suffragists witness Kentucky governor Edwin P. Morrow signing the Nineteenth Amendment in January 1920. By June of that year, enough states had ratified the amendment to make it part of the Constitution. American women, after generations of struggle, had finally won the right to vote.

ANALYSIS SKILL **ANALYZING INFORMATION**

What right did the Nineteenth Amendment grant?

Amendment XIX

Passed by Congress June 4, 1919. Ratified August 18, 1920.

1. Voting Rights The right of citizens of the United States to vote shall not be denied or abridged by the United States or by any State on account of sex.

2. Enforcement Congress shall have power to enforce this article by appropriate legislation.

Amendment XX

Passed by Congress March 2, 1932. Ratified January 23, 1933.

1. Presidential Terms The terms of the President and the Vice President shall end at noon on the 20th day of January, and the terms of Senators and Representatives at noon on the 3d day of January, of the years in which such terms would have ended if this article had not been ratified; and the terms of their successors shall then begin.

> **Women's Suffrage**
>
> Abigail Adams and others were disappointed that the Declaration of Independence and the Constitution did not specifically include women. It took many years and much campaigning before suffrage for women was finally achieved.

2. Meeting of Congress The Congress shall assemble at least once in every year, and such meeting shall begin at noon on the 3d day of January, unless they shall by law appoint a different day.

3. Succession of Vice President If, at the time fixed for the beginning of the term of the President, the President elect shall have died, the Vice President elect shall become President. If a President shall not have been chosen before the time fixed for the beginning of his term, or if the President elect shall have failed to qualify, then the Vice President elect shall act as President until a President shall have qualified; and the Congress may by law provide for the case wherein neither a President elect nor a Vice President shall have qualified, declaring who shall then act as President, or the manner in which one who is to act shall be selected, and such person shall act accordingly until a President or Vice President shall have qualified.

4. Succession by Vote of Congress The Congress may by law provide for the case of the death of any of the persons from whom the House of Representatives may choose a President whenever the right of choice shall have devolved upon them, and for the case of the death of any of the persons from whom the Senate may choose a Vice President whenever the right of choice shall have devolved upon them.

5. Ratification Sections 1 and 2 shall take effect on the 15th day of October following the ratification of this article.

6. Ratification This article shall be inoperative unless it shall have been ratified as an amendment to the Constitution by the legislatures of three-fourths of the several States within seven years from the date of its submission.

Amendment XXI

Passed by Congress February 20, 1933. Ratified December 5, 1933.

1. 18th Amendment Repealed The eighteenth article of amendment to the Constitution of the United States is hereby repealed.

2. Liquor Allowed by Law The transportation or importation into any State, Territory, or Possession of the United States for delivery or use therein of intoxicating liquors, in violation of the laws thereof, is hereby prohibited.

3. Ratification This article shall be inoperative unless it shall have been ratified as an amendment to the Constitution by conventions in the several States, as provided in the Constitution, within seven years from the date of the submission hereof to the States by the Congress.

Amendment XXII

Passed by Congress March 21, 1947. Ratified February 27, 1951.

1. Term Limits No person shall be elected to the office of the President more than twice, and no person who has held the office of President, or acted as President, for more than two years of a term to which some other person was elected President shall be elected to the office of President more than once. ~~But this Article shall not apply to any person holding the office of President when this Article was proposed by Congress, and shall not prevent any person who may be holding the office of President, or acting as President, during the term within which this Article becomes operative from holding the office of President or acting as President during the remainder of such term.~~

2. Ratification ~~This article shall be inoperative unless it shall have been ratified as an amendment to the Constitution by the legislatures of three-fourths of the several States within seven years from the date of its submission to the States by the Congress.~~

After Franklin D. Roosevelt was elected to four consecutive terms, limits were placed on the number of terms a president could serve.

EXPLORING THE DOCUMENT From the time of President George Washington's administration, it was a custom for presidents to serve no more than two terms in office. Franklin D. Roosevelt, however, was elected to four terms. The Twenty-second Amendment restricted presidents to no more than two terms in office. **Why do you think citizens chose to limit the power of the president in this way?**

Amendment XXIII

Passed by Congress June 16, 1960. Ratified March 29, 1961.

1. District of Columbia Represented The District constituting the seat of Government of the United States shall appoint in such manner as Congress may direct:

A number of electors of President and Vice President equal to the whole number of Senators and Representatives in Congress to which the District would be entitled if it were a State, but in no event more than the least populous State; they shall be in addition to those appointed by the States, but they shall be considered, for the purposes of the election of President and Vice President, to be electors appointed by a State; and they shall meet in the District and perform such duties as provided by the twelfth article of amendment.

2. Enforcement The Congress shall have power to enforce this article by appropriate legislation.

Voting Rights

Until the ratification of the Twenty-third Amendment, the people of Washington, D.C., could not vote in presidential elections.

Poll Tax Amendment

Poll taxes were used to deny many poor Americans, including African Americans and Hispanic Americans, their right to vote. These taxes were made unconstitutional by the Twenty-fourth Amendment.

The American GI Forum **Says:** BUY YOUR **POLL TAX**

1939 **Poll Tax Receipt**

ANALYSIS SKILL **ANALYZING INFORMATION**

How did poll taxes deny poor Americans the opportunity to vote?

Presidential Disability

The illness of President Eisenhower in the 1950s and the assassination of President Kennedy in 1963 were the events behind the Twenty-fifth Amendment. The Constitution did not provide a clear-cut method for a vice president to take over for a disabled president or upon the death of a president. This amendment provides for filling the office of the vice president if a vacancy occurs, and it provides a way for the vice president—or someone else in the line of succession—to take over if the president is unable to perform the duties of that office.

Amendment XXIV

Passed by Congress August 27, 1962. Ratified January 23, 1964.

1. Voting Rights The right of citizens of the United States to vote in any primary or other election for President or Vice President, for electors for President or Vice President, or for Senator or Representative in Congress, shall not be denied or abridged by the United States or any State by reason of failure to pay poll tax or other tax.

2. Enforcement The Congress shall have power to enforce this article by appropriate legislation.

Amendment XXV

Passed by Congress July 6, 1965. Ratified February 10, 1967.

1. Sucession of Vice President In case of the removal of the President from office or of his death or resignation, the Vice President shall become President.

2. Vacancy of Vice President Whenever there is a vacancy in the office of the Vice President, the President shall nominate a Vice President who shall take office upon confirmation by a majority vote of both Houses of Congress.

3. Written Declaration Whenever the President transmits to the President pro tempore of the Senate and the Speaker of the House of Representatives his written declaration that he is unable to discharge the powers and duties of his office, and until he transmits to them a written declaration to the contrary, such powers and duties shall be discharged by the Vice President as Acting President.

4. Removing the President Whenever the Vice President and a majority of either the principal officers of the executive departments or of such other body as Congress may by law provide, transmit to the President pro tempore of the Senate and the Speaker of the House of Representatives their written declaration that the President is unable to discharge the powers and duties of his office, the Vice President shall immediately assume the powers and duties of the office as Acting President.

Thereafter, when the President transmits to the President pro tempore of the Senate and the Speaker of the House of Representatives his written declaration that no inability exists, he shall resume the powers and duties of his office unless the Vice President and a majority of either the principal officers of the executive department or of such other body as Congress may by law provide, transmit within four days to the President pro tempore of the Senate and the Speaker of the House of Representatives their written declaration that the President is unable to discharge the powers and duties of his office. Thereupon Congress shall decide the issue, assembling within forty-eight hours for that purpose if not in session. If the Congress, within twenty-one days after receipt of the latter written declaration, or, if Congress is not in session, within twenty-one days after Congress is required to assemble, determines by two-thirds vote of both Houses that the President is unable to discharge the powers and duties of his office, the Vice President shall continue to discharge the same as Acting President; otherwise, the President shall resume the powers and duties of his office.

Amendment XXVI

Passed by Congress March 23, 1971. Ratified July 1, 1971.

1. Voting Rights The right of citizens of the United States, who are eighteen years of age or older, to vote shall not be denied or abridged by the United States or by any State on account of age.

2. Enforcement The Congress shall have power to enforce this article by appropriate legislation.

Amendment XXVII

Originally proposed September 25, 1789. Ratified May 7, 1992.

No law, varying the compensation for the services of the Senators and Representatives, shall take effect, until an election of representatives shall have intervened.

Expanded Suffrage

The Voting Rights Act of 1970 tried to set the voting age at 18. However, the Supreme Court ruled that the act set the voting age for national elections only, not for state or local elections. The Twenty-sixth Amendment gave 18-year-old citizens the right to vote in all elections.

The Bill of Rights

Main Ideas

1. The First Amendment guarantees basic freedoms to individuals.
2. Other amendments focus on protecting citizens from certain abuses.
3. The rights of the accused are an important part of the Bill of Rights.
4. The rights of states and citizens are protected by the Bill of Rights.

The Big Idea

The Bill of Rights was added to the Constitution to define clearly the rights and freedoms of citizens.

Key Terms and People

James Madison, *p. 216*
majority rule, *p. 216*
petition, *p. 217*
search warrant, *p. 218*
due process, *p. 218*
indict, *p. 218*
double jeopardy, *p. 218*
eminent domain, *p. 218*

TAKING NOTES As you read, take notes on the freedoms protected by the Bill of Rights and which amendment protects each. The first right has been filled in for you as an example.

Rights/Freedoms	Amendment
1. Freedom of religion	

 8.2.1, 8.2.2, 8.2.6, 8.2.10

If YOU were there...

Your father runs a bookshop in colonial Boston in 1770. Your family lives in a very small brick house. You and your sisters must share one small room. One day, a red-coated British officer knocks on your door and strides into the parlor. He says that your family will have to provide a room and meals for two British soldiers. "We're already crowded!" you protest, but he insists.

Would you support the British government's requirement that colonists provide food and shelter for troops? Why?

BUILDING BACKGROUND People in the American colonies resented the British soldiers stationed in their towns. They objected to sudden searches and to soldiers being housed in private homes. They disliked censorship of their newspapers. When the Constitution was written, Americans remembered those wrongs. They insisted on adding a bill of rights to the document.

First Amendment

Federalist **James Madison** promised that a bill of rights would be added to the Constitution. This promise allowed the Constitution to pass. In 1789 Madison began writing down a huge list of proposed amendments. He then presented a shorter list to the House of Representatives. Of those, the House approved 12. The states ratified 10, which took effect December 15, 1791. Those 10 amendments, called the Bill of Rights, protect U.S. citizens' individual liberties.

The protection of individual liberties is important in a representative democracy. Without safeguards, people's rights would not always be protected because of **majority rule**. This is the idea that the greatest number of people in society can make policies for everyone. While this means that most people agree on what the law should be, it also means that smaller groups, or minorities, might lose their rights. The Bill of Rights ensures that the rights of all citizens are protected.

The ideas spelled out in the First Amendment form the most basic rights of all U.S. citizens. These rights include freedom of religion, freedom of the press, freedom of speech, freedom of assembly, and the right to petition.

In the spirit of Thomas Jefferson's Virginia Statute for Religious Freedom, the First Amendment begins, "Congress shall make no law respecting an establishment of religion, or prohibiting the free exercise thereof." In other words, the government cannot support or interfere with the practice of a religion. This amendment keeps the government from favoring one religion over any other or establishing an official religion.

The First Amendment also guarantees freedom of speech and of the press. This means that Americans have the right to express their own ideas and views. They also have the right to hear the ideas and views of others. Former senator Margaret Chase Smith discussed why these freedoms are important. "The key to security," she once said, "is public information."

Freedom of speech does not mean that people can say anything they want to, however. The Constitution does not protect slander—false statements meant to damage someone's reputation. Libel, or intentionally writing a lie that harms another person, is not protected, either. The Supreme Court has also ruled that speech that endangers public safety is not protected. For example, Justice Oliver Wendell Holmes declared in 1919 that falsely shouting "Fire" in a crowded theater is not protected as free speech.

Americans also have freedom of assembly, or of holding meetings. Any group may gather to discuss issues or conduct business. If people gather peacefully and do not engage in illegal activities, the government cannot interfere. The right to **petition**, or make a request of the government, is another right of the American people. Any American can present a petition to a government official. This right lets Americans show dissatisfaction with a law. They can also suggest new laws.

THE IMPACT TODAY

Free-speech protection has also been applied to "symbolic" speech—or nonverbal communication that expresses an idea, such as wearing a protest button.

READING CHECK **Summarizing** What rights does the First Amendment guarantee to Americans?

Amendment I

Congress shall make no law respecting an establishment of religion, or prohibiting the free exercise thereof; or abridging the freedom of speech, or of the press; or the right of the people peaceably to assemble, and to petition the Government for a redress of grievances.

Workers use the right of assembly to protest a proposed budget in New York City.

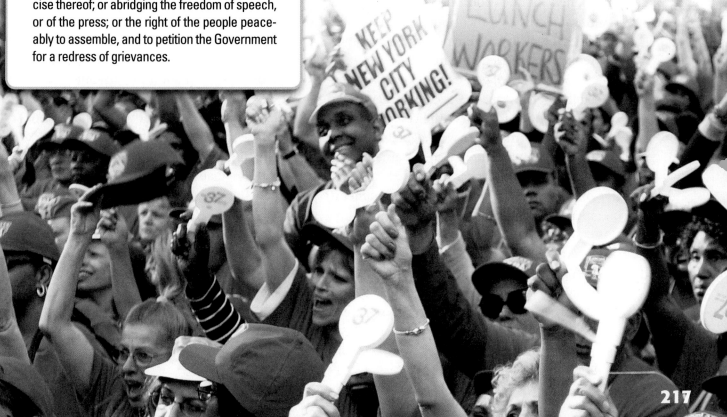

Amendment II

A well regulated Militia, being necessary to the security of a free State, the right of the people to keep and bear Arms, shall not be infringed.

Amendment III

No Soldier shall, in time of peace be quartered in any house, without the consent of the Owner, nor in time of war, but in a manner to be prescribed by law.

Amendment IV

The right of the people to be secure in their persons, houses, papers, and effects, against unreasonable searches and seizures, shall not be violated, and no Warrants shall issue, but upon probable cause, supported by Oath or affirmation, and particularly describing the place to be searched, and the persons or things to be seized.

Protecting Citizens

The Second, Third, and Fourth Amendments relate to colonial disputes with Britain and reflect many of the ideals outlined in the Declaration of Independence. The Second Amendment deals with state militias and the right to bear arms. Colonial militias played a big role in the Revolutionary War. The framers of the Constitution thought that the states needed their militias for emergencies. Today the National Guard has largely replaced organized state militias.

Supporters of gun-control laws have generally argued that the Second Amendment was intended to protect the collective right of states to maintain well-regulated militia units. Opponents hold that the amendment was meant to protect an individual's right of self-defense. The meaning of the amendment continues to be debated.

The Third Amendment prevents the military from forcing citizens to house soldiers. Before the Revolution, the British pressured colonists to shelter and feed British soldiers. British leaders also forced colonists to submit to having their property searched for illegal goods. Anger over such actions led to the

Fourth Amendment rule against "unreasonable searches and seizures." Before a citizen's property can be searched, authorities must now get a **search warrant**. This order gives authorities permission to search someone's property. A judge issues this order only when it seems likely that a search might uncover evidence relating to a crime. In emergencies, however, police can make an emergency search. This may preserve evidence needed to prove possible illegal activity.

READING CHECK Finding Main Ideas
Why were the Third and Fourth Amendments matters of great importance to Americans when the Bill of Rights was written?

Rights of the Accused

The Fifth, Sixth, Seventh, and Eighth Amendments provide guidelines for protecting the rights of the accused. According to the Fifth Amendment, the government cannot punish anyone without **due process** of law. This means that the law must be fairly applied. A grand jury decides if there is enough evidence to **indict** (en-DYT), or formally accuse, a person. Without an indictment, the court cannot try anyone for a serious crime. The Fifth Amendment also protects people from having to testify at their own criminal trial. To keep from testifying, a person need only "take the Fifth." In addition, anyone found not guilty in a criminal trial cannot face **double jeopardy**. In other words, he or she cannot be tried again for the same crime.

The final clause of the Fifth Amendment states that no one can have property taken without due process of law. There is one exception: the government's power of **eminent domain**. This is the power to take personal property to benefit the public. One example would be taking private land to build a public road. However, the government must pay the owners a fair price for the property. If the property was gained illegally, then the owners are not paid.

The Sixth Amendment protects the rights of a person who has been indicted. It guarantees that person a speedy public trial. Public trials ensure that laws are being followed by allowing the public to witness the proceedings. Accused people have the right to know the charges against them and can hear and question witnesses testifying against them. Accused people have the right to an attorney. If they cannot pay for legal service, the government must provide it. Sometimes accused persons refuse their Sixth Amendment rights. For example, some defendants refuse the services of an attorney, while others choose to have a trial in front of a judge alone instead of before a jury. In many cases, defendants can forgo trial and agree to a plea bargain. This means that a defendant pleads guilty to a lesser charge and avoids risking conviction for a crime with a greater sentence.

The Seventh Amendment states that juries can decide civil cases. It is possible to harm another person without committing a crime. In such cases, the injured party may sue, or seek justice, in a civil court. Civil cases usually involve disputes over money or property. For example, someone might bring a civil suit against a person who refuses to repay a debt.

Amendment V

No person shall be held to answer for a capital, or otherwise infamous crime, unless on a presentment or indictment of a Grand Jury, except in cases arising in the land or naval forces, or in the Militia, when in actual service in time of War or public danger; nor shall any person be subject for the same offence to be twice put in jeopardy of life or limb; nor shall be compelled in any criminal case to be a witness against himself, nor be deprived of life, liberty, or property, without due process of law; nor shall private property be taken for public use, without just compensation.

Amendment VI

In all criminal prosecutions, the accused shall enjoy the right to a speedy and public trial, by an impartial jury of the State and district wherein the crime shall have been committed, which district shall have been previously ascertained by law, and to be informed of the nature and cause of the accusation; to be confronted with the witnesses against him; to have compulsory process for obtaining witnesses in his favor, and to have the Assistance of Counsel for his defence.

Amendment VII

In suits at common law, where the value in controversy shall exceed twenty dollars, the right of trial by jury shall be preserved, and no fact tried by a jury, shall be otherwise reexamined in any Court of the United States, than according to the rules of the common law.

A judge and jury listen to a witness in a courtroom in Orange County, California.

A Right to Bail

The Eighth Amendment allows for bail. Bail is a set amount of money that defendants promise to pay the court if they fail to appear in court at the proper time.

By posting, or paying, bail, a defendant can avoid staying in jail before and during a trial. If a defendant does not show up in court for trial, the court demands the bail money be paid and issues a warrant for arrest.

The Eighth Amendment keeps courts from setting unfairly high bail. However, in cases of very serious crimes, a judge may refuse to set bail altogether. This can be the case, for example, if the court regards a defendant as being potentially dangerous to the public by being left free. A judge can also deny bail if he or she thinks the defendant will not show up for trial. In such cases the defendant must remain in jail through the trial.

> **Amendment VIII**
> Excessive bail shall not be required, nor excessive fines imposed, nor cruel and unusual punishments inflicted.

FOCUS ON INDIANA
Indiana is one of 36 states that allow the death penalty.

"Cruel and Unusual Punishments"

The Eighth Amendment also bans "cruel and unusual punishments" against a person convicted of a crime. For many years, Americans have debated the question of what exactly constitutes cruel and unusual punishment. The debate has often centered on the issue of capital punishment. In 1972 the Supreme Court ruled that the way in which most states carried out the death penalty was cruel and unusual. The Court also found that the ways in which many states sentenced people to death were unfair. However, a few years later, the Court ruled that not all executions were in themselves cruel and unusual.

Most states still allow the death penalty. Those that do must follow the Supreme Court's rules. To do so, many states have changed the ways in which they carry out the death penalty.

READING CHECK **Summarizing** What is the purpose of the Eighth Amendment?

Rights of States and Citizens

The final two amendments in the Bill of Rights give a general protection for other rights not addressed by the first eight amendments. These amendments also reserve some governmental powers for the states and the people.

Ninth Amendment

The Ninth Amendment says that the rights listed in the Constitution are not the only rights that citizens have. This amendment has allowed the courts and Congress to decide other basic rights of citizens.

The Constitution does not address the question of education. However, most Americans believe that it is a basic and essential right. This seems especially true in view of the fact that American citizens must be able to vote for the people who represent them in government. "Education is not just another

> **Amendment IX**
> The enumeration in the Constitution, of certain rights, shall not be construed to deny or disparage others retained by the people.
>
> **Amendment X**
> The powers not delegated to the United States by the Constitution, nor prohibited by it to the States, are reserved to the States respectively, or to the people.

consumer item. It is the bedrock [foundation] of our democracy," explained educational leader Mary Hatwood Futrell. Today state governments offer free education from elementary to high school—to all citizens.

Tenth Amendment

The Tenth Amendment recognizes that the states and the people have additional powers. These powers are any ones that the Constitution does not specifically give to Congress—the delegated powers. The Tenth Amendment makes it clear that any powers not either delegated to the federal government or prohibited to the states belong to the states and the people. Thus, the last amendment in the Bill of Rights protects citizens' rights and helps keep the balance of power between the federal and state governments.

READING CHECK **Summarizing** How does the Tenth Amendment protect the rights of citizens?

SUMMARY AND PREVIEW In this section you learned about the Bill of Rights. In the next section you will learn about the responsibilities of citizenship.

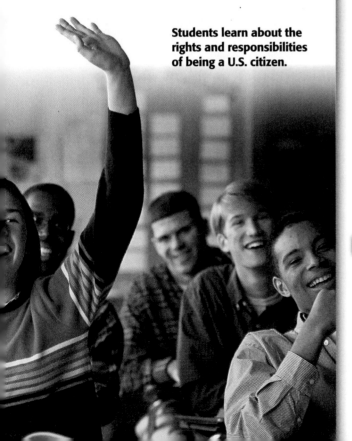

Students learn about the rights and responsibilities of being a U.S. citizen.

Section 2 Assessment

Reviewing Ideas, Terms, and People

1. **a. Identify** What basic rights are protected by the First Amendment?
   b. Explain What does the right to **petition** the government mean?
   c. Elaborate Why is freedom of the press an important right?
2. **a. Describe** How are citizens protected under the Third and Fourth Amendments?
   b. Draw Conclusions In what ways did British actions before the Revolution lead to the Second, Third, and Fourth Amendments?
3. **a. Identify** What protections does the Eighth Amendment provide for people accused of crimes?
   b. Elaborate Why is it important that the Bill of Rights protects people accused of crimes?
4. **a. Recall** What is the purpose of the final two amendments in the Bill of Rights?
   b. Analyze How does the Tenth Amendment balance power between national and state governments?

Critical Thinking

5. **Summarizing** Copy the chart below. Use it to summarize the rights guaranteed to citizens by each amendment in the Bill of Rights.

Amendment	Rights
1	
2	
3	
4	
5	
6	
7	
8	
9	
10	

FOCUS ON WRITING

6. **Gathering Information about the Bill of Rights** What freedoms are guaranteed by the Bill of Rights? Make a list of the most important freedoms. You'll list those freedoms on the third page of your pamphlet.

What You Will Learn...

Main Ideas

1. Citizenship in the United States is determined in several ways.
2. Citizens are expected to fulfill a number of important duties.
3. Active citizen involvement in government and the community is encouraged.

The Big Idea

American citizenship involves great privileges and serious responsibilities.

Key Terms

naturalized citizens, *p. 222*
deport, *p. 222*
draft, *p. 223*
political action committees, *p. 224*
interest groups, *p. 224*

 TAKING NOTES As you read, look for information on three ways a person can become a U.S. citizen. Take notes in a graphic organizer like the one below.

U.S. Citizenship

 8.1.28, 8.1.29, 8.1.30, 8.2.1, 8.2.2, 8.2.3, 8.2.6, 8.2.7, 8.2.8, 8.2.9

Rights and Responsibilities of Citizenship

If YOU were there...

Your older brother and his friends have just turned 18. That means they must register with selective service. But it also means that they are old enough to vote in national elections. You are interested in the upcoming elections and think it would be exciting to have a real voice in politics. But your brother and his friends don't even plan to register to vote.

How would you persuade your brother that voting is important?

BUILDING BACKGROUND Whether you are born an American citizen or become one later, citizenship brings many rights and privileges. But it also brings duties and responsibilities. Voting is both a right and a responsibility.

Gaining U.S. Citizenship

People become U.S. citizens in several ways. First, anyone born in the United States or a territory it controls is a citizen. People born in a foreign country are U.S. citizens if at least one parent is a U.S. citizen. Foreign-born people whose parents are not citizens must move to the United States to become **naturalized citizens**. Once in the United States, they go through a long process before applying for citizenship. If they succeed, they become naturalized citizens, giving them most of the rights and responsibilities of other citizens.

In the United States, legal immigrants have many of the rights and responsibilities of citizens but cannot vote or hold public office. The U.S. government can **deport**, or return to the country of origin, immigrants who break the law.

Legal immigrants over age 18 may request naturalization after living in the United States for five years. All legal immigrants have to support themselves financially. If not, someone must assume financial responsibility for them. Immigrants must be law-abiding and support the U.S. Constitution. They must demonstrate understanding of written and spoken English. They also must show basic knowledge of U.S. history and government.

When this is done, candidates go before a naturalization court and take an oath of allegiance to the United States. They then get certificates of naturalization.

Only two differences between naturalized and native-born citizens exist. Naturalized citizens can lose their citizenship, and they cannot become president or vice president. Many famous Americans have been naturalized citizens, including German Jewish scientist Albert Einstein and former secretary of state Madeleine Albright, originally from Czechoslovakia.

READING CHECK ▶ **Drawing Conclusions**
Why does U.S. law have such demanding requirements for people to become naturalized citizens?

Duties of Citizenship

For a representative democracy to work, Americans need to fulfill their civic duties. "The stakes … are too high for government to be a spectator sport," former Texas congresswoman Barbara Jordan once said.

Citizens elect officials to make laws for them. In turn, citizens must obey those laws and respect the authorities who enforce them. Obeying laws includes knowing what they are and staying informed about any changes to the law. Ignorance of a law will not prevent a person from being punished for breaking it.

Another duty is paying taxes for services such as public roads, police, and public schools. People pay sales taxes, property taxes, and tariffs. Many Americans also pay a tax on their income to the federal, and sometimes state, government.

Citizens have the duty to defend the nation. Men 18 years or older must register with selective service. In the event of a

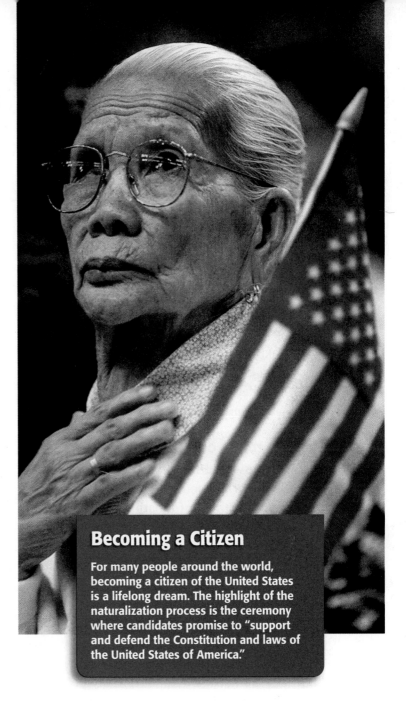

Becoming a Citizen

For many people around the world, becoming a citizen of the United States is a lifelong dream. The highlight of the naturalization process is the ceremony where candidates promise to "support and defend the Constitution and laws of the United States of America."

draft, or required military service, those able to fight are already registered. Although women do not register, many serve in the armed forces.

Americans have the right to a trial by jury under the Sixth Amendment. To protect this right, citizens should be willing to serve on a jury when they are called. Otherwise, fulfilling each person's Sixth Amendment rights would be difficult.

READING CHECK ▶ **Making Inferences** Why does citizenship carry with it certain responsibilities?

For representative democracy to work, citizens must do their part. Each activity pictured here serves an important role in the community.

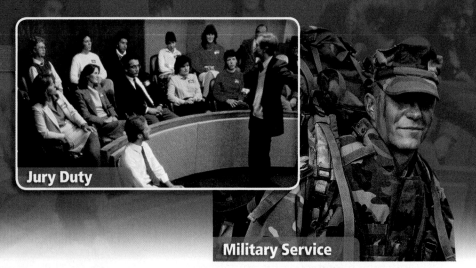

Jury Duty

Military Service

Citizens and Government

Taking part in the elections process by voting may be a citizen's most vital duty. Through free elections, U.S. citizens choose who will lead their government.

Function of Elections

FOCUS ON INDIANA
Citizens also take part in elections by working at voting stations.

It is essential for citizens to learn as much as they can about the issues and candidates before voting. Information is available from many sources: the Internet, newspapers, television, and other media. However, voters should also be aware that some material may be propaganda or material that is biased deliberately to help or harm a cause.

In addition to voting, many Americans choose to campaign for candidates or issues. Anyone can help campaign, even if he or she is not eligible to vote. Many people also help campaigns by giving money directly or through **political action committees** (PACs), groups that collect money for candidates who support certain issues.

Influencing Government

ACADEMIC VOCABULARY
influence
change or have an effect on

Even after an election, people can **influence** officials. Political participation is part of our nation's identity and tradition. When colonists protested British rule in the 1700s, they formed committees and presented their views to political leaders.

As the new American nation grew, so did political participation. French diplomat

Alexis de Tocqueville visited the United States in 1831 to study American democracy. He was amazed at the large number of political groups Americans participated in. He wrote about them:

*"*What political power could ever carry on the vast multitude [large number] of lesser undertakings which the American citizens perform every day, with the assistance of the principle of association [joining a group]? Nothing, in my opinion, is more deserving of our attention than the intellectual and moral associations of America.*"*
—Alexis de Tocqueville, *Democracy in America*

U.S. citizens sometimes work with **interest groups**. These groups of people share a common interest that motivates them to take political action. Interest groups organize speeches and rallies to support their cause. However, citizens need not join a group to influence government. They can write letters to leaders of government or attend city council meetings. Active political participation is an important duty for U.S. citizens and immigrants alike.

Helping the Community

Commitment to others moves many Americans to volunteer in community service groups. Some small communities rely on volunteers for services such as fire protection and law enforcement.

Volunteer groups also help government-sponsored agencies. For example, Citizens on

Community Service

Voting

Obey the Law

Patrol and Neighborhood Watch groups ask volunteers to walk their neighborhoods and tell police if they observe possible criminal activity in the area. The American Red Cross helps citizens in times of natural disasters or other emergencies. The Boy Scouts and Girl Scouts plan many projects such as planting trees to improve the environment. Even simple acts such as picking up trash in parks or serving food in shelters help a community.

READING CHECK **Summarizing** In what ways do volunteer groups benefit the community?

SUMMARY AND PREVIEW In this section you learned about citizens' duties toward their nation and their communities. In the next chapter you will learn about the first government formed under the Constitution.

Section 3 Assessment

Reviewing Ideas, Terms, and People

1. a. Identify What are the different ways in which a person can become a U.S. citizen?
b. Make Inferences Why do you think the law requires an immigrant to live in the United States at least five years before he or she can apply to become a **naturalized citizen**?

2. a. Describe What are three duties expected of U.S. citizens?
b. Evaluate In your opinion, which duty expected of citizens is the most important? Why?

3. a. Identify In what ways can citizens participate in the election process?
b. Draw Conclusions Why do you think it is important that citizens participate in the political process?

Critical Thinking

4. Categorizing Review your notes on becoming a

U.S. citizen. Then add the responsibilities of citizenship to your graphic organizer.

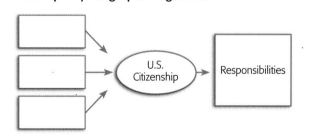

U.S. Citizenship → Responsibilities

FOCUS ON WRITING

5. Thinking about Citizenship The last page of your pamphlet will have two parts—one part on requirements for citizenship and one part on the responsibilities of citizens. Look back through this section and make two lists, one on requirements and one on responsibilities.

Social Studies Skills

Analysis **Critical Thinking** **Civic Participation** **Study**

Determining the Context of Statements

Define the Skill

A *context* is the circumstances under which something happens. *Historical context* includes values, beliefs, conditions, and practices that were common in the past. At times, some of these were quite different from what they are today. To truly understand a historical statement or event, you have to take its context into account. It is not right to judge what people in history did or said based on present-day values alone. To be fair, you must also consider the historical context of the statement or event.

Learn the Skill

To better understand something a historical figure said or wrote, use the following guidelines to determine the context of the statement.

1. Identify the speaker or writer, the date, and the topic and main idea of the statement.

2. Determine the speaker's or writer's attitude and point of view about the topic.

3. Review what you know about beliefs, conditions, or practices related to the topic that were common at the time. Find out more about the times in which the statement was made, if you need to.

4. Decide how well the statement reflects the values, attitudes, and practices of people living at that time. Then, determine how well it reflects values, attitudes, and practices related to the topic today.

Applying these guidelines will give you a better understanding of statements made by the Constitution's framers. You read in Chapter 6 that the Constitution created a representative democracy. However, the original Constitution gave most Americans little voice in choosing their leaders. Only the House of Representatives was elected by the voters. Alexander Hamilton, one of the Constitutional Convention's leaders, told the delegates:

" The people are turbulent and changing; they seldom judge or determine right. Give therefore to the first [upper] class a distinct, permanent share in government. They will check the unsteadiness of the second [the masses]. "

By modern standards, Hamilton's remark is undemocratic. But think about the times in which it was made. Shays's Rebellion had recently occurred. In addition, in those days most Americans had little or no education. Many could not even read or write. When its historical context is considered, the statement seems less harsh and extreme.

Practice the Skill

Read the following statement made by Patrick Henry in 1788. Then answer the questions to determine its context and better understand it.

" The Constitution is said to have beautiful features, but … they appear to me horribly frightful … Your dearest rights may be sacrificed by what may be a small minority … [that] … may continue forever unchangeably this government, although horribly defective. "

1. What was Henry's opinion of the Constitution?

2. How might Americans' recent experience in the Revolution have caused him to feel that way?

Chapter Review

HOLT
History's Impact
▶ video series
Review the video to answer the closing question:
Why did James Madison think the Tenth Amendment was important for the Bill of Rights?

Visual Summary

Use the visual summary below to help you review the main ideas of the chapter.

QUICK FACTS

The U.S. Constitution sets up a federal system of government, with powers divided between the federal government and state governments.

The powers of government are divided among three branches: the legislative, executive, and judicial branches.

A system of checks and balances prevents any one branch from becoming too powerful.

The Bill of Rights guarantees important rights and freedoms for American citizens.

Along with rights, citizens have duties: to obey laws, pay taxes, register for the draft, sit on juries, perform community service, and vote.

GOVERNMENT   CONSTITUTION   RIGHTS

Reviewing Vocabulary, Terms, and People

1. Who promised to add a bill of rights to the U.S. Constitution?
   a. Benjamin Franklin
   c. Alexander Hamilton
   b. Thomas Jefferson
   d. James Madison

2. What is the term for a person born in another country who becomes a citizen of the United States?
   a. immigrant
   c. naturalized citizen
   b. partial citizen
   d. separatist

3. What are powers granted to the states called?
   a. reserved powers
   c. stately powers
   b. concurrent powers
   d. delegated powers

4. What is the permission to look for evidence of a crime in a particular location called?
   a. petition
   c. indictment
   b. impeachment
   d. search warrant

5. Who was the first female Supreme Court justice?
   a. Abigail Adams
   c. Barbara Jordan
   b. Susan B. Anthony
   d. Sandra Day O'Connor

Comprehension and Critical Thinking

SECTION 1 *(Pages 182–186)*

6. a. Describe Name each branch of government and explain the duties of each.

b. Analyze What checks and balances exist between the branches of government?

c. Evaluate Do you think the three branches of government share their power equally? Explain your answer.

SECTION 2 *(Pages 216–221)*

7. a. Identify What is the Bill of Rights, and why was it added to the Constitution?

b. Analyze In what ways does the Bill of Rights protect individuals from the power of government?

c. Elaborate Which of the amendments in the Bill of Rights do you think is the most important? Why?

SECTION 3 *(Pages 222–225)*

8. a. Describe What are the ways in which a person can gain U.S. citizenship?

b. Analyze How are citizens able to influence their government?

c. Predict What might result if individuals failed to fulfill their duties as citizens?

Reading Skills

Summarizing Historical Texts *Use the Reading Skills taught in this chapter to answer the question about the reading selection below.*

> "The judicial power of the United States shall be vested in one supreme Court, and in such inferior Courts as the Congress may from time to time … establish. The Judges, both of the supreme and inferior Courts, shall hold their Offices during good Behavior, and … receive for their Services a Compensation…"

9. Which of the following is the best summary of the selection?

a. The U.S. judiciary consists of the Supreme Court and lower courts, and judges are paid.

b. Congress creates lower courts.

Reviewing Themes

10. Politics What important ideas has the U.S. Constitution contributed to government?

11. Politics Why is active political participation an important responsibility for people in the United States?

Social Studies Skills

Determining the Context of Statements *Use the Social Studies Skills taught in this chapter to answer the questions about the quotation below.*

> "What political power could ever carry on the vast multitude [large number] of lesser undertakings which the American citizens perform every day, with the assistance of the principle of association [joining a group]? Nothing, in my opinion, is more deserving of our attention than the intellectual and moral associations of America."
>
> —Alexis de Tocqueville, *Democracy in America*

12. De Tocqueville wrote this about his trip to the United States in 1831. What is his main idea?

a. Governments can fill every need of citizens.

b. American organizations cannot accomplish much.

c. American organizations get too much attention.

d. American organizations fill important needs of citizens that government cannot.

13. Do you think that de Tocqueville's statement accurately describes modern America? Why or why not?

FOCUS ON WRITING

14. Creating a Pamphlet You have gathered information about the Constitution, Bill of Rights, and citizenship. Use that information to create your pamphlet. On the first page, write a title and a phrase that will get your audience's attention. On each of the following pages, you can use this format: (1) a heading and sentence at the top of the page identifying the topic of the page, and (2) the list of the most important points for that topic. Remember that page 2 is on the Constitution, page 3 is on the Bill of Rights, and page 4 is on citizenship.

Standardized Test Practice

8.1.9, 8.2.1, 8.2.2, 8.2.4, 8.2.6, 8.2.8

DIRECTIONS: Read each question and write the letter of the best response.

1 Which of the following rights is a right protected in the First Amendment?

A the right to bear arms

B the right to public education

C the right to jury trials

D the right to free speech

2 The right of every American to be a member of a political party is an example of

A the principle of dual sovereignty.

B the First Amendment right to freedom of assembly.

C the principle of majority rule.

D the Fifth Amendment right to due process of law.

3 Obeying laws, paying taxes, and willingness to serve on a jury are all

A methods of gaining U.S. citizenship.

B duties of U.S. citizens.

C ways in which citizens can influence their government.

D protected by the Second Amendment.

4 The First Amendment would protect

A a reporter that knowingly spreads lies about someone.

B an individual who peacefully protests a government policy.

C an individual who falsely shouts, "Fire" in a crowded theater.

D a hunter who keeps a rifle at home.

5 Which of the following is an example of a check that the executive branch has on the legislative branch?

A The president may declare laws unconstitutional.

B The vice president serves as president of the Senate.

C The president may veto bills passed by Congress.

D The president may appoint members of Congress.

6 Which of the following protects the rights of the accused?

A the guarantee of a speedy trial

B the right to vote cannot be denied because of sex

C the right to sign a petition

D the right to keep and bear arms

7 Read the following quote from President Lyndon Johnson and use it to answer the question below.

> "What a president says and thinks is not worth five cents unless he has the people and Congress behind him. Without Congress, I'm just a six-feet-four Texan. With Congress, I'm President of the United States in the fullest sense."
>
> — President Lyndon Johnson, quoted in *The Macmillan Dictionary of Political Quotations*

Document-Based Question What point about government was President Johnson making in this remark?

Launching the Nation

IN Indiana Standards

Social Studies Standards

8.1.6 Identify the steps in the implementation of the federal government under the United States Constitution, including the First and Second Congresses of the United States (1789–1792).

8.1.7 Describe the origin and development of political parties, the Federalists and the Democratic Republicans (1793–1801) and examine points of agreement and disagreement between these parties.

8.4.5 Analyze contributions of entrepreneurs and inventors in the development of the United States economy.

8.4.8 Examine the development of the banking system in the United States.

go.hrw.com
Indiana
KEYWORD: SF10 IN

FOCUS ON WRITING

A Nobel Nomination Every year a few people are nominated for a Nobel Prize for their work to improve the world. In this chapter you will read about four great Americans— Washington, Hamilton, Jefferson, and Adams. Then you'll choose one of these great leaders and write a Nobel Prize nomination for him.

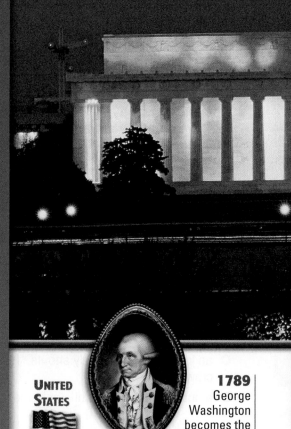

UNITED STATES

1789
George Washington becomes the first president.

1785

WORLD

1789
The French Revolution begins.

HOLT
History's Impact
▶ video series
Watch the video to under-
stand the impact of
political parties on the
new United States.

What You Will Learn...

In this chapter you will learn about the first
presidency and how it affected the country.
George Washington began many presidential
as well as national traditions. He is honored
with statues and memorials across the country,
including the Washington Monument in
Washington, D.C.

1794
After defeating a group
of Native Americans
led by Tecumseh,
General Anthony Wayne
establishes Fort Wayne.

1794
The Whiskey
Rebellion begins
in Pennsylvania.

1795
Native American
leaders sign
the Treaty of
Greenville.

1796
John Adams is
elected president
on December 7.

1799
George Washington dies
at Mount Vernon, Virginia,
on December 14.

1790

1795

1800

1793
French
revolutionaries
behead King
Louis XVI.

1799
The Rosetta Stone is discovered
in Egypt. Inscriptions on the stone
make it possible for researchers
to read Egyptian hieroglyphics.

Reading Social Studies

by Kylene Beers

Economics | Geography | Politics | Society and Culture | Science and Technology

Focus on Themes This chapter, titled "Launching the Nation," describes how the early leaders established this nation's **political** and **economic** systems. You will read about Washington's presidency, Hamilton's plan for financial security for the nation, the establishment of two parties to elect the president, and Jefferson's struggles with both Washington and Hamilton. Throughout the chapter, you will see that disagreement often defined these early days.

Inferences about History

Focus on Reading What's the difference between a good guess and a weak guess? A good guess is an *educated* guess. In other words, the guess is based on some knowledge or information. That's what an **inference** is, an educated guess.

Making Inferences About What You Read To make an inference, combine information from your reading with what you already know, and make an educated guess about what it all means. Once you have made several inferences, you may be able to draw a conclusion that ties them all together.

Question What kind of person was Alexander Hamilton?

Inside the Text

- Hamilton ran a company when he was just a teenager.
- He had a career as a lawyer.
- He became the secretary of the treasury under Washington.

Outside the Text

- Running a company takes intelligence and cleverness.
- Becoming a lawyer takes dedication.
- Washington probably wanted someone clever and capable.

Inference Alexander Hamilton was an intelligent, clever, and dedicated man.

Steps for Making Inferences

1. Ask a question.
2. Note information "Inside the Text."
3. Note information "Outside the Text."
4. **Use both sets of information to make an educated guess, or inference.**

You Try It!

Read the following passage and answer the questions that follow.

Economic Differences

Hamilton wanted new forms of economic growth. He wanted to promote manufacturing and business. He even suggested that the government award a prize to companies that made excellent products.

From Chapter 7, p. 240–241

In addition, Hamilton wanted to pass higher tariffs. Known as protective tariffs, these taxes would raise the prices of foreign products. Hamilton hoped this would cause Americans to buy U.S. goods. As a result, American manufacturing would be protected from foreign competition.

Jefferson worried about depending too much on business and manufacturing. He believed that farmers were the most independent voters . . . Jefferson wanted to help farmers by keeping the costs of the goods they bought low. Lower tariffs would help keep prices low.

After you read the passage, answer the following questions.

1. Which two questions can be answered directly from the text above and which one requires that you make an inference?

   a. Who wanted higher tariffs, Hamilton or Jefferson?
   b. Why do you think Hamilton and Jefferson had different views on the importance of manufacturing?
   c. Which man wanted to help the farmers?

2. To answer question b, it might help to know that Hamilton lived in New York City, and Jefferson was from the more rural area of Virginia. Use that information and information in the passage to explain why one man might have valued manufacturing more than the other.

As you read **Chapter 7**, remember that you need to combine what you already know with the information in the chapter to make inferences.

Washington Leads a New Nation

If YOU were there...

You are a seamstress in New York City in 1789. You've joined the excited crowd in the streets for inauguration day. Church bells are ringing, and people are cheering. Even though you were just a young child during the Revolution, Washington is your hero. Now you watch as he takes the oath of office. You are proud to see that he is wearing a suit of American–made cloth.

What do you think America's future will be like under President Washington?

BUILDING BACKGROUND George Washington was more than just a popular war hero. People naturally looked to him as a national leader. He had taken part in the Continental Congresses and in creating the Constitution. He helped establish and strengthen the new national government.

The First President

Americans believed in **George Washington**. They saw him as an honest leader and a hero of the Revolution. Many believed he should be the first U.S. president. Washington had been looking forward to retirement and a quiet life on his Virginia farm. When he hesitated at becoming a candidate for the presidency, his friends convinced him to run. Fellow politician Gouverneur Morris told him, "Should the idea prevail [win] that you would not accept the presidency, it should prove fatal . . . to the new government." Morris concluded confidently, "Of all men, you are the best fitted to fill that office."

In January 1789 each of the 11 states that had passed the Constitution sent electors to choose the first president. These delegates formed a group called the **electoral college**—a body of electors who represent the people's vote in choosing the president. The electoral college selected Washington unanimously, and John Adams became his vice president.

Washington's wife, First Lady **Martha Washington**, entertained guests and attended social events with her husband. She described the scene to her niece: "I have not had one half-hour to myself since the day of my arrival." She ran the presidential household with style.

Other women of the time period, such as author Judith Sargent Murray, believed that women needed to play a greater role in the new nation than Martha Washington did. Murray, Abigail Adams, and others believed in Republican Motherhood, the idea that women played an important role in teaching their children to be good citizens.

Some promoters of Republican Motherhood did not expect women to participate in politics or business. Other people, however, hoped that Republican Motherhood would lead to greater opportunities for women. They hoped more women would receive an education. Only a few families were willing to provide much education for their daughters, and adult women rarely had the time or money to get an education later in life. Most women in the early republic faced long days managing their households and working hard inside or outside the home to support their families.

READING CHECK **Analyzing** Why was Washington selected to be president?

Organizing the Government

Hard work also lay ahead for members of the new government. The new federal government had to create policies and procedures that would determine the future of the country. As President Washington noted in a letter to James Madison, "The first of everything in our situation will serve to establish a precedent." A **precedent** is an action or decision that later serves as an example.

The First Congress created departments in the executive branch for different areas of national policy. Washington met with the department heads, or cabinet members, who advised him.

Today we know that presidents have cabinet meetings with their top advisers. This practice started during Washington's presidency and was common by 1792.

For two of his most important cabinet positions, Washington chose carefully. He picked Alexander Hamilton as secretary of the treasury and Thomas Jefferson as secretary of state. Henry Knox served as secretary of war, and Samuel Osgood was chosen as postmaster general. Hamilton was a gifted

The First Cabinet
Washington's cabinet members kept him informed on political matters and debated important issues with one another. Each of the men chosen had experience that made him a wise choice to advise the nation's first president. By 1792 cabinet meetings were a common practice.

ANALYSIS SKILL **ANALYZING VISUALS**

How do you think a modern cabinet meeting might look different from the one shown here?

❶ Henry Knox, secretary of war
❷ Thomas Jefferson, secretary of state
❸ Edmund Randolph, attorney general
❹ Alexander Hamilton, secretary of the treasury
❺ George Washington, president

A Rural Nation

Urban vs. Rural Population, 1790

Urban
5%

Rural
95%

FOCUS ON INDIANA

The First Congress, which met from 1789 to 1791 in New York City and Philadelphia, passed legislation that organized the court system, levied the first federal tax, and created the first Bank of the United States. The Second Congress, which met from 1791 to 1793 in Philadelphia, passed legislation that created the U.S. Post Office and provided for the minting of currency.

economic planner, and Jefferson had served as ambassador to France. Knox had helped Washington run the Continental Army, and Osgood had government experience.

To set up the federal court system and the courts' location, Congress passed the **Judiciary Act of 1789.** This act created three levels of federal courts and defined their powers and relationship to the state courts. It set up federal district courts and circuit courts of appeals. The president nominated candidates for federal judgeships. Those candidates then had to be approved or rejected by the Senate. Washington wrote about the importance of these duties:

"I have always been persuaded that the stability and success of the national government ... would depend in a considerable degree on the interpretation and execution of its laws. In my opinion, therefore, it is important that the judiciary system should not only be independent in its operations, but as perfect as possible in its formation."

—George Washington, quoted in *The Real George Washington*, edited by Parry et al.

The basic parts of the federal government were now in place. Leaders began to face the challenges of the new nation. Hard work lay ahead.

READING CHECK Finding Main Ideas
What two important precedents were established for the federal government?

Americans' Expectations for the Nation

Most Americans had high expectations for the new country. They wanted improved trade, free from too many restrictions. But they also expected the government to protect them and to keep the economy stable. However, the idea of belonging to one united nation was new to them.

In 1790 the United States was home to almost 4 million people. Most Americans lived in the countryside and worked on farms. Farmers wanted fair tax laws and the right to settle western lands. They did not want the government to interfere with their daily lives.

Other Americans worked in towns as craftspeople, laborers, or merchants. These people looked to the government to help their businesses. Most merchants wanted simpler trade laws established. Manufacturers wanted laws to protect them from foreign competitors.

Some Americans lived in growing cities like New York, shown above. However, the new republic was overwhelmingly rural. Most Americans lived and worked on farms.

Why might rural Americans and urban Americans want different things from their new government?

Most cities were small. Only New York City and Philadelphia had populations larger than 25,000. New York City was the first capital of the United States, and it represented the spirit of the new nation. Although badly damaged during the Revolution, the city had already begun to recover. Citizens got rid of many signs of British rule.

New York City had a bustling economy. International trade and business became more active. A French visitor to New York City noted the city's energy.

"Everything in the city is in motion; everywhere the shops resound [ring out] with the noise of workers ... one sees vessels arriving from every part of the world."
—A French visitor to New York, quoted in *New York in the American Revolution* by Wilbur Abbott

In 1792 some 24 stockbrokers signed an **agreement** under a buttonwood tree on Wall Street. This agreement was the foundation for what later became the New York Stock Exchange. It cemented Wall Street's image as the economic hub of the United States.

By 1790 the city's population had topped 33,000 and was growing rapidly. To many officials, this vibrant city reflected the potential future of the new nation. It was thus a fitting place for the capital.

READING CHECK Analyzing Why was New York City chosen as the first capital of the United States?

SUMMARY AND PREVIEW Americans, led by President George Washington, set up their new government. In the next section you will read about Alexander Hamilton's economic plan.

ACADEMIC VOCABULARY
agreement
a decision reached by two or more people or groups

THE IMPACT TODAY

Today the New York Stock Exchange is the largest market for securities, or stocks, in the world.

Section 1 Assessment

go.hrw.com
Online Quiz
KEYWORD: SF7 HP7

Reviewing Ideas, Terms, and People

1. **a. Describe** What role did the electoral college play in **George Washington**'s election to the presidency?
   b. Summarize What were some of **Martha Washington**'s duties as First Lady?
2. **a. Describe** What **precedent** did President Washington and Congress establish regarding the executive branch?
   b. Explain What was the purpose of the **Judiciary Act of 1789**?
   c. Evaluate What do you think was the most important element of the Judiciary Act of 1789? Why?
3. **a. Recall** What city served as the first capital of the United States? Why?
   b. Draw Conclusions What expectations did most Americans have for the new nation?
   c. Make Judgments Do you think New York City should still be the capital city of the United States? Explain your answer.

Critical Thinking

4. **Comparing** Review your notes on George Washington. Then copy the chart below and use it to compare how Washington and Congress organized the new government.

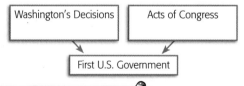

Washington's Decisions	Acts of Congress

First U.S. Government

FOCUS ON WRITING

5. **Thinking about Washington's Contributions** In this section you learned some things about George Washington as president. Jot down one or two things you could use to support his nomination for a Nobel Prize.

Hamilton and National Finances

What You Will Learn...

Main Ideas

1. Hamilton tackled the problem of settling national and state debt.
2. Thomas Jefferson opposed Hamilton's views on government and the economy.
3. Hamilton created a national bank to strengthen the U.S. economy.

The Big Idea

Treasury secretary Alexander Hamilton developed a financial plan for the national government.

Key Terms and People

Alexander Hamilton, *p. 238*
national debt, *p. 238*
bonds, *p. 238*
speculators, *p. 239*
Thomas Jefferson, *p. 239*
loose construction, *p. 242*
strict construction, *p. 242*
Bank of the United States, *p. 242*

TAKING NOTES As you read, take notes on the economic problems facing the nation when Alexander Hamilton became secretary of the treasury, as well as Hamilton's solutions to the problems.

Economic Problems	Solutions
	1.
	2.
	3.
	4.
	5.
	6.

8.1.6, 8.1.9, 8.1.28, 8.1.30, 8.2.1, 8.2.4, 8.2.10, 8.4.4, 8.4.5, 8.4.8

If YOU were there...

You live on a plantation in North Carolina in the 1790s. You have just heard that the federal government plans to pay most of the northern states' debts from the war. Your neighbors are outraged about this idea. It means more taxes and tariffs! New York and Massachusetts are far away, they say. Why should North Carolina farmers have to pay northern debts?

Would you pay other states' war debts? Why?

BUILDING BACKGROUND Some of the new nation's biggest problems were economic. The national and state governments had run up huge debts during the war. But the proposed solutions to these problems revealed differences in regional viewpoints. Southern planters and northern businesspeople had very different ideas about how the national economy should develop.

Settling the Debt

Alexander Hamilton seemed born with a head for economics. While still in his teens, he helped run a shipping company in his native British West Indies. Family friends then sent him to the American colonies for an education. Hamilton eventually married into a wealthy New York family and began practicing law. He served as Washington's aide and as a delegate to four Continental Congresses.

National Debt

As secretary of the treasury, Hamilton's biggest challenge was paying off the **national debt**—money owed by the United States—from the Revolutionary War. The United States owed about $11.7 million to foreign countries and about $40.4 million to U.S. citizens. During the war the government raised money with bonds. **Bonds** are certificates of debt that carry a promise to buy back the bonds at a higher price. The new government could not afford to keep this promise. Bondholders who needed money sold

Hamilton's Economic Plan

QUICK FACTS

Alexander Hamilton developed a three-point plan to solve the nation's financial problems.

Total Debt

- Domestic debt $40.4 million
- State debt $25 million
- Foreign debt $11.7 million

1 Deal with the Debt
- Take on the foreign and domestic debt by replacing creditors' old, low-value bonds with new, interest-bearing bonds → would build investor confidence in the stability of the new nation
- Take over most of the states' $25 million Revolutionary War debts → would free up state money for business and trade

2 Gain Revenue
- Pass a tariff to both bring in money and help American manufacturers

3 Stabilize the Banking System
- Create a national bank
- Create a national mint

their bonds for less than the original value to **speculators**, or people who buy items at low prices in the hope that the value will rise and they can sell the items for a profit.

Hamilton wanted to pay the foreign debt immediately and gradually repay the total value of all bonds. The second part of his plan caused disagreements because paying full value would allow speculators to make a profit. Hamilton thought this was fair. He said, "He [the speculator] paid what the commodity [bond] was worth . . . and took the risks."

Thomas Jefferson disagreed. He thought the idea cheated bondholders who had sold their bonds at low prices. Jefferson wrote, "Immense sums were thus filched [stolen] from the poor and ignorant." But more politicians agreed with Hamilton. In 1790 the government exchanged old bonds for new, more reliable ones that were guaranteed.

States' Debts

The states owed $25 million for Revolutionary War expenses. Hamilton wanted the federal government to pay for $21.5 million of this debt. Hamilton believed that this action would help the federal government. He thought that paying the states' debts would help the national economy. Debtor states would not have to spend so much on repayment and would have money to develop business and trade. Increased business and trade would put more money back into the national economy.

The South, however, did not want to help the federal government pay the debts of other states. States such as Virginia and North Carolina did not have many war debts. They thought Hamilton's idea was unfair. Patrick Henry said he did not believe that the Constitution gave Congress the power to pay state debts. Hamilton knew that he needed the help of southern representatives to get his plan approved.

Moving the Capital

Hamilton also knew that he had something to bargain with. Southern officials wanted to change the location of the nation's capital. Many southerners thought that having the capital in New York gave the northern states too much influence over national policy. Hamilton, Jefferson, and James Madison met in June 1790. Hamilton promised to convince northern members of Congress to move the capital. Jefferson and Madison then agreed to gather support in the South for Hamilton's debt plan.

The compromise worked. The national capital was moved to Philadelphia in 1791 for 10 years. For the capital's permanent location, Washington chose a place on the Potomac River that included part of both Maryland and Virginia. The land was made up of swamps and farms. This site would eventually become the city of Washington, D.C.

THE IMPACT TODAY

Washington, D.C., and the surrounding areas are home to more than 7 million people today. The city is not only the nation's capital but also a major tourist attraction.

READING CHECK **Identifying Points of View** How did southerners feel about the federal government paying state war debts, and how did Hamilton change their minds?

BIOGRAPHY

Benjamin Banneker (1731–1806)

Benjamin Banneker was born to a free African American family in rural Maryland. He attended a Quaker school but was largely self-educated. He was a skilled mathematician and scientist. His mathematical skills prompted Thomas Jefferson to give him a job surveying the land for the new national capital.

Draw Conclusions How was Benjamin Banneker's life different from most African Americans' of the time?

Jefferson Opposes Hamilton

Hamilton and Jefferson did not cooperate for long. Instead, they began to disagree about how to define the authority of the central government. Hamilton believed in a strong federal government. Jefferson wanted to protect the powers of the states. Their conflict reflected basic differences in their opinions about democracy. Hamilton had little faith in the average individual. He once said that "the people . . . seldom judge or determine [decide] right."

Differing Views

Hamilton wanted a strong central government that balanced power between the "mass of the people" and wealthier citizens. He believed that his approach would protect everyone's liberties while keeping the people from having too much power.

Jefferson disagreed strongly with Hamilton's views of the average citizen's ability to make decisions for the country. He admitted that "the people can not be all, and always, well informed." However, Jefferson believed that it was the right of the people to rule the country.

Economic Differences

Hamilton and Jefferson also fought over how the country's economy should grow. Hamilton wanted new forms of economic growth. He wanted to promote manufacturing and business. He even suggested that the

U.S. Capitol in Washington, D.C.

POINTS OF VIEW
Role of a Citizen

Alexander Hamilton thought that the average citizen had no interest in public affairs.

❝We must take man as we find him, and if we expect him to serve the public, [we] must interest his passions in doing so. A reliance on pure patriotism has been the source of many of our errors.❞

–Alexander Hamilton,
quoted in *Odd Destiny: The Life of Alexander Hamilton* by Marie B. Hecht

Thomas Jefferson believed that each citizen could work to better society.

❝It is my principle that the will of the Majority should always prevail [win] . . . Above all things I hope the education of the common people will be attended to; [I am] convinced that on their good sense we may rely with the most security for the preservation of a due degree of liberty.❞

–Thomas Jefferson,
from *Thomas Jefferson: A Biography in His Own Words*

ANALYSIS SKILL **ANALYZING POINTS OF VIEW**

How did the views of Hamilton and Jefferson differ?

government award a prize to companies that made excellent products.

In addition, Hamilton wanted to pass higher tariffs. Known as protective tariffs, these taxes would raise the prices of foreign products. Hamilton hoped this would cause Americans to buy U.S. goods. As a result, American manufacturing would be protected from foreign competition.

Jefferson worried about depending too much on business and manufacturing. He believed that farmers were the most independent voters. They did not depend on other people's work to make a living.

Jefferson wrote, "Our governments will remain virtuous [pure] for many centuries; as long as they are chiefly agricultural." Jefferson wanted to help farmers by keeping the costs of the goods they bought low. Lower tariffs would help keep prices low.

READING CHECK **Summarizing** What were the main differences between Hamilton and Jefferson concerning the power of the nation's government?

A National Bank

Hamilton's and Jefferson's differences became more and more public in early 1791. The two men had very different opinions about how the government should approach its economic problems.

Hamilton's Plan for a National Bank

Hamilton wanted to start a national bank where the government could safely deposit its money. The bank would also make loans to the government and businesses. Hamilton also thought that the United States should build a national mint, a place to make coins. Then the country could begin issuing its own money.

Hamilton knew that people who wanted to protect states' rights might have a strong reaction to the idea of a national bank, so he suggested limiting it to a 20-year charter. After that time Congress could decide whether to extend the charter. Hamilton also asked each state to start its own bank so the national bank would not have a monopoly.

THE IMPACT TODAY

The U.S. Mint was established in 1792 and now produces more than 15 billion coins each year.

Jefferson Opposes the Bank

Both Jefferson and Madison believed that Hamilton's plans for the economy gave too much power to the federal government. They also thought the U.S. Constitution did not give Congress the power to create a bank. But Hamilton quoted the elastic clause, which states that Congress can "make all laws which shall be necessary and proper" to govern the nation.

Hamilton declared that the clause allowed the government to create a national bank. Hamilton believed in loose construction of the Constitution. **Loose construction** means that the federal government can take reasonable actions that the Constitution does not specifically forbid.

Jefferson thought that the elastic clause should be used only in special cases. He wrote to President Washington, "The Constitution allows only the means which are 'necessary,' not those which are merely 'convenient.'"

Jefferson believed in strict construction of the Constitution. People who favor **strict construction** think that the federal government should do only what the Constitution specifically says it can do.

President Washington and Congress agreed with Hamilton. They hoped a bank would offer stability for the U.S. economy. In February 1791 Congress enacted the charter for the **Bank of the United States**—the country's first national bank. The bank played an important role in making the U.S. economy more stable.

READING CHECK Drawing Conclusions
Why did Congress and the president agree to create a national bank?

SUMMARY AND PREVIEW Washington and Hamilton developed plans for paying the national debt. In the next section you will read about the U.S. neutrality policy.

go.hrw.com
Online Quiz
KEYWORD: SF7 HP7

Section 2 Assessment

Reviewing Ideas, Terms, and People

1. **a. Describe** What economic problems did the new government face?
   b. Summarize What compromise did **Alexander Hamilton**, **Thomas Jefferson**, and James Madison reach regarding repayment of state debts?
2. **a. Identify** What disagreement did Jefferson and Hamilton have over the central government?
   b. Draw Conclusions Hamilton was a New Yorker, while Jefferson was from Virginia. How do you think that affected their views on the economy?
   c. Elaborate Do you agree with Hamilton or Jefferson regarding the average citizen's ability to make decisions for the country? Explain your answer.
3. **a. Recall** Why did Jefferson oppose the creation of the **Bank of the United States**?
   b. Contrast What is the difference between **loose construction** and **strict construction** of the Constitution?
   c. Elaborate Defend Alexander Hamilton's stance in favor of the creation of a national bank.

Critical Thinking

4. **Identifying Solutions** Review your notes on U.S. economic problems and Hamilton's solutions. Then copy the chart below and use it to show how Hamilton's views on the economy differed from those of Thomas Jefferson.

	Hamilton	Jefferson
Bonds		
Economy		
Tariffs		
National Bank		

FOCUS ON WRITING

5. **Gathering Information about Hamilton and Jefferson** Both Hamilton and Jefferson were strong leaders who helped shape the government of the young United States. What could you say about either of them to support a nomination for a Nobel Prize?

Challenges for the New Nation

If YOU were there...

You are the captain of an American merchant ship in the 1790s. Your ship has just picked up cargo in the French West Indies. You are headed back to your home port of Philadelphia. Suddenly, a British warship pulls alongside your ship. Marines swarm aboard. They order you into the nearest harbor and seize your goods.

How would this incident affect your views of Great Britain?

> **BUILDING BACKGROUND** As the new nation tried to get organized, it faced economic problems and internal divisions. Even more difficult challenges came from conflicts in Europe. The United States could not avoid being caught up in fighting between France and Great Britain.

Remaining Neutral

Tensions between France and Britain began to build after the French people rebelled against their king. On July 14, 1789, citizens of Paris attacked and captured the Bastille, a hated fortress and prison that stood as a mighty symbol of royal power.

The storming of the Bastille was one of the first acts of the **French Revolution**—a rebellion of French people against their king in 1789. The French people overthrew their king and created a republican government.

French revolutionaries storm the Bastille.

What You Will Learn...

Main Ideas
1. The United States tried to remain neutral regarding events in Europe.
2. The United States and Native Americans came into conflict in the Northwest Territory.
3. The Whiskey Rebellion tested Washington's administration.
4. In his Farewell Address, Washington advised the nation.

The Big Idea
The United States faced significant foreign and domestic challenges under Washington.

Key Terms and People
French Revolution, *p. 243*
Neutrality Proclamation, *p. 244*
privateers, *p. 244*
Jay's Treaty, *p. 245*
Pinckney's Treaty, *p. 245*
Little Turtle, *p. 246*
Battle of Fallen Timbers, *p. 247*
Treaty of Greenville, *p. 247*
Whiskey Rebellion, *p. 247*

TAKING NOTES As you read, take notes on the challenges faced by the new nation during Washington's administration.

Challenges

8.1.9, 8.1.30, 8.2.1, 8.2.4, 8.4.4

243

FOCUS ON READING

What can you tell about France before 1793 using this paragraph and what you already know about democracies?

ACADEMIC VOCABULARY

neutral
unbiased, not favoring either side in a conflict

Many French citizens had been inspired to take action by the American Revolution. Many Americans, in turn, supported the French Revolution. They thought that France was creating the same kind of democracy as the United States.

Some Americans worried about the French Revolution's violent riots and attacks on traditional authority. Revolutionaries shocked many Americans by beheading King Louis XVI in January 1793 and Queen Marie-Antoinette later that year.

A few years after the French Revolution started, France and Great Britain went to war. Some Americans supported the French, while others backed the British. Some wanted to remain **neutral**.

The Neutrality Proclamation

The debate divided Congress and Washington's cabinet. Washington presented his opinion to Congress on April 22, 1793:

"The duty and interest of the United States require that they should with sincerity and good faith adopt and pursue a conduct friendly and impartial [unbiased] towards the belligerent [fighting] powers."

—George Washington, quoted in *The Real George Washington* by Parry et al.

This **Neutrality Proclamation** stated that the United States would not take sides with any European countries that were at war. Washington believed his plan was the safest for the long run, but not everyone agreed.

Some members of Congress criticized Washington's ideas. James Madison believed that the president had gone beyond his authority. He questioned Washington's right to issue the proclamation without the approval of Congress.

The French Question

France's new representative to the United States, Edmond Genet (zhuh-NAY), asked American sailors to help France fight England by commanding **privateers**. Privateers were private ships hired by a country to attack its enemies. Washington told Genet that using American privateers violated U.S. neutrality. Jefferson wanted the French revolutionaries to succeed, but even he agreed that allowing France to use American privateers against England was a bad idea.

Jefferson was still upset by U.S. policy toward France. He believed that the United States should back France because France had supported the United States during the Revolutionary War. Hamilton, on the other hand, was pro-British. He hoped to strengthen trading ties with Britain—the most powerful trading nation in the world at the time. Jefferson thought that Hamilton had too much influence on the president's foreign policy and that Hamilton consequently interfered with Jefferson's role as secretary of state. Jefferson decided to resign from Washington's cabinet in 1793.

Time Line

The Struggle for Neutrality

April 1789 George Washington becomes president.

April 1793 President Washington issues the Neutrality Proclamation.

1789

July 1789 French citizens storm the Bastille.

October 1790 British-backed Little Turtle defeats U.S. forces under General Josiah Harmar.

1793

November 1794 Jay's Treaty sparks protest throughout the United States.

Jay's Treaty

There were other threats to U.S. neutrality. In late 1793 the British seized ships carrying food to the French West Indies. Hundreds of the ships were neutral American merchant ships. Also, British officers were helping Native Americans fight settlers.

Washington wanted to prevent another war with the British. He sent Chief Justice John Jay to London to work out a compromise. The British knew the United States lacked a strong navy and that U.S. businesses relied heavily on British trade. However, the British did not want to fight another war in America.

In November 1794 the two sides signed Jay's Treaty. **Jay's Treaty** settled the disputes that had arisen between the United States and Great Britain in the early 1790s. The British would pay damages on seized American ships and abandon their forts on the northwestern frontier. The United States agreed to pay debts it owed the British.

The treaty was unpopular and sparked violent protests. Citizens and congressional leaders thought the treaty hurt trade and did not punish Britain enough for some of its actions. Southerners were especially angry that the treaty did not ask Britain to repay them for slaves that Britain had set free during the Revolutionary War. Washington did not like the treaty but believed it was the most that could be done. At his urging the Senate approved the treaty.

Pinckney's Treaty

American businesses faced problems as well. The Spanish disputed the border between the United States and Florida. Spain closed the port of New Orleans to U.S. trade in 1784. This hurt the American economy because all goods moving down the Mississippi to places in the East or overseas had to pass through New Orleans.

Washington asked Ambassador Thomas Pinckney to meet with Spanish officials to discuss the problem. He asked the Spaniards to reopen New Orleans to U.S. trade. Pinckney also asked for the right of deposit in New Orleans. This right would allow American boats to transfer goods in New Orleans without paying cargo fees.

Spanish minister Manuel de Godoy (goh-THOY) tried to delay reaching an agreement, hoping Pinckney would become desperate and sign a treaty that favored the Spanish. He was worried that the United States and Great Britain might join against Spain after signing Jay's Treaty. Pinckney was patient, however, and his patience was rewarded.

In October 1795, Godoy agreed to **Pinckney's Treaty**, which settled the border and trade disputes with Spain. Under the treaty Spain agreed to recognize the U.S. southern boundary as 31°N latitude. Spain's government also reopened the port at

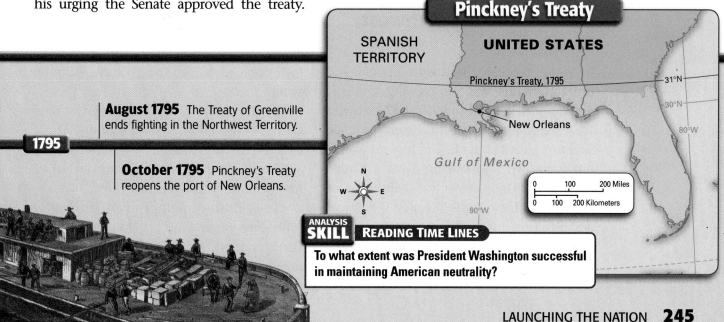

August 1795 The Treaty of Greenville ends fighting in the Northwest Territory.

1795

October 1795 Pinckney's Treaty reopens the port of New Orleans.

Pinckney's Treaty

SPANISH TERRITORY

UNITED STATES

Pinckney's Treaty, 1795

31°N

30°N

80°W

New Orleans

Gulf of Mexico

N
W E
S

| 0 | 100 | 200 Miles |
| 0 | 100 | 200 Kilometers |

90°W

ANALYSIS SKILL **READING TIME LINES**

To what extent was President Washington successful in maintaining American neutrality?

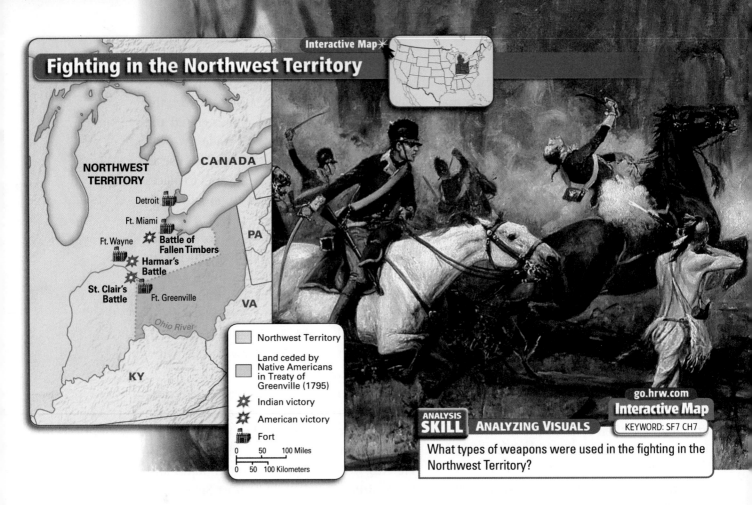

Fighting in the Northwest Territory

Interactive Map

NORTHWEST TERRITORY

CANADA

Detroit

Ft. Miami

Ft. Wayne ✦ **Battle of Fallen Timbers**

✦ **Harmar's Battle**

PA

St. Clair's Battle 🏰 Ft. Greenville

VA

Ohio River

KY

☐ Northwest Territory

☐ Land ceded by Native Americans in Treaty of Greenville (1795)

✦ Indian victory

✦ American victory

🏰 Fort

0   50   100 Miles

0   50   100 Kilometers

ANALYSIS SKILL **ANALYZING VISUALS**

go.hrw.com
Interactive Map
KEYWORD: SF7 CH7

What types of weapons were used in the fighting in the Northwest Territory?

New Orleans to American ships and gave them the right of deposit. Because it opened the frontier to more expansion, Washington and most other Americans believed that Pinckney's Treaty was a successful compromise.

READING CHECK **Summarizing** Why did President Washington want the United States to remain neutral?

Conflict in the Northwest Territory

As the United States dealt with international conflicts, trouble was also brewing at home. Americans continued to settle the Northwest Territory despite Native Americans' protests. Supplied by British traders with guns, Native Americans went to war. In 1790 a Native American alliance under the command of Miami chief **Little Turtle** defeated U.S. forces under General Josiah Harmar. Then in 1791, Native Americans defeated General Arthur St. Clair's troops.

General Wayne Takes Command

In 1792 President Washington gave command of the army in the West to General Anthony Wayne. Wayne's task was to bring troops to the frontier to fight against the Indians. In 1793 General Wayne arrived in Ohio. Many of his men were ill from smallpox and influenza, so they were unable to fight well.

Wayne's troops moved north and built Fort Greenville, where they remained during the winter. They built additional forts for protection and to have supplies at hand.

As the summer of 1794 neared, several Native American groups led by Little Turtle attacked a supply train near the fort. Wayne and his men responded. They attacked Native American towns and burned crops.

The British no longer aided the Native Americans after this defeat, and Little Turtle realized that he was outmatched. He urged his people to seek peace.

> "The trail has been long and bloody; it has no end. The [whites] … are many. They are like the leaves of the trees. When the frost comes they fall and are blown away. But when the sunshine comes again they come back more plentiful than ever before."
>
> —Little Turtle, quoted in *The Ohio Frontier* by Douglas Hurt

The End of Conflict

On August 20, 1794, Native Americans fought Wayne's troops in the **Battle of Fallen Timbers** and were defeated. The battle was named for an area where many trees had been destroyed by a tornado. Wayne's forces burned Indians' villages and fields. The strength of Indian forces in the region was broken.

The frontier war soon ended. In August 1795, Native American leaders signed the **Treaty of Greenville**, which gave the United States claim to most Indian lands in the Northwest Territory. The treaty also guaranteed the safety of citizens there. In exchange, Native Americans received $20,000 worth of goods and an acknowledgment of their claim to the lands they still held.

READING CHECK **Finding Main Ideas** What conflicts did the United States face in the late 1700s?

The Whiskey Rebellion

Other conflicts occurred on the frontier. Congress passed a tax on American-made whiskey in March 1791. The tax was part of Hamilton's plan to raise money to help pay the federal debt. He was also testing the power of the federal government to control the states' actions.

Reaction in the West

People in areas such as western Pennsylvania were bitter about the tax. They were already angry with the federal government, which they believed did not protect settlers from Native American attacks and did not allow settlers enough opportunities for trade. The farmers' corn crops were often made into whiskey, which was easier to transport than the corn. Because cash was rare, whiskey became like money in their region. The farmers believed that the tax was aimed specifically at them.

Farmers who produced small amounts of whiskey for trade argued that they could not afford the tax. They believed they should be able to keep the money they had made from a product they created themselves. Protests in 1792 led President Washington to issue a proclamation saying that people had to obey the law.

Westerners also disliked the fact that cases about the law were to be tried in a district court. These courts were usually far away from the people they affected and were a great inconvenience to them.

Whiskey Rebellion Is Crushed

The complaints of western Pennsylvanians were at first expressed peacefully. But by 1794 fighting had broken out. In what became known as the **Whiskey Rebellion**, farmers lashed out against the tax on whiskey. Protesters refused to pay the tax. They even tarred and feathered tax collectors. Some called themselves the new Sons of Liberty.

Incidents of violence spread to other states. President Washington feared that the rebels threatened the federal government's authority. He believed he needed to make people understand that the Constitution gave Congress the right to pass and enforce the tax.

Washington declared that he could "no longer remain a passive [inactive] spectator" in the event. He personally led the army in military action against the rebellion—the first and only time an American president has done so. The army of about 13,000 men approached western Pennsylvania in November 1794. By this time most of the rebels had fled. The Whiskey Rebellion ended without a battle.

READING CHECK **Supporting a Point of View** Defend the viewpoint of the Pennsylvania farmers who did not want to pay the whiskey tax.

FOCUS ON INDIANA After the Treaty of Greenville in 1795, more American settlers began to enter Indiana. By 1800 there were about 5,000 settlers there, and they often came into violent conflict with the Native Americans in the region.

HISTORICAL DOCUMENT
Washington's Farewell Address

On September 19,1796, President George Washington's Farewell Address first appeared in a Philadelphia newspaper. In it, Washington wrote about the nation's economy, political parties, and foreign policy.

While, then, every part of our country . . . feels an immediate and particular interest in union, all the parts combined cannot fail to find in the united mass . . . greater strength, greater resource, proportionally greater security from external danger, [and] a less frequent interruption of their peace by foreign nations; . . .

I have already **intimated**[1] to you the danger of [political] parties in the state, with particular reference to the founding of them on geographical **discriminations**[2]. Let me now take a more **comprehensive**[3] view, and warn you in the most solemn manner against the **baneful**[4] effects of the spirit of party, generally.

If, in the opinion of the people, the distribution or **modification**[5] of the constitutional powers be in any particular wrong, let it be corrected by an amendment . . .

Promote, then, as an object of primary importance, institutions for the general **diffusion**[6] of knowledge . . . As the structure of a government gives force to public opinion, it is essential that public opinion should be enlightened . . .

[Avoid] likewise the accumulation of debt, . . . not ungenerously throwing upon **posterity**[7] the burden, which we ourselves ought to bear . . .

Observe good faith and justice towards all nations; **cultivate**[8] peace and harmony with all . . .

The great rule of conduct for us, in regard to foreign nations, is . . . to have with them as little political connection as possible.

It is our true policy to steer clear of permanent alliances with any portion of the foreign world . . . There can be no greater error than to expect, or **calculate**[9] upon real favors from nation to nation. It is an illusion, which experience must cure, which a just pride ought to discard.

The duty of holding a neutral conduct may be inferred . . . from the obligation which justice and humanity impose on every nation . . . to maintain **inviolate**[10] the relations of peace and **amity**[11] towards other nations.

Washington lists the benefits of uniting the states under one government.

In this phrase, Washington emphasizes his warning against the dangers of political parties.

Washington points out the need for education.

This is Washington's advice to the new nation about foreign policy.

[1] **intimated**: told
[2] **discriminations**: differences
[3] **comprehensive**: complete
[4] **baneful**: destructive
[5] **modification**: change
[6] **diffusion**: spreading
[7] **posterity**: future generations

[8] **cultivate**: seek
[9] **calculate**: plan
[10] **inviolate**: unchanging
[11] **amity**: friendship

ANALYSIS SKILL ANALYZING PRIMARY SOURCES

1. What events happened before Washington left office that might have led to his warning against political parties?
2. Why did Washington suggest neutrality as a foreign policy?

Washington Says Farewell

In 1796 Washington decided not to run for a third presidential term. He wrote that he was "tired of public life" and "devoutly [strongly] wished for retirement." He also wanted to remind Americans that the people were the country's true leaders.

With the help of Alexander Hamilton and James Madison, Washington wrote his Farewell Address. In it he spoke about what he believed were the greatest dangers to the American republic. Among these were the dangers of foreign ties and political conflicts at home. Washington warned against forming permanent ties with other countries because choosing sides could draw the United States into war.

He also worried about growing political conflicts within the nation. Washington believed that disagreements between political groups weakened government. Political unity, he said, was a key to national success.

Washington left office warning the nation to work out its differences and protect its independence. Washington also warned against too much public debt. He thought the government should try not to borrow money. He wanted future generations to be protected from debt.

He concluded his speech by looking forward to his retirement and praising his country. "I anticipate . . . the sweet enjoyment . . . of good laws under a free government, the ever favorite object of my heart."

READING CHECK **Finding Main Ideas**
What issues did Washington believe were most dangerous to the future of the new nation?

SUMMARY AND PREVIEW Americans responded to foreign and domestic conflict during Washington's presidency. In the next section you will read about the formation of political parties in the United States and the presidency of John Adams.

Section 3 Assessment

go.hrw.com
Online Quiz
KEYWORD: SF7 HP7

Reviewing Ideas, Terms, and People

1. **a. Describe** What did Washington's **Neutrality Proclamation** state?
   b. Compare and Contrast In what ways were **Jay's Treaty** and **Pinckney's Treaty** similar and different?
2. **a. Identify** Who were the leaders of American Indian and U.S. forces in the conflict in the Northwest Territory?
   b. Predict What are some possible consequences of the **Treaty of Greenville** for American Indians in the Northwest Territory?
3. **a. Recall** Why did Congress tax American-made whiskey?
   b. Explain How did the tax lead to the **Whiskey Rebellion**?
   c. Elaborate Why do you think that President Washington personally led the army against westerners in the Whiskey Rebellion?
4. **a. Describe** What warnings did Washington give the nation in his Farewell Address?
   b. Draw Conclusions Why did Washington not run for a third term as president?

Critical Thinking

5. **Categorizing** Review your notes on the challenges the young United States faced. Then categorize those challenges as either foreign or domestic in a graphic organizer like this one.

Challenges	
Foreign	
Domestic	

FOCUS ON WRITING

6. **Thinking about Washington, Hamilton, and Jefferson** In this section you read about the activities of these three men during a difficult time for our country. What did you learn that you could add to a Nobel Prize nomination for any of these leaders?

John Adams's Presidency

Main Ideas

1. The rise of political parties created competition in the election of 1796.
2. The XYZ affair caused problems for President John Adams.
3. Controversy broke out over the Alien and Sedition Acts.

The Big Idea

The development of political parties in the United States contributed to differing ideas about the role of the federal government.

Key Terms

political parties, *p. 250*
Federalist Party, *p. 250*
Democratic-Republican Party, *p. 250*
XYZ affair, *p. 252*
Alien and Sedition Acts, *p. 253*
Kentucky and Virginia Resolutions, *p. 253*

TAKING NOTES As you read, take notes on the two political parties that emerged during the election of 1796, their views on government, their candidates in the 1796 election, and the outcome of the election. Use a graphic organizer like the one below for your notes.

Election of 1796	
Political Parties	
Views on Government	
Candidates	
Outcome	

8.1.6, 8.1.7, 8.1.9, 8.1.28, 8.2.1, 8.2.4, 8.2.7, 8.2.10, 8.4.4, 8.4.8

If YOU were there...

You are a newspaper editor in Virginia in 1798. You've joined Jefferson's political party, which opposes the new president. In fact, your paper has printed many articles that criticize him, calling him greedy and foolish. You believe that's your right in a free country. But now Congress has passed a law that makes it illegal to criticize the government. You could be arrested for your articles!

Would you stop criticizing the government? Why?

BUILDING BACKGROUND People within the new United States had differing viewpoints on many issues. Personal rivalries among political leaders also created divisions in the new nation. Trying to limit dissent in the country, the federal government passed several unpopular laws.

The Election of 1796

The election of 1796 began a new era in U.S. politics. For the first time, more than one candidate ran for president. **Political parties**, groups that help elect people and shape policies, had begun to form during Washington's presidency. Despite Washington's warnings about political parties, the rivalry between two parties dominated the 1796 election.

Alexander Hamilton helped found the **Federalist Party**, which wanted a strong federal government and supported industry and trade. The Federalists chose John Adams and Thomas Pinckney as candidates. Adams knew he was not well liked in the South or the West, but he hoped people would support him after they thought about his years of loyal public service.

Thomas Jefferson and James Madison founded the **Democratic-Republican Party**. Its members, called Republicans, wanted to limit the federal government's power. (This party is not related to today's Republican Party.) They chose Thomas Jefferson and Aaron Burr as their candidates.

The First Political Parties, 1796

Federalists/North

Alexander Hamilton

John Adams

John Jay

Republicans/South

Thomas Jefferson

James Madison

Albert Gallatin

TERRITORY
NORTHWEST
OF OHIO RIVER

SOUTHWEST
TERRITORY

VT 4
NH 6
MA 16
NY 12
RI 4
CT 9
PA DR-14 F-1
NJ 7
DE 3
MD DR-4 F-7
VA DR-20 F-1
KY 4
NC DR-11 F-1
TN 3
SC 8
GA 4

70°W
90°W

Federalist (Adams)

Democratic-Republican (Jefferson)

11   Number of electoral votes

0   150   300 Miles
0   150   300 Kilometers

N E S W

GEOGRAPHY SKILLS   **INTERPRETING MAPS**

Region Which political party had more electoral votes in 1796?

Party differences were based partly on where and how people lived. Businesspeople in the cities tended to support the Federalists. Farmers in more isolated areas generally favored the Democratic-Republicans. Both sides attacked each other. Republicans called Adams a royalist—an insult to a man so involved in the Revolution. The Federalists accused the Republicans of favoring the French.

In the end, Adams defeated Jefferson. At the time, the person who came in second in a presidential election became vice president. So, after months of campaigning against one another, Adams and Jefferson took office together.

READING CHECK   **Finding Main Ideas**
How did the election of 1796 change the nature of politics in the United States?

President Adams and the XYZ Affair

John Adams had the challenging task of following Washington as president. The people had adored Washington. Adams would have to work hard to win the people's trust.

A New President

At first glance, John Adams did not appear well suited for the presidency. Although Adams had been a leading Patriot during the American Revolution and had later served as a foreign diplomat, he lacked Washington's dignity, and most people saw him as a cold and distant person. Still, many people—even those who opposed him—respected Adams. They recognized his hard work, honesty, and intelligence.

POLITICAL CARTOON
The XYZ Affair

After the XYZ affair, French ships continued to attack American merchant ships. In this cartoon, the United States is represented by the woman. The men, symbolizing the French, are taking valuables from her. The people in the distance are other European nations.

Why do you think this man is encouraging the woman to look away?

These people aren't helping the woman. What do you think the cartoon is suggesting by this?

ANALYSIS SKILL | **INTERPRETING POLITICAL CARTOONS**

How does the cartoon show that America is being preyed upon by the French?

The United States and France

One of Adams's first goals as president was to improve the relationship between the United States and France. You may remember that the French had once tried to hire American privateers to help them fight Great Britain, a practice Washington frowned upon. Adams sent U.S. diplomats to Paris to smooth over the conflict and to negotiate a treaty to protect U.S. shipping.

When the diplomats arrived in France, they learned that French foreign minister Talleyrand would not speak to them. Instead, they had a strange and secret visit from three French agents. Shockingly, the agents said that Talleyrand would discuss a treaty only in exchange for a $250,000 bribe. The French government also wanted a loan of $12 million. The amazed diplomats refused these demands.

In March 1798 President Adams told Congress that the peace-seeking mission had failed. He described the French terms, substituting the letters X, Y, and Z for the names of the French agents. Upon hearing the disgraceful news, Federalists in Congress called for war with France.

The **XYZ affair**, as the French demand for a bribe came to be called, outraged the American public. "Millions for defense, but not one cent for tribute!" became the rallying cry of the American people.

Preparations for War

Fearing war, Adams asked Congress to expand the navy to a fleet of more than 30 ships. He thought war with France might be unavoidable. He also decided the United States should keep a peacetime army. Congress approved both measures.

Although Adams had asked Congress for military support, he did not want to go to war with France. He was worried about its cost. So he did not ask Congress to declare war. Instead, he tried to reopen peace talks with France.

Peace Efforts

Adams's decision not to declare war stunned Federalists. Despite intense pressure from members of his own party, Adams refused to change his mind.

American and French ships, however, began fighting each other in the Caribbean. Adams sent a representative to France to engage in talks to try to end the fighting. The United States and France eventually signed a treaty. Adams then forced two members of his cabinet to resign for trying to block his peace efforts.

READING CHECK Identifying Points of View
What did Americans mean when they said "Millions for defense, but not one cent for tribute"?

The Alien and Sedition Acts

Many Democratic-Republicans continued to sympathize with France. Federalists, angered by their stand, called them "democrats, mobocrats, and all other kinds of rats."

In 1798 the Federalist-controlled Congress passed four laws known together as the **Alien and Sedition Acts**. These laws were said to protect the United States, but the Federalists intended them to crush opposition to war. The most controversial was the Sedition Act, which forbade anyone from publishing or voicing criticism of the federal government. In effect, this cancelled basic protections of freedom of speech and freedom of the press.

The two main Democratic-Republican leaders, Thomas Jefferson and James Madison, viewed these acts as a misuse of the government's power. Attacking the problem at the state level, they wrote resolutions passed by the Kentucky legislature in 1798 and in Virginia in 1799. Known as the **Kentucky and Virginia Resolutions**, these documents argued that the Alien and Sedition Acts were unconstitutional. They stated that the federal government could not pass these acts because they interfered with state government. Madison and Jefferson pressured Congress to repeal the Alien and Sedition Acts. Congress did not, although it allowed the acts to expire within a few years.

The Kentucky and Virginia Resolutions did not have the force of national law, but they supported the idea that states could challenge the federal government. This idea would grow to have a tremendous impact on American history later in the 1800s.

READING CHECK **Analyzing** How did the Kentucky and Virginia Resolutions support the rights of states?

SUMMARY AND PREVIEW Political parties formed to reflect different viewpoints. In the next chapter you will read about Thomas Jefferson's presidency.

Section 4 Assessment

go.hrw.com
Online Quiz
KEYWORD: SF7 HP7

Reviewing Ideas, Terms, and People

1. a. Recall What two **political parties** emerged before the election of 1796? Who were the founders of each party?
b. Analyze What effect did political parties have on the election of 1796?
c. Elaborate Do you think it was difficult for Adams and Jefferson to serve together as president and vice president? Explain your answer.

2. a. Recall What was one of Adams's first goals as president?
b. Make Inferences Why were Federalists shocked by Adams's decision to resume peace talks with the French?

3. a. Identify What did the **Alien and Sedition Acts** state?
b. Explain What idea regarding states' rights did the **Kentucky and Virginia Resolutions** support?
c. Elaborate Would you have supported the Alien and Sedition Acts? Explain your answer.

Critical Thinking

4. Contrasting Review your notes on the election of 1796 and the formation of political parties. Then create a chart like this one identifying how each of the terms listed below reflected party disagreements.

XYZ Affair	
Alien and Sedition Acts	
Kentucky and Virginia Resolutions	

FOCUS ON WRITING

5. Gathering Information about John Adams Take some notes about John Adams's contributions that would support his nomination for the Nobel Prize. Then begin to compare and contrast all four leaders you have studied in this chapter. Which one will you nominate?

Social Studies Skills

Analysis | Critical Thinking | Civic Participation | Study

Making Group Decisions

Define the Skill

Democracy is one of the most valued principles of American society. It is based on the idea that the members of society, or representatives they choose, make the decisions that affect society. Decision-making would be much more efficient if just one person decided what to do and how to do it. However, that method is not at all democratic.

Making decisions as a group is a complicated and difficult skill. However, it is an important one at all levels of society—from governing the nation to making group decisions at school, in the community, and with your friends. At every level, the skill is based on the ability of the group's members to interact in effective and cooperative ways.

Learn the Skill

Think about the job the first Congress faced after the Constitution was ratified. The nation was still millions of dollars in debt from the Revolutionary War. Congress had to find a way to pay these debts as well as raise money to run the government.

Leaders like Jefferson and Hamilton had ideas about how to accomplish these goals. However, neither man could act alone. In a democracy the group—in this case Congress—must make the decisions and take action.

This task was complicated by the fact that Jefferson and Hamilton disagreed on what to do. Each man's supporters in Congress pushed his point of view. Fortunately, its members were able to overcome their differences, compromise on goals and actions, and accept group decisions they might not have agreed with personally. Had they not possessed this ability and skill, the nation's early years might have been even more difficult than they were.

Like that first Congress, being part of an effective group requires that you behave in certain ways.

1 **Be an active member.** Take part in setting the group's goals and in making its decisions. Participate in planning and taking group action.

2 **Take a position.** State your views and work to persuade other members to accept them. However, also be open to negotiating and compromising to settle differences within the group.

3 **Be willing to take charge if leadership is needed.** But also be willing to follow the leadership of other members.

Practice the Skill

Suppose that you are a member of the first Congress. With a group of classmates, you must decide what and who should be taxed to raise the money the government needs. Remember that you are an elected official. If you do something to upset the people, you could lose your job. When your group has finished, answer the following questions.

1. Did your group have a plan for completing its task? Did it discuss what taxes to pass? Compared to other members, how much did you take part in those activities?

2. How well did your group work together? What role did you play in that? Was it a positive contribution or a negative one? Explain.

3. Was your group able to make a decision? If not, why? If so, was compromise involved? Do you support the decision? Explain why or why not.

Chapter Review

Visual Summary

QUICK FACTS

Use the visual summary below to help you review the main ideas of the chapter.

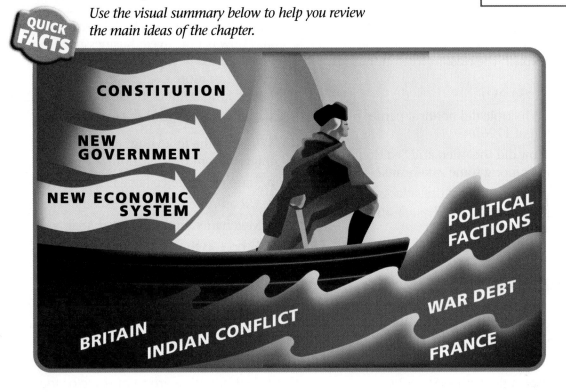

CONSTITUTION

NEW GOVERNMENT

NEW ECONOMIC SYSTEM

POLITICAL FACTIONS

BRITAIN   INDIAN CONFLICT

WAR DEBT

FRANCE

Reviewing Vocabulary, Terms, and People

Complete each sentence by filling in the blank with the correct term or person.

1. The _____ established the structure of the federal court system and its relationship to state courts.

2. Federalists angered many Republicans when they passed the _____ to protect the United States from traitors.

3. As president, Washington was able to establish several _____, or decisions that serve as examples for later action.

4. Farmers in western Pennsylvania protested taxes in the _____.

5. The _____ was created in order to strengthen the U.S. economy.

Comprehension and Critical Thinking

SECTION 1 *(Pages 234–237)*

6. **a. Recall** What precedents did President Washington and Congress establish for the executive and judicial branches?

   b. Draw Conclusions Why did Americans select George Washington as their first president?

   c. Evaluate Do you think the newly established government met the expectations of its citizens? Why or why not?

SECTION 2 *(Pages 238–242)*

7. **a. Identify** What changes did Alexander Hamilton make to the national economy?

   b. Contrast In what ways did Hamilton and Jefferson disagree on the economy?

   c. Evaluate Which of Hamilton's economic plans do you think was the most important to the new nation? Why?

SECTION 3 (Pages 243–249)

8. a. Describe What challenges did the nation face during Washington's presidency?

b. Make Inferences Why did Washington believe that it was important for the United States to remain neutral in foreign conflicts?

c. Evaluate Rate the success of Washington's presidency. Explain the reasons for your rating.

SECTION 4 (Pages 250–253)

9. a. Describe What role did political parties play in the election of 1796?

b. Analyze How did the Alien and Sedition Acts create division among some Americans?

c. Predict How might the political attacks between the Federalist and Democratic-Republican parties lead to problems in the future?

Reviewing Themes

10. Economics What economic problems troubled the nation at the beginning of Washington's presidency? How were they solved?

11. Politics How did the creation of political parties change politics in the United States?

Using the Internet

go.hrw.com
KEYWORD: SF7 CH7

12. Activity: Creating a Poster In 1798 war with France seemed on the horizon. The Federalist-controlled Congress passed a law that made it a crime to criticize the government in print. In 1971 war raged in Vietnam and the president used a court order to stop publication of information critical of the government's actions in Vietnam. What do these events have in common? Enter the activity keyword. Then research the Alien and Sedition Acts and the Pentagon Papers case during the Vietnam War. Create a poster to display your information and to illustrate the connection between a free press and a democratic society.

Reading Skills

Inferences about History *Use the Reading Skills taught in this chapter to answer the question about the reading selection below.*

> Party differences were based partly on where and how people lived. Businesspeople in the cities tended to support the Federalists. Farmers in more isolated areas generally favored the Democratic-Republicans. *(p. 251)*

13. Which of the following statements can be inferred from the selection?

a. Farmers wanted a large federal government.

b. Urban Americans were usually Republicans.

c. Merchants supported John Adams.

d. People in the cities had different concerns than did the rural population.

Social Studies Skills

Making Group Decisions *Use the Social Studies Skills taught in this chapter to answer the questions below.*

Get together with a group of three or four students and discuss the Alien and Sedition Acts. Answer the following questions individually and as a group.

14. Do you think that limits should have been put on Americans' speeches and printed articles?

15. What other ideas might Congress have considered to resolve the tensions over the issue?

FOCUS ON WRITING

16. Writing a Nobel Nomination Now that you've chosen your nominee for the Nobel Prize, you can start to write your nomination. Begin with a sentence that identifies the person you are nominating. Then give at least three reasons for your nomination. Each reason should include a specific achievement or contribution of this person. End your nomination with a sentence that sums up your reasons for nominating this person for the Nobel Prize. Be persuasive. You need to convince the Nobel Prize committee that this person deserves the prize more than anyone else in the world.

Standardized Test Practice

8.1.6, 8.1.7, 8.4.5, 8.4.8

DIRECTIONS: Read each question and write the letter of the best response.

1 In the 1790s, most Americans

   A lived in the countryside and worked on family farms.

   B lived in small towns and worked as laborers or craftspeople.

   C lived in cities and worked as laborers, craftspeople, or merchants.

   D lived west of the Appalachian Mountains or wanted to move West.

2 In his Farewell Address in 1796, President Washington advised Americans of

   A the nation's need for a national bank.

   B his fear of a British invasion to end American independence.

   C his wish that the office of president be given more power.

   D the dangers of ties with foreign nations.

3 President Washington demonstrated the government's power under the new Constitution to enforce federal law in the way he handled the

   A Whiskey Rebellion.

   B Alien and Sedition Acts.

   C XYZ affair.

   D Judiciary Act of 1789.

4 The two-party system that exists in American politics today first arose during the election of which president?

   A George Washington

   B John Adams

   C Thomas Jefferson

   D James Madison

5 Why did George Washington issue the Neutrality Proclamation?

   A He feared that involvement in the war between France and Britain was dangerous.

   B He hoped to show the world that the United States was a peaceful nation.

   C He wanted to concentrate on internal problems that faced the nation.

   D Jefferson persuaded Washington to stay neutral toward France.

6 Which of the following was an issue on which Alexander Hamilton and Thomas Jefferson had differing views?

   A protective tariffs

   B national bank

   C role of the central government

   D all of the above

7 Examine the following passage from a description of the Alien Act and then use it to answer the question below.

> "The Alien Law has been bitterly criticized as a direct attack upon our liberties. In fact, it affects only foreigners who are plotting against us, and has nothing to do with American citizens. It gives authority to the President to order out of the country all aliens he judges dangerous to the peace and safety of the United States, or whom he suspects of treason or secret plots against the government."
>
> — Timothy Pickering, adapted from *Life of Timothy Pickering,* Vol. 3

Document-Based Question What is the author's point of view toward the Alien Law?

Assignment

Write a paper explaining how the federal system balances power among the legislative, executive, and judicial branches of government.

Explaining a Political Process

How do you register to vote? What is the difference between a civil court and a federal court? When we want to know about a process or system of our government, we often turn to written explanations.

1. Prewrite

Considering Purpose and Audience

In this assignment, you will be writing for an audience of middle school students. You'll need to

- identify questions they might have about the process or system
- identify factors or details that might confuse them

As you plan your paper, keep your audience in mind.

TIP **Using a Graphic Organizer**
A chart like the following can help you organize the body of your explanation.

Legislative	Executive	Judicial

Collecting and Organizing the Information

The big idea, or thesis, of your explanation will be that the federal system balances the power among the three branches of government. To collect information about each branch and its powers, you can use a chart like the one on the left. Be sure to note the relationships among the parts. Also, note the important characteristics of each part. When you have completed the chart, you will have the basic organization of your paper.

2. Write

You can use this framework to help you write your first draft.

A Writer's Framework

Introduction	Body	Conclusion
■ State the big idea of your paper. ■ Explain briefly why this topic is important to the reader.	■ Identify the important characteristics of each part of the process or system. ■ Explain any relationships between or among the parts. ■ Define terms your readers might not know. ■ Where appropriate, include graphics to illustrate your explanation.	■ Restate your big idea in different words. ■ Summarize your main points.

3. Evaluate and Revise

Evaluating

Clear, straightforward language is important when explaining how things work. Use the following questions to discover ways to improve your paper.

Evaluation Questions for an Explanation of a Process or System

- Does your big-idea statement accurately reflect your explanation of the process or system?
- Do you discuss each part of the process or system in logical order?
- Do you include details and information to explain each part of the process or system?
- If you used bulleted or numbered lists, are the items parallel—that is, do they have the same grammatical forms or structures?
- Does your conclusion restate your big idea and explain the importance of your topic?

TIP Using Bulleted Lists The items in a bulleted list should be in the **same** grammatical forms or structures.

Not the same:
Duties of the judicial branch include
- interpret laws
- overseeing lower courts

The same:
Duties of the judicial branch include
- interpreting laws
- overseeing lower courts

Revising

Sometimes a complex explanation sounds even more complex when you try to explain it in a paragraph. In those cases, a bulleted list of facts or examples may make it easier for your readers to understand the information you are presenting. As you revise your paper, consider whether you have any information you should put in a bulleted list.

4. Proofread and Publish

Proofreading

If you use special formatting in your paper, it is important to make sure that it is consistent. Here are some things to check:

- If you have used boldface or italic type, have you always used it in the same way—for important information, for a heading, for a technical term?
- If you have used a list of items, have you consistently used numbers or bullets?

Publishing

Since you are writing this paper for students, you might find a student in the sixth or seventh grade to read it. Find out whether your explanation seems clear and interesting.

5. Practice and Apply

Use the steps and strategies outlined in this workshop to write your explanation of a process or system.

The New Republic

What You Will Learn...

By the time the country had experienced two presidential terms, people had begun to think of themselves as Americans. A new sense of pride and unity influenced all areas of American society, from politics to art, from economics to religion. Settlers began moving deeper into the continent and the United States began to grow. In the next four chapters, you will learn about the first expansion of the young nation.

Explore the Art

In this picture, Lewis and Clark are shown asking advice from Sacagawea, a teenaged Shoshone Indian who helped them on their exploration of the continent. How does this picture show the challenges facing the explorers?

The Jefferson Era

Indiana Standards

Social Studies Standards

8.1.8 Evaluate the significance of the presidential and congressional election of 1800 and the transfer of political authority and power to the Democratic-Republican party led by the new president, Thomas Jefferson (1801).

8.1.11 Explain the events leading up to and the significance of the Louisiana Purchase (1803) and the expedition of Lewis and Clark (1803–1806).

8.1.12 Explain the main issues, decisions, and consequences of landmark Supreme Court cases.

8.3.9 Analyze human and physical factors that have influenced migration and settlement patterns and relate them to the economic development of the United States.

go.hrw.com
Indiana
KEYWORD: SF10 IN

FOCUS ON WRITING

A Letter of Recommendation Americans love lists—the five best books of the year, the 10 best video games, the three best soccer players. As you read this chapter you will gather some information about Thomas Jefferson. Then you will write a letter to your newspaper telling why Jefferson should be on the newspaper's "Top Ten American Presidents" list.

UNITED STATES

1801 Thomas Jefferson takes office.

1803 U.S. Senate approves the Louisiana Purchase.

1800

WORLD

1802 An army of former slaves led by Toussaint-Louverture defeats a French army in Haiti.

HOLT

History's Impact

▶ video series

Watch the video to understand the impact of expanding frontiers on the United States.

What You Will Learn...

In this chapter you will learn about the presidency of Thomas Jefferson. A man of many talents, Jefferson looked back to classical architecture to design his Virginia home, Monticello.

1808
Tecumseh and his brother, known as the Prophet, found Prophetstown.

1804
Lewis and Clark begin their westward journey.

1807
Congress passes the Embargo Act.

1812
Congress declares war against Great Britain.

1815
The Battle of New Orleans is fought.

1805

1810

1815

1807
The slave trade is abolished in the British Empire.

1814
Kurozumi Munetada founds an influential Shinto religious sect that stresses patriotism in Japan.

THE JEFFERSON ERA **263**

Reading Social Studies

by Kylene Beers

| Economics | Geography | Politics | Society and Culture | Science and Technology |

Focus on Themes In this chapter you will learn about Thomas Jefferson's presidency. You will read what happened when Jefferson's first run to be president ended in a tie. After that, you will learn about his decision to buy Louisiana from the French, see how he encouraged the exploration of the West, and discover why, during his second term, America found itself at war with Great Britain. You will see how America's expanding **geography** and **politics** were intertwined.

Public Documents in History

Focus on Reading Historians use many types of documents to learn about the past. These documents can often be divided into two types—private and public. Private documents are those written for a person's own use, such as letters, journals, or notebooks. Public documents, on the other hand, are available for everyone to read and examine. They include such things as laws, tax codes, and treaties.

Studying Public Documents Studying public documents from the past can tell us a great deal about the politics and society of the time. However, public documents can often be confusing or difficult to understand. When you read such a document, you may want to use a list of questions like the one below to be sure you understand what you're reading.

You can often figure out the topic of a public document from the title and introduction.

Public documents often use unfamiliar words or use familiar words in unfamiliar ways. For example, the document on the next page uses the word *augmented*. Do you know what the word means in this context? If not, you should look it up.

Many public documents deal with several issues and will therefore have several main ideas.

Question Sheet for Public Documents

1. What is the topic of the document?
2. Do I understand what I'm reading?
3. Is there any vocabulary in the document that I do not understand?
4. What parts of the document should I re-read?
5. What are the main ideas and details of the document?
6. What have I learned from reading this document?

You Try It!

The passage below was taken from a Post Office notice from 1815. Read the passage and then answer the questions that follow.

Rates of Postage

Postmasters will take notice, that by an act of Congress, passed on the 23d instant, the several rates of postage are augmented fifty per cent; and that after the first of February next, the Rates of Postage for single Letters will be,
For any distance not exceeding 40 miles, 12 cents
    Over 40 miles and not exceeding 90 miles, 15 cents
    Over 90 miles and not exceeding 150 miles, 18 1/2 cents
    Over 150 miles and not exceeding 300 miles, 25 1/2 cents
    Over 300 miles and not exceeding 500 miles, 30 cents
    Over 500 miles, 37 1/2 cents
    Double letters, or those composed of two pieces of paper, double those rates.
    Triple letters, or those composed of three pieces of paper, triple those rates.
    Packets, or letters composed of four or more pieces of paper, and weighing one ounce or more, avoirdupois, are to be rated equal to one single letter for each quarter ounce.

After reading the document above, answer the following questions.

1. What is this document about?

2. What was the main idea or ideas of this document? What supporting details were included?

3. Look at the word *packets* in the last paragraph of the document. The word is not used here in the same way we usually use *packets* today. What does the word mean in this case? How can you tell?

4. Are there any other words in this passage with which you are unfamiliar? How might not knowing those words hinder your understanding of the passage?

As you read Chapter 8, look for passages from other public documents. What can these documents teach you about the past?

Jefferson Becomes President

What You Will Learn...

Main Ideas

1. The election of 1800 marked the first peaceful transition in power from one political party to another.
2. President Jefferson's beliefs about the federal government were reflected in his policies.
3. *Marbury* v. *Madison* increased the power of the judicial branch of government.

The Big Idea

Thomas Jefferson's election began a new era in American government.

Key Terms and People

John Adams, *p. 266*
Thomas Jefferson, *p. 266*
John Marshall, *p. 270*
Marbury v. *Madison*, p. 270
judicial review, *p. 270*

TAKING NOTES As you read, take notes in a graphic organizer like this one. List the details of the election of 1800, Jefferson's beliefs and policies, and how the power of the judicial branch changed during his time in office.

Election of 1800	
Jefferson's Beliefs and Policies	
Power of the Judical Branch	

 8.1.7. 8.1.8, 8.1.9, 8.1.12, 8.1.30, 8.2.1, 8.2.3

If **YOU** were there...

You are a Maryland voter from a frontier district—and you are tired! For days, you and your friends have been wrangling over the presidential election. Who shall it be—John Adams or Thomas Jefferson? Your vote depends on your personal judgment.

Which candidate would you choose for president?

BUILDING BACKGROUND John Adams had not been a popular president, but many still admired his ability and high principles. Both he and Thomas Jefferson had played major roles in winning independence and shaping the new government. Now, political differences sharply divided the two men and their supporters. In the election of 1800, voters were also divided.

The Election of 1800

In the presidential election of 1800, Federalists **John Adams** and Charles C. Pinckney ran against Democratic-Republicans **Thomas Jefferson** and Aaron Burr. Each party believed that the American republic's survival depended upon the success of their candidates. With so much at stake, the election was hotly contested.

Unlike today, candidates did not travel around giving speeches. Instead, the candidates' supporters made their arguments in letters and newspaper editorials. Adams's supporters claimed that Jefferson was a pro-French radical. Put Jefferson in office, they warned, and the violence and chaos of the French Revolution would surely follow in the United States. Plus, Federalists argued, Jefferson's interest in science and philosophy proved that he wanted to destroy organized religion.

Democratic-Republican newspapers responded that Adams wanted to crown himself king. What else, they asked, could be the purpose of the Alien and Sedition Acts? Republicans also hinted that Adams would use the newly created permanent army to limit Americans' rights.

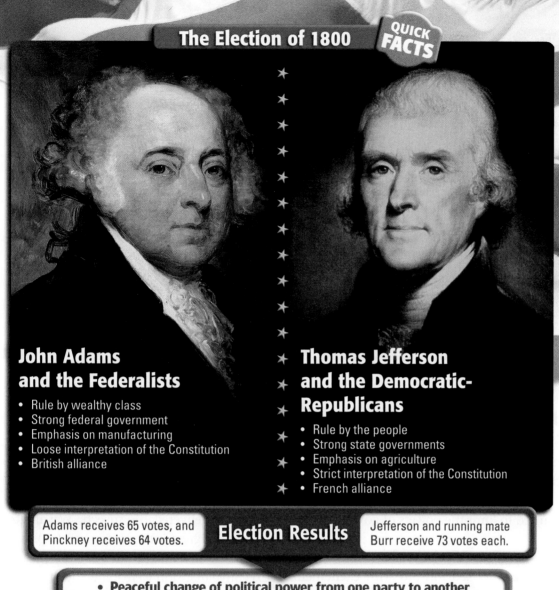

The Election of 1800

QUICK FACTS

John Adams and the Federalists

- Rule by wealthy class
- Strong federal government
- Emphasis on manufacturing
- Loose interpretation of the Constitution
- British alliance

Thomas Jefferson and the Democratic-Republicans

- Rule by the people
- Strong state governments
- Emphasis on agriculture
- Strict interpretation of the Constitution
- French alliance

Election Results

Adams receives 65 votes, and Pinckney receives 64 votes.

Jefferson and running mate Burr receive 73 votes each.

- **Peaceful change of political power from one party to another**
- **The tied race led to the Twelfth Amendment (1804), which created a separate ballot for president and vice president.**

When the election results came in, Jefferson and Burr had won 73 electoral votes each to 65 for Adams and 64 for Pinckney. The Democratic-Republicans had won the election, but the tie between Jefferson and Burr caused a problem. Under the Constitution at that time, the two candidates with the most votes became president and vice president. The decision went to the House of Representatives, as called for in the Constitution.

The House, like the electoral college, also deadlocked. Days went by as vote after vote was called, each ending in ties. Exhausted lawmakers put their heads on their desks and slept between votes. Some napped on the floor.

Jefferson finally won on the thirty-sixth vote. The election marked the first time that one party had replaced another in power in the United States.

The problems with the voting system led Congress to propose the Twelfth Amendment. This amendment created a separate ballot for president and vice president.

READING CHECK Analyzing Information
What was significant about Jefferson's victory?

SPEECH

Jefferson's Inaugural Address

On March 4, 1801, Thomas Jefferson gave his first inaugural address. In the following excerpt, Jefferson describes his thoughts on the nation's future.

> By using phrases like these, Jefferson tries to reassure his political opponents.

> Here Jefferson states his opinion of what is essential to good government.

> This phrase shows Jefferson's determination to keep government small.

"Let us, then, fellow citizens, unite with one heart and one mind . . . [E]very difference of opinion is not a difference of principle. We have called by different names brethren[1] of the same principle. We are all republicans; we are all federalists.**"**

"Still one thing more, fellow citizens, a wise and frugal[2] Government, which shall restrain men from injuring one another, shall leave them otherwise free to regulate their own pursuits of industry and improvement, and shall not take from the mouth of labor the bread it has earned. This is the sum of good government . . .**"**

1. **brethren**: brothers 2. **frugal**: thrifty

ANALYSIS SKILL | ANALYZING PRIMARY SOURCES

What words and phrases indicate Jefferson's support for a small national government?

Jefferson's Policies

When Jefferson took office, he brought with him a style and political ideas different from those of Adams and Washington. Jefferson was less formal than his predecessors, and he wanted to limit the powers of government.

Jefferson Is Inaugurated

THE IMPACT TODAY

A monument to Thomas Jefferson was completed in 1943 and is one of the most frequently visited sites in Washington, D.C.

Americans looked forward with excitement to Jefferson's first speech as president. People from across the nation gathered in the new capital, Washington, D.C., to hear him. Curious travelers looked with pride at the partially completed Capitol building and at the executive mansion (not yet called the White House). The two buildings dominated the surrounding homes and forests.

Small businesses dotted the landscape. At one of these, a modest boardinghouse, the president-elect was putting the finishing touches on his speech. On the morning of March 4, 1801, he left the boardinghouse and walked to the Capitol. The leader of a republic, Jefferson believed, should not ride in fancy carriages.

Jefferson read his speech in a quiet voice. He wanted to make it clear that he supported the will of the majority. He also stressed the need for a limited government and the protection of civil liberties.

From these humble surroundings in which Jefferson delivered his speech, Washington eventually grew into a large and impressive city. Over the years, the Capitol and the executive mansion were joined by other state buildings and monuments. Jefferson, who had long dreamed of a new national capital that would be independent of the interests of any one state, was pleased to be a part of this process of building a federal city.

Jefferson in Office

President Jefferson faced the task of putting his republican ideas into practice. One of his first actions was to select the members of his cabinet. His choices included James Madison as secretary of state and Albert Gallatin as secretary of the treasury.

Jefferson would also benefit from the Democratic-Republican Party's newly won control of both houses of Congress. At Jefferson's urging, Congress allowed the hated Alien and Sedition Acts to expire. Jefferson lowered military spending and reduced the size of the army. The navy was cut to seven active ships. Jefferson and Gallatin hoped that saving this money would allow the government to repay the national debt. Jefferson also asked Gallatin to find ways to get rid of domestic taxes, like the tax on whiskey. The Democratic-Republican–led Congress passed the laws needed to carry out these policies.

The entire national government in 1801 consisted only of several hundred people. Jefferson preferred to keep it that way. He believed that the primary **functions** of the federal government were to protect the nation from foreign threats, deliver the mail, and collect customs duties.

Jefferson did recognize that some of the Federalist policies—such as the creation of the Bank of the United States—should be kept. Although Jefferson had battled Hamilton over the Bank, as president he agreed to leave it in place.

READING CHECK **Summarizing** What policy changes did Democratic-Republicans introduce, and which Federalist policies did Jefferson keep?

Marbury v. Madison

Although Republicans controlled the presidency and Congress, Federalists dominated the federal judiciary. In an effort to continue their control over the judiciary, Federalist legislators passed the Judiciary Act of 1801 shortly before their terms of office ended. This act created 16 new federal judgeships that President Adams filled with Federalists before leaving office. The Republican press called these people midnight judges, arguing that Adams had packed the judiciary with Federalists the night before he left office.

Some of these appointments were made so late that the documents that authorized them had not been delivered by the time Adams left office. This led to controversy once Jefferson took office. William Marbury, named as a justice of the peace by President Adams, did not receive his documents before Adams left office. When Jefferson took office, Marbury demanded the documents. On Jefferson's advice, however, the new secretary of state, James Madison, refused to deliver them. Jefferson argued that the appointment of the midnight judges was not valid.

ACADEMIC VOCABULARY
functions
uses or purposes

SUPREME COURT DECISIONS

Marbury v. Madison (1803)

Background of the Case Shortly before Thomas Jefferson took office, John Adams had appointed William Marbury to be a justice of the peace. Adams had signed Marbury's commission, but it was never delivered. Marbury sued to force Madison to give him the commission.

The Court's Ruling
The Court ruled that the law Marbury based his claim on was unconstitutional.

The Court's Reasoning
The Judiciary Act of 1789 gave the Supreme Court the authority to hear a wide variety of cases, including those like Marbury's. But the Supreme Court ruled that Congress did not have the power to make such a law. Why? Because the Constitution limits the types of cases the Supreme Court can hear. Thus, the law was in conflict with the Constitution and had to be struck down.

Why It Matters
Marbury v. Madison was important for several reasons. It confirmed the Supreme Court's power to declare acts of Congress unconstitutional. By doing so, it established the Court as the final authority on the Constitution. This helped make the judicial branch of government equal to the other two branches. Chief Justice John Marshall and later federal judges would use this power of judicial review as a check on the legislative and executive branches.

ANALYSIS SKILL **ANALYZING INFORMATION**

1. What do you think it means to be the final authority on the Constitution?
2. How did *Marbury* v. *Madison* affect the Constitution's system of checks and balances?

Marbury brought suit, asking the Supreme Court to order Madison to deliver the appointment papers. Marbury claimed that the Judiciary Act of 1789 gave the Supreme Court the power to do so.

John Marshall, a Federalist appointed by John Adams, was the chief justice of the United States. Chief Justice Marshall and President Jefferson disagreed about many political issues. When Marshall agreed to hear Marbury's case, Jefferson protested, saying that the Federalists "have retired into the judiciary as a stronghold." Marshall wrote the Court's opinion in **Marbury v. Madison**, a case that helped establish the Supreme Court's power to check the power of the other branches of government. The Constitution, Chief Justice Marshall noted, gave the Supreme Court authority to hear only certain types of cases. A request like Marbury's was not one of them. The law that Marbury's case depended upon was, therefore, unconstitutional.

John Marshall served as chief justice of the United States for 34 years.

In denying Marbury's request in this way, the Court avoided a direct confrontation with Jefferson's administration. But more importantly, it established the Court's power of **judicial review**, the power to declare an act of Congress unconstitutional. Marshall and later federal judges would use this power of judicial review to make the judiciary a much stronger part of the national government.

READING CHECK Analyzing Information
Why was *Marbury* v. *Madison* an important ruling?

SUMMARY AND PREVIEW A peaceful transfer of power took place in Washington after the election of 1800. In the next section you will read about the Louisiana Purchase.

go.hrw.com
Online Quiz
KEYWORD: SF7 HP8

Section 1 Assessment

Reviewing Ideas, Terms, and People

1. **a. Identify** What were the political parties in the election of 1800, and who were their candidates?
   b. Analyze Why was the election of 1800 significant?
2. **a. Describe** What ideas for government did **Thomas Jefferson** stress in his inaugural address?
   b. Compare and Contrast What similarities and differences did Jefferson's Republican government have with the previous Federalist one?
   c. Elaborate Defend Jefferson's preference for keeping the national government small.
3. **a. Identify** Who was **John Marshall**?
   b. Draw Conclusions Why is the power of **judicial review** important?
   c. Predict How might the **Marbury v. Madison** ruling affect future actions by Congress?

Critical Thinking

4. **Categorizing** Review your notes on Jefferson's beliefs and policies. Then copy the graphic organizer below and show how Jefferson brought change through his policies.

Jefferson as President

Federalist Policies	Republican Policies

FOCUS ON WRITING

5. **Gathering Ideas about a Person's Accomplishments** Look back through what you have just read to see what you have learned about Jefferson's decisions in office. Make a list of the traits you think each decision shows in Jefferson.

Thomas Jefferson

How would you inspire people to seek freedom?

When did he live? He was born on April 13, 1743. He died on July 4, 1826, within hours of the death of President John Adams, his rival and friend. The date was also the fiftieth anniversary of the Declaration of Independence.

Where did he live? He was born in Albemarle County, Virginia, where he inherited a large estate from his father. At age 26 he began building his elegant lifetime home, Monticello, which he designed himself. He spent much of his life away from home, in Philadelphia; Washington, D.C.; and Europe. Yet he always longed to return to his peaceful home.

What did he do? Jefferson wanted only three of his accomplishments listed on his tomb: author of the Declaration of American Independence, author of the Virginia Statute for Religious Freedom, and Father of the University of Virginia. What did he *not* mention? Governor of Virginia, lawyer, Revolutionary leader, writer, philosopher, inventor, architect, plant scientist, book collector, musician, astronomer, ambassador, secretary of state—and, of course, president of the United States.

Why is he important? Jefferson's powerful words in the Declaration of Independence have inspired people throughout the world to seek freedom, equality, and self-rule. His most celebrated achievement as president (1801–1809) was the purchase of the Louisiana Territory from France. The Louisiana Purchase of 1803 nearly doubled the size of the United States. Jefferson then sponsored the Lewis and Clark expedition to explore this new territory.

Evaluating Why has Thomas Jefferson been a hero to generations of Americans?

Thomas Jefferson wrote the Declaration of Independence and later served as president of the United States.

KEY EVENTS

1767 Begins practicing law in Virginia

1769–1776 Serves in Virginia House of Burgesses

1776 Drafts the first version of the Declaration of Independence

1789 Appointed secretary of state by George Washington

1801 Inaugurated as president

1803 Authorizes the purchase of Louisiana from France

1809 Retires to Monticello

The Louisiana Purchase

What You Will Learn...

Main Ideas

1. As American settlers moved West, control of the Mississippi River became more important to the United States.
2. The Louisiana Purchase almost doubled the size of the United States.
3. Expeditions led by Lewis, Clark, and Pike increased Americans' understanding of the West.

The Big Idea

Under President Jefferson's leadership, the United States added the Louisiana Territory.

Key Terms and People

Louisiana Purchase, *p. 274*
Meriwether Lewis, *p. 275*
William Clark, *p. 275*
Lewis and Clark expedition, *p. 275*
Sacagawea, *p. 276*
Zebulon Pike, *p. 276*

TAKING NOTES As you read, take notes in a graphic organizer like the one below on the events leading up to the Louisiana Purchase and the exploration that followed.

Events Leading to Louisiana Purchase	Exploration that Followed Louisiana Purchase

8.1.11, 8.1.15, 8.3.1, 8.3.2, 8.3.5, 8.3.7, 8.3.9

If YOU were there...

You and your family live on a small farm in Kentucky in about 1800. Raised on the frontier, you are a skillful hunter and trapper. One day at the trading post, you see a poster calling for volunteers to join the Corps of Discovery. This expedition will explore the vast region west of the Mississippi River. You think it would be exciting—but dangerous. You might never come home.

Would you volunteer to join the Corps of Discovery?

BUILDING BACKGROUND As the 1800s began, the United States was expanding steadily westward. More lands were opened, and settlers moved in to occupy them. Americans were also curious about the vast lands that lay farther West. Adventurous explorers organized expeditions to find out more about those lands.

American Settlers Move West

By the early 1800s, thousands of Americans settled in the area between the Appalachians and the Mississippi River. As the region's population grew, Kentucky, Tennessee, and Ohio were admitted to the Union. Settlers in these states depended upon the Mississippi and Ohio rivers to move their products to eastern markets.

New Orleans, located at the mouth of the Mississippi, was a very important port. Its busy docks were filled with settlers' farm products and valuable furs bought from American Indians. Many of these cargoes were then sent to Europe. At the same time, manufactured goods passed through the port on their way upriver. As American dependence on the river grew, Jefferson began to worry that a foreign power might shut down access to New Orleans.

"There is on the globe one single spot, the possessor of which is our natural and habitual enemy. It is New Orleans, through which the produce of three-eighths of our territory must pass to market."

—Thomas Jefferson, quoted in *Annals of America, Volume 4, 1797–1820*

The Louisiana Purchase and Western Expeditions

Interactive Map

Fort Clatsop

Bitterroot Mtns.

LEWIS'S RETURN

CLARK'S RETURN

Fort Mandan

LEWIS AND CLARK'S EXPEDITION

BRITISH TERRITORY

Lake Superior

OREGON COUNTRY (Claimed by Britain, Russia, Spain, and the United States)

LOUISIANA PURCHASE (Purchased in 1803)

GREAT PLAINS

MICHIGAN TERRITORY

INDIANA TERRITORY

OH

St. Charles
St. Louis

KY

TN

MISSISSIPPI TERRITORY

ATLANTIC OCEAN

APPALACHIAN MOUNTAINS

Pikes Peak 14,110 ft. (4,301 m)

Santa Fe

SPANISH TERRITORY

PIKE'S EXPEDITION

New Orleans

Gulf of Mexico

PACIFIC OCEAN

Continental Divide

Legend:
- U.S. states and territories in 1804
- Louisiana Purchase
- Disputed by United States and Britain
- Lewis and Clark's Expedition, 1804–1806
- Pike's Expedition, 1806–1807

0   200   400 Miles
0   200   400 Kilometers

New Orleans was founded by the French in 1718. Over time, it became home to many languages and cultures.

GEOGRAPHY SKILLS INTERPRETING MAPS

go.hrw.com
Interactive Map
KEYWORD: SF7 CH8

1. **Location** What major port city was located at the southern tip of the Louisiana Territory?
2. **Human-Environment Interaction** Why might Lewis and Clark have followed the Missouri River?

Spain controlled both New Orleans and Louisiana. This region stretched west from the mighty Mississippi River to the great Rocky Mountains. Although Spain owned Louisiana, Spanish officials found it impossible to keep Americans out of the territory. "You can't put doors on open country," the foreign minister said in despair.

Years of effort failed to improve Spain's position. Under a secret treaty, Spain agreed to trade Louisiana to France, passing the problem on to someone else. One Spanish officer expressed his relief. "I can hardly wait to leave them [the Americans] behind me," he said.

READING CHECK Analyzing Information
Why was New Orleans important to settlers in the western regions of the United States?

Louisiana

In 1802, just before handing over Louisiana to France, Spain closed New Orleans to American shipping. Angry farmers worried about what this would do to the economy. President Jefferson asked the U.S. ambassador to France, Robert R. Livingston, to try to buy New Orleans. Jefferson sent James Monroe to help Livingston.

Napoléon and Louisiana

France was led by Napoléon (nuh-POH-lee-uhn) Bonaparte, a powerful ruler who had conquered most of Europe. He wished to rebuild France's empire in North America.

Napoléon's strategy was to use the French colony of Haiti, in the Caribbean, as a supply

THE JEFFERSON ERA **273**

base. From there he could send troops to Louisiana. However, enslaved Africans had revolted and freed themselves from French rule. Napoléon sent troops to try to regain control of the island, but they were defeated in 1802. This defeat ended his hopes of rebuilding a North American empire.

Jefferson Buys Louisiana

FOCUS ON INDIANA

The Louisiana Territory was briefly governed along with the Indiana Territory from its capital at Vincennes.

The American ambassador got a surprising offer during his negotiations with French foreign minister Charles Talleyrand. When the Americans tried to buy New Orleans, Talleyrand offered to sell all of Louisiana.

With his hopes for a North American empire dashed, Napoléon had turned his attention back to Europe. France was at war with Great Britain, and Napoléon needed money for military supplies. He also hoped that a larger United States would challenge British power.

Livingston and Monroe knew a bargain when they saw one. They quickly accepted the French offer to sell Louisiana for $15 million.

The news pleased Jefferson. But as a strict constructionist, he was troubled. The Constitution did not mention the purchase of foreign lands. He also did not like spending large amounts of public money. Nevertheless, Jefferson agreed to the purchase in the belief that doing so was best for the country.

On October 20, 1803, the Senate approved the **Louisiana Purchase** agreement, which roughly doubled the size of the United States. With the $15 million in the French treasury, Napoléon boasted, "I have given England a rival who, sooner or later, will humble her pride."

READING CHECK **Making Inferences**
Why was the Louisiana Purchase important to the future of the United States?

The Journey West

The time line and photographs you see here show some of the key events and places of the Lewis and Clark expedition. Read the journal entries to get an idea of what the explorers faced.

A large keelboat and two smaller boats were needed to get the supply-heavy expedition moving west.

Small boats helped the travelers move supplies across the Great Plains.

May 14, 1804
The expedition begins near St. Louis.

August 3, 1804
The first official council between representatives of the United States and Plains Indians is held.

October 1804 – April 1805
The expedition establishes Fort Mandan to spend the winter. There, the explorers meet a French fur trader and his wife, Sacagawea.

April 7, 1805 We are about to penetrate a country at least 2,000 miles in width, on which the foot of civilized man had never trodden (walked upon).
—Meriwether Lewis

Explorers Head West

Americans knew little about western Native Americans or the land they lived on. President Jefferson wanted to learn more about the people and land of the West. He also wanted to see if there was a river route that could be taken to the Pacific Ocean.

Lewis and Clark Expedition

In 1803 the president asked Congress to fund an expedition to explore the West. To lead it, he chose former army captain **Meriwether Lewis**. Lewis then chose his friend Lieutenant **William Clark** to be the co-leader of the expedition.

To prepare for the journey, Lewis spent weeks studying with experts about plants, surveying, and other subjects. This knowledge would allow him to take careful notes on what he saw. With Clark, Lewis carefully selected about 50 skilled frontiersmen to join the Corps of Discovery, as they called their group.

In May 1804 the **Lewis and Clark expedition** began its long journey to explore the Louisiana Purchase. The Corps of Discovery traveled up the Missouri River to the village of St. Charles. Once past this village the men would receive no more letters, fresh supplies, or reinforcements.

Lewis and Clark used the Missouri River as their highway through the unknown lands. As they moved upstream, a lookout on the boats kept a sharp eye out for sandbars and for tree stumps hidden underwater. When darkness fell, the weary explorers would pull their boats ashore. They cooked, wrote in their journals, and slept. Swarms of gnats, flies, and mosquitoes often interrupted their sleep.

The explorers paddled down the Columbia River toward the Pacific in five canoes.

The expedition relied on 24 horses to cross the Rocky Mountains.

August 12, 1805

Lewis climbs the first ridge to the Continental Divide.

September 1805

The expedition nearly starves. Local peoples help the explorers.

November 7, 1805

The expedition reaches a bay of the Pacific Ocean.

August 23, 1805 The hills or mountains were not like those I had seen, but like the side of a tree straight up.

— William Clark

ANALYSIS SKILL READING TIME LINES

On what date did the explorers reach the westernmost point of their journey?

JOURNAL ENTRY
September 17, 1804, Great Plains

While traveling across the Great Plains, Meriwether Lewis marveled at the richness of the land.

"The shortness . . . of grass gave the plain the appearance throughout its whole extent of beautiful bowling-green in fine order . . . this scenery, already rich, pleasing, and beautiful was still farther heightened by immense herds of Buffaloe, deer Elk and Antelopes which we saw in every direction feeding on the hills and plains. I do not think I exaggerate when I estimate the number of Buffalo which could be compre[hend]ed at one view to amount to 3000."

—Meriwether Lewis, quoted in *Original Journals of the Lewis and Clark Expedition*, edited by Reuben Bold Theraites

ANALYSIS SKILL **ANALYZING PRIMARY SOURCES**

What did Lewis find so impressive about the Great Plains?

Insects were not the only cause of sleeplessness for the Corps of Discovery. As weeks passed without seeing any Native Americans, the explorers wondered what their first encounter would be like.

Contact with Native Americans

During the summer of 1804 the Corps of Discovery had pushed more than 600 miles upriver without seeing any Native Americans. But when the men spotted huge buffalo herds in the distance, they guessed that Indian groups would be nearby. Many Indian groups depended on the buffalo for food, clothing, and tools.

Lewis used interpreters to talk to the leaders of each of the peoples they met. He told them that the United States now owned the land on which the Native Americans lived. Yet the explorers relied on the goodwill of the people they met. **Sacagawea** (sak-uh-juh-WEE-uh),

a Shoshone from the Rocky Mountains, accompanied the group with her husband, a French fur trader who lived with the Mandan Indians and served as a guide and interpreter. Sacagawea helped the expedition by naming plants and by gathering edible fruits and vegetables for the group. At one point, the group met with Sacagawea's brother, who provided horses and a guide to lead the expedition across the mountains.

After crossing the Rocky Mountains, Lewis and Clark followed the Columbia River. Along the way they met the powerful Nez Percé. Like the Shoshone, the Nez Percé provided the expedition with food. At last, in November 1805, Lewis and Clark reached the Pacific Ocean. The explorers stayed in the Pacific Northwest during the rough winter. In March 1806 Lewis and Clark set out on the long trip home.

Lewis and Clark had not found a river route across the West to the Pacific Ocean. But they had learned much about western lands and paths across the Rockies. The explorers also established contact with many Native American groups and collected much valuable information about western plants and animals.

Pike's Exploration

In 1806 a young army officer named **Zebulon Pike** was sent on another mission to the West. He was ordered to find the starting point of the Red River. This was important because the United States considered the Red River to be a part of the Louisiana Territory's western border with New Spain.

Heading into the Rocky Mountains, in present-day Colorado, Pike tried to reach the summit of the mountain now known as Pikes Peak. In 1807 he traveled into Spanish-held lands until Spanish cavalry arrested him. They suspected Pike of being a spy. When he was finally released, he returned to the United States and reported on his trip. Despite his imprisonment, he praised the opportunities for doing business with the Spanish in the Southwest. Pike's

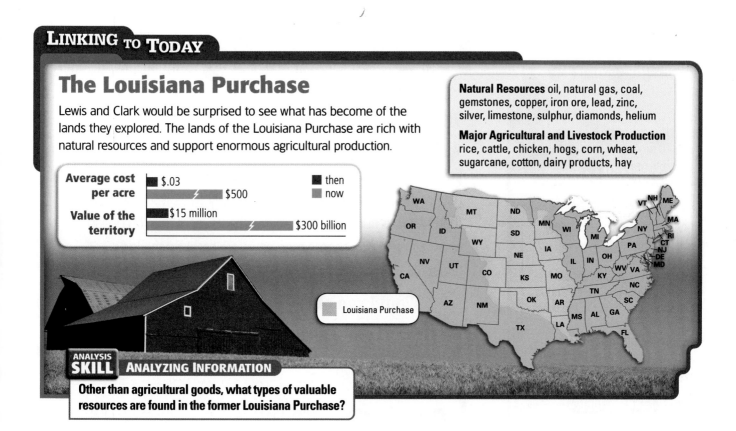

The Louisiana Purchase

Lewis and Clark would be surprised to see what has become of the lands they explored. The lands of the Louisiana Purchase are rich with natural resources and support enormous agricultural production.

Natural Resources oil, natural gas, coal, gemstones, copper, iron ore, lead, zinc, silver, limestone, sulphur, diamonds, helium

Major Agricultural and Livestock Production rice, cattle, chicken, hogs, corn, wheat, sugarcane, cotton, dairy products, hay

Average cost per acre ■ $.03 then ■ $500 now

Value of the territory $15 million ■ $300 billion

ANALYSIS SKILL **ANALYZING INFORMATION**

Other than agricultural goods, what types of valuable resources are found in the former Louisiana Purchase?

report offered many Americans their first description of the Southwest.

READING CHECK **Supporting a Point of View** What would you do if you were Pike and found yourself in Spanish territory?

SUMMARY AND PREVIEW The Louisiana Purchase nearly doubled the size of the United States. In the next section you will learn about increasing tensions between the United States and Great Britain.

Section 2 Assessment

go.hrw.com
Online Quiz
KEYWORD: SF7 HP8

Reviewing Ideas, Terms, and People

1. **a. Identify** What new states were added to the Union by the early 1800s?
   b. Explain Why were New Orleans and the Mississippi River important to settlers in the West?
2. **a. Recall** What two reasons did Napoléon have for selling Louisiana to the United States?
   b. Summarize Why was the **Louisiana Purchase** important to the United States?
   c. Predict What are some possible results of expansion into the Louisiana Purchase?
3. **a. Describe** What areas did the **Lewis and Clark expedition** and the Pike expedition explore?
   b. Draw Conclusions Why were **Meriwether Lewis** and **William Clark** chosen to lead the exploration of the Louisiana Purchase?

Critical Thinking

4. **Sequencing** Review your notes on the Louisiana Purchase. Then copy the graphic organizer below and use it to rank the three most important effects of the Louisiana Purchase, from most important to least important, and explain why you chose that order.

Importance	Why
1.	
2.	
3.	

FOCUS ON WRITING

5. **Gathering Information about a Person's Actions** Make a list of Jefferson's actions—the ones that would put him on that top-ten list. Add any new character traits you have discovered.

The Coming of War

What You Will Learn...

Main Ideas

1. Violations of U.S. neutrality led Congress to enact a ban on trade.
2. Native Americans, Great Britain, and the United States came into conflict in the West.
3. The War Hawks led a growing call for war with Great Britain.

The Big Idea

Challenges at home and abroad led the United States to declare war on Great Britain.

Key Terms and People

USS *Constitution*, p. 278
impressment, p. 279
embargo, p. 279
Embargo Act, p. 279
Non-Intercourse Act, p. 280
Tecumseh, p. 280
Battle of Tippecanoe, p. 282
War Hawks, p. 282
James Madison, p. 283

TAKING NOTES Create a graphic organizer like the one below. As you read, take notes on the challenges that led the United States to declare war on Great Britain.

8.1.13, 8.1.12, 8.2.4

If YOU were there...

You are a tea merchant in Boston in 1807, but right now your business is at a standstill. A new law forbids trading with European nations. Now, Boston Harbor is full of empty ships. It seems to you that the law is hurting American merchants more than European ones! You know that some merchants are breaking the law and smuggling goods, just to stay in business.

Would you obey the law or turn to smuggling?

BUILDING BACKGROUND The United States tried to stay neutral in the conflicts between France and Great Britain, but it was impossible to avoid getting involved. French and British ships interfered with American trade across the Atlantic. The British also caused trouble along the western frontier. Many Americans began to urge war with Great Britain.

Violations of Neutrality

During the late 1700s and early 1800s, American merchant ships fanned out across the oceans. The overseas trade, while profitable, was also risky. Ships had to travel vast distances, often through violent storms. Merchant ships sailing in the Mediterranean risked capture by pirates from the Barbary States of North Africa, who would steal cargo and hold ships' crews for ransom. Attacks continued until the United States sent the **USS *Constitution***, a large warship, and other ships to end them.

The Barbary pirates were a serious problem, but an even larger threat soon loomed. When Great Britain and France went to war in 1803, each country wanted to stop the United States from supplying goods to the other. Each government passed laws designed to prevent American merchants from trading with the other. In addition, the British and French navies captured many American merchant ships searching for war supplies.

The real trouble, however, started when Britain began stopping and searching American ships for sailors who had run away from the British navy, forcing the sailors to return to British ships.

The USS *Constitution*

CONNECT TO SCIENCE AND TECHNOLOGY

In the early years of the republic, foreign trade was critical to the nation's survival. In 1797 Congress decided to create a navy to protect American merchant ships. The powerful warship USS *Constitution* was a key part of the new navy and was undefeated in battle. It is the oldest commissioned warship in the world.

The main mast is 220 feet high.

Copper sheathing supplied by Paul Revere protected the hull.

People on the spar, or top, deck were exposed to enemy fire.

ANALYSIS SKILL **ANALYZING DIAGRAMS**

1. Why do you think gunpowder was stored on the bottom deck?
2. What was the purpose of the copper sheathing?

The crew slept and ate on the berth deck.

Most of the ship's cannons were located on the gun deck.

Boys called "powder monkeys" carried gunpowder from the orlop, or lowest, deck up to the gunners.

Sometimes U.S. citizens were captured by accident. This **impressment**, or the practice of forcing people to serve in the army or navy, continued despite American protests.

Soon Britain was even targeting American navy ships. In June 1807, for example, the British ship *Leopard* stopped the U.S. Navy ship *Chesapeake* and tried to remove sailors. When the captain of the *Chesapeake* refused, the British took the sailors by force. The brazen attack on the *Chesapeake* stunned Americans.

The Embargo Act

Great Britain's violations of U.S. neutrality sparked intense debate in America about how to respond. Some people wanted to go to war. Others favored an **embargo**, or the banning of trade, against Britain.

Jefferson, who had easily won re-election in 1804, supported an embargo. At his urging, in late 1807 Congress passed the **Embargo Act**. The law essentially banned trade with all foreign countries. American ships could not sail to foreign ports. American ports were also closed to British ships. Congress hoped that the embargo would punish Britain and France and protect American merchant ships from capture.

The effect of the law was devastating to American merchants. Without foreign trade, they lost enormous amounts of money. Northern states that relied heavily on trade were especially hard hit by the embargo. Congressman Josiah Quincy of Massachusetts, in a speech before Congress, described the situation. "All the business of the nation is in disorder. All the nation's industry is at a standstill," he said.

The embargo damaged Jefferson's popularity and strengthened the Federalist Party. Angry merchants sent Jefferson hundreds of petitions demanding the Embargo Act's repeal. One New Englander said the embargo was like "cutting one's throat to stop the nosebleed." Even worse, the embargo had little effect on Britain and France.

Non-Intercourse Act

In 1809 Congress tried to revive the nation's trade by replacing the unpopular act with the **Non-Intercourse Act**. This new law banned trade only with Britain, France, and their colonies. It also stated that the United States would resume trading with the first side that stopped violating U.S. neutrality. In time, however, the law was no more successful than the Embargo Act.

READING CHECK **Comparing and Contrasting** In what ways were the Embargo Act and the Non-Intercourse Act similar and different?

Conflict in the West

Disagreements between Great Britain and the United States went beyond the neutrality issue. In the West, the British and Native Americans again clashed with American settlers over land.

The Conflict over Land

In the early 1800s, Native Americans in the old Northwest Territory continued to lose land as thousands of settlers poured into the region. The United States had gained this land in the Treaty of Greenville, but Indian leaders who had not agreed to the treaty protested the settlers' arrival. Frustrated Indian groups considered what to do. In the meantime, Britain saw an opportunity to slow America's westward growth. British agents from Canada began to arm Native Americans who were living along the western frontier. Rumors of British activity in the old Northwest Territory quickly spread, filling American settlers with fear and anger.

Tecumseh Resists U.S. Settlers

Soon an Indian leader emerged who seemed more than capable of halting the American settlers. **Tecumseh** (tuh-KUHM-suh), a Shawnee chief, had watched angrily as Native Americans were pushed off their land. A brilliant speaker, he warned other Indians about the dangers they faced from settlers. He believed that the Native Americans had to do what white Americans had done: unite.

Time Line

America's Road to War

June 22, 1807 The British navy takes sailors from the U.S. Navy ship *Chesapeake*.

1807

December 22, 1807 The United States responds to impressment by passing the Embargo Act.

1809

January 9, 1809 Congress passes the Non-Intercourse Act.

POLITICAL CARTOON
The Embargo Act

The unpopularity of the Embargo Act prompted political cartoonists to show visually how the act was hurting American trade.

What do you think the turtle represents?

What is the turtle preventing this man from doing?

ANALYSIS SKILL ANALYZING PRIMARY SOURCES

How does the cartoonist emphasize the unpopularity of the Embargo Act?

What is "ograbme" spelled backward?

Tecumseh hoped to unite the Native Americans of the northwestern frontier, the South, and the eastern Mississippi Valley. He was helped by his brother, a religious leader called the Prophet. They founded a village called Prophetstown for their followers near the Wabash and Tippecanoe rivers.

The Battle of Tippecanoe

The governor of the Indiana Territory, William Henry Harrison, watched Tecumseh's activities with alarm. Harrison called him "one of those uncommon geniuses which spring up occasionally to . . . overturn the established order." The governor was convinced that Tecumseh had British backing. If true, Tecumseh could be a serious threat to American power in the West.

In 1810 Tecumseh met face to face with Harrison. The governor urged him to follow the Treaty of Greenville that had been signed in 1795. Tecumseh replied, "The white people have no right to take the land from the Indians, because the Indians had it first." No single chief, he insisted, could sell land belonging to all American Indians who used it. In response, Harrison warned Tecumseh not to resist the power of the United States.

FOCUS ON INDIANA

Today, the site of the Battle of Tippecanoe is a national historic landmark near the town of Battle Ground, Indiana. The memorial includes an 85-foot-tall obelisk dedicated to the American forces that fought there.

June 18, 1812
The United States declares war against Britain.

1810

1812

November 4, 1811
When the twelfth Congress convenes, Kentucky representative Henry Clay leads the call for war against Britain.

ANALYSIS SKILL READING TIME LINES

What events led to war against Great Britain?

POINTS OF VIEW
Views of War

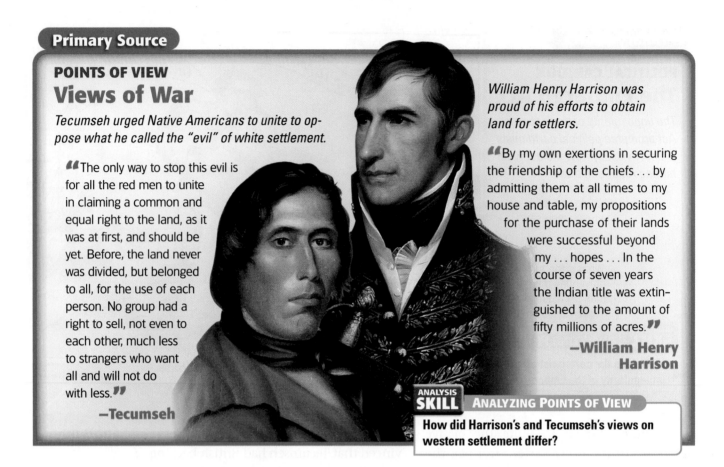

Tecumseh urged Native Americans to unite to oppose what he called the "evil" of white settlement.

❝The only way to stop this evil is for all the red men to unite in claiming a common and equal right to the land, as it was at first, and should be yet. Before, the land never was divided, but belonged to all, for the use of each person. No group had a right to sell, not even to each other, much less to strangers who want all and will not do with less.**❞**

—**Tecumseh**

William Henry Harrison was proud of his efforts to obtain land for settlers.

❝By my own exertions in securing the friendship of the chiefs . . . by admitting them at all times to my house and table, my propositions for the purchase of their lands were successful beyond my . . . hopes . . . In the course of seven years the Indian title was extinguished to the amount of fifty millions of acres.**❞**

—**William Henry Harrison**

ANALYSIS SKILL **ANALYZING POINTS OF VIEW**

How did Harrison's and Tecumseh's views on western settlement differ?

Tecumseh traveled south to ask the Creek nation to join his forces. In his absence, Harrison attacked. Harrison raised an army and marched his troops close to Prophetstown. Fighting broke out when the Prophet ordered an attack on Harrison's camp on November 7, 1811.

The Indians broke through army lines, but Harrison kept a "calm, cool, and collected" manner, according to one observer. During the all-day battle, Harrison's soldiers forced the Indian warriors to retreat and then destroyed Tecumseh's village. Said Chief Shabbona, "With the smoke of that town and loss of that battle, I lost all hope." Although Tecumseh was safe, U.S. forces defeated Tecumseh and his followers in the **Battle of Tippecanoe**. The defeat destroyed Tecumseh's dream of a great Indian confederation. He fled to Canada.

FOCUS ON READING

What words did Calhoun use that had strong emotions tied to them for Americans? (See "The War Hawks" section.)

READING CHECK **Finding Main Ideas**
Why were U.S. officials worried about Tecumseh's actions?

Call for War

The evidence of British support for Tecumseh further inflamed Americans. A Democratic-Republican newspaper declared, "The war on the Wabash [River] is purely BRITISH." Many Americans felt that Britain had encouraged Tecumseh to attack settlers in the West.

The War Hawks

Several young members of Congress—called **War Hawks** by their opponents—took the lead in calling for war against Britain. These legislators, most of whom were from the South and West, were led by Henry Clay of Kentucky, John C. Calhoun of South Carolina, and Felix Grundy of Tennessee. They saw war as the only answer to British insults. "If we submit," Calhoun warned, "the independence of this nation is lost." Calls for war grew. Leaders wanted to put a stop to British influence among Native Americans. They also wanted to invade

Canada and gain more land for settlement. Others were angered by British trade restrictions that hurt southern planters and western farmers. War Hawks gave emotional speeches urging Americans to stand up to Great Britain.

The Opposition

The strongest opponents of the War Hawks were New England Federalists. British trade restrictions and impressment had hurt New England's economy. People there wanted to renew friendly business ties with Britain instead of fighting another war.

Other politicians argued that war with Great Britain would be foolish. They feared that the United States was not yet ready to fight powerful Britain. America's army and navy were small and poorly equipped compared to Britain's military. In addition, Americans could produce only a fraction of the military supplies Britain could. Senator Obadiah German of New York pleaded with the War Hawks to be patient: "Prior to any declaration of war . . . my plan would be, and my first wish is, to prepare for it—to put the country in complete armor."

Declaring War

Republican **James Madison** was elected president in 1808. He faced the difficulty of continuing an unpopular trade war begun by Jefferson. He also felt growing pressure from the War Hawks. By 1812 he decided that Congress must vote on war. Speaking to Congress, Madison blasted Great Britain's conduct. He asked Congress to decide how the nation should respond.

When Congress voted a few days later, the War Hawks won. For the first time in the nation's brief history, Congress had declared war. Months later, Americans elected Madison to a second term. He would serve as commander in chief during the War of 1812.

READING CHECK **Summarizing** Why did the United States declare war in 1812?

SUMMARY AND PREVIEW Conflicts on the frontier and with Great Britain dominated U.S. foreign policy under Jefferson and Madison. In the next section you will read about the War of 1812.

Section 3 Assessment

go.hrw.com
Online Quiz
KEYWORD: SF7 HP8

Reviewing Ideas, Terms, and People

1. **a. Describe** In what ways did the war between France and Britain cause problems for the United States?
   b. Make Inferences What were the reasons for the failure of the **Embargo Act**?
   c. Elaborate Why do you think **embargoes** against Britain and France failed?
2. **a. Describe** What was **Tecumseh**'s goal?
   b. Explain What role did Great Britain play in the conflict between the United States and American Indians on the western frontier?
3. **a. Identify** Who were the **War Hawks**? Why did they support war with Britain?
   b. Elaborate Would you have supported going to war against Great Britain? Explain your answer.

Critical Thinking

4. **Categorizing** Review your notes on the challenges that led to the War of 1812. Were most challenges foreign or domestic? Categorize them in a chart like the one below.

Foreign	Domestic

FOCUS ON WRITING

5. **Taking Notes** Take notes about any of Jefferson's actions and character traits you can identify during the buildup to war with Britain. Save this information for the top-ten list you will create at the end of the chapter.

The War of 1812

What You Will Learn...

Main Ideas

1. American forces held their own against the British in the early battles of the war.
2. U.S. forces stopped British offensives in the East and South.
3. The effects of the war included prosperity and national pride.

The Big Idea

Great Britain and the United States went to battle in the War of 1812.

Key Terms and People

Oliver Hazard Perry, *p. 285*
Battle of Lake Erie, *p. 285*
Andrew Jackson, *p. 286*
Treaty of Fort Jackson, *p. 286*
Battle of New Orleans, *p. 286*
Hartford Convention, *p. 287*
Treaty of Ghent, *p. 287*

TAKING NOTES Create a graphic organizer like the one below. As you read, take notes on the sequence of events in the War of 1812, from beginning to end.

Sequence of Events
1.
2.
3.
4.
5.
6.
7.

 8.1.8, 8.1.9, 8.1.11, 8.1.13, 8.1.15, 8.1.29, 8.1.30, 8.2.1, 8.2.4, 8.3.1, 8.3.2, 8.3.5, 8.3.7, 8.3.9, 8.3.10

If YOU were there...

It's 1812, and the United States and Great Britain are at war. You are a sailor on an American merchant ship that has been licensed as a privateer. Your ship's mission will be to chase and capture ships of the mighty British navy. Even with the help of merchant ships like yours, the American navy is badly outnumbered. You know you face danger and may not survive.

Do you think your mission will succeed?

BUILDING BACKGROUND Anger against Great Britain's actions finally provoked the United States into the War of 1812. Britain's great navy gave it a clear advantage at sea, but the war was also fought on several other fronts. Victories in major battles along the frontier gave Americans a new sense of unity.

Early Battles

In the summer of 1812 the United States found itself in a war with one of the world's most powerful nations. Despite the claims by the War Hawks, the War of 1812 would not be a quick and easy fight.

War at Sea

When the war began, the British navy had hundreds of ships. In contrast, the U.S. Navy had fewer than 20 ships. None of them was as powerful as the greatest British warships.

Most of the British navy's ships, however, were scattered around the globe. Although small, the U.S. Navy had well-trained sailors and powerful new warships such as the USS *Constitution*. American vessels defeated British ships several times in one-on-one duels. Such victories embarrassed the British and raised American morale. Eventually, the British ships blockaded America's seaports.

Battles Along the Canadian Border

American leaders hoped to follow up victories at sea with an overland invasion of Canada. Three attacks were planned—from Detroit, from Niagara Falls, and from up the Hudson River valley toward Montreal.

The War of 1812

BRITISH TERRITORY

Disputed

Lake Superior

Disputed

ME (PART OF MA)

Montreal

Plattsburg VT

St. Lawrence River

ILLINOIS TERRITORY

Lake Michigan

Lake Huron

Lake Ontario

NH

Boston

UNITED STATES AND TERRITORIES

MICHIGAN TERR.

Fort Detroit

York

Thames

Fort Niagara

NY

MA

CT RI

40°N

Lake Erie

PERRY

HARRISON

PA

New York City

NJ

Philadelphia

DE

MD

Fort Dearborn

HULL

Lake Erie

Baltimore

MISSOURI TERRITORY

INDIANA TERRITORY

OH

Washington, D.C.

VA

KY

35°N

NC

TN

JACKSON

SC

N

W E

S

MISSISSIPPI TERRITORY

Tallapoosa River

Horseshoe Bend

30°N

Alabama River

GA

Fort Mims

LA

SPANISH TERRITORY

Disputed

New Orleans

ATLANTIC OCEAN

75°W

Legend

- American forces
- ✸ American victories
- British forces
- ✸ British victories
- ııı British blockades
- ✸ Creek victory

0 150 300 Miles
0 150 300 Kilometers

Gulf of Mexico

25°N

90°W 85°W 80°W

GEOGRAPHY SKILLS INTERPRETING MAPS

1. **Location** According to the map, what major southern port was affected by the British blockade?
2. **Region** Which battles took place in the Great Lakes region?

The attack from Detroit failed when British soldiers and Indians led by Tecumseh captured Fort Detroit. The other American attacks failed when state militia troops refused to cross the Canadian border, arguing that they did not have to fight in a foreign country.

In 1813 the United States went on the attack again. A key goal was to break Britain's control of Lake Erie. The navy gave the task to Commodore **Oliver Hazard Perry**. After building a small fleet, Perry sailed out to meet the British on September 10, beginning the **Battle of Lake Erie**. The battle ended

when the British surrendered. Perry sent a message to General William Henry Harrison: "We have met the enemy and they are ours." Perry's brilliant victory forced the British to withdraw, giving the U.S. Army control of the lake and new hope.

With American control of Lake Erie established, General Harrison marched his army into Canada. At the Battle of the Thames River in October 1813, he defeated a combined force of British troops and Native Americans. Harrison's victory ended British power in the Northwest. Tecumseh's death during the fighting also dealt a blow to the British alliance with Native Americans in the region.

The Creek War

Meanwhile, war with American Indians erupted in the South. Creek Indians, angry at American settlers for pushing into their lands, took up arms in 1813. A large force attacked Fort Mims on the Alabama River, destroying the fort and killing close to 250 of its defenders. In response, the commander of the Tennessee militia, **Andrew Jackson**, gathered about 2,000 volunteers to move against the Creek nation.

In the spring of 1814 Jackson attacked the Creek along the Tallapoosa River in Alabama. Jackson's troops won this battle, the Battle of Horseshoe Bend. The **Treaty of Fort Jackson**, signed late in 1814, ended the Creek War and forced the Creek to give up millions of acres of their land.

READING CHECK **Comparing** What advantages did Great Britain and the United States have at the start of the war?

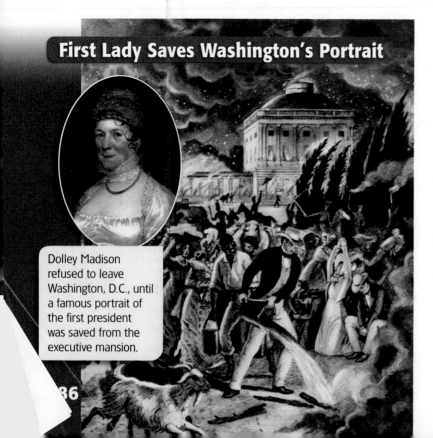

First Lady Saves Washington's Portrait

Dolley Madison refused to leave Washington, D.C., until a famous portrait of the first president was saved from the executive mansion.

Great Britain on the Offensive

Despite U.S. success on the western and southern frontiers, the situation in the East grew worse. After defeating France in April 1814, the British sent more troops to America.

British Attacks in the East

Now reinforced, the British attacked Washington, D.C. President Madison was forced to flee when the British broke through U.S. defenses. The British set fire to the White House, the Capitol, and other government buildings.

The British sailed on to Baltimore, Maryland, which was guarded by Fort McHenry. They shelled the fort for 25 hours. The Americans refused to surrender Fort McHenry. The British chose to retreat instead of continuing to fight.

The Battle of New Orleans

After the attack on Washington, the British moved against New Orleans. British commanders hoped to capture the city and thus take control of the Mississippi River.

Andrew Jackson commanded the U.S. forces around New Orleans. His troops were a mix of regular soldiers, including two battalions of free African Americans, a group of Choctaw Indians, state militia, and pirates led by Jean Lafitte.

The battle began on the morning of January 8, 1815. Some 5,300 British troops attacked Jackson's force of about 4,500. The British began marching toward the U.S. defenses, but they were caught on an open field. The British were cut down with frightening speed. More than 2,000 British soldiers were killed or wounded. The Americans, for their part, had suffered about 70 casualties. The **Battle of New Orleans** made Andrew Jackson a hero and was the last major conflict of the War of 1812.

READING CHECK **Finding Main Ideas**
What happened at the Battle of New Orleans?

Causes of the War
• Impressment of American sailors
• Interference with American shipping
• British military aid to Native Americans

Effects of the War
• Increased sense of national pride
• American manufacturing boosted
• Native American resistance weakened

Effects of the War

Before the battle of New Orleans, a group of New England Federalists gathered secretly at Hartford, Connecticut. At the **Hartford Convention**, Federalists agreed to oppose the war and send delegates to meet with Congress. Before the delegates reached Washington, however, news arrived that the war had ended. Some critics now laughed at the Federalists, and the party lost much of its political power.

Slow communications at the time meant that neither the Federalists nor Jackson knew about the **Treaty of Ghent**. The treaty, which had been signed in Belgium on December 24, 1814, ended the War of 1812.

Though each nation returned the territory it had conquered, the fighting did have several **consequences**. The war produced feelings of patriotism in Americans for having stood up to the mighty British. Some even called it the second war for independence. The war also broke the power of many Native American groups. Finally, a lack of goods caused by the interruption in trade boosted American manufacturing.

READING CHECK Analyzing Information
What were the main effects of the War of 1812?

SUMMARY AND PREVIEW The War of 1812 showed Americans that the nation would survive. In the next chapter you will see how the United States continued to grow.

ACADEMIC VOCABULARY

consequences the effects of a particular event or events

Section 4 Assessment

go.hrw.com
Online Quiz
KEYWORD: SF7 HP8

Reviewing Ideas, Terms, and People

1. **a. Identify** What losses did American forces face in the early battles of the War of 1812? What victories did they win?
   b. Make Generalizations What role did American Indians play in the war?
2. **a. Describe** What attacks did the British lead against American forces?
   b. Evaluate What do you think were the two most important battles of the war? Why?
3. **a. Identify** What was the purpose of the **Hartford Convention**?
   b. Draw Conclusions How did the United States benefit from the War of 1812?

Critical Thinking

4. **Comparing and Contrasting** Review your notes on the battle dates. Then compare and contrast the details of the major battles during the War of 1812 in a chart like this one.

Battle	Details (Winner, Location, Importance)

FOCUS ON WRITING

5. **Organizing Your Ideas** Reorder the items on your lists from least important to most important.

America's Growth 1820

In 1803 the United States made the biggest land purchase in its history—the Louisiana Purchase. With this purchase, the country stretched west all the way to the Rocky Mountains. In 1819 the United States acquired Florida from Spain, gaining even more new territory. By 1820, the young American republic had roughly doubled in size, as you can see on the map. Explorers, traders, and settlers began to pour into the new lands in search of wealth, land, and a place to call home.

British Territory

Claimed by United States, ceded to Great Britain in 1818

49th Parallel

Oregon Country

42nd Parallel

The Oregon Country Both the United States and Great Britain claimed the Oregon Country.

ROCKY MOUNTAINS

PACIFIC OCEAN

Spanish Territory

America's Population, 1820: 10.1 million

4%   1%
18%
77%

Ethnic Groups, 1820
- White/European
- African American
- Native American
- Other

1%   <1%   4%
94%

Religions, 1820
- Protestant
- Catholic
- Jewish
- Other

- ☐ Louisiana Purchase, 1803
- ▨ Claimed by United States and Great Britain, 1818
- ▬ Convention of 1818
- ■ From Britain to United States, 1818
- ☐ Adams-Onís Treaty of 1819
- ☐ From Spain to United States, 1819

0   150   300 Miles
0   150   300 Kilometers

120° W   110° W

Early Traders Soon after Lewis and Clark explored the Louisiana Territory, American fur trappers and traders began setting up trading posts there. Many of these posts became towns later as settlers arrived.

Through the Gaps Settlers crossed the Appalachians through valleys called gaps. In time, roads were built through the gaps, making it easier for Americans to head west.

Unorganized Territory

Missouri River

ATLANTIC OCEAN

40° N

Delaware Gap

APPALACHIAN MTS

Cumberland Gap

Missouri Territory

Arkansas Territory

Red River

Mississippi River

The Mighty Mississippi The Mississippi River was the great highway of the central United States. Americans west of the Appalachians shipped farm goods and supplies up and down the Mississippi and its major port, New Orleans.

Louisiana

New Orleans

Gulf of Mexico

Unorganized Territory (Florida)

go.hrw.com
Interactive Map
KEYWORD: SF7 CH8

GEOGRAPHY SKILLS INTERPRETING MAPS

1. **Movement** In which main directions did the United States expand before 1820?
2. **Region** Based on the map, why do you think the United States was interested in claiming the Oregon Country?

70° W

N W E S

Social Studies Skills

Analysis   Critical Thinking   Civic Participation   Study

Working in Groups to Solve Issues

Define the Skill

You already know that the decision-making process is more difficult in a group than it is if just one person makes the decisions. However, group decision-making becomes an even greater challenge when controversial issues are involved.

Group members must have additional skills for the group to function effectively when conflict exists within it. These include respect for differing views, the arts of persuasion and negotiation, and an ability to compromise. A group may not be able to find solutions to controversial problems unless its members have these skills.

Learn the Skill

Some of the biggest challenges Congress faced in the early 1800s were related to the war between Great Britain and France. Some Americans supported the British, while others favored the French. Both countries hoped for American help. When the United States would not take sides, they each began interfering with U.S. ships on the open seas.

As you read in this chapter, Congress tried to solve this problem by passing the Embargo Act. That solution was controversial, however. The northern states were hard hit by the law's ban on overseas trade. Their representatives in Congress demanded a less extreme action. The result was the Non-Intercourse Act. This law was a compromise between members who wanted to lift the trade ban and those who wanted to continue it. Congress was able to solve this problem because its members were able to work around their differences.

The skills Congress needed to reach its solution are valuable ones for any group that must make decisions involving controversial issues. They include the following attitudes and behaviors.

1 **Willingness to take a position.** If an issue is controversial, it is likely that group members will have differing opinions about it. You have a right to state your views and try to persuade others that you are correct.

2 **Willingness to listen to differing views.** Every other member has the same right you do. You have a duty to listen to their views, even if you do not agree. Disrespect for those whose views differ from yours makes it more difficult for the group to reach a solution.

3 **Willingness to debate.** Debate is a form of "healthy" argument because it defends and attacks ideas instead of the people who hold them. Debating the group's differences of opinion is an important step in reaching a solution.

4 **Willingness to negotiate and compromise.** If debate does not produce agreement, a compromise may be needed. Often it is better to have a solution that members may not like, but can accept, than to have no agreement at all.

Practice the Skill

Check your understanding of the skill by answering the following questions.

1. Why would refusing to listen to other members make group decision-making more difficult?

2. Why is compromise often a better solution than forcing a decision on members who disagree?

HOLT
History's Impact
▶ video series
Review the video to answer the closing question:
How do the background, value system, and character of the United States reflect its spirit of exploration?

Visual Summary

Use the visual summary below to help you review the main ideas of the chapter.

QUICK FACTS

The Nation at War and Peace

1803
Marbury v. *Madison* gives the Supreme Court the power of judicial review.

1803
The United States doubles its size by making the Louisiana Purchase.

1807–09
Congress passes the Embargo and Non-Intercourse Acts.

1811
William Henry Harrison defeats Tecumseh's forces at the Battle of Tippecanoe.

1814
Federalists hold the Hartford Convention to protest the War of 1812.

1812
The War of 1812 begins between Great Britain and the United States.

1814
The Treaty of Ghent ends the War of 1812.

1815
Andrew Jackson wins the Battle of New Orleans.

Reviewing Vocabulary, Terms, and People

Complete each sentence by filling in the blank with the correct term or person.

1. The War of 1812 ended soon after the U.S. victory over the British at the _____.

2. After winning the election of 1800, _____ became the third president of the United States.

3. The power of the Supreme Court to declare acts of Congress unconstitutional is known as _____.

4. After U.S. neutrality was violated, the United States issued an _____ against trade with foreign nations.

5. In 1803 Congress approved the _____ , which added former French territory in the West to the United States.

Comprehension and Critical Thinking

SECTION 1 *(Pages 266–270)*

6. a. Recall What were the key issues in the election of 1800?

b. Analyze In what ways did *Marbury* v. *Madison* affect the power of the judicial branch?

c. Evaluate Which of Jefferson's new policies do you think was most important? Why?

SECTION 2 *(Pages 272–277)*

7. a. Describe What was the purpose of the Lewis and Clark expedition?

b. Draw Conclusions What are three ways in which the United States benefited from the Louisiana Purchase?

c. Evaluate Do you think that Napoléon made a wise decision when he sold Louisiana to the United States? Explain your answer.

SECTION 3 (Pages 278–283)

8. a. Identify What group led the call for war with Great Britain?

b. Contrast What arguments were given in favor of war with Great Britain? What arguments were given against war with Britain?

c. Elaborate In your opinion, why were the Embargo Act and the Non-Intercourse Act unsuccessful?

SECTION 4 (Pages 284–287)

9. a. Identify What role did Andrew Jackson play in the War of 1812?

b. Make Inferences Why did the British want to capture the cities of Washington and New Orleans?

c. Predict In what ways might the U.S. victory over Great Britain in the war affect the status of the United States in the world?

Reviewing Themes

10. Geography Through what geographic regions did the Lewis and Clark expedition travel?

11. Politics What impact did the Hartford Convention have on American politics?

Using the Internet

go.hrw.com
KEYWORD: SF7 CH8

12. Activity: Journal Entry Prior to Lewis and Clark's expedition, some thought that woolly mammoths, unicorns, and seven-foot-tall beavers lived in the uncharted West. The Corps of Discovery set off to find out the truth about this uncharted land. Its members also wanted to search for a Northwest Passage that would speed commerce and bring wealth to the young nation. Enter the activity keyword. Research the Web sites and take the point of view of one of the explorers. Write a series of journal entries outlining the thoughts, feelings, discoveries, and events surrounding the journey. Include drawings of what you might have seen in the West in your journal entries.

Reading Skills

Public Documents in History *Use the Reading Skills taught in this chapter to answer the question below.*

13. Which of the following is an example of a public document?

a. the Constitution

b. the current president's journal

c. a tax return

d. an ambassador's letter to the president

Social Studies Skills

Working in Groups to Solve Issues *Use the Social Studies Skills taught in this chapter to answer the questions below.*

14. Organize into groups of two or three students. Decide which of the following reasons for the War of 1812 you think might have been most important in Congress's decision to declare war.

a. impressment of American sailors

b. trade barriers with Britain and France

c. battles with Native Americans on the frontier

d. gaining land in Canada

FOCUS ON WRITING

15. Writing Your Letter of Recommendation You already have a main idea and an opinion statement for your letter: Thomas Jefferson deserves to be on the list of the top-ten American presidents. Now, look at all your information and pick out three or four points—actions or character traits—that you think are the most important. Write a sentence on each of those points to add to your letter. Put the sentences in order, from the least important to the most important. Finally, conclude with one or two sentences that sum up why you think Thomas Jefferson was such an important president.

Standardized Test Practice

8.1.8, 8.1.11, 8.1.12, 8.3.9

DIRECTIONS: Read each question and write the letter of the best response.

1 The Supreme Court's decision in the 1803 case *Marbury* v. *Madison* is an example of

- A checks and balances.
- B reserved powers.
- C delegated powers.
- D dual sovereignty.

2 Most of the fighting in the War of 1812 took place

- A in Europe.
- B in Canada.
- C in the United States.
- D at sea.

3 Why did President Jefferson agree to buy Louisiana from France?

- A He wanted to learn more about the lands and peoples east of the Mississippi River.
- B He believed that the United States would benefit from the purchase.
- C He wanted to end the French threat in North America.
- D He hoped to increase the president's constitutional powers.

4 The United States went to war with Britain in 1812 for which of the following reasons?

- A to strengthen the alliance between Britain and France
- B to endanger the rights of U.S. ships on the high seas
- C to allow British influence among Indian groups on the frontier
- D to stop trade restrictions against American merchants

5 The Lewis and Clark expedition was significant because it

- A introduced the United States to valuable raw materials such as coal.
- B improved America's knowledge of the West.
- C led to U.S. settlement of the Southwest.
- D opened trade between the United States and Native Americans in the West.

6 During the War of 1812, trade interruptions resulted in

- A the repeal of the Embargo Act.
- B a rise in unemployment.
- C an increase in the production of cotton in the South.
- D a boost to U.S. manufacturing.

7 Read the following passage from Thomas Jefferson's inaugural address and use it to answer the question below.

> "Though the will of the majority is in all cases to prevail, that will, to be rightful, must be reasonable . . . [T]he minority possess their equal rights, which equal laws must protect . . . Let us then, fellow citizens, unite with one heart and one mind . . . We have been called by different names brethren of the same principle. We are all republicans; we are all federalists."
>
> —President Thomas Jefferson, Inaugural Address, 1801

Document-Based Question What did Jefferson mean in making this statement?

CHAPTER 9 1812–1830

A New National Identity

Indiana Standards

Social Studies Standards

8.1.14 Examine the international problem that led to the Monroe Doctrine (1823) and assess its consequences.

8.1.31 Obtain historical data from a variety of sources to compare and contrast examples of art, music, and literature during the nineteenth century and explain how these reflect American culture during this time period., Examine the development of the banking system in the United States.

8.4.9 Explain and evaluate examples of domstic and international interdependence throughout United States history.

go.hrw.com
Indiana
KEYWORD: SF10 IN

FOCUS ON WRITING

A Character Sketch Nations, like people, have characters. For example, a nation might be described as peaceful or aggressive, prosperous or struggling. In this chapter you'll read about the United States as a new nation with a new identity, or character. Then you'll write a paragraph describing that character.

UNITED STATES
1816
James Monroe is elected president.

1815

WORLD
1815
Napoléon returns to power in France but is defeated at the Battle of Waterloo.

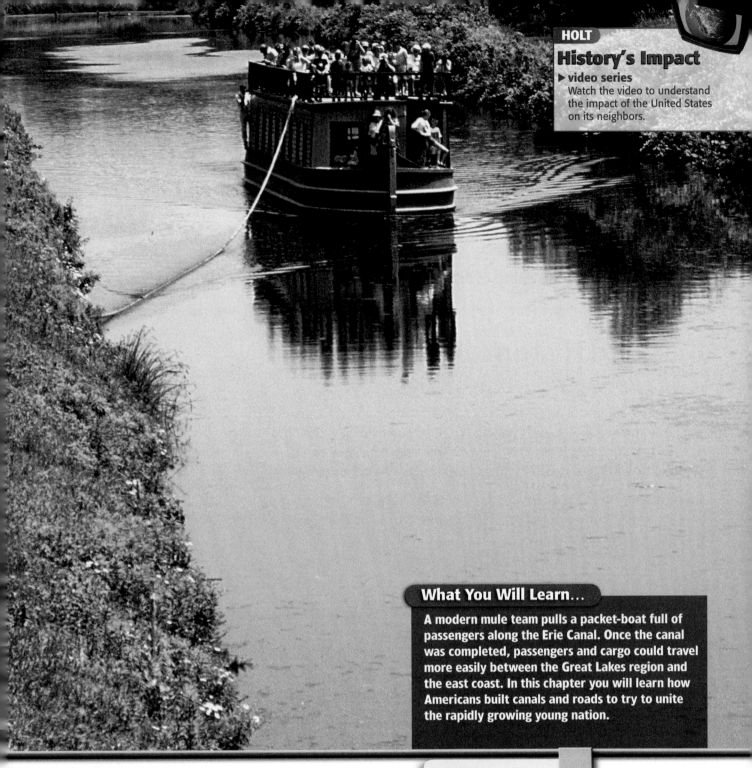

What You Will Learn...

A modern mule team pulls a packet-boat full of passengers along the Erie Canal. Once the canal was completed, passengers and cargo could travel more easily between the Great Lakes region and the east coast. In this chapter you will learn how Americans built canals and roads to try to unite the rapidly growing young nation.

1825
Indianapolis becomes the capital of Indiana.

1820
The Missouri Compromise allows Maine and Missouri to become states.

1823
The Monroe Doctrine is issued.

1824
John Quincy Adams is elected president.

1820

1825

1830

1821
Mexico and Peru gain their independence from Spain.

1824
Liberia is founded by freed American slaves.

1829
The Ottoman Empire recognizes the independence of Greece.

The Granger Collection, New York

Focus on Themes This chapter is titled "A New National Identity" because it explains how the United States government established relations with European powers and how Americans developed a strong sense of national pride even as they struggled with important state issues. You will learn about the Monroe Doctrine, the Missouri Compromise, the Cumberland Road project, and the rise of American music, literature, and public schools—events that changed the country's **culture** and **politics**.

Bias and Historical Events

Focus on Reading As you read this chapter, you will find that some people supported the idea of using federal dollars to create new and better roads. Others, however, did not think federal dollars should be used that way. People who can only see one side of an issue or situation may become biased, or prejudiced against the opposite view.

Recognizing Bias To understand the events and people in history, you have to be able to recognize a speaker's or writer's bias. Here are some steps you can take to do that.

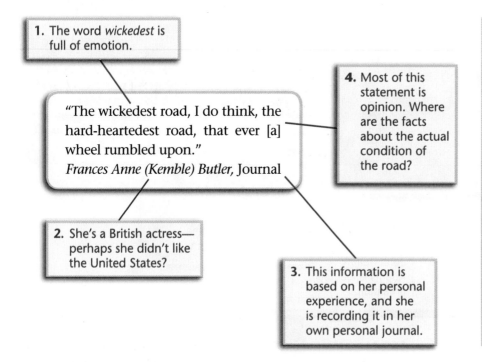

1. The word *wickedest* is full of emotion.

"The wickedest road, I do think, the hard-heartedest road, that ever [a] wheel rumbled upon."
Frances Anne (Kemble) Butler, Journal

2. She's a British actress—perhaps she didn't like the United States?

3. This information is based on her personal experience, and she is recording it in her own personal journal.

4. Most of this statement is opinion. Where are the facts about the actual condition of the road?

Steps to Recognize Bias

1. **Look at the words and images.** Are they emotionally charged? Do they present only one side or one point of view?

2. **Look at the writer.** What's the writer's background and what does that tell you about the writer's point of view?

3. **Look at the writer's sources.** Where does the writer get his or her information? Does the writer rely on sources who only support one point of view?

4. **Look at the information.** How much is fact and how much is opinion? Remember, facts can be proven. Opinions are personal beliefs—they can easily be biased.

You Try It!

The following passage is from the chapter you are getting ready to read. As you read the passage, think about living during the early to mid-1800s when there were no public schools.

Architecture and Education

Americans also embraced educational progress. Several early American political leaders expressed a belief that democracy would only succeed in a country of educated and enlightened people. But there was no general agreement on who should provide that education.

Eventually, the idea of a state-funded public school gathered support. In 1837 Massachusetts lawmakers created a state board of education. Other states followed this example, and the number of public schools slowly grew.

From Chapter 9, p. 311

After you read the passage, answer the following questions.

1. You are the editor of your town's newspaper in the year 1835. You think schools should be financed by the state government rather than the federal government. You decide to write an editorial to express your opinion. Which of the phrases below would reveal your personal bias to your readers? Why? What words in each statement create bias?

   a. Overbearing federal government
   b. Protecting state interests
   c. Powerful federal government
   d. Concerned state citizens

2. If you were going to write the editorial described in question 1, how could you avoid biased statements? How do you think this might affect people's reactions to your writing?

Key Terms and People

Chapter 9

Section 1
Rush-Bagot Agreement *(p. 298)*
Convention of 1818 *(p. 298)*
James Monroe *(p. 299)*
Adams-Onís Treaty *(p. 299)*
Simon Bolívar *(p. 300)*
Monroe Doctrine *(p. 300)*

Section 2
nationalism *(p. 302)*
Henry Clay *(p. 302)*
American System *(p. 302)*
Cumberland Road *(p. 303)*
Erie Canal *(p. 303)*
Era of Good Feelings *(p. 303)*
sectionalism *(p. 304)*
Missouri Compromise *(p. 305)*
John Quincy Adams *(p. 305)*

Section 3
Washington Irving *(p. 308)*
James Fenimore Cooper *(p. 309)*
Hudson River school *(p. 310)*
Thomas Cole *(p. 310)*
George Caleb Bingham *(p. 310)*

Academic Vocabulary

Success in school is related to knowing academic vocabulary— the words that are frequently used in school assignments and discussions. In this chapter, you will learn the following academic words:

circumstances *(p. 300)*
incentive *(p. 303)*

As you read Chapter 9, study the primary source documents carefully. Do you see any examples of bias?

American Foreign Policy

What You Will Learn...

Main Ideas

1. The United States and Great Britain settled their disputes over boundaries and control of waterways.
2. The United States gained Florida in an agreement with Spain.
3. With the Monroe Doctrine, the United States strengthened its relationship with Latin America.

The Big Idea

The United States peacefully settled disputes with foreign powers.

Key Terms and People

Rush-Bagot Agreement, *p. 298*
Convention of 1818, *p. 298*
James Monroe, *p. 299*
Adams-Onís Treaty, *p. 299*
Simon Bolívar, *p. 300*
Monroe Doctrine, *p. 300*

TAKING NOTES Create a chart like the one below. As you read, take notes on the foreign policy issues the United States had to deal with between 1817 and 1823.

Foreign Policy Issues
•
•
•
•
•
•
•

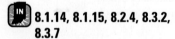 8.1.14, 8.1.15, 8.2.4, 8.3.2, 8.3.7

If YOU were there...

You are a Spanish settler living in West Florida in 1820. Your family has lived in Florida for many years. Only a few years ago, people in Spanish Florida were furious when American soldiers occupied the town of Pensacola. Now you hear that Spain has signed a treaty with the United States—Florida is no longer Spanish territory but rather part of the United States.

How would you feel about living under a new government?

BUILDING BACKGROUND The War of 1812 left the United States stronger and more self-confident. The new nation had remained strong against a great European power. The United States then turned to diplomacy as a way to settle international issues.

Settling Disputes with Great Britain

The Treaty of Ghent had ended the War of 1812, yet there were issues left unresolved. The United States and British Canada both wanted to keep their navies and fishing rights on the Great Lakes. In the spring of 1817, the two sides compromised by establishing the **Rush-Bagot Agreement**, which limited naval power on the Great Lakes for both the United States and British Canada.

Another treaty with Britain gave the United States fishing rights off parts of the Newfoundland and Labrador coasts. This treaty, known as the **Convention of 1818**, also set the border between the United States and Canada at 49°N latitude as far west as the Rocky Mountains. Interest in the valuable fur trade in the Oregon Country was another issue resolved by this treaty. Both countries agreed to occupy the Pacific Northwest together, an agreement that would be tested in the years to come.

READING CHECK **Summarizing** What were the main disputes between the United States and Britain?

U.S. Boundary Changes, 1818–1819

BRITISH TERRITORY

49th Parallel

OREGON COUNTRY

ROCKY MOUNTAINS

42nd Parallel

UNORGANIZED TERRITORY

MICHIGAN TERRITORY

Great Lakes

Mississippi River

ME

VT NH

MA

NY

RI CT

PA

NJ

DE

MD

OH

IL IN

70°W

VA

MISSOURI TERRITORY

KY

APPALACHIAN MOUNTAINS

Arkansas River

ARKANSAS TERRITORY

TN

NC

SC

Red River

SPANISH TERRITORY

Sabine River

MS AL GA

LA

Legend
— U.S.–Canadian border, Convention of 1818
— U.S.–Spanish territory border, Adams-Onís Treaty of 1819
☐ From Britain to United States, 1818
☐ From Spain to United States, 1819
☐ Disputed by United States and Great Britain, 1818

0   200   400 Miles
0   200   400 Kilometers

PACIFIC OCEAN

120°W

UNORGANIZED TERRITORY (FLORIDA)

Gulf of Mexico

ATLANTIC OCEAN

80°W

GEOGRAPHY SKILLS | **INTERPRETING MAPS**

1. Place What territory did the United States acquire from Spain in 1819?

2. Region What western region was claimed by both the United States and Great Britain?

United States Gains Florida

The United States also had a dispute over its southern border with Spanish Florida. In 1818 Secretary of State John Quincy Adams, son of John and Abigail Adams, held talks with Spanish diplomat Luis de Onís about letting Americans settle in Florida. Meanwhile, President **James Monroe**, elected in 1816, had sent U.S. troops to secure the U.S.–Florida border. General Andrew Jackson led these soldiers.

At the same time, conflicts arose between the United States and the Seminole Indians of Florida. The Seminole often helped runaway slaves and sometimes raided U.S. settlements. In April 1818 Jackson's troops invaded Florida to capture Seminole raiders. This act began the First Seminole War. During the war Jackson took over most of Spain's

important military posts. Then he overthrew the governor of Florida. He carried out these acts against Spain without receiving direct orders from President Monroe. Jackson's actions upset Spanish leaders. Most Americans, however, supported Jackson.

Jackson's presence in Florida convinced Spanish leaders to negotiate. In 1819 the two countries signed the **Adams-Onís Treaty**, which settled all border disputes between Spain and the United States. Under this treaty, Spain gave East Florida to the United States. In return, the United States gave up its claims to what is now Texas. U.S. leaders also agreed to pay up to $5 million of U.S. citizens' claims against Spain.

THE IMPACT TODAY

Florida was admitted as a U.S. state in 1845 and is now home to about 16 million people.

READING CHECK **Summarizing** How were the disagreements between the United States and Spanish Florida settled?

HISTORIC DOCUMENT
The Monroe Doctrine

President James Monroe established the foundation for U.S. foreign policy in Latin America in the Monroe Doctrine of 1823.

> In this phrase, Monroe warns European nations against trying to influence events in the Western Hemisphere.

> Monroe notes here the difference between existing colonies and newly independent countries.

The occasion has been judged proper for asserting . . . that the American continents . . . are henceforth not to be considered as subjects for future colonization by any European powers . . .

The political system of the allied powers is essentially different . . . from that of America. We . . . declare that we should consider any attempt on their part to extend their system to any portion of this hemisphere as dangerous to our peace and safety . . .

With the existing colonies . . . we have not interfered and shall not interfere. But with the governments who have declared their independence and maintained it, and whose independence we have . . . acknowledged, we could not view any interposition[1] for the purpose of oppressing them . . . by any European power in any other light than as the manifestation[2] of an unfriendly disposition[3] toward the United States.

ANALYSIS SKILL — **ANALYZING PRIMARY SOURCES**

1. What warning did President Monroe give to European powers in the Monroe Doctrine?
2. How does Monroe say the United States will treat existing European colonies?

[1] **interposition:** interference
[2] **manifestation:** evidence
[3] **disposition:** attitude

Monroe Doctrine

Meanwhile, Spain had other problems. By the early 1820s most of the Spanish colonies in the Americas had declared independence. Revolutionary fighter **Simon Bolívar**, called the Liberator, led many of these struggles for independence. The political **circumstances** surrounding the revolutions reminded most American leaders of the American Revolution. As a result, they supported these struggles.

After Mexico broke free from Spain in 1821, President Monroe grew worried. He feared that rival European powers might try to take control of newly independent Latin American countries. He was also concerned about Russia's interest in the northwest coast of North America.

Secretary of State Adams shared President Monroe's concerns. In a Fourth of July speech before Congress, Adams said that the United States had always been friendly with European powers, and that the country did not want to be involved in wars with them. He implied that he supported the newly independent countries but said the United States would not fight their battles.

Great Britain was also interested in restraining the influence of other European nations in the Americas. This was because Britain had formed close trading ties with most of the independent Latin American countries. Britain wanted to issue a joint statement with the United States to warn the rest of Europe not to interfere in Latin America.

Instead, Secretary of State Adams and President Monroe decided to put together a document protecting American interests. The **Monroe Doctrine** was an exclusive statement of American policy warning European powers not to interfere with the Americas.

ACADEMIC VOCABULARY

circumstances surrounding situation

The doctrine was issued by the president on December 2, 1823, during his annual message to Congress.

The Monroe Doctrine had four basic points.

1. The United States would not interfere in the affairs of European nations.
2. The United States would recognize, and not interfere with, European colonies that already existed in North and South America.
3. The Western Hemisphere was to be off-limits to future colonization by any foreign power.
4. The United States would consider any European power's attempt to colonize or interfere with nations in the Western Hemisphere to be a hostile act.

Some Europeans strongly criticized the Monroe Doctrine, but few European countries challenged it. The doctrine has remained important to U.S. foreign policy. The United States has continued to consider Latin America within its sphere of influence—the area a nation claims some control over. At times, it has intervened in Latin American affairs when its own interests, such as national security, were at risk.

READING CHECK Analyzing What effect did the revolutions in Latin America have on U.S. foreign policy?

SUMMARY AND PREVIEW In this section you learned that U.S. foreign policy was characterized by both compromise and strong leadership in the years following the War of 1812. In the next section you will learn about the rising sense of national pride that developed as the United States grew and expanded.

Section 1 Assessment

go.hrw.com
Online Quiz
KEYWORD: SF7 HP9

Reviewing Ideas, Terms, and People

1. a. **Identify** What issues were settled between the United States and Great Britain in 1817 and 1818?
   b. **Make Inferences** Why would the United States and Britain agree to occupy the Pacific Northwest together?
   c. **Elaborate** Why were the **Rush-Bagot Agreement** and the **Convention of 1818** compromises?
2. a. **Recall** What problems existed between Spain and the United States?
   b. **Analyze** Why was the **Adams-Onís Treaty** important?
   c. **Evaluate** Do you think that Andrew Jackson was right to act without orders? Explain your answer.
3. a. **Describe** What did the **Monroe Doctrine** state?
   b. **Contrast** How did the Monroe Doctrine differ from Adams's Fourth of July Address?
   c. **Elaborate** What do you think the newly independent Latin American countries thought of the Monroe Doctrine?

Critical Thinking

4. **Identifying Cause and Effect** Review your notes regarding U.S. foreign policy issues. Create a new chart and, for each issue, identify the nations involved, the agreement or doctrine, and the effects.

Nations	Agreement/Doctrine	Issue	Effects

FOCUS ON WRITING

5. **Determining Relationships** One of the main ways you can learn about someone's character is by how he or she treats others. As you read this section, start a list of words and phrases that describe how the United States acted in relationships with other nations. For example, lists might include words and phrases like "willing to compromise" and "firm."

Nationalism and Sectionalism

Main Ideas

1. Growing nationalism led to improvements in the nation's transportation systems.
2. The Missouri Compromise settled an important regional conflict.
3. The outcome of the election of 1824 led to controversy.

The Big Idea

A rising sense of national unity allowed some regional differences to be set aside and national interests to be served.

Key Terms and People

nationalism, *p. 302*
Henry Clay, *p. 302*
American System, *p. 302*
Cumberland Road, *p. 303*
Erie Canal, *p. 303*
Era of Good Feelings, *p. 303*
sectionalism, *p. 304*
Missouri Compromise, *p. 305*
John Quincy Adams, *p. 305*

TAKING NOTES As you read, take notes on how each of the following contributed to national unity.

8.1.10, 8.1.12, 8.1.16, 8.2.3, 8.2.4, 8.3.1, 8.3.2, 8.3.5, 8.3.7, 8.3.8, 8.3.9, 8.3.10, 8.3.11, 8.4.4, 8.4.8, 8.4.9

If YOU were there...

You live near the western end of the newly completed Erie Canal in New York State in 1831. In fact, your older brothers helped build the canal. Every day you watch as mules pull the canal boats along the still water of the canal. Sometimes the boats carry passengers traveling from city to city. You have never been far from your home, and you are curious about their journey.

What would you like to ask the travelers on the canal boat?

BUILDING BACKGROUND Peace, prosperity, and a growing country gave Americans a sense of national unity. In practical terms, building roads and canals also helped unify the nation. They made travel easier, linking people from different regions of the country. Nevertheless, some regional conflicts continued.

Growing Nationalism

Pleased by successful negotiations with foreign powers, Americans enjoyed a rising sense of nationalism. **Nationalism** is feelings of pride and loyalty to a nation. This new national unity found a strong supporter in U.S. representative **Henry Clay** from Kentucky.

Clay believed that a strong national economy would promote national feeling and reduce regional conflicts. He developed a plan eventually known as the **American System** —a series of measures intended to make the United States economically self-sufficient. To build the economy, he pushed for a national bank that would provide a single currency, making interstate trade easier. Clay wanted the money from a protective tariff to be used to improve roads and canals. These internal improvements would unite the country.

Some members of Congress believed that the Constitution did not permit the federal government to spend money on internal improvements. Clay argued that the possible gains for the country justified federal action.

Roads and Canals

In the early 1800s most roads in the United States were made of dirt, making travel difficult. British actress Frances Kemble described one New York road she had struggled along during a visit in the 1830s.

> "The wickedest road, I do think, the cruellest, hard-heartedest road, that ever [a] wheel rumbled upon."
>
> —Frances Anne (Kemble) Butler, *Journal*

To improve the nation's roads, Congress agreed with Clay and invested in road building. The **Cumberland Road** was the first road built by the federal government. It ran from Cumberland, Maryland, to Wheeling, a town on the Ohio River in present-day West Virginia. Construction began in 1815. Workers had to cut a 66-foot-wide band, sometimes through forest, to make way for the road. Then they had to use shovels and pickaxes to dig a 12- to 18-inch roadbed, which they filled with crushed stone. All of the work had to be done without the benefit of today's bulldozers and steamrollers.

By 1818 the road reached Wheeling. By 1833 the National Road, as the expansion was called, stretched to Columbus, Ohio. By 1850 it reached all the way to Illinois.

Meanwhile, Americans tried to make water transportation easier by building canals. One of the largest projects was the **Erie Canal**, which ran from Albany to Buffalo, New York.

Construction of the canal began in 1817 and was completed in 1825. Using shovels, British, German, and Irish immigrants dug the entire canal by hand. The canal cost millions of dollars, but it proved to be worth the expense. The Erie Canal allowed goods and people to move between towns on Lake Erie and New York City and the east coast. Its success served as an **incentive** for a canal-building boom across the country.

Era of Good Feelings

From 1815 to 1825 the United States enjoyed the **Era of Good Feelings**, a time of peace, pride, and progress. The phrase was coined

FOCUS ON INDIANA

The path of the Cumberland Road crossed Indiana by 1839, but the road existed in various stages of completion in the state. The Wabash and Erie Canal ran through Terre Haute, linking Indiana to markets in the east.

ACADEMIC VOCABULARY

incentive something that leads people to follow a certain course of action

U.S. Roads and Canals, 1850

Roads — — Canals

0   100   200 Miles
0   100   200 Kilometers

Americans used flatboats, like this one, to travel the country's canals.

Travelers on the National Road stopped at inns to eat and rest from a long day's journey.

GEOGRAPHY SKILLS **INTERPRETING MAPS**

1. Region In what region of the United States were most canals located?

2. Movement About how long was the National Road?

The Missouri Compromise, 1820

The Missouri Compromise banned slavery in the region north of 36°30'N.

Free state
Free territory
Slave state
Slave territory

Missouri Compromise line (36°30'N)

MAINE
VT
NH
MA
NY
RI
CT
PA
NJ
DE
MD
MICHIGAN TERRITORY
UNORGANIZED TERRITORY
IL
IN
OH
VA
KY
MISSOURI
TN
NC
ARKANSAS TERRITORY
SC
MS
AL
GA
LA
UNORGANIZED TERRITORY (FLORIDA)

BIOGRAPHY

Henry Clay
1777–1852

Known as the silver-tongued Kentuckian, Henry Clay was a gifted speaker. He became involved in local politics early in his life, and by age 29 he was appointed to the U.S. Senate. Throughout his career in the Senate, he was dedicated to preserving the Union. The Missouri Compromise and a later agreement, the Compromise of 1850, helped to ease sectional tensions, at least temporarily.

Analyzing Why did Henry Clay work for compromises between regions?

by a Boston editor in 1817 during James Monroe's visit to New England early in his presidency.

The emphasis on national unity was strengthened by two Supreme Court case decisions that reinforced the power of the federal government. In the 1819 case *McCulloch* v. *Maryland*, the Court asserted the implied powers of Congress in allowing for the creation of a national bank. In the 1824 case *Gibbons* v. *Ogden*, the Court said that the states could not interfere with the power of Congress to regulate interstate commerce.

READING CHECK Drawing Inferences How did new roads and canals affect the economy?

Missouri Compromise

Even during the Era of Good Feelings, disagreements between the different regions—known as **sectionalism**—threatened the Union. One such disagreement arose in 1819 when Congress considered Missouri's application to enter the Union as a slave state. At the time, the Union had 11 free states and 11 slave states. Adding a new slave state would have tipped the balance in the Senate in favor of the South.

To protect the power of the free states, the House passed a special amendment. It declared that the United States would accept Missouri as a slave state, but importing enslaved Africans into Missouri would be illegal. The amendment also set free the children of Missouri slaves. Southern politicians angrily opposed this plan.

North Carolina senator Nathaniel Macon wanted to continue adding slave states. "Why depart from the good old way, which has kept us in quiet, peace, and harmony?" he asked. Eventually, the Senate rejected the amendment. Missouri was still not a state.

Henry Clay convinced Congress to agree to the **Missouri Compromise**, which settled the conflict that had arisen from Missouri's application for statehood. This compromise had three main conditions:

1. Missouri would enter the Union as a slave state.
2. Maine would join the Union as a free state, keeping the number of slave and free states equal.
3. Slavery would be prohibited in any new territories or states formed north of 36°30' latitude—Missouri's southern border.

Congress passed the Missouri Compromise in 1820. Despite the success of the compromise, there were still strong disagreements between the North and South over the expansion of slavery.

READING CHECK **Drawing Conclusions** Why did Henry Clay propose the Missouri Compromise to resolve the issue of Missouri statehood?

The Election of 1824

Soon, a presidential election also brought controversy. Andrew Jackson won the most popular votes in 1824. However, he did not have enough electoral votes to win office. Under the Constitution, the House of Representatives had to choose the winner. When the House chose **John Quincy Adams** as president, Jackson's supporters claimed that Adams had made a <u>corrupt bargain</u> with Henry Clay. These accusations grew after Adams chose Clay to be secretary of state. The controversy weakened Adams's support.

READING CHECK **Drawing Inferences** Why did Adams have weak support during his presidency?

SUMMARY AND PREVIEW Strong nationalistic feeling contributed to the development of America's politics and economy. In the next section you will read about the development of a new national culture.

FOCUS ON READING

How is the term **corrupt bargain** an example of semantic slanting?

Section 2 Assessment

go.hrw.com
Online Quiz
KEYWORD: SF7 HP9

Reviewing Ideas, Terms, and People

1. **a. Describe** What was the **Era of Good Feelings**?
   b. Analyze Explain the impact the *McCulloch* v. *Maryland* and *Gibbons* v. *Ogden* decisions had on the federal government.
   c. Predict How would transportation improvements eventually aid the economy of the United States?
2. **a. Recall** What role did **Henry Clay** play in the debate over Missouri's statehood?
   b. Explain What problem did Missouri's request for statehood cause?
   c. Elaborate Was the **Missouri Compromise** a good solution to the debate between free states and slave states? Explain your answer.
3. **a. Identify** Who were the candidates in the presidential election of 1824? How was the winner determined?
   b. Draw Conclusions Why did **John Quincy Adams** lose popular support following the election of 1824?

Critical Thinking

4. **Evaluating** Review your notes on nationalism during the Era of Good Feelings. Then copy the following graphic organizer, and use it to identify how threats to nationalism were resolved by the Missouri Compromise.

Sectional differences → Missouri Compromise →

Outcome
1.
2.
3.

FOCUS ON WRITING

5. **Judging Self-Esteem** Another way you can tell about people's characters is by how they view themselves. Are they self-confident? Do they make healthy choices? As you read this section, think of the United States as a person and jot down notes about the view the United States had of itself. Is the new nation pleased with itself? Does it feel confident or confused?

The Erie Canal

In 1825 New York opened the Erie Canal, which connected Buffalo on Lake Erie to Albany on the Hudson River. With the new canal, boats and barges could travel from New York Harbor in the east to the Great Lakes region in the west. Trade boomed, new cities formed, and settlers moved farther west as the Erie Canal helped open up the Midwest region to farming and settlement.

363 miles

Profile of the Erie Canal

572.4 feet

Buffalo

370 feet

From this elevation profile you can tell that the canal rises almost 600 feet as it winds its way westward from Albany to Buffalo. Barges move along a steep route through a series of locks along the canal. The diagram below shows you how locks work.

1.3 feet

Albany

Tow path

Lock

Main gate

Sluice gate

HOW Canal Locks WORK

❶ The barge enters the lock through the main gate.

❷ Water flows into the lock through the sluice gate to raise the boat to the next level.

❸ The barge leaves the lock as mules help pull it across the water.

Lake Superior

Lake Huron

Lake Michigan

Lake Ontario

The Erie Canal

Albany

VT

NH

ME

MA

RI

CT

NY

Hudson River

Buffalo

New York

Lake Erie

MI

Later canals extended west into Ohio and Indiana.

Toledo Cleveland

Chicago

IL

OH

IN

KY

PA

NJ

VA

NC

SC

GA

FL

ATLANTIC OCEAN

VI

Settlers and goods moved west.

FLOUR FLOUR

Agricultural products moved east.

Trade through New York Harbor boomed as goods flowed along the Erie Canal to overseas markets and back to settlers and cities in the West.

EFFECTS OF THE CANAL

Thanks to the canal, the cost of shipping dropped. Lower costs led to increases in shipping and in city populations.

Cost of Shipping

1824: $100 per ton by road

1825: $10 per ton by canal

Population Growth

Population (Thousands)

40

30

20

10

0

Albany

Buffalo

Chicago

Cleveland

1820 1830 1840

Year

GEOGRAPHY SKILLS **INTERPRETING MAPS**

1. **Region** How did the Erie Canal affect western lands?
2. **Location** What effect do you think the Erie Canal had on New York City?

American Culture

If YOU were there...

You live in Philadelphia in 1830. Though you've lived in the city all your life, you dream about the West and the frontier. Now you've discovered a wonderful writer whose stories tell about frontier life and events in American history. You can't wait to read his next exciting adventure. You think that perhaps someday you could be a frontier hero, too.

Why would the frontier seem so exciting?

BUILDING BACKGROUND Until the early 1800s, Americans took most of their cultural ideas from Great Britain and Europe. But as American politics and the economy developed, so too did a new national culture. Writers and artists were inspired by American history and the American landscape.

American Writers

Like many people the world over, Americans expressed their thoughts and feelings in literature and art and sought spiritual comfort in religion and music. Developments in education and architecture also reflected the growing national identity.

One of the first American writers to gain international fame was **Washington Irving**. Born in 1783, he was named after George Washington. Irving's works often told about American

American Arts

Early to mid-1800s

American architects are inspired by ancient Greece and Rome.

history. Through a humorous form of writing called satire, Irving warned that Americans should learn from the past and be cautious about the future.

Irving shared this idea in one of his best-known short stories, "Rip Van Winkle." This story describes a man who falls asleep during the time of the American Revolution. He wakes up 20 years later to a society he does not recognize. Irving published this and another well-known tale, "The Legend of Sleepy Hollow," in an 1819–20 collection.

In some of his most popular works, Irving combined European influences with American settings and characters. His work served as a bridge between European literary traditions and a new type of writer who focused on authentically American characters and society.

Perhaps the best known of these new writers was **James Fenimore Cooper**. Cooper was born to a wealthy New Jersey family in 1789. Stories about the West and the Native Americans who lived on the frontier fascinated him. These subjects became the focus of his best-known works.

Cooper's first book was not very successful, but his next novel, *The Spy*, was a huge success. Published in 1821, it was an adventure story set during the American Revolution. It appealed to American readers' patriotism and desire for an exciting, action-filled story.

In 1823 Cooper published *The Pioneers*, the first of five novels featuring the heroic character Natty Bumppo. Cooper's novels told of settling the western frontier and included historical events. For example, his novel *The Last of the Mohicans* takes place during the French and Indian War. By placing fictional characters in a real historical setting, Cooper popularized a type of writing called historical fiction.

Some critics said that Cooper's characters were not interesting. They particularly criticized the women in his stories; one writer labeled them "flat as a prairie." Other authors of historical fiction, such as Catharine Maria Sedgwick, wrote about interesting heroines. Sedgwick's characters were inspired by the people of the Berkshire Hills region of Massachusetts, where she lived. Her works include *A New-England Tale* and *Hope Leslie*.

READING CHECK **Analyzing** How did American writers such as Irving and Cooper help create a new cultural identity in the United States?

A New Style of Art

The writings of Irving and Cooper inspired painters. These artists began to paint landscapes that showed the history of America and the beauty of the land. Earlier American painters had mainly painted portraits. By the

1827
John Audubon begins publishing *The Birds of America*, which is highly admired in England.

1830s the Hudson River school had emerged. The artists of the **Hudson River school** created paintings that reflected national pride and an appreciation of the American landscape. They took their name from the subject of many of their paintings—the Hudson River valley.

Landscape painter **Thomas Cole** was a founder of the Hudson River school. He had moved to the United States from Britain in 1819. He soon recognized the unique qualities of the American landscape. As his work gained fame, he encouraged other American artists to show the beauty of nature. "To walk with nature as a poet is the necessary condition of a perfect artist," Cole once said.

By the 1840s the style of American painting was changing. More artists were trying to combine images of the American landscape with scenes from people's daily lives. Painters like **George Caleb Bingham** and Alfred Jacob Miller travelled west to paint scenes of the American frontier, including trappers, traders, settlers, and Native Americans.

READING CHECK **Finding Main Ideas** How did the style of American art change to reflect the American way of life in the early 1800s?

Religion and Music

Through the early and mid-1800s, several waves of religious revivalism swept the United States. During periods of revivalism, meetings were held for the purpose of reawakening religious faith. These meetings sometimes lasted for days and included large sing-alongs.

At many revival meetings people sang songs called spirituals. Spirituals are a type of folk hymn found in both white and African American folk-music traditions. This type of song developed from the practice of calling out text from the Bible. A leader would call out the text one line at a time, and the congregation would sing the words using a familiar tune. Each singer added his or her own style to the tune. The congregation of singers sang freely as inspiration led them.

While spirituals reflected the religious nature of some Americans, popular folk music of the period reflected the unique views of the growing nation in a different way. One of the most popular songs of the era was "Hunters of Kentucky," which celebrated the Battle of New Orleans. It became an anthem for the spirit of nationalism in the United States and was used successfully in Andrew Jackson's campaign for the presidency in 1828.

READING CHECK **Summarizing** How did music reflect American interests in the early to mid-1800s?

Architecture and Education

American creativity extended to the way in which people designed buildings. Before the American Revolution, most architects followed the style used in Great Britain. After the

American Arts (continued)

1828
Noah Webster publishes his first dictionary of American— not British— English.

1830
George Catlin travels widely to paint images of Native American ways of life before they are lost.

1836
Painters of the Hudson River school prove American landscapes are worthy of art. (Thomas Cole's *The Oxbow*, 1836)

Revolution, leaders such as Thomas Jefferson called for Americans to model their architecture after the styles used in ancient Greece and Rome. Many Americans admired the ancient civilization of Greece and the Roman Republic because they contained some of the same democratic and republican ideals as the new American nation did.

As time went by, more architects followed Jefferson's ideas. Growing American cities soon had distinctive new buildings designed in the Greek and Roman styles. These buildings were usually made of marble or other stone and featured large, stately columns.

Americans also embraced educational progress. Several early American political leaders expressed a belief that democracy would only succeed in a country of educated and enlightened people. But there was no general agreement on who should provide that education.

Eventually, the idea of a state-funded public school gathered support. In 1837 Massachusetts lawmakers created a state board of education. Other states followed this example, and the number of public schools slowly grew.

READING CHECK Identifying Points of View
Why did some Americans call for new architectural styles and more education after the American Revolution?

ANALYSIS SKILL **ANALYZING INFORMATION**
How do these artistic developments show Americans' increasing sense of identity?

SUMMARY AND PREVIEW As the United States grew, so did a unique national identity. In Chapter 10 you will read about the changing face of American democracy.

go.hrw.com
Online Quiz
KEYWORD: SF7 HP9

Section 3 Assessment

Reviewing Ideas, Terms, and People
1. **a. Describe** What topics interested American writers in the early 1800s?
   b. Draw Conclusions Why is **Washington Irving** considered an important American writer?
2. **a. Identify** What influence did **Thomas Cole** have on American painters?
   b. Describe How did American painting styles change from the early period to the mid-1800s?
3. **a. Describe** What effect did religious revivalism have on American music?
   b. Elaborate Why do you think folk songs like "Hunters of Kentucky" were popular?
4. **a. Identify** On what historical examples did many American architects model their buildings?
   b. Predict What might be some possible results of the growing interest in education in the United States?

Critical Thinking
5. **Categorizing** Review your notes about new developments in American culture. Copy the graphic organizer below and use it to show how these cultural developments reflected a new American identity.

Cultural Development	⟶	New Identity
Cultural Development	⟶	New Identity
Cultural Development	⟶	New Identity
Cultural Development	⟶	New Identity
Cultural Development	⟶	New Identity

FOCUS ON WRITING

6. **Identifying Values** You can tell much about someone's values by what that person makes. For instance, you could guess that a person who creates a collage of personal mementos for a friend's birthday is creative and values personal relationships. As you read this section, make note of what the United States created and what it valued.

Literature of the American Frontier

from *The Last of the Mohicans*

by James Fenimore Cooper (1789–1851)

About the Reading *The Last of the Mohicans* is one of five novels known as the *Leatherstocking Tales. These novels follow the life and adventures of American pioneer Natty Bumppo (also known as Leatherstocking, Hawkeye, and the Deerslayer). Bumppo is the perfect woodsman: resourceful, honest, kind to both his friends and his enemies, but always a loner at heart.*

AS YOU READ **Try to imagine what Natty Bumppo looks like.**

On that day, two men were lingering on the banks of a small but rapid stream . . . While one of these loiterers showed the red skin and wild accoutrements of a native of the woods, the other exhibited, through the mask of his rude and nearly savage equipments, the brighter though sunburnt and long-faded complexion of one who might claim descent from a European parentage. ❶

The frame of the white man, judging by such parts as were not concealed by his clothes, was like that of one who had known hardships and exertion from his earliest youth. His person, though muscular, was rather attenuated than full; but every nerve and muscle appeared strung and indurated by unremitted exposure and toil. He wore a hunting shirt of forest green, fringed with faded yellow, and a summer cap of skins which had been shorn of their fur. He also bore a knife in a girdle of wampum, ❷ like that which confined the scanty garments of the Indian, but no tomahawk. His moccasins were ornamented after the . . . fashion of the natives, while the only part of his underdress which appeared below the hunting frock was a pair of buckskin leggings that laced at the sides, and which were gartered above the knees with the sinews of a deer. A pouch and horn completed his personal accoutrements, though a rifle of great length, which the theory of the more ingenious whites had taught them was the most dangerous of all firearms, leaned against a neighboring sapling.

GUIDED READING

WORD HELP

accoutrements dress and gear

rude crude, rough

attenuated made thin

indurated hardened

unremitted ongoing

gartered fastened

ingenious clever

❶ *What do you learn about Natty Bumppo in the first paragraph?*

❷ A "girdle of wampum" is a belt strung with beads. Wampum were used by Native Americans for both money and decoration.

Make a list of the items Bumppo wears and carries. What does each item suggest about him?

from *The Legend of Sleepy Hollow*

by Washington Irving (1783–1859)

About the Reading *"The Legend of Sleepy Hollow" has been called one of the first American short stories. Even though it is based on an old German folktale, its setting, a small village in the Hudson River valley, is American through and through. Irving's knack for capturing the look and the feel of the region made the story instantly popular—as did the tale's eerie central character, a horseman without a head.*

AS YOU READ **Try to picture both the ghost and the setting.**

GUIDED READING

WORD HELP

dominant prevailing; ruling
apparition a ghostlike form that appears suddenly
collating comparing
spectre ghost
allege to firmly state
purport sense; gist

❶ A Hessian trooper is a German mercenary soldier from the American Revolution.

How and when is the horseman said to have died?

❷ *Why does the horseman ride forth each night?*

❸ *What is happening "at all the country firesides"? What does this suggest about how early Americans entertained themselves?*

The dominant spirit, however, that haunts this enchanted region, and seems to be commander in chief of all the powers of the air, is the apparition of a figure on horseback without a head. It is said by some to be the ghost of a Hessian trooper, ❶ whose head had been carried away by a cannon ball, in some nameless battle during the revolutionary war, and who is ever and anon seen by the country folk, hurrying along in the gloom of night, as if on the wings of the wind. His haunts are not confined to the valley, but extend at times to the adjacent roads, and especially to the vicinity of a church at no great distance. Indeed, certain of the most authentic historians of those parts, who have been careful in collecting and collating the floating facts concerning this spectre, allege, that the body of the trooper having been buried in the church yard, the ghost rides forth to the scene of battle in nightly quest of his head, ❷ and that the rushing speed with which he sometimes passes along the hollow, like a midnight blast, is owing to his being belated, and in a hurry to get back to the church yard before day break.

Such is the general purport of this legendary superstition, which has furnished materials for many a wild story in that region of shadows; and the spectre is known, at all the country firesides, by the name of The Headless Horseman of Sleepy Hollow. ❸

CONNECTING LITERATURE TO HISTORY

1. **Drawing Inferences** The writing of the period reflects a new national culture and identity. What do these passages suggest about the thoughts, feelings, or lives of early Americans?
2. **Making Predictions** *The Last of the Mohicans* takes place during the French and Indian War. Whose side do you think Natty Bumppo would most likely take—that of the French and Indians, that of the English, or neither? Explain.
3. **Drawing Conclusions** Both of these stories were very popular in their time. Why do you think these stories were so popular? What is it about the stories that makes them entertaining?

Social Studies Skills

Identifying Central Issues

Define the Skill

The reasons for historical events are often complex and difficult to determine. An accurate understanding of them requires the ability to identify the central issues involved. A *central issue* is the main topic of concern in a discussion or dispute. In history, these issues are usually matters of public debate or concern. They generally involve political, social, moral, economic, or territorial matters.

Being able to identify central issues lets you go beyond what the participants in an event said and gain a more accurate understanding of it. The skill is also useful for understanding issues today, and for evaluating the statements of those involved.

Learn the Skill

In this chapter you learned about the dispute that arose over Missouri's admission to the Union. Yet that was not what this controversy was really about. Recognizing the central issue in this dispute helps you understand why each side fought so hard over just one state.

Use the following steps to identify central issues when you read about historical events.

1. Identify the main subject of the information.

2. Determine the nature and purpose of what you are reading. Is it a primary source or a secondary one? Why has the information been provided?

3. Find the strongest or most forceful phrases or statements in the material. These are often clues to the issues or ideas the speaker or writer thinks most central or important.

4. Determine how the information might be connected to the major events or controversies that were concerning the nation at the time.

Practice the Skill

Soon after the Missouri Compromise passed, Secretary of State John Quincy Adams wrote:

"The impression produced upon my mind by the progress of this discussion [the dispute over Missouri] is that the bargain between freedom and slavery contained in the Constitution … is morally and politically vicious, … cruel and oppressive. … I have favored this Missouri Compromise, believing it to be all that can be effected [accomplished] under the present Constitution, and from an extreme unwillingness to put the Union at hazard [risk]. But perhaps it would have been a … bolder course to have persisted in the restriction upon Missouri till it should have terminated [ended] in a convention of the states to … amend the Constitution. This would have produced a new Union of thirteen or fourteen states unpolluted with slavery … If the Union must be dissolved, slavery is precisely the question upon which it ought to break. For the present, however, this contest [issue] is laid to sleep."

Apply the steps to identifying central issues to analyze Adams's statement and answer the following questions:

1. About what subject was Adams writing? What was his reason for making these remarks?

2. What did Adams believe was the most important issue in the dispute? What strong language does he use to indicate this?

3. What evidence suggests Adams did not think the breakup of the Union the central issue?

Chapter Review

History's Impact
▶ video series
Review the video to answer the closing question:
How did the Roosevelt Corollary change the Monroe Doctrine?

Visual Summary

Use the visual summary below to help you review the main ideas of the chapter.

QUICK FACTS

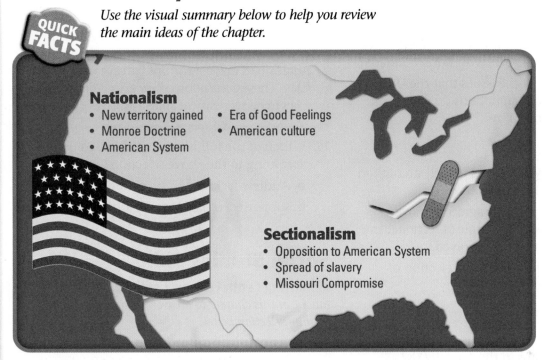

Nationalism
- New territory gained
- Monroe Doctrine
- American System
- Era of Good Feelings
- American culture

Sectionalism
- Opposition to American System
- Spread of slavery
- Missouri Compromise

Reviewing Vocabulary, Terms, and People

Match the word in the left column with the correct definition in the right column.

1. American System

2. George Caleb Bingham

3. Simon Bolívar

4. Henry Clay

5. Erie Canal

6. Hudson River school

7. James Monroe

8. Monroe Doctrine

9. nationalism

10. Rush-Bagot Agreement

a. an agreement that limited naval power on the Great Lakes for both the United States and British Canada

b. American artist known for his focus on the American landscape and people

c. sense of pride and devotion to a nation

d. a group of American artists in the mid-1800s who focused on the American landscape

e. a leader of independence movements in Latin America, known as the Liberator

f. the plan to raise tariffs in order to finance internal improvements such as roads and canals

g. president who promoted the acquisition of Florida, closer ties to Latin America, and presided during the Era of Good Feelings

h. project that connected the Hudson River to Lake Erie and improved trade and transportation

i. representative from Kentucky who promoted improvements in transportation and the Missouri Compromise

j. U.S. declaration that any attempt by a foreign nation to establish colonies in the Americas would be viewed as a hostile act

Comprehension and Critical Thinking

SECTION 1 *(Pages 298–301)*

11. a. Identify What were the four main points of the Monroe Doctrine?

b. Draw Conclusions How did the United States compromise in its disputes with British Canada?

c. Evaluate Which of the issues that the United States faced with foreign nations do you think was most important? Why?

SECTION 2 *(Pages 302–305)*

12. a. Recall What developments helped strengthen national unity in this period?

b. Analyze How was the disagreement over Missouri's statehood an example of sectionalism? How was the disagreement resolved?

c. Predict What effect might the election of 1824 have on national unity? Why?

SECTION 3 *(Pages 308–311)*

13. a. Describe How did popular music show the interests of Americans in the early 1800s?

b. Make Inferences Why do you think new American styles of art and literature emerged?

c. Elaborate Which element of American culture of the early 1800s do you find most appealing? Why?

Reviewing Themes

14. Politics How did the relations of the United States with foreign nations lead to a rise in nationalism?

15. Society and Culture What led to the creation of a uniquely American culture?

Using the Internet

go.hrw.com
KEYWORD: SF7 CH9

16. Activity: Researching In this chapter, you learned about the development of a new, creative spirit in American arts. Artists created works that featured American scenes and characters. Enter the activity keyword and research the development of American culture in art and literature. Then create a visual display.

Reading Skills

Bias and Historical Events *Use the Reading Skills taught in this chapter to answer the question about the reading selection below.*

> When the House chose John Quincy Adams as president, Jackson's supporters claimed that Adams had made a corrupt bargain with Henry Clay. These accusations grew after Adams chose Clay to be secretary of state. *(p. 305)*

17. Which of the following used a biased definition, according to the above selection?

a. Andrew Jackson   **c.** Henry Clay

b. supporters of Jackson   **d.** John Quincy Adams

Social Studies Skills

Identifying Central Issues *Use the Social Studies Skills taught in this chapter to answer the question about the reading selection below.*

> [Henry Clay] developed a plan that came to be known as the American System—a series of measures intended to make the United States economically self-sufficient. To build the economy, he pushed for a national bank that would provide a single currency, making interstate trade easier. Clay wanted the money from a protective tariff to be used to improve roads and canals. *(p. 302)*

18. Which of the following is the central issue addressed by the American System?

a. economic unity

b. protective tariff

c. national bank

d. improving roads and canals

FOCUS ON WRITING

19. Writing a Character Sketch Write a paragraph describing your overall impression of the nation's character. Write one sentence describing each of these aspects of the United States: its relationships with others, its feelings about itself, and its values.

8.1.14, 8.1.31, 8.4.8, 8.4.9

DIRECTIONS: Read each question and write the letter of the best response.

1 Use the map below to answer the following question.

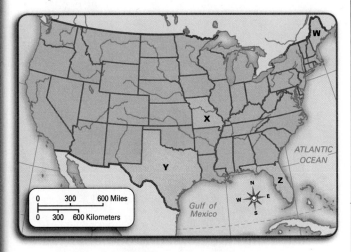

The present-day state that became part of the United States in the Adams-Onís Treaty of 1819 is shown on the map by the letter

A W.

B X.

C Y.

D Z.

2 The principle that European nations could establish no more colonies in North and South America was set forth in the

A Missouri Compromise.

B Rush-Bagot Agreement.

C Monroe Doctrine.

D Convention of 1818.

3 The Missouri Compromise had a significant effect on the United States because it

A established the present border with Canada.

B prohibited slavery north of Missouri's southern border.

C led to the expansion of roads and canals.

D settled conflicts between Native Americans in the West and the federal government.

4 Greek- and Roman-style architecture became common in the United States in the early 1800s because of

A the popularity of President George Washington, who liked the building style.

B Americans' admiration for the ideals of Greek democracy and republicanism.

C the nation's desire to build as strong a military as the Greeks and Romans had.

D Americans' great feeling of nationalism after the War of 1812.

5 Which painting would have been typical of an artist of the Hudson River school in the 1830s and 1840s?

A a portrait of a famous American

B a Native American hunting game

C a portrait of an ancient Greek or Roman lawmaker

D a scene showing America's natural beauty

6 Examine the following passage from a letter about American education and then use it to answer the question below.

> "A lady asked me one day, 'What state is Virginia in?' Another asked, 'Is Canada in Kentucky?' Another supposed that 'Joe Graphy [geography] was very hard to learn.' Such is the cause of all our mistakes in religion, morals, and politics. When we are educated we can cast off prejudice and superstition. Education improves our judgments and restrains our passions. In short, it enables us to discover what is best for our welfare."
>
> — Anne Newport Royall, adapted from *Letters from Alabama, 1817-1822*

Document-Based Question Why might Royall and others try to make education available to more Americans? Explain.

The Age of Jackson

Indiana Standards

Social Studies Standards

8.1.17 Identify the key ideas of Jacksonian democracy and explain their influence on political participation, political parties, and constitutional government.

8.3.6 Identify the agricultural regions of the United States and be able to give reasons for the type of land use and subsequent land development during different historical periods.

8.4.4 Explain the basic economic functions of the government in the economy of the United States.

8.4.8 Examine the development of the banking system in the United States.

go.hrw.com
Indiana
KEYWORD: SF10 IN

FOCUS ON WRITING

An Interview You are a reporter for a large city newspaper in the year 1837. Andrew Jackson has just left office, and you have been given the assignment of interviewing him about his presidency and his role in American politics. As you read this chapter, you will write interview questions for your interview with Jackson.

1828
UNITED STATES
Andrew Jackson is elected president.

Sequoya finishes a written language for the Cherokee.

183

1829
WORLD
Louis Braille publishes a reading system for the blind.

What You Will Learn...

In this chapter you will learn about how President Andrew Jackson helped shape the United States. He was so influential that historians refer to his presidency as the Age of Jackson. This statue of Jackson has stood in Washington, D.C., for more than 150 years and captures the drive and spirit of the seventh president of the United States.

Jackson Ticket.
FOR PRESIDENT,
Andrew Jackson.
FOR VICE-PRESIDENT,
John C. Calhoun.
FOR GOVERNOR,
MARTIN VAN BUREN.
For Lieutenant Governor,
ENOS T. THROOP,
For Presidential Elector,
John B. Russell.
FOR SENATOR,
Samuel Roxford.
FOR ASSEMBLY,
Charles G. De Witt,
Derick Dubois,

1832
Andrew Jackson vetoes the charter renewal of the national Bank of the United States.

1836
Martin Van Buren is elected president.

1838
The Trail of Tears begins when U.S. troops remove the Cherokee from Georgia.

1840
A treaty with the Miami cedes the last Native American lands in Indiana to the United States.

1835

1832 A British reform bill doubles the number of British men who can vote.

1833 Slavery is abolished in the British Empire.

1838 Dutch colonists known as Boers clash with the Zulu in southern Africa.

1839 The Opium War breaks out between Great Britain and China.

319

Reading Social Studies

by Kylene Beers

| Economics | Geography | Politics | Society and Culture | Science and Technology |

Focus on Themes In this chapter you will read about the events that shaped the United States from 1828 to 1838. You will see how **political** and **economic** decisions were intertwined. For instance, you will read about the tensions between southern and northern states over tariff regulations. You will also read about the forced relocation of many Native Americans to the West. Understanding how economic issues led to political decisions will help you understand this time.

Drawing Conclusions about the Past

Focus on Reading Writers don't always tell you everything you need to know about a subject. Sometimes you need to think critically about what they have said and make your own decisions about what you've read.

Drawing Conclusions Earlier in this book, you learned how to make inferences. Sometimes when you read, you will need to make several inferences and put them together. The result is a **conclusion**, an informed judgment that you make by combining information.

Election of 1828

The 1828 campaign focused a great deal on the candidates' personalities. Jackson's campaigners described him as a war hero who had <u>been born poor and rose to success through his own hard work.</u>

<u>Adams was a Harvard graduate whose father had been the second U.S. president.</u> Jackson's supporters described Adams as being out of touch with everyday people . . . When the ballots were counted, <u>Jackson had defeated Adams, winning a record number of popular votes.</u> *(pp. 323–324)*

Inference: Jackson shared many qualities with American voters.

+

Inference: Adams enjoyed many privileges that most Americans did not.

+

Inference: Jackson easily won the election by a huge majority.

Conclusion: In 1828, Americans chose a president to whom they could relate.

You Try It!

The following passage is from the chapter you are getting ready to read. As you read the passage, look for the facts of the situation.

The Election of 1834

In 1834 a new political party formed to oppose Jackson. Its members called themselves Whigs, after an English political party that opposed the monarchy, to make the point that Jackson was using his power like a king. The Whig Party favored the idea of a weak president and a strong Congress. Unable to agree on a presidential candidate, the Whigs nominated four men to run against Vice President Martin Van Buren. With strong backing from Jackson, Van Buren won the election.

From Chapter 10, p. 330

After you read the passage, answer the following questions.

1. From this passage, what can you infer about President Jackson's popularity with the Whig Party?

2. The Whigs could not choose a single presidential candidate, so they nominated four men. Based on what you know about elections from your studies and your past experiences, how do you think this affected the votes each man received?

3. Jackson's backing helped Van Buren win the presidency. From this, what can you infer about Jackson's popularity with the American people as a whole?

4. Using the inferences you made answering questions 1 through 3, draw a conclusion about why Van Buren won the election of 1834.

As you read **Chapter 10**, use your personal background knowledge and experience to draw conclusions about what you are reading.

Academic Vocabulary

Success in school is related to knowing academic vocabulary—the words that are frequently used in school assignments and discussions. In this chapter, you will learn the following academic words:

criteria *(p. 328)*
contemporary *(p. 333)*

Jacksonian Democracy

If YOU were there...

It's 1829, and you live in Washington, D.C. You've come with a friend to the party for Andrew Jackson's inauguration as president. Your friend admires Jackson as a man of the people. You are less sure about his ability. Jackson's inauguration soon turns into a rowdy party, as mobs crowd into the White House. They break glasses and overturn the furniture.

How would you feel about having Jackson as your president?

BUILDING BACKGROUND In the early years of the United States, the right to vote belonged mainly to a few—free white men who owned property. As the country grew, more men were given the right to vote. This expansion of democracy led to the election of Andrew Jackson, a war hero. But not everyone approved of Jackson.

Expansion of Democracy

America in the early 1800s was changing fast. In the North, workshops run by the craftspeople who owned them were being replaced by large-scale factories owned by businesspeople and staffed by hired workers. In the South, small family farms began to give way to large cotton plantations, owned by wealthy white people and worked by enslaved African Americans. Wealth seemed to be concentrating into fewer hands. Many ordinary Americans felt left behind.

These same people also began to believe they were losing power in their government. In the late 1700s some Americans thought that government was best managed by wealthy, property-owning men. Government policies seemed targeted to help build the power of these people. The result was a growing belief that the wealthy were tightening their grip on power in the United States.

Hoping for change, small farmers, frontier settlers, and slaveholders rallied behind reform-minded Andrew Jackson, the popular hero of the War of 1812 and presidential candidate in the 1824 election. They believed Jackson would defend the rights of the common

Democracy in Action

Democracy spread in the early 1800s as more people became active in politics. Many of these people lived in the new western states. In these mostly rural areas, a political rally could be as simple as neighboring farmers meeting to talk about the issues of the day, as the farmers in the painting on the right are doing.

During the early 1800s democracy and demonstrations blossomed in the United States. The demonstrators of today owe much to the Americans of Andrew Jackson's time. Today, political rallies are a familiar sight in communities all over the country.

ANALYSIS SKILL **ANALYZING INFORMATION**

How are the people in both pictures practicing democracy?

people and the slave states. And they had been bitterly disappointed in the way Jackson had lost the 1824 election because of the decision in the House of Representatives.

During the time of Jackson's popularity, many democratic reforms were made. Some states changed their qualifications for voters to grant more white males suffrage. The revised rules, however, usually excluded free blacks from voting as they had been allowed under original state constitutions. Political parties began holding public **nominating conventions**, where party members choose the party's candidates instead of the party leaders. This period of expanding democracy in the 1820s and 1830s later became known as **Jacksonian Democracy**.

READING CHECK **Finding Main Ideas**

How did voting rights change in the early 1800s?

Election of 1828

Jackson supporters were determined that their candidate would win the 1828 election. They formed the **Democratic Party** to support Jackson's candidacy. Many people who backed President Adams began calling themselves National Republicans.

The 1828 presidential contest was a rematch of the 1824 election. Once again, John Quincy Adams faced Andrew Jackson. Jackson chose **John C. Calhoun** as his vice presidential running mate.

The Campaign

The 1828 campaign focused a great deal on the candidates' personalities. Jackson's campaigners described him as a war hero who had been born poor and rose to success through his own hard work.

THE IMPACT TODAY

Just as they did in the 1820s, presidential campaigns today frequently focus on personal image—strong versus weak or government-insider versus newcomer, for example.

LETTER
People's President

Washington resident Margaret Bayard Smith was surprised by the chaos surrounding Jackson's inauguration.

❝What a scene did we witness! . . . a rabble, a mob, of boys, . . . women, children, scrambling, fighting, romping . . . Cut glass and china to the amount of several thousand dollars had been broken . . . But it was the people's day, and the people's President, and the people would rule.**❞**

—Margaret Bayard Smith, quoted in *Eyewitness to America*, edited by David Colbert

ANALYSIS SKILL **ANALYZING PRIMARY SOURCES**

How does the author view the people that support Jackson?

Adams was a Harvard graduate whose father had been the second U.S. president. Jackson's supporters described Adams as being out of touch with everyday people. Even a fan of Adams agreed that he was "as cold as a lump of ice." In turn, Adams's supporters said Jackson was hot tempered, crude, and ill-equipped to be president of the United States. When the ballots were counted, Jackson had defeated Adams, winning a record number of popular votes.

Jackson's Inauguration

Jackson's supporters saw his victory as a win for the common people. A crowd cheered outside the Capitol as he took his oath of office. The massive crowd followed Jackson to a huge party on the White House lawn. The few police officers on hand had difficulty controlling the partygoers.

As president, Jackson rewarded some of his supporters with government jobs. This **spoils system**—the practice of giving government jobs to political backers—comes from the saying "to the victor belong the spoils [valued goods] of the enemy."

Secretary of State **Martin Van Buren** was one of Jackson's strongest allies in his official cabinet. President Jackson also relied a great deal on his **Kitchen Cabinet**, an informal group of trusted advisers who sometimes met in the White House kitchen.

READING CHECK **Analyzing** How might the spoils system cause disputes?

SUMMARY AND PREVIEW The expansion of democracy swept Andrew Jackson into office. In the next section you will read about the increasing regional tensions that occurred during Jackson's presidency.

Section 1 Assessment

go.hrw.com
Online Quiz
KEYWORD: SF7 HP10

Reviewing Ideas, Terms, and People

1. **a. Recall** What changes did the new western states make that allowed more people to vote?
   b. Draw Conclusions How did **nominating conventions** allow the people more say in politics?
   c. Predict How might changes to the voting process brought about by **Jacksonian Democracy** affect politics in the future?

2. **a. Recall** What two new political parties faced off in the election of 1828? Which candidate did each party support?
   b. Make Inferences Why did **Andrew Jackson** have more popular support than did Adams?
   c. Evaluate Do you think the **spoils system** was an acceptable practice? Explain your answer.

Critical Thinking

3. **Identifying Effect** Review your notes on the election of Andrew Jackson to the presidency. Then use a cause-and-effect chart like this one to show the ways in which Jacksonian Democracy increased Americans' political power.

   | Jacksonian Democracy | → increased Americans' political power → | |

FOCUS ON WRITING ✎

4. **Noting Significance** As you read this section, note things that made Jackson's political campaign and election significant in the history of American politics.

Andrew Jackson

If you were president, how would you use your powers?

When did he live? 1767–1845

Where did he live? Jackson was born in Waxhaw, a region along the border of the North and South Carolina colonies. In 1788 he moved to Nashville, Tennessee, which was still a part of North Carolina. There he built a mansion called the Hermitage. He lived in Washington as president, then retired to the Hermitage, where he died.

What did he do? Jackson had no formal education, but he taught himself law and became a successful lawyer. He became Tennessee's first representative to the U.S. Congress and also served in the Senate. Jackson became a national hero when his forces defeated the Creek and Seminole Indians. He went on to battle the British in the Battle of New Orleans during the War of 1812. Jackson was elected as the nation's seventh president in 1828 and served until 1837.

Why is he so important? Jackson's belief in a strong presidency made him both loved and hated. He vetoed as many bills as the six previous presidents together. Jackson also believed in a strong Union. When South Carolina tried to nullify, or reject, a federal tariff, he threatened to send troops into the state to force it to obey.

Identifying Cause and Effect Why did Jackson gain loyal friends and fierce enemies?

KEY EVENTS

1796–1797
Served in the U.S. House of Representatives

1797–1798
Served in the U.S. Senate

1798–1804
Served on the Tennessee Supreme Court

1821
Governor of Florida Territory

1823–1825
Served in the U.S. Senate

1829–1837
Served as president of the United States

1832
Vetoed rechartering the Second Bank of the United States. Threatened to send troops to South Carolina when it tried to nullify a federal tariff

Jackson received a scar from a British officer as a boy.

Jackson's Administration

What You Will Learn...

Main Ideas

1. Regional differences grew during Jackson's presidency.
2. The rights of the states were debated amid arguments about a national tariff.
3. Jackson's attack on the Bank sparked controversy.
4. Jackson's policies led to the Panic of 1837.

The Big Idea

Andrew Jackson's presidency was marked by political conflicts.

Key Terms and People

Tariff of Abominations, *p. 327*
states' rights doctrine, *p. 328*
nullification crisis, *p. 328*
Daniel Webster, *p. 328*
McCulloch v. *Maryland*, *p. 330*
Whig Party, *p. 330*
Panic of 1837, *p. 331*
William Henry Harrison, *p. 331*

 TAKING NOTES As you read, use a diagram like the one below to show the conflicts facing Andrew Jackson during his administration. Add more ovals to your organizer as necessary.

Three distinct regions emerge.

Congress passes Tariff of Abominations.

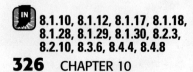 8.1.10, 8.1.12, 8.1.17, 8.1.18, 8.1.28, 8.1.29, 8.1.30, 8.2.3, 8.2.10, 8.3.6, 8.4.4, 8.4.8

If YOU were there...

You live on a small farm in South Carolina in 1829. Your family grows corn and cotton to sell, as well as vegetables for your own table. Although you grow your own food, you also depend on imported wool, flax, iron, and hemp to make ropes. But the government has just put new taxes on these products from Europe. Now they're too expensive for you to buy!

How would you feel about the new taxes on imports?

BUILDING BACKGROUND Even though Americans had a new feeling of national unity, different sections of the country still had very different interests. The industrial North competed with the agricultural South and the western frontier. As Congress favored one section over another, political differences grew.

Sectional Differences Increase

Regional differences had a major effect on Andrew Jackson's presidency. Americans' views of Jackson's policies were based on where they lived and the economy of those regions.

Three Regions Emerge

There were three main U.S. regions in the early 1800s. The North, first of all, had an economy based on trade and on manufacturing. Northerners supported tariffs because tariffs helped them compete with British factories. Northerners also opposed the federal government's sale of public land at cheap prices. Cheap land encouraged potential laborers to move from northern factory towns to the West.

The second region was the South. Its economy was based on farming. Southern farmers raised all types of crops, but the most popular were the cash crops of cotton and tobacco. Southerners sold a large portion of their crops to foreign nations.

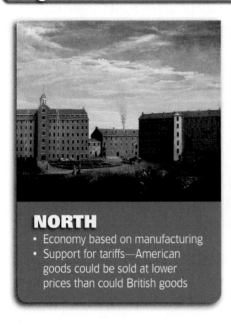

NORTH
- Economy based on manufacturing
- Support for tariffs—American goods could be sold at lower prices than could British goods

SOUTH
- Economy based on agriculture
- Opposition to tariffs, which increased the cost of imported goods

WEST
- Emerging economy
- Support for internal improvements and the sale of public lands

Southerners imported their manufactured goods. Tariffs made imported goods more expensive for southern farmers. In addition, high tariffs angered some of the South's European trading partners. These trading partners would likely raise their own tariffs in retaliation. To avoid this situation, southerners called for low tariffs.

Southerners also relied on enslaved African Americans to work the plantations. The issue of slavery would become increasingly controversial between the North and South.

In the third region, the West, the frontier economy was just emerging. Settlers favored policies that boosted their farming economy and encouraged further settlement. Western farmers grew a wide variety of crops. Their biggest priority was cheap land and internal improvements such as better roads and water transportation.

Tariff of Abominations

Tariffs became one of the first issues that President Jackson faced. In 1827, the year before Jackson's election, northern manufacturers began to demand a tariff on imported woolen goods. Northerners wanted the tariff to protect their industries from foreign competition, especially from Great Britain.

British companies were driving American ones out of business with their inexpensive manufactured goods. The tariff northerners supported, however, was so high that importing wool would be impossible. Southerners opposed the tariff, sayng it would hurt their economy.

Before Andrew Jackson took office, Congress placed a high tariff on imports. Angry southerners called it the **Tariff of Abominations**. (An abomination is a hateful thing.) Southern voters were outraged.

President John Quincy Adams signed the tariff legislation, though he did not fully support it. In early U.S. history, presidents tended to reserve veto power for legislation that they believed violated the Constitution. Signing the tariff bill meant Adams would surely be defeated in his re-election bid. The new tariff added fuel to the growing sectional differences plaguing the young nation.

READING CHECK **Summarizing** Describe the sectional economic differences in the United States during the early 1800s.

FOCUS ON INDIANA

Although Jackson won Indiana's electoral votes in 1824, 1828, and 1832, his party lost support in the state because of his economic policies. Sectional differences resulted in the state voting for Whig candidate and former Indiana Territory governor William Henry Harrison in 1836. Harrison lost the election, however.

States' Rights Debate

When Andrew Jackson took office in 1829, he was forced to respond to the growing conflict over tariffs. At the core of the dispute was the question of an individual state's right to disregard a law that had been passed by the U.S. Congress.

Nullification Crisis

ACADEMIC
VOCABULARY
criteria
basic requirements

Early in his political career, Vice President John C. Calhoun had supported the **criteria** of a strong central government. But in 1828 when Congress passed the Tariff of Abominations, Calhoun joined his fellow southerners in protest. Economic depression and previous tariffs had severely damaged the economy of his home state, South Carolina. It was only beginning to recover in 1828. Some leaders in the state even spoke of leaving the Union over the issue of tariffs.

In response to the tariff, Calhoun drafted the *South Carolina Exposition and Protest*. It said that Congress should not favor one state or region over another. Calhoun used the *Protest* to advance the **states' rights doctrine**, which said that since the states had formed the national government, state power should be greater than federal power. He believed states had the right to nullify, or reject, any federal law they judged to be unconstitutional.

FOCUS ON
READING
What conclusions can you draw about the importance of the states' rights debate after reading this section?

Calhoun's theory was controversial, and it drew some fierce challengers. Many of them were from the northern states that had benefited from increased tariffs. These opponents believed that the American people, not the individual states, made up the Union. Conflict between the supporters and the opponents of nullification deepened. The dispute became known as the **nullification crisis**.

Although he chose not to put his name on his *Exposition and Protest*, Calhoun did resign from the vice presidency. He was then elected to the Senate, where he continued his arguments in favor of nullification. Martin Van Buren replaced Calhoun as vice president when Jackson was re-elected president.

The Hayne-Webster Debate

The debate about states' rights began early in our nation's history. Thomas Jefferson and James Madison supported the states' power to disagree with the federal government in the Virginia and Kentucky Resolutions of 1798–99. Some of the delegates at the Hartford Convention supported states' rights. But Calhoun's theory went further. He believed that states could judge whether a law was or was not constitutional. This position put the power of the Supreme Court in question.

The issue of nullification was intensely debated on the floor of the Senate in 1830. Robert Y. Hayne, senator from South Carolina, defended states' rights. He argued that nullification gave states a way to lawfully protest federal legislation. **Daniel Webster** of Massachusetts argued that the United States was one nation, not a pact among independent states. He believed that the welfare of the nation should override that of individual states.

Jackson Responds

Although deeply opposed to nullification, Jackson was concerned about economic problems in the southern states. In 1832 he urged Congress to pass another tariff that lowered the previous rate. South Carolina thought the slight change was inadequate. The state legislature took a monumental step; it decided to test the doctrine of states' rights.

South Carolina's first action was to pass the Nullification Act, which declared the 1828 and 1832 tariffs "null, void … [and not] binding upon this State, its officers or citizens." South Carolina threatened to withdraw from the Union if federal troops were used to collect duties. The legislature also voted to form its own army. Jackson was enraged.

The president sternly condemned nullification. Jackson declared that he would enforce the law in South Carolina. At his request, Congress passed the Force Bill, approving use of the army if necessary. In light of Jackson's determined position, no other state chose to support South Carolina.

Early in 1833, Henry Clay of Kentucky had proposed a compromise that would gradually lower the tariff over several years. As Jackson's intentions became clear, both the U.S. Congress and South Carolina moved quickly to approve the compromise. The Congress would decrease the tariff, and South Carolina's leaders would enforce the law.

Despite the compromise, neither side changed its beliefs about states' rights. The argument continued for years, ending in the huge conflict known as the Civil War.

READING CHECK **Summarizing** What led to the nullification crisis, and why was it important?

Jackson Attacks the Bank

President Jackson upheld federal authority in the nullification crisis. He did not, however, always support greater federal power. For example, he opposed the Second Bank of the United States, founded by Congress in 1816.

The Second Bank of the United States was given a 20-year charter. This charter gave it the power to act exclusively as the federal government's financial agent. The Bank held federal deposits, made transfers of federal funds between states, and dealt with any payments or receipts involving the federal government. It also issued bank notes, or paper currency. Some 80 percent of the Bank was privately owned, but its operations were supervised by Congress and the president.

Many states, particularly in the South, had opposed the Bank. Small farmers believed that the Bank only helped wealthy businesspeople. Jackson also questioned the legality of the Bank. He believed it was an unconstitutional extension of the power of Congress. The states, he thought, should have the power to control the banking system.

Some states decided to take action. Maryland tried to pass a tax that would limit the

POINTS OF VIEW
States' Rights vs. the Union

The framers of the Constitution created a document that was remarkable in its scope. But a few issues were unresolved. One of the most controversial was the matter of states' rights versus the authority of the federal government. Daniel Webster insisted that the interests of the Union should prevail. John C. Calhoun believed that the powers of the states were greater.

"While the Union lasts we have high, exciting, gratifying [rewarding] prospects spread out before us, for us and our children. God grant that in my day . . . my eyes shall be turned to behold the gorgeous ensign [flag] of the republic . . . bearing for its motto . . . Liberty and Union, now and forever one and inseparable."

–Daniel Webster

from the Hayne-Webster debate, 1830

"If there be no protective power in the reserved rights of the states, they must in the end be forced to rebel . . ."

–John C. Calhoun

from a letter to Virgil Maxcy, September 11, 1830

ANALYSIS SKILL **ANALYZING PRIMARY SOURCES**

Finding Main Ideas How did the views of Calhoun and Webster differ?

POLITICAL CARTOON
Jackson against the Bank

Andrew Jackson's fight with the Bank was the subject of many political cartoons, like this one.

In this scene, Jackson is shown fighting a hydra that represents the national bank. The hydra is a mythological monster whose heads grow back when cut off. The heads of the hydra are portraits of politicians who opposed Jackson's policies.

Nicholas Biddle is at the center of the hydra. Why?

Andrew Jackson fights the hydra with a cane labeled "veto."

Why do you think the cartoonist chose this monster to represent the Bank?

ANALYSIS SKILL **ANALYZING PRIMARY SOURCES**

How does this image show the difficulty Jackson had politically?

Bank's operations. James McCulloch, cashier of the Bank's branch in Maryland, refused to pay this tax. The state took him to court, and the resulting case went all the way to the U.S. Supreme Court. In **McCulloch v. Maryland,** the Court ruled that the national bank was constitutional.

Nicholas Biddle, the Bank's director, decided to push for a bill to renew the Bank's charter in 1832. Jackson campaigned for the bill's defeat. "I will kill it," he promised. True to his word, Jackson vetoed the legislation when Congress sent it to him.

Congress could not get the two-thirds majority needed to override Jackson's veto. Jackson also weakened the Bank's power by moving most of its funds to state banks. In many cases, these banks used the funds to offer easy credit terms to people buying land. While this practice helped expansion in the West, it also led to inflation.

In the summer of 1836 Jackson tried to slow this inflation. He ordered Americans to use only gold or silver—instead of paper state-bank notes—to buy government-owned

land. This policy did not help the national economy as Jackson had hoped. Jackson did improve the economy by lowering the national debt. However, his policies opened the door for approaching economic troubles.

READING CHECK **Analyzing** Why did critics of the Second Bank of the United States oppose it?

Panic of 1837

Jackson was still very popular with voters in 1836. He chose not to run in 1836, however, and the Democrats nominated Vice President Martin Van Buren.

In 1834 a new political party had formed to oppose Jackson. Its members called themselves Whigs, after an English political party that opposed the monarchy, to make the point that Jackson was using his power like a king. The **Whig Party** favored the idea of a weak president and a strong Congress. Unable to agree on a candidate, the Whigs chose four men to run against Van Buren. Because of this indecision, and with backing from Jackson, Van Buren won the election.

The Supreme Court and Capitalism

During the early 1800s, the Supreme Court made several rulings that helped define federal power over contracts and commerce. These rulings reinforced capitalism as the ruling economic system in the United States.

What effect did the Supreme Court have on economic development?

1810

1819

1824

Fletcher v. Peck
State legislatures could not pass laws violating existing contracts.

Dartmouth College v. Woodward
State legislatures could not pass laws to change the charters of institutions or businesses.

McCulloch v. Maryland
States do not have the power to tax federal institutions.

Gibbons v. Ogden
Only the federal government has the power to regulate interstate and foreign commerce.

Shortly after Van Buren took office, the country experienced the **Panic of 1837**, a severe economic depression. Jackson's banking policies and his unsuccessful plan to curb inflation contributed to the panic. But people blamed Van Buren.

In 1840 the Whigs united against the weakened Van Buren to stand behind one candidate, **William Henry Harrison**, an army general. Harrison won in an electoral landslide. The Whigs had achieved their goal of winning the presidency.

READING CHECK Identifying Cause and Effect
What contributed to the Panic of 1837, and how did it affect the 1840 election?

SUMMARY AND PREVIEW The states' rights debate dominated much of Jackson's presidency. In the next section you will learn about the removal of American Indians from the southeastern United States.

Section 2 Assessment

Reviewing Ideas, Terms, and People

1. **a. Recall** On what were the economies of the northern, southern, and western states based?
   b. Predict How might the sectional issues involved in the dispute over the **Tariff of Abominations** lead to future problems between North and South?
2. **a. Describe** What roles did **Daniel Webster** and John C. Calhoun play in the **nullification crisis**?
   b. Summarize What idea did supporters of the **states' rights doctrine** promote?
3. **a. Describe** What problems resulted from weakening the Bank?
   b. Draw Conclusions Why did Jackson veto the bill to renew the Second Bank of the United States?
4. **a. Recall** What caused the **Panic of 1837**?
   b. Summarize How did the **Whig Party** win the election of 1840?
   c. Elaborate Why do you think Jackson chose not to run for the presidency in 1836? Do you think he made the right decision? Why?

Critical Thinking

5. **Identifying Cause and Effect** Review your notes on the political conflicts during Jackson's administration. Then use a graphic organizer like the one below to show how some of Jackson's policies dealing with conflicts led to the Panic of 1837.

FOCUS ON WRITING

6. **Identifying Important Conflicts** Stories about conflict sell newspapers. As you read this section, list important conflicts that occurred during Jackson's presidency and note the role Jackson played in creating or resolving the conflicts.

Indian Removal

What You Will Learn...

Main Ideas

1. The Indian Removal Act authorized the relocation of Native Americans to the West.
2. Cherokee resistance to removal led to disagreement between Jackson and the Supreme Court.
3. Other Native Americans resisted removal with force.

The Big Idea

President Jackson supported a policy of Indian removal.

Key Terms and People

Indian Removal Act, *p. 332*
Indian Territory, *p. 332*
Bureau of Indian Affairs, *p. 332*
Sequoya, *p. 333*
Worcester v. *Georgia, p. 334*
Trail of Tears, *p. 334*
Black Hawk, *p. 335*
Osceola, *p. 335*

TAKING NOTES As you read, use a graphic organizer like the one below to show the steps Andrew Jackson and the U.S. government took toward Indian removal.

Indian removal

8.1.12, 8.1.15, 8.1.17, 8.1.18, 8.1.24, 8.1.30, 8.2.3, 8.2.10, 8.3.1, 8.4.4, 8.4.8

If YOU were there...

You belong to the Cherokee nation. Your family has farmed rich lands in Georgia for as long as anyone can remember. You've learned some new ways from white settlers, too. At school you've learned to read both English and Cherokee. But now that doesn't seem important. The U.S. government is sending you and your people far away to unknown places in the West.

How would you feel about being taken away from your home?

BUILDING BACKGROUND President Andrew Jackson had become famous as an American Indian fighter. He had no sympathy with Native Americans' claim to the lands where they had always lived. With public support, he reversed the government's pledge to respect Indian land claims. The result was the brutal removal of the southeastern peoples to empty lands in the West.

Indian Removal Act

Native Americans had long lived in settlements stretching from Georgia to Mississippi. However, President Jackson and other political leaders wanted to open this land to settlement by American farmers. Under pressure from Jackson, Congress passed the **Indian Removal Act** in 1830, authorizing the removal of Native Americans who lived east of the Mississippi River to lands in the West.

Congress then established **Indian Territory**—U.S. land in what is now Oklahoma—and planned to move Native Americans there. Some supporters of this plan, like John C. Calhoun, argued that removal to Indian Territory would protect Indians from further conflicts with American settlers. "One of the greatest evils to which they are subject is that incessant [constant] pressure of our population," he noted. "To guard against this evil . . . there ought to be the strongest . . . assurance that the country given [to] them should be theirs." To manage Indian removal to western lands, Congress approved the creation of a new government agency, the **Bureau of Indian Affairs**.

Indian Removal

During the Trail of Tears, thousands of Cherokee died from disease, starvation, and harsh weather. They were forced to walk hundreds of miles to their new land in the West. Other Native Americans were also moved, with similar results.

What can you see in this painting that indicates this was a difficult journey?

The Choctaw were the first Indians sent to Indian Territory. The Mississippi legislature abolished the Choctaw government and then forced the Choctaw leaders to sign the Treaty of Dancing Rabbit Creek. This treaty gave more than 7.5 million acres of their land to the state. The Choctaw moved to Indian Territory during a disastrous winter trip. Federal officials in charge of the move did not provide enough food or supplies to the Choctaw, most of whom were on foot. About one-fourth of the Choctaw died of cold, disease, or starvation.

News of the Choctaw's hardships caused other Indians to resist removal. When the Creek resisted in 1836, federal troops moved in and captured some 14,500 of them. They led the Creek, many in chains, to Indian Territory. One Creek woman remembered the trip being filled with "the awful silence that showed the heartaches and sorrow at being taken from the homes and even separation from loved ones." The Chickasaw, who lived in upper Mississippi, negotiated a treaty for better supplies on their trip to Indian Territory. Nevertheless, many Chickasaw lives were also lost during removal.

READING CHECK **Finding Main Ideas** What major changes did President Jackson make to U.S. policy regarding Native Americans?

Cherokee Resistance

Many Cherokee had believed that they could prevent conflicts and avoid removal by adopting the **contemporary** culture of white people. In the early 1800s they invited missionaries to set up schools where Cherokee children learned how to read and write in English. The Cherokee developed their own government modeled after the U.S. Constitution with an election system, a bicameral council, and a court system. All of these were headed by a principal chief.

A Cherokee named **Sequoya** used 86 characters to represent Cherokee syllables to create a writing system for their own complex language. In 1828 the Cherokee began publishing a newspaper printed in both English and Cherokee.

The adoption of white culture did not protect the Cherokee. After gold was discovered on their land in Georgia, their treaty rights

ACADEMIC VOCABULARY

contemporary existing at the same time

were ignored. Georgia leaders began preparing for the Cherokee's removal. When they refused to move, the Georgia militia began attacking Cherokee towns. In response, the Cherokee sued the state. They said that they were an independent nation and claimed that the government of Georgia had no legal power over their lands.

In 1832 the Supreme Court, under the leadership of Chief Justice John Marshall, agreed. In **Worcester v. Georgia** the Court ruled that the Cherokee nation was a distinct community in which the laws of Georgia had no force. The Court also stated that only the federal government, not the states, had authority over Native Americans.

Georgia, however, ignored the Court's ruling, and President Jackson took no action to make Georgia follow the ruling. "John Marshall has made his decision; now let him enforce it," Jackson supposedly said. By not enforcing the Court's decision, Jackson violated his presidential oath to uphold the laws of the land. However, most members of Congress and American citizens did not protest the ways Jackson removed Native Americans.

In the spring of 1838, U.S. troops began to remove all Cherokee to Indian Territory. A few were able to escape and hide in the mountains of North Carolina. After the Cherokee were removed, Georgia took their businesses, farms, and property.

The Cherokee's 800-mile forced march became known as the **Trail of Tears**. During the march, the Cherokee suffered from disease, hunger, and harsh weather. Almost one-fourth of the 18,000 Cherokee died on the march.

READING CHECK **Finding Main Ideas**
What was the *Worcester* v. *Georgia* ruling, and what was Jackson's response?

THE IMPACT TODAY
Today more than 150,000 Cherokee or Cherokee descendants live in present-day Oklahoma.

Primary Source

PERSONAL ACCOUNTS
Trail of Tears

The Cherokee knew that they would be forced to march West, but they did not know that so many of their people would die on the way. Here are two accounts of the Trail of Tears, one written before it started and one written after, both by Cherokee who made the trip.

March 10, 1838
Beloved Martha, I have delayed writing to you so long ... If we Cherokees are to be driven to the west by the cruel hand of oppression to seek a new home in the west, it will be impossible ... It is thus all our rights are invaded."

—Letter from Jenny, a Cherokee girl, just before her removal

"Long time we travel on way to new land. People feel bad when they leave Old Nation. Women cry and make sad wails, Children cry and many men cry ... but they say nothing and just put heads down and keep on go towards West. Many days pass and people die very much."

—Recollections of a survivor of the Trail of Tears

ANALYSIS SKILL **ANALYZING POINTS OF VIEW**

1. What is different about the concerns of the Cherokee before and after the Trail of Tears?
2. How do you think the survivors of the Trail of Tears felt when they reached Indian Territory?

Other Native Americans Resist

Other Native Americans decided to fight U.S. troops to avoid removal. Chief **Black Hawk**, a leader of Fox and Sauk Indians, led his people in a struggle to protect their lands in Illinois. By 1832, however, the Sauk forces were running out of food and supplies, and by 1850 they had been forced to leave.

In Florida, Seminole leaders were forced to sign a removal treaty that their followers decided to ignore. A leader named **Osceola** called upon his people to resist with force, and the Second Seminole War began. Osceola was captured and soon died in prison. His followers, however, continued to fight. Some 4,000 Seminole were removed and hundreds of others killed. Eventually, U.S. officials decided to give up the fight. Small groups of Seminole had resisted removal, and their descendants live in Florida today.

READING CHECK **Evaluating** How effective was Native American resistance to removal?

Second Seminole War

FLORIDA TERRITORY
Clinch's Battle 1835
Fort Mellon 1837
ATLANTIC OCEAN
Dade's Massacre 1835
Fort Armstrong 1836
Okeechobee 1837
Gulf of Mexico
Fort Jupiter 1838
Lake Okeechobee
Fort Lauderdale 1842

Indian lands given up by treaty
Battles
0   50   100 Miles
0   50   100 Kilometers

GEOGRAPHY SKILLS **INTERPRETING MAPS**

1. **Location** In what parts of Florida was the Second Seminole War fought?
2. **Place** Where was the last battle of the Second Seminole War fought?

SUMMARY AND PREVIEW President Jackson supported the removal of thousands of Native Americans from their traditional lands to the federal territory in the West. In the next chapter you will learn about the westward growth of the nation as farmers, ranchers, and other settlers moved West.

FOCUS ON INDIANA

The treaty that resulted in the Black Hawk War had been negotiated by William Henry Harrison when he was the governor of Indiana Territory.

go.hrw.com
Online Quiz
KEYWORD: SF7 HP10

Section 3 Assessment

Reviewing Ideas, Terms, and People

1. **a. Identify** What Native American groups were affected by the **Indian Removal Act**? Where were they relocated?
   b. Explain Why did government officials want to relocate Native Americans to the West?
   c. Predict What are some possible effects that the Indian Removal Act might have on Native Americans already living in the West?
2. **a. Identify** What was the **Trail of Tears**?
   b. Analyze Why did the state of Georgia want to relocate the Cherokee, and what did the Cherokee do in response?
   c. Elaborate What do you think of President Jackson's refusal to enforce the **Worcester v. Georgia** ruling?
3. **a. Describe** What led to the Second Seminole War?
   b. Compare and Contrast How were the Seminole and the Sauk resistance efforts similar and different?

Critical Thinking

4. **Comparing and Contrasting** Review your notes on Indian removal. Then copy the chart below and use it to identify the Native American groups and their responses to removal.

Native American Group	Response to Removal

FOCUS ON WRITING

5. **Understanding Causes and Effects** As you read, identify the causes and effects of the Jackson administration's policy of Indian relocation.

The Indian Removal Treaties

MO

KS

Trail of Tears, 1838–39

Cherokee

Creek

AR

Seminole

OK

Chickasaw

Chocktaw

TX

LA

In 1830 President Andrew Jackson signed the Indian Removal Act into law. As its name implies, the purpose of the act was to remove Native Americans from land that white settlers wanted for themselves. Five tribes were forced to leave their traditional lands and walk to a territory west of the Mississippi River. The land in the new Indian Territory was land white settlers did not want. It was poor and not good for farming. The poor land made life very difficult for newly arrived Indians. Many died from malnutrition and disease. Within 10 years, about 60,000 Indians had been relocated.

Treaty	Date	Indian Group	Results for United States	Results for Indian Groups	Outcome
Treaty of Greenville	1795	12 Groups	Ended battles in Northwest Territory	Payment of $20,000; acknowledgment of lands	Indian land claims disregarded by American settlers
Treaty at Holston River	1798	Cherokee	Received land promised to Cherokee	Payment of $5,000, followed by annual payments	Cherokee lands reduced
Treaty at St. Louis	1804	Sauk and Fox	Received land from Sauk and Fox	Annual payment of $1,000	Indians claimed their leaders acted without permission; conflicts arose as settlers moved to Sauk and Fox land
Treaty at Ft. Jackson	1814	Creek	Ended battles with Red Eagle; received 23 million acres of land in Georgia	Received small amount of land in Alabama	Conflicts between settlers and Creek led to removal of Creek to Indian Territory
Treaty of Dancing Rabbit Creek	1830	Choctaw	Received all Choctaw lands east of Mississippi River	Received land in Indian Territory	Choctaw became first tribe moved from southeast to land in Indian Territory

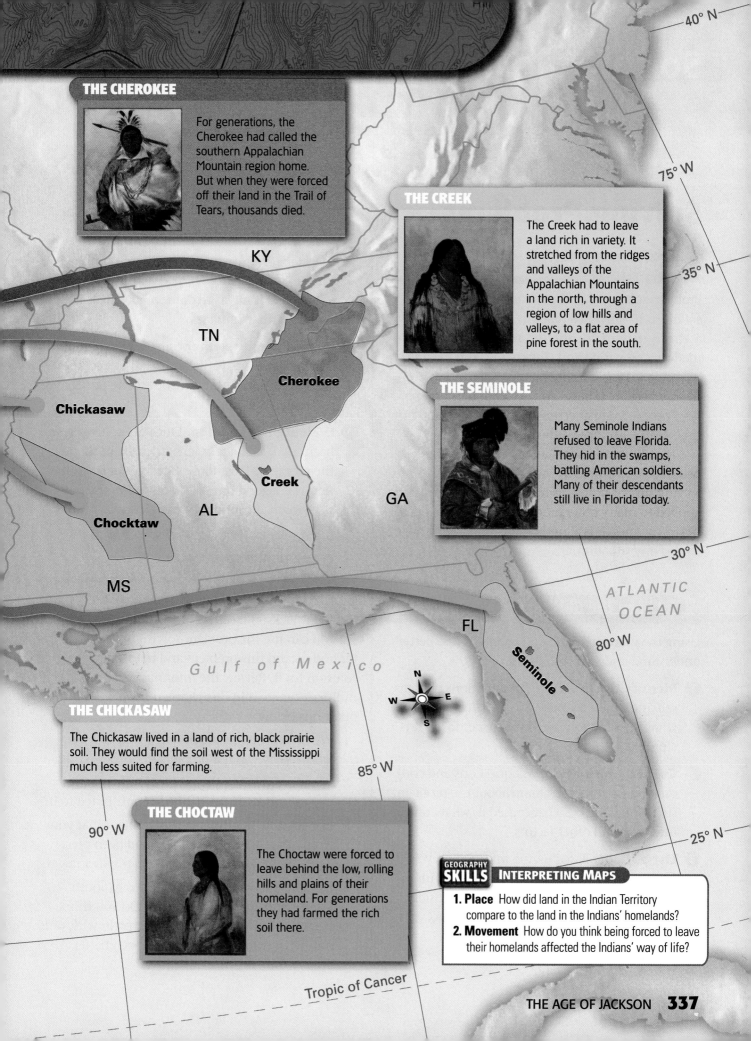

THE CHEROKEE

For generations, the Cherokee had called the southern Appalachian Mountain region home. But when they were forced off their land in the Trail of Tears, thousands died.

THE CREEK

The Creek had to leave a land rich in variety. It stretched from the ridges and valleys of the Appalachian Mountains in the north, through a region of low hills and valleys, to a flat area of pine forest in the south.

THE SEMINOLE

Many Seminole Indians refused to leave Florida. They hid in the swamps, battling American soldiers. Many of their descendants still live in Florida today.

THE CHICKASAW

The Chickasaw lived in a land of rich, black prairie soil. They would find the soil west of the Mississippi much less suited for farming.

THE CHOCTAW

The Choctaw were forced to leave behind the low, rolling hills and plains of their homeland. For generations they had farmed the rich soil there.

KY

TN

Cherokee

Chickasaw

Chocktaw

AL

Creek

GA

MS

FL

Seminole

Gulf of Mexico

ATLANTIC OCEAN

Tropic of Cancer

40° N

75° W

35° N

30° N

80° W

85° W

90° W

25° N

GEOGRAPHY SKILLS INTERPRETING MAPS

1. **Place** How did land in the Indian Territory compare to the land in the Indians' homelands?
2. **Movement** How do you think being forced to leave their homelands affected the Indians' way of life?

Social Studies Skills

Analysis | Critical Thinking | Civic Participation | Study

Solving Problems

Define the Skill

Problem solving is a process for finding workable solutions to difficult situations. The process involves asking questions, identifying and evaluating information, comparing and contrasting, and making judgments. Problem solving is useful in studying history because it helps you better understand problems people faced at certain points in time and how they dealt with those difficulties.

The ability to understand and evaluate how people solved problems in the past also can help in solving similar problems today. The skill can also be applied to many other kinds of difficulties besides historical ones. It is a method for thinking through almost any situation.

Learn the Skill

Using the following steps will enable you to better understand and solve problems.

1 **Identify the problem.** Ask questions of yourself and others to make sure you know exactly what the situation is and understand why it is a problem.

2 **Gather information.** Ask questions and conduct research to learn more about the problem, such as its history, what caused it, what contributes to it, and other factors.

3 **List options.** Based on the information you have gathered, identify possible options for solving the problem that you might consider. Be aware that your final solution will probably be better and easier to reach if you have as many options as possible to consider.

4 **Evaluate the options.** Weigh each option you are considering. Think of and list the advantages it has as a solution, as well as its potential disadvantages.

5 **Choose and implement a solution.** After comparing the advantages and disadvantages of each possible solution, choose the one that seems best and apply it.

6 **Evaluate the solution.** Once the solution has been tried, evaluate its effectiveness in solving the problem. This step will tell you if the solution was a good one, or if another of the possible solutions should be tried instead.

Practice the Skill

One of the most challenging situations that President Jackson faced was the nullification crisis. You can use the problem-solving skills to better understand this problem and to evaluate his solution for it. Review the information about the nullification crisis in this chapter. Then answer the questions below.

1. What was the specific problem that Jackson faced? Why was it a problem?

2. What event led to the problem? What earlier circumstances and conditions contributed to it?

3. List possible solutions to the problem that you would have considered if you had been president, along with advantages and disadvantages.

4. Jackson threatened to send troops to South Carolina to enforce federal law. Do you think his solution was the best one? Explain why, or if not, what solution would have been better.

HOLT
History's Impact
▶ video series
Review the video to answer
the closing question:

*How may the U.S. government's
early treatment of Native
Americans have contributed
to the reservations' current
situation?*

Visual Summary

QUICK FACTS

*Use the visual summary below to help you review
the main ideas of the chapter.*

SLAM!

Jackson's Policies Shut the Door on Key Issues

Second Bank of the United States Jackson
vetoed the legislation to renew the Bank's charter
and removed federal funds from the Bank.

Indian Removal Jackson pressured Congress to
pass a law to move Native Americans out of the
Southeast and into Indian Territory.

Nullification Crisis Jackson threatened to send
federal troops into South Carolina to enforce
federal law.

Reviewing Vocabulary, Terms, and People

*Complete each sentence by filling in the blank with the
correct term or person.*

1. In the Supreme Court case of _____,
   the Court ruled that the federal government, not
   the states, had authority over the Cherokee.

2. President Jackson's group of advisers was known
   as the _____ because of where its members met in the White House.

3. _____ served as Andrew Jackson's vice
   president until he resigned due to the dispute
   over nullification.

4. The _____ supported the power of the
   states over the federal government.

5. The practice of rewarding supporters with positions in government is known as the _____.

Comprehension and Critical Thinking

SECTION 1 *(Pages 322–324)*

6. **a. Identify** What changes took place in the
   early 1800s that broadened democracy in the
   United States?

   b. Analyze How was Jackson's victory in the
   election of 1828 a reflection of a change in
   American politics?

   c. Evaluate Do you think the changes brought
   about by Jacksonian Democracy went far
   enough in expanding democracy? Why or why
   not?

SECTION 2 *(Pages 326–331)*

7. **a. Describe** What conflicts troubled the Jackson administration?

b. Draw Conclusions What were the results of the conflict over the Second Bank of the United States?

c. Predict How might sectional differences and the debate over states' rights lead to future problems for the United States?

SECTION 3 *(Pages 332–335)*

8. a. Identify Who was Sequoya? What important contribution did he make?

b. Contrast In what different ways did the Cherokee and the Seminole attempt to resist removal to Indian Territory?

c. Elaborate Do you agree with Jackson's refusal to enforce the *Worcester* v. *Georgia* ruling? Why or why not?

Reviewing Themes

9. Politics What new political party rose in opposition to President Andrew Jackson? What was the party's attitude toward the power of the president?

10. Economics What economic factors influenced the policy of Indian removal?

Social Studies Skills

Solving Problems *Use the Social Studies Skills taught in this chapter to answer the question about the reading selection below.*

> Northerners wanted the tariff to protect their industries from foreign competition, especially from Great Britain.
>
> British companies were driving American ones out of business because they could manufacture goods more cheaply than American businesses could . . . Southerners opposed the tariff, claiming it would hurt their economy. *(p. 327)*

11. Which of the following might be a reasonable solution to the problem discussed above?

a. passing a low tariff

b. passing a high tariff only in the South

c. Britain passing a tariff

d. selling northern and British goods for a higher price

Reading Skills

Drawing Conclusions about the Past *Use the Reading Skills taught in this chapter to answer the question about the reading selection below.*

> Native Americans had long lived in settlements stretching from Georgia to Mississippi. However, President Jackson and other political leaders wanted to open this land to settlement by American farmers. *(p. 332)*

12. Which statement below can you conclude from the passage above?

a. Farmers moved onto the Native Americans' land after removal.

b. Native Americans wanted to move from their lands.

c. Native Americans resisted removal.

d. Government officials had to use force to remove Native Americans from their land.

Using the Internet

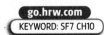
go.hrw.com
KEYWORD: SF7 CH10

13. Activity: Writing a newspaper Enter the activity keyword and research Jackson's presidency. Then create a party newspaper, using the template provided, that supports or criticizes Jackson's policies. Use evidence to support your articles either in favor of or against his policies. Write from the point of view of a supporter or from the point of view of a political enemy.

FOCUS ON WRITING

14. Writing Interview Questions Review the notes you have taken about Jackson's political significance, the conflicts he was involved in, and the causes and effects of his policies toward Indians. Then, based on your notes, begin writing questions for your interview with Jackson. What will the readers of your newspaper want to learn more about? Write at least 10 interview questions that your readers will want answered.

DIRECTIONS: Read each question and write the letter of the best response.

1 The era surrounding the presidency of Andrew Jackson is *best* known for an expansion in

A freedom of speech.

B religious toleration.

C states' rights.

D voting rights.

2 Which of the following was important to the South's economy in the 1830s?

A manufacturing

B plantation agriculture

C shipbuilding

D weaving

3 What action did the Cherokee take to resist their removal from Georgia and North Carolina to the West?

A sued the state of Georgia in the courts

B destroyed neighbors' farms and businesses

C went to war against the U.S. government

D staged a protest called the Trail of Tears

4 The debate between John C. Calhoun and Daniel Webster over states' rights was *most like* the debate between

A the Patriots and the Loyalists.

B the Antifederalists and the Federalists.

C England and France during the French and Indian War.

D the large states and the small states during the Constitutional Convention.

5 President Jackson's weakening of the Second Bank of the United States resulted in

A inflation and other economic problems.

B the nullification crisis.

C the rise of the Democratic Party.

D increasing sectionalism.

6 The ruling in the Supreme Court case of *Worcester* v. *Georgia*

A established the policy of Indian removal.

B determined that Georgia laws did not apply to the Cherokee.

C was enforced by President Andrew Jackson.

D established protective tariffs for imported goods.

7 Read the following quote from Daniel Webster's "Seventh of March" speech and use it to answer the question below.

"The people have preserved . . . their . . . Constitution, for forty years, and have seen their happiness, prosperity, and renown grow with its growth, and strengthen with its strength . . . I have not coolly weighed the chances of preserving liberty when the bonds that unite us together shall be broken . . . [Let us not have] 'Liberty first and Union afterwards,' but . . . that other sentiment, dear to every true American heart,—Liberty and Union, now and forever, one and inseparable!"

–Daniel Webster, Seventh of March Speech, 1830

Document-Based Question How does Webster appeal to listeners to preserve the Union?

Expanding West

Indiana Standards

Social Studies Standards

8.1.15 Explain the concept of Manifest Destiny and describe its impact on westward expansion of the United States.

8.1.25 Give examples of how immigration affected American culture in the decades before and after the Civil War, including growth of industrialism in the North; religious differences; tensions between middle-class and working-lcass people, particularly in the Northeast; and intensification of cultural differences between the North and the South.

8.3.8 Gather information on ways people changed the physical environment of the United States in the nineteenth century using primary sources and secondary sources including digitized photo collections and historic maps.

8.3.10 Create maps, graphs, and charts showing the distribution of natural resources—such as forests, water sources, and wildlife—in the United States at the beginning of the nineteenth century and give examples of how people exploited these resources as the country became more indisturalized and people moved westward.

go.hrw.com
Indiana
KEYWORD: SF10 IN

 FOCUS ON WRITING

Outline for a Documentary Film Many documentary films have been made about the history of the United States, but there is always room for one more. In this chapter you will read about the westward expansion of the United States, a period filled with excitement and challenge. Then you will create an outline for a documentary film to be used in middle–school history classes.

UNITED STATES

1811
John Jacob Astor founds the fur-trading post Astoria on the Columbia River.

1810

WORLD

What You Will Learn...

In this chapter you will learn about how the United States expanded west. The country acquired vast amounts of territory in a short time. Lured by land and gold, hundreds of thousands of Americans followed trails west in search of a better life. However, many Californio families, like the one pictured here, had already lived in California for generations.

1827
The United States and Great Britain agree to continue joint occupation of Oregon Country.

1841
Pro-expansionist John Tyler becomes president after William Henry Harrison dies in office.

1846
The United States declares war against Mexico.

1848
Gold is discovered in California on January 24.

1820

1830

1840

1850

1821
Mexico wins its independence from Spain.

1838
Californios revolt unsuccessfully against the Mexican government.

1842
China gives Great Britain control of the island of Hong Kong.

1854
Commodore Matthew Perry negotiates a trade treaty with Japan.

Reading Social Studies

by Kylene Beers

| Economics | Geography | Politics | Society and Culture | Science and Technology |

Focus on Themes In this chapter you will read about the American people as they continued to move west. You will find out about the famous Oregon and Santa Fe trails, Texas's fight for independence from Mexico, and Mexico's war with the United States. Finally, you will read about the California gold rush that brought thousands of people west. As you read each section, you will see how **economic** issues affected the growth of different **geographic** areas.

Vocabulary in Context

Focus on Reading In Chapter 3 you learned how writers sometimes give you clues to a word's meaning in the same or a nearby sentence. Those clues are usually definitions, restatements in different words, or comparisons or contrasts. But what do you do if you do not know the word and the writer doesn't think to give you a direct clue?

Using Broader Context Clues If the writer does not give you one of those direct clues, you have to try to figure out the meaning of the word for yourself.

1. Read the whole paragraph and look for information that will help you figure out the meaning.

2. Look up the word in the dictionary to be sure of its meaning.

Notice how a student used information from the whole paragraph to learn the meaning of two unknown words.

In 1844, the Whig Party passed up Tyler and chose Senator Henry Clay of Kentucky as its presidential candidate. At first opposing *annexation,* Clay changed his mind due to pressure from southern politicians. The Democratic Party chose former Tennessee governor James K. Polk to oppose Clay. Both candidates strongly favored *acquiring* Texas and Oregon. *(p. 355)*

I'm not sure about *annexation*. The southerners convinced Clay to be for it. Maybe I'll understand if I read some more.

Oh, both presidential candidates favored acquiring Texas and Oregon. Maybe annexation means almost the same thing as acquiring. I'll check the dictionary.

You Try It!

The following passage is from the chapter you are about to read. Read the passage and then answer the questions.

American Settlement in the Mexican Cession

From Chapter 11, p. 361

The war ended after Scott took Mexico City. In February 1848, the United States and Mexico signed the Treaty of Guadalupe Hidalgo, which officially ended the war and forced Mexico to turn over much of its northern territory to the United States. Known as the Mexican Cession, this land included the present-day states of California, Nevada, and Utah . . .

In exchange for this vast territory, the United States agreed to pay Mexico $15 million. In addition, the United States assumed claims of more than $3 million held by American citizens against the Mexican government.

Refer to the passage to answer the following questions.

1. Do you know what the word *cession* means? What clues in the first paragraph can help you figure out what the word might mean? Use those clues to write a definition of *cession*.

2. Look *cession* up in a dictionary. How does your definition compare to the dictionary definition?

3. In your experience, what does the word *assume* usually mean? Do you think that meaning is the one used in the second paragraph? If not, what do you think *assume* means in this case?

4. Look *assume* up in a dictionary. Does one of its meanings match the one you came up with?

As you read Chapter 11, use context clues to figure out the meanings of unfamiliar words. Check yourself by looking the words up in a dictionary.

Key Terms and People

Academic Vocabulary

Success in school is related to knowing academic vocabulary—the words that are frequently used in school assignments and discussions. In this chapter, you will learn the following academic words:

explicit *(p. 351)*
element *(p. 357)*

Trails to the West

What You Will Learn...

Main Ideas

1. During the early 1800s, Americans moved west of the Rocky Mountains to settle and trade.
2. The Mormons traveled west in search of religious freedom.

The Big Idea

The American West attracted a variety of settlers.

Key Terms and People

John Jacob Astor, *p. 346*
mountain men, *p. 346*
Oregon Trail, *p. 348*
Santa Fe Trail, *p. 349*
Mormons, *p. 349*
Brigham Young, *p. 349*

TAKING NOTES Create a diagram like the one below. As you read, take notes on the different groups that settled in the American West, the trails they took, and their motives for moving West.

Trails	Travelers	Motives

8.1.15, 8.3.2, 8.3.5, 8.3.7, 8.3.9

If YOU were there...

You live in Ohio in 1840. A few months ago, you and your family heard stories about a wonderful land in the Northwest, with sparkling rivers and fertile valleys. You all decide to pull up stakes and head West. You travel to Independence, Missouri, planning to join a wagon train on the Oregon Trail. In Missouri, you're surprised to find hundreds of other people planning to make the trip.

What would you expect your journey West to be like?

BUILDING BACKGROUND Many Americans in the Jacksonian Era were restless, curious, and eager to be on the move. The American West drew a variety of settlers. Some looked for wealth and adventure. Others, like this family on its way to the Northwest, dreamed of rich farmland and new homes.

Americans Move West

In the early 1800s, Americans pushed steadily westward, moving even beyond the territory of the United States. They traveled by canoe and flatboat, on horseback, and by wagon train. Some even walked much of the way.

The rush to the West occurred, in part, because of a hat. The "high hat," made of water-repellent beaver fur, was popular in the United States and Europe. While acquiring fur for the hats, French, British, and American companies gradually killed off the beaver population in the East. Companies moved west in search of more beavers. Most of the first non-Native Americans who traveled to the Rocky Mountains and the Pacific Northwest were fur traders and trappers.

American merchant **John Jacob Astor** created one of the largest fur businesses, the American Fur Company. His company bought skins from western fur traders and trappers who became known as **mountain men**. These adventurers were some of the first easterners to explore and map the Rocky Mountains and lands west of them. Mountain men lived lonely and often dangerous lives. They trapped animals on their own, far from towns and settlements. Mountain men such as Jedediah Smith, Manuel Lisa, Jim Bridger, and Jim

Trails Leading West

Trails, Distances, and Travel Times

◄ **California** 2,000 miles, 6 months
◄ **Santa Fe** 1,200 miles, 2 months
◄ **Mormon** 1,300 miles, 4 months
◄ **Old Spanish** 700 miles, 7 weeks
◄ **Oregon** 2,000 miles, 6 months
🏠 Fort or trading post

0   200   400 Miles
0   200   400 Kilometers

Jim Beckwourth was an African American fur trapper and explorer of the West in the early 1800s.

GEOGRAPHY SKILLS | **INTERPRETING MAPS**

1. **Movement** Which trails took the longest to travel?
2. **Human-Environment Interaction** What difficulties do you think travelers on the trails faced?

Beckwourth survived many hardships during their search for wealth and adventure. To survive on the frontier, mountain men adopted Native American customs and clothing. In addition, they often married Native American women. The Indian wives of trappers often worked hard to contribute to their success.

Pioneer William Ashley saw that frequently bringing furs out of the Rocky Mountains was expensive. He asked his traders to stay in the mountains and meet once a year to trade and socialize. This practice helped make the fur trade more profitable. The yearly meeting was known as the rendezvous. At the rendezvous, mountain men and Native American trappers sold their fur to fur-company agents. It was thus important to bring as many furs as possible. One trapper described the people at a typical rendezvous in 1837. He saw Americans, Canadian French, some Europeans, and "Indians, of nearly every tribe in the Rocky Mountains."

The rendezvous was filled with celebrating and storytelling. At the same time, the meeting was also about conducting business. Western artist Alfred Jacob Miller described how trade was begun in the rendezvous camp.

"The Fur Company's great tent is raised; the Indians erect their picturesque [beautiful] white lodges; the accumulated [collected] furs of the hunting season are brought forth and the Company's tent is a ... busy place."
—Alfred Jacob Miller, quoted in *The Fur Trade of the American West*, by David J. Wishart

In 1811, John Jacob Astor founded a fur-trading post called Astoria at the mouth of the Columbia River. Astoria was one of the first American settlements in what became known as Oregon Country. American Indians occupied the region, which was rich in forests, rivers, and wildlife. However, Britain, Russia, Spain, and the United States all claimed the land. The United States based its claim on

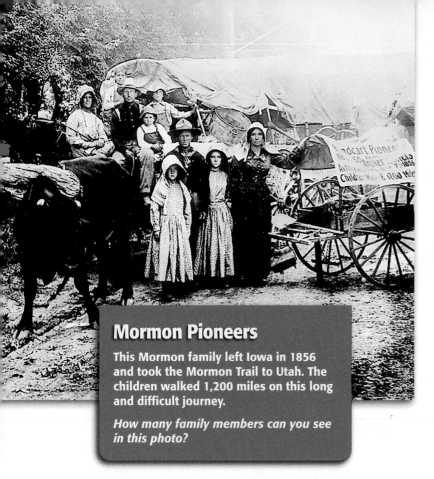

Mormon Pioneers

This Mormon family left Iowa in 1856 and took the Mormon Trail to Utah. The children walked 1,200 miles on this long and difficult journey.

How many family members can you see in this photo?

The Oregon Trail

Many settlers moving to Oregon Country and other western areas followed the 2,000-mile-long **Oregon Trail**, which stretched from places such as Independence, Missouri, or Council Bluffs, Iowa, west into Oregon Country. The trail followed the Platte and Sweetwater Rivers over the Plains. After it crossed the Rocky Mountains, the trail forked. The northern branch led to the Willamette Valley in Oregon. The other branch went to California and became known as the California Trail.

Traveling the trail challenged the strength and determination of pioneer families. The journey usually began after the rainy season ended in late spring and lasted about six months. The cost, about $600 for a family of four, was high at a time when a typical worker usually made about $1.50 per day. Young families made up most groups of settlers. They gathered in wagon trains for the trip. There could be as few as 10 wagons or as many as several dozen in a wagon train.

The wagons were pulled by oxen, mules, or horses. Pioneers often walked to save their animals' strength. They kept up a tiring pace, traveling from dawn until dusk. Settler Jesse Applegate recalled the advice he received from one experienced Oregon pioneer: "Travel, *travel*, TRAVEL . . . Nothing is good that causes a moment's delay."

Some pioneers brought small herds of cattle with them on the trail. They faced severe hardships, including shortages of food, supplies, and water. Rough weather and geographic barriers, such as rivers and mountains, sometimes forced large numbers of pioneers to abandon their wagons. In the early days of the Oregon Trail, many Native Americans helped the pioneers, acting as guides and messengers. They also traded goods for food. Although newspapers sometimes reported Native American "massacres" of pioneers, few settlers died from Indian attacks.

The settlers who arrived safely in Oregon and California found generally healthy

the exploration of merchant captain Robert Gray, who had reached the mouth of the Columbia River in 1792.

Recognizing the huge economic value of the Pacific Northwest, the United States made treaties in which Spain and Russia gave up their claims to various areas. The United States also signed treaties with Britain allowing both countries to occupy Oregon Country, the Columbia River, and its surrounding lands.

By the 1840s, the era of American fur trading in the Pacific Northwest was drawing to a close. The demand for beaver furs had fallen because fashions changed. Too much trapping had also greatly reduced the number of beavers. Some mountain men gave up their work and moved back east. Their daring stories, however, along with the treaties made by the U.S. government, inspired other Americans to move West. Lured by rich resources and a mild climate, easterners poured into Oregon Country in the 1840s. These new settlers soon replaced the mountain men on the frontier.

and pleasant climates. By 1845 some 5,000 settlers occupied the Willamette Valley.

The Santa Fe Trail

The **Santa Fe Trail** was another important path west. It led from Independence, Missouri, to Santa Fe, New Mexico. It followed an ancient trading route first used by Native Americans. American traders loaded their wagon trains with cloth and other manufactured goods to exchange for horses, mules, and silver from Mexican traders in Santa Fe.

The long trip across blazing deserts and rough mountains was dangerous. But the lure of high profits encouraged traders to take to the trail. One trader reported a 2,000 percent profit on his cargo. The U.S. government helped protect traders by sending troops to ensure that Native Americans were not a threat.

READING CHECK Contrasting How were the Oregon and Santa Fe trails different?

Mormons Travel West

One large group of settlers traveled to the West in search of religious freedom. In 1830 a young man named Joseph Smith founded the Church of Jesus Christ of Latter-day Saints in western New York. The members of Joseph Smith's church became known as **Mormons**. Smith told his followers that he had found and translated a set of golden tablets containing religious teachings. The writings were called the *Book of Mormon*.

Church membership grew rapidly, but certain beliefs and practices caused Mormons to be persecuted. For example, beginning in the 1850s some Mormon men practiced polygamy—a practice in which one man is married to several women at the same time. This practice was outlawed by the church in 1890.

In the early 1830s Smith and his growing number of converts left New York. They formed new communities, first in Ohio, then in Missouri, and finally in Illinois. All three communities eventually failed, and an anti-Mormon mob murdered Smith in 1844. Following Smith's murder, **Brigham Young** became head of the Mormon Church. Young chose what is now Utah as the group's new home, and thousands of Mormons took the Mormon Trail to the area near the Great Salt Lake, where they prospered. By 1860 there were about 40,000 Mormons in Utah.

READING CHECK Finding Main Ideas Why did Mormons move west?

SUMMARY AND PREVIEW Some of the first Americans to move West were fur traders and trappers. Settlers soon followed. In the next section you will learn about the Texas Revolution.

Section 1 Assessment

Reviewing Ideas, Terms, and People

1. **a. Identify** What was the **Oregon Trail**?
   b. Elaborate Would you have chosen to leave your home to travel west? Why?
2. **a. Identify** Who are the **Mormons**?
   b. Summarize What difficulties led Mormons to move to Utah?

Critical Thinking

3. **Drawing Conclusions** Review your notes on early American settlement in the West. Then copy the chart below and use it to identify challenges of the trip that western travelers faced.

Travelers	Challenges Faced

FOCUS ON WRITING

4. **Describing Trails West** As you read this section, note important topics that you might want to cover in your documentary film. In addition, write down ideas about how you might present information about each topic. For example, will you use a narrator to tell the life story of Joseph Smith, or will you have actors present it dramatically?

The Texas Revolution

What You Will Learn...

Main Ideas

1. Many American settlers moved to Texas after Mexico achieved independence from Spain.
2. Texans revolted against Mexican rule and established an independent nation.

The Big Idea

In 1836, Texas gained its independence from Mexico.

Key Terms and People

Father Miguel Hidalgo y Costilla, *p. 350*

empresarios, *p. 350*

Stephen F. Austin, *p. 351*

Antonio López de Santa Anna, *p. 351*

Alamo, *p. 352*

Battle of San Jacinto, *p. 352*

TAKING NOTES As you read, take notes on the events that led to the independence of Texas. Write your notes in steps, as shown below.

1. Mexican government hires empresarios.
2. _____
   3. _____
      4. _____

 8.1.15, 8.3.7, 8.3.9

If YOU were there...

You are the father of a large farm family in Missouri. There is not enough land for everyone, so you're looking for another opportunity. One day, a Mexican government official comes to town. He is looking for people to settle in Texas. The Mexican government is offering generous tracts of land to colonists. However, you have to become a citizen of Mexico and follow Mexican laws.

Would you decide to move your family to Texas? Why?

BUILDING BACKGROUND Spain controlled a vast amount of territory in what would later become the American Southwest. The Spanish built missions and forts in Texas to establish control of that region. But the settlements were far apart, and conflicts with Native Americans discouraged Spanish settlers from moving to Texas. When Mexico became an independent republic, it actively looked for more settlers.

American Settlers Move to Texas

Mexico had a long, unprotected border that stretched from Texas to California. Mexico's Spanish rulers worried constantly about attacks from neighbors. They also were concerned about threats from within Mexico.

Their fears were justified. Mexicans moved to overthrow Spanish rule in the early 1800s. In September 1810 **Father Miguel Hidalgo y Costilla**, a Mexican priest, led a rebellion of about 80,000 poor Indians and mestizos, or people of Indian and Spanish ancestry. They hoped that if Mexico became independent from the Spanish monarchy, their lives would improve.

Hidalgo's revolt failed, but the rebellion he started grew. In 1821 Mexico became independent. In 1824 it adopted a republican constitution that declared rights for all Mexicans. The new Mexican government hired **empresarios**, or agents, to bring settlers to Texas. They paid the agents in land.

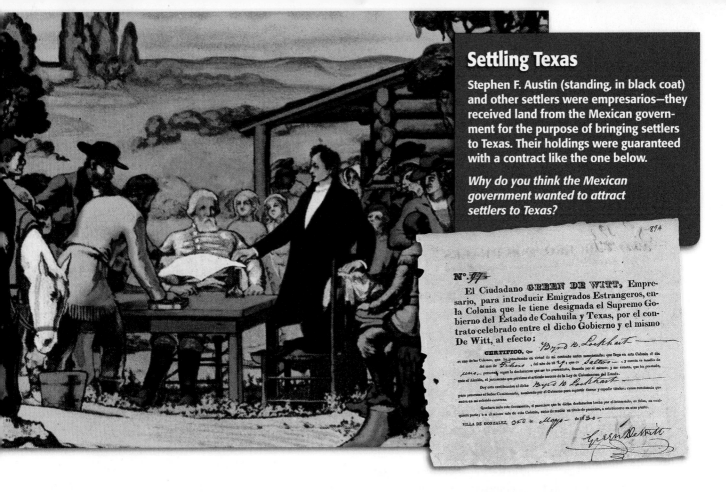

Settling Texas

Stephen F. Austin (standing, in black coat) and other settlers were empresarios—they received land from the Mexican government for the purpose of bringing settlers to Texas. Their holdings were guaranteed with a contract like the one below.

Why do you think the Mexican government wanted to attract settlers to Texas?

In 1822 one young agent, **Stephen F. Austin**, started a Texas colony on the lower Colorado River. The first 300 families became known as the Old Three Hundred. Austin's successful colony attracted other agents, and American settlers flocked to the region.

In exchange for free land, settlers had to obey Mexican laws. But some settlers often **explicitly** ignored these laws. For example, despite the ban on slavery, many brought slaves. Concerned that it was losing control of the growing American population, Mexico responded. In 1830, it banned further settlement by Americans. Angry about the new law, many Texans began to think of gaining independence from Mexico.

Meanwhile, Mexico had come under the rule of General **Antonio López de Santa Anna**. He soon suspended Mexico's republican constitution and turned his attention to the growing unrest in Texas.

READING CHECK **Finding Main Ideas** Why did settlers move to Texas?

Texans Revolt against Mexico

In October 1835 the Mexican army tried to remove a cannon from the town of Gonzales, Texas. Rebels stood next to the cannon. Their flag read, "Come and take it." In the following battle, the rebels won. The Texas Revolution, also known as the Texas War for Independence, had begun.

Texas Independence

On March 2, 1836, Texans declared their independence from Mexico. The new Republic of Texas was born. Both the declaration and the constitution that shortly followed were modeled after the U.S. documents. The Texas constitution, however, made slavery legal.

Delegates to the new Texas government chose politician David Burnet as president and Lorenzo de Zavala as vice president. Another revolutionary, Sam Houston, was named to head the Texas army. Austin went to the United States to seek money and troops.

ACADEMIC VOCABULARY
explicit fully revealed without vagueness

Battle at the Alamo

FOCUS ON READING

Use this section to summarize the events of the battle at the Alamo.

The Texans' actions angered Santa Anna. He began assembling a force of thousands to stop the rebellion.

A hastily created army of Texas volunteers had been clashing with Mexican troops for months. Under Colonel William Travis, a small force took the town of San Antonio. It then occupied the **Alamo**, an abandoned mission near San Antonio that became an important battle site in the Texas Revolution. Volunteers from the United States, including frontiersman Davy Crockett and Colonel Jim Bowie, joined the Alamo's defense.

The rebels, numbering fewer than 200, hoped to stall the huge Mexican force while a larger Texas army assembled. For almost two weeks, from February 23 to March 6, 1836, the Texans held out. Travis managed to get a message to other Texans through enemy lines:

> "I call on you in the name of Liberty, of patriotism, and everything dear to the American character, to come to our aid with all dispatch [speed] …VICTORY OR DEATH."
>
> —William Travis, from a letter written at the Alamo, 1836

Before dawn on March 6, the Mexican army attacked. Despite heavy losses, the army overcame the Texans. All the defenders of the Alamo were killed, though some civilians survived. Following a later battle, at Goliad, Santa Anna ordered the execution of 350 prisoners who had surrendered. Texans were enraged by the massacres.

Battle of San Jacinto

Santa Anna now chased the untrained forces of Sam Houston. Outnumbered, the Texans fled east. Finally, they reorganized at the San Jacinto River, near Galveston Bay. There, the Texans took a stand.

Santa Anna was confident of victory, but he was careless in choosing the site for his camp. On the afternoon of April 21, 1836, while Mexican troops were resting, Houston's forces swarmed the camp, shouting, "Remember the Alamo! Remember Goliad!"

The fighting ended swiftly. Santa Anna's army was destroyed. In the **Battle of San Jacinto**, the Texans captured Santa Anna and forced him to sign a treaty giving Texas its independence.

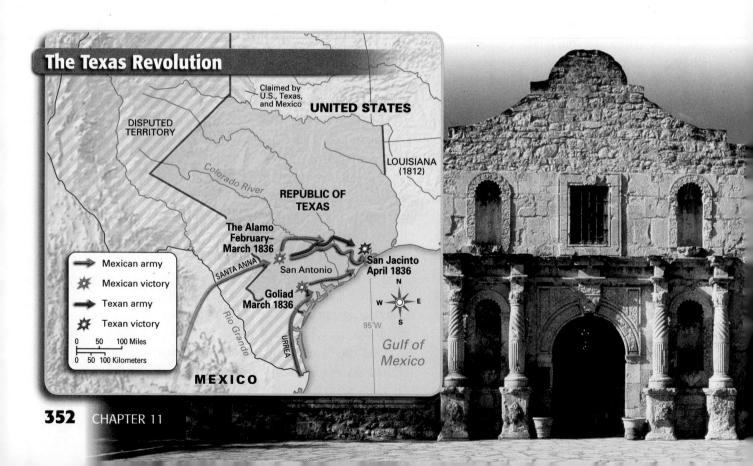

The Texas Revolution

DISPUTED TERRITORY

Claimed by U.S., Texas, and Mexico

UNITED STATES

LOUISIANA (1812)

Colorado River

REPUBLIC OF TEXAS

The Alamo February–March 1836

SANTA ANNA

San Antonio

Goliad March 1836

San Jacinto April 1836

URREA

Rio Grande

Gulf of Mexico

MEXICO

→ Mexican army
✦ Mexican victory
→ Texan army
✦ Texan victory

0   50   100 Miles
0   50   100 Kilometers

An Independent Nation

Sam Houston was the hero of the new independent nation of Texas. The republic created a new town named Houston and made it the capital. Voters elected Sam Houston as president. Stephen F. Austin became secretary of state.

To increase the population, Texas offered land grants. American settlers came from nearby southern states, often bringing slaves with them to help grow and harvest cotton.

Most Texans hoped that the United States would annex, or take control of, Texas, making it a state. The U.S. Congress also wanted to annex Texas. But President Andrew Jackson refused. He was concerned that admitting Texas as a slave state would upset the fragile balance of free and slave states. The president also did not want to have a war with Mexico over Texas.

Finally, Jackson did recognize Texas as an independent nation. France did so in 1839. Britain, which wanted to halt U.S. expansion, recognized Texas in 1840.

The Mexican government, however, did not recognize Santa Anna's forced handover of Texas. For this reason, in 1837 the republic organized the Texas Rangers to guard its long frontier from Mexican and Native American attacks. Finally, in 1844 Texas and Mexico signed a peace treaty.

READING CHECK **Finding Main Ideas** What issues did the new nation of Texas face?

SUMMARY AND PREVIEW American settlers in Texas challenged the Mexican government and won their independence. In the next section you will learn about the war between Mexico and the United States.

On March 6, 1836, Texans fought and lost the Battle of the Alamo. A rallying cry for the Texans at the Battle of San Jacinto was "Remember the Alamo!" The single star of the flag represents the Republic of Texas, also called the Lone Star Republic.

Why do you think "Remember the Alamo!" was a rallying cry for Texas troops at San Jacinto?

go.hrw.com
Online Quiz
KEYWORD: SF7 HP11

Section 2 Assessment

Reviewing Ideas, Terms, and People

1. **a. Identify** What role did **Stephen F. Austin** play in the settlement of Texas?
   b. Make Inferences Why did Mexican officials want to bring more settlers to Texas?
   c. Evaluate Do you think Mexico's requirements for foreign immigrants were reasonable or unreasonable? Explain.
2. **a. Describe** What were the important battles in the War for Texas Independence? Why was each important?
   b. Make Inferences Why did Texas offer land grants to settlers?
   c. Predict What problems might the Republic of Texas face?

Critical Thinking

3. **Sequencing** Review your notes on American settlement in Texas. Then copy the graphic organizer below and use it to show the significant events in the history of the Republic of Texas.

Significant Events
1. Houston is founded and made the capital.
2.
3.
4.
5.
6.
7.

FOCUS ON WRITING

4. **Explaining the Texas Revolution** As you read this section, make note of the most important players and events in the story of how Texas gained independence from Mexico. Consider also how you will present information about these people and events to your film's audience. What words, images, and sounds will make the story of the revolution come alive for the audience?

The Mexican-American War

What You Will Learn...

Main Ideas

1. Many Americans believed that the nation had a manifest destiny to claim new lands in the West.
2. As a result of the Mexican-American War, the United States added territory in the Southwest.
3. American settlement in the Mexican Cession produced conflict and a blending of cultures.

The Big Idea

The ideals of manifest destiny and the outcome of the Mexican-American War led to U.S. expansion to the Pacific Ocean.

Key Terms and People

manifest destiny, *p. 354*
James K. Polk, *p. 355*
vaqueros, p. 357
Californios, *p. 357*
Bear Flag Revolt, *p. 358*
Treaty of Guadalupe Hidalgo, *p. 361*
Gadsden Purchase, *p. 361*

 Create a graphic organizer like the one below. Use it to define *manifest destiny* and then list the events in the expansion of the United States.

| Manifest Destiny is | → | Events 1. 2. |

 8.1.15, 8.3.1, 8.3.7, 8.3.9, 8.3.10

If YOU were there...

Your family are Californios, Spanish settlers who have lived in California for many years. You raise horses on your ranch. So far, you have gotten along with American settlers. But it has become clear that the American government wants to take over California. You hear that fighting has already started between American and Mexican troops.

How might life change under American rule?

BUILDING BACKGROUND Mexican independence set the stage for conflict and change in the West and Southwest. At the same time, American settlers continued to move westward, settling in the Mexican territories of Texas and California. American ambitions led to clashes with Mexico and the people who already lived in Mexico's territories.

Manifest Destiny

"We have it in our power to start the world over again."
—Thomas Paine, from his pamphlet *Common Sense*

Americans had always believed they could build a new, better society founded on democratic principles. In 1839 writer John O'Sullivan noted, "We are the nation of human progress, and who will, what can, set limits to our onward march?"

Actually, there was one limit: land. By the 1840s the United States had a booming economy and population. Barely 70 years old, the nation already needed more room for farms, ranches, businesses, and ever-growing families. Americans looked West to what they saw as a vast wilderness, ready to be taken.

Some people believed it was America's **manifest destiny**, or obvious fate, to settle land all the way to the Pacific Ocean in order to spread democracy. O'Sullivan coined the term in 1845. He wrote that it was America's "manifest destiny to overspread and to possess the whole continent which Providence [God] has given us for the development of the great experiment of liberty . . . "

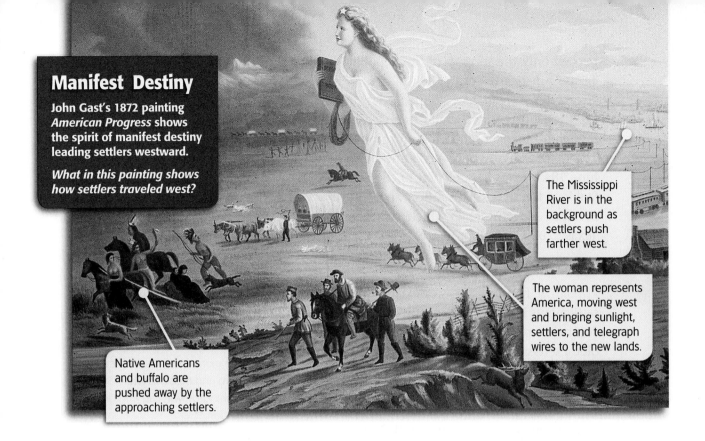

Manifest Destiny

John Gast's 1872 painting *American Progress* shows the spirit of manifest destiny leading settlers westward.

What in this painting shows how settlers traveled west?

The Mississippi River is in the background as settlers push farther west.

The woman represents America, moving west and bringing sunlight, settlers, and telegraph wires to the new lands.

Native Americans and buffalo are pushed away by the approaching settlers.

In the 1840s and 1850s, manifest destiny was tied up with the slavery issue. If America expanded, would slavery be allowed in the new territories? Several presidents became involved in the difficult issue. Among them was President John Tyler. A pro-slavery Whig, Tyler wanted to increase the power of the southern slave states by annexing Texas. His fellow Whigs disagreed.

In 1844, the Whig Party passed up Tyler and chose Senator Henry Clay of Kentucky as its presidential candidate. At first opposing annexation, Clay changed his mind due to pressure from southern politicians. The Democratic Party chose former Tennessee governor **James K. Polk** to oppose Clay. Both candidates strongly favored acquiring Texas and Oregon.

Southerners feared the loss of Texas, a possible new slave state. Others worried that Texas might become an ally of Britain. These concerns helped Polk narrowly defeat Clay.

Acquiring New Territory

President Polk quickly set out to fulfill his campaign promise to annex Oregon and Texas. By the 1820s, Russia and Spain had given up their claims to Oregon Country. Britain and the United States had agreed to occupy the territory together.

As more Americans settled there, they began to ask that Oregon become part of the United States. Polk wanted to protect these settlers' interests. Some politicians noted that Oregon Country would provide a Pacific port for the growing U.S. trade with China.

Meanwhile, Britain and the United States disagreed over how to draw the United States–Canadian border. American expansionists cried, "Fifty-four forty or fight!" This slogan referred to 54°40' north latitude, the line to which Americans wanted their northern territory to extend.

Neither side really wanted a war, though. In 1846 Great Britain and the United States signed a treaty that gave the United States all Oregon land south of the forty-ninth parallel. This treaty drew the border that still exists today. Oregon became an organized U.S. territory in February 1848.

Texas came next. By March 1845, Congress had approved annexation and needed only the support of the Republic of Texas. Americans continued to pour into Texas. Texas politicians hoped that joining the United States would help solve the republic's financial and military problems. The Texas Congress approved annexation in June 1845. Texas became part of the United States in December. This action angered the Mexican government, which considered Texas to be a "stolen province."

California under Mexico

Though it had lost Texas, Mexico still had settlements in other areas of the present-day Southwest to govern. New Mexico was the oldest settled area, with its capital at Santa Fe. Mexico also controlled present-day Arizona, Nevada, and California.

During early Spanish rule, the mission system had dominated much of the present-day Southwest. Over time, it had become less important there, especially in New Mexico, where settlers lived in small villages. In California, however, missions remained the focus of everyday life. Missions under later Spanish rule carried out huge farming and ranching operations using the labor of Native Americans. Some of the Indians came willingly to the missions. Others were brought by force. Usually, they were not allowed to leave the mission once they had arrived. They had to adopt the clothing, food, and religion of the Spanish priests.

Missions often sold their goods to local pueblos, or towns, that arose near the missions and presidios. One wealthy California settler, Mariano Guadalupe Vallejo, remembered the early days.

“We were the pioneers of the Pacific coast, building towns and missions while General [George] Washington was carrying on the war of the Revolution.”

—Mariano Guadalupe Vallejo, quoted in *Eyewitnesses and Others*

After winning independence from Spain in 1821, Mexico began to change old Spanish

Ranch Life

Spanish and Mexican *vaqueros*, or cowboys, were expert horse riders. They used their horses to herd cattle on the ranches of the Spanish Southwest.

Leather chaps protected riders from dust and scrapes.

Vaqueros were known for their specially designed hats.

Saddles like these were highly prized by *vaqueros*.

ANALYSIS SKILL **ANALYZING VISUALS**

What features of the *vaqueros'* life are shown in this painting?

policies toward California and Texas. In 1833, for example, Mexico ended the mission system in California. Mission lands were broken up, and huge grants were given to some of the wealthiest California settlers, including Vallejo. They created vast ranchos, or ranches, with tens of thousands of acres of land. *Vaqueros*, or cowboys, managed the large herds of cattle and sheep. Cowhides were so valuable that they were called "California banknotes." Hides were traded for household items and luxury goods with ship captains from the eastern United States. Some settlers also made wine and grew citrus fruits.

Although they had been freed from the missions, for most California Indians the **elements** of life changed very little. They continued to herd animals and do much of the hard physical labor on ranches and farms. Some, however, ran away into the wilderness or to the nearby towns of San Diego and Los Angeles.

The Californios

Because of the great distance between California and the center of Mexico's government, by the early 1820s California had only around 3,200 colonists. These early California settlers, called **Californios**, felt little connection to their faraway government.

Californios developed a lasting reputation for hospitality and skilled horse riding. In *Two Years Before the Mast*, American novelist Richard Henry Dana Jr. wrote about his encounters with Californio culture. He described, for example, what happened after a Californio served a feast to Dana and a friend.

"We took out some money and asked him how much we were to pay. He shook his head and crossed himself, saying that it was charity—that the Lord gave it to us."

—Richard Henry Dana Jr., from *Two Years Before the Mast*

In addition to traders and travelers, a small number of settlers also arrived from the United States. They were called Anglos by the Californios. Although there were few

Anglo settlers in California, their calls for independence increased tensions between Mexico and the United States.

READING CHECK Drawing Inferences How did manifest destiny affect Spanish and Mexican rule in California?

ACADEMIC VOCABULARY
element a basic part of an individual's surroundings

Mexican-American War

Diplomatic relations between Mexico and the United States became increasingly strained. U.S. involvement in California and Texas contributed to this tension.

Conflict Breaks Out

Mexico had long insisted that its northern border lay along the Nueces River. The United States said the border was farther south, along the Rio Grande. In June 1845 President Polk ordered General Zachary Taylor to lead an army into the disputed region.

Polk sent diplomat John Slidell to Mexico City to try to settle the border dispute. Slidell came with an offer to buy New Mexico and California for $30 million. Mexican officials refused to speak to him.

In March 1846, General Taylor led his troops to the Rio Grande. He camped across from Mexican forces stationed near the town of Matamoros, Mexico. In April, the Mexican commander told Taylor to withdraw from Mexican territory. Taylor refused. The two sides clashed, and several U.S. soldiers were killed.

In response, President Polk said to Congress:

"Mexico has passed the boundary of the United States, has invaded our territory, and shed American blood upon the American soil...The two nations are now at war."

—James K. Polk, from his address to Congress, May 11, 1846

Polk's war message was persuasive. Two days later, Congress declared war on Mexico.

War Begins

At the beginning of the war with Mexico, the U.S. Army had better weapons and equipment. Yet it was greatly outnumbered and poorly prepared. The government put out a call for 50,000 volunteers. About 200,000 responded. Many were young men who thought the war would be a grand adventure in a foreign land.

On the home front, many Americans supported the war. However, many Whigs thought the war was unjustified and avoidable. Northern abolitionists also opposed the conflict. They feared the spread of slavery into southwestern lands.

While Americans debated the war, fighting proceeded. General Taylor's soldiers won battles south of the Nueces River. Taylor then crossed the Rio Grande and occupied Matamoros, Mexico. While Taylor waited for more men, Polk ordered General Stephen Kearny to attack New Mexico. On August 18, 1846, Kearny took Santa Fe, the capital city, without a fight. He claimed the entire province of New Mexico for the United States and marched west to California, where another conflict with Mexico was already under way.

The Bear Flag Revolt

In 1846, only about 500 Americans lived in the huge province of California, in contrast to about 12,000 Californios. Yet, in the spirit of manifest destiny, a small group of American settlers seized the town of Sonoma, north of San Francisco, on June 14. Hostilities began between the two sides when the Americans took some horses that were intended for the Mexican militia. In what became known as the **Bear Flag Revolt**, the Americans declared California to be an independent nation. Above the town, the rebels hoisted a hastily made flag of a grizzly bear facing a red star. Californios laughed at the roughly-made bear, thinking it "looked more like a pig than a bear."

John C. Frémont, a U.S. Army captain, was leading a mapping expedition across the Sierra Nevada when he heard of the possible war with Mexico. Frémont went to Sonoma and quickly joined the American settlers in their revolt against the Californios. Because war had already broken out between the United States and Mexico, Frémont's actions were seen as beneficial to the American cause in the region. His stated goal, however, was Californian independence, not to annex California to the United States. During the revolt, several important Californios were taken prisoner, including Mariano Vallejo. Vallejo and his brother were held at an Anglo settlement for two months without any formal charges being brought against them. Long after his release, Vallejo wrote a history of California that included an account of his time as a bear flag prisoner.

But the bear flag was quick to fall. In July, U.S. naval forces came ashore in California and raised the stars and stripes. Kearny's army arrived from the East. The towns of San Diego, Los Angeles, and San Francisco fell rapidly. In August, U.S. Navy commodore Robert Stockton claimed California for the United States. Some Californios continued to resist until early 1847, when they surrendered.

Mexican-American War, 1846–1847

The Bear Flag Revolt

American settlers took over Sonoma, the regional headquarters of the Mexican army. They captured Mexican general Mariano Vallejo and declared California a new country: the California Republic.

CALIFORNIA REPUBLIC

OREGON COUNTRY

Great Salt Lake

Bear Flag Revolt, June 1846
Sutter's Fort
Sonoma
San Francisco
Monterey
SIERRA NEVADA
FRÉMONT
CA
San Gabriel, Jan. 1847
STOCKTON
Los Angeles
San Pasqual, Dec. 1846
San Diego
KEARNY
120°W
30°N

Colorado River

UNORGANIZED TERRITORY

Bent's Fort
KEARNY
Fort Leavenworth
KEARNY

UNITED STATES

NEW MEXICO
Santa Fe

Arkansas River

DISPUTED TERRITORY

Red River

Gila River
DONIPHAN
Rio Grande

TEXAS

San Antonio

Mississippi River

New Orleans
90°W

Nueces River

Chihuahua

WOOL

Corpus Christi
Palo Alto, May 1846
TAYLOR
Resaca de la Palma, May 1846
Matamoros

Monterrey, Sept . 1846

PACIFIC OCEAN

SLOAT

Mazatlán

110°W

Buena Vista, Feb. 1847

SANTA ANNA

MEXICO

Gulf of Mexico
Tropic of Cancer

Tampico
SCOTT

End of the War

General Winfield Scott landed at Veracruz and defeated troops in the Mexican fortress there. He then marched inland, toward Mexico City. Scott's capture of the Mexican capital led to the end of the war.

Mexico City, Sept. 1847
SCOTT
SANTA ANNA
Cerro Gordo, April 1847
Veracruz, Mar. 1847
20°N

Legend:
- → American forces
- ✸ American victory
- → Mexican forces
- ✸ Mexican victory
- 🏰 Fort
- — Modern-day state boundaries

0   100   200 Miles
0   100   200 Kilometers

N
W   E
S

go.hrw.com
Interactive Map
KEYWORD: SF7 CH11

GEOGRAPHY SKILLS | **INTERPRETING MAPS**

1. **Location** What Mexican city did Scott's forces attack in March 1847?
2. **Movement** Which U.S. commander led forces from Santa Fe to San Diego?

American soldier

**FOCUS ON
INDIANA**

Most of the volunteer U.S. troops in the Mexican-American War came from western states, including Indiana. A volunteer regiment from Indiana was the first to meet Santa Anna's troops at the Battle of Buena Vista.

War's End

In Mexico General Taylor finally got the reinforcements he needed. He drove his forces deep into enemy lands. Santa Anna, thrown from office after losing Texas, returned to power in Mexico in September 1846. He quickly came after Taylor.

The two armies clashed at Buena Vista in February 1847. After a close battle with heavy casualties on both sides, the Mexican Army retreated. The next morning, the cry went up: "The enemy has fled! The field is ours!"

Taylor's success made him a war hero back home. The general's popularity troubled President Polk, and when Taylor's progress stalled, Polk gave the command to General Winfield Scott. A beloved leader, he was known by his troops as "Old Fuss and Feathers" because of his strict military discipline.

Scott sailed to the port of Veracruz, the strongest fortress in Mexico. On March 29, after an 88-hour artillery attack, Veracruz fell.

Scott moved on to the final goal, Mexico City, the capital. Taking a route similar to one followed by Spanish conquistador Hernán Cortés in 1519, the Americans pushed 200 or so miles inland. Santa Anna tried to stop the U.S. forces at Cerro Gordo in mid-April, but failed. By August 1847, U.S. troops were at the edge of Mexico City.

After a truce failed, Scott ordered a massive attack on Mexico City. Mexican soldiers and civilians fought fierce battles in and around the capital. At a military school atop the steep, fortified hill of Chapultepec, young Mexican cadets bravely defended their hopeless position. At least one soldier jumped to his death rather than surrender to the invading forces. Finally, on September 14, 1847, Mexico City fell. Santa Anna soon fled the country.

READING CHECK **Sequencing** In chronological order, list the key battles of the Mexican-American War.

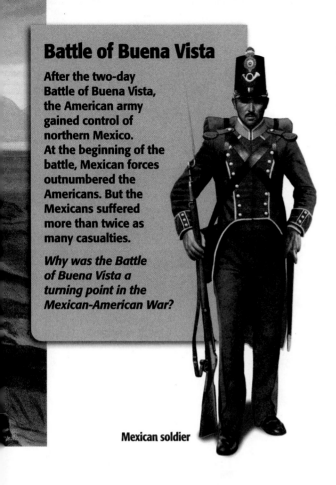

Battle of Buena Vista

After the two-day Battle of Buena Vista, the American army gained control of northern Mexico. At the beginning of the battle, Mexican forces outnumbered the Americans. But the Mexicans suffered more than twice as many casualties.

Why was the Battle of Buena Vista a turning point in the Mexican-American War?

Mexican soldier

American Settlement in the Mexican Cession

The war ended after Scott took Mexico City. In February 1848, the United States and Mexico signed the **Treaty of Guadalupe Hidalgo**, which officially ended the war and forced Mexico to turn over much of its northern territory to the United States. Known as the Mexican Cession, this land included the present-day states of California, Nevada, and Utah. In addition, it included most of Arizona and New Mexico and parts of Colorado and Wyoming. The United States also won the area claimed by Texas north of the Rio Grande. The Mexican Cession totaled more than 500,000 square miles and increased the size of the United States by almost 25 percent.

Agreements and Payments

In exchange for this vast territory, the United States agreed to pay Mexico $15 million. In addition, the United States assumed claims of more than $3 million held by American citizens against the Mexican government. The treaty also addressed the status of Mexicans in the Mexican Cession. The treaty provided that they would be "protected in the free enjoyment of their liberty and property, and secured in the free exercise of their religion." The Senate passed the treaty in March 1848.

After the war with Mexico, some Americans wanted to guarantee that any southern railroad to California would be built completely on American soil. James Gadsden, U.S. minister to Mexico, negotiated an important agreement with Mexico in December 1853. Under the terms of the **Gadsden Purchase**, the U.S. government paid Mexico $10 million. In exchange, the United States received the southern parts of what are now Arizona and New Mexico. With this purchase, the existing boundary with Mexico was finally fixed.

Surge of American Settlers

After the Mexican-American War, a flood of Americans moved to the Southwest. American newcomers struggled against longtime residents to control the land and other valuable resources, such as water and minerals. Most Mexicans, Mexican Americans, and Native Americans faced legal, economic, and social discrimination. As a result, they found it difficult to protect their rights.

The Treaty of Guadalupe Hidalgo promised to protect Mexican American residents' property rights. Yet differences between Mexican and U.S. land laws led to great confusion. The U.S. government often made Mexican American landowners go to court to prove that they had titles to their land. Landowners had to pay their own travel costs as well as those of witnesses and interpreters. They also had to pay attorneys' and interpreters' fees. These legal battles often bankrupted landowners. New settlers also tended to ignore Mexican legal concepts, such as community property or community water rights.

Mexican Americans Today

Today Mexican Americans are about 9 percent of the U.S. population. More than 26 million Mexican Americans live in all 50 states. Many who live in the West are descended from people who lived there long before the region became part of the United States.

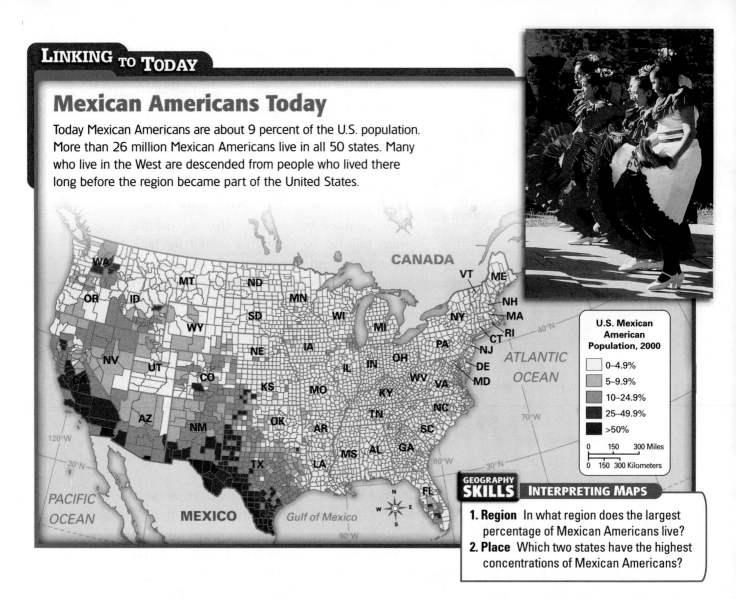

U.S. Mexican American Population, 2000

- 0–4.9%
- 5–9.9%
- 10–24.9%
- 25–49.9%
- >50%

0   150   300 Miles
0   150   300 Kilometers

GEOGRAPHY SKILLS INTERPRETING MAPS

1. **Region** In what region does the largest percentage of Mexican Americans live?
2. **Place** Which two states have the highest concentrations of Mexican Americans?

White settlers also battled with American Indians over property rights. In some areas, for example, new white settlers soon outnumbered southwestern Native Americans. The Anglo settlers often tried to take control of valuable water resources and grazing lands. In addition, settlers rarely respected Indian holy places. Native American peoples such as the Navajo and the Apache tried to protect their land and livestock from the settlers. Indians and settlers alike attacked one another to protect their interests.

THE IMPACT TODAY

Mexican holidays like Cinco de Mayo and Día de los Muertos are still popular holidays in the Southwest.

Cultural Encounters

Despite conflicts, different cultures shaped one another in the Southwest. In settlements with large Mexican populations, laws were often printed in both English and Spanish.

Names of places—such as San Antonio, San Diego, and Santa Barbara—show Hispanic heritage. Other place-names, such as Taos and Tesuque, are derived from Native American words. Communities throughout the Southwest regularly celebrated both Mexican and American holidays.

Mexican and Native American knowledge and traditions also shaped many local economies. Mexican Americans taught Anglo settlers about mining in the mountains. Many ranching communities were first started by Mexican settlers. In addition, Mexican Americans introduced new types of saddles and other equipment to American ranchers. Adobe, developed by the Anasazi Indians, was adopted from the Pueblo people by the Spanish. It is still commonly used by American residents in New Mexico, Arizona, and California.

Trade also changed the Southwest. For example, the Navajo created handwoven woolen blankets to sell to Americans. Americans in turn brought manufactured goods and money to the Southwest. Due to exchanges like these, the economies of many Mexican American and Native American communities in the Southwest began to change.

Water Rights

Eastern water-use laws commonly required owners whose land bordered streams or rivers to maintain a free flow of water. These restrictions generally prevented landowners from constructing dams because doing so would infringe upon the water rights of neighbors downstream.

In the typically dry climate of the West, large-scale agriculture was not possible without irrigation. Dams and canals were required to direct scarce water to fields. This need conflicted with the accepted eastern tradition of equal access to water.

Brigham Young established a strict code regulating water rights for the Mormon community. In any dispute over water use, the good of the community would outweigh the interests of individuals. Young's approach stood as an example for modern water laws throughout the West.

READING CHECK **Summarizing** What were some of the early important agreements between the United States and Mexico, and why were they significant?

SUMMARY AND PREVIEW America's westward expansion continued rapidly after the Mexican-American War. In the next section you will learn about the California gold rush.

Section 3 Assessment

Reviewing Ideas, Terms, and People

1. **a. Define** What was **manifest destiny**?
   b. Make Inferences Why was westward expansion such an important issue in the election of 1844?
   c. Evaluate Do you think California benefited from Mexican independence? Why or why not?
2. **a. Recall** Why did the United States declare war on Mexico?
   b. Summarize What was General Winfield Scott's strategy for winning the war with Mexico?
   c. Elaborate Would you have sided with those who opposed the war with Mexico or with those who supported it? Why?
3. **a. Describe** What conflicts did American settlers, Native Americans, and Mexican Americans in the Mexican Cession experience?
   b. Draw Conclusions Why were water rights so important in the American Southwest?
   c. Evaluate In your opinion, what was the most important effect of the annexation of the Mexican Cession?

Critical Thinking

4. **Identifying Cause and Effect** Review your notes on manifest destiny and U.S. territorial expansion. Then use the graphic organizer below to show how Americans' expansion into California caused war, as well as the effects of the war.

FOCUS ON WRITING

5. **Explaining the Mexican-American War** How will you convey ideas, such as manifest destiny, in a film? How will you explain to your audience the Mexican-American War's role in expansion of the United States? Consider these questions as you read this section.

The California Gold Rush

What You Will Learn...

Main Ideas

1. The discovery of gold brought settlers to California.
2. The gold rush had a lasting impact on California's population and economy.

The Big Idea

The California gold rush changed the future of the West.

Key Terms and People

John Sutter, *p. 365*

Donner party, *p. 365*

forty-niners, *p. 365*

prospect, *p. 366*

placer miners, *p. 366*

TAKING NOTES As you read, take notes on the California gold rush in a chart like the one below.

Gold Rush	
How was gold first discovered?	
How was a stake claimed?	
What was life like in camps?	
Who came to California for gold?	

8.1.15, 8.1.25, 8.3.1, 8.3.2, 8.3.5, 8.3.7, 8.3.8, 8.3.9, 8.3.10

If YOU were there...

You are a low–paid bank clerk in New England in early 1849. Local newspaper headlines are shouting exciting news: "Gold Is Discovered in California! Thousands Are on Their Way West." You enjoy having a steady job. However, some of your friends are planning to go west, and you are being influenced by their excitement. Your friends are even buying pickaxes and other mining equipment. They urge you to go west with them.

Would you go west to seek your fortune in California? Why?

BUILDING BACKGROUND At the end of the Mexican-American War, the United States gained control of Mexican territories in the West, including all of the present-day state of California. American settlements in California increased slowly at first. Then, the discovery of gold brought quick population growth and an economic boom.

Discovery of Gold Brings Settlers

In the 1830s and 1840s, Americans who wanted to move to California started up the Oregon Trail. At the Snake River in present-day Idaho, the trail split. People bound for California took the southern route, which became known as the California Trail. This path ran through the Sierra Nevada mountain range. American emigrants and traders on the California Trail tried to cross these mountains before the season's first snows.

Although many Americans traveled along the California Trail, few actually settled in California. American merchants were usually more interested in trading goods made in factories than in establishing settlements. They traded for gold and silver coins, hides, and tallow (animal fat used to make soap and candles) from Mexico. California became a meeting ground for traders from Mexico and the United States.

Before the Mexican-American War, California's population consisted mostly of Mexicans and Native Americans. When Mexico controlled California, Mexican officials did not want many Americans to settle there. However, in 1839 they did give Swiss immigrant **John Sutter** permission to start a colony. Sutter's Fort, located near the Sacramento River, soon became a popular rest stop for many American emigrants. These new arrivals praised Sutter's hospitality and helpfulness. By the mid-1840s some Anglo Californians were publishing newspaper advertisements and guidebooks encouraging other settlers to move West.

The **Donner party** was a group of western travelers who went to California but were stranded in the Sierra Nevada Mountains during winter. The party began its journey West in the spring of 1846. Trying to find a shortcut, the group left the main trail and got lost. When the Donner party reached the Sierra Nevada Mountains, they became trapped by heavy snows. They were stuck and had almost no food.

A rescue party found the starving and freezing group in February 1847. Of the original 87 travelers, 42 had died.

Gold in California

In January 1848, Sutter sent a carpenter named James Marshall to build a sawmill beside a nearby river. While working near Sutter's Mill, Marshall glanced at the ground. "I reached my hand down and picked it up; it made my heart thump, for I was certain it was gold."

Sutter and Marshall agreed to keep the discovery a secret. However, when they examined the work site the next day, they met a Spanish-speaking Native American worker holding a nugget and shouting, "Oro [gold]! Oro! Oro!"

Sutter's workers soon quit to search for gold. Stories of the discovery rapidly spread across the country. President Polk added to the national excitement by confirming the California gold strike in his farewell message to Congress in December 1848. In 1849 about 80,000 gold-seekers came to California, hoping to strike it rich. These gold-seeking migrants to California were called **forty-niners**. As one Iowa woman who

"Gold Fever"

"Gold fever" brought 80,000 people, like this miner, to California in 1849 alone. One California newspaper captured the excitement: "The whole country, from San Francisco to Los Angeles, and from the sea shore to the base of the Sierra Nevadas, resounds with the cry of 'gold, GOLD, GOLD!' while the field is left half planted, the house half built, and everything neglected but the manufacture of shovels and pickaxes." Below is a piece of jewelry made from nuggets found in California.

Why was everything neglected except for "the manufacture of shovels and pickaxes"?

Staking a Claim

California State Library

left to find gold recalled, "At that time the 'gold fever' was contagious, and few, old or young, escaped the malady [sickness]." Nearly 80 percent of the forty-niners were Americans, while the rest came from all over the world.

Most forty-niners braved long and often dangerous journeys to reach California. Many easterners and Europeans arrived via sea routes. Midwestern gold-seekers usually traveled West in wagon trains. Most forty-niners first arrived in San Francisco. This port town became a convenient trade center and stopping point for travelers. As a result, its population increased from around 800 in March 1848 to more than 25,000 by 1850.

Staking a Claim

Few of the forty-niners had any previous gold-mining experience. The work was difficult and time-consuming. The forty-niners would **prospect**, or search for gold, along the banks of streams or in shallow surface mines.

The early forty-niners worked an area that ran for 70 miles along rivers in northern California.

The first person to arrive at a site would "stake a claim." Early miners frequently banded together to prospect for gold. The miners agreed that each would keep a share of whatever gold was discovered. When one group abandoned a claim, more recent arrivals often took it over, hoping for success. Sometimes, two or more groups arrived in an area at the same time. In the early gold-rush days, before courts were established, this competition often led to conflict. Occasionally, violent disputes arose over competing claims.

Mining methods varied according to the location. The most popular method, placer (PLA-suhr) mining, was done along rivers and streams. **Placer miners** used pans or other devices to wash gold nuggets out of loose rock and gravel. To reach gold deposits buried in

Miners came to California from around the world to make their fortune. In the photo on the left, Anglo and Chinese miners work together in Auburn Ravine in 1852. Above, a woman joins men to look for gold. Fewer women than men moved west to search for gold, but the ones that did often found greater social and economic opportunity than they had in the east.

Why might people leave their homes and travel long distances in search of gold?

the hills, miners had to dig shafts and tunnels. These tasks were usually pursued by mining companies, rather than by individuals.

In 1853 California's yearly gold production peaked at more than $60 million. Individual success stories inspired many miners. One lucky man found two and a half pounds of gold after only 15 minutes of work. Two African American miners found a rich gold deposit that became known as Negro Hill in honor of their discovery. The vast majority of miners, however, did not become rich. Forty-niner Alonzo Delano commented that the "lean, meager [thin], worn-out and woe-begone [sorrowful] miner…might daily be seen at almost every point in the upper mines."

Life in the Mining Camps

Mining camps sprang up wherever enough people gathered to look for gold. These camps had colorful names, such as Hangtown or Poker Flat.

Miners in the camps came from many cultures and backgrounds. Most miners were young, unmarried men in search of adventure. Only around 5 percent of gold-rush immigrants were women or children. The hardworking women generally made good money by cooking meals, washing clothes, and operating boardinghouses. One such woman, Catherine Haun, recalled her first home in California.

"We were glad to settle down and go house-keeping in a shed that was built in a day of lumber purchased with the first fee …For neighbors, we had a real live saloon. I never have received more respectful attention than I did from these neighbors."

—Catherine Haun, quoted in *Ordinary Americans*, edited by Linda R. Monk

Haun's husband was a lawyer. He concluded that he could make more money practicing law than he could panning for gold. He was one of many people who made a good living supplying miners with food, clothing, equipment, and other services. Miners paid high prices for basic necessities because the large amounts of gold in circulation caused severe inflation in California. A loaf of bread, for example, might cost 5 cents in the East, but it would sell for 50 to 75 cents in San Francisco. Eggs sometimes sold for $1 apiece.

Some settlers took full advantage of these conditions for free enterprise. Biddy Mason and her family, for instance, had arrived in California as slaves. A Georgia slaveholder had brought them during the gold-rush years. Mason quickly discovered that most Californians opposed slavery, particularly in the gold mines. She and her family gained their freedom and moved to the small village of Los Angeles. There she saved money until she could purchase some land. Over time, Mason's property increased in value from $250 to $200,000. She became one of the wealthiest landowners in California, a community leader, and a well-known supporter of charities.

Westward Movement in the United States

QUICK FACTS

Causes
- Americans believe in the idea of manifest destiny.
- The United States acquires vast new lands in the West.
- Pathfinders open trails to new territories.
- Gold is discovered in California.

Effects
- Native Americans are forced off lands.
- Americans travel west to settle new areas.
- The United States stretches to the Pacific Ocean.
- California experiences a population boom.

Immigrants to California

THE IMPACT TODAY

Today California is the nation's most populous state.

The lure of gold in California attracted miners from around the world. Many were from countries that had seen few immigrants to the United States in the past. They were drawn to California by the lure of wealth. For example, famine and economic hardship in southeastern China caused many Chinese men to leave China for America. Most hoped to find great wealth, and then return home to China. These immigrants were known in Chinese as *gam saan haak*, or "travelers to Gold Mountain." Between 1849 and 1853 about 24,000 Chinese men moved to California. "From far and near we came and were pleased," wrote merchant Lai Chun-chuen in 1855.

Chinese immigrants soon discovered that many Americans did not welcome them, however. In 1852, California placed a high monthly tax on all foreign miners. Chinese miners had no choice but to pay this tax if they wanted to prospect for gold in California. Some Chinese workers were the targets of violent attacks. If the Chinese

miners dared to protest the attacks, the legal system favored Americans over immigrants.

Despite such treatment, many Chinese immigrants still worked in the gold mines. Some looked for other jobs. Others opened their own businesses. A newspaper reported Chinese working as "ploughmen, laundrymen, placer miners, woolen spinners and weavers, domestic servants, cigar makers, [and] shoemakers."

In 1849 alone, about 20,000 immigrants arrived in California not only from China but also from Europe, Mexico, and South America. Like most Americans who sought gold, these new arrivals intended to return home after they had made their fortunes. However, many decided to stay. Some began businesses. For example, Levi Strauss, a German Jewish immigrant, earned a fortune by making tough denim pants for miners.

READING CHECK **Categorizing** What types of people came to California hoping to benefit from the gold rush?

Impact on California

During the Spanish and Mexican periods of settlement, California's population grew slowly. The arrival of the forty-niners changed this dramatically.

Population Boom

California's population explosion made it eligible for statehood only two years after being acquired by the United States. In 1850 California became the 31st state.

However, fast population growth had negative consequences for many Californios and California Native Americans. One early observer of the gold rush described why.

"The Yankee regarded every man but [his own kind] as an interloper [trespasser], who had no right to come to California and pick up the gold of 'free and enlightened citizens.'"

—W. Kelly, quoted in *The Other Californians,* by Robert F. Heizer and Alan F. Almquist

San Francisco Grows

San Francisco boomed in the early years of the gold rush.

What factors led to San Francisco's population growth?

San Francisco Population, 1847–1850

Economic Growth

In addition to rapid population growth, a flood of new businesses and industries transformed California's economy. Gold mining remained an important part of the state's early economy. But Californians soon discovered other ways to make a living. Farming and ranching, for example, became industries for those willing to do the necessary hard labor.

California faced an obstacle to growth, though. The state was isolated from the rest of the country. It was difficult to bring in and ship out goods. The answer to the isolation problem was to bring the railroad all the way to California. Californians would have to wait almost 20 years for that. Completion of the transcontinental railroad in 1869 at last gave Californians the means to grow a stronger economy.

READING CHECK Analyzing Information
What political effect resulted from California's rapid population growth?

SUMMARY AND PREVIEW Americans moved west to create new lives and seize new opportunities. In the next chapter you will learn about the Industrial Revolution in America.

go.hrw.com

Section 4 Assessment

Online Quiz
KEYWORD: SF7 HP11

Reviewing Ideas, Terms, and People
1. **a. Recall** Why was Sutter's Mill important?
   b. Summarize What types of people participated in the California gold rush, and how did they take part in it?
   c. Elaborate What are some possible problems caused by the arrival of so many new settlers to California?
2. **a. Describe** How did some people hope to solve the problem of California's isolation from the rest of the country?
   b. Draw Inferences What effect did California's rapid population growth have on Californios and Native Americans?
   c. Evaluate Overall, do you think that the gold rush had a positive or negative effect on California? Explain.

Critical Thinking
3. **Evaluating** Review your notes on the gold rush. Then copy the graphic organizer below. Use it to show how the discovery of gold changed California.

Discovery of Gold

FOCUS ON WRITING

4. **Describing the California Gold Rush** As you read this section, take note of significant events and effects of the gold rush. Consider also how your film can convey the excitement of that time in American history.

America's Growth 1850

In the 1830s, a new dream began to shape the American mind—manifest destiny. Manifest destiny was the belief that the United States should extend all the way to the Pacific Ocean. By 1850, that dream had become a reality. In 1845, the United States annexed Texas. In 1848, it acquired Oregon and the huge Mexican Cession. By 1853, with the Gadsden Purchase, the United States had taken the basic shape it still has today.

CANADA

Washington Territory

Oregon Territory

California

Utah Territory

•San Francisco

New Mexico Territory

ROCKY MOUNTAINS

PACIFIC OCEAN

MEXI

America's Population, 1850: 23.6 million

Ethnic Groups, 1850

2% <1% <1%
16%
80%

- ■ White/European
- ■ African American
- ■ Native American
- ■ Asian
- ■ Mexican American

Religions, 1850

1% 3%
5%
91%

- ■ Protestant
- ■ Catholic
- ■ Jewish
- ■ Other

Gold Fever

The discovery of gold in California in 1848 set off a massive migration. In 1849 some 80,000 forty-niners headed toward California. San Francisco, located on an excellent natural port, grew quickly as a result.

Texas annexation, 1845
Claim recognized in Oregon Treaty, 1848
Mexican Cession, 1848
Gadsden Purchase, 1853

| 0 | 150 | 300 Miles |
| 0 | 150 | 300 Kilometers |

120° W   120° W   110° W

Water Rights Water was critical in the dry West. Bitter disputes arose over who had the water rights to streams. Gold rush miners developed a simple system: whoever used the water first owned the rights to it. In other parts of the West, the community as a whole had a right to use the water source.

Manifest Destiny Supporters of manifest destiny believed it was God's will that the United States should expand and spread democracy across North America. Huge numbers of settlers headed West to tame new lands.

The Rocky Mountains The Rocky Mountains were a gigantic obstacle to settlers on their way West. Pathfinders like Lt. John C. Frémont traveled widely in the region, making maps and noting possible trails. The South Pass, through which the Oregon Trail ran, was one of the few easy ways through the great chain of mountains.

GREAT PLAINS

Oregon Trail

Missouri River

Mississippi River

Unorganized Territory

Indian Territory

Claimed by Texas

Texas

Gulf of Mexico

ATLANTIC OCEAN

30° N

70° W

90° W

Tropic of Cancer

GEOGRAPHY SKILLS INTERPRETING MAPS

1. **Movement** Why did San Francisco grow so rapidly?
2. **Human-Environment Interaction** Why was water so important in the West?

Social Studies Skills

Interpreting Maps: Expansion

Define the Skill

Maps show features on Earth's surface. These can be physical features, such as mountains and rivers, or human features, such as roads and settlements. Historical maps show an area as it was in the past. Some show how a nation's boundaries changed over time. Interpreting maps can answer questions about history as well as geography.

Learn the Skill

Follow these steps to gain information from a map.

1 Read the title to determine what the map is about and the time period it covers.

2 Study the legend or key to understand what the colors or symbols on the map mean. Note the map scale, which is used to measure distances.

3 Note the map's other features. Maps often contain labels and other information in addition to what is explained in the legend or key.

Practice the Skill

Interpret the map below to answer the following questions about the expansion of the United States.

1. The addition of which territory almost doubled the size of the United States?

2. What was the smallest expansion of U.S. borders, and when did it take place?

3. According to the map, when did California become part of the United States?

4. What choice of overland routes did a traveler have for getting to California?

5. What physical obstacles does the map show such a traveler would face?

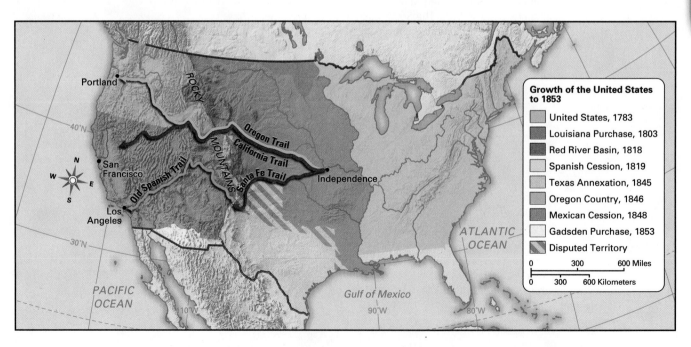

Growth of the United States to 1853

- United States, 1783
- Louisiana Purchase, 1803
- Red River Basin, 1818
- Spanish Cession, 1819
- Texas Annexation, 1845
- Oregon Country, 1846
- Mexican Cession, 1848
- Gadsden Purchase, 1853
- Disputed Territory

HOLT
History's Impact
▶ video series
Review the video to answer the closing question:
What does the modern success of Silicon Valley have in common with the California gold rush? How is it different?

Visual Summary

Use the visual summary below to help you review the main ideas of the chapter.

QUICK FACTS

U.S. Expansion

1839 Sutter's Fort established.

1840 Pioneers begin traveling West on the Oregon Trail.

1845 United States annexes Texas.

1846 Mexican War begins.

1848 United States wins the Mexican War and gains the Mexican Cession. Oregon becomes a U.S. territory.

1849 California gold rush begins.

1853 Gadsden Purchase establishes the southwestern U.S. border.

Reviewing Vocabulary, Terms, and People

Identify the correct term or person from the chapter that best fits each of the following descriptions.

1. Mexican priest who led a rebellion for independence from Spain

2. Spanish cowboys in California

3. A group of pioneers who were stranded in the Sierra Nevada Mountains and struggled to survive the winter

4. Agents hired by the Mexican government to attract settlers to Texas

5. The belief that the United States was meant to expand across the continent to the Pacific Ocean

6. Members of the Church of Jesus Christ of Latter-day Saints

7. Fur traders and trappers who lived west of the Rocky Mountains and in the Pacific Northwest

8. Mexican ruler who fought to keep Texas from gaining independence

9. Swiss immigrant who received permission from Mexico to start a colony in California

10. Western trail from Missouri to New Mexico that was an important route for trade between American and Mexican merchants

Comprehension and Critical Thinking

SECTION 1 *(Pages 346–349)*

11. **a. Identify** What different groups of people traveled West?

    b. Draw Conclusions Why did Brigham Young move the Mormon community to Utah?

    c. Predict What are some possible problems that might result from American settlement in the West?

SECTION 2 *(Pages 350–353)*

12. a. Identify Who were Stephen F. Austin and Antonio López de Santa Anna?

b. Draw Conclusions Why did settlers in Texas rebel against Mexican rule?

c. Elaborate In what ways was the Texas struggle for independence similar to that of the United States?

SECTION 3 *(Pages 354–363)*

13. a. Recall Why were some Americans opposed to the annexation of new territories?

b. Draw Conclusions What economic and cultural influences did Native Americans and Mexican Americans have on American settlers in the Mexican Cession?

c. Predict What are some possible problems the acquisition of so much territory might cause the United States?

SECTION 4 *(Pages 364–369)*

14. a. Identify What roles did women and immigrants play in the California gold rush?

b. Make Inferences Why were most gold-rush settlers young, unmarried men?

c. Predict What long-term effects might the gold rush have on California's future?

Reviewing Themes

15. Economics What role did economics play in the desire of Americans to go west?

16. Geography What were the main trails to the West, and what areas did they pass through?

Reading Skills

Vocabulary in Context *Use the Reading Skills taught in this chapter to answer the question about the reading selection below.*

> Texas politicians hoped that joining the United States would help solve the republic's financial and military problems. The Texas Congress approved annexation in June 1845. Texas became part of the United States in December. *(p. 356)*

17. Determine the definition of *annexation* using context clues.

Social Studies Skills

Interpreting Maps: Expansion *Use the Social Studies Skills taught in this chapter to answer the question about the map below.*

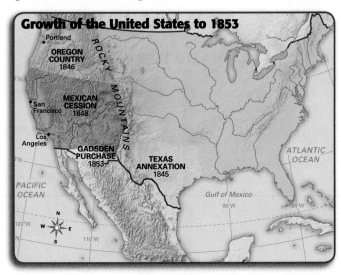

Growth of the United States to 1853

18. Place the expansions in the order in which they were acquired by the United States, according to the map.

FOCUS ON WRITING

19. Writing an Outline for a Documentary Film Look back through all your notes, and choose one topic from this chapter that you think would make a good 10-minute documentary. Your outline should be organized by scene (no more than 3 scenes), in chronological order. For each scene, give the following information: main idea of scene, costumes and images to be used, audio to be used, and length of scene. As you plan, remember that the audience will be students your own age.

DIRECTIONS: Read each question and write the letter of the best response.

1 *Use the map below to answer the following question.*

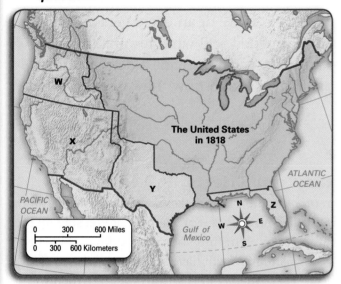

The part of the present-day United States that was once claimed by Britain, Spain, and Russia is shown on the map by which letter?

A W

B X

C Y

D Z

2 In general, what position did Californios take toward the Mexican-American War?

A They supported the war because they wanted independence from Mexico.

B They supported the war because they wanted to become U.S. citizens.

C They opposed the war because they feared it might bring an end to slavery.

D They opposed the war because they did not want to lose control of California.

3 What was the *main* reason John Jacob Astor founded Astoria at the mouth of the Columbia River in 1811?

A Plenty of freshwater and salt-water fish were available for residents to eat.

B The soil there was rich and good for farming.

C Trappers could use the river to bring furs from the mountains to trade.

D The location offered easy protection from attacks by Native Americans or the French.

4 The *main* attraction of Texas for many Americans in the 1820s and 1830s was the

A freedom to practice the Catholic faith.

B availability of cheap or free land.

C desire to become citizens of Mexico.

D Mexican rebellion against Spain.

5 Which of the following occurred after the Mexican-American War?

A Mexican foods and festivals became more important to American culture.

B Prosperity of Mexican landowners in the Southwest increased under U.S. rule.

C Mexican Americans left the United States.

D The size of the United States was reduced.

6 Examine the following flier about cheap land available in the Dakota Territory and then use it to answer the question below.

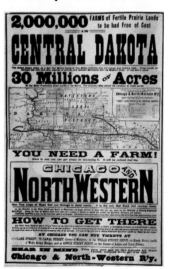

Document-Based Question Who might have been attracted by this description of Dakota? Why?

Assignment

Write a paper explaining the causes or the effects of the War of 1812.

Cause and Effect in History

Historians try to make sense of an event by considering why the event happened and what resulted from it. Exploring causes and effects can provide a deeper understanding of historical events and how they are connected to one another.

1. Prewrite

Identifying Causes and Effects

A **cause** is an action or a situation that makes something else happen. What happens is called an **effect**. For example, if you stay up too late watching TV (cause), you might find yourself nodding off in class (effect). Often an event or situation will have several causes as well as several effects. In those cases, we may look at the order in which the causes or effects occurred, or we may look at their relative importance.

Researching and Organizing

For this paper, you will write about the causes or the effects of the event —the War of 1812. Gather information from the chapter in this textbook, an encyclopedia, or another source recommended by your teacher.

- Look for two or three reasons (causes) why the War of 1812 (the event or situation) occurred.
- At the same time, consider the war as a cause. Look for two or three effects of the war.

Then choose whether to write about the causes or the effects.

TIP **Using a Graphic Organizer**

Use a graphic organizer like this to organize your research.

Cause 1
↓
Cause 2
↓
Event or Situation
↓
Effect
↓
Effect

2. Write

You can use this framework to help you write your first draft.

A Writer's Framework

Introduction	Body	Conclusion
■ Begin with a quote or interesting fact about the event. ■ Identify the event you will discuss. [The War of 1812] ■ Identify whether you will be discussing the causes or the effects.	■ Present the causes or effects in chronological (time) order or order of importance. ■ Explain each cause or effect in its own paragraph, providing support with facts and examples.	■ Summarize your ideas about the causes or the effects of the event [the war].

3. Evaluate and Revise

Evaluating

Drawing clear, logical connections is the key to writing about causes and effects. Use these questions to evaluate and revise your paper.

Evaluation Questions for an Explanation of Causes or Effects

- Does the introduction begin with an interesting quotation or fact?
- Does the introduction identify the event [the war] and the causes or events to be discussed?
- Is each cause or effect explained in its own paragraph?

- Do facts and examples help to explain each cause or effect and connect it to the event [the war]?
- Are the causes or effects organized clearly—by chronological order or order of importance?
- Does the conclusion summarize the causes or effects and their importance?

Revising

Make sure the connections between the war and its causes or effects are clear by sharing your paper with a classmate. If your classmate is confused, add background information. If he or she disagrees with your conclusions, add evidence or rethink your reasoning.

4. Proofread and Publish

Proofreading

Some transitional words and phrases need to be set off from the sentence with commas. Here are two examples:

- The Louisiana Territory was a huge region of land. *As a result,* the size of the United States almost doubled when the land was purchased.
- Jefferson wanted to know more about the land he had purchased. *Therefore,* he asked Congress to fund an expedition.

Check your paper to see if you need to add commas after or around any transitional words or phrases.

Publishing

Get together with a classmate and share causes and/or effects. Compare your lists to see whether you have identified different causes or effects. Share your findings with your class.

5. Practice and Apply

Use the steps and strategies outlined in this workshop to write your explanation of the causes or effects of the War of 1812.

TIP **Recognizing False Cause-and-Effect** In planning your essay, be careful to avoid false cause-and-effect relationships. The fact that one thing happened before or after another doesn't mean one caused the other. For example, the fact that James Madison was elected in 1808, just four years before the War of 1812, does not mean his election caused the War of 1812.

TIP **Using Transitions** Here are some transitional words and phrases that show cause or effect relationships: *because, as a result, therefore, for, since, so, consequently, for this reason.*

The Nation Expands

The United States continued to grow in size and wealth, experiencing revolutions in technology and business as did other parts of the world. During the earliest phases of expansion, regions of the United States developed differently from each other. Citizens differed in their ideas of progress, government, and religion. For the success of the nation, they tried to compromise on their disagreements. In the next four chapters, you will learn about two regions in the United States, and how they were alike and different.

Explore the Art

This painting shows a bustling street scene in New York City around 1797. What does the scene indicate about business in the city during this period?

The North

IN Indiana Standards

Social Studies Standards

8.1.10 Compare differences in ways of life in the northern and osuthern states, including the growth of towns and cities in the North and the growing dependence on slavery in the South.

8.4.5 Analyze contributions of entrepreneurs and inventors in the development of the United States economy.

8.4.6 Relate technological change and inventions to changes in labor productivity in the United States in the eighteenth and nineteenth centuries.

8.4.9 Explain and evaluate examples of domstic and international interdependence throughout United States history.

go.hrw.com
Indiana
KEYWORD: SF10 IN

FOCUS ON WRITING

Newspaper Advertisement The Industrial Revolution was a time when a great many new inventions were introduced. You work for an advertising agency, and your job is to design an advertisement for one of the inventions mentioned in this chapter. As you read, take notes on the inventions, their inventors, and how they changed life in the United States. Then choose one invention and design a newspaper advertisement to persuade readers to buy or use the invention.

1807
Robert Fulton's *Clermont* becomes the first commercially successful steamboat.

UNITED STATES

1790

1790
The first steam-powered mill opens in Great Britain.

WORLD

Textile mill workers were often women.

What You Will Learn...

New machinery led to the construction of new mills, often along rivers. In this chapter you will learn about changes in the lives of Americans in the North as a result of rapid industrialization.

1838
The first steam locomotive in Indiana travels from North Madison to Graham's Ford.

1830
The *Tom Thumb* becomes the first locomotive in the United States to carry passengers.

1840
Federal government employees receive a 10-hour workday.

1845
Sarah Bagley is appointed secretary of the New England Working Men's Association.

1856
Gail Borden patents a method of condensing milk so that it can be safely stored in cans.

Borden's
UNSWEETENED
EVAPORATED
MILK
NET WEIGHT 1 POUND

1830

1840

1850

1860

1838
The *Sirius* becomes the first ship to cross the Atlantic Ocean entirely under steam power.

1846
German astronomer Johann Galle observes that Neptune is a planet.

1851
London's Great Exhibition displays inventions from around the world in the Crystal Palace.

381

Reading Social Studies

by Kylene Beers

Economics   Geography   Politics   Society and Culture   Science and Technology

Focus on Themes As you read this chapter, you will learn about how developments in **science and technology** brought about what is called the Industrial Revolution. As a result of the Industrial Revolution, you will see how American **economic** patterns changed. Next, you will read about how family life changed as more and more people went to work in factories. Finally, you will see how new methods of transportation changed where people lived and how new inventions affected daily life and work.

Causes and Effects in History

Focus on Reading Have you heard the saying, "We have to understand the past to avoid repeating it."? That is one reason we look for causes and effects in history.

Cause and Effect Chains You might say that all of history is one long chain of causes and effects. It may help you to understand the course of history better if you draw out such a chain as you read.

Since the 1790s, <u>wars between European powers</u> had interfered with U.S. trade. <u>American customers were no longer able to get all the manufactured goods</u> they were used to buying from British and European manufacturers . . . <u>Americans began to buy the items they needed from American manufacturers</u> instead of from foreign suppliers. As <u>profits for American factories grew</u>, <u>manufacturers began to spend more money expanding their factories</u> . . .

At the same time, many <u>Americans began to realize that the United States had been relying too heavily on foreign goods.</u> *(p. 389)*

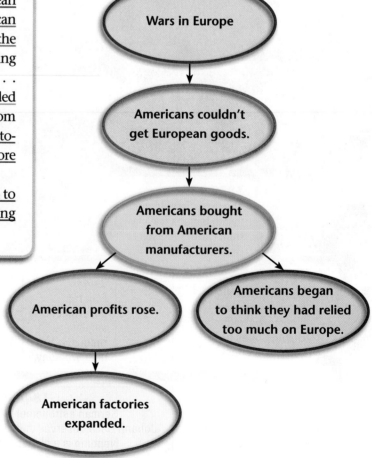

You Try It!

The following passage is from the chapter you are about to read. As you read each paragraph, ask yourself what is the cause and what is the effect of what is being discussed.

Workers Organize

Factories continued to spread in the 1800s. Craftspeople, who made goods by hand, felt threatened. Factories quickly produced low-priced goods. To compete with factories, shop owners had to hire more workers and pay them less . . .

From Chapter 12, p. 394

The wages of factory workers also went down as people competed for jobs. A wave of immigration in the 1840s brought people from other, poorer countries. They were willing to work for low pay. More immigrants came to the Northeast, where the mills were located, than to the South. Competition for jobs also came from people unemployed during the financial Panic of 1837.

After you have read the passage, answer the following questions.

1. What cause is being discussed in the first paragraph? What were its effects?

2. Draw a cause and effect chain that shows the events described in the first paragraph.

3. What main effect is discussed in the second paragraph? How many causes are given for it?

4. Draw a cause and effect chain that shows the events described in the second paragraph.

As you read Chapter 12, look for words that signal causes or effects. Picture these causes and effects as the links in a cause and effect chain.

Academic Vocabulary

Success in school is related to knowing academic vocabulary—the words that are frequently used in school assignments and discussions. In this chapter, you will learn the following academic words:

efficient *(p. 385)*
concrete *(p. 395)*

The Industrial Revolution in America

What You Will Learn...

Main Ideas

1. The invention of new machines in Great Britain led to the beginning of the Industrial Revolution.
2. The development of new machines and processes brought the Industrial Revolution to the United States.
3. Despite a slow start in manufacturing, the United States made rapid improvements during the War of 1812.

The Big Idea

The Industrial Revolution transformed the way goods were produced in the United States.

Key Terms and People

Industrial Revolution, *p. 385*
textiles, *p. 385*
Richard Arkwright, *p. 385*
Samuel Slater, *p. 386*
technology, *p. 387*
Eli Whitney, *p. 387*
interchangeable parts, *p. 387*
mass production, *p. 387*

 TAKING NOTES As you read, make a list of the key contributions of the Industrial Revolution and who initiated them. Write your notes in a chart like the one below.

Contributor	Invention/improvement

 8.1.10, 8.3.5, 8.3.8, 8.3.9, 8.3.10, 8.3.11, 8.4.2, 8.4.3, 8.4.5, 8.4.6, 8.4.9

If **YOU** were there...

You live in a small Pennsylvania town in the 1780s. Your father is a blacksmith, but you earn money for the family, too. You raise sheep and spin their wool into yarn. Your sisters knit the yarn into warm wool gloves and mittens. You sell your products to merchants in the city. But now you hear that someone has invented machines that can spin thread and make cloth.

Would you still be able to earn the same amount of money for your family? Why?

BUILDING BACKGROUND In the early 1700s making goods depended on the hard work of humans and animals. It had been that way for hundreds of years. Then new technology brought a change so radical that it is called a revolution. It began in Great Britain and soon spread to the United States.

The Industrial Revolution

At the beginning of the 1700s, the majority of people in Europe and the United States were farmers. They made most of what they needed by hand. For example, female family members usually made clothing. First, they used a spinning wheel to spin raw materials, such as cotton or wool, into thread. Then they used a hand loom to weave the thread into cloth.

Some families produced extra cloth to sell to merchants, who sold it for a profit. In towns, a few skilled workers made goods by hand in their own shops. These workers included blacksmiths, carpenters, and shoemakers. Their ways of life had stayed the same for generations.

A Need for Change

By the mid-1700s, however, changes in Great Britain led to a greater demand for manufactured goods. As agriculture and roads

Textile Mill and Water Frame

CONNECT TO SCIENCE AND TECHNOLOGY

A water frame adapts the power of flowing water into energy that moves wheels and gears through a system of belts. These wheels and gears then move parts of machines such as looms and spinning wheels.

5 After the thread was spun, it moved to the loom to be woven into cloth. Workers called spoolers watched the looms and made sure that the spools of thread were kept straight.

4 Then the raw cotton was spun into thread on a spinning frame.

3 A machine for cleaning the raw cotton was the first step.

1 Flowing water from a river turned the waterwheel. The giant wheel turned smaller gears connected to belts. **2** These belts moved parts of the machinery in the mill.

ANALYSIS SKILL | **ANALYZING VISUALS**

What provided the power for the machines in the mill?

---

improved, cities and populations grew. Overseas trade also expanded. Traditional manufacturing methods did not produce enough goods to meet everyone's needs.

People began creating ways to use machines to make things more **efficient**. These developments led to the **Industrial Revolution**, a period of rapid growth in using machines for manufacturing and production that began in the mid-1700s.

Textile Industry

The first important breakthrough of the Industrial Revolution took place in how **textiles**, or cloth items, were made. Before the Industrial Revolution, spinning thread took much more time than making cloth. Several workers were needed to spin enough thread to supply a single weaver.

In 1769 Englishman **Richard Arkwright** invented a large spinning machine called a water frame. The water frame could produce dozens of cotton threads at the same time. It lowered the cost of cotton cloth and increased the speed of textile production.

The water frame used flowing water as its source of power. Merchants began to build large textile mills, or factories, near rivers and streams. The mills were filled with spinning machines. Merchants began hiring people to work in the mills.

Additional improvements also speeded up the spinning process. Britain soon had the world's most productive textile manufacturing industry.

READING CHECK **Drawing Conclusions** How did machines speed up textile manufacturing?

ACADEMIC VOCABULARY
efficient
productive and not wasteful

New Machines and Processes

New machines encouraged the rise of new processes in business and manufacturing. As the machines used to make products became more efficient, the processes involved changed dramatically.

Slater and His Secrets

The new textile machines allowed Great Britain to produce cloth more quickly and inexpensively than other countries could. To protect British industry, the British Parliament had made it illegal for skilled mechanics or machine plans to leave the country. Disguised as a farmer, **Samuel Slater**, a skilled British mechanic, immigrated to the United States after carefully memorizing the designs of textile mill machines. Soon after arriving, he sent a letter to Moses Brown, who owned a textile business in New England. Slater claimed he could improve the way textiles were manufactured in the United States.

Brown had one of his workers test Slater's knowledge of machinery. Slater passed. Brown's son, Smith Brown, and son-in-law, William Almy, formed a partnership with Slater. In 1793 they opened their first mill in Pawtucket, Rhode Island. The production of cotton thread by American machines had begun. Slater ran the mill and the machinery. He was confident that his new machines would work well.

" If I do not make as good yarn as they do in England, I will have nothing for my services, but will throw the whole of what I have attempted over the bridge. "

—Samuel Slater, quoted in *The Ingenious Yankees,* by Joseph and Francis Gies

Slater's machines worked, and the Pawtucket mill became a success. Slater's wife also invented a new cotton thread for sewing. In 1798 Slater formed his own company to build a mill. By the time he died in 1835, he owned all or part of 13 textile mills.

Other Americans began building textile mills. Most were located in the Northeast. In New England in particular, merchants had the money to invest in new mills. More importantly, this region had many rivers and streams that provided a reliable supply of power. Fewer mills were built in the South, partly because investors in the South concentrated on expanding agriculture. There, agriculture was seen as an easier way to make money.

Elements of Mass Production

CONNECT TO ECONOMICS

Mass-production techniques allow manufacturers to efficiently create more goods for the marketplace. Mass production requires the use of interchangeable parts, machine tools, and the division of labor.

Why are interchangeable parts important?

Interchangeable Parts

Eli Whitney developed the idea of using interchangeable parts. Interchangeable, or identical, parts are needed so each part does not have to be custom-made by hand.

Machine Tools

Machine tools like this one make parts that are identical and therefore interchangeable.

A Manufacturing Breakthrough

Despite these great changes, most manufacturing was still done by hand. In the late 1790s the U.S. government worried about a possible war with France, so it wanted more muskets for the army. Skilled workers made the parts for each weapon by hand. No two parts were exactly alike, and carefully fitting all the pieces together took much time and skill.

As a result, American gun makers could not produce the muskets quickly enough to satisfy the government's demand. Factories needed better **technology**, the tools used to produce items or to do work.

In 1798 inventor **Eli Whitney** tried to address some of these problems. Whitney gave officials a proposal for mass-producing guns for the U.S. government using water-powered machinery. Whitney explained the benefits of his ideas.

"I am persuaded that machinery moved by water [and] adapted to this business would greatly reduce the labor and facilitate [ease] the manufacture of this article."

—Eli Whitney, quoted in *Technology in America*, edited by Carroll W. Pursell

Whitney also came up with the idea of using **interchangeable parts**—parts of a machine that are identical. Using interchangeable parts made machines easier to assemble and broken parts easier to replace. Whitney promised to build 10,000 muskets in two years. The federal government gave him money to build his factory, and in 1801 Whitney was called to Washington, D.C., to give a demonstration.

Whitney stood before President John Adams and his secretary of war. He had an assortment of parts for 10 guns. He then randomly chose parts and quickly assembled them into muskets. To the audience's amazement, he repeated the process several times.

Whitney's Influence

Whitney had proven that American inventors could improve upon the new British technology. Machines that produced matching parts soon became standard in industry. Interchangeable parts sped up **mass production**, the efficient production of large numbers of identical goods.

READING CHECK **Summarizing** How did Eli Whitney influence American manufacturing?

Division of Labor

Mass production uses a division of labor in which the work is divided among several people, each doing a specific task, like the worker shown here.

Mass-Produced Goods

The end result is goods that have been mass-produced. Eli Whitney used mass-production techniques to manufacture firearms.

Modern Manufacturing

The word *manufacture* comes from Latin words that mean "to make by hand." Yet in modern manufacturing, machines—not human hands—do most of the work.

A key feature of modern manufacturing is the assembly line. An assembly line is a long conveyer belt. As the product moves along the belt, or "down the line," workers assemble it. Often, the workers use machines to help them. On a growing number of assembly lines, there are no workers at all: the product is assembled by computer-controlled robots.

Although a far cry from Eli Whitney's factory, modern factories use the same elements of mass production that Whitney did more than 200 years ago.

ANALYSIS SKILL ANALYZING INFORMATION

How do interchangeable parts help the modern assembly line work?

Manufacturing Grows Slowly

Despite the hard work of people such as Samuel Slater and Eli Whitney, manufacturing in the United States grew slowly. In 1810 Secretary of the Treasury Albert Gallatin suggested some reasons why there were so few factories in the United States.

> "[The reasons include] . . . the superior attractions of agricultural pursuits [farming], . . . the abundance of land compared with the population, the high price of labor, and the want [lack] of sufficient capital [investment]."
>
> —Albert Gallatin, quoted in *Who Built America?* by Bruce Levine et al.

Gallatin and others believed that few people would choose to work in a factory if they could own their own farm instead. In Great Britain, on the other hand, land was more scarce and more expensive than in the United States. As a result, fewer people were able to own farms. British factory workers generally were willing to work for lower wages than factory workers in the United States were.

Because British manufacturers had plenty of factory workers with technical skills, they could produce large amounts of goods less expensively than most American businesses could. As a result, they could charge lower prices for the goods. Lower British prices made it difficult for many American manufacturers to compete with British companies. This situation in turn discouraged American investors from spending the money needed to build new factories and machinery. As a result, only a few industries had found a place in the American economy. These included cotton goods, flour milling, weapons, and iron production.

These circumstances began to change around the time of the War of 1812. Since the 1790s, wars between European powers had interfered with U.S. trade. American customers were no longer able to get all the manufactured goods they were used to buying from British and European manufacturers. Then, during the War of 1812, British ships blockaded eastern seaports, preventing foreign ships from delivering goods. Americans began to buy the items they needed from American manufacturers instead of from foreign suppliers. As profits for American factories grew, manufacturers began to spend more money expanding their factories. State banks and private investors began to lend money to manufacturers for their businesses.

At the same time, many Americans began to realize that the United States had been relying too heavily on foreign goods. If the United States could not meet its own needs, it might be weak and open to attack. Former president Thomas Jefferson, who had once opposed manufacturing, changed his mind. He, too, realized that the United States was too dependent on imports.

"To be independent for the comforts of life we must fabricate [make] them ourselves. We must now place the manufacturer by the side of the agriculturalist [farmer]."
—Thomas Jefferson, from *The Writings of Thomas Jefferson*, edited by P. L. Ford

In February 1815, New Yorkers celebrated the end of the War of 1812 and the return of free trade. The streets were decorated and filled with merchants whose ships were loaded with goods. "With Peace and Commerce, America Prospers," declared one display. Eager businesspeople prepared to lead the United States into a period of industrial growth. They urged northern politicians to pass higher tariffs on foreign goods to protect American companies.

READING CHECK **Analyzing** How did the War of 1812 aid the growth of American manufacturing?

SUMMARY AND PREVIEW The Industrial Revolution started with the textile industry in England but soon spread to the United States. In the next section you will learn about how the spread of factories changed the working lives of many Americans.

THE IMPACT TODAY
American dependence on some foreign goods, such as oil, is still being debated today.

go.hrw.com
Online Quiz
KEYWORD: SB7 HP12

Section 1 Assessment

Reviewing Ideas, Terms, and People
1. **a. Identify** What was the first industry to begin to use machines to manufacture goods?
   b. Predict In what ways might life for workers change as a result of the **Industrial Revolution**?
2. **a. Recall** In what part of the United States were most mills located? Why?
   b. Draw Conclusions How did the ideas of **Samuel Slater** and **Eli Whitney** affect manufacturing in the United States?
   c. Evaluate Whose contributions do you think were more important—Slater's textile machines or Whitney's **interchangeable parts**? Why?
3. **a. Identify** What event encouraged the growth of American manufacturing? Why?
   b. Contrast Why was manufacturing in Great Britain in the early years more successful than that in the United States?

Critical Thinking
4. **Drawing Conclusions** Review your notes on key inventions and improvements during the Industrial Revolution. Then copy the chart below and use it to show how each contribution affected manufacturing.

Invention/improvement	Effect on Manufacturing

FOCUS ON WRITING

5. **Noting Inventions** In your notebook, create a three-column chart. In the first column, list any inventions mentioned in this section. In the second column, identify the inventor. In the third column, describe the invention and its benefits.

Changes in Working Life

What You Will Learn...

Main Ideas

1. The spread of mills in the Northeast changed workers' lives.
2. The Lowell System revolutionized the textile industry in the Northeast.
3. Workers organized to reform working conditions.

The Big Idea

The introduction of factories changed working life for many Americans.

Key Terms and People

Rhode Island system, p. 391
Francis Cabot Lowell, p. 392
Lowell system, p. 392
trade unions, p. 394
strikes, p. 394
Sarah G. Bagley, p. 395

TAKING NOTES As you read, take notes on how mills changed workers' lives, and how workers organized to fight many of these changes.

Changes to workers' lives → Workers' reaction

8.1.26, 8.4.2, 8.4.3, 8.4.6

If YOU were there...

You live on a dairy farm in Massachusetts in about 1820. On the farm, you get up at dawn to milk the cows, and your work goes on until night. But now you have a chance at a different life. A nearby textile mill is hiring young people. You would leave the farm and live with other workers. You could go to classes. Most important, you could earn money of your own.

Would you go to work in the textile mill? Why?

BUILDING BACKGROUND As factories and mills were established, the way people worked changed drastically. One dramatic change was the opportunity that factory work gave to young women. For young women in farm families, it was almost the only chance they had to earn their own money and a measure of independence.

Mills Change Workers' Lives

Workers no longer needed the specific skills of craftspeople to run the machines of the new mills. The lives of workers changed along with their jobs. Resistance to these changes sometimes sparked protests.

Many mill owners in the United States could not find enough people to work in factories because other jobs were available. At first, Samuel Slater and his two partners used apprentices—young men who worked for several years to learn the trade. However, they often were given only simple work. For example, their jobs might include feeding cotton into the machines and cleaning the mill equipment. They grew tired of this work and frequently left. Apprentice James Horton, for example, ran away from Slater's mill. "Mr. Slater ... keep me always at one thing ...," Horton complained. "I might have stayed there until this time and never knew nothing."

Eventually, Slater began to hire entire families who moved to Pawtucket to work in the mills. This practice allowed Slater to fill his labor needs at a low cost. Children as well as adults worked in the mills.

NEWSPAPER ADVERTISEMENT
Family Wanted

This advertisement appeared in a Massachusetts newspaper in 1823. In it, a company requests that families come to work at a factory. The practice of hiring entire families was common at the time, especially in Britain. In America, it became known as the Rhode Island system.

The advertisement requests more than one family.

Why do you think Blackstone wants large families?

FAMILIES WANTED.

THREE or four Families of large size, and good characters, may find employment at Blackstone Manufactory.
STEPHEN TRIPP,
Agent Blackstone Manufacturing Co.
Mendon, Nov. 27.
tf.

ANALYSIS SKILL ANALYZING PRIMARY SOURCES

Drawing Conclusions Do you think advertisements like this one had the effect the companies wanted?

On most farms children worked to help their families. Therefore, few people complained about the hiring of children to work in factories. H. Humphrey, an author of books on raising children, told parents that children needed to be useful. Humphrey wrote, "If he [a child] will not study, put him on to a farm, or send him into the shop, or in some other way provide regular employment for him." The machines made many tasks in the mill simple enough for children to do. Mill owners profited because they paid children low wages. Adults usually earned as much in a day as most children did in a week.

To attract families to his mill, Slater built housing for the workers. He also provided them with a company store where they could buy necessities. In addition, he started the practice of paying workers with credit at the company store. Instead of paying the full price for an item all at once, small payments could be made over a period of time. This practice allowed Slater to reinvest his money in his business.

Slater's strategy of hiring families and dividing factory work into simple tasks became known as the **Rhode Island system**. Mill owners throughout the Northeast copied Slater's methods. Owners advertised with "Men with growing families wanted." They also sent recruiters to poor communities to find new workers. For many people, the chance to work in a factory was a welcome opportunity to earn money and to learn a new skill.

One of the earliest of the mill towns, Slatersville, was named after Samuel Slater. The town was built by Slater and his brother John. It included two houses for workers and their families, the owner's house, the company store, and the Slatersville Mill. The mill was the largest and most modern industrial building of its time.

The mills employed not only the textile workers who operated the machinery but also machine part makers and dam builders. Although the company store sold food and necessary items to workers, mill towns supported the same variety of businesses any other town needed to thrive. These included tailors and dressmakers, butchers, and other small workshops.

READING CHECK **Summarizing** What problem did Slater have in his mills, and how did he solve it?

The Lowell System

Not all mill owners followed this system. **Francis Cabot Lowell**, a businessman from New England, developed a very different approach. His ideas completely changed the textile industry in the Northeast.

The **Lowell system** was based on water-powered textile mills that employed young, unmarried women from local farms. The system included a loom that could both spin thread and weave cloth in the same mill. Lowell constructed boardinghouses for the women. Boardinghouse residents were given a room and meals along with their jobs.

With financial support from investors of the Boston Manufacturing Company, Lowell's first textile mill opened in Waltham, Massachusetts, in 1814. "From the first starting of the first power loom there was not . . . doubt about the success," wrote one investor. In 1822, the company built a larger mill in a Massachusetts town later named Lowell. Visitors to Lowell were amazed by the clean factories and neatly kept boardinghouses as well as the new machinery.

The young millworkers soon became known as Lowell girls. The mills paid them between $2 and $4 each week. The workers paid $1.25 for room and board. These wages were much better than those women could earn per week in other available jobs, such as domestic work.

Many young women came to Lowell from across New England. They wanted the chance to earn money instead of working on the family farm. "I must of course have something of my own before many more years have passed over my head," wrote one young woman. The typical Lowell girl worked at the mills for about four years.

Unlike other factory workers, the Lowell girls were encouraged to use their free time to take classes and form women's clubs. They even wrote their own magazine, the *Lowell Offering*. Lucy Larcom, who started working at Lowell at age 11, later praised her fellow workers.

No record exists today of the name of this girl, who worked in a mill around 1850. Judging from the photograph, if she were in school today, she would probably be in the seventh or eighth grade. Although hard to see in this photograph, her hands and arms are scratched and swollen—telltale signs of the hard labor required of young girls who worked up to 14 hours per day.

TIME TABLE OF THE LOWELL MILLS

Morning Bells

First bell . . . . 4:30 AM

Second bell . . . . 5:30 AM

Third bell . . . . 6:20 AM

Dinner (Lunch) Bells

Ring out . . . . 12:00 PM

Ring in . . . . 12:35 PM

Evening Bells

Ring out . . . . 6:30 PM

Except on Saturday Evenings

—*The Table of the Lowell Mills, October 21, 1851*

Life of a Mill Girl

Girls had to keep their hair pulled back so it did not get caught in the machines, resulting in serious injury—or death.

Windows were rarely opened, to prevent air from blowing the threads. The result is a hot, stuffy room.

The air is dirty and causes breathing problems. One visitor remarked, "The atmosphere . . . is charged with cotton filaments and dust, which . . . are very injurious to the lungs."

This girl is straightening threads as they enter the power loom, a job that cut her hands.

Girls must shout to be heard above the noise of the power looms. Visitors to the mill routinely referred to the sound of the machines as "deafening."

ANALYSIS SKILL **ANALYZING VISUALS**

Judging from the photograph on page 392, what might be the condition of the girl's hands in this illustration? Why?

MAGAZINE ARTICLE
Sarah G. Bagley and Workers' Rights

Lowell girl Sarah G. Bagley wrote magazine articles and made speeches about working in the mills. She organized workers to help change conditions.

> Bagley believes that most mill girls would leave their jobs if they could.

> Bagley says that mill girls work to help their family members.

"Is anyone such a fool as to suppose that out of six thousand factory girls in Lowell, sixty would be there if they could help it? Whenever I raise the point that it is immoral to shut us up in a close room twelve hours a day in the most monotonous and tedious of employment I am told that we have come to the mills voluntarily and we can leave when we will. Voluntarily! . . . the whip which brings us to Lowell is necessity. We must have money; a father's debts are to be paid, an aged mother to be supported, a brother's ambition to be aided and so the factories are supplied. Is this to act from free will?. . . Is this freedom? To my mind it is slavery."

—Sarah G. Bagley, quoted in *The Belles of New England: The Women of the Textile Mills and the Families Whose Wealth They Wove,* by William Moran

ANALYSIS SKILL **ANALYZING PRIMARY SOURCES**

How did Bagley view the idea that workers must endure poor conditions?

"I regard it as one of the privileges [advantages] of my youth that I . . . [grew] up among those active, interesting girls, whose lives . . . had principle [ideals] and purpose distinctly their own."

—Lucy Larcom, from *A New England Girlhood*

Mill life was hard, however. The workday was between 12 and 14 hours long, and daily life was carefully controlled. Ringing bells ordered workers to breakfast or lunch. Employees had to work harder and faster to keep up with new equipment. Cotton dust also began to cause health problems, such as chronic cough, for workers.

THE IMPACT TODAY

In the 1950s, labor union membership reached its peak; about 40 percent of the workforce belonged to unions. Today only about 12 percent of the working population belongs to a labor union.

READING CHECK **Contrasting** How was the Lowell system different from the Rhode Island system?

Workers Organize

Factories continued to spread in the 1800s. Craftspeople, who made goods by hand, felt threatened. Factories quickly produced low-priced goods. To compete with factories, shop owners had to hire more workers and pay them less. Shoemaker William Frazier complained about the situation in the mid-1840s. "We have to sit on our seats from twelve to sixteen hours per day, to earn one dollar."

The wages of factory workers also went down as people competed for jobs. A wave of immigration in the 1840s brought people from other, poorer countries. They were willing to work for low pay. More immigrants came to the Northeast, where the mills were located, than to the South. Competition for jobs also came from people unemployed during the financial Panic of 1837. For example, about 50,000 workers in New York City alone lost their jobs.

The Beginning of Trade Unions

Facing low wages and the fear of losing their jobs, skilled workers formed **trade unions**, groups that tried to improve pay and working conditions. Eventually, unskilled factory workers also formed trade unions. Most employers did not want to hire union workers. Employers believed that the higher cost of union employees prevented competition with other manufacturers.

Sometimes labor unions staged protests called **strikes**. Workers on strike refuse to work until employers meet their demands. Most early strikes were not successful, however. Courts and police usually supported companies, not striking union members.

Labor Reform Efforts

A strong voice in the union movement was that of millworker **Sarah G. Bagley**. She founded the Lowell Female Labor Reform Association in 1844 and publicized the struggles of factory laborers. The association's two main goals were to influence an investigation of working conditions by the Massachusetts state legislature and to obtain a 10-hour workday. Members of the association passed out pamphlets and circulated petitions.

President Martin Van Buren had granted a 10-hour workday in 1840 for many federal employees. Bagley wanted this rule to apply to employees of private businesses. These men and women often worked 12 to 14 hours per day, six days per week.

Many working men and women supported the 10-hour-workday campaign, despite the opposition of business owners. In 1845 Sarah Bagley was elected vice president of the New England Working Men's Association. She was the first woman to hold such a high-ranking position in the American labor movement.

Over time, the unions achieved some <u>concrete</u> legal victories. Connecticut, Maine, New Hampshire, Ohio, Pennsylvania, and a few other states passed 10-hour-workday laws.

For factory workers in other states, long hours remained common. One witness described how children were "summoned by the factory bell before daylight" and worked until eight o'clock at night "with nothing but [a] recess of forty-five minutes to get their dinner." Union supporters continued to fight for work reforms such as an end to child labor in factories during the 1800s.

ACADEMIC VOCABULARY

concrete
specific, real

READING CHECK Finding Main Ideas
Why did workers form unions, and what were the main goals of union reformers?

SUMMARY AND PREVIEW With the growth of factories, workers faced new opportunities and challenges. In the next section you will learn about how the Transportation Revolution brought changes to commerce and the daily lives of Americans.

Section 2 Assessment

go.hrw.com
Online Quiz
KEYWORD: SF7 HP12

Reviewing Ideas, Terms, and People

1. **a. Identify** What problems did many mill owners have in finding workers?
   b. Analyze How did Samuel Slater's **Rhode Island system** change employment practices in mills?
2. **a. Describe** What was life like for mill workers in the **Lowell system**?
   b. Make Inferences Why would young women have wanted to go to work in the Lowell mills?
3. **a. Recall** Why did workers form **trade unions**?
   b. Predict What are some possible problems that might arise between factory owners and trade unions?

Critical Thinking

4. **Drawing Conclusions** Review your notes on mills and workers' reactions to them. Then copy the graphic organizer to the right and use it to show how Slater, Lowell, and Sarah G. Bagley affected workers' lives.

FOCUS ON WRITING

5. **Examining Working Conditions** This section tells about mill life and conditions for workers. In the chart you started for the first section, list the two labor systems used by mills, the person who developed each, and the benefits of each system.

The Transportation Revolution

What You Will Learn...

Main Ideas

1. The Transportation Revolution affected trade and daily life.
2. The steamboat was one of the first developments of the Transportation Revolution.
3. Railroads were a vital part of the Transportation Revolution.
4. The Transportation Revolution brought many changes to American life and industry.

The Big Idea

New forms of transportation improved business, travel, and communication in the United States.

Key Terms and People

Transportation Revolution, *p. 396*
Robert Fulton, *p. 397*
Clermont, *p. 397*
Gibbons v. *Ogden*, *p. 397*
Peter Cooper, *p. 398*

TAKING NOTES Create a time line like the one below. As you read, fill in the time line with the key events in the development of the steamboat and the locomotive as vital forms of transportation.

	1824	1840	
1807	1830		1860

8.1.12, 8.1.27, 8.3.1, 8.3.2, 8.3.6, 8.3.7, 8.3.8, 8.3.9, 8.3.10, 8.3.11, 8.4.3, 8.4.4, 8.4.5, 8.4.9

If YOU were there...

You live in a small town in Iowa in the 1860s. You've never been more than 30 miles from home and have always traveled by wagon or on horseback. Now there are plans to build a railroad westward from Chicago, 200 miles to the east. The tracks will come through your town! Twice a week, trains will bring goods from the city and take people farther west.

How would the coming of the railroad change your life?

BUILDING BACKGROUND The Industrial Revolution changed how goods were made. It brought great changes in the ways that many Americans lived. But developments in technology led to major changes in other areas of life, too. New forms of transportation would bring remote parts of America closer together.

Trade and Daily Life

During the 1800s the United States was transformed by a **Transportation Revolution**—a period of rapid growth in the speed and convenience of travel because of new methods of transportation. The Transportation Revolution created a boom in business across the country, particularly by reducing shipping time and costs. As one foreign observer declared in 1835, "The Americans . . . have joined the Hudson to the Mississippi, and made the Atlantic Ocean communicate with the Gulf of Mexico."

These improvements were made possible largely by the invention of two new forms of transportation: the steamboat and steam-powered trains. They enabled goods, people, and information to travel rapidly and efficiently across the United States.

READING CHECK **Finding Main Ideas** What benefits did the Transportation Revolution bring to trade and daily life?

Steamboats

American and European inventors had developed steam-powered boats in the late 1700s. However, they were not in wide use until the early 1800s.

Steamboat Era

In 1803 American **Robert Fulton** tested his first steamboat design in France. Several years later, he tested the first full-sized commercial steamboat, called the *Clermont*, in the United States. On August 9, 1807, the *Clermont* traveled against the current up the Hudson River without trouble. Demand for steamboat ferry service soon arose.

The steamboat was well suited for river travel. It could move upriver and did not rely on wind power. Steamboats increased trade and profits because goods could be moved quickly and thus more cheaply. More than 500 steamboats were in use in the United States by 1840. By the 1850s, steamboats were also being used to carry people and goods across the Atlantic Ocean.

Mississippi River Steamboats

Deckhands load a Mississippi River steamboat in Memphis, Tennessee. By the mid-1800s, hundreds of steamboats traveled up and down American rivers. Steamboats enabled Americans to ship more goods farther, faster, and for less money than ever before.

Upstream River Rates

(graph: Dollars (per 100 pounds) vs. Year, 1800–1830, showing decline from 9 to near 0)

Gibbons v. *Ogden*

Increased steamboat shipping led to conflict over waterway rights. In 1819 Aaron Ogden sued Thomas Gibbons for operating steamboats in New York waters that Ogden said he owned. Gibbons did not have a license to operate in New York, but argued that his federal license gave him the right to use New York waterways.

In the case of **Gibbons v. Ogden**, which reached the Supreme Court in 1824, the Court reinforced the federal government's authority to regulate trade between the states by ending monopolistic control over waterways in several states. The ruling freed up waters to even greater trade and shipping.

READING CHECK **Summarizing** Explain the effects of the *Gibbons* v. *Ogden* ruling.

American Railroads

What the steamboat did for water travel, the train did for overland travel. Steam-powered trains had first been developed in Great Britain in the early 1800s. However, they did not become popular in the United States until the 1830s. In 1830 **Peter Cooper** built a small but powerful locomotive called the *Tom Thumb*. He raced the locomotive against a horse-drawn railcar. Eyewitness John Latrobe later described the race, in which *Tom Thumb* had a slow start and fell behind. Latrobe wrote, "The pace increased, the passengers shouted, the engine gained on the horse . . . then the engine passes the horse, and a great hurrah hailed the victory." Unfortunately for Cooper, victory was spoiled when *Tom Thumb* broke down and lost the race near the end.

Despite the defeat, the contest showed the power and speed of even a small locomotive. Railroad fever soon spread. By 1840 railroad companies had laid about 2,800 miles of track—more than existed in all of Europe. French economist Michel Chevalier described Americans as having "a perfect passion for railroads."

As more railroads were built, engineers and mechanics overcame many tough challenges. Most British railroads, for example, ran on straight tracks across flat ground. In the United States, however, many railroads had to run up and down steep mountains, around tight curves, and over swift rivers. Railroad companies also built the tracks quickly and often with the least expensive materials available. As time went on, engineers and mechanics built heavier, faster, and more powerful steam locomotives.

By 1860 about 30,000 miles of railroad linked almost every major city in the eastern United States. As a result, the economy surged forward. For example, American locomotives hauled more freight than those in any other country. The railroad companies quickly became some of the most powerful businesses in the nation. As the railroad

The Steam Train

CONNECT TO SCIENCE AND TECHNOLOGY

Boiling water produces steam, which pushes pistons back and forth in a steam engine. These pistons are connected to rods that rotate the wheels of the locomotive.

Why does the train have a firebox?

Piston

❶ As steam follows the path of the white arrows into the cylinder, the pressure pushes the piston in the direction of the large blue arrow. Connecting rods turn the wheel half a turn.

❷ When the small valve rod moves, the other valve is blocked, pushing steam into the other side of the cylinder. The pressure moves the piston in the direction of the large blue arrow and the wheel completes a turn.

system grew, manufacturers and farmers could send their goods to distant markets.

In addition to their tremendous economic impact, the railroads made a powerful impression on the senses of passengers and observers. Trains were the fastest form of transportation most people had ever experienced. While wagons often traveled less than 2 miles per hour, locomotives averaged about 20 miles per hour. Writer George Templeton Strong of New York City described the thrill of a steam train passing by in the night:

" Whizzing and rattling and panting, with its fiery furnace gleaming in front, its chimney vomiting fiery smoke above, and its long train of cars rushing along behind like the body and tail of a gigantic dragon— . . . and all darting forward at the rate of twenty miles an hour. Whew! "

—George Templeton Strong, quoted in *The Market Revolution* by Charles Sellers

Riding on the early trains was often an adventure, but it could also be quite dangerous. Engineers trying to stay on time sometimes traveled too fast. English citizen Charles Richard Weld was on a railroad car that flew off the tracks. To his amazement, the other passengers did not complain about the accident. Instead, they praised the engineer for trying to keep on schedule!

Passengers accepted such risks because the railroads reduced travel time dramatically. Railroads also helped tie communities together. In 1847 Senator Daniel Webster spoke for many people in the United States when he declared that the railroad "towers above all other inventions of this or the preceding age."

READING CHECK **Drawing Inferences** In what ways did railroads affect the economy of the United States?

Chimney

Regulator

Boiler

Firebox

Fire doors

Water

Smoke box

Piston

By 1850 the United States already had about 9,000 miles of railroad track. Timber was needed for railroad ties, cars, and bridges and as fuel for steam locomotives.

Railroad

Coal   **Timber**

0   150   300 Miles
0   150   300 Kilometers

GEOGRAPHY SKILLS   INTERPRETING MAPS

go.hrw.com
Interactive Map
KEYWORD: SF7 CH12

1. **Region** Where were most railroads located in 1850?
2. **Human-Environment Interaction** How does this map suggest that people modified the landscape?

Transportation Revolution Brings Changes

The Transportation Revolution brought many changes to America. Steamboats and railroads made getting goods to distant markets much easier and less costly. People in all areas of the nation now had access to products made and grown far away. More than ever before, there was a national economy. The wealth, however, was centered in the North.

Railroads contributed to the expansion of the borders of the nation and guided population growth. Towns sprang up at railroad junctions. Those towns that did not have railroads nearby suffered. Cities grew as trains brought new residents and raw materials for industry and construction. The growing prosperity of the nation, especially in the North, encouraged Americans to take pride in their country.

A New Fuel

The Transportation Revolution also increased the use of certain natural resources that had not been important until then. Throughout the early Transportation Revolution, wood was the primary source of fuel for trains and steamboats, as well as for cooking, light, and heat. As faster locomotives were built, coal replaced wood as the main source of power. A half ton of coal produces as much energy as two tons of wood but at half the cost. Coal also became popular for heating homes. Railroads transported the coal from mines to towns and cities.

As the demand for coal increased, a coal-mining industry developed in many states, including Pennsylvania, western Virginia, and Illinois. Coal mining changed the landscape in a number of ways. New towns, such as Coal City and Carbondale in Illinois, sprang up in places where coal deposits could be mined. Miners made deep gashes in the earth removing the coal.

Later, in the 1870s, the demand for coal increased as the demand for steel grew. Steel is made through a smelting process—heating iron ore to very high temperatures. Coal was used to fire the furnaces. Steel, which is much stronger than iron, was increasingly used to build factories and the machines they produced. Steel was also used to make the rails that trains ride on.

The growing market for steel helped fuel the need for more railroads. Railroads transported steel to places where new factories were being built. Railroads also brought new steel farming tools and machines to farmers in the Midwest. Using the new equipment, farmers produced more crops. Railroads then transported their harvests to markets.

Effects of Railroads

The railroads also played a role in the growth of other businesses. The logging industry expanded as people in the growing towns and cities needed wood for houses and furniture. As newspaper publishing increased, demand for paper grew. Lumber items became the primary product of New England. Settlers spreading out across the Midwest cut down trees and plowed up prairies to make farmland. Deforestation, or cutting down and removing trees, took place on a large scale.

Railroads also caused cities to grow. Some cities became transportation hubs. Chicago was one such city. Its location on Lake Michigan made it an ideal transportation hub, linking the Midwest to the East and South.

READING CHECK **Analyzing Information**
What role did railroads play in the growth of the coal industry?

SUMMARY AND PREVIEW The Transportation Revolution changed the way business was done. In the next section you will learn about more technological advances.

FOCUS ON READING
What causes and effects do you see in this section?

Section 3 Assessment

go.hrw.com
Online Quiz
KEYWORD: SF7 HP12

Reviewing Ideas, Terms, and People

1. **a. Identify** What forms of transportation were improved or invented at this time?
   b. Explain What effect did the **Transportation Revolution** have on the United States?
2. **a. Describe** What were the benefits of steamboat travel?
   b. Analyze What effect did the ruling in the *Gibbons v. Ogden* case have on federal government?
3. **a. Describe** What event showed the power and speed of locomotives?
   b. Draw Conclusions How did railroads affect trade and business in the United States?
   c. Elaborate Why do you think Americans were fascinated by railroads?
4. **a. Describe** What physical obstacles did railroad construction in the United States face?
   b. Analyze What effects did the Transportation Revolution have on the U.S. economy?
   c. Elaborate Do you think the Transportation Revolution played a role in deforestation? Explain.

Critical Thinking

5. **Identifying Effects** Review your time line on the steamboat and the locomotive. Then copy the chart below and use it to show how they affected business, travel, and communication in the United States.

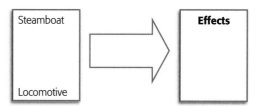

FOCUS ON WRITING

6. **Describing Travel Inventions** Add the steamboat and locomotive to your list. Note the individuals involved in their development as well as how these new methods of travel changed life for people in the United States.

More Technological Advances

What You Will Learn...

Main Ideas

1. The telegraph made swift communication possible from coast to coast.
2. With the shift to steam power, businesses built new factories closer to cities and transportation centers.
3. Improved farm equipment and other labor-saving devices made life easier for many Americans.
4. New inventions changed lives in American homes.

The Big Idea

Advances in technology led to new inventions that continued to change daily life and work.

Key Terms and People

Samuel F. B. Morse, *p. 402*
telegraph, *p. 402*
Morse code, *p. 403*
John Deere, *p. 404*
Cyrus McCormick, *p. 404*
Isaac Singer, *p. 405*

TAKING NOTES As you read, take notes on the new advances in technology listed in the section. Create a graphic organizer like the one shown below that identifies the effects of each.

Inventions	Effects
Telegraph	
Steam Power	
Mass Production	
Home Inventions	

IN 8.1.10, 8.1.20, 8.1.26, 8.1.27, 8.1.29, 8.1.30, 8.3.8, 8.3.9, 8.3.11, 8.4.2, 8.4.3, 8.4.5, 8.4.6

If YOU were there...

You own a small shop in Chicago, Illinois, in the 1850s. You sell ladies' hats and gowns. When you need more hats, you send a letter to the manufacturer in New York. Sometimes it takes weeks for the letter to get there. One day, the owner of the shop next door tells you about a wonderful new machine. It can send orders from Chicago to New York in just minutes!

How would a machine like this change your business?

BUILDING BACKGROUND The Industrial and Transportation Revolutions had far-reaching effects on Americans' lives. They led to still more innovations in technology. Some of the new machines and devices speeded up processes for business owners. Others made life easier for people at home.

Telegraph Speeds Communication

In 1832 **Samuel F. B. Morse** perfected the **telegraph**—a device that could send information over wires across great distances. To develop the telegraph, Morse studied electricity and magnetism. In

Time Line

American Inventions

1798 Eli Whitney proposed the idea of mass producing guns. Machines like this one made it possible for workers to make interchangeable parts efficiently.

1831 Cyrus McCormick invents the mechanical reaper. Harvesting grain becomes eight times more efficient.

time, Morse put the work of other scientists together in a practical machine.

The telegraph sent pulses, or surges, of electric current through a wire. The telegraph operator tapped a bar, called a telegraph key, that controlled the length of each pulse. At the other end of the wire, these pulses were changed into clicking sounds. A short click was called a dot. A long click was called a dash. Morse's partner, Alfred Lewis Vail, developed a system known as **Morse code**—different combinations of dots and dashes that represent each letter of the alphabet. For example, *dot dot dot, dash dash dash, dot dot dot* is the distress signal called SOS. Skilled telegraph operators could send and receive many words per minute.

Several years passed before Morse was able to connect two locations with telegraph wires. Despite that achievement, people doubted his machine. Some people did not think that he was reading messages sent from miles away. They claimed that he was making lucky guesses.

Morse's break came during the 1844 Democratic National Convention in Baltimore, Maryland. A telegraph wired news of the presidential candidate's nomination to politicians in Washington. The waiting politicians responded, "Three cheers for the telegraph!" Telegraphs were soon sending and receiving information for businesses, the government, newspapers, and private citizens.

BIOGRAPHY

Samuel F. B. Morse
(1791–1872)

Like steamboat creator Robert Fulton, Samuel F. B. Morse began his career as a painter rather than as an inventor. In 1832 Morse was a widower struggling to raise his three children alone. He became interested in the idea of sending messages electrically. Morse hoped he could invent a device that would earn him enough money to support his family. Eventually, earnings from the telegraph made Morse extremely wealthy.

Drawing Conclusions What motivated Morse to invent the telegraph?

The telegraph grew with the railroad. Telegraph companies strung their wires on poles along railroads across the country. They established telegraph offices in many train stations. Thousands of miles of telegraph line were added every year in the 1850s. The first transcontinental line was finished in 1861. By the time he died in 1872, Morse was famous across the United States.

READING CHECK **Identifying Cause and Effect** What event led to the widespread use of the telegraph, and what effect did the telegraph have on cross-country communications?

1837 John Deere invents the steel plow. The tough prairie sod can be cut and the thick soil ploughed without having to constantly clean the plow.

1832 Samuel F. B. Morse invents the telegraph. Long-distance communication becomes almost instantaneous.

FOCUS ON INDIANA

An improvement on John Deere's plow design was introduced by James Oliver in South Bend, Indiana. Oliver's "chilled plow" was made of strong iron, but the face was smooth.

Steam Power and New Factories

At the start of the Industrial Revolution, most factories ran on waterpower. In time, however, factory owners began using steam power. This shift brought major changes to the nation's industries. Water-powered factories had to be built near streams or waterfalls. In contrast, steam power allowed business owners to build factories almost anywhere. Yet the Northeast was still home to most of the nation's industry. By 1860 New England alone had as many factories as the entire South did.

Some companies decided to build their factories closer to cities and transportation centers. This provided easier access to workers, allowing businesses to lower wages. Being closer to cities also reduced shipping costs. Cities soon became the center of industrial growth. People from rural areas as well as foreign countries flocked to the cities for factory jobs.

Factory workers improved the designs of many kinds of machines. Mechanics invented tools that could cut and shape metal, stone, and wood with great precision. By the 1840s this new machinery was able to produce interchangeable parts. Within a short period of time, the growing machine-tool industry was even making customized equipment.

READING CHECK **Finding Main Ideas** What changes resulted from the shift to steam power?

Improved Farm Equipment

During the 1830s, technology began transforming the farm as well as the factory. In 1837 blacksmith **John Deere** saw that friends in Illinois had difficulty plowing thick soil with iron plows. He thought a steel blade might work better. His design for a steel plow was a success. By 1846 Deere was selling 1,000 plows per year.

In 1831 **Cyrus McCormick** developed a new harvesting machine, the mechanical reaper, which quickly and efficiently cut down wheat. He began mass producing his reapers in a Chicago factory. McCormick used new methods to encourage sales. His company advertised, gave demonstrations, and provided a repair and spare parts department. He also let customers buy on credit.

The combination of Deere's plow and McCormick's reaper allowed Midwestern farmers to plant and harvest huge crop fields. By 1860, U.S. farmers were producing more than 170 million bushels of wheat and more than 800 million bushels of corn per year.

READING CHECK **Summarizing** What marketing methods did McCormick use to help sell his farm equipment?

American Inventions (continued)

1849 Walter Hunt invents the safety pin.

W. Hunt.
Pin.
№ 6281. *Patented Apr. 10. 1849.*
Fig. 1.
Fig. 2.

UNITED STATES PATENT OFFICE.

WALTER HUNT, OF NEW YORK, N. Y., ASSIGNOR TO WM. RICHARDSON AND JNO. RICHARDSON.

DRESS-PIN.

Specification of Letters Patent No. 6,281, dated April 10, 1849.

To all whom it may concern:
Be it known that I, WALTER HUNT, of the city, county, and State of New York, have invented a new and useful Improvement in the Make or Form of Dress-Pins, of which the following is a faithful and accurate

to the bar C, (see Figs. 6, 7 and 8,) which combined with the advantages of the spring and catch, renders it equally ornamental, and at the same time more secure and durable than any other plan of a clasp pin, heretofore in use, there being no joint to break or pivot to wear or get loose as in other plans.

1851 Isaac Singer improves the sewing machine. The production and repair of clothing becomes much easier.

Changing Life at Home

Many inventions of the Industrial Revolution simply made life easier. When Alexis de Tocqueville of France visited the United States in the early 1830s, he identified what he called a very American quality.

" [Americans want] to be always making life more comfortable and convenient, to avoid trouble, and to satisfy the smallest wants [desires] without effort and almost without cost. "
—Alexis de Tocqueville, from *Democracy in America*

The sewing machine, first invented by Elias Howe, a factory apprentice in Lowell, Massachusetts, was one of these conveniences. **Isaac Singer** then made improvements to Howe's design. Like McCormick, Singer allowed customers to buy his machines on credit and provided service. By 1860 Singer's company was the world's largest maker of sewing machines.

Other advances improved on everyday items. In the 1830s, iceboxes cooled by large blocks of ice became available. Iceboxes stored fresh food safely for longer periods. Iron cookstoves began replacing cooking fires and stone hearths.

Companies also began to mass produce earlier inventions. This allowed many families to buy household items, such as clocks, that they could not afford in the past. For example, a clock that cost $50 in 1800 was selling for only $1.50 by the 1850s. Additional useful items created during this period

include matches, introduced in the 1830s, and the safety pin, invented in 1849. All of these inventions helped make life at home more convenient for an increasing number of Americans.

READING CHECK Analyzing How did labor-saving inventions affect daily life?

SUMMARY AND PREVIEW New machines and inventions changed the way Americans lived and did business in the early 1800s. In the next section you will learn how agricultural changes affected the South.

THE IMPACT TODAY

New inventions, such as cell phones, laptop computers, and microwave ovens, continue to make life easier and more convenient for people today.

---

go.hrw.com
Online Quiz
KEYWORD: SF7 HP12

Section 4 Assessment

Reviewing Ideas, Terms, and People

1. **a. Describe** How did the **telegraph** work?
   b. Predict What impact might the telegraph have on the future of the United States?
2. **a. Describe** How did waterpowered factories differ from steam-powered factories?
   b. Explain How did the shift to steam power lead to the growth of cities?
3. **a. Identify** What contributions did **Cyrus McCormick** and **John Deere** make to farming?
   b. Analyze What effect did new inventions have on agriculture in the United States?
4. **a. Identify** What inventions improved life at home?
   b. Evaluate Which invention do you think had the greatest effect on the daily lives of Americans? Why?

Critical Thinking

5. **Supporting a Point of View** Review your notes on technological advances and their effects. Then create a graphic organizer like the one below that shows the top three advances you think are most important and why.

Most Important	Why

FOCUS ON WRITING

6. **Describing Technological Advances** Add notes about the inventions mentioned in this section to your chart. Think about which invention you will use for your newspaper advertisement.

1859 Manufactured goods become more valuable than agricultural goods in the country's economy for the first time. The United States is becoming a modern industrial nation.

ANALYSIS SKILL **READING TIME LINES**

Which two inventions improved American agriculture?

Social Studies Skills

Analysis   Critical Thinking   **Civic Participation**   Study

Personal Conviction and Bias

Define the Skill

Everyone has *convictions,* or firmly held beliefs. However, when we let our beliefs automatically slant or shape our point of view on topics, we may be showing bias. *Bias* is a fixed idea or opinion about someone or something. Some bias is based on a set of ideas about a group to which the person or thing belongs. This type of bias is called a *stereotype*. If the group is defined by race, religion, age, gender, or similar characteristics, the bias is known as *prejudice*.

Bias, stereotypes, and prejudice are not always negative in nature. They include favorable opinions too. For example, the belief that a student is good at math because that person is male is a bias that shows both stereotyping and prejudice.

We should always be on guard for the presence of personal bias. Eliminating stereotyping and prejudice is particularly important. However, even "good" biases can slant how we view, judge, and communicate information. Honest and accurate communication requires that the information and ideas we express be as free of bias as possible.

Learn the Skill

Not all beliefs are biases, even if those beliefs are strongly held. Biases are beliefs that have little or no evidence to support them. The more unreasonable a person's view is in light of facts and evidence, the more likely it is that the belief is a bias.

Another characteristic of bias is the person's reluctance to question his or her belief if it is challenged by evidence. Sometimes people stubbornly cling to views that overwhelming evidence proves wrong. This is why bias is defined as a "fixed" idea or opinion. One of the most damaging effects of bias, and a good reason for trying to avoid it, is that it can prevent us from learning new things.

The following precautions can help you to reduce the amount of bias you hold and express.

1. When discussing a topic, keep in mind beliefs and experiences in your own background that might affect how you feel about the topic.

2. Try to not mix statements of fact with statements of opinion. Clearly separate and indicate what you *know* to be true from what you *believe* to be true.

3. Avoid using emotional, positive, or negative words when communicating factual information.

Practice the Skill

In 1834 Tennessee congressman Davy Crockett visited the textile mills at Lowell, Massachusetts. Read his account of the "Lowell girls" who worked in the factory and complete the activity below.

" Here are thousands [of young women], useful to others, . . . with the prospect before them of future comfort and respectability . . . There are more than five thousand females employed in Lowell; and when you come to see the amount of labour performed by them, in superintending [operating] the different machinery, you will be astonished. "

Suppose that you were a "Lowell girl" who has just read this account of Crockett's visit. Write a letter to the editor of the *Lowell Offering* reacting to the biases and stereotypes about women that Crockett shows in his account.

HOLT
History's Impact
▶ video series
Review the video to answer the closing question:
How do you think ease of travel has affected U.S. population centers?

Visual Summary

Use the visual summary below to help you review the main ideas of the chapter.

INDUSTRIAL REVOLUTION
• Mass production
• Interchangeable parts
• The Lowell and Rhode Island systems

TRANSPORTATION REVOLUTION

Water- and Steam Power

Railroad and Steamboat

Telegraph

Factories

New Farm Machinery

To Growing Cities

Reviewing Vocabulary, Terms, and People

Complete each sentence below by filling in the blank with the correct term or person from the chapter.

1. The system of _____ was developed to represent letters of the alphabet when sending telegraph messages.

2. The first American woman to hold a high-ranking position in the labor movement was _____.

3. The _____ was a period of rapid growth in the use of machines and manufacturing.

4. The first locomotive in the United States was built by _____.

5. Workers would sometimes go on _____ to force factory owners to meet their demands for better pay and working conditions.

6. The _____ industry, which produced cloth items, was the first to use machines for manufacturing.

Comprehension and Critical Thinking

SECTION 1 *(Pages 384–389)*

7. **a. Identify** What ideas did Eli Whitney want to apply to the manufacture of guns?

   b. Analyze How did the War of 1812 lead to a boom in manufacturing in the United States?

   c. Elaborate Why do you think the Industrial Revolution began in Great Britain rather than in the United States?

SECTION 2 *(Pages 390–395)*

8. **a. Describe** What was mill life like?

   b. Draw Conclusions How did the Rhode Island system and the Lowell system change the lives of American workers?

   c. Evaluate Were reformers such as Sarah G. Bagley effective in improving labor conditions? Why?

9. **a. Describe** How were Americans affected by the introduction of steamboats?

   b. Make Inferences How did railroad companies become some of the most powerful businesses in the country?

   c. Elaborate What was the most important result of the Transportation Revolution? Why?

SECTION 4 *(Pages 402–405)*

10. **a. Recall** What important change took place in how factories were powered?

    b. Draw Conclusions How did the telegraph affect communication in the United States?

    c. Evaluate Do you think moving factories close to cities helped or hurt working life? Explain.

Reviewing Themes

11. **Science and Technology** What are the three most important inventions of the Industrial Revolution? Why?

12. **Economics** What was the overall effect of the Industrial Revolution on the U.S. economy?

Using the Internet

go.hrw.com
KEYWORD: SF7 CH12

13. **Activity: Marketing Plan** The Industrial Revolution changed the way goods were produced. New inventions created easier, faster, or completely new ways of doing things. Enter the activity keyword and research inventions made between 1790 and 1860. Then create a plan for how to sell one of the inventions. In your plan, identify the problems the invention will fix, your target audience, and how the invention should be advertised and sold.

Reading Skills

Causes and Effects in History *Use the Reading Skills taught in this chapter to answer the question about the reading selection below.*

> Many young women came to Lowell from across New England. They wanted the chance to earn money instead of working on the family farm. *(p. 392)*

14. According to the passage above, what was a cause for moving to Lowell?

    a. working long hours

    b. earning money

    c. meeting people

    d. working on a farm

Social Studies Skills

Personal Conviction and Bias *Use the Social Studies Skills taught in this chapter to answer the question about the reading selection below.*

> "Is anyone such a fool as to suppose that out of six thousand factory girls in Lowell, sixty would be there if they could help it?"
>
> —Sarah G. Bagley, quoted in *The Belles of New England* by William Moran

15. Do you think that Bagley's opposition to the Lowell system was unfairly biased? Why or why not?

FOCUS ON WRITING

16. **Writing Your Newspaper Advertisement** Look over your chart, and choose one invention for your advertisement. Then answer these questions to help you plan your advertisement: Who is your audience? Who will buy this invention? How will the invention benefit this audience? What words or phrases will best persuade this audience? Once you have answered these questions, design your advertisement. To draw readers' attention to your ad, include an illustration, a catchy heading, and a few lines of text.

Standardized Test Practice

8.1.10, 8.4.5, 8.4.6, 8.4.9

DIRECTIONS: Read each question and write the letter of the best response.

1 **The first machines of the Industrial Revolution were powered by**

A electricity.

B water.

C animals.

D coal.

2 **The earliest important evidence of the Industrial Revolution in America was found in**

A the way cotton was processed for market.

B the production of tobacco products.

C the manufacture of cloth and thread.

D the construction of the first steam railroads.

3 **Which of the following was a development of the Transportation Revolution of the mid-1800s?**

A automobiles

B wind-powered boats

C diesel freighters

D steam-powered trains

4 **What change in technology allowed business owners to sell their goods in markets across the country?**

A the Lowell system

B the growth of railroads

C the invention of the telegraph

D the Arkwright system

5 **Eli Whitney's idea of interchangeable parts resulted in**

A the dominance of American manufacturing.

B the beginning of the Industrial Revolution.

C a rapid expansion of railroads.

D the mass production of goods.

6 **The inventions of John Deere and Cyrus McCormick**

A improved communication.

B introduced two new factory labor systems.

C helped increase agricultural production in the United States.

D led to manufacturing breakthroughs in the textile industry.

7 **Read the following passage written by a textile worker and use it to answer the question below.**

> *"*The little money I could earn—one dollar a week, besides the price of my board—was needed in the family, and I must return [from home] to the mill . . . I began to reflect on life rather seriously for a girl of twelve or thirteen. What was I here for? What would I make of myself? . . . We did not forget that we were working girls . . . clearing away a few weeds from the overgrown track of independent labor for other women . . . [so that] no real odium [disrespect] could be attached to any honest toil that any self-respecting woman might undertake.*"*
>
> —from *A New England Girlhood* by Lucy Larcom (1824–1893)

Document-Based Question **How did Larcom see the role of women changing in the workforce?**

The South

IN Indiana Standards

Social Studies Standards

8.1.10 Compare differences in ways of life in the northern and osuthern states, including the growth of towns and cities in the North and the growing dependence on slavery in the South.

8.3.1 Read maps to interpret symbols and determine the land forms and human features that represent physical and cultural characteristics of areas in the United States. 1 Identify ways people modified the physical environment as the United States developed and describe the impacts that resulted.

8.4.6 Relate technological change and inventions to changes in labor productivity in the United States in the eighteenth and nineteenth centuries.

8.4.9 Explain and evaluate examples of domstic and international interdependence throughout United States history.

go.hrw.com
Indiana
KEYWORD: SF10 IN

FOCUS ON WRITING

Biographical Sketch In this chapter you will learn about life in the South during the first half of the nineteenth century. Read the chapter, and then write a two-paragraph biographical sketch about a day in the life of a person living on a large cotton farm in the South. You might choose to write about a wealthy male landowner, his wife, or an enslaved man or woman working on the farm. As you read, think about what life would have been like for the different people who lived and worked on the farm. Take notes about farm life in your notebook.

UNITED STATES

1793 Eli Whitney invents the cotton gin.

1800

1794 France ends slavery in its colonies.

WORLD

History's Impact

▶ **video series**
Watch the video to understand the impact of regional economies on the nation.

What You Will Learn...

These enslaved people were photographed on a South Carolina plantation in the year 1861. The issue of slavery would have a serious and dramatic impact on the history of the entire United States. In this chapter you will learn how the South developed an agricultural economy, and how that economy was dependent on the labor of enslaved people.

1851
Indiana voters approve a new constitution banning African Americans from moving into the state.

1808 A congressional ban on importing slaves into the United States takes effect.

1831 Nat Turner's Rebellion leads to fears of further slave revolts in the South.

1848 Joseph R. Anderson becomes the owner of the Tredegar Iron Works, the South's only large iron factory.

1820

1840

1860

1807 Parliament bans the slave trade in the British Empire.

1835 Alexis de Tocqueville publishes *Democracy in America*.

1837 Victoria is crowned queen of Great Britain.

1858 A treaty at Tianjin, China, gives Hong Kong to the United Kingdom.

THE SOUTH **411**

Reading Social Studies

by Kylene Beers

Focus on Themes This chapter takes you into the heart of the South from 1800 through the mid-1800s. As you read, you will discover that the South depended on cotton as its **economic** backbone, especially after the invention of the cotton gin. You will also read about the slave system in the South during this time and about the harsh living conditions slaves endured. As you will see, the South was home to a variety of **societies and cultures**.

Online Research

Focus on Reading Researching history topics on the Web can give you access to valuable information. However, just because the information is on the Web doesn't mean it is automatically valuable.

Evaluating Web Sites Before you use information you find online, you need to evaluate the site it comes from. The checklist below can help you determine if the site is worth your time.

Evaluating Web Sites

Site: _____ URL: _____ Date of access: _____

Rate each item on this 1–3 scale. Then add up the total score.

	No	Some	Yes
I. Authority			
a. Authors are clearly identified by name.	1	2	3
b. Contact information is provided for authors.	1	2	3
c. Authors' qualifications are clearly stated.	1	2	3
d. Site has been updated recently.	1	2	3
II. Content			
a. Site's information is useful to your project.	1	2	3
b. Information is clear and well-organized.	1	2	3
c. Information appears to be at the right level.	1	2	3
d. Links to additional important information are provided.	1	2	3
e. Information can be verified in other sources.	1	2	3
f. Graphics are helpful, not just decorative.	1	2	3
III. Design and Technical Elements			
a. Pages are readable and easy to navigate.	1	2	3
b. Links to other sites work.	1	2	3

Total Score _____

36–28 = very good site   27–20 = average site   below 20 = poor site

---

You Try It!

The passage below is from the chapter you are about to read.

Cotton Becomes Profitable

Cotton had been grown in the New World for centuries, but it had not been a very profitable crop. Before cotton could be spun into thread for weaving into cloth, the seeds had to be removed from the cotton fibers.

From Chapter 13, pp. 414–415

Long-staple cotton, also called black-seed cotton, was fairly easy to process. Workers could pick the seeds from the cotton with relative ease. But long-staple cotton grew well in only a few places in the South. More common was short-staple cotton, which was also known as green-seed cotton. Removing the seeds from this cotton was difficult and time consuming. A worker could spend an entire day picking the seeds from a single pound of short-staple cotton.

After you read the passage, complete the following activity.

Suppose that after reading this passage you decide to do some research on cotton growing. You use a search engine that directs you to a site. At that site, you find the information described below. Using the evaluation criteria listed on the previous page, decide if this is a site you would recommend to others.

a. The authors of the site are listed as "Bob and Mack, good friends who enjoy working together."

b. The site was last updated on "the last time we got together."

c. The title of the site is "Cotton Pickin'." There are few headings.

d. This ten-page site includes nine pages about the authors' childhood on a cotton farm. No illustrations are included.

e. Pages are very long, but they load quickly, as there are no graphics. There is one link to a site selling cotton clothing.

As you read Chapter 13, think about what topics would be interesting to research on the Web. If you do some research on the Web, remember to use the evaluation list to analyze the Web site.

Growth of the Cotton Industry

What You Will Learn...

Main Ideas

1. The invention of the cotton gin revived the economy of the South.
2. The cotton gin created a cotton boom in which farmers grew little else.
3. Some people encouraged southerners to focus on other crops and industries.

The Big Idea

The invention of the cotton gin made the South a one-crop economy and increased the need for slave labor.

Key Terms and People

cotton gin, *p. 415*
planters, *p. 416*
cotton belt, *p. 416*
factors, *p. 417*
Tredegar Iron Works, *p. 419*

TAKING NOTES As you read, take notes on the causes of the cotton boom in the South. Record your notes in a graphic organizer like the one shown below.

IN 8.1.10, 8.3.1, 8.3.6, 8.3.7, 8.3.8, 8.3.9, 8.3.11, 8.4.3, 8.4.5, 8.4.6, 8.4.9

If YOU were there...

You are a field-worker on a cotton farm in the South in about 1800. Your job is to separate the seeds from the cotton fibers. It is dull, tiring work because the tiny seeds are tangled in the fibers. Sometimes it takes you a whole day just to clean one pound of cotton! Now you hear that someone has invented a machine that can clean cotton 50 times faster than by hand.

How might this machine change your life?

BUILDING BACKGROUND Sectional differences had always existed between different regions of the United States. The revolutionary changes in industry and transportation deepened the differences between North and South. The South remained mainly agricultural. New technology helped the region become the Cotton Kingdom.

Reviving the South's Economy

Before the American Revolution, three crops dominated southern agriculture—tobacco, rice, and indigo. These crops, produced mostly by enslaved African Americans, played a central role in the southern economy and culture.

After the American Revolution, however, prices for tobacco, rice, and indigo dropped. When crop prices fell, the demand for and the price of slaves also went down. In an effort to protect their incomes, many farmers tried, with little success, to grow other crops that needed less labor. Soon, however, cotton would transform the southern economy and greatly increase the demand for slave labor.

Cotton Becomes Profitable

Cotton had been grown in the New World for centuries, but it had not been a very profitable crop. Before cotton could be spun into thread for weaving into cloth, the seeds had to be removed from the cotton fibers.

Cotton Gin

❶ The operator turned the crank.

❷ The crank turned a roller with teeth that stripped the seeds away from the cotton fiber.

❸ Brushes on a second roller lifted the seed-less cotton off the teeth of the first cylinder and dropped it out of the machine.

❹ A belt connected the rollers so that they would both turn when the crank was turned.

Long-staple cotton, also called black-seed cotton, was fairly easy to process. Workers could pick the seeds from the cotton with relative ease. But long-staple cotton grew well in only a few places in the South. More common was short-staple cotton, which was also known as green-seed cotton. Removing the seeds from this cotton was difficult and time consuming. A worker could spend an entire day picking the seeds from a single pound of short-staple cotton.

By the early 1790s the demand for American cotton began increasing rapidly. For instance, in Great Britain, new textile factories needed raw cotton that could be used for making cloth, and American cotton producers could not keep up with the high demand for their cotton. These producers of cotton needed a machine that could remove the seeds from the cotton more rapidly.

Eli Whitney's Cotton Gin

Northerner Eli Whitney finally patented such a machine in 1793. The year before, Whitney had visited a Georgia plantation owned by Catherine Greene where workers were using a machine that removed seeds from long-staple cotton. This machine did not work well on short-staple cotton, and Greene asked Whitney if he could improve it. By the next spring, Whitney had perfected his design for the **cotton gin**, a machine that removes seeds from short-staple cotton. ("Gin" is short for engine.) The cotton gin used a hand-cranked cylinder with wire teeth to pull cotton fibers from the seeds.

Whitney hoped to keep the design of the gin a secret, but the machine was so useful that his patent was often ignored by other manufacturers. Whitney described how his invention would improve the cotton business.

THE IMPACT TODAY

The same patent law that protected Whitney's invention of the cotton gin protects the rights of inventors today.

> "One man will clean ten times as much cotton as he can in any other way before known and also clean it much better than in the usual mode [method]. This machine may be turned by water or with a horse, with the greatest ease, and one man and a horse will do more than fifty men with the old machines."
>
> —Eli Whitney, quoted in *Eli Whitney and the Birth of American Technology* by Constance McLaughlin Green

Whitney's gin revolutionized the cotton industry. **Planters**—large-scale farmers who held more than 20 slaves—built cotton gins that could process tons of cotton much faster than hand processing. A healthy crop almost guaranteed financial success because of high demand from the textile industry.

READING CHECK Drawing Conclusions
What effects did the cotton gin have on the southern economy?

The Cotton Boom

Whitney's invention of the cotton gin made cotton so profitable that southern farmers abandoned other crops in favor of growing cotton. The removal of Native Americans opened up more land, while the development of new types of cotton plants helped spread cotton production throughout the South as far west as Texas. This area of high cotton production became known as the **cotton belt**.

Production increased rapidly—from about 2 million pounds in 1791 to roughly a billion pounds by 1860. As early as 1840, the United States was producing more than half of the cotton grown in the entire world. The economic boom attracted new settlers, built up wealth among wealthy white southerners, and firmly put in place the institution of slavery in the South.

The Cotton Kingdom

After the invention of the cotton gin, the amount of cotton produced each year in the United States soared, as the chart below shows. The area of land devoted to growing cotton also increased dramatically between 1820 and 1860, as shown on the map.

U.S. Cotton Production, 1800–1860

Cotton (in 100,000 bales) vs. Year (1800, 1820, 1840, 1860)

Extent of cotton growing by 1820
Extent of cotton growing by 1860

0   150   300 Miles
0   150   300 Kilometers

ANALYSIS SKILL INTERPRETING CHARTS

1. In what region of the United States was the cotton belt?
2. How many bales of cotton were produced in 1860?

Cotton Belt

Cotton had many advantages as a cash crop. It cost little to market. Unlike food staples, harvested cotton could be stored for a long time. Because cotton was lighter than other staple crops, it also cost less to transport long distances.

Farmers eager to profit from growing cotton headed west to find land. Farmers also began to apply scientific methods to improve crop production. Cotton had one disadvantage as a crop—it rapidly used up the nutrients in the soil. After a few years, cotton could make the land useless for growing anything. Some agricultural scientists recommended crop rotation—changing the crop grown on a particular plot of land every few years. Different crops needed different nutrients, so crop rotation would keep the land fertile longer. Other agricultural scientists began to study soil chemistry, in an effort to keep the land rich and productive.

As the cotton belt grew, farmers continued trying to improve the crop. Agricultural scientists worked at crossbreeding short-staple cotton with other varieties. As a result, new, stronger types of cotton were soon growing throughout the cotton belt. This led to expansion of the cotton industry through the 1860s.

The cotton boom involved much more than growing and harvesting cotton. Harvested cotton had to be ginned, pressed into bales, and then shipped to market or to warehouses. Special agents helped do everything from marketing cotton to customers to insuring crops against loss or damage. Factories were built to produce items needed by cotton farmers, such as ropes to bale cotton.

Growing and harvesting cotton required many field hands. Rather than pay wages to free workers, planters began to use more slave labor. Congress had made bringing slaves into the United States illegal in 1808. However, the growing demand for slaves led to an increase in the slave trade within the United States.

Cotton Trade

In an 1858 speech before the U.S. Senate, South Carolina politician James Henry Hammond declared, "Cotton is King!" Without cotton, Hammond claimed, the global economy would fail. He believed that southern cotton was one of the most valuable resources in the world. Southern cotton was used to make cloth in England and the North. Many southerners shared Hammond's viewpoints about cotton. Southerner David Christy declared, "King cotton is a profound [learned] statesman, and knows what measures will best sustain [protect] his throne."

The cotton boom made the South a major player in world trade. Great Britain became the South's most valued foreign trading partner. Southerners also sold tons of cotton to the growing textile industry in the northeastern United States. This increased trade led to the growth of major port cities in the South, including Charleston, South Carolina; Savannah, Georgia; and New Orleans, Louisiana.

In these cities, crop brokers called **factors** managed the cotton trade. Farmers sold their cotton to merchants, who then made deals with the factors. Merchants and factors also arranged loans for farmers who needed to buy supplies. They often advised farmers on how to invest profits. Once farmers got their cotton to the port cities, factors arranged for transportation aboard trading ships.

However, shipping cotton by land to port cities was very difficult in the South. The few major road projects at the time were limited to the Southeast. Most southern farmers had to ship their goods on the region's rivers. On the Ohio and Mississippi rivers, flatboats and steamboats carried cotton and other products to port. Eventually, hundreds of steamboats traveled up and down the mighty Mississippi River each day.

THE IMPACT TODAY

The Port of New Orleans remains a major seaport. It handles about 85 million tons of cargo annually.

READING CHECK Identifying Cause and Effect
What effect did the cotton boom have on the slave trade within the United States?

Eli Whitney's cotton gin began the cotton boom. Soon, the Cotton Kingdom stretched across the South. For the cotton planters to succeed, they had to get their cotton to market.

Enslaved African Americans did most of the planting, harvesting, and processing of cotton.

Cotton was shipped on river steamboats to major ports such as Charleston.

From southern ports, sailing ships carried the cotton to distant textile mills.

Other Crops and Industries

Some leaders worried that the South was depending too much on cotton. They wanted southerners to try a variety of cash crops and investments.

ACADEMIC VOCABULARY

primary
main, most important

Food and Cash Crops

One such crop was corn, the **primary** southern food crop. By the late 1830s the top three corn-growing states in the nation were all in the South. The South's other successful food crops included rice, sweet potatoes, wheat, and sugarcane.

Production of tobacco, the South's first major cash crop, was very time consuming because tobacco leaves had to be cured, or dried, before they could be shipped to market. In 1839 a slave discovered a way to improve the drying process by using heat from burning charcoal. This new, faster curing process increased tobacco production.

Partly as a result of the cotton boom, hemp and flax also became major cash crops. Their fibers were used to make rope and sackcloth. Farmers used the rope and sackcloth to bundle cotton into bales.

Industry

Many of the first factories in the South were built to serve farmers' needs by processing crops such as sugarcane. In 1803 the nation's first steam-powered sawmill was built in Donaldsonville, Louisiana. This new technology enabled lumber companies to cut, sort, and clean wood quickly.

By the 1840s, entrepreneurs in Georgia began investing in cotton mills. In 1840, there were 14 cotton mills; by the mid-1850s, there were more than 50. A few mill owners followed the model established by Francis Cabot Lowell. However, most built small-scale factories on the falls of a river for waterpower. A few steam-powered mills were built in towns without enough waterpower.

Southerners such as Hinton Rowan Helper encouraged industrial growth in the South.

"We should . . . keep pace with the progress of the age. We must expand our energies, and acquire habits of enterprise and industry; we should rouse ourselves from the couch of lassitude [laziness] and inure [set] our minds to thought and our bodies to action."

— Hinton Rowan Helper, *The Impending Crisis of the South: How to Meet It*

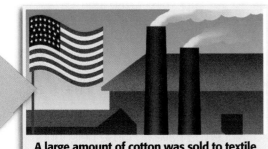

A large amount of cotton was sold to textile mills in the northeastern United States.

Textile mills in Great Britain were the largest foreign buyers of southern cotton.

ANALYSIS SKILL **DRAWING CONCLUSIONS**

Why do you think cotton was so important to the South's economy?

Joseph R. Anderson followed Helper's advice. In 1848 Anderson became the owner of the **Tredegar Iron Works** in Richmond, Virginia—one of the most productive iron works in the nation. It was the only factory to produce bridge materials, cannons, steam engines, and other products.

Industry, however, remained a small part of the southern economy. Southern industry faced stiff competition from the North and from England, both of which could produce many goods more cheaply. And as long as agricultural profits remained high, southern investors preferred to invest in land.

READING CHECK **Making Inferences** Why were there fewer industries in the South?

SUMMARY AND PREVIEW You have read about how southern farmers worked to improve farming methods. In the next section you will read about the structure of southern society.

FOCUS ON READING

What kind of Web site would you look for to learn more about the Tredegar Iron Works?

go.hrw.com
Online Quiz
KEYWORD: SF7 HP13

Section 1 Assessment

Reviewing Ideas, Terms, and People

1. a. Describe How did the **cotton gin** make processing cotton easier?
b. Draw Conclusions Why had slavery been on the decline before the invention of the cotton gin? How did slavery change as a result of the cotton gin?
c. Predict How might the rise of cotton production and slavery affect Southern society?
2. a. Identify What areas of the United States made up the **cotton belt**?
b. Evaluate Do you think the South should have paid more attention to its industrial growth? Why?
3. a. Describe What other crops and industries were encouraged in the South?
b. Make Inferences Why were some southern leaders worried about the South's reliance on cotton?

Critical Thinking

4. Identifying Cause and Effect Review your notes on the causes of the cotton boom. Then add to your graphic organizer by identifying the effects of the cotton boom on the South.

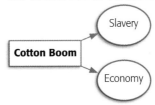

FOCUS ON WRITING

5. Noting Life on the Cotton Farm In your notebook, note how Whitney's gin changed life on the farm. Also note other details about cotton farming you could include in your sketch.

Southern Society

SECTION 2

What You Will Learn...

Main Ideas

1. Southern society and culture consisted of four main groups.
2. Free African Americans in the South faced a great deal of discrimination.

The Big Idea

Southern society centered around agriculture.

Key Term

yeomen, *p. 422*

TAKING NOTES As you read, take notes on the different segments of southern society. Record the information you find in a graphic organizer like the one below.

Group	Life
Planters	
Yeomen	
Poor Whites	
Free African Americans	

 8.1.26

If YOU were there...

Your family owns a small farm in Georgia in the 1840s. Sometimes you work in the fields, but more often you tend the vegetable garden and peach orchard. Since you have no close neighbors, you look forward to Sundays. Going to church gives you a chance to socialize with other young people. Sometimes you wonder what it would be like to live in a city like Savannah.

How would life be different if you left the farm for the city?

BUILDING BACKGROUND Although the South had some industry, agriculture was the heart of the southern economy. Cotton was king. As a result, wealthy plantation families were the most prominent social class in southern society. Small farmers, however, made up the largest part of the population.

Southern Society and Culture

Popular fiction often made it seem that all white southerners had many slaves and lived on large plantations. Many fiction writers wrote about wealthy southern families who had frequent, grand parties. The ideal image of the Antebellum (before the war) South included hospitality and well-treated slaves on beautiful plantations that almost ran themselves.

This romantic view was far from the reality. During the first half of the 1800s, only about one-third of white southern families had slaves. Fewer families had plantations. Despite their small numbers, these planters had a powerful influence over the South. Many served as political leaders. They led a society made up of many different kinds of people, including yeomen farmers, poor whites, slaves, and free African Americans. Each of these segments of society contributed to the economic success of the South.

Planters

As the wealthiest members of southern society, planters also greatly influenced the economy. Some showed off their wealth by living in beautiful mansions. Many others chose to live more simply. A visitor described wealthy planter Alexander Stephens's estate as "an old wooden house" surrounded by weeds. Some planters saved all of their money to buy more land and slaves.

Male planters were primarily concerned with raising crops and supervising slave laborers. They left the running of the plantation household to their wives. The planter's wife oversaw the raising of the children and supervised the work of all slaves within the household. Slave women typically cooked, cleaned, and helped care for the planter's children. Wives also took on the important social duties of the family. For example, many southern leaders discussed political issues at the dances and dinners hosted by their wives.

Planters often arranged their children's marriages based on business interests. Lucy Breckinridge, the daughter of a wealthy Virginia planter, was married by arrangement in 1865. Three years earlier, she had described in her journal how she dreaded the very thought of marriage. "A woman's life after she is married, unless there is an immense amount of love, is nothing but suffering and hard work." How Breckinridge's life in her own arranged marriage would have turned out cannot be known. She died of typhoid fever just months after her wedding.

History Close-up

A Southern Plantation

A typical plantation had fields as well as many buildings where different work was done. This picture shows some of the more important buildings that were a part of the plantation system.

Slave Cabins
Slaves lived crowded together in small cabins. Cabins are crude, wooden structures with dirt floors.

Fields

Barn

Warehouse

Cotton-Ginning Shed
This sizable plantation had several large cotton gins. The vital machines were housed in a shed to protect them from the weather.

Smokehouse

Overseer's House

Plantation House
The planter and his family lived in the plantation house. The planter's wife was in charge of running the household.

Stable

Fields

ANALYSIS SKILL **ANALYZING VISUALS**

How can you tell that the owner of this plantation was wealthy?

Free African Americans in the South

In 1860 about 1 out of 50 African Americans in the South was free. Many worked in skilled trades, like this barber in Richmond, Virginia. In Charleston, South Carolina, a system of badges was set up to distinguish between free African Americans and slaves.

How would the work of the free African American in this picture be different from that of slaves in the South?

Yeomen and Poor Whites

Most white southerners were **yeomen**, owners of small farms. Yeomen owned few slaves or none at all. The typical farm averaged 100 acres. Yeomen took great pride in their work. In 1849 a young Georgia man wrote, "I desire above all things to be a 'Farmer.' It is the most honest, upright, and sure way of securing all the comforts of life."

Yeoman families, including women and children, typically worked long days at a variety of tasks. Some yeomen held a few slaves but worked alongside them.

The poorest of white southerners lived on land that could not grow cash crops. They survived by hunting, fishing, raising small gardens, and doing odd jobs for money.

Religion and Society

Most white southerners shared similar religious beliefs. Because of the long distances between farms, families often saw their neighbors only at church events, such as revivals or socials. Rural women often played volunteer roles in their churches. Wealthy white southerners thought that their religion justified their position in society and the institution of slavery. They argued that God created some people, like themselves, to rule others. This belief opposed many northern Christians' belief that God was against slavery.

Urban Life

Many of the largest and most important cities in the South were strung along the Atlantic coast and had begun as shipping centers. Although fewer in number, the southern cities were similar to northern cities. City governments built public water systems and provided well-maintained streets. Public education was available in a few places. Wealthy residents occasionally gave large sums of money to charities, such as orphanages and public libraries. Southern urban leaders wanted their cities to appear as modern as possible.

As on plantations, slaves did much of the work in southern cities. Slaves worked as domestic servants, in mills, in shipyards, and at skilled jobs. Many business leaders held slaves or hired them from nearby plantations.

READING CHECK **Summarizing** What different groups made up southern society?

Free African Americans and Discrimination

Although the vast majority of African Americans in the South were enslaved, more than 250,000 free African Americans lived in the region by 1860. Some were descendants of slaves who were freed after the American Revolution. Others were descendants of refugees from Toussaint L'Ouverture's Haitian Revolution in the late 1790s. Still others were former slaves who had run away, been freed by their slaveholder, or earned enough money to buy their freedom.

Free African Americans lived in both rural and urban areas. Most lived in the countryside and worked as paid laborers on plantations or farms. Free African Americans in cities often worked a variety of jobs, mostly as skilled artisans. Some, like barber William Johnson of Natchez, Mississippi, became quite successful in their businesses. Frequently, free African Americans, especially those in the cities, formed social and economic ties with one another. Churches often served as the center of their social lives.

Free African Americans faced constant discrimination from white southerners. Many governments passed laws limiting the rights of free African Americans. Most free African Americans could not vote, travel freely, or hold certain jobs. In some places, free African Americans had to have a white person represent them in any business transaction. In others, laws restricted where they were allowed to live or conduct business.

Many white southerners argued that free African Americans did not have the ability to take care of themselves, and they used this belief to justify the institution of slavery. "The status of slavery is the only one for which the African is adapted," wrote one white Mississippian. To many white southerners, the very existence of free African Americans threatened the institution of slavery.

READING CHECK **Finding Main Ideas** What challenges did free African Americans face in the South?

SUMMARY AND PREVIEW Southern society was led by rich planters but included groups of small farmers, slaves, and free African Americans as well. These groups each had their own culture. In the next section you will read about life under slavery.

Section 2 Assessment

go.hrw.com
Online Quiz
KEYWORD: SF7 HP13

Reviewing Ideas, Terms, and People

1. **a. Identify** What was the largest social group in the South? How did its members make a living?
   b. Compare In what ways were southern cities similar to northern cities?
   c. Elaborate Which southern social class do you think had the most difficult life? Why?
2. **a. Describe** What jobs were available to free African Americans in the South? Why were these jobs the only ones available?
   b. Analyze Why did many white southerners fear free African Americans?
   c. Elaborate Why do you think that discrimination against free African Americans was harsher in the South than in the North?

Critical Thinking

3. **Comparing and Contrasting** Review your notes on the different kinds of people who lived in the South. Then use a graphic organizer like the one below to identify the similarities and differences of the lives of planters, yeomen, and free African Americans.

   Similarities

   Planters Free African Americans Yeomen

FOCUS ON WRITING

4. **Describing the Life of Cotton Farmers** In your notebook, describe the different roles played by male planters and their wives. What challenges would female planters have faced? When would the planters have had a chance to socialize?

The Slave System

What You Will Learn...

Main Ideas

1. Slaves worked at a variety of jobs on plantations.
2. Life under slavery was difficult and dehumanizing.
3. Slave culture centered around family, community, and religion.
4. Slave uprisings led to stricter slave codes in many states.

The Big Idea

The slave system in the South produced harsh living conditions and occasional rebellions.

Key Terms and People

folktales, *p. 427*
spirituals, *p. 427*
Nat Turner's Rebellion, *p. 428*
Nat Turner, *p. 428*

TAKING NOTES As you read, take notes on the slavery system in a graphic organizer like the one shown below.

	Life as an Enslaved Person
Work	
Life	
Culture	

8.1.10, 8.1.16, 8.1.18, 8.1.20, 8.1.28, 8.1.29, 8.1.31, 8.2.9, 8.3.9, 8.4.3, 8.4.5, 8.4.6, 8.4.9

If **YOU** were there...

You are a reporter for a newspaper in Philadelphia in the 1850s. You are writing a series of articles about the slave system in the South. To get background for your stories, you are planning to interview some former slaves who now live in Philadelphia. Some have bought their freedom, while others have successfully escaped from slavery.

What questions will you ask in your interviews?

BUILDING BACKGROUND While most white southern families were not slaveholders, the southern economy depended on the work of slaves. This was true not only on large plantations but also on smaller farms and in the cities. Few chances existed for enslaved African Americans to escape their hard lives.

Slaves and Work

Most enslaved African Americans lived in rural areas where they worked on farms and plantations. Enslaved people on small farms usually did a variety of jobs. On large plantations, most slaves were assigned to specific jobs, and most worked in the fields. Most slaveholders demanded that slaves work as much as possible. Supervisors known as drivers, who were sometimes slaves themselves, made sure that slaves followed orders and carried out punishments.

Working in the Field

Most plantation owners used the gang-labor system. In this system, all field hands worked on the same task at the same time. They usually worked from sunup to sundown. Former slave Harry McMillan had worked on a plantation in South Carolina. He recalled that the field hands usually did not even get a break to eat lunch. "You had to get your victuals [food] standing at your hoe," he remembered.

Men, women, and even children older than about 10 usually did the same tasks. Sickness and poor weather rarely stopped the work. "The times I hated most was picking cotton when the frost was on the bolls [seed pods]," recalled former Louisiana slave Mary Reynolds. "My hands git sore and crack open and bleed."

Working in the Planter's Home

Some slaves worked as butlers, cooks, or nurses in the planter's home. These slaves often had better food, clothing, and shelter than field hands did, but they often worked longer hours. They had to serve the planter's family 24 hours a day.

Working at Skilled Jobs

On larger plantations, some enslaved African Americans worked at skilled jobs, such as blacksmithing or carpentry. Sometimes planters let these slaves sell their services to other people. Often planters collected a portion of what was earned but allowed slaves to keep the rest. In this way, some skilled slaves earned enough money to buy their freedom from their slaveholders. For example, William Ellison earned his freedom in South Carolina by working for wages as a cotton gin maker. For years, he worked late at night and on Sundays. He bought his freedom with the money he earned. Eventually, he was also able to buy the freedom of his wife and daughter.

READING CHECK **Summarizing** What were some types of work done by enslaved people on plantations?

Life Under Slavery

Generally, slaveholders viewed slaves as property, not as people. Slaveholders bought and sold slaves to make a profit. The most common method of sale was at an auction. The auction itself determined whether families would be kept together or separated. Sometimes a buyer wanted a slave to fill a specific job, such as heavy laborer, carpenter, or blacksmith. The buyer might be willing to pay for the slave who could do the work, but not for that slave's family. Families would then be separated with little hope of ever getting back together.

Slave traders sometimes even kidnapped free African Americans and then sold them into slavery. For example, Solomon Northup, a free African American, was kidnapped in Washington, D.C. He spent 12 years as a slave until he finally proved his identity and gained his release.

Living Conditions

Enslaved people often endured poor living conditions. Planters housed them in dirt-floor cabins with few furnishings and often leaky roofs. The clothing given to them was usually simple and made of cheap, coarse fabric. Some slaves tried to brighten up their

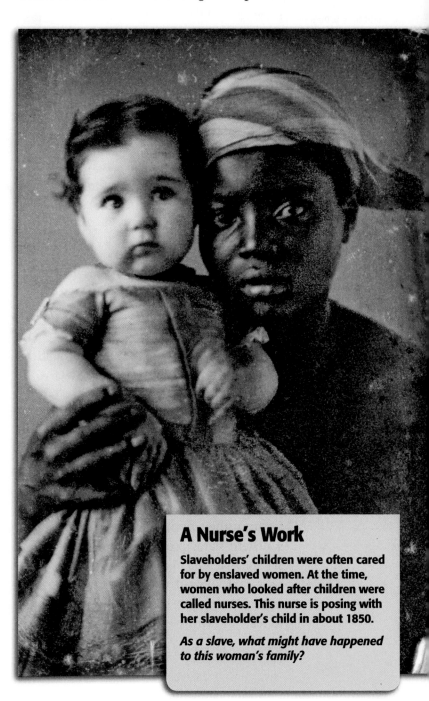

A Nurse's Work

Slaveholders' children were often cared for by enslaved women. At the time, women who looked after children were called nurses. This nurse is posing with her slaveholder's child in about 1850.

As a slave, what might have happened to this woman's family?

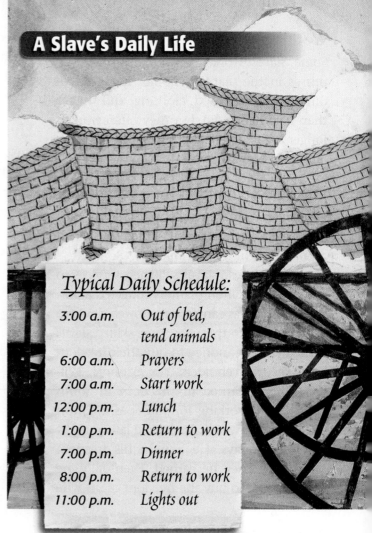

Typical Daily Schedule:

3:00 a.m.	Out of bed, tend animals
6:00 a.m.	Prayers
7:00 a.m.	Start work
12:00 p.m.	Lunch
1:00 p.m.	Return to work
7:00 p.m.	Dinner
8:00 p.m.	Return to work
11:00 p.m.	Lights out

FOCUS ON INDIANA

Although the Northwest Ordinance declared slavery illegal in Indiana and the rest of the Northwest Territory, many residents owned slaves anyway. Many early Indianans were from the southern states, and they brought the slave system with them. The territorial government tried repeatedly to have the antislavery portion of the Northwest Ordinance suspended, but the efforts failed.

clothing by sewing on designs from discarded scraps of material. In this way, they expressed their individuality and personalized the clothing assigned to them by the planters.

Likewise, many slaves did what they could to improve their small food rations. Some planters allowed slaves to keep their own gardens for vegetables, and chickens for eggs. Other slaves were able to add a little variety to their diet by fishing or picking wild berries.

Punishment and Slave Codes

Some planters offered more food or better living conditions to encourage slaves' obedience. However, most slaveholders used punishment instead. Some would punish one slave in front of others as a warning to them all. Harry McMillan recalled some of the punishments he had witnessed.

" The punishments were whipping, putting you in the stocks [wooden frames to lock people in] and making you wear irons and a chain at work. Then they had a collar to put round your neck with two horns, like cows' horns, so that you could not lie down … Sometimes they dug a hole like a well with a door on top. This they called a dungeon keeping you in it two or three weeks or a month, or sometimes till you died in there. "

—Harry McMillan, quoted in *Major Problems in the History of the American South, Volume I,* edited by Paul D. Escott and David R. Goldfield

ACADEMIC VOCABULARY

aspect   part

To further control slaves' actions, many states passed strict laws called slave codes. Some laws prohibited slaves from traveling far from their homes. Literacy laws in most southern states prohibited the education of slaves. Alabama, Virginia, and Georgia had laws that allowed the fining and whipping of anyone caught teaching enslaved people to read and write.

READING CHECK **Summarizing** How did slaveholders control slaves?

Slave Culture

Many enslaved Africans found comfort in their community and culture. They made time for social activity, even after exhausting workdays, in order to relieve the hardship of their lives.

Family and Community

Family was the most important **aspect** of slave communities, and many slaves feared separation more than they feared punishment. Josiah Henson never forgot the day that he and his family were auctioned. His mother begged the slaveholder who bought her to buy Josiah, too. The slaveholder refused, and Henson's entire family was separated. "I must have been then between five or six years old," he recalled years later. "I seem to see and hear my poor weeping mother now."

The lives of slaves revolved around the work that was required of them. For many, this meant doing the backbreaking work of harvesting and loading tons of cotton. Most slaves found hope and a short escape from their daily misery in Sunday church services. Others sought to escape permanently and ran away, hoping to reach the freedom of the North. A failed escape attempt, however, could result in a cruel whipping—or worse.

What different aspects of slavery are shown in these pictures?

Hauling the Whole Week's Pickings by William Henry Brown, The Historic New Orleans Collection

Enslaved parents kept their heritage alive by passing down family histories as well as African customs and traditions. They also told **folktales**, or stories with a moral, to teach lessons about how to survive under slavery. Folktales often included a clever animal character called a trickster. The trickster—which often represented slaves—defeated a stronger animal by outwitting it. Folktales reassured slaves that they could survive by outsmarting more powerful slaveholders.

Religion

Religion also played an important part in slave culture. By the early 1800s many slaves were Christians. They came to see themselves, like the slaves in the Old Testament, as God's chosen people, much like the Hebrew slaves in ancient Egypt who had faith that they would someday live in freedom.

Some slaves sang **spirituals**, emotional Christian songs that blended African and European music, to express their religious beliefs. For example, "The Heavenly Road" reflected slaves' belief in their equality in the eyes of God.

" Come, my brother, if you never did pray,
I hope you pray tonight;
For I really believe I am a child of God
As I walk on the heavenly road. "

—Anonymous, quoted in *Afro-American Religious History*, edited by Milton C. Sernett

Slaves blended some aspects of their traditional African religions with those of the Christianity that the slaveholders followed. They worshiped in secret, out of sight of slaveholders. Some historians have called slave religion the invisible institution.

FOCUS ON INDIANA
Much of the art, music, and writing created by white Americans during this period depicted African Americans as unequal to whites. Some white Americans, however, chose to depict African American subjects as they would any other subject. One such painter was Winslow Homer, whose painting *At the Cabin Door* is considered a rare example of a true portrait of African American life of the time.

Nat Turner's Rebellion

Slave Nat Turner led a revolt against white slaveholders in 1831. This is a map of his route and a depiction of his capture.

VIRGINIA

Nat Turner's route
House or plantation
Hiding place

0   3   6 Miles
0   3   6 Kilometers

ATLANTIC OCEAN

Captured
October 30, 1831

Second cave

First cave

Cypress Bridge

August 23, 1831
Most of the rebelling slaves are captured or killed at James Parker's plantation. Turner escapes.

August 21, 1831
Turner meets with other slaves and plans to revolt.

SOUTHAMPTON COUNTY

NORTH CAROLINA

ANALYSIS SKILL ANALYZING VISUALS

1. **Location** Where did Nat Turner's Rebellion take place?
2. **Movement** How many days did it take to capture Nat Turner?

Seeds of Rebellion

Maintaining their own religious beliefs and practices was only one way in which enslaved people resisted slaveholders' attempts to control them completely. In small ways, slaves rebelled against the system daily. Sometimes they worked slower to protest long hours in the fields. Other times they ran away for a few days to avoid an angry slaveholder. Some slaves tried to escape permanently, but most left only for short periods, often to go and visit relatives.

Gaining freedom by escaping to the North was hard. If discovered, slaves were captured and sent back to their slaveholders, where they faced certain punishment or death. However, thousands of enslaved people succeeded in escaping.

READING CHECK Summarizing How did slaves' religious beliefs affect their attitudes toward slavery?

Slave Uprisings

Although violent slave revolts were relatively rare, white southerners lived in fear of them. Two planned rebellions were stopped before they began. Gabriel Prosser planned a rebellion near Richmond, Virginia, in 1800. Denmark Vesey planned one in Charleston, South Carolina, in 1822. Local authorities executed most of those involved in planning these rebellions. Though Vesey was executed as the leader of the Charleston conspiracy, several accounts written after his death by anti-slavery writers claimed he was a hero.

The most violent slave revolt in the country occurred in 1831 and is known as **Nat Turner's Rebellion**. **Nat Turner**, a slave from Southampton County, Virginia, believed that God had told him to end slavery. On an August night in 1831, Turner led a group of slaves in a plan to kill all of the slaveholders and their families in the county. First, they attacked the family that held Turner as a slave. Soon they had killed about 60 white people in the community.

More than 100 innocent slaves who were not part of Turner's group were killed in an attempt to stop the rebellion. Turner himself led authorities on a chase around the country-side for six weeks. He hid in caves and in the woods before he was caught and brought to trial. Before his trial, Turner made a confession. He expressed his belief that the revolt was justified and worth his death: "I am willing to suffer the fate that awaits me." Turner was executed on November 11, 1831. After the rebellion, many states strengthened their slave codes. The new codes placed stricter control on enslaved people. Despite resistance, slavery continued to spread.

READING CHECK Finding Main Ideas
What was Nat Turner's Rebellion, and what happened as a result?

SUMMARY AND PREVIEW Several groups of African Americans attempted to end slavery by rebellion. All of the attempts failed. In the next chapter you will read about efforts to reform American society.

Primary Source

LETTER
Nat Turner's Rebellion

In 1831 a white southerner who had escaped the rebellion wrote a letter describing the mood of the area where Nat Turner had killed slaveholders.

> The author believes no one in the county has been through a worse event.

❝The oldest inhabitants of our county have never experienced such a distress-ing [terrible] time, as we have had since Sunday night last. The [slaves], about fifteen miles from this place, have massa-cred from 50 to 75 women and children, and some 8 or 10 men. Every house, room and corner in this place is full of women and children, driven from home, who had to take to the woods, until they could get to this place. We are worn out with fatigue [tiredness].**❞**

> The author says that many people went into hiding when the rebellion began.

—*Richmond Enquirer*, quoted in
The Southampton Slave Revolt of 1831
by Henry I. Tragle

ANALYSIS SKILL **ANALYZING PRIMARY SOURCES**
What emotions do you think the author of this letter was feeling?

Section 3 Assessment

go.hrw.com
Online Quiz
KEYWORD: SF7 HP13

Reviewing Ideas, Terms, and People
1. **a. Identify** What different types of work were done by slaves on plantations?
   b. Elaborate Do you think that skilled slaves had advantages over other slaves? Why or why not?
2. **a. Describe** What were living conditions like for most slaves?
   b. Summarize In what different ways did slave-holders encourage obedience from their slaves?
3. **a. Recall** What was the purpose of African American **folktales**?
   b. Explain How did slaves try to maintain a sense of community?
4. **a. Describe** What was the outcome of **Nat Turner's Rebellion**?
   b. Elaborate What do you think were some rea-sons why slaves rebelled?

Critical Thinking
5. **Evaluating** Review your notes on the slavery system. Then use a graphic organizer like the one shown below to identify the two most important reasons enslaved people challenged the system as well as how they did so.

Reasons for Challenging Slavery	Ways of Challenging Slavery

FOCUS ON WRITING

6. **Describing the Life of Slaves** Add notes about the life of slaves to your notebook. What would it have been like to be a slave? How would it have felt to have been separated from your family?

Social Studies Skills

Analysis | Critical Thinking | Civic Participation | Study

Interpreting Graphs

Define the Skill

Graphs are drawings that classify and display data in a clear, visual format. There are three basic types of graphs. *Line graphs* and *bar graphs* plot changes in quantities over time. Bar graphs are also used to compare quantities within a category at a particular time. *Circle graphs,* also called *pie graphs,* have a similar use. The circle represents the whole of something, and the slices show what proportion of the whole is made by each part.

Being able to interpret graphs accurately lets you see and understand relationships more easily than in tables or in written explanations. This is especially true if the information is detailed or the relationships are complicated.

Learn the Skill

The following guidelines will help you interpret data that is presented as a graph.

1. Read the title to identify the subject and purpose of the graph. Note the kind of graph, remembering what each type is designed to indicate. Also note how the graph's subject relates to any printed material that accompanies it.

2. Study the graph's parts. Place close attention to the labels that define each axis. Note the units of measure. Identify the categories used. If there are different colors on bars or lines in the graph, determine what those differences mean.

3. Analyze the data in the graph. Note any increases or decreases in quantities. Look for trends, changes, and other relationships in the data.

4. Apply the information in the graph. Use the results of your analysis to draw conclusions. Ask yourself what generalizations can be made about the trends, changes, or relationships shown in the graph.

Practice the Skill

The graph below is a double-line graph. It shows both changes and relationships over time. This type of graph allows you to see how changes in one thing compare with changes in something else. Apply the guidelines to interpret the graph and answer the questions that follow.

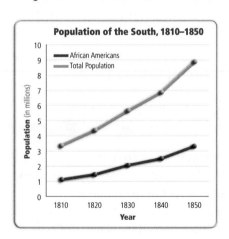

Population of the South, 1810–1850

1. What is shown on each axis of this graph? What are the units of measure on each axis?

2. What do each of the lines represent?

3. What was the total population of the South in 1810? in 1850? By how much did the African American population grow during that period?

4. Was the white population or the African American population growing faster? Explain how you know.

HOLT
History's Impact
▶ video series
Review the video to answer the closing question:
What could Silicon Valley learn from the economic and industrial past (and present) of the South?

Visual Summary

QUICK FACTS

Use the visual summary below to help you review the main ideas of the chapter.

Southern Society Planters were at the top of southern society.

Cotton Economy In addition to cotton, southern farmers grew other cash crops and staple crops.

Slavery The strength of the southern economy depended on slave labor.

Reviewing Vocabulary, Terms, and People

Match the definition on the left with the correct term on the right.

1. A region of cotton-producing areas that stretched from South Carolina to Texas

2. Emotional songs that mixed African and European music and expressed religious beliefs

3. Owners of small farms who made up the largest social class in the South

4. Crop brokers who often managed the cotton trade in the South

5. Wealthy farmers and plantation owners

a. cotton belt

b. factors

c. planters

d. spirituals

e. yeomen

Comprehension and Critical Thinking

SECTION 1 *(Pages 414–419)*

6. **a. Describe** How did the cotton gin lead to a cotton boom in the South?

b. Analyze What were the positive and negative results of the cotton boom?

c. Evaluate Do you think that the South suffered as a result of its reliance on cotton? Why or why not?

SECTION 2 *(Pages 420–423)*

7. **a. Describe** What three groups made up white southern society?

b. Compare and Contrast In what ways were the lives of free African Americans and white southerners similar and different?

c. Predict What might have been the attitude of yeomen and poor white southerners toward slavery? Why?

SECTION 3 *(Pages 424–429)*

8. a. Identify What are some small ways in which slaves tried to challenge the slave system?

b. Make Inferences How did religion and family help slaves cope with their lives?

c. Predict What could be some possible results of stronger strengthening of slave codes in the South?

Reading Skills

Online Research *Use the Reading Skills taught in this chapter to answer the question below.*

9. Which of the following would be the best Web site to find information about life in the South before the Civil War?

a. a Civil War historian's homepage

b. a collection of autobiographies written by slaves

c. a site with information about how to grow cotton

d. a collection of biographies of inventors

Using the Internet

go.hrw.com
KEYWORD: SF7 CH13

10. Activity: Writing Diary Entries Enslaved African Americans faced harsh working and living conditions. Many tried to escape the slave system. Enter the activity keyword and research the attempts by enslaved African Americans to reach the North and the people who assisted them. Imagine you were trying to help slaves travel to freedom. Write four entries into a diary. In each entry, describe your experiences. Include thumbnail maps to trace their trip.

Reviewing Themes

11. Society and Culture How were the different social classes in the South affected by the cotton boom?

12. Economics How did the cotton boom affect the economy of the South?

Social Studies Skills

Interpreting Graphs *Use the Social Studies Skills taught in this chapter to answer the questions about the graph below.*

13. What span of time saw the largest increase in cotton production?

a. 1800 to 1820   **c.** 1840 to 1860

b. 1820 to 1840   **d.** after 1860

14. About what year did cotton production reach 1.2 million bales per year?

a. 1800   **c.** 1840

b. 1820   **d.** 1860

FOCUS ON WRITING

15. Writing Your Biographical Sketch Look over your notes about life on a cotton farm. Then choose an imaginary person to write about. Think about what life would have been like for this person. What might he or she have looked like? How might he or she have spoken? What might a typical day have been like? Once you have answered these questions, write two paragraphs about a day in the life of this person.

Standardized Test Practice

8.1.10, 8.3.11, 8.4.6, 8.4.9

DIRECTIONS: Read each question and write the letter of the best response.

1

U.S. Cotton Production, 1795–1805

The *main* reason for the changes shown in the graph was

A the invention and use of the cotton gin.

B a decline in the number of slaves.

C the end of the international slave trade.

D a switch from food crops to cash crops.

2 Which of the following helped enslaved African Americans to endure and survive slavery?

A their work

B spirituals

C slave codes

D rebellions

3 Because some southerners feared farmers had become too reliant on cotton, they encouraged farmers to

A stop using the cotton gin.

B try growing a variety of cash crops.

C demand higher tariffs.

D introduce cotton and slavery to the West.

4 Which statement accurately describes southern society in the mid-1800s?

A Very few white southerners owned slaves.

B Few white southerners owned the land they farmed.

C Many African Americans in the South owned land.

D Most white southerners were small farmers.

5 Free African Americans in the South in the early and mid-1800s

A had the same rights and freedoms as white southerners.

B had few rights and freedoms.

C usually had escaped from slavery.

D could travel freely in their home states.

6 Examine the following passage from a northern woman's journal of her stay in Georgia and then use it to answer the question below.

> *"On my return from the river I had a long and painful talk with Mr. Butler on the subject of the whipping of Teresa [a slave worn out from childbearing and field work, who asked the author to try to get her workload reduced]. Those discussions are terrible. They throw me into great distress [worry] for the slaves, whose position is completely hopeless; for myself, whose efforts on their behalf sometimes seem to me worse than useless; and for Mr. Butler, whose part in this horrible system fills me by turns with anger and pity."*
>
> –Frances Anne Kemble, adapted from *Journal of a Residence on a Georgian Plantation in 1838–1839*

Document-Based Question What might be the differences between Kemble and Butler on the question of slavery?

New Movements in America

IN Indiana Standards

Social Studies Standards

8.1.18 analyze different interests and points of view of individuals and groups involved in the abolitionist, feminist, and social reform movements and in sectional conflicts.

8.1.19 Explain the influence of early individual social reformers and movements.

8.1.24 Identify the influence of individuals on poltical and social events and movements, such as the abolition movement, the Dred Scott case, women's rights, and Native American Indian removal.

8.1.31 Obtain historical data from a variety of sources to compare and contrast examples of art, music, and literature during the nineteenth century and explain how these reflect American culture during this time period.

8.3.6 Identify the agricultural regions of the United States and be able to give reasons for the type of land use and subsequent land development during different historical periods.

> go.hrw.com
> **Indiana**
> KEYWORD: SF10 IN

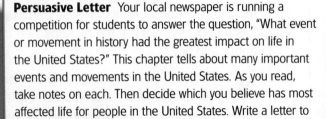

FOCUS ON WRITING

Persuasive Letter Your local newspaper is running a competition for students to answer the question, "What event or movement in history had the greatest impact on life in the United States?" This chapter tells about many important events and movements in the United States. As you read, take notes on each. Then decide which you believe has most affected life for people in the United States. Write a letter to the newspaper arguing your position.

UNITED STATES

1817
Thomas Gallaudet founds a school for people who have hearing impairments.

1820

WORLD

1824
British laws making trade unions illegal are repealed.

What You Will Learn...

In this chapter you will learn about dramatic changes in the United States in the early to mid-1800s. Ships filled with goods sailed back and forth across the Atlantic Ocean between Europe and the United States, as this painting of a busy port city shows. Many of these ships also brought people. The United States experienced a dramatic increase in immigration during this time period, particularly from Europe. Irish immigrants, forced from their homes by the potato famine, moved to the United States and built thriving communities. The photograph above shows a modern parade on Saint Patrick's Day, an Irish celebration day.

1831 William Lloyd Garrison begins publishing the abolitionist newspaper the *Liberator.*

1842 The University of Notre Dame is founded in South Bend.

1848 A major meeting for women's rights—the Seneca Falls Convention—is held in New York.

1850 Nathaniel Hawthorne publishes *The Scarlet Letter.*

1830

1840

1850

1829 French educator Louis Braille creates a writing system of raised dots for people who are blind.

1845 A potato famine in Ireland increases Irish immigration to the United States.

1848 Revolutionaries attempt to unify German-speaking peoples in central Europe.

Reading Social Studies

by Kylene Beers

Economics Geography Politics Society and Culture Science and Technology

Focus on Themes The mid-1800s was a time of change in America. **Society and culture** changed for several reasons: thousands of immigrants arrived in America; women began to work hard for equal rights; and the North and South debated more and more over the slavery issue. Religious beliefs helped shape people's views toward abolition—the move to end slavery—and women's suffrage—the move to give women the right to vote. This chapter discusses these issues.

Information and Propaganda

Focus on Reading Where do you get information about historical events and people? One source is this textbook and others like it. You can expect the authors of your textbook to do their best to present the facts objectively and fairly. But some sources of historical information may have a totally different purpose in mind. For example, advertisements in political campaigns may contain information, but their main purpose is to persuade people to act or think in a certain way.

Recognizing Propaganda Techniques Propaganda is created to change people's opinions or get them to act in a certain way. Learn to recognize propaganda techniques, and you will be able to separate propaganda from the facts.

"People who don't support public education are greedy monsters who don't care about children!" → **Name Calling** Using loaded words, words that create strong positive or negative emotions, to make someone else's ideas seem inappropriate or wrong

"People all around the country are opening free public schools. It's obviously the right thing to do." → **Bandwagon** Encouraging people to do something because "everyone else is doing it"

"If we provide free education for all children, everyone will be able to get jobs. Poverty and unemployment will disappear." → **Oversimplification** Making a complex situation seem simple, a complex problem seem easy to solve

You Try It!

The flyer below was published in 1837. Read it and then answer the questions that follow.

Flyer from 1837

OUTRAGE.

Fellow Citizens, AN **ABOLITIONIST,** of the most revolting character is among you, exciting the feelings of the North against the South. A seditious Lecture is to be delivered **THIS EVENING,** at 7 o'clock, at the Presbyterian Church in Cannon-street. You are requested to attend and unite in putting down and silencing by peaceable means this tool of evil and fanaticism. Let the rights of the States guaranteed by the Constitution be protected. **Feb. 27, 1837.** *The Union forever!*

After studying the flyer, answer the following questions.

1. What is the purpose of this flyer?

2. Who do you think distributed this flyer?

3. Do you think this flyer is an example of propaganda? Why or why not? If you think it is propaganda, what kind is it?

4. If you were the subject of this flyer, how would you feel? How might you respond to it?

As you read **Chapter 14,** look carefully at all the primary sources. Do any of them include examples of propaganda?

Immigrants and Urban Challenges

What You Will Learn...

Main Ideas

1. Millions of immigrants, mostly German and Irish, arrived in the United States despite anti-immigrant movements.
2. Industrialization led to the growth of cities.
3. American cities experienced urban problems due to rapid growth.

The Big Idea

The population of the United States grew rapidly in the early 1800s with the arrival of millions of immigrants.

Key Terms

nativists, *p. 440*
Know-Nothing Party, *p. 440*
middle class, *p. 440*
tenements, *p. 442*

TAKING NOTES As you read, take notes on the causes of immigration and urban growth. Record your notes in a graphic organizer like the one shown below.

Immigration

Urban Growth

IN 8.1.10, 8.1.16, 8.1.25, 8.3.11

If **YOU** were there...

It is 1850, and you are a German immigrant standing on the deck of a steamboat, crossing Lake Erie. Other immigrants are on board, but they are strangers to you. Soon, you will arrive at your new home in Cleveland, Ohio. You've been told that other Germans have settled there. You hope to find friends and work as a baker. Right now, America seems very big and very strange.

What would you expect from your new life in America?

BUILDING BACKGROUND The revolutions in industry, transportation, and technology were not the only major changes in the United States in the mid-1800s. Millions of immigrants, mostly from Europe, swelled the population. Some settled in the rich farmland of the Midwest, while others moved to cities.

Millions of Immigrants Arrive

In the mid-1800s, large numbers of immigrants crossed the Atlantic Ocean to begin new lives in the United States. More than 4 million of them settled in the United States between 1840 and 1860, most from Europe. More than 3 million of these immigrants arrived from Ireland and Germany. Many of them were fleeing economic or political troubles in their native countries.

Fleeing the Irish Potato Famine

Most immigrants from the British Isles during that period were Irish. In the mid-1840s, potato blight, a disease that causes rot in potatoes, left many families in Ireland with little food. More than a million Irish people died of starvation and disease. Even more fled to the United States.

Most Irish immigrants were very poor. Many settled in cities in Massachusetts, New Jersey, New York, and Pennsylvania. They worked at unskilled jobs in the cities or on building canals and

Push-Pull Factors of Immigration

QUICK FACTS

Pull Factors
- Jobs
- Greater freedom and equality
- Abundant land

Push Factors
- Starvation
- Poverty
- Lack of political freedom

Starvation and poverty pushed many Irish families such as this one from their homes, while economic opportunities pulled them toward the United States.

ANALYSIS SKILL   ANALYZING VISUALS

How was freedom a push factor and a pull factor?

---

railroads. Irish women often worked as domestic servants for wealthy families, laboring 16 or more hours per day. In 1849 a Boston health committee reported that low wages forced most Irish immigrants to live in poor housing.

Still, many immigrants enjoyed a new feeling of equality. Patrick Dunny wrote home to his family about this situation.

"People that cuts a great dash [style] at home ... think it strange [in the United States] for the humble class of people to get as much respect as themselves."

—Patrick Dunny, quoted in *Who Built America?* by Bruce Levine et al.

A Failed German Revolution

Many Germans also came to the United States during this time. In 1848 some Germans had staged a revolution against harsh rule. Some educated Germans fled to the United States to escape persecution caused by their political activities. Most German immigrants, however, were working class, and they came for economic reasons. The United States seemed to offer both greater economic opportunity and more freedom from government control. While most Irish immigrants were Catholics, German immigrant groups included Catholics, Jews, and Protestants.

German immigrants were more likely than the Irish to become farmers and live in rural areas. They moved to midwestern states where more land was available. Unlike the Irish, a high percentage of German immigrants arrived in the United States with money. Despite their funds and skills, German immigrants often were forced to take low-paying jobs. Many German immigrants worked as tailors, seamstresses, bricklayers,

THE IMPACT TODAY

Many immigrants still come to the United States today. More than 13 million entered the United States between 1990 and 2000.

servants, clerks, cabinetmakers, bakers, and food merchants.

Anti-Immigration Movements

Industrialization and the waves of people from Europe greatly changed the American labor force. While many immigrants went to the Midwest to get farmland, other immigrants filled the need for cheap labor in towns and cities. Industrial jobs in the Northeast attracted many people.

Yet a great deal of native-born Americans feared losing their jobs to immigrants who might work for lower wages. Some felt **implicitly** threatened by the new immigrants' cultures and religions. For example, before Catholic immigrants arrived, most Americans were Protestants. Conflicts between Catholics and Protestants in Europe caused American Protestants to mistrust Catholic immigrants. Those Americans and others who opposed immigration were called **nativists**.

In the 1840s and 1850s some nativists became politically active. An 1844 election flyer gave Americans this warning.

"Look at the . . . thieves and vagabonds [tramps] roaming our streets . . . monopolizing [taking] the business which properly belongs to our own native and true-born citizens."

—Election flyer, quoted in *Who Built America?* by Bruce Levine et al.

In 1849 nativists founded a political organization, the **Know-Nothing Party**, that supported measures making it difficult for foreigners to become citizens or hold office. Its members wanted to keep Catholics and immigrants out of public office. They also wanted to require immigrants to live in the United States for 21 years before becoming citizens. Know-Nothing politicians had some success getting elected during the 1850s. Later, disagreements over the issue of slavery caused the party to fall apart.

READING CHECK **Understanding Cause and Effect** Why did the Know-Nothing Party try to limit the rights of immigrants?

ACADEMIC VOCABULARY

implicit
understood though not clearly put into words

FOCUS ON READING

Look carefully at the quotation to the right from an election flyer. Does it include any examples of propaganda?

Rapid Growth of Cities

The Industrial Revolution led to the creation of many new jobs in American cities. These city jobs drew immigrants from many nations as well as migrants from rural parts of the United States. The Transportation Revolution helped connect cities and made it easier for people to move to them. As a result of these two trends, American cities grew rapidly during the mid-1800s. Cities in the northeastern and Middle Atlantic states grew the most. By the mid-1800s, three-quarters of the country's manufacturing jobs were in these areas.

The rise of industry and the growth of cities changed American life. Those who owned their own businesses or worked in skilled jobs benefited most from those changes. The families of these merchants, manufacturers, professionals, and master craftspeople made up a growing social class. This new **middle class** was a social and economic level between the wealthy and the poor. Those in the new middle class built large, dignified homes that demonstrated their place in society.

In the growing cities, people found entertainment and an enriched cultural life. Many enjoyed visiting places such as libraries and clubs, or attending concerts or lectures. In the mid-1800s people also attended urban theaters. Favorite pastimes included bowling, boxing, and playing cards. The rules of baseball were formalized in 1845, and the game became increasingly popular.

Cities during this time were compact and crowded. Many people lived close enough to their jobs that they could walk to work. Wagons carried goods down streets paved with stones, making a noisy, busy scene. One observer noted that the professionals in New York City always had a "hurried walk."

READING CHECK **Summarizing** How did the Industrial Revolution affect life in American cities?

History Close-up

New York City, Mid-1800s

In the mid-1800s, cities such as New York City lured thousands of people in search of jobs and a better life. Many city dwellers found life difficult in the crowded urban conditions.

Many city residents, particularly immigrants, lived in crowded, unsafe conditions.

Many immigrants and other poor city dwellers worked long hours in factories at dangerous jobs.

Women—and frequently children—labored all day in small rooms making clothing to be sold to the wealthy.

City streets were crowded with people buying, selling, and transporting goods.

The first floor of the building served many purposes—living quarters, kitchen, and work space. Here, garments were finished for sale.

PICKLES 1c

ANALYSIS SKILL ANALYZING VISUALS

How is this scene similar to one you might see in a large American city today? How is it different?

Urban Problems

American cities in the mid-1800s faced many challenges due to rapid growth. Because public and private transportation was limited, city residents had to live near their workplaces. In addition, there was a lack of safe housing. Many city dwellers, particularly immigrants, could afford to live only in **tenements**—poorly designed apartment buildings that housed large numbers of people. These structures were often dirty, overcrowded, and unsafe.

Public services were also poor. The majority of cities did not have clean water, public health regulations, or healthful ways to get rid of garbage and human and animal waste. Under these conditions, diseases spread easily, and epidemics were common. In 1832 and 1849, for example, New York City suffered cholera epidemics that killed thousands.

City life held other dangers. As urban areas grew, they became centers of criminal activity. Most cities—including New York, Boston, and Philadelphia—had no permanent or organized force to fight crime. Instead, they relied on volunteer night watches, which offered little protection.

Fire was another constant and serious danger in crowded cities. There was little organized fire protection. Most cities were served by volunteer fire companies. Firefighters used hand pumps and buckets to put out fires. In addition, there were not enough sanitation workers and road maintenance crews. These shortages and flaws caused health and safety problems for many city residents.

READING CHECK **Analyzing** Why did so many American cities have problems in the mid-1800s?

SUMMARY AND PREVIEW Immigrants expected a better life in America, but not all Americans welcomed newcomers. The rapid growth of cities caused many problems. In the next section you will read about how America developed its own style of art and literature.

Section 1 Assessment

Reviewing Ideas, Terms, and People

1. a. **Identify** Who were the **nativists**?
   b. **Compare and Contrast** In what ways were Irish and German immigrants to the United States similar and different?
   c. **Predict** How might the rise of anti-immigrant groups lead to problems in the United States?
2. a. **Describe** What led to the growth of cities?
   b. **Analyze** How did the rise of industrialization and the growth of cities change American society?
3. a. **Describe** What were **tenements**?
   b. **Summarize** What problems affected American cities in the mid-1800s?
   c. **Evaluate** What do you think was the biggest problem facing cities in the United States? Why?

Critical Thinking

4. **Identifying Cause and Effect** Review your notes on the causes of immigration and urban growth. Then add the effects of each to your graphic organizer.

   Immigration → Effects

   Urban Growth → Effects

FOCUS ON WRITING

5. **Identifying Important Events** In your notebook, create a two-column chart. In the first column, list events described in this section. In the second column, write a description of each event and a note about how it changed life in the United States.

American Arts

If YOU were there...

You are a teacher living in Massachusetts in the 1840s. Some of your neighbors have started an experimental community. They want to live more simply than present-day society allows. They hope to have time to write and think, while still sharing the work. Some people will teach, others will raise food. You think this might be an interesting place to live.

What would you ask the leaders of the community?

BUILDING BACKGROUND Great changes were taking place in American culture. The early 1800s brought a revolution in American thought. Artists, writers, and philosophers pursued their ideals and developed truly American styles.

Transcendentalists

Some New England writers and philosophers found spiritual wisdom in **transcendentalism**, the belief that people could transcend, or rise above, material things in life. Transcendentalists also believed that people should depend on themselves and their own insights, rather than on outside authorities. Important transcendentalists included **Ralph Waldo Emerson**, **Margaret Fuller**, and **Henry David Thoreau**.

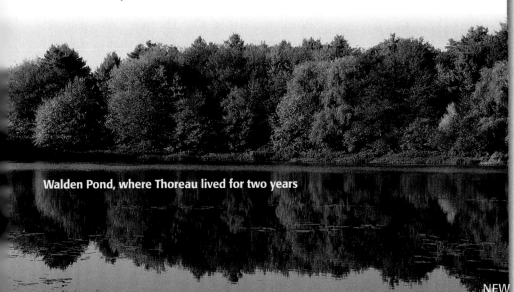

Walden Pond, where Thoreau lived for two years

What You Will Learn...

Main Ideas

1. Transcendentalists and utopian communities withdrew from American society.
2. American Romantic painters and writers made important contributions to art and literature.

The Big Idea

New movements in art and literature influenced many Americans in the early 1800s.

Key Terms and People

transcendentalism, *p. 443*
Ralph Waldo Emerson, *p. 443*
Margaret Fuller, *p. 443*
Henry David Thoreau, *p. 443*
utopian communities, *p. 444*
Nathaniel Hawthorne, *p. 444*
Edgar Allan Poe, *p. 445*
Emily Dickinson, *p. 445*
Henry Wadsworth Longfellow, *p. 445*
Walt Whitman, *p. 445*

TAKING NOTES Create a graphic organizer like the one shown below. Use it to take notes on the new movements in art and literature.

	Transcendentalism	Romanticism
What		
Who		

 8.1.19, 8.1.24, 8.1.31

Emerson was a popular writer and thinker who argued that Americans should disregard institutions and follow their own beliefs. "What I must do is all that concerns me, not what the people think," he wrote in an essay called "Self-Reliance." Fuller edited the famous transcendentalist publication *The Dial*. Thoreau advised even stronger self-reliance and simple living away from society in natural settings. He wrote his book *Walden* after living for two years at Walden Pond.

Some transcendentalists formed a community at Brook Farm, Massachusetts, in the 1840s. It was one of many experiments with **utopian communities**, groups of people who tried to form a perfect society. People in utopian communities pursued **abstract** spirituality and cooperative lifestyles. Communities sprang up in New Harmony, Oneida, and many other places. However, few communities lasted for long.

READING CHECK Drawing Inferences
Why did utopian communities last a short time?

American Romanticism

Ideas about the simple life and nature also inspired painters and writers in the early and mid-1800s. Some joined the Romantic movement that had begun in Europe. Romanticism involved a great interest in nature, an emphasis on individual expression, and a rejection of many established rules. These painters and writers felt that each person brings a unique view to the world. They believed in using emotion to guide their creative output. Some Romantic artists, like Thomas Cole, painted the American landscape. Their works showed the beauty and wonder of nature in the United States. Their images contrasted with the huge cities and corruption of nature that many Americans saw as typical of Europe.

Many female writers, like Ann Sophia Stephens, wrote historical fiction that was popular in the mid-1800s. New England writer **Nathaniel Hawthorne** wrote *The Scarlet Letter* during that period. One of the greatest classics of Romantic literature, it explored Puritan

Artists of the Romantic movement celebrated nature in their dramatic paintings. Their work was made popular by their leader, Thomas Cole. Other important painters of the era were Frederick Church and Asher Durand.

What words would you use to describe this painting?

❶ The light in the painting has a delicate, glowing quality. Artists of the Romantic movement pioneered this technique.

❷ The human presence in this scene is dwarfed by nature but is in harmony with it.

Asher Durand's *The First Harvest in the Wilderness*

American Romantic authors also wrote a great deal of poetry. The poet **Edgar Allan Poe**, also a short story writer, became famous for a haunting poem called "The Raven." Other gifted American poets included **Emily Dickinson**, **Henry Wadsworth Longfellow**, and **Walt Whitman**. Most of Dickinson's short, thoughtful poems were not published until after her death. Longfellow, the best-known poet of the mid-1800s, wrote popular story-poems, like *The Song of Hiawatha*. Whitman praised American individualism and democracy in his simple, unrhymed poetry. In his poetry collection *Leaves of Grass,* he wrote, "The United States themselves are essentially the greatest poem."

READING CHECK Summarizing Who were some American Romantic authors, and why were they important?

life in the 1600s. Hawthorne's friend Herman Melville, a writer and former sailor, wrote novels about the sea, such as *Moby-Dick* and *Billy Budd*. Many people believe that *Moby-Dick* is one of the finest American novels ever written.

SUMMARY AND PREVIEW American Romantic artists and authors were inspired by ideas about the simple life, nature, and spirituality. In the next section you will learn about ideas that changed American society.

Section 2 Assessment

Reviewing Ideas, Terms, and People

1. **a. Identify** What were the main teachings of **transcendentalism**?
   b. Summarize What was one **utopian community** established in the United States, and what was its goal?
   c. Elaborate Do you agree with transcendentalists that Americans put too much emphasis on institutions and traditions? Explain your answer.
2. **a. Recall** Who were some important American authors and poets at this time?
   b. Explain What ideas did artists in the Romantic movement express?
   c. Evaluate Do you think the Romantic movement was important to American culture? Explain.

Critical Thinking

3. **Comparing and Contrasting** Review your notes on art and literature. Then copy the graphic organizer below and use it to show the similarities and differences between the two movements.

   Transcendentalism — Similarities — Romanticism

FOCUS ON WRITING

4. **Describing Artistic Movements** Two artistic movements are described in this section, transcendentalism and romanticism. Write these two movements in the first column of your chart. Then in the second column, write a brief description of each and explain how writings from each either described or influenced life in the United States.

WORD HELP

belfry bell tower

muster gathering

barrack building where soldiers meet

grenadiers a soldier that throws grenades

❶ When the poem was written, there were still a few people alive who had lived during the Revolution.

❷ Longfellow uses poetic language to make Revere's story more dramatic.

❸ The sounds of the night are described to help the reader feel the excitement.

Literature of the Young Nation:
Romanticism and Realism

from "The Midnight Ride of Paul Revere"

by Henry Wadsworth Longfellow (1807–1882)

About the Reading *"The Midnight Ride of Paul Revere" was published in a book called* Tales of a Wayside Inn. *The book is a collection of poems that tell well-known stories from history and mythology. By including the story of Paul Revere with other famous stories, Longfellow helped increase the importance of Paul Revere's ride.*

AS YOU READ **Notice how Longfellow describes Revere as a hero.**

Listen my children and you shall hear
Of the midnight ride of Paul Revere,
On the eighteenth of April, in Seventy-five;
Hardly a man is now alive
Who remembers that famous day and year. ❶

He said to his friend, "If the British march
By land or sea from the town to-night,
Hang a lantern aloft in the belfry arch
Of the North Church tower as a signal light,—
One if by land, and two if by sea;
And I on the opposite shore will be,
Ready to ride and spread the alarm
Through every . . . village and farm,
For the country folk to be up and to arm." ❷
. . . .
Meanwhile, his friend, through alley and street
Wanders and watches with eager ears,
Till in the silence around him he hears
The muster of men at the barrack door,
The sound of arms, and the tramp of feet,
And the measured tread of the grenadiers,
Marching down to their boats on the shore. ❸

from *Little Women*

by Louisa May Alcott (1832–1888)

About the Reading Little Women *is a novel about four sisters living in a small New England town before the Civil War. Still popular with young people today,* Little Women *describes a family much like the one Louisa May Alcott grew up in. Alcott based the main character, Jo March, on herself. Like Alcott, Jo was different from most women of her time. She was outspoken, eager for adventure, and in conflict with the role her society expected her to play.*

AS YOU READ Try to understand how Jo is different from Aunt March.

Jo happened to suit Aunt March, who was lame and needed an active person to wait upon her. The childless old lady had offered to adopt one of the girls when the troubles came, and was much offended because her offer was declined . . .

The old lady wouldn't speak to them for a time, but happening to meet Jo at a friend's, . . . she proposed to take her for a companion.❶ This did not suit Jo at all, but she accepted the place since nothing better appeared, and to everyone's surprise, got on remarkably well with her irascible relative . . .

I suspect that the real attraction was a large library of fine books, which was left to dust and spiders since Uncle March died . . . The dim, dusty room, with the busts staring down from the tall bookcases, the cozy chairs, the globes, and, best of all, the wilderness of books, in which she could wander where she liked, made the library a region of bliss to her . . . ❷

Jo's ambition was to do something very splendid. What it was she had no idea, as yet, but left it for time to tell her, and, meanwhile, found her greatest affliction in the fact that she couldn't read, run, and ride as much as she liked.❸ A quick temper, sharp tongue, and restless spirit were always getting her into scrapes, and her life was a series of ups and downs, which were both comic and pathetic. But the training she received at Aunt March's was just what she needed, and the thought that she was doing something to support herself made her happy in spite of the perpetual "Josy-phine!"

GUIDED READING

WORD HELP

lame disabled
irascible difficult
bliss happiness
ambition hope for the future
affliction problem
pathetic very sad
perpetual constant

❶ *Some women kept companions to help entertain them and perform small chores. Why might Jo not want to be a companion?*

❷ *How does Jo differ from ideas about women in the 1880s?*

❸ *What might Jo be able to do for work in the 1800s?*

CONNECTING LITERATURE TO HISTORY

1. **Drawing Conclusions** Henry Wadsworth Longfellow was the most popular American poet of his time. How does his version of Paul Revere's ride increase the importance of the story?

2. **Comparing and Contrasting** The lives of women in the 1800s were very different from the lives of women today. How does this excerpt of *Little Women* show some similarities and differences between now and then?

Reforming Society

Main Ideas

1. The Second Great Awakening sparked interest in religion.
2. Social reformers began to speak out about temperance and prison reform.
3. Improvements in education reform affected many segments of the population.
4. Northern African American communities became involved in reform efforts.

The Big Idea

Reform movements in the early 1800s affected religion, education, and society.

Key Terms and People

Second Great Awakening, *p. 448*
Charles Grandison Finney, *p. 448*
Lyman Beecher, *p. 448*
temperance movement, *p. 449*
Dorothea Dix, *p. 450*
common-school movement, *p. 450*
Horace Mann, *p. 450*
Catharine Beecher, *p. 451*
Thomas Gallaudet, *p. 451*

TAKING NOTES Create a time line like the one shown below. As you read, list the important events of the reform movements next to the appropriate date on the time line. Some dates might have more than one event.

1817 1821 1835 1837 1841

8.1.16, 8.1.18, 8.1.19, 8.1.24, 8.1.26, 8.1.31, 8.2.7

If YOU were there...

You live in New York State in the 1850s. You are the oldest daughter in your family. Since childhood you have loved mathematics, which puzzles your family. Your sisters are happy learning to sew and cook and run a household. You want more. You know that there is a female seminary nearby, where you could study and learn much more. But your parents are undecided.

How might you persuade your parents to send you to the school?

BUILDING BACKGROUND Along with changes in American culture, changes were also taking place in American society. A religious revival swept the country. Reform-minded men and women tried to improve all aspects of society, from schools to taverns. Reforms in education opened up new opportunities for young women.

Second Great Awakening

During the 1790s and early 1800s, some Americans took part in a Christian renewal movement called the **Second Great Awakening**. It swept through towns across upstate New York and through the frontier regions of Kentucky, Ohio, Tennessee, and South Carolina. By the 1820s and 1830s, this new interest in religion had spread to New England and the South.

Charles Grandison Finney was one of the most important leaders of the Second Great Awakening. After experiencing a dramatic religious conversion in 1821, Finney left his career as a lawyer and began preaching. He challenged some traditional Protestant beliefs, telling congregations that each individual was responsible for his or her own salvation. He also believed that sin was avoidable. Finney held revivals, emotional prayer meetings that lasted for days. Many people converted to Christianity during these revivals. Finney told new converts to prove their faith by doing good deeds.

Finney's style of preaching and his ideas angered some traditional ministers, like Boston's **Lyman Beecher**. Beecher wanted to prevent Finney from holding revivals in his city. "You mean to carry a streak of fire to Boston. If you attempt it, as the Lord liveth, I'll meet you . . . and fight every inch of the way." Despite the opposition of Beecher and other traditional ministers, Finney's appeal remained powerful. Also, the First Amendment guarantee of freedom of religion prevented the government from passing laws banning the new religious practices. Ministers were therefore free to spread their message of faith and salvation to whomever wished to listen.

Due to the efforts of Finney and his followers, church membership across the country grew a great deal during the Second Great Awakening. Many new church members were women and African Americans. The African Methodist Episcopal Church spread across the Middle Atlantic states. Although the movement had begun in the Northeast and on the frontier, the Second Great Awakening renewed some people's religious faith throughout America.

READING CHECK **Drawing Conclusions**
What impact did the Second Great Awakening have on religion in America?

Social Reformers Speak Out

Renewed religious faith often led to involvement in movements to fix the problems created by urban growth. One solution was political action. For example, in 1844 New York City created the first city police force.

Members of the growing middle class, especially women, often led the efforts. Many of the women did not work outside the home and hired servants to care for their households. This gave them time to work in reform groups.

Temperance Movement

Many social reformers worked to prevent alcohol abuse. They believed that Americans drank too much. In the 1830s, on average, an American consumed seven gallons of alcohol per year. Countless Americans thought that alcohol abuse caused social problems, such as family violence, poverty, and criminal behavior.

Americans' worries about the effects of alcohol led to the growth of a **temperance movement**. This reform effort urged people to use self-discipline to stop drinking hard liquor.

Reform Movements

Reform movements in America included religious meetings called revivals, where preachers urged huge crowds of people to seek salvation. The temperance movement, an effort to convince people to avoid drinking alcohol, promoted posters like the one shown here.

How might the scenes in this poster encourage people to stop drinking?

449

Reformers asked people to limit themselves to beer and wine in small amounts. Groups like the American Temperance Society and the American Temperance Union helped to spread the message. Minister Lyman Beecher spoke widely about the evils of alcohol. He claimed that people who drank alcohol were "neglecting the education of their families—and corrupting their morals."

Prison Reform

Another target of reform was the prison system. **Dorothea Dix** was a middle-class reformer who visited prisons through-out Massachusetts beginning in 1841. Dix reported that mentally ill people frequently were jailed with criminals. They were some-times left in dark cells without clothes or heat and were chained to the walls and beaten. Dix spoke of what she saw to the state legislature.

In response, the Massachusetts gov-ernment built facilities for the mentally ill. Dix's work had a nationwide effect. Eventually, more than 100 state hospitals were built to give mentally ill people pro-fessional care.

Prisons also held runaway children and orphans. Some had survived only by beg-ging or stealing, and they got the same pun-ishment as adult criminals. Boston mayor Josiah Quincy asked that young offenders receive different punishments than adults. In the 1820s, several state and local govern-ments founded reform schools for children who had been housed in prisons. There, children lived under strict rules and learned useful skills.

Some reformers also tried to end the overcrowding and cruel conditions in pris-ons. Their efforts led to the creation of houses of correction. These institutions did not use punishment alone to change behav-ior. They also offered prisoners education.

READING CHECK **Summarizing** How did reformers change the punishment of criminals?

THE IMPACT TODAY

McGuffey's Readers were among the first "graded" text-books. Organizing classes by grades was a new idea that is standard practice today.

Improvements in Education

Another challenge facing America in the early 1800s was poor public education. Dur-ing this era, childhood was beginning to be viewed as a separate stage of life in which education was of the utmost importance in creating responsible citizens. However, many children worked in factories or on farms to help support their families. If children could read the Bible, write, and do simple math, that was often considered to be enough.

Education in the Early 1800s

The availability of education varied widely. New England had the most schools, while the South and West had the fewest. Few teachers were trained. Schoolhouses were small, and students of all ages and levels worked in one room.

McGuffey's Readers were the most pop-ular textbooks. William Holmes McGuffey, an educator and minister, put selections from British and American literature in them as well as instruction in moral and social values.

Social background and wealth affected the quality of education. Rich families sent children to private schools or hired tutors. However, poor children had only public schools. Girls could go to school, but parents usually thought that girls needed little edu-cation and kept them home. Therefore, few girls learned to read.

Common-School Movement

People in the **common-school movement** wanted all children taught in a common place, regardless of background. **Horace Mann** was a leader of this movement.

In 1837 Mann became Massachusetts's first secretary of education. He convinced the state to double its school budget and raise teachers' salaries. He lengthened the school year and began the first school for teacher training. Mann's success set a standard for education reform throughout the country.

Women's Education

Education reform created greater opportunities for women. **Catharine Beecher** started an all-female academy in Hartford, Connecticut. The first college-level educational institution available to women was the Troy Female Seminary, opened by Emma Willard in 1821. Several other women's colleges opened during the 1830s, including Mount Holyoke College. The first medical college for women, who were barred from men's medical schools, opened in Boston in 1848.

Teaching People with Special Needs

Efforts to improve education also helped people with special needs. In 1831 Samuel Gridley Howe opened the Perkins School for the Blind in Massachusetts. Howe traveled widely, talking about teaching people with visual impairment. **Thomas Gallaudet** improved the education and lives of people with hearing impairments. He founded the first free American school for hearing-impaired people in 1817.

READING CHECK **Summarizing** What were Horace Mann's achievements?

BIOGRAPHY

Horace Mann
1796-1859

Born in Franklin, Massachusetts, Mann had little schooling, but he educated himself well enough at the local library to get into Brown University and attend law school. Despite a busy law practice, he served in the Massachusetts legislature for 10 years. He was also an outspoken advocate for public education. In 1837 the state created the post of secretary of education for him. His achievements in that office made him famous. He later served in the U.S. House of Representatives and as president of Antioch College in Ohio. His influence on education is reflected by the fact that many American schools are named for him.

Analyzing Information How do you think Mann's own education influenced his desire for public schools?

Primary Source

SPEECH
Horace Mann to the Board of Education

In a speech to the newly created Massachusetts Board of Education, Horace Mann, the board's first secretary, described the purpose of the public school system.

❝[T]here should be a free district school, sufficiently safe, and sufficiently good, for all of the children... where they may be well instructed in the rudiments [basics] of knowledge, formed to propriety of demeanor [good behavior], and imbued [filled] with the principles of duty... It is on this common platform, that a general acquaintanceship [friendship] should be formed between the children of the same neighborhood. It is here, that the affinities [qualities] of a common nature should unite them together.❞

—Horace Mann, quoted in *The Republic and the School*, edited by Lawrence A. Cremin

Mann believed all students should receive free education.

Neighborhood children should attend school together to form a common bond.

ANALYSIS SKILL **ANALYZING PRIMARY SOURCES**

Besides knowledge, what purpose did Mann believe the public schools had?

Though African Americans faced racial discrimination during the 1800s, many became successful entreprenuers, scholars, and artists. Edmonia Lewis, a sculptor, Paul Dunbar, a poet, and Edward Bannister and Henry Ossawa Tanner, both painters, became renowned for their work. Their successes combatted the idea that African Americans were unable to produce intellectual and artistic creations that rivaled those of other races.

African American Communities

Free African Americans usually lived in segregated, or separate, communities in the North. Most of them lived in cities such as New York, Boston, and Philadelphia. Community leaders were often influenced by the Second Great Awakening and its spirit of reform.

Founded by former slave Richard Allen, the Free African Religious Society became a model for other groups that pressed for racial equality and the education of blacks. In 1816 Allen became the first bishop of the African Methodist Episcopal Church, or AME Church. This church broke away from white Methodist churches after African Americans were treated poorly in some white congregations.

Other influential African Americans of the time, such as Alexander Crummel, pushed for the creation of schools for black Americans. The New York African Free School in New York City educated hundreds of children, many of whom became brilliant scholars and important African American leaders. Philadelphia also had a long history of educating African Americans. This was largely because Philadelphia was a center of Quaker influence, and the Quakers believed strongly in equality. The city ran seven schools for African American students by the year 1800. In 1820 Boston followed Philadelphia's lead and opened a separate elementary school for African American children. The city began allowing them to attend school with whites in 1855.

African Americans rarely attended college because few colleges would accept them. In 1835 Oberlin College became the first to do so. Harvard University soon admitted African Americans, too. Several African American colleges were founded beginning in the 1840s. In 1842 the Institute for Colored Youth opened in Philadelphia. Avery College, also in Pennsylvania, was founded in 1849.

This photograph (left) of the 1855 class at Oberlin College shows the slow integration of African Americans into previously white colleges. Some churches also became more integrated, and preachers like the one pictured above began calling for equality between races.

Why might preachers have been particularly influential in calls for greater integration?

While free African Americans had some opportunities to attend school in the North and Midwest, few had this chance in the South. Laws in the South barred most enslaved people from getting any education, even at the primary school level. While some slaves learned to read on their own, they almost always did so in secret. Slaveholders were fearful that education and knowledge in general might encourage a spirit of revolt among enslaved African Americans.

READING CHECK **Drawing Conclusions**
Why was it difficult for African Americans to get an education in the South in the early 1800s?

SUMMARY AND PREVIEW The efforts of reformers led to improvements in many aspects of American life in the early to mid-1800s. In the next section you will learn about reform-minded people who opposed the practice of slavery.

Section 3 Assessment

Reviewing Ideas, Terms, and People

1. **a. Identify** What was the **Second Great Awakening**, and who was one of its leaders?
   b. Summarize What effects did the Second Great Awakening have on religion in the United States?
2. **a. Identify** What role did **Dorothea Dix** play in social reforms of the early 1800s?
   b. Summarize What different reforms helped improve the U.S. prison system?
   c. Elaborate How might the Second Great Awakening have led to the growth of social reform movements?
3. **a. Identify** What was the **common-school movement**, and who was one of its leaders?
   b. Analyze Why did reformers set out to improve education in the United States?
   c. Evaluate Do you think **Horace Mann**'s ideas for educational reform were good ones? Explain.
4. **a. Recall** In what cities were the first public schools for African Americans located?
   b. Draw Conclusions How did free African Americans benefit from educational reforms?

Critical Thinking

5. **Categorizing** Review the reform-movement events on the time line in your notes. Then use a chart like the one below to identify the leaders and accomplishments of each reform movement.

Movement	Leaders	Accomplishments
Prison and Mental Health Reform		
Temperance		
Education		

FOCUS ON WRITING

6. **Choosing Important Events** This section covers the reform of social issues such as religion, prisons, and education. Write the reforms described in your chart. Then write a note about each reform and about the important people involved in it. Think about how each one influenced life in the United States.

The Movement to End Slavery

What You Will Learn...

Main Ideas

1. Americans from a variety of backgrounds actively opposed slavery.
2. Abolitionists organized the Underground Railroad to help enslaved Africans escape.
3. Despite efforts of abolitionists, many Americans remained opposed to ending slavery.

The Big Idea

In the mid-1800s, debate over slavery increased as abolitionists organized to challenge slavery in the United States.

Key Terms and People

abolition, *p. 454*
William Lloyd Garrison, *p. 455*
American Anti-Slavery
   Society, *p. 455*
Angelina and Sarah Grimké, *p. 455*
Frederick Douglass, *p. 456*
Sojourner Truth, *p. 456*
Underground Railroad, *p. 456*
Harriet Tubman, *p. 458*

TAKING NOTES As you read, take notes on the different abolitionist movements that existed, the leaders of each movement, and the methods used by each group to oppose slavery. Write your notes in a chart like the one below.

Movement	Members	Methods

8.1.16, 8.1.18, 8.1.19. 8.1.20, 8.1.24, 8.1.28, 8.1.31, 8.2.7

If **YOU** were there...

You live in southern Ohio in the 1850s. A friend who lives across the river in Kentucky has asked you to join a network that helps escaping slaves. She reminds you that your house has a secret cellar where you could easily hide fugitives for a few days. You are opposed to slavery. But you know this might get you in trouble with your neighbors—and with the law.

Would you become an agent for the Underground Railroad? Why?

BUILDING BACKGROUND The early 1800s brought many movements for social reform in the United States. Perhaps the most important and far-reaching was the movement for the abolition of slavery. While reformers worked to end slavery, many also took risks to help slaves to escape.

Americans Oppose Slavery

Some Americans had opposed slavery since before the country was founded. Benjamin Franklin was the president of the first antislavery society in America, the Pennsylvania Society for Promoting the Abolition of Slavery. In the 1830s, Americans took more organized action supporting **abolition**, or a complete end to slavery.

Differences among Abolitionists

Abolitionists came from many different backgrounds and opposed slavery for various reasons. The Quakers were among the first groups to challenge slavery on religious grounds. Other religious leaders gave speeches and published pamphlets that moved many Americans to support abolition. In one of these, abolitionist Theodore Weld wrote that "everyman knows that slavery is a curse." Other abolitionists referred to the Declaration of Independence. They reminded people that the American Revolution had been fought in the name of liberty.

Antislavery reformers did not always agree on the details, however. They differed over how much equality they thought African Americans should have. Some believed that African Americans should receive the same treatment as white Americans. In contrast, other abolitionists were against full political and social equality.

Some abolitionists wanted to send freed African Americans to Africa to start new colonies. They thought that this would prevent conflicts between the races in the United States. In 1817 a minister named Robert Finley started the American Colonization Society, an organization dedicated to establishing colonies of freed slaves in Africa. Five years later, the society founded the colony of Liberia on the west coast of Africa. About 12,000 African Americans eventually settled in Liberia. However, many abolitionists who once favored colonization later opposed it. Some African Americans also opposed it. David Walker was one such person. In his 1829 essay, *Appeal to the Colored Citizens of the World*, Walker explained his opposition to colonization.

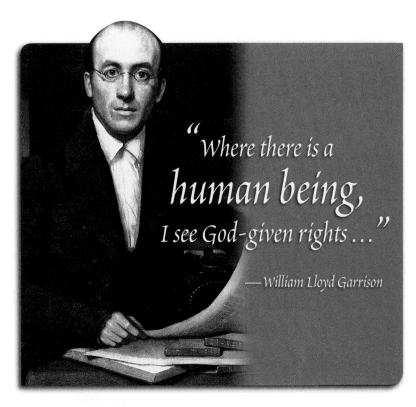

"*Where there is a* **human being**, *I see God-given rights…*"

—William Lloyd Garrison

"The greatest riches in all America have arisen from our blood and tears: and they [whites] will drive us from our property and homes, which we have earned with our blood."

—David Walker, quoted in *From Slavery to Freedom* by John Hope Franklin and Alfred A. Moss Jr.

Spreading the Abolitionist Message

Abolitionists found many ways to further their cause. Some went on speaking tours or wrote pamphlets and newspaper articles. John Greenleaf Whittier wrote abolitionist poetry and literature. **William Lloyd Garrison** published an abolitionist newspaper, the *Liberator*, beginning in 1831. In 1833 he also helped found the **American Anti-Slavery Society**. Its members wanted immediate emancipation and racial equality for African Americans. Garrison later became its president.

Both the *Liberator* and the Anti-Slavery Society relied on support from free African Americans. Society members spread antislavery literature and petitioned Congress to end federal support of slavery. In 1840 the American Anti-Slavery Society split. One group wanted immediate freedom for enslaved African Americans and a bigger role for women. The others wanted gradual emancipation and for women to play only minor roles in the movement.

Angelina and Sarah Grimké, two white southern women, were antislavery activists of the 1830s. They came from a South Carolina slaveholding family but disagreed with their parents' support of slavery. Angelina Grimké tried to recruit other white southern women in a pamphlet called *Appeal to the Christian Women of the South* in 1836.

"I know you do not make the laws, but …if you really suppose you can do nothing to overthrow slavery you are greatly mistaken …Try to persuade your husband, father, brothers, and sons that slavery is a crime against God and man."

—Angelina Grimké, quoted in *The Grimké Sisters from South Carolina*, edited by Gerda Lerner

This essay was very popular in the North. In 1839 the Grimké sisters wrote *American Slavery As It Is*. The book was one of the most important antislavery works of its time.

Indiana became an important part of the Underground Railroad since it shared a border with the slave state of Kentucky. Although many Indianans supported slavery and worked to return escaped slaves to the South, others helped escaped slaves to reach freedom in the North or in Canada. Levi Coffin's house in Fountain City helped so many slaves escape that it was called "the Grand Central Station" of the Underground Railroad.

African American Abolitionists

Many former slaves were active in the anti-slavery cause. **Frederick Douglass** escaped from slavery when he was 20 and went on to become one of the most important African American leaders of the 1800s. Douglass secretly learned to read and write as a boy, despite a law against it. His public-speaking skills impressed members of the Anti-Slavery Society. In 1841 they asked him to give regular lectures.

At a Fourth of July celebration in 1852, he captured the audience's attention with his powerful voice.

"The blessings in which you, this day, rejoice, are not enjoyed in common ... This Fourth of July is yours, not mine. You may rejoice, I must mourn."

—Frederick Douglass, quoted in *From Slavery to Freedom* by John Hope Franklin and Alfred A. Moss Jr.

In addition to his many speaking tours in the United States and Europe, Douglass published a newspaper called the *North Star* and wrote several autobiographies. His autobiographies were intended to show the injustices of slavery.

Another former slave, **Sojourner Truth**, also contributed to the abolitionist cause. She claimed God had called her to travel through the United States and preach the truth about slavery and women's rights. With her deep voice and quick wit, Truth became legendary in the antislavery movement for her fiery and dramatic speeches.

Other African Americans wrote narratives about their experiences as slaves to expose the cruelties that many slaves faced. In 1861 Harriet Jacobs published *Incidents in the Life of a Slave Girl*, one of the few slave narratives by a woman. William Wells Brown wrote an anti-slavery play as well as a personal narrative in the form of a novel called *Clotel*.

READING CHECK **Finding Main Ideas** In what ways did African Americans participate in the abolition movement?

The Underground Railroad

By the 1830s, a loosely organized group had begun helping slaves escape from the South. Free African Americans, former slaves, and a few white abolitionists worked together. They created what became known as the **Underground Railroad**. The organization was not an actual railroad but was a network of people who arranged transportation and hiding places for fugitives, or escaped slaves.

Fugitives would travel along "freedom trails" that led them to northern states or sometimes into Canada. At no time did the Railroad have a central leadership. No one person, or group of people, was ever officially in charge. Despite the lack of any real structure, the Underground Railroad managed to achieve dramatic results.

Often wearing disguises, fugitives moved along the "railroad" at night, led by people known as conductors. Many times, the fugitives had no other guideposts but the stars. They stopped to rest during the day at "stations," often barns, attics, or other places on property owned by abolitionists known as station masters. The station masters hid and fed the fugitives.

Harriet Tubman was a courageous conductor on the Underground Railroad.

The Underground Railroad

Enslaved African Americans followed many routes to escape from southern slavery. Once in the free states, however, fugitive slaves could not be certain of their freedom. U.S. law still considered them as property, and bounty hunters were paid to capture and return any fugitive slaves they found.

CANADA

Montreal

ME

VT   NH

70°W

Boston

Collingwood

Lake Huron

Lake Ontario

NY

MA

RI

Niagara Falls

CT

New York City

MI

Detroit

Lake Erie

Erie

40°N

Brooklyn

NJ

Chicago

PA

OH

IA

Baltimore

MD

DE

Washington, D.C.

IL

IN

Cincinnati

ATLANTIC OCEAN

St. Louis

Evansville

Ohio River

Mississippi River

MO

KY

Cairo

Fugitive slaves hid behind a secret door in this Indiana house on the Underground Railroad.

TN

N
W   E
S

AR

AL

Charleston

Atlanta

| Free states | | Slave states |
| Routes of the Underground Railroad | | |

0   75   150 Miles
0   75   150 Kilometers

MS

GA

Savannah

LA

80°W

30°N

This painting, *A Ride for Liberty— The Fugitive Slaves* by Eastman Johnson, shows an African American family riding toward freedom.

FL

GEOGRAPHY SKILLS INTERPRETING MAPS

1. **Place** Which northern cities were destinations for escaped slaves?
2. **Movement** Which rivers were routes for the Underground Railroad?

HANDBILL
Anti-Abolitionist Rally

Members of an anti-abolitionist group used this flyer to call people together in order to disrupt a meeting of abolitionists in 1837.

Seditious means "guilty of rebelling against lawful authority."

The group believes abolition violates the Constitution.

OUTRAGE.

Fellow Citizens,

AN ABOLITIONIST,

of the most revolting character is among you, exciting the feelings of the North against the South. A seditious Lecture is to be delivered

THIS EVENING,

at **7** o'clock, at the Presbyterian Church in Cannon-street. You are requested to attend and unite in putting down and silencing by peaceable means this tool of evil and fanaticism. Let the rights of the States guaranteed by the Constitution be protected.

Feb. 27, 1837. *The Union forever!*

ANALYSIS SKILL ANALYZING PRIMARY SOURCES

What emotional language does this handbill use to get its message across?

The most famous and daring conductor on the Underground Railroad was **Harriet Tubman**. When Tubman escaped slavery in 1849, she left behind her family. She swore that she would return and lead her whole family to freedom in the North. Tubman returned to the South 19 times, successfully leading her family and more than 300 other slaves to freedom. At one time the reward for Tubman's capture reportedly climbed to $40,000, a huge amount of money at that time.

READING CHECK Drawing Inferences
Why were the operations of the Underground Railroad kept secret?

Opposition to Ending Slavery

Although the North was the center of the abolitionist movement, many white northerners agreed with the South and supported slavery. Others disliked slavery but opposed equality for African Americans.

Newspaper editors and politicians warned that freed slaves would move north and take jobs from white workers. Some workers feared losing jobs to newly freed African Americans, whom they believed would accept lower wages. Abolitionist leaders were threatened with violence as some northerners joined mobs. Such a mob killed abolitionist Elijah Lovejoy in 1837 in Alton, Illinois.

The federal government also obstructed abolitionists. Between 1836 and 1844, the U.S. House of Representatives used what was called a gag rule. Congress had received thousands of antislavery petitions. Yet the gag rule forbade members of Congress from discussing them. This rule violated the First Amendment right of citizens to petition the government. But southern members of Congress did not want to debate slavery. Many northern members of Congress preferred to avoid the issue.

Eventually, representative and former president John Quincy Adams was able to get the gag rule overturned. His resolution to enact a constitutional amendment halting the expansion of slavery never passed, however.

Many white southerners saw slavery as vital to the South's economy and culture. They also felt that outsiders should not

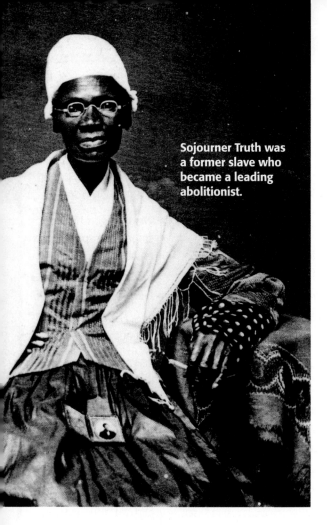

Sojourner Truth was a former slave who became a leading abolitionist.

interfere with their way of life. After Nat Turner's Rebellion in 1831, when Turner led some slaves to kill slaveholders, open talk about slavery disappeared in the South. It became dangerous to voice antislavery sentiments in southern states. Abolitionists like the Grimké sisters left rather than air unpopular views to hostile neighbors. Racism, fear, and economic dependence on slavery made emancipation all but impossible in the South.

READING CHECK Drawing Conclusions

Why did many northern workers oppose the abolition movement?

SUMMARY AND PREVIEW The issue of slavery grew more controversial in the United States during the first half of the nineteenth century. In the next section you will learn about women's rights.

Section 4 Assessment

Reviewing Ideas, Terms, and People

1. **a. Identify** What contributions did **William Lloyd Garrison** make to the **abolition** movement?
   b. Draw Conclusions In what ways did contributions from African Americans aid the struggle for abolition?
   c. Elaborate What do you think about the American Colonization Society's plan to return free African Americans to Liberia?
2. **a. Describe** How did the **Underground Railroad** work?
   b. Explain Why did **Harriet Tubman** first become involved with the Underground Railroad?
   c. Evaluate Do you think the Underground Railroad was a success? Why or why not?
3. **a. Describe** What action did Congress take to block abolitionists?
   b. Analyze Why did some Americans oppose equality for African Americans?
   c. Predict How might the debate over slavery lead to conflict in the future?

Critical Thinking

4. **Identifying Cause and Effect** Review your notes on the abolitionist movement. Then use a graphic organizer like the one below to show the reasons for opposition to the movement and the effects of that opposition.

Reasons for Opposing the End of Slavery	Effects of Opposition to the Movement

FOCUS ON WRITING

5. **Describing Abolition** Add notes about the abolitionist movement and its leaders to your chart. Be sure to note how abolitionists influenced life in the United States. What were they fighting for? Who opposed them, and why?

Frederick Douglass

As a freed slave, how would you help people still enslaved?

When did he live? 1817–1895

Where did he live? Frederick Douglass was born in rural Maryland. At age six he was sent to live in Baltimore, and at age 20 he escaped to New York City. For most of his life, Douglass lived in Rochester, New York, making his home into a stop along the Underground Railroad. He traveled often, giving powerful antislavery speeches to audiences throughout the North and in Europe.

What did he do? After hearing the abolitionist William Lloyd Garrison speak in 1841, Douglass began his own speaking tours about his experiences as a slave. In midlife he wrote an autobiography and started an abolitionist newspaper called the *North Star*. During the Civil War, Douglass persuaded black soldiers to fight for the North.

Why is he important? Douglass was the most famous African American in the 1800s. His personal stories and elegant speaking style helped the abolitionist movement to grow. His words remain an inspiration to this day.

Drawing Conclusions What made Frederick Douglass's speeches and writings so powerful?

KEY EVENTS

1817 Born a slave in Maryland

1837 Escapes slavery disguised as a sailor

1841 Begins his career as a speaker on abolition

1845 Writes *Narrative of the Life of Frederick Douglass*, his first autobiography

1847 Publishes first issue of the *North Star*

1863 Meets President Lincoln and becomes an adviser

1889 Named American consul general to Haiti

1895 Dies in Washington, D.C.

Frederick Douglass began publishing the *North Star*, an abolitionist newspaper, in 1847.

THE NORTH STAR.

ROCHESTER, N. Y. FRIDAY, JUNE 2, 1848.

Women's Rights

If YOU were there...

You are a schoolteacher in New York State in 1848. Although you earn a small salary, you still live at home. Your father does not believe that unmarried women should live alone or look after their own money. One day in a shop, you see a poster about a public meeting to discuss women's rights. You know your father will be angry if you go to the meeting. But you are very curious.

Would you attend the meeting? Why?

BUILDING BACKGROUND Women were active in the movements to reform prisons and schools. They fought for temperance and worked for abolition. But with all their work for social change, women still lacked many rights and opportunities of their own. Throughout the 1800s, the women's rights movement gradually became stronger and more organized.

Women's Struggle for Equal Rights

Fighting for the rights of African Americans led many female abolitionists to fight for women's rights. In the mid-1800s, these women found that they had to defend their right to speak in public, particularly when a woman addressed both men and women. For example, members of the press, the clergy, and even some male abolitionists criticized the Grimké sisters. These critics thought that the sisters should not give public speeches. They did not want women to leave their traditional female roles. The Grimkés protested that women had a moral duty to lead the antislavery movement.

Early Writings for Women's Rights

In 1838 Sarah Grimké published a pamphlet arguing for equal rights for women. She titled it *Letters on the Equality of the Sexes and the Condition of Women.*

"I ask no favors for my sex ... All I ask our brethren [brothers] is that they will take their feet from off our necks, and permit us to stand upright on that ground which God designed us to occupy."
—Sarah Grimké, quoted in *The Grimké Sisters from South Carolina,* edited by Gerda Lerner

---

What You Will Learn...

Main Ideas

1. Influenced by the abolition movement, many women struggled to gain equal rights for themselves.
2. Calls for women's rights met opposition from men and women.
3. The Seneca Falls Convention launched the first organized women's rights movement in the United States.

The Big Idea

Reformers sought to improve women's rights in American society.

Key Terms and People

Elizabeth Cady Stanton, *p. 464*
Lucretia Mott, *p. 464*
Seneca Falls Convention, *p. 464*
Declaration of Sentiments, *p. 464*
Lucy Stone, *p. 465*
Susan B. Anthony, *p. 465*

TAKING NOTES Create a graphic organizer like the one shown below. Use it to show some of the significant events in the struggle for women's rights.

Date	Events
1838	
1848	
1851	
1860	

 8.1.10, 8.1.16, 8.1.18, 8.1.19, 8.1.24, 8.1.26, 8.1.28, 8.1.29, 8.1.30, 8.2.7, 8.2.9, 8.3.6, 8.3.11

Sarah Grimké also argued for equal educational opportunities. She pointed out laws that negatively affected women. In addition, she demanded equal pay for equal work.

Sarah Grimké never married. She explained that the laws of the day gave a husband complete control of his wife's property. Therefore, she feared that by marrying, she would become more like a slave than a wife. Her sister, Angelina, did marry, but she refused to promise to obey her husband during their marriage ceremony. She married Theodore Weld, an abolitionist. Weld agreed to give up his legal right to control her property after they married. For the Grimkés, the abolitionist principles and women's rights principles were identical.

In 1845 the famous transcendentalist Margaret Fuller published *Woman in the Nineteenth Century*. This book used well-known sayings to explain the role of women in American society. Fuller used democratic and transcendentalist principles to stress the importance of individualism to all people, especially women. The book influenced many leaders of the women's rights movement.

Sojourner Truth

Sojourner Truth was another powerful supporter of both abolition and women's rights.

She had been born into slavery in about 1797. Her birth name was Isabella Baumfree. She took the name Sojourner Truth because she felt that her mission was to be a sojourner, or traveler, and spread the truth. Though she never learned to read or write, she impressed many well-educated people. One person who thought highly of her was the author Harriet Beecher Stowe. Stowe said that she had never spoken "with anyone who had more . . . personal presence than this woman." Truth stood six feet tall and was a confident speaker.

In 1851 Truth gave a speech that is often quoted to this day.

"That man over here says that women need to be helped into carriages and lifted over ditches, and to have the best place everywhere. Nobody ever helps me into carriages or over mud puddles, or gives me any best place … Look at me! I have ploughed and planted and … no man could head [outwork] me. And ain't I a woman?"

—Sojourner Truth, quoted in *A History of Women in America* by Carol Hymowitz and Michaele Weissman

Truth, the Grimké sisters, and other supporters of the women's movement were determined to be heard.

READING CHECK **Drawing Inferences**
Why would reformers link the issues of abolition and women's rights?

Time Line

Women's Rights

1848 The Seneca Falls Convention is held, and the Declaration of Sentiments is written.

1776 Abigail Adams asks her husband, John Adams, to "remember the ladies" and their rights in the Declaration of Independence.

Opposing the Call for Women's Rights

Publications about women's rights first appeared in the United States shortly after the American Revolution. However, women's concerns did not become a national issue with strong opposition for many more years.

The Movement Grows

The change took place when women took a more active and leading role in reform and abolition. Other social changes also led to the rise of the women's movement. Women took advantage of better educational opportunities in the early 1800s. Their efforts on behalf of reform groups helped them learn how to organize more effectively and to work together.

Another benefit of reform-group work was that some men began to fight for women's rights. Many activists, both men and women, found it unacceptable that women were not allowed to vote or sit on juries. They were also upset that married women in many states had little or no control over their own property.

Opposition to Women's Rights

Like the abolitionist movement, the struggle for women's rights faced opposition. Many people did not agree with some of the goals of the women's rights movement. Some women believed that they did not need new rights. They said that women were not unequal to men, only different. Some critics believed that women should not try to work in public for social changes. Women were welcome to work for social change, but only from within their homes. "Let her not look away from her own little family circle for the means of producing moral and social reforms," wrote T. S. Arthur. His advice appeared in a popular women's magazine called *The Lady at Home*.

Some people also thought that women lacked the physical or mental strength to survive without men's protection. They believed that a woman should go from the protection of her father's home to that of her husband's. They also thought that women could not cope with the outside world; therefore, a husband should control his wife's property. Despite opposition, women continued to pursue their goal of greater rights.

READING CHECK **Drawing Conclusions**
Why did some men and women think that the women's rights movement was misguided?

"There never will be complete equality until women themselves help to make laws and elect lawmakers."

Susan B. Anthony

1872 Susan B. Anthony is arrested while trying to vote in New York.

1890 Wyoming's new state constitution includes women's suffrage.

1911 The National Association Opposed to Woman Suffrage is formed.

1920 On August 26, the Nineteenth Amendment is declared ratified by Congress, giving women the right to vote.

ANALYSIS SKILL **READING TIME LINES**
Women in Wyoming could vote how many years before women in the rest of the country could?

HISTORIC DOCUMENT
Declaration of Sentiments

At the 1848 Seneca Falls Convention, 100 people signed the Declaration of Sentiments, a document declaring the rights of women. The wording of the document purposely echoed the Declaration of Independence.

> The authors use the same words that are in the Declaration of Independence, but include women.

> Here the women demand that they become a part of government.

We hold these truths to be self-evident: that all men and women are created equal; that they are endowed by their Creator with certain inalienable[1] rights; that among these are life, liberty, and the pursuit of happiness; that to secure these rights governments are instituted, deriving their just powers from the consent of the governed. Whenever any form of government becomes destructive of these ends, it is the right of those who suffer from it to refuse allegiance[2] to it, and to insist upon the institution of a new government, laying its foundation on such principles, and organizing its powers in such form, as to them shall seem most likely to effect their safety and happiness.

1. **inalienable** not able to be taken away 2. **allegiance** loyalty

ANALYSIS SKILL | **ANALYZING PRIMARY SOURCES**

Why would women want to use the Declaration of Independence as a source for their own declaration?

FOCUS ON INDIANA

FOCUS ON INDIANA

Women's rights reformers in Indiana called a meeting in 1851, and the next year they became the Indiana Woman's Rights Association. Members of this group worked for property rights as well as suffrage for women.

Seneca Falls Convention

In 1840 **Elizabeth Cady Stanton** attended the World's Anti-Slavery Convention in London, England, while on her honeymoon. She discovered that, unlike her husband, she was not allowed to participate. All women in attendance had to sit behind a curtain in a separate gallery of the convention hall. William Lloyd Garrison, who had helped found the American Anti-Slavery Society, sat with them in protest.

The treatment of women abolitionists at the convention angered Stanton and her new friend, **Lucretia Mott**. Apparently, even many abolitionists did not think that women were equal to men. Stanton and Mott wanted to change this, so they planned to "form a society to advance the rights of women." Eight years passed before Stanton and Mott finally announced the **Seneca Falls Convention**, the first public meeting about women's rights held in the United States. It opened on July 19, 1848, in Seneca Falls, New York.

Declaration of Sentiments

The convention organizers wrote a **Declaration of Sentiments**. This document detailed beliefs about social injustice toward women. They used the Declaration of Independence as the basis for the language for their Declaration of Sentiments. The authors included 18 charges against men—the same number that had been charged against King George III. The Declaration of Sentiments was signed by some 100 people.

About 240 people attended the Seneca Falls Convention, including men such as abolitionist Frederick Douglass. Many other reformers who also worked in the temperance and abolitionist movements were present. Several women who participated in the convention worked in nearby factories. One of them, 19-year-old Charlotte Woodward, signed the Declaration of Sentiments. She worked long hours in a factory, making gloves. Her wages were very low, and she could not even keep her earnings. She had to turn her wages over to her father.

Women's Rights Leaders

After the convention, the struggle continued. Women's rights activists battled many difficulties and much opposition. Still, they kept working to obtain greater equality for women. Among the many women working for women's rights, three became important leaders: Lucy Stone, Susan B. Anthony, and Elizabeth Cady Stanton. Each brought different strengths to the fight for women's rights.

Lucy Stone was a well-known spokesperson for the Anti-Slavery Society. In the early years of the women's rights movement, Stone became known as a gifted speaker. Elizabeth Cady Stanton called her "the first who really stirred the nation's heart on the subject of women's wrongs."

Susan B. Anthony brought strong organizational skills to the women's rights movement. She did much to turn the fight for women's rights into a political movement. Anthony argued that women and men should receive equal pay for equal work. She also believed that women should be allowed to enter traditionally male professions, such as religion and law. Anthony was especially concerned with laws that affected women's control of money and property.

Anthony led a campaign to change laws regarding the property rights of women. She wrote in her diary that no woman could ever be free without "a purse of her own." After forming a network to cover the entire state of New York, she collected more than 6,000 signatures to petition for a new property-rights law. In 1860, due largely to the efforts of Anthony, New York finally gave married women ownership of their wages and property. Other states in the Northeast and Midwest soon created similar laws.

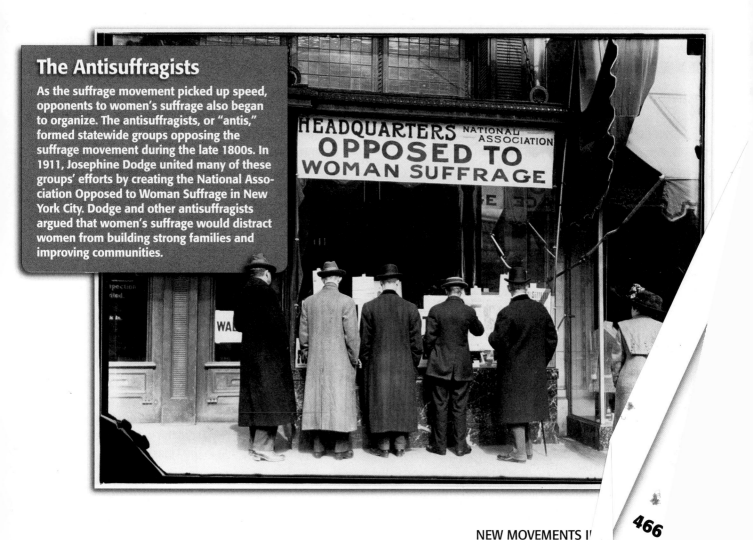

The Antisuffragists

As the suffrage movement picked up speed, opponents to women's suffrage also began to organize. The antisuffragists, or "antis," formed statewide groups opposing the suffrage movement during the late 1800s. In 1911, Josephine Dodge united many of these groups' efforts by creating the National Association Opposed to Woman Suffrage in New York City. Dodge and other antisuffragists argued that women's suffrage would distract women from building strong families and improving communities.

Elizabeth Cady Stanton wrote many of the documents and speeches of the movement, which were often delivered by Anthony. Stanton was a founder and important leader of the National Woman Suffrage Association. This organization was considered one of the more radical groups because of its position that abolition was not a more important cause than women's rights.

Not every battle was won. Other major reforms, such as women's right to vote, were not achieved at this time. Still, more women than ever before became actively involved in women's rights issues. This increased activity was one of the movement's greatest accomplishments.

READING CHECK Identifying Points of View What did Susan B. Anthony mean when she said that no woman could be free without "a purse of her own"?

Lucy Stone worked for equal rights for women and African Americans.

SUMMARY AND PREVIEW Women's rights became a major issue in the mid-1800s, as women began to demand a greater degree of equality. In the next chapter you will read about western expansion.

Section 5 Assessment

go.hrw.com
Online Quiz
KEYWORD: SF7 HP14

Reviewing Ideas, Terms, and People

1. **a. Identify** What role did Sojourner Truth play in both the abolition and women's rights movements?
   b. Analyze How did the abolition movement influence women to demand equal rights?
2. **a. Identify** What limitations on women's rights did many activists find unacceptable?
   b. Summarize Why did many Americans oppose equal rights for women?
   c. Elaborate What arguments might you use to counter the arguments of men and women who opposed equal rights for women?
3. **a. Recall** Who were the three main leaders of the women's rights movement, and how did they each contribute to the movement?
   b. Draw Conclusions Why might working-class women like Charlotte Woodward have supported the **Seneca Falls Convention** and the **Declaration of Sentiments**?
   c. Evaluate Do you agree with **Susan B. Anthony** that women should receive equal pay for equal work? Explain your answer.

Critical Thinking

4. **Analyzing** Review your notes on events in the women's rights movement. Then copy the graphic organizer shown below and use it to show the goals of the movement, as well as the arguments against it.

Goals	Opponents' Arguments

FOCUS ON WRITING

5. **Describing Women's Suffrage** Add notes about the women's suffrage movement to your chart. Note important leaders and describe what they were fighting for. Ask yourself, "How did the women's suffrage movement change life in the United States?"

Elizabeth Cady Stanton

What steps would you take to bring about nationwide change?

When did she live? 1815–1902

Where did she live? Elizabeth Cady Stanton was born in Johnstown, New York. She married a prominent abolitionist and settled in Seneca Falls, New York, where she had seven children. Later in life she traveled widely, giving lectures and speeches across the country.

What did she do? Stanton and fellow activist Lucretia Mott organized the nation's first women's rights convention, at Seneca Falls in 1848. She and Susan B. Anthony founded the National Woman Suffrage Association in 1869. For nearly six decades, she spoke and wrote passionately about women's rights.

Why is she important? Stanton helped author the Declaration of Sentiments, which demanded equal rights for women, including the right to vote. A brilliant speaker and debater, Stanton spoke out against laws that kept married women from owning property, earning wages, and keeping custody of their children.

Finding Main Ideas What problems did Stanton try to correct? What problems did she face in accomplishing her goals?

Elizabeth Cady Stanton helped author the Declaration of Sentiments at the Seneca Falls Convention.

KEY EVENTS

1815 Born in Johnstown, New York

1840 Meets Lucretia Mott at the World's Anti-Slavery Convention, where they are barred from participating

1848 Helps organize the first national meeting of women's suffrage reformers at Seneca Falls, New York

1851 Meets Susan B. Anthony, with whom she will later lead the National Woman Suffrage Association

1895 Publishes the Woman's Bible

1902 Dies in New York City

A WOMAN'S DECLARATION OF INDEPENDENCE 1848

467

Social Studies Skills

Analysis | Critical Thinking | **Civic Participation** | Study

Accepting Social Responsibility

Define the Skill

A *society* is an organized group of people who share a common set of activities, traditions, and goals. You are part of many societies—your school, community, and nation are just three. Every society's strength depends on the support and contributions of its members. *Social responsibility* is the obligation that every person has to the societies in which he or she is a member.

Learn the Skill

As a part of your school, community, and nation, you have obligations to the people around you. The most obvious is to do nothing to harm your society. You also have a duty to be part of it. At the very least, this means exercising the rights and responsibilities of membership. These include being informed about issues in your society.

Another level of social responsibility is support of change to benefit society. This level of involvement goes beyond being informed about issues to trying to do something about them. If you take this important step, here are some points to consider.

1 Few efforts to change society have everyone's support. Some people will want things to stay the same. They may treat you badly if you work for change. You must be prepared for this possibility if you decide to take action.

2 Sometimes efforts to improve things involve opposing laws or rules that need to be changed. No matter how just your cause is, if you break law or rules, you must be willing to accept the consequences of your behavior.

3 Remember that violence is *never* an acceptable method for change. People who use force in seeking change are not behaving in a socially responsible manner, even if their cause is good.

This chapter was filled with the stories of socially responsible people. Many of them devoted their lives to changing society for the better. Some did so at great personal risk. Boston abolitionist William Lloyd Garrison barely escaped with his life from a local mob that tried to lynch him because of his views.

Garrison and the other reformers you read about demonstrated the highest level of social responsibility. They saw an issue they believed to be a problem in society, and they worked tirelessly to change it and make society better.

Practice the Skill

Review the "If you were there" scene on page 454. Imagine yourself as that Ohioan. You believe slavery to be wrong. However, you also respect the law, and it is illegal to help an escaped slave. In addition, you know that most of your neighbors do not feel as you do about slavery. They might harm you or your property if you take this stand against it.

1. Would agreeing to your friend's request help benefit society? Explain why or why not.

2. Are you willing to risk the anger of your neighbors? Why or why not?

3. Is the idea of breaking the law or possibly going to jail a factor in your decision? Explain.

4. Would agreeing to your friend's request be a socially responsible thing to do? Explain why or why not.

HOLT
History's Impact
▶ **video series**
Review the video to answer the closing question:
Why does it make sense that the women's suffrage movement originated from the abolitionist movement?

Visual Summary

QUICK FACTS

Use the visual summary below to help you review the main ideas of the chapter.

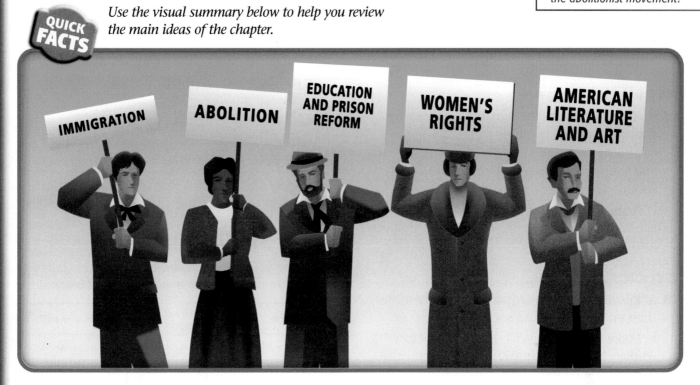

Reviewing Vocabulary, Terms, and People

1. Which of the following authors wrote about Puritan life in *The Scarlet Letter*?

a. Emily Dickinson **c.** Thomas Gallaudet

b. Herman Melville **d.** Nathaniel Hawthorne

2. Which document expressed the complaints of supporters of women's rights?

a. Declaration of the Rights of Women **c.** Letters on Women's Rights

b. Declaration of Sentiments **d.** Seneca Falls Convention

3. As leader of the common-school movement, who worked to improve free public education?

a. Walt Whitman **c.** Lyman Beecher

b. Horace Mann **d.** Sojourner Truth

Comprehension and Critical Thinking

SECTION 1 *(Pages 438–442)*

4. a. Identify What political party was founded by nativists, and what policies did it support?

b. Analyze What factors caused U.S. cities to grow so fast?

c. Evaluate Do you think that the benefits of city life outweighed its drawbacks? Explain.

SECTION 2 *(Pages 443–445)*

5. a. Describe Who were some important transcendentalists, and what ideas did they promote?

b. Compare and Contrast In what ways were transcendentalists and Romantics similar and different?

c. Elaborate Which movement appeals to you more—American transcendentalism or Romanticism? Why?

SECTION 3 (Pages 448–453)

6. a. Identify What important reform movements became popular in the early 1800s?

b. Analyze Why did education become an important topic for reformers in the 1800s?

c. Evaluate Which reform movement do you think had the greatest effect on the United States? Why?

SECTION 4 (Pages 454–459)

7. a. Recall What are the different reasons why people supported abolition?

b. Make Inferences How did northerners and southerners differ in their opposition to abolition?

c. Evaluate Which of the methods used by abolitionists to oppose slavery do you think was most successful? Why?

SECTION 5 (Pages 461–466)

8. a. Recall What led many women to question their place in American society?

b. Make Inferences Why did female factory workers like Charlotte Woodward support the women's rights movement?

c. Evaluate By 1860 do you think the women's movement had been successful? Explain your answer.

Using the Internet

go.hrw.com
KEYWORD: SF7 CH14

9. Activity: Creating Visuals The *Liberator* and *North Star* were two newspapers that encouraged the end of slavery. Enter the activity keyword and research the influence of abolitionist newspapers, such as those written by William Lloyd Garrison and Frederick Douglass. Then create a visual display that illustrates how each newspaper represented the abolitionist point of view.

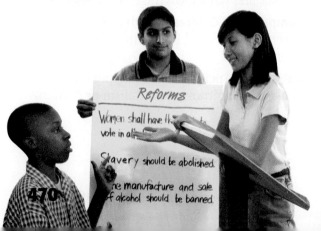

Reading Skills

Information and Propaganda *Use the Reading Skills taught in this chapter to answer the question below.*

10. Which of the following is *not* an example of propaganda?

a. a flyer protesting new tax laws

b. an ad about a political candidate

c. a radio announcement sponsored by an interest group

d. a list of camping rules from a park

Reviewing Themes

11. Society and Culture What social and cultural changes took place from 1800 to the mid-1800s?

Social Studies Skills

Accepting Social Responsibility *Use the Social Studies Skills taught in this chapter to fill in the chart below.*

12.

Action	Is it socially responsible?	Why or why not?
Removing litter from a park		
Voting		
Reading a political magazine		
Running a red light		

FOCUS ON WRITING ✏️

13. Writing Your Persuasive Letter You've described a number of important events and political, religious, and artistic movements in your notebook. Now, it's time to choose the one you consider most important. Think about how it changed life for people in the United States. Then write a two-paragraph persuasive letter to the newspaper, arguing for the event or movement you chose. In the first paragraph, identify the event or movement you chose as well as a thesis explaining why it is important. In the second paragraph, include details about the event or movement that support your thesis. Close with one or two sentences that sum up your points.

470

DIRECTIONS: Read each question and write the letter of the best response.

1 A potato blight in Europe brought a large number of immigrants to the United States who were

A Jewish.

B German.

C Irish.

D Protestant.

2 The author of *The Raven* was

A James Fenimore Cooper.

B Edgar Allan Poe.

C Walt Whitman.

D Emily Dickinson.

3 The most famous leader of the Underground Railroad was

A Frederick Douglass.

B Harriet Tubman.

C William Lloyd Garrison.

D Harriet Beecher Stowe.

4 African American students in the North

A had less opportunity for education than those in the South.

B did not benefit from educational reforms.

C had opportunities to attend black colleges formed in the 1840s.

D usually attended the same schools as white students.

5 The temperance movement, efforts at prison reform, and the abolition movement were all elements of

A social reforms of the mid-1800s.

B the Second Great Awakening.

C transcendentalism.

D the women's rights movement.

6 Which of the following people would *most likely* have supported a law prohibiting foreigners from holding public office?

A an antisuffragist

B a nativist

C an abolitionist

D a transcendentalist

7 Examine the following cartoon about women breaking kegs of liquor and then use it to answer the question below.

Document-Based Question What does the shield of the woman on horseback represent? How can you tell?

A Divided Nation

IN Indiana Standards

Social Studies Standards

8.1.16 Describe the abolition of slavery in the northern states, conflict and compromises associated with westward expansion of slavery, such as the Missouri Compromise (1820), the Compromise of 1850, Kansas-Nebraska Act (1854); and the continued resistance to slavery by people such as Frederick Douglass, Harriet Tubman, William Lloyd Garrison, and Harriet Beecher Stowe.

8.1.20 analyze the causes and effects of events leading to the Civil War, including development of sectional conflict over slavery.

8.3.2 Identify and create maps showing the physical growth and development of the United States from settlement of the original thirteen colonies through Reconstruction (1877) including transportation routes used during the period.

8.3.7 Using maps identify changes influenced by growth, economic development, and human migration in the eighteenth and nineteenth centuries.

go.hrw.com
Indiana
KEYWORD: SF10 IN

FOCUS ON WRITING

Writing an Autobiographical Sketch When you read about history, it can be difficult to imagine how the events you read about affected ordinary people. In this chapter you will read about slavery in the United States. Then you will write an autobiography of a fictional character, telling how these events affected him or her. Your fictional character can live in any part of the United States. He or she might be an enslaved African, a southern plantation owner, a northern abolitionist, or a settler in one of the new territories. Your classmates are your audience.

 UNITED STATES

1848
The Free-Soil Party is formed on August 9.

1848

 WORLD

1848
Revolutionary movements sweep across Europe.

SURVIVAL OF SPIRIT

We bake de bread,
Dey gib us de crust.
We sif de meat,
Dey gib us de huss.
We peel de meat,
Dey gib us de skin.
And dat's de way
Dey take us in:
We skim de pot,
Dey gib us de liquor,
And say dat's good
enough for nigger.

There was one or two things I had a right to, liberty, or death: if I could not have one, I would have the other; for no man should take me

Harriet Tubman, who returned to the South 19 times, helping more than three hundred enslaved

HOLT

History's Impact
▶ video series
Watch the video to understand the impact of the states' rights debate on national unity.

STOCKHOLDERS
R. R. COMPANY
Hold on to Your Stock!!

What You Will Learn...

Two women look at a display called "Survival of Spirit" at the Museum of African American History in Detroit, Michigan. The display shows a history of resistance to slavery. In this chapter you will learn about how the debate over slavery increasingly divided Americans during the mid-1800s.

1851
Indiana's constitutional convention supports the Fugitive Slave Law, urging Indianans to turn in escaped slaves.

CHARLESTON
MERCURY
EXTRA:

UNION
DISSOLVED!

1850
Congress passes the Fugitive Slave Act on September 18.

1852
Uncle Tom's Cabin is published by Harriet Beecher Stowe.

1856 In the Sack of Lawrence, pro-slavery forces attack the town of Lawrence, Kansas, on May 21.

1859
John Brown takes control of the federal arsenal at Harpers Ferry, Virginia.

1860
On December 20, South Carolina votes to secede from the United States.

1850

1855

1860

1852
Louis-Napoléon declares himself Emperor Napoléon III of France.

1856
British and French forces defeat Russia in the Crimean War.

1857 Indian soldiers in the British army begin the Sepoy Mutiny against British control of India.

Reading Social Studies

by Kylene Beers

Focus on Themes This chapter describes the growing tension between the North and the South over the slavery issue. You will read what happened as more states were admitted to the Union and people argued if they should be slave states or not. You will read about events that widened the division between the North and South so that the South finally chose to secede from the Union. Throughout the chapter you will see that **cultural** differences influenced **political** decisions.

Facts, Opinions, and the Past

Focus on Reading When you are trying to learn about history, separating facts from opinions helps you know what really happened.

Identifying Facts and Opinions Something is a **fact** if there is a way to prove it. For example, research can prove or disprove the following statement: "Abraham Lincoln belonged to the Republican Party." But research can't prove the following statement because it is just an **opinion**, or someone's belief: "Lincoln was the greatest president in American history."

Use the process below to decide whether a statement is fact or opinion.

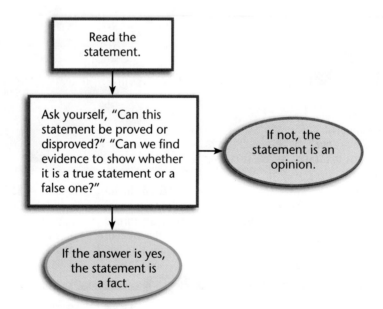

Read the statement.

Ask yourself, "Can this statement be proved or disproved?" "Can we find evidence to show whether it is a true statement or a false one?"

If not, the statement is an opinion.

If the answer is yes, the statement is a fact.

You Try It!

The following passage tells about the debates that Abraham Lincoln had with Stephen Douglas. All the statements in this passage are facts. What makes them facts and not opinions?

The Lincoln-Douglas Debates

In 1858 Illinois Republicans nominated Abraham Lincoln for the U.S. Senate. His opponent was Democrat Stephen Douglas, who had represented Illinois in the Senate since 1847. Lincoln challenged Douglas in what became the historic Lincoln-Douglas debates.

From Chapter 15, p. 491

In each debate, Lincoln stressed that the central issue of the campaign was the spread of slavery in the West. He said that the Democrats were trying to spread slavery across the nation.

Lincoln talked about the *Dred Scott* decision. He said that African Americans were "entitled to all the natural rights" listed in the Declaration of Independence, specifically mentioning "the right to life, liberty, and the pursuit of happiness."

Identify each of the following as a fact or an opinion and then explain your choice.

1. Lincoln accused the Democrats of trying to spread slavery across the nation.

2. The Lincoln-Douglas debates were the most important debates in the history of the nation.

3. Stephen Douglas was a U.S. senator from Illinois.

4. Abraham Lincoln ran against Douglas in the 1858 Senate election.

5. Most Americans believed that the *Dred Scott* decision was a good one.

6. Lincoln was the best debater people from Illinois had ever heard.

Academic Vocabulary

In this chapter, you will learn the following academic words:

implications *(p. 485)*
complex *(p. 489)*

As you read Chapter 15, look closely at quotes from historical figures. Are these quotes showing you facts or opinions?

The Debate over Slavery

What You Will Learn...

Main Ideas

1. The addition of new land in the West renewed disputes over the expansion of slavery.
2. The Compromise of 1850 tried to solve the disputes over slavery.
3. The Fugitive Slave Act caused more controversy.
4. Abolitionists used antislavery literature to promote opposition.

The Big Idea

Antislavery literature and the annexation of new lands intensified the debate over slavery.

Key Terms and People

popular sovereignty, *p. 476*
Wilmot Proviso, *p. 476*
sectionalism, *p. 477*
Free-Soil Party, *p. 477*
secede, *p. 478*
Compromise of 1850, *p. 479*
Fugitive Slave Act, *p. 479*
Anthony Burns, *p. 480*
Uncle Tom's Cabin, p. 481
Harriet Beecher Stowe, *p. 481*

TAKING NOTES Copy the graphic organizer below. As you read, take notes on the sequence of events in the debate over slavery. Be sure to describe the effects of each event.

Significant Events in the Slavery Debate	
Event	Effect
1.	
2.	
3.	
4.	
5.	
6.	

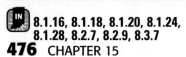

If YOU were there...

You live in a crowded neighborhood in New York City in 1854. Your apartment building is home to a variety of people—long-time residents, Irish immigrants, free African Americans. One day federal marshals knock on your door. They claim that one of your neighbors is a fugitive slave. The marshals say you must help them find her. If you don't, you will be fined or even sent to jail.

What would you tell the federal marshals?

BUILDING BACKGROUND Some reform movements of the 1800s drew stubborn and often violent opposition. This was especially true of the abolitionist movement. Pro-slavery supporters fought for laws to protect slavery and extend the slave system. These laws were a threat to African Americans in the North.

New Land Renews Slavery Disputes

The United States added more than 500,000 square miles of land as a result of winning the Mexican-American War in 1848. The additional land caused bitter debate about slavery. The Missouri Compromise of 1820 had divided the Louisiana Purchase into either free or slave regions. It prohibited slavery north of latitude 36°30′ but let Missouri become a slave state. In the 1840s President James K. Polk wanted to extend the 36°30′ line to the West coast, dividing the Mexican Cession into two parts—one free and one enslaved. Some leaders, including Senator Lewis Cass of Michigan, encouraged **popular sovereignty**, the idea that political power belongs to the people, who should decide on banning or allowing slavery.

Regional Differences about Slavery

Some northerners wanted to outlaw slavery in all parts of the Mexican Cession. During the war, Representative David Wilmot offered the **Wilmot Proviso**, a document stating that "neither slavery nor involuntary servitude shall ever exist in any part of [the] territory."

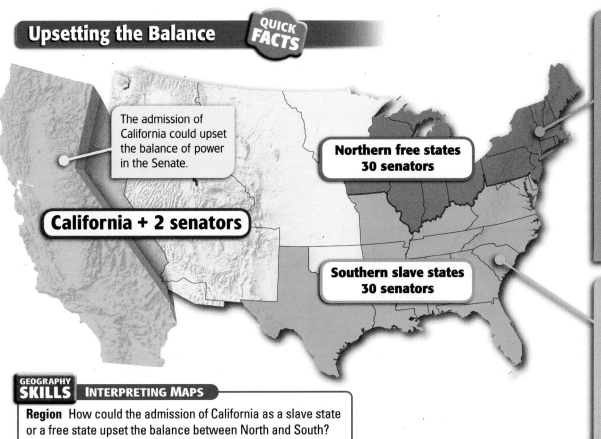

Upsetting the Balance — QUICK FACTS

The admission of California could upset the balance of power in the Senate.

California + 2 senators

Northern free states 30 senators

Southern slave states 30 senators

Free States
Connecticut
Illinois
Indiana
Iowa
Maine
Massachusetts
Michigan
New Hampshire
New Jersey
New York
Ohio
Pennsylvania
Rhode Island
Vermont
Wisconsin

Slave States
Alabama
Arkansas
Delaware
Florida
Georgia
Kentucky
Louisiana
Maryland
Mississippi
Missouri
North Carolina
South Carolina
Tennessee
Texas
Virginia

GEOGRAPHY SKILLS **INTERPRETING MAPS**

Region How could the admission of California as a slave state or a free state upset the balance between North and South?

The northern-controlled House passed the document, but in the Senate, the South had more power. The Wilmot Proviso did not pass. Before this time, politicians had usually supported the ideas of their political parties. However, the Wilmot Proviso spurred a debate that showed growing **sectionalism**, or favoring the interests of one section or region over the interests of the entire country.

To attract voters, the Democrats and the Whigs did not take a clear position on slavery in the presidential campaign of 1848. In response, antislavery northerners formed a new party, the **Free-Soil Party**, which supported the Wilmot Proviso. They worried that slave labor would mean fewer jobs for white workers. Party members chose former president Martin Van Buren as their candidate. The new party won 10 percent of the popular vote, drawing away votes from Democrat Lewis Cass. Whig candidate Zachary Taylor won a narrow victory.

The California Question

The California gold rush caused such rapid population growth that California applied to join the Union as a state instead of as a territory. But would California enter the Union as a free state or a slave state?

Most Californians opposed slavery, which had been illegal when the state was part of Mexico. Also, many forty-niners had come from free states. But if California became a free state, the balance between free and slave states would change, favoring the free states.

In the South, an imbalance was unacceptable. "We are about permanently to destroy the balance of power between the sections," said Senator Jefferson Davis of Mississippi. He and many other southerners did not want California to enter the Union as a free state.

READING CHECK **Drawing Inferences**
Why did sectionalism in the United States increase in the late 1840s?

THE IMPACT TODAY
Small parties still affect presidential elections in a similar way today.

Compromise of 1850

Senator Henry Clay of Kentucky had helped to settle the Missouri crisis of 1819–20 and the nullification crisis of 1832–33 by proposing compromises. He now had another plan to help the nation maintain peace. His ideas were designed to give both sides things that they wanted:

1. California would enter the Union as a free state.
2. The rest of the Mexican Cession would be federal land. In this territory, popular sovereignty would decide on slavery.
3. Texas would give up land east of the upper Rio Grande. In return, the government would pay Texas's debts from when it was an independent republic.
4. The slave trade—but not slavery—would end in the nation's capital.
5. A more effective fugitive slave law would be passed.

Clay's plan drew attack, especially regarding California. Senator William Seward of New York defended antislavery views and wanted California admitted "directly, without conditions, without qualifications, and without compromise." However, Senator John C. Calhoun of South Carolina argued that letting California enter as a free state would destroy the nation's balance. He warned people of issues that would later start the Civil War. Calhoun asked that the slave states be allowed to **secede**—formally withdraw—from the Union.

SPEECH
The Seventh of March Speech

On March 7, 1850, Daniel Webster spoke on the floor of the Senate in favor of the Compromise of 1850.

I hear with distress and anguish the word "secession." Secession! Peaceable secession! Sir, your eyes and mine are never destined to see the miracle. The dismemberment [taking apart] of this vast country without convulsion! The breaking up of the fountains of the great deep without ruffing the surface! Who is so foolish, I beg every body's pardon, as to expect to see any such thing? . . . There can be no such thing as peaceable secession.

—quoted in *Daniel Webster: The Completest Man,*
edited by Kenneth Shewmaker

> Webster is upset by talk of secession.

> Webster is saying that just as it is impossible to move water in the ocean without making waves, it is impossible for states to peacefully secede.

ANALYSIS SKILL **ANALYZING PRIMARY SOURCES**

Why did Webster support the Compromise of 1850?

Henry Clay introduced the Compromise of 1850 on the Senate floor.

Daniel Webster spoke eloquently in support of the compromise.

In contrast, Senator Daniel Webster of Massachusetts favored Clay's plan:

"I wish to speak today, not as a Massachusetts man, nor as a Northern man, but as an American … I speak today for the preservation of the Union. Hear me for my cause."

—Daniel Webster, quoted in *Battle Cry of Freedom* by James M. McPherson

Webster criticized northern abolitionists and southerners who talked of secession.

A compromise was enacted that year and seemed to settle most disputes between free and slave states. It achieved the majority of Clay's proposals. With the **Compromise of 1850**, California was able to enter the Union as a free state. The rest of the Mexican Cession was divided into two territories—Utah and New Mexico—where the question of whether to allow slavery would be decided by popular sovereignty.

Texas agreed to give up its land claims in New Mexico in exchange for financial aid from the federal government. The compromise outlawed the slave trade in the District of Columbia and established a new fugitive slave law.

READING CHECK **Analyzing** How was Texas affected by the Compromise of 1850?

Fugitive Slave Act

The newly passed **Fugitive Slave Act** made it a crime to help runaway slaves and allowed officials to arrest those slaves in free areas. Slaveholders were permitted to take suspected fugitives to U.S. commissioners, who decided their fate.

Details of the Fugitive Slave Act

Slaveholders could use testimony from white witnesses, but enslaved African Americans accused of being fugitives could not testify. Nor could people who hid or helped a runaway slave—they faced six months in jail and a $1,000 fine. Commissioners who rejected a slaveholder's claim earned $5 while those who returned suspected fugitives to slaveholders earned $10. Clearly, the commissioners benefited from helping slaveholders.

Reactions to the Fugitive Slave Act

Enforcement of the Fugitive Slave Act began immediately. In September 1850—the same month the law was passed—federal marshals arrested African American James Hamlet. They returned him to a slaveholder in

John C. Calhoun was weak and near death. He had his speech in support of slavery read to the Senate for him.

Primary Source

SPEECH
Southern View of the Compromise of 1850

John C. Calhoun from South Carolina wrote a speech saying that the proposed compromise did not go far enough to satisfy the South.

"I have, senators, believed from the first that the agitation of the subject of slavery would, if not prevented by some timely and effective measure, end in disunion … The South asks for justice, simple justice, and less she ought not to take. She has no compromise to offer but the Constitution, and no concession or surrender to make."

Agitation means "unrest."

Calhoun believes the South's position was supported by the Constitution.

ANALYSIS SKILL **ANALYZING PRIMARY SOURCES**

Why did Calhoun urge southern senators to vote against the compromise?

PHOTOGRAPH
A Fugitive Slave Convention

The Fugitive Slave Act enraged abolition-ists. To protest the new law, they held many meetings to publicly denounce it. One such meeting was held in 1850 in the small town of Cazenovia in central New York, a center for abolitionist activity. About 2,000 people—including many former slaves—attended the convention. They listened to speeches, made plans, and raised their voices for freedom. This photo was a point of pride for the delegates, but it also was used by opponents of the movement as a symbol of the poor morals of abolitionists: Not only were whites allowed to mix with African Americans, women and men were allowed to mix as well. This angered many people.

Gerrit Smith organized the convention.

Frederick Douglass spoke to the crowd.

The Edmonson sisters, Mary (left) and Emily, tried to escape from slavery but were captured. Abolitionists later purchased their freedom.

ANALYSIS SKILL **ANALYZING PRIMARY SOURCES**

Why would the abolitionists want a photograph of their convention?

Maryland, although he had lived in New York City for three years.

Thousands of northern African Americans fled to Canada in fear. In the 10 years after Congress passed the Fugitive Slave Act, some 343 fugitive slave cases were reviewed. The accused fugitives were declared free in only 11 cases.

The Fugitive Slave Act upset northern-ers, who were uncomfortable with the commissioners' power. Northerners disliked the idea of a trial without a jury. They also disapproved of commissioners' higher fees for returning slaves. Most were horrified that some free African Americans had been captured and sent to the South.

Most northerners opposed to the Act peacefully resisted, but violence did erupt. In 1854 **Anthony Burns**, a fugitive slave from Virginia, was arrested in Boston. Abolitionists used force while trying to rescue him from jail, killing a deputy marshal. A federal ship was ordered to return Burns to Virginia after his trial. Many people in the North, particularly in Massachusetts, were outraged. The event persuaded many to join the abolitionist cause.

READING CHECK **Drawing Conclusions**
What concerns did northerners have about the Fugitive Slave Act?

Antislavery Literature

Abolitionists in the North used the stories of fugitive slaves like James Hamlet and Anthony Burns to gain sympathy for their cause. Slave narratives also educated people about their hardships.

Fiction also informed people about the evils of slavery. **Uncle Tom's Cabin**, the antislavery novel written by **Harriet Beecher Stowe**, spoke out powerfully against slavery. Stowe, the daughter of Connecticut minister Lyman Beecher, moved to Ohio when she was 21. There she met fugitive slaves and learned about the cruelties of slavery. The Fugitive Slave Act greatly angered Stowe. She decided to write a book that would educate northerners about the realities of slavery.

Uncle Tom's Cabin was published in 1852. The main character, a kindly enslaved African American named Tom, is taken from his wife and sold "down the river" in Louisiana. Tom becomes the slave of cruel Simon Legree. In a rage, Legree has Tom beaten to death.

The novel electrified the nation and sparked outrage in the South. Louisa McCord, a famous southern writer, questioned the "foul imagination which could invent such scenes."

Within a decade, more than 2 million copies of *Uncle Tom's Cabin* had been sold in the United States. The book's popularity caused one northerner to remark that Stowe and her book had created "two millions of abolitionists." Stowe later wrote *A Key to Uncle Tom's Cabin* to answer those who had criticized her book.

The impact of Stowe's book is suggested by her reported meeting with Abraham Lincoln in 1862, a year after the start of the Civil War. Lincoln supposedly said to Stowe that she was "the little lady who made this big war." Her book is still widely read today as a source of information about the harsh realities of slavery.

READING CHECK Identifying Cause and Effect Why did abolitionists use antislavery literature to promote their cause, and what effect did it have on the slavery debate?

SUMMARY AND PREVIEW The United States experienced increasing disagreement over the issue of slavery. The Compromise of 1850 and the Fugitive Slave Act tried to address these disagreements with legislation. In the next section you will read about another disputed law concerning slavery, the Kansas-Nebraska Act, and the violence it sparked.

go.hrw.com
Online Quiz
KEYWORD: SF7 HP15

Section 1 Assessment

Reviewing Ideas, Terms, and People

1. a. Describe What ideas did the **Free-Soil Party** promote?
   b. Predict What are some possible results of the growing sectional debate over slavery?

2. a. Describe What were the major points of the **Compromise of 1850**?
   b. Contrast What differing opinions emerged toward Henry Clay's proposed compromise?

3. a. Identify What were the effects of the **Fugitive Slave Act**?
   b. Draw Conclusions Why did some Americans believe the Fugitive Slave Act was unfair?

4. a. Identify What are three examples of antislavery literature?
   b. Elaborate Do you think literature was an effective tool against slavery? Why or why not?

Critical Thinking

5. Evaluating Review your notes on the debate over slavery. Then evaluate how the Compromise of 1850, the Fugitive Slave Act, and antislavery literature affected the slavery debate. Use a graphic organizer like the one below.

FOCUS ON WRITING

6. Taking Notes on the Debate over Slavery Make some notes on the Wilmot Proviso, the Free-Soil Party, the Compromise of 1850, and the Fugitive Slave Act. Decide how your character feels about each of these. How do the Compromise of 1850 and the Fugitive Slave Act affect your character?

Antislavery Literature

from Uncle Tom's Cabin

WORD HELP

conceive imagine
desolate alone
forlorn unhappy
slacking slowing down
thither there

❶ *What detail tells you how long Eliza has walked up to this point?*

❷ *Why do you think she chooses that escape route?*

by Harriet Beecher Stowe (1811–1896)

About the Reading *Published nine years before the outbreak of the Civil War,* Uncle Tom's Cabin *focused the nation's attention on the cruelties of slavery. In the following section, Stowe describes how a slave named Eliza is trying to escape to save her son from being sold.*

AS YOU READ Look for details that appeal to your feelings.

It is impossible to conceive of a human creature more wholly desolate and forlorn than Eliza when she turned her footsteps from Uncle Tom's cabin . . .

The boundaries of the farm, the grove, the wood lot passed by her dizzily as she walked on; and still she went, leaving one familiar object after another, slacking not, pausing not, till reddening daylight found her many a long mile from all traces of any familiar objects upon the open highway. ❶

She had often been, with her mistress, to visit some connections in the little town of T—, not far from the Ohio River, and knew the road well. ❷ To go thither, to escape across the Ohio River, were the first hurried outlines of her plan of escape; beyond that she could only hope in God . . .

CONNECTING LITERATURE TO HISTORY

1. **Slaves had no legal rights. They were considered to be property, not human beings.** How do the actions and description in this passage contradict these ideas about slaves?

2. **Frederick Douglass, Sojourner Truth, and other former slaves wrote narratives about their experiences. Yet these true stories did not have as much impact as Stowe's novel.** Why do you think this fictional story about slavery had more impact than true slave narratives?

Trouble in Kansas

If YOU were there...

You live on a New England farm in 1855. You often think about moving West. But the last few harvests have been bad, and you can't afford it. Now the Emigrant Aid Society offers to help you get to Kansas. To bring in antislavery voters like you, they'll give you a wagon, livestock, and farm machines. Still, you know that Kansas might be dangerous.

Would you decide to risk settling in Kansas?

BUILDING BACKGROUND The argument over the extension of slavery grew stronger and more bitter. It dominated American politics in the mid-1800s. Laws that tried to find compromises ended by causing more violence. The bloodiest battleground of this period was in Kansas.

Election of 1852

Four leading candidates for the Democratic presidential nomination emerged in 1852. It became clear that none of them would win a majority of votes. Frustrated delegates at the Democratic National Convention turned to **Franklin Pierce**, a little-known politician from New Hampshire. Pierce promised to honor the Compromise

What You Will Learn...

Main Ideas

1. The debate over the expansion of slavery influenced the election of 1852.
2. The Kansas-Nebraska Act allowed voters to allow or prohibit slavery.
3. Pro-slavery and antislavery groups clashed violently in what became known as "Bleeding Kansas."

The Big Idea

The Kansas-Nebraska Act heightened tensions in the conflict over slavery.

Key Terms and People

Franklin Pierce, *p. 483*
Stephen Douglas, *p. 484*
Kansas-Nebraska Act, *p. 485*
Pottawatomie Massacre, *p. 487*
Charles Sumner, *p. 487*
Preston Brooks, *p. 487*

TAKING NOTES As you read, take notes on Stephen Douglas's plan for a railroad to the Pacific Ocean, southern congressmembers' views of his plan, and the resulting Kansas-Nebraska Act. Write details about each in a graphic organizer like the one shown below.

Douglas's plan		Kansas-Nebraska Act
Southern Congress members' reaction		

 8.1.16, 8.1.18, 8.1.20, 8.1.24, 8.3.2, 8.3.7

This political cartoon shows pro-slavery politicians forcing slavery on a settler in Kansas who is a member of the antislavery Free-Soil political party.

MURDER !!! help— neighbors help. O my poor Wife and Children.

FORCING SLAVERY DOWN THE THROAT OF A FREESOILER

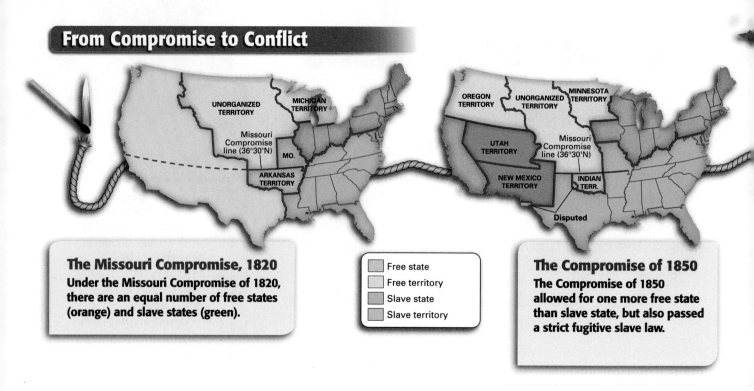

The Missouri Compromise, 1820
Under the Missouri Compromise of 1820, there are an equal number of free states (orange) and slave states (green).

Free state
Free territory
Slave state
Slave territory

The Compromise of 1850
The Compromise of 1850 allowed for one more free state than slave state, but also passed a strict fugitive slave law.

FOCUS ON READING

What facts and what opinions are mentioned in this paragraph?

FOCUS ON INDIANA

The Kansas-Nebraska Act was opposed by many Indianans. The Indiana Fusionist movement tried to unite voters from the Whig Party, Free Soilers, Know-Nothings, and other viewpoints. The Fusionists won many state elections in 1854, but by 1856 their power had dwindled. Many of them joined the newly emerging Republican Party.

of 1850 and the Fugitive Slave Act. Therefore, southerners trusted Pierce on the issue of slavery.

The opposing Whigs also held their convention in 1852. In other presidential elections, they had nominated well-known former generals such as William Henry Harrison and Zachary Taylor. This had been a good strategy, as both men had won. The Whigs decided to choose another war hero. They passed over the current president, Millard Fillmore, because they believed that his strict enforcement of the Fugitive Slave Act would cost votes. Instead, they chose Winfield Scott, a Mexican War hero. Southerners did not trust Scott, however, because he had not fully supported the Compromise of 1850.

Pierce won the election of 1852 by a large margin. Many Whigs viewed the election as a painful defeat, not just for their candidate, but for their party.

READING CHECK Drawing Conclusions
What issues determined the outcome of the presidential election of 1852?

The Kansas-Nebraska Act

In his inaugural address, President Pierce expressed his hope that the slavery issue had been put to rest "and that no sectional . . . excitement may again threaten the durability [stability] of our institutions." Less than a year later, however, a proposal to build a railroad to the West coast helped revive the slavery controversy and opened a new period of sectional conflict.

Douglas and the Railroad

Ever since entering Congress in the mid-1840s, **Stephen Douglas** had supported the idea of building a railroad to the Pacific Ocean. Douglas favored a line running from Chicago. The first step toward building such a railroad would be organizing what remained of the Louisiana Purchase into a federal territory. The Missouri Compromise required that this land be free territory and eventually free states.

Southerners in Congress did not support Douglas's plan, recommending a southern route for the railroad. Their preferred line

The Kansas-Nebraska Act

As a result of the Kansas-Nebraska Act, the question of slavery is to be decided by popular sovereignty—by the people who vote in the elections there—in the newly organized territories of Kansas and Nebraska. The act sparked violent conflict between pro-slavery and antislavery groups.

Map labels: WASH. TERR., OREGON TERRITORY, NEBRASKA TERRITORY, MINNESOTA TERRITORY, UTAH TERRITORY, KANSAS TERRITORY, NEW MEXICO TERRITORY, INDIAN TERR., Disputed

Legend:
- Free state
- Free territory
- Slave state
- Slave territory
- Popular sovereignty

GEOGRAPHY SKILLS INTERPRETING MAPS

1. **Region** In what part of the United States were the slave states located?
2. **Place** What free state was added with the Compromise of 1850?

ran from New Orleans, across Texas and New Mexico Territory, to southern California. Determined to have the railroad start in Chicago, Douglas asked a few key southern senators to support his plan. They agreed to do so if the new territory west of Missouri was opened to slavery.

Two New Territories

In January 1854, Douglas introduced what became the **Kansas-Nebraska Act**, a plan that would divide the remainder of the Louisiana Purchase into two territories—Kansas and Nebraska—and allow the people in each territory to decide on the question of slavery. The act would eliminate the Missouri Compromise's restriction on slavery north of the 36° 30' line.

Antislavery northerners were outraged by the **implications**. Some believed the proposal was part of a terrible plot to turn free territory into a "dreary region . . . inhabited by masters and slaves." All across the North, citizens attended protest meetings and sent anti-Nebraska petitions to Congress.

Even so, with strong southern support—and with Douglas and President Pierce pressuring their fellow Democrats to vote for it—the measure passed both houses of Congress and was signed into law on May 30, 1854. Lost amid all the controversy over the territorial bill was Douglas's proposed railroad to the Pacific Ocean. Congress would not approve the construction of such a railroad until 1862.

Kansas Divided

Antislavery and pro-slavery groups rushed their supporters to Kansas. One of the people who spoke out strongly against slavery in Kansas was Senator Seward.

" Gentlemen of the Slave States ... I accept [your challenge] in ... the cause of freedom. We will engage in competition for ... Kansas, and God give the victory to the side which is stronger in numbers as it is in right. "
—William Henry Seward, quoted in
The Impending Crisis, 1848–1861 by David M. Potter

Elections for the Kansas territorial legislature were held in March 1855. Almost 5,000

ACADEMIC VOCABULARY

implications
things that are inferred or deduced

pro-slavery voters crossed the border from Missouri, voted in Kansas, and then returned home. As a result, the new legislature had a huge pro-slavery majority. The members of the legislature passed strict laws that made it a crime to question slaveholders' rights and said that those who helped fugitive slaves could be put to death. In protest, antislavery Kansans formed their own legislature 25 miles away in Topeka. President Pierce, however, only recognized the pro-slavery legislature.

READING CHECK Analyzing Why did northerners dislike the Kansas-Nebraska Act?

Bleeding Kansas

By early 1856 Kansas had two opposing governments, and the population was angry. Settlers had moved to Kansas to homestead in peace, but the controversy over slavery began to affect everyone.

In April 1856, a congressional committee arrived in Kansas to decide which government was legitimate. Although committee members declared the election of the pro-slavery legislature to be unfair, the federal government did not agree.

Attack on Lawrence

The new pro-slavery settlers owned guns, and antislavery settlers received weapons shipments from friends in the East. Then, violence broke out. In May 1856 a pro-slavery grand jury in Kansas charged leaders of the antislavery government with treason. About 800 men rode to the city of Lawrence to arrest the antislavery leaders, but they had fled. The posse took its anger out on Lawrence by setting fires, looting buildings, and destroying presses used to print antislavery newspapers. One man was killed in the pro-slavery attack that became known as the Sack of Lawrence.

John Brown's Response

Abolitionist John Brown was from New England, but he and some of his sons had moved to Kansas in 1855. The Sack of Lawrence made him determined to "fight fire with fire" and to "strike terror in the hearts of the pro-slavery people." On the night of May 24, 1856, along Pottawatomie Creek,

"Bleeding Kansas"

Abolitionists and pro-slavery forces clashed in Kansas, killing many people. Shown here is a group of abolitionists who took the law into their own hands to free one of their group from prison.

Why might these men have fought against slavery?

John Doy was imprisoned for his abolitionist activities but was freed by other abolitionists.

486

Brown and his men killed five pro-slavery men in Kansas in what became known as the **Pottawatomie Massacre**. Brown and his men dragged the pro-slavery men out of their cabins and killed them with swords. The abolitionist band managed to escape capture. Brown declared that his actions had been ordered by God.

Kansas collapsed into civil war, and about 200 people were killed. The events in "Bleeding Kansas" became national front-page stories. In September 1856, a new territorial governor arrived and began to restore order.

Brooks Attacks Sumner

Congress also reacted to the violence of the Sack of Lawrence. Senator **Charles Sumner** of Massachusetts criticized pro-slavery people in Kansas and personally insulted Andrew Pickens Butler, a pro-slavery senator from South Carolina. Representative **Preston Brooks**, a relative of Butler's, responded strongly.

On May 22, 1856, Brooks used a walking cane to beat Sumner unconscious in the Senate chambers. Dozens of southerners sent Brooks new canes, but northerners were out-

raged and called the attacker "Bully Brooks." Brooks only had to pay a $300 fine to the federal court. It took Sumner three years before he was well enough to return to the Senate.

READING CHECK **Summarizing** What were some of the results of the intense division in Kansas?

SUMMARY AND PREVIEW The Kansas-Nebraska Act produced a national uproar. In the next section you will read about divisions in political parties.

The cartoon above shows Preston Brooks beating Charles Sumner with his cane. Sumner's only protection is a quill pen symbolically representing the law.

Section 2 Assessment

Reviewing Ideas, Terms, and People

1. **a. Identify** What issues influenced the outcome of the election of 1852?
   b. Draw Conclusions Why did northern and southern Democrats support **Franklin Pierce**?
2. **a. Recall** What did the **Kansas-Nebraska Act** do?
   b. Explain Why did antislavery and pro-slavery groups encourage people to move to Kansas?
   c. Evaluate Would you have supported or opposed the Kansas-Nebraska Act? Why?
3. **a. Describe** What was the **Pottawatomie Massacre**?
   b. Analyze How did **Charles Sumner's** views on "Bleeding Kansas" create conflict?
   c. Elaborate Do you think **Preston Brooks's** punishment was reasonable? Why or why not?

Critical Thinking

4. **Sequencing** Review your notes on the Kansas-Nebraska Act. Then copy the graphic organizer

shown below and use it to show how the act and later events led to violence in Kansas.

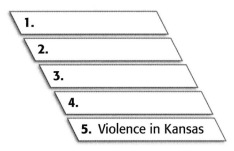

1.
2.
3.
4.
5. Violence in Kansas

FOCUS ON WRITING

5. **Taking Notes on the Trouble in Kansas** Make some notes on the election of 1852, the Kansas-Nebraska Act, and the events in Kansas. Decide how your character feels about each of these. How do these events affect your character?

Political Divisions

If **YOU** were there...

You are traveling through Michigan in July 1854. As you pass through the town of Jackson, you see a crowd of several hundred people gathered under the trees. You join them and find that it is a political rally. Antislavery supporters from different parties are meeting to form a new political party. Speakers promise to fight slavery "until the contest be terminated."

How do you think this new party will affect American politics?

BUILDING BACKGROUND The slavery question continued to divide the country and lead to violence. The issue not only dominated American politics in the mid-1800s but also brought changes in the makeup of American political parties.

Political Parties Undergo Change

Democrat Stephen Douglas had predicted that the Kansas-Nebraska Act would "raise a . . . storm." He was right. The Kansas-Nebraska Act brought the slavery issue back into the national spotlight. Some Whigs, Democrats, Free-Soilers, and abolitionists joined in 1854 to form the **Republican Party**, a political party united against the spread of slavery in the West.

Democrats were in trouble. Those who supported the Kansas-Nebraska Act were not re-elected. The Whig Party also fell apart when northern and southern Whigs refused to work together. A senator from Connecticut complained, "The Whig Party has been killed off . . . by that miserable Nebraska business." Some Whigs and Democrats joined the American Party, also known as the Know-Nothing Party. At the party's convention, delegates argued over slavery, then chose former president Millard Fillmore as their candidate for the election of 1856.

The Democrats knew they could not choose a strong supporter of the Kansas-Nebraska Act, such as President Pierce or Senator Douglas. They nominated **James Buchanan** of Pennsylvania. Buchanan had a great deal of political experience as Polk's secretary of state. Most

What You Will Learn...

Main Ideas

1. Political parties in the United States underwent change due to the movement to expand slavery.
2. The *Dred Scott* decision created further division over the issue of slavery.
3. The Lincoln-Douglas debates brought much attention to the conflict over slavery.

The Big Idea

The split over the issue of slavery intensified due to political division and judicial decisions.

Key Terms and People

Republican Party, *p. 488*
James Buchanan, *p. 488*
John C. Frémont, *p. 489*
Dred Scott, *p. 489*
Roger B. Taney, *p. 490*
Abraham Lincoln, *p. 490*
Lincoln-Douglas debates, *p. 491*
Freeport Doctrine, *p. 492*

TAKING NOTES As you read, take notes on the effects of political divisions and the *Dred Scott* case on the debate over slavery. Write your notes in a graphic organizer like the one below.

8.1.18, 8.1.20, 8.1.24, 8.1.28, 8.1.29, 8.2.3

importantly, he had been in Great Britain as ambassador during the Kansas-Nebraska Act dispute and had not been involved in the debate.

At their first nominating convention, the Republicans chose explorer **John C. Frémont** as their candidate. He had little political experience, but he stood against the spread of slavery. The public saw Republicans as a single-issue party. They had almost no supporters outside of the free states.

On election day, Buchanan won 14 of the 15 slave states and became the new president. Frémont won 11 of the 16 free states. Fillmore won only one state—Maryland. Buchanan had won the election.

READING CHECK Summarizing What were the major political parties in the election of 1856, and who was the candidate for each party?

Dred Scott Decision

Just two days after Buchanan became president, the Supreme Court issued a historic ruling about slavery. News of the decision threw the country back into crisis. The Court reviewed and decided the **complex** case involving an enslaved man named **Dred Scott**.

Dred Scott Sues for Freedom

Dred Scott was the slave of Dr. John Emerson, an army surgeon who lived in St. Louis, Missouri. In the 1830s, Emerson had taken Scott on tours of duty in Illinois and the Wisconsin Territory. After they returned to Missouri, the doctor died, and Scott became the slave of Emerson's widow. In 1846 Scott sued for his freedom in the Missouri state courts, arguing that he had become free when he lived in free territory. Though a lower court ruled in

ACADEMIC VOCABULARY
complex
difficult, not simple

SUPREME COURT DECISIONS

Dred Scott v. *Sandford* (1857)

Background of the Case Born a slave in Virginia, Dred Scott moved with his slaveholder to the free state of Illinois and then to the Wisconsin Territory. After returning to the South, Scott sued for his freedom. He claimed that because he had lived in a state that banned slavery, he was no longer a slave.

The Court's Ruling
The Court ruled that African Americans, whether free or slave, were not considered citizens of the United States, and therefore had no right to sue in federal court. It also decided that the Missouri Compromise was unconstitutional.

The Court's Reasoning
Chief Justice Roger B. Taney wrote in the majority opinion that the Court did not believe that African Americans were included in the Constitution's definition of citizens and that they "had no rights which the white man was bound to respect." Addressing a side issue in the case, the opinion also stated that Congress could not outlaw slavery in the territories. This struck down the Missouri Compromise, which had made slavery illegal in territories north of the 36°30′ dividing line.

Why It Matters
The *Dred Scott* case was seen as a setback to abolitionist ideas against slavery. It reduced the status of free African Americans and upheld the view of slaves as property without rights or protection under the Constitution. It also took from Congress the power to ban slavery in its territories, which would aid the spread of slavery in new states. Because of its pro-slavery decision, the reputation of the Court suffered greatly in parts of the North.

ANALYSIS SKILL ANALYZING INFORMATION
1. Why do you think the Court ruled that African Americans had no access to federal courts?
2. How did this case affect abolitionist efforts?

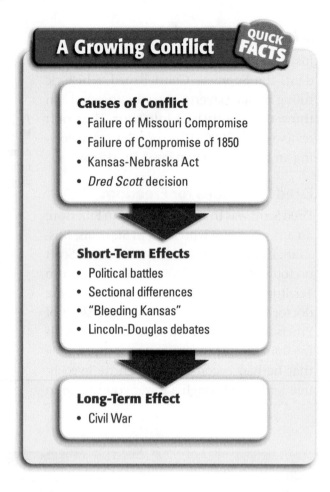

A Growing Conflict

Causes of Conflict
- Failure of Missouri Compromise
- Failure of Compromise of 1850
- Kansas-Nebraska Act
- *Dred Scott* decision

Short-Term Effects
- Political battles
- Sectional differences
- "Bleeding Kansas"
- Lincoln-Douglas debates

Long-Term Effect
- Civil War

his favor, the Missouri Supreme Court overturned this ruling.

Scott's case reached the U.S. Supreme Court 11 years later, in 1857. The justices—a majority of whom were from the South—had three key issues before them. First, the Court had to rule on whether Scott was a citizen. Only citizens could sue in federal court. Second, the Court had to decide if his time living on free soil made him free. Third, the Court had to determine the constitutionality of prohibiting slavery in parts of the Louisiana Purchase.

The Supreme Court's Ruling

Chief Justice **Roger B. Taney** (TAW-nee), himself from a slaveholding family in Maryland, wrote the majority opinion in the *Dred Scott* decision in March 1857. First, he addressed the issue of Dred Scott's citizenship. Taney said the nation's founders believed that African Americans "had no rights which a white man was bound to respect." He therefore concluded that all African Americans, whether slave or free, were not citizens under the U.S. Constitution. Thus, Dred Scott did not have the right to file suit in federal court.

Taney also ruled on the other issues before the Court. As to whether Scott's residence on free soil made him free, Taney flatly said it did not. Because Scott had returned to the slave state of Missouri, the chief justice said, "his *status,* as free or slave, depended on the laws of Missouri."

Finally, Taney declared the Missouri Compromise restriction on slavery north of 36°30′ to be unconstitutional. He pointed out that the Fifth Amendment said no one could "be deprived of life, liberty, or property without due process of law." Because slaves were considered property, Congress could not prohibit someone from taking slaves into a federal territory. Under this ruling, Congress had no right to ban slavery in any federal territory.

Most white southerners cheered this decision. It "covers every question regarding slavery and settles it in favor of the South," reported a Georgia newspaper. Another newspaper, the New Orleans *Picayune,* assured its readers that the ruling put "the whole basis of the . . . Republican organization under the ban of law."

The ruling stunned many northerners. The Republicans were particularly upset because their platform in 1856 had argued that Congress held the right to ban slavery in the federal territories. Now the nation's highest court had ruled that Congress did not have this right.

Indeed, some northerners feared that the spread of slavery would not stop with the federal territories. Illinois lawyer **Abraham Lincoln** warned that a future Court ruling, or what he called "the next *Dred Scott* decision," would prohibit states from banning slavery.

SPEECH

A House Divided

In 1858 Abraham Lincoln gave a passionate speech to Illinois Republicans about the dangers of the disagreement over slavery. Some considered it a call for war.

> This line is a paraphrase of a line in the Bible.

❝In my opinion, it [disagreement over slavery] will not cease [stop], until a crisis shall have been reached and passed. "A house divided against itself cannot stand." I believe this government cannot endure permanently half slave and half free. I do not expect the Union to be dissolved—I do not expect the house to fall—but I do expect it will cease to be divided.**❞**

—**Abraham Lincoln,**
quoted in *Abraham Lincoln: Speeches and Writings 1832–1858*
edited by Don E. Fehrenbacher

> Lincoln expresses confidence that the Union will survive.

ANALYSIS SKILL **ANALYZING PRIMARY SOURCES**

What do you think Lincoln meant by "crisis"?

❝We shall *lie down* pleasantly dreaming that the people of *Missouri* are on the verge of [close to] making their state *free;* and we shall *awake* to the *reality,* instead, that the 90 Supreme Court has made *Illinois* a *slave state.* **❞**

—Abraham Lincoln, quoted in *The Collected Works of Abraham Lincoln*, edited by Roy P. Basler

READING CHECK **Summarizing** What were the major rulings of the *Dred Scott* decision?

Lincoln-Douglas Debates

In 1858 Illinois Republicans nominated Abraham Lincoln for the U.S. Senate. His opponent was Democrat Stephen Douglas, who had represented Illinois in the Senate since 1847. Lincoln challenged Douglas in what became the historic **Lincoln-Douglas debates**.

In each debate, Lincoln stressed that the central issue of the campaign was the spread of slavery in the West. He said that the Democrats were trying to spread slavery across the nation.

Lincoln talked about the *Dred Scott* decision. He said that African Americans were "entitled to all the natural rights" listed in the Declaration of Independence, specifically mentioning "the right to life, liberty, and the pursuit of happiness." However, Lincoln believed that African Americans were not necessarily the social or political equals of whites. Hoping to cost Lincoln votes, Douglas charged that Lincoln "thinks that the Negro is his brother . . ."

Douglas also criticized Lincoln for saying that the nation could not remain "half slave and half free." Douglas said that the statement revealed a Republican desire to make every state a free state. This, he warned, would only lead to "a dissolution [destruction] of the Union" and "warfare between the North and the South."

At the second debate, in the northern Illinois town of Freeport, Illinois, Lincoln pressed Douglas on the apparent contradiction between the Democrats' belief in popu-

THE IMPACT TODAY

Today political debates are televised and can be seen around the world.

Lincoln-Douglas Debates

Lincoln ran for the U.S. Senate in Illinois against Douglas in 1858. The two men debated seven times at various locations around the state. Lincoln lost the election but gained national recognition.

Abraham Lincoln   **Stephen Douglas**

they please, for the reason that slavery cannot exist a day or an hour anywhere, unless it is supported by local police regulations."

This notion that the police would enforce the voters' decision if it contradicted the Supreme Court's decision in the Dred Scott case became known as the **Freeport Doctrine**.

The Freeport Doctrine put the slavery question back in the hands of American citizens. It helped Douglas win the Senate seat. Lincoln, while not victorious, made a strong, important leader of the Republican Party.

READING CHECK **Drawing Inferences** Why did Abraham Lincoln make slavery's expansion the central issue of the Lincoln-Douglas debates?

lar sovereignty and the *Dred Scott* decision. Lincoln asked Douglas to explain how, if Congress could not ban slavery from a federal territory, Congress could allow the citizens of that territory to ban it.

Douglas responded that it did not matter what the Supreme Court decided about slavery. He argued that "the people have the lawful means to introduce it or exclude it as

SUMMARY AND PREVIEW The *Dred Scott* decision and the Lincoln-Douglas debates dealt with the conflict over slavery in the western territories. In the next section you will read about how the conflict broke apart the Union.

go.hrw.com
Online Quiz
KEYWORD: SF7 HP15

Section 3 Assessment

Reviewing Ideas, Terms, and People

1. a. Identify What was the major issue of the newly formed **Republican Party**?
 b. Draw Conclusions How did the Kansas-Nebraska Act affect political parties?
 c. Elaborate Why do you think **James Buchanan** won the election of 1856?
2. a. Identify Who was **Roger B. Taney**, and why was he important?
 b. Draw Conclusions How did the *Dred Scott* decision affect the Missouri Compromise and the expansion of slavery?
 c. Predict What problems might result from the Supreme Court's ruling in the *Dred Scott* case?
3. a. Recall What was the major issue of the **Lincoln-Douglas debates**?
 b. Make Inferences Despite his loss in the election, how did Lincoln become the leader of the Republican Party?

Critical Thinking

4. Identifying Points of View Review your notes on political divisions and the Dred Scott decision. Then copy the graphic organizer below and use it to identify the views of Abraham Lincoln and Stephen Douglas on slavery.

Lincoln	Douglas
vs.	

FOCUS ON WRITING

5. Taking Notes on the Political Divisions Make some notes on the Republican Party, the *Dred Scott* decision, and the Lincoln-Douglas debates. Decide how your character feels about each of these. How do these events affect your character?

The Nation Divides

If YOU were there...

You work for the weekly newspaper in Harpers Ferry, Virginia. You strongly oppose slavery, but you think the question ought to be resolved by laws, not bloodshed. Now your paper has sent you to interview the famous abolitionist John Brown in prison. His raids in "Bleeding Kansas" killed several people. Now he is in jail for attacking a federal arsenal and taking weapons.

What questions would you ask John Brown?

BUILDING BACKGROUND Unpopular compromises and court decisions deepened the divisions between pro-slavery and antislavery advocates. The Lincoln-Douglas debates attracted more attention to the issue. As the disagreements grew, violence increased, though many Americans hoped to avoid it. But it was too late to keep the nation unified.

Raid on Harpers Ferry

In 1858 John Brown tried to start an uprising. He wanted to attack the federal arsenal in Virginia and seize weapons there. He planned to arm local slaves. Brown expected to kill or take hostage white southerners who stood in his way. He urged abolitionists to give him money so that he could support a small army. But after nearly two years, Brown's army had only about 20 men.

On the night of October 16, 1859, **John Brown's raid** began when he and his men took over the arsenal in Harpers Ferry, Virginia, in hopes of starting a slave rebellion. He sent several of his men into the countryside to get slaves to join him. However, enslaved African Americans did not come to Harpers Ferry, fearing punishment if they took part. Instead, local white southerners attacked Brown. Eight of his men and three local men were killed. Brown and some followers retreated to a firehouse.

Federal troops arrived in Harpers Ferry the following night. The next morning, Colonel Robert E. Lee ordered a squad of marines to storm the firehouse. In a matter of seconds, the marines killed two more of Brown's men and captured the rest—including Brown.

What You Will Learn...

Main Ideas

1. John Brown's raid on Harpers Ferry intensified the disagreement between free states and slave states.
2. The outcome of the election of 1860 divided the United States.
3. The dispute over slavery led the South to secede.

The Big Idea

The United States broke apart due to the growing conflict over slavery.

Key Terms and People

John Brown's raid, *p. 493*
John C. Breckinridge, *p. 495*
Constitutional Union Party, *p. 495*
John Bell, *p. 495*
John J. Crittenden, *p. 496*
Confederate States of America, *p. 497*
Jefferson Davis, *p. 497*

TAKING NOTES Create a chart like the one below. As you read, take notes on the significance of each of the people listed in the chart and his relationship to the events of the section.

Person	Significance
John Brown	
John C. Breckinridge	
John Bell	
Abraham Lincoln	
Jefferson Davis	
John J. Crittenden	

 8.1.16, 8.1.18, 8.1.20, 8.1.21, 8.1.24, 8.1.28, 8.1.29, 8.1.30. 8.2.3, 8.3.2, 8.3.7

SPEECH
John Brown's Last Speech

At his trial, after being pronounced guilty, John Brown spoke in his own defense about his plan to free slaves.

Brown says he never meant to start a rebellion.

> **"**I intended certainly to have made a clean thing of that matter [freeing slaves] . . . I never did intend murder or treason, or the destruction of property, or to excite or incite the slaves to rebellion, or to make insurrection [revolt] . . . Had I interfered in the manner which I admit . . . in behalf of the rich, the powerful, the intelligent, the so-called great . . . it would have been all right, and every man in this Court would have deemed it an act worthy of reward rather than punishment . . . I believe that to have interfered as I have done . . . in behalf of His despised poor, is no wrong, but right.**"**
>
> **—John Brown,**
> quoted in *The Life, Trial and Execution of Captain John Brown*

By *His*, Brown means God's.

ANALYSIS SKILL   ANALYZING PRIMARY SOURCES

How does Brown contrast his ideas with the Court's ideas?

Brown was quickly convicted of treason, murder, and conspiracy. Some of his men received death sentences. John A. Copeland, a fugitive slave, defended his actions. "If I am dying for freedom, I could not die for a better cause." Convinced that he also would be sentenced to death, Brown delivered a memorable speech.

> *"* Now, if it is deemed [thought] necessary that I should forfeit [give up] my life for the furtherance of the ends of justice, and mingle [mix] my blood . . . with the blood of millions in this slave country whose rights are disregarded by wicked, cruel, and unjust enactments, I say, let it be done. *"*
>
> —John Brown, quoted in *John Brown, 1800–1859* by Oswald Garrison Villard

As expected, the judge ordered Brown to be hanged. The sentence was carried out one month later on December 2, 1859.

Many northerners mourned John Brown's death, but some abolitionists criticized his extreme actions. Abraham Lincoln said Brown "agreed with us in thinking slavery wrong." However, Lincoln continued, "That cannot excuse violence, bloodshed, and treason."

Most southern whites—both slaveholders and non-slaveholders—felt threatened by the actions of John Brown. They worried that a "John Brown the Second" might attack. One South Carolina newspaper voiced these fears: "We are convinced the safety of the South lies only outside the present Union." Another newspaper stated that "the sooner we get out of the Union, the better."

READING CHECK **Drawing Conclusions**
Why did John Brown's raid lead some southerners to talk about leaving the Union?

Election of 1860

In this climate of distrust, Americans prepared for another presidential election in 1860. The northern and southern Democrats could not agree on a candidate. Northern Democrats chose Senator Stephen Douglas. Southern Democrats backed the current vice president, **John C. Breckinridge** of Kentucky, who supported slavery in the territories.

Meanwhile, a new political party emerged. The **Constitutional Union Party** recognized "no political principles other than the Constitution of the country, the Union of the states, and the enforcement of the laws." Members of this new party met in Baltimore, Maryland, and selected **John Bell** of Tennessee as their candidate. Bell was a slaveholder, but he had opposed the Kansas-Nebraska Act in 1854.

Senator William Seward of New York was the Republicans' leading candidate at the start of their convention. But it turned out that Lincoln appealed to more party members. A moderate who was against the spread of slavery, Lincoln promised not to abolish slavery where it already existed.

Douglas, Breckinridge, and Bell each knew he might not win the election. They hoped to win enough electoral votes to prevent Lincoln from winning in the electoral college. But with a unified Republican Party behind him, Lincoln won. Although he received the highest number of votes, he won only about 40 percent of the overall popular vote.

Lincoln won 180 of 183 electoral votes in free states. Douglas had the second-highest number of popular votes, but he won only one state. He earned just 12 electoral votes. Breckinridge and Bell split electoral votes in other slave states.

The election results angered southerners. Lincoln did not campaign in their region and did not carry any southern states, but he became the next president. The election signaled that the South was losing its national political power.

READING CHECK **Analyzing** Why was Lincoln viewed by many as a moderate candidate during his campaign for the presidency?

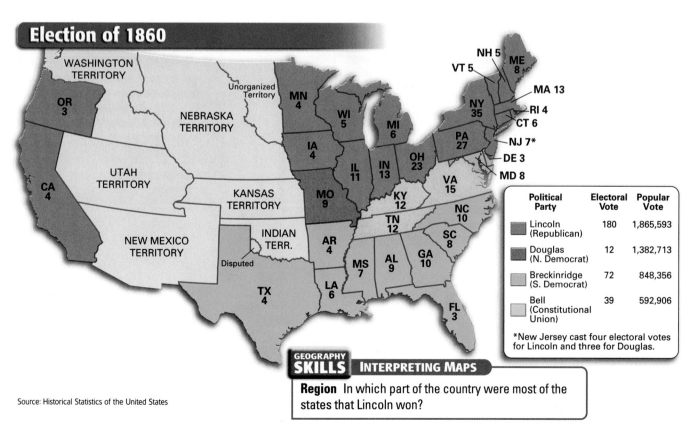

Election of 1860

Political Party	Electoral Vote	Popular Vote
Lincoln (Republican)	180	1,865,593
Douglas (N. Democrat)	12	1,382,713
Breckinridge (S. Democrat)	72	848,356
Bell (Constitutional Union)	39	592,906

*New Jersey cast four electoral votes for Lincoln and three for Douglas.

GEOGRAPHY SKILLS **INTERPRETING MAPS**

Region In which part of the country were most of the states that Lincoln won?

Source: Historical Statistics of the United States

The South Secedes

Lincoln insisted that he would not change slavery in the South. However, he said that slavery could not expand and thus would eventually die out completely. That idea angered many southerners.

Southerners' Reactions

People in the South believed their economy and way of life would be destroyed without slave labor. They reacted immediately. Within a week of Lincoln's election, South Carolina's legislature called for a special convention. The delegates considered secession. Southern secessionists believed that they had a right to leave the Union. They pointed out that each of the original states had voluntarily joined the Union by holding a special convention that had ratified the Constitution. Surely, they reasoned, states could leave the Union by the same process.

Critics of secession thought this argument was ridiculous. President Buchanan said the Union was not "a mere voluntary association of States, to be dissolved at pleasure by any one of the contracting parties." President-elect Abraham Lincoln agreed, saying, "No State, upon its own mere motion, can lawfully get out of the Union." Lincoln added, "They can only do so against [the] law, and by revolution."

While the South Carolina representatives were meeting in Charleston to discuss secession, Congress examined a plan to save the Union. Senator **John J. Crittenden** of Kentucky proposed a series of constitutional amendments that he believed would satisfy the South by protecting slavery. Crittenden hoped the country could avoid secession and a civil war.

Lincoln disagreed with Crittenden's plan. He believed there could be no compromise about the extension of slavery. Lincoln wrote, "The tug has to come and better now than later." A Senate committee voted on Crittenden's plan, and every Republican rejected it, as Lincoln had requested.

Jefferson Davis takes the oath of office for president of the Confederate States of America.

Rebel Government

This photograph is of the inauguration of Jefferson Davis as the president of the Confederate States of America. A former U.S. secretary of war, Davis was elected president of the confederacy in 1861.

How does this photo show the state of the southern government?

The Confederate States of America

South Carolina elected to dissolve "the union now subsisting [existing] between South Carolina and other States" on December 20, 1860. Mississippi, Florida, Alabama, Georgia, Louisiana, and Texas also seceded to form the **Confederate States of America**, also called the Confederacy. Its new constitution guaranteed citizens the right to own slaves.

Delegates from seceded states elected **Jefferson Davis** of Mississippi as president of the Confederacy. Davis had hoped to be the commanding general of Mississippi's troops. He responded to the news of his election with reluctance.

When the southern states seceded, the question of who owned federal property in the South arose. For instance, the forts in the harbor of Charleston, South Carolina, were federal property. However, Confederate president Davis and the Confederacy were ready to prevent the federal army from controlling the property.

Lincoln Takes Office

President Lincoln was inaugurated on March 4, 1861. In writing his inaugural address, Lincoln looked to many of the nation's founding documents. Referring to the idea that governments receive "their just powers from the consent of the governed," a line from the Declaration of Independence, Lincoln stated, "This country, with its institutions, belongs to the people who inhabit it. Whenever they grow weary of the existing Government, they can exercise their *constitutional* right of amending it or their *revolutionary* right to dismember [take apart] or overthrow it. I can not be ignorant of the fact that many worthy and patriotic citizens are desirous [wanting] of having the National Constitution amended . . ."

While he believed that U.S. citizens had the power to change their government through majority consent, he opposed the idea that southern states could leave the Union because they were unhappy with the government's position on slavery.

He announced in his inaugural address that he would keep all government property in the seceding states. However, he also tried to convince southerners that his government would not provoke a war. He hoped that, given time, southern states would return to the Union.

READING CHECK Drawing Conclusions Why did some southern states secede from the Union?

SUMMARY AND PREVIEW The secession of the southern states hinted at the violence to come. In the next chapter you will read about the Civil War.

go.hrw.com
Online Quiz
KEYWORD: SF7 HP15

Section 4 Assessment

Reviewing Ideas, Terms, and People

1. **a. Recall** Why did John Brown want to seize the federal arsenal at Harpers Ferry?
   b. Explain Why did some abolitionists disagree with Brown's actions?
2. **a. Identify** List the candidates in the presidential election of 1860, and what party each supported.
   b. Predict How might Abraham Lincoln's victory in the election of 1860 lead to future problems?
3. **a. Identify** What states made up the **Confederate States of America**?
   b. Explain Why did Lincoln disagree with **John J. Crittenden**'s plan to keep the Union together?
   c. Elaborate Do you believe that the southern states had the right to secede? Why or why not?

Critical Thinking

4. **Summarizing** Review your notes on the significant people in the section. Then copy the graphic organizer below and use it to summarize the causes of secession.

Causes → Secession

FOCUS ON WRITING

5. **Taking Notes on Secession** Make some notes on the raid on Harpers Ferry, the election of 1860, and the secession of the South. Decide how your character feels about each of these. How do these events affect your character?

Social Studies Skills

Analysis | Critical Thinking | Civic Participation | Study

Assessing Primary and Secondary Sources

Define the Skill

All historical information comes from primary and secondary sources. *Primary sources* are documents written by someone who witnessed or took part in an event. They include diaries, letters, autobiographies, and newspaper reports. *Secondary sources* are accounts of events written after the events have occurred by someone who did not witness or take part in them. They retell, interpret, and summarize information from primary sources. History books and biographies are examples of secondary sources.

Historical sources often disagree. One writer's version of an event may be different from another writer's version. You must assess the reliability of a primary or secondary source in order to weigh its value to you as a source of accurate information.

Learn the Skill

Use these guidelines to analyze and evaluate primary and secondary sources.

1. Identify the nature of the material. Is it a first-hand, eyewitness account or is it based on information provided by others?

2. Evaluate the author. If the material is a secondary source, what qualifications does the author have to interpret the sources from which it came? If the material is a primary source, what was the author's connection to the event he or she is writing about?

3. Determine the audience. Was the source meant to be seen by the public? Was it meant for a friend, or for the writer alone? The intended audience can influence a source's content.

4. Determine the purpose. Even authors of primary sources can have reasons to distort the truth to suit their own purposes. Look for evidence of emotion, exaggeration, opinion, or bias that may have influenced the account.

5. Look for documentation. Look for other information or evidence that supports the source's account. Compare sources whenever possible.

Practice the Skill

The passage below concerns the attack on Lawrence, Kansas, that you read about in this chapter. The passage contains both a primary and a secondary source. The secondary account was written by John A. Garraty, a well-known historian. Review the information on page 486, analyze the passage, and answer the questions that follow.

" Sheriff Jones, at the head of an army of Missourians, marched into Lawrence. In broad daylight they threw the printing presses of two newspapers into a river. They burned down the Free State Hotel and other buildings. Antislavery Kansans seethed with rage. Here is how one eyewitness described the attack:

"Sheriff Jones, after looking at the flames rising from the hotel and saying that it was 'the happiest day of his life,' dismissed the troops and they began their lawless destruction. "

1. Did the author of the primary source likely support the attackers or the people of Lawrence? What clues in the passage suggest this?

2. For whom was the primary source likely written?

3. Which source is more reliable for information about this incident? Explain why.

HOLT
History's Impact
▶ video series
Review the video to answer the closing question:
What do the Tenth Amendment and the Civil Rights Act indicate about the powers of the federal and state governments?

Visual Summary

QUICK FACTS

Use the visual summary below to help you review the main ideas of the chapter.

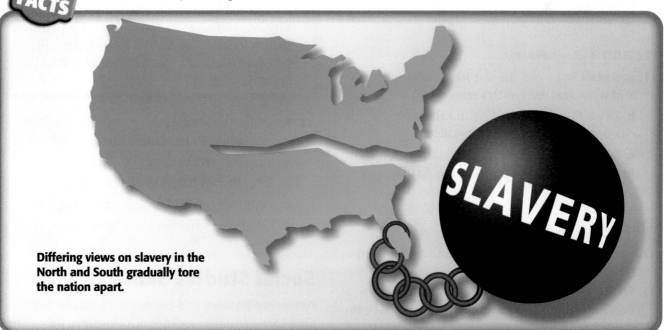

Differing views on slavery in the North and South gradually tore the nation apart.

Reviewing Vocabulary, Terms, and People

Identify the correct term or person from the chapter that best fits each of the following descriptions.

1. belief that voters should be given the right to decide if slavery would be permitted or banned

2. chief justice of the Supreme Court who wrote the majority opinion for the *Dred Scott* decision

3. Democratic candidate for president in 1852 who promised to enforce the Compromise of 1850 and the Fugitive Slave Act

4. a fugitive slave whose arrest led to violence between government officials and abolitionists

5. Republican candidate for the presidency in 1856 who opposed the spread of slavery in the West

6. slave who sued for freedom, claiming that by living in free territory, he had earned his freedom

7. Stephen Douglas's claim that states and territories should determine the issue of slavery through popular sovereignty

Comprehension and Critical Thinking

SECTION 1 *(Pages 476–481)*

8. **a. Describe** How did literature aid the antislavery movement?

b. Draw Conclusions How did the issue of slavery promote sectionalism?

c. Evaluate Do you think the Compromise of 1850 was a good solution? Explain your answer.

SECTION 2 *(Pages 483–487)*

9. **a. Identify** Who were the candidates in the presidential election of 1852, and what issues did each support?

b. Analyze How did the Kansas-Nebraska Act lead to growing hostility between pro-slavery and antislavery supporters?

c. Elaborate Why do you think "Bleeding Kansas" produced intense controversy between many Americans?

SECTION 3 (Pages 488–492)

10. a. Identify Who was Dred Scott, and why was his case important?

b. Analyze How were political parties affected by the debate over slavery?

c. Elaborate Why do you think Republicans challenged Stephen Douglas's run for the Senate?

SECTION 4 (Pages 493–497)

11. a. Recall Why did the southern states secede, and what was the North's response?

b. Draw Conclusions Why did the results of the election of 1860 anger southerners?

c. Evaluate Do you think John Brown was right to use violence to protest slavery? Explain.

Reviewing Themes

12. Politics How did sectionalism affect American politics?

13. Society and Culture What effect did Harriet Beecher Stowe's book *Uncle Tom's Cabin* have on the debate over slavery?

Using the Internet

go.hrw.com
KEYWORD: SF7 CH15

14. Activity: Creating a Newspaper Harriet Beecher Stowe's novel and John Brown's raids were two important events that created more debate over slavery and heightened tension between sides. Enter the activity keyword and learn more about antislavery actions. Then create a newspaper with which to display your research. Remember to write from the point of view of someone from the mid-1800s.

Reading Skills

Facts, Opinions, and the Past *Use the Reading Skills taught in this chapter to answer the question about the reading selection below.*

> In 1858 John Brown tried to start an uprising. He wanted to attack the federal arsenal in Virginia and seize weapons there. He planned to arm local slaves. Brown expected to kill or take hostage white southerners who stood in his way. *(p. 493)*

15. Based on the reading selection above, which of the following statements is an opinion?

a. John Brown's raid was in 1858.

b. John Brown hated all slaveholders.

c. John Brown's raid took place in Virginia.

d. Local slaves helped John Brown.

Social Studies Skills

Assessing Primary and Secondary Sources *Use the Social Studies Skills taught in this chapter to answer the question below.*

16. Which of the following is *not* an example of a primary source used in this chapter?

a. *A People's History of the United States* by Howard Zinn

b. The Seventh of March speech by Daniel Webster

c. Abraham Lincoln's A House Divided speech

d. John Brown's last speech

FOCUS ON WRITING

17. Writing Your Autobiography Review your notes. Then write your autobiography, being sure to mention each of the events from your notes. Tell how your character heard about each event, what he or she was doing at the time, how he or she felt about the event, and how it affected him or her. What are your character's hopes and fears for the future?

Standardized Test Practice

DIRECTIONS: Read each question and write the letter of the best response.

1 Use the map below to answer the following question.

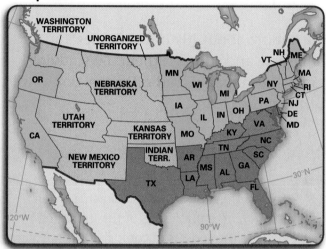

From the information in this map, you can conclude that it shows

A the provisions of the Compromise of 1850.

B the results of the election of 1860.

C the formation of the Confederacy.

D the results of the *Dred Scott* decision.

2 Which leader was responsible for settling the dispute over the expansion of slavery that arose after the Mexican War?

A David Wilmot

B Henry Clay

C Abraham Lincoln

D Jefferson Davis

3 California's admission as a free state after the Mexican War aroused controversy because

A many Californians already held slaves.

B it would upset the balance between free states and slave states.

C Mexico still claimed that California was part of Mexico's territory.

D most Californians wanted independence.

4 Widespread violence erupted in Kansas over slavery in the mid-1850s *mainly* due to

A the practice of popular sovereignty.

B the Pottawatomie Massacre.

C the Missouri Compromise.

D the threat of secession.

5 The election of 1852 led directly to which of the following?

A the Compromise of 1850

B the collapse of the Whig Party

C the collapse of the Republican Party

D the Missouri Compromise.

6 The Compromise of 1850 was *most* similar to what earlier compromise between free states and slave states?

A the Great Compromise

B the Rush-Bagot Agreement

C the Northwest Ordinance

D the Missouri Compromise

7 Examine the following passage written by a southerner before secession and then use it to answer the question below.

> "As we sat around the long table today the talk turned to the [secession] convention, so soon to meet in Tallahassee [Florida]. Father said he considered this the most important year in the history of the South. He is for secession, and he does not think that war will necessarily [certainly] follow. Brother Junius is a strong Union man, and he thinks we will certainly have war. If the South secedes, the North will fight to keep us. If we do not secede, all property rights will be taken from us and we will be forced to fight to hold our own."
>
> —Susan Bradford, adapted from *Heroines of Dixie,* edited by Katharine Jones

Document-Based Question What might be the outcome of this convention? Why?

Assignment

Write a paper comparing and contrasting one of the following: (1) America before and after the Industrial Revolution, (2) the lives of free blacks in the North with the lives of free blacks in the South.

Comparing People and Events

One way to learn more about historical figures and events is to compare and contrast them. By studying how the figures or events are alike and different, you can begin to see each one more clearly.

1. Prewrite

Getting Started

"How are they alike?" "How are they different?" Jot down answers to these questions as you research the presidents or the Industrial Revolution. Group your answers into points of comparison. For example, points of comparison for the lives of free blacks might be work, education, etc. Points of comparison for the Industrial Revolution might be factories or farming.

Organizing Your Information

There are two ways to organize a compare-and-contrast paper.

- **Block Style** Say everything you have to say about one subject. Then say everything you have to say about the second subject. Discuss the points of comparison in the same order for each subject.
- **Point-by-Point Style** Discuss the points of comparison one at a time. Explain how the subjects are alike and different on one point of comparison, then another, and so on. Discuss the subjects in the same order for each point of comparison.

2. Write

You can use this framework with your notes to help you write your first draft.

TIP Using Graphic Organizers
Venn diagrams help you focus on similarities and differences. Write details the subjects have in common in the overlapping area. Write details that make each subject different in the sections that do not overlap.

Differences Similarities Differences

A Writer's Framework

Introduction	Body	Conclusion
■ Identify the two subjects and give background information to help readers understand your comparisons. ■ State your big idea, or main purpose, in comparing and contrasting them.	■ Use block or point-by-point organization. ■ Use three points of comparison. ■ Support your points with specific historical facts, details, and examples.	■ Restate your big idea. ■ Summarize the points you made. ■ Expand on your big idea, perhaps by relating it to later historical events or other historical figures.

3. Evaluate and Revise

Evaluating

Use these questions to discover ways to improve your paper.

Evaluation Questions for a Comparison/Contrast Paper

- Do you introduce both subjects in the first paragraph?
- Do you provide relevant background information in a clear and concise manner?
- Do you state your big idea in the introduction?
- Do you include three points of comparison between the subjects?

- Do you use either the block style or point-by-point style to organize your points of comparison?
- Do you support your points of comparison with appropriate historical facts, details, and examples?
- Do you restate your big idea and summarize your points?

TIP **Making Meaning Clear**

One way to make relationships between ideas clear is to repeat key or similar words and phrases in your writing. For example, you can use similar wording when comparing two historical figures on the same point of comparison.

EXAMPLE

Samuel Slater filled his labor needs by hiring entire families to work in the mills. Francis Lowell filled his labor needs by hiring young, unmarried women to work in the mills.

Revising

As you reread your paper, look for sentences that start with *There was* or *There were*. Sentences beginning with *There was/There were* tend to be weak: The verbs *was* and *were* do not convey any action.

Weak

There was a decline in southern agriculture after the American Revolution.

Stronger

Southern agriculture declined after the American Revolution.

4. Proofread and Publish

Proofreading

In a research report, you may be referring to the titles of your sources of information. Check to see whether you have punctuated any titles according to these guidelines.

- Underlining (if you are writing) or italics (if you are using a computer) for books, movies, TV programs, Internet sites, and magazines or newspapers
- Quotation marks for magazine articles, newspaper articles, chapters in a book

Publishing

Share your paper with one or more classmates. After reading each other's papers, you can compare and contrast them.

5. Practice and Apply

Use the steps and strategies outlined in this workshop to write your paper comparing and contrasting two people or events.

The Nation Breaks Apart

What You Will Learn...

When compromise after compromise failed, the United States was divided by war. The American Civil War tested the strength of the bond between the states. During the Civil War, Americans fought each other on battlefields and in government. Ideas about slavery and sovereignty led many soldiers to fight. Eventually the nation was reunited, but deep scars remained. In the next two chapters, you will learn about the war and the period after when rebuilding the South became a priority.

Explore the Art

This painting is titled *Fight for the Colors*. It shows Union and Confederate troops at the Battle of Gettysburg, which began in Pennsylvania on July 1, 1863. This 3-day battle was the largest and bloodiest in the Civil War.

What aspects of the Civil War does this picture show?

505

CHAPTER 16 1861–1865

The Civil War

Indiana Standards

Social Studies Standards

8.1.21 Describe the importance of key events and individuals in the Civil War.

8.1.29 Differentiate betweenfacts and historical interpretations recognizing that the historian's narrative reflects his or her judgment about the significance of particular facts.

8.2.10 Research and defend positions on issues in which fundamental values and principles related to the United States Constitution are in conflict, using a variety of information resources.

go.hrw.com
Indiana
KEYWORD: SF10 IN

FOCUS ON WRITING

Writing a Newspaper Article For most of this nation's history, newspapers have been an important way for citizens to learn about what is happening in the United States. In this chapter you will read about the main events of the Civil War. Then you will choose one of these events and write a newspaper article about it.

UNITED STATES

1861 Confederate guns open fire on Fort Sumter on April 12. Confederates win the first battle of the Civil War on July 21 at Bull Run in Virginia.

1861

WORLD

1861 Great Britain and France decide to buy cotton from Egypt instead of from the Confederacy.

HOLT

History's Impact
▶ video series
Watch the video to understand the impact of the Civil War.

What You Will Learn...

In this chapter you will learn how the resources of the North enabled it to defeat the South in the Civil War. Among those who marched off to war were these drummer boys of the Union army.

1863
Confederate general John Hunt Morgan leads a raid into Indiana.

1862 The *Monitor* fights the *Virginia* on March 9.

1863 The Emancipation Proclamation is issued on January 1.

1865 General Robert E. Lee surrenders to General Ulysses S. Grant on April 9.

| 1862 | 1863 | 1864 | 1865 |

1862 An imperial decree expels foreigners from Japan.

1864 With the support of French troops, Archduke Maximilian of Austria becomes emperor of Mexico.

1864 The Taiping Rebellion in China ends after the capture of Nanjing in July.

Reading Social Studies

by Kylene Beers

Economics	Geography	Politics	Society and Culture	Science and Technology

Focus on Themes As you read this chapter about the Civil War, you will see that this was a time in our history dominated by two major concerns: **politics** and **society and culture**. You will not only read about the political decisions made during this war, but also you will see how the war affected all of American society. You will read about the causes and the key events during the war and the many consequences of this war. This chapter tells of one of the most important events in our history.

Supporting Facts and Details

Focus on Reading Main ideas and big ideas are just that, ideas. How do we know what those ideas really mean?

Understanding Ideas and Their Support A main idea or big idea may be a kind of summary statement, or it may be a statement of the author's opinion. Either way, a good reader looks to see what support—facts and various kinds of details—the writer provides. If the writer doesn't provide good support, the ideas may not be trustworthy.

Notice how the passage below uses facts and details to support the main idea.

Civil War armies fought in the ancient battlefield formation that produced massive casualties. Endless rows of troops fired directly at one another, with cannonballs landing amid them. When the order was given, soldiers would attach bayonets to their guns and rush toward their enemy. Men died to gain every inch of ground. . .

Despite the huge battlefield losses, the biggest killer in the Civil War was not the fighting. It was diseases such as typhoid, pneumonia, and tuberculosis. Nearly twice as many soldiers died of illnesses as died in combat.

From Chapter 16, p. 533

> The main idea is stated first.

> These sentences provide details about the challenges soldiers faced.

> The writer concludes with some facts as support.

Writers support propositions with . . .

1. **Facts and statistics**—statements that can be proved; facts in number form
2. **Examples**—specific instances that illustrate the facts
3. **Anecdotes**—brief stories that help explain the facts
4. **Definitions**—explanation of unusual terms or words
5. **Comments from the experts or eyewitnesses**—statements from reliable sources

You Try It!

The following passage is from the chapter you are about to read. As you read it, look for the writer's main idea and support.

In February 1862, Grant led an assault force into Tennessee. With help from navy gunboats, Grant's Army of the Tennessee took two outposts on key rivers in the west. On February 6, he captured Fort Henry on the Tennessee River. Several days later he took Fort Donelson on the Cumberland River.

From Chapter 16, pp. 522–523

Fort Donelson's commander asked for the terms of surrender. Grant replied, "No terms except an unconditional and immediate surrender can be accepted." The fort surrendered. The North gave a new name to Grant's initials: "Unconditional Surrender" Grant.

After you read the passage, answer the following questions.

1. Which sentence best states the writer's main idea?
   a. The fort surrendered.
   b. In February 1862, Grant led an assault force into Tennessee.
   c. Fort Donelson's commander asked for the terms of surrender.

2. Which method of support is not used to support the main idea?
   a. facts
   b. comments from experts or eyewitnesses
   c. anecdotes

3. Which sentence in this passage provides a comment from an expert or eyewitness?

As you read Chapter 16, pay attention to the details that the writers have chosen to support their main ideas.

Key Terms and People

Chapter 16

Section 1
Fort Sumter *(p. 511)*
border states *(p. 512)*
Winfield Scott *(p. 513)*
cotton diplomacy *(p. 513)*

Section 2
Thomas "Stonewall" Jackson *(p. 517)*
First Battle of Bull Run *(p. 517)*
George B. McClellan *(p. 517)*
Robert E. Lee *(p. 518)*
Seven Days' Battles *(p. 518)*
Second Battle of Bull Run *(p. 518)*
Battle of Antietam *(p. 519)*
ironclads *(p. 520)*

Section 3
Ulysses S. Grant *(p. 522)*
Battle of Shiloh *(p. 523)*
David Farragut *(p. 524)*
Siege of Vicksburg *(p. 524)*

Section 4
emancipation *(p. 529)*
Emancipation Proclamation *(p. 529)*
contrabands *(p. 531)*
54th Massachusetts Infantry *(p. 531)*
Copperheads *(p. 532)*
habeas corpus *(p. 532)*
Clara Barton *(p. 534)*

Section 5
Battle of Gettysburg *(p. 537)*
George Pickett *(p. 539)*
Pickett's Charge *(p. 539)*
Gettysburg Address *(p. 540)*
Wilderness Campaign *(p. 540)*
William Tecumseh Sherman *(p. 541)*
total war *(p. 542)*
Appomattox Courthouse *(p. 542)*

Academic Vocabulary

In this chapter, you will learn the following academic words:

innovation *(p. 520)*
execute *(p. 540)*

THE CIVIL WAR **509**

The War Begins

If YOU were there...

You are a college student in Charleston in early 1861. Seven southern states have left the Union and formed their own government. All-out war seems unavoidable. Your friends have begun to volunteer for either the Union or the Confederate forces. You are torn between loyalty to your home state and to the United States.

Would you join the Union or the Confederate army?

BUILDING BACKGROUND The divisions within the United States reached a breaking point with the election of Abraham Lincoln in 1860. Several southern states angrily left the Union to form a new confederation. In border states such as Virginia and Kentucky, people were divided. The question now was whether the United States could survive as a disunified country.

Americans Choose Sides

Furious at Lincoln's election and fearing a federal invasion, seven southern states had seceded. The new commander in chief tried desperately to save the Union.

In his inaugural address, Lincoln promised not to end slavery where it existed. The federal government "will not assail [attack] you. You can have no conflict without being yourselves the aggressors," he said, trying to calm southerners' fears. However, Lincoln also stated his intention to preserve the Union. He believed that saving the Union would help to save democracy. If the Union and its government failed, then monarchs could say that people were unable to rule themselves. As a result, Lincoln refused to recognize secession, declaring the Union to be "unbroken."

In fact, after decades of painful compromises, the Union was badly broken. From the lower South, a battle cry was arising, born out of fear, rage—and excitement. Confederate officials began seizing branches of the federal mint, arsenals, and military outposts. In a last ditch effort to avoid war between the states, Secretary of State Seward suggested a united effort of threatening war against Spain and France for interfering in Mexico and the Caribbean. In the highly charged atmosphere, it would take only a spark to unleash the heat of war.

What You Will Learn...

Main Ideas

1. Following the outbreak of war at Fort Sumter, Americans chose sides.
2. The Union and the Confederacy prepared for war.

The Big Idea

Civil war broke out between the North and the South in 1861.

Key Terms and People

Fort Sumter, *p. 511*
border states, *p. 512*
Winfield Scott, *p. 513*
cotton diplomacy, *p. 513*

TAKING NOTES As you read, take notes on the Civil War and how Americans chose sides and how each side prepared for the war.

	Choosing Sides	Preparing for War
North		
South		

History Close-up
Fort Sumter

Charleston

In Charleston, all activity came to a complete stop. Citizens crowded rooftops to watch the battle.

Castle Pinckney

Charleston Harbor

Charleston

ATLANTIC OCEAN

Shots fired at the ironclad battery did little damage.

The first shot fired on Fort Sumter was fired from Fort Johnson.

Fort Johnson

Fort Sumter

Fort Moultrie

Cummings Point

Fort Sumter was strategically placed to control Charleston Harbor.

Atlantic Ocean

The first shots of the Civil War were fired at Fort Sumter, South Carolina. Although no one was killed there, the bloodiest war in the country's history had begun.

GEOGRAPHY SKILLS | **INTERPRETING MAPS**

1. **Human-Environment Interaction** Why would the Union Army need to resupply Fort Sumter?
2. **Place** What advantages would a floating battery have?

In 1861, that spark occurred at **Fort Sumter**, a federal outpost in Charleston, South Carolina, that was attacked by Confederate troops, beginning the Civil War. Determined to seize the fortress—which controlled the entrance to Charleston harbor—the Confederates ringed the harbor with heavy guns. Instead of surrendering the fort, Lincoln decided to send in ships to provide badly needed supplies to defend the fort. Confederate officials demanded that the federal troops evacuate. The fort's commander, Major Robert Anderson, refused.

Before sunrise on April 12, 1861, Confederate guns opened fire on Fort Sumter. A witness wrote that the first shots brought "every soldier in the harbor to his feet, and every man, woman, and child in the city of Charleston from their beds." The Civil War had begun.

The fort, although massive, stood little chance. Its heavy guns faced the Atlantic Ocean, not the shore. After 34 hours of cannon blasts, Fort Sumter surrendered. "The last ray of hope for preserving the Union has expired at the assault upon Fort Sumter . . ." Lincoln wrote.

Reaction to Lincoln's Call

The fall of Fort Sumter stunned the North. Lincoln declared the South to be in a state of rebellion and asked state governors for 75,000 militiamen to put down the rebellion. States now had to choose: Would they secede, or would they stay in the Union? Democratic Senator Stephen Douglas, speaking in support of Lincoln's call for troops, declared, "There can be no neutrals in this war, *only patriots—or traitors.*"

FOCUS ON INDIANA

Of the 75,000 troops that Lincoln called for, Indiana was to provide 7,500. Although many more than this volunteered, they were turned away. Most people thought extra troops would not be needed since they expected the rebellion to be put down quickly.

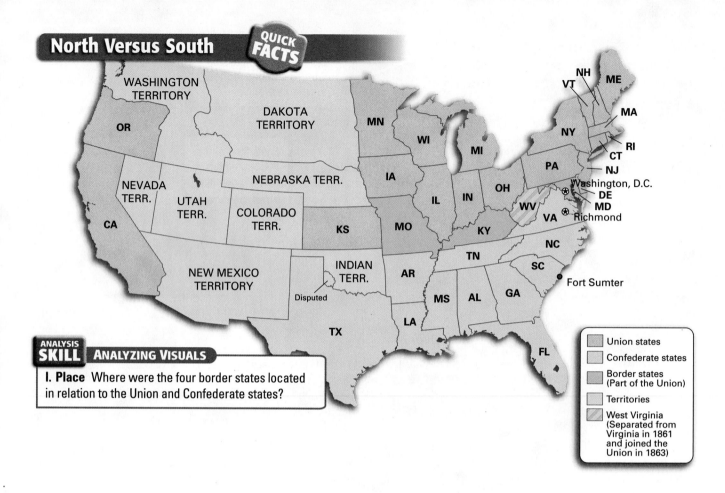

North Versus South

QUICK FACTS

WASHINGTON TERRITORY

OR

DAKOTA TERRITORY

MN

WI

MI

NY

NH

VT

ME

MA

RI

CT

NJ

PA

NEVADA TERR.

UTAH TERR.

NEBRASKA TERR.

IA

IL

IN

OH

WV

Washington, D.C.

DE

MD

CA

COLORADO TERR.

KS

MO

KY

VA

Richmond

NC

NEW MEXICO TERRITORY

INDIAN TERR.

AR

TN

SC

Fort Sumter

Disputed

MS

AL

GA

TX

LA

FL

Union states

Confederate states

Border states (Part of the Union)

Territories

West Virginia (Separated from Virginia in 1861 and joined the Union in 1863)

ANALYSIS SKILL ANALYZING VISUALS

1. Place Where were the four border states located in relation to the Union and Confederate states?

Pennsylvania, New Jersey, and the states north of them rallied to the president's call. The crucial slave states of the Upper South—North Carolina, Tennessee, Virginia, and Arkansas—seceded. They provided soldiers and supplies to the South. Mary Boykin Chesnut, whose husband became a Confederate congressman, wrote in her diary:

"I did not know that one could live in such days of excitement…Everybody tells you half of something, and then rushes off…to hear the last news."

—Mary Boykin Chesnut, quoted in *Mary Chesnut's Civil War*, edited by C. Vann Woodward

Wedged between the North and the South were the key **border states** of Delaware, Kentucky, Maryland, and Missouri—slave states that did not join the Confederacy. Kentucky and Missouri controlled parts of important rivers. Maryland separated the Union capital, Washington, D.C., from the North.

People in the border states were deeply divided on the war. The president's own wife, Mary Todd Lincoln, had four brothers from Kentucky who fought for the Confederacy. Lincoln sent federal troops into the border states to help keep them in the Union. He also sent soldiers into western Virginia, where Union loyalties were strong. West Virginia set up its own state government in 1863.

Northern Resources

Numbers tell an important story about the Civil War. Consider the North's advantages. It could draw soldiers and workers from a population of 22 million. The South had only 5.5 million people to draw from. One of the greatest advantages in the North was the region's network of roads, canals, and railroads. Some 22,000 miles of railroad track could move soldiers and supplies throughout the North. The South had only about 9,000 miles of track.

In the North, the Civil War stimulated economic growth. To supply the military, the production of coal, iron, wheat, and wool increased. Also, the export of corn, wheat, beef, and pork to Europe doubled. In the South, the export of resources decreased because of the Union blockade.

Finally, the Union had money. It had a more developed economy, banking system, and a currency called greenbacks. The South had to start printing its own Confederate dollars. Some states printed their own money, too. This led to financial chaos.

Taking advantage of the Union's strengths, General **Winfield Scott** developed a two-part strategy: (1) destroy the South's economy with a naval blockade of southern ports; (2) gain control of the Mississippi River to divide the South. Other leaders urged an attack on Richmond, Virginia, the Confederate capital.

Southern Resources

The Confederacy had advantages as well. With its strong military tradition, the South put many brilliant officers into battle. Southern farms provided food for its armies. The South's best advantage, however, was strategic. It needed only to defend itself until the North grew tired of fighting.

The North had to invade and control the South. To accomplish this, the Union army had to travel huge distances. For example, the distance from northern Virginia to central Georgia is about the length of Scotland and England combined. Because of distances such as this, the North had to maintain long supply lines.

In addition, wilderness covered much of the South. Armies found this land difficult to cross. Also, in Virginia, many of the rivers ran from east to west. Because of this, they formed a natural defense against an army that attacked from the north to the south. As a result, Northern generals were often forced to attack Confederate troops from the side rather than from the front. Furthermore, because southerners fought mostly on their home soil, they were often familiar with the area.

The South hoped to wear down the North and to capture Washington, D.C. Confederate president Jefferson Davis also tried to win foreign allies through **cotton diplomacy**. This was the idea that Great Britain would support the Confederacy because it needed the South's raw cotton to supply its booming textile industry. Cotton diplomacy did not work as the South had hoped. Britain had large supplies of cotton, and it got more from India and Egypt.

READING CHECK **Comparing** What advantages did the North and South have leading up to the war?

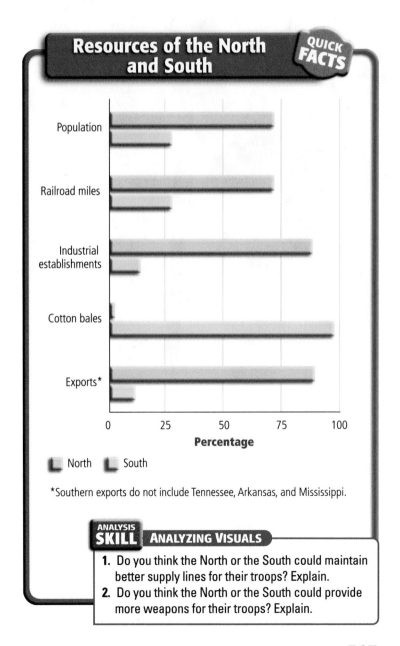

Resources of the North and South QUICK FACTS

North   South

*Southern exports do not include Tennessee, Arkansas, and Mississippi.

ANALYSIS SKILL **ANALYZING VISUALS**

1. Do you think the North or the South could maintain better supply lines for their troops? Explain.
2. Do you think the North or the South could provide more weapons for their troops? Explain.

Union and Confederate Soldiers

Early in the war, uniforms differed greatly, especially in the Confederate army. Uniforms became simpler and more standard as the war dragged on.

The soldiers carried food, extra ammunition, and other items in their haversacks.

Each soldier was armed with a bayonet, a knife that can be attached to the barrel of a rifle. The bayonets were stored in scabbards on their belts.

Confederate Soldier

Both soldiers were also armed with single-shot, muzzle-loading rifles.

Union Soldier

ANALYSIS SKILL **ANALYZING VISUALS**

How are the Union and Confederate uniforms and equipment similar and different?

Preparing for War

The North and the South now rushed to war. Neither side was prepared for the tragedy to come.

Volunteer Armies

Volunteer militias had sparked the revolution that created the United States. Now they would battle for its future. At the start of the war, the Union army had only 16,000 soldiers. Within months that number had swelled to a half million. Southern men rose up to defend their land and their ways of life. Virginian Thomas Webber came to fight "against the invading foe [enemy] who now pollute the sacred soil of my beloved native state." When Union soldiers asked one captured rebel why he was fighting, he replied, "I'm fighting because you're down here."

Helping the Troops

Civilians on both sides helped those in uniform. They raised money, provided aid for soldiers and their families, and ran emergency hospitals. Dr. Elizabeth Blackwell, the first woman to receive a license to practice medicine, organized a group that pressured President Lincoln to form the U.S. Sanitary Commission in June 1861. The Sanitary, as it was called, was run by clergyman Henry Bellows. Tens of thousands of volunteers worked with the U.S. Sanitary Commission to send bandages, medicines, and food to Union army camps and hospitals. Some 3,000 women served as nurses in the Union army.

Training the Soldiers

Both the Union and Confederate armies faced shortages of clothing, food, and even rifles. Most troops lacked standard uniforms and simply wore their own clothes. Eventually, each side chose a color for their uniforms. The Union chose blue. The Confederates wore gray.

The problem with volunteers was that many of them had no idea how to fight. Schoolteachers, farmers, and laborers all had to learn the combat basics of marching, shooting, and using bayonets.

In a letter to a friend, a Union soldier described life in the training camp.

" We have been wading through mud knee deep all winter ... For the last two weeks we have been drilled almost to death. Squad drill from 6 to 7 A.M. Company drill from 9 to 11 A.M. Batallion Drill from 2 to 4 1/2 P.M. Dress Parade from 5 to 5 1/2 P.M. and non-commissioned officers' school from 7 to 8 in the evening. If we don't soon become a well drilled Regiment, we ought to. "
—David R. P. Shoemaker, 1862

With visions of glory and action, many young soldiers were eager to fight. They would not have to wait long.

Discipline and drill were used to turn raw volunteers into an efficient fighting machine. During a battle, the success or failure of a regiment often depended on its discipline—how well it responded to orders.

Volunteers also learned how to use rifles. Eventually, soldiers were expected to be able to load, aim, and fire their rifles three times in one minute. The quality of the weapons provided varied greatly. Most soldiers favored the Springfield and Enfield rifles for their accuracy. On the other hand, soldiers often complained about their Austrian and Belgian rifles. A soldier remarked, "I don't believe one could hit the broadside of a barn with them."

The Union army provided the infantry with two-person tents. However, soldiers often discarded these tents in favor of more portable ones. The Confederate army did not usually issue tents. Instead, Confederates often used tents that were captured from the Union army.

READING CHECK **Summarizing** How did soldiers and civilians prepare for war?

SUMMARY AND PREVIEW As citizens chose sides in the Civil War, civilians and soldiers alike became involved in the war effort. In the next section you will learn about some early battles in the war, both on land and at sea.

go.hrw.com
Online Quiz
KEYWORD: SF7 HP16

Section 1 Assessment

Reviewing Ideas, Terms, and People

1. **a. Identify** What event triggered the war between the Union and the Confederacy?
   b. Contrast How did the Union's strategy differ from that of the Confederacy?
   c. Evaluate Which side do you believe was best prepared for war? Explain your answer.
2. **a. Describe** How did women take part in the war?
   b. Summarize In what ways were the armies of the North and South unprepared for war?
   c. Elaborate Why did men volunteer to fight in the war?

Critical Thinking

3. **Comparing and Contrasting** Review your notes on the preparations for war by the North and the South.

Then copy the graphic organizer shown below and use it to show the strengths and weaknesses of each side in the war.

	Union	Confederacy
Strengths		
Weaknesses		

FOCUS ON WRITING

4. **Taking Notes on the War's Beginning** As you read this section, take notes on the crisis at Fort Sumter and on the recruiting and training of the armies. Be sure to answer the following questions: Who? Where? When? Why? and How?

The War in the East

What You Will Learn...

Main Ideas

1. Union and Confederate forces fought for control of the war in Virginia.
2. The Battle of Antietam gave the North a slight advantage.
3. The Confederacy attempted to break the Union naval blockade.

The Big Idea

Confederate and Union forces faced off in Virginia and at sea.

Key Terms and People

Thomas "Stonewall" Jackson, *p. 517*
First Battle of Bull Run, *p. 517*
George B. McClellan, *p. 517*
Robert E. Lee, *p. 518*
Seven Days' Battles, *p. 518*
Second Battle of Bull Run, *p. 518*
Battle of Antietam, *p. 519*
ironclads, *p. 520*

TAKING NOTES As you read, take notes on the battles in the east and at sea and the winners of each. Write your notes in a chart like the one below.

Battle	Winner

 8.1.21, 8.1.29

If YOU were there...

You live in Washington, D.C., in July 1861. You and your friends are on your way to Manassas, near Washington, to watch the battle there. Everyone expects a quick Union victory. Your wagon is loaded with food for a picnic, and people are in a holiday mood. You see some members of Congress riding toward Manassas, too. Maybe this battle will end the war!

Why would you want to watch this battle?

BUILDING BACKGROUND The shots fired at Fort Sumter made the war a reality. Neither the North nor the South was really prepared. Each side had some advantages—more industry and railroads in the North, a military tradition in the South. The war in the East centered in the region around the two capitals: Washington, D.C., and Richmond, Virginia.

War in Virginia

The troops that met in the first major battle of the Civil War found that it was no picnic. In July 1861, Lincoln ordered General Irvin McDowell to lead his 35,000-man army from the Union capital, Washington, to the Confederate capital, Richmond. The soldiers were barely trained. McDowell complained that they "stopped every moment to pick blackberries or get water; they would not keep in the ranks." The first day's march covered only five miles.

Bull Run/Manassas

McDowell's army was headed to Manassas, Virginia, an important railroad junction. If McDowell could seize Manassas, he would control the best route to the Confederate capital. Some 22,000 Confederate troops under the command of General Pierre G. T. Beauregard were waiting for McDowell and his troops along a creek called Bull Run. For two days, Union troops tried to find a way around the Confederates. During that time, Beauregard requested assistance, and

General Joseph E. Johnston headed toward Manassas with another 10,000 Confederate troops. By July 21, 1861, they had all arrived.

That morning, Union troops managed to cross the creek and drive back the left side of the Confederate line. Yet one unit held firmly in place.

"There is Jackson standing like a stone wall!" cried one southern officer. "Rally behind the Virginians!" At that moment, General **Thomas "Stonewall" Jackson** earned his famous nickname.

A steady stream of Virginia volunteers arrived to counter the attack. The Confederates surged forward, letting out their terrifying "rebel yell." One eyewitness described the awful scene.

"There is smoke, dust, wild talking, shouting; hissings, howlings, explosions. It is a new, strange, unanticipated experience to the soldiers of both armies, far different from what they thought it would be."

—Charles Coffin,
quoted in *Voices of the Civil War* by Richard Wheeler

The battle raged through the day, with rebel soldiers still arriving. Finally, the weary Union troops gave out. They tried to make an orderly retreat back across the creek, but the roads were clogged with the fancy carriages of panicked spectators. The Union army scattered in the chaos.

The Confederates lacked the strength to push north and capture Washington, D.C. But clearly, the rebels had won the day. The **First Battle of Bull Run** was the first major battle of the Civil War, and the Confederates' victory. The battle is also known as the First Battle of Manassas. It shattered the North's hopes of winning the war quickly.

More Battles in Virginia

The shock at Bull Run persuaded Lincoln of the need for a better trained army. He put his hopes in General **George B. McClellan**. The general assembled a highly disciplined force of 100,000 soldiers called the Army of the Potomac. The careful McClellan spent months training. However, because

Interactive Map

Battles in the East

PENNSYLVANIA

Antietam Sep. 1862

MARYLAND

WEST VIRGINIA

Shenandoah Valley

Potomac

LEE

McCLELLAN River

POPE

Washington, D.C.

Manassas Junction

LEE

Bull Run July 1861 & Aug. 1862

Chesapeake Bay

Fair Oaks May – June 1862

Richmond

James River

Seven Days June 1862

York R.

McCLELLAN

Yorktown

VIRGINIA

ATLANTIC OCEAN

Union state

West Virginia (Separated from Virginia in 1861 and joined the Union in 1863)

Confederate state

→ Union forces

✶ Union victory

→ Confederate forces

✶ Confederate victory

0   15   30 Miles
0   15   30 Kilometers

N W E S

go.hrw.com
Interactive Map
KEYWORD: SF7 CH16

GEOGRAPHY SKILLS | **INTERPRETING MAPS**

1. **Location** Which battle was fought in Maryland?
2. **Human-Environment Interaction** How did geography influence the movement of forces?

he overestimated the size of the Confederate army, McClellan hesitated to attack. Lincoln grew impatient. Finally, in the spring of 1862, McClellan launched an effort to capture Richmond called the "Peninsular Campaign." Instead of marching south for a direct assault, McClellan slowly brought his force through the peninsula between the James and York rivers. More time slipped away.

The South feared that McClellan would receive reinforcements from Washington. To prevent this, Stonewall Jackson launched an attack toward Washington. Although the attack was pushed back, it prevented the Union from sending reinforcements to McClellan.

THE IMPACT TODAY

Many Americans continue to be fascinated by the Civil War. Some history buffs regularly stage re-enactments of famous battles, complete with uniforms, guns, and bayonets.

In June 1862, with McClellan's force poised outside Richmond, the Confederate army in Virginia came under the command of General **Robert E. Lee**. A graduate of the U.S. Military Academy at West Point, Lee had served in the Mexican War and had led federal troops at Harpers Ferry. Lee was willing to take risks and make unpredictable moves to throw Union forces off balance.

During the summer of 1862, Lee strengthened his positions. On June 26, he attacked, launching a series of clashes known as the **Seven Days' Battles** that forced the Union army to retreat from near Richmond. Confederate General D. H. Hill described one failed attack. "It was not war—it was murder," he said. Lee saved Richmond and forced McClellan to retreat.

A frustrated Lincoln ordered General John Pope to march directly on Richmond from Washington. Pope told his soldiers, "Let us look before us and not behind. Success and glory are in the advance."

Jackson wanted to defeat Pope's army before it could join up with McClellan's larger Army of the Potomac. Jackson's troops met Pope's Union forces on the battlefield in August in 1862. The three-day battle became known as the **Second Battle of Bull Run**, or the Second Battle of Manassas.

The first day's fighting was savage. Captain George Fairfield of the 7th Wisconsin regiment later recalled, "What a slaughter! No one appeared to know the object of the fight, and there we stood for one hour, the men falling all around." The fighting ended in a stalemate.

On the second day, Pope found Jackson's troops along an unfinished railroad grade. Pope hurled his men against the Confederates. But the attacks were pushed back with heavy casualties on both sides.

On the third day, the Confederates crushed the Union army's assault and forced it to retreat in defeat. The Confederates had won a major victory, and General Robert E. Lee decided it was time to take the war to the North.

READING CHECK **Sequencing** List in order the events that forced Union troops out of Virginia.

Eyewitness at Antietam

Battle of Antietam

Confederate leaders hoped to follow up Lee's successes in Virginia with a major victory on northern soil. On September 4, 1862, some 40,000 Confederate soldiers began crossing into Maryland. General Robert E. Lee decided to divide his army. He sent about half of his troops, under the command of Stonewall Jackson, to Harpers Ferry. There they defeated a Union force and captured the town. Meanwhile, Lee arrived in the town of Frederick and issued a Proclamation to the People of Maryland, urging them to join the Confederates. However, his words would not be enough to convince Marylanders to abandon the Union. Union soldiers, however, found a copy of Lee's battle plan, which had been left at an abandoned Confederate camp. General McClellan learned that Lee had divided his army in order to attack Harpers Ferry. However, McClellan hesitated to attack. As a result, the Confederates had time to reunite.

James Hope was a professional artist who joined the Union army. Too sick to fight at Antietam, Hope was reassigned to work as a scout and a mapmaker. He sketched scenes from the battle as it happened and later used his sketches to make paintings like this one. This scene is of early morning on the battlefield. This painting doesn't represent a particular moment, but is meant to show a series of events.

ANALYSIS SKILL **ANALYZING VISUALS**

How is this painting different from modern war reporting?

BIOGRAPHY

Robert E. Lee
(1807–1870)

Robert E. Lee was born into a wealthy Virginia family in 1807. Lee fought in the Mexican-American War, helping to capture Veracruz. When the Civil War began, President Lincoln asked Lee to lead the Union army. Lee declined and resigned from the U.S. Army to become a general in the Confederate army.

Drawing Conclusions How did Lee's choice reflect the division of the states?

The two armies met along Antietam Creek in Maryland on September 17, 1862. The battle lasted for hours. By the end of the day, the Union had suffered more than 12,000 casualties. The Confederates endured more than 13,000 casualties. Union officer A. H. Nickerson later recalled, "It seemed that everybody near me was killed." The **Battle of Antietam,** also known as the Battle of Sharpsburg, was the bloodiest single-day battle of the Civil War—and of U.S. history. More soldiers were killed and wounded at the Battle of Antietam than the deaths of all Americans in the American Revolution, War of 1812, and Mexican-American War combined.

During the battle, McClellan kept four divisions of soldiers in reserve and refused to use them to attack Lee's devastated army. McClellan was convinced that Lee was massing reserves for a counterattack. Those reserves did not exist. Despite this blunder, Antietam was an important victory. Lee's northward advance had been stopped.

READING CHECK **Analyzing** Why was the Battle of Antietam significant?

POLITICAL CARTOON
Anaconda Plan

This cartoon shows visually the North's plan to cut off supplies to the South through naval blockades, a strategy called the Anaconda Plan.

Why is the snake's head red, white, and blue?

How does the cartoonist show what the snake represents?

ANALYSIS SKILL ANALYZING PRIMARY SOURCES

Why do you think the plan was called the Anaconda Plan?

SCOTT'S GREAT SNAKE.

Breaking the Union's Blockade

While the two armies fought for control of the land, the Union navy controlled the sea. The North had most of the U.S. Navy's small fleet, and many experienced naval officers had remained loyal to the Union. The North also had enough industry to build more ships. The Confederacy turned to British companies for new ships.

The Union's Naval Strategy

The Union navy quickly mobilized to set up a blockade of southern ports. The blockade largely prevented the South from selling or receiving goods, and it seriously damaged the southern economy.

The blockade was hard to maintain because the Union navy had to patrol thousands of miles of coastline from Virginia to Texas. The South used small, fast ships to outrun the larger Union warships. Most of these blockade runners traveled to the Bahamas or Nassau to buy supplies for the Confederacy. These ships, however, could not make up for the South's loss of trade. The Union blockade reduced the number of ships entering southern ports from 6,000 to 800 per year.

Clash of the Ironclads

Hoping to take away the Union's advantage at sea, the Confederacy turned to a new type of warship—**ironclads**, or ships heavily armored with iron. The British government neglected to stop these ships from being delivered, in violation of its pledge of neutrality. The Confederates had captured a Union steamship, the *Merrimack*, and turned it into an ironclad, renamed the *Virginia*. One Union sailor described the **innovation** as "a huge half-submerged crocodile." In early March 1862, the ironclad sailed into Hampton Roads, Virginia, an important waterway guarded by Union ships. Before nightfall, the *Virginia* easily sank two of the Union's wooden warships, while it received minor damage.

ACADEMIC VOCABULARY

innovation a new idea or way of doing something

Union Blockade

Union states
Confederate states
Union blockade

0   100   200 Miles
0 100 200 Kilometers

Washington, D.C.

Hampton Roads

Richmond

Monitor battles Virginia at Hampton Roads.

Ohio

Mississippi River

Charleston

80°W

30°N

ATLANTIC OCEAN

New Orleans

Gulf of Mexico

N
W   E
S

90°W

Tropic of Cancer

GEOGRAPHY SKILLS **INTERPRETING MAPS**

Location What major port cities in the South were affected by the blockade?

The Union navy had already built its own ironclad, the *Monitor*, designed by Swedish-born engineer John Ericsson. Ericsson's ship had unusual new features, such as a revolving gun tower. One Confederate soldier called the *Monitor* "a tin can on a shingle!" Although small, the *Monitor* carried powerful guns and had thick plating.

When the *Virginia* returned to Hampton Roads later that month, the *Monitor* was waiting. After several hours of fighting, neither ship was seriously damaged, but the *Monitor* forced the *Virginia* to withdraw. This success saved the Union fleet and continued the blockade. The clash of the ironclads also signaled a revolution in naval warfare. The days of wooden warships powered by wind and sails were drawing to a close.

READING CHECK **Evaluating** How effective was the Union blockade?

SUMMARY AND PREVIEW The early battles of the Civil War were centered in the East. In the next section you will read about battles in the West.

Section 2 Assessment

go.hrw.com
Online Quiz
KEYWORD: SF7 HP16

Reviewing Ideas, Terms, and People

1. **a. Identify** List the early battles in the East and the outcome of each battle.
   b. Elaborate Why do you think the Union lost the **First Battle of Bull Run**?
2. **a. Describe** What costly mistake did the Confederacy make before the **Battle of Antietam**?
   b. Analyze What was the outcome of the Battle of Antietam, and what effect did it have on both the North and the South?
   c. Elaborate Why do you think General **George B. McClellan** did not finish off General **Robert E. Lee**'s troops when he had the chance?
3. **a. Describe** What was the Union's strategy in the war at sea?
   b. Draw Conclusions Why were **ironclads** more successful than older, wooden ships?

Critical Thinking

4. **Supporting a Point of View** Review your notes on the battles in the east and at sea. Then copy the graphic organizer below and use it to show which three conflicts you think were the most significant and why.

Most Significant	Why

FOCUS ON WRITING

5. **Taking Notes on the War in the East** As you read this section, take notes on the First Battle of Bull Run, the Seven Days' Battles, the Second Battle of Bull Run, and the Battle of Antietam. Be sure to answer the following questions: Who? Where? When? Why? and How?

The War in the West

What You Will Learn...

Main Ideas

1. Union strategy in the West centered on control of the Mississippi River.
2. Confederate and Union troops struggled for dominance in the Far West.

The Big Idea

Fighting in the Civil War spread to the western United States.

Key Terms and People

Ulysses S. Grant, *p. 522*
Battle of Shiloh, *p. 523*
David Farragut, *p. 524*
Siege of Vicksburg, *p. 524*

TAKING NOTES As you read, take notes on Civil War battles in the West. Write your notes in a graphic organizer like the one below.

Battles in the West
1.
2.
3.
4.
5.
6.

 8.1.21

If YOU were there...

You live in the city of Vicksburg, set on high bluffs above the Mississippi River. Vicksburg is vital to the control of the river, and Confederate defenses are strong. But the Union general is determined to take the town. For weeks, you have been surrounded and besieged. Cannon shells burst overhead, day and night. Some have fallen on nearby homes. Supplies of food are running low.

How would you survive this siege?

BUILDING BACKGROUND The Civil War was fought on many fronts, all across the continent and even at sea. In the East, fighting was at first concentrated in Virginia. In the West, cities and forts along the Mississippi River were the main target of Union forces. Northern control of the river would cut off the western states of the Confederacy.

Union Strategy in the West

While Lincoln fumed over the cautious, hesitant General McClellan, he had no such problems with **Ulysses S. Grant**. Bold and restless, Grant grew impatient when he was asked to lead defensive maneuvers. He wanted to be on the attack. As a commander of forces in the Union's western campaign, he would get his wish.

The western campaign focused on taking control of the Mississippi River. This strategy would cut off the eastern part of the Confederacy from sources of food production in Arkansas, Louisiana, and Texas. From bases on the Mississippi, the Union army could attack southern communication and transportation networks.

In February 1862, Grant led an assault force into Tennessee. With help from navy gunboats, Grant's Army of the Tennessee took two outposts on key rivers in the west. On February 6, he captured Fort Henry on the Tennessee River. Several days later he took Fort Donelson on the Cumberland River.

Fort Donelson's commander asked for the terms of surrender. Grant replied, "No terms except an unconditional and immediate

The War in the West

Interactive Map

- Union state or territory
- Union occupied 1863
- Confederate state
- → Union forces
- ↑↑ Union blockade
- ✸ Union victory
- → Confederate forces
- ✸ Confederate victory

0   100   200 Miles
0   100   200 Kilometers

Ft. Donelson
Feb. 1862
Paducah
Nashville
Ft. Henry
Feb. 1862
Murfreesboro
Dec. 1862–Jan. 1863
Shiloh
April 1862
TN
Chattanooga
Nov. 1863
Memphis
Corinth
Chickamauga
Sept. 1863
JOHNSTON
Atlanta
MS
AL
GA
Vicksburg
May–July 1863
Jackson
LA
Natchez
Port Hudson
May–July 1863
Mobile
Baton Rouge
New Orleans
April 1862
FARRAGUT
UNION BLOCKADE
Gulf of Mexico
FL

Louisville
Ohio River
KY
IL
VA
NC
SC
KS
INDIAN TERRITORY
AR
Arkansas River
Sabine River
Mississippi R.

90°W
80°W
30°N

go.hrw.com
Interactive Map
KEYWORD: SF7 CH16

GEOGRAPHY SKILLS | **INTERPRETING MAPS**

1. **Location** What river did Union forces fight to control?
2. **Human-Environment Interaction** Why do you think so many battles took place along rivers?

---

surrender can be accepted." The fort surrendered. The North gave a new name to Grant's initials: "Unconditional Surrender" Grant.

Advancing south in Tennessee, General Grant paused near Shiloh Church to await the arrival of the Army of Ohio. Grant knew that the large rebel army of General A. S. Johnston was nearby in Corinth, Mississippi, but he did not expect an attack. Instead of setting up defenses, he worked on drilling his new recruits.

In the early morning of April 6, 1862, the rebels sprang on Grant's sleepy camp. This began the **Battle of Shiloh**, in which the Union army gained greater control of the Mississippi River valley.

During the bloody two-day battle, each side gained and lost ground. Johnston was killed on the first day. The arrival of the Ohio force helped Grant regain territory and push the enemy back into Mississippi. The armies finally gave out, each with about 10,000 casualties. Both sides claimed victory, but, in fact, the victor was Grant.

The Fall of New Orleans

As Grant battled his way down the Mississippi, the Union navy prepared to blast its way upriver to meet him. The first obstacle was the port of New Orleans, the largest city in the Confederacy and the gateway to the Mississippi River.

BIOGRAPHY

David Farragut
(1801–1870)

David Farragut was born in Tennessee to a Spanish father and an American mother. At age seven Farragut was adopted by a family friend who agreed to train the young boy for the navy. Farragut received his first navy position—midshipman at large—at age nine and commanded his first vessel at 12. He spent the rest of his life in the U.S. Navy. Farragut led key attacks on the southern ports of Vicksburg and New Orleans.

Drawing Inferences How did Farragut help the war effort of the North?

THE CIVIL WAR **523**

With 18 ships and 700 men, Admiral **David Farragut** approached the two forts that guarded the entrance to New Orleans from the Gulf of Mexico. Unable to destroy the forts, Farragut decided to race past them.

The risky operation would take place at night. Farragut had his wooden ships wrapped in heavy chains to protect them like ironclads. Sailors slapped Mississippi mud on the ships' hulls to make them hard to see. Trees were tied to the masts to make the ships look like the forested shore.

Before dawn on April 24, 1862, the warships made their daring dash. The Confederates fired at Farragut's ships from the shore and from gunboats. They launched burning rafts, one of which scorched Farragut's own ship. But his fleet slipped by the twin forts and made it to New Orleans. The city fell on April 29.

Farragut sailed up the Mississippi River, taking Baton Rouge, Louisiana, and Natchez, Mississippi. He then approached the city of Vicksburg, Mississippi.

The Siege of Vicksburg

Vicksburg's geography made invasion all but impossible. Perched on 200-foot-high cliffs above the Mississippi River, the city could rain down firepower on enemy ships or on soldiers trying to scale the cliffs. Deep gorges surrounded the city, turning back land assaults. Nevertheless, Farragut ordered Vicksburg to surrender.

> "Mississippians don't know, and refuse to learn, how to surrender … If Commodore Farragut … can teach them, let [him] come and try."
>
> —Colonel James L. Autry,
> military commander of Vicksburg

Farragut's guns had trouble reaching the city above. It was up to General Grant. His solution was to starve the city into surrender.

General Grant's troops began the **Siege of Vicksburg** in mid-May 1863, cutting off the city and shelling it repeatedly. As food ran out, residents and soldiers survived by eating horses, dogs, and rats. "We are utterly cut off from the world, surrounded by a circle of fire," wrote one woman. "People do nothing

The Union navy played an important part in the Civil War. Besides blockading and raiding southern ports, the navy joined battles along the Mississippi River, as in this painting of Vicksburg.

but eat what they can get, sleep when they can, and dodge the shells."

The Confederate soldiers were also sick and hungry. In late June a group of soldiers sent their commander a warning.

"The army is now ripe for mutiny [rebellion], unless it can be fed. If you can't feed us, you'd better surrender us, horrible as the idea is."
—Confederate soldiers at Vicksburg to General John C. Pemberton, 1863

On July 4, Pemberton surrendered. Grant immediately sent food to the soldiers and civilians. He later claimed that "the fate of the Confederacy was sealed when Vicksburg fell."

READING CHECK Summarizing How did the Union gain control of the Mississippi River?

Struggle for the Far West

Early on in the war, the Union halted several attempts by Confederate armies to control lands west of the Mississippi. In August 1861, a Union detachment from Colorado turned back a Confederate force at Glorieta Pass. Union volunteers also defeated rebel forces at Arizona's Pichaco Pass.

Confederate attempts to take the border state of Missouri also collapsed. Failing to seize the federal arsenal at St. Louis in mid-1861, the rebels fell back to Pea Ridge in northwest Arkansas. There, in March 1862, they attacked again, aided by some 800 Cherokee. The Indians hoped the Confederates would give them greater freedom. In addition, slavery was legal in Indian Territory, and some Native Americans who were slaveholders supported the Confederacy. Despite being outnumbered, Union forces won the Battle of Pea Ridge. The Union defense of Missouri held.

Pro-Confederate forces remained active in the region throughout the war. They attacked Union forts and raided towns in Missouri and Kansas, forcing Union commanders to keep valuable troops stationed in the area.

READING CHECK Analyzing What was the importance of the fighting in the Far West?

SUMMARY AND PREVIEW The North and the South continued their struggle with battles in the West. A number of key battles took place in the Western theater, and several important Union leaders emerged from these battles. One, Ulysses S. Grant, would soon become even more important to the Union army. In the next section you will learn about the lives of civilians, enslaved Africans, and soldiers during the war.

go.hrw.com
Online Quiz
KEYWORD: SF7 HP16

Section 3 Assessment

Reviewing Ideas, Terms, and People

1. a. **Identify** What role did **Ulysses S. Grant** play in the war in the West?
   b. **Explain** Why was the **Battle of Shiloh** important?
   c. **Elaborate** Do you think President Lincoln would have approved of Grant's actions in the West? Why or why not?
2. a. **Describe** How did the Union take New Orleans, and why was it an important victory?
   b. **Draw Conclusions** How were civilians affected by the **Siege of Vicksburg**?
   c. **Predict** What might be some possible results of the Union victory at Vicksburg?

Critical Thinking

3. **Identifying Cause and Effect** Review your notes on Union strategy in the West. Then copy this graphic organizer and use it to show the causes and effects of each battle.

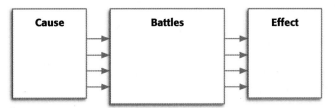

| Cause | Battles | Effect |

FOCUS ON WRITING

4. **Taking Notes on the War in the West** As you read this section, take notes on the fight for the Mississippi River and the Siege of Vicksburg. Be sure to answer the following questions: Who? Where? When? Why? and How?

The Vicksburg Strategy

"Vicksburg is the key!" President Abraham Lincoln declared. "The war can never be brought to a close until that key is in our pocket." Vicksburg was so important because of its location on the Mississippi River, a vital trade route and supply line. Union ships couldn't get past the Confederate guns mounted on the high bluffs of Vicksburg. Capturing Vicksburg would give the Union control of the Mississippi, stealing a vital supply line and splitting the Confederacy in two. The task fell to General Ulysses S. Grant.

5 The Siege of Vicksburg Grant now had 30,000 Confederate troops trapped in Vicksburg. After two assaults on the city failed, Grant was forced to lay siege. After six weeks of bombardment, the Confederates surrendered on July 4, 1863. Grant's bold campaign had given the Union control of the Mississippi River.

Vicksburg

1 Grant Crosses into Louisiana General Grant planned to attack Vicksburg from the North, but the swampy land made attack from that direction difficult. So, Grant crossed the Mississippi River into Louisiana and marched south.

Port Gibson

2 Grant Moves East Grant's troops met up with their supply boats here and crossed back into Mississippi. In a daring gamble, Grant decided to move without a supply line, allowing his army to move quickly.

3 Port Gibson A skirmish at Port Gibson proved that the Confederates could not defend the Mississippi line.

UNION
CONTROL

CONFEDERATE
CONTROL

Ironclads

Union ironclads were vital to the Vicksburg campaign. These gunboats protected Grant's troops when they crossed the Mississippi. Later, they bombarded Vicksburg during the siege of the city.

Jackson

④

The Battle of Jackson Grant defeated a Confederate army at Jackson and then moved on to Vicksburg. This prevented Confederate forces from reinforcing Vicksburg.

BIOGRAPHY

Ulysses S. Grant
(1822–1885)

Ulysses S. Grant was born in April 1822 in New York. Grant attended West Point and fought in the Mexican-American War. He resigned in 1854 and worked at various jobs in farming, real estate, and retail. When the Civil War started, he joined the Union army and was quickly promoted to general. After the Civil War, Grant rode a wave of popularity to become president of the United States.

GEOGRAPHY SKILLS INTERPRETING MAPS

1. **Location** Why was Vicksburg's location so important?
2. **Place** What natural features made Vicksburg difficult to attack?

Daily Life during the War

If **YOU** were there...

You live in Maryland in 1864. Your father and brothers are in the Union army, and you want to do your part in the war. You hear that a woman in Washington, D.C., is supplying medicines and caring for wounded soldiers on the battlefield. She is looking for volunteers. You know the work will be dangerous, for you'll be in the line of fire. You might be shot or even killed.

Would you join the nurses on the battlefield?

BUILDING BACKGROUND The Civil War touched almost all Americans. Some 3 million men fought in the two armies. Thousands of other men and women worked behind the lines, providing food, supplies, medical care, and other necessary services. Civilians could not escape the effects of war, as the fighting destroyed farms, homes, and cities.

Emancipation Proclamation

Emancipation Proclamation

At the heart of the nation's bloody struggle were millions of enslaved African Americans. Abolitionists urged President Lincoln to free them.

In an 1858 speech, Lincoln declared, "There is no reason in the world why the negro is not entitled to all the natural rights numerated in the Declaration of Independence—the right to life, liberty, and the pursuit of happiness." Yet as president, Lincoln found **emancipation**, or the freeing of slaves, to be a difficult issue. He did not believe he had the constitutional power. He also worried about the effects of emancipation.

Lincoln Issues the Proclamation

Northerners had a range of opinions about abolishing slavery.

- The Democratic Party, which included many laborers, opposed emancipation. Laborers feared that freed slaves would come north and take their jobs at lower wages.
- Abolitionists argued that the war was pointless if it did not win freedom for African Americans. They warned that the Union would remain divided until the problem was resolved.

The painting at left shows Lincoln and his cabinet after the signing of the Emancipation Proclamation. Above is a photo of former slaves who were freed by the proclamation.

How do you think the Emancipation Proclamation would affect the Civil War?

Emancipation Proclamation

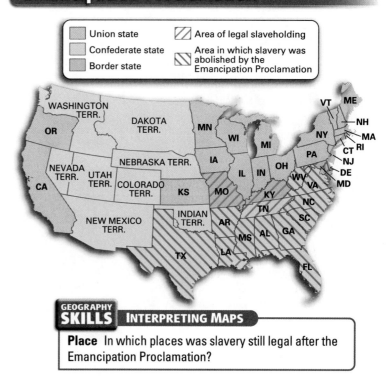

Union state
Confederate state
Border state
Area of legal slaveholding
Area in which slavery was abolished by the Emancipation Proclamation

GEOGRAPHY SKILLS **INTERPRETING MAPS**

Place In which places was slavery still legal after the Emancipation Proclamation?

- Lincoln worried about losing support for the war. Previous wartime Confiscation Acts that had attempted to free the slaves had been unpopular in the border states.
- Others, including Secretary of War Edwin Stanton, agreed with Lincoln that the use of slave labor was helping the Confederacy make war. Therefore, as commander in chief, the president could free the slaves in all rebellious states. Freed African Americans could then be recruited into the Union army.

For several weeks in 1862, Lincoln worked intensely, thinking, writing, and rewriting. He finally wrote the **Emancipation Proclamation**, the order to free the Confederate slaves. The proclamation declared that:

"…all persons held as slaves within any State or designated part of a State the people whereof shall then be in rebellion against the United States shall be then, thenceforward, and forever free."
—Emancipation Proclamation, 1862

The Emancipation Proclamation was a military order that freed slaves only in areas

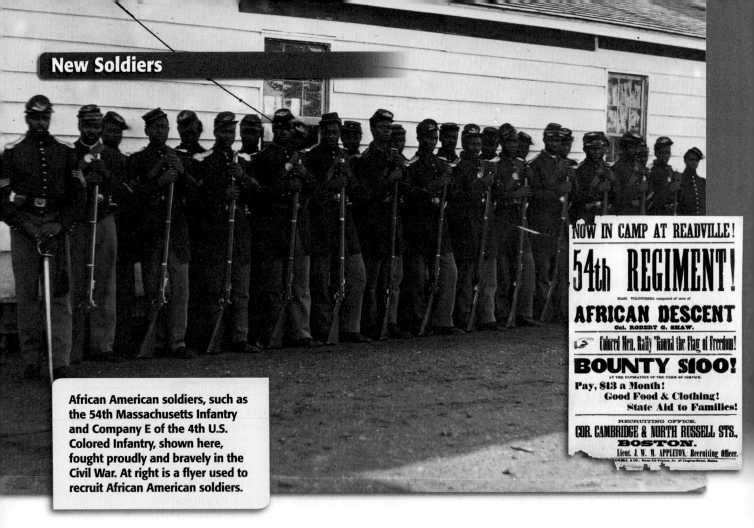

New Soldiers

African American soldiers, such as the 54th Massachusetts Infantry and Company E of the 4th U.S. Colored Infantry, shown here, fought proudly and bravely in the Civil War. At right is a flyer used to recruit African American soldiers.

NOW IN CAMP AT READVILLE!

54th REGIMENT!

MASS. VOLUNTEERS, composed of men of

AFRICAN DESCENT

Col. ROBERT G. SHAW.

Colored Men, Rally 'Round the Flag of Freedom!

BOUNTY $100!

AT THE EXPIRATION OF THE TERM OF SERVICE.

Pay, $13 a Month!
Good Food & Clothing!
State Aid to Families!

RECRUITING OFFICE,

COR. CAMBRIDGE & NORTH RUSSELL STS.,

BOSTON.

Lieut. J. W. M. APPLETON, Recruiting Officer.

controlled by the Confederacy. In fact, the proclamation had little immediate effect. It was impossible for the federal government to enforce the proclamation in the areas where it actually applied—the states in rebellion that were not under federal control. The proclamation did not stop slavery in the border states, where the federal government would have had the power to enforce it. The words written in the Emancipation Proclamation were powerful, but the impact of the document was more symbolic than real. It defined what the Union was fighting against, and discouraged Britain from aiding the Confederacy.

Lincoln wanted to be in a strong position in the war before announcing his plan. The Battle of Antietam gave him the victory he needed. He issued the Emancipation Proclamation on September 22, 1862. The proclamation went into effect on January 1, 1863.

Reaction to the Proclamation

New Year's Eve, December 31, 1862: In "night watch" meetings at many African American churches, worshippers prayed, sang, and gave thanks. When the clocks struck midnight, millions were free. Abolitionists rejoiced. Frederick Douglass called January 1, 1863, "the great day which is to determine the destiny not only of the American Republic, but that of the American Continent."

William Lloyd Garrison was quick to note, however, that "slavery, as a system" continued to exist in the loyal slave states. Yet where slavery remained, the proclamation encouraged many enslaved Africans to escape when the Union troops came near. They flocked to the Union camps and followed them for protection. The loss of slaves crippled the South's ability to wage war.

READING CHECK Finding Main Ideas How did northerners view the Emancipation Proclamation?

LETTER
June 23, 1863

Joseph E. Williams, an African American soldier and recruiter from Pennsylvania, wrote this letter describing why African Americans fought for the Union.

"We are now determined to hold every step which has been offered to us as citizens of the United States for our elevation [benefit], which represent justice, the purity, the truth, and aspiration [hope] of heaven. We must learn deeply to realize the duty, the moral and political necessity for the benefit of our race...Every consideration of honor, of interest, and of duty to God and man, requires that we should be true to our trust."

—quoted in *A Grand Army of Black Men*, edited by Edwin S. Redkey

ANALYSIS SKILL **ANALYZING PRIMARY SOURCES**

Why did Williams think being soldiers was so important for African Americans?

African Americans Participate in the War

As the war casualties climbed, the Union needed even more troops. African Americans were ready to volunteer. Not all white northerners were ready to accept them, but eventually they had to. Frederick Douglass believed that military service would help African Americans gain rights.

"Once let the black man get upon his person the brass letters, U.S.; ... and a musket on his shoulder and bullets in his pocket, and there is no power on earth which can deny that he has earned the right to citizenship."

—Frederick Douglass, quoted in
The Life and Writings of Frederick Douglass, Vol. 3

Congress began allowing the army to sign up African American volunteers as laborers in July 1862. The War Department also gave **contrabands**, or escaped slaves, the right to join the Union army in South Carolina. Free African Americans in Louisiana and Kansas also formed their own units in the Union army. By the spring of 1863, African American army units were proving themselves in combat. They took part in a Union attack on Port Hudson, Louisiana, in May.

One unit stood out above the others. The **54th Massachusetts Infantry** consisted mostly of free African Americans. In July 1863 this regiment led a heroic charge on South Carolina's Fort Wagner. The 54th took heavy fire and suffered huge casualties in the failed operation. About half the regiment was killed, wounded, or captured. Edward L. Pierce, a correspondent for the *New York Tribune*, wrote, "The Fifty-fourth did well and nobly...They moved up as gallantly as any troops could, and with their enthusiasm they deserved a better fate." The bravery of the 54th regiment made it the most celebrated African American unit of the war.

About 180,000 African Americans served with the Union army. They received $10 a month, while white soldiers got $13. They were usually led by white officers, some from abolitionist families.

African Americans faced special horrors on the battlefield. Confederates often killed their black captives or sold them into slavery. In the 1864 election, Lincoln suggested rewarding African American soldiers by giving them the right to vote.

READING CHECK **Analyzing Information**
How did African Americans support the Union?

Growing Opposition

The deepening shadows in Lincoln's face reflected the huge responsibilities he carried. Besides running the war, he had to deal with growing tensions in the North.

Copperheads

As the months rolled on and the number of dead continued to increase, a group of northern Democrats began speaking out against the war. Led by U.S. Representative Clement L. Vallandigham of Ohio, they called themselves Peace Democrats. Their enemies called them Copperheads, comparing them to a poisonous snake. The name stuck.

Many **Copperheads** were midwesterners that sympathized with the South and opposed abolition. They believed the war was not necessary and called for its end. Vallandigham asked what the war had gained, and then said, "Let the dead at Fredericksburg and Vicksburg answer."

Lincoln saw the Copperheads as a threat to support of the war effort. To silence them, he suspended the right of habeas corpus.

Habeas corpus is a constitutional protection against unlawful imprisonment. Ignoring this protection, Union officials jailed their enemies, including some Copperheads, without evidence or trial. Lincoln's action greatly angered Democrats and some Republicans.

Northern Draft

In March 1863, war critics erupted again when Congress approved a draft, or forced military service. For $300, men were allowed to buy their way out of military service. For an unskilled laborer, however, that was nearly a year's wages. Critics of the draft called the Civil War a "rich man's war and a poor man's fight."

In July 1863, riots broke out when African Americans were brought into New York City to replace striking Irish dock workers. The city happened to be holding a war draft at the same time. The two events enraged rioters, who attacked African Americans and draft offices. More than 100 people died.

In this tense situation, the northern Democrats nominated former General George McClellan for president in 1864. They called

Infantry Family

While wealthy civilians could avoid military service, poorer men were drafted to serve in the Union army. This member of the 31st Pennsylvania Infantry brought his family along with him. His wife probably helped the soldier with many daily chores such as cooking and laundry.

Why would soldiers bring their families to live with them in camp?

for an immediate end to the war. Lincoln defeated McClellan in the popular vote, winning by about 400,000 votes out of 4 million cast. The electoral vote was not even close. Lincoln won 212 to 21.

READING CHECK **Identifying Cause and Effect**
Who opposed the war, and how did Lincoln respond to the conflict?

Life for Soldiers and Civilians

Young, fresh recruits in both armies were generally eager to fight. Experienced troops, however, knew better.

On the Battlefield

Civil War armies fought in the ancient battlefield formation that produced massive casualties. Endless rows of troops fired directly at one another, with cannonballs landing amid them. When the order was given, soldiers would attach bayonets to their guns and rush toward their enemy. Men died to gain every inch of ground.

Doctors and nurses in the field saved many lives. Yet they had no medicines to stop infections that developed after soldiers were wounded. Many soldiers endured the horror of having infected legs and arms amputated without painkillers. Infections from minor injuries caused many deaths.

Despite the huge battlefield losses, the biggest killer in the Civil War was not the fighting. It was diseases such as typhoid, pneumonia, and tuberculosis. Nearly twice as many soldiers died of illnesses as died in combat.

Prisoners of War

Military prisoners on both sides lived in unimaginable misery. In prison camps, such as Andersonville, Georgia, and Elmira, New York, soldiers were packed into camps designed to hold only a fraction of their number. Soldiers had little shelter, food, or clothing. Starvation and disease killed thousands of prisoners.

LINKING TO TODAY

Battlefield Communications

The drummer was an essential member of every Civil War unit. Drummers served army commanders by drumming specific beats that directed troop movements during battle. Different beats were used to order troops to prepare to attack, to fire, to cease fire, and to signal a truce. Drummers had to stay near their commanders to hear orders. This meant that the drummers—some as young as nine years old—often saw deadly combat conditions.

The Civil War gave birth to the Signal Corps, the army unit devoted to communications. Today battlefield communications are primarily electronic. Radio, e-mail, facsimile, and telephone messages, often relayed by satellites, enable orders and other information to be transmitted nearly instantaneously all over the globe.

Union Signal Corps

Modern battlefield communications

ANALYSIS SKILL **ANALYZING INFORMATION**
Why is communication so important on the battlefield?

Life as a Civilian

The war effort involved all levels of society. Women as well as people too young or too old for military service worked in factories and on farms. Economy in the North boomed as production and prices soared. The lack of workers caused wages to rise by 43 percent between 1860 and 1865.

Women were the backbone of civilian life. On the farms, women and children performed the daily chores usually done by men. One visitor to Iowa in 1862 reported that he "met more women . . . at work in the fields than men." Southern women also managed farms and plantations.

One woman brought strength and comfort to countless wounded Union soldiers. Volunteer **Clara Barton** organized the collection of medicine and supplies for delivery to the battlefield. At the field hospitals,

Clara Barton founded the American Red Cross.

the "angel of the battlefield" soothed the wounded and dying and assisted doctors as bullets flew around her. Barton's work formed the basis for the future American Red Cross.

In the South, Sally Louisa Tompkins established a small hospital in Richmond, Virginia. By the end of the war, it had grown into a major army hospital. Jefferson Davis recognized her value to the war effort by making her a captain in the Confederate army.

READING CHECK **Analyzing** How did women help the war effort on both sides?

SUMMARY AND PREVIEW Many lives were changed by the war. In the next section you will learn about the end of the war.

Section 4 Assessment

Reviewing Ideas, Terms, and People

1. **a. Recall** Why did some Americans want to end slavery?
   b. Contrast How did reactions to the **Emancipation Proclamation** differ?
   c. Elaborate Do you think that the **emancipation** of slaves should have extended to the border states? Explain your answer.
2. **a. Recall** Why did some northerners want to recruit African Americans into the Union army?
   b. Contrast In what ways did African American soldiers face more difficulties than white soldiers did?
3. **a. Identify** Who were **Copperheads**, and why did they oppose the war?
   b. Evaluate Should President Lincoln have suspended the right to **habeas corpus**? Why?
4. **a. Describe** What were conditions like in military camps?
   b. Draw Conclusions How did the war change life on the home front?

Critical Thinking

5. **Identifying Effects** Review your notes. Then copy the graphic organizer below. Use it to summarize the reasons for the Emancipation Proclamation, its main points, and its effects on different people.

Reasons for the Emancipation Proclamation
Main points of the Proclamation
Effect on People's Lives

FOCUS ON WRITING

6. **Taking Notes on Life During the War** As you read this section, take notes on the emancipation of the slaves, African American soldiers, and women who provided medical care for soldiers. Answer the following questions: Who? Where? When? Why? and How?

Abraham Lincoln

What would you do to save the struggling Union?

When did he live? 1809–1865

Where did he live? Abraham Lincoln was born in a log cabin to a poor family in Kentucky. Growing up in Kentucky and Illinois, Lincoln went to school for less than a year. He taught himself law and settled in Springfield, where he practiced law and politics. As president he lived in Washington, D.C. There, at age 56, his life was cut short by an assassin, John Wilkes Booth.

What did he do? The issue of slavery defined Lincoln's political career. He was not an abolitionist, but he strongly opposed extending slavery into the territories. In a series of famous debates against Senator Stephen Douglas of Illinois, Lincoln championed his views on slavery and made a brilliant defense of democracy and the Union. As president, Lincoln led the nation through the Civil War.

Why is he important? Lincoln is one of the great symbols of American democracy. "A house divided against itself cannot stand," he declared in a debate with Douglas. In 1863 Lincoln issued the Emancipation Proclamation. His address to commemorate the bloody battlefield at Gettysburg is widely considered to be one of the best political speeches in American history.

Summarizing Why is Lincoln such an important figure in American history?

KEY EVENTS

- **1834** Elected to the Illinois legislature

- **1842** Marries Mary Todd

- **1858** Holds series of famous debates with U.S. Senator Stephen Douglas

- **1860** Elected president on November 6

- **1863** Issues the Emancipation Proclamation on January 1

- **1863** Gives the Gettysburg Address on November 19

- **1865** Gives second inaugural address on March 4

- **1865** Shot on April 14; dies the next day

Lincoln's address at the dedication of the Gettysburg National Cemetery.

The Tide of War Turns

What You Will Learn...

Main Ideas

1. The Union tried to divide the Confederate Army at Fredericksburg, but the attempt failed.
2. The Battle of Gettysburg in 1863 was a major turning point in the war.
3. During 1864, Union campaigns in the East and South dealt crippling blows to the Confederacy.
4. Union troops forced the South to surrender in 1865, ending the Civil War.

The Big Idea

Union victories in 1863, 1864, and 1865 ended the Civil War.

Key Terms and People

Battle of Gettysburg, *p. 537*
George Pickett, *p. 539*
Pickett's Charge, *p. 539*
Gettysburg Address, *p. 540*
Wilderness Campaign, *p. 540*
William Tecumseh Sherman, *p. 541*
total war, *p. 542*
Appomattox Courthouse, *p. 542*

TAKING NOTES Copy the graphic organizer. Use it to recall the events that led to the end of the Civil War.

| July 1–3, 1863 |
| May–June, 1864 |
| September 2, 1864 |
| December 10, 1864 |
| April 2, 1865 |
| April 9, 1865 |

8.1.21, 8.1.29, 8.1.30

If YOU were there...

You live in southern Pennsylvania in 1863, near a battlefield where thousands died. Now people have come from miles around to dedicate a cemetery here. You are near the front of the crowd. The first speaker impresses everyone with two hours of dramatic words and gestures. Then President Lincoln speaks—just a few minutes of simple words. Many people are disappointed.

Why do you think the president's speech was so short?

BUILDING BACKGROUND Many people, especially in the North, had expected a quick victory, but the war dragged on for years. The balance of victories seemed to seesaw between North and South, and both sides suffered terrible casualties. The last Confederate push into the North ended at Gettysburg in one of the bloodiest battles of the war.

Fredericksburg and Chancellorsville

Frustrated by McClellan's lack of aggression, Lincoln replaced him with General Ambrose E. Burnside as leader of the Army of the Potomac. Burnside favored a swift, decisive attack on Richmond by way of Fredericksburg. In November 1862, he set out with 120,000 troops.

Burnside's tactics surprised General Lee. The Confederate commander had divided his force of 78,000 men. Neither section of the Confederate army was in a good position to defend Fredericksburg. However, Burnside's army experienced delays in crossing the Rappahannock River. These delays allowed Lee's army to reunite and entrench themselves around Fredericksburg. Finally, the Union army crossed the Rappahannock and launched a series of charges. These attacks had heavy casualties and failed to break the Confederate line. Eventually, after suffering about 12,600 casualties, Burnside ordered a retreat. The Confederates had about 5,300 casualties.

Soon Burnside stepped down from his position. Lincoln made General Joseph Hooker the commander of the Army of the Potomac. At the end of April 1863, Hooker and his army of about 138,000 men launched a frontal attack on Fredericksburg. Then Hooker ordered about 115,000 of his troops to split off and approach the Confederate's flank, or side. Hooker's strategy seemed about to work. But for some reason he hesitated and had his flanking troops take a defensive position at Chancellorsville. This town was located a few miles west of Fredericksburg.

The following day, Lee used most of his army (about 60,000 men) to attack Hooker's troops at Chancellorsville. Stonewall Jackson led an attack on Hooker's flank while Lee commanded an assault on the Union front. The Union army was almost cut in two. They managed to form a defensive line, which they held for three days. Then Hooker ordered a retreat.

Lee's army won a major victory. But this victory had severe casualties. During the battle, Lee's trusted general, Stonewall Jackson, was accidentally shot by his own troops. He died a few days later.

READING CHECK **Comparing** What did generals McClellan, Burnside, and Hooker have in common?

Battle of Gettysburg

General Lee launched more attacks within Union territory. As before, his goal was to break the North's will to fight. He also hoped that a victory would convince other nations to recognize the Confederacy.

First Day

In early June 1863, Lee cut across northern Maryland into southern Pennsylvania. His forces gathered west of a small town called Gettysburg. Lee was unaware that Union soldiers were encamped closer to town. He had been suffering from lack of enemy information for three days because his cavalry chief "Jeb" Stuart was not performing his duties. Stuart and his cavalry had gone off on their own raiding party, disobeying Lee's orders.

Another Confederate raiding party went to Gettysburg for boots and other supplies. There, Lee's troops ran right into Union general George G. Meade's cavalry, triggering the **Battle of Gettysburg**, a key battle that finally turned the tide against the Confederates. The battle began on July 1, 1863, when the

FOCUS ON INDIANA

At the same time that the Battle of Gettysburg was tipping the tide of war to the Union, Brigadier General John Hunt Morgan was leading a Confederate raid into Indiana and through to Ohio. On July 9, 1863, his forces clashed with Indiana militia at Corydon, the only Civil War battle on Indiana soil.

Three Days at Gettysburg

Gettysburg was the largest and bloodiest battle of the Civil War. In three days, more than 51,000 soldiers were killed, wounded, captured, or went missing. It was an important victory for the Union, and it stopped Lee's plan of invading the North.

Artillery played a key role in the Battle of Gettysburg on July 1, 1863.

Day One: July 1, 1863

Confederate raiding party and the Union forces began exchanging fire. The larger Confederate forces began to push the Union troops back through Gettysburg.

The Union soldiers regrouped along the high ground of Cemetery Ridge and Culp's Hill. General Lee wanted to prevent the Union forces from entrenching themselves. He therefore ordered General Ewell to attack immediately. However, Ewell hesitated and thereby gave the Federals time to establish an excellent defensive position.

In fact, Confederate General James Longstreet thought that the Union position was almost impossible to overrun. Instead of attacking, he felt that the Confederate army should move east, take a strong defensive position themselves, and wait for the Union forces to attack them. However, General Lee was not convinced. He believed that his troops were invincible.

The Confederates camped at Seminary Ridge, which ran parallel to the Union forces. Both camps called for their main forces to reinforce them and prepare for combat the next day.

Second Day

On July 2, Lee ordered an attack on the left side of the Union line. Lee knew that he could win the battle if his troops captured Little Round Top from the Union forces. From this hill, Lee's troops could easily fire down on the line of Union forces. Union forces and Confederate troops fought viciously for control of Little Round Top. The fighting was particularly fierce on the south side of the hill. There the 20th Maine led by Colonel Joshua Chamberlain battled the 15th Alabama led by Colonel William Oates. Later, when describing the conflict, Oates said, "The blood stood in puddles in some places in the rocks." Eventually, the Union forced the Confederates to pull back from Little Round Top.

Then the Confederates attacked Cemetery Hill and Culp's Hill. The fighting lasted until nightfall. The assault on Cemetery Hill was unsuccessful. The Confederates did manage to take a few trenches on Culp's Hill. Even so, the Union forces still held a strong defensive position by the day's end.

Three Days at Gettysburg (continued)

Day Two: July 2, 1863, 10 a.m.

Union soldiers desperately defended Little Round Top from a fierce Confederate charge.

Pickett's Charge

On the third day of battle, Longstreet again tried to convince Lee not to attack. But Lee thought that the Union forces were severely battered and ready to break. Because of this, he planned to attack the center of the Union line on Cemetery Ridge. Such a tactic, he felt, would not be expected. Indeed, General Meade left only about 5,750 troops to defend the center.

For over an hour, the Confederates shelled Cemetery Ridge with cannon fire. For a while, the Union cannons fired back. Then they slacked off. The Confederates assumed that they had seriously damaged the Union artillery. In reality, the Confederate barrage did little damage.

The task of charging the Union center fell to three divisions of Confederate soldiers. General **George Pickett** commanded the largest unit. In late afternoon, nearly 15,000 men took part in **Pickett's Charge**. For one mile, the Confederates marched slowly up toward Cemetery Ridge. Showered with cannon and rifle fire, they suffered severe losses. But eventually, some of them almost reached their destination. Then Union reinforcements added to the barrage on the rebels. Soon the

Pickett's Charge, July 3, 1863

Interactive Map

General George Pickett led his troops across Emmitsburg Road to attack the Union position. He lost more than half of his men in the 50-minute battle.

GEOGRAPHY SKILLS | **INTERPRETING MAPS**

go.hrw.com
Interactive Map
KEYWORD: SF7 CH16

1. **Human-Environment Interaction** How do you think geography affected Pickett's Charge?
2. **Movement** In which direction did Pickett's soldiers charge?

Pickett's Charge

Pickett's Charge proved a disaster for the Confederate attackers. Fewer than half of them survived.

Day Three: July 3, 1863, 3 p.m.

Confederates retreated, leaving about 7,500 casualties on the field of battle. Distressed by this defeat, General Lee rode among the survivors and told them, "It is all my fault."

On the fourth day, Lee began to retreat to Virginia. In all, nearly 75,000 Confederate soldiers and 90,000 Union troops had fought during the Battle of Gettysburg.

General Meade decided not to follow Lee's army. This decision angered Lincoln. He felt that Meade had missed an opportunity to crush the Confederates and possibly end the war.

Aftermath of Gettysburg

Gettysburg was a turning point in the war. Lee's troops would never again launch an attack in the North. The Union victory at Gettysburg took place on the day before Grant's capture of Vicksburg, Mississippi. These victories made northerners believe that the war could be won.

In addition, the Union win at Gettysburg helped to end the South's search for foreign influence in the war. After Gettysburg, Great Britain and France refused to provide aid to the Confederacy. The South's attempt at cotton diplomacy failed.

The Gettysburg Address

On November 19, 1863, at the dedicating ceremony of the Gettysburg battlefield cemetery, President Lincoln gave a speech called the **Gettysburg Address**, in which he praised the bravery of Union soldiers and renewed his commitment to winning the Civil War. This short but moving speech is one of the most famous in American history. In one of its frequently quoted lines, Lincoln referenced the Declaration of Independence and its ideals of liberty, equality, and democracy. He reminded listeners that the war was being fought for those reasons.

Lincoln rededicated himself to winning the war and preserving the Union. A difficult road still lay ahead.

READING CHECK Analyzing Why was Gettysburg a turning point?

Union Campaigns Cripple the Confederacy

Lincoln had been impressed with General Grant's successes in capturing Vicksburg. He transferred Grant to the East and gave him command of the Union army. In early 1864, Grant forced Lee to fight a series of battles in Virginia that stretched Confederate soldiers and supplies to their limits.

Wilderness Campaign in the East

From May through June, the armies fought in northern and central Virginia. Union troops launched the **Wilderness Campaign**—a series of battles designed to capture the Confederate capital at Richmond, Virginia. The first battle took place in early May, in woods about 50 miles outside of Richmond. Grant then ordered General Meade to Spotsylvania, where the fighting raged for five days.

Over the next month, Union soldiers moved the Confederate troops back toward Richmond. However, Grant experienced his worst defeat at the Battle of Cold Harbor in early June, just 10 miles northeast of Richmond. In only a few hours the Union army suffered 7,000 casualties. The battle delayed Grant's plans to take the Confederate capital.

Union forces had suffered twice as many casualties as the Confederates had, yet Grant continued his strategy. He knew he would be getting additional soldiers, and Lee could not. Grant slowly but surely advanced his troops through Virginia. He told another officer, "I propose to fight it out on this line if it takes all summer."

After Cold Harbor, General Grant moved south of Richmond. He had hoped to take control of the key railroad junction at Petersburg, Virginia. Lee's army, however, formed a solid defense, and Grant could not **execute** his attack. Grant was winning the war, but he still had not captured Richmond. Facing re-election, Lincoln was especially discouraged by this failure.

Final Campaigns

Nashville
Dec. 15–16, 1864

Raleigh
April 13, 1865

Atlanta
Sept. 2, 1864

Wilmington
Feb. 22, 1865

Savannah
Dec. 21, 1864

Pensacola

Gettysburg,
July 1–3, 1863

Washington, D.C.

The Wilderness,
May 5–7, 1864

Chancellorsville,
May 1–5, 1863

Spotsylvania
Courthouse,
May 8–19, 1864

Richmond

Appomattox
Courthouse,
Apr. 9, 1865–
Lee surrenders
to Grant

Petersburg,
June 1864–
April 1865

Cold Harbor,
June 3, 1864

0   20   40 Miles
0   20   40 Kilometers

ATLANTIC OCEAN

Gulf of Mexico

Union state
Union occupied, 1865
Confederate state
Union forces
Union victory
Confederate forces
Confederate victory

0   100   200 Miles
0   100   200 Kilometers

GEOGRAPHY SKILLS INTERPRETING MAPS

1. **Movement** About how long was Sherman's March to the Sea from Atlanta to Savannah?
2. **Movement** What challenges do you think Sherman faced on his southern attacks?

Sherman Strikes the South

Lincoln needed a victory for the Union army to help him win re-election in 1864. The bold campaign of General **William Tecumseh Sherman** provided this key victory. Sherman carried out the Union plan to destroy southern railroads and industries.

In the spring of 1864, Sherman marched south from Tennessee with 100,000 troops. His goal was to take Atlanta, Georgia, and knock out an important railroad link. From May through August, Sherman's army moved steadily through the Appalachian Mountains toward Atlanta. Several times, Sherman avoided defenses set up by Confederate general Joseph Johnston.

In July, Sherman was within sight of Atlanta. Confederate president Jefferson Davis gave General John Hood command of Confederate forces in the region. Hood repeatedly attacked Sherman in a final attempt to

save Atlanta, but the Union troops proved stronger. The Confederate troops retreated as Sherman held Atlanta under siege.

Atlanta fell to Sherman's troops on September 2, 1864. Much of the city was destroyed by artillery and fire. Sherman ordered the residents who still remained to leave. Responding to his critics, Sherman later wrote, "War is war, and not popularity-seeking." The loss of Atlanta cost the South an important railroad link and its center of industry.

Many people in the North had been upset with the length of the war. However, the capture of Atlanta showed that progress was being made in defeating the South. This success helped to convince Union voters to re-elect Lincoln in a landslide.

Sherman did not wait long to begin his next campaign. His goal was the port city of Savannah, Georgia. In mid-November 1864,

Sherman left Atlanta with a force of about 60,000 men. He said he would "make Georgia howl!"

During his March to the Sea, Sherman practiced **total war**—destroying civilian and economic resources. Sherman believed that total war would ruin the South's economy and its ability to fight. He ordered his troops to destroy railways, bridges, crops, livestock, and other resources. They burned plantations and freed slaves.

Sherman's army reached Savannah on December 10, 1864. They left behind a path of destruction 60 miles wide. Sherman believed that this march would speed the end of the war. He wanted to break the South's will to fight by marching Union troops through the heart of the Confederacy. In the end, Sherman's destruction of the South led to anger and resentment toward the people of the North that would last for generations.

READING CHECK **Drawing Conclusions**
How did Sherman hope to help the Union with his total-war strategy?

QUICK FACTS

Causes and Effects of the Civil War

Causes
• Disagreement over the institution of slavery
• Economic differences
• Political differences

Effects
• Slavery ends
• 620,000 Americans killed
• Military districts created
• Southern economy in ruins

ANALYSIS SKILL **INTERPRETING CHARTS**
How important was slavery to the Civil War?

The South Surrenders

In early April, Sherman closed in on the last Confederate defenders in North Carolina. At the same time, Grant finally broke through the Confederate defenses at Petersburg. On April 2, Lee was forced to retreat from Richmond.

Fighting Ends

By the second week of April 1865, Grant had surrounded Lee's army and demanded the soldiers' surrender. Lee hoped to join other Confederates in fighting in North Carolina, but Grant cut off his escape just west of Richmond. Lee tried some last minute attacks but could not break the Union line. Lee's forces were running low on supplies. General James Longstreet told about the condition of Confederate troops. "Many weary soldiers were picked up . . . some with, many without, arms [weapons],—all asking for food."

Trapped by the Union army, Lee recognized that the situation was hopeless. "There is nothing left for me to do but go and see General Grant," Lee said, "and I would rather die a thousand deaths."

On April 9, 1865, the Union and Confederate leaders met at a home in the small town of **Appomattox Courthouse** where Lee surrendered to Grant, thus ending the Civil War.

During the meeting, Grant assured Lee that his troops would be fed and allowed to keep their horses, and they would not be tried for treason. Then Lee signed the surrender documents. The long, bloody war had finally ended. Grant later wrote that he found the scene at Appomattox Courthouse more tragic than joyful.

"I felt . . . sad and depressed at the downfall of a foe [enemy] who had fought so long and valiantly [bravely], and had suffered so much for a cause, though that cause was, I believe, one of the worst for which a people ever fought."
—Ulysses S. Grant, *Battle Cry of Freedom*

Surrender at Appomattox

Union general Grant rose to shake hands with Confederate general Lee after the surrender. Grant allowed Lee to keep his sword and Lee's men to keep their horses.

Was it important for Grant and Lee to shake hands? Why or why not?

As General Lee returned to his troops, General Grant stopped Union forces from cheering their victory. "The war is over," Grant said with relief. "The rebels are our countrymen again."

The Effects of the War

The Civil War had deep and long-lasting effects. Almost 620,000 Americans lost their lives during the four years of fighting.

The defeat of the South ended slavery there. The majority of former slaves, however, had no homes or jobs. The southern economy was in ruins.

A tremendous amount of hostility remained, even after the fighting had ceased. The war was over, but the question remained: How could the United States be united once more?

READING CHECK **Predicting** What problems might the Union face following the Civil War?

SUMMARY AND PREVIEW After four long years of battles, the Civil War ended with General Lee's surrender at Appomattox Courthouse. In the next chapter you will read about the consequences of the war in the South.

go.hrw.com
Online Quiz
KEYWORD: SF7 HP16

Section 5 Assessment

Reviewing Ideas, Terms, and People

1. **a. Identify** What Confederate general died from his wounds at Chancellorsville?
   b. Draw Conclusions Why was the Union army defeated at Chancellorsville?
2. **a. Identify** What was the **Gettysburg Address**?
   b. Analyze Why was geography important to the outcome of the Battle of Gettysburg?
3. **a. Recall** What was the purpose of the **Wilderness Campaign**?
   b. Draw Conclusions In what way was the capture of Atlanta an important victory for President Lincoln?
4. **a. Identify** What events led to Lee's surrender at **Appomattox Courthouse**?
   b. Summarize What problems did the South face at the end of the war?

Critical Thinking

5. **Supporting a Point of View** Review your notes on the end of the Civil War. Then copy the graphic organizer below. Use it to show the three events in this section that you think contributed most to the end of the Civil War and explain why.

FOCUS ON WRITING

6. **Taking Notes on the End of the War** As you read this section, take notes on the Battle of Gettysburg, the Wilderness Campaign, the fall of Atlanta, and the South's surrender. Be sure to answer the following questions: Who? Where? When? Why? and How?

Social Studies Skills

Analysis   **Critical Thinking**   Civic Participation   Study

Interpreting Political Cartoons

Define the Skill

Political cartoons are drawings that express views on important issues. They have been used throughout history to influence public opinion. The ability to interpret political cartoons will help you understand issues and people's attitudes about them.

Learn the Skill

Political cartoons use both words and images to convey their message. They often contain caricatures or symbolism. A caricature is a drawing that exaggerates the features of a person or object. Symbolism is the use of one thing to represent something else. Cartoonists use these techniques to help make their point clear. They also use titles, labels, and captions to get their message across.

Use these steps to interpret political cartoons.

1 Read any title, labels, and caption to identify the cartoon's general topic.

2 Identify the people and objects. Determine if they are exaggerated and, if so, why. Identify any symbols and analyze their meaning.

3 Draw conclusions about the message the cartoonist is trying to convey.

The following cartoon was published in the North in 1863. The cartoonist has used symbols to make his point. Lady Liberty, representing the Union, is being threatened by the Copperheads. The cartoonist has expressed his opinion of these people by drawing them as the poisonous snake for which they were named. This cartoon clearly supports the Union's continuing to fight the war.

Practice the Skill

Apply the guidelines to interpret the cartoon below and answer the questions that follow.

1. What do the tree and the man in it symbolize?

2. What policy or action of President Lincoln is this cartoon supporting?

LINCOLN'S LAST WARNING.
"Now, if you don't come down, I'll cut the Tree from under you."

Chapter Review

HOLT
History's Impact
▶ **video series**
Review the video to answer the closing question:
How do you think the age of a country relates to its citizens' national pride?

Visual Summary

Use the visual summary below to help you review the main ideas of the chapter.

QUICK FACTS

Union — 1861 — Confederacy

FORT SUMTER

1ST BATTLE OF BULL RUN

SHILOH

SEVEN DAYS' BATTLES

ANTIETAM

2ND BATTLE OF BULL RUN

VICKSBURG

GETTYSBURG

1865
Surrender at Appomattox Courthouse

Reviewing Vocabulary, Terms, and People

Match the numbered definitions with the correct terms from the list below.

  a. contrabands
  b. cotton diplomacy
  c. Second Battle of Bull Run
  d. Siege of Vicksburg
  e. Thomas "Stonewall" Jackson

1. Attack by Union general Ulysses S. Grant that gave the North control of the Mississippi River

2. Confederate general who held off Union attacks and helped the South win the First Battle of Bull Run

3. Important Confederate victory in which General Robert E. Lee defeated Union troops and pushed into Union territory for the first time

4. Southern strategy of using cotton exports to gain Britain's support in the Civil War

5. Term given to escaped slaves from the South

Comprehension and Critical Thinking

SECTION 1 *(Pages 510–515)*

  6. a. Identify When and where did fighting in the U.S. Civil War begin?

    b. Analyze How did civilians help the war effort in both the North and the South?

    c. Elaborate Why do you think the border states chose to remain in the Union despite their support of slavery?

SECTION 2 *(Pages 516–521)*

  7. a. Identify What was the first major battle of the war? What was the outcome of the battle?

    b. Analyze What was the Union army hoping to accomplish when it marched into Virginia at the start of the war?

    c. Evaluate Was the Union's naval blockade of the South successful? Why or why not?

SECTION 3 *(Pages 522–525)*

8. a. Identify Which side did the Cherokee support in the fighting at Pea Ridge? Why?

b. Draw Conclusions What progress did Union leaders make in the war in the West?

c. Evaluate Which victory in the West was most valuable to the Union? Why?

SECTION 4 *(Pages 528–534)*

9. a. Describe What responsibilities did women take on during the war?

b. Analyze What opposition to the war did President Lincoln face, and how did he deal with that opposition?

c. Predict What might be some possible problems that the newly freed slaves in the South might face?

SECTION 5 *(Pages 536–543)*

10. a. Recall When and where did the war finally end?

b. Compare and Contrast How were the efforts of Generals Grant and Sherman at the end of the war similar and different?

c. Elaborate What do you think led to the South's defeat in the Civil War? Explain.

Social Studies Skills

Interpreting Political Cartoons *Use the Social Studies Skills taught in this chapter to answer the question about the political cartoon below.*

11. What do you think the artist is saying about politicians with this cartoon?

Reading Skills

Supporting Facts and Details *Use the Reading Skills taught in this chapter to answer the question about the reading selection below.*

> Lee was unaware that Union soldiers were encamped closer to town. He had been suffering from lack of enemy information for three days because his cavalry chief "Jeb" Stuart was not performing his duties. Stuart and his cavalry had gone off on their own raiding party, disobeying Lee's orders. *(p. 537)*

12. What is the main idea of the above reading selection?

a. "Jeb" Stuart was not performing his duties.

b. Stuart and his cavalry had gone off on their own.

c. Stuart and his cavalry disobeyed Lee's orders.

d. Lee was suffering from a lack of enemy information.

Reviewing Themes

13. Society and Culture What effects did the Civil War have on American society?

14. Politics What political difficulties did the Emancipation Proclamation cause for President Lincoln?

Using the Internet

15. Activity: Writing a Poem Soldiers in the Civil War came from all walks of life. Despite the hope for glory and adventure, many encountered dangerous and uncomfortable conditions. Enter the activity keyword to learn more about Civil War soldiers. After viewing photographs and reading letters, write a poem describing the life of a soldier. Your poem should reflect on the soldier's emotions and experiences.

FOCUS ON WRITING

16. Write Your Newspaper Article Review your notes. Then choose the subject you think would make the best newspaper article. Write an attention-grabbing headline. Then write your article, giving as many facts as possible.

DIRECTIONS: Read each question and write the letter of the best response.

1 Use the map below to answer the following question.

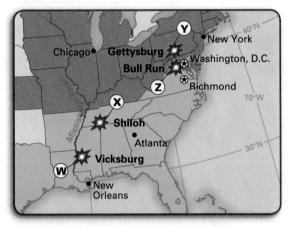

The place where two major battles of the Civil War were fought is indicated on the map by which letter?

A W

B X

C Y

D Z

2 The Battle of Gettysburg was an important battle of the Civil War because

A it was an overwhelming Confederate victory.

B the Union army's advance on the Confederate capital was stopped.

C it ended Lee's hopes of advancing into northern territory.

D it enabled the Union to control the Mississippi River.

3 Overall command of Confederate forces in Virginia during most of the Civil War was held by

A Jefferson Davis.

B William Tecumseh Sherman.

C Thomas "Stonewall" Jackson.

D Robert E. Lee.

4 Which of Lincoln's speeches and writings reflected the statement that "all men are created equal"?

A the Emancipation Proclamation

B the first inaugural address (1861)

C the second inaugural address (1865)

D the Gettysburg Address

5 The tactics that Sherman used against Confederate armies in the South were based on what strategy?

A cutting off troops from their officers

B a naval blockade of southern ports

C destroying the South's resources and economy

D hit-and-run attacks on major southern cities

6 In the War of 1812 the British navy blockaded American seaports in the hope that the U.S. economy would suffer and the United States would surrender. Which Civil War strategy was similar?

A Scott's plan to destroy the southern economy

B Sherman's March to the Sea

C General Ulysses S. Grant's capture of Vicksburg

D Admiral David Farragut's defeat of New Orleans

7 Read the following quote from Grant about Lee's surrender and use it to answer the question below.

> "What General Lee's feelings were I do not know. He was a man of much dignity, without expression on his face. It was impossible to say whether he felt inwardly glad that the end had finally come, or felt sad over the result, and was too manly to show it. Whatever his feelings, they were entirely hidden from me."
>
> –Ulysses S. Grant, adapted from *Personal Memoirs of U.S. Grant, Vol. 2*

Document-Based Question What is your opinion about what Lee might have been feeling during his surrender?

Reconstruction

Indiana Standards

Social Studies Standards

8.1.22 Explain and evaluate the policies, practices, and consequences of Reconstruction, including the Thirteenth, Fourteenth, and Fifteenth Amendments to the Constitution.

8.1.26 Give examples of the changing role of women and minorities in the northern, southern, and western parts of the United States in the mid-nineteenth century, and examine possible causes for these changes.

8.2.3 Explain how and why legislative, executive, and judicial powers are distributed, shared, and limited in the constitutional government of the United States.

8.2.7 Explain the importance in a democratic republic of responsible participation by citizens in voluntary civil associations/nongovernmental organizations that comprise civil society.

go.hrw.com
Indiana
KEYWORD: SF10 IN

FOCUS ON WRITING

Job History When the Civil War ended, it was time to rebuild. People were ready to get back to work. But life had changed for many people and would continue to change. As you read this chapter, think about jobs people may have had during Reconstruction.

UNITED STATES

1865
Abraham Lincoln is assassinated.

1865

WORLD

1865
Black Jamaicans rebel against the wealthy planter class.

What You Will Learn...

The ruins of this Virginia plantation stand as a bleak reminder of the changes brought to the South by the Civil War. In this chapter you will learn about the challenges that faced the nation after the Civil War and attempts to meet those challenges.

1868
President Andrew Johnson is impeached and almost removed from office.

1869
Indiana becomes the 14th state to ratify the Fifteenth Amendment.

1870
Hiram Revels becomes the first African American to serve in the U.S. Senate.

1877
The Compromise of 1877 ends Reconstruction.

1870

1875

1880

1868
The Meiji dynasty returns to power in Japan.

1869
The Suez Canal opens, linking the Mediterranean and Red seas.

1871
Otto von Bismarck and Wilhelm I unite Germany.

RECONSTRUCTION   **549**

Reading Social Studies

by Kylene Beers

Economics	Geography	Politics	Society and Culture	Science and Technology

Focus on Themes In this chapter you will read about the time immediately after the Civil War. You will see how the government tried to rebuild the South and will learn about how life changed for African Americans after slavery was declared illegal. You will read about the **political** conflicts that emerged as southern leadership worked to gain control of Reconstruction efforts. Throughout the chapter, you will read how the **culture** of the South changed after the War.

Analyzing Historical Information

Focus on Reading History books are full of information. As you read, you are confronted with names, dates, places, terms, and descriptions on every page. You don't want to have to deal with anything unimportant or untrue.

Identifying Relevant and Essential Information
Information in a history book should be relevant to the topic you're studying. It should also be essential to understanding the topic and be verifiable. Anything else distracts from the material you are studying.

The first passage below includes several pieces of irrelevant and nonessential information. In the second, this information has been removed. Note how much easier the revised passage is to comprehend.

First Passage

President Abraham Lincoln, who was very tall, wanted to reunite the nation as quickly and painlessly as possible. He had proposed a plan for readmitting the southern states even before the war ended, which happened on a Sunday. Called the Ten Percent Plan, it offered southerners amnesty, or official pardon, for all illegal acts supporting the rebellion. Today a group called Amnesty International works to protect the rights of prisoners. Lincoln's plan certainly would have worked if it would have been implemented.

Lincoln's appearance and the day on which the war ended are not essential facts.

Amnesty International is not relevant to this topic.

There is no way to prove the accuracy of the last sentence.

Revised Passage

President Abraham Lincoln wanted to reunite the nation as quickly and painlessly as possible. He had proposed a plan for readmitting the southern states even before the war ended. Called the Ten Percent Plan, it offered southerners amnesty, or official pardon, for all illegal acts supporting the rebellion.

From Chapter 17, p. 553

You Try It!

The following passage is adapted from the chapter you are about to read. As you read, look for irrelevant, nonessential, or unverifiable information.

The Freedmen's Bureau

From Chapter 17, p. 556

In 1865 Congress established the Freedmen's Bureau, an agency providing relief for freedpeople and certain poor people in the South. The Bureau had a difficult job. It may have been one of the most difficult jobs ever. At its high point, about 900 agents served the entire South. All 900 people could fit into one hotel ballroom today. Bureau commissioner Oliver O. Howard eventually decided to use the Bureau's limited budget to distribute food to the poor and to provide education and legal help for freedpeople. One common food in the South at that time was salted meat. The Bureau also helped African American war veterans. Today the Department of Veterans' Affairs assists American war veterans.

After you read the passage, answer the following questions.

1. Which sentence in this passage is unverifiable and should be cut?

2. Find two sentences in this passage that are irrelevant to the discussion of the Freedmen's Bureau. What makes those sentences irrelevant?

3. Look at the last sentence of the passage. Do you think this sentence is essential to the discussion? Why or why not?

As you read Chapter 17, ask yourself what makes the information you are reading essential to a study of Reconstruction.

Key Terms and People

Chapter 17

Section 1
Reconstruction *(p. 552)*
Ten Percent Plan *(p. 553)*
Thirteenth Amendment *(p. 554)*
Freedmen's Bureau *(p. 556)*
Andrew Johnson *(p. 557)*

Section 2
Black Codes *(p. 558)*
Radical Republicans *(p. 559)*
Civil Rights Act of 1866 *(p. 560)*
Fourteenth Amendment *(p. 561)*
Reconstruction Acts *(p. 561)*
impeachment *(p. 562)*
Fifteenth Amendment *(p. 563)*

Section 3
Hiram Revels *(p. 565)*
Ku Klux Klan *(p. 566)*
Compromise of 1877 *(p. 567)*
poll tax *(p. 568)*
segregation *(p. 568)*
Jim Crow laws *(p. 568)*
Plessy v. *Ferguson (p. 569)*
sharecropping *(p. 569)*

Academic Vocabulary

Success in school is related to knowing academic vocabulary—the words that are frequently used in school assignments and discussions. In this chapter, you will learn the following academic words:

procedure *(p. 553)*
principle *(p. 560)*

Rebuilding the South

What You Will Learn...

Main Ideas

1. President Lincoln and Congress differed in their views as Reconstruction began.
2. The end of the Civil War meant freedom for African Americans in the South.
3. President Johnson's plan began the process of Reconstruction.

The Big Idea

The nation faced many problems in rebuilding the Union.

Key Terms and People

Reconstruction, *p. 552*
Ten Percent Plan, *p. 553*
Thirteenth Amendment, *p. 554*
Freedmen's Bureau, *p. 556*
Andrew Johnson, *p. 557*

TAKING NOTES As you read, take notes on the different ways the U.S. government attempted to reconstruct the south after the Civil War. Write your notes in a graphic organizer like the one below.

Rebuilding and Reconstruction
1.
2.
3.
4.
5.
6.
7.

 8.1.22, 8.1.24, 8.1.26, 8.2.7

If YOU were there...

You are a young soldier who has been fighting in the Civil War for many months. Now that the war is over, you are on your way home. During your journey, you pass plantation manor homes, houses, and barns that have been burned down. No one is doing spring planting in the fields. As you near your family's farm, you see that fences and sheds have been destroyed. You wonder what is left of your home and family.

What would you think your future on the farm would be like?

BUILDING BACKGROUND When the Civil War ended, much of the South lay in ruins. Like the young soldier above, many people returned to destroyed homes and farms. Harvests of corn, cotton, rice, and other crops fell far below normal. Many farm animals had been killed or were roaming free. These were some of the challenges in restoring the nation.

Reconstruction Begins

After the Civil War ended in 1865, the U.S. government faced the problem of dealing with the defeated southern states. The challenges of **Reconstruction**, the process of readmitting the former Confederate states to the Union, lasted from 1865 to 1877.

Damaged South

Tired southern soldiers returned home to find that the world they had known before the war was gone. Cities, towns, and farms had been ruined. Because of high food prices and widespread crop failures, many southerners faced starvation. The Confederate money held by most southerners was now worthless. Banks failed, and merchants had gone bankrupt because people could not pay their debts.

Former Confederate general Braxton Bragg was one of many southerners who faced economic hardship. He found that *"all, all* was lost, except my debts." In South Carolina, Mary Boykin Chesnut wrote in her diary about the isolation she experienced after the war. "We are shut in here . . . All RR's [railroads] destroyed—bridges gone. We are cut off from the world."

Lincoln's Plan

President Abraham Lincoln wanted to reunite the nation as quickly and painlessly as possible. He had proposed a plan for readmitting the southern states even before the war ended. Called the **Ten Percent Plan**, it offered southerners amnesty, or official pardon, for all illegal acts supporting the rebellion. To receive amnesty, southerners had to do two things. They had to swear an oath of loyalty to the United States. They also had to agree that slavery was illegal. Once 10 percent of voters in

a state made these pledges, they could form a new government. The state then could be readmitted to the Union.

Louisiana quickly elected a new state legislature under the Ten Percent Plan. Other southern states that had been occupied by Union troops soon followed Louisiana back into the United States.

Wade-Davis Bill

Some politicians argued that Congress, not the president, should control the southern states' return to the Union. They believed that Congress had the power to admit new states. Also, many Republican members of Congress thought the Ten Percent Plan did not go far enough. A senator from Michigan expressed their views.

*"*The people of the North are not such fools as to ... turn around and say to the traitors, 'all you have to do [to return] is ... take an oath that henceforth you will be true to the Government.'*"*

–Senator Jacob Howard, quoted in *Reconstruction: America's Unfinished Revolution, 1863–1877,* by Eric Foner

Two Republicans—Senator Benjamin Wade and Representative Henry Davis—had an alternative to Lincoln's plan. Following **procedures** of the Wade-Davis bill, a state had to meet two conditions before it could rejoin the Union. First, it had to ban slavery. Second, a majority of adult males in the state had to take the loyalty oath.

ACADEMIC VOCABULARY

procedure
a series of steps taken to accomplish a task

War destroyed Richmond, Virginia, once the capital of the Confederacy.

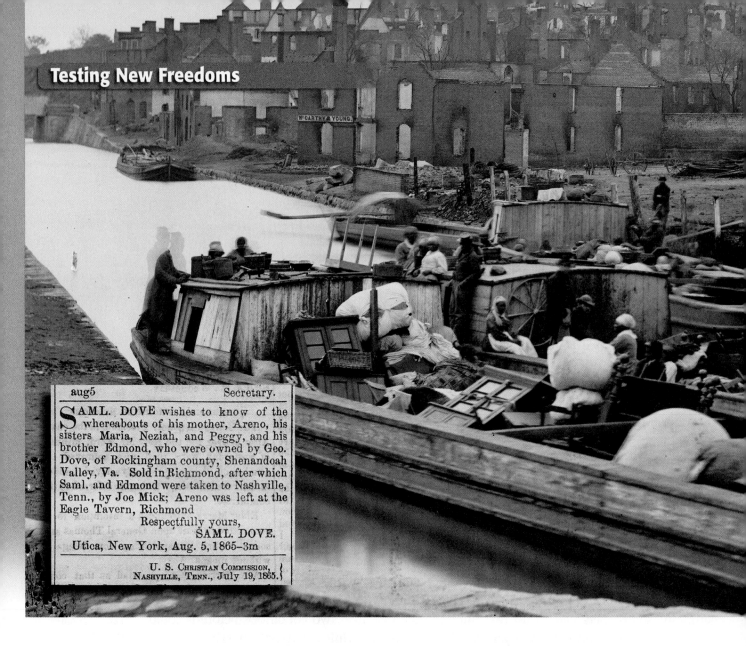

aug5   Secretary.

SAML. DOVE wishes to know of the
whereabouts of his mother, Areno, his
sisters Maria, Neziah, and Peggy, and his
brother Edmond, who were owned by Geo.
Dove, of Rockingham county, Shenandoah
Valley, Va. Sold in Richmond, after which
Saml. and Edmond were taken to Nashville,
Tenn., by Joe Mick; Areno was left at the
Eagle Tavern, Richmond
                    Respectfully yours,
                              SAML. DOVE.
Utica, New York, Aug. 5, 1865–3m

          U. S. CHRISTIAN COMMISSION,
          NASHVILLE, TENN., July 19, 1865.

Under the Wade-Davis bill, only southerners who swore that they had never supported the Confederacy could vote or hold office. In general, the bill was much stricter than the Ten Percent Plan. Its provisions would make it harder for southern states to rejoin the Union quickly.

President Lincoln therefore refused to sign the bill into law. He thought that few southern states would agree to meet its requirements. He believed that his plan would help restore order more quickly.

READING CHECK **Contrasting** How was the Ten Percent Plan different from the Wade-Davis bill?

Freedom for African Americans

One thing Republicans agreed on was abolishing slavery. The Emancipation Proclamation had freed slaves only in areas that had not been occupied by Union forces, not in the border states. Many people feared that the federal courts might someday declare the proclamation unconstitutional.

Slavery Ends

On January 31, 1865, at President Lincoln's urging, Congress proposed the **Thirteenth Amendment**. This amendment made slavery illegal throughout the United States.

The freedpeople at left have packed their household belongings and are leaving Richmond. Many people traveled in search of relatives. Others placed newspaper advertisements looking for long-lost relatives. For other freedpeople, like the couple above, freedom brought the right to marry.

In what ways did former slaves react to freedom?

The amendment was ratified and took effect on December 18, 1865. When abolitionist William Lloyd Garrison heard the news, he declared that his work was now finished. He called for the American Anti-Slavery Society to break up. Not all abolitionists agreed that their work was done, however. Frederick Douglass insisted that "slavery is not abolished until the black man has the ballot [vote]."

Freedom brought important changes to newly freed slaves. Many couples held ceremonies to legalize marriages that had not been recognized under slavery. Many freedpeople searched for relatives who had been sold away from their families years earlier. Others placed newspaper ads seeking information about their children. Many women began to work at home instead of in the fields. Still others adopted children of dead relatives to keep families together. Church members established voluntary associations and mutual-aid societies to help those in need.

Now that they could travel without a pass, many freedpeople moved from mostly white counties to places with more African Americans. Other freedpeople traveled simply to test their new freedom of movement. A South Carolina woman explained this need. "I must go, if I stay here I'll never know I'm free."

For most former slaves, freedom to travel was just the first step on a long road toward equal rights and new ways of life. Adults took new last names and began to insist on being called Mr. or Mrs. as a sign of respect, rather than by their first names or by nicknames. Freedpeople began to demand the same economic and political rights as white citizens. Henry Adams, a former slave, argued that "if I cannot do like a white man I am not free."

Forty Acres to Farm?

Many former slaves wanted their own land to farm. Near the end of the Civil War, Union general William Tecumseh Sherman had issued an order to break up plantations in coastal South Carolina and Georgia. He wanted to divide the land into 40-acre plots and give them to former slaves as compensation for their forced labor before the war.

Many white planters refused to surrender their land. Some freedpeople pointed out that it was only fair that they receive some of this land because their labor had made the plantations prosper. In the end, the U.S. government returned the land to its original owners. At this time, many freedpeople were unsure about where they would live, what kind of work they would do, and what rights they had. Freedoms that were theirs by law were difficult to enforce.

Freedmen's Bureau

In 1865 Congress established the **Freedmen's Bureau**, an agency providing relief for freedpeople and certain poor people in the South. The Bureau had a difficult job. At its high point, about 900 agents served the entire South. Bureau commissioner Oliver O. Howard eventually decided to use the Bureau's limited budget to distribute food to the poor and to provide education and legal help for freedpeople. The Bureau also helped African American war veterans.

The Freedmen's Bureau played an important role in establishing more schools in the South. Laws against educating slaves meant that most freedpeople had never learned to read or write. Before the war ended, however, northern groups, such as the American Missionary Association, began providing books and teachers to African Americans. The teachers were mostly women who were committed to helping freedpeople. One teacher said of her students, "I never before saw children so eager to learn . . . It is wonderful how [they] . . . can have so great a desire for

knowledge, and such a capacity for attaining [reaching] it."

After the war, some freedpeople organized their own education efforts. For example, Freedmen's Bureau agents found that some African Americans had opened schools in abandoned buildings. Many white southerners continued to believe that African Americans should not be educated. Despite opposition, by 1869 more than 150,000 African American students were attending more than 3,000 schools. The Freedmen's Bureau also helped establish a number of universities for African Americans, including Howard and Fisk universities.

Students quickly filled the new classrooms. Working adults attended classes in the evening. African Americans hoped that education would help them to understand and protect their rights and to enable them to find better jobs. Both black and white southerners benefited from the effort to provide greater access to education in the South.

READING CHECK **Analyzing** How did the Freedmen's Bureau help reform education in the South?

Helping the Freedpeople

Congress created the Freedmen's Bureau to help freedpeople and poor southerners recover from the Civil War. The Bureau assisted people by:

- providing supplies and medical services
- establishing schools
- supervising contracts between freedpeople and employers
- taking care of lands abandoned or captured during the war

What role did the Freedmen's Bureau play during Reconstruction?

President Johnson's Reconstruction Plan

While the Freedmen's Bureau was helping African Americans, the issue of how the South would politically rejoin the Union remained unresolved. Soon, however, a tragic event ended Lincoln's dream of peacefully reuniting the country.

A New President

On the evening of April 14, 1865, President Lincoln and his wife attended a play at Ford's Theater in Washington, D.C. During the play, John Wilkes Booth, a southerner who opposed Lincoln's policies, sneaked into the president's theater box and shot him. Lincoln was rushed to a boardinghouse across the street, where he died early the next morning. Vice President **Andrew Johnson** was sworn into office quickly. Reconstruction had now become his responsibility. He would have to win the trust of a nation shocked at its leader's death.

Johnson's plan for bringing southern states back into the Union was similar to Lincoln's plan. However, he decided that wealthy southerners and former Confederate officials would need a presidential pardon to receive amnesty. Johnson shocked Radical Republicans by eventually pardoning more than 7,000 people by 1866.

New State Governments

Johnson was a Democrat whom Republicans had put on the ticket in 1864 to appeal to the border states. A former slaveholder, he was a stubborn man who would soon face a hostile Congress.

Johnson offered a mild program for setting up new southern state governments. First, he appointed a temporary governor for each state. Then he required that the states revise their constitutions. Next, voters elected state and federal representatives. The new state government had to declare that secession was illegal. It also had to ratify the Thirteenth Amendment and refuse to pay Confederate debts.

By the end of 1865, all the southern states except Texas had created new governments. Johnson approved them all and declared that the United States was restored. Newly elected representatives came to Washington from each reconstructed southern state. However, Republicans complained that many new representatives had been leaders of the Confederacy. Congress therefore refused to readmit the southern states into the Union. Clearly, the nation was still divided.

READING CHECK **Summarizing** What was President Johnson's plan for Reconstruction?

SUMMARY AND PREVIEW In this section you learned about early plans for Reconstruction. In the next section, you will learn that disagreements about Reconstruction became so serious that the president was almost removed from office.

go.hrw.com
Online Quiz
KEYWORD: SF7 HP17

Section 1 Assessment

Reviewing Ideas, Terms, and People

1. a. **Identify** What does **Reconstruction** mean?
   b. **Summarize** What was President Lincoln's plan for Reconstruction?
2. a. **Recall** What is the **Thirteenth Amendment**?
   b. **Elaborate** In your opinion, what was the most important accomplishment of the **Freedmen's Bureau**? Explain.
3. a. **Recall** Why was President Lincoln killed?
   b. **Analyze** Why did some Americans oppose President Johnson's Reconstruction plan?

Critical Thinking

4. **Summarizing** Review your notes on Reconstruction. Then copy the graphic organizer below and use it to show how African Americans were affected by the end of the war.

   African Americans and Reconstruction — Marriages are legalized.

FOCUS ON WRITING

5. **Considering Historical Context** Many people planned to continue doing what they had done before the war. Others planned to start a new life. How do you think events and conditions you just read about might have affected their plans?

The Fight over Reconstruction

What You Will Learn...

Main Ideas

1. Black Codes led to opposition to President Johnson's plan for Reconstruction.
2. The Fourteenth Amendment ensured citizenship for African Americans.
3. Radical Republicans in Congress took charge of Reconstruction.
4. The Fifteenth Amendment gave African Americans the right to vote.

The Big Idea

The return to power of the pre-war southern leadership led Republicans in Congress to take control of Reconstruction.

Key Terms and People

Black Codes, *p. 558*
Radical Republicans, *p. 559*
Civil Rights Act of 1866, *p. 560*
Fourteenth Amendment, *p. 561*
Reconstruction Acts, *p. 561*
impeachment, *p. 562*
Fifteenth Amendment, *p. 563*

TAKING NOTES As you read, take notes on how Republicans in Congress took over Reconstruction and how they changed Reconstruction policies. Write your notes in a graphic organizer like the one below.

Issues that Concerned Republicans	Changes by the Republican Congress

8.1.22, 8.1.24, 8.1.28

If YOU were there...

A member of Congress, you belong to the same political party as the president. But you strongly disagree with his ideas about Reconstruction and civil rights for African Americans. Now some of the president's opponents are trying to remove him from office. You do not think he is a good president. On the other hand, you think removing him would be bad for the unity of the country.

Will you vote to remove the president?

BUILDING BACKGROUND Americans were bitterly divided about what should happen in the South during Reconstruction. They disagreed about ending racial inequality and guaranteeing civil rights for African Americans. These conflicts split political parties. They led to showdowns between Congress and the president. Political fights even threatened the president's job.

Opposition to President Johnson

In 1866 Congress continued to debate the rules for restoring the Union. Meanwhile, new state legislatures approved by President Johnson had already begun passing laws to deny African Americans' civil rights. "This is a white man's government, and intended for white men only," declared Governor Benjamin F. Perry of South Carolina.

Black Codes

Soon, every southern state passed **Black Codes**, or laws that greatly limited the freedom of African Americans. They required African Americans to sign work contracts, creating working conditions similar to those under slavery. In most southern states, any African Americans who could not prove they were employed could be arrested. Their punishment might be one year of work without pay. African Americans were also prevented from owning guns. In addition, they were not allowed to rent property except in cities.

The Black Codes alarmed many Americans. As one Civil War veteran asked, "If you call this freedom, what do you call slavery?"

African Americans organized to oppose the codes. One group sent a petition to officials in South Carolina.

" We simply ask …that the same laws which govern *white men* shall govern *black men* …that, in short, we be dealt with as others are—in equity [equality] and justice. "

—Petition from an African American convention held in South Carolina, quoted in *There Is a River: The Black Struggle for Freedom in America* by Vincent Harding

Radical Republicans

The Black Codes angered many Republicans. They thought the South was returning to its old ways. Most Republicans were moderates who wanted the South to have loyal state governments. They also believed that African Americans should have rights as citizens. They hoped that the government would not have to force the South to follow federal laws.

Radical Republicans, on the other hand, took a harsher stance. They wanted the federal government to force change in the South. Like the moderates, they thought the Black Codes were cruel and unjust. The Radicals, however, wanted the federal government to be much more involved in Reconstruction. They feared that too many southern leaders remained loyal to the former Confederacy and would not enforce the new laws. Thaddeus Stevens

Primary Source

POLITICAL CARTOON
Supporting Radical Republican Ideas

Republicans were outraged to see former Confederates return to power as leaders of the Democratic Party. This 1868 political cartoon shows former Confederates Raphael Semmes and Nathan Bedford Forrest. Semmes was a Confederate admiral who had captured 62 Union merchant ships during the Civil War. Forrest was a cavalry officer known for brutality who later founded the Ku Klux Klan.

How do the actions of the people in these illustrations support the artist's point of view?

How do events in the background of these illustrations support the artist's point of view?

ANALYSIS
SKILL ANALYZING PRIMARY SOURCES

Why do you think that the men are shown in their Confederate uniforms?

"Captain Semmes ordered the captains of both ships on board the Alabama, examined their papers, and allowing them to take a small quantity of clothing, burned their ships, and sent them adrift in their boats without any water or provisions."—*Report of the burning of the American ships Sonora and Highlander, near Singapore, East Indies.*

"I drew my sword...

"Forrest says: 'No quarter! no quarter! Kill 'em! kill 'em! damn 'em!' That's Forrest's orders, not to leave one alive."—*May's Official Report.*

"In closing my report, I desire to acknowledge the prompt action of Brigadier General Chal... ...ding the forces at Fort Pillow. His faithful execution of all movements...

POINTS OF VIEW
Johnson vs. Stevens

President Andrew Johnson argued that the South should not be placed under military control.

❝Military governments . . . established for an indefinite period, would have divided the people into the vanquishers and the vanquished, and would have envenomed [made poisonous] hatred rather than have restored affection.❞

—Andrew Johnson

Thaddeus Stevens believed that Congress had the power to treat the South as conquered territory.

❝The future condition of the conquered power depends on the will of the conqueror. They must come in as new states or remain as conquered provinces. Congress . . . is the only power that can act in the matter.❞

—Thaddeus Stevens

ANALYSIS SKILL **IDENTIFYING POINTS OF VIEW**

How did Johnson's and Stevens's views on the South differ?

FOCUS ON INDIANA

Radical Republicans also held power in state legislatures, including Indiana's. Some Democratic members of the Indiana assembly resigned their offices in a failed attempt to prevent ratification of the Fifteenth Amendment.

ACADEMIC VOCABULARY

principle basic belief, rule, or law

of Pennsylvania and Charles Sumner of Massachusetts were the leaders of the Radical Republicans.

A harsh critic of President Johnson, Stevens was known for his honesty and sharp tongue. He wanted economic and political justice for both African Americans and poor white southerners. Sumner had been a strong opponent of slavery before the Civil War. He continued to argue tirelessly for African Americans' civil rights, including the right to vote and the right to fair laws.

Both Stevens and Sumner believed that President Johnson's Reconstruction plan was a failure. Although the Radicals did not control Congress, they began to gain support among moderates when President Johnson ignored criticism of the Black Codes. Stevens believed the federal government could not allow racial inequality to survive.

READING CHECK **Comparing and Contrasting** How were Radical Republicans and moderate Republicans similar and different?

Fourteenth Amendment

Urged on by the Radicals in 1866, Congress proposed a new bill. It would give the Freedmen's Bureau more powers. The law would allow the Freedmen's Bureau to use military courts to try people accused of violating African Americans' rights. The bill's supporters hoped that these courts would be fairer than local courts in the South.

Johnson versus Congress

Surprising many members of Congress, Johnson vetoed the Freedmen's Bureau Bill. He insisted that Congress could not pass any new laws until the southern states were represented in Congress. Johnson also argued that the Freedmen's Bureau was unconstitutional.

Republicans responded with the **Civil Rights Act of 1866**. This act provided African Americans with the same legal rights as white Americans. President Johnson once again used his veto power. He argued that the act gave too much power to the federal government. He also rejected the **principle** of equal rights for African Americans. Congress, however, overrode Johnson's veto.

Many Republicans worried about what would happen when the southern states were readmitted. Fearing that the Civil Rights Act might be overturned, the Republicans proposed the **Fourteenth Amendment** in the summer of 1866. The Fourteenth Amendment included the following provisions.

1. It defined all people born or naturalized within the United States, except Native Americans, as citizens.
2. It guaranteed citizens the equal protection of the laws.
3. It said that states could not "deprive any person of life, liberty, or property, without due process of law."
4. It banned many former Confederate officials from holding state or federal offices.
5. It made state laws subject to federal court review.
6. It gave Congress the power to pass any laws needed to enforce it.

1866 Elections

President Johnson and most Democrats opposed the Fourteenth Amendment. As a result, civil rights for African Americans became a key issue in the 1866 congressional elections. To help the Democrats, Johnson traveled around the country defending his Reconstruction plan. Johnson's speaking tour was a disaster. It did little to win votes for the Democratic Party. Johnson even got into arguments with people in the audiences of some of his speaking engagements.

Two major riots in the South also hurt Johnson's campaign. On May 1, 1866, a dispute in Memphis, Tennessee, took place between local police and black Union soldiers. The dispute turned into a three-day wave of violence against African Americans. About three months later, another riot took place during a political demonstration in New Orleans. During that dispute, 34 African Americans and three white Republicans were killed.

READING CHECK **Summarizing** What issue did the Fourteenth Amendment address, and how did it affect the congressional elections of 1866?

Congress Takes Control of Reconstruction

The 1866 elections gave the Republican Party a commanding two-thirds majority in both the House and the Senate. This majority gave the Republicans the power to override any presidential veto. In addition, the Republicans became united as the moderates joined with the Radicals. Together, they called for a new form of Reconstruction.

Reconstruction Acts

In March 1867, Congress passed the first of several **Reconstruction Acts**. These laws divided the South into five districts. A U.S. military commander controlled each district.

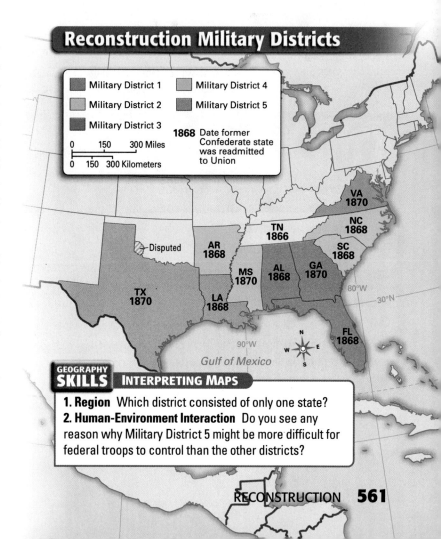

Reconstruction Military Districts

- Military District 1
- Military District 2
- Military District 3
- Military District 4
- Military District 5

1868 Date former Confederate state was readmitted to Union

0   150   300 Miles
0 150 300 Kilometers

VA 1870
NC 1868
TN 1866
SC 1868
AR 1868
Disputed
MS 1870
AL 1868
GA 1870
TX 1870
LA 1868
FL 1868
Gulf of Mexico

GEOGRAPHY SKILLS **INTERPRETING MAPS**
1. **Region** Which district consisted of only one state?
2. **Human-Environment Interaction** Do you see any reason why Military District 5 might be more difficult for federal troops to control than the other districts?

The military would remain in control of the South until the southern states rejoined the Union. To be readmitted, a state had to write a new state constitution supporting the Fourteenth Amendment. Finally, the state had to give African American men the right to vote.

Thaddeus Stevens was one of the new Reconstruction Acts' most enthusiastic supporters. He spoke in Congress to defend the acts.

" Have not loyal blacks quite as good a right to choose rulers and make laws as rebel whites? Every man, no matter what his race or color . . .

has an equal right to justice, honesty, and fair play with every other man; and the law should secure him those rights. "

–Thaddeus Stevens, quoted in *Sources of the American Republic*, edited by Marvin Meyers et al.

President on Trial

President Johnson strongly disagreed with Stevens. He argued that African Americans did not deserve the same treatment as white people. The Reconstruction Acts, he said, used "powers not granted to the federal government or any one of its branches." Knowing that Johnson did not support its Reconstruction policies, Congress passed a law limiting his power. This law prevented the president from removing cabinet officials without Senate approval. Johnson quickly broke the law by firing Edwin Stanton, the secretary of war.

For the first time in United States history, the House of Representatives responded by voting to impeach the president. **Impeachment** is the process used by a legislative body to bring charges of wrongdoing against a public official. The next step, under Article I of the Constitution, was a trial in the Senate. A two-thirds majority was required to find Johnson guilty and remove him from office.

Although Johnson was unpopular with Republicans, some of them believed he was being judged unfairly. Others did not trust the president pro tempore of the Senate, Benjamin Wade. He would become president if Johnson were removed from office. By a single vote, Senate Republicans failed to convict Johnson. Even so, the trial weakened his power as president.

Election of 1868

Johnson did not run for another term in 1868. The Democrats chose

The Reconstruction Amendments

QUICK FACTS

Thirteenth Amendment (1865)
Banned slavery throughout the United States

Fourteenth Amendment (1868)
Overturned the *Dred Scott* case by granting citizenship to all people born in the United States (except for Native Americans)

Fifteenth Amendment (1870)
Gave African American men the right to vote

This Reconstruction-era painting shows African American men voting after passage of the Fifteenth Amendment.

What right did the Fifteenth Amendment protect?

former New York governor Horatio Seymour as their presidential candidate. The Republicans chose Ulysses S. Grant. As a war hero, Grant appealed to many northern voters. He had no political experience but supported the congressional Reconstruction plan. He ran under the slogan "Let Us Have Peace."

Shortly after Grant was nominated, Congress readmitted seven southern states—Alabama, Arkansas, Florida, Georgia, Louisiana, North Carolina, and South Carolina. (Tennessee had already been readmitted in 1866.) Under the terms of readmission, these seven states approved the Fourteenth Amendment. They also agreed to let African American men vote. However, white southerners used violence to try to keep African Americans away from the polls.

Despite such tactics, hundreds of thousands of African Americans voted for Grant and the "party of Lincoln." The *New Orleans Tribune* reported that many former slaves "see clearly enough that the Republican party [is] their political life boat." African American votes helped Grant to win a narrow victory.

READING CHECK **Analyzing** To what voters did Grant appeal in the presidential election of 1868?

Fifteenth Amendment

After Grant's victory, Congressional Republicans wanted to protect their Reconstruction plan. They worried that the southern states might try to keep black voters from the polls in future elections. Also, some Radical Republicans argued that it was not fair that many northern states still had laws preventing African Americans from voting. After all, every southern state was required to grant suffrage to African American men.

In 1869 Congress proposed the **Fifteenth Amendment**, which gave African American men the right to vote. Abolitionist William Lloyd Garrison praised what he saw as "this wonderful, quiet, sudden transformation of four millions of human beings from . . . the auction block to the ballot-box." The amendment went

into effect in 1870 as one of the last Reconstruction laws passed at the federal level.

The Fifteenth Amendment did not please every reformer, however. Many women were angry because the amendment did not also grant them the right to vote.

READING CHECK **Finding Main Ideas** How did Radical Republicans take control of Reconstruction?

SUMMARY AND PREVIEW In this section you learned that Congress took control of Reconstruction and took steps to protect the rights of African Americans. In the next section you will learn about increasing opposition to Reconstruction.

FOCUS ON INDIANA

Schuyler Colfax, an Indianan and the Speaker of the House of Representatives, was elected as Grant's vice president in 1868. Colfax was nominated for vice president in 1872 but was defeated.

---

go.hrw.com
Online Quiz
KEYWORD: SF7 HP17

Section 2 Assessment

Reviewing Ideas, Terms, and People

1. **a. Describe** What were **Black Codes**?
   b. Make Inferences Why did Republicans think Johnson's Reconstruction plan was a failure?
2. **a. Recall** What was the **Civil Rights Act of 1866**?
   b. Summarize Why was the **Fourteenth Amendment** important?
3. **a. Recall** Why was President Johnson impeached?
   b. Evaluate Which element of the **Reconstruction Acts** do you believe was most important? Why?
4. **a. Recall** What does the **Fifteenth Amendment** state?
   b. Elaborate Do you think that women should have been included in the Fifteenth Amendment? Explain.

Critical Thinking

5. **Identify** Review your notes on the issues that led Republicans to take over Reconstruction. Then copy the graphic organizer below and use it to identify the main provisions of the Fourteenth Amendment and their effects.

Provisions	Effects

FOCUS ON WRITING

6. **Recognizing Cause-and-Effect Relationships** As you have read in this section, social and political unrest continued long after the war ended. How could this unrest cause people to leave their jobs? What new jobs might they find?

Reconstruction in the South

What You Will Learn...

Main Ideas

1. Reconstruction governments helped reform the South.
2. The Ku Klux Klan was organized as African Americans moved into positions of power.
3. As Reconstruction ended, the rights of African Americans were restricted.
4. Southern business leaders relied on industry to rebuild the South.

The Big Idea

As Reconstruction ended, African Americans faced new hurdles and the South attempted to rebuild.

Key Terms and People

Hiram Revels, *p. 565*
Ku Klux Klan, *p. 566*
Compromise of 1877, *p. 567*
poll tax, *p. 568*
segregation, *p. 568*
Jim Crow laws, *p. 568*
Plessy v. *Ferguson, p. 569*
sharecropping, *p. 569*

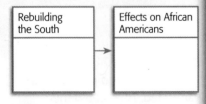

TAKING NOTES As you read, look for information related to the South's efforts to rebuild and the effects on African Americans.

Rebuilding the South	Effects on African Americans

8.1.22, 8.1.24, 8.1.26, 8.1.28, 8.1.30, 8.2.3

If **YOU** were there...

You live on a farm in the South in the 1870s. Times are hard because you do not own your farm. Instead, you and your family work in a landowner's cotton fields. You never seem to earn enough to buy land of your own. Some of your neighbors have decided to give up farming and move to the city. Others are going to work in the textile mills. But you have always been a farmer.

Will you decide to change your way of life?

BUILDING BACKGROUND Reconstruction affected politics and economics in the South. Republican and Democratic politicians fought over policies and programs. New state governments began reforms, but later leaders ended many of them. Some parts of the southern economy improved. However, many farmers, like the family above, went through hard times.

Reconstruction Governments

After Grant became president in 1869, the Republicans seemed stronger than ever. They controlled most southern governments, partly because of the support of African American voters. However, most of the Republican officeholders were unpopular with white southerners.

Carpetbaggers and Scalawags

Some of these office-holders were northern-born Republicans who had moved South after the war. Many white southerners called them carpetbaggers. Supposedly, they had rushed South carrying all their possessions in bags made from carpeting. Many southerners resented these northerners, accusing them—often unfairly—of trying to profit from Reconstruction.

Southern Democrats cared even less for white southern Republicans. They referred to them as scalawags, or greedy rascals. Democrats believed that these southerners had betrayed the South by

African American Representation in the South, 1870

Hiram Revels was the son of former slaves and helped organize African American regiments in the Civil War. Revels was selected to fill the U.S. Senate seat formerly held by Jefferson Davis, president of the Confederacy.

Blanche K. Bruce escaped from slavery and began a school for African Americans before the Civil War. Bruce was the first African American elected to a full six-year term in the U.S. Senate.

● Member of U.S. Congress
○ State legislator

GEOGRAPHY SKILLS **INTERPRETING MAPS**

1. **Location** Which state had the most African American state legislators?
2. **Region** Which states had the least African American representation?

voting for the Republican Party. Many southern Republicans were small farmers who had supported the Union during the war. Others, like Mississippi governor James Alcorn, were former members of the Whig Party. They preferred to become Republicans rather than join the Democrats.

African American Leaders

African Americans were the largest group of southern Republican voters. During Reconstruction, more than 600 African Americans won election to state legislatures. Some 16 of these politicians were elected to Congress. Other African Americans held local offices in counties throughout the South.

African American politicians came from many backgrounds. **Hiram Revels** was born free in North Carolina and went to college in Illinois. He became a Methodist minister and served as a chaplain in the Union army. In 1870 Revels became the first African American in the U.S. Senate. He took over the seat previously held by Confederate president Jefferson Davis. Unlike Revels, Blanche K. Bruce grew up in slavery in Virginia. Bruce became an important Republican in Mississippi and served one term as a U.S. senator.

State Governments Change Direction

Reconstruction governments provided money for many new programs and organizations in the South. They helped to establish some of the first state-funded public school systems in the South. They also built new hospitals, prisons, and orphanages and passed laws prohibiting discrimination against African Americans.

Southern states under Republican control spent large amounts of money. They aided the construction of railroads, bridges, and public buildings. These improvements were intended to help the southern economy recover from the war. To get the money for these projects, the Reconstruction governments raised taxes and issued bonds.

READING CHECK **Summarizing** What reforms did Reconstruction state governments carry out?

FOCUS ON READING
How does the heading of this section tell you about what you will learn?

Ku Klux Klan

As more African Americans took office, resistance to Reconstruction increased among white southerners. Democrats claimed that the Reconstruction governments were corrupt, illegal, and unjust. They also disliked having federal soldiers stationed in their states. Many white southerners disapproved of African American officeholders. One Democrat noted, "'A white man's government' [is] the most popular rallying cry we have."

In 1866 a group of white southerners in Tennessee created the **Ku Klux Klan**. This secret society opposed civil rights, particularly suffrage, for African Americans. The Klan used violence and terror against African Americans. The group's membership grew rapidly as it spread throughout the South.

Klan members wore robes and disguises to hide their identities. They attacked—and even murdered—African Americans, white Republican voters, and public officials, usually at night.

Local governments did little to stop the violence. Many officials feared the Klan or were sympathetic to its activities. In 1870 and 1871 the federal government took action. Congress passed laws that made it a federal crime to interfere with elections or to deny citizens equal protection under the law.

Within a few years, the Klan was no longer an organized threat. But groups of whites continued to assault African Americans and Republicans throughout the 1870s.

READING CHECK **Drawing Conclusions** Why did southerners join the Ku Klux Klan?

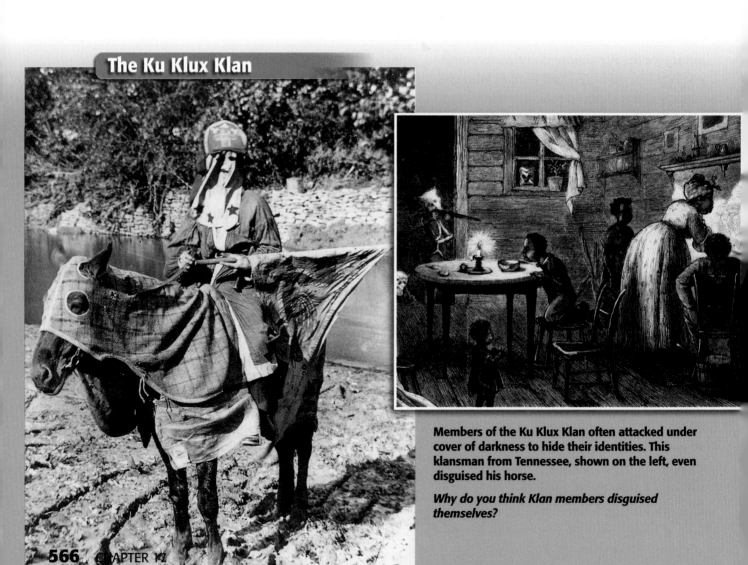

The Ku Klux Klan

Members of the Ku Klux Klan often attacked under cover of darkness to hide their identities. This klansman from Tennessee, shown on the left, even disguised his horse.

Why do you think Klan members disguised themselves?

Reconstruction Ends

The violence of the Ku Klux Klan was not the only challenge to Reconstruction. Republicans slowly lost control of southern state governments to the Democratic Party. The General Amnesty Act of 1872 allowed former Confederates, except those who had held high ranks, to serve in public office. Many of these former Confederates, most of whom were Democrats, were soon elected to southern governments.

The Republican Party also began losing its power in the North. Although President Grant was re-elected in 1872, financial and political scandals in his administration upset voters. In his first term, a gold-buying scheme in which Grant's cousin took a leading role led to a brief crisis on the stock market called Black Friday. During his second term, his personal secretary was involved in the Whiskey Ring scandal, in which whiskey distillers and public officials worked together to steal liquor taxes from the federal government. Furthermore, people blamed Republican policies for the Panic of 1873.

Panic of 1873

This severe economic downturn began in September 1873 when Jay Cooke and Company, a major investor in railroads and the largest financier of the Union's Civil War effort, declared bankruptcy. The company had lied about the value of land along the side of the Northern Pacific Railroad that it owned and was trying to sell. When the truth leaked out, the company failed.

The failure of such an important business sent panic through the stock market, and investors began selling shares of stock more rapidly than people wanted to buy them. Companies had to buy their shares back from the investors. Soon, 89 of the nation's 364 railroads had failed as well. The failure of almost 18,000 other businesses followed within two years, leaving the nation in an economic crisis. By 1876 unemployment had risen to 14 percent, with an estimated 2 million people out of work. The high unemployment rate set off numerous strikes and protests around the nation, many involving railroad workers. In 1874 the Democrats gained control of the House of Representatives. Northerners were becoming less concerned about southern racism and more concerned about their financial well-being.

Election of 1876

Republicans could tell that northern support for Reconstruction was fading. Voters' attention was shifting to economic problems. In 1874 the Republican Party lost control of the House of Representatives to the Democrats. The Republicans in Congress managed to pass one last civil rights law. The Civil Rights Act of 1875 guaranteed African Americans equal rights in public places, such as theaters and public transportation. But as Americans became increasingly worried about economic problems and government corruption, the Republican Party began to abandon Reconstruction.

Republicans selected Ohio governor Rutherford B. Hayes as their 1876 presidential candidate. He believed in ending federal support of the Reconstruction governments. The Democrats nominated New York governor Samuel J. Tilden. During the election, Democrats in the South again used violence at the polls to keep Republican voters away.

The election between Hayes and Tilden was close. Tilden appeared to have won. Republicans challenged the electoral votes in Oregon and three southern states. A special commission of members of Congress and Supreme Court justices was appointed to settle the issue.

The commission narrowly decided to give all the disputed votes to Hayes. Hayes thus won the presidency by one electoral vote. In the **Compromise of 1877**, the Democrats agreed to accept Hayes's victory. In return, they wanted all remaining federal troops removed from the South. They also asked for funding for internal improvements in the South and

SUPREME COURT DECISIONS

Plessy v. *Ferguson* (1896)

Background of the Case In 1892, Homer Plessy took a seat in the "whites only" car of a train in Louisiana. He was arrested, put on trial, and convicted of violating Louisiana's segregation law. Plessy argued that the Louisiana law violated the Thirteenth Amendment and denied him the equal protection of the law as guaranteed.

The Court's Ruling

The Court ruled that the Louisiana "separate-but-equal" law was constitutional.

The Court's Reasoning

The Court stated that the Thirteenth and Fourteenth Amendments did not apply. The Court decided that the case had nothing to do with the abolition of slavery mentioned in the Thirteenth Amendment. The justices also ruled that the Fourteenth Amendment was not designed to eliminate social barriers to equality between the races, only political barriers.

Justice John Marshall Harlan disagreed with the Court's ruling. In a dissenting opinion, he wrote that "in respect of civil rights, all citizens are equal before the law."

Why It Matters

Plessy was important because it approved the idea of separate-but-equal facilities for people based on race. The doctrine of separate-but-equal led to segregation in trains, buses, schools, restaurants, and many other social institutions.

The separate-but-equal doctrine led to unequal treatment of minority groups for decades. It was finally struck down by another Supreme Court ruling, *Brown* v. *Board of Education,* in 1954.

ANALYSIS SKILL **ANALYZING INFORMATION**

1. Why did the Court reject Plessy's arguments?
2. Why was *Plessy* v. *Ferguson* an important Supreme Court case?

---

the appointment of a southern Democrat to the president's cabinet. Shortly after he took office in 1877, President Hayes removed the last of the federal troops from the South.

Redeemers

Gradually, Democrats regained control of state governments in the South. In each state, they moved quickly to get rid of the Reconstruction reforms.

Democrats who brought their party back to power in the South were called Redeemers. They came from a variety of backgrounds. For instance, U.S. senator John T. Morgan of Alabama was a former general in the Confederate army. Newspaper editor Henry Grady of Georgia was interested in promoting southern industry.

Redeemers wanted to reduce the size of state government and limit the rights of African Americans. They lowered state budgets and got rid of a variety of social programs. The Redeemers cut property taxes and cut public funding for schools. They also succeeded in limiting African Americans' civil rights.

African Americans' Rights Restricted

Redeemers set up the poll tax in an effort to deny the vote to African Americans. The **poll tax** was a special tax people had to pay before they could vote.

Some states also targeted African American voters by requiring them to pass a literacy test. A so-called grandfather clause written into law affected men whose fathers or grandfathers could vote before 1867. In those cases, a voter did not have to pay a poll tax or pass a literacy test. As a result, almost every white man could escape the voting restrictions.

Redeemer governments also introduced legal **segregation**, the forced separation of whites and African Americans in public places. **Jim Crow laws**—laws that enforced segregation—became common in southern states in the 1880s.

African Americans challenged Jim Crow laws in court. In 1883, however, the U.S. Supreme Court ruled that the Civil Rights Act of 1875 was unconstitutional. The Court also ruled that the Fourteenth Amendment applied only to the actions of state governments. This ruling allowed private individuals and businesses to practice segregation.

Plessy v. Ferguson

In 1896 the U.S. Supreme Court returned to the issue of segregation. When Homer Plessy, an African American, refused to leave the whites-only Louisiana train car he was riding on, he was arrested and accused of breaking a state law requiring separate cars for blacks and whites. Plessy sued the railroad company and lost. His lawyers argued that the law violated his right to equal treatment under the Fourteenth Amendment. He then appealed to the U.S. Supreme Court. The Supreme Court ruled against Plessy in **Plessy v. Ferguson**. Segregation was allowed, said the Court, if "separate-but-equal" facilities were provided. Among the justices, only John Marshall Harlan disagreed with the Court's decision. He explained his disagreement in a dissenting opinion:

" In the eye of the law, there is in the country no superior, dominant [controlling], ruling class of citizens … Our constitution is color-blind, and neither knows nor tolerates classes among citizens. In respect of civil rights, all citizens are equal before the law. "

—John Marshall Harlan, quoted in *Plessy v. Ferguson: A Brief History with Documents*, edited by Brook Thomas

Despite Harlan's view, segregation became widespread across the country. African Americans were forced to use separate public schools, libraries, and parks. When they existed, these facilities were usually of poorer quality than those created for whites. In practice, these so-called separate-but-equal facilities were separate and unequal.

Farming in the South

Few African Americans in the South could afford to buy or even rent farms. Moving West also was costly. Many African Americans therefore remained on plantations. Others tried to make a living in the cities.

African Americans who stayed on plantations often became part of a system known as **sharecropping**, or sharing the crop. Landowners provided the land, tools, and supplies, and sharecroppers provided the labor. At harvest time, the sharecropper usually had to give most of the crop to the landowner. Whatever remained belonged to the sharecropper. Many sharecroppers hoped to save enough money from selling their share of the crops to one day be able to buy a farm. Unfortunately, only a few ever achieved this dream.

Instead, most sharecroppers lived in a cycle of debt. When they needed food, clothing, or supplies, most families had to buy goods on credit because they had little cash.

Hopes Raised and Denied — QUICK FACTS

Slavery

- No rights
- Forced labor
- No freedom of movement without permission
- Family members sold away from one another
- No representation in government

Freedom

- Slavery banned
- Free to work for wages
- Could move and live anywhere
- Many families reunited
- Could serve in political office

Rights Denied

- Sharecropping system put in place
- Ability to vote and hold office restricted
- White leadership regained control of southern state governments

When sharecroppers sold their crops, they hoped to be able to pay off these debts. However, bad weather, poor harvests, or low crop prices often made this dream impossible.

Sharecroppers usually grew cotton, one of the South's most important cash crops. When too many farmers planted cotton, however, the supply became excessive. As a result, the price per bale of cotton dropped. Many farmers understood the drawbacks of planting cotton. However, farmers felt pressure from banks and others to keep raising cotton. A southern farmer explained why so many sharecroppers depended on cotton:

" Cotton is the thing to get credit on in this country ... You can always sell cotton ... [Y]ou load up your wagon with wheat or corn ...and I doubt some days whether you could sell it. "

–Anonymous farmer quoted in *The Promise of the New South,* by Edward L. Ayers

READING CHECK **Finding Main Ideas** How were African Americans' rights restricted?

Rebuilding Southern Industry

The southern economy suffered through cycles of good and bad years as cotton prices went up and down. Some business leaders hoped industry would strengthen the southern economy and create a New South.

Southern Industry

Henry Grady, an Atlanta newspaper editor, was a leader of the New South movement. "The new South presents . . . a diversified [varied] industry that meets the complex needs of this complex age," he wrote. Grady and his supporters felt that with its cheap and abundant labor, the South could build factories and provide a workforce for them.

The most successful industrial development in the South involved textile production. Businesspeople built textile mills in many small towns to produce cotton fabric. Many people from rural areas came to work in the mills, but African Americans were not allowed to work in most of them.

"The New South...is stirred with the breath of a new life."

—Henry Grady

Atlanta rebuilt quickly after the war, becoming a leading railroad and industrial center. Newspaper editor Henry Grady gave stirring speeches about the need for industry in the South. He became one of the best-known spokesmen of the "New South."

Why might Grady point to Atlanta as a model for economic change?

Southern Mill Life

Work in the cotton mills appealed to farm families who had trouble making ends meet. As one mill worker explained, "It was a necessity to move and get a job, rather than depend on the farm." Recruiters sent out by the mills promised good wages and steady work.

Entire families often worked in the same cotton mill. Mills employed large numbers of women and children. Many children started working at about the age of 12. Some children started working at an even earlier age. Women did most of the spinning and were valued workers. However, few women had the opportunity to advance within the company.

Many mill workers were proud of the skills they used, but they did not enjoy their work. One unhappy worker described it as "the same thing over and over again . . . The more you do, the more they want done." Workers often labored 12 hours a day, six days a week. Cotton dust and lint filled the air, causing asthma and an illness known as brown-lung disease. Fast-moving machinery caused injuries and even deaths. Despite the long hours and dangerous working conditions, wages remained low. However, mill work did offer an alternative to farming.

READING CHECK **Finding Main Ideas** What did southern business leaders hope industry would do?

SUMMARY AND PREVIEW In this section you learned about the end of Reconstruction. In the next chapter you will learn about America's continued westward expansion.

go.hrw.com
Online Quiz
KEYWORD: SF7 HP17

Section 3 Assessment

Reviewing Ideas, Terms, and People

1. **a. Identify** Who were some prominent African American leaders during Reconstruction?
   b. Evaluate What do you think was the most important change made by Reconstruction state governments? Explain your answer.
2. **a. Recall** For what reasons did some local governments not stop the **Ku Klux Klan**?
   b. Draw Conclusions How did the Ku Klux Klan's use of terror interfere with elections in the South?
3. **a. Recall** How did Reconstruction come to an end?
   b. Explain What was the relationship between **Jim Crow laws** and **segregation**?
4. **a. Identify** Who was Henry Grady, and why was he important?
   b. Predict What are some possible results of the rise of the "New South"?

Critical Thinking

5. **Identifying Causes and Effects** Review your notes on Reconstruction governments. Then copy the graphic organizer below and use it to show why Reconstruction ended, as well as the results of its end.

| Causes | → | Effect/Cause
End of
Reconstruction | → | Effects |

WRITING JOURNAL

6. **Relating Historical Change to Individual Choice** Despite the difficulties of Reconstruction, the Freedmen's Bureau and plans to bring industry to the "New South" did create new jobs. What might have led people to leave their jobs for new ones?

Social Studies Skills

Analysis | Critical Thinking | Civic Participation | Study

Chance, Oversight, and Error in History

Understand the Skill

Sometimes, history can seem very routine. One event leads to others which, in turn, lead to still others. You learn to look for cause-and-effect relationships among events. You learn how point of view and bias can influence decisions and actions. These approaches to the study of history imply that the events of the past are orderly and predictable.

In fact, many of the events of the past *are* orderly and predictable! They may seem even more so since they're over and done with, and we know how things turned out. Yet, predictable patterns of behavior *do* exist throughout history. Recognizing them is one of the great values and rewards of studying the past. As the philosopher George Santayana once famously said, "Those who cannot remember the past are condemned to repeat it."

At its most basic level, however, history is people, and people are "human." They make mistakes. Unexpected things happen to them, both good things and bad. This is the unpredictable element of history. The current phrase "stuff happens" is just as true of the past as it is today. Mistakes, oversights, and just plain "dumb luck" have shaped the course of history—and have helped to make the study of it so exciting.

Learn the Skill

California merchant John Sutter decided to build a sawmill along a nearby American river in 1848. He planned to sell the lumber it produced to settlers who were moving into the area. Sutter put James W. Marshall to work building the mill. To install the large water wheel that would power the saw, Marshall first had to deepen the river bed next to the mill. During his digging, he noticed some shiny bits of yellow metal in the water. The result of this accidental find was the California gold rush, which sent thousands of Americans to California, and speeded settlement of the West.

In 1863 the army of Confederate General Robert E. Lee invaded Maryland. The Civil War had been going well for the South. Lee hoped a southern victory on Union soil would convince the British to aid the South in the war. However, a Confederate officer forgot his cigars as his unit left its camp in the Maryland countryside. Wrapped around the cigars was a copy of Lee's battle plans. When a Union soldier came upon the abandoned camp, he spotted the cigars. This chance discovery enabled the Union army to defeat Lee at the Battle of Antietam. The Union victory helped keep the British out of the war. More importantly, it allowed President Lincoln to issue the Emancipation Proclamation and begin the process of ending slavery in the United States.

Practice the Skill

In April 1865 President Lincoln was assassinated while attending the theater in Washington, D.C. Bodyguard John Parker was stationed outside the door of the president's box. However, Parker left his post to find a seat from which he could watch the play. This allowed the killer to enter the box and shoot the unprotected president.

Write an essay about how this chance event altered the course of history. How might Reconstruction, North–South relations, and African Americans' struggle for equality have been different had Lincoln lived?

Chapter Review

HOLT
History's Impact
▶ video series
Review the video to answer the closing question:
Name three ways the Thirteenth, Fourteenth, and Fifteenth Amendments are related.

Visual Summary

QUICK FACTS

Use the visual summary below to help you review the main ideas of the chapter.

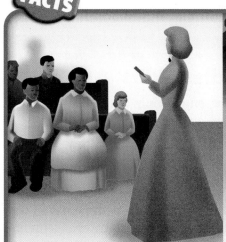

Reform During Reconstruction, the Freedmen's Bureau opened schools for former slaves and performed other services to help the poorest southerners.

Dispute Differing ideas about how to govern the South led to conflicts between African Americans and white southerners, as well as between Republicans and Democrats.

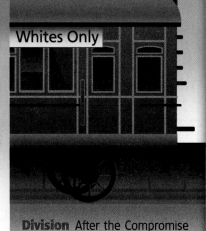

Whites Only

Division After the Compromise of 1877 ended Reconstruction, segregation laws were enacted by southern governments and upheld by the U.S. Supreme Court.

Reviewing Vocabulary, Terms, and People

Complete each sentence by filling in the blank with the correct term or person from the chapter.

1. _____ were laws that allowed racial segregation in public places.
2. The Radical Republicans were led by _____, a member of Congress from Pennsylvania.
3. The period from 1865 to 1877 that focused on reuniting the nation is known as _____.
4. Following the Civil War, many African Americans in the South made a living by participating in the _____ system.
5. After opposing Congress, Andrew Johnson became the first president to face _____ proceedings.
6. The _____ Amendment made slavery in the United States illegal.
7. In 1870 _____ became the first African American to serve in the U.S. Senate.

Comprehension and Critical Thinking

SECTION 1 *(Pages 552–557)*

8. **a. Describe** How did the lives of African Americans change after the Civil War?

   b. Compare and Contrast How was President Johnson's Reconstruction plan similar and different from President Lincoln's Ten Percent Plan?

   c. Evaluate Which of the three Reconstruction plans that were originally proposed do you think would have been the most successful? Why?

SECTION 2 *(Pages 558–563)*

9. **a. Identify** Who were the Radical Republicans, and how did they change Reconstruction?

   b. Analyze How did the debate over the Fourteenth Amendment affect the election of 1866?

   c. Elaborate Do you think Congress was right to impeach President Andrew Johnson? Explain.

10. a. Describe What reforms did Reconstruction governments in the South support?

b. Draw Conclusions In what ways did southern governments attempt to reverse the accomplishments of Reconstruction?

c. Evaluate Do you think the South was successful or unsuccessful in its rebuilding efforts? Explain your answer.

Reviewing Themes

11. Politics Explain the political struggles that took place during Reconstruction.

12. Society and Culture How were the lives of ordinary southerners affected in the years after Reconstruction?

Using the Internet

13. Activity: Drawing Conclusions A challenge for anyone trying to understand Reconstruction is drawing conclusions from primary and secondary sources from the time period. This activity will help you see how complex this can be. Enter the activity keyword, and then rate the credibility of the sources provided. Make sure you explain whether the source is a primary or secondary source, whether or not you think the source is credible, and the reasons for your thoughts.

Reading Skills

Analyzing Historical Information *Use the Reading Skills taught in this chapter to answer the question about the reading selection below.*

> Radical Republicans, on the other hand, took a harsher stance. They wanted the Federal government to force change in the South. Like the moderates, they thought the Black Codes were cruel and unjust. *(p. 559)*

14. Which of the following is relevant information for the passage above?

a. Thaddeus Stevens was a Radical Republican.

b. Andrew Johnson was a Democrat.

c. Radical Republicans wanted the federal government to make major changes in the South.

d. Radical Republicans were eventually removed from power.

Social Studies Skills

Chance, Oversight, and Error in History *Use the Social Studies Skills taught in this chapter to answer the question about the reading selection below.*

> Johnson's speaking tour was a disaster. It did little to win votes for the Democratic Party. Johnson even got into arguments with people in the audiences of some of his speaking engagements. *(p. 561)*

15. Which of the following is an example of chance, oversight, or error that affected history?

a. Johnson got into arguments with audiences.

b. The tour was a disaster.

c. The tour did not win votes.

d. Johnson spoke for the Democratic Party.

FOCUS ON WRITING

16. Writing a Job History Review your notes about the changing job scene during Reconstruction. Put yourself in the shoes of a person living then. It could be anyone—a returning soldier, a shopkeeper, a schoolteacher, or a politician. What jobs would that person seek? Why would he or she leave one job for another?

Write a brief job history for that person during Reconstruction. Include at least four jobs. Make each job description two to four sentences long. End each one with a sentence or two about why the person left that job. Add one sentence explaining why he or she took the next job. Be sure to include specific historical details.

DIRECTIONS: Read each question and write the letter of the best response.

1 Use the map below to answer the following question.

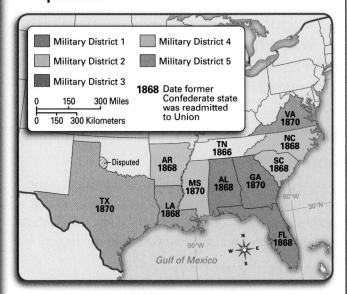

Military District 1

Military District 2

Military District 3

Military District 4

Military District 5

1868 Date former Confederate state was readmitted to Union

0   150   300 Miles

0   150   300 Kilometers

VA 1870

NC 1868

TN 1866

AR 1868

SC 1868

Disputed

MS 1870

AL 1868

GA 1870

TX 1870

LA 1868

80°W

30°N

FL 1868

90°W

Gulf of Mexico

Which military district contained the largest number of states?

A Military District 2

B Military District 3

C Military District 4

D Military District 5

2 What can you infer from the map information?

A South Carolina was difficult to reconstruct.

B The largest number of troops was in Military District 1.

C Military District 5 was the last district to end Reconstruction.

D Tennessee was readmitted to the Union before the other southern states.

3 The quickest approach to reuniting the nation was proposed by the

A Ten Percent Plan.

B Wade-Davis Bill.

C Civil Rights Act of 1866.

D Compromise of 1877.

4 What development convinced Republicans in Congress to take control of Reconstruction from the president?

A President Abraham Lincoln was assassinated by a southern sympathizer.

B President Andrew Johnson vetoed the Wade-Davis bill.

C Southern states began passing Black Codes to restrict African Americans' freedoms.

D White southern women refused to support the Fifteenth Amendment.

5 Which of the following limited opportunities for African Americans in the South after Reconstruction ended?

A Ten Percent plan

B Radical Republicans

C Jim Crow laws

D carpetbaggers

6 Examine the following passage from a northern schoolteacher's letter home and then use it to answer the question.

> "Wishing to work where there was the most need—there are so many places where nothing has been done for the freedmen, and where they are sorely persecuted—we came here. A schoolhouse built by the soldiers had just been destroyed by the citizens. The feeling is intensely bitter against anything northern. The affairs of the [Freedmen's] Bureau have been very much mismanaged in Columbus, and our government has been disgraced by the troops who were stationed here."
>
> —Sarah Chase, from *Dear Ones at Home*

Document-Based Question What were some of the problems facing the Freedmen's Bureau in the South?

Assignment

Collect information and write an informative report on a topic related to the Civil War.

A Social Studies Report

All research begins with a question. Why did the North win the Civil War? Why did Abraham Lincoln choose Ulysses S. Grant? In a research report, you find answers to questions like these and share what you learn with your reader.

1. Prewrite

Choosing a Subject

Since you will spend a lot of time researching and writing about your topic, pick one that interests you. First, think of several topics related to the Civil War. Narrow your list to one topic by thinking about what interests you and where you can find information about the topic.

Developing a Research Question

A guiding question related to your topic will help focus your research. For example, here is a research question for the topic "Robert E. Lee's Role in the Civil War": *How did Lee's decision to turn down the leadership of the Union army affect the Civil War?* The answer to this question becomes the thesis, or the big idea of your report.

Finding Historical Information

Use at least three sources of historical information besides your text-book. Good sources include

- books, maps, magazines, newspapers
- television programs, movies, Internet sites, CD-ROMs.

For each source, write down the kinds of information shown below. When taking notes, put a circled number next to each source.

> **Encyclopedia article**
> ① "Title of Article." <u>Name of Encyclopedia</u>. Edition or year published.
> **Book**
> ② Author. <u>Title</u>. City of Publication: Publisher, year published.
> **Magazine or newspaper article**
> ③ Author. "Title of Article." <u>Publication name</u>. Date: page number(s).
> **Internet site**
> ④ Author (if known). "Document title." <u>Web site</u>. Date of electronic publication. Date information was accessed <url>.

> **TIP** **Narrowing the Task** The key to a successful research report is picking a topic that is broad enough that you can find information, but narrow enough that you can cover it in detail. To narrow a subject, focus on one aspect of the larger subject. Then think about whether that one aspect can be broken down into smaller parts. Here's an example of how to narrow a topic:
> **Too Broad:** Civil War Leaders
> **Less Broad:** Civil War Generals
> **Narrower:** Robert E. Lee's Role in the Civil War

Taking Notes

As you read the source material, take thorough notes on facts, statistics, comparisons, and quotations. Take special care to spell names correctly and to record dates and facts accurately. If you use a direct quotation from a source, copy it word for word and enclose it in quotation marks. Along with each note, include the number of its source and its page number.

Organizing Your Ideas and Information

Informative research reports are usually organized in one of these ways:

- Chronological order (the order in which events occurred)
- Order of importance
- Causes (actions or situations that make something else happen) and effects (what happened as a result of something else).

Use one of these orders to organize your notes in an outline. Here is a partial outline for a paper on Robert E. Lee.

> The Thesis/Big Idea: Robert E. Lee's decision to decline the leadership of the Union army had serious consequences for the path of the Civil War.
>
> I. Lee's Military Expertise
>   A. Achievements at the U.S. Military Academy
>   B. Achievements during the Mexican War
> II. Lee's Personality and Character
>   A. Intelligence and strength
>   B. Honesty and fairness
>   C. Daring and courage
> III. Lee's Military Victories
>   A. Battle of Fredericksburg
>   B. Battle of Chancellorsville

TIP **Seeing Different Viewpoints** Consult a variety of sources, including those with different points of view on the topic. Reading sources with different opinions will give you a more complete picture of your subject. For example, reading articles about Robert E. Lee written by a southern writer as well as a northern writer may give you a more balanced view of Lee.

TIP **Recording Others' Ideas** You will be taking three types of notes. **Paraphrases** Restatements of all the ideas in your own words. **Summaries** Brief restatements of only the most important parts. **Direct quotations** The writer's exact words inside quotation marks.

2. Write

You can use this framework to help you write your first draft.

A Writer's Framework

Introduction
- Start with a quote or an interesting historical detail to grab your reader's attention.
- State the main idea of your report.
- Provide any historical background readers need to understand your main idea.

Body
- Present your information under at least three main ideas, using logical order.
- Write at least one paragraph for each of these main ideas.
- Add supporting details, facts, or examples to each paragraph.

Conclusion
- Restate your main idea, using slightly different words.
- Include a general comment about your topic.
- You might comment on how the historical information in your report relates to later historical events.

Studying a Model

Here is a model of a research report. Study it to see how one student developed a paper. The first and the concluding paragraphs are shown in full. The paragraphs in the body of the paper are summarized.

INTRODUCTORY PARAGRAPH

Attention grabber

Statement of thesis

"I cannot raise my hand against my birthplace, my home, my children." With these words, Robert E. Lee changed the course of the Civil War. Abraham Lincoln had turned to Lee as his first choice for commander of the Union army. However, Lee turned Lincoln down, choosing instead to side with his home state of Virginia and take command of the Confederate army. Lee's decision to turn Lincoln down weakened the North and strengthened the Confederates, turning what might have been an easy victory for the North into a long, costly war.

BODY PARAGRAPHS

In the first part of the body, the student points out that Lee graduated from the U.S. Military Academy at West Point, served in the Mexican War, and was a member of the Union army. She goes on to explain that he would have been a strong leader for the North, and his absence made the North weaker.

In the middle of the report, the writer discusses Lee's personality and character. She includes information about the strength of character he showed while in the military academy and while leading the Confederate army. She discusses and gives examples of his intelligence, his daring, his courage, and his honesty.

In the last part of the body of the report, the student provides examples of Lee leading the outnumbered Confederate army to a series of victories. The student provides details of the battles of Fredericksburg and Chancellorsville and explains how a lesser general than Lee may have lost both battles.

CONCLUDING PARAGRAPH

Summary of main points

Restatement of big idea

Lee's brilliant and resourceful leadership bedeviled a series of Union generals. He won battles that most generals would have lost. If Lee had used these skills to lead the larger and more powerful Union army, the Civil War might have ended in months instead of years.

3. Evaluate and Revise

Evaluating and Revising Your Draft

Evaluate your first draft by carefully reading it twice. Ask the questions below to decide which parts of your first draft should be revised.

Evaluation Questions for an Informative Report

- Does the introduction attract the readers' interest and state the big idea/thesis of your report?
- Does the body of your report have at least three paragraphs that develop your big idea? Is the main idea in each paragraph clearly stated?
- Have you included enough information to support each of your main ideas? Are all facts, details, and examples accurate? Are all of them clearly related to the main ideas they support?

- Is the report clearly organized? Does it use chronological order, order of importance, or cause and effect?
- Does the conclusion restate the big idea of your report? Does it end with a general comment about the importance or significance of your topic?
- Have you included at least three sources in your bibliography? Have you included all the sources you used and not any you did not use?

TIP Organizing Your Time By creating a schedule and following it, you can avoid that panicky moment when the due date is near and you haven't even started your research. To create your schedule and manage your time, include these six steps.

1. Develop a question and research your topic (10% of your total time).
2. Research and take notes (25%).
3. Write your main idea statement and create an outline (15%).
4. Write a first draft (25%).
5. Evaluate and revise your first draft (15%).
6. Proofread and publish your report (10%).

4. Proofread and Publish

Proofreading

To improve your report before sharing it, check the following:

- The spelling and capitalization of all proper names for people, places, things, and events.
- Punctuation marks around any direct quotation.
- Your list of sources (Works Cited or Bibliography) against a guide to writing research papers. Make sure you follow the examples in the guide when punctuating and capitalizing your source listings.

Publishing

Choose one or more of these ideas to publish your report.

- Share your report with your classmates by turning it into an informative speech.
- Submit your report to an online discussion group that focuses on the Civil War and ask for feedback.
- With your classmates, create a magazine that includes reports on several different topics or post the reports on your school Web site.

5. Practice and Apply

Use the steps and strategies outlined in this workshop to research and write an informative report on the Civil War.

A Growing America

What You Will Learn...

After the American Civil War, the United States began a process of building a new economy and political structure. Events in the rest of the world began affecting the nation more noticeably.

During this period of expansion, the U.S. population spread across the continent. New immigrants and new technology began to change life in many parts of the country, especially in cities. In the next three chapters, you will learn about changes in the United States that helped the country increase its size, wealth, and power.

Explore the Art

In this picture, a teenage Buffalo Bill Cody flees from bandits on his Pony Express route. How does this picture show the importance of communication in the expansion of the United States?

Americans Move West

IN Indiana Standards

Social Studies Standards

8.1.23 Describe the conflicts between native american Indians and settlers of the Great Plains.

8.1.24 Identify the influence of individuals on poltical and social events and movements, such as the abolition movement, the Dred Scott case, women's rights, and Native American Indian removal.

8.2.4 Examine functions of the national government in the lives of people., Trace the development of different kinds of money used in the United States and explain how money helps make saving easier.

8.4.8 Examine the development of the banking system in the United States.

go.hrw.com
Indiana
KEYWORD: SF10 IN

FOCUS ON WRITING

Writing a Letter Before telephones and e-mail, one way to communicate with people far away was by letter. In this chapter, you will read about the settlement of the West by European Americans. Suppose you were an Irish immigrant working on a railroad that crossed the Great Plains. What might you have seen or experienced? After you read the chapter, you will write a letter to your sister in Ireland telling her about your experiences.

UNITED STATES

1860 The Pony Express begins delivering mail between East and West.

1850   1860

WORLD

1855 Paris holds a World's Fair.

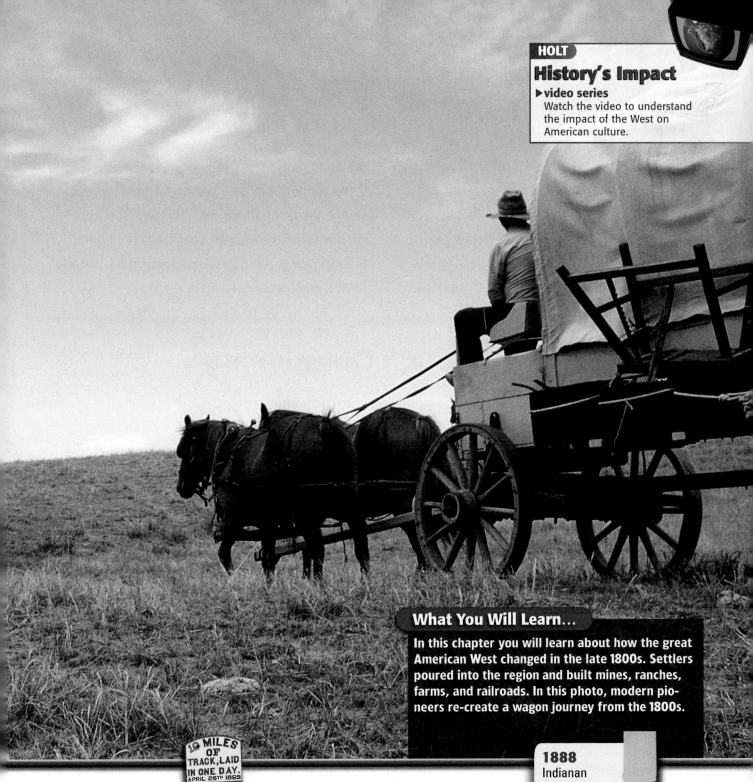

What You Will Learn...

In this chapter you will learn about how the great American West changed in the late 1800s. Settlers poured into the region and built mines, ranches, farms, and railroads. In this photo, modern pioneers re-create a wagon journey from the 1800s.

1888 Indianan Benjamin Harrison is elected the 23rd president

1869 The first transcontinental railroad is completed.

1874 Gold is discovered in the Black Hills of the Dakotas.

1879 Thousands of African Americans migrate from the South to Kansas.

1890 The Massacre at Wounded Knee occurs.

1870

1880

1890

1864 French scientist Louis Pasteur invents the purification process of pasteurization.

1883 The Orient Express railway makes its first run from Paris to Istanbul.

1888 Brazil abolishes slavery.

Reading Social Studies

by Kylene Beers

Focus on Themes In this chapter you will follow the development of the United States from the mid-1800s through the 1890s. You will learn that California was admitted to the Union in 1850. You will find out about the struggles that people faced as the movement West continued and people settled the Great Plains. You will learn about the **technological** advancements made during this time as well as the difficult **geographical** obstacles miners and ranchers faced in the West.

Understanding through Questioning

Focus on Reading When newspaper reporters want to get to the heart of a story, they ask certain questions: who, what, when, where, why, and how. When you are reading a history book, you can use the same questions to get to the heart of what happened in the past.

Hypothetical Questions You can also use questions to dig deeper than what is in the text. You can ask hypothetical, or what if, questions. These questions ask what might have happened had events occurred differently. Sometimes asking such questions can help history come alive.

Who?
Congress

Where?
the West

How?
Congress gave land to anyone who agreed to settle on it for five years.

In 1862 Congress passed two important land acts that helped open the West to settlers. The Homestead Act gave government-owned land to small farmers. Any adult who was a U.S. citizen or planned to become one could receive 160 acres of land. In exchange, homesteaders promised to live on the land for five years. The Morrill Act granted more than 17 million acres of federal land to the states. *(p. 600)*

What if?
If Congress had not passed these laws, U.S. citizens might not have moved West. The United States might not have grown as quickly as it did.

What?
encouraged new settlement

When?
1862

Why?
Perhaps Congress feared what would happen to western lands if they remained unsettled by U.S. citizens.

You Try It!

Read the following passage and then answer the questions below.

Building Communities

Women were an important force in the settlement of the frontier. They joined in the hard work of farming and ranching and helped build communities out of the widely spaced farms and small towns. Their role in founding communities facilitated a strong voice in public affairs. Wyoming women, for example, were granted the vote in the new state's constitution, which was approved in 1869. Annie Bidwell, one of the founders of Chico, California, used her influence to support a variety of moral and social causes such as women's suffrage and temperance.

From Chapter 18, p. 602

Answer these questions based on the passage you just read.

1. Who is this passage about?

2. What did they do?

3. When did they do this?

4. How do you think they accomplished it?

5. Why do you think they were able to accomplish so much?

6. How can knowing this information help you understand the past?

7. What if women in the West had been given more rights? Fewer rights? How might the West have been different?

Key Terms and People

Chapter 18

Section 1
frontier *(p. 586)*
Comstock Lode *(p. 587)*
boomtowns *(p. 588)*
Cattle Kingdom *(p. 589)*
cattle drive *(p. 589)*
Chisholm Trail *(p. 589)*
Pony Express *(p. 590)*
transcontinental railroad *(p. 590)*

Section 2
Treaty of Fort Laramie *(p. 594)*
reservations *(p. 595)*
Crazy Horse *(p. 595)*
Treaty of Medicine Lodge *(p. 595)*
buffalo soldiers *(p. 596)*
George Armstrong Custer *(p. 596)*
Sitting Bull *(p. 596)*
Battle of the Little Bighorn *(p. 596)*
Massacre at Wounded Knee *(p. 597)*
Long Walk *(p. 597)*
Geronimo *(p. 597)*
Ghost Dance *(p. 598)*
Sarah Winnemucca *(p. 598)*
Dawes General Allotment Act *(p. 598)*

Section 3
Homestead Act *(p. 600)*
Morrill Act *(p. 600)*
Exodusters *(p. 601)*
sodbusters *(p. 601)*
dry farming *(p. 601)*
Annie Bidwell *(p. 602)*
National Grange *(p. 603)*
deflation *(p. 604)*
William Jennings Bryan *(p. 604)*
Populist Party *(p. 604)*

Academic Vocabulary

In this chapter, you will learn the following academic words:

establish *(p. 588)*
facilitate *(p. 602)*

As you read Chapter 18, ask questions like *who, what, when, where, why, how,* and *what if* to help you analyze what you are reading.

Miners, Ranchers, and Railroads

What You Will Learn...

Main Ideas

1. A mining boom brought growth to the West.
2. The demand for cattle created a short-lived Cattle Kingdom on the Great Plains.
3. East and West were connected by the transcontinental railroad.

The Big Idea

As more settlers moved West, mining, ranching, and railroads soon transformed the western landscape.

Key Terms

frontier, *p. 586*
Comstock Lode, *p. 587*
boomtowns, *p. 588*
Cattle Kingdom, *p. 589*
cattle drive, *p. 589*
Chisholm Trail, *p. 589*
Pony Express, *p. 590*
transcontinental railroad, *p. 590*

 TAKING NOTES As you read the following section, take notes on the kinds of economic opppportunities that people found in the West. Organize your notes in a table like the one below.

Opportunities in the West

 8.1.25, 8.1.26, 8.1.27, 8.3.1, 8.3.2, 8.3.6, 8.3.8, 8.3.9, 8.3.10, 8.3.11, 8.4.4

If YOU were there...

You are a cowboy in Texas in 1875. You love life on the open range, the quiet nights, and the freedom. You even like the hard work of the long cattle drives to Kansas. But you know that times are changing. Homesteaders are moving in and fencing off their lands. Some of the older cowboys say it's time to settle down and buy a small ranch. You hope that they're not right.

What would make you give up a cowboy's life?

BUILDING BACKGROUND In the years following the Civil War, the U.S. population grew rapidly. Settlements in the West increased. More discoveries of gold and silver attracted adventurers, while the open range drew others. Thousands of former Civil War soldiers also joined the move West.

Mining Boom Brings Growth

During the years surrounding the War, most Americans had thought of the Great Plains and other western lands as the Great American Desert. In the years following the Civil War, Americans witnessed the rapid growth of the U.S. population and the spread of settlements throughout the West. With the admission of the state of California to the Union in 1850, the western boundary of the American **frontier**—an undeveloped area—had reached the Pacific Ocean.

The frontier changed dramatically as more and more people moved westward. Settlers built homes, fenced off land, and laid out ranches and farms. Miners, ranchers, and farmers remade the landscape of the West as they adapted to their new surroundings. The geography of the West was further changed by the development and expansion of a large and successful railroad industry that moved the West's natural resources to eastern markets. Gold and silver were the most valuable natural resources, and mining companies used the growing railroad network to bring these precious metals to the East.

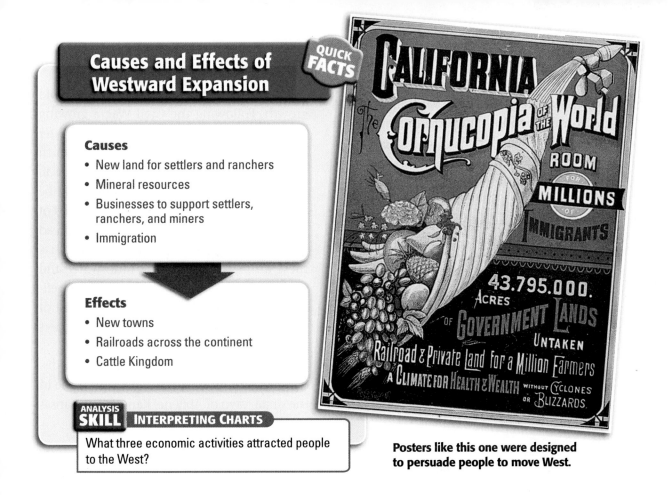

Causes and Effects of Westward Expansion

QUICK FACTS

Causes
- New land for settlers and ranchers
- Mineral resources
- Businesses to support settlers, ranchers, and miners
- Immigration

Effects
- New towns
- Railroads across the continent
- Cattle Kingdom

ANALYSIS SKILL INTERPRETING CHARTS

What three economic activities attracted people to the West?

Posters like this one were designed to persuade people to move West.

Big Business

Most of the precious metals were located in western Nevada. In 1859 miner Henry Comstock discovered a huge deposit of gold and silver in Nevada that became called the **Comstock Lode**. The deposit was incredibly rich and deep. In just the first year after its discovery, the Comstock Lode lured thousands of California miners to Nevada. Over the next 20 years, the Comstock Lode produced more than $500 million worth of gold and silver.

Expensive equipment was needed to remove the silver and gold that were trapped within quartz rock. Larger mining companies bought up land claims from miners who could not afford this machinery. As a result, mining became a big business in the West.

As companies dug bigger and deeper mines, the work became more dangerous. Miners had to use unsafe equipment, such as elevator platforms without protective walls. They worked in dark tunnels and breathed hot, stuffy air. They suffered from lung disease caused by dusty air. Miners often were injured or killed by poorly planned explosions or by cave-ins. Fire was also a great danger. Mining was therefore one of the most dangerous jobs in the country. In the West, worries about safety and pay led miners to form several unions in the 1860s.

Settlers

People from all over the world came to work in the western mines. Some miners came from the eastern United States. Others emigrated from Europe, Central and South America, and Asia. Many Mexican immigrants and Mexican Americans were experienced miners. They were skilled in assaying, or testing, the contents of valuable ore. One newspaper reporter wrote, "Here were congregated the most varied elements of humanity . . . belonging to almost every nationality and every status of life."

New Towns

Mining booms also produced **boomtowns**, communities that grew suddenly when a mine opened. They disappeared just as quickly when the mine closed. Most boomtowns had general stores, saloons, and boardinghouses.

Few women or families lived in boomtowns. "I was never so lonely and homesick in all my life," wrote one young woman. Women washed, cooked, made clothes, and chopped wood. They also raised families, <u>established</u> schools, and wrote for newspapers. Their work helped turn some mining camps into successful, permanent towns.

ACADEMIC VOCABULARY
establish to set up or create

READING CHECK **Summarizing** What risks did miners face?

The Cattle Kingdom

The cattle industry was another area of rapid growth. Following the Civil War, a growing economy and population created a greater demand for beef in the East. Cattle worth $3 to $6 each in Texas could be sold for $38 each in Kansas. In New York, they could be sold for $80 each. The most popular breed of cattle was the longhorn. The longhorn spread quickly throughout western Texas. Because these animals needed very little water and could survive harsh weather, they were well-suited to the dry, desert-like environment of western Texas. But how could Texas ranchers move the longhorns to eastern markets?

In 1867 businessman Joseph McCoy discovered a solution. He built pens for cattle in the small town of Abilene, Kansas. The Kansas

Myth and Reality in the Wild West

No episode in American history has given rise to as many myths as the Wild West. Writers of dime novels, popular in the East, helped created the myths in the years after the Civil War. Even today, popular books, television shows, and movies continue to portray the West in ways that are more myth than reality.

Myth: The cowboy was a free-spirited individual.

Reality: Most cowboys were employees. Many joined labor unions and even went on strike.

Myth: Western cowtowns were wild places where cowboys had gunfights, and there was little law and order.

Reality: Most were orderly cities with active law enforcement. Showdowns rarely, if ever, occurred.

Myth: Almost all cowboys were Anglo Americans.

Reality: About 25 percent of cowboys were African Americans, and 12 percent were Hispanic.

Pacific Railroad line went through Abilene. As a result, cattle could be shipped by rail from there. Soon, countless Texas ranchers were making the trip north to Abilene to sell their herds of cattle.

Around the same time, cattle ranching began to expand in the Midwest. The Great Plains from Texas to Canada, where many ranchers raised cattle in the late 1800s, became known as the **Cattle Kingdom**. Ranchers grazed huge herds on public land called the open range. The land had once been occupied by Plains Indians and buffalo herds.

Importance of Cowboys

The workers who took care of the ranchers' cattle were known as cowhands or cowboys. They borrowed many techniques and tools from vaqueros (bah-KER-ohs), Mexican ranch

Marshal Wyatt Earp

Deadwood, South Dakota

hands who cared for cattle and horses. From vaqueros came the western saddle and the lariat—a rope used for lassoing cattle. The cowboys also borrowed the vaqueros' broad felt hat. However, they changed it into the familiar high-peaked cowboy hat.

One of the cowboy's most important and dangerous duties was the **cattle drive**. On these long journeys, cowboys herded cattle to the market or to the northern Plains for grazing. The trips usually lasted several months and covered hundreds of miles. The **Chisholm Trail**, which ran from San Antonio, Texas, to the cattle town of Abilene, Kansas, was one of the earliest and most popular routes for cattle drives. It was blazed, or marked, by Texas cowboy Jesse Chisholm in the late 1860s.

At times, rowdy cowboys made life in cattle towns rough and violent. There were rarely shoot-outs in the street, but there was often disorderly behavior. Law officials such as Wyatt Earp became famous for keeping the peace in cattle towns.

End of the Open Range

As the cattle business boomed, ranchers faced more competition for use of the open range. Farmers began to buy range land on the Great Plains where cattle had once grazed. Small ranchers also began competing with large ranchers for land. Then in 1874, the invention of barbed wire allowed westerners to fence off large amounts of land cheaply. The competition between farmers, large ranchers, and small ranchers increased. This competition led to range wars, or fights for access to land.

Making matters worse, in 1885 and 1886, disaster struck the Cattle Kingdom. The huge cattle herds on the Plains had eaten most of the prairie grass. Unusually severe winters in both years made the ranching situation even worse. Thousands of cattle died, and many ranchers were ruined financially. The Cattle Kingdom had come to an end.

READING CHECK **Drawing Conclusions**
Why did the Cattle Kingdom come to an end?

FOCUS ON READING
Ask yourself questions about the information in this paragraph to help you understand the competition between farmers and ranchers.

The Transcontinental Railroad

As more Americans began moving West, the need to send goods and information between the East and West increased. Americans searched for ways to improve communication and travel across the country.

In 1860 a system of messengers on horseback called the **Pony Express** began to carry messages west. The messengers carried mail between relay stations on a route about 2,000 miles long. However, telegraph lines, which sent messages faster, quickly put the Pony Express out of business.

Some Americans wanted to build a **transcontinental railroad**—a railroad that would cross the continent and connect the East to the West. The federal government, therefore, passed the Pacific Railway Acts in 1862 and in 1864. These acts gave railroad companies loans and large land grants that could be sold to pay for construction costs. Congress had granted more than 131 million acres of public land to railroad companies. In exchange, the government asked the railroads to carry U.S. mail and troops at a lower cost. Many railroad companies were inspired to begin laying miles of tracks.

Great Race

Two companies, the Central Pacific and the Union Pacific, led the race to complete the transcontinental railroad. In February 1863, the Central Pacific began building east from Sacramento, California. At the end of the year, the Union Pacific started building west from Omaha, Nebraska.

The Union Pacific hired thousands of railroad workers, particularly Irish immigrants. Chinese immigrants made up some 85 percent of the Central Pacific workforce. The railroad's part-owner Leland Stanford praised them, but he paid them less than other laborers. Chinese crews also were given the most dangerous tasks and had to work longer hours than other railroad laborers. They took the job, however, because the $30 a month

Routes West, 1870

When the two lines of the transcontinental railroad met in Promontory, Utah, Leland Stanford drove a celebratory golden spike into the rails.

GEOGRAPHY SKILLS   INTERPRETING MAPS

Movement According to the map, what was the westernmost city on the transcontinental railroad?

that the Central Pacific paid was as much as 10 times what they could earn in China.

Railroad companies faced many geographic challenges. For example, workers for Central Pacific struggled to cross the Sierra Nevada mountain range in California. Breaking apart its rock formations required setting carefully controlled explosions using large amounts of blasting powder and the explosive nitroglycerin. And in the winter of 1866, snowdrifts more than 60 feet high trapped and killed dozens of workers. Faced with these obstacles, the Central Pacific took four years to lay the first 115 miles of track.

Meanwhile, Union Pacific workers faced harsh weather on the Great Plains. In addition, the company pressured them to work at a rapid pace—at times laying 250 miles of track in six months.

For both railroad companies, providing food and supplies for workers was vital. This job became more difficult in remote areas. The railroad companies consequently often relied on local resources. Professional hunters, such as William "Buffalo Bill" Cody, shot thousands of buffalo to feed Union Pacific workers.

Golden Spike

Congress required the two completed rail lines to connect at Promontory, Utah. On May 10, 1869, a golden spike was used to connect the railroad tie joining the two tracks. Alexander Toponce witnessed the event.

" Governor Stanford, president of the Central Pacific, took the sledge [hammer], and the first time he struck he missed the spike and hit the rail. What a howl went up! Irish, Chinese, Mexicans, and everybody yelled with delight. 'He missed it' . . . Then Stanford tried it again and tapped the spike. "

—Alexander Toponce, quoted in
A Treasury of Railroad Folklore,
edited by B. A. Botkin and Alvin F. Harlo

The railroad companies were not finished, though. Following completion of the transcontinental railroad, companies continued building railroads until the West was crisscrossed with rail lines.

The Central Pacific and Union Pacific connected their tracks at Promontory, Utah, in 1869, completing the transcontinental railroad.

Effects of the Transcontinental Railroad

- Increased settlement of the West
- Increased business activity and East-West trade
- Helped make the railroad industry one of the most powerful in the country

Results of the Railroad

The transcontinental railroad increased both economic growth and the population in the West. Railroad companies provided better transportation for people and goods. They also sold land to settlers, which encouraged people to move West.

New railroads helped businesses. Western timber companies, miners, ranchers, and farmers shipped wood, metals, meat, and grain east by railroad. In exchange, eastern businesses shipped manufactured goods to the West. As trade between regions increased, the idea that the U.S. economy was inter-dependent became more widespread. Even perceptions of time became more formal as railroad schedules began to unite areas that had before existed under different times. Four continental time zones were established in 1883.

Railroad companies encouraged people to put their money into the railroad business, which they did—sometimes unwisely. Railroad speculation and the collapse of railroad owner Jay Cooke's banking firm helped start the Panic of 1873. By the 1880s, many small western railroads were deeply in debt. Despite such setbacks, Americans remained interested in railroad investments. By 1890 there were about 164,000 more miles of track in operation than in 1865. Railroads had become one of the biggest industries in the United States.

READING CHECK Finding Main Ideas How did the railroad affect the development of the West?

SUMMARY AND PREVIEW In this section you learned about the increased settlement of the West. In the next section you will learn about conflicts with Native Americans.

Section 1 Assessment

Reviewing Ideas, Terms, and People

1. **a. Recall** Why did Americans move West in the years following the Civil War?
   b. Draw Conclusions What effect did the discovery of the **Comstock Lode** have on the West?
   c. Evaluate Do you think women were important to the success of mining towns? Why or why not?
2. **a. Recall** What led to the cattle boom in the West?
   b. Analyze Why was there competition between ranchers and farmers to settle in the Great Plains?
   c. Evaluate What played the biggest role in ending the **Cattle Kingdom**? Why?
3. **a. Recall** When and where did the Union Pacific and Central Pacific lines meet?
   b. Make Generalizations How do you think the **transcontinental railroad** improved people's lives?

Critical Thinking

4. **Comparing** Review your notes about opportunities in the West. Then use a graphic organizer like the one below to list the effects of these opportunities.

Opportunity	Effect

FOCUS ON WRITING

5. **Taking Notes on Mining, Ranching, and the Railroads** As you read this section, take notes on how mining, ranching, and railroads changed the West. How might a railroad worker feel about these changes?

Wars for the West

If YOU were there...

You are a member of the Sioux nation, living in Dakota Territory in 1875. These lands are sacred to your people, and the U.S. government has promised them to you. But now gold has been found here, and the government has ordered you to give up your land. Some Sioux leaders want to fight. Others say that it is of no use, that the soldiers will win.

Would you fight to keep your lands? Why?

BUILDING BACKGROUND Miners, ranchers, and farmers all moved West in the years after the Civil War. The arrival of settlers and the U.S. army to the Great Plains meant the end of the way of life of the Indians who lived there. The coming of the railroad began this destruction, with the killing of thousands of buffalo. Treaties were made but did not protect Indian lands from settlers.

Settlers Encounter the Plains Indians

As miners and settlers began crossing the Great Plains in the mid-1800s, they pressured the federal government for more access to western lands. To protect these travelers, U.S. officials sent agents to negotiate treaties with the Plains Indians.

The Plains Indians lived in the Great Plains, which stretch north into Canada and south into Texas. Indian groups such as the Apache and the Comanche lived in and around Texas and

The Plains Indians depended on two animals—the horse and the buffalo.

What You Will Learn...

Main Ideas

1. As settlers moved to the Great Plains, they encountered the Plains Indians.
2. The U.S. Army and Native Americans fought in the northern plains, the Southwest, and the Far West.
3. Despite efforts to reform U.S. policy toward Native Americans, conflict continued.

The Big Idea

Native Americans and the U.S. government came into conflict over land in the West.

Key Terms and People

Treaty of Fort Laramie, *p. 594*
reservations, *p. 595*
Crazy Horse, *p. 595*
Treaty of Medicine Lodge, *p. 595*
buffalo soldiers, *p. 596*
George Armstrong Custer, *p. 596*
Sitting Bull, *p. 596*
Battle of the Little Bighorn, *p. 596*
Massacre at Wounded Knee, *p. 597*
Long Walk, *p. 597*
Geronimo, *p. 597*
Ghost Dance, *p. 598*
Sarah Winnemucca, *p. 598*
Dawes General Allotment Act, *p. 598*

TAKING NOTES As you read this section, take notes on the major events in Native Americans' loss of land rights. Organize them in a chart like the one below.

Date	Event

8.1.23, 8.1.24, 8.1.30, 8.3.1, 8.3.9, 8.3.10, 8.3.11

what is now Oklahoma. The Cheyenne and the Arapaho lived in different regions across the central Plains. The Pawnee lived in parts of Nebraska. To the north were the Sioux. These groups spoke many different languages. However, they used a common sign language to communicate and they shared a similar lifestyle.

Hunting Buffalo

For survival, Plains Indians depended on two animals—the horse and the buffalo. The Spanish brought horses to America in the 1500s. Plains Indians learned to ride horses, and hunters used them to follow buffalo herds year-round. While on horseback, most Plains Indian hunters used a short bow and arrows to shoot buffalo from close range.

Plains Indians used buffalo for food, shelter, clothing, utensils, and tools. Women dried buffalo meat to make jerky. They made tepees and clothing from buffalo hides, and cups and tools from buffalo horns. As one Sioux explained, "When our people killed a buffalo, all of the animal was utilized [used] in some manner; nothing was wasted." The Plains Indians prospered. By 1850, some 75,000 Native Americans lived on the Plains.

Struggle to Keep Land

Miners and settlers were also increasing in numbers—and they wanted Indians' land. The U.S. government tried to avoid disputes by negotiating the **Treaty of Fort Laramie**, the first major treaty between the U.S. government and Plains Indians. Two years later, several southern Plains nations signed a treaty at Fort Atkinson in Nebraska. These treaties recognized Indian claims to most of the Great Plains. They also allowed the United States to build forts and roads and to travel across Indian homelands. The U.S. government promised to pay for any damages to Indian lands.

★ Interactive Map

Native American Land Loss in the West, 1850–1890

Land lost by Native Americans
- 1850–1870
- 1870–1890
- Reservations in 1890
- UTE Native American group

0   200   400 Miles
0   200   400 Kilometers

Battles and Treaties of the Indian Wars

1. Treaties at Fort Laramie, 1851 and 1868
2. Treaty at Fort Atkinson, 1853
3. Sand Creek Massacre, 1864
4. Fetterman Massacre, 1866
5. Treaty of Medicine Lodge, 1867
6. Battle of the Little Bighorn, 1876
7. Battle of the Rosebud, 1876
8. Wounded Knee Massacre, 1890

GEOGRAPHY **SKILLS**   **INTERPRETING MAPS**

go.hrw.com
Interactive Map
KEYWORD: SF7 CH18

Region In what regions did Native Americans lose land in the late 1800s?

Tribal Councils

Native Americans have long held tribal councils to make decisions on behalf of the group. Today this tradition of Native American government continues. There are more than 500 tribal governments in the United States. Tribal governments provide a wide range of services, including law enforcement, health care, and education. Here, a member of the Blackfoot Tribal Council addresses the Montana state legislature.

ANALYSIS SKILL **ANALYZING INFORMATION**

What types of services do tribal governments provide?

The treaties did not keep the peace for long. In 1858 the discovery of gold in what is now Colorado brought thousands of miners to the West. They soon clashed with the Cheyenne and the Arapaho. In 1861 the U.S. government negotiated new treaties with Plains Indians. These treaties created **reservations**, areas of federal land set aside for Native Americans. The government expected Indians to stay on the reservations, which made hunting buffalo almost impossible.

Pioneers and miners continued to cross the Great Plains. Many miners used the Bozeman Trail. To protect them, the U.S. Army built forts along the trail, which ran through favored Sioux hunting grounds. The Sioux responded with war. In late 1866, **Crazy Horse** and a group of Sioux ambushed and killed 81 cavalry troops.

In 1868, under the Second Treaty of Fort Laramie, the government agreed to close the Bozeman Trail, abandon the forts, and provide reservation land to the Sioux.

The U.S. government also negotiated for southern Plains Indians to move off their land. In the 1867 **Treaty of Medicine Lodge**, most southern Plains Indians agreed to live on reservations. However, many Indians did not want to give up their hunting grounds. Fighting soon broke out between the Comanche and Texans. The U.S. Army and the Texas Rangers were unable to defeat the Comanche, so they cut off the Comanche's access to food and water. In 1875 the last of the Comanche war leaders surrendered.

READING CHECK **Summarizing** What was the federal policy toward the Plains Indians in the 1860s and 1870s?

Two Views of a Historic Battle

Art historians have identified about 1,000 paintings of the Battle of the Little Bighorn. The painting on this page was painted in 1899. The painting on the next page is one of the many colored-pencil drawings of the battle done by Red Horse, who participated in the fight. He drew them five years after the battle.

How do these paintings show the influences of different cultures?

The Native Americans are shown surrounding a small force of U.S. soldiers.

General Custer is shown standing among his men as he fires.

Fighting on the Plains

In the northern Plains, Southwest, and Far West, Native Americans continued to resist being moved to and confined on reservations. The U.S. government sent troops, including African American cavalry, who the Indians called **buffalo soldiers**, into the area to force the Indians to leave.

Battles on the Northern Plains

As fighting on the southern Plains came to an end, new trouble started in the north. In 1874 Lieutenant Colonel **George Armstrong Custer**'s soldiers discovered gold in the Black Hills of the Dakotas. **Sitting Bull**, a leader of the Lakota Sioux, protested U.S. demands for the land.

" What treaty that the whites have kept has the red man broken? Not one. What treaty that the white man ever made with us have they kept? Not one."
—Sitting Bull, quoted in *Touch the Earth* by T. C. McLuhan

Other Sioux leaders listened to Sitting Bull and refused to give up land. Fighting soon broke out between the army and the Sioux.

On June 25, 1876, Custer's scouts found a Sioux camp along the Little Bighorn River in Montana Territory. Leading 264 of his soldiers, Custer raced ahead without waiting for any supporting forces. In the **Battle of the Little Bighorn**, Sioux forces led by Crazy Horse and Sitting Bull surrounded and defeated Custer and his troops. Newspapers called the battle "Custer's Last Stand" because his entire command was killed. It was the worst defeat the U.S. Army suffered in the West. The Battle of the Little Bighorn was also the Sioux's last major victory.

In 1881 Sitting Bull and a few followers returned from Canada where they had moved. They had run out of food during the hard winter. They joined the Sioux on Standing Rock Reservation in Dakota Territory.

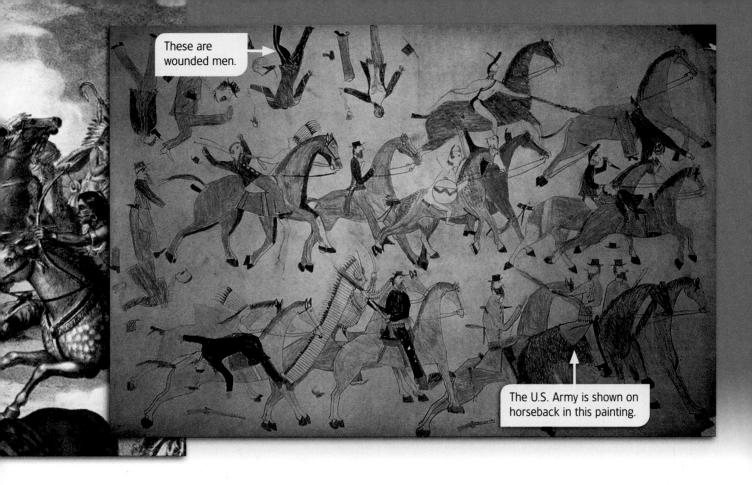

These are wounded men.

The U.S. Army is shown on horseback in this painting.

Almost a decade later, in 1890, while following orders to arrest Sitting Bull, reservation police killed him. Many Sioux left the reservations in protest. Later that year, the U.S. Army shot and killed about 150 Sioux near Wounded Knee Creek in South Dakota. This **Massacre at Wounded Knee** was the last major incident on the Great Plains.

Southwest

The Navajo lived in what became Arizona and New Mexico. In 1863 the Navajo refused to settle on a reservation. In response, U.S. troops made raids on the Navajo's fields, homes, and livestock.

When the Navajo ran out of food and shelter, they started surrendering to the U.S. Army. In 1864 the army led Navajo captives on the **Long Walk**. On this 300-mile march the Navajo were forced to walk across the desert to a reservation in Bosque Redondo, New Mexico. Along the way, countless Navajo died.

Far West

The United States had promised to let the peaceful Nez Percé keep their land in Oregon. Within a few years, however, the government ordered the Nez Percé to a reservation in what is now Idaho. Before leaving, a few angry Nez Percé killed some local settlers and tried to escape to Canada. Near the border, U.S. troops overtook them and sent them to a reservation in what is now Oklahoma.

Final Battles

By the 1880s, most Native Americans had stopped fighting. The Apache of the Southwest, however, continued to battle the U.S. Army. A Chiricahua Apache named **Geronimo** and his band of raiders avoided capture for many years. In September 1886 Geronimo surrendered, ending the Apache armed resistance.

READING CHECK Contrasting How did the Apache resistance differ from that of the Navajo?

Conflict Continues

By the 1870s, many Native Americans lived on reservations, where land was usually not useful for farming or buffalo hunting. Many Indians were starving.

A Paiute Indian named Wovoka began a religious movement, the **Ghost Dance**, that predicted the arrival of paradise for Native Americans. In this paradise, the buffalo herds would return and the settlers would disappear.

U.S. officials did not understand the meaning of the Ghost Dance. They feared it would lead to rebellion, so they tried to end the movement, which had spread to other groups, including the Sioux. After the massacre in 1890 at Wounded Knee, the Ghost Dance movement gradually died out.

In the late 1870s, a Paiute Indian named **Sarah Winnemucca** called for reform. She gave lectures on problems of the reservation system. Writer Helen Hunt Jackson published a book that pushed for reform of U.S. Indian policy in 1881.

Sarah Winnemucca spoke out for the fair treatment of her people.

Some reformers believed that Native Americans should adopt the ways of white people. The **Dawes General Allotment Act** of 1887 tried to lessen traditional influences on Indian society by making land ownership private rather than shared. The act also promised—but failed to deliver—U.S. citizenship to Native Americans. After breaking up reservation land, the government sold the acreage remaining. The Act took about two-thirds of Indian land.

READING CHECK **Evaluating** How did reformers try to influence Native Americans' lives?

SUMMARY AND PREVIEW In this section you read about conflict in the settlement of the West. In the next section you will learn more about Great Plains settlers.

Section 2 Assessment

Reviewing Ideas, Terms, and People

1. **a. Describe** What animals did Plains Indians depend on, and how did they use those animals?
   b. Analyze How did U.S. policy toward the Plains Indians change in the late 1850s?
   c. Elaborate Would you have agreed to move to a **reservation**? Why or why not?
2. **a. Describe** What events led to the **Battle of the Little Bighorn**?
   b. Elaborate Why do you think most Indian groups eventually stopped resisting the United States?
3. **a. Describe** How did the **Dawes General Allotment Act** affect American Indians?
   b. Predict What effect do you think the **Massacre at Wounded Knee** would have on relations between Plains Indians and the United States?

Critical Thinking

4. **Identifying Cause and Effect** Review your notes about Native American land losses. Organize the events in a time line like the one below.

1851   1864   1867   1887

FOCUS ON WRITING

5. **Reading about the Wars for the West** As you read this section, take notes on the wars between the U.S. government and the Plains Indians. How might a railroad worker have experienced these conflicts?

Chief Joseph

What would you do to protect your home and your ways of life?

When did he live? 1840–1904

Where did he live? Chief Joseph lived in the Wallowa Valley, the Nez Percé homeland, in present-day Oregon.

What did he do? Chief Joseph led his people in an effort to hold on to the Nez Percé homeland and to avoid war with the United States. For years, Joseph and a band of Nez Percé refused to move as white settlers moved into the valley. Finally, after being threatened with attack, Joseph gave in. An army led by General Oliver Otis Howard eventually chased the Nez Percé across Idaho, Wyoming, and Montana. They were sent to a reservation in what is now Oklahoma, where many died.

Why is he so important? Chief Joseph's surrender speech earned him a place in American history. The band of 700 people, including only 200 warriors, made a courageous three-month, 1,400-mile trek, hoping to cross into Canada for protection. Exhausted, hungry, and freezing, Joseph's people collapsed just short of the Canadian border. In later years, the chief spoke about what had happened.

Cause and Effect What brought suffering to Chief Joseph and his people?

Chief Joseph of the Nez Percé nation tried to protect his people from the advancement of white settlers.

Speech

"I am tired of fighting. Our chiefs are killed …The old men are all dead …It is cold, and we have no blankets. The little children are freezing to death. My people, some of them, have run away to the hills, and have no blankets, no food. No one knows where they are—perhaps freezing to death. I want to have time to look for my children, and see how many of them I can find. Maybe I shall find them among the dead. Hear me, my chiefs! I am tired. My heart is sick and sad. From where the sun now stands I will fight no more forever."

—Chief Joseph of the Nez Percé, surrender speech, October 5, 1877

Farming and Populism

What You Will Learn...

Main Ideas

1. Many Americans started new lives on the Great Plains.
2. Economic challenges led to the creation of farmers' political groups.
3. By the 1890s, the western frontier had come to an end.

The Big Idea

Settlers on the Great Plains created new communities and unique political groups.

Key Terms and People

Homestead Act, *p. 600*
Morrill Act, *p. 600*
Exodusters, *p. 601*
sodbusters, *p. 601*
dry farming, *p. 601*
Annie Bidwell, *p. 602*
National Grange, *p. 603*
deflation, *p. 604*
William Jennings Bryan, *p. 604*
Populist Party, *p. 604*

TAKING NOTES As you read this section, take notes on the reasons for the rise of populism. Organize your notes in a graphic organizer like the one below.

8.1.23, 8.1.24, 8.1.25, 8.1.26, 8.1.30, 8.2.3, 8.2.4, 8.2.8, 8.3.1, 8.3.6, 8.3.7, 8.3.8, 8.3.9, 8.3.10, 8.3.11, 8.4.7, 8.4.8

If YOU were there...

You are a female schoolteacher in Wisconsin in 1880. You live and teach in a small town, but you grew up on a farm and are used to hard work. Now you are thinking about moving West to claim free land from the government. You could teach in a school there, too. You think it would be an exciting adventure, but your family is horrified that a single woman would move West on her own.

Would you decide to become a homesteader?

BUILDING BACKGROUND By the 1870s and 1880s, the Great Plains had been "tamed" and made more welcoming to settlers. The end of the open cattle range was coming, and the Indian wars were nearly over. The government moved to encourage permanent settlements in the West by offering land to homesteaders.

New Lives on the Plains

In 1862 Congress passed two important land grant acts that helped open the West to settlers. The **Homestead Act** gave government-owned land to small farmers. Any adult who was a U.S. citizen or planned to become one could receive 160 acres of land. In exchange, homesteaders promised to live on the land for five years. The **Morrill Act** granted more than 17 million acres of federal land to the states. The act required each state to sell this land and to use the money to build colleges to teach agriculture and engineering.

Settling the Plains

People from all over the country moved West. Many farming families moved from areas where farmland was becoming scarce or expensive, such as New England. Many single women moved West. The Homestead Act granted land to unmarried women, which was unusual for the time.

The promise of land and a life free of discrimination also drew a large group of African Americans West. In 1879 some

20,000 to 40,000 southern African Americans moved to Kansas. Known as **Exodusters**, these southerners made a mass exodus, or departure, from the South. A number of black communities soon developed.

Western homesteads also were attractive to immigrants. Norwegian, Swedish, Danish, German, and Czech immigrants formed many small communities on the Great Plains.

Farming the Plains

Plains farmers had many unique challenges. The seasons were extreme. Weather could be extreme. Also, the root-filled sod, or dirt, beneath the Plains grass was very tough. The hard work of breaking up the sod earned Plains farmers the nickname **sodbusters**.

In the 1890s western Plains farmers began **dry farming**, a new method of farming that shifted the focus away from water-dependent crops such as corn. Instead, farmers grew more hardy crops like red wheat. In addition, by the 1880s mechanical farming was becoming common. By using machinery, farmers could work much more quickly on large fields with fewer workers. Farmers shipped their harvest east by train. From there, crops were shipped overseas. The Great Plains soon became known as the breadbasket of the world.

Primary Source

LETTER
Letter from the Plains, 1863

In a letter to her family in Norway, immigrant Gro Svendsen describes her new life as a farmer on the plains of Iowa.

"I remember I used to wonder when I heard that it would be impossible to keep the milk here as we did at home. Now I have learned that it is indeed impossible because of the heat here in the summertime . . . It's difficult, too, to preserve the butter. One must pour brine [salt water] over it or salt it.

The thunderstorms are so violent that one might think it was the end of the world . . . Quite often the lightning strikes down both cattle and people, damages property, and splinters sturdy oak trees into many pieces."

—quoted in *Sources in American History*

 ANALYSIS SKILL **ANALYZING PRIMARY SOURCES**

What might be some of the differences between Norway and Svendsen's new home in Iowa?

Pioneers like this family often lived in houses made of sod because there were few trees for lumber on the Plains.

Building Communities

ACADEMIC VOCABULARY
facilitate to make easier

Women were an important force in the settlement of the frontier. They joined in the hard work of farming and ranching and helped build communities out of the widely spaced farms and small towns. Their role in founding communities **facilitated** a strong voice in public affairs. Wyoming women, for example, were granted the vote in the new state's constitution, which was approved in 1869. **Annie Bidwell**, one of the founders of Chico, California, used her influence to support a variety of moral and social causes such as women's suffrage and temperance.

Many early settlers found life on their remote farms to be extremely difficult. Farmers formed communities so that they could assist one another in times of need. One of the first things that many pioneer communities did was establish a local church and school.

Children helped with many chores around the farm. Author Laura Ingalls Wilder was one of four children in a pioneer family. Wilder's books about settlers' lives on the prairie are still popular today.

READING CHECK Comparing and Contrasting
How were settlers' lives alike and different from their lives in the East?

Farmers' Political Groups

From 1860 to 1900, the U.S. population more than doubled. To feed this growing population, the number of farms tripled. With modern machines, farmers in 1900 could harvest a bushel of wheat almost 20 times faster than they could in 1830.

Farm Incomes Fall

The combination of more farms and greater productivity, however, led to overproduction. Overproduction resulted in lower prices for crops. As their incomes decreased, many farmers found it difficult to pay bills. Farmers who could not make their mortgage payments lost their farms and homes. Many of these homeless farmers became tenant farmers who worked land owned by others. By 1880 one-fourth of all farms were rented by tenants, and the number continued to grow.

The National Grange

Many farmers blamed businesspeople—wholesalers, brokers, grain buyers, and especially railroad owners—for making money at their expense. As economic conditions worsened, farmers began to follow the example of other workers. They formed associations to protect and help their interests.

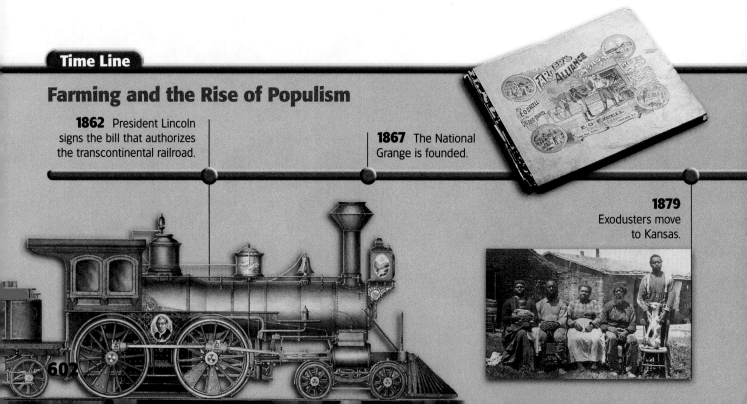

Time Line

Farming and the Rise of Populism

1862 President Lincoln signs the bill that authorizes the transcontinental railroad.

1867 The National Grange is founded.

1879 Exodusters move to Kansas.

602

One such organization was founded by Oliver Hudson Kelley, who toured the South in 1866 for the U.S. Department of Agriculture. Kelley saw firsthand how the country's farmers suffered. Afterward, Kelley and several government clerks formed the National Grange of the Patrons of Husbandry in 1867. The **National Grange** was a social and educational organization for farmers. (*Grange* is an old word for granary.) Local chapters were quickly founded, and membership grew rapidly.

The Grange campaigned for political candidates who supported farmers' goals. The organization also called for laws that regulated rates charged by railroads. The U.S. Supreme Court ruled in 1877 that the government could regulate railroads because they affected the public interest. In 1886 the Court said that the federal government could only regulate companies doing business across state lines. Rate regulation for railroad lines within states fell to the state governments.

In February 1887 Congress passed the Interstate Commerce Act, providing national regulations over trade between states and creating the Interstate Commerce Commission to ensure fair railroad rates. However, the commission lacked power to enforce its regulations.

Agricultural Supply and Demand

CONNECT TO ECONOMICS

Supply is the amount of a good that is available. *Demand* is the amount of a good that people want to buy. When supply exceeds demand, prices fall.

What happened to the price of wheat as the supply increased?

Wheat Production, 1866–1880

Wheat (in millions of bushels)

Wheat Prices, 1866–1880

Cost ($ per bushel of wheat)

W. McKINLEY.

1887 The Interstate Commerce Commission is formed to regulate railroad prices.

1892 The national Populist Party is formed.

1896 The Populist Party backs William Jennings Bryan as the Democratic presidential candidate.

ANALYSIS SKILL READING TIME LINES

How many years after the authorization of the transcontinental railroad was the Interstate Commerce Commission created?

Free Silver Debate

Money issues also caused problems for farmers. Many farmers hoped that help would come from new laws affecting the money supply.

Since 1873 the United States had been on the gold standard, meaning that all paper money had to be backed by gold in the treasury. As a result, the money supply grow more slowly than the nation's population and led to **deflation**—a decrease in the money supply and overall lower prices. One solution was to allow the unlimited coining of silver and to back paper currency with silver. This was the position of those in the Free Silver movement.

During the late 1870s, there was a great deal of support for the Free Silver movement. Many farmers began backing political candidates who favored free silver coinage. One such candidate was **William Jennings Bryan** of Nebraska.

The two major political parties, however, largely ignored the money issue. After the election of 1888, the Republican-controlled Congress passed the Sherman Silver Purchase Act. The act increased the amount of silver purchased for coinage. However, this did not help farmers as much as they had hoped.

BIOGRAPHY

William Jennings Bryan
1860–1925

William Jennings Bryan was born in Illinois but moved to Nebraska when he finished law school. He was elected Nebraska's first Democratic Congress member in 1890. Through his political campaigns and work as a newspaper editor, he became one of the best-known supporters of Populist ideas. After a dramatic speech at the 1896 Democratic National Convention, Bryan was nominated for the presidency. He was the youngest presidential candidate up to that time. Although he lost the election, he continued to be an influential speaker.

Making Inferences Why was Bryan's support of Populist ideas important?

Populist Party

To have greater power, many farmers organized to elect candidates that would help them. These political organizations became known as the Farmers' Alliances.

In the 1890 elections the Alliances were a strong political force. State and local wins raised farmers' political hopes. At a conference in Cincinnati, Ohio, in 1891, Alliance leaders met with labor and reform groups. Then, at a convention in St. Louis in February 1892, the Alliances formed a new national political party.

The new party was called the **Populist Party**, and it called for the government to own railroads and telephone and telegraph systems. It also favored the "free and unlimited coinage of silver." To gain the votes of workers, the Populists backed an eight-hour workday and limits on immigration.

The concerns of the Populists were soon put in the national spotlight. During the Panic of 1893, the U.S. economy experienced a crisis that some critics blamed on the shortage of gold. The failure of several major railroad companies also contributed to the economic problems.

The Panic of 1893 led more people to back the Populist call for economic reform. In 1896 the Republicans nominated William McKinley for president. McKinley was firmly against free coinage of silver. The Democrats nominated William Jennings Bryan, who favored free coinage.

The Populists had to decide between running their own candidate, and thus splitting the silver vote, or supporting Bryan. They decided to support Bryan. The Republicans had a well-financed campaign, and they won the election. McKinley's victory in 1896 marked the end of both the Populist Party and the Farmers' Alliances.

READING CHECK **Summarizing** Why did farmers, laborers, and reformers join to form the Populist Party?

Guthrie, Oklahoma

Oklahoma Land Rush

- The rush began at noon on April 22, 1889.
- Some witnesses said they could feel the ground shake as 50,000 people raced to claim land.
- Single women and widows could claim land on an equal basis with men.
- Many settlers were dismayed to find some people had claimed land before the rush legally began. These people were called sooners.

End of the Frontier

By 1870 only small portions of the Great Plains remained unsettled. For most of the next two decades, this land remained open range.

In March 1889, government officials announced that homesteaders could file claims on land in what is now the state of Oklahoma. This land had belonged to Creek and Seminole Indians. Within a month, about 50,000 people rushed to Oklahoma to stake their claims.

In all, settlers claimed more than 11 million acres of former Indian land in the famous Oklahoma land rush. This huge wave of pioneers was the last chapter of the westward movement. By the early 1890s, the frontier had ceased to exist in the United States.

READING CHECK Finding Main Ideas
What event signaled the closing of the frontier?

SUMMARY AND PREVIEW In this section you read about the challenges settlers faced. In the next chapter you will read about the growth of America's industrial power and how that growth affected American lives.

Section 3 Assessment

Reviewing Ideas, Terms, and People

1. **a. Describe** What groups settled in the Great Plains?
   b. Explain How did the U.S. government make lands available to western settlers?
   c. Elaborate Would you have chosen to settle on the frontier? Why or why not?
2. **a. Recall** What was the goal of the **National Grange**?
   b. Make Inferences Why did the **Populist Party** want the government to own railroads and telegraph and telephone systems?
   c. Evaluate Do you think farmers were successful in bringing about economic and political change? Explain.
3. **a. Recall** What was the Oklahoma land rush?
   b. Explain Why did the frontier cease to exist in the United States?

Critical Thinking

4. **Comparing and Contrasting** Look back over your notes about the rise of populism. Use them to explain why Populists sought the changes they did in a chart like the one below.

Change sought	Reason why

FOCUS ON WRITING

5. **Farming the Great Plains** As you read this section, take notes on the growth of farming on the Great Plains. How did farmers interact with the railroads? What changes might have been apparent to a railroad worker?

AMERICANS MOVE WEST **605**

Social Studies Skills

Comparing Migration Maps

Define the Skill

One of the best ways of using geography to learn history is by comparing maps. This skill allows you to see changes over time. It also helps you see relationships between one factor, such as population growth, and another factor, such as transportation routes or economic activities in an area.

Learn the Skill

Follow these steps to compare information on maps.

① Apply basic map skills by reading the title and studying the legend and symbols for each map.

② Note the date of each map and the area it covers. Maps compared for changes over time should include the same areas. Those used to look for relationships should have similar dates.

③ Note similarities or differences. Closely examine and compare each map's patterns and symbols.

④ Apply critical thinking skills. Make generalizations and draw conclusions about the relationships you find.

Practice the Skill

Use the maps below to answer the following questions.

1. What present-day state was unsettled by Americans in 1850 and almost completely settled in 1890?

2. Which other two present-day states show the most settlement by Americans from 1850 to 1890?

3. Why do you think the West coast was settled before the interior of the United States?

4. According to the maps, how might rivers have shaped the settlement of the West?

Chapter Review

HOLT
History's Impact
▶ video series
Review the video to answer the closing question:
How was a cowboy's job essential to the American economy?

Visual Summary

QUICK FACTS

Use the visual summary below to help you review the main ideas of the chapter.

The American West

As settlers moved West, they came into conflict with American Indians. The U.S. government defeated Indian resistance and moved many tribes to reservations.

The completion of the transcontinental railroad in 1869 opened the West to more settlement. Gold and silver strikes also drew people hoping to get rich.

The railroads helped make the rise of the Cattle Kingdom possible. Cowboys drove huge herds of cattle from ranches to railway stations to be shipped to the East.

Farmers settled the Great Plains in large numbers. They overcame many hardships to make the Plains the breadbasket of America.

Reviewing Vocabulary, Terms, and People

1. Who was the leader of the 7th Cavalry in the Battle of the Little Bighorn?
   - **a.** Cyrus McCormick
   - **b.** Leland Stanford
   - **c.** William Jennings Bryan
   - **d.** George Armstrong Custer

2. What act gave millions of acres of federal lands to the states, which were to sell them and use those funds to build agricultural and engineering colleges?
   - **a.** Morrill Act
   - **b.** Sherman Act
   - **c.** Pacific Railway Act
   - **d.** Interstate Commerce Act

3. Which frontier woman was instrumental in supporting reform efforts in the West?
   - **a.** Sarah Winnemucca
   - **b.** Laura Ingalls Wilder
   - **c.** Annie Bidwell
   - **d.** Lucretia Mott

Comprehension and Critical Thinking

SECTION 1 *(Pages 586–592)*

4. **a. Recall** Why were many Americans eager to move to the western frontier?

   b. Analyze How did railroads and ranching change the landscape of the West?

   c. Elaborate In your opinion, which made the greatest changes to the West—mining, ranching, or railroads? Explain your answer.

SECTION 2 *(Pages 593–598)*

5. **a. Describe** What was life like for the Plains Indians before and after the arrival of large numbers of American settlers?

   b. Draw Conclusions Why did the spread of the Ghost Dance movement cause concern for U.S. officials?

   c. Elaborate What do you think about the reservation system established by the United States?

6. a. Identify What political organizations did western farmers create? Why did farmers create these organizations?

b. Analyze How did women participate in the settling of the American frontier?

c. Predict How might the end of the frontier in the United States affect the nation?

Reviewing Themes

7. Geography What geographic obstacles did miners, ranchers, and railroad workers face in the West?

8. Science and Technology What types of technology did farmers on the Great Plains use, and how did it benefit them?

Using the Internet

go.hrw.com
KEYWORD: SF7 CH18

9. Activity: Creating a Presentation Our view of the settlement of the West is heavily influenced by popular culture. Writers, painters, and illustrators provided a steady flow of words and images that sensationalized life in the American West. Later, film makers and television producers also contributed to the myth of the Wild West. "When legend becomes fact," said one actor in the classic western movie *The Man Who Shot Liberty Valance*, "print the legend." How does legend affect our view of this part of our history? Enter the activity keyword. Analyze the myths and realities of the West and the ways in which they shaped our view of that time period. Then create a visual display or PowerPoint presentation to present your research.

Reading Skills

Understanding Through Questioning *Use the Reading Skills taught in this chapter to answer the question about the reading selection below.*

> For survival, Plains Indians depended on two animals—the horse and the buffalo. The Spanish brought horses to America in the 1500s. Plains Indians learned to ride horses, and hunters used them to follow buffalo herds year-round. *(p. 594)*

10. Write two or three questions you have about the information in the passage above. Remember to use the five W's—Who? What? When? Where? and Why?

Social Studies Skills

Comparing Migration Maps *Use the Social Studies Skills taught in this chapter to answer the questions about the map below.*

11. According to the map above, for what reasons did settlers migrate to the West?

a. for mining, ranching, and farming

b. for jobs in manufacturing

c. for the homes in the major cities there

d. for the fishing industry

FOCUS ON WRITING

12. Writing Your Letter Review your notes. Then write a letter to your sister back in Ireland about your experiences on the Great Plains. Describe all the changes you have seen. Use colorful language and precise details to make your sister feel as though she were there.

DIRECTIONS: Read each question and write the letter of the best response.

1

> • Government ownership of railroads
>
> • Free and unlimited coinage of silver
>
> • An eight-hour day for industrial workers
>
> • Strict limits on foreign immigration
>
> • Election of officials who will help farmers

Which of the following intended to accomplish the changes listed above in American society?

A the Morrill Act

B the Populist Party

C the National Grange

D the Homestead Act

2 The goal of many reformers who wanted to help Native Americans in the late 1800s was to

A get Indians to adopt the ways of white people.

B return to Indians all the land that had been taken from them.

C relocate all the nations to create an American Indian state in Oklahoma.

D negotiate treaties to bring peace to the frontier.

3 What played the *most* important part in the growth of the West's population and economy between 1865 and 1900?

A the mining industry

B the Cattle Kingdom

C the Populist Party

D the railroad

4 In general, the policy of the United States government toward Native Americans in the West was to

A send the army to track them down and engage them in battle.

B move them onto reservations and open their homelands to white settlers.

C kill all the buffalo so that they could not continue their traditional way of life.

D drive them into Canada or Mexico to settle.

5 The biggest problem facing western farmers in the late 1800s was

A a scarcity of good, cheap land to farm.

B their lack of organization to achieve change.

C overproduction and low crop prices.

D the threat of attacks by Native Americans.

6 Read the following speech from Comanche chief Ten Bears and use it to answer the question below.

> *"*You said that you wanted to put us upon a reservation, to build us houses and make us medicine lodges [places of religious practice]. I do not want them. I was born upon the prairie, where the wind blew free and there was nothing to break the light of the sun. I was born where there were no enclosures and where everything drew a free breath. I want to die there and not within walls.*"*
>
> —Ten Bears, quoted in *Eyewitnesses and Others*

Document-Based Question Why does Ten Bears not want to move to a reservation?

The Industrial Age

Indiana Standards

Social Studies Standards

8.1.27 Give examples of scientific and technolgoical developments that changed cultural life in the nineteenth-century United States, such as the use of photography, growth in the use of the telegraph, the completion of the transcontinental railroad, and, the invention of the telephone.

8.4.3 Evaluate how the characteristics of a market economy have affected the economic and labor development of the United States.

8.4.5 Analyze contributions of entrepreneurs and inventors in the development of the United States economy.

8.4.6 Relate technological change and inventions to changes in labor productivity in the United States in the eighteenth and nineteenth centuries.

go.hrw.com
Indiana
KEYWORD: SF10 IN

FOCUS ON WRITING

A Business Plan You are an inventor in the late 1800s, and you want to start a business to sell your new inventions. Write a business plan for investors that will encourage them to lend you money to start your business. As you read this chapter, gather information about the new business practices that you can use to run your business. Then write your plan. Include information about what you will sell, how you will make it, and how you can avoid conflicts with the workers who make your product.

UNITED STATES

1879
Thomas Edison invents the first lightbulb.

1870

WORLD

1876
German engineer Nikolaus A. Otto perfects a gasoline-powered engine.

What You Will Learn...

In this chapter you will learn about how the United States became an industrial power in the late 1800s. A new wave of immigrants provided the labor, and the combination of industry and immigration led to increased urbanization of the country. Cities like San Francisco, shown here, began to take the shape that they still have today. In fact, much of what we know as modern America developed during this important period.

1886
Natural gas is discovered near Portland.

1886
The American Federation of Labor is formed on December 8.

1890
Congress passes the Sherman Antitrust Act.

1892
On June 29 the Homestead strike begins. Carnegie Steel Company refuses to negotiate with the union.

1880

1890

1900

1883 The island volcano of Krakatau in the Pacific Ocean erupts in one of the world's greatest natural disasters.

1889 The Eiffel Tower is built in Paris.

1898 French scientists Pierre and Marie Curie discover radium.

611

Reading Social Studies

by Kylene Beers

Focus on Themes In this chapter, you will read about the advancements in transportation and communication made during what is called the Second Industrial Revolution. You will learn about the rise of powerful corporations. You will also read about the workers who organized in the late 1800s and will see what happened as unions began demanding better treatment for workers. Throughout the chapter, you will see how **society** was affected by the changing **economy**.

Organization of Facts and Information

Focus on Reading How are clothes organized in a department store? How are files arranged in a file cabinet? Clear organization helps us find the product we need, and it also helps us find facts and information.

Understanding Structural Patterns Writers use structural patterns to organize information in sentences or paragraphs. What's a structural pattern? It's simply a way of organizing information. Learning to recognize those patterns will make it easier for you to read and understand social studies texts.

Patterns of Organization		
Pattern	**Clue Words**	**Graphic Organizer**
Cause-effect shows how one thing leads to another.	as a result, therefore, because, this led to	Cause → Effect → Effect, Effect
Chronological order shows the sequence of events or actions.	after, before, first, then, not long after, finally	First → Next → Last
Comparison-contrast points out similarities and/or differences.	although, but, however, on the other hand, similarly, also	Differences / Similarities
Listing presents information in categories such as size, location, or importance.	also, most important, for example, in fact	Category • Fact • Fact • Fact

To use text structure to improve your understanding, follow these steps:

1. Look for the main idea of the passage you are reading.
2. Then look for clues that signal a specific pattern.
3. Look for other important ideas and think about how the ideas connect. Is there any obvious pattern?
4. Use a graphic organizer to map the relationships among the facts and details.

You Try It!

The following passages are from the chapter you are about to read. As you read each set of sentences, ask yourself what structural pattern the writer used to organize the information.

Recognizing Structural Patterns

(A) Great advances in communication technologies took place in the late 1800s. By 1861, telegraph wires connected the East and West coasts. Five years later, a telegraph cable on the floor of the Atlantic Ocean connected the United States and Great Britain. *(p. 617)*

(B) Many business leaders justified their business methods through their belief in social Darwinism . . . Other business leaders, however, believed that the rich had a duty to aid the poor. *(p. 621)*

(C) During the late 1800s, several factors led to a decline in the quality of working conditions. Machines run by unskilled workers were eliminating the jobs of many skilled craftspeople. These low-paid workers could be replaced easily. *(p. 624)*

After you read the passages, answer the questions below:

1. Reread passage A. What structural pattern did the writer use to organize this information? How can you tell?

2. Reread passage B. What structural pattern did the writer use to organize this information? How can you tell? Why do you think the writer chose this pattern?

3. Reread passage C. What structural pattern did the writer use to organize this information? How can you tell? Why do you think the writer chose this pattern?

As you read Chapter 19, think about the organization of the ideas. Ask yourself why the writer chose to organize the information in this way.

Key Terms and People

Chapter 19

Section 1
Second Industrial Revolution *(p. 615)*
Bessemer process *(p. 615)*
Thomas Edison *(p. 616)*
patents *(p. 616)*
Alexander Graham Bell *(p. 617)*
Henry Ford *(p. 617)*
Wilbur and Orville Wright *(p. 618)*

Section 2
corporations *(p. 619)*
Andrew Carnegie *(p. 620)*
vertical integration *(p. 620)*
John D. Rockefeller *(p. 620)*
horizontal integration *(p. 621)*
trust *(p. 621)*
Leland Stanford *(p. 621)*
social Darwinism *(p. 621)*
monopoly *(p. 622)*
Sherman Antitrust Act *(p. 622)*

Section 3
Frederick W. Taylor *(p. 624)*
Knights of Labor *(p. 625)*
Terence V. Powderly *(p. 625)*
American Federation of Labor *(p. 625)*
Samuel Gompers *(p. 625)*
collective bargaining *(p. 626)*
Mary Harris Jones *(p. 626)*
Haymarket Riot *(p. 626)*
Homestead strike *(p. 627)*
Pullman strike *(p. 627)*

Academic Vocabulary

In this chapter, you will learn the following academic words:
implement *(p. 617)*
acquire *(p. 620)*

The Second Industrial Revolution

What You Will Learn...

Main Ideas

1. Breakthroughs in steel processing led to a boom in railroad construction.
2. Advances in the use of oil and electricity improved communications and transportation.
3. A rush of inventions changed Americans' lives.

The Big Idea

The Second Industrial Revolution led to new sources of power and advances in transportation and communication.

Key Terms and People

Second Industrial Revolution, *p. 615*
Bessemer process, *p. 615*
Thomas Edison, *p. 616*
patents, *p. 616*
Alexander Graham Bell, *p. 617*
Henry Ford, *p. 617*
Wilbur and Orville Wright, *p. 618*

TAKING NOTES As you read this section, take notes on the inventors of the Second Industrial Revolution. Organize your notes in a table like the one below.

Inventor

IN 8.1.27, 8.3.6, 8.3.8, 8.4.1, 8.4.3, 8.4.5

If YOU were there...

You live in a small town but are visiting an aunt in the city in the 1890s. You are amazed when your aunt pushes a button on the wall to turn on electric lights. At home you still use kerosene lamps. You hear a clatter outside and see an electric streetcar traveling down the street. You are shocked when a telephone rings, and your aunt speaks to someone miles away!

Which of these inventions would you find most amazing?

BUILDING BACKGROUND The first Industrial Revolution in America began in the early 1800s. It changed the way products were made, from handwork to machines. It moved the workplace from cottages to factories. Later, it brought advances in transportation and communication. The Second Industrial Revolution built on these changes, introducing new technology and new sources of power.

Breakthroughs in Steel Processing

Technological advances were important to the **Second Industrial Revolution**, a period of rapid growth in U.S. manufacturing in the late 1800s. By the mid-1890s, the United States had become the world's industrial leader.

The Steel Industry

Some of the most important advances in technology happened in the steel industry. Steel is iron that has been made stronger by heat and the addition of other metals. In the mid-1850s Henry Bessemer invented the **Bessemer process**, a way to manufacture steel quickly and cheaply by blasting hot air through melted iron to quickly remove impurities. Before, turning several tons of iron ore into steel took a day or more. The Bessemer process took only 10 to 20 minutes.

The Bessemer process helped increase steel production. U.S. mills had produced 77,000 tons of steel in 1870. By 1879 production had risen to more than 1 million tons in one year.

Riding the Rails

As steel dropped in price, so did the cost of building railroads. Companies built thousands of miles of new steel track. The design of elegant passenger and sleeping cars improved passenger service. Manufacturers and farmers sent products to market faster than ever by rail in newly invented refrigerated shipping cars. Cities where major rail lines crossed, such as Chicago, grew rapidly. Railroads also increased western growth by offering free tickets to settlers. Finally, as rail travel and shipping increased, railroads and related industries began employing more people.

READING CHECK **Identifying Cause and Effect** How did steel processing change in the 1850s, and how did this affect the United States?

Factors Affecting Industrial Growth

- Greater ability to use natural resources
- A growing population
- Transportation advances
- Rising immigration
- Inventions and innovations
- Increasing business investment
- Government policies assisting business, such as protective tariffs

Homestead Steel Mill

Steel mills like this one in Homestead, Pennsylvania, were the center of the new steel industry that led to advancements in rail travel. Workers used the Bessemer process to make steel more quickly.

How do you think mills like this one affected the surrounding area?

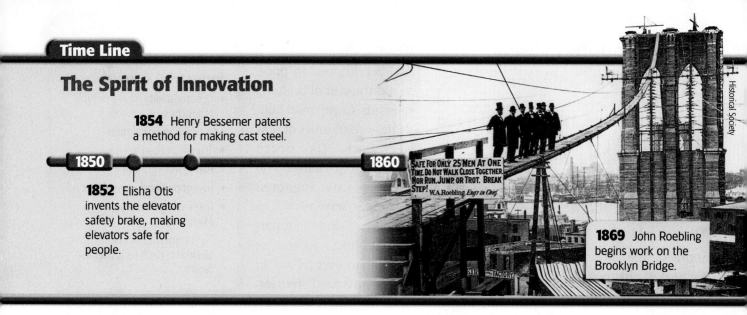

The Spirit of Innovation

1854 Henry Bessemer patents a method for making cast steel.

1850

1860

1852 Elisha Otis invents the elevator safety brake, making elevators safe for people.

SAFE FOR ONLY 25 MEN AT ONE TIME. DO NOT WALK CLOSE TOGETHER, NOR RUN, JUMP, OR TROT. BREAK STEP! W.A. Roebling, *Eng'r in Chief*

1869 John Roebling begins work on the Brooklyn Bridge.

Historical Society

FOCUS ON INDIANA

Natural gas also helped fuel the steel industry and light cities and homes. The Trenton Field in western Indiana, discovered in 1886, was the largest know field of natural gas at the time. Natural gas wells in the region contributed to the rise of a "gas belt" in the state, but overuse of the field resulted in diminishing output by the early 1900s.

FOCUS ON READING

How does this paragraph show the cause and effect structure?

Use of Oil and Electricity

The Second Industrial Revolution was characterized by dramatic developments in the use and distribution of oil and electricity. These power sources fueled other changes.

Oil as a Power Source

An important technological breakthrough in the late 1800s was the use of petroleum, or oil, as a power source. People had known about oil for many years but had discovered few ways to use it. However, in the 1850s, chemists invented a way to convert crude, or unprocessed, oil into a fuel called kerosene. Kerosene could be used for cooking, heating, and lighting. Suddenly there was a demand for oil.

As demand grew, people began searching for a reliable source for oil. In 1859 Edwin L. Drake proved that it was possible to pump crude oil from the ground. Soon, wildcatters, or oil prospectors, drilled for oil in Ohio, Pennsylvania, and West Virginia. Oil became a big business as these states began producing millions of barrels per year. Oil companies built refineries to turn the crude oil into finished products like kerosene. One oil company supervisor referred to oil workers as "men who are supplying light for the world."

Electricity Spreads

In addition to kerosene, electricity became a critical source of light and power during the Second Industrial Revolution. The possible uses of electricity interested inventors like **Thomas Edison**. His research center in Menlo Park, New Jersey, was called an invention factory. Edison explained his practical approach to science.

" I do not regard myself as a pure scientist, as so many persons have insisted that I am. I do not search for the laws of nature ...for the purpose of learning truth. I am only a professional inventor ...with the object [goal] of inventing that which will have commercial utility [use]. "

—Thomas Edison, quoted in *American Made*, by Harold C. Livesay

Edison eventually held more than 1,000 **patents**, exclusive rights to make or sell inventions. Patents allowed inventors to protect their inventions from being manufactured by others.

In 1878 Edison announced that he would soon invent a practical electric light. By the end of 1879 Edison and his team of inventors had created the electric lightbulb. The public was excited. However, Edison had a problem. At the time, few homes or businesses could get electricity. Edison therefore built a power plant that began supplying electricity to dozens of New York City buildings in

1872 Elijah McCoy receives the patent for his device that oiled machine engines.

1876 Alexander Graham Bell invents the telephone.

1879 Thomas Edison creates a durable electric lightbulb.

1887 Harriet Strong receives a patent for her advances in dam and reservoir construction.

1893 J. Frank and Charles Duryea successfully test their first gasoline-powered automobile.

1870

1880

1890

September 1882. The *New York Times* reported that with electric lighting in the newspaper offices, "it seemed almost like writing by daylight." However, Edison's equipment could not send electricity over long distances. As a result, his power company, Edison Electric, provided electricity mainly to central cities.

In the late 1880s, George Westinghouse built a power system that could send electricity across many miles. As Edison and Westinghouse competed, the use of electricity spread rapidly in the nation's cities. After a while, electricity soon lit homes and businesses and powered city factories. Electricity also was used to power streetcars in cities across the nation.

READING CHECK Drawing Conclusions

Why did people begin to pump oil from the ground?

Rush of Inventions

In the late 1800s, inventors focused on finding solutions to practical problems. Communication and transportation took the lead.

Advances in Communication

Great advances in communication technologies took place in the late 1800s. By 1861, telegraph wires connected the East and West coasts. Five years later, a telegraph cable on the floor of the Atlantic Ocean connected the United States and Great Britain.

However, the telegraph carried only written messages and was difficult for untrained people to use. These problems were solved in March 1876, when inventor **Alexander Graham Bell** patented the telephone. Bell was a Scottish-born speech teacher who studied the science of sound. He called the telephone a "talking telegraph."

Telephone companies raced to lay thousands of miles of phone lines. By 1880 there were about 55,000 telephones in the United States, and by 1900 there were almost 1.5 million.

Automobiles and Planes

In 1876 a German engineer invented an engine powered by gasoline, another fuel made from oil. In 1893 Charles and J. Frank Duryea used a gasoline engine to build the first practical motorcar in the United States. By the early 1900s, thousands of cars were being built in the United States.

At first, only the wealthy could buy these early cars. **Henry Ford** introduced the Model T in 1908. Ford was the first to **implement** the moving assembly line in manufacturing, a process that greatly reduced the cost of building a product, thus making cars more affordable.

THE IMPACT TODAY

AT&T Corporation is a direct descendant of Bell's original company. AT&T pioneered the use of telephone cables across the oceans, satellite communications, and a radar system for the U.S. Defense Department.

ACADEMIC VOCABULARY

implement to put in place

THE INDUSTRIAL AGE **617**

The Spirit of Innovation

1903 Orville Wright makes the first flight in a motorized airplane.

1893 George Ferris displays the first Ferris wheel at the World's Columbian Exposition in Chicago.

1900

ANALYSIS SKILL **READING TIME LINES**

When was the telephone invented?

New engine technology helped make another breakthrough in transportation possible—air flight. Brothers **Wilbur and Orville Wright** built a lightweight airplane that used a small, gas-powered engine. In Kitty Hawk, North Carolina, Orville Wright made the first piloted flight in a gas-powered plane on December 17, 1903. This invention would change the way that many Americans traveled in the future and would increase the demand for oil production.

READING CHECK **Comparing** What new inventions excited the public in the 1800s, and how were they used?

SUMMARY AND PREVIEW The Second Industrial Revolution led to advances in energy sources, communication, and transportation. In the next section you will learn about the growth of big business.

go.hrw.com
Online Quiz
KEYWORD: SF7 HP19

Section 1 Assessment

Reviewing Ideas, Terms, and People

1. **a. Describe** What was the **Bessemer process**?
   b. Summarize How did improvements to railroads affect the economy and transportation in the United States?
   c. Elaborate What do you think was the most important effect of the Bessemer process? Why?

2. **a. Identify** What is kerosene, and for what could it be used?
   b. Explain What problem did **Thomas Edison** face regarding the use of electricity, and how did he solve it?

3. **a. Recall** What contribution did **Wilbur and Orville Wright** make to transportation?
   b. Draw Conclusions How did **Alexander Graham Bell**'s invention improve life in the United States?
   c. Elaborate Why do you think there was a rush of inventions in the late 1800s?

Critical Thinking

4. **Analyzing** Look over your notes on inventors. Use them to complete a table like the one below about inventors and their inventions.

Inventor	Invention

FOCUS ON WRITING

5. **Information on a Product** In your notes, list what kinds of new products became available at this time. What do you think would be a good thing to make and sell during the late 1800s?

Big Business

If YOU were there...

It is 1895, and your town is home to a large corporation. The company's founder and owner, a wealthy man, lives in a mansion on a hill. He is a fair employer but not especially generous. Many townspeople work in his factory. You and other town leaders feel that he should contribute more to local charities and community organizations.

How could this business leader help the town more?

> **BUILDING BACKGROUND** Advanced technology along with the use of oil and electric power helped American businesses grow. Soon the shape of the American economy changed. Some companies grew so large that they began to dominate entire industries.

Dominance of Big Business

In the late 1800s many entrepreneurs formed their businesses as **corporations**, or businesses that sell portions of ownership called stock shares. The leaders of these corporations were some of the most widely respected members of American society in the late 1800s. Political leaders praised prosperous businesspeople as examples of American hard work, talent, and success.

New sales techniques like those taught by John H. Patterson helped change business practices.

What You Will Learn...

Main Ideas

1. The rise of corporations and powerful business leaders led to the dominance of big business in the United States.
2. People and the government began to question the methods of big business.

The Big Idea

The growth of big business in the late 1800s led to the creation of monopolies.

Key Terms and People

corporations, *p. 619*
Andrew Carnegie, *p. 620*
vertical integration, *p. 620*
John D. Rockefeller, *p. 620*
horizontal integration, *p. 621*
trust, *p. 621*
Leland Stanford, *p. 621*
social Darwinism, *p. 621*
monopoly, *p. 622*
Sherman Antitrust Act, *p. 622*

TAKING NOTES As you read this section, take notes on the new business practices you learn about. Keep them organized in a chart like the one below.

New Business Practice

 8.2.4, 8.4.2, 8.4.3, 8.4.4, 8.4.5

Corporations Generate Wealth

Successful corporations reward not only the people who found them but also investors who hold stock. Stockholders in a corporation typically get a percentage of profits based on the amount of stock they own. Although stockholders actually own the corporation, they do not run its day-to-day business. Instead, they elect a board of directors that chooses the corporation's main leaders, such as the president.

Corporations provided several important advantages over earlier business forms. Stockholders in a corporation are not responsible for business debts. If a corporation fails financially, the stockholders lose only the money that they invested. Stockholders are also usually free to sell their stock to whomever they want, whenever they want. As a result, corporations encouraged more investment in businesses. By 1900 more than 100 million shares per year were being traded on the New York Stock Exchange.

Business Leaders

Countless business leaders became wealthy, powerful, and famous because of the business boom. **Andrew Carnegie** was one of the most admired businesspeople of the time. Born in Scotland, Carnegie came to the United States as a poor immigrant. As a teenager he took a job with a railroad company and quickly worked his way up to the position of railroad superintendent.

In 1873 he focused his efforts on steelmaking. Carnegie expanded his business by buying out competitors when steel prices were low. By 1901 Carnegie's mills were producing more steel than all of Great Britain's mills combined. Carnegie's businesses succeeded largely through **vertical integration**, or ownership of businesses involved in each step of a manufacturing process. For example, to lower production costs, Carnegie **acquired** the iron ore mines, coalfields, and railroads needed to supply and support his steel mills.

John D. Rockefeller was also successful in consolidating, or combining, businesses. By age 21, while a partner in a wholesale business, he decided to start an oil-refining company. In only 10 years Rockefeller's Standard Oil Company was the country's largest oil refiner. Like Carnegie, Rockefeller used ver-

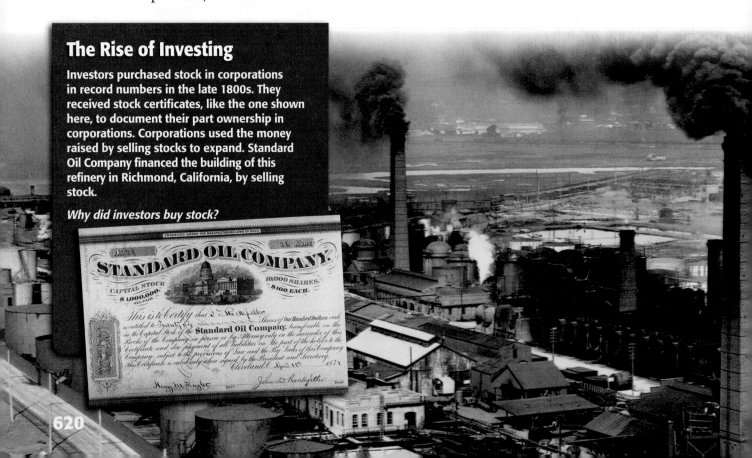

The Rise of Investing

Investors purchased stock in corporations in record numbers in the late 1800s. They received stock certificates, like the one shown here, to document their part ownership in corporations. Corporations used the money raised by selling stocks to expand. Standard Oil Company financed the building of this refinery in Richmond, California, by selling stock.

Why did investors buy stock?

POLITICAL CARTOON
Trusts

The wealth and size of trusts such as Standard Oil made many Americans fear the influence of business leaders over government.

What do you think the smokestacks on the Capitol building represent?

What does the position of the White House suggest?

ANALYSIS SKILL **ANALYZING PRIMARY SOURCES**

How does the cartoonist show Rockefeller's power?

tical integration. For example, the company controlled most of the pipelines it used.

Rockefeller's company also developed **horizontal integration**, or owning all businesses in a certain field. By 1880 Rockefeller's companies controlled about 90 percent of the oil refining business in the United States. Rockefeller also formed a **trust**, a legal arrangement grouping together a number of companies under a single board of directors. To earn more money, trusts often tried to get rid of competition and to control production.

Leland Stanford was another important business leader of the late 1800s. He made a fortune selling equipment to miners. While governor of California, he became one of the founders of the state's Central Pacific railroad. Stanford also founded Stanford University.

Late in life, Stanford argued that industries should be owned and managed cooperatively by workers. He believed this would be the fulfillment of democracy.

READING CHECK **Comparing and Contrasting**
Why did Andrew Carnegie use vertical integration?

Questioning the Methods of Big Business

By the late 1800s, people and the government were becoming uncomfortable with child labor, low wages, and poor working conditions. They began to view big business as a problem.

Social Darwinism

Many business leaders justified their business methods through their belief in **social Darwinism**, a view of society based on scientist Charles Darwin's theory of natural selection. Social Darwinists thought that Darwin's "survival of the fittest" theory decided which human beings would succeed in business and in life in general.

Other business leaders, however, believed that the rich had a duty to aid the poor. These leaders tried to help the less fortunate through philanthropy, or giving money to charities. Carnegie, Rockefeller, Stanford, and other business leaders gave away large sums. Carnegie gave away more than $350 million to charities, about $60 million of which went to fund public libraries to expand access to books. By the late 1800s, various charities had received millions of dollars from philanthropists.

The Antitrust Movement

Critics of big business said that many business leaders earned their fortunes through unfair business practices. These criticisms grew stronger in the 1880s as corporations became more powerful. Large corporations often used their size and strength to drive smaller competitors out of business. Carnegie and Rockefeller, for example, pressured railroads to charge their companies lower shipping rates. Powerful trusts also arranged to sell goods and services below market value. Smaller competitors went out of business trying to match those prices. Then the trusts raised prices again.

Some people became concerned when a trust gained a **monopoly**, or total ownership of a product or service. Critics argued that monopolies reduced necessary competition. They believed competition in a free market economy kept prices low and the quality of goods and services high.

Some Americans also worried about the political power of wealthy trusts. Many citizens and small businesses wanted the government to help control monopolies and trusts. People who favored trusts responded that trusts were more efficient and gave the consumer dependable products or services.

Many members of Congress favored big business. However, elected officials could not ignore the concerns of voters. In July 1890 Congress passed the **Sherman Antitrust Act**, a law that made it illegal to create monopolies or trusts that restrained trade. It stated that any "attempt to monopolize . . . any part of the trade or commerce among the several States" was a crime. However, the act did not clearly define a trust in legal terms. The antitrust laws were therefore difficult to enforce. Corporations and trusts kept growing in size and power.

READING CHECK **Analyzing** How did concerns about trusts lead to the Sherman Antitrust Act?

SUMMARY AND PREVIEW In the late 1800s some corporations became monopolies that dominated industries such as oil. In the next section you will learn about how industrial workers organized to improve working conditions.

Section 2 Assessment

Reviewing Ideas, Terms, and People

1. **a. Identify** What are **horizontal** and **vertical integration**?
   b. Explain What are the benefits of investing in **corporations**?
   c. Evaluate What do you think about the business methods of **Carnegie, Rockefeller,** and **Stanford**?
2. **a. Describe** What is **social Darwinism**?
   b. Summarize What concerns did critics of big business have regarding **trusts**?
   c. Evaluate Was the **Sherman Antitrust Act** successful? Why or why not?

Critical Thinking

3. **Contrasting** Look back over your notes about new business practices. Find examples of the new business practices. Use them to complete a graphic organizer like the one below.

New Practices	Example

FOCUS ON WRITING

4. **Gathering Information on Business** Look back over your notes and determine what new practices helped businesses expand during this time. Which practices could you use to start your business? Where would you try to sell your product?

Andrew Carnegie, John D. Rockefeller, and Leland Stanford

How would you go about building an industry?

Andrew Carnegie (1835–1919) Born in Scotland, Carnegie rose to become a multibillionaire in the steel industry. He brought new technologies to his steel mills and made them extremely efficient. In 1901 he sold Carnegie Steel Company for $250 billion, making him the richest man in the world.

John D. Rockefeller (1839–1937) Rockefeller got his start in the oil business in Cleveland, Ohio. Rockefeller's Standard Oil Company quickly bought out its competitors throughout the United States. To better control oil production and delivery, Rockefeller also bought railroad rights, terminals, and pipelines.

Leland Stanford (1825–1893) Leland Stanford was born to a New York farming family that sent him to excellent private schools. After practicing law in Wisconsin, he made his career in California. Stanford was instrumental in building the western section of the transcontinental railroad. He then plunged into politics, serving one term as governor. His political connections helped him obtain huge state land grants and other benefits for his railroad companies. As president of Central Pacific and Southern Pacific, he oversaw the laying of thousands of miles of track throughout the West.

Why are they so important? Carnegie, Rockefeller, and Stanford helped make America the world's greatest industrial power by the end of the 1800s. They built giant industries that made goods cheaply by keeping workers' wages low. They also engaged in ruthless business practices to defeat their competition and create monopolies. The Sherman Antitrust Act was passed in reaction to the Standard Oil monopoly. Later in life, all three men became philanthropists, people devoted to charity work. Rockefeller's philanthropies gave out $500 million in his lifetime. Carnegie spent $350 million, funding educational grants, concert halls, and nearly 3,000 public libraries. Stanford founded Stanford University in 1884.

Finding Main Ideas
Why are these three men important figures in U.S. history?

Carnegie

Rockefeller   Stanford

Industrial Workers

If YOU were there...

You run a button machine in a clothing factory in the 1890s. You work from 7:00 in the morning until 6:00 at night, every day except Sunday. Your only break is 15 minutes for lunch. Now you hear about a movement to start a workers' union to bargain with your employer. Union members will ask for an eight-hour workday. But you think your employer might fire you if you join.

Would you join the union?

BUILDING BACKGROUND The rise of corporations and the establishment of monopolies gave big business a great deal of power. An antitrust movement arose to try to limit the power of trusts. Workers themselves began to organize and take action against bad working conditions and other problems.

Maximizing Profits and Efficiency

During the late 1800s, several factors led to a decline in the quality of working conditions. Machines run by unskilled workers were eliminating the jobs of many skilled craftspeople. These low-paid workers could be replaced easily. Factories began to focus on specialization, or workers repeating a single step again and again. Specialization brought costs down and caused production to rise. But it also made workers tired, bored, and more likely to be injured. Specialization allowed for Henry Ford's idea of a moving assembly line to speed production. Ford's use of the moving assembly line allowed automobiles to be made more quickly and cheaply. Automobiles soon became available to a wider segment of the population than ever before.

In 1909 **Frederick W. Taylor**, an efficiency engineer, published a popular book called *The Principles of Scientific Management*. He encouraged managers to view workers as interchangeable parts of the production process. In factories, managers influenced by Taylor paid less attention to working conditions. Injuries increased, and as conditions grew worse, workers looked for ways to bring about change.

READING CHECK Identifying Cause and Effect Why did companies begin to use scientific management, and how did it affect workers?

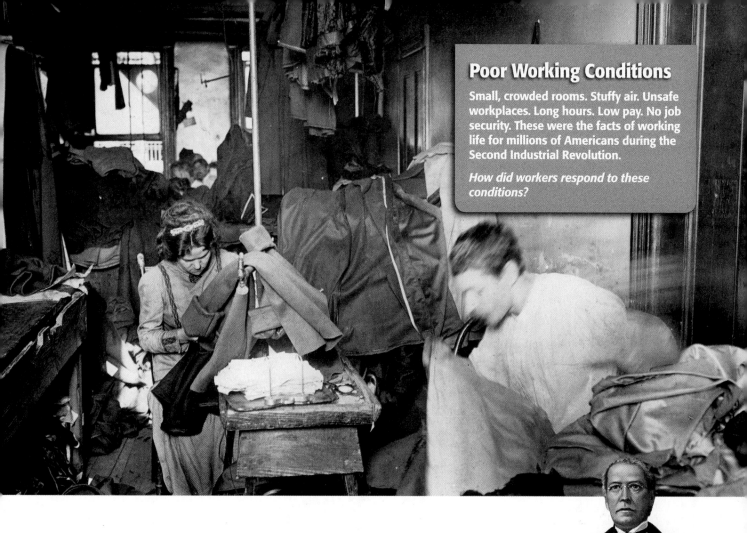

Workers Organize

Workers formed labor unions to get better wages and working conditions for all workers in a factory or industry. The first national labor union, the **Knights of Labor**, was founded in the 1870s. It pushed for an eight-hour workday, equal pay for equal work, and an end to child labor. Union members also wanted the government to regulate trusts. Unlike most unions at the time, the Knights included both skilled and unskilled workers. The Knights of Labor was originally organized much like a secret society. In 1879 **Terence V. Powderly** became leader of the Knights. He ended all secrecy, creating the first truly national labor union in the United States.

Another early labor union was the **American Federation of Labor (AFL)**, led by **Samuel Gompers**. Unlike the Knights, the American Federation of Labor organized individual national unions, such as the mineworkers' and steelworkers' unions. The AFL

BIOGRAPHY

Samuel Gompers
1850–1924

Samuel Gompers was a Jewish immigrant born in London. He came to the United States with his parents in 1863 at age 13. He worked as a cigar maker and joined a local union, eventually becoming its president. The Cigarmakers Union was reorganized and later joined the American Federation of Labor. Gompers became the AFL's first president and remained so, except for the year 1895, until his death. He campaigned for basic trade-union rights, such as the right to picket and to organize boycotts and strikes. His efforts on behalf of workers helped organized labor to gain respect.

Summarizing How did Samuel Gompers help the labor-union movement?

Interactive Map

Major Labor Strikes, Late 1800s

1 Haymarket Riot In May 1886 the Haymarket Riot erupted between protesters and police in Chicago. It resulted in the decline of the Knights of Labor.

2 Homestead Strike In 1892 a strike occurred at Carnegie Steel Company in Homestead, Pennsylvania. The resulting fight left workers and Pinkerton guards dead.

3 Colorado Miners' Strike In the summer of 1893, gold miners at Cripple Creek, Colorado, went on strike for higher wages and a shorter workday.

4 Pullman Strike The Pullman strike of 1894 began with workers who made Pullman train cars. It soon spread to workers who worked on trains pulling the sleeper cars.

5 California Railroad Strike In 1894 railroad workers in Oakland went on strike in the Bay Area's first major strike. Supporting Chicago Pullman workers, they halted passenger, freight, and mail trains for months.

Union Membership, 1880–1900

(Haymarket Riot) (Pullman Strike)

Number of workers (in thousands)

- Knights of Labor
- American Railway Union
- AFL (Organized in 1886)

ANALYSIS SKILL **ANALYZING INFORMATION**

go.hrw.com
Interactive Map
KEYWORD: SF7 CH19

How did conflicts between striking workers and authorities affect union membership?

In 1955 the AFL merged with the Congress of Industrial Organizations to become the AFL-CIO. Today the organization has more than 10 million members.

also limited its membership to skilled workers. This gave the union great bargaining power but left out most workers. The AFL tried to get better wages, hours, and working conditions for laborers. By 1890 the AFL's membership was larger than that of the Knights. With **collective bargaining**—all workers acting collectively, or together—workers had a much greater chance of success in negotiating with management. Most employers opposed collective bargaining. One company president said, "I shall never give in. I would rather go out of business."

Many women took active roles in unions. For example, **Mary Harris Jones**, an Irish immigrant, worked for better conditions for miners. A fiery speaker, she organized strikes and helped educate workers.

READING CHECK **Contrasting** How did the Knights of Labor and the AFL differ?

Labor Strikes

By the late 1800s, other unions were gaining strength. Major workers' strikes swept the country and included miners in Colorado, steel workers in Pennsylvania, and railroad workers in Illinois and California. The first major labor strike began in 1886 in Chicago.

In May 1886, thousands of union members in Chicago went on strike because they wanted an eight-hour workday. Two strikers were killed in a fight with police. The next night, workers met at Haymarket Square to protest the killings. In what became known as the **Haymarket Riot**, someone threw a bomb that wounded many police officers and killed eight. The police fired into the crowd, killing several people and wounding 100 others.

Eight people, some of whom were not at the riot, were arrested and convicted of conspiracy. One of them had a Knights of Labor membership card. Though Knights leadership had not supported the strike, several local chapters had. Membership in the Knights fell quickly.

Sometimes, business owners succeeded in breaking up unions. In 1892 a violent strike called the **Homestead strike** took place at Andrew Carnegie's Homestead steel factory in Pennsylvania. Union members there protested a plan to buy new machinery and cut jobs. The company refused to negotiate with the union and locked workers out of the plant, hiring strike breakers to perform their jobs. The workers responded by seizing control of the plant. Gunfire erupted on July 6, when Pinkerton detectives hired by the company tried to enter the plant. A fierce battle raged for 14 hours, leaving 16 people dead. The governor called out the state militia to restore order. Continuing for four more months, the union was eventually defeated.

Another major strike happened at George Pullman's Pullman Palace Car Company in the company town of Pullman, Illinois. Most of the company workers lived there, paying high rents. During a financial depression that began in 1893, Pullman laid off about half of the workers and cut pay for those that were left, without lowering their rents. On May 11, 1894, workers began the **Pullman strike**, which stopped traffic on many railroad lines until federal courts ordered the workers to return to their jobs. President Grover Cleveland sent federal troops to Chicago to stop the strike. Such defeats seriously damaged the labor movement for years.

READING CHECK **Analyzing** What were the effects of early major strikes on workers?

SUMMARY AND PREVIEW Workers formed unions to fight for better conditions and to keep their jobs. In the next section, you will learn about a new wave of immigrants in the late 1800s.

Section 3 Assessment

Reviewing Ideas, Terms, and People

1. **a. Recall** Why did conditions in factories begin to decline?
   b. Draw Conclusions How were workers affected by specialization and scientific management?
   c. Evaluate Do you think scientific management made businesses more successful? Explain.
2. **a. Identify** What role did **Mary Harris Jones** play in the labor movement?
   b. Analyze Why did workers demand **collective bargaining**, and why did business owners oppose it?
   c. Elaborate Do you think the demands made by labor unions were reasonable? Explain your answer.
3. **a. Describe** What major labor strikes took place in the late 1800s?
   b. Evaluate Do you think President Cleveland was right to use federal troops to end the **Pullman strike**? Explain.

Critical Thinking

4. **Analyzing** Review your notes about the problems workers faced. Use them to complete a table like the one below about how workers tried to solve the problems they faced.

Problem	Solution

FOCUS ON WRITING

5. **Taking Notes on Working Conditions** In your notebook, list some reasons why industrial workers were unhappy with working conditions. Can you think of ways to run your business so that you can avoid the problem of strikes?

THE INDUSTRIAL AGE **627**

Analyzing Costs and Benefits

Define the Skill

Everything you do has both costs and benefits connected to it. *Benefits* are things that you gain from something. *Costs* are what you give up to obtain benefits. For example, if you buy a video game, the benefits of your action include the game itself and the enjoyment of playing it. The most clear cost is what you pay for the game. However, there are other costs that do not involve money. One is the time you spend playing the game. This is a cost because you give up something else, such as doing your homework or watching a TV show, when you choose to play the game.

The ability to analyze costs and benefits is a valuable life skill as well as a useful tool in the study of history. Weighing an action's benefits against its costs can help you decide whether or not to take it.

Learn the Skill

Analyzing the costs and benefits of historical events will help you to better understand and evaluate them. Follow these guidelines to do a cost-benefit analysis of an action or decision in history.

1. First determine what the action or decision was trying to accomplish. This step is needed in order to determine which of its effects were benefits and which were costs.

2. Then look for the positive or successful results of the action or decision. These are its benefits.

3. Consider the negative or unsuccessful effects of the action or decision. Also think about what positive things would have happened if it had *not* occurred. All these things are its costs.

4. Making a chart of the costs and benefits can be useful. By comparing the list of benefits to the list of costs you can better understand the action or decision and evaluate it.

For example, you learned in Chapter 19 about the Second Industrial Revolution and its effects on the American economy. A cost-benefit analysis of the changes in American businesses might produce a chart like this one:

Benefits	Costs
New inventions made life easier.	New business methods ran smaller companies out of business.
Communication became easier with new technologies.	Workers received lower wages.
Efficient management reduced costs of products.	Strikes resulted in violence and deaths.
Workers began to organize for better conditions.	

Based on this chart, one might conclude that the Second Industrial Revolution was beneficial to the nation's economy.

Practice the Skill

Among the changes that occurred in the early 1900s was an increase in specialization and efficiency in the workplace. Use information from the chapter and the guidelines above to do a cost-benefit analysis of this development. Then write a paragraph explaining whether or not it was a wise one.

HOLT

History's Impact
▶ video series
Review the video to answer the closing question:
What advantages and disadvantages did the assembly line create? Do you think assembly lines still exist today?

Visual Summary

Use the visual summary below to help you review the main ideas of the chapter.

Inventions
- Bessemer process
- Lightbulb
- Automobile

Big Business
- Growth of corporations
- Wealthy business owners
- Antitrust movements

Labor Movement
- Knights of Labor
- American Federation of Labor
- Haymarket Riot
- Homestead Strike

Reviewing Vocabulary, Terms, and People

Identify the descriptions below with the correct term or person from the chapter.

1. Labor organization that represented both skilled and unskilled laborers and was the first national labor union in the United States

2. Inventor who patented the telephone in 1876

3. A way of making steel quickly and cheaply by blasting hot air through melted iron to quickly remove waste

4. A system of business in which one company owns businesses in each step of the manufacturing process

5. Powerful business leader who helped to found the Central Pacific Railroad

6. Union speaker who worked to better the lives of mine workers

7. A method of negotiating for better wages or working conditions in which all workers act together to ensure a better chance for success

Comprehension and Critical Thinking

SECTION 1 *(Pages 614–618)*

8. **a. Identify** What was the Second Industrial Revolution?

b. Draw Conclusions Why were advances in transportation and communication important to the Second Industrial Revolution?

c. Elaborate Which invention do you think had the greatest effect on people's lives in the late 1800s? Explain your answer.

SECTION 2 *(Pages 619–622)*

9. **a. Recall** What criticisms were made of business leaders and trusts?

b. Analyze How did the rise of corporations and powerful business leaders lead to the growth of big business?

c. Evaluate Do you think the growth of big business helped or hurt ordinary Americans? Explain your answer.

10. a. Recall What led to poor working conditions in factories during the Second Industrial Revolution?

b. Make Inferences Why did labor unions have a better chance of improving working conditions than laborers did on their own?

c. Evaluate Did the strikes of the 1880s and 1890s hurt or help the labor movement in the long run? Explain your answer.

Reviewing Themes

11. Economics How did the rise of big business affect consumers in the United States?

12. Society and Culture What changes in society were brought about by the organization of labor?

Using the Internet

go.hrw.com
KEYWORD: SF7 CH19

13. Activity: Creating a Time Line Technology in some sense has been part of human history since we began to write history. All tools are, in a sense, technology. In this chapter you read about new scientific discoveries that had positive and negative effects. Enter the activity keyword. Then choose one technological innovation mentioned in the chapter and trace its development to the present day. Create an illustrated time line to present your research.

Reading Skills

Organization of Facts and Information *Use the Reading Skills taught in this chapter to answer the question about the reading selection below.*

> Corporations provided several important advantages over earlier business forms. Stockholders in a corporation are not responsible for business debts. If a corporation fails financially, the stockholders lose only the money that they invested. Stockholders are also usually free to sell their stock to whomever they want, whenever they want. *(p. 620)*

14. By which structural pattern is the above passage organized?

a. Listing

b. Cause-effect

c. Chronological order

d. Comparison-contrast

Social Studies Skills

Analyzing Costs and Benefits *Use the Social Studies Skills taught in this chapter to answer the question below.*

15. Write two costs and two benefits of the Pullman strike from the point of view of the workers who participated.

FOCUS ON WRITING

16. Writing Your Business Plan Collect your notes and determine a good product to sell during the late 1800s. Decide which business practices you would use and which you would not. Write two to three paragraphs in which you explain why your product would sell, which business practices you can use to make your product, and how to avoid conflicts with workers. Remember to explain to the investors why your plan will work.

Standardized Test Practice

IN **8.1.27, 8.4.3, 8.4.5, 8.4.6**

DIRECTIONS: Read each question and write the letter of the best response. Use the map below to answer question 1.

1

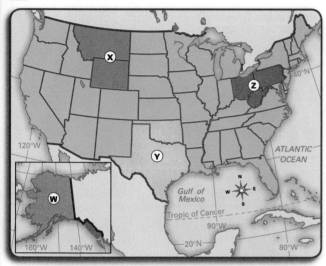

Which area on the map provided the petroleum for the oil-refining industry that arose in the United States in the mid- to late 1800s?

A the area labeled W

B the area labeled X

C the area labeled Y

D the area labeled Z

2 **The person *most* responsible for making the steel industry a big business in the United States is**

A John D. Rockefeller.

B Andrew Carnegie.

C Henry Bessemer.

D Leland Stanford.

3 **The exclusive right to make or sell an invention or product is called**

A a corporation.

B a patent.

C vertical integration.

D a trust.

4 **The development of corporations in America was helped by**

A suburbs.

B vertical integration.

C the Sherman Antitrust Act.

D social Darwinism.

5 **Which of the following was an inventor of the late 1800s?**

A Andrew Carnegie

B Thomas Edison

C Leland Stanford

D John D. Rockefeller

6 **One cause of labor strikes in the late 1800s was that workers sought**

A shorter workdays.

B vertical integration.

C social Darwinism.

D lower wages.

7 **Read the following excerpt from the 1889 book *Recent Economic Changes* and use it to answer the question below.**

❝Machinery is now recognized as essential to cheap production. Nobody can produce effectively and economically without it, and what was formerly known as domestic manfacture is now almost obsolete. But machinery is one of the most expensive of all products, and its extensive purchase and use require an amount of capital far beyond the capacity [ability] of the ordinary individual to furnish.❞

—David Wells, quoted in *Voices of the American Past*

Document-Based Question How might the large amounts of money needed for machinery affect the future of business?

Immigrants and Urban Life

IN Indiana Standards

Social Studies Standards

8.1.25 Give examples of how immigration affected American culture in the decades before and after the Civil War, including growth of industrialism in the North; religious differences; tensions between middle-class and working-lcass people, particularly in the Northeast; and intensification of cultural differences between the North and the South.

8.3.9 Analyze human and physical factors that have influenced migration and settlement patterns and relate them to the economic development of the United States.

8.4.5 Analyze contributions of entrepreneurs and inventors in the development of the United States economy.

go.hrw.com
Indiana
KEYWORD: SF10 IN

FOCUS ON WRITING

A Memo You are a writer at a television network, and you have an idea for a TV drama series set in the late 1800s. Draft a memo telling your boss about your story idea. As you read this chapter, gather information about the people, places, and events of this time period. Tell about the cast of characters, the setting, and the basic plot of your series.

UNITED STATES

1873 Olmsted designs the U.S. Capitol grounds.

1876 The Centennial Exposition opens in Philadelphia.

1870

WORLD

1878 Electric streetlights are introduced in London.

HOLT

History's Impact
► video series
Watch the video to understand the impact of immigrants on the United States.

What You Will Learn...

Millions of immigrants from Europe came through Ellis Island, shown here. They came in search of jobs, freedom, and better lives for their families. Most settled in New York, Chicago, and other growing cities. American cities began to take the shape they still have today. In this chapter you will learn about the wave of immigration that changed the United States in the late 1800s and early 1900s.

1886 Workers complete the Statue of Liberty.

1889 Jane Addams founds Hull House in Chicago.

1893 The Ferris Wheel is introduced at the 1893 Columbian Exposition in Chicago.

1906 The United States Steel Corporation founds the town of Gary, Indiana.

1880 — 1890 — 1900 — 1910

1886 Impressionists' exhibit opens in Paris.

1891 Construction begins on Russia's Trans-Siberian Railroad.

1901 The first Nobel Prizes are awarded in Stockholm, Sweden.

IMMIGRANTS AND URBAN LIFE **633**

Focus on Themes In this chapter, you will read about the changes in **society and culture** in the late 1800s. Among these changes was an increase in immigration. New immigrants to America found a society full of **economic** opportunities and hardships. Immigration and technology combined to change the way of life in cities.

Understanding Historical Fact versus Historical Fiction

Focus on Reading When you read a book like *The Red Badge of Courage* or see a movie about World War II, do you ever wonder how much is fiction and how much is fact?

Distinguishing Fact from Fiction Historical fiction gives readers a chance to meet real historical people and real historical events in the framework of a made-up story. Some of what you read in historical fiction could be verified in an encyclopedia, but other parts existed only in the author's mind until he or she put it on paper. As a good reader of history, you should know the difference between facts, which can be proved or verified, and fiction.

Notice how one reader determined which details could be verified or proved.

> That was a *woman filling her pail by the hydrant* you just bumped against. The *sinks are in the hallway,* that all the tenants may have access—and all be poisoned alike by their summer stenches. Hear the pump squeak! It is the lullaby of tenement house babes. In summer, when *a thousand thirsty throats pant for a cooling drink in this block,* it is worked in vain ...
> — From *How the Other Half Lives,* by Jacob Riis

The woman filling her pail isn't a fact I can check. He's just using her as an example of what women did.

We could probably check city records to see whether the buildings really had sinks in the hallways.

The writer is generalizing here. We probably can't prove 1,000 thirsty throats. We could find out whether the city's water pumps actually went dry in the summer. That's verifiable.

You Try It!

The following passage is from *Bread Givers* by Anzia Yezierska, a young immigrant to New York. After you read it, answer the questions below.

> Mashah [Anzia's sister] came home with stories that in rich people's homes they had silver knives and forks, separate, for each person. And new-ironed tablecloths and napkins every time they ate on them. And rich people had marble bathtubs in their own houses, with running hot and cold water all day and night long so they could take a bath any time they felt like it, instead of having to stand on a line before the public bath-house, as we had to do when we wanted a bath for the holidays. But these millionaire things were so far over our heads that they were like fairy tales.
>
> That time when Mashah had work hemming towels in an uptown house, she came home with another new-rich idea, another money-spending thing, which she said she had to have. She told us that by those Americans, everybody in the family had a toothbrush and a separate towel for himself.
>
> —Anzia Yezierska, *Bread Givers*

1. Which facts from the paragraph above can be confirmed?

2. What sources might you check to confirm some of these facts?

3. List two things from the passage that could not be confirmed.

4. Why are these two things not able to be confirmed?

As you read **Chapter 20**, notice which facts you could easily confirm.

A New Wave of Immigration

What You Will Learn...

Main Ideas

1. U.S. immigration patterns changed during the late 1800s as new immigrants arrived from Europe, Asia, and Mexico.
2. Immigrants worked hard to adjust to life in the United States.
3. Some Americans opposed immigration and worked to restrict it.

The Big Idea

A new wave of immigration in the late 1800s brought large numbers of immigrants to the United States.

Key Terms and People

old immigrants, *p. 636*
new immigrants, *p. 636*
steerage, *p. 637*
benevolent societies, *p. 639*
tenements, *p. 639*
sweatshops, *p. 640*
Chinese Exclusion Act, *p. 641*

 TAKING NOTES As you read, look for information about new immigrants' lives in the United States. Take notes on the benefits and challenges immigrants found. Use a diagram like the one below.

Benefits   Challenges

If **YOU** were there...

You live with your family on a small farm in Italy in the 1890s. You want to earn some money to help your parents, but there are not many jobs nearby. You have heard that jobs are easy to find in the booming factories of the United States. But you speak no English and know no one in America.

Would you travel to the United States in search of new opportunities?

BUILDING BACKGROUND From its beginnings, America has attracted people from many parts of the world. They came for many reasons, including land, religious freedom, and the chance to start new lives. In the late 1800s, jobs created by the rapid growth of the U.S. economy drew millions of new immigrants.

Changing Patterns of Immigration

Millions of immigrants came to the United States from northern Europe in the mid-1800s. They came mainly from Great Britain, Germany, Ireland, and the countries of Scandinavia. Except for the Irish, who were Roman Catholics, most were Protestants. Many were skilled workers. Others settled in rural areas and became farmers. By the late 1800s immigrants from northern Europe were known as **old immigrants**. A newer and larger wave of immigration—from different parts of the world—was arriving in the United States.

New Immigrants

During the 1880s more than 5 million immigrants arrived in the United States—about the same number of people as had arrived during the six decades from 1800 to 1860 combined. The majority of these **new immigrants** were from southern and eastern Europe. Thousands of Czechs, Greeks, Hungarians, Italians, Poles, Russians, and Slovaks came to the United States to find new opportunities and better lives. A young woman from Russia spoke for many of her fellow immigrants when she said she hoped "for all manner of miracles in a strange, wonderful land!"

New immigrants came from many different cultural and religious backgrounds. They included Orthodox Christians, Roman Catholics, and Jews. Some were escaping political or religious persecution. They were eager for the job opportunities created by the U.S. industrial boom of the late 1800s.

Arriving in a New Land

Immigrants usually faced a difficult journey by ship to America. Most traveled in **steerage**—an area below a ship's deck where steering mechanisms were located. Steerage tickets were inexpensive, but the cabins were hot, cramped, and foul-smelling. Many passengers were seasick for the entire journey. Some even died of diseases contracted along the way.

Once in the United States, new arrivals were processed through government-run immigration centers. The busiest center on the East Coast was Ellis Island, which opened in New York Harbor in 1892. The first immigrant processed through Ellis Island was Annie Moore Schayer, a 14 year old from Ireland. Over the next 40 years, millions of European immigrants came through Ellis Island.

At immigration centers officials interviewed and examined immigrants to decide whether to let them enter the country. People with contagious diseases or legal problems could be turned away. "There was this terrible anxiety that one of us might be rejected," remembered one immigrant traveling with his family. "And if one of us was, what would the rest of the family do?" This rarely happened, however. Less than 2 percent of the people who arrived at Ellis Island were not allowed into the country.

On the West Coast, many Chinese immigrants entered the United States through Angel Island, which opened near San Francisco in 1910. Because laws limited immigration from China, only people whose fathers were

AUTOBIOGRAPHY
An Immigrant's Story

Mary Antin and her family were Jewish. They moved from Russia to Boston in the 1890s to find religious freedom. Here, Antin writes about their journey.

> What do you think *fugitive* means here?

For sixteen days the ship was our world ... [It] pitched and rolled so that people were thrown from their berths [beds] ... All this while the seasickness lasted. Then came happy hours on deck, with fugitive sunshine, birds atop the crested waves, band music and dancing and fun ... And so suffering, fearing, brooding [worrying], rejoicing, we crept nearer and nearer to the coveted [wished for] shore, until, on a glorious May morning, six weeks after our departure from Polotzk our eyes beheld the Promised Land [the United States].

—Mary Antin, *The Promised Land*

> Antin describes a mix of emotions.

ANALYSIS SKILL   **ANALYZING PRIMARY SOURCES**

Why do you think Antin was both "fearing" and "rejoicing" during her trip?

U.S. citizens were allowed into the country. Chinese immigrants were often kept at Angel Island for weeks or months while officials investigated their families.

Mexican immigrants also came to the United States in large numbers in the late 1800s. The main processing center for immigrants from Mexico was in El Paso, Texas. Most settled in the Southwest. They found work in construction, steel mills, and mines, and on large commercial farms.

READING CHECK **Contrasting** How was the experience of immigrants at Ellis Island different from that of immigrants at Angel Island?

THE IMPACT TODAY

Almost half of all Americans today are related to someone who passed through Ellis Island. Visitors can now research their family origins at the Ellis Island Immigration Museum.

ASIA

PACIFIC OCEAN

Equator

160°W

40°N

NORTH AMERICA

San Francisco

New York City

El Paso

SOUTH AMERICA

In this photo, Japanese men and Chinese women leave the detention center on Angel Island in San Francisco Bay. Angel Island was the processing center for many immigrants from Asia.

Augustin and Maria Lozano and their two children are shown after moving from Mexico to California. Many Mexican immigrants moved into the Southwest.

Adjusting to a New Life

Once they entered the United States, immigrants began the hard work of adjusting to life in a new country. They needed to find homes and jobs. They had to learn a new language and get used to new customs. This was all part of building a new life.

Immigrant Neighborhoods

FOCUS ON READING

How could you verify the facts in this paragraph?

Many immigrants moved into neighborhoods with others from the same country. In these neighborhoods, they could speak their native language and eat foods that reminded them of home. Immigrants could also practice the customs that their families had passed down from generation to generation. An Italian immigrant remembered that in his new neighborhood, "cheeses from Italy, sausage, salamis were all hanging in the window."

In their newly adopted neighborhoods, many immigrant groups published newspapers in their own languages. They founded schools, clubs, and places of worship to help preserve their customs. In New York City, for example, Jewish immigrants founded a theater that gave performances in Yiddish—the language spoken by Jews from central and eastern Europe.

Immigrants often opened local shops and small neighborhood banks. Business owners helped new arrivals by offering credit and giving small loans. Such aid was important for newcomers because there were few commercial banks in immigrant neighborhoods. In 1904 Italian immigrant Amadeo Peter Giannini started the Bank of Italy in San Francisco. This bank later grew and became the Bank of America.

Shifting Patterns of Immigration

Where Immigrants Came From, 1840–1860: 93%, 1%, 1%, 2%, 3%

Where Immigrants Came From, 1880–1900: 61%, 31%, 6%, .5%, 1.5%

- ■ Northern and western Europe
- ■ Eastern and southern Europe
- ■ North and South America
- ■ Asia
- ■ All other areas

Swedish immigrant Swan August Swanson followed his father to Wisconsin to help with the family farm. Like many new Americans, he married within the immigrant community.

During the late 1800s the places people came from began to change. The charts above show the percentages of people who moved from different places. The total number of immigrants reached a peak in the 1880s, when about 5 million people came to the United States.

By how much did the percentage of immigrants from northern and western Europe change from 1840 to 1900?

The son of Italian immigrants, Amadeo Peter Giannini founded the Bank of Italy in San Francisco in 1904. Due to his guidance and perseverance, it became the largest privately owned bank in the world.

Some immigrant communities formed **benevolent societies**. These aid organizations offered immigrants help in cases of sickness, unemployment, or death. At that time, few national government agencies provided such aid.

Even with neighborhood support, however, immigrants often found city life difficult. Many immigrants lived in **tenements**—poorly built, overcrowded apartment buildings. One young woman in New York City described the difference between her hopes and reality in the new land:

"[I dreamed] of the golden stairs leading to the top of the American palace where father was supposed to live. [I] went 'home' to ...an ugly old tenement in the heart of the Lower East Side. There were stairs to climb but they were not golden."

– Miriam Shomer Zusner, *Yesterday: A Memoir of a Russian Jewish Family*

Immigrants worked hard to adjust to their new country. Children often learned American customs more quickly than their parents. In public schools immigrant children learned English from McGuffey's Readers—illustrated textbooks that taught reading and writing.

Finding Work

Many new immigrants had worked on farms in their homelands. Few could afford to buy land in the United States, however. Instead, they found jobs in cities, where most of the country's manufacturing took place.

Having come from rural areas, few new immigrants were skilled in modern manufacturing or industrial work. They often had no choice but to take low-paying, unskilled jobs in garment factories, steel mills, or construction. Long hours were common.

Not all industrial labor took place in large factories. Some immigrants worked for little pay in small shops or mills located in their own neighborhoods. Often associated with the clothing industry, these workplaces were called **sweatshops** because of long hours and hot, unhealthy working conditions. One young immigrant worker remembered:

"When the shirtwaists were finished at the machine … we were given scissors to cut the threads off. It wasn't heavy work, but it was monotonous [boring], because you did the same thing from seven-thirty in the morning till nine at night."

– Pauline Newman, quoted in *American Mosaic: The Immigrant Experience in the Words of Those Who Lived It,* by Joan Morrison and Charlotte Fox Zabusky

Immigrants with skills that were in demand sometimes found work outside factories and sweatshops. For example, some immigrants worked as bakers, carpenters, masons, or skilled machinists. Others saved or borrowed money to open small businesses such as laundries, barbershops, or street vending carts. New immigrants often opened the same types of businesses in which other immigrants from the same country were already succeeding. They worked hard for long hours to become successful themselves.

READING CHECK **Summarizing** How did new immigrants help themselves and others to try to make successful lives in the United States?

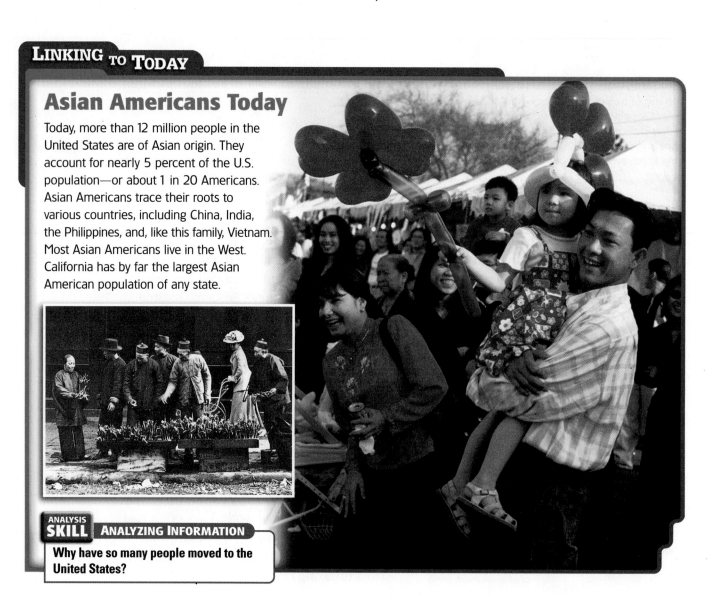

LINKING TO TODAY

Asian Americans Today

Today, more than 12 million people in the United States are of Asian origin. They account for nearly 5 percent of the U.S. population—or about 1 in 20 Americans. Asian Americans trace their roots to various countries, including China, India, the Philippines, and, like this family, Vietnam. Most Asian Americans live in the West. California has by far the largest Asian American population of any state.

ANALYSIS SKILL **ANALYZING INFORMATION**
Why have so many people moved to the United States?

Opposition to Immigration

Some Americans welcomed new immigrants. Many business leaders, for example, wanted immigrant workers who were willing to work for low pay. In general, however, anti-immigrant feelings grew along with the rise in immigration in the late 1800s. Some labor unions opposed immigration because their members believed immigrants would take jobs away from native-born Americans.

Other Americans called nativists also feared that too many new immigrants were being allowed into the country. Many nativists held racial and ethnic prejudices. They thought that the new immigrants would not learn American customs, which might harm American society.

Some nativists were violent toward immigrants. Others **advocated** laws to stop or limit immigration. For example, in 1880 about 105,000 Chinese immigrants lived in the United States. Two years later, Congress passed the **Chinese Exclusion Act**, banning Chinese people from immigrating to the United States for 10 years. This law marked the first time a nationality was banned from entering the country. Although the law violated treaties with China, Congress continued to renew the law for decades to come. In 1892 another law was passed restricting convicts, immigrants with certain diseases, and those likely to need public assistance from entering the country.

Despite such opposition immigrants continued to arrive in large numbers. They worked for low pay in factories and built buildings, highways, and railroads. Their labor helped power the continuing industrial growth of the late 1800s and early 1900s. Although they did not always achieve their dreams as quickly as they had hoped, most immigrants were still confident about the future for themselves and their families in the United States. A Russian immigrant named Abraham Hyman expressed this idea, saying, "Your feeling is that a better time is coming, if not for yourself, for your families, for your children."

READING CHECK **Analyzing** Why did nativists oppose immigration?

ACADEMIC VOCABULARY

advocate to plead in favor of

SUMMARY AND PREVIEW Immigrants helped build the nation's economy and cities, but they met resistance from some native-born Americans. In the next section you will learn about what life was like in urban America.

Section 1 Assessment

go.hrw.com
Online Quiz
KEYWORD: SF7 HP20

Reviewing Ideas, Terms, and People

1. a. **Identify** What was Ellis Island?
   b. **Contrast** What differences existed between the **old immigrants** and the **new immigrants**?
2. a. **Identify** What job opportunities were available to new immigrants?
   b. **Summarize** How did immigrants attempt to adapt to their new lives in the United States?
   c. **Elaborate** Why do you think many immigrants tolerated difficult living and working conditions?
3. a. **Recall** What was the purpose of the **Chinese Exclusion Act**?
   b. **Explain** Why did some labor unions oppose immigration?
   c. **Predict** How might the growing opposition to immigration lead to problems in the United States?

Critical Thinking

4. **Categorizing** Review your notes on the benefits and challenges new U.S. immigrants faced. Then use the following graphic organizer to categorize the challenges into different areas of life.

Education:

Work:

Challenges faced by new immigrants

Culture:

Living Conditions:

FOCUS ON WRITING

5. **Writing about Immigrants and Their Lives** Make a list of potential characters for your TV series, and be sure to include new immigrants. Take notes about what life was like for them.

The Growth of Cities

If **YOU** were there...

The year is 1905 and you have just come to the city of Chicago from the small town where you grew up. People rush past as you stop to stare up at the skyscrapers. Elevated trains roar overhead, and electric streetcars clatter along streets already crowded with pushcarts and horse-drawn wagons.

Will you stay and look for work in this big city?

BUILDING BACKGROUND Industrial growth and a new wave of immigration swelled the populations of American cities in the late 1800s. Cities changed quickly to accommodate so many new people, offering urban residents excitement and new kinds of entertainment.

Growth of Urban Areas

In 1850 New York City was the only U.S. city with a population of more than 500,000. By 1900 New York City, Chicago, Philadelphia, St. Louis, Boston, and Baltimore all had more than half a million residents. More than 35 U.S. cities had populations greater than 100,000. About 40 percent of Americans now lived in urban areas.

As you have read, new immigrants were responsible for a lot of this urban growth. So were families from rural areas in the United States. As farm equipment replaced workers in the countryside, large numbers of rural residents moved to the cities in search of work. African Americans from the rural South also began moving to northern cities in the 1890s. They hoped to escape discrimination and find better educational and economic opportunities. Cities such as Chicago; Cleveland, Ohio; Detroit, Michigan; and New York saw large increases in their African American populations during the late 1800s and early 1900s.

Perhaps the most dramatic example of urban growth was the rise of Chicago. The city's population exploded from 30,000 in 1850 to 1.7 million in 1900. Chicago passed St. Louis as the

POSTCARD
Chicago, 1900

Postcards like this one were one way people shared the experience of visiting or living in a big city like Chicago. This scene shows a bustling street corner at which modern transportation like streetcars mingle with horse-drawn carts.

Streetcars move large numbers of people through the crowded cities.

ANALYSIS SKILL **ANALYZING PRIMARY SOURCES**

What changes does this picture show taking place in cities at the time?

Population Growth of Chicago, 1870–1900

biggest city in the Midwest. Along with the large numbers of African Americans moving to the city, many of Chicago's new residents were immigrants from southern and eastern Europe. In 1900 immigrants and their children made up three quarters of Chicago's population.

Chicago's location was another **factor** in its rapid growth. Many of the new railroad lines connecting the East and West coasts ran through Chicago. This put Chicago at the heart of the nation's trade in lumber, grain, and meat. Thousands of new Chicago residents found work in the city's huge slaughterhouses and meatpacking plants. Here, meat from the West and Midwest was packed into refrigerated train cars and shipped to the growing cities of the East, where it could be sold in shops to customers.

READING CHECK Identifying Cause and Effect
What factors led to massive population growth in urban areas during the late 1800s and early 1900s?

Changing Cities

American cities such as Chicago were ill-prepared for the rapid urban growth of the late 1800s and early 1900s. Where was everyone going to live? How were people going to get from home to work on crowded city streets? Several new technologies helped cities meet these challenges. These technologies forever changed the look and function of U.S. cities.

ACADEMIC
VOCABULARY
factor cause

Building Skyscrapers

With so many people moving to urban areas, cities quickly ran out of building space in downtown areas. One solution would be to build taller buildings. Typical city buildings in the mid-1800s were only five stories tall, but taller structures were impossible to construct because the building materials available were either too weak or too heavy.

This changed with the rise of the American steel industry in the late 1800s.

THE IMPACT TODAY

Skyscrapers today use much of the same technology that was developed in the late 1800s—steel skeletons and elevators. Chicago's Sears Tower, with 110 stories, is one of the tallest buildings in the world.

Mills began producing tons of strong and inexpensive steel. Soon, architects such as Louis Sullivan of Chicago began designing multistory buildings called skyscrapers. Architects used steel beams to make sturdy frames that could support the weight of tall buildings. This allowed builders to use limited city space more efficiently.

The safety elevator, patented by Elisha Otis in the 1850s, helped make skyscrapers practical. Previous elevators had been unsafe because they would crash to the ground if the elevator cable snapped. Otis's safety elevator included a device to hold the elevator in place if the cable broke.

Getting Around

Taller buildings made it possible for more people to live and work in city centers. This increased the need for **mass transit**, or public transportation designed to move many people. By the late 1860s New York City had elevated trains running on tracks above the streets. Chicago followed in the 1890s.

Some cities built underground railroads, known as subways. In 1897 the first subway in the United States opened in Boston. In 1904 the first line of the New York City subway system began operation. Cable cars and electric trolleys also became common. These streetcars cheaply and quickly carried people in the cities to and from work.

Many Americans who could afford it moved to **suburbs**, residential neighborhoods outside of downtown areas that had begun springing up before the Civil War. Mass transit networks made such moves possible. People could live in the suburbs and take trolleys, subways, or trains into the cities.

New Ideas

In the late 1800s the United States also began to develop forms of **mass culture**, or leisure and cultural activities shared by many people. One factor contributing to mass culture was a boom in publishing. The invention of the Linotype, an automatic typesetting machine, greatly reduced the time and cost of printing. In 1850

Frederick Law Olmsted

Olmsted intentionally placed the pond near busy streets, hoping that it would attract walkers.

People can walk, ride, or roller skate on the many trails through Central Park.

CONNECT TO THE ARTS

Frederick Law Olmsted designed Central Park to serve as a place where New York City residents could relax, exercise, and enjoy nature. Olmsted included areas for horseback riding, ice-skating, boating, and baseball. The Children's District was designed as a place where parents could bring children to stay cool in the summer.

Why do you think a city dweller might be attracted to Central Park?

there were fewer than 300 daily newspapers in the country. Because of the use of Linotype machines, by 1900 there were more than 2,000 newspapers.

Big cities often had many newspapers, so publishers had to compete for readers. In 1896 **Joseph Pulitzer** added a color comic to his *New York World* newspaper. More people started buying Pulitzer's paper. **William Randolph Hearst**, publisher of the *New York Journal*, saw that comics helped sell newspapers. So he added a color comic strip to the *Journal*. Soon, newspapers across the country were adding comic strips.

Mass culture affected how people shopped as well. Giant retail shops, or **department stores**, appeared in some cities during the late 1800s. One of the earliest was Marshall Field in Chicago, which offered low prices and large quantities of products. It also was the first department store to offer its customers a restaurant where they could eat while shopping. Newspaper advertising was used to bring in customers. The public was also attracted by fancy window displays.

World fairs were another example of mass culture. Fairs brought merchants together, which sometimes resulted in new ideas and products. At the 1904 St. Louis World's Fair, for example, a Syrian food vendor began making cones for a nearby ice cream vendor who had run out of dishes. Ice cream cones became popular throughout the country.

The demand for public entertainment also led to the creation of amusement parks, such as New York's Coney Island. The inexpensive entry tickets made Coney Island a favorite destination for children and families. For a nickel, visitors could ride a new invention called the Switchback Railway—the country's first roller coaster.

As cities grew, people became aware of the need for open public space. Landscape architect **Frederick Law Olmsted** became nationally famous. He designed Central Park in New York City, as well as many state and national parks. Some of his other well-known projects include Prospect Park in Brooklyn, New York, and the U.S. Capitol grounds, which he worked on between 1874 and 1895.

READING CHECK **Summarizing** What forms of mass culture were available in urban areas?

SUMMARY AND PREVIEW Immigration and new technology helped cities grow in the late 1800s. In the next section you will learn about some of the problems caused by rapid urban growth.

Section 2 Assessment

go.hrw.com
Online Quiz
KEYWORD: SF7 HP20

Reviewing Ideas, Terms, and People

1. **a. Identify** What groups of people began moving to cities in the late 1800s?
   b. Explain Why did African Americans begin to move to northern cities in the 1890s?
   c. Predict Do you think cities such as Chicago continued to grow in the 1900s? Why or why not?
2. **a. Define** What is **mass transit**? What made mass transit necessary?
   b. Explain How did new inventions make it possible for people to build skyscrapers?
   c. Evaluate Which improvement to urban living do you think had the greatest impact on people's lives? Explain your answer.

Critical Thinking

3. **Identifying Cause and Effect** Review your notes on the causes for the growth of cities. Then copy the following graphic organizer and use it to identify the effects of city growth. You may need to add more circles.

FOCUS ON WRITING

4. **Describing Setting** A city like those you have read about could serve as the setting of your TV series. How could you describe the city?

City Life

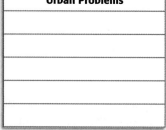

TAKING NOTES As you read, take notes on problems facing city residents. You can organize your notes in a table like this one.

Urban Problems

8.1.25, 8.3.8, 8.3.9, 8.3.11

If YOU were there...

You live in a fast-growing city in 1895. When you walk the streets, you meet families that are packed into run-down apartments in crowded, filthy neighborhoods. You meet immigrants who want to study English but have no money for classes. You are determined to help these city residents improve their lives.

What would you do to help improve life in your city?

BUILDING BACKGROUND Despite the new public parks, skyscrapers, and mass transit systems, many cities were not ready for the rapid population growth that began taking place in the late 1800s. Overcrowding and poor living conditions forced people to search for solutions to these problems.

Urban Problems

In the late 1800s and early 1900s, shortages of affordable housing forced many poor families to squeeze into tiny tenement apartments, which were frequently unsafe and unsanitary. Journalist and photographer **Jacob Riis** became famous for exposing the horrible conditions in New York City tenements. Riis wrote about one typical tenement family:

" There were nine in the family: husband, wife, an aged grandmother, and six children ... All nine lived in two rooms, one about ten feet square that served as parlor, bedroom, and eating-room, the other a small hall-room made into a kitchen. "

— Jacob Riis, *How the Other Half Lives*

This kind of overcrowding caused sanitation problems. Most cities did not have a good system for collecting trash, so garbage often piled up outside apartment buildings. An article in the *New York Tribune* described the garbage in front of one tenement as a "mass of air poisoning, death-breeding filth, reeking in the fierce sunshine."

Unsafe conditions were also common in tenements. Before 1900 most cities did not have laws requiring landlords to fix their tenements or to maintain safety standards. A fire on one floor could easily spread, and fire escapes were often blocked or broken.

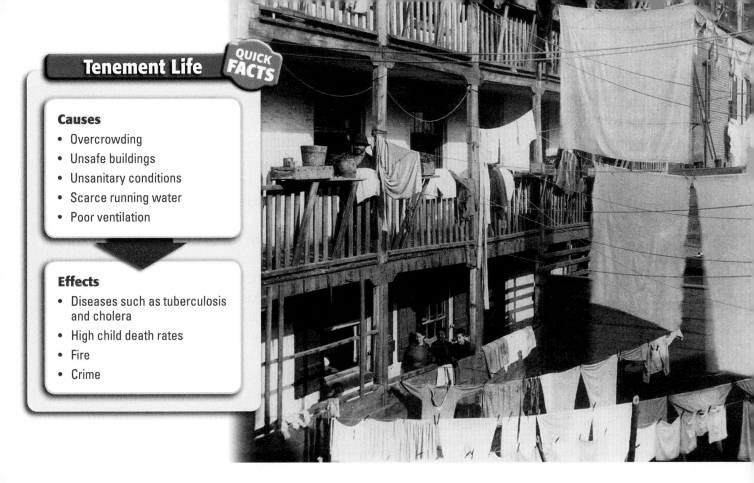

Tenement Life · QUICK FACTS

Causes
- Overcrowding
- Unsafe buildings
- Unsanitary conditions
- Scarce running water
- Poor ventilation

Effects
- Diseases such as tuberculosis and cholera
- High child death rates
- Fire
- Crime

Tenement rooms had few or no windows to let in fresh air and sunshine. Comfort was also scarce, with so many people crowded into such small spaces. Running water and indoor plumbing were also scarce. So was clean water—cities often dumped garbage into local rivers that were used for drinking water.

Disease-causing bacteria grew easily in these conditions. Diseases such as cholera, typhoid, influenza, and tuberculosis spread quickly in crowded neighborhoods. Children were the most vulnerable to these diseases. For example, babies born in Chicago in 1870 had only a 50 percent chance of living to the age of five.

Air pollution was also a serious problem in many growing cities. This was a time when many business leaders were building huge oil refineries, steel mills, and other factories. The steel mills of Andrew Carnegie, for example, helped make Pittsburgh the nation's steel-making center in the late 1800s. Steel mills brought jobs and wealth to Pittsburgh, but they also caused some of the nation's worst air pollution. "Every street appears to end in a huge, black cloud," said one writer. "Pittsburgh is smoke, smoke, smoke—everywhere smoke." The air was so polluted at times that the city had to turn on outdoor lighting during the day.

The work of many city governments slowly helped to lessen some of these urban problems. By the late 1800s new sewage and water purification systems improved city sanitation. Many major cities also were hiring full-time firefighters and police officers. Police officers in cities were typically placed in one neighborhood. They knew the local residents and were frequently involved in local activities. They could spot local problems and, in many cases, provide help to immigrants.

READING CHECK **Summarizing** What challenges did many city residents face in the late 1800s?

THE IMPACT TODAY

Like many industrial cities, Pittsburgh has made great progress in cleaning its air and water. Today, Pittsburgh is ranked as one of the cleanest American cities.

Many immigrants came to Indiana from eastern and southern Europe to work in the steel mills and other heavy industries there. Groups in cities such as Indianapolis and Gary founded settlement houses that helped immigrants adjust to life in the United States.

Improving City Life

Jacob Riis hoped his book *How the Other Half Lives* would shock many Americans—and it did. A reformer named Lawrence Veiller helped lead the effort to improve conditions in tenements. Describing the effects of tenement living on children, he wrote:

" A child living its early years in dark rooms, without sunlight or fresh air, does not grow up to be a normal, healthy person … It is not of such material that strong nations are made. "

– Lawrence Veiller, quoted in *Readings in American History, Vol. 2*

Veiller worked with an organization called the Charity Organization Society (COS) to get changes made to New York laws. In 1900 he and the COS sponsored an exhibit of photographs and maps graphically showing the conditions of New York tenements. More than 10,000 people visited the exhibit, and they were shocked by what they saw. The work of Veiller and the COS helped to get the 1901 New York State Tenement House Act passed. This law required new buildings to have better ventilation and running water. The act became a model for housing reform in other states.

Because there was little government aid available in the 1800s, private organizations generally took on the task of helping the urban poor. Some individuals set up **settlement houses**, or neighborhood centers in poor areas that offered education, recreation, and social activities.

Settlement houses were staffed by professionals and volunteers. Many were educated women who came from wealthy families. In 1886 Charles B. Stover and Stanton Coit established the first settlement house in the United States. It was called Neighborhood Guild and was located on the Lower East Side in New York City. In 1889 **Jane Addams** and Ellen Gates Starr moved into a run-down building in a poor Chicago neighborhood and turned it into **Hull House**, the most famous settlement house of the period.

The Hull House staff focused on the needs of immigrant families, and by 1893 Hull House was serving 2,000 people a week. It provided services such as English classes, day care, and cooking and sewing classes. Children and adults came to take part in club meetings, art classes, plays, and sports.

Jane Addams and the staff at Hull House also worked for reforms. They studied the problems facing immigrants and poor city dwellers, then searched for ways to improve conditions. **Florence Kelley** was one important reformer at Hull House. She visited sweatshops and wrote about the problems there. Her work helped convince lawmakers to take action. Illinois passed a law in 1893 to limit working hours for women and to prevent child labor.

Kelley became the state's chief factory inspector and helped enforce the law. Although she believed more reforms were needed, she did report some improvements:

Hull House

Neighborhood children attended kindergarten at Hull House. Their parents typically had low-paying jobs, and many were children of immigrants. Children like these had few other options for education.

How did Hull House try to improve the lives of children?

"Previous to the passage of the factory law of 1893, it was the rule of [a candy] factory to work the children ...from 7 A.M. to 9 P.M., with twenty minutes for lunch, and no supper, a working week of eighty-two hours ...Since the enactment of the factory law, their working week has consisted of six days of eight hours each, a reduction of thirty-four hours a week."

– Florence Kelley and Alzina P. Stevens, from *Hull House Maps and Papers*

As Hull House gained recognition, the settlement house movement spread to other cities. Most settlement houses continued to provide programs and services for city dwellers through the early 1900s. Some, such as Germantown Settlement in Pennsylvania, remain active today.

READING CHECK **Drawing Conclusions**
How did Hull House help improve city life?

SUMMARY AND PREVIEW Reformers in the late 1800s worked to solve urban problems. In the next chapter you will learn how Progressives pushed for further reforms.

BIOGRAPHY

Jane Addams
1860–1935

Jane Addams was born in Cedarville, Illinois. Like many upper-class women of the era, she received a college education but found few jobs open to her. In 1888, on a visit to England with classmate Ellen Gates Starr, she visited a London settlement house. On their return to the United States, Addams and Starr opened a settlement house in Chicago. They started a kindergarten and a public playground. Addams also became involved in housing safety and sanitation issues, factory inspection, and immigrants' rights. In 1931 she shared the Nobel Peace Prize for her work with the Women's International League for Peace and Freedom.

Summarizing How did Jane Addams try to improve the lives of workers?

go.hrw.com
Online Quiz
KEYWORD: SF7 HP20

Section 3 Assessment

Reviewing Ideas, Terms, and People

1. **a. Describe** What were conditions like in tenements?
   b. Summarize What problems resulted from the rapid growth of cities?
   c. Draw Conclusions Why do you think people lived in tenements?
2. **a. Define** What is a **settlement house**?
   b. Explain How did settlement houses help city dwellers?
   c. Evaluate Do you think settlement houses were successful? Why or why not?

Critical Thinking

3. **Categorizing** Review your notes on urban problems. Then copy the chart to the right onto your own sheet of paper and use it to identify the responses to those problems.

Urban Problems	→	Responses to Urban Problems

FOCUS ON WRITING

4. **Writing about Urban Problems** Finding solutions to problems is an important part of the plot of many stories. Take notes on scenes you could include in your TV series in which characters deal with the problems of urban life.

Social Studies Skills

Analysis | Critical Thinking | Civic Participation | Study

Making Comparisons

Define the Skill

Understanding similarities is important when studying history. Comparing two or more people, things, events, or ideas highlights the similarities between them. Making comparisons can help clarify larger historical issues. This is true when comparing different time periods or when comparing different things from the same time period. Making comparisons is important in identifying historical connections.

Learn the Skill

When you encounter similar people, things, events, or ideas in history, use the following guidelines to make comparisons.

1 Identify who or what you are going to compare.

2 Look for similarities between them. Find examples of what makes them alike. Note any differences as well.

3 Use comparison words such as "like," "both," and "similar" to point out similarities.

In this chapter, you have learned about several reformers, including Lawrence Veiller and Florence Kelley. Veiller helped lead the effort to improve conditions in tenements. Kelley was a reformer who worked at Hull House.

Lawrence Veiller and Florence Kelley were alike in many ways. Although Veiller focused on tenements and Kelley concentrated on factory work, both were concerned with problems that affected children. Both did research about their issues. Both then wrote about the poor conditions they found.

Both Veiller and Kelley worked successfully for laws that would improve those conditions. Kelley's work helped convince Illinois lawmakers to pass a law to limit child labor. Similarly, Veiller helped to get the 1901 New York State Tenement House Act passed.

Practice the Skill

Review the chapter to find two people, things, events, or ideas that are similar. Then apply the guidelines to answer the following questions.

1 Which people, events, or ideas will you compare? Why is each of them important?

2 How are they alike? How are they different?

Chapter Review

Visual Summary

QUICK FACTS

Use the visual summary below to help you review the main ideas of the chapter.

People Arrived
- New immigrants, mostly from southern and eastern Europe
- Came for new opportunities and better lives
- Mostly found jobs in cities
- Faced opposition from some Americans

Cities Grew
- Massive urban growth
- New technologies emerged—skyscrapers and mass transit
- New urban culture

Problems Developed
- Overcrowded tenements
- Unsanitary conditions

Reviewing Vocabulary, Terms, and People

Identify the descriptions below with the correct term or person from the chapter.

1. Public transportation systems built to move many people and ease traffic in crowded cities

2. Founded Hull House with Ellen Gates Starr in 1889

3. Organizations created by immigrants to help each other in times of sickness, unemployment, or other troubles

4. Law banning Chinese people from moving to the United States

5. Neighborhood centers in poor urban areas that offered education, recreation, and social activities

6. Landscape architect who designed New York City's Central Park

7. Small shops or mills where immigrants worked for long hours in hot, unhealthy conditions

Comprehension and Critical Thinking

SECTION 1 *(Pages 636–641)*

8. **a. Identify** From what parts of the world did the wave of new immigrants come?

   b. Analyze In what ways did immigration patterns in the United States change in the late 1800s?

   c. Elaborate In your opinion, were the difficulties that immigrants faced worth the benefits of life in the United States? Explain.

SECTION 2 *(Pages 642–645)*

9. **a. Recall** Why did U.S. cities experience such rapid growth in the late 1800s?

   b. Analyze How did new technologies help cities deal with population growth?

   c. Elaborate Would you have preferred to live in a city or in a suburb? Why?

SECTION 3 *(Pages 646–649)*

10. a. Recall What were conditions like in tenements in the late 1800s?

b. Make Inferences Why did rapid population growth cause problems in cities?

c. Elaborate Why do you think the settlement house movement grew in the late 1800s and early 1900s?

Reviewing Themes

11. Economics What role did economics play in the growth of cities?

12. Society and Culture How did the lives of city dwellers change with the rise of mass culture?

Reading Skills

Understanding Historical Fact versus Historical Fiction *Use the Reading Skills taught in this chapter to answer the question about the reading selection below.*

> Mass culture affected how people shopped as well. Giant retail shops, or department stores, appeared in some cities during the late 1800s. One of the earliest was Marshall Field in Chicago, which offered low prices and large quantities of products. It also was the first department store to offer its customers a restaurant where they could eat while shopping. Newspaper advertising was used to bring in customers. The public was also attracted by fancy window displays. *(p. 645)*

13. Which facts above can be verified? Where would you look to verify them?

Social Studies Skills

Making Comparisons *Use the Social Studies Skills taught in this chapter to answer the question below.*

14. Choose two reforms that were discussed in this chapter. Make a comparison between the two.

Using the Internet

go.hrw.com
KEYWORD: SF7 CH20

15. Activity: Investigating Culture Mass culture developed in the late 1800s and early 1900s as a result of new and broader forms of communication taking root. Enter the activity keyword and explore some of the early influences on mass culture. Then research the ways in which modern culture is influenced by the media, the Internet, and other forms of mass communication. How does today's society experience mass culture? Create a visual display or computer-based presentation that compares mass culture then and now.

FOCUS ON WRITING

16. Writing Your Memo Look back over your notes about the people, places, and events of the late 1800s. Decide which of these you will include in your television drama series. Then draft a one- to two-paragraph memo to your boss describing the series. Remember to describe the basic plot, setting, and characters.

DIRECTIONS: Read each question and write the letter of the best response.

1 Which of the following is associated with providing a better life for urban immigrants in the late 1800s and early 1900s?

A the department store

B the suburb

C the tenement

D the settlement house

2 Immigrants to the United States in the late 1800s and early 1900s came *mainly* from

A southern and eastern Europe.

B Japan, China, and the rest of Asia.

C Mexico and Central America.

D northern and western Europe.

3 Ellis Island and Angel Island were both

A locations of settlement houses.

B immigration processing centers.

C centers of shipping and industry.

D amusement parks.

4 Which of the following is an example of mass culture?

A newspaper comics

B immigrant neighborhoods

C Yiddish-language theaters

D subways

5 The *main* goal of Hull House was to

A provide jobs for wealthy women.

B pass the Tenement House Act of 1901.

C help poor immigrants.

D oppose the Chinese Exclusion Act.

6 Anti-immigrant feeling resulted in

A benevolent societies.

B the Chinese Exclusion Act.

C tenements.

D the Tenement House Act.

7 Which of the following groups moved from the southern United States to the North in large numbers during the 1890s?

A Chinese immigrants

B Mexican Americans

C African Americans

D Irish immigrants

8 Read this 1896 newspaper article describing poor conditions faced by many people and use it to answer the question below.

> "lack of family privacy … lack of light and air, and of sanitary accommodations, insuring a large death rate, and danger from fire … [These places are] infested with vermin [insects] and infected with disease germs, they are a disgrace to humanity and a menace, not only to the health of the unfortunate residents therein, but to the health of the whole community."
>
> —*The New York Times*, 1896

Document-Based Question Based on this description, to what was this article most likely referring?

Assignment

Write a persuasive essay either for or against one of these statements.

1. New laws should have limited immigration in the late 1800s.
2. The government should have done more to improve conditions in tenements.

TIP **Using Order of Importance**

How do you know whether to start or end with your most important or most convincing reason? If you are worried about getting your readers to read your entire paper, you might try to catch their attention by starting with the most convincing reason. If you are concerned that your readers remember one point after they finish reading, you may want to place that point, or reason, at the end of your paper.

Persuasion and History

You have probably heard people disagree about current political events—perhaps a new law or a government leader. People also disagree about events of the past. When we disagree about historical events, those of the past or those of the present, we can use persuasive arguments to convince others to agree with our opinion.

1. Prewrite

Stating Your Opinion

Persuasion starts with an opinion or a position on a topic. Choose one of the statements in the assignment and decide on your opinion, either for or against. Write your opinion in a statement: it will be the big idea of your persuasive paper. For example, here is an opinion statement about the first topic:

The government should not have limited immigration in the late 1800s.

Building and Organizing a Logical Argument

A strong persuasive essay includes a logical argument, sound reasoning, and proof in support of an opinion. Reasons tell *why* you have an opinion. Proof, or evidence, includes facts, examples, or expert opinions.

- **Opinion:** *Reformers' work improved Americans' lives.*
- **Reason:** *Reforms improved life in cities.*
- **Evidence:** *Lawrence Veiller influenced the passage of the 1901 New York State Tenement House Act.*

Persuasive writing is usually organized by order of importance.

2. Write

Here is a framework to help you write your first draft.

A Writer's Framework

Introduction	Body	Conclusion
■ Start with an interesting opener, such as a quotation or a surprising fact. ■ Include your opinion statement, or big idea, for the paper.	■ Present one reason and its supporting evidence in each body paragraph. ■ Address your reasons by order of importance.	■ Restate your opinion in different words. ■ Summarize your reasons. ■ Make a connection to a current event.

3. Evaluate and Revise

Evaluating

Use these questions to discover ways to improve your draft.

Evaluation Questions for a Persuasive Essay

- Does your introduction include a clear statement of your opinion on the topic?
- Do you present your reasons by order of importance in the body paragraphs?
- Do you provide at least three reasons to support your opinion?
- Do you include facts, examples, or expert opinions to support each reason?
- Do you restate your opinion in different words in your conclusion?
- Does your conclusion include a summary of the reasons that support your opinion?

TIP **Fact vs. Opinion** Knowing the difference between a fact and an opinion is important for both writers and readers of persuasive essays.

- **Facts** are statements that can be proven true or false. *Jane Addams founded Hull House in 1889.*

- **Opinions** are statements of personal belief and cannot be proven. *Jane Addams was the greatest American woman of her time.*

Revising

Your essay will be more forceful if you write in the active voice.

Passive voice: *New parks were designed by Frederick Law Olmsted.*

Active voice: *Frederick Law Olmsted designed new parks.*

Active voice is more forceful, and often clearer, because it makes a stronger connection between the action and the actor. However, we may use passive voice because we do not know, or do not want to say, who the actor is or was.

Example: *New parks were designed in the late 1800s.*

4. Proofread and Publish

Proofreading

If you are writing your paper on a computer, you should use the spell-check feature to look for spelling errors. However, the spell-check feature will not help much if you have used the wrong word. Here are some examples to look for: *their/they're, its/it's, accept/except, affect/effect, advice/advise, altar/alter, capitol/capital.* When you spot one of these words in your paper, check your dictionary to make sure you have used the correct word.

Publishing

Share your essay with a classmate who took an opinion opposed to yours. Review each other's reasons. Can one of you persuade the other?

● 5. Practice and Apply

Use the steps and strategies in this workshop to write a persuasive essay.

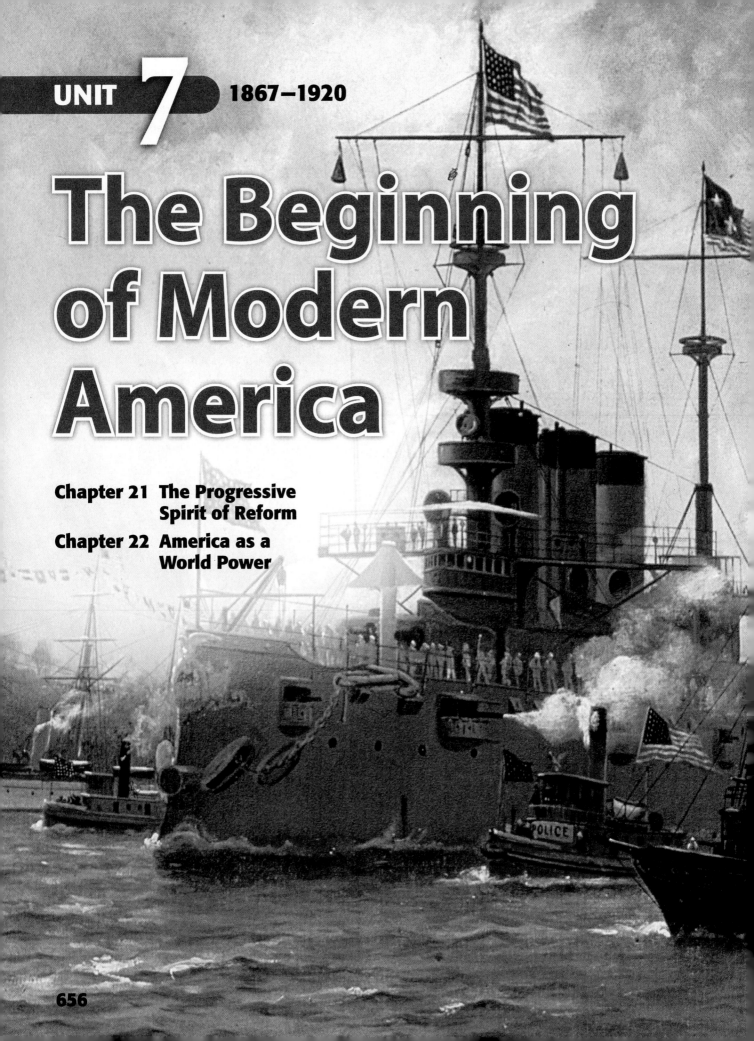

The Beginning of Modern America

656

What You Will Learn...

As cities in the United States became more prosperous, people began to examine the inequalities in American society. A progressive spirit emerged that led to changes in American culture. The United States also began to expand its influence overseas.

Presidents were called upon to deal with many domestic and foreign challenges, including two wars that changed the landscape of international politics. During the Spanish-American War, the United States acquired overseas territories. During World War I, Americans fought in Europe for the first time.

Explore the Art

This painting shows the Great White Fleet, a group of U.S. ships that toured the world from 1907 to 1909. How might a tour of American ships affect foreign views of the United States?

The Progressive Spirit of Reform

Indiana Standards

Social Studies Standards

8.2.9 Explain how citizens can monitor and inluence the development and implementatiion of public policies at local, state, and national levels of government.

8.4.2 Illustrate elements of the three types of economic systems, using cases from United States history.

8.4.4 Explain the basic economic functions of the government in the economy of the United States.

8.4.5 Analyze contributions of entrepreneurs and inventors in the development of the United States economy.

go.hrw.com
Indiana
KEYWORD: SF10 IN

FOCUS ON SPEAKING

Campaign Promises In this chapter you will read about the political corruption of the Gilded Age and the reform movements that followed. Serious problems face the nation, and you must convince voters that you should be the one to tackle those problems. Create and present a list of campaign promises that you would make if you were a politician running for office in the United States in the late 1800s or early 1900s.

UNITED STATES

1868 Ulysses S. Grant is elected president.

1865 — 1870

WORLD

1871 The British Parliament legalizes labor unions.

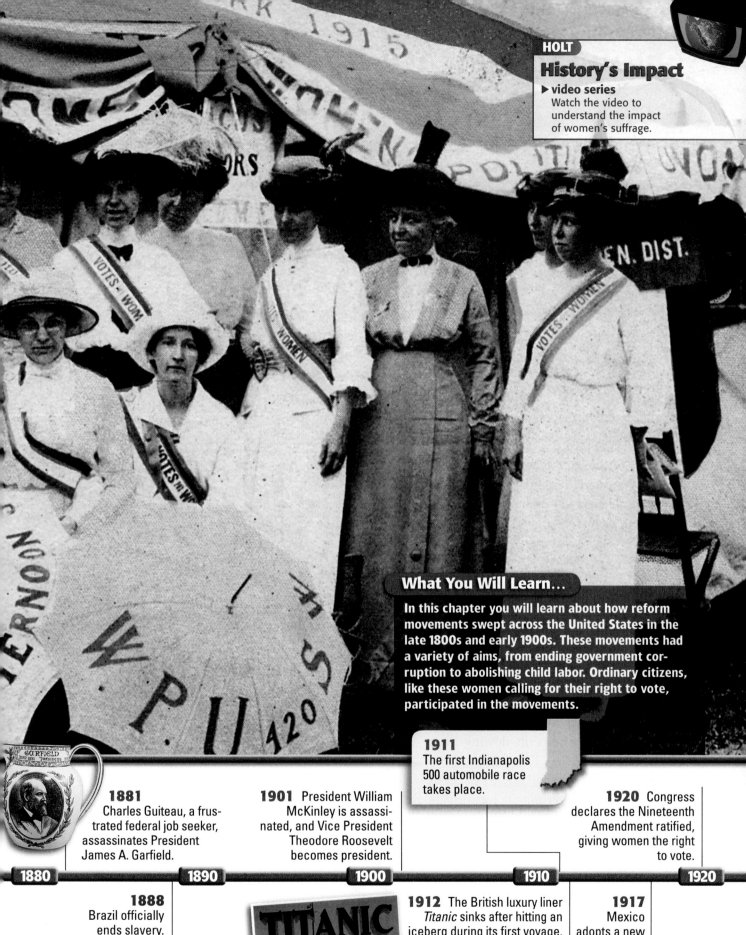

History's Impact

▶ **video series**
Watch the video to understand the impact of women's suffrage.

What You Will Learn...

In this chapter you will learn about how reform movements swept across the United States in the late 1800s and early 1900s. These movements had a variety of aims, from ending government corruption to abolishing child labor. Ordinary citizens, like these women calling for their right to vote, participated in the movements.

1911
The first Indianapolis 500 automobile race takes place.

1881
Charles Guiteau, a frustrated federal job seeker, assassinates President James A. Garfield.

1901 President William McKinley is assassinated, and Vice President Theodore Roosevelt becomes president.

1920 Congress declares the Nineteenth Amendment ratified, giving women the right to vote.

1880   **1890**   **1900**   **1910**   **1920**

1888
Brazil officially ends slavery.

1912 The British luxury liner *Titanic* sinks after hitting an iceberg during its first voyage. About 1,500 passengers die.

1917
Mexico adopts a new constitution.

TITANIC
The World's Largest Liner
WHITE STAR LINE

THE PROGRESSIVE SPIRIT OF REFORM   **659**

Reading Social Studies

by Kylene Beers

| Economics | Geography | Politics | Society and Culture | Science and Technology |

Focus on Themes In this chapter, you will read about the corrupt **politics** of the Gilded Age, a time marked by attempts at reform. You will learn how **society and culture** reacted and responded to the problems of corruption and inequality. Finally, you will read about several presidents of the early 1900s who supported ideas and initiatives that promoted social reform.

Evaluating Sources

Focus on Reading Historical texts and current history books are good sources of information about the past. However, some sources can be more reliable than others to learn the truth.

Evaluating Texts Sometimes people write texts with a specific purpose or viewpoint in mind. Determining what the author's goal was in writing a passage can help you evaluate whether to believe all of the text, or merely some of it. Knowing which parts you can believe and which you cannot will help you understand what really happened in history.

Notice how one reader evaluated the source below.

The man, therefore, who as the owner of newspapers, <u>would corrupt public opinion is the most dangerous enemy of the State.</u> We may talk about the perils incident [dangers attached] to the <u>concentration of wealth,</u> about the perils flowing from a <u>disregard of fiduciary [financial] responsibility,</u> about <u>abuses of privilege,</u> about <u>exploiting the government for private advantage</u>; but all of these menaces, great as they are, are nothing compared with a deliberate, persistent, artful, purchased endeavor to [change and direct] the public judgment.

—*Harper's Weekly*, October 20, 1906, quoted in *Yellow Journalism* by W. Joseph Campbell

> The author is using strong words to describe his viewpoint. Maybe he isn't being as objective as he should be.

> The article lists several ideas that the author seems to think are bad. Are these things really bad? Can that help me determine the author's viewpoint?

> This magazine was widely read when the article appeared. I think that makes the article a good source for some viewpoints of the time.

You Try It!

Read the passage below and evaluate whether you would use it as a source for a paper.

> Space is no intervention now between communication. [N]ot only do the wires of copper bind the world together in closer communication, but with the telephone it is possible to converse [talk] with friends a thousand miles away, hearing distinctly every word and recognizing the individual voice. Closer acquaintance has thus wrought [created] vast changes in public opinions and policies. The entire civilized world has been drawn more closely together, old ideas and prejudices have been wiped out.
>
> –*Cincinnati Times-Star*, January 1, 1900, quoted in *Yellow Journalism* by W. Joseph Campbell

1. What viewpoint of new technology is the author taking in this article? How can you tell?

2. Do you believe that the telephone brought about "changes in public opinions and policies"? Why or why not? Why might the author say this?

3. Can you trust the author when he says that "old ideas and prejudices have been wiped out"? Why or why not? Why might the author say this?

4. Did this article appear in a well-known newspaper? Does this make it more trustworthy or less?

5. Would you use this article as a source for writing a paper about how new inventions affected life in the early 1900s? Explain your answer.

As you read Chapter 21, evaluate the primary sources for their usefulness in understanding history.

Academic Vocabulary

In this chapter you will learn the following academic words:

motive *(p. 666)*
various *(p. 682)*

The Gilded Age and the Progressive Movement

What You Will Learn...

Main Ideas

1. Political corruption was common during the Gilded Age.
2. Progressives pushed for reforms to improve living conditions.
3. Progressive reforms expanded the voting power of citizens.

The Big Idea

From the late 1800s through the early 1900s, the Progressive movement addressed problems in American society.

Key Terms and People

political machines, *p. 662*
Progressives, *p. 664*
muckrakers, *p. 664*
Seventeenth Amendment, *p. 666*
recall, *p. 666*
initiative, *p. 666*
referendum, *p. 666*
Robert M. La Follette, *p. 667*

TAKING NOTES As you read, take notes on progressive reforms and the problems they addressed. Organize your notes in a chart like the one below.

Progressive reform	Problem it addressed

 8.2.8, 8.2.9, 8.3.8, 8.3.11

If YOU were there...

You live in a big-city neighborhood in the 1890s. You and your brother are both looking for jobs. You know that the man down the street is the "ward boss." He can always get city jobs for his friends and neighbors. But in return you'll have to promise to vote the way he tells you to in the upcoming election.

Would you ask the ward boss for a job? Why or why not?

BUILDING BACKGROUND The late 1800s were a time of contrasts in American life. Great wealth created through business ventures existed alongside poverty and the difficulties of tenement life. In politics, money led to corruption and dishonesty. Reacting to these conditions, reformers worked to improve many areas of American life.

Political Corruption

The late 1800s in the United States are often called the Gilded Age. The term came from a novel by that name. *The Gilded Age* highlights the inequality between wealthy business owners, who profited from the Industrial Revolution, and workers, who often labored under terrible conditions for little pay. Many people began to believe that the government should help fix this inequality. The first step was to get rid of corruption in politics.

Political Machines

In the late 1800s city and county politics were dominated by **political machines**—powerful organizations that used both legal and illegal methods to get their candidates elected to public office. For example, members of political machines sometimes stuffed ballot boxes with extra votes for their candidates. They also paid people to vote a certain way and then bribed vote counters. Through such actions, political machines could control local governments.

POLITICAL CARTOON
The Tammany Ring

This political cartoon shows a ring of corrupt politicians known as Tammany Hall. The cartoonist shows how each person blames the one next to him for the corruption in government. As a result of political machines like Tammany Hall, many Americans began demanding political reforms.

The men have labels on their backs that show they represent different interests.

The Granger Collection, New York

ANALYSIS SKILL **ANALYZING PRIMARY SOURCES**

Why are the men shown standing in a circle?

Political machines were run by leaders called bosses. The machine's boss frequently traded favors for votes. For example, the boss might hand out city jobs to unqualified people or allow an illegal business to operate. The bosses drew much of their support from immigrants. They became popular among poor families because of the services they provided, including jobs and social services such as a fire brigade. A Boston politician said that the role of the machine boss was "to be . . . somebody that any bloke [man] can come to . . . and get help."

New York City's political machine, Tammany Hall, was one of the most notorious. After winning city elections in 1888, members of Tammany Hall rewarded their supporters with about 12,000 jobs. As boss of Tammany Hall, William Marcy Tweed may have stolen up to $200 million from the city. One man remembered how Tammany Hall stayed in power by intimidating voters:

"Father used to say, 'They know how you're voting. You can't fool them.' He was a Republican at heart, but he had to vote Democratic in order that they didn't find out and make it difficult for him."

—Henry Fenner, quoted in *You Must Remember This*, edited by Jeff Kisseloff

Cleaning Up Political Corruption

Corruption was also a problem in the federal government. Many people thought that the corruption extended to the presidential administration of Ulysses S. Grant. During Grant's second term, federal officials were jailed for taking bribes from whiskey makers in exchange for allowing them to avoid paying taxes. Another scandal involved members of Congress who had taken bribes to allow the Union Pacific Railway to receive government funds. These scandals and others caused many Americans to question the honesty of national leaders.

In response, Americans began calling for changes in the civil service, the government job system. They disliked the spoils system, the practice of giving jobs to the winning candidates' supporters. Thomas Jefferson was the first to reward supporters with jobs. After his administration, each time a new party took power, it replaced many government officials. Many new employees were unqualified and untrained.

By the late 1800s government corruption was so widespread that reformers demanded that only qualified people be given government jobs. In response, President Rutherford B. Hayes

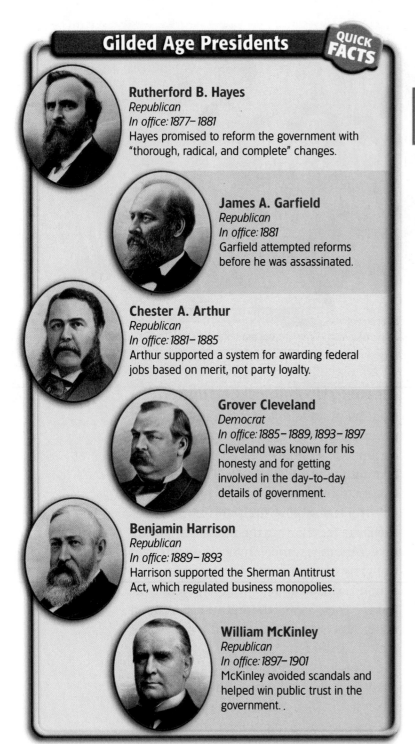

Gilded Age Presidents

QUICK FACTS

Rutherford B. Hayes
Republican
In office: 1877–1881
Hayes promised to reform the government with "thorough, radical, and complete" changes.

James A. Garfield
Republican
In office: 1881
Garfield attempted reforms before he was assassinated.

Chester A. Arthur
Republican
In office: 1881–1885
Arthur supported a system for awarding federal jobs based on merit, not party loyalty.

Grover Cleveland
Democrat
In office: 1885–1889, 1893–1897
Cleveland was known for his honesty and for getting involved in the day-to-day details of government.

Benjamin Harrison
Republican
In office: 1889–1893
Harrison supported the Sherman Antitrust Act, which regulated business monopolies.

William McKinley
Republican
In office: 1897–1901
McKinley avoided scandals and helped win public trust in the government. .

THE IMPACT TODAY

Tests are still required for many federal jobs, including secretarial positions, air traffic control, and law enforcement.·

made minor reforms, such as firing a powerful member of the New York Republican political machine. President James A. Garfield also attempted reforms. But on July 2, 1881, Garfield was attacked and shot twice by a mentally unstable federal job seeker named Charles Guiteau. The president later died from his wounds, and Vice President Chester A. Arthur became president.

Arthur continued the push for reforms by backing the Pendleton Civil Service Act, which was passed in 1883. This law set up a merit system for awarding federal jobs. Under the Pendleton Act, more than 10 percent of government job applicants had to pass an exam before they could be hired. It was a start to reforming other government practices.

READING CHECK **Analyzing** What factors led to civil-service reform?

Progressives Push for Reforms

A group of reformers known as **Progressives** were also working to improve society in the late 1800s. Progressives tried to solve problems caused by rapid industrial and urban growth. Their goals were to eliminate the causes of problems such as crime, disease, and poverty. They fought for reforms ranging from better working conditions to education programs in poor neighborhoods.

Muckrakers at Work

Some journalists urged Progressives to action by writing stories that vividly described problems in U.S. society. These journalists were nicknamed **muckrakers** because they "raked up" and exposed the muck, or filth, of society. Muckrakers wrote about troubling issues such as child labor, racial discrimination, slum housing, and corruption in business and politics.

In 1902 and 1903 Lincoln Steffens wrote a series of articles in *McClure's Magazine* exposing corruption in city government. In one article, he described how government officials in St. Louis, Missouri, used their positions to earn extra money illegally:

❝Men empowered to issue peddlers' licenses and permits to citizens who wished to erect awnings or use a portion of the sidewalk for storage purposes charged an amount in excess of the prices stipulated [set] by law, and pocketed the difference.❞

—Lincoln Steffens, *The Shame of the Cities*

PHOTOGRAPH
The Other Half

In 1890 Jacob Riis published How the Other Half Lives. *The book was a collection of photographs of residents and workers in New York City tenement buildings, including families and immigrants. The conditions of life that Riis showed in his photographs, like this one, shocked many wealthier Americans.*

Sweatshops turned out large amounts of clothing at low prices.

Sweatshops were located in tenements to avoid the labor laws that affected factories. Workers crowded into the small, stuffy spaces.

This 12-year-old boy said he was 16 in order to keep his job of pulling threads.

ANALYSIS SKILL **ANALYZING PRIMARY SOURCES**

How might this photograph encourage people to become reformers?

Another muckraker, Ida B. Tarbell, wrote articles criticizing the unfair business practices of the Standard Oil Company. Upton Sinclair exposed unsanitary practices in the meat-processing industry in his novel *The Jungle.*

Although such writing angered many politicians and business leaders, it also helped to unite Progressives. Muckrakers influenced voters, causing them to pressure politicians into backing reforms.

Reform Successes

A major goal of Progressive reformers was to help the urban poor. You have read about the work of housing reformers, which led to the 1901 New York State Tenement House Act. Other Progressives started settlement houses similar to Jane Addams's Hull House. People usually started settlement houses in poor areas in order to improve education, housing, and sanitation there.

The movement for urban reform also led to new professions, such as city planning

and civil engineering. City planners helped design safer building codes and opened new public parks. Civil engineers improved transportation by paving streets and building bridges. Sanitation engineers tried to solve problems concerning pollution, waste disposal, and impure water supplies. Death rates dropped dramatically in areas where planners and engineers addressed these problems.

Progressives also believed that improving education would lead to a better society. In response to their demands for reform, states passed laws requiring all children to attend school. Some Progressives started kindergarten programs to help young city children learn basic social skills. In 1873 reformer Susan Blow opened the first American public kindergarten in St. Louis. By 1898 more than 4,000 kindergartens had opened in the United States.

Philosopher John Dewey was a key supporter of early childhood education. His

<u>motive</u> was to help children learn problem-solving skills, not just memorize facts. This, he thought, would help them in everyday life. Dewey's teaching methods became a model for progressive education across the country.

Progressives also worked to improve the education of medical professionals. In the late 1800s the United States lacked a ready supply of well-trained and professionally organized doctors. Researchers knew the causes of diseases such as pneumonia and tuberculosis. However, there were few medical organizations that could help spread this knowledge.

Under the leadership of Joseph McCormack, the American Medical Association (AMA) brought together local medical organizations in 1901. The AMA supported laws designed to protect public health and showed how Progressives could organize to help improve society. Other organizations followed the AMA's lead.

READING CHECK **Finding Main Ideas** How did progressive reforms improve society?

BIOGRAPHY

Robert M. La Follette
1855–1925

Born in rural Wisconsin, Robert M. La Follette began his political career at a young age. He was elected to the U.S. House of Representatives in 1884, becoming the youngest member of Congress. He soon earned the nickname "Fighting Bob" for his energetic speaking style and his active support for progressive reforms.

After serving as Wisconsin's governor and as U.S. senator, La Follette ran for president as the Progressive Party candidate in 1924. He won his home state and received about 16 percent of the popular vote.

Drawing Conclusions Why might La Follette have been proud of the nickname "Fighting Bob"?

Expansion of Voting Power

Some Progressives worked to change state and local governments in order to reduce the power of political machines. In many places, reformers replaced corrupt ballots that listed only one party's candidates with government-prepared ballots that listed all candidates. Under pressure from reformers, many states adopted secret ballots, a measure that ensured the privacy of every voter.

Voting Reforms

Reformers also hoped to expand voting power. For example, they favored the **Seventeenth Amendment**, which allowed Americans to vote directly for U.S. senators. Before the constitutional amendment was passed in 1913, state legislatures had elected senators. Reformers also favored the direct primary, in which voters choose candidates for public office directly. Previously, party leaders had selected which candidates would run for office.

Other reform measures allowed voters to take action against corrupt politicians. Some states and cities gave unhappy voters the right to sign a petition asking for a special vote. The purpose of that vote was to **recall**, or remove, an official before the end of his or her term. If enough voters signed the petition, the vote took place. The official could then be removed from office if there was a majority of recall votes.

In California, Oregon, and states in the Midwest, Progressives worked on reforms to give voters direct influence over new laws. A procedure called the **initiative** allowed voters to propose a new law by collecting signatures on a petition. If enough signatures were collected, the proposed law was voted on at the next election. Another measure, called the **referendum**, permitted voters to approve or reject a law that had already been proposed or passed by a government body. This process gave voters a chance to overrule laws that they opposed.

Government Reforms

In addition to working for greater voter participation, Progressives attempted to change the way city government operated. Some reformers wanted city government to be run like a business. As a result of their efforts, several cities changed to council-manager governments. Under this system, voters elect a city council. The council then appoints a professional manager to run the city. Other business-minded reformers supported the commission form of government. Under this system, the city is headed by a group of elected officials. Each official manages a major city agency, such as housing or transportation.

One of the leaders of the effort to reform state government was Wisconsin's Republican governor **Robert M. La Follette**. La Follette decreased the power of political machines and used university professors and other experts to help write new laws and work in state agencies. He also made available to the public information on how politicians voted. That way, voters would know if leaders had

kept their campaign promises. Called the Wisconsin Idea, La Follette's plan became a model for progressive reforms in other states.

Expanding Democracy	QUICK FACTS
Direct Primaries	Voters choose candidates.
Recall	Voters can remove an official from office.
Initiatives	Voters can propose laws by petition.
Referendum	Voters can overrule a law.
17th Amendment	Senators are elected directly by voters.

READING CHECK **Evaluating** How did Progressives work to change voting procedures?

SUMMARY AND PREVIEW Progressives worked to reform government and improve city life. In the next section you will learn about reforms in working conditions.

go.hrw.com

Section 1 Assessment

Online Quiz
KEYWORD: SF7 HP21

Reviewing Ideas, Terms, and People

1. **a. Recall** What was the main goal of **political machines** during the Gilded Age?
   b. Draw Conclusions Why do you think some immigrants supported political machines?
   c. Predict Do you think the system of testing created by the Pendleton Civil Service Act would work to reduce corruption in the spoils system? Why or why not?
2. **a. Identify** Who were **muckrakers**, and what effect did they have on reform?
   b. Explain How did **Progressives** try to improve education?
   c. Evaluate Which progressive reform do you think was most important? Why?
3. **a. Describe** What new ideas and practices were introduced to give voters more power?
   b. Draw Conclusions How did progressive reforms limit the power of political machines?

Critical Thinking

4. **Categorizing** Review your notes on the problems that progressive reforms addressed. Then copy the chart below and use it to categorize the various progressive reforms.

Progressive Reforms		
Social	Political	Urban

FOCUS ON SPEAKING

5. **Addressing Political and Social Problems** How would you address the problems of political corruption and urban growth during the late 1800s? Jot down notes about campaign promises you might make to assure voters that you would make the necessary reforms.

Reform Literature

from *How the Other Half Lives*
by Jacob Riis (1849–1914)

About the Reading *How the Other Half Lives de-scribes the tenement houses where immigrants lived in New York City. Its author, Jacob Riis, was a newspaper reporter. His nonfiction book made Americans aware of the extremes of poverty suffered by working people. Riis believed that every human being deserved a decent, safe place to live.* How the Other Half Lives *led to reforms and new laws that improved housing conditions.*

AS YOU READ Look for details that help you see, hear, and smell Cherry Street.

Cherry Street. Be a little careful, please! ❶ The hall is dark and you might stumble over the children pitching pennies back there. Not that it would hurt them; kicks and cuffs are their daily diet. They have little else. Here where the hall turns and dives into utter darkness is a step, and another, another. A flight of stairs. You can feel your way, if you cannot see it. Close? Yes! What would you have? All the fresh air that ever enters these stairs comes from the hall door that is for-ever slamming, and from the windows of dark bedrooms that in turn receive from the stairs their sole supply of the elements God meant to be free . . . That was a woman filling her pail by the hydrant you just bumped against. The sinks are in the hallway, that all the tenants may have access—and all be poisoned alike by their summer stenches. Hear the pump squeak! It is the lullaby of tenement house babes. In sum-mer, when a thousand thirsty throats pant for a cooling drink in this block, it is worked in vain . . . ❷

The sea of a mighty population, held in galling fetters, heaves uneasily in the tenements . . . If it rise once more, no human power may avail to check it. The gap between the classes in which it surges, unseen, unsuspected by the thoughtless, is widening day by day . . . I know of but one bridge that will carry us over safe, a bridge founded upon justice and built of human hearts.

GUIDED READING

WORD HELP

cuffs punches

utter complete

close stuffy

sole only

access right to use

stenches bad smells

in vain without success

galling causing pain; irritating

fetters chains

heaves rises and falls

avail help

❶ *The writer wants you to imagine that he is taking you on a tour of the building. Why do you think he chooses this way to describe the place?*

❷ *Find one detail that appeals to each sense: sight, sound, smell, taste, and touch. How would you sum up, in one sentence, the place that Riis describes?*

from *The Jungle*

by Upton Sinclair (1878–1968)

THE JUNGLE
BY
UPTON SINCLAIR

DOUBLEDAY, PAGE & Cº
NEW YORK

About the Reading *The Jungle focused the nation's attention on immigrant workers in the meatpacking industry. Upton Sinclair's novel showed bosses forcing human beings to live and work like animals. He also described, in shocking detail, how meat was handled. Sinclair published his book in 1906. Later that same year, the U.S. government passed the Pure Food and Drug Act and the Meat Inspection Act. Many Americans even gave up eating meat for a while.*

AS YOU READ Look for details that create one overwhelming effect.

There was never the least attention paid to what was cut up for sausage; there would come back from Europe old sausage that had been rejected, and that was mouldy and white—it would be dosed with borax and glycerine, and dumped into hoppers, and made over again for home consumption. There would be meat that had tumbled out on the floor, in the dirt and sawdust, where the workers had tramped and spit uncounted billions of consumption germs. ❶ There would be meat stored in great piles in rooms and the water from leaky roofs would drip over it, and thousands of rats would race about on it. It was too dark in these storage places to see well, but a man would run his hand over these piles of meat and sweep off handfuls of the dried dung of rats. ❷ These rats were nuisances, and the packers would put poisoned bread out for them; they would die, and then rats, bread, and meat would go into the hoppers together . . . ❸ There was no place for the men to wash their hands before they ate their dinner, and so they made a practice of washing them in the water that was to be ladled into the sausage. ❹

CONNECTING LITERATURE TO HISTORY

1. **Identify Cause and Effect** Jacob Riis and Upton Sinclair were both muckraking journalists. Why do you think so much muck existed in the tenements and in the meatpacking business? Why had people ignored those conditions for so long?

2. **Identify Cause and Effect** Both Riis and Sinclair believed that improving conditions for immigrants would benefit all of society. Explain how one specific change in the tenements might have a favorable effect on everyone. Then explain how one specific change in meat handling might affect everyone.

3. **Compare and Contrast** Both *How the Other Half Lives* and *The Jungle* inspired Progressives to work for reform. Which work do you think had the greater effect on its readers? Use details from each passage to explain your answer.

Reforming the Workplace

What You Will Learn...

Main Ideas

1. Reformers attempted to improve conditions for child laborers.
2. Unions and reformers took steps to improve safety in the workplace and to limit working hours.

The Big Idea

In the early 1900s, Progressives and other reformers focused on improving conditions for American workers.

Key Terms and People

Triangle Shirtwaist Fire, *p. 673*
workers' compensation laws, *p. 673*
capitalism, *p. 674*
socialism, *p. 674*
William "Big Bill" Haywood, *p. 674*
Industrial Workers of the World, *p. 674*

TAKING NOTES As you read, take notes on important labor problems and the workers they affected. You can organize your notes in a table like this one.

Problems in the Workplace

 8.2.3, 8.4.2

If YOU were there...

You have been working in a hat factory since 1900, when you were eight years old. Now you are experienced enough to run one of the sewing machines. You don't earn as much as older workers, but your family needs every penny you bring home. Still, the long hours make you very tired. One day you hear that people are trying to stop children from doing factory work. They think that children should be at school or playing.

Would you be for or against this social reform? Why?

BUILDING BACKGROUND Since the Second Industrial Revolution, more and more people were working long hours in difficult conditions. With adult workers earning low wages, many children had to work full time to help support their families. Progressive reformers began to focus on these problems.

Improving Conditions for Children

In the early 1900s a reformer named Marie Van Vorst took a series of jobs in factories and clothing mills around the country. She wanted to investigate working conditions for children by living and working alongside them. In a South Carolina textile mill, Van Vorst met children as young as seven years old. She described working with one young child:

❝Through the looms I catch sight of ... my landlord's little child. She is seven; so small that they have a box for her to stand on ... I can see only her fingers as they clutch at the flying spools.❞
– Marie Van Vorst, quoted in *A History of Women in America,* edited by Carol Hymowitz

This girl—and other children like her—provided cheap labor for manufacturers. Some children were paid as little as 40 cents per day. Marie Van Vorst helped focus attention on the problem of child labor. Eliminating the problems of child labor became a major issue for Progressives and other reformers.

Children at Work

Children did many jobs in the late 1800s. Boys sold newspapers and shined shoes on the streets. Girls often cooked or cleaned for boarders staying with their families. Girls also worked at home with their mothers, sewing clothes or making handicrafts.

Like the child Van Vorst encountered, many children worked in industry. In 1900 more than 1.75 million children age 15 and under worked in factories, mines, and mills, earning very low wages.

Calls for Reform

As reporters published shocking accounts of working conditions for children, more people became aware of the problem. Progressives began to call for new reforms. You have read about Florence Kelley's work against child labor in Illinois. Kelley also served as a board member of the National Consumers' League, the major lobbying group for women's and children's labor issues. A lobbying group works to influence legislators in favor of a cause.

During the early 1900s, reformers finally succeeded in getting some laws passed to ease the conditions of child laborers. In 1912 the state of Massachusetts passed the first minimum wage law, and a commission was created to establish rates for child workers.

In 1916 and 1919 Congress passed federal child labor laws. The laws banned products made with child labor from being shipped from one state to another. The Supreme Court, however, ruled that the laws were unconstitutional. The Court argued that the laws went beyond the federal government's legal power to regulate interstate commerce.

In any case, laws alone could not end child labor. Some parents ignored child labor laws so that their children could continue contributing to the family income. Children were often instructed to lie about their age to government inspectors and tell them they were older than they really were.

FOCUS ON READING
What do you think the author's goal is in this paragraph?

READING CHECK **Finding Main Ideas** How did reformers try to improve child labor conditions?

Child Labor

Young children did much of the work in the American factories of the late 1800s. They were paid less than adult workers.

Why did some parents want their children to work?

Working Conditions for Children, Early 1900s

This illustration shows some of the jobs that children did in glass factories in the early 1900s. You can see that there were many ways for young workers to be injured on the job.

Hot air blew from the glass ovens into the working space.

Adult workers closely supervised child workers.

Workers wore no protection against the fires and machinery.

Temperatures in the ovens used to make glass were more than 2,000° Fahrenheit.

Bending and lifting often left young workers tired and sore after their long day's work.

ANALYSIS SKILL **ANALYZING VISUALS**

Using the illustration, what can you tell about the life and work of these boys?

Safety and Working Conditions

Child labor reform was only part of the progressive effort to help American workers. Many Progressives also favored laws to ensure workers' safety, limit working hours, and protect workers' rights.

Workplace Safety

Workplace accidents were common in the 1800s and early 1900s. In 1900 some 35,000 people were killed in industrial accidents. About 500,000 suffered injuries. One child described how her sister was injured using a machine in a string factory. "You see you mustn't talk or look off a minute," she explained. "My sister was like me. She forgot and talked, and just that minute her finger was off, and she didn't even cry till she picked it up."

Accidents like this were not big news in the early 1900s, but in 1911 a much greater workplace tragedy shocked the nation. It took place at the Triangle Shirtwaist Company, a New York City clothing factory that employed mostly Jewish and Italian teenage immigrant women. On the afternoon of March 25, a fire started on the eighth floor of the factory. Workers tried to escape, but factory owners had locked the exit doors—to reduce theft of materials, they said.

By the time firefighters brought the fire under control, 146 workers had died. At a memorial service for the victims, union leader Rose Schneiderman called for action. "It is up to the working people to save themselves," she said. The **Triangle Shirtwaist Fire** and similar accidents led to the passage of laws improving factory safety standards.

Labor leaders and reformers also fought for **workers' compensation laws**, which guaranteed a portion of lost wages to workers injured on the job. In 1902 Maryland became the first state to pass such a law. However, new laws were not always strictly enforced. Working conditions remained poor in many places.

TRIAL TRANSCRIPT
Triangle Shirtwaist Fire

Ethel Monick was one of the teenage factory workers at the Triangle Shirtwaist Company. In the trial that followed the disaster, she described her experience in the fire. Rose Freedman, pictured, was the longest living survivor of the fire. She died in 2001.

I seen the fire and then I seen all the girls rushing down to the place to escape. So I tried to go through the Greene Street door, and there were quick girls there and I seen I can't get out there, so I went to the elevator, and then I heard the elevator fall down, so I ran through to the Washington Place side . . . I tried the door and I could not open it, so I thought I was not strong enough to open it, so I hollered girls here is a door, and they all rushed over and they tried to open it, but it was locked and they hollered "the door is locked and we can't open it!"

—Testimony of Ethel Monick, age 16

ANALYSIS **SKILL** ANALYZING PRIMARY SOURCES

According to Monick, what is the feeling in the factory?

The Courts and Labor

Not everyone supported the new workplace regulations. Some business leaders believed that the economy should operate without any government interference. They went to court to block new labor laws.

One important case began in New York in 1897, after the state passed a law limiting bakers to a 10-hour workday. Joseph Lochner, a bakery owner, challenged the law. The case eventually went to the U.S. Supreme Court in 1905. In *Lochner* v. *New York*, the Court ruled that states could not restrict the rights of employers and workers to enter into any type of labor agreement. The New York law was declared unconstitutional.

The Supreme Court did uphold some limits on working hours for women and children. In the 1908 *Muller* v. *Oregon* case, the Court upheld laws restricting women's work hours. The justices stated that such laws protected women's health, which was of public concern.

Labor Organizations

Labor unions were also a strong force for improving working conditions. Union membership rose from about 800,000 in 1900 to about 5 million in 1920. Led by Samuel Gompers, the American Federation of Labor (AFL) remained one of the strongest labor unions. The AFL focused on better working conditions and pay for skilled workers. Gompers supported the American system of **capitalism**, an economic system in which private businesses run most industries and competition determines the price of goods.

Some union members, however, believed in **socialism**—a system in which the government owns and operates a country's means of production. Socialists, led by Eugene V. Debs, hoped that the government would protect workers.

In 1905 a group of socialists and union leaders founded a union that welcomed immigrants, women, African Americans, and others not welcome in the AFL. Led by **William "Big Bill" Haywood**, this socialist union was called the **Industrial Workers of the World** (IWW). Its goal was to organize all workers into one large union that would overthrow capitalism. Staging strikes across the country, the IWW frightened many Americans with its aggressive tactics. Strong opposition led to its decline by 1920.

READING CHECK **Analyzing** How did reforms change the workplace?

SUMMARY AND PREVIEW Progressive reformers fought to improve working conditions. In the next section you will learn about how women and minorities struggled for their rights.

Section 2 Assessment

go.hrw.com
Online Quiz
KEYWORD: SF7 HP21

Reviewing Ideas, Terms, and People

1. **a. Recall** What jobs did child laborers often hold?
   b. Explain Why did businesses employ children in factories?
   c. Elaborate Why do you think reformers began to demand improvements to child labor conditions?
2. **a. Identify** What events led to the movement to improve workplace safety?
   b. Make Inferences Why did the **Industrial Workers of the World** frighten some people?
   c. Predict What conflicts might arise between supporters of **capitalism** and **socialism**?

Critical Thinking

3. **Analyzing** Review your notes on labor reforms and workers. Then copy the graphic organizer shown below. Use it to give specific examples of how Progressives tried to reform child labor, women's labor, and workplace conditions.

Labor Reform	Child labor:
	Women's labor:
	Workplace conditions:

FOCUS ON SPEAKING

4. **Addressing Problems in the Workplace** How would you address problems in the workplace? Make notes on campaign promises you might make to assure voters that you would address issues of child labor and workplace safety.

The Rights of Women and Minorities

If YOU were there...

You are a member of the graduating class of 1912 from an excellent women's college. You have always been interested in science, especially biology. You would like to be a doctor, but you know that medical schools accept very few women. One career path for you is to go into social work. Yet that's not what you really want to do.

How would you want to use your education?

BUILDING BACKGROUND The Progressives had a wide variety of goals. Besides attacking social problems such as child labor, they worked to reform government and make it more democratic. Changes in women's education affected the movement, as college-educated women often became leaders in working for reforms.

Women Fight for Temperance and Voting Rights

New educational opportunities drew more women into the Progressive movement. In the late 1800s, women began attending women's colleges, such as Smith College in Massachusetts and Vassar College in New York, in record numbers. In 1870 only about 20 percent of college students were women. By 1910 that number had doubled. The goal of female students was "to develop as fully as may be the powers of womanhood," said Sophia Smith, founder of Smith College.

Many women graduates entered fields such as social work and teaching. They found it much harder to enter professions such as law and medicine, which were dominated by men. Denied access to such professions, women often put their education to use by becoming active in reform. Women's clubs campaigned for causes such as temperance, women's suffrage, child welfare, and political reform.

What You Will Learn...

Main Ideas
1. Women fought for temperance and the right to vote.
2. African American reformers challenged discrimination and called for equality.
3. Progressive reforms failed to benefit all minorities.

The Big Idea
The Progressive movement made advances for the rights of women and some minorities.

Key Terms and People
Eighteenth Amendment, *p. 676*
National American Woman Suffrage Association, *p. 676*
Alice Paul, *p. 677*
Nineteenth Amendment, *p. 677*
Booker T. Washington, *p. 677*
Ida B. Wells, *p. 677*
W. E. B. Du Bois, *p. 678*
National Association for the Advancement of Colored People, *p. 678*

TAKING NOTES As you read, take notes on the causes supported by different groups of progressive reformers. In each circle of a diagram like the one below, fill in details about one cause or goal. You may need to add more circles.

Progressive Reforms

8.2.9, 8.4.5

The Temperance Movement

In the mid-1800s many of these reformers blamed social problems such as family violence and criminal behavior on a number of factors, including urbanization and immigration. They also blamed problems on alcohol consumption. As a result, many groups took up the cause of temperance, or avoidance of alcohol.

In 1874, reformers from many different backgrounds formed the Woman's Christian Temperance Union (WCTU), which fought for adoption of local and state laws restricting the sale of alcohol. Under the leadership of Frances Willard, the organization started 10,000 branches. More than 1,000 saloons were forced to shut down as a result of temperance supporters' efforts.

One especially radical temperance fighter chose more aggressive methods to fight for her cause. In the 1890s Carry Nation became famous for storming into saloons with a hatchet and smashing liquor bottles. Nation described destroying a Kansas saloon with bricks and rocks:

"I threw as hard, and as fast as I could, smashing mirrors and bottles and glasses and it was astonishing how quickly this was done."

—Carry Nation, quoted in *Witnessing America: The Library of Congress Book of Firsthand Accounts of Life in America, 1600–1900*

In 1919 many years of temperance efforts led to the passage of the **Eighteenth Amendment**, banning the production, sale, and transportation of alcoholic beverages throughout the United States.

The Right to Vote

Women reformers also fought for suffrage, or the right to vote. Many people at this time opposed giving women the vote. Political bosses, for instance, worried about the anti-corruption efforts of women. Some business leaders worried that women voters would support minimum wage and child labor laws. Other people believed that women should only be homemakers and mothers and not politically active citizens.

In spite of such opposition, the women's suffrage movement began to gain national support in the 1890s. Elizabeth Cady Stanton and Susan B. Anthony founded the **National American Woman Suffrage Association** (NAWSA) in 1890 to promote the cause of women's suffrage. That same year, women

Time Line

The Nineteenth Amendment

Women had been seeking the right to vote since 1776. Finally, in 1920 they achieved success with the passage of the Nineteenth Amendment.

1919

May 21, 1919 The House of Representatives passes the Nineteenth Amendment by a vote of 304 to 89.

June 4, 1919 The Senate passes the Nineteenth Amendment by a vote of 56 to 25.

June 10, 1919 Illinois, Michigan, and Wisconsin become the first states to ratify the Nineteenth Amendment.

won the right to vote in Wyoming. Colorado, Idaho, and Utah followed.

Carrie Chapman Catt became president of the NAWSA in 1900. Catt mobilized more than 1 million volunteers for the movement. She argued that women should have a voice in creating laws that affected them. "We women demand an equal voice," she said. "We shall accept nothing less."

Some women believed that NAWSA did not go far enough. In 1913 **Alice Paul** founded what would become the National Woman's Party (NWP). The NWP used parades, public demonstrations, picketing, hunger strikes, and other means to draw attention to the suffrage cause. Paul even organized picketing in front of the White House. Paul and other NWP leaders were jailed for their actions.

Suffragists finally succeeded in gaining the vote. In 1919 the U.S. Congress passed the **Nineteenth Amendment**, granting American women the right to vote. The Nineteenth Amendment was ratified by the states the following year, making it law.

READING CHECK **Analyzing** How did reformers draw attention to the temperance and women's suffrage movements?

African Americans Challenge Discrimination

White reformers often overlooked issues such as racial discrimination and segregation. African American reformers took the lead in addressing these problems.

One of the most important African American leaders was **Booker T. Washington**. Born into slavery, he became a respected educator while in his twenties. Washington's strategy was not to fight discrimination directly. Instead, he encouraged African Americans to improve their educational and economic well-being. This, he believed, would eventually lead to the end of discrimination.

Other African Americans spoke out more directly against discrimination. Journalist **Ida B. Wells** wrote articles about the unequal education available to African American children. In her Memphis newspaper *Free Speech*, Wells also drew attention to the lynching of African Americans. During lynchings people were murdered by mobs instead of receiving a trial after being accused of a crime, or even for breaking social codes. More than 3,000 African Americans were lynched between 1885 and 1915.

Although death threats forced Wells to move to the North, she continued campaigning against lynching. In 1900 she wrote:

"Our country's national crime is *lynching* … In fact, for all kinds of offenses—and, for no offenses— from murders to misdemeanors, men and women are put to death without judge or jury."
—Ida B. Wells, from her article "Lynch Law in America"

1920

August 18, 1920 Tennessee becomes the thirty-sixth state to ratify the Nineteenth Amendment.

August 26, 1920 The secretary of state officially declares the Nineteenth Amendment ratified by three-fourths of the states, making it law.

November 2, 1920 The first national election in which all women can vote is held.

1921

THE PROGRESSIVE SPIRIT OF REFORM **677**

Like Wells, **W. E. B. Du Bois** took a direct approach to fighting racial injustice. Born in Massachusetts, Du Bois was a college graduate who earned a doctorate from Harvard University. As part of his research, he studied and publicized cases of racial prejudice. Du Bois believed that African Americans should protest unjust treatment and demand equal rights.

In 1909 Du Bois and other reformers founded the **National Association for the Advancement of Colored People** (NAACP), an organization that called for economic and educational equality for African Americans. The NAACP attacked discrimination by using the courts. In 1915 it won the important case of *Guinn* v. *United States,* which made grandfather clauses illegal. These laws were used in the South to keep African Americans

THE IMPACT TODAY

Today the NAACP claims around 2,200 adult branches and 1,700 branches for young people.

from voting. Grandfather clauses imposed strict qualifications on voters unless their grandfathers had been allowed to vote. Many white voters met this requirement and were therefore automatically permitted to vote in elections. However, most African Americans' grandfathers had been enslaved and could not vote.

Another important organization, the National Urban League, was formed in 1911 by Dr. George Edmund Haynes. This organization aided many African Americans moving from the South by helping them find jobs and housing in northern cities. The League addressed many of the same problems faced by other Progressives, such as health, sanitation, and education.

READING CHECK **Finding Main Ideas** What was the purpose of the NAACP?

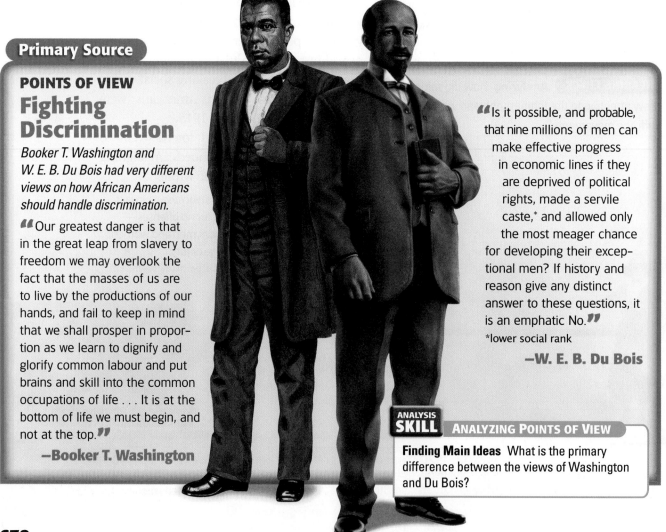

Primary Source

POINTS OF VIEW
Fighting Discrimination

Booker T. Washington and W. E. B. Du Bois had very different views on how African Americans should handle discrimination.

❝Our greatest danger is that in the great leap from slavery to freedom we may overlook the fact that the masses of us are to live by the productions of our hands, and fail to keep in mind that we shall prosper in proportion as we learn to dignify and glorify common labour and put brains and skill into the common occupations of life . . . It is at the bottom of life we must begin, and not at the top.❞

—Booker T. Washington

❝Is it possible, and probable, that nine millions of men can make effective progress in economic lines if they are deprived of political rights, made a servile caste,* and allowed only the most meager chance for developing their exceptional men? If history and reason give any distinct answer to these questions, it is an emphatic No.❞

*lower social rank

—W. E. B. Du Bois

ANALYSIS SKILL **ANALYZING POINTS OF VIEW**

Finding Main Ideas What is the primary difference between the views of Washington and Du Bois?

Failures of Reform

Other minority groups felt left behind by the Progressive movement. Although some reformers tried to aid such groups, the aim of many was to encourage other ethnicities to adopt the ways of European society. The Society of American Indians, formed in 1911, was one such attempt. Started by Native American doctors Carlos Montezuma and Charles Eastman, the society believed that integration into white society would end Native American poverty. Many Native Americans, however, wanted to preserve their traditional culture. They resisted the movement toward adopting white culture.

Immigrant groups from non-European countries also formed groups to help support their members. Chinese immigrants, for example, organized neighborhood associations in the communities in which they lived. District associations, cultural groups, churches, and temples provided public services that white reformers ignored. Such groups provided the money for building San Francisco's Chinese hospital in 1925. Chinese immigration dropped, however, due in part to anti-Chinese riots that occurred in some western towns and cities.

While fewer Chinese immigrants came to the United States, the number of Mexican immigrants increased. The northern and southern borders between the United States and its neighbors were fairly easy to cross in this period. Many Mexican immigrants moved to the South and Southwest, where they became an important part of the societies and economies of these regions. Many Mexican immigrants found jobs in the mining and railroad industries. Others began farms or became migrant workers. Progressive labor laws and factory reforms did nothing to improve the poor living and working conditions of migrant farm workers.

READING CHECK **Summarizing** What were the limitations of progressive reforms?

SUMMARY AND PREVIEW Many U.S. citizens worked for progressive reforms. In the next section you will read about presidents who also worked for progressive goals.

go.hrw.com
Online Quiz
KEYWORD: SF7 HP21

Section 3 Assessment

Reviewing Ideas, Terms, and People

1. **a. Identify** What did the **Eighteenth** and **Nineteenth Amendments** accomplish?
   b. Summarize How did **Alice Paul** and the National Woman's Party try to draw attention to the issue of women's suffrage?

2. **a. Identify** What role did **Ida B. Wells** play in reform efforts for African Americans?
   b. Contrast How did **Booker T. Washington** differ from other African American leaders?
   c. Evaluate Do you think the **National Association for the Advancement of Colored People** was successful in fighting discrimination? Explain.

3. **a. Describe** What discrimination did Chinese Americans face?
   b. Summarize How were some minority groups overlooked by the Progressive movement?

Critical Thinking

4. **Analyzing** Review your notes on Progressives' causes. Then copy the diagram shown and use it to identify the progressive reforms introduced by the temperance movement, the women's suffrage movement, and African Americans.

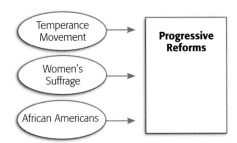

FOCUS ON SPEAKING

5. **Addressing the Rights of Women and Minorities** Review this section's material on education for women, women's suffrage, temperance, racial discrimination, and segregation. As a politician, what promises would you make regarding these issues? Think about how you would make your ideas acceptable to the American public. Would you be willing to compromise your ideals?

The Progressive Presidents

What You Will Learn...

Main Ideas

1. Theodore Roosevelt's progressive reforms tried to balance the interests of business, consumers, and laborers.
2. William Howard Taft angered Progressives with his cautious reforms, while Woodrow Wilson enacted far-reaching banking and antitrust reforms.

The Big Idea

American presidents in the early 1900s did a great deal to promote progressive reforms.

Key Terms and People

Theodore Roosevelt, *p. 680*
Pure Food and Drug Act, *p. 681*
conservation, *p. 681*
William Howard Taft, *p. 682*
Progressive Party, *p. 682*
Woodrow Wilson, *p. 682*
Sixteenth Amendment, *p. 683*

TAKING NOTES As you read, take notes on the achievements of each of the progressive presidents. Use a table like the one below to organize your notes.

Roosevelt	Taft	Wilson

8.2.4, 8.2.9, 8.3.8, 8.3.10, 8.3.11, 8.4.2, 8.4.4

If YOU were there...

It is 1912 and you're voting in your first presidential election. This election is unusual—there are three major candidates. One is the popular former president Theodore Roosevelt, who is running as a third-party candidate. He thinks the Republican candidate will not make enough progressive reforms. But the Democratic candidate is a progressive reformer too.

How will you decide which candidate to support?

BUILDING BACKGROUND Political corruption was one early target of the progressive reformers. Some politicians who joined them believed that government—local, state, and national—should play an active role in improving society and people's lives.

Roosevelt's Progressive Reforms

During a summer tour after his second inauguration in 1901, President William McKinley met a friendly crowd in Buffalo, New York. Suddenly, anarchist Leon Czolgosz stepped forward and shot the president. A little more than a week later, McKinley died. Vice President **Theodore Roosevelt** took office.

Roosevelt's Square Deal

Roosevelt believed that the interests of businesspeople, laborers, and consumers should be balanced for the public good. He called this policy the Square Deal. He put the policy to the test in 1902 when faced by a coal miners' strike. Roosevelt knew the strike might leave the country without heating fuel for the coming winter. He threatened to take over the mines unless managers and strikers agreed to arbitration—a formal process to settle disputes. He felt this was the only fair way to protect Americans.

"The labor unions shall have a square deal, and the corporations shall have a square deal, and in addition all private citizens shall have a square deal."

—President Theodore Roosevelt, quoted in *The Presidency of Theodore Roosevelt*, by Lewis L. Gould

The National Park System

In 1872 Yellowstone National Park, located mostly in Wyoming, became the first national park in the United States—and the world. Today there are 55 national parks in the United States. They are managed by the National Park Service (NPS), an agency of the federal government established in 1916. The National Park Service administers almost 84 million acres (133,000 square miles) of land.

President Theodore Roosevelt and conservationist John Muir in Yosemite National Park in California

Cathedral Rocks, Yosemite National Park

Regulating Big Business

Roosevelt made regulating big business a top goal of his administration. Muckrakers helped build support for this regulation. The public was shocked, for instance, after reading Upton Sinclair's description of the meatpacking industry in *The Jungle*. Roosevelt opened an investigation and later convinced Congress to pass a meat inspection law.

In 1906 Congress passed the **Pure Food and Drug Act**. This law prohibited the manufacture, sale, and transport of mislabeled or contaminated food and drugs. Roosevelt also was the first president to successfully use the 1890 Sherman Antitrust Act to break up a monopoly. He persuaded Congress to regulate railroad shipping rates. The public largely supported this expansion of federal regulatory powers.

Conservation

Roosevelt's love of the outdoors inspired him to join other Progressives in supporting **conservation**, or the protection of nature and its resources. Roosevelt was the first president to consider conservation an important national priority.

People believed in conservation for various reasons. Preservationists such as John Muir thought that nature should be left untouched so that people could enjoy its beauty:

"Thousands of tired, nerve-shaken, over-civilized people are beginning to find out that going to the mountains is going home; that wildness is a necessity; and that mountain parks and reservations are useful not only as fountains of timber and irrigating rivers, but as fountains of life."
—John Muir, *Our National Parks*

Other conservationists wanted to make sure the nation used its natural resources efficiently. Gifford Pinchot, the first head of the newly created Forest Service, valued forests for the resources they provided to build "prosperous homes." The disagreement between the two ideals of conservation eventually widened.

While Roosevelt was in office, the Forest Service gained control of nearly 150 million acres of public land. Roosevelt doubled the number of national parks, created 18 national monuments, and started 51 bird sanctuaries.

READING CHECK **Summarizing** What reforms did Roosevelt support?

Reforms of Taft and Wilson

Theodore Roosevelt hoped that his secretary of war, **William Howard Taft**, would take his place as president in 1908. Like Roosevelt, Taft favored business regulation and opposed socialism. With Roosevelt's assistance, Taft defeated William Jennings Bryan in the election of 1908.

Taft Angers Progressives

Despite their friendship, Roosevelt and Taft held different ideas about how a president should act. Taft thought Roosevelt had claimed more power than a president was constitutionally allowed.

ACADEMIC VOCABULARY

various
of many types

As president, therefore, Taft chose to move cautiously toward reform and regulation. This upset Roosevelt and **various** Progressives, who supported stricter regulation of big business. Although Taft's administration started twice as many antitrust lawsuits as Roosevelt's had, Progressives were not satisfied.

Taft angered Progressives further by signing the Payne-Aldrich Tariff of 1909. This tariff reduced some rates on imported goods, but it raised others. Progressives wanted all tariffs to be lowered, in order to lower prices for consumers.

Furious with Taft, Roosevelt decided to run for president again in 1912. After Taft won the Republican nomination, Roosevelt and his followers formed the **Progressive Party**. It was nicknamed the Bull Moose Party because Roosevelt said he was "as strong as a bull moose." The split between Taft and Roosevelt divided the Republican vote, and Democratic candidate **Woodrow Wilson** won the electoral vote by a wide margin.

Wilson's Reforms

In his inaugural address, Wilson spoke of the terrible social conditions under which many working-class Americans lived. "We have been proud of our industrial achievements," he said, "but we have not hitherto [yet] stopped thoughtfully enough to count the human cost." Passing reform legislation was Wilson's top goal. He pushed for two measures soon after taking office: tariff revision and banking reform.

Wilson backed the Underwood Tariff Act of 1913, which lowered tariffs. The act also introduced a version of the modern

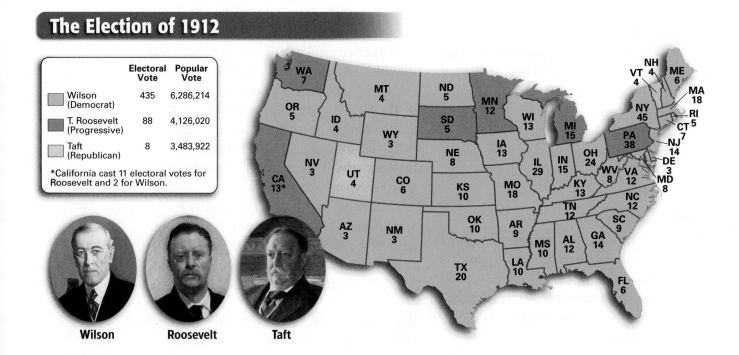

The Election of 1912

	Electoral Vote	Popular Vote
Wilson (Democrat)	435	6,286,214
T. Roosevelt (Progressive)	88	4,126,020
Taft (Republican)	8	3,483,922

*California cast 11 electoral votes for Roosevelt and 2 for Wilson.

WA 7 | OR 5 | ID 4 | MT 4 | WY 3 | NV 3 | CA 13* | UT 4 | CO 6 | AZ 3 | NM 3 | ND 5 | SD 5 | NE 8 | KS 10 | OK 10 | TX 20 | MN 12 | IA 13 | MO 18 | AR 9 | LA 10 | WI 13 | IL 29 | MS 10 | AL 12 | MI 15 | IN 15 | KY 13 | TN 12 | GA 14 | FL 6 | OH 24 | WV 8 | VA 12 | NC 12 | SC 9 | PA 38 | NY 45 | MD 8 | DE 3 | NJ 14 | CT 7 | RI 5 | MA 18 | VT 4 | NH 4 | ME 6

Wilson   Roosevelt   Taft

The Progressive Amendments, 1909–1920

QUICK FACTS

Number	Description	Proposed by Congress	Ratified by States
16th	Federal income tax	1909	1913
17th	Senators elected by people rather than state legislatures	1912	1913
18th	Manufacture, sale, and transport of alcohol prohibited	1917	1919
19th	Women's suffrage	1919	1920

income tax. The new tax was made possible in 1913 by the ratification of the **Sixteenth Amendment**. This amendment allows the federal government to impose direct taxes on citizens' incomes.

President Wilson next addressed banking reform with the 1913 Federal Reserve Act. This law created a national banking system called the Federal Reserve to regulate the economy.

Wilson also pushed for laws to regulate big business. The Clayton Antitrust Act of 1914 strengthened federal laws against monopolies. The Federal Trade Commission, created in 1914, had the power to investigate and punish unfair trade practices. Wilson's success in guiding reform programs through Congress helped him to win re-election in 1916.

READING CHECK **Analyzing** Why did Wilson win the election of 1912?

SUMMARY AND PREVIEW The progressive presidents tried to change American society for the better. In the next chapter you will learn how they also helped the United States become a world power.

Section 4 Assessment

go.hrw.com
Online Quiz
KEYWORD: SF7 HP21

Reviewing Ideas, Terms, and People

1. **a. Describe** How did **Theodore Roosevelt** support progressive reforms?
   b. Analyze Why did many Americans support **conservation**?
   c. Evaluate Do you think Roosevelt's reforms benefited the nation? Why or why not?
2. **a. Identify** What was the **Progressive Party**? Why was it created?
   b. Compare and Contrast How were the administrations of **William Howard Taft** and Roosevelt similar, and how were they different?
   c. Evaluate Which president do you think had the biggest influence on progressive reform—Roosevelt, Taft, or **Woodrow Wilson**? Explain your choice.

Critical Thinking

3. **Comparing and Contrasting** Review your notes on the progressive presidents. Then copy the diagram below and use it to compare and contrast the reforms of the progressive presidents.

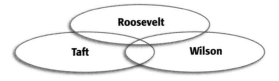

FOCUS ON SPEAKING

4. **The Ideas of Roosevelt, Taft, and Wilson** Do you agree or disagree with Presidents Roosevelt, Taft, and Wilson? Take notes on any of their ideas that you would include in your campaign promises.

Social Studies Skills

Analysis   Critical Thinking   Civic Participation   Study

Short- and Long-term Causal Relationships

Define the Skill

Most historical events are the result of other events. When something happens as a result of other things that occur, it is an effect of those things. Some events take place soon after the things that cause them. Such events are called *short-term effects*. In contrast, *long-term effects* can occur years, decades, or even hundreds of years after the events that caused them. Being able to recognize short-term and long-term cause-and-effect relationships will help you to better understand historical events.

Learn the Skill

Clue words can sometimes reveal a cause-and-effect relationship between events. Often, however, such language clues may not be present. Therefore, when you study history, you should always look for other clues that might explain why an action or event occurred.

Short-term effects are usually fairly easy to identify. In historical writing they are often closely linked to the event that caused them. For example, consider this passage from Chapter 21.

" Some Progressives worked to change state and local governments in order to reduce the power of political machines. In many places, reformers replaced corrupt ballots that listed only one party's candidates with government-prepared ballots that listed all candidates. Under pressure from reformers, many states adopted secret ballots, giving every voter a private vote. "

This passage contains no clue words. Yet it is clear that cause-and-effect relationships exist. The power of political machines created corrupt voting practices. Reformers wanted to change this. One effect of this situation was the government-prepared ballot, and another was the secret ballot.

Recognizing long-term causal relationships is often more difficult. Since long-term effects take place well after the event that caused them, they may not be discussed at the same time as their cause. This is why you should always question why an event occurred as you learn about it. For example, in 1971 Congress passed the first federal law to protect the health and safety of all workers. This law was a long-term result of efforts begun years earlier by the progressives you read about in this chapter.

Many long-term effects result from major forces running through history that make things happen. They include economics, science and technology, expansion, conflict and cooperation among people, cultural clashes and differences, and moral and religious issues. Ask yourself if one of these forces is involved in the event being studied. If so, the event may have long-term effects that you should be on the lookout for when studying later events.

Practice and Apply the Skill

Review the information in Chapter 21 and answer these questions to practice recognizing short- and long-term causal relationships.

1. All packaged food today must have its contents listed on the container. This requirement is a long-term effect of what progressive reform?

2. Write a paragraph explaining the effects of the muckrakers on the news media today.

Chapter Review

HOLT

History's Impact

▶ **video series**
Review the video to answer the closing question:

How did the rights of women in individual states play a role in the women's suffrage movement?

Visual Summary

Use the visual summary below to help you review the main ideas of the chapter.

Progressives hoped to improve society through reform. Their goals included

- Temperance
- Women's suffrage
- Big business regulation
- Conservation
- Tariff and banking reform

PROSPERITY

Reviewing Vocabulary, Terms, and People

Complete each sentence by filling in the blank with the correct term or person from the chapter.

1. Some Americans supported a _____ system, which proposed government ownership of the country's means of production.

2. Republican _____ began a program to reform state politics in Wisconsin.

3. The _____ granted women in the United States the right to vote.

4. The _____ prohibited the manufacture, sale, and transport of mislabeled or contaminated food and drugs.

5. During the Gilded Age, _____ often dominated local politics and used corruption to get their candidates elected.

6. _____ were journalists who wrote about troubling issues such as child labor, tenement housing, and political corruption.

Comprehension and Critical Thinking

SECTION 1 *(Pages 662–667)*

7. **a. Describe** What tactics did bosses and political machines use to gain control of local governments?

b. Analyze What changes did Progressives make to city life?

c. Elaborate Which progressive reform do you think had the greatest effect on Americans?

SECTION 2 *(Pages 670–674)*

8. **a. Identify** What reforms were made to improve working conditions, and who was affected by these reforms?

b. Contrast What are the differences between capitalism and socialism?

c. Elaborate If you were a business owner, would you have supported the progressive workplace reforms? Explain your answer.

SECTION 3 (Pages 675–679)

9. a. Recall What minority groups were overlooked by progressive reform efforts?

b. Analyze How did women's involvement in the Progressive movement lead to constitutional change?

c. Elaborate Do you agree with Booker T. Washington's approach to improving life for African Americans? Explain your answer.

SECTION 4 (Pages 680–683)

10. a. Describe How did William Howard Taft disappoint Progressives?

b. Compare In what ways were the reforms of Presidents Roosevelt, Taft, and Wilson similar?

c. Elaborate Would you have supported Wilson's progressive reforms? Explain your answer.

Reviewing Themes

11. Politics What role did political machines play in local politics during the Gilded Age?

12. Society and Culture How were children affected by the movement for workplace reforms?

Reading Skills

Evaluating Sources *Use the Reading Skills taught in this chapter to answer the question about the reading selection below.*

> The next day Rose went to town [Chicago] alone. The wind had veered [turned] to the south, the dust blew, and the whole terrifying panorama [view] of life in the street seemed some way blurred together, and forms of men and animals were like figures in tapestry. The grind and clang and clatter and hiss and howl of the traffic was all about her . . .
>
> —Hamlin Garland, from his novel *Rose of Dutcher's Coolly*, 1895

13. Is this a good source for understanding the experiences of Chicago in the late 1800s? Why or why not?

Social Studies Skills

Short- and Long-Term Causal Relationships *Use the Social Studies Skills taught in this chapter to answer the question about the reading selection below.*

> Despite their friendship, Roosevelt and Taft held different ideas about how a president should act. Taft thought Roosevelt had claimed more power than a president was constitutionally allowed.
>
> As president, therefore, Taft chose to move cautiously toward reform and regulation. *(p. 682)*

14. According to the passage above, what was a long-term cause of Taft's cautious reforms?

Using the Internet

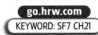
go.hrw.com
KEYWORD: SF7 CH21

15. Activity: Researching Progressives Rapid industrial and urban growth in America in the late 1800s resulted in a number of problems. Progressives worked to address these issues in many ways, including efforts to clean up political corruption, improve working conditions, and enact social reforms. Enter the activity keyword and explore the lives of some of the leaders of the Progressive movement. Then write a profile of a Progressive leader that outlines his or her life and impact on American reform.

FOCUS ON SPEAKING

16. Share Your Campaign Promises Review your notes about possible campaign promises. Which promises will be most helpful in getting you elected? Look at your promises to see whether they focus on issues important to voters. Then write a speech including your campaign promises that you can deliver to your class.

DIRECTIONS: Read each question and write the letter of the best response.

1

The people in this photograph would probably have been *most* interested in which of the following reforms?

A secret ballots

B the Pure Food and Drug Act

C child labor laws

D elimination of political machines

2 **One direct result of immigration and urban growth was the rise of**

A political machines.

B the civil-service system.

C the spoils system.

D primary elections.

3 **What was the *main* idea behind the creation of the civil-service system in the late 1800s?**

A Government jobs should be awarded to people who support the party in power.

B Government workers should be required to support the elected officials who hire them.

C Government employees should be qualified to do the jobs for which they were hired.

D Government jobs should not be filled with employees who serve in those jobs for life.

4 **The Nineteenth Amendment to the Constitution increased democracy in the United States by**

A granting women the right to vote.

B allowing the people of each state to elect their senators.

C establishing direct primary elections.

D enabling voters to remove elected officials from office before the end of their terms.

5 **Earlier in the book you learned how Frederick Douglass wrote and spoke against slavery and unfair treatment of African Americans. What later reformer also spoke out for equal rights for African Americans?**

A John Dewey

B W. E. B. Du Bois

C William Howard Taft

D Upton Sinclair

6 **Read the following excerpt from an interview with a boss at Tammany Hall and use it to answer the question below.**

> There's only one way to hold a district: you must study human nature and act accordin' . . . To learn real human nature you have to go among the people, see them and be seen. I know every man, woman, and child in the Fifteenth District, except them that's been born this summer—and I know some of them, too. I know what they like and what they don't like, what they are strong at and what they are weak in, and I reach them by approachin' at the right side.
>
> —George Washington Plunkitt, quoted in *Eyewitnesses and Others*

Document-Based Question **How did Plunkitt say he kept his position in the political machine?**

America as a World Power

IN Indiana Standards

Social Studies Standards

8.3.9 Analyze human and physical factors that have influenced migration and settlement patterns and relate them to the economic development of the United States.

8.4.2 Illustrate elements of the three types of economic systems, using cases from United States history.

8.4.10 Examine the importance of borrowing and lending (the use of credit) in the United States and list the advantages and disadvantages of using credit.

go.hrw.com
Indiana
KEYWORD: SF10 IN

FOCUS ON WRITING

A List of Pros and Cons In the last half of the 1800s, the United States became more involved in international affairs. As you read this chapter, you will analyze the nation's new role and use the results of your analysis to guide U.S. policy in the future. In order to analyze the advantages and disadvantages of an aggressive foreign policy, you will need to create a list of the pros and cons of U.S. involvement with other nations in the late 1800s and early 1900s. As you create your list, note which items are facts and which are opinions—either yours or someone else's.

UNITED STATES

1867 The United States buys Alaska.

1867

1868 Japan begins a time of modernization known as the Meiji Restoration.

WORLD

HOLT

History's Impact
▶ video series
Watch the video to understand the impact of the United States as a world power.

What You Will Learn...

In this chapter you will learn about how the United States became a global power in the late 1800s and early 1900s. Through a combination of economic strength, military might, and aggressive foreign policy, America made its presence known in many parts of the world. One such place was Panama, where the United States built the Panama Canal, shown here. The United States has remained a powerful force on the international stage to this day.

1898
Within 24 hours of the call for troops, Indiana becomes the first state to fulfill a request for volunteers to fight in the Spanish-American War.

1890 Congress passes the McKinley Tariff, which gives a subsidy to U.S. sugar producers.

1898 The United States wins the Spanish-American War, gaining the Philippine Islands and Puerto Rico.

1914
The Panama Canal officially opens.

1880   1890   1900   1910   1920

1885 The Indian National Congress is formed in British-controlled India.

1895 Cubans rebel against Spanish rule.

1900 The Boxer Rebellion erupts in China.

1903 Panama declares itself an independent nation.

1910 The Mexican Revolution begins.

Reading Social Studies

by Kylene Beers

| Economics | Geography | Politics | Society and Culture | Science and Technology |

Focus on Themes In this chapter, you will learn about how the physical **geography** of the United States changed as it acquired overseas territories. You will also read about how national and international **politics** affected foreign policy and brought new responsibilities to the government of the United States.

Comparing Historical Texts

Focus on Reading A good way to learn what people in the past thought is to read what they wrote. However, most documents will only tell you one side of the story. By comparing writings by different people, you can learn a great deal about various sides of a historical issue or debate.

Comparing Texts When you compare historical texts, you should consider two things: who wrote the documents and what the documents were meant to achieve. To do this, you need to find the writers' main point or points.

Document 1

"We have cherished the policy of non-interference with affairs of foreign governments wisely inaugurated [begun] by Washington, keeping ourselves free from entanglement, either as allies or foes, content to leave undisturbed with them the settlement of their own domestic concerns."

–President William McKinley,
First Inaugural Address, 1897

Document 2

"Therefore, Mr. President, here is a war with terrible characteristics flagrant [obvious] at our very doors [in Cuba]. We have the power to bring it to an end. I believe that the whole American people would welcome steps in that direction."

–Senator Henry Cabot Lodge,
Speech in Congress, 1896

Document 1	Document 2
Writer	
President William McKinley	Senator Henry Cabot Lodge
Main point	
The United States should not involve itself in the affairs of other countries.	The United States should go to war in Cuba.
Both Sides of the Issue	
Americans were torn over the war in Cuba. Some thought the United States should remain uninvolved as it always had. Others thought it was time for a change in foreign policy.	

You Try It!

Read the following passages, both taken from presidential addresses to Congress. As you read, look for the main point each president makes in his address.

Foreign Policy

In treating of our foreign policy and of the attitude that this great Nation should assume in the world at large, it is absolutely necessary to consider the Army and the Navy, and the Congress, through which the thought of the Nation finds its expression, should keep ever vividly in mind the fundamental fact that it is impossible to treat our foreign policy, whether this policy takes shape in the effort to secure justice for others or justice for ourselves, save as conditioned upon the attitude we are willing to take toward our Army, and especially toward our Navy.

—President Theodore Roosevelt,
Message to Congress, 1904

The diplomacy of the present administration has sought to respond to modern ideas of commercial intercourse [involvement]. This policy has been characterized as substituting dollars for bullets. It is one that appeals alike to idealistic humanitarian sentiments [feelings], to the dictates [rules] of sound policy and strategy, and to legitimate [make real] commercial aims.

—President William Howard Taft,
Message to Congress, 1912

After you read the passages, answer the following questions.

1. What was the main point Roosevelt made in his address?

2. What was the main point Taft made in his address?

3. How can a comparison of Roosevelt's and Taft's addresses to Congress help you understand the issues that shaped U.S. foreign policy in the early 1900s?

Chapter 22

Section 1
imperialism *(p. 692)*
isolationism *(p. 693)*
William H. Seward *(p. 693)*
Liliuokalani *(p. 694)*
spheres of influence *(p. 695)*
Open Door Policy *(p. 695)*
Boxer Rebellion *(p. 695)*

Section 2
yellow journalism *(p. 697)*
Teller Amendment *(p. 698)*
Emilio Aguinaldo *(p. 699)*
Anti-Imperialist League *(p. 700)*
Platt Amendment *(p. 701)*

Section 3
Panama Canal *(p. 705)*
Roosevelt Corollary *(p. 707)*
dollar diplomacy *(p. 708)*
Mexican Revolution *(p. 708)*
John J. Pershing *(p. 709)*
Francisco "Pancho" Villa *(p. 709)*

Academic Vocabulary

In this chapter, you will learn the following academic words:

process *(p. 695)*
role *(p. 707)*

As you read Chapter 22, organize your notes to help you point out the similarities and differences among events or policies.

The United States Gains Overseas Territories

What You Will Learn...

Main Ideas

1. The United States ended its policy of isolationism.
2. Hawaii became a U.S. territory in 1898.
3. The United States sought trade with Japan and China.

The Big Idea

In the last half of the 1800s, the United States joined the race for control of overseas territories.

Key Terms and People

imperialism, *p. 692*
isolationism, *p. 693*
William H. Seward, *p. 693*
Liliuokalani, *p. 694*
spheres of influence, *p. 695*
Open Door Policy, *p. 695*
Boxer Rebellion, *p. 695*

 TAKING NOTES As you read, make a list of examples of U.S. expansion in a chart like this one.

Areas or Trade Rights Gained

 8.3.6, 8.3.9

If YOU were there...

You are a Hawaiian living on Maui, one of the Hawaiian Islands, in 1890. Your parents work in a sugar mill owned by American planters. Although the mill supplies jobs, you don't trust the sugar planters. They have already made your king sign a treaty that gives them a lot of power in the islands. You are afraid they will take over the government.

What would you do if the planters took over your islands?

BUILDING BACKGROUND In the mid-1800s, most Americans had little interest in being involved with the rest of the world diplomatically. The Civil War and Reconstruction kept their focus on challenges at home. In the meantime, though, European nations were busily acquiring overseas territories. The United States would soon join them.

End of Isolation

In the 1800s powerful Western nations were busy building naval bases to protect their shipping routes around the world. This was an aspect of **imperialism**—building an empire by founding colonies or conquering other nations. Between 1870 and 1914, Europeans extended their colonial empires until they controlled most of Africa and Southeast Asia.

Roots of Imperialism

Several forces drove this wave of European imperialism. Countries wanted sources of raw materials—such as copper, rubber, and tin—to fuel industrial growth. Businesspeople wanted new markets for their manufactured goods. And many

Europeans saw colonies as a source of power and national pride.

In contrast, the United States followed a limited policy of **isolationism**—avoiding involvement in the affairs of other countries. In 1789 President George Washington had warned Americans "to steer clear of permanent alliances" with other countries. American leaders tried to follow this advice by staying out of overseas conflicts.

By the late 1800s, however, some Americans believed the United States needed to expand to keep its economy strong. In his 1890 book *The Influence of Sea Power upon History*, Alfred T. Mahan argued that the United States needed a strong navy to protect its economic interests. Mahan also explained that a strong navy needed overseas bases and coaling stations—places for ships to take on coal for fuel.

Seward's Folly

In 1867 the United States greatly expanded its North American territory when Secretary of State **William H. Seward** arranged the purchase of Alaska from Russia for $7.2 million. Some people thought Alaska was a frozen wasteland, calling the deal "Seward's Folly" [foolish act]. But Seward had purchased an area more than twice the size of Texas for two cents an acre. And as he had hoped, Alaska became a source of valuable natural resources such as fur, timber, and minerals. Gold was found in Alaska in the 1890s, bringing miners and settlers to the area.

Based on Seward's belief that the United States "must continue to move on westward," the nation also annexed the Midway Islands in 1867. The islands' location about halfway between the U.S. West Coast and Japan made Midway an excellent coaling station for the U.S. Navy.

The United States wanted the island group of Samoa for similar reasons. The United States and Germany agreed to divide Samoa in 1899.

READING CHECK **Analyzing** Why did U.S. leaders end isolationist policies in the late 1800s?

U.S. Territories in the Pacific, 1856–1899

United States and possessions

1898 Date of acquisition

0   1,000   2,000 Miles

0   1,000   2,000 Kilometers

RUSSIA

ALASKA 1867

Boundary disputed until 1903

CANADA

Sea of Okhotsk

Bering Sea

Beijing

KOREA

CHINA

JAPAN

Tokyo

TAIWAN

PHILIPPINES 1898

Manila

GUAM 1898

WAKE ISLAND 1898

40°N

MIDWAY 1867

PACIFIC OCEAN

UNITED STATES

MEXICO

60°W

Tropic of Cancer

Honolulu

HAWAII 1898

JOHNSTON ISLAND 1858

0° Equator

HOWLAND ISLAND 1856

DUTCH EAST INDIES

Pago Pago

AMERICAN SAMOA 1899

AUSTRALIA

Tropic of Capricorn

100°E

180°

40°S

GEOGRAPHY SKILLS **INTERPRETING MAPS**

Between 1856 and 1898, Alaska and many Pacific islands, including Hawaii, became U.S. territories.
1. What U.S. territory was located below the equator?
2. In what year did the United States acquire the most territories?

693

Hawaii Becomes a Territory

Even more appealing than Samoa were the Hawaiian Islands. Hawaiians first saw Europeans in 1778. Trading and whaling ships in the Pacific soon began stopping in Hawaii. In the early 1800s American missionaries came and attempted to convert Hawaiians to Christianity. Missionaries opened businesses and raised crops, such as sugarcane. Some Americans became rich sugar planters.

By the 1840s most shops and shipyards in Hawaii were owned by Americans. Sugar became a leading export of the Hawaiian economy. An 1875 treaty allowed Hawaiian sugar to be shipped duty-free to the United States. (A duty is a tax on imported items.) This agreement helped the Hawaiian sugar industry prosper.

The planters used their power to force the Hawaiian king to sign a new constitution in 1887. It became known as the Bayonet Constitution because the king was forced to sign it at gunpoint. The constitution granted more power to the planter-controlled legislature. Many Hawaiians feared the foreigners' increase in power.

THE IMPACT TODAY

Today, sugarcane is Hawaii's most valuable crop.

In 1891 the king died, and his sister, **Liliuokalani** (li-LEE-uh-woh-kuh-LAHN-ee), became queen. She proposed a new constitution that would return power to the monarchy. The planters revolted. John L. Stevens, U.S. minister to Hawaii, called 150 marines ashore to support the revolt, and it succeeded without a battle. The planters formed a new government. Congress voted to annex the Hawaiian Islands in 1898.

READING CHECK **Identifying Cause and Effect** What effect did the growing power of the planters have on the Hawaiian monarchy?

United States Seeks Trade with Japan and China

Economic interest also drew the United States to Japan and China. The United States wanted to open and secure trade markets in both Asian countries.

Opening Trade with Japan

By the mid-1800s European powers had formed strong trade ties with most East Asian countries. However, the island nation of Japan had isolated itself from the rest of the world for hundreds of years.

The United States wanted to open up trade with Japan before Europeans arrived. President Millard Fillmore sent Commodore Matthew Perry to Japan to secure "friendship, commerce, [and] a supply of coal and provisions." Perry attempted a peaceful alliance in 1853, but he was not successful.

Perry returned to Japan in 1854 with seven warships. He gave Japanese leaders gifts and tried to show some of the benefits that Japanese-American trade would have. For instance, Perry presented them with a telegraph transmitter and a model train. This effort—and the presence of U.S. naval power—persuaded Japanese officials to open trade with the United States. The two countries signed a trade agreement in 1858.

BIOGRAPHY

Liliuokalani
(1838–1917)

Born in Honolulu, Queen Liliuokalani was proud of Hawaiian traditions. Even after being driven from power in 1883, she continued speaking out on behalf of native-born Hawaiians. In 1887 she traveled to Washington, D.C., meeting with President Grover Cleveland to argue against the annexation of Hawaii by the United States. Until her death, Liliuokalani served as a symbol of Hawaiian pride and a reminder of the islands' history as an independent nation.

Drawing Conclusions Why do you think Liliuokalani was a symbol of Hawaiian pride?

Perry Arrives in Japan

How might the Japanese have felt seeing these ships arrive?

CONNECT TO THE ARTS

This painting from 1854 shows Commodore Perry landing at Yokohama, Japan. He staged a parade to disembark and meet the imperial commissioners that represented the emperor. This meeting was the first official meeting between an agent of the United States and officials from Japan.

How does this picture show U.S. imperialism and its effects on Japan?

Some Japanese leaders welcomed trade with the United States. In 1868 people who favored the industrialization **process** came to power in Japan, beginning a 40-year period of modernization. By the 1890s Japan was becoming a major imperial power. It defeated China in the Sino-Japanese War from 1894 to 1895. As a result, Japan gained new territory and enjoyed the same trading privileges in China as European countries. In 1904 Japan attacked Russian forces stationed in China. President Theodore Roosevelt helped to negotiate a peace treaty to end the Russo-Japanese War a year later. Japan gained control of Korea, a lease on Port Arthur in China, and other rights. Japan had become a world power.

Foreign Powers in China

After Japan defeated China, other countries took advantage of China's weakness by seizing **spheres of influence**—areas where foreign nations controlled resources. Germany, Great Britain, France, Japan, and Russia all took control of areas within China.

Some U.S. leaders feared that the United States would be closed out of Chinese markets. In 1899 Secretary of State John Hay sent notes to Japan and many European countries announcing the **Open Door Policy**. This policy stated that all nations should have equal access to trade in China. The policy was neither rejected nor accepted by European powers and Japan but made U.S. intentions clear.

Meanwhile, many Chinese resented the power and control held by foreign nations. This hostility sparked the **Boxer Rebellion**. The Boxers were Chinese nationalists who were angered by foreign involvement in China. In their language, the group was called the Fists of Righteous Harmony. Westerners called them Boxers because they used a clenched fist as their symbol. Although officially denounced, they were secretly supported by the Chinese government.

In June 1900 the Boxers took to the streets of Beijing, China's capital, and laid siege to the walled settlement where foreigners lived. They killed more than 200 people.

ACADEMIC VOCABULARY

process a series of steps by which a task is accomplished

The siege continued for two months. Foreign military forces, including United States Marines, fought their way from the port of Tianjin to Beijing, where they invaded the Forbidden City. The Boxers were soon defeated. China was forced to make a cash payment of $333 million to foreign governments, $25 million of which went to the United States. Secretary of State Hay then sent another Open Door note to Japan and the European nations. The Open Door Policy remained in effect until World War II again closed China's borders to foreign influence.

READING CHECK **Identifying Cause and Effect** What factors led to the Boxer Rebellion, and what was the result?

SUMMARY AND PREVIEW The United States greatly expanded its territory and influence in the Pacific. In the next section, you will learn about the causes and effects of the Spanish-American War.

Chinese nationalists attack the foreigners' compound in Beijing in this illustration of China's Boxer Rebellion.

Section 1 Assessment

Reviewing Ideas, Terms, and People

1. **a. Describe** What policy had the United States followed regarding other countries before the late 1800s?
   b. Analyze Why did the United States expand to Alaska and to islands in the Pacific?
   c. Evaluate Do you think **William H. Seward**'s purchase of Alaska was a good decision? Explain.

2. **a. Recall** What became Hawaii's leading export?
   b. Sequence What events led to Hawaii's annexation as a U.S. territory?
   c. Elaborate What do you think about the planters' revolt against Queen **Liliuokalani**?

3. **a. Describe** How did the United States persuade Japanese leaders to sign a trade treaty?
   b. Contrast How was the U.S. experience establishing trade with China different from U.S. attempts to open trade with Japan?
   c. Evaluate Do you think Japan made the right decision in agreeing to open trade with the United States? Explain your answer.

Critical Thinking

4. **Generalizing** Review your notes on the areas or trade rights gained by the United States. Then use the chart below to identify the benefits of these areas and trade rights.

American Expansion

Areas or Trade Rights Gained	Benefits for United States

FOCUS ON WRITING

5. **Identifying Pros and Cons of U.S. Involvement Overseas** What did the United States gain from its involvement in these areas of the world? What were the disadvantages? As you read this section, identify pros and cons to add to your list.

The Spanish-American War

If YOU were there...

You live in New York City in 1898. Newspaper headlines are screaming about the start of war in Cuba. You hear that Theodore Roosevelt wants volunteers for a cavalry troop called the Rough Riders. You know how to ride a horse, and you've admired Roosevelt ever since he was New York's police commissioner. You know it will be dangerous, but it also sounds like a great adventure.

Would you join the Rough Riders? Why?

BUILDING BACKGROUND While the United States, Japan, and several European powers were gaining colonies, Spain's empire was declining. By the late 1800s Spain's once-extensive American empire was reduced to two island colonies—Cuba and Puerto Rico. Eager for independence, some Cubans revolted against Spanish rule. Many Americans sympathized with Cuba's fight for independence.

War with Spain

You read earlier that newspaper publishers Joseph Pulitzer and William Randolph Hearst were in a fierce competition for readers. In the late 1890s their newspapers published stories from Cuba, where Cuban rebels were fighting for independence from Spain. To attract readers, Pulitzer and Hearst printed sensational, often exaggerated news stories. This technique is called **yellow journalism**. Vivid stories about Spanish brutality in Cuba convinced many Americans that the U.S. military should support the Cuban rebels.

Newspapers such as this one encouraged Americans to seek war with Spain.

What You Will Learn...

Main Ideas

1. In 1898 the United States went to war with Spain in the Spanish-American War.
2. The United States gained territories in the Caribbean and Pacific.

The Big Idea

The United States expanded into new parts of the world as a result of the Spanish-American War.

Key Terms and People

yellow journalism, *p. 697*
Teller Amendment, *p. 698*
Emilio Aguinaldo, *p. 699*
Anti-Imperialist League, *p. 700*
Platt Amendment, *p. 701*

TAKING NOTES As you read, use a graphic organizer like this one to list the results of the Spanish-American War.

Spanish-American War

↓

Results

697

Despite growing support for military action in Cuba, President Grover Cleveland was opposed to U.S. involvement. In 1896 William McKinley, a supporter of Cuban independence, was elected president. Several events soon led to war.

In February 1898 Hearst's newspaper published a letter written by the Spanish minister to the United States, Enrique Dupuy de Lôme. In it, de Lôme called McKinley "weak and a bidder for the admiration of the crowd." Many Americans were outraged.

In January 1898, even before de Lôme's letter became public, the United States sent the battleship USS *Maine* to Havana Harbor. The *Maine*'s mission was to protect U.S. citizens and economic interests in Cuba. On February 15 the *Maine* exploded and

sank, with a loss of 266 men. Although the cause of the explosion was unclear, the American press immediately blamed Spain. "Remember the *Maine*!" became a rallying cry for angry Americans.

President McKinley requested $50 million to prepare for war. Congress approved the money. Although Cuba was not a U.S. territory, Congress issued a resolution on April 20 declaring Cuba independent and demanding that Spain leave the island within three days. Attached to the resolution was the **Teller Amendment**, which stated that the United States had no interest in taking control of Cuba. In response to the resolution, Spain declared war on the United States. The next day, Congress passed, and McKinley signed, a declaration of war against Spain.

"Remember the *Maine*!"

Most of the men aboard the USS *Maine* were sleeping when a terrible explosion demolished the forward third of the ship at 9:40 P.M. on February 15, 1898. The rest of the ship sank quickly. Some 266 men were killed.

Who did the United States blame for the explosion?

War in the Philippines

While attention was focused on Cuba, the U.S. Navy won a quick victory nearly half-way around the world in the Philippines, a Spanish colony in the Pacific. Filipinos, like Cubans, were rebelling against Spanish rule.

As soon as the Spanish-American War began, American commodore George Dewey raced to the Philippines with four large warships and two small gunboats. On May 1, ignoring reports that mines beneath the water barred his way, he sailed into Manila Bay and destroyed the Spanish Pacific fleet stationed there. Dewey's forces sank or captured 10 ships. The Spanish lost 381 lives, but none of Dewey's men were killed.

Dewey had defeated the Spanish, but he did not have enough troops to occupy and secure the Philippines. Troops eventually arrived, and on August 13, U.S. troops and Filipino rebels led by **Emilio Aguinaldo** (ahg-ee-NAHL-doh) took control of the Philippine capital, Manila.

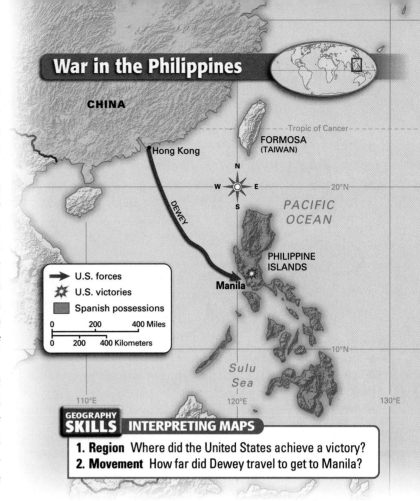

War in the Philippines

GEOGRAPHY SKILLS | **INTERPRETING MAPS**

1. **Region** Where did the United States achieve a victory?
2. **Movement** How far did Dewey travel to get to Manila?

War in the Caribbean

In contrast to the navy, the U.S. Army was unprepared for war. At the start of the conflict, the entire U.S. Army had only 28,000 soldiers. New volunteers quickly raised that figure to more than 280,000. The army did not have enough rifles or bullets for these soldiers. It did not even have appropriate clothing for the troops. Many soldiers received warm woolen uniforms to wear in Cuba's tropical heat.

The soldiers faced harsh living conditions in Cuba. They ate canned meat that one general called "embalmed beef," and many were stricken with yellow fever and other deadly diseases. More than 2,000 Americans died from diseases they contracted in Cuba. Fewer than 400 were killed in battle.

The most colorful group of soldiers was the Rough Riders. Second in command of this group was Lieutenant Colonel Theodore Roosevelt. Roosevelt had organized the Rough Riders to fight in Cuba. Volunteers included Native Americans, college athletes, cowboys, miners, and ranchers. Newspaper stories of their heroism earned the Rough Riders Americans' admiration. Four privates of the African American 10th Cavalry, who served with the Rough Riders, received the Congressional Medal of Honor.

Landing on June 22, 1898, the U.S. troops captured the hills around the main Spanish forces at Santiago. At the village of El Caney on July 1, some 7,000 U.S. soldiers, aided by Cuban rebels, overwhelmed about 600 Spanish defenders.

The main U.S. force then attacked and captured San Juan Hill. The Rough Riders and the African American 9th and 10th cavalries captured nearby Kettle Hill. The many accounts of the battle became popular with the American public back home. A journalist on the scene described the soldiers' charge:

FOCUS ON READING

How might accounts of the war written by these various soldiers have been different?

War in the Caribbean

UNITED STATES

ATLANTIC OCEAN

Tampa

FLORIDA

Gulf of Mexico

30°N

BAHAMAS (BR.)

USS *Maine* sunk, February, 1898

Tropic of Cancer

Havana

CUBA

Santiago

San Juan Hill, July, 1898

20°N

HAITI

DOMINICAN REPUBLIC

PUERTO RICO

JAMAICA (BR.)

Caribbean Sea

70°W

→ U.S. forces
✳ U.S. victories
⟋ U.S. blockade
▨ Spanish possessions

0   200   400 Miles
0   200   400 Kilometers

The Battle of San Juan Hill, shown in this painting, became a symbol of American courage in the Spanish–American War.

GEOGRAPHY SKILLS | **INTERPRETING MAPS**

1. **Location** About how far is Havana from Tampa?
2. **Place** When was the victory at San Juan Hill?

"It was a miracle of self-sacrifice, a triumph of bulldog courage ...The fire of the Spanish riflemen ...doubled and trebled [tripled] in fierceness, the crests of the hills crackled and burst in amazed roars and rippled with waves of tiny flame. But the blue line [of United States soldiers] crept steadily up and on."

—Richard Harding Davis, quoted in *The American Reader*, edited by Paul M. Angle

On July 3 the commander of the Spanish fleet decided to try breaking through the U.S. blockade. Though every Spanish ship was destroyed in the battle, American forces suffered only two casualties. Santiago surrendered two weeks later. President McKinley began peace negotiations with Spain, which was assured of defeat. A few days later, U.S. troops invaded Spanish-held Puerto Rico, which surrendered with little resistance. Spain signed a cease-fire agreement on August 12, 1898.

READING CHECK **Comparing** How was fighting in the Pacific and the Caribbean similar?

United States Gains Territories

The peace treaty placed Cuba, Guam, Puerto Rico, and the Philippines under U.S. control. In reaction, some Americans formed the **Anti-Imperialist League**, a group that opposed the treaty and the creation of an American colonial empire. They argued that the treaty threatened democracy because it denied self-government to the people living in the newly acquired territories. The Senate approved the peace treaty by a vote of 57 to 27—just one vote more than the two-thirds majority needed to ratify treaties.

Cuba

The Teller Amendment had declared that the United States would not annex Cuba. However, McKinley wanted to create stability and increase U.S. economic activity there, so he set up a military government. He appointed Leonard Wood, who had commanded the Rough Riders during the war, as governor.

Wood quickly began building schools and a sanitation system.

Even with the new sanitation system, disease remained a major problem. Dr. Walter Reed, head of the army's Yellow Fever Commission, was sent to Cuba in 1900 to help fight the disease. He and his volunteers conducted experiments, including allowing themselves to be bitten by infected insects. They soon proved that yellow fever was transmitted by mosquitoes. Getting rid of the standing water where mosquitoes lived helped health officials to control the disease.

Governor Wood also oversaw the writing of a Cuban constitution. The document included the **Platt Amendment**, which limited Cuba's right to make treaties and allowed the United States to intervene in Cuban affairs. It also required Cuba to sell or lease land to the United States. Cuban leaders compared the Platt Amendment to "handing over the keys to our house so that they [the Americans] can enter it at any time, whenever the desire seizes them." The Cubans reluctantly accepted the amendment, and U.S. troops withdrew. The amendment remained in force until 1934, and the U.S. government stayed actively involved in Cuban affairs until the late 1950s.

Puerto Rico

Like Cubans, Puerto Ricans had hoped for independence after the war. Instead, the U.S. government made the island a territory. On April 12, 1900, the Foraker Act established a civil government in Puerto Rico. It was headed by a governor and included a two-house legislature.

A debate over the new territory soon arose. People who lived in Puerto Rico were

LINKING TO TODAY

Puerto Ricans Today

Today about 3.7 million Puerto Ricans live on the mainland United States. This is the second-largest Hispanic population in the country, behind people of Mexican descent. Puerto Ricans live throughout the United States, but about one-third live in New York State.

Puerto Rican culture is very strong in New York— the National Puerto Rican Day Parade in New York City is one of the largest parades for any ethnic group in the city.

Puerto Ricans in the Mainland United States

(line graph: Puerto Rican Population in millions, Years 1970, 1980, 1990, 2000)

ANALYSIS SKILL **ANALYZING INFORMATION**

How are the people in the picture showing support for Puerto Rican culture?

considered citizens of the island but not of the United States. In 1917 the Jones Act gave Puerto Ricans U.S. citizenship and made both houses of the legislature elective. However, another 30 years passed before Puerto Ricans could elect their own governor. Today the island has its own constitution and elected officials but remains associated with the United States as what is known as a commonwealth.

The Philippines

Spain had surrendered the Philippines in return for a $20 million payment from the United States. Many Americans agreed with President McKinley, who said that the United States would benefit from the islands' naval and commercial value and that annexing the islands would keep Europeans from seizing them.

Filipino rebels, however, had expected to gain independence after the war. They had helped U.S. forces to capture Manila. When the United States decided instead to keep the islands, rebels led by Emilio Aguinaldo started a guerrilla war against the American forces. More than 4,200 U.S. soldiers and hundreds of thousands of Filipinos died before the conflict ended in 1902.

That same year, Congress passed the Philippine Government Act. It provided that an appointed governor and a two-house legislature would rule the Philippines. In 1946 the United States granted full independence to the Philippines.

READING CHECK **Summarizing** What areas did the United States control as a result of the war?

SUMMARY AND PREVIEW The United States fought a war with Spain and gained new territories in the Pacific and Caribbean regions. In the next section you will learn about U.S. interests in Latin America.

Section 2 Assessment

go.hrw.com
Online Quiz
KEYWORD: SF7 HP22

Reviewing Ideas, Terms, and People

1. **a. Recall** What was the cause of the conflict between Cuba and Spain?
   b. Analyze How did **yellow journalism** affect public support for U.S. military action in Cuba?
   c. Elaborate Why do you think the United States was so successful in defeating Spain? Explain your answer.
2. **a. Identify** What territories did the United States gain as a result of the war?
   b. Analyze Why did some Americans oppose the annexation of the Philippines?

Critical Thinking

3. **Categorizing** Review your notes on the results of the Spanish-American War. Then copy the graphic organizer to the right. Use your notes to identify arguments for and against taking control of foreign territories.

Arguments for Imperialism		Arguments against Imperialism
	vs.	

FOCUS ON WRITING

4. **Identifying Pros and Cons of the Spanish-American War** As you read this section, add to your pros and cons list by identifying American losses and gains as a result of the Spanish-American War. What were the costs in human lives? What were the gains in territory? Can you identify any other losses and gains? For example, how did the United States handle the issues of self-rule involved in the war?

Theodore Roosevelt

What would you do to reform your country and make it stronger?

When did he live? 1858–1919

Where did he live? Theodore Roosevelt was born into a wealthy family in New York City. He spent two years on a ranch in the Dakota Territory, where he became an avid hunter and conservationist. His political career then took him to Albany, New York, where he served as state governor, and Washington, D.C., where he served as vice president and president.

What did he do? Roosevelt became a national hero while leading the Rough Riders in the Spanish-American War. After serving less than a year as vice president, the 42-year-old Roosevelt became the youngest president in U.S. history when President William McKinley was killed in 1901. As president, Roosevelt fought for progressive reforms and set aside millions of acres as national parks and forests. Roosevelt's aggressive foreign policy expanded American power in the world.

Why is he so important? "I believe in a strong executive," Roosevelt once declared. "While president, I have been president, emphatically [forcefully]; I have used every ounce of power there was in the office." As this quote suggests, Roosevelt was a strong leader who set a precedent for a more active and powerful presidency.

Drawing Conclusions What characteristics made Theodore Roosevelt a successful leader?

KEY EVENTS

1882
Elected to the New York State Assembly at age 23

1898
Becomes a hero in the Spanish-American War; elected governor of New York

1900
Elected vice president

1901
Becomes president when McKinley is assassinated

1903
Gains Panama Canal Zone for the United States

1906
Visits Panama, becoming the first president to travel outside the country while in office

1919
Dies at home in New York

President Theodore Roosevelt and the Rough Riders

The United States and Latin America

What You Will Learn...

Main Ideas

1. The United States built the Panama Canal in the early 1900s.
2. Theodore Roosevelt changed U.S. policy toward Latin America.
3. Presidents Taft and Wilson promoted U.S. interests in Latin America.

The Big Idea

The United States expanded its role in Latin America in the early 1900s.

Key Terms and People

Panama Canal, *p. 705*
Roosevelt Corollary, *p. 707*
dollar diplomacy, *p. 708*
Mexican Revolution, *p. 708*
John J. Pershing, *p. 709*
Francisco "Pancho" Villa, *p. 709*

TAKING NOTES As you read, take notes on changing U.S. policies toward Latin America. List each policy in an outer circle of a web like this one.

U.S. policies toward Latin America

8.3.7, 8.3.9, 8.4.2, 8.4.9, 8.4.10

If **YOU** were there...

You are an engineer, and you've been working on the Panama Canal for almost eight years. Your work crews used huge steam shovels to slice through a ridge of mountains and built a huge artificial lake. You planned a system to move ships through different water levels. Now your work is done. You can watch massive ships travel from the Atlantic to the Pacific.

Which part of the work on the canal was the most challenging?

BUILDING BACKGROUND When the Spanish-American War began in 1898, the U.S. battleship *Oregon* set out from Washington State to join the fighting in Cuba. The approximately 12,000-mile trip around the southern tip of South America took more than two months. This delay convinced many U.S. leaders that the United States needed to build a canal linking the Atlantic and Pacific oceans.

Building the Panama Canal

A canal across the narrow neck of Central America would link the Atlantic and Pacific oceans and cut some 8,000 miles off the voyage by ship from the West to the East coasts of the United States. It would also allow the U.S. Navy to link its Atlantic and Pacific naval fleets quickly.

Revolution in Panama

No one was a stronger supporter of a Central American canal than President Theodore Roosevelt. Roosevelt knew that the best spot for the canal was the Isthmus of Panama, which at the time was part of the nation of Colombia. But he was unable to convince the Colombian senate to lease a strip of land across Panama to the United States.

Roosevelt considered other ways to gain control of the land. He learned that Panamanian revolutionaries were planning a revolt against Colombia. On November 2, 1903, a U.S. warship arrived outside Colón, Panama. The next day the revolt began. Blocked by the U.S. warship, Colombian forces could not reach Panama to stop the rebellion. Panama declared itself an independent country. The United States then recognized the new nation.

The new government of Panama supported the idea of a canal across its land. The United States agreed to pay Panama $10 million plus $250,000 a year for a 99-year lease on a 10-mile-wide strip of land across the isthmus.

Building the Canal

Canal construction began in 1904. The first obstacle to overcome was tropical disease. The canal route ran through 51 miles of forests and swamps filled with mosquitoes, many of which carried the deadly diseases malaria and yellow fever.

Dr. William C. Gorgas, who had helped Dr. Walter Reed stamp out yellow fever in Cuba, organized a successful effort to rid the canal route of disease-carrying mosquitoes. If Gorgas had not been successful, the canal's construction would have taken much longer. It also would have cost much more in terms of both lives and money.

Even with the reduced risk of disease, the work was very dangerous. Most of the canal had to be blasted out of solid rock with explosives. Workers used dozens of steam shovels to cut a narrow, eight-mile-long channel through the mountains of central Panama. Sometimes workers died when their shovels struck explosive charges. "The flesh of men flew in the air like birds every day," recalled one worker from the West Indies.

Some 6,000 lives were lost during the American construction of the **Panama Canal**. It was finally opened to ships on August 15, 1914, linking the Atlantic and Pacific oceans. An opening ceremony was held the next year. It had taken 10 years to complete, and the cost was $375 million. In the end, however, the world had its "highway between the oceans."

READING CHECK **Drawing Conclusions** Why did building the canal cost so many lives?

THE IMPACT TODAY

Today the Panama Canal Zone is threatened by deforestation and erosion because of heavy use. Decreased rainfall is also hurting the canal.

The massive Gatun Locks, shown here under construction in 1914, raise ships 85 feet onto Gatun Lake, an inland waterway on the Panama Canal.

The Panama Canal

CONNECT TO ECONOMICS

Increasing Exports The Panama Canal did not just increase trade between the East and West coasts of the United States. By shortening the trip from many U.S. ports to other parts of the world, the canal also led to increased exports of agricultural and manufactured goods.

By how many miles did the Panama Canal shorten the shipping distance between New York City and San Francisco?

NORTH AMERICA

UNITED STATES

ATLANTIC OCEAN

San Francisco

New York City

Gulf of Mexico

Tropic of Cancer

Caribbean Sea

Panama Canal

5,200 Miles (8,370 Kilometers)

CENTRAL AMERICA

PACIFIC OCEAN

13,000 Miles (20,900 Kilometers)

0° Equator

SOUTH AMERICA

Canal zone
Canal route
Railroad
⋊ Locks

Colón
Cristobal

Caribbean Sea

Gatun Locks

Gatun Lake

Gaillard Cut

Pedro Miguel Locks
Miraflores Locks

Panama City

PANAMA

Balboa

Bay of Panama

0 10 20 Miles
0 10 20 Kilometers

go.hrw.com
Interactive Map
KEYWORD: SF7 CH22

GEOGRAPHY SKILLS **INTERPRETING MAPS**

1. **Place** Why was Panama chosen as the site for a canal?
2. **Movement** How many locks did ships have to travel through from Balboa to Colón?

0 400 800 Miles
0 400 800 Kilometers

U.S. Policy Toward Latin America

As president, Theodore Roosevelt actively pursued progressive reforms at home. He also believed the United States should play a more active role in the Western Hemisphere. In 1900 Roosevelt said, "I have always been fond of the West African proverb: 'Speak softly and carry a big stick; you will go far.'" Roosevelt wanted everyone to know he would use a "big stick"—meaning U.S. military force—to protect U.S. interests in Latin America.

This was a change from the policies of previous presidents. In the 1823 Monroe Doctrine, President James Monroe had warned European nations not to interfere in the Western Hemisphere. And while the Monroe Doctrine became a major principle of U.S. foreign policy, the United States did not have the military strength to enforce it. By the time Roosevelt became president, however, this situation was changing. The United States was growing stronger and expanding its influence. The United States was becoming a world power.

How should the United States use its new power in Latin America? This question came up often in the early 1900s. European banks had made loans to a number of Latin American countries. Venezuela, for example, fell deeply in debt to British and German investors. Venezuela refused to repay these debts in 1902. A similar situation arose in the Caribbean nation of the Dominican Republic in 1904. European powers prepared to use military force to collect the debts.

Roosevelt insisted the countries must repay their debts. But he did not want to allow Europeans to intervene in Latin America. The presence of European forces there would violate the Monroe Doctrine and threaten U.S. power in the region.

Roosevelt knew that U.S. officials would have to force debtor nations to repay their loans in order to keep European nations from directly intervening in Latin America. In December 1904 he announced what became known as the **Roosevelt Corollary** to the Monroe Doctrine. This addition warned that in cases of "wrongdoing" by Latin American countries, the United States might exercise "international police power."

The Roosevelt Corollary asserted a new **role** for the United States as an "international police power" in the Western Hemisphere. Roosevelt actively enforced the corollary throughout the rest of his presidency.

READING CHECK Finding Main Ideas Why did Roosevelt announce the Roosevelt Corollary?

Primary Source

POLITICAL CARTOON
Roosevelt's Imperialism

Theodore Roosevelt's foreign policy is shown visually in this cartoon. Roosevelt is the giant leading a group of ships that represent debt collection. The U.S. president is patrolling the Caribbean Sea and Latin American countries, trying to enforce the payment of debts to European countries.

What do you think this stick represents?

Why are these vessels warships?

ANALYSIS SKILL ANALYZING PRIMARY SOURCES

Analyzing How does the cartoonist portray the parts of the Roosevelt Corollary?

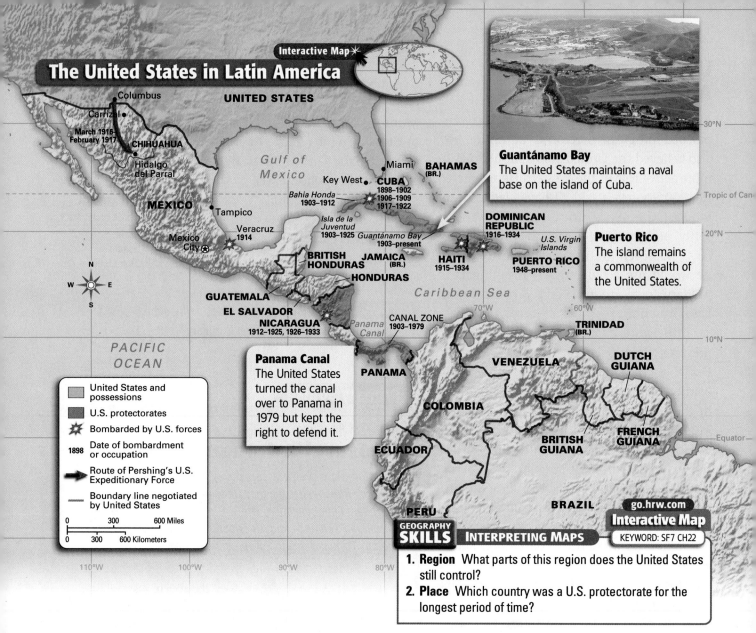

The United States in Latin America

Interactive Map

Guantánamo Bay
The United States maintains a naval base on the island of Cuba.

Puerto Rico
The island remains a commonwealth of the United States.

Panama Canal
The United States turned the canal over to Panama in 1979 but kept the right to defend it.

UNITED STATES

Columbus
Carrizal
March 1916–February 1917
CHIHUAHUA
Hidalgo del Parral
MEXICO
Tampico
Veracruz 1914
Mexico City
Gulf of Mexico
Key West
Miami
BAHAMAS (BR.)
CUBA 1898–1902 1906–1909 1917–1922
Bahia Honda 1903–1912
Isla de la Juventud 1903–1925
Guantánamo Bay 1903–present
DOMINICAN REPUBLIC 1916–1934
U.S. Virgin Islands
HAITI 1915–1934
PUERTO RICO 1948–present
BRITISH HONDURAS
JAMAICA (BR.)
HONDURAS
Caribbean Sea
GUATEMALA
EL SALVADOR
NICARAGUA 1912–1925, 1926–1933
Panama Canal
CANAL ZONE 1903–1979
PANAMA
TRINIDAD (BR.)
VENEZUELA
DUTCH GUIANA
COLOMBIA
BRITISH GUIANA
FRENCH GUIANA
ECUADOR
PERU
BRAZIL
PACIFIC OCEAN

30°N
Tropic of Can
20°N
10°N
Equator
70°W 60°W

Legend
- United States and possessions
- U.S. protectorates
- Bombarded by U.S. forces
- 1898 Date of bombardment or occupation
- Route of Pershing's U.S. Expeditionary Force
- Boundary line negotiated by United States

0   300   600 Miles
0   300   600 Kilometers

110°W   100°W   90°W   80°W

go.hrw.com
Interactive Map
KEYWORD: SF7 CH22

GEOGRAPHY SKILLS | **INTERPRETING MAPS**

1. **Region** What parts of this region does the United States still control?
2. **Place** Which country was a U.S. protectorate for the longest period of time?

U.S. Interests in Latin America

William Howard Taft, who became president in 1909, also acted to protect U.S. interests in Latin America. Taft used a policy called **dollar diplomacy**—influencing governments through economic, not military, intervention.

President Taft described dollar diplomacy as "substituting dollars for bullets. It is . . . directed to the increase of American trade." He wanted to encourage stability and keep Europeans out of Latin America by expanding U.S. business interests there.

For example, in 1911 Nicaragua failed to repay a loan from British investors. American bankers lent Nicaragua $1.5 billion in return for control of the National Bank of Nicaragua and the government-owned railway. When local anger over this deal led to revolt in Nicaragua, Taft sent U.S. Marines to protect American interests.

When President Woodrow Wilson took office in 1913, he rejected Taft's dollar diplomacy. He believed the United States had a moral obligation to promote democracy in Latin America. Like Roosevelt, Wilson was willing to use military force to protect U.S. interests in the region.

In 1910 many Mexicans revolted against the harsh rule of Mexican dictator Porfirio Díaz. This was the start of the **Mexican Revolution**, a long, violent struggle for power in Mexico. The war affected U.S. interests

U.S. Foreign Policy

QUICK FACTS

Departing from the example set by the nation's first president, George Washington, future presidents increased U.S. involvement around the world, particularly in Latin America.

Washington's Farewell Address
The United States will not become involved in European affairs.

Monroe Doctrine
The United States will defend its interests in the Western Hemisphere and keep European powers out.

Roosevelt Corollary
The United States will police wrongdoing by nations in the Western Hemisphere.

Taft's Dollar Diplomacy
The United States will use economic means to aid its interests in Latin America.

Wilson and Democracy
The United States will promote and protect democracy in the Western Hemisphere.

because Americans had invested more than $1 billion in Mexican land, mining, oil, and railways. American business leaders feared they would lose their investments.

In 1914 President Wilson learned that a German ship carrying weapons was headed to the port of Veracruz, Mexico. To keep the weapons from reaching the rebels, Wilson ordered the navy to seize Veracruz. Wilson acted again in 1916, sending General **John J. Pershing** and 15,000 U.S. soldiers into Mexico. Pershing's mission was to catch the rebel leader **Francisco "Pancho" Villa**, who had killed 17 Americans in New Mexico. Pershing failed to capture Villa, and Wilson recalled the troops.

In 1917 a new constitution began to bring order to Mexico. The violence caused more than 120,000 Mexicans to flee to the United States between 1905 and 1915.

READING CHECK Summarizing How did Wilson respond to events in Mexico?

SUMMARY AND PREVIEW The United States and Latin America established relationships through both conflicts and agreements. In the next chapter, you will learn how the United States became involved in conflict in Europe.

Section 3 Assessment

go.hrw.com
Online Quiz
KEYWORD: SF7 HP22

Reviewing Ideas, Terms, and People

1. **a. Recall** Why did the United States want to build a canal?
   b. Analyze What challenges did the builders of the **Panama Canal** face, and how did they overcome them?
   c. Elaborate Defend or criticize the U.S. decision to support the revolution in Panama.
2. **a. Describe** What problem was causing conflict between European and Latin American nations?
   b. Summarize How and why did Theodore Roosevelt change U.S. policy toward Latin America?
3. **a. Recall** What did Woodrow Wilson believe was the United States's obligation to Latin America?
   b. Compare and Contrast How were the policies of Taft and Wilson toward Latin America similar, and how were they different?

Critical Thinking

4. **Categorizing** Review your notes on U.S. policies toward Latin America. Then copy the web diagram below. Use it to identify American policies toward Latin America.

FOCUS ON WRITING

5. **Identifying Pros and Cons of U.S. Intervention**
   What were the pros and cons of the construction of the Panama Canal and interventionist U.S. policies toward Latin America? Take notes for your list as you read this section.

AMERICA AS A WORLD POWER **709**

America's Global Influence 1900

By 1900 most of the current boundaries of the United States had been established. But the world had become a much smaller place. American inventions were spreading, changing daily life in countries around the world. In addition, U.S. troops stationed in China were displaying the increasing importance of the United States in global affairs.

ASIA

PACIFIC OCEAN

On July 5, 1900, William Jennings Bryan spoke out against U.S. involvement in China, saying, "Imperialism is the most dangerous of the evils now menacing [threatening] our country."

Asia Before 1898, U.S. troops had never been sent outside the Western Hemisphere. But in 1900, some 5,000 troops were in Asia, fighting alongside European troops.

Paris The Paris Exposition of 1900 showcased many U.S. inventions. One British writer claimed the exposition displayed "the Americanization of the world."

London

EUROPE

Paris

London In August 1900, English farmers protested in London against new farm equipment introduced from the United States that they feared would cause farmers to lose their jobs.

UNITED STATES

New York

ATLANTIC OCEAN

New York City Nearly 500,000 people immigrated to the United States in 1900. By 1920 more than 16 million had come. Many arrived in New York City.

AFRICA

SOUTH AMERICA

GEOGRAPHY SKILLS **INTERPRETING MAPS**

1. **Region** By 1900, what role was the U.S. military playing in China?
2. **Movement** In what ways did the U.S. influence other countries?

AMERICA AS A WORLD POWER **711**

Social Studies Skills

Continuity and Change in History

Define the Skill

A well-known saying claims that "the more things change, the more they stay the same." Nowhere does this observation apply better than to the study of history. Any examination of the past will show many changes—nations expanding or shrinking, empires rising and falling, changes in leadership, or people on the move, for example.

The reasons for change have not changed, however. The same general forces have driven the actions of people and nations across time. These forces are the threads that run through history and give it continuity, or connectedness. They are the "sameness" in a world of continuous change.

Learn the Skill

You can find the causes of all events of the past in one or more of these major forces or themes that connect all history.

1. **Cooperation and Conflict** Throughout time, people and groups have worked together to achieve goals. They have also opposed others who stood in the way of their goals.

2. **Cultural Invention and Interaction** The values and ideas expressed in peoples' art, literature, customs, and religion have enriched the world. But the spread of cultures and their contact with other cultures have produced conflict as well.

3. **Geography and Environment** Physical environment and natural resources have shaped how people live. Efforts to gain, protect, or make good use of land and resources have been major causes of cooperation and conflict in history.

4. **Science and Technology** *Technology,* or the development and use of tools, has helped humans across time make better use of their environment. Science has changed their knowledge of the world, and changed their lives, too.

5. **Economic Opportunity and Development** From hunting and gathering to herding, farming, manufacturing, and trade, people have tried to make the most of their resources. The desire for a better life has also been a major reason people have moved from one place to another.

6. **The Impact of Individuals** Political, religious, military, business, and other leaders have been a major influence in history. The actions of many ordinary people have also shaped history

7. **Nationalism and Imperialism** *Nationalism* is the desire of a people to have their own country. *Imperialism* is the desire of a nation to influence or control other nations. Both have existed across time.

8. **Political and Social Systems** People have always been part of groups—families, villages, nations, or religious groups, for example. The groups to which people belong shape how they relate to others around them.

Practice the Skill

Check your understanding of continuity and change in history by answering the following questions.

1. What forces of history are illustrated by the events in Chapter 22? Explain with examples.

2. How do the events in this chapter show continuity with earlier periods in U.S. history?

Chapter Review

HOLT
History's Impact
▶ video series
Review the video to answer the closing question:
How would you characterize the current policy of the United States: isolationist or imperialist?

Visual Summary

QUICK FACTS

Use the visual summary below to help you review the main ideas of the chapter.

- Platt Amendment
- Occupation of Puerto Rico
- Roosevelt Corollary
- Dollar Diplomacy

- Open Door Policy
- Boxer Rebellion
- Trade with Japan
- Annexation of Hawaii
- Occupation of the Philippines
- Purchase of Alaska

- Mexican Revolution
- Panama Canal
- Spanish-American War

Reviewing Vocabulary, Terms, and People

1. In which of the following did the United States declare that it had no interest in taking control of Cuba?
   a. Roosevelt Corollary   **c.** Open Door Policy
   b. Monroe Doctrine   **d.** Teller Amendment

2. Which leader upset sugar planters in Hawaii by proposing a plan to return power to the monarchy?
   a. Liliuokalani   **c.** Millard Fillmore
   b. John L. Stevens   **d.** Woodrow Wilson

3. Which president supported Panama's revolt against Colombia in 1903?
   a. Woodrow Wilson   **c.** William Howard Taft
   b. William McKinley   **d.** Theodore Roosevelt

4. Who led U.S. forces into Mexico after attacks against U.S. citizens by Mexican rebels?
   a. John Hay   **c.** John J. Pershing
   b. William H. Seward   **d.** Theodore Roosevelt

Comprehension and Critical Thinking

SECTION 1 *(Pages 692–696)*

5. **a. Identify** Into what areas did the United States expand in the late 1800s?

   b. Draw Conclusions How did the United States benefit from contact with foreign nations and territories?

   c. Elaborate Which policy would you have supported—isolationism or imperialism? Explain your answer.

SECTION 2 *(Pages 697–702)*

6. **a. Describe** What events led the United States to declare war on Spain?

   b. Analyze How did the United States benefit from the Spanish-American War?

   c. Predict How might foreign countries view the actions of the United States in the Spanish-American War?

7. a. Identify In what ways did the United States become involved in Latin American affairs?

b. Draw Conclusions Why did the United States expand its role in Latin America in the early 1900s?

c. Elaborate Do you think the United States should have been as actively involved in Latin America as it was? Explain your answer.

Reviewing Themes

8. Geography How did the geography of the United States change after the end of its policy of isolationism?

9. Politics How did the policy of imperialism affect American politics in the late 1800s and early 1900s?

Reading Skills

Comparing Historical Texts *Use the Reading Skills taught in this chapter to answer the question about the reading selections below.*

A. "Sad to say, this most precious and sublime feature of the Yosemite National Park (Hetch Hetchy Valley), one of the greatest of all our natural resources for the uplifting joy and peace and health of the people, is in danger of being dammed and made into a reservoir to help supply San Francisco with water and light . . ."
—John Muir, *The Yosemite*, 1912

B. "As we all know, there is no use of water that is higher than the domestic use. Then, if there is, as the engineers tell us, no other source of supply that is anything like so reasonably available as this one; if this is the best, and, within reasonable limits of cost, the only means of supplying San Francisco with water, we come straight to the question of whether the advantage of leaving this valley in a state of nature is greater than the advantage of using it for the benefit of the city of San Francisco."
—Gifford Pinchot, address to Congress, 1913

10. How do the two men quoted above differ on the issue of building a dam in the Hetch Hetchy Valley?

Social Studies Skills

Continuity and Change in History *Use the Social Studies Skills taught in this chapter to answer the question below.*

11. Pick three of the themes listed on page 712. Explain how the themes connect to the history of the Panama Canal.

Using the Internet

go.hrw.com
KEYWORD: SF7 CH22

12. Activity: Creating a Poster The Panama Canal was opened on August 15, 1914. It took 10 years to build, cost a total of over $600 million, and had a death toll of some 6,000 lives. Human and geographic factors had a huge impact on the people and machines that worked on the canal project. Research the effects of human and geographic factors on the construction of the Panama Canal. Physical factors include landforms, climate, and weather. Human factors should focus on the use of technology and the reasons humans modified the environment, along with the hazards they faced. Then create a poster about the canal, highlighting the most important details.

FOCUS ON WRITING

13. Writing Your List of Pros and Cons Review your notes and choose the pros and cons to include in your final list. Decide whether you want to include only facts, only opinions, or some of each. How can your analysis of history help guide U.S. foreign policy in the future? When you have finished your list, use it as the basis for a paragraph recommending either that the United States continue to involve itself in the affairs of other nations or that it pull back from such involvement.

DIRECTIONS: Read each question and write the letter of the best response. Use the map below to answer question 1.

1

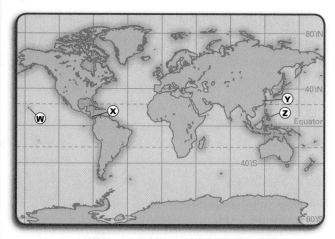

The only area in which the United States did not control territory in the late 1800s and early 1900s is shown on the map by which letter?

A W

B X

C Y

D Z

2 The practice of using U.S. businesses and economic aid to influence foreign governments and achieve U.S. goals in Latin America is known as

A imperialism.

B dollar diplomacy.

C isolationism.

D the big stick.

3 During the Mexican Revolution, President Wilson sent U.S. forces to Veracruz, Mexico. Which U.S. policy did this act best express?

A Roosevelt Corollary

B dollar diplomacy

C Teller Amendment

D isolationism

4 Which two nations did the United States hope to trade with rather than annex in the late 1800s?

A Hawaii and Japan

B Japan and China

C China and Cuba

D Cuba and Hawaii

5 How did American newspapers respond to the explosion of the USS *Maine* in Havana Harbor?

A They refused to report the story.

B They reported that the explosion was an accident.

C They blamed the explosion on Spain.

D They blamed the explosion on Cuban rebels.

6 In his book *The Influence of Sea Power upon History,* Alfred T. Mahan argued that the United States should

A avoid foreign conflicts.

B sell its naval bases.

C build a strong navy.

D remain isolationist.

7 Read the following passage from a letter from President Fillmore and use it to answer the question below.

> "I am desirous that our two countries should trade with each other, for the benefit of both Japan and the United States. We know that the ancient laws of your imperial majesty's government do not allow of foreign trade, except with the Chinese and the Dutch; but as the state of the world changes . . . it seems to be wise, from time to time, to make new laws."
>
> —Letter from U.S. President Millard Fillmore to Japan, 1852

Document-Based Question What is President Fillmore asking the Japanese to do?

Assignment

Find a primary source about the Triangle Shirtwaist Factory Fire and write an analysis of it.

Analyzing a Primary Source

Primary sources are often the best sources of information available to historians. Primary sources provide answers to questions about the past. They also provide a unique point of view from the past. Analyzing a primary source allows you to share that information.

TIP **Using the Internet** If you find a primary source on the Internet, make sure it is accurate. You should be able to identify the person or institution that runs the Web site and make sure that person or institution is trustworthy. The Web site should include basic information about the source, such as its author, when it was written, and where it first appeared. University and library Web sites are excellent places to find primary sources.

1. Prewrite

Locating Primary Sources

Many primary sources are available in libraries and on the Internet. Letters, diaries, autobiographies, memoirs, newspaper articles, public speeches, and legal documents are good examples of primary sources.

Reading the Primary Source

Take notes on these questions to better understand the document.

- Who wrote the document?
- What kind of document is it?
- When was it written? Where did it originally appear?
- What was the author's point of view? What was his or her experience during the fire?
- Why did the author write the document?

As you read the primary source, take notes on these questions.

- Why is the document important? The answer to this question will be the main idea of your essay.
- What questions about the fire does it answer? Answering this question will help you write your body paragraphs.

2. Write

You can use this framework to help you write your first draft.

A Writer's Framework

Introduction	Body	Conclusion
■ Introduce your primary source and its main purpose. ■ Introduce the author of the source and include the date it was written. ■ State your main idea, explaining why this source is important.	■ Explain how the source answers at least two questions about the fire. ■ Include examples from the document.	■ Summarize the information in the source. ■ Restate why the document is important for historians.

3. Evaluate and Revise

Evaluating

Use these questions to discover ways to improve your paper.

Evaluation Questions for Analyzing a Primary Source

- Do you introduce your primary source with its main purpose?
- Do you introduce the author of the source and the document's date?
- Do you state a main idea explaining why this source is important?

- Do you explain how the source answers at least two questions about the fire?
- Do you include examples from the document?
- Do you summarize the information in the source?

Revising

Make sure each paragraph has a topic sentence at the beginning. Then check the information in the paragraph. It should all relate to the topic sentence. If it does not, there are several ways to fix the paragraph. First, you can remove unrelated information. If the information is related but not clearly explained, add a more detailed explanation. You can also change the topic sentence to include all the information in the paragraph.

4. Proofread and Publish

Proofreading

Reread your paper carefully to make sure all the verbs are in the same tense. The past tense is usually best for history writing. Summaries of primary sources should also be in the past tense. A direct quotation from a primary source, however, should remain in its original tense.

Publishing

Share your paper with a classmate. Read each other's papers. Then write a one-paragraph summary of the new information you each learned.

5. Practice and Apply

Use the steps and strategies in this workshop to analyze your primary source.

TIP Using Pronouns Effectively

Use pronouns such as *he, she, they,* and *it* to replace frequently used nouns and proper nouns. This will help you vary your sentences. Make sure that the person or thing to which each pronoun refers is clear. If it is not, repeat the original noun or name.

EXAMPLE

Workers at the factory were trapped inside. They tried to escape, but the doors were locked.

Modern America

America Since 1914

The United States of America is a very different place today than it was in 1914. The nation is now bigger, more powerful, and more involved in world affairs. It has changed from a nation where most people lived in small towns to one in which most people live in cities, many with populations of more than 1 million people. The nation is also a more democratic place today—more Americans have access to the privileges and responsibilities of citizenship than at any other time in the country's history.

Despite these differences, America faces many of the same challenges that it faced in 1914. For example, Americans still debate questions about civil rights, religion, taxes, and the role of government in their lives. They also worry about the health of the environment, children, and the poor.

Americans do not always agree on these issues. But they do believe strongly in their right to debate and to disagree. The freedom to do so—in peaceful and productive ways—is a testament to the strength of the founding fathers' plan for government.

America became a global power in the 1900s as U.S. troops fought in two world wars.

America as a Global Power

The United States continued to expand its influence in global affairs after the Spanish-American War. In 1914 World War I began in Europe, involving millions of people in the first modern war. Although the United States was at first divided over joining the faraway struggle, by 1917 the country had entered the war on the side of the Allies. American soldiers fought and died on the battlefields of Europe and helped defeat the Central Powers. The experience forever changed the United States and its citizens. America had stepped onto the world stage with its military and industrial might.

War tore Europe apart again in the 1930s and 1940s during World War II. When Japan attacked the United States at Pearl Harbor in late 1941, the country entered the global struggle. Again American soldiers helped the Allied Powers defeat their enemies. Global politics would change dramatically after the conclusion of World War II with the emergence of new countries and powerful new weapons.

Martin Luther King, Jr., (center) helped lead the fight for civil rights in America.

The Civil Rights Era

The U.S. victory in World War II had other consequences as well. Millions of World War II veterans returned home ready to start new lives in peacetime. These veterans enrolled in college in record numbers, settled into the nation's cities and new suburbs, and started families.

Soldiers who had fought on the side of democracy abroad also fought for democracy at home. This was especially true of the nation's African American and Mexican American soldiers. Their efforts to seek greater access to the rights of citizenship helped invigorate the civil rights movement. They were joined in these efforts by Americans from all walks of life—people who believed that America worked best when the promises of freedom were open to all.

By the 1960s, the push for greater civil rights had become a true social movement in America. It was a grassroots effort on the part of ordinary Americans to change both people's attitudes and federal laws. This movement for greater civil, educational, and political rights among racial and ethnic groups helped spur the women's rights movement of the 1960s and 1970s as well.

HE FINAL FROST BARRIER!

IT'S HERE!
A FROST-PROOF
FOOD FREEZER!
NO FROST!
NO FROST-LOCKED
FOODS!
NO DEFROSTING!

America's economy boomed following World War II as middle-class Americans enjoyed the benefits of modern conveniences like refrigerators.

Economic Changes and Challenges

The U.S. economy has also changed dramatically since 1914. In the 1930s, millions of Americans were affected by the huge economic collapse known as the Great Depression. After World War II, the U.S. economy recovered and the nation enjoyed a long period of prosperity. Many Americans joined the middle class for the first time. During the 1950s and 1960s they bought homes, televisions and appliances, and cars in record numbers.

Since the 1970s, the economy has had more ups and downs. Industrial jobs, which were once so plentiful in America, have become far less important in recent decades. Many American companies have moved their factories overseas to take advantage of lower wages in other countries. As a result, the U.S. economy is now becoming more of a service economy—one in which most workers provide services (like banking or law) instead of actually making products.

Immigration

Immigration has been an important feature of the United States ever since the country first began. After 1914, the number of immigrants began to fall, reaching a low in 1940. Since 1940, however, numbers of immigrants have continued to rise. According to the 2000 census, an estimated 31 million Americans are immigrants from foreign countries. The largest percentage comes from Latin America, but many come from Asia, Africa, and Europe as well. These new immigrants help keep the United States a diverse blend of cultures, people, and ideas.

With its long history of immigration, America is one of the most ethnically diverse places in the world. Here, Sikhs celebrate their culture at a parade in New York.

America Then and Now

In the years since 1914, the United States has faced many difficult challenges that have drawn citizens together. The terrorist attacks of September 11, 2001, are one of the latest of these challenges. Since 2001, a War on Terror has been ongoing as the United States tries to effectively end the threat of terrorism around the world. Parts of this War on Terror have been a military action in Afghanistan and Operation Iraqi Freedom.

Terrorism in Iraq and other foreign countries continues to be a danger to all citizens. Kidnappings and bombings threaten peace efforts across the world. In late 2008 attacks on luxury hotels in Mumbai, India, left more than 150 people dead. Concerns about the nuclear programs of Iran and North Korea also shape the international relationships of the United States.

In the final years of President Bush's second term of office, his approval rating dropped dramatically. One contributing factor to this decline was criticism of the federal government's response to the disaster left by Hurricane Katrina, which hit New Orleans and the Gulf Coast in 2005. During the 2008 presidential campaign, both Democrats and Republicans made historic choices for their candidates. Democrat Barack Obama, a U.S. senator from Illinois, became the first African American presidential nominee of a major party, while Republican Sarah Palin, governor of Alaska, became the second woman to gain a major-party nomination for vice president. The campaign focused on issues such as the war in Iraq, health care, and repairing the economy. Obama won, the first African American to be elected president of the United States.

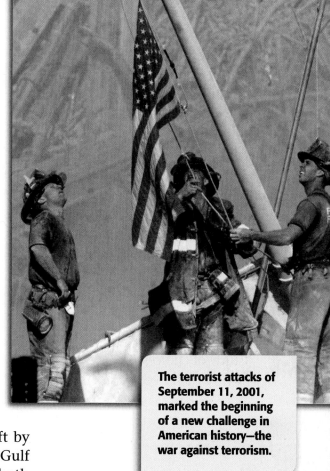

The terrorist attacks of September 11, 2001, marked the beginning of a new challenge in American history—the war against terrorism.

Cities such as St. Louis, shown here, are part of America's past, present, and future. Once a small town known as the Gateway to the West, St. Louis has grown into a large and modern American city.

Economics Handbook

What Is Economics?

Economics may sound dull, but it touches almost every part of your life. Here are some examples of the kinds of economic choices you may have made yourself:

- Which pair of shoes to buy—the ones on sale or the ones you really like, which cost much more
- Whether to continue saving your money for the DVD player you want or use some of it now to go to a movie
- Whether to give some money to a fundraiser for a new park or to housing for the homeless

As these examples show, we can think of economics as a study of choices. These choices are the ones people make to satisfy their needs or their desires.

Glossary of Economic Terms

Here are some of the words we use to talk about economics:

ECONOMIC SYSTEMS

Countries have developed different economic systems to help them make choices, such as what goods and services to produce, how to produce them, and for whom to produce them. The most common economic systems in the world are market economies and mixed economies.

capitalism See market economy.

command economy an economic system in which the central government makes all economic decisions, such as in the countries of Cuba and North Korea

communism a political system in which the government owns all property and runs a command economy

free enterprise a system in which businesses operate with little government involvement, such as in a country with a market economy

market economy an economic system based on private ownership, free trade, and competition; the government has little to say about what, how, or for whom goods and services are produced; examples include Germany and the United States

mixed economy an economy that is a combination of command, market, and traditional economies

traditional economy an economy in which production is based on customs and tradition, and in which people often grow their own food, make their own goods, and use barter to trade

THE ECONOMY AND MONEY

People, businesses, and countries obtain the items they need and want through economic activities such as producing, selling, and buying goods or services. Countries differ in the amount of economic activity that they have and in the strength of their economies.

consumer a person who buys goods or services for personal use

consumer good a finished product sold to consumers for personal or home use

corporation a business in which a group of owners share in the profits and losses

currency paper or coins that a country uses for its money supply

demand the amount of goods and services that consumers are willing and able to buy at a given time

depression a severe drop in overall business activity over a long period of time

developed countries countries with strong economies and a high quality of life; often have high per capita GDPs and high levels of industrialization and technology

developing countries countries with less productive economies and a lower quality of life; often have less industrialization and technology

economic development the level of a country's economic activity, growth, and quality of life

economy the structure of economic life in a country

goods objects or materials that humans can purchase to satisfy their wants and needs

gross domestic product (GDP) total market value of all goods and services produced in a country in a given year; *per capita GDP* is the average value of goods and services produced per person in a country in a given year

industrialization the process of using machinery for all major forms of production

inflation an increase in overall prices

investment the purchase of something with the expectation that it will gain in value; usually property, stocks, etc.

money any item, usually coins or paper currency, that is used in payment for goods or services

producer a person or group that makes goods or provides services to satisfy consumers' wants and needs

productivity the amount of goods or services that a worker or workers can produce within a given amount of time

profit the gain or excess made by selling goods or services over their costs

purchasing power the amount of income that people have available to spend on goods and services

services any activities that are performed for a fee

standard of living how well people are living; determined by the amount of goods and services they can afford

stock a share of ownership in a corporation

supply the amount of goods and services that are available at a given time

INTERNATIONAL TRADE

Countries trade with each other to obtain resources, goods, and services. Growing global trade has helped lead to the development of a global economy.

balance of trade the difference between the value of a country's exports and imports

barter the exchange of one good or service for another

black market the illegal buying and selling of goods, often at high prices

comparative advantage the ability of a company or country to produce something at a lower cost than other companies or countries

competition rivalry between businesses selling similar goods or services; a condition that often leads to lower prices or improved products

e-commerce the electronic trading of goods and services, such as over the Internet

exports goods or services that a country sells and sends to other countries

free trade trade among nations that is not affected by financial or legal barriers; trade without barriers

imports goods or services that a country brings in or purchases from another country

interdependence a relationship between countries in which they rely on one another for resources, goods, or services

market the trade of goods and services

market clearing price the price of a good or service at which supply equals demand

one-crop economy an economy that is dominated by the production of a single product

opportunity cost the value of the next-best alternative that is sacrificed when choosing to consume or produce another good or service

scarcity a condition of limited resources and unlimited wants by people

specialization a focus on only one or two aspects of production in order to produce a product more quickly and cheaply; for example, one worker washes the wheels of the car, another cleans the interior, and another washes the body

trade barriers financial or legal limitations to trade; prevention of free trade

trade-offs the goods or services sacrificed in order to consume or produce another good or service

underground economy illegal economic activities and unreported legal economic activities

PERSONAL ECONOMICS

Individuals make personal choices in how they manage and use their money to satisfy their needs and desires. Individuals have the choice to spend, save, or invest their money. Individuals can also borrow money or buy goods and services on credit.

budget a plan listing the expenses and income of an individual or organization

credit a system that allows consumers to pay for goods and services over time

debt an amount of money that is owed

financial institutions businesses that keep and invest people's money and loan money to people; include banks and credit unions

income a gain of money that comes typically from labor or capital

interest the money that a borrower pays to a lender in return for a loan

loan money given on the condition that it will be paid back, often with interest

savings money or income that is not used to purchase goods or services

tax a required payment to a local, state, or national government; different kinds of taxes include sales taxes, income taxes, and property taxes

wage the payment a worker receives for his or her labor

RESOURCES

People and businesses need resources—such as land, labor, and money—to produce goods and services.

capital generally refers to wealth, in particular wealth that can be used to finance the production of goods or services

human capital sometimes used to refer to human skills and education that affect the production of goods and services in a company or country

labor force all people who are legally old enough to work and are either working or looking for work

natural resource any material in nature that people use and value

nonrenewable resource a resource that cannot be replaced naturally, such as coal or petroleum

raw material a natural resource used to make a product or good

renewable resource a resource that Earth replaces naturally, such as water, soil, and trees

ORGANIZATIONS

Countries have formed many organizations to promote economic cooperation, growth, and trade. These organizations are important in today's global economy.

European Union (EU) an organization that promotes political and economic cooperation in Europe

International Monetary Fund (IMF) a UN agency that promotes international cooperation and stability in trade and the exchange of countries' currencies

Organization of Economic Cooperation and Development (OECD) an organization of countries that promotes democracy and market economies

United Nations (UN) an organization of countries that promotes peace and security around the globe

World Bank a UN agency that provides loans to countries for development and recovery

World Trade Organization (WTO) an international organization dealing with trade between nations

Economic Handbook Review

Reviewing Vocabulary and Terms

On a separate sheet of paper, fill in the blanks in the following sentences:

ECONOMIC SYSTEMS

1. **A.** Businesses are able to operate with little government involvement in a _____ system.
   B. In a _____, a central government makes all economic decisions.
   C. _____ is a political system in which the government owns all property and runs a command economy.
   D. Economies that combine elements of command, market, and traditional economies are called _____.
   E. _____ is another name for a market economy.

THE ECONOMY AND MONEY

2. **A.** _____ are objects or materials that humans can buy to satisfy their needs and wants.
   B. A _____ is any activity that is performed for a fee.
   C. A person who buys goods or services is a _____.
   D. The amount of goods and services that consumers are willing and able to buy at any given time is known as _____.
   E. The total value of all the goods and services produced in the United States in one year is its _____.

INTERNATIONAL TRADE

3. **A.** If we have an unlimited demand for a natural resource, such as oil, and there is only so much oil in the ground, we have a condition called _____.
   B. Goods or services that a country sells to other countries are _____.
   C. Rivalry between producers that provide the same good or service is called _____.
   D. If a country is able to produce a good or service at a lower cost than other countries, it is said to have a _____.
   E. Trade among nations that is not limited by legal or economic barriers is called _____.

PERSONAL ECONOMICS

4. **A.** A _____ is a required payment to a local, state, or national government.
   B. The money we do not spend on goods or services is our _____.
   C. You can use _____ to pay for goods and services over time.
   D. The payment that a worker receives for his or her labor is called a _____.
   E. Individuals and companies use _____ to plan and manage their expenses and their income.

RESOURCES

5. A. Diamonds and gold are examples of _____, which are any materials in nature that people use and value.

B. The _____ consists of all people who are legally able to work and are working or looking for work.

C. Wealth that can be used to finance the production of goods and services is called _____.

D. Oil is an example of a _____, which is a resource that cannot be replaced naturally.

E. Water, soil, and trees are examples of _____, which are resources that Earth replaces naturally.

ORGANIZATIONS

6. A. Many European countries have joined the _____ to help promote political and economic cooperation across Europe.

B. The _____ consists of many agencies that promote peace and security around the world.

C. The _____ is a UN agency that provides loans to countries to help them develop their economies.

D. The _____ is a UN agency that helps protect the stability of countries' currencies.

E. Many democratic countries promote market economies through their membership in the _____.

Activities

1. With a partner, compare prices in two grocery stores. Create a chart showing the price of five items in the two stores. Also, figure the average price of the items in each store. How do you think the fact that the stores are near each other affects prices? How might prices be different if one store went out of business? How might the prices be different or similar if the United States had a command economy? Present what you have learned about prices and competition to your class.

2. With a group, choose five countries from a unit region to research. Look up the per capita GDP and the life expectancy rates for each of these countries in the regional atlas. Then use your textbook, go to your library, or use the Internet to research the literacy rate and the number of TVs per 1,000 people for each of these countries. Organize this information in a five-column chart like the one shown here. Study the information to see if you can find any patterns. Write a brief paragraph explaining what you have learned about the five countries.

Region				
Country	Per Capita GDP (U.S. $)	Life Expectancy at Birth	Literacy Rate	TVs per 1,000 People

3. Work with a partner to identify some of the types of currency used in Europe. Then imagine that you are the owners of a business in the United States. You have created a new product that you want to sell in Europe, but people there do not use the same currency as you do. To sell your product, you will need to be able to exchange one type of currency for another. Search the Internet or look in a newspaper to find a list of currency exchange rates. If your product sells for 1,000 dollars, what should the cost be in euros? In British pounds? In Russian rubles? In Norwegian kroner?

725

References

The United States of America: Political

CANADA

WASHINGTON
Seattle
Tacoma
Olympia ★
Spokane
45°N
Portland
★ Salem
Eugene
OREGON
125°W

MONTANA
Great Falls
Helena ★
Billings
Franklin D. Roosevelt Lake
Pend Oreille
Flathead Lake
Fort Peck Lake
Missouri River
Yellowstone River

NORTH DAKOT
Lake Sakakawea
Bismarck

IDAHO
Boise ★
Sun Valley
Pocatello
Snake River

WYOMING
Yellowstone Lake
Cheyenne ★

SOUTH DAKOTA
Pierre ★
Rapid City
Lake Oahe

Cape Mendocino
40°N
Goose Lake
Shasta Lake
Sacramento River

NEVADA
Pyramid Lake
Reno
★ Carson City
Lake Tahoe

Great Salt Lake
Ogden
★ Salt Lake City
Provo
Utah Lake
UTAH

COLORADO
Boulder
Vail
★ Denver
Aspen
Colorado Springs
Pueblo
Arkansas River

NEBRASKA
Platte River

KANS

125°W
San Francisco Bay
Berkeley
Oakland
San Francisco
★ Sacramento
San Jose
Monterey Bay
San Joaquin River

Fresno
CALIFORNIA
35°N

Las Vegas

Lake Powell

Santa Barbara
Ventura
Los Angeles
Long Beach
Anaheim
Santa Ana
San Diego
Riverside
Palm Springs
Salton Sea
Channel Islands

120°W

PACIFIC OCEAN

Lake Mead
Colorado

Flagstaff
ARIZONA
Phoenix ★
Casa Grande
Tucson
Gila River

Taos
Santa Fe ★
Albuquerque
NEW MEXICO
Las Cruces
El Paso
Pecos River

OKLAHO
Amarillo
Oklahoma
Lav
Canadian River

Lubbock
Abilene
Fort W
Midland
Odessa
TEXA
Brazos River

30°N

Gulf of California

To understand the relative locations of Alaska and Hawaii, as well as the vast distances separating them from the rest of the United States, see the world map.

22°N
Kauai
Niihau
Oahu
HAWAII
Honolulu
Molokai
Lanai
Maui
Kahoolawe
PACIFIC OCEAN
160°W
155°W
N
W E
S
Hilo
Hawaii
19°N

0   75   150 Miles
0   75   150 Kilometers
Projection: Mercator

170°E
55°N
Attu Island
PACIFIC OCEAN
50°N
180°
Bering Sea

ARCTIC OCEAN
Arctic Circle
Bering Strait
RUSSIA
N
W E
S
Nome
Yukon River
St. Lawrence Island
St. Matthew Island
Nunivak Island
ALASKA
Fairbanks
Anchorage
Valdez
Kodiak Island
Gulf of Alaska
Skagway
Juneau
Alexander Archipelago
55°N
CANADA
40°W
150°W
160°W
170°W

0   250   500 Miles
0   250   500 Kilometers
Projection: Albers Equal Area

MEXICO

Austin
San Antonio
Corpus Ch
Laredo

Amistad Reservoir

CANADA

MINNESOTA

Grand Forks
Fargo
Red River
Minnesota River
Duluth
Superior
Marquette
Sault Ste. Marie
Lake Superior

WISCONSIN
Minneapolis
St. Paul
Green Bay
Madison
Milwaukee
Mississippi River

MICHIGAN
Lake Michigan
Lake Huron
Grand Rapids
Saginaw
Lansing
Detroit
Ann Arbor

Sioux Falls
Sioux City

IOWA
Cedar Rapids
Davenport
Des Moines
omaha
ncoln

Rockford
Chicago
Gary
South Bend
Fort Wayne
Peoria

ILLINOIS
Springfield
Indianapolis

INDIANA

OHIO
Toledo
Cleveland
Youngstown
Akron
Columbus
Dayton
Cincinnati
Lake Erie

MISSOURI
Kansas City
Kansas City
opeka
St. Louis
East St. Louis
Jefferson City
Lake of the Ozarks
ichita
Springfield

KENTUCKY
Louisville
Evansville
Frankfort
Lexington
Ohio River
Lake Barkley
Kentucky Lake

MAINE
Augusta
Portland

St. Lawrence River
Lake Champlain
Burlington
Montpelier
VT
NH
Concord
Manchester
Hudson R.
Rochester
Syracuse
Albany
Springfield
MA
Boston
Worcester
Providence
Cape Cod

NEW YORK
Buffalo
Hartford
CT
RI
Bridgeport
New Haven
Long Island Sound
Long Island

PENNSYLVANIA
Allentown
Jersey City
Newark
Yonkers
New York City
Trenton
Harrisburg
Camden
Pittsburgh
Philadelphia
NJ
Atlantic City
Susquehanna River

Baltimore
DE
Dover
MD
Annapolis
Washington, D.C.

WEST VIRGINIA
Charleston

VIRGINIA
Richmond
Newport News
Norfolk
Virginia Beach
Chesapeake Bay
Delaware Bay

ATLANTIC OCEAN

40°N
70°W
35°N

Greensboro
Durham
Raleigh
Cape Hatteras
Winston-Salem
NORTH CAROLINA
Charlotte

Tulsa
Fayetteville
Keystone Lake

TENNESSEE
Nashville
Knoxville
Asheville
Chattanooga
Memphis
Kentucky Lake
Mississippi River

ufaula Lake
Lake Texoma

ARKANSAS
Little Rock
Pine Bluff
Huntsville

Greenville

SOUTH CAROLINA
Columbia
Charleston
Sea Islands
Savannah River

MISSISSIPPI
Vicksburg
Jackson
Meridian
Montgomery

ALABAMA
Birmingham

GEORGIA
Atlanta
Macon
Columbus

Mobile
Pensacola
Tallahassee
Jacksonville

Dallas
aco

Shreveport
Toledo Bend Reservoir

LOUISIANA
Baton Rouge
Beaumont
Houston
New Orleans
Biloxi
Chandeleur Islands
Galveston

Gainesville

FLORIDA
Orlando
Cape Canaveral
Tampa
St. Petersburg
Lake Okeechobee
Fort Myers
Fort Lauderdale
Miami
Cape Sable
Florida Keys
Straits of Florida

THE BAHAMAS

Gulf of Mexico

25°N
30°N
25°N
75°W
80°W
85°W
90°W
95°W

Legend	
⊛	National capital
★	State capitals
•	Other cities

0   100   200 Miles
0   100   200 Kilometers
Projection: Albers Equal Area

The United States of America: Physical

CANADA

ROCKY

Mount Rainier
14,410 ft.
(4,392 m)

Puget Sound

Franklin D.
Roosevelt Lake

Pend
Oreille

Flathead River

Flathead Lake

Milk River

Missouri River

Fort Peck
Lake

Lake
Sakakawea

CASCADE RANGE

COAST RANGES

Columbia River

Willamette River

Bitterroot Range

Salmon
River
Mts.

Clark Fork

Salmon River

Sawtooth
Mts.

CONTINENTAL

Lewis Range

Yellowstone River

Lake
Oahe

Cape
Mendocino

Klamath
River

Goose
Lake

Columbia Plateau

Snake River

Grand
Tetons

Yellowstone
Lake

Bighorn Mts.

Bighorn River

Powder River

Black
Hills

Cheyenne
River

White River

James River

Shasta
Lake

Pyramid
Lake

Gannett Peak
13,804 ft.
(4,207 m)

Wind River
Range

Wind
River

North Platte River

Niobrara River

San Francisco Bay

SIERRA NEVADA

Central Valley

Lake Tahoe

GREAT
BASIN

Great
Salt
Lake

Utah
Lake

Wasatch Range

Uinta
Mts.

Green River

DIVIDE

Front Range

South Platte River

Platte River

Republican River

Monterey
Bay

San Joaquin River

Mount Whitney
14,494 ft.
(4,419 m)

Death Valley

COLORADO

Lake
Powell

Silverton

Mount Elbert
14,433 ft.
(4,400 m)

Pikes Peak
14,110 ft.
(4,301 m)

Smoky Hill River

Coast Ranges

Mojave
Desert

Colorado River

Lake
Mead

Grand
Canyon

PLATEAU

Painted Desert

San Juan River

San Luis
Valley

Sangre De Cristo Mts.

MOUNTAINS

PLAINS

GREAT

INTERIOR

**PACIFIC
OCEAN**

Channel
Islands

Salton
Sea

Imperial
Valley

DIVIDE

Rio Grande

CONTINENTAL

Canadian River

Gila River

Sonoran
Desert

Gulf of
California

Pecos River

Colorado River

Amistad
Reservoir

Rio Grande

Nueces River

MEXICO

45°N

40°N

35°N

30°N

125°W

120°W

To understand the relative locations of Alaska and Hawaii,
as well as the vast distances separating them from the rest
of the United States, see the world map.

HAWAII

Kauai

Niihau

Oahu

Molokai

Lanai

Maui

Kahoolawe

Mauna Kea
13,796 ft.
(4,206 m)

Hawaii

PACIFIC
OCEAN

22°N

155°W

160°W

19°N

0	75	150 Miles
0	75	150 Kilometers

Projection: Mercator

ARCTIC OCEAN

RUSSIA

Arctic Circle

Bering Strait

BROOKS RANGE

Yukon River

CANADA

St. Lawrence
Island

St. Matthew
Island

Nunivak
Island

Kuskokwim River

Tanana River

ALASKA RANGE

Mount McKinley
20,320 ft.
(6,194 m)

Bering Sea

Attu Island

Yukon River

Gulf of Alaska

Kodiak Island

Alexander
Archipelago

PACIFIC
OCEAN

170°E

180°

170°W

160°W

150°W

140°W

55°N

50°N

40°N

55°N

0	250	500 Miles
0	250	500 Kilometers

Projection: Albers Equal Area

CANADA

Red River

Isle Royale

Mesabi Range

Lake Superior

Minnesota River

Mississippi River

Wisconsin River

Lake Michigan

Lake Huron

St. Lawrence Seaway

St. Lawrence River

Lake Champlain

Adirondack Mts.

Green Mts.

White Mts.

Longfellow Mts.

Penobscot River

St. John River

Connecticut River

Lake Ontario

Cape Cod

Long Island Sound

Long Island

Lake Erie

ALLEGHENY PLATEAU

Catskill Mts.

Hudson R.

Allegheny R.

Susquehanna River

Delaware River

40°N

70°W

Des Moines River

Missouri River

Illinois River

Scioto River

Wabash River

P L A I N S

Kansas R.

Ohio River

Monongahela R.

Potomac River

Delaware Bay

James River

APPALACHIAN MOUNTAINS

P I E D M O N T

Chesapeake Bay

ATLANTIC OCEAN

Lake of the Ozarks

OZARK PLATEAU

White River

Kentucky Lake

Lake Barkley

Cumberland River

Cumberland Plateau

Kanawha River

BLUE RIDGE MOUNTAINS

Roanoke River

Pamlico Sound

Cape Hatteras

35°N

Keystone Lake

Arkansas River

Great Smoky Mts.

ufaula Lake

Ouachita Mts.

Lake Texoma

Tennessee River

Tombigbee River

Coosa River

Oconee River

Savannah River

ELEVATION

Feet | Meters

13,120 | 4,000

6,560 | 2,000

1,640 | 500

656 | 200

(Sea level) 0 | 0 (Sea level)

Below sea level | Below sea level

0 — 100 — 200 Miles

0 — 100 — 200 Kilometers

Projection: Albers Equal Area

Trinity River

Red River

Sabine River

Mississippi River

Pearl River

Alabama R.

Chattahoochee River

Altamaha River

Sea Islands

C O A S T A L   P L A I N

ns River

Toledo Bend Reservoir

Okefenokee Swamp

FLORIDA PENINSULA

Cape Canaveral

80°W

ULF

Chandeleur Islands

Mississippi Delta

N
W   E
S

Gulf of Mexico

85°W

90°W

95°W

25°N

Lake Okeechobee

THE BAHAMAS

25°N

The Everglades

Cape Sable

Florida Keys

Straits of Florida

75°W

ATLAS

Boundaries
⊛ National capitals
• Other cities

0   500   1,000 Miles
0 500 1,000 Kilometers
Projection: Mollweide

0   200   400 Miles
0   200   400 Kilometers
Projection: Mercator

	COUNTRY	CAPITAL
1	Antigua and Barbuda	St. Johns
2	St. Kitts and Nevis	Basseterre
3	Dominica	Roseau
4	St. Lucia	Castries
5	St. Vincent and the Grenadines	Kingstown
6	Barbados	Bridgetown
7	Grenada	St. George's

COUNTRY	CAPITAL
1 Czech Republic	Prague
2 Slovakia	Bratislava
3 Slovenia	Ljubljana
4 Croatia	Zagreb
5 Bosnia and Herzegovina	Sarajevo
6 Macedonia	Skopje
7 Serbia	Belgrade
8 Montenegro	Podgorica
9 Lithuania	Vilnius
10 Latvia	Riga
11 Estonia	Tallinn
12 Kosovo	Pristina

North America: Political

ARCTIC OCEAN

EUROPE

ASIA

North Pole

ICELAND

160°E

170°E

180°

170°W

St. Lawrence Island

Bering Sea

Bering Strait

Nunivak Island

Point Barrow

Beaufort Sea

Queen Elizabeth Islands

Ellesmere Island

Greenland (DENMARK)

10°E

10°W

Arctic Circle

ALASKA (U.S.)

Yukon River

Banks Island

Baffin Bay

Denmark Strait

20°W

Anchorage

Kodiak Island

Gulf of Alaska

Mackenzie River

Great Bear Lake

Victoria Island

Baffin Island

Davis Strait

Cape Farewell

30°W

Juneau

Alexander Archipelago

Great Slave Lake

Southampton Island

Hudson Strait

Labrador Sea

160°W

50°N

Queen Charlotte Islands

Peace River

Coats Island

Mansel Island

Newfoundland

40°W

PACIFIC OCEAN

Edmonton

CANADA

Hudson Bay

Anticosti Island

St. Pierre and Miquelon (FRANCE)

Vancouver Island

Vancouver

Calgary

Lake Winnipeg

Gulf of St. Lawrence

Prince Edward Island

Cape Breton Island

150°W

Seattle

Winnipeg

St. Lawrence R.

Quebec

50°W

Portland

Columbia

Lake Superior

Lake Michigan

Lake Huron

Ottawa

Montreal

40°N

Cape Mendocino

Snake River

Minneapolis

Milwaukee

Detroit

Lake Ontario

Lake Erie

Toronto

Boston

Cape Cod

San Francisco

Great Salt Lake

Salt Lake City

Missouri River

Platte River

Chicago

Cleveland

Columbus

New York City

Philadelphia

ATLANTIC OCEAN

San Jose

Denver

Indianapolis

St. Louis

Baltimore

Washington, D.C.

30°N

140°W

San

Colorado River

Kansas City

Ohio R.

Norfolk

Los Angeles

San Diego

Tijuana

Phoenix

UNITED STATES

Memphis

Red River

Atlanta

Birmingham

Cape Hatteras

Bermuda (U.K.)

30°N

Dallas

Mississippi River

Jacksonville

Austin

Rio Grande

New Orleans

Cape Canaveral

Tropic of Cancer

San Antonio

Houston

Miami

THE BAHAMAS

Turks and Caicos Islands (U.K.)

Puerto Rico (U.S.)

ST. KITTS & NEVIS

20°N

Gulf of California

Gulf of Mexico

Florida Keys

Nassau

San Juan

ANTIGUA & BARBUDA

Monterrey

Havana

Straits of Florida

DOMINICAN REPUBLIC

Virgin Is. (U.S., U.K.)

Guadeloupe (FRANCE)

20°N

MEXICO

CUBA

HAITI

Santo Domingo

Martinique (FRANCE)

DOMINICA

Guadalajara

Mexico City

Mérida

Cayman Is. (U.K.)

Kingston

Port-au-Prince

ST. LUCIA

BARBADOS

130°W

Puebla

Balsas R.

JAMAICA

ST. VINCENT AND THE GRENADINES

GRENADA

10°N

Belmopan

BELIZE

Caribbean Sea

Netherlands Antilles (NETHERLANDS)

GUATEMALA

HONDURAS

Tegucigalpa

Aruba (NETHERLANDS)

120°W

Guatemala City

NICARAGUA

Panama Canal

TRINIDAD AND TOBAGO

San Salvador

Managua

EL SALVADOR

San José

Panama City

10°N

COSTA RICA

PANAMA

SOUTH AMERICA

110°W

100°W

90°W

80°W

70°W

60°W

Legend

- ▨ Boundaries
- ⊛ National capitals
- • Other cities

0 300 600 Miles

0 300 600 Kilometers

Projection: Azimuthal Equal Area

N W E S

10°N

0° Equator

South America: Political

CENTRAL
AMERICA

Caribbean Sea

Barranquilla
Cartagena
Caracas

VENEZUELA

Georgetown
Paramaribo
Cayenne

GUYANA

SURINAME
FRENCH
GUIANA
(FRANCE)

Medellín

Bogotá

COLOMBIA

Cali

Malpelo
Island
(COLOMBIA)

Orinoco River

Río Negro

Amazon River

Amazon River

Belém

Quito

ECUADOR

Guayaquil

Galápagos
Islands
(ECUADOR)

Equator 0°

BRAZIL

Recife

PERU

Marañón River

Ucayali River

Trujillo

São Francisco River

Callao
Lima

Arequipa

Lake
Titicaca

La Paz

Lake
Poopó

BOLIVIA

Sucre

Brasília

Salvador

PACIFIC
OCEAN

Belo Horizonte

Paraguay River

PARAGUAY

Campinas
São Paulo

Rio de Janeiro

Asunción

Curitiba

San Ambrosio
Island
(CHILE)

San Félix Island
(CHILE)

CHILE

Paraná River

Uruguay River

Pôrto Alegre

Córdoba

Juan Fernández
Islands
(CHILE)

Valparaíso
Santiago

Rosario

URUGUAY

ATLANTIC
OCEAN

Buenos Aires
Montevideo

Río de la Plata

ARGENTINA

ATLANTIC
OCEAN

Boundaries
National capitals
Other cities

0   250   500 Miles

0   250   500 Kilometers

Projection: Azimuthal Equal Area

Strait of
Magellan

Falkland
Islands (U.K.)

South Georgia
Island
(U.K.)

Tierra del
Fuego

Europe: Political

Boundaries
⊛ National capitals
• Other cities

| 0 | 150 | 300 Miles |
| 0 | 150 | 300 Kilometers |

Projection: Azimuthal Equal Area

ASIA

URAL MOUNTAINS

RUSSIA

Nizhny Novgorod

Moscow ⊛

Caspian Sea

SOUTHWEST ASIA

Barents Sea

White Sea

St. Petersburg

North Cape

Volga River

Don River

Black Sea

Dnipro River

FINLAND

Helsinki ⊛

Gulf of Bothnia

ESTONIA
Tallinn ⊛

LATVIA
Riga ⊛

LITHUANIA
Vilnius ⊛

RUSSIA

Minsk ⊛
BELARUS

Kiev ⊛
UKRAINE

MOLDOVA
Chişinău ⊛

ROMANIA
Bucharest ⊛

BULGARIA
Sofia ⊛

Skopje ⊛
MACEDONIA

GREECE

Rhodes

Crete

Athens ⊛

Aegean Sea

SWEDEN

Stockholm ⊛

Göteborg

Baltic Sea

Warsaw ⊛
POLAND

Krakow

SLOVAKIA
Bratislava ⊛

Budapest ⊛
HUNGARY

Zagreb ⊛

Belgrade ⊛
SERBIA

BOSNIA AND
HERZEGOVINA
Sarajevo ⊛

KOSOVO
Priština ⊛

MONTENEGRO
Podgorica ⊛

Tiranë ⊛
ALBANIA

Adriatic Sea

Danube River

NORWAY

Oslo ⊛

Bergen

ARCTIC OCEAN

Arctic Circle

Shetland Islands

Faeroe Islands (DENMARK)

ICELAND
Reykjavík ⊛

North Sea

DENMARK
Copenhagen ⊛

Hamburg

Berlin ⊛
GERMANY

Dresden

Prague ⊛
CZECH REPUBLIC

Vienna ⊛
AUSTRIA

SLOVENIA
Ljubljana ⊛

CROATIA

SAN MARINO
San Marino

ITALY
Rome ⊛

VATICAN CITY

Naples

Sicily

MALTA
Valletta ⊛

Elbe River

Cologne
Bonn

Munich

LIECHTENSTEIN
Vaduz

SWITZERLAND
Bern ⊛

Milan

MONACO
Monaco

Corsica (FRANCE)

Sardinia (ITALY)

Mediterranean Sea

AFRICA

NETHERLANDS
The Hague ⊛
Amsterdam ⊛

Brussels ⊛
BELGIUM

LUXEMBOURG
Luxembourg ⊛

Paris ⊛
FRANCE

Lyon

Marseille

PYRENEES

ANDORRA
Andorra la Vella ⊛

Barcelona

Balearic Islands (SPAIN)

SCOTLAND
Edinburgh ⊛

Liverpool

ENGLAND
London ⊛

WALES

NORTHERN IRELAND
Belfast ⊛

UNITED KINGDOM

IRELAND
Dublin ⊛

British Isles

Channel Islands (U.K.)

English Channel

Bay of Biscay

ATLANTIC OCEAN

SPAIN
Madrid ⊛

Seville

Valencia

Gibraltar (U.K.)

Strait of Gibraltar

PORTUGAL
Lisbon ⊛

Tagus River

N
E
W
S

R10 ATLAS

Asia: Political

Boundaries
⊛ National capitals
• Other cities

250 500 750 Kilometers
250 500 750 Miles

Projection: Two-Point Equidistant

North Pole
Arctic Circle

EUROPE

RUSSIA
Moscow
URAL MOUNTAINS
Ob River
Yekaterinburg
Chelyabinsk
Omsk
Astana
Novosibirsk
Yakutsk
Irkutsk
Lake Baykal
Ulaanbaatar
Lena River
Yenisey River
Angara River
Amur River
Vladivostok
Sakhalin Island
Kuril Islands (RUSSIA)
Sea of Okhotsk
Bering Sea
Aleutian Islands
Barents Sea
Kara Sea
Laptev Sea

KAZAKHSTAN
Lake Balkhash
Almaty
Bishkek
KYRGYZSTAN
Tashkent
UZBEKISTAN
TURKMENISTAN
Ashgabat
TAJIKISTAN
Dushanbe
Ural River
Caspian Sea

GEORGIA
T'bilisi
ARMENIA
Yerevan
AZERBAIJAN
Baku
Black Sea
Istanbul
Izmir
Ankara
TURKEY
CYPRUS
Nicosia
LEBANON
Beirut
ISRAEL
Tel Aviv
Jerusalem
SYRIA
Aleppo
Damascus
Amman
JORDAN
Mediterranean Sea
Tabriz
Mosul
IRAQ
Baghdad
Basra
Tehran
Mashhad
Isfahan
IRAN
Shiraz
KUWAIT
Kuwait City
BAHRAIN
Manama
QATAR
Doha
Riyadh
UNITED ARAB EMIRATES
Abu Dhabi
OMAN
Muscat (Masqat)
SAUDI ARABIA
Mecca
Jidda
Medina
YEMEN
Sanaa
Red Sea
Gulf of Aden
Socotra (YEMEN)
Persian Gulf
Tigris River
Euphrates River

AFGHANISTAN
Kabul
PAKISTAN
Islamabad
Lahore
Faisalabad
Karachi
Indus River
Arabian Sea

CHINA
Great Wall of China
Beijing
Xi'an
Chengdu
Chongqing
Wuhan
Nanjing
Shanghai
Qingdao
Harbin
Changchun
Fushun
Dalian
Huang (Yellow) River
Chang (Yangtze) River
Hong Kong
Macao
Guangzhou
Yellow Sea
East China Sea

MONGOLIA

NORTH KOREA
P'yongyang
SOUTH KOREA
Seoul
Pusan
JAPAN
Tokyo
Yokohama
Nagoya
Kyoto
Osaka
Hiroshima
Nagasaki
Sapporo
Sea of Japan (East Sea)

INDIA
New Delhi
Delhi
Jaipur
Ahmadabad
Bhopal
Nagpur
Kolkata (Calcutta)
Mumbai (Bombay)
Hyderabad
Bangalore
Chennai (Madras)
Ganges River
Brahmaputra River
NEPAL
Kathmandu
BHUTAN
Thimphu
BANGLADESH
Dhaka
Chittagong
Bay of Bengal
SRI LANKA
Colombo
MALDIVES
Male
Lakshadweep Islands (INDIA)
Andaman Islands (INDIA)
Nicobar Islands (INDIA)

MYANMAR (BURMA)
Yangon (Rangoon)
Mandalay
THAILAND
Bangkok
LAOS
Vientiane
VIETNAM
Hanoi
Ho Chi Minh City
CAMBODIA
Phnom Penh
Gulf of Thailand
Andaman Sea

MALAYSIA
Kuala Lumpur
SINGAPORE
Singapore
BRUNEI
Bandar Seri Begawan
Medan
INDONESIA
Jakarta
Bandung
Semarang
Surabaya
Ujung Pandang
Java Sea
Celebes Sea
EAST TIMOR

PHILIPPINES
Manila
South China Sea
Luzon Strait
Hainan (CHINA)
TAIWAN
Taipei
Ryukyu Islands (JAPAN)
Tropic of Cancer

PACIFIC OCEAN
INDIAN OCEAN

AUSTRALIA
New Guinea
Arafura Sea
Equator

AFRICA

N 20°E 40°E 60°E 80°E 100°E 120°E 140°E 150°E 160°E 170°E 180° 170°W
0° 10°S 10°N 20°N 30°N 40°N 50°N 60°N 70°N

ATLAS

EUROPE

SOUTHWEST ASIA

40°N

Azores (PORTUGAL)

Madeira (PORTUGAL)

Strait of Gibraltar

Algiers Tunis

Casablanca Rabat

30°N

Canary Islands (SPAIN)

El Aaiún

TUNISIA

Tripoli

Mediterranean Sea

Alexandria

MOROCCO

ALGERIA

LIBYA

Giza Cairo

Suez Canal

EGYPT

WESTERN SAHARA (Claimed by Morocco)

Tropic of Cancer

20°N

MAURITANIA

Nouakchott

MALI

NIGER

CHAD

Khartoum

Lake Nasser

Nile River

Red Sea

ERITREA

Asmara

Gulf of Aden

CAPE VERDE

Praia

SENEGAL

Dakar

GAMBIA

Banjul

Bissau

Bamako

BURKINA FASO

Niamey

Lake Chad

N'Djamena

SUDAN

DJIBOUTI

Djibouti

GUINEA-BISSAU

Conakry

GUINEA

Ouagadougou

BENIN

NIGERIA

ETHIOPIA

Addis Ababa

10°N

Freetown

SIERRA LEONE

Monrovia

LIBERIA

CÔTE D'IVOIRE

GHANA

Yamoussoukro

Abidjan

Accra

TOGO

Lomé

Abuja

Porto-Novo

Lagos

CENTRAL AFRICAN REPUBLIC

CAMEROON

Bangui

SOMALIA

Mogadishu

10°N

Gulf of Guinea

Malabo

Yaoundé

UGANDA

KENYA

EQUATORIAL GUINEA

SÃO TOMÉ AND PRÍNCIPE

São Tomé

Libreville

GABON

REPUBLIC OF THE CONGO

Congo River

Kisangani

Kampala

RWANDA

Kigali

Nairobi

INDIAN OCEAN

Victoria

0° Equator

Equator 0°

SEYCHELLES

N W E S

Brazzaville

DEMOCRATIC REPUBLIC OF THE CONGO

Bujumbura

BURUNDI

TANZANIA

Mombasa

Pemba

Zanzibar

CABINDA (ANGOLA)

Kinshasa

Dodoma

Dar es Salaam

Luanda

ATLANTIC OCEAN

10°S

Lubumbashi

MALAWI

Lilongwe

COMOROS

Moroni

10°S

ANGOLA

ZAMBIA

Lusaka

Zambezi River

Lake Malawi (Nyasa)

St. Helena (U.K.)

Harare

ZIMBABWE

Bulawayo

MOZAMBIQUE

Antananarivo

MAURITIUS

20°S

NAMIBIA

BOTSWANA

Windhoek

Gaborone

Pretoria

Maputo

MADAGASCAR

Port Louis

Réunion (FRANCE)

Tropic of Capricorn

Johannesburg

Bloemfontein

Mbabane

SWAZILAND

Maseru

LESOTHO

30°S

SOUTH AFRICA

Cape Town

40°S

Tropic of Cancer

20°N

10°N

0° Equator

10°S

20°S

Tropic of Capricorn

30°S

40°S

Boundaries

National capitals

Other cities

0   250   500 Miles

0   250   500 Kilometers

Projection: Azimuthal Equal Area

Australia and New Zealand: Political

ATLAS

NORTH PACIFIC OCEAN

SOUTH PACIFIC OCEAN

POLYNESIA

Marquesas Islands (FRANCE)

Tuamotu Archipelago (FRANCE)

French Polynesia

Rapa Island (FRANCE)

Tubuai Islands (FRANCE)

Society Islands (FRANCE)

Tahiti (FRANCE)

Papeete

Easter Island (CHILE)

Pitcairn (U.K.)

Pitcairn Island

Ducie Island

Starbuck Island

KIRIBATI

Manihiki Island

Cook Islands (NEW ZEALAND)

Rarotonga Island

Hawaiian Islands

Hawaii (U.S.)

Kingman Reef (U.S.)

Palmyra Island (U.S.)

Fanning Island

Washington Island

Jarvis I. (U.S.)

Howland I. (U.S.)

Baker I. (U.S.)

Phoenix Islands

Gardner

McKean I.

Tokelau (N.Z.)

American Samoa

Pago Pago

Niue (N.Z.)

SAMOA Apia

Wallis & Futuna (FR.)

TONGA Nuku'alofa

Midway Island (U.S.)

Johnston Island (U.S.)

International Date Line

Wake Island (U.S.)

MARSHALL ISLANDS

Eniwetok I.

Kwajalein Island

Majuro

Tarawa

Gilbert Islands

TUVALU Funafuti

NAURU Yaren

SOLOMON ISLANDS

MELANESIA

FIJI Suva

VANUATU Port-Vila

Espiritu Santo I.

Malekula I.

New Caledonia (FRANCE)

Nouméa

Loyalty Islands (FRANCE)

MICRONESIA

Truk Is.

FEDERATED STATES OF MICRONESIA Palikir

Northern Marianas (U.S.)

Bonin Islands (JAPAN)

Volcano Islands (JAPAN)

Guam (U.S.) Agana

PALAU Koror

Bismarck Archipelago

PAPUA NEW GUINEA

Port Moresby

Honiara

Guadalcanal I.

New Guinea

Kermadec Islands (N.Z.)

Norfolk Island (AUSTRALIA)

Auckland

Wellington

Christchurch

NEW ZEALAND

North Island

South Island

Chatham Islands (N.Z.)

Bounty Islands (N.Z.)

Auckland Islands (NEW ZEALAND)

Tropic of Capricorn

Tropic of Cancer

Equator

N E S W

ASIA

Philippine Sea

South China Sea

Christmas Island (AUSTRALIA)

Coral Sea

Arafura Sea

Timor Sea

Tasman Sea

AUSTRALIA

Brisbane

Sydney

Canberra

Hobart

Melbourne

Adelaide

Perth

Darwin

Flinders R.

Darling R.

Lachlan R.

Murray R.

INDIAN OCEAN

Boundaries

⊛ National capitals

• Other cities

0 500 1,000 Miles

0 500 1,000 Kilometers

Projection: Mercator

Indiana: Physical

MICHIGAN

Lake Michigan

GREAT   LAKES   PLAINS

Lake
Wawasee

Kankakee   River

Tippecanoe

River

Eel   River

St. Joseph R.

St. Marys River

Huntington
Lake

ILLINOIS

Iroquois

River

Wabash

Mississinewa
Lake

Salamonie
Lake

Wabash
R.

Mississinewa   River

N
W   E
S

River

Sugar   Creek

White   River

OHIO

TILL   PLAINS

Highest Point:
Hoosier Hill
1,257 ft (383 m) ▲

Cecil M.
Harden
Lake

Eel   River

White   River

Blue   River

Wabash   River

Cagles
Mill Lake

White

Big

River

Brookville
Lake

Whitewater   River

Monroe
Lake

Salt R.

Muscatatuck River

River

SOUTHERN   HILLS
AND
LOWLANDS

Fork

White

River

River

River

White

East

Patoka   R.

Wabash   River

Patoka
Lake

Ohio   River

ELEVATION

Feet	Meters
984	300
656	200
(Sea level) 0	0 (Sea level)

0   15   30 Miles

0   15   30 Kilometers

Projection: Albers Equal Area

Ohio   River

Lowest Point:
Ohio River
320 ft (98 m)

KENTUCKY

Indiana: Political

Lake Michigan

MICHIGAN

• Michigan City
Hammond •
Gary • Portage
• Valparaiso
• Elkhart
South Bend • Mishawaka
• Goshen

Lake Wawasee

Kankakee River
Iroquois River
Tippecanoe River
Eel River
St. Joseph R.
Fort Wayne •
St. Marys River

ILLINOIS

Wabash River
Huntington Lake
Salamonie Lake
Mississinewa Lake
West Lafayette •
• Kokomo
Marion •
Mississinewa River
Lafayette •
Wabash R.

Sugar Creek
Muncie •
White River
Noblesville •
Anderson •

OHIO

Carmel •
• Fishers
Cecil M. Harden Lake
• Lawrence
Richmond •
★ Indianapolis
Blue River
Whitewater River
Greenwood •
Big River
River
Terre Haute •
Cagles Mill Lake
White River
Eel River
Brookville Lake

Columbus •
Muscatattuck River
Bloomington •
Monroe Lake
River
White River

	State boundary
★	State capital
•	Other cities

0   15   30 Miles
0   15   30 Kilometers
Projection: Albers Equal Area

Fork
White River
East River
New Albany • Jeffersonville •
Patoka R.
Patoka Lake
Ohio River

Wabash River
Evansville •
Ohio River

KENTUCKY

W — E
N
S

ATLAS

Indiana Governors

Jonathan Jennings (1784-1834)
November 7, 1816-September 12, 1822

Ratliff Boon (1781-1844)
September 12-December 5, 1822

William Hendricks (1782-1850)
December 5, 1822-February 12, 1825

James Brown Ray (1794-1848)
February 12, 1825-December 7, 1831

Noah Noble (1794-1844)
December 7, 1831-December 6, 1837

David Wallace (1799-1859)
December 6, 1837-December 9, 1840

Samuel Bigger (1802-1846)
December 9, 1840-December 6, 1843

James Whitcomb (1795-1852)
December 6, 1843-December 26, 1848

Paris Chipman Dunning (1806-1884)
December 26, 1848-December 5, 1849

Joseph Albert Wright (1810-1867)
December 5, 1849-January 12, 1857

Ashbel Parsons Willard (1820-1860)
January 12, 1857-October 4, 1860

Abram Adams Hammond (1814-1874)
October 4, 1860-January 14, 1861

Henry Smith Lane (1811-1881)
January 14-16, 1861

Oliver Perry Morton (1823-1877)
January 16, 1861-January 23, 1867

Conrad Baker (1817-1885)
January 23, 1867-January 13, 1873

Thomas Andrews Hendricks (1819-1885)
January 13, 1873-January 8, 1877

James Douglas Williams (1808-1880)
January 8, 1877-November 20, 1880

Isaac Pusey Gray (1825-1895)
November 20, 1880-January 10, 1881

Albert Gallatin Porter (1824-1897)
January 10, 1881-January 12, 1885

Isaac Pusey Gray (1825-1895)
January 12, 1885-January 14, 1889

Alvin Peterson Hovey (1821-1891)
January 14, 1889-November 23, 1891

Ira Joy Chase (1834-1895)
November 23, 1891-January 9, 1893

Claude Matthews (1845-1898)
January 9, 1893-January 11, 1897

James Atwell Mount (1843-1901)
January 11, 1897-January 14, 1901

Winfield Taylor Durbin (1847-1928)
January 14, 1901-January 9, 1905

James Frank Hanly (1863-1920)
January 9, 1905-January 11, 1909

Thomas Riley Marshall (1854-1925)
January 11, 1909-January 13, 1913

Samuel Moffett Ralston (1857-1925)
January 13, 1913-January 8, 1917

James Putnam Goodrich (1864-1940)
January 8, 1917-January 10, 1921

Warren Terry McCray (1865-1938)
January 10, 1921-April 30, 1924

Emmett Forrest Branch (1874-1932)
April 30, 1924-January 12, 1925

Edward L. Jackson (1873-1954)
January 12, 1925-January 14, 1929

Harry Guyer Leslie (1878-1937)
January 14, 1929-January 9, 1933

Paul Vories McNutt (1891-1955)
January 9, 1933-January 11, 1937

Maurice Clifford Townsend (1884-1954)
January 11, 1937-January 13, 1941

Henry Frederick Schricker (1883-1966)
January 13, 1941-January 8, 1945

Ralph F. Gates (1893-1978)
January 8, 1945-January 10, 1949

Henry Frederick Schricker (1883-1966)
January 10, 1949-January 12, 1953

George N. Craig (1909-1992)
January 12, 1953-January 14, 1957

Harold W. Handley (1909-1972)
January 14, 1957-January 9, 1961

Matthew E. Welsh (1912-1995)
January 9, 1961-January 11, 1965

Roger D. Branigin (1902-1975)
January 11, 1965-January 13, 1969

Edgar D. Whitcombe (b. 1917)
January 13, 1969-January 9, 1973

Otis R. Bowen (b. 1918)
January 9, 1973-January 13, 1981

Robert D. Orr (1917-2004)
January 13, 1981-January 9, 1989

Evan Bayh (b. 1955)
January 9, 1989-January 13, 1997

Frank O'Bannon (1930-2003)
January 13, 1997-September 13, 2003

Joseph E. Kernan (b. 1946)
September 13, 2003-January 10, 2005

Mitchell E. Daniels, Jr. (b. 1949)
January 10, 2005-

Indiana Government

Executive Branch

Carries out the laws and policies of state government

Governor

- Elected by voters to a four-year term
- Can only serve eight years in any twelve-year period

Lieutenant Governor

- Elected by voters to four-year term

Other Elected Officials

- Attorney General
- Auditor
- Secretary of State
- Treasurer
- Superintendent of Public Instruction

Legislative Branch

Makes state laws

Bicameral System

- The General Assembly has two houses—a House of Representatives and a Senate
- Both houses take part in law-making
- Legislature can override the governor's veto with a majority in each house

State Senate

- 50 senators
- Elected by voters to four-year terms
- Must be at least 25 years old

House of Representatives

- 100 representatives
- Elected by voters to two-year terms
- Must be at least 25 years old

Judicial Branch

Interprets the meaning of state laws

Trial Courts

- Hear civil and criminal cases

Appellate Courts

- Indiana Court of Appeals consists of 15 judges
- Indiana Tax Court has only one judge

Indiana Supreme Court

- Consists of five judges
- Highest court in the state

Indiana Facts

State tree	Tulip tree
State bird	Cardinal
State flower	Peony
State stone	Salem limestone
Capital	Indianapolis
Nickname	Hoosier State
Year of Statehood	1816 (19th state)
Motto	The Crossroads of America
Song	*On the Banks of the Wabash, Far Away*
Highest Elevation	Hoosier Hill, 1,257 feet above sea level
Lowest Elevation	Ohio River, 320 feet above sea level
Total area	36,420 sq. miles
National rank in total area	38th largest
Largest city	Indianapolis
Largest lake	Lake Michigan
Number of counties	92 counties
Bordering states	Michigan, Ohio, Kentucky, Illinois
Population (2006)	6,313,520
National rank in population	14th largest

The Cardinal is the Indiana state bird.

Indianapolis skyline

Gazetteer

A

Africa Second-largest continent. Lies in both the northern and the southern hemispheres. p. 16

Alabama (AL) State in the southern United States. Admitted as a state in 1819. Capital: Montgomery. (33°N 87°W) p. 426

Alaska (AK) U.S. state in northwestern North America. Purchased from Russia in 1867. Became a territory in 1912. Admitted as a state in 1959. Capital: Juneau. (64°N 150°W) p. 6

Albany Capital of New York. (42°N 74°W) p. 96

Andes Mountains Mountain range along the west coast of South America. p. 8

Appalachian Mountains Mountain system in eastern North America that extends from Canada to central Alabama. p. 48

Arctic Region around the North Pole including the Arctic Ocean and parts of Alaska, Canada, Russia, and the Scandinavian countries. (90°N 0°E) p. 12

Arizona (AZ) State in the southwestern United States. Organized into a territory in 1863. Admitted as a state in 1912. Capital: Phoenix. (34°N 113°W) p. 10

Arkansas (AR) State in the south-central United States. Admitted as a state in 1836. Capital: Little Rock. (35°N 93°W) p. 55

Asia Largest continent. Occupies the same land mass as Europe. p. 6

Athens Ancient city and modern capital of Greece; the world's first democracy developed in Athens around 500 BC. (38°N 24°E) p. 23

Atlanta Capital of Georgia. (33°N 84°W) p. 541

Atlantic Ocean Vast body of water separating North and South America from Europe and Africa. p. 44

B

Baltimore Maryland city northeast of Washington, D.C., on the Chesapeake Bay. (39°N 76°W) p. 286

Bering Land Bridge Land bridge that once connected what is now Alaska with Siberia. p. 6

Boston Capital of Massachusetts. (42°N 71°W) p. 100

Buena Vista City in northeastern Mexico. (33°N 117°W) p. 360

Brazil Country in eastern South America. Capital: Brasília. (10°S 55°W) p. 60

Bull Run Creek in northeastern Virginia where the Confederates won two major battles during the Civil War. p. 516

Bunker Hill Hill in Boston, Massachusetts. Site of an early Revolutionary War battle. p. 115

Cahokia Site in modern-day Missouri where the Mississippian culture built large settlements. (38°N 90°W) p. 11

California (CA) State in the western United States. Admitted as a state in 1850. Capital: Sacramento. (38°N 121°W) p. 12

Canada Country in northern North America. Capital: Ottawa. (50°N 100°W) p. 6

Cape of Good Hope Southern tip of Africa. p. 40

Caribbean Sea Arm of the Atlantic Ocean between North and South America. p. 48

Central America Region of land connecting North and South America. p. 8

Charleston Port city in southeastern South Carolina. Originally called Charles Town. (33°N 80°W) p. 136

Chesapeake Bay Inlet of the Atlantic Ocean in Virginia and Maryland. p. 75

Chicago Large U.S. city in northeastern Illinois on Lake Michigan. Major port. (41°N 87°W) p. 401

Chile Country in western South America; the Inca Empire stretched into central Chile. Capital: Santiago. p. 9

China Country in East Asia with the world's largest population. Capital: Beijing. (Official name: People's Republic of China) p. 25

Colombia Country in northwest South America. Capital: Bogotá. (4°N 72°W) p. 705

Columbia River River in the northwestern United States and southwestern Canada. Forms part of boundary between Oregon and Washington. p. 276

Colorado (CO) State in the southwestern United States. Admitted as a state in 1876. Capital: Denver. (39°N 107°W) p. 10

Concord One of two northeastern Massachusetts towns (along with Lexington) where the first fighting of the American Revolution took place in 1775. (42°N 71°W) p. 113

Connecticut (CT) State in the northeastern United States. One of the original thirteen colonies. Admitted as a state in 1788. Capital: Hartford. (41°N 73°W) p. 57

Cuba Westernmost country of the West Indies, an island republic in the northern Caribbean Sea. Capital: Havana. (23°N 82°W) p. 697

Cuzco City in Peru; it was the capital of the Inca Empire. (14°S 72°W) p. 8

Delaware (DE) State in the eastern United States. One of the original thirteen colonies. Capital: Dover. (38°N 75°W) p. 57

Detroit Largest city in Michigan. (42°N 83°W) p. 642

District of Columbia Federal district between Maryland and Virginia where the capital of the United States is located. (39°N 77°W) p. 240

Dominican Republic West Indies country that occupies approximately the eastern two-thirds of Hispaniola. Capital: Santo Domingo. (19°N 71°W) p. 707

Ecuador Country in northwest South America. Capital: Quito. (2°S 78°W) p. 9

Ellis Island New York Bay island. Part of Statue of Liberty National Monument. U.S. immigration center. Entry point for millions of people from 1892–1954. (41°N 74°W) p. 637

England Region of the United Kingdom that makes up most of the southern part of the island of Great Britain. Capital: London. (51°N 1°W) p. 53

Erie Canal Early 1800s building project created a waterway between New York cities of Albany, the capital, and Buffalo, on Lake Erie. p. 303

Europe Continent occupying the same land mass as Asia. p. 22

Florence City in Italy; ruled by the Medici family in the 1400s, it was a major center for culture and trade. (44°N 11°E) p. 27

Florida (FL) State in the southeastern United States. Organized as a territory in 1822. Admitted as a state in 1845. Capital: Tallahassee. (30°N 84°W) p. 299

Fort McHenry U.S. fort that guarded Baltimore, Maryland. The British attacked the fort in the War of 1812. p. 286

Fort Necessity Site where the French defeated British colonists in 1754, in what was the first battle of the French and Indian War. p. 96

Fort Sumter Fort on Charleston Harbor, South Carolina. Attack by Confederate forces here began the American Civil War. p. 511

France Country in Western Europe. Capital: Paris. (46°N 0°W) p. 24

Georgia (GA) State in the southeastern United States. Admitted as a state in 1788. One of the original thirteen colonies. Capital: Atlanta. (32°N 84°W) p. 76

Germany Country in Western Europe. Capital: Berlin. (51°N 8°E) p. 53

Gettysburg Town in southern Pennsylvania. (40°N 77°W) p. 537

Ghana West African country located between the Niger and Senegal Rivers; it was the site of a powerful empire established around AD 300. Capital: Accra. p. 16

Great Basin Elevated region made up of parts of California, Idaho, Nevada, Oregon, Utah, and Wyoming that was home to many Native American nations. p. 12

Great Britain Country in western Europe that includes England, Scotland, and Wales. Capital: London. p. 93

Great Lakes Chain of lakes located in central North America that extends across the U.S.-Canada border. Includes Lake Superior, Lake Michigan, Lake Huron, Lake Erie, and Lake Ontario. p. 55

Great Plains Region of central North America that lies between the Mississippi River and the Rocky Mountains. p. 14

Greece Country in southern Europe with mountains, rugged coastlines, and scenic islands; the country is called the birthplace of democracy. Capital: Athens. p. 22

Greenland Island in the North Atlantic that was settled by the Vikings. Capital: Godthåb. p. 38

Guam Unincorporated U.S. territory that is the southernmost and largest of the Mariana Islands in the west Pacific Ocean. Capital: Agana. (13°N 145°E) p. 700

Gulf of Mexico Gulf on the southeastern coast of North America, bordered by the United States, Mexico, and Cuba. p. 48

Hartford Capital of Connecticut. (41°N 72°W) p. 287

Hawaii Largest of group of eight large and many smaller Hawaiian Islands in the Pacific Ocean admitted to the Union in 1959 as the 50th state. Capital: Honolulu. (21°N 158°W) p. 694

Hispaniola Island that includes the countries of Haiti and the Dominican Republic. p. 43

Hudson Bay Inland sea in east-central Canada. Explored by Henry Hudson in 1610. p. 96

Hudson River River flowing from northeastern to southern New York. p. 57

Idaho (ID) State in the northwestern United States. Admitted as a state in 1890. Capital: Boise. (44°N 115°W) p. 364

Illinois (IL) State in the north-central United States. Admitted as a state in 1819. Capital: Springfield. (40°N 90°W) p. 11

India Large country in southern Asia. Capital: New Delhi. (28°N 77°E) p. 40

Indiana (IN) State in the north-central United States. Admitted as a state in 1816. Capital: Indianapolis. (40°N 86°W) p. 155

Indian Ocean Vast body of water east of Africa, south of Asia, west of Australia, and north of Antarctica. p. 44

Iowa (IA) State in the north-central United States. Admitted as a state in 1846. Capital: Des Moines. (42°N 94°W) p. 348

Ireland Island in the British Isles. Divided into Northern Ireland (Capital: Belfast), and the Republic of Ireland (Capital: Dublin). (54°N 8°W) p. 438

Italy Country in southern Europe. Capital: Rome. (44°N 11°E) p. 26

GAZETTEER

Jamestown First successful English colony in America. Established in eastern Virginia in 1607. p. 72

Japan Island chain nation of East Asia. Japan in Chinese means "Land of the rising sun." Capital: Tokyo. (36°N 140°E) p. 694

Kansas (KS) State in the central United States. Organized as a territory in 1854. Admitted as a state in 1861. Capital: Topeka. (38°N 99°W) p. 483

Kentucky (KY) State in the east-central United States. Admitted as a state in 1792. Capital: Frankfort. (37°N 87°W) p. 253

Lake Erie One of the Great Lakes. Located in the United States and Canada. p. 285

Latin America Spanish-speaking countries of North and South America that were once claimed by Spain and Portugal. p. 60

Lexington One of two northeastern Massachusetts towns (along with Concord) where the first fighting of the American Revolution took place in 1775. (42°N 71°W) p. 114

Liberia Country on the west coast of Africa. Capital: Monrovia. (6°N 10°W) p. 455

London Capital of the United Kingdom, in England. (52°N 0°W) p. 72

Los Angeles Large city in southern California. (34°N 118°W) p. 367

Louisiana (LA) State in the southeastern United States carved out of the Louisiana Territory. Admitted as a state in 1812. Capital: Baton Rouge. (31°N 92°W) p. 273

M

Maine (ME) State in the northeastern United States. Admitted as a state in 1820. Capital: Augusta. (45°N 70°W) p. 305

Mali West African country located on the Niger River; it was the location of an empire that reached its height around 1300. Capital: Bamako. p. 18

Manhattan Island Island at the north end of New York Bay. One of the five boroughs that make up New York City. p. 57

Maryland (MD) State in the east-central United States. One of the original thirteen colonies. Admitted as a state in 1788. Capital: Annapolis. (39°N 76°W) p. 75

Massachusetts (MA) State in the northeastern United States. One of the original thirteen colonies. Admitted as a state in 1788. Capital: Boston. (42°N 72°W) p. 79

Mecca Ancient city in Arabia and the birthplace of Muhammad. (21°N 40°E) p. 18

Mediterranean Sea Large sea bordered by southern Europe, Southwest Asia, and northern Africa. p. 25

Mesoamerica Area from Mexico to North Central American during pre-Spanish culture. p. 8

Mexico Country in southern North America. Capital: Mexico City. (23°N 104°W) p. 6

Michigan (MI) State in the north-central United States. Admitted as a state in 1837. Capital: Lansing. (46°N 87°W) p. 155

Minnesota (MN) State in the north-central United States. Admitted as a state in 1858. Capital: St. Paul. (46°N 90°W) p. 155

Mississippi (MS) State in the southeastern United States. Admitted as a state in 1817. Capital: Jackson. (32°N 89°W) p. 332

Mississippi River River that flows from Minnesota south to the Gulf of Mexico. p. 11

Missouri (MO) State in the central United States. Admitted as a state in 1821. Capital: Jefferson City. (38°N 93°W) p. 11

Missouri River River that flows from southern Montana and joins the Mississippi River. p. 11

Montana (MT) State in the northwestern United States. Admitted as a state in 1889. Capital: Helena. (47°N 112°W) p. 599

Montreal City in southeastern Canada founded by the French in 1642. (46°N 74°W) p. 128

Morocco Country in northwest Africa bounded by the western Sahara, the Mediterranean Sea, and the Atlantic Ocean. Capital: Rabat. (34°N 07°W). p. 18

Nebraska (NE) State in the central United States. Admitted as a state in 1867. Capital: Lincoln. (41°N 101°W) p. 484

Netherlands Country in northwestern Europe. Capital: Amsterdam. (52°N 5°E) p. 53

Nevada (NV) State in the western United States. Organized as a territory in 1861. Admitted as a state in 1864. Capital: Carson City. (39°N 117°W) p. 356

New Amsterdam Dutch settlement on the island of Manhattan. Founded in 1626. p. 57

New England Northeastern section of the United States. Made up of Connecticut, Maine, Massachusetts, New Hampshire, Rhode Island, and Vermont. p. 81

New Hampshire (NH) State in the northeastern United States. One of the original thirteen colonies. Admitted as a state in 1788. Capital: Concord. (44°N 71°W) p. 83

New Jersey (NJ) State in the northeastern United States. One of the original thirteen colonies. Admitted as a state in 1787. Capital: Trenton. (40°N 75°W) p. 57

New Mexico (NM) State in the southwestern United States. Admitted as a state in 1912. Capital: Santa Fe. (34°N 107°W) p. 10

New Orleans Port city in southeastern Louisiana. (30°N 90°W) p. 57

New Spain Vast area of North America controlled by Spain. p. 47

New Sweden Swedish colony in North America that was located along the Delaware River. p. 57

New York (NY) State in the northeastern United States. One of the original thirteen colonies. Admitted as a state in 1788. Capital: Albany. (42°N 78°W) p. 57

New York City Largest city in the United States. (41°N 74°W) p. 57

Nicaragua Country between Caribbean Sea and Pacific Ocean in Central America. Capital: Managua. (12°N 86°W) p. 708

Niger River Major river in West Africa. p. 18

North America Continent in the northern Western Hemisphere. p. 6

North Carolina (NC) State in the southeastern United States. One of the original thirteen colonies. Admitted as a state in 1789. Capital: Raleigh. p. 76

Ohio (OH) State in the north-central United States. Originally part of the Northwest Territory. Admitted as a state in 1803. Capital: Columbus. (40°N 83°W) p. 155

Ohio River River that flows through Pennsylvania, Ohio, Indiana, and Illinois. p. 11

Oklahoma (OK) State in the south-central United States. Organized as a territory in 1890. Admitted as a state in 1907. Capital: Oklahoma City. (36°N 98°W) p. 48

Oregon (OR) State in the northwestern United States. Admitted as a state in 1859. Capital: Salem. (43°N 122°W) p. 348

Pacific Ocean Body of water extending from the Arctic Circle to Antarctica and from western North and South America to Australia, the Malay Archipelago, and East Asia. p. 44

Panama Country in southern Central America. Location of the Panama Canal. Capital: Panama City. (8°N 81°W) p. 49

Pennsylvania (PA) State in the eastern United States. One of the original thirteen colonies. Admitted as a state in 1787. Capital: Harrisburg. (41°N 78°W) p. 86

Peru Country in western South America. Capital: Lima. (10°S 75°W) p. 47

Philadelphia City in southeastern Pennsylvania. Capital of the United States from 1790 to 1800. (40°N 75°W) p. 86

Philippines Country in the western Pacific Ocean. Made up of about 7,100 islands. Capital: Manila. (14°N 125°E) p. 44

Pittsburgh Second largest city and major port in Pennsylvania. (40°N 80°W) p. 647

Plymouth Site in Massachusetts where the Pilgrims first landed in North America in 1620. (42°N 70°W) p. 79

Portugal Country in southwestern Europe on the western Iberian Peninsula. Capital: Lisbon. (38°N 8°W) p. 39

Providence Capital of Rhode Island. (42°N 71°W) p. 82

Puerto Rico Island east of Cuba and southeast of Florida. A U.S. territory acquired in the Spanish-American War. Capital: San Juan. (18°N 67°W) p. 48

Rhode Island (RI) State in the northeastern United States. One of the original thirteen colonies. Admitted as a state in 1790. Capital: Providence. (41°N 71°W) p. 82

Richmond Capital of Virginia. Capital of the Confederate States of America during the Civil War. (37°N 7°W) p. 428

Rio Grande Spanish for *Great River*. Forms the border between Texas and Mexico. p. 357

Roanoke Island Island off the coast of North Carolina. Site of Britain's first settlement in North America. p. 56

Rocky Mountains Mountain range in western North America that extends from Alaska south to New Mexico. p. 14

Rome A city in Italy near the Mediterranean Sea; it was the capital of the Roman Empire. (42°N 13°E) p. 22

Russia Vast country that extends from Eastern Europe through northwestern Asia. Capital: Moscow. (61°N 60°E) p. 347

Sacramento River River in northwest California. Sacramento, capital of California, sits at its head. (38°N 121°W) p. 365

Sahara The world's largest desert, located in northern Africa. p. 16

St. Louis City in Missouri on the Mississippi River. (39°N 90°W) p. 642

San Antonio City in southern Texas. Site of the Mexican victory over Texas forces at the Alamo during the Texas Revolution. (29°N 99°W) p. 362

San Diego City in southern California. Located on San Diego Bay. (33°N 117°W) p. 358

San Francisco City in western California on a peninsula between the Pacific Ocean and San Francisco Bay. (37°N 122°W) p. 358

San Juan Hill Hill close to the city of Santiago, Cuba. Site of a battle in the Spanish-American War. p. 699

Santa Fe Capital of New Mexico. (35°N 106°W) p. 349

Saratoga Site in eastern New York of the Revolutionary War's Battle of Saratoga, the turning point of the war. p. 129

Savannah Port city in southeastern Georgia. Founded by James Oglethorpe in 1733. (32°N 81°W) p. 136

Scandinavia Large peninsula in northern Europe. p. 38

Seneca Falls Village in west-central New York State. Site of the first women's rights convention in the United States in 1848. (43°N 77°W) p. 464

Sierra Nevada Large mountain range in eastern California. p. 12

Songhai Large and powerful empire in West Africa during the 1400s and 1500s. p. 19

South America Continent in the southern Western Hemisphere. p. 6

South Carolina (SC) State in the southeastern United States. One of the original thirteen colonies. Admitted as a state in 1788. Capital: Columbia. (34°N 81°W) p. 76

South Dakota (SD) State in the north-central United States. Organized as part of the Dakota Territory in 1861. Admitted as a state in 1889. Capital: Pierre. (44°N 102°W) p. 597

GAZETTEER

Spain Country in southwestern Europe that occupies the greater part of the Iberian Peninsula. Capital: Madrid. (40°N 4°W) p. 43

Tennessee (TN) State in the south-central United States. Admitted as a state in 1796. Capital: Nashville. (36°N 88°W) p. 282

Tenochtitlán Aztec island-city that was located on the site of what is now Mexico City. p. 8

Texas (TX) State in the south-central United States. Independent republic from 1836 to 1845. Admitted as a state in 1845. Capital: Austin. (31°N 101°W) p. 350

Timbuktu City in West Africa that began as a camp for traders around AD 1100 and became a major center of culture and learning. (17°N 3°W) p. 18

United States of America Country in central North America. Capital: Washington, D.C. (38°N 110°W) p. 6

Utah (UT) State in the western United States. Admitted as a state in 1896. Capital: Salt Lake City. (39°N 112°W) p. 10

Valley Forge Site in southeastern Pennsylvania where General George Washington and his troops spent the harsh winter of 1777–1778. p. 132

Venezuela Country in South America. Capital: Caracas. (11°N 67°W) p. 707

Vermont (VT) State in the northeastern United States. Admitted as a state in 1791. Capital: Montpelier. (44°N 73°W) p. 89

Vicksburg City in western Mississippi on the bluffs above the Mississippi River. (42°N 85°W) p. 522

Virginia (VA) State in the eastern United States. One of the original thirteen colonies. Admitted as a state in 1788. Capital: Richmond. (37°N 80°W) p. 72

Washington (WA) State in the northwestern United States. Admitted as a state in 1889. Capital: Olympia. (47°N 121°W) p. 362

Washington, D.C. Capital of the United States. Located on the Potomac River between Virginia and Maryland. (39°N 77°W) p. 240

West Virginia (WV) State in the east-central United States. Part of Virginia until the area refused to join the Confederacy in 1861. Admitted as a state in 1863. Capital: Charleston. (39°N 81°W) p. 303

Western Hemisphere Term given to that half of the earth's sphere that contains the Americas. p. 707

Wisconsin (WI) State in the north-central United States. Became part of the Northwest Territory in 1787. Admitted as a state in 1848. Capital: Madison. (44°N 91°W) p. 155

Wyoming (WY) State in the northwestern United States. Admitted as a state in 1890. Capital: Cheyenne. (43°N 108°W) p. 361

Presidents

1 **GEORGE WASHINGTON**
Born: 1732 **Died:** 1799
Years in Office: 1789–97
Political Party: None
Home State: Virginia
Vice President: John Adams

2 **JOHN ADAMS**
Born: 1735 **Died:** 1826
Years in Office: 1797–1801
Political Party: Federalist
Home State: Massachusetts
Vice President: Thomas Jefferson

3 **THOMAS JEFFERSON**
Born: 1743 **Died:** 1826
Years in Office: 1801–09
Political Party: Republican*
Home State: Virginia
Vice Presidents: Aaron Burr,
George Clinton

4 **JAMES MADISON**
Born: 1751 **Died:** 1836
Years in Office: 1809–17
Political Party: Republican
Home State: Virginia
Vice Presidents: George Clinton,
Elbridge Gerry

5 **JAMES MONROE**
Born: 1758 **Died:** 1831
Years in Office: 1817–25
Political Party: Republican
Home State: Virginia
Vice President: Daniel D. Tompkins

6 **JOHN QUINCY ADAMS**
Born: 1767 **Died:** 1848
Years in Office: 1825–29
Political Party: Republican
Home State: Massachusetts
Vice President: John C. Calhoun

7 **ANDREW JACKSON**
Born: 1767 **Died:** 1845
Years in Office: 1829–37
Political Party: Democratic
Home State: Tennessee
Vice Presidents: John C. Calhoun,
Martin Van Buren

8 **MARTIN VAN BUREN**
Born: 1782 **Died:** 1862
Years in Office: 1837–41
Political Party: Democratic
Home State: New York
Vice President: Richard M. Johnson

* The Republican Party of the third through sixth presidents is not the party of Abraham Lincoln, which was founded in 1854.

9 WILLIAM HENRY HARRISON
Born: 1773 **Died:** 1841
Years in Office: 1841
Political Party: Whig
Home State: Ohio
Vice President: John Tyler

10 JOHN TYLER
Born: 1790 **Died:** 1862
Years in Office: 1841–45
Political Party: Whig
Home State: Virginia
Vice President: None

11 JAMES K. POLK
Born: 1795 **Died:** 1849
Years in Office: 1845–49
Political Party: Democratic
Home State: Tennessee
Vice President: George M. Dallas

12 ZACHARY TAYLOR
Born: 1784 **Died:** 1850
Years in Office: 1849–50
Political Party: Whig
Home State: Louisiana
Vice President: Millard Fillmore

13 MILLARD FILLMORE
Born: 1800 **Died:** 1874
Years in Office: 1850–53
Political Party: Whig
Home State: New York
Vice President: None

14 FRANKLIN PIERCE
Born: 1804 **Died:** 1869
Years in Office: 1853–57
Political Party: Democratic
Home State: New Hampshire
Vice President: William R. King

15 JAMES BUCHANAN
Born: 1791 **Died:** 1868
Years in Office: 1857–61
Political Party: Democratic
Home State: Pennsylvania
Vice President: John C. Breckinridge

16 ABRAHAM LINCOLN
Born: 1809 **Died:** 1865
Years in Office: 1861–65
Political Party: Republican
Home State: Illinois
Vice Presidents: Hannibal Hamlin,
Andrew Johnson

17 ANDREW JOHNSON
Born: 1808 **Died:** 1875
Years in Office: 1865–69
Political Party: Democratic
Home State: Tennessee
Vice President: None

18 ULYSSES S. GRANT
Born: 1822 **Died:** 1885
Years in Office: 1869–77
Political Party: Republican
Home State: Illinois
Vice Presidents: Schuyler Colfax,
Henry Wilson

19 RUTHERFORD B. HAYES
Born: 1822 **Died:** 1893
Years in Office: 1877–81
Political Party: Republican
Home State: Ohio
Vice President: William A. Wheeler

20 JAMES A. GARFIELD
Born: 1831 **Died:** 1881
Years in Office: 1881
Political Party: Republican
Home State: Ohio
Vice President: Chester A. Arthur

21 CHESTER A. ARTHUR
Born: 1829 **Died:** 1886
Years in Office: 1881–85
Political Party: Republican
Home State: New York
Vice President: None

22 GROVER CLEVELAND
Born: 1837 **Died:** 1908
Years in Office: 1885–89
Political Party: Democratic
Home State: New York
Vice President: Thomas A. Hendricks

23 BENJAMIN HARRISON
Born: 1833 **Died:** 1901
Years in Office: 1889–93
Political Party: Republican
Home State: Indiana
Vice President: Levi P. Morton

24 GROVER CLEVELAND
Born: 1837 **Died:** 1908
Years in Office: 1893–97
Political Party: Democratic
Home State: New York
Vice President: Adlai E. Stevenson

25 WILLIAM MCKINLEY
Born: 1843 **Died:** 1901
Years in Office: 1897–1901
Political Party: Republican
Home State: Ohio
Vice Presidents: Garret A. Hobart,
Theodore Roosevelt

26 THEODORE ROOSEVELT
Born: 1858 **Died:** 1919
Years in Office: 1901–09
Political Party: Republican
Home State: New York
Vice President: Charles W. Fairbanks

27 WILLIAM HOWARD TAFT
Born: 1857 **Died:** 1930
Years in Office: 1909–13
Political Party: Republican
Home State: Ohio
Vice President: James S. Sherman

28 WOODROW WILSON
Born: 1856 **Died:** 1924
Years in Office: 1913–21
Political Party: Democratic
Home State: New Jersey
Vice President: Thomas R. Marshall

29 WARREN G. HARDING
Born: 1865 **Died:** 1923
Years in Office: 1921–23
Political Party: Republican
Home State: Ohio
Vice President: Calvin Coolidge

30 CALVIN COOLIDGE
Born: 1872 **Died:** 1933
Years in Office: 1923–29
Political Party: Republican
Home State: Massachusetts
Vice President: Charles G. Dawes

31 HERBERT HOOVER
Born: 1874 **Died:** 1964
Years in Office: 1929–33
Political Party: Republican
Home State: California
Vice President: Charles Curtis

32 FRANKLIN D. ROOSEVELT
Born: 1882 **Died:** 1945
Years in Office: 1933–45
Political Party: Democratic
Home State: New York
Vice Presidents: John Nance Garner, Henry Wallace, Harry S Truman

33 HARRY S. TRUMAN
Born: 1884 **Died:** 1972
Years in Office: 1945–53
Political Party: Democratic
Home State: Missouri
Vice President: Alben W. Barkley

34 DWIGHT D. EISENHOWER
Born: 1890 **Died:** 1969
Years in Office: 1953–61
Political Party: Republican
Home State: Kansas
Vice President: Richard M. Nixon

35 JOHN F. KENNEDY
Born: 1917 **Died:** 1963
Years in Office: 1961–63
Political Party: Democratic
Home State: Massachusetts
Vice President: Lyndon B. Johnson

36 **Lyndon B. Johnson**
Born: 1908 **Died:** 1973
Years in Office: 1963–69
Political Party: Democratic
Home State: Texas
Vice President: Hubert H. Humphrey

37 **Richard M. Nixon**
Born: 1913 **Died:** 1994
Years in Office: 1969–74
Political Party: Republican
Home State: California
Vice Presidents: Spiro T. Agnew, Gerald R. Ford

38 **Gerald R. Ford**
Born: 1913 **Died:** 2006
Years in Office: 1974–77
Political Party: Republican
Home State: Michigan
Vice President: Nelson A. Rockefeller

39 **Jimmy Carter**
Born: 1924
Years in Office: 1977–81
Political Party: Democratic
Home State: Georgia
Vice President: Walter F. Mondale

40 **Ronald Reagan**
Born: 1911 **Died:** 2004
Years in Office: 1981–89
Political Party: Republican
Home State: California
Vice President: George Bush

41 **George Bush**
Born: 1924
Years in Office: 1989–93
Political Party: Republican
Home State: Texas
Vice President: J. Danforth Quayle

42 **Bill Clinton**
Born: 1946
Years in Office: 1993–2001
Political Party: Democratic
Home State: Arkansas
Vice President: Albert Gore Jr.

43 **George W. Bush**
Born: 1946
Years in Office: 2001–2009
Political Party: Republican
Home State: Texas
Vice President: Richard B. Cheney

44 **Barack Obama**
Born: 1961
Years in Office: 2009–
Political Party: Democratic
Home State: Illinois
Vice President: Joe Biden

Facts about the States

State	Year of Statehood	2006 Population	Area (Sq. Mi.)	Population Density (Sq Mi.)	Capital
Alabama	1819	4,599,030	50,744	88.7	Montgomery
Alaska	1959	670,053	571,951	1.1	Juneau
Arizona	1912	6,166,318	113,635	49.1	Phoenix
Arkansas	1836	2,810,872	52,068	52.3	Little Rock
California	1850	36,457,549	155,959	227.5	Sacramento
Colorado	1876	4,753,377	103,718	43.9	Denver
Connecticut	1788	3,504,809	4,845	719.0	Hartford
Delaware	1787	853,476	1,954	418.4	Dover
District of Columbia	—	581,530	61	9,235.8	—
Florida	1845	18,089,888	53,927	315.6	Tallahassee
Georgia	1788	9,363,941	57,906	150.0	Atlanta
Hawaii	1959	1,285,498	6,423	195.8	Honolulu
Idaho	1890	1,466,465	82,747	16.5	Boise
Illinois	1818	12,831,970	55,584	227.6	Springfield
Indiana	1816	6,313,520	35,867	172.7	Indianapolis
Iowa	1846	2,982,085	55,869	52.7	Des Moines
Kansas	1861	2,764,075	81,815	33.3	Topeka
Kentucky	1792	4,206,074	39,728	103.7	Frankfort
Louisiana	1812	4,287,768	43,562	103.2	Baton Rouge
Maine	1820	1,321,574	30,862	42.3	Augusta
Maryland	1788	5,615,727	9,774	563.6	Annapolis
Massachusetts	1788	6,437,193	7,840	820.6	Boston
Michigan	1837	10,095,643	56,804	177.5	Lansing
Minnesota	1858	5,167,101	79,610	63.6	St. Paul

State	Year of Statehood	2006 Population	Area (Sq. Mi.)	Population Density (Sq Mi.)	Capital
Mississippi	1817	2,910,540	46,907	61.4	Jackson
Missouri	1821	5,842,713	68,886	82.8	Jefferson City
Montana	1889	944,632	145,552	6.3	Helena
Nebraska	1867	1,768,331	76,872	22.6	Lincoln
Nevada	1864	2,495,529	109,826	20.4	Carson City
New Hampshire	1788	1,314,895	8,968	143.6	Concord
New Jersey	1787	8,724,560	7,417	1,164.7	Trenton
New Mexico	1912	1,954,599	121,356	15.4	Santa Fe
New York	1788	19,306,183	47,214	406.4	Albany
North Carolina	1789	8,856,505	48,711	172.6	Raleigh
North Dakota	1889	635,867	68,976	9.2	Bismarck
Ohio	1803	11,478,006	40,948	279.3	Columbus
Oklahoma	1907	3,579,212	68,667	51.1	Oklahoma City
Oregon	1859	3,700,758	95,997	37.1	Salem
Pennsylvania	1787	12,440,621	44,817	275.9	Harrisburg
Rhode Island	1790	1,067,610	1,045	1,029.8	Providence
South Carolina	1788	4,321,249	30,109	137.7	Columbia
South Dakota	1889	781,919	75,885	10.1	Pierre
Tennessee	1796	6,038,803	41,217	141.7	Nashville
Texas	1845	23,507,783	261,797	84.5	Austin
Utah	1896	2,550,063	82,144	28.6	Salt Lake City
Vermont	1791	623,908	9,250	66.9	Montpelier
Virginia	1788	7,642,884	39,594	186.6	Richmond
Washington	1889	6,395,798	66,544	92.1	Olympia
West Virginia	1863	1,818,470	24,078	75.2	Charleston
Wisconsin	1848	5,556,506	54,310	100.8	Madison
Wyoming	1890	515,004	97,100	5.2	Cheyenne

American Flag

The American flag is a symbol of the nation. It is recognized instantly, whether as a big banner waving in the wind or a tiny emblem worn on a lapel. The flag is so important that it is a major theme of the national anthem, "The Star-Spangled Banner." One of the most popular names for the flag is the Stars and Stripes. It is also known as Old Glory.

The American flag has 13 stripes—7 red and 6 white. In the upper-left corner of the flag is the union—50 white five-pointed stars against a blue background.

The 13 stripes stand for the original 13 American states, and the 50 stars represent the states of the nation today. According to the U.S. Department of State, the colors of the flag also are symbolic:

Red stands for courage.

White symbolizes purity.

Blue is the color of vigilance, perseverance, and justice.

DISPLAYING THE FLAG

It is customary not to display the American flag in bad weather. It is also customary for the flag to be displayed outdoors only from sunrise to sunset, except on certain occasions. In a few special places, however, the flag is always flown day and night. When flown at night, the flag should be illuminated.

Near a speaker's platform, the flag should occupy the place of honor at the speaker's right. When carried in a parade with other flags, the American flag should be on the marching right or in front at the center. When flying with the flags of the 50 states, the national flag must be at the center and the highest point. In a group of national flags, all should be of equal size and all should be flown from staffs, or flagpoles, of equal height.

The flag should never touch the ground or the floor. It should not be marked with any insignia, pictures, or words. Nor should it be used in any disrespectful way—as an advertising decoration, for instance. The flag should never be dipped to honor any person or thing.

SALUTING THE FLAG

The United States, like other countries, has a flag code, or rules for displaying and honoring the flag. For example, all those present should stand at attention facing the flag and salute it when it is being raised or lowered or when it is carried past them in a parade or procession. A man wearing a hat should take it off and hold it with his right hand over his heart. All women and hatless men should stand with their right hands over their hearts to show their respect for the flag. The flag should also receive these honors during the playing of the national anthem and the reciting of the Pledge of Allegiance.

THE PLEDGE OF ALLEGIANCE

The Pledge of Allegiance was written in 1892 by Massachusetts magazine (*Youth's Companion*) editor Francis Bellamy. (Congress added the words "under God" in 1954.)

> *I pledge allegiance to the flag of the United States of America and to the republic for which it stands, one nation under God, indivisible, with liberty and justice for all.*

Civilians should say the Pledge of Allegiance with their right hands placed over their hearts. People in the armed forces give the military salute. By saying the Pledge of Allegiance, we promise loyalty ("pledge allegiance") to the United States and its ideals.

"THE STAR-SPANGLED BANNER"

"The Star-Spangled Banner" is the national anthem of the United States. It was written by Francis Scott Key during the War of 1812. While being detained by the British aboard a ship on September 13–14, 1814, Key watched the British bombardment of Fort McHenry at Baltimore. The attack lasted 25 hours. The smoke was so thick that Key could not tell who had won. When the air cleared, Key saw the American flag that was still flying over the fort. "The Star-Spangled Banner" is sung to music written by British composer John Stafford Smith. In 1931 Congress designated "The Star-Spangled Banner" as the national anthem.

I

Oh, say, can you see, by the dawn's early light,
What so proudly we hailed at the twilight's last gleaming,
Whose broad stripes and bright stars through the perilous fight,
O'er the ramparts we watched were so gallantly streaming?
And the rockets' red glare, the bombs bursting in air,
Gave proof through the night that our flag was still there.
Oh, say, does that star-spangled banner yet wave
O'er the land of the free, and the home of the brave?

II

On the shore, dimly seen through the mists of the deep,
Where the foe's haughty host in dread silence reposes,
What is that which the breeze, o'er the towering steep,
As it fitfully blows, half conceals, half discloses?
Now it catches the gleam of the morning's first beam,
In full glory reflected, now shines on the stream.
'Tis the star-spangled banner; oh, long may it wave
O'er the land of the free, and the home of the brave!

III

And where is that band who so vauntingly swore
That the havoc of war and the battle's confusion
A home and a country should leave us no more?
Their blood has washed out their foul footsteps' pollution.
No refuge could save the hireling and slave
From the terror of flight, or the gloom of the grave:
And the star-spangled banner in triumph doth wave
O'er the land of the free, and the home of the brave!

IV

Oh! thus be it ever when freemen shall stand
Between their loved homes and the war's desolation!
Blest with victory and peace, may the heaven-rescued land
Praise the Power that hath made and preserved us a nation!
Then conquer we must, for our cause it is just,
And this be our motto: "In God is our trust!"
And the star-spangled banner in triumph shall wave,
O'er the land of the free, and the home of the brave!

Sheet music to the national anthem

"AMERICA, THE BEAUTIFUL"

One of the most beloved songs celebrating our nation is "America, the Beautiful." Katharine Lee Bates first wrote the lyrics to the song in 1893 after visiting Colorado. The version of the song we know today is set to music by Samuel A. Ward. The first and last stanzas of "America, the Beautiful" are shown below.

O beautiful for spacious skies,
For amber waves of grain,
For purple mountain majesties
Above the fruited plain!
America! America!
God shed his grace on thee
And crown thy good with brotherhood
From sea to shining sea!

O beautiful for patriot dream
That sees beyond the years
Thine alabaster cities gleam
Undimmed by human tears!
America! America!
God shed his grace on thee
And crown thy good with brotherhood
From sea to shining sea!

Supreme Court Decisions

Marbury v. Madison (1803)

Significance This ruling established the Supreme Court's power of judicial review, by which the Court decides whether laws passed by Congress are constitutional. This decision greatly increased the prestige of the Court and gave the judiciary branch a powerful check against the legislative and executive branches.

Background William Marbury and several others were commissioned as judges by Federalist president John Adams during his last days in office. This act angered the new Democratic-Republican president, Thomas Jefferson. Jefferson ordered his secretary of state, James Madison, not to deliver the commissions. Marbury took advantage of a section in the Judiciary Act of 1789 that allowed him to take his case directly to the Supreme Court. He sued Madison, demanding the commission and the judgeship.

Decision This case was decided on February 24, 1803, by a vote of 5 to 0. Chief Justice John Marshall spoke for the Court, which decided against Marbury. The court ruled that although Marbury's commission had been unfairly withheld, he could not lawfully take his case to the Supreme Court without first trying it in a lower court. Marshall said that the section of the Judiciary Act that Marbury had used was actually unconstitutional and that the Constitution must take priority over laws passed by Congress.

McCulloch v. Maryland (1819)

Significance This ruling established that Congress had the constitutional power to charter a national bank. The case also established the principle of national supremacy, which states that the Constitution and other laws of the federal government take priority over state laws. In addition, the ruling reinforced the loose-construction interpretation of the Constitution favored by many Federalists.

Background In 1816 the federal government set up the Second Bank of the United States to stabilize the economy following the War of 1812. Many states were opposed to the competition provided by the new national bank. Some of these states passed heavy taxes on the Bank. The national bank refused to pay the taxes. This led the state of Maryland to sue James McCulloch, the cashier of the Baltimore, Maryland, branch of the national bank.

Decision This case was decided on March 6, 1819, by a vote of 7 to 0. Chief Justice John Marshall spoke for the unanimous Court, which ruled that the national bank was constitutional because it helped the federal government carry out other powers granted to it by the Constitution. The Court declared that any attempt by the states to interfere with the duties of the federal government could not be permitted.

Gibbons v. Ogden (1824)

Significance This ruling was the first case to deal with the clause of the Constitution that allows Congress to regulate interstate and foreign commerce. This case was important because it reinforced both the authority of the federal government over the states and the division of powers between the federal government and the state governments.

Background Steamboat operators who wanted to travel on New York waters had to obtain a state license. Thomas Gibbons had a federal license to travel along the coast, but not a state license for New York. He wanted the freedom to compete with state-licensed Aaron Ogden for steam travel between New Jersey and the New York island of Manhattan.

Decision This case was decided on March 2, 1824, by a vote of 6 to 0. Chief Justice John Marshall spoke for the Court, which ruled in favor of Gibbons. The Court stated that the congressional statute (Gibbons's federal license) took priority over the state statute (Ogden's state-monopoly license). The ruling also defined commerce as more than simply the exchange of goods, broadening it to include the transportation of people and the use of new inventions (such as the steamboat).

Supreme Court Building, Washington, D.C.

Worcester v. *Georgia* (1832)

Significance This ruling made Georgia's removal of the Cherokee illegal. However, Georgia, with President Andrew Jackson's support, defied the Court's decision. By not enforcing the Court's ruling, Jackson violated his constitutional oath as president. As a result, the Cherokee and other American Indian tribes continued to be forced off of lands protected by treaties.

Background The state of Georgia wanted to remove Cherokee Indians from lands they held by treaty. Samuel Worcester, a missionary who worked with the Cherokee Nation, was arrested for failing to take an oath of allegiance to the state and to obey a Georgia militia order to leave the Cherokee's lands. Worcester sued, charging that Georgia had no legal authority on Cherokee lands.

Decision This case was decided on March 3, 1832, by a vote of 5 to 1 in favor of Worcester. Chief Justice John Marshall spoke for the Supreme Court, which ruled that the Cherokee were an independent political community. The Court decided that only the federal government, not the state of Georgia, had authority over legal matters involving the Cherokee people.

Scott v. *Sandford* (1857)

Significance This ruling denied enslaved African Americans U.S. citizenship and the right to sue in federal court. The decision also invalidated the Missouri Compromise, which had prevented slavery in territories north of the 36° 30' line of latitude. The ruling increased the controversy over the expansion of slavery in new states and territories.

Background John Emerson, an army doctor, took his slave Dred Scott with him to live in Illinois and then Wisconsin Territory, both of which had banned slavery. In 1842 the two moved to Missouri, a slave state. Four years later, Scott sued for his freedom according to a Missouri legal principle of "once free, always free." The principle meant that a slave was entitled to freedom if he or she had once lived in a free state or territory.

Decision This case was decided March 6-7, 1857, by a vote of 7 to 2. Chief Justice Roger B. Taney spoke for the Court, which ruled that slaves did not have the right to sue in federal courts because they were considered property, not citizens. In addition, the Court ruled that Congress did not have the power to abolish slavery in territories because that power was not strictly defined in the Constitution. Furthermore, the Court overturned the once-free, always-free principle.

Civil Rights Cases (1883)

Significance This ruling struck down the Civil Rights Act of 1875. It allowed private businesses to discriminate based on race or color. The Court ruled that Congress could only make laws preventing states, not private individuals or companies, from discriminating.

Background Five separate cases were combined under this one decision. After the Civil Rights Act of 1875 was passed, individuals and private businesses continued to discriminate against former slaves and other African Americans. In the five separate cases, African Americans were denied the same accommodations that whites were provided.

Decision The case was decided on October 15, 1883, by a vote of 8 to 1. Justice Joseph P. Bradley wrote the opinion, which said of the 14th Amendment, "Individual invasion of individual rights is not the subject-matter of the amendment." Justice John Marshall Harlan was the lone dissenter, claiming that the 13th Amendment gave Congress the right to make the law. "The letter of the law is the body," he said. "[T]he sense and reason of the law is the soul."

Wabash, St. Louis & Pacific Railroad v. Illinois (1886)

Significance This ruling reversed an earlier decision in *Munn* v. *Illinois* and removed the power from the states to regulate railroad rates. It reasserted the authority of Congress over interstate commerce and led to the creation of the Interstate Commerce Commission.

Background The state of Illinois passed a law attempting to regulate the shipping rates of railroads that passed through the state, including the Wabash, St. Louis & Pacific line. In an attempt to operate without regulation, the railroad company sued the state.

Decision The Court struck down the Illinois law, saying that the state was able to regulate businesses that operated only within its boundaries. Businesses that operated between states were subject to regulation by the national government.

United States v. E.C. Knight Co. (1895)

Significance This ruling effectively put most monopolies out of the reach of the Sherman Antitrust Act of 1890. It declared that local manufacturing was out of the scope of the interstate-commerce regulatory power of Congress.

Background The E. C. Knight Company enjoyed a virtual monopoly of sugar refining within the United States. The federal government sued the company under the Sherman Antitrust Act in an attempt to break this monopoly and allow other companies to refine sugar.

Decision The court ruled that although the act was legal, it did not apply to manufacturing. Justice Melville Fuller said that manufacturing was not interstate commerce and could therefore not be regulated by Congress.

In Re Debs (1895)

Significance In this ruling the Court upheld the right of the federal government to halt strikes organized by union workers. After losing his case, Debs ran for president from his jail cell.

Background Railway union official Eugene V. Debs had organized a strike of union workers. The government petitioned him to halt the strike, and a court held him in contempt when he refused. Debs fought his conviction.

Decision In a unanimous decision, the Court declared that the federal government did have the power to order Debs to halt the strike. Justice David J. Brewer wrote the opinion of the Court, which stated the U.S. government "acts directly upon each citizen."

Plessy v. Ferguson (1896)

Significance This case upheld the constitutionality of racial segregation by ruling that separate facilities for different races were legal as long as those facilities were equal to one another. This case provided a legal justification for racial segregation for nearly 60 years until it was overturned by *Brown* v. *Board of Education* in 1954.

Background An 1890 Louisiana law required that all railway companies in the state use "separate-but-equal" railcars for white and African American passengers. A group of citizens in New Orleans banded together to challenge the law and chose Homer Plessy to test the law in 1892. Plessy took a seat in a whites-only coach, and when he refused to move, he was arrested. Plessy eventually sought review by the U.S. Supreme Court, claiming that the Louisiana law violated his Fourteenth Amendment right to equal protection.

Decision This case was decided on May 18, 1896, by a vote of 7 to 1. Justice Henry Billings Brown spoke for the Court, which upheld the constitutionality of the Louisiana law that segregated railcars. Justice John M. Harlan dissented, arguing that the Constitution should not be interpreted in ways that recognize class or racial distinctions.

Northern Securities Co. v. *United States* (1904)

Significance In this ruling the Court declared that the federal government had the right to break up companies if their formation was illegal, whether or not dissolving the company would have a harmful impact on the business community.

Background The Northern Securities Company held stock in several major railroads. Although President Theodore Roosevelt claimed the company was a trust and therefore illegal under the Sherman Antitrust Act, some disagreed that the idea of trusts extended into the realm of owning stocks.

Decision In a 5-to-4 decision, the Court ruled that the formation of the company was illegal, and that the federal government had the power to disband it. Writing for the majority, Justice John Marshall Harlan said, "every corporation created by a state is necessarily subject to the supreme law of the land," meaning the federal government.

Lochner v. *New York* (1905)

Significance This decision established the Supreme Court's role in overseeing state regulations. For more than 30 years, Lochner was often used as a precedent in striking down state laws such as minimum-wage laws, child labor laws, and regulations placed on the banking and transportation industries.

Background In 1895 the state of New York passed a labor law limiting bakers to working no more than 10 hours per day or 60 hours per week. The purpose of the law was to protect the health of bakers, who worked in hot and damp conditions and breathed in large quantities of flour dust. In 1902 Joseph Lochner, the owner of a small bakery in New York, claimed that the state law violated his Fourteenth Amendment rights by unfairly depriving him of the liberty to make contracts with employees. This case went to the U.S. Supreme Court.

Decision This case was decided on April 17, 1905, by a vote of 5 to 4 in favor of Lochner. The Supreme Court judged that the Fourteenth Amendment protected the right to sell and buy labor, and that any state law restricting that right was unconstitutional. The Court rejected the argument that the limited workday and workweek were necessary to protect the health of bakery workers.

Muller v. *Oregon* (1908)

Significance A landmark for cases involving social reform, this decision established the Court's recognition of social and economic conditions (in this case, women's health) as a factor in making laws.

Background In 1903 Oregon passed a law limiting workdays to 10 hours for female workers in laundries and factories. In 1905 Curt Muller's Grand Laundry was found guilty of breaking this law. Muller appealed, claiming that the state law violated his freedom of contract (the Supreme Court had upheld a similar claim that year in *Lochner* v. *New York*). When this case came to the Court, the National Consumers' League hired lawyer Louis D. Brandeis to present Oregon's argument. Brandeis argued that the Court had already defended the state's police power to protect its citizens' health, safety, and welfare.

Decision This case was decided on February 24, 1908, by a vote of 9 to 0 upholding the Oregon law. The Court agreed that women's well-being was in the state's public interest and that the 10-hour law was a valid way to protect their well-being.

Schechter Poultry Corporation v. United States (1935)

Significance This ruling declared that the United States could not regulate businesses that operated only within one state. It dealt a severe blow to President Franklin Roosevelt's New Deal.

Background In an attempt to lessen the effects of the Great Depression, Roosevelt encouraged Congress to pass a Recovery Act that set a minimum wage and restricted working hours. The Schechter Poultry Corporation, which operated only within New York City, maintained that the federal government did not have a constitutional right to regulate its businesses practices.

Decision In a unanimous decision, the Court upheld the Schechter Corporation's claim. Chief Justice Charles Evans Hughes wrote the opinion, which stated that the transactions in the case—wages, salaries, and working hours—were a local concern outside of the scope of federal regulation.

Korematsu v. United States (1944)

Significance This case addressed the question of whether government action that treats a racial group differently from other people violates the Equal Protection Clause of the Fourteenth Amendment. The ruling in the case held that distinctions based on race are "inherently suspect," and that laws and rules based on race must withstand "strict scrutiny" by the courts. The Court still applies the "strict scrutiny" standard today to cases involving race and other groups.

Background When the United States declared war on Japan in 1941, about 112,000 Japanese Americans lived on the West Coast. About 70,000 of these Japanese Americans were citizens. In 1942 the U.S. military was afraid that these people could not be trusted in wartime. They ordered most of the Japanese Americans to move to special camps far from their homes. Fred Korematsu, a Japanese American and an American citizen, did not go to the camps as ordered. He stayed in California and was arrested. He was sent to a camp in Utah. Korematsu then sued, claiming that the government acted illegally when it sent people of Japanese descent to camps.

Decision By a 6-to-3 margin, the Supreme Court said the orders moving the Japanese-Americans into the camps were constitutional. Justice Hugo Black wrote the opinion for the Court. He said that the unusual demands of wartime security justified the orders. However, he made it clear that distinctions based on race are "inherently suspect," and that laws based on race must withstand "strict scrutiny" by the courts. Justice Robert H. Jackson dissented; he wrote that Korematsu was "convicted of an act not commonly a crime … being present in the state [where] he is a citizen, near where he was born, and where all his life he has lived." Justice Frank Murphy, another dissenter, said the military order was based on racial prejudice.

Brown v. Board of Education (1954)

Significance This ruling reversed the Supreme Court's earlier position on segregation set by *Plessy* v. *Ferguson* (1896). The decision also inspired Congress and the federal courts to help carry out further civil rights reforms for African Americans.

Background Beginning in the 1930s, the National Association for the Advancement of Colored People (NAACP) began using the courts to challenge racial segregation in public education. In 1952 the NAACP took a number of school segregation cases to the Supreme Court. These included the Brown family's suit against the school board of Topeka, Kansas, over its "separate-but-equal" policy.

Decision This case was decided on May 17, 1954, by a vote of 9 to 0. Chief Justice Earl Warren spoke for the unanimous Court, which ruled that segregation in public education created inequality. The Court held that racial segregation in public schools was by nature unequal, even if the school facilities were equal. The Court noted that such segregation created feelings of inferiority that could not be undone. Therefore, enforced separation of the races in public education is unconstitutional.

Watkins v. United States (1957)

Significance The decision limited the inquiry powers of Congress. It was expected not to engage in law enforcement (an executive function), nor to act as a trial agency (a judicial function), but to inquire only as far as was necessary for the functioning of Congress.

Background Watkins was a labor union officer who appeared before the House Un-American Activities Committee during the 1950s Red Scare. Although he was willing to answer personal questions about himself and others whom he knew to be members of the Communist Party, he would not answer questions about past members of the Communist Party. He was therefore held in contempt of Congress.

Decision In a vote of 6 to 1 handed down on June 17, 1957, the Court threw out the charge of contempt against Watkins. Congress, it said, did not have the right to invade the private lives of individuals.

Mapp v. Ohio (1961)

Significance In this ruling the Court declared that evidence discovered in the process of an illegal search could not be used in state courts.

Background While searching for a bombing suspect, police found evidence of a separate crime in the house of Dollree Mapp. The police did not have permission to enter the home, nor did they have a search warrant. Upon conviction for the separate crime, Mapp appealed her case to the Supreme Court.

Decision In a 5-to-3 decision, the Court stated that convictions based on illegally obtained evidence must be overturned. Justice Tom Clark wrote for the majority, "all evidence obtained by searches and seizures in violation of the Constitution is … inadmissible in a state court."

Baker v. Carr (1962)

Significance Through this decision, the Court ruled that the judiciary branch may involve itself in hearing cases about political matters.

Background Voters from Tennessee sued their state in federal court, arguing that the way the state drew the boundary lines between representative districts created unequal representation within the legislature, and therefore unequal protection under the laws of the state. Tennessee argued that the federal court did not have the jurisdiction to hear the case.

Decision By a 6-to-2 margin, the Court decided that the federal court did have the right to hear the case and that the voters had the right to sue over the issue. Writing for the majority, Justice William Brennan said that the voters "are entitled to a trial and a decision" on whether they were denied equal protection.

Engel v. Vitale (1962)

Significance This case deals with the specific issue of organized prayer in schools and the broader issue of the proper relationship between government and religion under the First Amendment. The question in the case was whether a state violates the First Amendment when it composes a prayer that students must say at the beginning of each school day.

Background The state of New York recommended that public schools in the state begin the day by having students recite a prayer written by the state government. A group of parents sued to stop the official prayer, saying that it was contrary to their beliefs and their children's beliefs. They believed the law was unconstitutional because it "established" (officially supported) religion. Though students were permitted to remain silent, the parents claimed that there would always be pressure on students to pray.

Decision By a 6-to-1 margin (two justices did not take part in the case), the Court agreed with the parents. It struck down the state law. Justice Hugo Black wrote for the decision for the majority. He pointed out that the prayer was clearly religious. He said that under the First Amendment, "it is no part of the business of government to compose official prayers for any group of American people to recite as part of a religious program carried on by government." Black, referring to Jefferson and Madison, said "These men knew that the First Amendment, which tried to put an end to governmental control of religion and prayer, was not written to destroy either."

Gideon v. Wainwright (1963)

Significance This ruling was one of several key Supreme Court decisions establishing free legal help for those who cannot otherwise afford representation in court.

Background Clarence Earl Gideon was accused of robbery in Florida. Gideon could not afford a lawyer for his trial, and the judge refused to supply him with one for free. Gideon tried to defend himself and was found guilty. He eventually appealed to the U.S. Supreme Court, claiming that the lower court's denial of a court-appointed lawyer violated his Sixth and Fourteenth Amendment rights.

Decision This case was decided on March 18, 1963, by a vote of 9 to 0 in favor of Gideon. The Court agreed that the Sixth Amendment (which protects a citizen's right to have a lawyer for his or her defense) applied to the states because it fell under the due process clause of the Fourteenth Amendment. Thus, the states are required to provide legal aid to those defendants in criminal cases who cannot afford to pay for legal representation.

Heart of Atlanta Motel v. United States (1964)

Significance This ruling upheld the public accommodations clause of the Civil Rights Act of 1964. It enforced the right of African Americans to receive access to the same accommodations as whites and gave Congress judicial backing for passing more civil rights legislation.

Background The owner of the Heart of Atlanta Motel routinely discriminated against African Americans. He claimed that his business was not an interstate business and therefore not subject to regulation by congressional acts.

Decision In a unanimous decision, the Court declared that as a business that served people from across state boundaries, the Heart of Atlanta Motel was in fact an interstate business and that, therefore, congressional acts did apply.

Miranda v. Arizona (1966)

Significance This decision ruled that an accused person's Fifth Amendment rights begin at the time of arrest. The ruling caused controversy because it made the questioning of suspects and collecting evidence more difficult for law enforcement officers.

Background In 1963 Ernesto Miranda was arrested in Arizona for a kidnapping. Miranda signed a confession and was later found guilty of the crime. The arresting police officers, however, admitted that they had not told Miranda of his right to talk with an attorney before his confession. Miranda appealed his conviction on the grounds that by not informing him of his legal rights the police had violated his Fifth Amendment right against self-incrimination.

Decision This case was decided on June 13, 1966, by a vote of 5 to 4. Chief Justice Earl Warren spoke for the Court, which ruled in Miranda's favor. The Court decided that an accused person must be given four warnings after being taken into police custody: (1) the suspect has the right to remain silent, (2) anything the suspect says can and will be used against him or her, (3) the suspect has the right to consult with an attorney and to have an attorney present during questioning, and (4) if the suspect cannot afford a lawyer, one will be provided before questioning begins.

Tinker v. Des Moines Independent Community School District (1969)

Significance This ruling established the extent to which American public school students can take part in political protests in their schools. The question the case raised is whether, under the First Amendment, school officials can prohibit students from wearing armbands to symbolize political protest.

Background Students in Des Moines, Iowa, decided to wear black armbands to protest the Vietnam War. Two days before the protest, the school board created a new policy. The policy stated that any student who wore an armband to school and refused to remove it would be suspended. Three students wore armbands and were suspended. They said that their First Amendment right to freedom of speech had been violated. In 1969 the United States Supreme Court decided their case.

The Decision By a 7-to-2 margin, the Court agreed with the students. Justice Abe Fortas wrote the decision for the majority. He said that students do not "shed their constitutional rights to freedom of speech ... at the schoolhouse gate." Fortas admitted that school officials had the right to set rules. However, their rules must be consistent with the First Amendment. In this case, Des Moines school officials thought their rule was justified. They feared that the protest would disrupt learning. Fortas's opinion held that wearing an armband symbolizing political protest was a form of speech called symbolic speech. Symbolic speech is conduct that expresses an idea. Symbolic speech is protected in the same manner as the spoken word. Fortas wrote that student symbolic speech could be punished only if it disrupts the learning process. Fortas also noted that school officials allowed other political symbols, such as campaign buttons, to be worn in school.

Reed v. Reed (1971)

Significance This ruling was the first in a century of Fourteenth Amendment decisions to say that gender discrimination violated the equal protection clause. This case was later used to strike down other statutes that discriminated against women.

Background Cecil and Sally Reed were separated. When their son died without a will, the law gave preference to Cecil to be appointed the administrator of the son's estate. Sally sued Cecil for the right to administer the estate, challenging the gender preference in the law.

Decision This case was decided on November 22, 1971, by a vote of 7 to 0. Chief Justice Warren Burger spoke for the unanimous Supreme Court. Although the Court had upheld laws based on gender preference in the past, in this case it reversed its position. The Court declared that gender discrimination violated the equal protection clause of the Fourteenth Amendment and therefore could not be the basis for a law.

New York Times v. United States (1971)

Significance In this ruling the Court dismissed the idea of "prior restraint," or attempting to stop an action before it happens, by the government as unconstitutional. The ruling allowed the *New York Times* to continue publishing documents that were critical of the government's handling of the Vietnam War.

Background The *New York Times* began publishing a series of papers called the Pentagon Papers that were critical of the government. The government attempted to stop publication of the papers with a court order, citing national security. Because of the national importance of the case, the Supreme Court agreed to hear the case quickly.

Decision In a 6-to-3 decision, the Court declared that the government could not stop publication of the Pentagon Papers. Although the government did have the right to stop publication if it could prove the danger to national security, the Court said that in this case the government had not met the burden of proof.

Roe v. Wade (1973)

Significance This ruling made abortions available to women during their first trimester of pregnancy, even when their health was not in danger.

Background The case was brought in the name of Jane Roe against the restrictive abortion laws of Texas. Until this case, states had widely varying laws about the availability of abortions, some restricting them altogether.

Decision With a 7 to 2 decision, the Court said that elective abortions must be available to any woman in her first three months of pregnancy. Because of the variety of moral opinions about when life begins, the court ruled that a fetus does not have the same rights as an infant.

United States v. Nixon (1974)

Significance This ruling forced President Nixon to turn over tapes of White House conversations to the congressional committee investigating his wrongdoing in the Watergate breakin. Nixon resigned shortly after.

Background Nixon had been secretly taping every conversation that took place in the Oval Office. After the president was implicated in the cover-up of the Watergate Hotel break in, Congress wanted to hear these tapes. Nixon refused to hand them over, claiming "executive privilege" to keep some information secret.

Decision In a unanimous decision, the Court ruled that Nixon must turn the tapes over to the prosecution as requested. Writing for the court, Chief Justice Warren Burger stated that finding the truth requires that courts have all the evidence they need, even if it includes presidential communication.

New Jersey v. TLO (1985)

Significance In this ruling, the Court declared that searches of juveniles on school grounds are not subject to the same standards of "reasonableness" and "probable cause" that protect other citizens.

Background T. L. O. was a fourteen year old who was caught smoking in the girls' bathroom of her school. A principal at the school questioned the girl and searched her purse, finding marijuana and other drug paraphernalia.

Decision In a 7 to 2 decision, the Court ruled that the suspension of the rules of "reasonable" search and seizure as defined by the Fourth Amendment and later court rulings applied only to school officials and not to law enforcement officers.

Texas v. Johnson (1989)

Significance This ruling answered the question of whether the First Amendment protects burning the U.S. flag as a form of symbolic speech. It deals with the limits of symbolic speech. This case is particularly important because it involves burning the flag, one of our national symbols.

Background At the 1984 Republican National Convention in Texas, Gregory Lee Johnson doused a U.S. flag with kerosene. He did this during a demonstration, as a form of protest. Johnson was convicted of violating a Texas law that made it a crime to desecrate [treat disrespectfully] the national flag. He was sentenced to one year in prison and fined $2,000. The Texas Court of Criminal Appeals reversed the conviction because, it said, Johnson's burning of the flag was a form of symbolic speech protected by the First Amendment. Texas then appealed to the U.S. Supreme Court.

Decision The Court ruled for Johnson, five to four. Justice William Brennan wrote for the majority. He said that Johnson was within his constitutional rights when he burned the U.S. flag in protest. As in Tinker v. Des Moines Independent Community School District (1969), the Court looked at the First Amendment and "symbolic speech." Brennan concluded that Johnson's burning the flag was a form of symbolic speech—like the students wearing armbands in Des Moines—is protected by the First Amendment. According to Brennan, "Government may not prohibit the expression of an idea [because it is] offensive." Chief Justice Rehnquist dissented. He said the flag is "the visible symbol embodying our Nation. It does not represent the views of any particular political party, and it does not represent any particular political philosophy. The flag is not simply another 'idea' or 'point of view' competing for recognition in the marketplace of ideas." Since this decision, several amendments banning flag burning have been proposed in Congress, but so far all have failed.

Cruzan v. Director, Missouri Department of Health (1990)

Significance This ruling helped define who may refuse medical treatment. Although the issue is still undecided, this case began a series of efforts to provide legislative and judicial guidelines for the "right to die."

Background The parents of comatose patient Nancy Cruzan wanted to remove her life support system. The Department of Health ruled that Cruzan had not previously made clear her desire to refuse medical treatment in the event of brain damage.

Decision By a 5-to-4 margin, the Court ruled that Cruzan's parents could not remove her from life support because she had not clearly expressed her desires previously. Writing for the majority, Chief Justice William Rehnquist stated that it was Nancy's demand to be removed from life support, not her parents' wishes, that the state must respect in such cases.

Planned Parenthood of Southeastern Pennsylvania, et al. v. Casey (1992)

Significance In this ruling the Court upheld its decision in *Roe* v. *Wade* of the right to elective abortion, but allowed the state of Pennsylvania to impose restrictions of notification and consent upon minors.

Background In 1988 and 1989, Pennsylvania revised its laws to require that, to receive an abortion, minors must receive consent from a parent, and married women must notify their husbands. The laws were challenged by several abortion clinics and physicians.

Decision In a 5-to-4 decision, the Court upheld its previous ruling of *Roe* v. *Wade* that women have the right to an abortion in the first trimester of pregnancy, but provided that a state may require that minors have the consent of one parent 24 hours before the procedure. The Court struck down the part of the Pennsylvania laws that required married women to notify their husbands, saying that it could be an "undue burden" upon women.

Vernonia School District v. Acton (1995)

Significance This ruling allowed random drug testing of minors on school property as a safety measure.

Background James Acton, a student athlete in the Vernonia School District, refused to participate in drug testing, stating that the policy invaded his right to privacy and was an illegal search and seizure.

Decision In a 6-to-3 decision, the Court ruled that while on school property, students are subject to greater control of personal rights than are free adults. Furthermore, concern over the safety of minors under governmental supervision outweighs the minimal intrusion into a student's privacy.

Bush v. *Gore* (2000)

Significance In this ruling, the question before the court was whether ballots that could not be read by voting machines should be recounted by hand. The broader issues were whether the Supreme Court can overrule state court decisions on state laws, and whether an appointed judiciary can affect the result of democratic elections.

Background The 2000 presidential election between Democrat Al Gore and Republican George Bush was very close. Ultimately, the outcome would be determined by votes in the state of Florida. People in Florida voted by punching a hole in a ballot card. The votes were counted by a machine that detected these holes. According to that count, Bush won the state of Florida by a few hundred votes. Florida's Election Commission declared that Bush had won Florida. However, about 60,000 ballots were not counted because the machines could not detect a hole in the ballot. Gore argued in the Florida Supreme Court that these votes should be recounted by hand. The Florida Supreme Court ordered counties to recount all those votes. Bush appealed to the United States Supreme Court, which issued an order to stop the recounts while it made a decision.

The Decision On December 12, 2000, the Supreme Court voted 5 to 4 to end the hand recount of votes ordered by the Florida Supreme Court. The majority said that the Florida Supreme Court had ordered a recount without setting standards for what was a valid vote. Different vote-counters might use different standards. The Court said that this inconsistency meant that votes were treated arbitrarily—based on a person's choice rather than on standards. This arbitrariness, said the Court, violated the due process clause and the equal protection clause of the Constitution. Also, the justices said that Florida law required the vote count to be finalized by December 12. The justices said that rules for recounts could not be made by that date, so they ordered election officials to stop recounting votes.

Gratz v. *Bollinger* and *Grutter* v. *Bollinger* (2003)

Significance These cases considered whether a university violates the Constitution by using race as a factor for admitting students to its undergraduate school and its law school. The ruling affects use of affirmative action programs in higher education. The decisions gave colleges guidelines as to what is permitted and what is not. The decisions were limited to higher education and may not apply to other affirmative action programs such as those for applying for a job or for a government contract.

Background Jennifer Gratz and Barbara Grutter are both white. They challenged the University of Michigan's affirmative action admissions policies. Gratz said that the university violated the Constitution by considering race as a factor in its undergraduate admissions programs. Grutter claimed that the University of Michigan Law School did so.

Decisions In Gratz, the Court ruled 6 to 3 that the undergraduate program—which gave each minority applicant an automatic 20 points toward admission—was unconstitutional. Chief Justice William Rehnquist's opinion held that the policy violated the equal protection clause because it did not consider each applicant individually. "The ... automatic distribution of 20 points has the effect of making 'the factor of race ... decisive' for virtually every minimally qualified underrepresented minority applicant." The result was different when the Court turned to the affirmative action policy of Michigan's Law School, however, which used race as one factor for admission. In Grutter, by a 5-to-4 margin, the Court held that this policy did not violate the equal protection clause. Justice Sandra Day O'Connor wrote for the majority. "Truly individualized consideration demands that race be used in a flexible, nonmechanical way ... Universities can ... consider race or ethnicity ... as a 'plus' factor [when individually considering] each and every applicant." Thus, the law school's policy was constitutional.

United States v. American Library Association (2003)

Significance This case deals with the constitutionality of a federal law called the Children's Internet Protection Act (CIPA). The law was designed to protect children from being exposed to pornographic Web sites while using computers in public libraries. The question before the court was this: Does a public library violate the First Amendment by installing Internet filtering software on its public computers?

Background CIPA applies to public libraries that accept federal money to help pay for Internet access. These libraries must install filtering software to block pornographic images. Some library associations sued to block these filtering requirements. They argued that by linking money and filters, the law required public libraries to violate the First Amendment's guarantees of free speech. The libraries argued that filters block some non-pornographic sites along with pornographic ones. That, they said, violates library patrons' First Amendment rights. CIPA does allow anyone to ask a librarian to unblock a specific Web site. It also allows adults to ask that the filter be turned off altogether. But, the libraries argued, people using the library would find these remedies embarrassing and impractical.

Decision In this case, Chief Justice William Rehnquist authored a plurality opinion. He explained that the law does not require any library to accept federal money. A library can choose to do without federal money. If the library makes that choice, it does not have to install Internet filters. And Rehnquist did not think that filtering software's tendency to overblock nonpornographic sites was a constitutional problem. Adult patrons could simply ask a librarian to unblock a blocked site or could have the filter disabled entirely.

The Dissents Justice John Paul Stevens viewed CIPA "as a blunt nationwide restraint on adult access to an enormous amount of valuable" and often constitutionally protected speech. Justice David Souter noted that he would have joined the plurality if the First Amendment interests raised in this case were those of children rather than those of adults.

Hamdi v. Rumsfeld and Rasul v. Bush (2004)

Significance These cases addressed the balance between the government's powers to fight terrorism and the Constitution's promise of due process. Each case raised a slightly different question:

1. Can the government hold American citizens for an indefinite period as "enemy combatants" and not permit them access to American courts, and

2. Do foreigners captured overseas and jailed at Guantánamo Bay, Cuba, have the right to take their cases to American courts to decide if they are being held legally?

Background In *Hamdi* v. *Rumsfeld*, Yaser Hamdi, an American citizen, was captured in Afghanistan in 2001. The U.S. military said Hamdi was an enemy combatant and claimed that "it has the authority to hold ... enemy combatants captured on the battlefield ... to prevent them from returning to the battle." Hamdi's attorney said that Hamdi deserved the due process rights that other Americans have, including a hearing in court to argue that he was not an enemy combatant.

The prisoners in *Rasul* v. *Bush* also claimed they were wrongly imprisoned. They wanted a court hearing, but Guantánamo Bay Naval Base is on Cuban soil. Cuba leases the base to the United States. In an earlier case, the Court had ruled that "if an alien is outside the country's sovereign territory, then ... the alien is not permitted access to the courts of the United States to enforce the Constitution."

Decision In *Hamdi*, the Court ruled 6 to 3 that Hamdi had a right to a hearing. Justice Sandra Day O'Connor wrote that the Court has "made clear that a state of war is not a blank check for the president when it comes to the rights of the nation's citizens." The government decided not to prosecute Hamdi. In *Rasul*, also decided 6 to 3, Justice John Paul Stevens wrote that the prisoners had been held for more than two years in territory under U.S. control. Thus, even though the prisoners are not on U.S. soil, they can ask U.S. courts if their detention is legal. The *Rasul* cases were still pending when this book was printed.

Historic Documents

Magna Carta

England's King John angered many people with high taxes. In 1215 a group of English nobles joined the archbishop of Canterbury to force the king to agree to sign Magna Carta. This document stated that the king was subject to the rule of law, just as other citizens of England were. It also presented the ideas of a fair and speedy trial and due process of law. These principles are still a part of the U.S. Bill of Rights.

1. In the first place have granted to God, and by this our present charter confirmed for us and our heirs for ever that the English church shall be free, and shall have its rights undiminished and its liberties unimpaired . . . We have also granted to all free men of our kingdom, for ourselves and our heirs for ever, all the liberties written below, to be had and held by them and their heirs of us and our heirs.

2. If any of our earls or barons or others holding of us in chief by knight service dies, and at his death his heir be of full age and owe relief he shall have his inheritance on payment of the old relief, namely the heir or heirs of an earl 100 for a whole earl's barony, the heir or heirs of a baron 100 for a whole barony, the heir or heirs of a knight 100s, at most, for a whole knight's fee; and he who owes less shall give less according to the ancient usage of fiefs.

3. If, however, the heir of any such be under age and a ward, he shall have his inheritance when he comes of age without paying relief and without making fine.

40. To no one will we sell, to no one will we refuse or delay right or justice.

41. All merchants shall be able to go out of and come into England safely and securely and stay and travel throughout England, as well by land as by water, for buying and selling by the ancient and right customs free from all evil tolls, except in time of war and if they are of the land that is at war with us . . .

42. It shall be lawful in future for anyone, without prejudicing the allegiance due to us, to leave our kingdom and return safely and securely by land and water, save, in the public interest, for a short period in time of war—except for those imprisoned or outlawed in accordance with the law of the kingdom and natives of a land that is at war with us and merchants (who shall be treated as aforesaid).

62. And we have fully remitted and pardoned to everyone all the ill–will, indignation and rancour that have arisen between us and our men, clergy and laity, from the time of the quarrel. Furthermore, we have fully remitted to all, clergy and laity, and as far as pertains to us have completely forgiven, all trespasses occasioned by the same quarrel between Easter in the sixteenth year of our reign and the restoration of peace. And, besides, we have caused to be made for them letters testimonial patent of the lord Stephen archbishop of Canterbury, of the lord Henry archbishop of Dublin and of the aforementioned bishops and of master Pandulf about this security and the aforementioned concessions.

63. An oath, moreover, has been taken, as well on our part as on the part of the barons, that all these things aforesaid shall be observed in good faith and without evil disposition. Witness the above–mentioned and many others. Given by our hand in the meadow which is called Runnymede between Windsor and Staines on the fifteenth day of June, in the seventeenth year of our reign.

From "English Bill of Rights." Britannica Online. Vers. 99.1. 1994–1999. Copyright © 1994–1999 Encyclopaedia Britannica, Inc.

The Mayflower Compact

In November 1620, the Pilgrim leaders aboard the Mayflower *drafted the Mayflower Compact. This was the first document in the English colonies to establish guidelines for self-government. This excerpt from the Mayflower Compact describes the principles of the Pilgrim colony's government.*

The Mayflower Compact

We whose names are underwritten, the loyal subjects of our dread Sovereign Lord King James, by the Grace of God of Great Britain, France and Ireland, King, Defender of the Faith, etc.

Having undertaken, for the Glory of God and advancement of the Christian Faith and Honour of our King and Country, a Voyage to plant the First Colony in the Northern Parts of Virginia, do by these presents solemnly and mutually in the presence of God and one of another, Covenant and Combine ourselves together into a Civil Body Politic, for our better ordering and preservation and furtherance of the ends aforesaid; and by virtue hereof to enact, constitute and frame such just and equal Laws, Ordinances, Acts, Constitutions and Offices, from time to time, as shall be thought most meet and convenient for the general good of the Colony, unto which we promise all due submission and obedience. In witness whereof we have hereunder subscribed our names at Cape Cod, the 11th of November, in the year of the reign of our Sovereign Lord King James, of England, France and Ireland the eighteenth, and of Scotland the fifty-fourth. Anno Domini 1620.

From William Bradford, *Of Plymouth Plantation, 1620–1647* (Samuel Eliot Morison, ed., 1952), 75–76.

Fundamental Orders of Connecticut

In January 1639, settlers in Connecticut led by Thomas Hooker drew up the Fundamental Orders of Connecticut—America's first written constitution. It is essentially a compact among the settlers and a body of laws.

Forasmuch as it hath pleased the All-mighty God by the wise disposition of his divyne pruvidence so to Order and dispose of things that we the Inhabitants and Residents of Windsor, Harteford and Wethersfield are now cohabiting and dwelling in and uppon the River of Conectecotte and the Lands thereunto adioyneing; As also in our Civell Affaires to be guided and governed according to such Lawes, Rules, Orders and decrees as shall be made, ordered & decreed, as followeth:—

1. It is Ordered . . . that there shall be yerely two generall Assemblies or Courts, the one the second thursday in Aprill, the other the second thursday in September, following; the first shall be called the Courte of Election, wherein shall be yerely Chosen . . . soe many Magestrats and other publike Officers as shall be found requisitte: which choise shall be made by all that are admitted freemen and have taken the Oath of Fidelity, and doe cohabitte within this Jurisdiction, (having beene admitted Inhabitants by the major part of the Towne wherein they live,) or the major parte of such as shall be then present . . .

From F. N. Thorpe, ed., *Federal and State Constitutions,* vol. 1 (1909), 519.

The English Bill of Rights

In 1689, after the Glorious Revolution, Parliament passed the English Bill of Rights, which ensured that Parliament would have supreme power over the monarchy. The bill also protected the rights of English citizens.

Whereas the late King James the Second, by the assistance of divers evil counsellors, judges and ministers employed by him, did endeavour to subvert and extirpate the Protestant religion and the laws and liberties of this kingdom;

By assuming and exercising a power of dispensing with and suspending of laws and the execution of laws without consent of Parliament;

By committing and prosecuting divers worthy prelates for humbly petitioning to be excused from concurring to the said assumed power;

By issuing and causing to be executed a commission under the great seal for erecting a court called the Court of Commissioners for Ecclesiastical Causes;

By levying money for and to the use of the Crown by pretence of prerogative for other time and in other manner than the same was granted by Parliament;

By raising and keeping a standing army within this kingdom in time of peace without consent of Parliament, and quartering soldiers contrary to law; . . .

By violating the freedom of election of members to serve in Parliament;

By prosecutions in the Court of King's Bench for matters and causes cognizable only in Parliament, and by divers other arbitrary and illegal courses;

And whereas of late years partial corrupt and unqualified persons have been returned and served on juries in trials, and particularly divers jurors in trials for high treason which were not freeholders;

And excessive bail hath been required of persons committed in criminal cases to elude the benefit of the laws made for the liberty of the subjects;

And excessive fines have been imposed;

And illegal and cruel punishments inflicted;

And several grants and promises made of fines and forfeitures before any conviction or judgment against the persons upon whom the same were to be levied;

All which are utterly and directly contrary to the known laws and statutes and freedom of this realm; ...

That the pretended power of suspending of laws or the execution of laws by regal authority without consent of Parliament is illegal;

That the pretended power of dispensing with laws or the execution of laws by regal authority, as it hath been assumed and exercised of late, is illegal;

That the commission for erecting the late Court of Commissioners for Ecclesiastical Causes, and all other commissions and courts of like nature, are illegal and pernicious;

That levying money for or to the use of the Crown by pretence of prerogative, without grant of Parliament, for longer time, or in other manner than the same is or shall be granted, is illegal;

That it is the right of the subjects to petition the king, and all commitments and prosecutions for such petitioning are illegal;

That the raising or keeping a standing army within the kingdom in time of peace, unless it be with consent of Parliament, is against law;

That the subjects which are Protestants may have arms for their defence suitable to their conditions and as allowed by law;

That election of members of Parliament ought to be free;

That the freedom of speech and debates or proceedings in Parliament ought not to be impeached or questioned in any court or place out of Parliament;

(continued next page)

That excessive bail ought not to be required, nor excessive fines imposed, nor cruel and unusual punishments inflicted;

That jurors ought to be duly impanelled and returned, and jurors which pass upon men in trials for high treason ought to be freeholders;

That all grants and promises of fines and forfeitures of particular persons before conviction are illegal and void;

And that for redress of all grievances, and for the amending, strengthening and preserving of the laws, Parliaments ought to be held frequently.

From "English Bill of Rights." Britannica Online. Vers. 99.1. 1994–1999. Copyright © 1994–1999 Encyclopaedia Britannica, Inc.

Articles of Confederation

After winning the Revolutionary War in 1777, the newly formed United States of America created a government under the Articles of Confederation. This government allowed the states to have more power than the central government, a situation that would lead to problems later.

Articles of Confederation and perpetual Union between the states of New Hampshire, Massachusetts-bay Rhode Island and Providence Plantations, Connecticut, New York, New Jersey, Pennsylvania, Delaware, Maryland, Virginia, North Carolina, South Carolina and Georgia.

I.
The Stile of this Confederacy shall be
"The United States of America".

II.
Each state retains its sovereignty, freedom, and independence, and every power, jurisdiction, and right, which is not by this Confederation expressly delegated to the United States, in Congress assembled.

III.
The said States hereby severally enter into a firm league of friendship with each other, for their common defense, the security of their liberties, and their mutual and general welfare, binding themselves to assist each other, against all force offered to, or attacks made upon them, or any of them, on account of religion, sovereignty, trade, or any other pretense whatever.

VI.
No State, without the consent of the United States in Congress assembled, shall send any embassy to, or receive any embassy from, or enter into any conference, agreement, alliance or treaty with any King, Prince or State; nor shall any person holding any office of profit or trust under the United States, or any of them, accept any present, emolument, office or title of any kind whatever from any King, Prince or foreign State; nor shall the United States in Congress assembled, or any of them, grant any title of nobility.

VIII.
All charges of war, and all other expenses that shall be incurred for the common defense or general welfare, and allowed by the United States in Congress assembled, shall be defrayed out of a common treasury, which shall be supplied by the several States in proportion to the value of all land within each State, granted or surveyed for any person, as such land and the buildings and improvements thereon shall be estimated according to such mode as the United States in Congress assembled, shall from time to time direct and appoint.

The taxes for paying that proportion shall be laid and levied by the authority and direction of the legislatures of the several States within the time agreed upon by the United States in Congress assembled.

Federalist Paper No. 51

In 1788 the newly written Constitution faced opponents who believed it gave too much power to the federal government. James Madison, Alexander Hamilton, and John Jay wrote, anonymously, a collection of essays that became known as the Federalist Papers. The following essay, written by James Madison, outlines reasons why the division of power written into the Constitution would keep the government from harming citizens.

In order to lay a due foundation for that separate and distinct exercise of the different powers of government, which to a certain extent is admitted on all hands to be essential to the preservation of liberty, it is evident that each department should have a will of its own; and consequently should be so constituted that the members of each should have as little agency as possible in the appointment of the members of the others. Were this principle rigorously adhered to, it would require that all the appointments for the supreme executive, legislative, and judiciary magistracies should be drawn from the same fountain of authority, the people, through channels having no communication whatever with one another. Perhaps such a plan of constructing the several departments would be less difficult in practice than it may in contemplation appear. Some difficulties, however, and some additional expense would attend the execution of it. Some deviations, therefore, from the principle must be admitted. In the constitution of the judiciary department in particular, it might be inexpedient to insist rigorously on the principle: first, because peculiar qualifications being essential in the members, the primary consideration ought to be to select that mode of choice which best secures these qualifications; secondly, because the permanent tenure by which the appointments are held in that department, must soon destroy all sense of dependence on the authority conferring them.

Washington's Farewell Address

In 1796 at the end of his second term as president, George Washington wrote his farewell address with the help of Alexander Hamilton and James Madison. In it he spoke of the dangers facing the young nation. He warned against the dangers of political parties and sectionalism, and he advised the nation against permanent alliances with other nations.

In contemplating the causes, which may disturb our Union, it occurs as matter of serious concern, that any ground should have been furnished for characterizing parties by geographical discriminations-Northern and Southern-Atlantic and Western . . .

No alliances, however strict, between the parts can be an adequate substitute; they must inevitably experience the infractions and interruptions which all alliances in all times have experienced . . .

The great rule of conduct for us, in regard to foreign nations, is, in extending our commercial relations, to have with them as little political connexion as possible. So far as we have already formed engagements, let them be fulfilled with perfect good faith. Here let us stop.

From *Annals of Congress*, 4th Congress, pp. 2869–2880. American Memory. Library of Congress. 1999.

Monroe Doctrine

In 1823 President James Monroe proclaimed the Monroe Doctrine. Designed to end European influence in the Western Hemisphere, it became a cornerstone of U.S. foreign policy.

With the existing colonies or dependencies of any European power we have not interfered and shall not interfere. But with the governments who have declared their independence and maintained it, and whose independence we have, on great consideration and on just principles, acknowledged, we could not view any interposition for the purpose of oppressing them, or controlling in any other manner their destiny, by any European power in any other light than as the manifestation of an unfriendly disposition toward the United States. . . .

Our policy in regard to Europe, which was adopted at an early stage of the wars which have so long agitated that quarter of the globe, nevertheless remains the same, which is not to interfere in the internal concerns of any of its powers; to consider the government de facto as the legitimate government for us; to cultivate friendly relations with it, and to preserve those relations by a frank, firm, and manly policy, meeting in all instances the just claims of every power, submitting to injuries from none.

From "The Monroe Doctrine" by James Monroe. Reprinted in *The Annals of America: Volume 5, 1821–1832*. Copyright © 1976 by Encyclopaedia Britannica.

Seneca Falls Declaration of Sentiments

One of the first documents to express the desire for equal rights for women is the Declaration of Sentiments, issued in 1848 at the Seneca Falls Convention in Seneca Falls, New York. Led by Elizabeth Cady Stanton and Lucretia Mott, the delegates adopted a set of resolutions modeled on the Declaration of Independence.

When, in the course of human events, it becomes necessary for one portion of the family of man to assume among the people of the earth a position different from that which they have hitherto occupied, but one to which the laws of nature and of nature's God entitle them, a decent respect to the opinions of mankind requires that they should declare the causes that impel them to such a course.

We hold these truths to be self–evident: that all men and women are created equal; that they are endowed by their Creator with certain inalienable rights; that among these are life, liberty, and the pursuit of happiness; that to secure these rights governments are instituted, deriving their just powers from the consent of the governed. Whenever any form of government becomes destructive of these ends, it is the right of those who suffer from it to refuse allegiance to it, and to insist upon the institution of a new government, laying its foundation on such principles, and organizing its powers in such form, as to them shall seem most likely to effect their safety and happiness.

From "Seneca Falls Declaration on Women's Rights." Reprinted in *The Annals of America: Volume 7, 1841–1849*. Copyright © 1976 by Encyclopaedia Britannica.

The Emancipation Proclamation

When the Union army won the Battle of Antietam, President Abraham Lincoln decided to issue the Emancipation Proclamation, which freed all enslaved people in states under Confederate control. The proclamation, which went into effect on January 1, 1863, was a step toward the Thirteenth Amendment (1865), which ended slavery in all of the United States.

That on the 1st day of January, in the year of our Lord 1863, all persons held as slaves within any state or designated part of a state, the people whereof shall then be in rebellion against the United States, shall be then, thenceforward, and forever free; and the executive government of the United States, including the military and naval authority thereof, will recognize and maintain the freedom of such persons and will do no act or acts to repress such persons, or any of them, in any efforts they may make for their actual freedom. . . .

And I further declare and make known that such persons of suitable condition will be received into the armed service of the United States to garrison forts, positions, stations, and other places, and to man vessels of all sorts in said service.

And upon this act, sincerely believed to be an act of justice, warranted by the Constitution upon military necessity, I invoke the considerate judgment of mankind and the gracious favor of Almighty God.

From "Emancipation Proclamation" by Abraham Lincoln. Reprinted in *The Annals of America: Volume 9, 1858–1865.* Copyright © 1976 by Encyclopaedia Britannica, Inc.

Lincoln's Gettysburg Address

On November 19, 1863, Abraham Lincoln addressed a crowd gathered to dedicate a cemetery at the Gettysburg battlefield. His short speech, which is excerpted below, reminded Americans of the ideals on which the Republic was founded.

FOUR SCORE AND SEVEN YEARS ago our fathers brought forth on this continent a new nation, conceived in liberty and dedicated to the proposition that all men are created equal.

Now we are engaged in a great civil war, testing whether that nation or any nation so conceived and so dedicated can long endure. We are met on a great battlefield of that war. We have come to dedicate a portion of that field as a final resting–place for those who here gave their lives that that nation might live. It is altogether fitting and proper that we should do this.

But in a larger sense, we cannot dedicate—we cannot consecrate—we cannot hallow—this ground. The brave men, living and dead, who struggled here have consecrated it far above our poor power to add or detract. The world will little note nor long remember what we say here, but it can never forget what they did here. It is for us, the living, rather, to be dedicated here to the unfinished work which they who fought here have thus far so nobly advanced.

It is rather for us to be here dedicated to the great task remaining before us—that from these honored dead we take increased devotion to that cause for which they gave the last full measure of devotion; that we here highly resolve that these dead shall not have died in vain; that this nation, under God, shall have a new birth of freedom; and that government of the people, by the people, for the people shall not perish from the earth.

From "The Gettysburg Address" by Abraham Lincoln. Reprinted in *The Annals of America: Volume 9, 1858–1865.* Copyright © 1976 by Encyclopaedia Britannica, Inc.

"I Will Fight No More Forever"

In 1877 Chief Joseph and his group of Nez Percé surrendered to General Oliver Otis Howard. With this surrender, the Nez Percé were removed from their native lands in Idaho to a reservation in Oklahoma.

Tell General Howard I know his heart. What he told me before I have in my heart. I am tired of fighting. Our chiefs are killed. Looking Glass is dead. Toohoolhoolzote is dead. The old men are all killed. It is the young men who say yes or no. He who led the young men is dead. It is cold and we have no blankets. The little children are freezing to death. My people, some of them, have run away to the hills, and have no blankets, no food; no one knows where they are -- perhaps freezing to death. I want time to look for my children and see how many of them I can find. Maybe I shall find them among the dead. Hear me, my chiefs. I am tired; my heart is sick and sad. From where the sun now stands, I will fight no more forever.

Wilson's Fourteen Points

Even before the end of World War I, President Woodrow Wilson announced a 14-point plan to help maintain peace throughout Europe and the world. The goal of his plan was to provide "peace without victory."

Gentlemen of the Congress:

It will be our wish and purpose that the processes of peace, when they are begun, shall be absolutely open and that they shall involve and permit henceforth no secret understandings of any kind. The day of conquest and aggrandizement is gone by; so is also the day of secret covenants entered into in the interest of particular governments and likely at some unlooked-for moment to upset the peace of the world. It is this happy fact, now clear to the view of every public man whose thoughts do not still linger in an age that is dead and gone, which makes it possible for every nation whose purposes are consistent with justice and the peace of the world to avow now or at any other time the objects it has in view.

We entered this war because violations of right had occurred which touched us to the quick and made the life of our own people impossible unless they were corrected and the world secured once for all against their recurrence. What we demand in this war, therefore, is nothing peculiar to ourselves. It is that the world be made fit and safe to live in; and particularly that it be made safe for every peace-loving nation which, like our own, wishes to live its own life, determine its own institutions, be assured of justice and fair dealing by the other peoples of the world as against force and selfish aggression. All the peoples of the world are in effect partners in this interest, and for our own part we see very clearly that unless justice be done to others it will not be done to us. The program of the world's peace, therefore, is our program; and that program, the only possible program, as we see it, is this:

I. Open covenants of peace, openly arrived at, after which there shall be no private international understandings of any kind but diplomacy shall proceed always frankly and in the public view.

II. Absolute freedom of navigation upon the seas, outside territorial waters, alike in peace and in war, except as the seas may be closed in whole or in part by international action for the enforcement of international covenants.

III. The removal, so far as possible, of all economic barriers and the establishment of an equality of trade conditions among all the nations consenting to the peace and associating themselves for its maintenance.

(continued next page)

IV. Adequate guarantees given and taken that national armaments will be reduced to the lowest point consistent with domestic safety.

V. A free, open-minded, and absolutely impartial adjustment of all colonial claims, based upon a strict observance of the principle that in determining all such questions of sovereignty the interests of the populations concerned must have equal weight with the equitable claims of the government whose title is to be determined.

VI. The evacuation of all Russian territory and such a settlement of all questions affecting Russia as will secure the best and freest cooperation of the other nations of the world in obtaining for her an unhampered and unembarrassed opportunity for the independent determination of her own political development and national policy and assure her of a sincere welcome into the society of free nations under institutions of her won choosing; and, more than a welcome, assistance also of every kind that she may need and may herself desire. The treatment accorded Russia by her sister nations in the months to come will be the acid test of their good will, of their comprehension of her needs as distinguished from their own interests, and of their intelligent and unselfish sympathy.

VII. Belgium, the whole world will agree, must be evacuated and restored, without any attempt to limit the sovereignty which she enjoys in common with all other free nations. No other single act will serve as this will serve to restore confidence among the nations in the laws which they have themselves set and determined for the government of their relations with one another. Without this healing act the whole structure and validity of international law is forever impaired.

VIII. All French territory should be freed and the invaded portions restored, and the wrong done to France by Prussia in 1871 in the matter of Alsace-Lorraine, which has unsettled the peace of the world for nearly fifty years, should be righted, in order that peace may once more be made secure in the interest of all.

IX. A readjustment of the frontiers of Italy should be effected along clearly recognizable lines of nationality.

X. The peoples of Austria-Hungary, whose place among the nations we wish to see safeguarded and assured, should be accorded the freest opportunity of autonomous development.

XI. Rumania, Serbia and Montenegro should be evacuated; occupied territories restored; Serbia accorded free and secure access to the sea; and the relations of the several Balkan states to one another determined by friendly counsel along historically established lines of allegiance and nationality; and international guarantees of the political and economic independence and territorial integrity of the several Balkan states should be entered into.

XII. The Turkish portions of the present Ottoman Empire should be assured a secure sovereignty, but the other nationalities which are now under Turkish rule should be assured an undoubted security of life and an absolutely unmolested opportunity of autonomous development, and the Dardanelles should be permanently opened as a free passage to the ships and commerce of all nations under international guarantees.

XIII. An independent Polish state should be erected which should include the territories inhabited by indisputably Polish populations, which should be assured a free and secure access to the sea, and whose political and economic independence and territorial integrity should be guaranteed by international covenant.

XIV. A general association of nations must be formed under specific covenants for the purpose of affording mutual guarantees of political independence and territorial integrity to great and small states alike.

In regard to these essential rectifications of wrong and assertions of right we feel ourselves to be intimate partners of all the governments and peoples associated together against the Imperialists. We cannot be separated in interest or divided in purpose. We stand together until the end.

Brown v. Board of Education

In 1954 a collection of cases came before the Supreme Court under the name Brown *v.* Board of Education. *These cases challenged segregation in public schools based on the equal protection clause of the Fourteenth Amendment. Chief Justice Earl Warren wrote the majority opinion, which reversed the earlier decision in* Plessy *v.* Ferguson *that instituted the "separate but equal" doctrine."*

In the instant cases, that question is directly presented. Here, unlike *Sweatt* v. *Painter*, there are findings below that the Negro and white schools involved have been equalized, or are being equalized, with respect to buildings, curricula, qualifications and salaries of teachers, and other "tangible" factors. Our decision, therefore, cannot turn on merely a comparison of these tangible factors in the Negro and white schools involved in each of the cases. We must look instead to the effect of segregation itself on public education.

In approaching this problem, we cannot turn the clock back to 1868 when the Amendment was adopted, or even to 1896 when *Plessy* v. *Ferguson* was written. We must consider public education in the light of its full development and its present place in American life throughout the Nation. Only in this way can it be determined if segregation in public schools deprives these plaintiffs of the equal protection of the laws.

Today, education is perhaps the most important function of state and local governments. Compulsory school attendance laws and the great expenditures for education both demonstrate our recognition of the importance of education to our democratic society. It is required in the performance of our most basic public responsibilities, even service in the armed forces. It is the very foundation of good citizenship. Today it is a principal instrument in awakening the child to cultural values, in preparing him for later professional training, and in helping him to adjust normally to his environment. In these days, it is doubtful that any child may reasonably be expected to succeed in life if he is denied the opportunity of an education. Such an opportunity, where the state has undertaken to provide it, is a right which must be made available to all on equal terms.

We come then to the question presented: Does segregation of children in public schools solely on the basis of race, even though the physical facilities and other "tangible" factors may be equal, deprive the children of the minority group of equal educational opportunities? We believe that it does.

We conclude that in the field of public education the doctrine of "separate but equal" has no place. Separate educational facilities are inherently unequal. Therefore, we hold that the plaintiffs and others similarly situated for whom the actions have been brought are, by reason of the segregation complained of, deprived of the equal protection of the laws guaranteed by the Fourteenth Amendment.

John F. Kennedy's Inaugural Address

John F. Kennedy became president in 1961, during the middle of the Cold War. In his inaugural address, he spoke to citizens of the United States and the world, asking for peace to be restored for the good of humanity.

[W]e observe today not a victory of party, but a celebration of freedom—symbolizing an end, as well as a beginning—signifying renewal, as well as change. For I have sworn before you and Almighty God the same solemn oath our forebears prescribed nearly a century and three quarters ago.

The world is very different now. For man holds in his mortal hands the power to abolish all forms of human poverty and all forms of human life. And yet the same revolutionary beliefs for which our forebears fought are still at issue around the globe—the belief that the rights of man come not from the generosity of the state, but from the hand of God.

We dare not forget today that we are the heirs of that first revolution. Let the word go forth from this time and place, to friend and foe alike, that the torch has been passed to a new generation of Americans—born in this century, tempered by war, disciplined by a hard and bitter peace, proud of our ancient heritage—and unwilling to witness or permit the slow undoing of those human rights to which this Nation has always been committed, and to which we are committed today at home and around the world.

Let every nation know, whether it wishes us well or ill, that we shall pay any price, bear any burden, meet any hardship, support any friend, oppose any foe, in order to assure the survival and the success of liberty.

This much we pledge—and more.

So let us begin anew—remembering on both sides that civility is not a sign of weakness, and sincerity is always subject to proof. Let us never negotiate out of fear. But let us never fear to negotiate.

Let both sides explore what problems unite us instead of belaboring those problems which divide us.

Let both sides, for the first time, formulate serious and precise proposals for the inspection and control of arms—and bring the absolute power to destroy other nations under the absolute control of all nations.

Let both sides seek to invoke the wonders of science instead of its terrors. Together let us explore the stars, conquer the deserts, eradicate disease, tap the ocean depths, and encourage the arts and commerce.

Let both sides unite to heed in all corners of the earth the command of Isaiah—to "undo the heavy burdens ... and to let the oppressed go free."

And so, my fellow Americans: ask not what your country can do for you—ask what you can do for your country.

My fellow citizens of the world: ask not what America will do for you, but what together we can do for the freedom of man.

I Have a Dream

In 1963 civil rights leaders organized a march on Washington, D.C., that brought attention to the difference between the ideals of the United States and the reality faced by millions of African American citizens. Martin Luther King, Jr. gave the following speech in front of the more than 200,000 demonstrators at the Lincoln Memorial.

I say to you today, my friends, that in spite of the difficulties and frustrations of the moment, I still have a dream. It is a dream deeply rooted in the American dream.

I have a dream that one day this nation will rise up and live out the true meaning of its creed: "We hold these truths to be self-evident; that all men are created equal."

I have a dream that one day on the red hills of Georgia the sons of former slaves and the sons of former slaveowners will be able to sit down together at a table of brotherhood.

I have a dream that one day even the state of Mississippi, a desert state sweltering with the heat of injustice and oppression, will be transformed into an oasis of freedom and justice.

I have a dream that my four children will one day live in a nation where they will not be judged by the color of their skin but by the content of their character.

I have a dream today.

I have a dream that one day the state of Alabama, whose governor's lips are presently dripping with the words of interposition and nullification, will be transformed into a situation where little black boys and black girls will be able to join hands with little white boys and white girls and walk together as sisters and brothers.

I have a dream today.

I have a dream that one day every valley shall be exalted, every hill and mountain shall be made low, the rough places will be made plain, and the crooked places will be made straight, and the glory of the Lord shall be revealed, and all flesh shall see it together.

This is our hope. This is the faith with which I return to the South. With this faith we will be able to hew out of the mountain of despair a stone of hope. With this faith we will be able to transform the jangling discords of our nation into a beautiful symphony of brotherhood.

With this faith we will be able to work together, to pray together, to struggle together, to go to jail together, to stand up for freedom together, knowing that we will be free one day.

This will be the day when all of God's children will be able to sing with a new meaning, "My country, 'tis of thee, sweet land of liberty, of thee I sing. Land where my fathers died, land of the Pilgrim's pride, from every mountainside, let freedom ring."

Let freedom ring from every hill and every molehill of Mississippi. From every mountainside, let freedom ring.

When we let freedom ring, when we let it ring from every village and every hamlet, from every state and every city, we will be able to speed up that day when all of God's children, black men and white men, Jews and Gentiles, Protestants and Catholics, will be able to join hands and sing in the words of the old Negro spiritual, "Free at last! Free at last! Thank God Almighty, we are free at last!"

President Bush's Address to the Nation

On September 11, 2001, terrorists hijacked four passenger planes and used them to attack sites in the United States, including the World Trade Center in New York City. President George W. Bush addressed the country's citizens that evening.

Good evening. Today, our fellow citizens, our way of life, our very freedom came under attack in a series of deliberate and deadly terrorist acts. The victims were in airplanes, or in their offices; secretaries, businessmen and women, military and federal workers; moms and dads, friends and neighbors. Thousands of lives were suddenly ended by evil, despicable acts of terror.

The pictures of airplanes flying into buildings, fires burning, huge structures collapsing, have filled us with disbelief, terrible sadness, and a quiet, unyielding anger. These acts of mass murder were intended to frighten our nation into chaos and retreat. But they have failed; our country is strong.

A great people has been moved to defend a great nation. Terrorist attacks can shake the foundations of our biggest buildings, but they cannot touch the foundation of America. These acts shattered steel, but they cannot dent the steel of American resolve.

America was targeted for attack because we're the brightest beacon for freedom and opportunity in the world. And no one will keep that light from shining.

Today, our nation saw evil, the very worst of human nature. And we responded with the best of America—with the daring of our rescue workers, with the caring for strangers and neighbors who came to give blood and help in any way they could.

Immediately following the first attack, I implemented our government's emergency response plans. Our military is powerful, and it's prepared. Our emergency teams are working in New York City and Washington, D.C. to help with local rescue efforts.

Our first priority is to get help to those who have been injured, and to take every precaution to protect our citizens at home and around the world from further attacks.

The functions of our government continue without interruption. Federal agencies in Washington which had to be evacuated today are reopening for essential personnel tonight, and will be open for business tomorrow. Our financial institutions remain strong, and the American economy will be open for business, as well.

The search is underway for those who are behind these evil acts. I've directed the full resources of our intelligence and law enforcement communities to find those responsible and to bring them to justice. We will make no distinction between the terrorists who committed these acts and those who harbor them.

I appreciate so very much the members of Congress who have joined me in strongly condemning these attacks. And on behalf of the American people, I thank the many world leaders who have called to offer their condolences and assistance.

America and our friends and allies join with all those who want peace and security in the world, and we stand together to win the war against terrorism. Tonight, I ask for your prayers for all those who grieve, for the children whose worlds have been shattered, for all whose sense of safety and security has been threatened. And I pray they will be comforted by a power greater than any of us, spoken through the ages in Psalm 23: "Even though I walk through the valley of the shadow of death, I fear no evil, for You are with me."

This is a day when all Americans from every walk of life unite in our resolve for justice and peace. America has stood down enemies before, and we will do so this time. None of us will ever forget this day. Yet, we go forward to defend freedom and all that is good and just in our world.

Thank you. Good night, and God bless America.

Biographical Dictionary

A

Adams, John (1735–1826) American statesman, he was a delegate to the Continental Congress, a member of the committee that drafted the Declaration of Independence, vice president to George Washington, and the second president of the United States. (p. 266)

Adams, John Quincy (1767–1848) Son of President John Adams and the secretary of state to James Monroe, he largely formulated the Monroe Doctrine. He was the sixth president of the United States and later became a representative in Congress. (p. 305)

Adams, Samuel (1722–1803) American revolutionary who led the agitation that led to the Boston Tea Party; he signed the Declaration of Independence. (p. 99)

Addams, Jane (1860–1935) American social worker and activist, she was the co-founder of Hull House, an organization that focused on the needs of immigrants. She helped found the American Civil Liberties Union and won the Nobel Peace Prize in 1931. (p. 648)

Aguinaldo (ahg-ee-NAHL-doh), Emilio (1869–1964) Filipino leader and commander of forces in rebellion against Spain, he led an insurrection against the authority of the United States. (p. 699)

Anthony, Susan B. (1820–1906) American social reformer, she was active in the temperance, abolitionist, and women's suffrage movements and was co-organizer and president of the National Woman Suffrage Association. (p. 465)

Aristotle (384 BC–322 BC) Greek philosopher, he thought that people should live in moderation and use reason. (p. 22)

Arkwright, Richard (1732–1792) English inventor, he patented the water-powered spinning frame, improving the production of cotton thread. (p. 385)

Askia the Great (c. 1443–1538) Songhai ruler, he overthrew Sunni Baru. Originally named Muhammad Ture, he took the military title askia and became known as Askia the Great. (p. 19)

Astor, John Jacob (1763–1848) American fur trader and financier, he founded the fur-trading post of Astoria and the American Fur Company. (p. 346)

Austin, Stephen F. (1793–1836) American colonizer in Texas, he was imprisoned for urging Texas statehood after Santa Anna suspended Mexico's constitution. After helping Texas win independence from Mexico, he became secretary of state for the Texas Republic. (p. 351)

B

Banneker, Benjamin (1731–1806) African American architect and city planner, he helped design the city of Washington, D.C. after the site was chosen by George Washington. (p. 240)

Barton, Clara (1821–1912) Founder of the American Red Cross, she obtained and administered supplies and care to the Union soldiers during the American Civil War. (p. 534)

Beckwourth, Jim (1798–1866?) African American explorer and mountain man who spent time in the unsettled western United States and later recounted his exciting life in a book. (p. 347)

Beecher, Catharine (1800–1878) American educator and the daughter of Lyman Beecher, she promoted education for women in such writings as An Essay on the Education of Female Teachers. She founded the first all-female academy. (p. 451)

Beecher, Lyman (1775–1863) American clergyman, he disapproved of the style of preaching of the Great Awakening ministers. He served as president of the Lane Theological Seminary and supported female higher education. (p. 448)

Bell, Alexander Graham (1847–1922) American inventor and educator, his interest in electrical and mechanical devices to aid the hearing-impaired led to the development and patent of the telephone. (p. 617)

BIOGRAPHICAL DICTIONARY

Bell, John (1797–1869) Senator from Tennessee, he supported the Union over slavery and helped found the Constitutional Union Party. (p. 495)

Bidwell, Annie (1839–1918) American pioneer activist, she worked for social and moral causes and for women's suffrage. (p. 602)

Bingham, George Caleb (1811–1879) American painter who specialized in painting scenes of everyday life in the West. (p. 310)

Black Hawk (1767–1838) Native American leader of Fox and Sauk Indians, he resisted the U.S.-ordered removal of Indian nations from Illinois and raided settlements and fought the U.S. Army. (p. 335)

Bolívar, Simon (1783–1830) South American revolutionary leader who was nicknamed the Liberator, he fought many battles for independence, winning the support of many U.S. leaders. (p. 300)

Breckinridge, John C. (1821–1875) Vice president under James Buchanan, he was also a senator from Kentucky. He later served as a general in the Confederate army. (p. 495)

Brooks, Preston (1819–1857) American congressman, he assaulted and beat Senator Charles Sumner for his antislavery speeches and for insulting a pro-slavery relative. He was nicknamed Bully Brooks by northerners. (p. 487)

Brown, John (1800–1859) American abolitionist who helped fuel the violence in Bleeding Kansas and was executed for his role in organizing a slave revolt at Harpers Ferry, Virginia. (p. 486)

Bryan, William Jennings (1860–1925) American lawyer and Populist politician, he favored free silver coinage, an economic policy expected to help farmers. He was a Democratic nominee for president in 1896 and was defeated by William McKinley. (p. 604)

Buchanan, James (1791–1868) American politician and fifteenth president of the United States, he was chosen as the Democratic nominee for president in 1854 for being politically experienced and not offensive to slave states. (p. 488)

Burns, Anthony (1834–1862) American enslaved African, he ran away and was arrested in Boston. His arrest became the center of violent protests by northern opponents of the Fugitive Slave Act. (p. 480)

 C

Calhoun, John C. (1782–1850) American politician and supporter of slavery and states' rights, he served as vice president to Andrew Jackson and was instrumental in the South Carolina nullification crisis. (p. 323)

Carnegie, Andrew (1835–1919) American industrialist and humanitarian, he focused his attention on steelmaking and made a fortune through his vertical integration method. (p. 620)

Cartier, Jacques (1491–1557) French navigator who made three voyages to Canada for France. He explored the St. Lawrence River. (p. 54)

Clark, George Rogers (1752–1818) American Revolutionary soldier and frontier leader, he captured the British trading village of Kaskaskia during the Revolution and encouraged Indian leaders to remain neutral. (p. 133)

Clark, William (1770–1838) American soldier and friend of Meriwether Lewis, he was invited to explore the Louisiana Purchase and joined what became known as the Lewis and Clark expedition. (p. 275)

Clay, Henry (1777–1852) American politician from Kentucky, he was known as the Great Pacificator because of his support of the Missouri Compromise. He developed the Compromise of 1850 to try to avoid civil war. (p. 302)

Cole, Thomas (1801–1848) American painter, he was the founder of the Hudson River school, a group of artists who emphasized the beauty of the American landscape, especially the Hudson River valley. (p. 310)

Columbus, Christopher (1451–1506) Italian explorer, he was convinced that he could reach Asia by sailing westward across the Atlantic Ocean. He gained the support of Spain's monarchs and commanded a small fleet that reached the so-called New World, setting off a tide of European exploration of the area. (p. 42)

Cooper, James Fenimore (1789–1851) Well-known Early American novelist, he wrote the *Last of the Mohicans* and many stories about the West. (p. 309)

Cooper, Peter (1791–1883) American ironworks manufacturer who designed and built Tom Thumb, the first American locomotive. (p. 398)

Cortés, Hernán (1485–1547) Spanish conquistador, he conquered Mexico and brought about the fall of the Aztec Empire. (p. 46)

Crazy Horse (1842?–1877) Native American chief of Oglala Sioux, he took part in the Battle of the Little Bighorn, in which General Custer was surrounded and killed. He was killed after surrendering and resisting imprisonment. (p. 595)

Crittenden, John J. (1787–1863) Kentucky senator, he attempted to save the Union by reconciling differences between northern and southern states in the Senate proposal known as Crittenden's Compromise. (p. 496)

Custer, George Armstrong (1839–1876) American army officer in the Civil War, he became a Native American fighter in the West and was killed with his troops in the Battle of the Little Bighorn. (p. 596)

da Vinci, Leonardo (1452–1519) Italian painter, sculptor, architect, engineer, scientist, and inventor. (p. 26)

Davis, Jefferson (1808–1889) First and only president of the Confederate States of America after the election of President Abraham Lincoln in 1860 led to the secession of many southern states. (p. 497)

Deere, John (1804–1886) American industrialist; he developed a steel plow to ease difficulty of turning thick soil on the Great Plains. (p. 404)

Dickinson, Emily (1830–1886) American poet, she lived a reclusive life, and her poems were not widely acclaimed until after her death. (p. 445)

Dix, Dorothea (1802–1887) American philanthropist and social reformer, she helped change the prison system nationwide by advocating the development of state hospitals for treatment for the mentally ill instead of imprisonment. (p. 450)

Douglas, Stephen (1813–1861) American politician and pro-slavery nominee for president, he debated Abraham Lincoln about slavery during the Illinois senatorial race. He proposed the unpopular Kansas-Nebraska Act, and he established the Freeport Doctrine, upholding the idea of popular sovereignty. (p. 484)

Douglass, Frederick (1817–1895) American abolitionist and writer, he escaped slavery and became a leading African American spokesman and writer. He published his biography, *The Narrative of the Life of Frederick Douglass,* and founded the abolitionist newspaper, the *North Star.* (p. 456)

Du Bois, W. E. B. (1868–1963) African American educator, editor, and writer, he led the Niagara Movement, calling for economic and educational equality for African Americans. He helped found the National Association for the Advancement of Colored People (NAACP). (p. 678)

E

Edison, Thomas Alva (1847–1931) American inventor of over 1,000 patents, he invented the lightbulb and established a power plant that supplied electricity to parts of New York City. (p. 616)

Edwards, Jonathan (1703–1758) Important and influential revivalist leader in the Great Awakening religious movement, he delivered dramatic sermons on the choice between salvation and damnation. (p. 94)

Emerson, Ralph Waldo (1803–1882) American essayist and poet, he was a supporter of the transcendentalist philosophy of self-reliance. (p. 443)

BIOGRAPHICAL DICTIONARY

Equiano, Olaudah (c.1750–1797) African American abolitionist, he was an enslaved African who was eventually freed and became a leader of the abolitionist movement and writer of *The Interesting Narrative of the Life of Olaudah Equiano.* (p. 77)

Eriksson, Lief (c. 1000) Norwegian explorer, son of Erik the Red, was first European to explore the Americas. (p. 38)

Farragut, David (1801–1870) American soldier, he was the first commissioned American admiral, and in the Civil War he captured New Orleans and maintained a blockade along the Gulf Coast against Confederate forces. (p. 524)

Finney, Charles Grandison (1792–1875) American clergyman and educator, he became influential in the Second Great Awakening after a dramatic religious experience and conversion. He led long revivals that annoyed conventional ministers. (p. 448)

Ford, Henry (1863–1947) Founder of Ford Motor Company, he created the moving assembly line and is often credited with helping to create a middle class in American culture. (p. 617)

Franklin, Benjamin (1706–1790) Early American politician and inventor, he took a central role in helping form the government of the new United States, and acted as a foreign diplomat on behalf of the new nation. (p. 169)

Frémont, John C. (1813–1890) American explorer, army officer, and politician, he was chosen as the first Republican candidate for president. He was against the spread of slavery, and he was rejected by all but the free states as a "single issue" candidate in the election of 1856. (p. 489)

Fuller, Margaret (1810–1850) A journalist, critic, and women's rights activist, she was a member of the Transcendentalist group of authors. (p. 443)

Fulton, Robert (1765–1815) American engineer and inventor, he built the first commercially successful full-sized steamboat, the Clermont, which led to the development of commercial steamboat ferry services for goods and people. (p. 397)

Gallaudet, Thomas (1787–1851) American educator, he studied techniques for instructing hearing impaired people and established the first American school for the hearing impaired. (p. 451)

Gálvez, Bernardo de (1746–1786) Governor of Spanish Louisiana, he captured key cities from the British, greatly aiding the American Patriot movement and enabling the Spanish acquisition of Florida. (p. 131)

Garrison, William Lloyd (1805–1879) American journalist and reformer; he published the famous antislavery newspaper, the Liberator, and helped found the American Anti-Slavery Society, promoting immediate emancipation and racial equality. (p. 455)

George III (1738–1820) King of England, 1760–1820, during the American Revolution. King against which American colonists claimed to be rebelling. (p. 97)

Geronimo (1829–1909) Chiricahua Apache leader, he evaded capture for years and led an extraordinary opposition struggle against white settlements in the American Southwest until his eventual surrender. (p. 597)

Gompers, Samuel (1850–1924) American labor leader, he helped found the American Federation of Labor to campaign for workers' rights, such as the right to organize boycotts. (p. 625)

Grant, Ulysses S. (1822–1885) Eighteenth president of the United States, he received a field promotion to lieutenant general in charge of all Union forces after leading a successful battle. He accepted General Lee's surrender of Confederate forces at Appomattox Courthouse, ending the Civil War. (p. 522)

Grimké, Angelina (1805–1879) and **Sarah** (1792–1873) American sisters and reformers, they were the daughters of a slaveholding family from South Carolina who became antislavery supporters and lecturers for the American Anti-Slavery Society. They also took up the women's rights campaign. (p. 455)

Gutenberg, Johannes (c. 1400–1468) Credited with the invention of the movable type printing press. (p. 27)

Hamilton, Alexander (1755–1804) American states-man and member of the Continental Congress and the Constitutional Convention, he was an author of the Federalist Papers, which support-ed ratification of the Constitution. He was the first secretary of treasury under George Washington and developed the Bank of the United States. (p. 238)

Harrison, William Henry (1773–1841) American politician, he served as the governor of Indian Territory and fought Tecumseh in the Battle of Tippecanoe. He was the ninth president of the United States. (p. 331)

Hawthorne, Nathaniel (1804–1864) American writer, he is famous for his many stories and books, including *The Scarlet Letter,* and he is recognized as one of the first authors to write in a uniquely American style. (p. 444)

Haywood, William "Big Bill" (1869–1928) One of the leaders of the International Workers of the World, a Socialist labor union active in the early 1900s. (p. 674)

Hearst, William Randolph (1863–1951) American journalist, he was famed for sensational news stories, known as yellow journalism, that stirred feelings of nationalism and formed public opinion for the Spanish-American War. (p. 645)

Henry the Navigator (1394–1460) King of Portugal who established a school of navigation and financed trips of exploration. (p. 39)

Hidalgo y Costilla, Father Miguel (1753–1811) Mexican priest and revolutionist, he led a rebellion of about 80,000 impoverished Indians and mestizos against Spain in the hope of improving living conditions; though defeated, the rebellion eventually grew and helped lead to Mexican independence. (p. 350)

Hutchinson, Anne (1591–1643) Puritan leader who angered other Puritans by claiming that people's relationship to God did not need guidance from ministers; she was tried and convicted of undermining church authorities and was banished from Massachusetts Bay Colony; she later established the colony of Portsmouth in present-day Rhode Island. (p. 82)

Irving, Washington (1783–1859) Early American satirical writer, he was the first American writer to gain international acclaim. His works include Rip Van Winkle and The Legend of Sleepy Hollow. He often used American history and authentic American settings and characters. (p. 308)

Jackson, Andrew (1767–1845) Nicknamed Old Hickory, he was an American hero in the Battle of New Orleans. As commander of the Tennessee militia, he defeated the Creek Indians, securing 23 million acres of land. His election as the seventh president of the United States marked an era of democracy called Jacksonian Democracy. (pp. 286, 325)

Jackson, Thomas "Stonewall" (1824–1863) American Confederate general, he led the Shenandoah Valley campaign and fought with Lee in the Seven Days' Battles and the First and Second Battles of Bull Run. (p. 517)

Jefferson, Thomas (1743–1826) American statesman, and member of two Continental Congresses, chairman of the committee to draft the Declaration of Independence, the Declaration's main author and one of its signers, and the third president of the United States. (pp. 119, 239, 266, 271)

Johnson, Andrew (1808–1875) American politician and the seventeenth president of the United States upon the assassination of Lincoln, he was impeached for his unpopular ideas about Reconstruction. He held onto the office by a one-vote margin. (p. 557)

Jones, John Paul (1747–1792) American naval officer famed for bravery, his most famous victory was the defeat of the British warship *Serapis,* during which he declared, "I have not yet begun to fight!" (p. 133)

Joseph (1840–1904) Native American chief of the Nez Percé group, he became involved in a war with the U.S. Army when his people were removed to a reservation in Idaho. (p. 599)

Kelley, Florence (1859–1932) American reformer, she was active in the settlement house movement and led progressive reforms in labor conditions for women and children. (p. 648)

Key, Francis Scott (1749–1843) American lawyer who was imprisoned on a British ship during the War of 1812. His poem written about the battle he witnessed has become the national anthem of the United States. (p. R31)

Lafayette, Marquis de (1757–1834) French statesman and officer who viewed the American Revolution as important to the world, he helped finance the Revolution and served as major general. p. 131)

La Follette, Robert M. (1855–1925) Progressive American politician, he was active in local Wisconsin issues and challenged party bosses. As governor, he began the reform program called the Wisconsin Idea to make state government more professional. (p. 667)

Las Casas, Bartolomé de (1474–1566) Spanish missionary and historian, he became the first ordained Catholic priest in the New World and advocated for the welfare and protection of Native Americans as well as preached against the slavery system. (p. 51)

Lee, Robert E. (1807–1870) American soldier, he refused Lincoln's offer to head the Union Army and agreed to lead Confederate forces. He successfully led several major battles until his defeat at Gettysburg, and he surrendered to the Union's commander General Grant at Appomattox Courthouse. (p. 518)

Lewis, Meriwether (1774–1809) Former army captain selected by President Jefferson to explore the Louisiana Purchase, he led the expedition that became known as the Lewis and Clark expedition. (p. 275)

Liliuokalani (li-lee-uh-woh-kuh-LAHN-ee) (1838–1917) Queen of the Hawaiian Islands, she opposed annexation by the United States but lost power in a U.S.-supported revolt by planters that led to a new government. (p. 694)

Lincoln, Abraham (1809–1865) Sixteenth president of the United States, he promoted equal rights for African Americans in the famed Lincoln-Douglas debates. He issued the Emancipation Proclamation and set in motion the Civil War, but he was determined to preserve the Union. He was assassinated in 1865. (p. 490)

Little Turtle (c. 1752–1812) Miami chief who led a Native American alliance that raided settlements in the Northwest Territory, he was defeated and forced to sign the Treaty of Greenville, and he later became an advocate for peace. (p. 246)

Locke, John (1632–1704) English philosopher during the Enlightenment who argued that there was a social contract between people and their government. His ideas influenced the writers of the Declaration of Independence and U.S. Constitution. (p. 95)

Longfellow, Henry Wadsworth (1807–1882) American poet in the mid-nineteenth century, he is best known for his story-poems, such as "Paul Revere's Ride" in Tales of a Wayside Inn and The Song of Hiawatha. (p. 445)

Lowell, Francis Cabot (1775–1817) American industrialist who developed the Lowell system, a mill system that included looms that could both weave thread and spin cloth. He hired young women to live and work in his mill. (p. 392)

M

Madison, James (1751–1836) American statesman, he was a delegate to the Constitutional Convention, the fourth president of the United States, the author of some of the Federalist Papers, and is called the father of the Constitution for his proposals at the Constitutional Convention. He led the United States through the War of 1812. (p. 164, 216, 283)

Magellan (muh-JEL-uhn), Ferdinand (1480–1521) Portuguese captain of a Spanish fleet that sought a western route to Asia via the "Southern Ocean", he found a passage through South America, now known as the Strait of Magellan, but died during the expedition. His crew of 18 people with one remaining ship successfully circumnavigated the world. (p. 44)

Mann, Horace (1796–1859) American educator, he is considered the father of American public education. He was a leader of the common-school movement, advocating education for all children. (p. 450)

Mansa Musa (d. 1332?) Emperor of Mali, grandson or grandnephew of Sundiata, made pilgrimage to Mecca in 1324. (p. 18)

Marion, Francis (1732?–1795) Revolutionary War commander of Marion's Brigade, a group of guerrilla soldiers in South Carolina that used surprise raids against British communications and supply lines. (p. 136)

Marshall, John (1755–1835) Federalist leader who served in the House of Representatives and as U.S. Secretary of State, he later became the Chief Justice of the U.S. Supreme Court, establishing in Marbury v. Madison the Supreme Court's power of judicial review. (p. 270)

Marshall, Thurgood (1908–1993) First African American U.S. Supreme Court Justice, he represented as a lawyer the National Association for the Advancement of Colored People and fought racial segregation. (p. 186)

Mason, George (1725–1792) American Patriot who became an Antifederalist and refused to sign the Constitution (p. 170)

McClellan, George B. (1826–1885) American army general put in charge of Union troops and later removed by Lincoln for failure to press Lee's Confederate troops in Richmond. (p. 517)

McCormick, Cyrus (1809–1884) American inventor and industrialist, he invented the mechanical reaper and harvesting machine that quickly cut down wheat. (p. 404)

Michelangelo (1475–1564) Italian sculptor, painter, architect, and poet. (p. 26)

Moctezuma II (1466–1520) Emperor of Mexico's Aztec Empire, he welcomed explorer Cortés as a god but was taken prisoner by him. He was later killed, and the Aztec capital was destroyed during the following Aztec uprising. (p. 46)

Monroe, James (1758–1831) Leading Revolutionary figure and negotiator of the Louisiana Purchase, he was the fifth president of the United States. He put forth the Monroe Doctrine establishing the U.S. sphere of influence in the Western Hemisphere that became the foundation of U.S. foreign policy. (p. 299)

Morse, Samuel F. B. (1791–1872) American artist and inventor, he applied scientists' discoveries of electricity and magnetism to develop the telegraph, which soon sent messages all across the country. (p. 402)

Mott, Lucretia (1793–1880) American reformer, she planned the Seneca Falls Convention with Elizabeth Cady Stanton, the first organized meeting for women's rights in the United States. (p. 464)

O'Connor, Sandra Day (1930–) Associate justice of the U.S. Supreme Court, she was the first woman appointed to the Court. (p. 186)

Olmsted, Frederick Law (1822–1903) American landscape architect who promoted the idea of recreational parks across the nation and helped design Central Park in New York City. (p. 645)

Osceola (c.1804–1838) Florida Seminole leader, he resisted removal by the U.S. government despite an earlier treaty that Seminole leaders had been forced to sign. He was eventually captured and died in prison. (p. 335)

Paine, Thomas (1737–1809) American political philosopher and author, he urged an immediate declaration of independence from England in his anonymously and simply written pamphlet, Common Sense. (p. 118)

Paul, Alice (1885–1977) American social reformer, suffragist, and activist, she was the founder of the organization that became the National Woman's Party (NWP) that worked to obtain women's suffrage. (p. 677)

Penn, William (1644–1718) Quaker leader who founded a colony for Quakers in Pennsylvania; the colony provided an important example of representative self-government and became a model of freedom and tolerance. (p. 86)

Perry, Oliver Hazard (1785–1819) American naval captain who put together the fleet that defeated the British at the Battle of Lake Erie in the War of 1812. (p. 285)

Pershing, John J. (1860–1948) American army commander, he commanded the expeditionary force sent into Mexico to find Pancho Villa. He was the major general and commander in chief of the American Expeditionary Forces in World War I. (p. 709)

Pickett, George (1825–1875) American general in the Confederate army, he was famed for Pickett's Charge, a failed but heroic effort at Cemetery Ridge in the Battle of Gettysburg, often considered a turning point of the Civil War. (p. 539)

Pierce, Franklin (1804–1869) Democratic candidate for president in 1852 and the fourteenth president of the United States, he made the Gadsden Purchase, which opened the Northwest for settlement, and passed the unpopular Kansas-Nebraska Act. (p. 483)

Pike, Zebulon (1779–1813) Army officer sent on a mission to explore the West, he was ordered to find the headwaters of the Red River. He attempted to climb what is now known as Pikes Peak in Colorado. (p. 276)

Pizarro (puh-ZAHR-oh), Francisco (c. 1475–1541) Spanish conquistador who sailed with Balboa on the discovery of the Pacific Ocean, he later pursued rumors of golden cities in the Andes Mountains of South America and conquered the Inca Empire. (p. 47)

Plato (c. 428–348 BC) Greek philosopher, student of Plato and teacher of Aristotle, wrote The Republic. (p. 22)

Pocahontas (c.1595–1617) American Indian princess, she saved the life of John Smith when he was captured and sentenced to death by the Powhatan. She was later taken prisoner by the English, converted to Christianity, and married colonist John Rolfe. (p. 73)

Poe, Edgar Allan (1809–1849) American writer, he is famed for his haunting poem "The Raven," as well as many other chilling or romantic stories and poems. He is credited with creating the first detective story, "The Gold Bug." (p. 445)

Polk, James K. (1795–1849) Eleventh president of the United States, he settled the Oregon boundary with Great Britain and successfully conducted the Mexican-American War. (p. 355)

Pontiac (c.1720–1769) Ottawa chief who united the Great Lakes' Indians to try to halt the advance of European settlements, he attacked British forts in a rebellion known as Pontiac's Rebellion; he eventually surrendered in 1766. (p. 97)

Powderly, Terence V. (1849–1924) American labor leader for the Knights of Labor, he removed the secrecy originally surrounding the organization, leading to its becoming the first truly national American labor union. (p. 625)

Pulitzer, Joseph (1847–1911) American journalist and newspaper publisher, he established the Pulitzer Prize for public service and advancement of education. (p. 645)

Revels, Hiram (1822–1901) American clergyman, educator, and politician, he became the first African American in the U.S. Senate. (p. 565)

Riis, Jacob (1849–1914) Photographer and journalist who took shocking pictures of the lives of poverty-stricken immigrants, sweatshop workers, and tenement dwellers. These photos were published in *How the Other Half Lives*. (p. 646)

Rochambeau, Comte de (1725–1807) French soldier who commanded the French troops in the American Revolutionary War. He was with General George Washington at the Battle of Yorktown. (p. 137)

Rockefeller, John D. (1839–1937) American industrialist and philanthropist, he made a fortune in the oil business and used vertical and horizontal integration to establish a monopoly on the steel business. (p. 620)

Roosevelt, Theodore (1858–1919) Twenty-sixth president of the United States after William McKinley was assassinated, he organized the first volunteer cavalry regiment known as the Rough Riders who fought in Cuba during the Spanish-American War. As President, he acquired the Panama Canal Zone, and announced the Roosevelt Corollary, making the United States the defender of the Western Hemisphere. (p. 680)

Sacagawea (sak-uh-juh-WEE-uh) (1786?–1812) Shoshone woman who, along with her French fur-trapper husband, accompanied and aided Lewis and Clark on their expedition. (p. 276)

Santa Anna, Antonio López de (1794–1876) Mexican general and politician, he was president of Mexico and became a dictator. He fought in the Texas Revolution and seized the Alamo but was defeated and captured by Sam Houston at San Jacinto. (p. 351)

Scott, Dred (1795?–1858) Enslaved African who filed suit for his freedom stating that his time living in a free state made him a free man; the Supreme Court ruling known as the Dred Scott decision upheld slavery and found the Missouri Compromise unconstitutional. (p. 489)

Scott, Winfield (1786–1866) American general, he served as commander in the Mexican War and used a two-part strategy against the South in the Civil War; he wanted to destroy the South's economy with a naval blockade and gain control of the Mississippi River. (p. 513)

Sequoya (between 1760 and 1770–1843) American Indian scholar and craftsman, he created a writing system for the Cherokee language and taught literacy to many Cherokee. (p. 333)

Seward, William H. (1801–1872) Secretary of state under Abraham Lincoln, he also was responsible for the purchase of Alaska from Russia. (p. 693)

Shays, Daniel (1747?–1825) Revolutionary War officer who led Shays's Rebellion, an uprising of farmers in western Massachusetts that shut down the courts so that farmers would not lose their farms for tax debts. He was defeated and condemned to death, but pardoned. (p. 161)

Sherman, William Tecumseh (1820–1891) American Union army officer, his famous March to the Sea captured Atlanta, Georgia, marking an important turning point in the war. (p. 541)

Singer, Isaac (1811–1875) American inventor; he patented an improved sewing machine and by 1860, was the largest manufacturer of sewing machines in the country. (p. 405)

Sitting Bull (c.1831–1890) American Indian leader who became the head chief of the entire Sioux nation, he encouraged other Sioux leaders to resist government demands to buy lands on the Black Hills reservations. (p. 596)

Slater, Samuel (1768–1835) English industrialist who brought a design for a textile mill to America, he is considered the founder of the American cotton industry. (p. 386)

Smith, John (c.1580–1631) English colonist to the Americas who helped found the Jamestown Colony and encouraged settlers to work harder and build better housing. (p. 73)

Socrates (c. 470–399 BC) Greek philosopher and teacher who wanted to make people question their own beliefs and think for themselves. (p. 22)

Squanto (?–1622) Patuxet Indian who was captured and enslaved in Spain but later escaped to England and then America; he taught the Pilgrims native farming methods and helped them establish relations with the Wampanoag, the Indians at the feast later known as Thanksgiving. (p. 79)

Stanford, Leland (1824–1893) American railroad builder and politician, he established the California Central Pacific Railroad and founded Stanford University. (p. 621)

Stanton, Elizabeth Cady (1815–1902) American woman suffrage leader, she organized the Seneca Falls Convention with Lucretia Mott. The convention was the first organized meeting for women's rights in the United States, which launched the suffrage movement. (p. 464)

Steuben, Baron Friedrich von (1730–1794) Prussian soldier who helped train American forces at Valley Forge during the American Revolutionary War. (p. 131)

Stone, Lucy (1818–1893) American woman suffragist, she was a well-known and accomplished antislavery speaker who supported the women's rights movement. (p. 465)

Stowe, Harriet Beecher (1811–1896) American author and daughter of Lyman Beecher, she was an abolitionist and author of the famous antislavery novel, *Uncle Tom's Cabin*. (p. 481)

Stuyvesant (STY-vi-suhnt), Peter (c.1610–1672) Director general of the Dutch New Netherland colony, he was forced to surrender New Netherland to the English. (p. 85)

Sumner, Charles (1811–1874) A Senator from Massachusetts, he was attacked by Preston Brooks with a cane over the issue of slavery. (p. 487)

Sutter, John (1803–1880) American pioneer who built Sutter's Fort, a trading post on the California frontier; gold was discovered leading to the California gold rush. (p. 365)

Taft, William Howard (1857–1930) Twenty-seventh president of the United States, he angered progressives by moving cautiously toward reforms and by supporting the Payne–Aldrich Tariff, which did not lower tariffs very much. He lost Roosevelt's support and was defeated for a second term. (p. 682)

Taney (TAW-nee), Roger B. (1777–1864) U.S. Supreme Court Chief Justice he wrote the majority opinion in the Dred Scott decision, stating that African Americans were not citizens and that the Missouri Compromise was unconstitutional. (p. 490)

Taylor, Frederick W. (1856–1915) American efficiency engineer, he introduced the manufacturing system known as scientific management that viewed workers as mechanical parts of the production process, not as human beings. (p. 624)

Tecumseh (1768–1813) Shawnee chief who attempted to form an Indian confederation to resist white settlement in the Northwest Territory. (p. 280)

Thoreau, Henry David (1817–1862) American writer and transcendentalist philosopher, he studied nature and published a magazine article, "Civil Disobedience," as well as his famous book, *Walden Pond*. (p. 443)

Truth, Sojourner (c.1797–1883) American evangelist and reformer, she was born an enslaved African but was later freed and became a speaker for abolition and women's suffrage. (p. 456)

Tubman, Harriet (c.1820–1913) American abolitionist who escaped slavery and assisted other enslaved Africans to escape; she is the most famous Underground Railroad conductor and is known as the Moses of her people. (p. 458)

Turner, Nat (1800–1831) American slave leader, he claimed that divine inspiration had led him to end the slavery system. Called Nat Turner's Rebellion, the slave revolt was the most violent one in U.S. history; he was tried, convicted, and executed. (p. 428)

Tweed, William Marcy (1823–1878) New York city politician known for his control of the corrupt political machine called the Tammany Ring. (p. 663)

Vallejo, Mariano Guadalupe (1808–1890) Californio leader who urged equal rights for Mexicans living in California after the state was captured in the Mexican-American War. (p. 357)

Van Buren, Martin (1782–1862) American politician and secretary of state under Andrew Jackson, he later became the eighth president of the United States. (p. 324)

Villa, Francisco "Pancho" (1878–1923) Mexican bandit and revolutionary leader, he led revolts against Carranza and Huerta. He was pursued by the U.S. but evaded General Pershing. (p. 709)

Washington, Booker T. (1856–1915) African American educator and civil rights leader, he was born into slavery and later became head of the Tuskegee Institute for career training for African Americans. He was an advocate for conservative social change. (p. 677)

Washington, George (1732–1799) Revolutionary War hero and Patriot leader, he served as a representative to the Continental Congresses, commanded the Continental Army, and was unanimously elected to two terms as president of the United States. (pp. 114, 234)

Washington, Martha (1731–1802) Wife of George Washington, she was the first First Lady. (p. 234)

Webster, Daniel (1782–1852) American lawyer and statesman, he spoke out against nullification and states' rights, believing that the country should stay unified. (p. 328)

Wells, Ida B. (1862–1931) African American journalist and anti-lynching activist, she was part owner and editor of the Memphis Free Speech. (p. 677)

Whitman, Walt (1819–1892) American poet, he gained recognition abroad and later at home for unrhymed works of poetry praising the United States, Americans, democracy, and individualism. (p. 445)

Whitney, Eli (1765–1825) American inventor whose cotton gin changed cotton harvesting procedures and enabled large increases in cotton production; he introduced the technology of mass production through the development of interchangeable parts in gun-making. (p. 387)

Willard, Frances (1839–1898) American reformer who helped found the Women's Christian Temperance Union and was also active in the Women's suffrage movement. (p. 676)

Winnemucca, Sarah (1844–1891) Paiute Indian reformer, she was an activist for Indian rights and lectured specifically about the problems of the reservation system. (p. 598)

Winthrop, John (1588–1649) Leader of the Massachusetts Bay Colony who led Puritan colonists to Massachusetts to establish an ideal Christian community; he later became the colony's first governor. (p. 80)

Wright, Orville (1871–1948) and **Wilbur** (1867–1912) American pioneers of aviation, they went from experiments with kites and gliders to piloting the first successful gas-powered airplane flight and later founded the American Wright Company to manufacture airplanes. (p. 618)

Young, Brigham (1801–1877) American religious leader who headed the Mormon Church after the murder of Joseph Smith, he moved the community to Utah, leading thousands along what came to be known as the Mormon Trail to the main settlement at Salt Lake City. (p. 349)

BIOGRAPHICAL DICTIONARY

English and Spanish Glossary

MARK	AS IN	RESPELLING	EXAMPLE
a	alphabet	a	*AL-fuh-bet
ā	Asia	ay	AY-zhuh
ä	cart, top	ah	KAHRT, TAHP
e	let, ten	e	LET, TEN
ē	even, leaf	ee	EE-vuhn, LEEF
i	it, tip, British	i	IT, TIP, BRIT-ish
ī	site, buy, Ohio	y	SYT, BY, oh-HY-oh
	iris	eye	EYE-ris
k	card	k	KAHRD
ō	over, rainbow	oh	OH-vuhr, RAYN-boh
ů	book, wood	ooh	BOOHK, WOOHD
ò	all, orchid	aw	AWL, AWR-kid
òi	foil, coin	oy	FOYL, KOYN
aů	out	ow	OWT
ə	cup, butter	uh	KUHP, BUHT-uhr
ü	rule, food	oo	ROOL, FOOD
yü	few	yoo	FYOO
zh	vision	zh	VIZH-uhn

*A syllable printed in small capital letters receives heavier emphasis than the other syllable(s) in a word.

Phonetic Respelling and Pronunciation Guide

Many of the key terms in this textbook have been respelled to help you pronounce them. The letter combinations used in the respelling throughout the narrative are explained in the following phonetic respelling and pronunciation guide. The guide is adapted from *Merriam-Webster's Collegiate Dictionary, 11th Edition; Merriam-Webster's Geographical Dictionary;* and *Merriam-Webster's Biographical Dictionary.*

A

abolition an end to slavery (p. 454)
abolición fin de la esclavitud (pág. 454)

Adams-Onís Treaty (1819) an agreement in which Spain gave East Florida to the United States (p. 299)
Tratado de Adams y Onís (1819) acuerdo en el que España le dio el territorio del este de Florida a Estados Unidos (pág. 299)

African Diaspora the population of displaced Africans and their descendants around the world (p. 60)
diáspora africana población de africanos desplazados y sus descendientes en todo el mundo (pág. 60)

Alamo Spanish mission in San Antonio, Texas, that was the site of a famous battle of the Texas Revolution in 1836 (p. 352)
El Álamo misión española en San Antonio, Texas; escenario de una famosa batalla durante la Revolución Texana de 1836 (pág. 352)

Alien and Sedition Acts (1798) laws passed by a Federalist-dominated Congress aimed at protecting the government from treasonous ideas, actions, and people (p. 253)
Leyes de No Intervención Extranjera y Sedición (1798) leyes aprobadas por un Congreso mayormente federalista para proteger al gobierno de la influencia de ideas, acciones y personas desleales (pág. 253)

amendment official change, correction, or addition to a law or constitution (p. 173)
enmienda cambio, corrección o adición oficial a una ley o constitución (pág. 173)

American Anti-Slavery Society an organization started by William Lloyd Garrison whose members wanted immediate emancipation and racial equality for African Americans (p. 455)
Sociedad Americana contra la Esclavitud organización fundada por William Lloyd Garrison cuyos miembros pedían la emancipación inmediata y la igualdad racial de los afroamericanos (pág. 455)

American Federation of Labor (AFL) an organization that united skilled workers into national unions for specific industries (p. 625)
Federación Americana del Trabajo (AFL, por sus siglas en inglés) organización que unió a obreros especializados en sindicatos nacionales para industrias específicas (pág. 625)

American System Henry Clay's plan for raising tariffs to pay for internal improvements such as better roads and canals (p. 302)
Sistema Estadounidense plan de alza de aranceles creado por Henry Clay para hacer mejoras internas como la reparación de caminos y canales (pág. 302)

Antifederalists people who opposed ratification of the Constitution (p. 170) antifederalistas personas que se oponían a la aprobación de la Constitución (pág. 170)

Anti-Imperialist League a group of citizens opposed to imperialism, and, specifically, to the peace treaty that gave the United States control of Cuba, Guam, Puerto Rico, and the Philippines (p. 700)
Liga Antiimperialista grupo de ciudadanos que se oponían al imperialismo y, más específicamente, al tratado de paz que daba a Estados Unidos el control de Cuba, Guam, Puerto Rico y Filipinas (pág. 700)

Appomattox Courthouse the location where General Robert E. Lee was forced to surrender, thus ending the Civil War (p. 542)
Appomattox Courthouse poblado de Virginia donde el general Robert E. Lee fue obligado a rendirse, dando fin a la Guerra Civil (pág. 542)

Articles of Confederation (1777) the document that created the first central government for the United States; was replaced by the Constitution in 1789 (p. 154)
Artículos de Confederación (1777) documento que creó el primer gobierno central en Estados Unidos; fue reemplazado por la Constitución en 1789 (pág. 154)

astrolabe a device that enabled navigators to learn their ship's location by charting the position of the stars (p. 40)
astrolabio aparato que permitía a los navegantes saber la ubicación de su barco al trazar la posición de las estrellas (pág. 40)

B

Bacon's Rebellion (1676) an atttack led by Nathaniel Bacon against American Indians and the colonial government in Virginia (p. 74)
Rebelión de Bacon (1676) ataque encabezado por Nathaniel Bacon contra los indígenas norteamericanos y el gobierno colonial en Virginia (pág. 74)

Bank of the United States a national bank chartered by Congress in 1791 to provide security for the U.S. economy (p. 242)
Banco de Estados Unidos banco nacional formado por el Congreso en 1791 para dar seguridad a la economía de Estados Unidos (pág. 242)

Battle of Antietam (1862) a Union victory in the Civil War that marked the bloodiest single-day battle in U.S. military history (p. 519)
batalla de Antietam (1862) victoria del ejército de la Unión durante la Guerra Civil en la batalla de un solo día más sangrienta de la historia militar de Estados Unidos (pág. 519)

Battle of Bunker Hill (1775) a Revolutionary War battle in Boston that demonstrated that the colonists could fight well against the British army (p. 115)

batalla de Bunker Hill (1775) batalla de la Guerra de Independencia estadounidense en Boston; en ésta se demostró que los colonos podían luchar bien contra el ejército británico (pág. 115)

Battle of Fallen Timbers (1794) a battle between U.S. troops and an American Indian confederation that ended Indian efforts to halt white settlement in the Northwest Territory (p. 247)
batalla de Fallen Timbers (1794) batalla entre las tropas estadounidenses y una confederación de indígenas norteamericanos que puso fin a los intentos de los indígenas para detener la emigración de personas de raza blanca al Territorio del Noroeste (pág. 247)

Battle of Gettysburg (1863) a Union Civil War victory that turned the tide against the Confederates at Gettysburg, Pennsylvania (p. 537)
batalla de Gettysburg (1863) victoria del ejército de la Unión durante la Guerra Civil que cambió el curso de la guerra en contra de los confederados en Gettysburg, Pensilvania (pág. 537)

Battle of Lake Erie (1813) U.S. victory in the War of 1812, led by Oliver Hazard Perry; broke Britain's control of Lake Erie (p. 285)
batalla del lago Erie (1813) victoria en la Guerra de 1812 en la que el ejército estadounidense, comandado por Oliver Hazard Perry, puso fin al control británico del lago Erie (pág. 285)

Battle of New Orleans (1815) the greatest U.S. victory in the War of 1812; actually took place two weeks after a peace treaty had been signed ending the war (p. 286)
batalla de Nueva Orleáns (1815) la mayor victoria del ejército estadounidense en la Guerra de 1812; tuvo lugar dos semanas después de la firma de un tratado de paz en el que se declaraba el final de la guerra (pág. 286)

Battle of San Jacinto (1836) the final battle of the Texas Revolution; resulted in the defeat of the Mexican army and independence for Texas (p. 352)
batalla de San Jacinto (1836) batalla final de la Revolución Texana en la que el ejército mexicano fue derrotado y Texas obtuvo su independencia (pág. 352)

Battle of Saratoga (1777) a Revolutionary War battle in New York that resulted in a major defeat of British troops; marked the Patriots' greatest victory up to that point in the war (p. 130)
batalla de Saratoga (1777) batalla de la Guerra de Independencia estadounidense que tuvo lugar en Nueva York y en la que las fuerzas británicas sufrieron una de sus mayores derrotas; los patriotas obtuvieron su mayor victoria hasta ese momento (pág. 130)

Battle of Shiloh (1862) a Civil War battle in Tennessee in which the Union army gained greater control over the Mississippi River valley (p. 523)
batalla de Shiloh (1862) batalla de la Guerra Civil en Tennessee en la que el ejército de la Unión adquirió mayor control sobre el valle del río Mississippi (pág. 523)

Battle of the Little Big Horn (1876) "Custer's Last Stand"; battle between U.S. soldiers, led by George Armstrong Custer, and Sioux warriors, led by Crazy Horse and Sitting Bull, that resulted in the worst defeat for the U.S. Army in the West (p. 596)
batalla de Little Big Horn (1876) última batalla del general Custer; esta batalla entre las tropas de George Armstrong Custer y los guerreros siux al mando de Caballo Loco y Toro Sentado produjo la mayor derrota del ejército estadounidense en el Oeste (pág. 596)

Battle of Tippecanoe (1811) U.S. victory over an Indian confederation that wanted to stop white settlement in the Northwest Territory; increased tensions between Great Britain and the United States (p. 282)
batalla de Tippecanoe (1811) victoria del ejército estadounidense sobre la confederación indígena que intentaba evitar el establecimiento de poblaciones de blancos en el Territorio del Noroeste; esta batalla aumentó las hostilidades entre Gran Bretaña y Estados Unidos (pág. 282)

Battle of Trenton (1776) a Revolutionary War battle in New Jersey in which Patriot forces captured more than 900 Hessian troops (p. 129)
batalla de Trenton (1776) batalla de la Guerra de Independencia estadounidense que tuvo lugar en Nueva Jersey; en esta batalla las fuerzas de los patriotas capturaron a más de 900 soldados hessianos (pág. 129)

Battle of Yorktown (1781) the last major battle of the Revolutionary War; site of British general Charles Cornwallis's surrender to the Patriots in Virginia (p. 137)
batalla de Yorktown (1781) la última batalla importante de la Guerra de Independencia estadounidense; lugar donde se rindió el general británico Charles Cornwallis ante los patriotas en Virginia (pág. 137)

Bear Flag Revolt (1846) a revolt against Mexico by American settlers in California who declared the territory an independent republic (p. 358)
Revuelta de Bear Flag (1846) rebelión iniciada por colonos estadounidenses en contra de México para declarar al territorio de California una república independiente (pág. 358)

benevolent society an aid organization formed by immigrant communities (p. 639)
sociedad de beneficencia organización de ayuda formada por comunidades de inmigrantes (pág. 639)

Berbers a group of people from northern Africa (p. 16)
bereberes grupo de habitantes del norte de África (pág. 16)

Bering Land Bridge a strip of land connecting Alaska with Russia that emerged from underwater around 38,000 BC (p. 6)
Puente de Tierra de Bering franja de tierra que conecta Alaska con Rusia y que surgió del agua alrededor del año 38,000 a.C. (pág. 6)

Bessemer process a process developed in the 1850s that led to faster, cheaper steel production (p. 615)
proceso de Bessemer proceso de producción de acero más económico y rápido, desarrollado en la década de 1850 (pág. 615)

Bill of Rights the first 10 amendments to the Constitution; ratified in 1791 (p. 173)
Declaración de Derechos primeras 10 enmiendas a la Constitución; aprobada en 1791 (pág. 173)

Black Codes laws passed in the southern states during Reconstruction that greatly limited the freedom and rights of African Americans (p. 558)
códigos de negros decretos aprobados en los estados sureños en la época de la Reconstrucción que limitaron en gran medida la libertad y los derechos de los afroamericanos (pág. 558)

Black Death a series of plagues that killed about 25 million people in Europe starting in 1347 (p. 25)
Peste Negra serie de plagas que mataron a unos 25 millones de personas en Europa a partir de 1347 (pág. 25)

bond a certificate that represents money the government has borrowed from private citizens (p. 238)
bono certificado que representa dinero que el gobierno toma prestado de los ciudadanos (pág. 238)

boomtown a Western community that grew quickly because of the mining boom and often disappeared when the boom ended (p. 588)
pueblo de rápido crecimiento comunidad del Oeste que se desarrolló con gran rapidez debido a la fiebre del oro, pero que desapareció cuando la fiebre terminó (pág. 588)

border states Delaware, Kentucky, Maryland, and Missouri; slave states that lay between the North and the South and did not join the Confederacy during the Civil War (p. 512)
estados fronterizos Delaware, Kentucky, Maryland y Missouri; estados esclavistas ubicados entre el Norte y el Sur y que no se unieron a la Confederación durante la Guerra Civil (pág. 512)

Boston Massacre (1770) an incident in which British soldiers fired into a crowd of colonists, killing five people (p. 101)
masacre de Boston (1770) incidente en el que los soldados británicos le dispararon a una multitud de colonos, dando muerte a cinco personas (pág. 101)

Boston Tea Party (1773) a protest against the Tea Act in which a group of colonists boarded British tea ships and dumped more than 340 chests of tea into Boston Harbor (p. 102)
Motín del Té de Boston (1773) protesta en contra de la Ley del Té en la que un grupo de colonos abordó barcos británicos que transportaban té y arrojó al mar alrededor de 340 baúles de té en el puerto de Boston (pág. 102)

Boxer Rebellion (1900) a siege of a foreign settlement in Beijing by Chinese nationalists who were angry at foreign involvement in China (p. 695)
rebelión de los boxers (1900) asedio a un asentamiento extranjero en Beijing por parte de un grupo de nacionalistas chinos que estaban enojados por la participación extranjera en China (pág. 695)

buffalo soldiers African American soldiers who served in the cavalry during the wars for the west (p. 596)
soldados búfalo soldados afroamericanos que sirvieron en la caballería durante las guerras del oeste (pág. 596)

Bureau of Indian Affairs a government agency created in the 1800s to oversee federal policy toward Native Americans (p. 332)
Oficina de Asuntos Indígenas agencia creada por el gobierno en el siglo XIX para supervisar las políticas federales en cuanto a los indígenas norteamericanos (pág. 332)

C

Californios Spanish colonists in California in the 1800s (p. 357)
californios colonos españoles que vivían en California en el siglo XIX (pág. 357)

capitalism an economic system in which private businesses run most industries (p. 674)
capitalismo sistema económico en el que las empresas privadas controlan la mayoría de las industrias (pág. 674)

caravels ships that used triangular sails to sail against the wind, and had rudders to improve steering (p. 40)
carabelas barcos con velas triangulares usadas para navegar contra el viento y que tenían timones para mejorar la dirección (pág. 40)

cattle drive a long journey on which cowboys herded cattle to northern markets or better grazing lands (p. 589)
arreo de ganado viaje largo en el que los vaqueros arreaban ganado para llevarlo a los mercados del Norte o a mejores pastos (pág. 589)

Cattle Kingdom an area of the Great Plains on which many ranchers raised cattle in the late 1800s (p. 589)
Reino del Ganado área de las Grandes Planicies en la que muchos rancheros criaban ganado a finales de siglo XIX (pág. 589)

charter an official document that gives a person the right to establish a colony (p. 54)
carta de constitución documento oficial que da a una persona el derecho de establecer una colonia (pág. 54)

checks and balances a system established by the Constitution that prevents any branch of government from becoming too powerful (p. 167)

equilibrio de poderes sistema establecido por la Constitución para evitar que cualquier poder del gobierno adquiera demasiada autoridad (pág. 167)

Chinese Exclusion Act (1882) a law passed by Congress that banned Chinese from immigrating to the United States for 10 years (p. 641)
Ley de Exclusión de Chinos (1882) ley aprobada por el Congreso que prohibió la inmigración de chinos a Estados Unidos por 10 años (pág. 641)

Chisholm Trail a trail that ran from San Antonio, Texas, to Abilene, Kansas, established by Jesse Chisholm in the late 1860s for cattle drives (p. 589)
Camino de Chisholm camino creado por Jesse Chisholm a finales de la década de 1860 que iba desde San Antonio, Texas hasta Abilene, Kansas, para arreos de ganado (pág. 589)

circumnavigate to travel all the way around the globe (p. 44)
circunnavegar darle la vuelta al planeta (pág. 44)

Civil Rights Act of 1866 a law that gave African Americans legal rights equal to those of white Americans (p. 560)
Ley de Derechos Civiles de 1866 ley que dio a los afroamericanos los mismos derechos legales que tenían los estadounidenses blancos (pág. 560)

Clermont the first full-sized U.S. commercial steamboat; developed by Robert Fulton and tested in 1807 (p. 397)
Clermont primer barco comercial de vapor de gran tamaño, diseñado por Robert Fulton y probado en 1807 (pág. 397)

collective bargaining a technique used by labor unions in which workers act collectively to change working conditions or wages (p. 626)
negociación colectiva método empleado por los sindicatos en el que los trabajadores actúan colectivamente para cambiar las condiciones laborales o los salarios (pág. 626)

Columbian Exchange the transfer of plants, animals, and diseases between the Americas and Europe, Asia, and Africa (p. 45)
intercambio colombino intercambio de plantas, animales y enfermedades entre las Américas y Europa, Asia y África (pág. 45)

Committees of Correspondence committees created by the Massachusetts House of Representatives in the 1760s to help towns and colonies share information about resisting British laws (p. 99)
comités de correspondencia comités creados por la Cámara de Representantes de Massachusetts en la década de 1760 para que los pueblos y colonias compartieran información sobra la resistencia a las leyes británicas (pág. 99)

common-school movement a social reform effort that began in the mid-1800s and promoted the idea of having all children educated in a common place regardless of social class or background (p. 450)

movimiento de escuelas comunes reforma social iniciada a mediados del siglo XIX para fomentar la idea de que todos los niños debían recibir educación en un mismo lugar sin importar su origen o clase social (pág. 450)

Common Sense (1776) a pamphlet written by Thomas Paine that criticized monarchies and convinced many American colonists of the need to break away from Britain (p. 118)
Sentido común (1776) folleto escrito por Thomas Paine en el que criticaba a las monarquías y convenció a muchos colonos norteamericanos de la necesidad de independizarse de Gran Bretaña (pág. 118)

Compromise of 1850 Henry Clay's proposed agreement that allowed California to enter the Union as a free state and divided the rest of the Mexican Cession into two territories where slavery would be decided by popular sovereignty (p. 479)
Compromiso de 1850 acuerdo propuesto por Henry Clay en que se permitía a California entrar en la Unión como estado libre y se proponía la división del resto del territorio de la Cesión Mexicana en dos partes donde la esclavitud sería reglamentada por soberanía popular (pág. 479)

Compromise of 1877 an agreement to settle the disputed presidential election of 1876; Democrats agreed to accept Republican Rutherford B. Hayes as president in return for the removal of federal troops from the South (p. 567)
Compromiso de 1877 acuerdo en el que se resolvieron las disputadas elecciones presidenciales de 1876; los demócratas aceptaron al republicano Rutherford B. Hayes como presidente a cambio del retiro de las tropas federales del Sur (pág. 567)

Comstock Lode Nevada gold and silver mine discovered by Henry Comstock in 1859 (p. 587)
veta de Comstock mina de oro y plata descubierta en Nevada por Henry Comstock en 1859 (pág. 587)

Confederate States of America the nation formed by the southern states when they seceded from the Union; also known as the Confederacy (p.497)
Estados Confederados de América nación formada por los estados del Sur cuando se separaron de la Unión; también conocida como Confederación (pág. 497)

conquistador a Spanish soldier and explorer who led military expeditions in the Americas and captured land for Spain (p. 46)
conquistador soldado y explorador español que encabezó expediciones militares en América y capturó territorios en nombre de España (pág. 46)

conservation the planned management of natural resources to prevent their destruction (p. 681)
conservación administración planificada de los recursos naturales para evitar su destrucción (pág. 681)

constitution a set of basic principles that determines the powers and duties of a government (p. 153)

constitución conjunto de principios básicos que determina los poderes y las obligaciones de un gobierno (pág. 153)

Constitutional Convention (1787) a meeting held in Philadelphia at which delegates from the states wrote the Constitution (p. 164)
Convención Constitucional (1787) reunión en Filadelfia en la que delegados de los estados redactaron la Constitución (pág. 164)

Constitutional Union Party a political party formed in 1860 by a group of northerners and southerners who supported the Union, its laws, and the Constitution (p. 495)
Partido Constitucional por la Unión partido político formado en 1860 por habitantes del Norte y del Sur en apoyo de la Unión, sus leyes y la Constitución (pág. 495)

Continental Army the army created by the Second Continental Congress in 1775 to defend the American colonies from Britain (p. 114)
Ejército Continental ejército creado por el Segundo Congreso Continental en 1775 para defender a las colonias norteamericanas del dominio británico (pág. 114)

contraband an escaped slave who joined the Union army during the Civil War (p. 531)
contrabando esclavo que escapó y se unió al ejército de la Unión durante la Guerra Civil (pág. 531)

Convention of 1818 an agreement between the United States and Great Britain that settled fishing rights and established new North American borders (p. 298)
Convención de 1818 acuerdo entre Estados Unidos y Gran Bretaña para definir los derechos de pesca y establecer las nuevas fronteras norteamericanas (pág. 298)

Copperheads a group of northern Democrats who opposed abolition and sympathized with the South during the Civil War (p. 532)
copperheads grupo de demócratas del Norte que se oponían a la abolición de la esclavitud y simpatizaban con las creencias sureñas durante la Guerra Civil (pág. 532)

corporation a business that sells portions of ownership called stock shares (p. 619)
corporación compañía que vende algunas partes en forma de acciones (pág. 619)

cotton belt a region stretching from South Carolina to east Texas where most U.S. cotton was produced during the mid-1800s (p. 416)
región algodonera zona que se extendía desde Carolina del Sur hasta el este de Texas, en la que se producía la mayor parte del algodón cosechado en Estados Unidos a mediados del siglo XIX (pág. 416)

cotton diplomacy Confederate efforts to use the importance of southern cotton to Britain's textile industry to persuade the British to support the Confederacy in the Civil War (p. 513)

diplomacia del algodón esfuerzos de la Confederación por aprovechar la importancia del algodón del Sur en la industria textil británica para convencer a Gran Bretaña de apoyar a la Confederación en la Guerra Civil (pág. 513)

cotton gin a machine invented by Eli Whitney in 1793 to remove seeds from short-staple cotton; revolutionized the cotton industry (p. 415)
desmotadora de algodón máquina inventada por Eli Whitney en 1793 para separar las fibras de algodón de las semillas; revolucionó la industria del algodón (pág. 415)

culture the common values and traditions of a society, such as language, government, and family relationships (p. 7)
cultura valores y tradiciones comunes de una sociedad, como el lenguaje, la forma de gobierno y las relaciones familiares (pág. 7)

Cumberland Road the first federal road project, construction of which began in 1815; ran from Cumberland, Maryland, to present-day Wheeling, West Virginia (p. 303)
camino de Cumberland primer proyecto federal de construcción de carreteras, iniciado en 1815 para crear un camino entre Cumberland, Maryland y el poblado que actualmente lleva el nombre de Wheeling, en Virginia Occidental (pág. 303)

Dawes General Allotment Act (1887) legislation passed by Congress that split up Indian reservation lands among individual Indians and promised them citizenship (p. 598)
Ley de Adjudicación General de Dawes (1887) ley aprobada por el Congreso que dividía el terreno de las reservas indígenas entre sus habitantes y les prometía la ciudadanía (pág. 598)

Declaration of Independence (1776) the document written to declare the colonies free from British rule (p. 119)
Declaración de Independencia (1776) documento redactado para declarar la independencia de las colonias del dominio británico (pág. 119)

Declaration of Sentiments (1848) a statement written and signed by women's rights supporters at the Seneca Falls Convention; detailed their beliefs about social injustice against women (p. 464)
Declaración de Sentimientos (1848) declaración redactada y firmada por partidarios de los derechos de la mujer durante la Convención de Seneca Falls; se describía con detalle su punto de vista sobre las injusticias sociales que afectaban a las mujeres (pág. 464)

deflation a decrease in money supply and overall lower prices (p. 604)
deflación reducción de la disponibilidad del dinero y baja general en los precios (pág. 604)

democracy a government in which people rule themselves (p. 23)
democracia gobierno en el que el pueblo se gobierna a sí mismo (pág. 23)

Democratic Party a political party formed by supporters of Andrew Jackson after the presidential election of 1824 (p. 323)
Partido Demócrata partido político formado por partidarios de Andrew Jackson después de las elecciones presidenciales de 1824 (pág. 323)

Democratic-Republican Party a political party founded in the 1790s by Thomas Jefferson, James Madison, and other leaders who wanted to preserve the power of the state governments and promote agriculture (p. 250)
Partido Demócrata Republicano partido político formado en la década de 1790 por Thomas Jefferson, James Madison y otros líderes políticos para preservar el poder de los gobiernos estatales y promover la agricultura (pág. 250)

department store giant retail shop (p. 645)
tiendas por departamentos grandes comercios de venta al público (pág. 645)

deport to send an immigrant back to his or her country of origin (p. 222)
deportar enviar a un inmigrante de regreso a su país de origen (pág. 222)

depression a steep drop in economic activity combined with rising unemployment (p. 161)
depresión bajón considerable en la actividad económica, combinado con un alza en el desempleo (pág. 161)

Donner party a group of western travelers who were stranded in the Sierra Nevada during the winter of 1846-47; only 45 of the party's 87 members survived (p. 365)
grupo Donner grupo de viajeros del Oeste perdidos en la Sierra Nevada durante el invierno de 1846-47; sólo 45 de los 87 viajeros sobrevivieron (pág. 365)

double jeopardy the act of trying a person twice for the same crime (p. 218)
doble proceso acto de juzgar a una persona dos veces por el mismo delito (pág. 218)

draft a system of required service in the armed forces (p. 223)
conscripción sistema de servicio obligatorio en las fuerzas armadas (pág. 223)

dry farming a method of farming used by Plains farmers in the 1890s that shifted focus from water-dependent crops to more hardy crops (p. 601)

ENGLISH AND SPANISH GLOSSARY

agricultura de secano método de cultivo que usaban los agricultores de las Planicies en la década de 1890 que provocó un cambio de los cultivos que dependían del agua a otros más resistentes (pág. 601)

due process the fair application of the law (p. 218)
debido proceso aplicación justa de la ley (pág. 218)

E

Eighteenth Amendment (1919) a constitutional amendment that outlawed the production and sale of alcoholic beverages in the United States; repealed in 1933 (p. 676)
Decimoctava Enmienda (1919) enmienda constitucional que prohibió la producción y venta de bebidas alcohólicas en Estados Unidos; revocada en 1933 (pág. 676)

electoral college a group of people selected from each of the states to cast votes in presidential elections (p. 234)
colegio electoral grupo de personas seleccionado en cada estado para votar en las elecciones presidenciales (pág. 234)

emancipation freeing of the slaves (p. 529)
emancipación liberación de los esclavos (pág. 529)

Emancipation Proclamation (1862) an order issued by President Abraham Lincoln freeing the slaves in areas rebelling against the Union; took effect January 1, 1863 (p. 529)
Proclamación de Emancipación (1862) orden emitida por el presidente Abraham Lincoln para liberar a los esclavos en las áreas que se rebelaban contra la Unión; entró en vigor el primero de enero de 1863 (pág. 529)

embargo the banning of trade with a country (p. 279)
embargo prohibición del comercio con un país (pág. 279)

Embargo Act (1807) a law that prohibited American merchants from trading with other countries (p. 279)
Ley de Embargo (1807) ley que prohibía a los comerciantes norteamericanos comerciar con otros países (pág. 279)

eminent domain the government's power to take personal property to benefit the public (p. 218)
derecho de expropiación poder otorgado al gobierno para tomar propiedades personales en beneficio del público (pág. 218)

empresarios agents who were contracted by the Mexican republic to bring settlers to Texas in the early l800s (p. 350)
empresarios agentes contratados por la República Mexicana para traer pobladores a Texas a principios del siglo XIX (pág. 350)

encomienda system a system in Spanish America that gave settlers the right to tax local Indians or to demand their labor in exchange for protecting them and converting them to Christianity (p. 50)
sistema de encomienda sistema adoptado en la América española que permitía a los colonos cobrar impuestos a los indígenas o exigirles trabajo a cambio de su protección y de convertirlos al cristianismo (pág. 50)

English Bill of Rights (1689) a shift of political power from the British monarchy to Parliament (p. 91)
Declaración de Derechos inglesa (1689) cambio del poder político de la monarquía británica al Parlamento inglés (pág. 91)

Enlightenment the Age of Reason; movement that began in Europe in the 1700s as people began examining the natural world, society, and government (p. 95)
Ilustración Era de la Razón; movimiento iniciado en Europa en el siglo XVIII cuando las personas empezaron a examinar la naturaleza, la sociedad y el gobierno (pág. 95)

environment the climate and landscape that surrounds living things (p. 7)
medio ambiente clima y paisaje donde habitan seres vivos (pág. 7)

Era of Good Feelings a period of peace, pride, and progress for the United States from 1815 to 1825 (p. 303)
Era de los Buenos Sentimientos período de paz, orgullo y progreso en Estados Unidos de 1815 a 1825 (pág. 303)

Erie Canal the canal that runs from Albany to Buffalo, New York; completed in 1825 (p. 303)
canal de Erie canal que va de Albany a Buffalo, Nueva York; completado en 1825 (pág. 303)

executive branch the division of the federal government that includes the president and the administrative departments; enforces the nation's laws (p. 167)
poder ejecutivo división del gobierno federal que incluye al presidente y a los departamentos administrativos; hace cumplir las leyes de la nación (pág. 167)

executive orders nonlegislative directives issued by the U.S. president in certain circumstances; executive orders have the force of congressional law (p. 185)
órdenes ejecutivas órdenes no legislativas dictadas por el presidente de Estados Unidos en circunstancias específicas; tienen la misma validez que las leyes del Congreso (pág. 185)

Exodusters African Americans who settled western lands in the late 1800s (p. 601)
Exodusters afroamericanos que se establecieron en el Oeste a finales del siglo XIX (pág. 601)

factor a crop broker who managed the trade between southern planters and their customers (p. 417)
agente agrícola persona que administraba el comercio entre las plantaciones del Sur y sus clientes (pág. 417)

federal system a system that divided powers between the states and the federal government (p. 182)
sistema federal sistema en el que se distribuye el poder entre los estados y el gobierno federal (pág. 182)

federalism U.S. system of government in which power is distributed between a central government and individual states (p. 167)
federalismo sistema de gobierno de Estados Unidos en el que el poder se divide entre una autoridad central y estados individuales (pág. 167)

Federalist Papers a series of essays that defended and explained the Constitution and tried to reassure Americans that the states would not be overpowered by the proposed national government (p. 171)
Federalist Papers serie de ensayos que defendían y explicaban la Constitución para convencer a los estadounidenses de que el gobierno nacional propuesto no tendría más poder que los estados (pág. 171)

Federalist Party a political party created in the 1790s and influenced by Alexander Hamilton that wanted to strengthen the federal government and promote industry and trade (p. 250)
Partido Federalista partido político creado en la década de 1790 e influenciado por las ideas de Alexander Hamilton para fortalecer al gobierno federal y fomentar la industria y el comercio (pág. 250)

Federalists people who supported ratification of the Constitution (p. 170)
federalistas personas que apoyaban la ratificación de la Constitución (pág. 170)

Fifteenth Amendment (1870) a constitutional amendment that gave African American men the right to vote (p. 563)
Decimoquinta Enmienda (1870) enmienda constitucional que daba a los hombres afroamericanos el derecho al voto (pág. 563)

54th Massachusetts Infantry African American Civil War regiment that captured Fort Wagner in South Carolina (p. 531)
54to Batallón de Infantería de Massachusetts regimiento afroamericano de la Guerra Civil que tomó el fuerte Wagner en Carolina del Sur (pág. 531)

First Battle of Bull Run (1861) the first major battle of the Civil War, resulting in a Confederate victory; showed that the Civil War would not be won easily (p. 517)
primera batalla de Bull Run (1861) primera batalla importante de la Guerra Civil, en la cual ganó el ejército confederado; demostró que la guerra no se ganaría fácilmente (pág. 517)

First Continental Congress (1774) a meeting of colonial delegates in Philadelphia to decide how to respond to the closing of Boston Harbor, increased taxes, and abuses of authority by the British government; delegates petitioned King George III, listing the freedoms they believed colonists should enjoy (p. 112)
Primer Congreso Continental (1774) reunión de delegados de las colonias en Filadelfia para decidir cómo responder al cierre del puerto de Boston, al alza de impuestos y a los abusos de la autoridad por parte del gobierno británico; los delegados hicieron peticiones al rey Jorge III, enumerando los derechos que consideraban justos para los colonos (pág. 112)

folktale a story that often provides a moral lesson (p. 427)
cuento popular narración que con frecuencia ofrece una moraleja (pág. 427)

Fort Sumter a federal outpost in Charleston, South Carolina, that was attacked by the Confederates in April 1861, sparking the Civil War (p. 511)
fuerte Sumter puesto de avanzada federal en Charleston, Carolina del Sur, cuyo ataque por parte de los confederados en abril de 1861 dio origen a la Guerra Civil (pág. 511)

forty-niner a gold-seeker who moved to California during the gold rush (p. 365)
del cuarenta y nueve buscador de oro que se mudó a California durante la fiebre del oro (pág. 365)

Fourteenth Amendment (1866) a constitutional amendment giving full rights of citizenship to all people born or naturalized in the United States, except for American Indians (p. 561)
Decimocuarta Enmienda (1866) enmienda constitucional que otorgaba derechos totales de ciudadanía a todas las personas nacidas en Estados Unidos o naturalizadas estadounidenses, con excepción de los indígenas americanos (pág. 561)

Freedmen's Bureau an agency established by Congress in 1865 to help poor people throughout the South (p. 556)
Oficina de Esclavos Libertos oficina creada por el Congreso en 1865 para ayudar a los pobres del Sur del país (pág. 556)

Freeport Doctrine (1858) a statement made by Stephen Douglas during the Lincoln-Douglas debates that pointed out how people could use popular sovereignty to determine if their state or territory should permit slavery (p. 492)
Doctrina de Freeport (1858) declaración hecha por Stephen Douglas durante los debates Lincoln-Douglas que señalaba que el pueblo podía usar la soberanía popular para decidir si su estado o territorio debía permitir la esclavitud (pág. 492)

Free-Soil Party a political party formed in 1848 by antislavery northerners who left the Whig and Democratic parties because neither addressed the slavery issue (p. 477)
Partido Tierra Libre partido político formado en 1848 por abolicionistas de los estados del Norte que habían abandonado el Partido Whig y el Partido Demócrata porque ninguno de los dos partidos tenía una postura sobre la esclavitud (pág. 477)

French Revolution French rebellion that began in 1789 in which the French people overthrew the monarchy and made their country a republic (p. 243)
Revolución Francesa rebelión francesa iniciada en 1789 en la que la población francesa derrocó a la monarquía y convirtió el país en una república (pág. 243)

frontier an undeveloped area (p. 586)
frontera área que no está siendo utilizada por el ser humano (pág. 586)

Fugitive Slave Act (1850) a law that made it a crime to help runaway slaves; allowed for the arrest of escaped slaves in areas where slavery was illegal, and required their return to slaveholders (p. 479)
Ley de Esclavos Fugitivos (1850) ley que hacía que ayudar a un esclavo a escapar de su amo fuera un delito; permitía la captura de esclavos fugitivos en zonas donde la esclavitud era ilegal para devolverlos a sus dueños (pág. 479)

G

Gadsden Purchase (1853) U.S. purchase of land from Mexico that included the southern parts of presentday Arizona and New Mexico (p. 361)
Compra de Gadsden (1853) compra por parte del gobierno de Estados Unidos de territorio mexicano que incluía la región ocupada actualmente por el sur de Arizona y Nuevo México (pág. 361)

Gettysburg Address (1863) a speech given by Abraham Lincoln in which he praised the bravery of Union soldiers and renewed his commitment to winning the Civil War (p. 540)
Discurso de Gettysburg (1863) discurso de Abraham Lincoln en el que alababa la valentía de las tropas de la Unión y renovaba su compromiso de triunfar en la Guerra Civil (pág. 540)

Ghost Dance a religious movement among Native Americans that spread across the Plains in the 1880s (p. 598)
Danza de los Espíritus movimiento religioso de los indígenas norteamericanos que se extendió por la región de las Planicies en la década de 1880 (pág. 598)

Gibbons v. *Ogden* (1824) a Supreme Court ruling that reinforced the federal government's authority over the states (p. 397)
Gibbons contra *Ogden* (1824) decisión de la Corte Suprema que reforzó la autoridad del gobierno federal sobre los estados (pág. 397)

Great Awakening a religious movement that became widespread in the American colonies in the 1730s and 1740s (p. 94)
Gran Despertar movimiento religioso que tuvo gran popularidad en las colonias norteamericanas en las décadas de 1730 y 1740 (pág. 94)

Great Compromise (1787) an agreement worked out at the Constitutional Convention establishing that a state's population would determine representation in the lower house of the legislature, while each state would have equal representation in the upper house of the legislature (p. 165)
Gran Compromiso (1787) acuerdo redactado durante la Convención Constitucional en el que se establece que la población de un estado debe determinar su representación en la cámara baja de la asamblea legislativa y que cada estado debe tener igual representación en la cámara alta de la asamblea. (pág. 165)

H

habeas corpus the constitutional protection against unlawful imprisonment (p. 532)
hábeas corpus protección constitucional contra el encarcelamiento ilegal (pág. 532)

hajj a pilgrimage to Mecca made by devout Muslims (p. 18)
hajj peregrinación a La Meca realizada por los musulmanes devotos (pág. 18)

Hartford Convention (1815) a meeting of Federalists at Hartford, Connecticut, to protest the War of 1812 (p. 287)
Convención de Hartford (1815) reunión de federalistas en Hartford, Connecticut, para protestar por la Guerra de 1812 (pág. 287)

Haymarket Riot a riot that broke out at Haymarket Square in Chicago over the deaths of two strikers (p. 626)
Revuelta de Haymarket revuelta que se originó en la Plaza Haymarket de Chicago por la muerte de dos huelguistas (pág. 626)

Homestead Act (1862) a law passed by Congress to encourage settlement in the West by giving government-owned land to small farmers (p. 600)
Ley de Colonización de Tierras (1862) ley aprobada por el Congreso para fomentar la colonización del Oeste mediante la cesión de tierras del gobierno a pequeños agricultores (pág. 600)

Homestead strike (1892) a labor-union strike at Andrew Carnegie's Homestead Steel factory in Pennsylvania that erupted in violence between strikers and private detectives (p. 627)
huelga de Homestead (1892) huelga sindical en la fábrica de acero Homestead de Andrew Carnegie en Pensilvania, que produjo violencia entre huelguistas y detectives privados (pág. 627)

horizontal integration owning all the businesses in a certain field (p. 621)
integración horizontal posesión de todas las empresas en un campo específico (pág. 621)

Hudson River school a group of American artists in the mid-1800s whose paintings focused on the American landscape (p. 310)
Escuela del Río Hudson grupo de artistas estadounidenses de mediados del siglo XIX que pintaban diversos paisajes del territorio estadounidense (pág. 310)

Hull House a settlement house founded by Jane Addams and Ellen Gates Starr in 1889 (p. 648)
Casa Hull casa de asistencia a la comunidad fundada por Jane Addams y Ellen Gates Starr en 1889 (pág. 648)

hunter-gatherer a person who hunts animals and gathers wild plants to provide for his or her needs (p. 6)
cazador y recolector persona que caza animales y recolecta plantas para satisfacer sus necesidades (pág. 6)

immigrant a person who moves to another country after leaving his or her homeland (p. 78)
inmigrante persona que abandona su país para establecerse en un país diferente (pág. 78)

immune having a natural resistance to disease (p. 58)
inmune la condición de tener resistencia natural contra la enfermedad (pág. 58)

impeach to bring charges against a public official (p. 184)
someter a juicio político presentar cargos en contra de un funcionario público (pág. 184)

impeachment the process used by a legislative body to bring charges of wrongdoing against a public official (p. 562)
juicio político proceso por el cual un cuerpo legislativo presenta cargos en contra de un funcionario público (pág. 562)

imperialism the practice of extending a nation's power by gaining territories for a colonial empire (p. 692)
imperialismo práctica en la que una nación amplía su poder adquiriendo territorios para un imperio colonial (pág. 692)

impressment the practice of forcing people to serve in the army or navy; led to increased tensions between Great Britain and the United States in the early 1800s (p. 279)
leva práctica que obligaba a las personas a servir en el ejército o la marina; aumentó las fricciones entre Gran Bretaña y Estados Unidos a principios del siglo XIX (pág. 279)

indentured servant a colonist who received free passage to North America in exchange for working without pay for a certain number of years (p. 74)
sirviente por contrato colono que recibía un pasaje gratuito a América del Norte a cambio de trabajar sin salario por varios años (pág. 74)

Indian Removal Act (1830) a congressional act that authorized the removal of Native Americans who lived east of the Mississippi River (p. 332)
Ley de Expulsión de Indígenas (1830) ley del Congreso que autorizaba la expulsión de los indígenas norteamericanos que vivían al este del río Mississippi (pág. 332)

Indian Territory an area covering most of present-day Oklahoma to which most Native Americans in the Southeast were forced to move in the 1830s (p. 332)
Territorio Indígena área que abarcaba la mayor parte del actual estado de Oklahoma a la que la mayoría de las tribus indígenas del sureste fueron obligadas a trasladarse durante la década de 1830 (pág. 332)

indict to formally accuse (p. 218)
acusar presentar cargos formales en contra de alguien (pág. 218)

Industrial Revolution a period of rapid growth in the use of machines in manufacturing and production that began in the mid-1700s (p. 385)
Revolución Industrial período de rápido desarrollo debido al uso de maquinaria en la fabricación y producción; comenzó a mediados del siglo XVIII (pág. 385)

Industrial Workers of the World (IWW) a union founded in 1905 by socialists and union leaders that included workers not welcomed in the AFL (p. 674)
Trabajadores Industriales del Mundo (IWW, por sus siglas en inglés) sindicato fundado en 1905 por socialistas y líderes sindicales que incluía a los trabajadores que no admitía la Federación Americana del Trabajo (pág. 674)

inflation increased prices for goods and services combined with the reduced value of money (p. 161)
inflación subida en los precios de los bienes al mismo tiempo que se reduce al valor del dinero (pág. 161)

initiative a method of allowing voters to propose a new law if enough signatures are collected on a petition (p. 666)
iniciativa método que permite a los votantes proponer una nueva ley si consiguen suficientes firmas para una petición (pág. 666)

interchangeable parts a process developed by Eli Whitney in the 1790s that called for making each part of a machine exactly the same (p. 387)
piezas intercambiables proceso desarrollado por Eli Whitney en la década de 1790 para que todas las piezas de una máquina fueran exactamente iguales (pág. 387)

interest group a group of people who share common interests for political action (p. 224)
grupo de interés grupo de personas que comparten intereses comunes en iniciativas políticas (pág. 224)

interstate commerce trade between two or more states (p. 160)
comercio interestatal intercambio comercial entre dos o más estados (pág. 160)

Intolerable Acts (1774) laws passed by Parliament to punish the colonists for the Boston Tea Party and to tighten government control of the colonies (p. 102)
Leyes Intolerables (1774) serie de leyes aprobadas por el Parlamento para castigar a los colonos que participaron en el Motín del Té de Boston y para aumentar su control sobre las colonias (pág. 102)

ironclad a warship that is heavily armored with iron (p. 520)
acorazado buque de guerra fuertemente protegido con hierro (pág. 520)

Iroquois League a political confederation of five northeastern Native American nations of the Seneca, Oneida, Mohawk, Cayuga, and Onondaga that made decisions concerning war and peace (p. 14)
Liga de Iroqueses confederación política formada por cinco naciones indígenas del noreste de Estados Unidos (los senecas, los oneidas, los mohawks, los cayugas y los onondagas) para tomar decisiones relacionadas con asuntos de guerra y paz (pág. 14)

isolationism a national policy of avoiding involvement in other countries' affairs (p. 693)
aislacionismo política nacional de evitar involucrarse en los asuntos de otras naciones (pág. 693)

Jacksonian Democracy an expansion of voting rights during the popular Andrew Jackson administration (p. 323)
democracia jacksoniana ampliación del derecho al voto durante el popular gobierno del presidente Andrew Jackson (pág. 323)

Jamestown the first colony in the United States; set up in 1607 along the James River in Virginia (p. 72)
Jamestown primera colonia en territorio estadounidense; fundada en 1607 a orillas del río James en Virginia (pág. 72)

Jay's Treaty (1794) an agreement negotiated by John Jay to work out problems between Britain and the United States over northwestern lands, British seizure of U.S. ships, and U.S. debts owed to the British (p. 245)
Tratado de Jay (1794) acuerdo negociado por John Jay para resolver los problemas entre Gran Bretaña y Estados Unidos por los territorios del noroeste, la confiscación británica de barcos estadounidenses, y las deudas que los estadounidenses les debían a los británicos (pág. 245)

Jim Crow law a law that enforced segregation in the southern states (p. 568)
ley de Jim Crow ley que imponía la segregación en los estados del Sur (pág. 568)

John Brown's raid (1859) an incident in which abolitionist John Brown and 21 other men captured a federal arsenal in Harpers Ferry, Virginia, in hope of starting a slave rebellion (p. 493)
ataque de John Brown (1859) incidente en el que el abolicionista John Brown y otros 21 hombres capturaron un arsenal federal en Harpers Ferry, Virginia, con la esperanza de iniciar una rebelión de esclavos (pág. 493)

joint-stock company a business formed by a group of people who jointly make an investment and share in the profits and losses (p. 27)
sociedad por acciones negocio formado por un grupo de personas que hacen una inversión juntos y comparten las ganancias y las pérdidas (pág. 27)

judicial branch the division of the federal government that is made up of the national courts; interprets laws, punishes criminals, and settles disputes between states (p. 167)
poder judicial división del gobierno federal formada por las cortes nacionales; interpreta las leyes, castiga a los delincuentes y resuelve las disputas entre estados (pág. 167)

judicial review the Supreme Court's power to declare acts of Congress unconstitutional (p. 270)
recurso de inconstitucionalidad poder de la Corte Suprema para declarar inconstitucionales las leyes del Congreso (pág. 270)

Judiciary Act of 1789 legislation passed by Congress that created the federal court system (p. 236)
Ley de Judicatura de 1789 ley aprobada por el Congreso para crear el sistema federal de cortes (pág. 236)

Kansas-Nebraska Act (1854) a law that allowed voters in Kansas and Nebraska to choose whether to allow slavery (p. 485)
Ley de Kansas y Nebraska (1854) ley que permitía a los votantes de Kansas y Nebraska decidir si permitían la esclavitud (pág. 485)

Kentucky and Virginia Resolutions (1798–1799) Republican documents that argued that the Alien and Sedition Acts were unconstitutional (p. 253)
Resoluciones de Kentucky y Virginia (1798–1799) documentos republicanos que argumentaban que las Leyes de No Intervención Extranjera y Sedición eran inconstitucionales (pág. 253)

Kitchen Cabinet President Andrew Jackson's group of informal advisers; so called because they often met in the White House kitchen (p. 324)
gabinete de la cocina grupo informal de consejeros del presidente Andrew Jackson; llamado así porque solían reunirse en la cocina de la Casa Blanca (pág. 324)

kivas underground ceremonial chambers at the center of Anasazi communities (p. 11)
kivas cámaras ceremoniales subterráneas en el centro de las comunidades anasazi (pág. 11)

knights warriors who fought on horseback in return for land from nobles (p. 24)
caballeros guerreros que luchaban a caballo a cambio de tierras de los nobles (pág. 24)

Knights of Labor secret society that became the first truly national labor union in the United States (p. 625)
Caballeros del Trabajo sociedad secreta que se convirtió en el primer sindicato verdaderamente nacional en Estados Unidos (pág. 625)

Know-Nothing Party a political organization founded in 1849 by nativists who supported measures making it difficult for foreigners to become citizens and to hold office (p. 440)
Partido de los Ignorantes organización política fundada en 1849 por un grupo de nativistas; apoyaba medidas que dificultaban que los extranjeros obtuvieran la ciudadanía y que tuvieran cargos públicos (pág. 440)

Ku Klux Klan a secret society created by white southerners in 1866 that used terror and violence to keep African Americans from obtaining their civil rights (p. 566)
Ku Klux Klan sociedad secreta creada en 1866 por blancos del Sur que usaba el terror y la violencia para impedir que los afroamericanos obtuvieran derechos civiles (pág. 566)

Land Ordinance of 1785 legislation passed by Congress authorizing surveys and the division of public lands in the western region of the country (p. 155)
Ordenanza de Territorios de 1785 legislación aprobada por el Congreso en la que se autorizaban las mediciones de terreno y la división de territorios públicos en el oeste del país (pág. 155)

legislative branch the division of the government that proposes bills and passes them into laws (p. 167)
poder legislativo división del gobierno que propone proyectos de ley y los aprueba para convertirlos en leyes (pág. 167)

Lewis and Clark expedition an expedition led by Meriwether Lewis and William Clark that began in 1804 to explore the Louisiana Purchase (p. 275)
expedición de Lewis y Clark expedición encabezada por Meriwether Lewis y William Clark que empezó en 1804 para explorar la Compra de Luisiana (pág. 275)

Lincoln-Douglas debates a series of debates between Republican Abraham Lincoln and Democrat Stephen Douglas during the 1858 U.S. Senate campaign in Illinois (p. 491)
debates Lincoln-Douglas serie de debates entre el republicano Abraham Lincoln y el demócrata Stephen Douglas durante la campaña de 1858 para el Senado estadounidense en Illinois (pág. 491)

Line of Demarcation boundary between Spanish and Portuguese territories in the New World (p. 44)
Línea de Demarcación límite entre los territorios españoles y portugueses en el Nuevo Mundo (pág. 44)

Long Walk (1864) a 300-mile march made by Navajo captives to a reservation in Bosque Redondo, New Mexico, that led to the deaths of hundreds of Navajo (p. 597)
Larga Marcha (1864) caminata de 300 millas que hizo un grupo de prisioneros navajos hasta una reserva indígena en Bosque Redondo, Nuevo México, en la que murieron cientos de ellos (pág. 597)

loose construction a way of interpreting the Constitution that allows the federal government to take actions that the Constitution does not specifically forbid it from taking (p. 242)
interpretación flexible interpretación de la Constitución que permite al gobierno federal tomar acciones que la Constitución no prohíbe de manera específica (pág. 242)

Louisiana Purchase (1803) the purchase of French land between the Mississippi River and the Rocky Mountains that doubled the size of the United States (p. 274)

ENGLISH AND SPANISH GLOSSARY

Compra de Luisiana (1803) adquisición del territorio francés localizado entre el río Mississippi y las montañas Rocallosas que duplicó el tamaño de Estados Unidos (pág. 274)

Lowell system the use of waterpowered textile mills that employed young, unmarried women in the 1800s (p. 392)

sistema de Lowell uso de molinos de agua en la industria textil, dando empleo a muchas mujeres jóvenes solteras en el siglo XIX (pág. 392)

Loyalists colonists who sided with Britain in the American Revolution (p. 119)

leales colonos que apoyaron la causa británica durante la Guerra de Independencia estadounidense (pág. 119)

M

Magna Carta (1215) a charter of liberties agreed to by King John of England, it made the king obey the same laws as citizens (p. 152)

Carta Magna (1215) carta de libertades firmada por el rey Juan de Inglaterra que decía que el rey debía obedecer las mismas leyes que los ciudadanos (pág. 152)

majority rule the idea that policies are decided by the greatest number of people (p. 216)

gobierno de la mayoría idea de que las políticas se adoptan según lo que decida el mayor número de personas (pág. 216)

manifest destiny a belief shared by many Americans in the mid-1800s that the United States should expand across the continent to the Pacific Ocean (p. 354)

destino manifiesto creencia de muchos ciudadanos estadounidenses a mediados del siglo XIX de que Estados Unidos debía expandirse por todo el continente hasta el océano Pacífico (pág. 354)

Marbury v. *Madison* (1803) U.S. Supreme Court case that established the principle of judicial review (p. 270)

Marbury contra *Madison* (1803) caso de la Corte Suprema de Estados Unidos que estableció recurso de inconstitucionalidad (pág. 270)

Massacre at Wounded Knee (1890) the U.S. Army's killing of approximately 150 Sioux at Wounded Knee Creek in South Dakota; ended U.S-Indian wars on the Plains (p. 597)

masacre de Wounded Knee (1890) matanza de aproximadamente 150 indios siux en Wounded Knee Creek, Dakota del Sur; dio por terminadas las guerras entre estadounidenses e indígenas en las Planicies (pág. 597)

mass culture leisure and cultural activities shared by many people (p. 644)

cultura de masas actividades culturales y del tiempo libre que les gustan a muchas personas (pág. 644)

mass production the efficient production of large numbers of identical goods (p. 387)

producción en masa producción eficiente de grandes cantidades de productos idénticos (pág. 387)

mass transit public transportation (p. 644)

transporte colectivo transporte público (pág. 644)

matrilineal related to ancestry traced through the maternal, or mother's, line (p. 14)

materno basado en linaje seguido por línea materna, o de la madre (pág. 14)

Mayflower Compact (1620) a document written by the Pilgrims establishing themselves as a political society and setting guidelines for self-government (p. 79)

Pacto del Mayflower (1620) documento redactado por los peregrinos en el que se establecían como sociedad política y establecían principios para gobernarse a sí mismos (pág. 79)

McCulloch v. *Maryland* (1819) U.S. Supreme Court case that declared the Second Bank of the United States was constitutional and that Maryland could not interfere with it (p. 330)

McCulloch contra *Maryland* (1819) caso de la Corte Suprema de Estados Unidos que declaraba que el Segundo Banco de la Nación era constitucional y que Maryland no podía intervenir en sus operaciones (pág. 330)

mercenaries hired foreign soldiers (p. 128)

mercenario s soldados extranjeros a sueldo (pág. 128)

Mexican Revolution a revolution led by Francisco Madero in 1910 that eventually forced the Mexican dictator Díaz to resign (p. 708)

Revolución Mexicana revolución iniciada en 1910 por Francisco Madero, que finalmente obligó al dictador mexicano Díaz a renunciar (pág. 708)

middle class the social and economic level between the wealthy and the poor (p. 440)

clase media nivel social y económico ubicado entre la clase rica y la clase pobre (pág. 440)

Middle Passage a voyage that brought enslaved Africans across the Atlantic Ocean to North America and the West Indies (p. 59)

Viaje Intermedio viaje a través del océano Atlántico para transportar esclavos africanos a América del Norte y a las Antillas (pág. 59)

migration the movement of people from one region to another (p. 6)

migración movimiento de personas de una región a otra (pág. 6)

minutemen American colonial militia members ready to fight at a minute's notice (p. 114)

minutemen milicanos norteamericanos en la época colonial que estaban preparados para combatir en cualquier momento si la situación lo requería (pág. 114)

Missouri Compromise (1820) an agreement proposed by Henry Clay that allowed Missouri to enter the Union as a slave state and Maine to enter as a free state and outlawed slavery in any territories or states north of 36°30´ latitude (p. 305)
Compromiso de Missouri (1820) acuerdo propuesto por Henry Clay en el que se aceptaba a Missouri en la Unión como estado esclavista y a Maine como estado libre, además de prohibir la esclavitud en los territorios o estados al norte del paralelo 36°30´ (pág. 305)

monopoly a complete control over the entire supply of goods or a service in a particular market (p. 622)
monopolio control absoluto de toda la oferta de bienes o de un servicio en un mercado en particular (pág. 622)

Monroe Doctrine (1823) President James Monroe's statement forbidding further colonization in the Americas and declaring that any attempt by a foreign country to colonize would be considered an act of hostility (p. 300)
Doctrina Monroe (1823) declaración hecha por el presidente James Monroe en la que se prohibía la colonización adicional de las Américas y se declaraba que cualquier intento de colonización por parte de otro país se consideraría un acto hostil (pág. 300)

Mormon a member of the Church of Jesus Christ of Latter-day Saints (p. 349)
mormón miembro de la Iglesia de Jesucristo de los Santos de los Últimos Días (pág. 349)

Morrill Act (1862) a federal law passed by Congress that gave land to western states to encourage them to build colleges (p. 600)
Ley de Morrill (1862) ley federal aprobada por el Congreso que otorgaba tierras a los estados del Oeste para fomentar la construcción de universidades (pág. 600)

Morse code a system developed by Alfred Lewis Vail for the telegraph that used a certain combination of dots and dashes to represent each letter of the alphabet (p. 403)
clave Morse sistema desarrollado por Alfred Lewis Vail para el telégrafo en el que una combinación de puntos y rayas representa cada letra del alfabeto (pág. 403)

mosques buildings used for Muslim prayer (p. 19)
mezquitas casas de oración musulmanas (pág. 19)

mountain men men hired by eastern companies to trap animals for fur in the Rocky Mountains and other western regions of the United States (p. 346)
montañeses hombres contratados por compañías del este para atrapar animales y obtener sus pieles en las montañas Rocallosas y en otras regiones del oeste de Estados Unidos (pág. 346)

muckrakers a term coined for journalists who "raked up" and exposed corruption and problems of society (p. 664)
muckrakers término acuñado para nombrar a los periodistas que se dedicaban a investigar y exponer la corrupción y los problemas de la sociedad (pág. 664)

National American Woman Suffrage Association (NAWSA) an organization founded by Elizabeth Cady Stanton and Susan B. Anthony in 1890 to obtain women's right to vote (p. 676)
Asociación Nacional Americana para el Sufragio Femenino (NAWSA, por sus siglas en inglés) organización fundada en 1890 por Elizabeth Cady Stanton y Susan B. Anthony para obtener el derecho al voto de las mujeres (pág. 676)

National Association for the Advancement of Colored People (NAACP) an organization founded in 1909 by W. E. B. Du Bois and other reformers to bring attention to racial inequality (p. 678)
Asociación Nacional para el Progreso de la Gente de Color (NAACP, por sus siglas en inglés) organización fundada en 1909 por W. E. B. Du Bois y otros reformadores para llamar la atención sobre la desigualdad racial (pág. 678)

national debt the total amount of money owed by a country to its lenders (p. 238)
deuda pública cantidad total de dinero que un país debe a quienes se lo prestaron (pág. 238)

National Grange a social and educational organization for farmers (p. 603)
National Grange organización social y educativa para los agricultores (pág. 603)

nationalism a sense of pride and devotion to a nation (p. 302)
nacionalismo sentimiento de orgullo y lealtad a una nación (pág. 302)

nativists U.S. citizens who opposed immigration because they were suspicious of immigrants and feared losing jobs to them (p. 440)
nativistas ciudadanos estadounidenses que se oponían a la inmigración porque sospechaban de los inmigrantes y temían que se apropiaran de sus empleos (pág. 440)

Nat Turner's Rebellion (1831) a rebellion in which Nat Turner led a group of slaves in Virginia in an unsuccessful attempt to overthrow and kill planter families (p. 428)
Rebelión de Nat Turner (1831) rebelión de un grupo de esclavos encabezados por Nat Turner en Virginia en un intento frustrado de derrocar y asesinar familias que eran dueñas de plantaciones (pág. 428)

naturalized citizen a person born in another country who has been granted citizenship in the United States (p. 222)
ciudadano naturalizado persona nacida en otro país que ha obtenido la ciudadanía estadounidense (pág. 222)

Neutrality Proclamation (1793) a statement made by President George Washington that the United States would not side with any of the nations at war in Europe following the French Revolution (p. 244)
Proclamación de Neutralidad (1793) declaración en la que el presidente George Washington anunció que Estados Unidos no sería aliado de ninguna de las naciones europeas en guerra después de la Revolución Francesa (pág. 244)

new immigrant a term often used for an immigrant who arrived in the United States beginning in the 1880s (p. 636)
nuevo inmigrante término empleado a menudo para referirse a los inmigrantes que llegaron a Estados Unidos a partir de la década de 1880 (pág. 636)

New Jersey Plan a proposal to create a unicameral legislature with equal representation of states rather than representation by population; rejected at the Constitutional Convention (p. 165)
Plan de Nueva Jersey propuesta para la creación de un gobierno de una cámara con la misma representación para cada estado sin importar el tamaño de su población; fue rechazada en la Convención Constitucional (pág. 165)

Nineteenth Amendment (1920) a constitutional amendment that gave women the vote (p. 677)
Decimonovena Enmienda (1920) enmienda constitucional que dio a la mujer el derecho al voto (pág. 677)

nominating conventions a meeting at which a political party selects its presidential and vice presidential candidate; first held in the 1820s (p. 323)
convenciones de nominación reunión en la que un partido político elige a sus candidatos a la presidencia y la vicepresidencia; se realizaron por primera vez en la década de 1820 (pág. 323)

Non-Intercourse Act (1809) a law that replaced the Embargo Act and restored trade with all nations except Britain, France, and their colonies (p. 280)
Ley de No Interacción (1809) ley que reemplazaba a la Ley de Embargo, restableciendo el comercio con todas las naciones, excepto Gran Bretaña, Francia y sus colonias (pág. 280)

Northwest Ordinance of 1787 legislation passed by Congress to establish a political structure for the Northwest Territory and create a system for the admission of new states (p. 155)
Ordenanza del Noroeste de 1787 legislación aprobada por el Congreso para establecer una estructura política en el Territorio del Noroeste y crear un proceso de admisión de nuevos estados (pág. 155)

Northwest Passage a nonexistent path through North America that early explorers searched for that would allow ships to sail from the Atlantic to the Pacific Ocean (p. 54)
Paso del Noroeste ruta inexistente buscada por muchos exploradores a lo largo de América del Norte para cruzar en barco del océano Atlántico al océano Pacífico (pág. 54)

Northwest Territory lands including present-day Illinois, Indiana, Michigan, Ohio, and Wisconsin; organized by the Northwest Ordinance of 1787 (p. 155)
Territorio del Noroeste región que incluía los actuales estados de Illinois, Indiana, Michigan, Ohio y Wisconsin; creado por la Ordenanza del Noroeste de 1787 (pág. 155)

nullification crisis a dispute led by John C. Calhoun that said that states could ignore federal laws if they believed those laws violated the Constitution (p. 328)
crisis de anulación controversia iniciada por John C. Calhoun que decía que los estados no tenían que hacer caso a las leyes federales si consideraban que desobedecían la Constitución (pág. 328)

O

old immigrant a term often used for an immigrant who arrived in the United States before the 1880s (p. 636)
antiguo inmigrante término empleado con frecuencia para referirse a los inmigrantes que llegaron a Estados Unidos antes de la década de 1880 (pág. 636)

Open Door Policy a policy established by the United States in 1899 to promote equal access for all nations to trade in China (p. 695)
política de puertas abiertas política establecida por Estados Unidos en 1899 para promover el acceso igualitario de todas las naciones al comercio con China (pág. 695)

Oregon Trail a 2,000-mile trail stretching through the Great Plains from western Missouri to the Oregon Territory (p. 348)
Camino de Oregón ruta de 2,000 millas que cruzaba las Grandes Planicies desde el oeste de Missouri hasta el Territorio de Oregón (pág. 348)

P

Paleo-Indians the first Americans who crossed from Asia into North America sometime between 38,000 and 10,000 BC (p. 6)
paleoindígenas primeros habitantes de América que cruzaron de Asia a América del Norte entre 38,000 y 10,000 a. C. (pág. 6)

Panama Canal an artificial waterway across the Isthmus of Panama; completed by the United States in 1914 (p. 705)

canal de Panamá canal artificial que atraviesa el istmo de Panamá; Estados Unidos completó su construcción en 1914 (pág. 705)

Panic of 1837 a financial crisis in the United States that led to an economic depression (p. 331)

Pánico de 1837 crisis financiera en Estados Unidos que provocó una depresión económica (pág. 331)

pardon freedom from punishment (p. 185)

indulto liberación de un castigo (pág. 185)

patent an exclusive right to make or sell an invention (p. 616)

patente derecho exclusivo para fabricar o vender un invento (pág. 616)

Patriots American colonists who fought for independence from Great Britain during the Revolutionary War (p. 113)

patriotas colonos norteamericanos que lucharon para independizarse de Gran Bretaña durante la Guerra de Independencia estadounidense (pág. 113)

petition to make a formal request of the government (p. 217)

peticionar hacer una solicitud formal al gobierno (pág. 217)

Pickett's Charge (1863) a failed Confederate attack during the Civil War led by General George Pickett at the Battle of Gettysburg (p. 539)

ataque de Pickett (1863) ataque fallido del ejército confederado, al mando del general George Pickett, en la batalla de Gettysburg durante la Guerra Civil (pág. 539)

Pilgrim a member of a Puritan Separatist sect that left England in the early 1600s to settle in the Americas (p. 78)

peregrino miembro de una secta separatista puritana que se fue de Inglaterra a principios del siglo XVII para establecerse en América (pág. 78)

Pinckney's Treaty (1795) an agreement between the United States and Spain that changed Florida's border and made it easier for American ships to use the port of New Orleans (p. 245)

Tratado de Pinckney (1795) acuerdo entre Estados Unidos y España que modificó los límites de Florida y facilitó a los barcos estadounidenses el uso del puerto de Nueva Orleáns (pág. 245)

placer miner a person who mines for gold by using pans or other devices to wash gold nuggets out of loose rock and gravel (p. 366)

buscador de oro con batea persona que busca oro con bateas u otros aparatos similares para lavar las pepitas de oro y separarlas de las piedras y la gravilla (pág. 366)

plantation a large farm that usually specialized in growing one kind of crop for profit (p. 50)

plantación gran finca que por lo general se especializaba en un cultivo específico para obtener ganancias (pág. 50)

planter a large-scale farmer who held more than 20 slaves (p. 416)

hacendado agricultor a gran escala que tenía más de 20 esclavos (pág. 416)

Platt Amendment a part of the Cuban constitution drafted under the supervision of the United States that limited Cuba's right to make treaties, gave the U.S. the right to intervene in Cuban affairs, and required Cuba to sell or lease land to the U.S (p. 701)

Enmienda Platt parte de la constitución cubana redactada bajo la supervisión de Estados Unidos que limitaba el derecho de Cuba a firmar tratados, le daba a Estados Unidos el derecho de intervenir en los asuntos cubanos y le exigía a Cuba vender o arrendar tierras a Estados Unidos (pág. 701)

Plessy v. Ferguson (1896) U.S. Supreme Court case that established the "separate-but-equal" doctrine for public facilities (p. 569)

Plessy contra *Ferguson* (1896) caso en el que la Corte Suprema de Estados Unidos estableció la doctrina de "separados pero iguales" en los lugares públicos (pág. 569)

political action committee (PAC) an organization that collects money to distribute to candidates who support the same issues as the contributors (p. 224)

comité de acción política (PAC, por sus siglas en inglés) organización que recolecta dinero para distribuirlo a los candidatos que apoyen los mismos asuntos que los contribuyentes (pág. 224)

political machine a powerful organization that influenced city and county politics in the late 1800s (p. 662)

maquinaria política organización poderosa que influía en la política municipal y del condado a finales del siglo XIX (pág. 662)

political party a group of people who organize to help elect government officials and influence government policies (p. 250)

partido político grupo de personas que se organiza para facilitar la elección de los funcionarios del gobierno e influye en las políticas del gobierno (pág. 250)

poll tax a special tax that a person had to pay in order to vote (p. 568)

impuesto electoral impuesto especial que tenía que pagar una persona para poder votar (pág. 568)

Pony Express a system of messengers that carried mail between relay stations on a route 2,000-miles long in 1860 and 1861 (p. 590)

Pony Express sistema de mensajeros que llevaban el correo entre estaciones de relevo a lo largo de una ruta de 2,000 millas en 1860 y 1861 (pág. 590)

popular sovereignty the idea that political authority belongs to the people (p. 167, 476)
soberanía popular idea de que la autoridad política pertenece al pueblo (pág. 167, 476)

Populist Party a political party formed in 1892 that supported free coinage of silver, work reforms, immigration restrictions, and government ownership of railroads and telegraph and telephone systems (p. 604)
Partido Populista partido político formado en 1892 que apoyaba la libre producción de monedas de plata, reformas laborales y restricciones de la inmigración, además de asignar al gobierno la propiedad de los sistemas ferroviario, telegráfico y telefónico (pág. 604)

Pottawatomie Massacre (1856) an incident in which abolitionist John Brown and seven other men murdered pro-slavery Kansans (p. 487)
masacre de Pottawatomie (1856) incidente en el que el abolicionista John Brown y siete hombres más asesinaron a habitantes esclavistas de Kansas (pág. 487)

precedent an action or decision that later serves as an example (p. 235)
precedente acción o decisión que más tarde sirve de ejemplo (pág. 235)

privateer a private ship authorized by a nation to attack its enemies (p. 244)
corsario barco privado autorizado por una nación para atacar a sus enemigos (pág. 244)

Progressives a group of reformers who worked to improve social and political problems in the late 1800s (p. 664)
progresistas grupo de reformistas que trabajaron para resolver problemas sociales y políticos a finales del siglo XIX (pág. 664)

Progressive Party a short-lived political party that attempted to institute social reforms (p. 682)
Partido Progresista partido político de poca duración que intentó establecer reformas sociales (pág. 682)

prospect to search for gold (p. 366)
prospectar buscar oro (pág. 366)

Protestant Reformation a religious movement begun by Martin Luther and others in 1517 to reform the Catholic Church (p. 53)
Reforma Protestante movimiento religioso iniciado por Martín Lutero y otros en 1517 para reformar la Iglesia católica (pág. 53)

Protestants reformers who protested certain practices of the Catholic Church (p. 53)
protestantes reformistas que protestaban por ciertas prácticas de la Iglesia católica (pág. 53)

pueblos above ground houses made of a heavy clay called adobe that were built by Native Americans of the southwestern United States (p. 11)

pueblos casas de arcilla gruesa, llamada adobe, construidas más arriba de la superficie por indígenas del suroeste de Estados Unidos (pág. 11)

Pullman strike (1894) a railroad strike that ended when President Grover Cleveland sent in federal troops (p. 627)
huelga de Pullman (1894) huelga del ferrocarril que terminó cuando el presidente Grover Cleveland envió a tropas federales (pág. 627)

Pure Food and Drug Act (1906) a law that set regulatory standards for industries involved in preparing food (p. 681)
Ley de Alimentos y Medicamentos Puros (1906) ley que estableció normas regulatorias para las industrias de preparación de productos alimenticios (pág. 681)

Puritans Protestants who wanted to reform the Church of England (p. 78)
puritanos protestantes que querían reformar la Iglesia anglicana (pág. 78)

Q

Quakers Society of Friends; Protestant sect founded in 1640s in England whose members believed that salvation was available to all people (p. 86)
cuáqueros Sociedad de Amigos; secta protestante fundada en la década de 1640 en Inglaterra cuyos miembros creían que la salvación estaba al alcance de todos (pág. 86)

Quartering Act (1774) One of the Coercive or Intolerable Acts that helped fan the flames of revolution in the English colonies. It required each colonist to provide a place in their home, or quarter, for British soldiers. (p. 92)
Ley de Acuartelamiento (1774) Uno de los actos coersitivos o intolerables que ayudó a inspirar la revolución en las colonias inglesas. Requería que cada colono proveyera alojamiento en su casa para los soldados británicos. (pág. 92)

R

Radical Republicans members of Congress who felt that southern states needed to make great social changes before they could be readmitted to the Union (p. 559)
republicanos radicales miembros del Congreso convencidos de que los estados del Sur necesitaban hacer grandes cambios sociales antes de volver a ser admitidos en la Unión (pág. 559)

ratification an official approval (p. 154)
ratificación aprobación formal (pág. 154)

reason clear and ordered thinking; Greek philosopher Aristotle believed it was the basis of a good life (p. 22)
razón ideas claras y ordenadas; el filósofo griego Aristóteles pensaba que la razón era la base de una vida buena (pág. 22)

recall a vote to remove an official from office (p. 666)
destitución votación para sacar a un funcionario de su cargo (pág. 666)

Reconstruction (1865–1877) the period following the Civil War during which the U.S. government worked to reunite the nation and to rebuild the southern states (p. 552)
Reconstrucción (1865–1877) período posterior a la Guerra Civil en el que el gobierno de Estados Unidos trabajó por reunificar de la nación y reconstruir los estados del Sur (pág. 552)

Reconstruction Acts (1867–1868) the laws that put the southern states under U.S. military control and required them to draft new constitutions upholding the Fourteenth Amendment (p. 561)
Leyes de Reconstrucción (1867–1868) leyes que declaraban a los estados del Sur territorio sujeto al control militar estadounidense y los obligaban a reformar sus constituciones de manera que defendieran la Decimocuarta Enmienda (pág. 561)

Redcoats British soldiers who fought against the colonists in the American Revolution; so called because of their bright red uniforms (p. 114)
casacas rojas soldados británicos que lucharon contra los colonos en la Guerra de Independencia estadounidense, llamados así por el color rojo fuerte de sus uniformes (pág. 114)

referendum a procedure that allows voters to approve or reject a law already proposed or passed by government (p. 666)
referéndum proceso que permite a los votantes aprobar o rechazar una ley previamente propuesta o aprobada por el gobierno (pág. 666)

Republican Party a political party formed in the 1850s to stop the spread of slavery in the West (p. 488)
Partido Republicano partido político formado en la década de 1850 para detener la expansión de la esclavitud en el Oeste (pág. 488)

reservations federal lands set aside for American Indians (p. 595)
reservas territorios federales reservados para los indígenas norteamericanos (pág. 595)

Rhode Island system a system developed by Samuel Slater in the mid-1800s in which whole families were hired as textile workers and factory work was divided into simple tasks (p. 391)
sistema de Rhode Island sistema desarrollado por Samuel Slater a mediados del siglo XIX mediante el cual se contrataba a familias completas para trabajar en la industria textil y en el que el trabajo de las fábricas estaba dividido en tareas sencillas (pág. 391)

Rush-Bagot Agreement (1817) an agreement that limited naval power on the Great Lakes for both the United States and British Canada (p. 298)
Acuerdo de Rush-Bagot (1817) acuerdo que limitaba el poder naval de Estados Unidos y la Canadá británica en los Grandes Lagos (pág. 298)

Santa Fe Trail an important trade trail west from Independence, Missouri, to Santa Fe, New Mexico (p. 349)
Camino de Santa Fe importante ruta comercial que va desde Independence, Missouri, hasta Santa Fe, Nuevo México (pág. 349)

search warrant a judge's order authorizing the search of a person's home or property to look for evidence of a crime (p. 218)
orden de registro orden de un juez que permite registrar el hogar y las pertenencias de una persona en busca de pruebas de un delito (pág. 218)

secede to formally withdraw from the Union (p. 478)
separarse salirse formalmente de la Unión (pág. 478)

Second Battle of Bull Run (1862) a Civil War battle in which the Confederate army forced most of the Union army out of Virginia (p. 518)
segunda batalla de Bull Run (1862) batalla de la Guerra Civil en la que el ejército confederado obligó a gran parte del ejército de la Unión a abandonar Virginia (pág. 518)

Second Continental Congress (1775) a meeting of colonial delegates in Philadelphia to decide how to react to fighting at Lexington and Concord (p. 114)
Segundo Congreso Continental (1775) reunión de delegados coloniales en Filadelfia para decidir cómo reaccionar ante la lucha en Lexington y Concord (pág. 114)

Second Great Awakening a period of religious evangelism that began in the 1790s and became widespread in the United States by the 1830s (p. 448)
Segundo Gran Despertar período de evangelización religiosa iniciado en la década de 1790 que se extendió por Estados Unidos para la década de 1830 (pág. 448)

Second Industrial Revolution a period of rapid growth in manufacturing and industry in the late 1800s (p. 615)
Segunda Revolución Industrial período de gran crecimiento en la manufactura y en la industria a finales del siglo XIX (pág. 615)

sectionalism a devotion to the interests of one geographic region over the interests of the country as a whole (p. 304, 477)

regionalismo lealtad a los intereses de una región geográfica más que a los del país entero (págs 304, 477)

segregation the forced separation of people of different races in public places (p. 568)

segregación separación obligada de personas de diferentes razas en lugares públicos (pág. 568)

Seneca Falls Convention (1848) the first national women's rights convention at which the Declaration of Sentiments was written (p. 464)

Convención de Seneca Falls (1848) primera convención nacional a favor de los derechos de la mujer, en la cual se redactó la Declaración de Sentimientos (pág. 464)

settlement houses neighborhood centers staffed by professionals and volunteers for education, recreation, and social activities in poor areas (p. 648)

organizaciones de servicio a la comunidad centros comunitarios atendidos por profesionales y voluntarios para ofrecer educación, recreación y actividades sociales en zonas pobres (pág. 648)

Seven Days' Battles (1862) a series of Civil War battles in which Confederate army successes forced the Union army to retreat from Richmond, Virginia, the Confederate capital (p. 518)

batallas de los Siete Días (1862) serie de batallas de la Guerra Civil en las que las victorias del ejército confederado obligaron a las tropas de la Unión a retirarse de Richmond, Virginia, la capital confederada (pág. 518)

Seventeenth Amendment (1913) a constitutional amendment allowing American voters to directly elect U.S. senators (p. 666)

Decimoséptima Enmienda (1913) enmienda constitucional que permite a los votantes estadounidenses elegir directamente a los senadores de Estados Unidos (pág. 666)

sharecropping a system used on southern farms after the Civil War in which farmers worked land owned by someone else in return for a small portion of the crops (p. 569)

cultivo de aparceros sistema usado en las granjas sureñas después de la Guerra Civil en el que los agricultores trabajaban las tierras de otra persona a cambio de una pequeña porción de la cosecha (pág. 569)

Shays's Rebellion (1786-87) an uprising of Massachusetts's farmers, led by Daniel Shays, to protest high taxes, heavy debt, and farm foreclosures (p. 161)

Rebelión de Shays (1786-87) rebelión de agricultores de Massachusetts, encabezados por Daniel Shays, para protestar por los altos impuestos, las grandes deudas y el embargo de las granjas (pág. 161)

Sherman Antitrust Act (1890) a law that made it illegal to create monopolies or trusts that restrained free trade (p. 622)

Ley Antimonopolio de Sherman (1890) ley que prohibía la creación de monopolios o consorcios que restringieran el libre comercio (pág. 622)

Siege of Vicksburg (1863) the Union army's six-week blockade of Vicksburg that led the city to surrender during the Civil War (p. 524)

Sitio de Vicksburg (1863) bloqueo de seis semanas realizado por el ejército de la Unión en Vicksburg para forzar la rendición de esa ciudad durante la Guerra Civil (pág. 524)

Sixteenth Amendment (1913) an amendment to the Constitution that allows personal income to be taxed (p. 683)

Decimosexta Enmienda (1913) enmienda constitucional que permite los impuestos sobre los ingresos personales (pág. 683)

slave codes laws passed in the colonies to control slaves (p. 77)

códigos de esclavos leyes aprobadas por las colonias para controlar a los esclavos (pág. 77)

social Darwinism a view of society based on Charles Darwin's scientific theory of natural selection (p. 621)

darwinismo social visión de la sociedad basada en la teoría científica de la selección natural de Charles Darwin (pág. 621)

socialism economic system in which the government owns and operates a country's means of production (p. 674)

socialismo sistema económico en el que el gobierno controla y maneja los medios de producción de un país (pág. 674)

sodbusters the name given to Plains farmers who worked hard to break up the region's tough sod (p. 601)

sodbusters nombre dado a los agricultores de las Planicies que se esforzaron mucho para trabajar el duro terreno de la región (pág. 601)

Spanish Armada a large Spanish fleet defeated by England in 1588 (p. 53)

Armada española gran flota española derrotada por las tropas de Inglaterra en 1588 (pág. 53)

speculator an investor who buys items at low prices in hope that their values will rise (p. 239)

especulador inversionista que compra artículos a precios bajos con la esperanza de que su valor aumente (pág. 239)

sphere of influence an area where foreign countries control trade or natural resources of another nation or area (p. 695)

esfera de influencia nación o lugar cuyos recursos naturales y comercio son controlados por otro país (pág. 695)

spirituals emotional Christian songs sung by enslaved people in the South that mixed African and European elements and usually expressed slaves' religious beliefs (p. 427)
espirituales canciones religiosas emotivas cantadas por los esclavos del Sur que combinaban elementos de origen africano y europeo y solían expresar sus creencias religiosas (pág. 427)

spoils system a politicians' practice of giving government jobs to his or her supporters (p. 324)
tráfico de influencias práctica de los políticos de ofrecer empleos a las personas que los apoyan (pág. 324)

Stamp Act of 1765 a law passed by Parliament that raised tax money by requiring colonists to pay for an official stamp whenever they bought paper items such as newspapers, licenses, and legal documents (p. 100)
Ley del Sello de 1765 ley aprobada por el Parlamento para recaudar impuestos en la que se obligaba a los colonos a pagar un sello oficial cada vez que compraran artículos de papel, como periódicos, licencias y documentos legales (pág. 100)

staple crop a crop that is continuously in demand (p. 87)
cultivo básico cultivo de demanda constante (pág. 87)

states' rights doctrine the belief that the power of the states should be greater than the power of the federal government (p. 328)
doctrina de los derechos estatales creencia de que el poder de los estados debe ser mayor que el del gobierno federal (pág. 328)

steerage the area on a ship in the lower levels where the steering mechanisms were located and where cramped quarters were provided for people who could only afford cheap passage (p. 637)
tercera clase nivel inferior un barco en el que se encontraban los mecanismos del timón y se ofrecían habitaciones reducidas para las personas que sólo podían comprar un pasaje barato (pág. 637)

strict construction a way of interpreting the Constitution that allows the federal government to take only those actions the Constitution specifically says it can take (p. 242)
interpretación estricta interpretación de la Constitución que sólo permite al gobierno federal hacer las acciones mencionadas específicamente en ella (pág. 242)

strike the refusal of workers to perform their jobs until employers meet their demands (p. 394)
huelga negativa de los empleados a trabajar hasta que sus empleadores satisfagan sus demandas (pág. 394)

suburb a neighborhood outside of a downtown area (p. 644)
suburbio vecindario en las afueras de una ciudad (pág. 644)

suffrage voting rights (p. 153)
sufragio derecho al voto (pág. 153)

sweatshops hot, stuffy workshops in which workers prepare materials for low wages (p. 640)
fábricas explotadoras talleres calurosos y con el aire cargado en los cuales los trabajadores preparan materiales por salarios reducidos (pág. 640)

tariff a tax on imports or exports (p. 159)
arancel impuesto pagado por las importaciones o exportaciones (pág. 159)

Tariff of Abominations (1828) the nickname given to a tariff by southerners who opposed it (p. 327)
Arancel de Abominaciones (1828) sobrenombre dado a un arancel por los habitantes del Sur que se oponían a éste (pág. 327)

Tea Act (1773) a law passed by Parliament allowing the British East India Company to sell its low-cost tea directly to the colonies, undermining colonial tea merchants; led to the Boston Tea Party (p. 102)
Ley del Té (1773) ley aprobada por el Parlamento británico que le permitía a la British East India Company vender té a bajo costo a las colonias directamente, afectando a los comerciantes de té coloniales; dio origen al Motín del Té de Boston (pág. 102)

technology the tools used to produce goods or to do work (p. 387)
tecnología herramientas utilizadas para producir bienes o realizar un trabajo (pág. 387)

teepees cone-shaped shelters made of buffalo skins used by Native Americans in the Plains region (p. 14)
tipis viviendas en forma de cono hechas de piel de búfalo que usaban los indígenas norteamericanos en la región de las Planicies (pág. 14)

telegraph a machine perfected by Samuel F. B. Morse in 1832 that uses pulses of electric current to send messages across long distances through wires (p. 402)
telégrafo máquina perfeccionada por Samuel F. B. Morse en 1832 que emplea impulsos eléctricos transmitidos por cables para enviar mensajes a grandes distancias (pág. 402)

Teller Amendment (1898) a congressional resolution stating that the U.S. had no interest in taking control of Cuba (p. 698)
Enmienda Teller (1898) resolución del Congreso en la que Estados Unidos declaró que no tenía intención de tomar el control de Cuba (pág. 698)

ENGLISH AND SPANISH GLOSSARY

ENGLISH AND SPANISH GLOSSARY

temperance movement a social reform effort begun in the mid-1800s to encourage people to drink less alcohol (p. 449)
movimiento de abstinencia movimiento de reforma social iniciado a mediados del siglo XIX para promover el que las personas bebieran menos alcohol (pág. 449)

tenements poorly built, overcrowded housing where many immigrants lived (p. 442)
casas de vecindad viviendas mal construidas y llenas de gente donde vivían muchos inmigrantes (pág. 442)

Ten Percent Plan President Abraham Lincoln's plan for Reconstruction; once 10 percent of voters in a former Confederate state took a U.S. loyalty oath, they could form a new state government and be readmitted to the Union (p. 553)
Plan del Diez por Ciento plan de Reconstrucción del presidente Abraham Lincoln; si el 10 por ciento de los votantes de un estado que había sido confederado juraba lealtad a la nación, podían formar un nuevo gobierno y ser readmitidos en la Unión (pág. 553)

textile cloth (p. 385)
textil tela (pág. 385)

Thirteenth Amendment (1865) a constitutional amendment that outlawed slavery (p. 554)
Decimotercera Enmienda (1865) enmienda constitucional que prohibió la esclavitud (pág. 554)

Three-Fifths Compromise (1787) an agreement worked out at the Constitutional Convention stating that only three-fifths of the slaves in a state would count when determining a state's population for representation in the lower house of Congress (p. 166)
Compromiso de las Tres Quintas Partes (1787) acuerdo negociado durante la Convención Constitucional en el que se estableció que solamente tres quintas de los esclavos en un estado contrarían para al determinar la representación de ese estado en la cámara baja del Congreso (pág. 166)

Toleration Act of 1649 a Maryland law that made restricting the religious rights of Christians a crime; the first law guaranteeing religious freedom to be passed in America (p. 75)
Ley de Tolerancia de 1649 ley de Maryland que calificaba como delito la restricción de los derechos religiosos de los cristianos; fue la primera ley que garantizó la libertad religiosa en América (pág. 75)

total war a type of war in which an army destroys its opponent's ability to fight by targeting civilian and economic as well as military resources (p. 542)
guerra total tipo de guerra en la que un ejército destruye la capacidad de lucha de su oponente mediante ataques a la población civil y a la economía así como a los recursos militares (pág. 542)

totems images of ancestors or animal spirits; often carved onto tall, wooden poles by Native American peoples of the Pacific Northwest (p. 12)

tótems imágenes de antepasados o espíritus de animales; a menudo talladas en altos troncos de madera por los indígenas americanos de la costa noroeste del Pacífico (pág. 12)

town meeting a political meeting at which people make decisions on local issues; used primarily in New England (p. 91)
reunión del pueblo reunión política en la que las personas toman decisiones sobre temas locales; se usan principalmente en Nueva Inglaterra (pág. 91)

trade unions workers' organizations that try to improve working conditions (p. 394)
sindicatos organizaciones de trabajadores que intentan mejorar sus condiciones laborales (pág. 394)

Trail of Tears (1838-39) an 800-mile forced march made by the Cherokee from their homeland in Georgia to Indian Territory; resulted in the deaths of almost one fourth of the Cherokee people (p. 334)
Ruta de las Lágrimas (1838-39) marcha forzada de 800 millas que hicieron los cheroquíes desde su territorio natal en Georgia hasta el Territorio Indígena, y en la que perdió la vida casi una cuarta parte del pueblo cheroquí (pág. 334)

transcendentalism the idea that people could rise above the material things in life; a popular movement among New England writers and thinkers in the mid-1800s (p. 443)
trascendentalismo creencia de que las personas podían prescindir de los objetos materiales en la vida; movimiento popular entre los escritores y pensadores de Nueva Inglaterra a mediados del siglo XIX (pág. 443)

transcontinental railroad a railroad system that crossed the continental United States; construction began in 1863 (p. 590)
tren transcontinental línea ferroviaria que cruzaba Estados Unidos de un extremo a otro; su construcción se inició en 1863 (pág. 590)

Transportation Revolution the rapid growth in the speed and convenience of transportation (p. 396)
Revolución del Transporte rápido desarrollo de la velocidad y comodidad de los medios de transporte (pág. 396)

Treaty of Fort Jackson (1814) a treaty signed after the U.S. victory at the Battle of Horseshoe Bend; the Creek were forced to give up 23 million acres of their land (p. 286)
Tratado del Fuerte Jackson (1814) tratado que se firmó tras la victoria de Estados Unidos en la batalla de Horseshoe Bend; los indígenas creek se vieron obligados a ceder 23 millones de acres de su territorio (pág. 286)

Treaty of Fort Laramie (1851) a treaty signed in Wyoming by the United States and northern Plains nations (p. 594)
Tratado del Fuerte Laramie (1851) tratado firmado en Wyoming por Estados Unidos y las naciones indígenas de las Planicies del norte (pág. 594)

Treaty of Ghent (1814) a treaty signed by the United States and Britain ending the War of 1812 (p. 287)
Tratado de Gante (1814) tratado firmado por Estados Unidos y Gran Bretaña para dar fin a la Guerra de 1812 (pág. 287)

Treaty of Greenville (1795) an agreement between Native American confederation leaders and the U.S. government that gave the United States Indian lands in the Northwest Territory and guaranteed that U.S. citizens could safely travel through the region (p. 247)
Tratado de Greenville (1795) acuerdo entre los líderes de la confederación de indígenas norteamericanos y el gobierno estadounidense que otorgó a Estados Unidos tierras indígenas en el Territorio del Noroeste y garantizó la seguridad a los ciudadanos estadounidenses que viajaran por la región (pág. 247)

Treaty of Guadalupe Hidalgo (1848) a treaty that ended the Mexican-American War and gave the United States much of Mexico's northern territory (p. 361)
Tratado de Guadalupe Hidalgo (1848) tratado que daba por terminada la Guerra contra México y daba a Estados Unidos gran parte del norte del territorio mexicano (pág. 361)

Treaty of Medicine Lodge (1867) an agreement between the U.S. government and southern Plains Indians in which the Indians agreed to move onto reservations (p. 595)
Tratado de Medicine Lodge (1867) acuerdo entre el gobierno de Estados Unidos y los indígenas de las Planicies del sur en el que los indígenas aceptaron irse a las reservas (pág. 595)

Treaty of Paris of 1783 a peace agreement that officially ended the Revolutionary War and established British recognition of the independence of the United States (p. 139)
Tratado de París de 1783 acuerdo de paz que oficialmente dio por terminada la Guerra de Independencia estadounidense y en el que Gran Bretaña reconocía la independencia de Estados Unidos (pág. 139)

Treaty of Tordesillas (1494) a treaty between Spain and Portugal that moved the Line of Demarcation (p. 44)
Tratado de Tordesillas (1494) tratado entre España y Portugal que modificó la Línea de Demarcación (pág. 44)

Tredegar Iron Works a large iron factory that operated in Richmond, Virginia, in the early to mid-1800s (p. 419)
Tredegar Iron Works gran fábrica de acero que operaba a mediados del siglo XIX en Richmond, Virginia (pág. 419)

Triangle Shirtwaist Fire a factory fire that killed 146 workers trapped in the building; led to new safety standard laws (p. 673)
incendio de Triangle Shirtwaist incendio de una fábrica en el que murieron 146 trabajadores atrapados en el edificio; este suceso obligó a crear nuevas leyes de seguridad (pág. 673)

triangular trade trading networks in which goods and slaves moved among England, the American colonies, and Africa (p. 93)
comercio triangular redes comerciales en las que los bienes y los esclavos se intercambiaban entre Inglaterra, las colonias americanas y África (pág. 93)

trust a number of companies legally grouped under a single board of directors (p. 621)
consorcio varias compañías agrupadas legalmente bajo el mando de una sola junta directiva (pág. 621)

Uncle Tom's Cabin (1852) an antislavery novel written by Harriet Beecher Stowe that showed northerners the violent reality of slavery and drew many people to the abolitionists' cause (p. 481)
La cabaña del tío Tom (1852) novela abolicionista escrita por Harriet Beecher Stowe que mostró a los habitantes del norte del país la violenta realidad de la esclavitud e hizo que muchos se unieran a la causa abolicionista (pág. 481)

Underground Railroad a network of people who helped thousands of enslaved people escape to the North by providing transportation and hiding places (p. 456)
Tren Clandestino red de personas que ayudó a miles de esclavos a escapar al Norte ofreciéndoles transporte y lugares para esconderse (pág. 456)

USS *Constitution* a large warship (p. 278)
USS *Constitution* gran buque de guerra (pág. 278)

utopian communities places where people worked to establish a perfect society; such communities were popular in the United States during the late 1700s and early to mid-1800s (p. 444)
comunidades utópicas lugares en los que un grupo de personas trabajaba para establecer una sociedad perfecta; se popularizaron en Estados Unidos a finales del siglo XVIII y principios y mediados del XIX (pág. 444)

vaqueros Mexican cowboys in the West who tended cattle and horses (p. 357)
vaqueros arrieros mexicanos que vivían en el Oeste y se ganaban la vida ocupándose del ganado y los caballos (pág. 357)

vertical integration the business practice of owning all of the businesses involved in each step of a manufacturing process (p. 620)
integración vertical práctica empresarial de poseer todas las empresas que participan en cada paso de un proceso de manufactura (pág. 620)

ENGLISH AND SPANISH GLOSSARY

veto to cancel a law (p. 184)
　vetar cancelar una ley (pág. 184)

Virginia Plan (1787) the plan for government proposed at the Constitutional Convention in which the national government would have supreme power and a legislative branch would have two houses with representation determined by state population (p. 164)
　Plan de Virginia (1787) plan de gobierno propuesto en la Convención Constitucional por el que el gobierno nacional tendría poder supremo y habría un poder legislativo con dos cámaras en las que la representación de cada estado sería determinada por su población (pág. 164)

Virginia Statute for Religious Freedom (1786) a document that gave people in Virginia freedom of worship and prohibited tax money from being used to fund churches (p. 153)
　Estatuto de Virginia para la Libertad Religiosa (1786) documento que reconocía a los habitantes de Virginia la libertad de culto y prohibía utilizar los impuestos para financiar iglesias (pág. 153)

W

War Hawks members of Congress who wanted to declare war against Britain after the Battle of Tippecanoe (p. 282)
　halcones de guerra miembros del Congreso que querían declarar la guerra a Gran Bretaña tras la batalla de Tippecanoe (pág. 282)

Whig Party a political party formed in 1834 by opponents of Andrew Jackson and who supported a strong legislature (p. 330)
　Partido Whig partido político formado en 1834 por oponentes de Andrew Jackson que apoyaba una asamblea legislativa con mucha autoridad (pág. 330)

Whiskey Rebellion (1794) a protest of small farmers in Pennsylvania against new taxes on whiskey (p. 247)
　Rebelión del Whisky (1794) protesta de pequeños agricultores de Pensilvania contra los nuevos impuestos sobre el whisky (pág. 247)

Wilderness Campaign (1864) a series of battles between Union and Confederate forces in northern and central Virginia that delayed the Union capture of Richmond (p. 540)
　Campaña de Wilderness (1864) serie de batallas entre la Unión y los confederados en el norte y el centro de Virginia que retrasaron la captura de Richmond por parte de la Unión (pág. 540)

Wilmot Proviso (1846) a proposal to outlaw slavery in the territory added to the United States by the Mexican Cession; passed in the House of Representatives but was defeated in the Senate (p. 476)
　Condición de Wilmot (1846) propuesta de prohibir la esclavitud en el territorio anexado a Estados Unidos por la Cesión Mexicana; aprobada por la Cámara de Representantes, pero rechazada por el Senado (pág. 476)

Worcester* v. *Georgia (1832) the Supreme Court ruling that stated that the Cherokee nation was a distinct territory over which only the federal government had authority; ignored by both President Andrew Jackson and the state of Georgia (p. 334)
　Worcester* contra *Georgia (1832) decisión de la Corte Suprema que establecía que la nación cheroquí era un territorio distinto sobre el que sólo el gobierno federal tenía autoridad; fue ignorada por el presidente Andrew Jackson y por el estado de Georgia (pág. 334)

X

XYZ affair (1797) an incident in which French agents attempted to get a bribe and loans from U.S. diplomats in exchange for an agreement that French privateers would no longer attack American ships; it led to an undeclared naval war between the two countries (p. 252)
　incidente XYZ (1797) incidente en el que funcionarios franceses intentaron obtener sobornos y préstamos de diplomáticos estadounidenses a cambio de un acuerdo por el cual sus corsarios no atacarían más a los barcos estadounidenses; provocó una guerra no declarada entre las fuerzas navales de ambas naciones (pág. 252)

Y

yellow journalism the reporting of exaggerated stories in newspapers to increase sales (p. 697)
　prensa amarillista publicación de noticias exageradas en los periódicos para aumentar las ventas (pág. 697)

yeomen owners of small farms (p. 422)
　pequeños terratenientes dueños de granjas pequeñas (pág. 422)

Index

INDEX

D

E

INDEX

INDEX

INDEX

INDEX

Z

Credits and Acknowledgments

For permission to reproduce copyrighted material, grateful acknowledgment is made to the following sources:

Norwegian-American Historical Association:
From quote by Gro Svendsen from *Frontier Mother: The Letters of Gro Svendsen,* translated and edited by Pauline Farseth and Theodore C. Blegen. Copyright © 1950 Norwegian-American Historical Association.

Sources Cited:

Quote by an Aztec messenger from *The Broken Spears: The Aztec Account of the Conquest of Mexico,* Expanded and Updated Edition, edited by Miguel León-Portilla. Published by Beacon Press, Boston, 1992.

From *Yesterday: A Memoir of a Russian Jewish Family* by Miriam Shomer Zunser, edited by Emily Wortis Leider. Published by HarperCollins Publishers, New York, 1978.

Quote by a Hungarian immigrant from *This Was America* by Oscar Handlin. Published by Harvard University Press, Cambridge, Mass., 1949.

Illustration and Photo Credits

Front Cover: © Wolfgang Kaehler/CORBIS.

Front Matter: Page ii (l) Seth Joel/HRW; (r) Michael Denora/HRW Photo; v (b), Mary Evans Picture Library; v (t), The Field Museum of Natural History, Neg. A108557-c, Photo by Ron Testa;; vi (l), © Dennis Degnan/CORBIS; vi (r), American Antiquarian Society; vii, © David Butow/CORBIS; viii, © 1993 Mickey Osterreischer/Black Star/ stockphoto.com; ix (l) (Art Reference) © Board of Trustees, National Gallery of Art, Washington; (r) The Hermitage, Home of Andrew Jackson; xi, National Museum of American History, Smithsonian Institution, Washington, DC. Photo by Kim Neilson, #83-2953; xiii, Nebraska State Historical Society, Photograph Collections; xv, The Granger Collection, New York; xvi (art ref) PRC Archive; xx, © Collection of the New-York Historical Society, [neg. 41800]; xxv, Picture Research Consultants & Archives; H2, ©Bettmann/CORBIS; H4, Laurie Platt Winfrey/Woodfin Camp &Associates; H6, Superstock; H7, The Granger Collection, New York; H8, Library of Congress, H9, The Granger Collection, New York; H25 (t) © Daily News Pix; (l) © Randy Wells/CORBIS; (cr) © Robert Maass/CORBIS; (b) © Glen Allison/Getty Images.

Unit 1: 00-01 © Burstein Collection/Corbis. **Chapter 1:** Pages 2-3 (t)© Annie Griffiths/CORBIS; 2 (br) The Art Archive/National Anthropological Museum Mexico/Dagli Orti; 3 (bc) ©Yoshio Tomii/SuperStock, (br) ©Rabatti - Dominigie/akg-images; 7 (t) Smithsonian Institution, Washington, DC. Photograph by Chip Clark # 90-14563, (c) PRC Archive, (b) Getty Images; 11 © David Muench/CORBIS; 13 (tr) From the Collection of Gilcrease Museum, Tulsa, 13 (bl) © 2000 The Art Institute of Chicago (detail), (tl) Ohio Historical Society; 14 (tl) Marilyn Wynn/Nativestock Pictures, 14 (tr) The Granger Collection, New York; 17 (tl) Carol Beckwith & Angela Fisher/HAGA/The Image Works, Inc., 17 (tl) © John Elk III Photography; 19 (bc) Reuters/Corbis, (br) AFP/Getty Images; 21 (br) The Granger Collection, New York;

23 (b) Ben Mangor/SuperStock; 24 (bc) © Archivo Iconografico, S.A./CORBIS, (bl) ©Christopher Groenhout/Lonely Planet Images; 25 (bl) © Bettmann/CORBIS, (br) ©G K & Vikki Hart/PhotoDisc, (bc) The Granger Collection, New York. **Chapter 2:** Pages 34-35 (all) © Rebecca Marvil/Index Stock Imagery, Inc.; 34 (b) National Maritime Museum; 35 (cl) SuperStock, (c) Tate Gallery, London/Art Resource, NY, (bl) Fundacion Miguel Mujica Gallo, Museo do Oro del Peru, (bc) G. Tortoli/Ancient Art & Architecture Collection, Ltd., (br) Victoria & Albert Museum, London/Art Resource, NY, (cr) David Muench/Corbis; 40 (bkgd) © Royalty Free/CORBIS; 44 SuperStock; 47 (br) © Scott Nelson/Getty Images; 49 The Granger Collection, New York; 51 (cr) PRC Archive; 52 (bl) Saint Bride Printing Library; 53 (bl) AKG-Images, (br) Mary Evans Picture Library; 54 (t) Tate Gallery, London/Art Resource, NY; 59 (br) Copyright The New York Public Library / Art Resource, NY; 60 (tr) **Chapter 3:** Pages 68-69 (t) Ted Curtin for Plimoth Plantation, (c) Courtesy of the Pilgrim Society, Plymouth, Massachusetts; 68 (bl) © David Ball/CORBIS; 69 (br) © Culver Pictures, Inc., (bl) © SuperStock, (cr) Courtesy of the Burton Historical Collection, Detroit Public Library; 75 (t) Colonial Williamsburg Foundation; 82 (t) Art Reference: PRC Archive; 85 (b) © SuperStock; 86 (bl) Art Reference: Historical Society of Pennsylvania; 88 (l) SuperStock, (t) NASA, (b) © SuperStock, Inc./SuperStock; 93 (r) Art Reference: Royal Albert Memorial Museum, Exeter, Devon, UK/Bridgeman Art Library, (l) Private Collection/www.bridgeman.co.uk; 94 (t) National Portrait Library, London/Bridgeman Art Library; 97 (tr) Art Reference: Courtesy of the Burton Historical Collection, Detroit Public Library; 99 (t) Virginia Historical Society; 101 (t) Peter Newark's American Pictures; 102 (tr) Courtesy of the Massachusetts Historical Society, (tl) © Hulton-Deutsch Collection/CORBIS; 103 (tl) © Bettmann/CORBIS, (tr) American Antiquarian Society. **Chapter 4:** Pages 108-109 (t) © James Lemass/Index Stock Imagery; 108 (cl) The Granger Collection, New York; 109 (br) © Christie's Images, (cr) North Wind Picture Archives; 113 (b) © Concord Museum/Photograph by Chip Fanelli, (t) The Granger Collection, New York; 117 (br) © Robert Llewellyn/SuperStock; 119 (br) The Granger Collection, New York, (bl) © 2003-2005 clipart.com; 120 (t) © Bettmann/CORBIS; 123 (br) The Granger Collection, New York; 127 (l) #1921.101, ©Collection of The New-York Historical Society, (r) ©Collection of The New-York Historical Society, neg. 31665; 128-129 (t) © SuperStock; 130 (r) Chateau de Versailles, France/Giraudon/ Bridgeman Art Library, (l) Saratoga National Historic Park; 131 (r) Hotel Galvez, Galveston, Texas, (l) Falmouth Art Gallery, Cornwall, UK/The Bridgeman Art Library; 132 © SuperStock, Inc. / SuperStock; 136 (t) The Granger Collection, New York; 138 The Granger Collection, New York.

Unit 2. Chapter 5: Pages 148-149 (t) © 2009 Jay Mallin; 148 (b) Library of Congress/PRC Archive; 149 (br) © Andrea Jemolo/CORBIS, (bl) © Nik Wheeler/CORBIS, (c) Collection of the American Numismatic Society, New York; 153 The Granger Collection, New York; 156 (t) © Bettmann/CORBIS, (b) © Bettmann/CORBIS; 157 (t) © Bettmann/CORBIS, (c) ©

Michael Nicholson/CORBIS , (br) © Archivo Iconografico, S.A./CORBIS; 160-161 (b) The Granger Collection, New York; 163 © Dennis Degnan/CORBIS; 164 (t) Hall of Representatives, Washington, DC/ Bridgeman Art Library, (bl) Independence National Historical Park , (bc) Stock MontageStrock, (br) Portrait by Robert S. Susan, Collection of the Supreme Court of the United States; 166 (l) South Carolina Legal History Collection, (r) City of Bristol Museum and Art Gallery/Bridgeman Art Library; 167 © Alex Wong/Getty Images; 169 (br) American Antiquarian Society; 171 (r) © Bettmann/CORBIS, (l) Stock Montage, Inc., (bkgd) © Alan Schein Photography/CORBIS. **Chapter 6:** Pages 178-179 (t) Sam Dudgeon/HRW Photo; 179 (b) © Bettmannn/CORBIS, (cl) PRC Archive, (cr) © Tony Freeman/PhotoEdit; 185 Getty Images; 187 (bc) National Archives (NARA), (br) National Archives/PRC Archive; 192 (br) Dennis Cook/AP/Wide World Photos; 192-193 (bc) © Mark Wilson/Getty Images, (t) © Miles Ertman/Masterfile; 193 (br) © Brooks Kraft/CORBIS; 194 © Royalty-Free/CORBIS; 204 (bl) © Yang Liu/CORBIS, (bc) Norm Detlaff, Las Cruces Sun-News/AP/Wide World Photos; 205 (bl) ©Alex Webb/Magnum Photos, (bc) © David Young-Wolff/PhotoEdit, (br) © Bettmann/CORBIS; © Royalty-Free/CORBIS; 209 (t) Library of Congress/PRC Archive; 211 (tr) Library of Congress; 213 (l) © Bettmann/CORBIS, (r) © Oscar White/CORBIS; 214 (tr) ©1978 Matt Herron/TakeStock, (tc) Texas State Library & Archives Commission, (tl) Dr. Hector P. Garcia Papers, Special Collections & Archives, Texas A&M University-Corpus Christi, Bell Library; 217 (b) © Daily News Pix; 219 © Spencer Grant/PhotoEdit; 220-221 (b) © Ariel Skelley/CORBIS; 223 (t) © David Butow/CORBIS; 224 (tl) ©James Pickerell/The Image Works, (tr) © Brownie Harris/CORBIS; 225 (l) © Ariel Skelly/CORBIS, (c) Janet Knott/The Boston Globe. Republished with permission of The Globe Newspaper Company, Inc., (r) © Jeff Greenberg/PhotoEdit. **Chapter 7:** Pages 230 (b) © Christie's Images; 231 (bl) Giraudon/Art Resource, NY ,(r) Art Resource, NY; 235 (r) Library of Congress/PRC Archive; 237 (inset) © Collection of The New-York Historical Society, 31907.32; 240 (b) © Joseph Sohm; Chromosohm, Inc./CORBIS, (c) Photo ©2004 Roger Foley; 241 (r) Stock Montage/Getty Images, (l) Stock Montage, Inc.; 243 (b) Réunion des Musées Nationaux/Art Resource, NY; 244 (l) Chicago Historical Society, (r) Library of Congress/PRC Archive, (c) Chicago Historical Society, #i35980aa; 245 (l) HRW Photo Research Library; 246 Courtesy Ohio Historical Society; 248 © Museum of the City of New York/CORBIS; 251 (tl) ©The New York Historical Society, New York, NY/ Bridgeman Art Library, (tc) The Art Archive/Chateau de Biernacourt/Dagli Orti, (bl) Independence National Historical Park Collection, (bc) The Henry Luce III Center for the Study of American Culture/SuperStock, (tr) ©The New-York Historical Society, New York, NY/ Bridgeman Art Library, (br) National Portrait Gallery, Smithsonian Institution, Washington, DC/Art Resource, NY; 252 Library of Congress/PRC Archive.

Unit 3. Chapter 8: Pages 262 (b) The Granger Collection, New York; 262-263 (t) Superstock; 263 (cl) Benninghoff Collection of the American Revolution, (cr) Portrait of the

Unit 6. Chapter 18: Pages 582-583 © James L. Amos/CORBIS; 582 (b) Courtesy Wells Fargo Bank; 583 (bl) The Art Archive / Musée d'Orsay Paris/ Dagli Orti, (cl) Southern Pacific Lines/PRC Archive, (cr) © CORBIS, (br) The Granger Collection, New York; 587 (tr) © Collection of the New-York Historical Society, [neg. 41800]; 588 (l) Denver Public Library, Western History Collection; 588-589 (r) Nebraska State Historical Society, Photograph Collections; 589 (inset) Bob Boze Bell, True West Magazine; 590 (inset) © James L. Amos/CORBIS; 591 Union Pacific Historical Collection; 592 (t) The Granger Collection, New York; 592-593 (b) SuperStock; 595 (t) George Lane/AP/Wide World Photos; 596 (t) © Bettmann/CORBIS; 597 (t) Western History Division, National Museum of American History/Smithsonian Institution, Washington, DC; 598 The Granger Collection, New York; 599 (l) (art Reference) all LOC -no credit needed, (r); 601 (b) Western History Collections, University of Oklahoma; 602 (bl) Library of Congress, (tr) Elias Carr Papers, East Carolina Manuscript Collection, J.Y. Joyner Library, East Carolina University, Greenville, NC. Photo by Dewane Frutiger., (br) Nebraska State Historical Society; 603 (l) Culver Pictures; 604 (art reference) LOC/PRC No credit needed; 605 (t) © CORBIS; 608 (bl) Sam Dudgeon/HRW. **Chapter 19:** Pages 610-611 (t) PRC Archive; 611 (bl) © Bettmann/CORBIS, (br) Archives Larousse, Paris, France/ Bridgeman Art Library, (c) George Meany Memorial Archives; 614-615 (b) Library of Congress; 616 (r) [neg. #40578] ©Collection of The New-York Historical Society, (l) Whittier Museum; 617 (l) Property of AT&T Archives. Printed with permission of AT&T., (r) © Hulton Archive/Getty Images; 618 (l) © CORBIS, (r) Library of Congress/PRC Archive; 619 (b) Montgomery County Historical Society; 620 (b) © CORBIS, (inset) Courtesy of the Rockefeller Archive Center; 621 (t) [#71880T] © Collection of The New-York Historical Society; 623 (l) (Art Reference) AP/Wide World Photos & © Bettmann/CORBIS, (c) (Art Reference) AP/Wide World Photos, (r) (Art Reference) Photo courtesy Union Pacific Historical Collection; 625 (b) (Art Reference) © Bettmann/CORBIS, (t) Brown Brothers. **Chapter 20:** Pages 632-633 © Bettmann/CORBIS; 633 (cl) © Joseph Sohm, Chromosohm, Inc./CORBIS, (cr) © CORBIS, (br) © Ted Spiegel/CORBIS; 637 (t) PictureHistory/NewsCom; 638 (cr) Shades of L.A. Archives/Los Angeles Public Library, (cl) National Archives, #90-G-152-2038; 639 (tc) Col. Ernest Swanson Papers, Swenson Swedish Immigration Research Center, Augustana College, Rock Island, IL, (cl) © CORBIS; 640 (bl) Library of Congress, Arnold Genthe Collections, #LC-G403-T01-0363, (br) Library of Congress, Arnold Genthe Collections, #LC-G403-T01-0363; 643 (t) Lake County (IL) Museum /Curt Teich Postcard Archives; 644 (bc) New York State Historical Association, (br) © David Bell/CORBIS; 647 The Granger Collection, New York; 648 Jane Addams Memorial Collection (JAMC neg 227), Special Collections, University Library, University of Illinois at Chicago.

Unit 7: 656-657 Courtesy of the U.S. Naval Academy Museum. **Chapter 21:** 658-659 (t) Elizabeth Cady Stanton Trust; 659 (cl, cr) Janice L. and David J. Frent Collection of Political Americana, (b) The Granger Collection, New York; 663 (t) The Granger Collection, New York; 664 (tl) PRC Archive, (tr) PRC Archive, (cl) PRC Archive, (cr) PRC Archive, (bl) PRC Archive, (br) PRC Archive; 665 (t) © Bettmann/CORBIS; 668 (t) Barnes & Noble, Inc.; 669 (t) Library of Congress/PRC Archive; 671 (b) National Archives/PRC Archive; 673 (t) Courtesy of Steve Latham; 676 (b) © Bettmann/CORBIS; 677 (b) Library of Congress, 681 (tc) Leroy Radanovich/Yosemite Museum, (tl) © W. Perry Conway/CORBIS; 682 (br) White House Collection, copyright White House Historical Association, (bl) White House Collection, copyright White House Historical Association, (bc) White House Collection, copyright White House Historical Association; 687 (t) Library of Congress. **Chapter 22:** Pages 688 (b) © Charles Sleicher; 688-689 (t) © Bettmann/CORBIS; 689 (bl) Press Information Bureau of India, (c) Denver Public Library, Western History Collection; 694 (c) © Douglas Peebles/CORBIS; 695 National Portrait Gallery, Smithsonian Institution/Art Resource, NY; 696 Trustees of the British Museum; 698 (b) © Bettmann/CORBIS, (c) PRC Archive; 700 (tr) Library of Congress; 701 (bl) © Richard Cohen/CORBIS; 703 (br) © CORBIS; 704-705 (b) Library of Congress; 707 The Granger Collection, New York; 708 (inset) © Bettmann/CORBIS; 710 (b) © Bettmann/CORBIS, (c) © Bettmann/CORBIS; 711 (tr, b) © Bettmann/CORBIS. R0-R1 (bkgd) © Royalty-free/CORBIS; R23 –R27 White House Historical Association (White House Collection); R27 (bc) The White House, photo by Eric Draper, (br), © Pete Souza. R30 © Getty Images; R31, The Granger Collection, New York; R33 (t) © Tom Brakefield/Digital Vision/Getty Images.

Staff Credits. The people who contributed to *Holt McDougal Social Studies: United States History, Beginnings to 1914* are listed below. They represent editorial, design, intellectual property resources, production, emedia, and permissions.

Lissa B. Anderson, Charles Becker, Ed Blake, Gillian Brody, Erin Cornett, Michelle Dike, Mescal Evler, Leanna Ford, Bob Fullilove, Rhonda Haynes, Wilonda Ieans, Cathy Jenevein, Shannon Johnston, Cathy Kuhles, Debbie Lofland, Bob McClellan, Joe Melomo, Richard Metzger, Mercedes Newman, Holly Norman, Nathan O'Neal, Karl Pallmeyer, Shelly Ramos, Gene Rumann, Kay Selke, Ken Shepardson, Michele Shukers, Chris Smith, Jeannie Taylor, Joni Wackwitz, Ken Whiteside, Nadyne Wood